W9-ADQ-472

Winner's Popular Vote Percent	Winner's Electoral College Vote Percent	Party of President	Congress	House		Senate	
				Majority Party	Minority Party	Majority Party	Minority Party
No popular vote	Not applicable	None	1st	38 Admin	26 Opp	17 Admin	9 Opp
			2nd	37 Fed	33 Dem-R	16 Fed	13 Dem-R
No popular vote	Not applicable		3rd	57 Dem-R	48 Fed	17 Fed	13 Dem-R
			4th	54 Fed	52 Dem-R	19 Fed	13 Dem-R
No popular vote	Not applicable	Fed	5th	58 Fed	48 Dem-R	20 Fed	12 Dem-R
			6th	64 Fed	42 Dem-R	19 Fed	13 Dem-R
No popular vote	Decided in House	Dem-R	7th	69 Dem-R	36 Fed	18 Dem-R	13 Fed
			8th	102 Dem-R	39 Fed	25 Dem-R	9 Fed
No popular vote	92.0		9th	116 Dem-R	25 Fed	27 Dem-R	7 Fed
			10th	118 Dem-R	24 Fed	28 Dem-R	6 Fed
No popular vote	69.7	Dem-R	11th	94 Dem-R	48 Fed	28 Dem-R	6 Fed
			12th	108 Dem-R	36 Fed	30 Dem-R	6 Fed
No popular vote	59.0		13th	112 Dem-R	68 Fed	27 Dem-R	9 Fed
			14th	117 Dem-R	65 Fed	25 Dem-R	11 Fed
No popular vote	84.3	Dem-R	15th	141 Dem-R	42 Fed	34 Dem-R	10 Fed
			16th	156 Dem-R	27 Fed	35 Dem-R	7 Fed
No popular vote	99.5		17th	158 Dem-R	25 Fed	44 Dem-R	4 Fed
			18th	187 Dem-R	26 Fed	44 Dem-R	4 Fed
39.1	Decided in House	Nat-R	19th	105 Admin	97 Dem-J	26 Admin	20 Dem-J
			20th	119 Dem-J	94 Admin	28 Dem-J	20 Admin
56.0	68.2	Dem	21st	139 Dem	74 Nat R	26 Dem	22 Nat R
			22nd	141 Dem	58 Nat R	25 Dem	21 Nat R
54.5	76.6		23rd	147 Dem	53 AntiMas	20 Dem	20 Nat R
			24th	145 Dem	98 Whig	27 Dem	25 Whig
50.9	57.8	Dem	25th	108 Dem	107 Whig	30 Dem	18 Whig
			26th	124 Dem	118 Whig	28 Dem	22 Whig
52.9	79.6	Whig					
52.9		Whig	27th	133 Whig	102 Dem	28 Whig	22 Dem
			28th	142 Dem	79 Whig	28 Whig	25 Dem
49.6	61.8	Dem	29th	143 Dem	77 Whig	31 Dem	25 Whig
			30th	115 Whig	108 Dem	36 Dem	21 Whig
47.3	56.2	Whig	31st	112 Dem	109 Whig	35 Dem	25 Whig
—	—	Whig	32nd	140 Dem	88 Whig	35 Dem	24 Whig
50.9	85.8	Dem	33rd	159 Dem	71 Whig	38 Dem	22 Whig
			34th	108 Rep	83 Dem	40 Dem	15 Rep
45.6	58.8	Dem	35th	118 Dem	92 Rep	36 Dem	20 Rep
			36th	114 Rep	92 Dem	36 Dem	26 Rep
39.8	59.4	Rep	37th	105 Rep	43 Dem	31 Rep	10 Dem
			38th	102 Rep	75 Dem	36 Rep	9 Dem
55.2	91.0						
—	—	Rep	39th	149 Union	42 Dem	42 Union	10 Dem
			40th	143 Rep	49 Dem	42 Rep	11 Dem
52.7	72.8	Rep	41st	149 Rep	63 Dem	56 Rep	11 Dem
			42nd	134 Rep	104 Dem	52 Rep	17 Dem
55.6	81.9		43rd	194 Rep	92 Dem	49 Rep	19 Dem
			44th	169 Rep	109 Dem	45 Rep	29 Dem
47.9	50.1	Rep	45th	153 Dem	140 Rep	39 Rep	36 Dem
			46th	149 Dem	130 Rep	42 Dem	33 Rep
48.3	58.0	Rep	47th	147 Rep	135 Dem	37 Rep	37 Dem
—	—	Rep	48th	197 Dem	118 Rep	38 Rep	36 Dem

The Dorsey
DICTIONARY *of*
AMERICAN GOVERNMENT
and POLITICS

The Dorsey
DICTIONARY *of*
AMERICAN GOVERNMENT
and POLITICS

Jay M. Shafritz
University of Pittsburgh

THE DORSEY PRESS

Chicago, Illinois 60604

Acquisitions editor: *Leo Wiegman*
Developmental editor: *Diane Hammond*
Project editor: *Gladys True*
Production manager: *Charles J. Hess*
Interior Design: *Harry Voight Design*
Cover Design: *Michael Warrell*
Photo researcher: *Stephen Forsling*
Compositor: *Weimer Typesetting Co., Inc.*
Typeface: *9/11 Times Roman*
Printer: *Arcata Graphics/Halliday*

Library of Congress Cataloging-in-Publication Data

Shafritz, Jay M.
   The Dorsey dictionary of American government and politics.

   Includes bibliographies.
   1. United States—Politics and government—Dictionaries.   I. Title.
JK9.S42 1988   320.973'03   87–72401
ISBN 0-256-05639-0
ISBN 0-256-05589-0 (pbk.)

Printed in the United States of America
1 2 3 4 5 6 7 8 9 0 H 5 4 3 2 1 0 9 8

Dedicated to
Mrs. Cora Hurwitz,
a wise counselor

Foreword

Justice Oliver Wendell Holmes once wrote that the life of the law was not logic but experience. So it is with a political system. Especially when it involves history and traditions extending back two hundred years or more, a political system like that of the United States cannot be comprehended outside of its particulars — its laws and folkways, its procedures and symbols, its heroes and villains. Such bits and pieces of knowledge do not add up to comprehensive understanding, but they are an indispensable foundation for such an understanding.

That is why experienced analysts of American government and politics insist on getting accurate information about the details of laws and practices. And that is why teachers fill the syllabi of their core courses with factual material about history and structure. Sometimes we speak patronizingly of "nuts and bolts" political science; but we must not forget that such appliances, small and insignificant as they seem, fasten together the superstructure of our more sophisticated concepts and theories about the political system.

A few examples will serve to bring home my point. Certain political commentators have gotten into the habit of lamenting the sad state of political participation in the United States. Each new election provides new ammunition for their viewpoint and leads to a spate of fresh articles about how few citizens go to the polls and what gloomy future that fact portends. Yet few of these writers stop to analyze the mundane factual elements of the phenomenon of voter turnout. Unlike some nations, the United States does not have universal or automatic voter registration. Thus, not all people of voting age are "eligible" to vote. Establishing one's eligibility demands initiative and effort. Moreover, voting rolls are kept by local governments operating under state laws. The states differ significantly in the way they keep their records; many do not regularly purge their lists of voters who have moved away or died. The result is turnout figures that may be based on erroneous estimates of eligible voters. Even if the election turnout statistics are conceded, people participate in politics in countless ways that are not captured by voting numbers, or indeed by any reliable numbers at all. So a detailed knowledge of the "nuts and bolts" of election administration is a prerequisite to a full understanding of the problem of voter turnout.

Another example. A few years ago I attended a panel at a professional meeting, the highlight of which was a paper applying formal mathematical modeling to a certain legislative procedure that I happened to know something about. The model was elegant, and the conclusions were tidy. The only problem was that the paper's author had not an inkling of how the procedure actually worked, and so the findings bore little resemblance to the phenomenon ostensibly being discussed. Again, a serious exercise was flawed because the investigator neglected the "nuts and bolts" of his topic.

No one would argue that these sophsticated forms of inquiry—conceptualization, theory building, model construction, and the like—are not worth doing. Indeed, they are for many

Foreword

of us most rewarding and useful activities, for they point us in the direction of a true science of politics. Rather, the point is that these "scientific" activities are based on the equally "scientific" work of gathering and verifying facts. It is true that scholarly reputations are far more likely to be made by theorizing than by studying the operating details of a system. But we must not forget that all science, however elegant and subtle, is based at some point on accurate, patient observation; and that the most complex theories must finally answer the test of conformity to observation. Again, "nuts and bolts" questions will always be with us.

Indeed, one indicator of the maturity of our ancient but imprecise science of politics is the state of our reference materials. We literally cannot go about our daily work of research without referring to sources of "nuts and bolts" information. The accuracy of our knowledge and of our intellectual products—lectures, articles, and books—depends upon plentiful sources of such facts.

The Dorsey Dictionary of American Government and Politics is full of the kind of basic information that we as students and scholars need on a daily basis to go about our work. It has far more entries than any similar volume. Its essays are supplemented by tabular and statistical material. A majority of its entries include references for further reading. It is even illustrated to render using it more pleasurable and more meaningful.

Those of us who have been involved in this project have attempted to produce a reference volume that is at once comprehensive, succinct, and useful. For undergraduate students it should be a helpful supplement to their initial study of American politics and government. For graduate students it should be a vehicle for refreshing and broadening their knowledge. For practicing scholars of all ages and levels, it should be a resource for checking out the facts pertaining to a given subject.

Like the science of politics itself, this dictionary is by no means an end product; rather, it is part of an ongoing process of factual collection and refinement. Naturally, therefore, we hope there will be many more editions of this work. We also hope that users of the volume will contribute by volunteering their comments and suggestions in the years to come. Such a work, reflecting as it does the state of knowledge within a discipline, is by its very nature a cooperative enterprise.

Roger H. Davidson
Professor of Government and Politics
University of Maryland

Barry D. Karl
Norman and Edna Freehling Professor of History
The University of Chicago

Preface

This dictionary is a tool for those who seek information on American national, state, or local government and politics. You will find here all commonly used terms and concepts of American government, such as the presidency, Congress, and the courts. Also included are the vocabularies of other key aspects of American governance, such as foreign policy, public administration, political economy, and taxation.

With more than four thousand entries, this dictionary is the most comprehensive and useful single-volume reference book on all of the concerns of governance in the United States. It captures and codifies the living language of American government and politics, although I realize it can never be absolutely complete. The language of government and politics constantly evolves and expands and does not wait on publishers' deadlines.

While this effort may be incomplete by its nature, it is nevertheless comprehensive in its design. This dictionary contains explanations of the terms, phrases, and processes essential for an understanding of American government and politics, and includes entries on significant Supreme Court cases, biographical identifications, laws, political slang, scholarly journals, and professional associations. The goal has been to capture the language, concerns, and professional literature of American governance in one volume. Because the concerns of government and politics are anything but pure and limited to one discipline, judgments constantly had to be made about how extensively to cover related fields such as economics, history, law, and sociology, among others. As a rule of thumb, if a term was found in any of several scores of standard texts on American government or its subspecialties, it is included here.

Writing the dictionary was akin to doing a gargantuan jigsaw puzzle in which you have to make up the pieces as you go along and have no idea how large it will be in the end. The first task in completing this jigsaw puzzle was to find the pieces. For a subject as commonly taught and written about as American government and politics, many terms were obvious entries. But as a check on comprehensiveness, I systematically reviewed each issue of all the scholarly journals in political science for the last three decades. If a political scientist took the trouble to write an article on a concept, theory, practice, court case, law, or person, I seriously considered including a definition of it. Next I roamed the stacks and reference sections of a variety of university libraries, finding new puzzle pieces here and there. Periodically I gathered up all my newfound pieces, gave them form and polish, compared them to like terms in my personal library of several hundred volumes in American governance, and then placed them on the puzzle board—in this case, the hard disk of my computer. I made extensive use of public domain materials published by a variety of federal government agencies, and I wish to acknowledge and thank the legions of anonymous public servants who have produced the various manuals, glossaries, analyses, directories, and guidelines that were so useful. Sometimes I would start with a definition from one of these public sources and research it and rework it until the original was no longer recognizable. But more commonly I had the more difficult task of writing a definition from scratch based on my own twenty years of experience in studying, teaching, and writing about American governance, as well as on the earlier work of thousands of authors and on the forbearance of my friends and colleagues whom I would call at odd hours and ask: "What do *you* think this means?"

Beyond listing generally accepted and established terms, I have specifically included political terms found in newspapers and mass market journals that have not yet found their way into text, reference, and scholarly books. Generally excluded were those terms whose meaning in the context of American governance did not differ from definitions to be found in any college-level dictionary of the English language. When a word had multiple meanings, I often thought it useful to provide a brief standard English meaning first. I excluded those terms that once were, but no longer are, part of the language of American politics. With minor exceptions, for entries considered historically important, a term had to be relevant to modern American governance in order to merit a place in this dictionary.

No one scholar writes a large reference book without considerable help from others. My intellectual debts are acknowledged in the citations that follow the entries. But there are some personal debts as well. In one way or another, each of the following colleagues made contributions to this book:

Harry A. Bailey, Jr., of Temple University

Elizabeth T. Boris of the Council on Foundations

James S. Bowman of Florida State University

Ronald S. Calinger of The Catholic University of America

Robert W. Gage of the University of Colorado at Denver

Donald Goldstein of the University of Pittsburgh

Albert C. Hyde of San Francisco State University

Alice E. Kaiser of the University of Pittsburgh

Samuel H. Kernell of the University of California at San Diego

William J. Keefe of the University of Pittsburgh

Kate Kelly of Facts on File, Inc.

Lawrence J. Korb of the University of Pittsburgh

Arthur I. Marsh of St. Edmund Hall, Oxford University

Dail A. Neugarten of the University of Colorado at Denver

Daniel Oran of The Foresight Corporation

J. Steven Ott of the University of Maine

David B. Robertson of St. Hugh's College, Oxford University

David H. Rosenbloom of Syracuse University

Noah J. Shafritz of Ingomar Middle School

Todd J. Shafritz of North Allegheny High School

Frederick C. Thayer of the University of Pittsburgh

Frank J. Thompson of the State University of New York at Albany

Tim J. Tieperman of the University of Pittsburgh

Eileen Tynan of the University of Colorado at Denver

David B. Walker of the University of Connecticut

But there are two intellectual debts that are far greater than all of the others combined. Professors Roger H. Davidson of the Congressional Research Service and the University of Maryland and Barry Dean Karl of The University of Chicago each spent many months reviewing multiple drafts of the complete manuscript. They reviewed every entry and made countless helpful suggestions for improvement and expansion. They were my severest critics; I answered their criticisms with constant revision until finally they were quiet and I was exhausted.

This book was not typed; it was "inputted" as a computerized data base. Thus my greatest single debt is to my wife, Luise Alexander Shafritz, who was my data base management consultant and "inputter." While I wrote this dictionary, it was she who physically created it. Never in the course of political lexicography have two people owed so much to a hard disk and a fast chip.

This work was designed to include definitions of everything that anyone interested in American government and politics might reasonably wish to have. If you do not find a term that you feel should be included, I can only mimic Samuel Johnson's explanation when a woman made a similar complaint about his 1755 English *Dictionary*: "Ignorance, Madam, pure ignorance." Naturally, all omissions, mistakes, or other flaws to be found herein are solely my responsibility. It is still true today as Johnson wrote in 1755 that while "every other author may aspire to praise; the lexicographer can only hope to escape reproach." Yet I remain hopeful that as the years go by, this work will warrant subsequent editions. I would therefore encourage those readers who might care enough to help me do it "right" the next time around to write to me. Suggestions for enhancements, new entries, and additional citations will always be welcome.

Jay M. Shafritz
Graduate School of Public and International Affairs
Forbes Quadrangle
University of Pittsburgh
Pittsburgh, Pennsylvania 15260

Contents

List of Boxes

List of Boxes

List of Boxes

List of Illustrations

List of Illustrations

List of Illustrations

How to Use This Book

This dictionary includes several features designed to make it easy for the reader to use.

Alphabetization

The dictionary is arranged in continuous alphabetical order. This organization is especially useful for comparing entries that sound similar. It also allows for quick comparison of terms with the same root. For example, the entry for *bill* is followed by more than a dozen variants of bill, such as "bill, companion"; "bill, deficiency"; "bill, omnibus"; and so on. The entry for *democracy* is followed by "democracy, direct"; "democracy, industrial"; "democracy, Jacksonian"; and so on. This format is followed as often as possible so that if the root of a term is known, all of its variants can readily be found. All terms that begin as numbers, such as the constitutional amendments, are alphabetized as if the number were spelled out; thus, the Second Amendment is under *S*, the Third under *T*, and so on.

Key Concept List

If you are not quite sure of the word you want but know that it has something to do with the Congress, examine the key concept list in Appendix E (pages 641–657) to see if something looks familiar. If not, find some key words that are close, look them up, and follow the cross references. The key concept list is also useful if you wish to examine all of the major concepts of an area of governance. Remember that the key concept list does not contain all of the definitions to be found in the dictionary, only the core terms in each of the following key concepts:

Bureaucracy

Civil liberties

Congress

The Constitution

Courts

Federalism

Foreign policy

Political economy

Political parties and interest groups

Political theory

Presidency

Public policy

State and local government

Voting and elections

Bibliography

Most entries are followed by citations of bibliographic sources giving examples of the usage of the term as well as sources for further information. For the most part the references cited can be found in any large public or small college library. "Fugitive" materials, those items that exist only in the most specialized collections, have been avoided—with the significant exception of law review articles.

The bibliographic references are grouped in chronological order after each entry. Older works are cited if they are classics in the field, if they were important to the development of thinking on the subject, or if they are the only references available. Specialized bibliographies and other reference materials are cited as often as practical. When an entry concerns something that has been a matter of controversy, I have sought to balance the accompanying citations with both supportive and critical sources.

These accompanying citations are in themselves a comprehensive bibliography of American government and politics. It is integrated with the dictionary for the usual reason of showing the reader the sources that have been used; but also because most users of this book, whether students, public officials, or politically active citizens, will sometimes want greater depth of information on a term, concept, court case, or individual. Because of this integrated bibliography, they need not spend hours searching in a library for just the right source; those hours have already been spent on their behalf.

Numbering

When an entry has more than one meaning, the definitions are numbered starting with the most common meaning as **1**. Correspondingly, the bibliographic citations that apply, if any, are given the same number after the entry. Thus, a book or article applying to meaning **1** will be preceded by a **1**; citations applying to meaning **2** will be preceded by a **2**. If an entry has more than one meaning and no numbers precede the citations that follow, it means the citations are generally applicable to all meanings of the term.

Cross References

No event or term of American government and politics is an island unto itself. No dictionary of more than four thousand terms would be optimally useful if it did not suggest the related terms, laws, court cases, or personalities significant to a fuller understanding of the initial term. The many hundreds of cross references provide threads the reader can use to follow the connections between and evolution of political concepts. Cross references usually follow at the end of an entry. When a cross reference was needed for a fuller understanding of a word within the body of the definition, the word was cross referenced by putting it in SMALL CAPITALS.

Biographical Entries

More than one hundred of the entries are identifications of people living and dead, who have been significant in the history, writing, and practice of American government. These entries are designed merely to identify individuals; they are not a substitute for reading their works. I readily concede that some notable individuals may have been excluded and other individuals may have been described in words too brief to do them justice. For the most part, biographical entries are limited to presidents, to the key actors in twentieth-century American government, and to those who have made an intellectual contribution to American political thought or to the practice of governance. This latter group ranges from Aristotle, a Greek philosopher; to Thomas Paine, a Revolutionary War pamphleteer; to Eleanor Roosevelt, the first politically active presidential wife; to Robert Dahl, a modern-day political scientist.

Court Cases

Among the entries are several hundred United States Supreme Court decisions. Often they will be integrated with a related entry. Such judicial decisions are originally many pages long, so be cautious! A brief summary of a case, no matter how succinct, may not be sufficient information upon which to base formal action. These summaries were written to identify the case and its significance to American governance, not to make less work for lawyers. The full legal citation is given with each court case so that the reader may readily locate the full text.

Journals

Because entries for all journals and magazines that bear upon American governance would be almost as large as this entire book, only those scholarly and professional journals that most consistently address the core concerns of American government and politics are included. Each of these thirty-seven periodical entries contains a statement of purpose as well as the journal's address and its Library of Congress call number. A master list of journals can be found under the entry "JOURNALS."

Federal Laws

Choosing from among thousands of federal legislative acts those most significant to contemporary government proved very difficult. Rather than attempt to compile an encyclopedia of federal law, I selected about one hundred of those laws that have had a major and continuing impact on American governance, such as the National Labor Relations Act of 1935, the Civil Rights Act of 1964, or the Tax Reform Act of 1986.

Associations and Organizations

Almost fifty professional and scholarly associations, interest groups, think tanks, unions, and research organizations have been included. In each entry, such as "Brookings Institution" or "American Bar Association," you will find a brief statement of the organization's origins and purpose, its current address and telephone number, and the name of its significant periodicals, if any.

Government Agencies

Close to a hundred entries on federal government agencies, from the Agency for International Development, to the National Railroad Passenger Corporation (AMTRAK), to the Tennessee Valley Authority, as well as all cabinet departments, have been included. Each agency entry provides background on the organization's origin and present purpose as well as a contact address and telephone number.

Slang

More than 150 slang terms (such as "big mo" and "teflon president") and informal processes (such as "logrolling" and "spin control") are described. Each entry includes the historical background, if one could be determined. Only those expressions that have developed a specialized meaning and usage in the practice of American politics were included.

Boxes

As the dictionary grew, many tidbits surfaced that seemed to deserve a spot of their own in the manuscript to help shed light on a preceding entry. These irresistible asides became the many boxes you will find on subjects as diverse as Henry David Thoreau's defense of anarchism, Edmund Burke's analysis of the role of an elected representative, and William Faulkner's letter of resignation as a Mississippi postmaster. Many boxes contain statistical summaries such as the number of black elected officials in 1970, 1980, and 1985; the number and kinds of governments in the United States, and so on. Other boxes contain lists of presidents, of vice presidents, of speakers of the House of Representatives, and so on. Each box is located near the entry for its key term.

Photographs and Illustrations

Distributed throughout the dictionary are more than one hundred photographs, prints, Thomas Nast engravings (see "bossism," "donkey," or "elephant"), cartoons, and drawings that help make the book more useful as a reference and more fun to browse through.

The Appendixes

Since the Constitution of the United States is the core document of American government, an annotated copy is provided in Appendix A. Appendix B offers a guide to federal government documents for those who desire a map through the complex world of national government publishing. Appendix C is a guide to statistical information on American government for those who would seek numerical data on any aspect of national, state, or local government. Appendix D is a brief review of the on-line data bases appropriate for research on American government and politics. Finally, Appendix E is the Key Concept List of the major concepts in the dictionary for each distinct area of American governance.

A

AAA *See* AGRICULTURAL ADJUSTMENT ADMINISTRATION.

ABA *See* AMERICAN BAR ASSOCIATION.

abdication **1** Historically, renunciation of a hereditary office; in recent decades, a voluntary resignation from high public office. For example, it has been said that Richard M. Nixon abdicated when he resigned as president of the United States in 1974. **2** The giving up of a public office by ceasing to perform its function rather than by formally resigning.

ability to pay **1** The principle of taxation that holds that the tax burden should be distributed according to a person's wealth. It is based on the assumption that, as a person's income increases, the person (whether an individual or a corporation) can and should contribute a larger percentage of income to support government activities. The progressive income tax is based on the ability-to-pay principle. **2** A concept from labor relations and collective bargaining that refers to an employer's ability to tolerate the costs of requested wage and benefit increases.
REFERENCE
1 For the first major analysis, see Adam Smith, *Wealth of Nations* (1776), book 5, chapter 2, part 2.

Abington School District v Schempp *See* SCHOOL DISTRICT OF ABINGTON TOWNSHIP V SCHEMPP.

Ableman v Booth 21 Howard 506 (1859) The U.S. Supreme Court case that held that a prisoner in federal custody could not be released by a writ of habeas corpus issued by a state court. This case helped establish the independence of the state and federal courts from each other by asserting that no judicial process can have any authority outside its own jurisdiction.

ABM Antiballistic missile; a missile designed to shoot down incoming missiles. In 1972 the United States signed an ABM treaty with the Soviet Union limiting ABM deployments. A 1974 protocol to the treaty restricts both sides to one ABM site each. The Soviets have deployed an ABM system around Moscow. The United States has yet to deploy an ABM system. However, President Reagan's STRATEGIC DEFENSE INITIATIVE seems to call for what amounts to ABMs in space. While the ABM treaty specifically limits "space-based" systems, it has, been contended by the Reagan administration that research and testing of exotic weapons (such as lasers) is allowed by the treaty. This has proved controversial because many members of the Senate feel that the treaty is unambiguous when it states that: "Each party undertakes not to develop, test, or deploy ABM systems or components which are sea-based, air-based, space-based, or mobile land-based."
REFERENCES
Abram Chayes and Antonia Handler Chayes, Testing and development of "exotic" systems under the ABM treaty: The great reinterpretation caper, *Harvard Law Review* 99 (June 1986);
Kevin C. Kennedy, Treaty interpretation by the executive branch: The ABM treaty and "Star Wars" testing and development, *American Journal of International Law* 80 (October 1986);
Alan B. Sherr, Sound legal reasoning or policy expedient? The "new interpretation" of the ABM treaty, *International Security* 11 (Winter 1986–87).

Abood v Detroit Board of Education *See* AGENCY SHOP.

abortion decision *See* ROE V WADE.

Abrams v United States 250 U.S. 616 (1919) The U.S. Supreme Court case that upheld the federal government's authority, under the Sedition Act of 1918, to restrict the circulation of pamphlets, during World War I, calling for munitions workers to strike. In doing this, the Court invoked the "bad tendency" rule, which holds that free speech and other First Amendment rights can be curtailed if their exercise might lead to such evils as sedition, riots, or rebellion. In a famous dissenting opinion, Justice Oliver Wendell Holmes, Jr., argued for the "free trade of ideas." It was in a previous decision, *Schenck v United States*, 249 U.S. 47 (1919), that Holmes, speaking for a unanimous Court, enunciated his famous CLEAR AND PRESENT DANGER doctrine. *Compare to* GITLOW V NEW YORK.

abrogation 1 The repeal of a law. 2 The termination of an agreement by the mutual consent of the parties involved. 3 The unilateral termination of a formal agreement. The founders of the United States abrogated their formal ties to England when they stated in the Declaration of Independence "that these United Colonies are, and of right ought to be free and independent states; that they are absolved from all allegiance to the British Crown, and that all political connection between them and the State of Great Britain, is and ought to be totally dissolved."
REFERENCE
Charles F. Wilkinson and John M. Volkman, Judicial review of Indian treaty abrogation: "As long as water flows, or grass grows upon the earth"—how long a time is that? *California Law Review* 63 (May 1975).

Abscam The 1979 FBI undercover operation (the scam) that had agents pose as Arab businessmen (the Ab) seeking to purchase favors unlawfully from U.S. congressmen. Six U.S. congressmen and one senator were convicted of accepting bribes and were sentenced to federal prison. *Compare to* ENTRAPMENT.
REFERENCES
James Q. Wilson, The changing FBI: The road to Abscam, *Public Interest* 59 (Spring 1980);
Bennett L. Gershman, Abscam, the judiciary, and the ethics of entrapment, *Yale Law Journal* 91 (July 1982);

Gerald M. Caplan, ed., *Abscam Ethics: Moral Issues and Deception in Law Enforcement* (Cambridge, MA: Ballinger, 1983).

absentee ballot *See* BALLOT, ABSENTEE.

absolute advantage An international trade concept, formulated by Adam Smith (1723–1790), that holds that one nation has an absolute advantage over another when it can produce more of a product than another can, using the same amount of resources. *Compare to* COMPARATIVE ADVANTAGE.
REFERENCE
Glenn M. MacDonald and James R. Markusen, A rehabilitation of absolute advantage, *Journal of Political Economy* 93 (April 1985).

absolute majority More than 50 percent of those eligible to vote, no matter how many of the potential voters are attending or voting. An absolute majority of one hundred potential voters, as in the U.S. Senate, is fifty-one.

absolute veto *See* VETO, ABSOLUTE.

absolutism A government with no limits to its power and under which the people have no guaranteed or constitutional rights. The concept was originally applied to the absolute monarchs of eighteenth-century Europe. *Compare to* AUTOCRACY; DICTATOR.

abstention 1 The policy of the federal courts of withholding jurisdiction, even though it may lawfully be claimed, until a state court has rendered judgment of those aspects of state law that bear on the case. *Compare to* COMITY. 2 Refraining to vote when one is entitled to do so.
REFERENCES
1 Martin H. Redish, Abstention, separation of powers, and the limits of the judicial function, *Yale Law Journal* 94 (November 1984).
2 William V. Gehrlein and Peter C. Fishburn, Effects of abstentions on voting procedures in three candidate elections, *Behavioral Science* 24 (September 1979);
Charles L. Davis and Kenneth M. Coleman, Who abstains? The situational

meaning of nonvoting, *Social Science Quarterly* 64 (December 1983).

abuse **1** The use of an existing authority for purposes that extend beyond or even contradict the intentions of the grantors of that authority. **2** The furnishing of excessive services to beneficiaries of government programs, violating program regulations, or performing improper practices, none of which involves prosecutable fraud. Fraud, a more serious offense, is the obtaining of something of value by unlawful means through willful misrepresentation.

REFERENCES

Amitai Etzioni, The fight against fraud and abuse: Analyzing constituent support, *Journal of Policy Analysis and Management* 2 (Fall 1982);

John D. Young, Reflections on the root causes of fraud, abuse, and waste in federal social programs, *Public Administration Review* 43 (July/August 1983);

Richard P. Kusserow, Fighting fraud, waste, and abuse, *Bureaucrat* 12 (Fall 1983);

Henry N. Pontell, Paul D. Jesilow, and Gilbert Geis, Practitioner fraud and abuse in medical benefit programs: Government regulation and professional white-collar crime, *Law and Policy* 6 (October 1984).

abuser fees Additional taxes on tobacco products or alcoholic beverages justified on basis that abusers of these products, in consequence of their abuse, use a disproportionate share of the nation's health care resources.

Academy of Political Science A nonpartisan organization founded in 1880 to promote the understanding of political science and its application to government, political, social, economic, and related problems; publishes the *Political Science Quarterly*.

Academy of Political Science
2852 Broadway
New York, NY 10025
(212) 866-6752

access **1** The ability to gain the attention and to influence the decisions of key political agents. Political party leaders, the heads of ma-

After deputy chief of staff Michael Deaver left the Reagan administration, he came under fire for abusing his access to the White House on behalf of foreign governments.

jor interest groups, and those who make large campaign contributions are typically said to have access. **2** Lobbying; getting information to key decision makers at critical times. This concept was extensively developed by DAVID B. TRUMAN.

acclamation Overwhelming approval by voice vote. At a political convention, when it becomes obvious that a particular candidate will win a nomination, it is often suggested that the nomination be approved by acclamation to create the appearance of party unity and to generate a sense of total enthusiasm.

accord **1** An informal diplomatic understanding. **2** An agreement reached by two previously conflicting parties (such as labor and management). **3** An agreement by one side to pay, and another side to accept, less than full payment for a debt or obligation.

accountability **1** The extent to which one must answer to higher authority—legal or organizational—for one's actions in society at large or within one's particular organizational position. Elected public officials are theoretically accountable to the political sovereignty of the voters. In this sense, appointed officials—from file clerks to cabinet secretaries—are less accountable than elected officials. The former are accountable mainly to their organizational supervisors, while the latter must answer to the people of their jurisdiction. **2** An obligation for keeping accurate records of property, documents, or funds. *See also* ADMINISTRATIVE ACCOUNTABILITY; BARR V MATTEO; BUTZ V ECONOMOU; SMITH V WADE; SPALDING V VILAS; WOOD V STRICKLAND.
REFERENCES
Bernard Rosen, *Holding Government Bureaucracies Accountable* (New York: Praeger, 1982);
Henry W. Chappell, Jr., and William R. Keech, A new view of political accountability for economic performance, *American Political Science Review* 79 (March 1985);
Bert A. Rockman, The modern presidency and theories of accountability: Old wine *and* old bottles, *Congress and the Presidency* 13 (Autumn 1986).

acid rain Rainfall contaminated by industrial pollution. Such rain, because of its acidity, adversely affects inland aquatic life and forests. Since the pollutants causing acid rain come from one place and the rain itself falls on another, this has become an important interregional and international environmental issue. Acid rain is an especially contentious problem between the United States and Canada.
REFERENCES
Jeffrey Maclure, North American acid rain and international law, *Fletcher Forum* 7 (Winter 1983);
Jon R. Luoma, *Troubled Skies, Troubled Waters: The Story of Acid Rain* (New York: Viking, 1984);
James L. Regens, The political economy of acid rain, *Publius* 15 (Summer 1985).

ACIR *See* ADVISORY COMMISSION ON INTERGOVERNMENTAL RELATIONS.

ACLU *See* AMERICAN CIVIL LIBERTIES UNION.

acquittal The judgment of a court, based on the verdict of either a jury or a judge, that a defendant is not guilty of the offense that was charged. *See* DOUBLE JEOPARDY.

act **1** A written BILL formally passed by a legislature, such as the U.S. Congress, and signed by an executive, such as the U.S. president. An act is a bill from its introduction until its passage by a legislature. An act becomes a law, becomes a formal statute, when it is signed by (or passed over the veto of) a chief executive, such as the U.S. president. **2** A bill that has been passed by only one house of a legislature.

acting Temporary. For example, someone might be the acting director of a government agency. Acting appointments are sometimes automatic, as when a lieutenant governor is the acting governor whenever the elected governor leaves the state.

ACTION The federal agency, created by the Domestic Volunteer Service Act of 1973, that coordinates and administers all domestic volunteer activities sponsored by the federal gov-

A senior citizen reads to schoolchildren under ACTION's Foster Grandparent Program.

ernment. ACTION is the administrative home of Volunteers in Service to America (VISTA), the Foster Grandparent Program, the Retired Senior Volunteer Program (RSVP), and related programs. While ACTION is correctly written with all capital letters, it is not an acronym— just a matter of federal government style. *Compare to* PEACE CORPS.

ACTION
806 Connecticut Avenue, N.W.
Washington, D.C. 20525
(202) 634-9380

actionable   Something that provides adequate reason for a grievance or lawsuit.

activism   *See* JUDICIAL ACTIVISM.

activist   **1** One who is seriously and passionately involved in politics by running for office, mobilizing support for issues, participating in campaigns, and so on.   **2** One who is so impatient with the normal or existing processes of political change that he or she resorts to more active methods, such as street demonstrations or sit-ins. Activists subscribe to the philosophy of Oliver Wendell Holmes, Jr., (1841–1935) which states that: "Life is action and passion. I think it is required of a man that he should share the action and passion of his time at peril of being judged not to have lived."
REFERENCES
1   Ronald B. Rapoport, Alan I. Abramowitz, and John McGlennon, eds., *The Life of the Parties: Activists in Presidential Politics* (Lexington: University Press of Kentucky, 1986).

2   Harry Boyte, Citizen activists in the public interest, *Social Policy* 10 (November/December 1979);
Stephen D. Shaffer, The policy biases of political activists, *American Politics Quarterly* 8 (January 1980).

act of Congress   A statute; a law passed by the U.S. Congress and signed (or passed over the veto of) the president. All of the acts passed by the Congress are published, in chronological order according to term and session of Congress in the *U.S. Statutes-at-Large*. The statutes are organized by subject in the *U.S. Code*.

act of state doctrine   The judicial policy that a court in one nation should not rule on the legality of the internal acts of a foreign country.
REFERENCES
Robert Delson, The act of state doctrine: Judicial deference or abstention? *American Journal of International Law* 66 (January 1972);
Michael J. Bazyler, Abolishing the act of state doctrine, *University of Pennsylvania Law Review* 134 (January 1986).

ADA   *See*   AMERICANS   FOR   DEMOCRATIC   ACTION.

Adams, Herbert Baxter (1850–1901)   The American historian who, after study in Germany, returned to the United States in 1876 to teach at the Johns Hopkins University and who helped revolutionize higher education with his introduction of the seminar method and his "germ theory of politics," which sought to trace American political institutions back to their roots in ancient Anglo-Saxon villages. Along with JOHN W. BURGESS at Columbia University, Adams stressed the historical-comparative approach, which called for scholars to use original sources. Adams, who viewed political science as just contemporary history, was a significant mentor and influence on the first generation of American doctoral candidates. Among his students were Woodrow Wilson, John Dewey, Thorstein Veblen, and Frederick Jackson Turner.

Adams, John

REFERENCE

Bert James Loewenberg, *American History in American Thought* (New York: Simon & Schuster, 1972), chapter 19, "Herbert Baxter Adams and American Historical Craftsmanship."

Adams, John (1735–1826) The first vice president (1789–1797) and the second president (1797–1801) of the United States. Adams, the lawyer who defended the British soldiers responsible for the Boston Massacre, represented Massachusetts in the Continental Congress. He was a major influence in the appointment of George Washington as the commander of the revolutionary forces, because he felt it was essential for national unity that the war, at first fought mainly in New England, actively involve all the colonies—especially Virginia.

Although Thomas Jefferson drafted the Declaration of Independence, many of its principles were formulated by Adams; and it was Adams who led the fight for its adoption by the Continental Congress. On July 3, 1776, Adams wrote to his wife:

> The second day of July, 1776, will be the most memorable epoch in the history of America. I am apt to believe that it will be celebrated by succeeding generations as the great anniversary festival. It ought to be commemorated as the day of deliverance, by solemn acts of devotion to God Almighty. It ought to be solemnized with pomp and parade, with shows, games, sports, guns, bells, bonfires, and illuminations, from one end of this continent to the other, from this time forward for evermore.

Nevertheless, Independence Day has been celebrated on July 4, because that was the day the final draft of the Declaration of Independence was approved.

Adams failed to win reelection to a second presidential term largely because of the controversy over the ALIEN AND SEDITION LAWS. His replacement by Thomas Jefferson is often hailed as the "real" American Revolution, because it was the first major instance of a party in power (the Federalists) peacefully yielding government control to its political opposition (the Democratic-Republicans). Adams's defeat also marks the beginning of a viable two-party

John Adams.

system in the United States. John Adams is the only president of the United States whose son became president: John Quincy Adams (1767–1848) was elected president in 1824.

REFERENCES

Catherine Drinker Bowen, *John Adams* (Boston: Little, Brown, 1950);

J. M. Porter and Stewart Farnell, John Adams and American constitutionalism, *American Journal of Jurisprudence* 21 (1976);

Harry C. Thomson, The second place in Rome: John Adams as vice-president, *Presidential Studies Quarterly* 10 (Spring 1980).

Adderly v Florida 385 U.S. 39 (1966) The U.S. Supreme Court case that upheld the authority of a state to restrict public demonstrations on the grounds of a county jail. The Court held that "nothing in the Constitution of the United States prevented Florida from even handed enforcement of its general trespass statute against those refusing to obey the sheriff's order to remove themselves from what amounted to the curtilage of the jailhouse." *Compare to* HAGUE V CIO.

ADEA *See* AGE DISCRIMINATION IN EMPLOYMENT ACT OF 1967.

ad hoc   A Latin term meaning temporarily; for this one time. It is sometimes used to criticize methods that substitute for standard procedures.

ad hoc committee   A committee created by the Speaker of the House of Representatives for a specific task or purpose, whose existence ceases with the attainment of its goal, and whose members are drawn from the several House committees having jurisdictional claims over the issue or question involved.

REFERENCE

David J. Vogler, Ad hoc committees in the House of Representatives and purposive models of legislative behavior, *Polity* 14 (Fall 1981).

ad hocracy   Alvin Toffler's term, in *Future Shock* (New York: Random House, 1970), for "the fast-moving, information-rich, kinetic organization of the future, filled with transient cells and extremely mobile individuals." Ad hocracy is a contraction of ad hoc (Latin term meaning to this; temporary) and bureaucracy.

REFERENCES

George A. Miller, Beyond ad-hocracy, *Pacific Sociological Review* 20 (January 1977);

Henry Mintzberg and Alexandra McHugh, Strategy formation in an adhocracy, *Administrative Science Quarterly* 30 (June 1985).

ad interim   A Latin term meaning in the meantime. A public official is ad interim when serving the unexpired term of a predecessor (who has died, resigned, or been removed) until a permanent official can be appointed or elected.

adjournment   The putting off of business to another time or place; the decision of a court, legislature, or other group to stop meeting either temporarily or permanently.

adjournment sine die   The adjournment of a legislature that does not fix a day for reconvening. (Sine die is a Latin term meaning without a day.) It is used to indicate the final adjournment of a session of the Congress or of a state legislature.

adjournment to a day certain   Legislative adjournment under a motion or resolution fixing the date for a next meeting. Neither house of the U.S. Congress can adjourn for more than three days without the concurrence of the other. *Compare to* RECESS.

adjudication   1 The resolution of a dispute by means of judicial or quasi-judicial proceedings in which the parties are able to present evidence and reasoned arguments.   2 The formal pronouncing and recording of the decision of a court or quasi-judicial entity.

REFERENCE

1   Meir Dan-Cohen, Bureaucratic organizations and the theory of adjudication, *Columbia Law Review* 85 (January 1985).

adjusted gross income   An income tax term referring, in general, to the money a person earns minus allowable deductions for certain expenses for travel, work, business, moving, and so on.

adjustment assistance   Federal financial and technical assistance for firms, workers, and communities to help them adjust to competition from imported products. Qualified workers adversely affected by imports can receive special unemployment compensation, retraining to develop new skills, and job search and relocation assistance; affected firms can receive technical assistance and loan guarantees to finance their modernization or shift to other product lines; and communities threatened by expanding imports can receive loans and other assistance to attract new industry or to enable existing plants to move into more competitive fields.

REFERENCES

Harold R. Williams, US trade adjustment assistance to mitigate injury from import competition, *American Journal of Economics and Sociology* 36 (October 1977);

C. Michael Aho and Thomas A. Bayard, American trade adjustment assistance after five years, *World Economy* 3 (November 1980);

James A. Dorn, Trade adjustment assistance: A case of government failure, *Cato Journal* 2 (Winter 1982).

For a comparative perspective, see Leslie Stein, Trade adjustment assistance as a means of achieving improved resource allocation through freer trade: An analysis of policies for aiding the import-injured in the U.S., Canada, and Australia, *American Journal of Economics and Sociology* 41 (July 1982).

Adkins v Children's Hospital See WEST COAST HOTEL V PARRISH.

administered prices Prices determined by other than market forces, such as those set by monopolies, cartels, or governments.

administration 1 The management and direction of the affairs of governments and institutions. 2 A collective term for all policymaking officials of a government. 3 The execution and implementation of public policy. 4 The time in office of a chief executive such as a president, governor, or mayor. Thus the Carter administration refers to those years (1977–1981) when Jimmy Carter was president of the United States. 5 The supervision of the estate of a dead person to pay taxes and assign assets to heirs. *Compare to* PUBLIC ADMINISTRATION.

REFERENCE

A. Dunsire, *Administration: The Word and the Science* (New York: Halsted, Wiley, 1973).

Administration & Society A quarterly published since 1969 that seeks to further the understanding of public and human service organizations, their administrative processes, and their impacts upon the larger society. Library of Congress no. JA3. J65.

Administration & Society
275 South Beverly Drive
Beverly Hills, CA 90212

administration of justice The management of the law enforcement, judicial, and correctional aspects of each level of government. The phrase most often refers to the total criminal justice system.

REFERENCE

J. Norman Swaton and Loren Morgan, *Administration of Justice: An Introduction*, 2d ed. (New York: Van Nostrand, 1980).

administrative accountability That aspect of administrative responsibility by which officials are held answerable for general notions of democracy and morality as well as for specific legal mandates. The two basic approaches to administrative accountability were first delineated by Carl J. Friedrich (1901–1984) and Herman Finer (1898–1969). Friedrich argued that administrative responsibility can be assured only internally, through professionalism or professional standards or codes, because the increasing complexities of modern policies require extensive policy expertise and specialized abilities on the part of bureaucrats. Finer, on the other hand, argued that administrative responsibility could be maintained only externally, through legislative or popular controls, because internal power or control would ultimately lead to corruption. *See also* ACCOUNTABILITY; ETHICS.

REFERENCES

Carl J. Friedrich, The nature of administrative responsibility, in *Public Policy,* ed. Carl J. Friedrich (Cambridge, MA: Harvard University Press, 1940);

Herman Finer, Administrative responsibility in democratic government, *Public Administration Review* 1 (Autumn 1941);

Ledivina V. Carino, Administrative accountability: A review of the evaluation, meaning and operationalization of a key concept in public administration, *Philippine Journal of Public Administration* 27 (January 1983);

B. B. Misra, Evolution of the concept of administrative accountability, *Indian Journal of Public Administration* 29 (July/September 1984).

administrative advocacy The presentation of alternative policies to an administrative agency. This practice recognizes that public administration is a highly political process involving significant differences of judgment. The most feasible course of action often emerges from the competition produced when each interested group pleads the cause it represents, whether that cause be more funds to carry out agency policies, the survival of a particular program, or the desire for a more efficient system of administrative decision making.

REFERENCES

Paul Davidoff, Advocacy and pluralism in planning, *Journal of the American Institute of Planners* (December 1965);

William W. Vosburgh and Drew Hyman, Advocacy and bureaucracy: The life and times of a decentralized citizen's advocacy program, *Administrative Science Quarterly* 18 (December 1973);

Nancy A. Moore, The public administrator as policy advocate, *Public Administration Review* 39 (September/October 1978);

Jeffrey M. Berry, Beyond citizen participation: Effective advocacy before administrative agencies, *Journal of Applied Behavioral Science* 17 (October/December 1981).

administrative agency 1 A government organization set up to implement a law. 2 Any civilian government body (board, bureau, department, or individual), other than a court or legislature, that deals with the rights of private parties by adjudication, rule making, investigation, prosecuting, and so on. 3 In the context of labor relations, any impartial private or government organization that oversees or facilitates the labor relations process.

Administrative Conference of the United States A permanent independent agency established by the Administrative Conference Act of 1964 that seeks to develop improvements in the legal procedures by which federal agencies administer regulatory, benefit, and other government programs. Members of the conference—agency heads, other federal officials, private lawyers, university professors, and other experts in administrative law and government—are provided with a forum in which they can conduct continuing studies of selected problems involving administrative procedures.

REFERENCE

Warner W. Gardner, The administrative conference of the United States, *Annals of the American Academy of Political and Social Science* 400 (March 1972).

Administrative Conference of the
  United States
2120 L Street, N.W.
Washington, D.C. 20037
(202) 254-7020

administrative discretion 1 The latitude that an individual bureaucrat has in interpreting and applying the law. 2 A public official's right to act in the spirit of a law in a situation not precisely covered by the law. 3 A concept from administrative law that requires that the actions of any public official be based upon specific legal authority, which establishes strict limits on official action. *Compare to* MINISTERIAL FUNCTION.

REFERENCES

Clark C. Havighurst, ed., *Administrative Discretion: Problems of Decision-Making by Governmental Agencies* (Dobbs Ferry, NY: Oceana, 1974);

Martin Shapiro, Administrative discretion: The next stage, *Yale Law Journal* 92 (July 1983);

William F. West, Structuring administrative discretion: The pursuit of rationality and responsiveness, *American Journal of Political Science* 28 (May 1984).

administrative due process Term encompassing a number of points in administrative law that require that the administrative procedures of government agencies and regulatory commissions, as they affect private parties, be based upon written guidelines that safeguard individual rights and protect against the arbitrary or inequitable exercise of government authority. *Compare to* DUE PROCESS.

administrative law 1 That branch of law concerned with the procedures by which administrative agencies make rules and adjudicate cases; the conditions under which these actions can be reviewed by courts. 2 The legislation that creates administrative agencies. 3 The rules and regulations promulgated by administrative agencies. 4 The law governing judicial review of administrative actions.

REFERENCES

Richard B. Stewart, The reformation of American administrative law, *Harvard Law Review* 88 (June 1975);

Kenneth F. Warren, *Administrative Law in the American Political System* (St. Paul, MN: West, 1982);

Richard C. Cortner, *The Bureaucracy in*

Court: Commentaries and Case Studies in Administrative Law (Port Washington, NY: Kennikat, 1982);

Lief H. Carter, Administrative Law and Politics: Cases and Comments (Boston: Little, Brown, 1983).

administrative law judge/hearing examiner/ hearing officer A government official who conducts hearings in the place of or on behalf of a more formal body, such as the National Labor Relations Board, the Merit Systems Protection Board, or the Social Security Administration.

REFERENCES

Jeffrey S. Lubbers, Federal administrative law judge: A focus on our invisible judiciary, Administrative Law Review (Winter 1981);

Daniel L. Skoler, The administrative law judiciary: Change, challenge and choices, Annals 462 (July 1982).

administrative morality The use of ethical, political, or social precepts to create standards by which the quality of public administration may be judged; in the main, the standards of honesty, responsiveness, efficiency, effectiveness, competence, effect on individual rights, adherence to democratic procedures, and social equity.

REFERENCES

Paul H. Appleby, Morality and Administration in American Government (Baton Rouge: Louisiana State University Press, 1952);

Joel L. Fleishman, Lance Liebman, and Mark H. Moore, eds., Public Duties: The Moral Obligations of Government Officials (Cambridge, MA: Harvard University Press, 1981).

administrative order A directive carrying the force of law issued by an administrative agency after adjudication.

administrative presidency Richard Nathan's descriptive term for the way President Richard M. Nixon sought to use administrative tactics (such as reorganization, decentralization, and impoundment) to assert presidential authority over the federal bureaucracy.

REFERENCES

Richard Nathan, The Plot that Failed: Nixon and the Administrative Presidency (New York: Wiley, 1975);

Richard Nathan, The administrative presidency, Public Interest 44 (Summer 1976).

Administrative Procedure Act of 1946 (APA) The basic law governing the way federal government agencies operate to safeguard agency clients and the general public. The APA specifies the conditions under which administrative agencies (1) publicize information about their operations; (2) make rules; (3) engage in adjudication; and (4) are subject to judicial review. Major amendments to the APA include the FREEDOM OF INFORMATION ACT OF 1966, the PRIVACY ACT OF 1974, and the Sunshine Act of 1976 (see SUNSHINE LAWS).

REFERENCES

Kenneth C. Davis, Revising the Administrative Procedure Act, Administrative Law Review 29 (Winter 1977);

Thomas R. Folk, The Administrative Procedure Act and the military departments, Military Law Review 108 (Spring 1985).

administrative remedy A means of enforcing a right by going to an administrative agency either for help or for a decision. People are often required to "exhaust all administrative remedies" by submitting their problems to the proper agency before taking their cases to court.

administrative reorganization See REORGANIZATION.

administrator 1 A manager. 2 The head of a government agency. 3 Someone appointed by a court to handle a deceased person's estate. 4 Anyone with a FIDUCIARY responsibility.

admiralty 1 Maritime law; the general laws of the sea as modified by the Congress and applicable on both the high seas and internal navigable waters. Article III, Section 2, of the U.S. Constitution provides that the federal courts will have exclusive jurisdiction in all cases of admiralty law. 2 A court that handles maritime cases, such as collisions at sea.

REFERENCES
Grant Gilmore and Charles L. Black, Jr., *The Law of Admiralty* (Mineola, NY: Foundation, 1975);
Gordon W. Paulsen, An historical overview of the development of uniformity in international maritime law, *Tulane Law Review* 57 (June 1983).

admonition of rights *See* MIRANDA RIGHTS.

ADO *See* ALLEGED DISCRIMINATORY OFFICIAL.

ad valorem tax *See* TAX BASE.

advance appropriation *See* APPROPRIATION, ADVANCE.

advance funding Budget authority provided in an appropriation act to obligate and disburse funds during a fiscal year from a succeeding year's appropriation.

advance man/advance woman A person who travels to a location in advance of a political candidate to arrange for campaign appearances, hotels, rental cars, publicity, and so on.

REFERENCE
Jerry Bruno and Jeff Greenfield, *The Advance Man* (New York: Morrow, 1971).

adversary proceeding Any formal hearing, trial, or legal contest in which both sides are appropriately represented and challenge each other's view of fact or law before an impartial decision maker or jury.

adversary system The Anglo-American system of law, in which a judge or jury acts as an impartial decision maker between opposite sides, each of which has an opportunity to prove its assertion of guilt or innocence. The adversary system contrasts with the inquisitional system, in which accused parties must exonerate themselves before a judge (or judges), who function as both judge and public prosecutor.

REFERENCES
Anne Strick, What's wrong with the adversary system: Paranoia, hatred, and suspicion, *Washington Monthly* 8 (January 1977);
Arthur R. Miller, The adversary system: Dinosaur or phoenix? *Minnesota Law Review* 69 (October 1984).

adverse action 1 An act against someone else's interests. 2 A personnel action unfavorable to an employee, such as discharge, suspension, or demotion. 3 A use of land that harms local property values, such as putting a gas station or a prison on land zoned for and occupied by single-family homes.

advice and consent The right of the U.S. Senate (provided for in Article II, Section 2 of the Constitution) to review treaties and major presidential appointments; for these to take effect they must be approved by two-thirds of the senators present or a simple majority, respectively. While much is made of the Senate's right to confirm designated presidential appointees, it is only on the rarest occasion that a nominee is rejected. (More often, a controversial nomination is withdrawn.) For example, during 1983–1984, President Ronald Reagan nominated 97,893 individuals for various offices. Over 99 percent (97,262) were confirmed, a typical rate. Historically, rejections have been based far more on questions of qualifications and scandals in the nominee's past than on disapproval of the nominee's political, judicial, or managerial philosophy. This attitude on the part of the Senate has had the effect of giving the president a relatively free hand in appointments. President Ronald Reagan used this freedom to great effect in getting through the Senate many appointees to federal judgeships whose political philosophy can reasonably be said to be outside the mainstream of American political thought.

REFERENCES
For evidence of how the Reagan administration has reshaped the federal bench, see Sheldon Goldman, Reorganizing the judiciary: The first-term appointments, *Judicature* 68 (April/May 1985).
Also see Joseph Pratt Harris, *The Advice and Consent of the Senate: A Study of the Confirmation of Appointments by the United States Senate* (New York: Greenwood, 1953, 1968);

Advisory Commission on Intergovernmental Relations (ACIR)

William F. Swindler, The politics of "advice and consent," *American Bar Association Journal* 56 (June 1970).

Advisory Commission on Intergovernmental Relations (ACIR) The federal commission created by the U.S. Congress in 1959 to monitor the operation of the federal system and to recommend improvements. The ACIR is a permanent national bipartisan body composed of twenty-six members, who serve two-year terms and are representative of the federal, state, and local governments and the public. As a continuing body, the commission approaches its work by addressing itself to specific issues and problems, the resolution of which would improve cooperation among the levels of government and the functioning of the federal system. One of the long-range efforts of the commission has been to seek ways to improve federal, state, and local government taxing practices and policies to achieve equitable allocation of resources, increased efficiency in collection and administration, and reduced compliance burdens upon the taxpayers.

REFERENCES

Maurice E. White, ACIR's model state legislation for strengthening local government financial management, *Governmental Finance* 8 (December 1979);

Samuel K. Gove, J. Fred Giertz, and James W. Fossett, ACIR: A mixed review, *Publius* 14 (Summer 1984).

Advisory Commission on Intergovernmental Relations
1111 20th Street, N.W.
Washington, D.C. 20575
(202) 653-5640

advisory opinion *See* OPINION, ADVISORY.

advocacy, administrative *See* ADMINISTRATIVE ADVOCACY.

AEI *See* AMERICAN ENTERPRISE INSTITUTE FOR PUBLIC POLICY RESEARCH.

AFDC *See* AID TO FAMILIES WITH DEPENDENT CHILDREN.

affidavit A written statement made under oath before a person permitted by law to ad-minister such an oath (a notary public, for example). Such statements are frequently used in legal proceedings, labor arbitrations, and other formal hearings.

affirmative action A term that first gained currency in the 1960s, when it meant the removal of "artificial barriers" to the employment of women and minority group members. Toward the end of that decade, however, the term was altered to mean compensatory opportunities for hitherto disadvantaged groups. In a formal, legal sense, affirmative action now refers to specific efforts to recruit, hire, and promote disadvantaged groups for the purpose of eliminating the present effects of past discrimination. *See also* EQUAL EMPLOYMENT OPPORTUNITY; REGENTS OF THE UNIVERSITY OF CALIFORNIA V ALLAN BAKKE; REVERSE DISCRIMINATION; RIGHTFUL PLACE; TITLE VII; UNITED STEELWORKERS OF AMERICA V WEBER ET AL; WYGANT V JACKSON BOARD OF EDUCATION.

REFERENCES

Paul J. Mishkin, The uses of ambivalence: Reflections on the Supreme Court and the constitutionality of affirmative action, *University of Pennsylvania Law Review* 131 (March 1983);

Nelson C. Dometrius and Lee Sigelman, Assessing progress toward affirmative action goals in state and local government: A new benchmark, *Public Administration Review* 44 (May/June 1984);

David H. Rosenbloom, The declining salience of affirmative action in federal personnel management, *Review of Public Personnel Administration* 4 (Summer 1984);

Cardell K. Jacobson, Resistance to affirmative action: Self-interest or racism? *Journal of Conflict Resolution* 29 (June 1985).

affirmative action plan An organization's written plan to remedy past discrimination against, or underutilization of, women and minorities. The plan itself usually consists of a statement of goals, timetables for achieving them, and specific program efforts.

affirmative action groups/protected groups Segments of the population that have been identified by federal, state, or local laws to be specifically protected from employment discrimination. Such groups include women, identified minorities, the elderly, and the handicapped.

affirmative gerrymandering *See* GERRYMANDERING, AFFIRMATIVE.

affirmative zoning *See* ZONING, AFFIRMATIVE.

AFGE *See* AMERICAN FEDERATION OF GOVERNMENT EMPLOYEES.

AFL-CIO *See* AMERICAN FEDERATION OF LABOR-CONGRESS OF INDUSTRIAL ORGANIZATIONS.

Afroyim v Rusk 387 U.S. 253 (1967) The U.S. Supreme Court case that held unconstitutional a portion of the Nationality Act of 1940, under which U.S. citizens would forfeit their citizenship by voting in a foreign election. This reversed *Perez v Brownell*, 356 U.S. 44 (1958), which held that certain acts in a foreign country could cause automatic forfeiture of U.S. citizenship. In *Afroyim*, the Court held that a citizen has a constitutional right to remain a citizen unless that right is specifically relinquished.
REFERENCES
Donald K. Duvall, Expatriation under United States law, *Perez* to *Afroyim:* The search for a philosophy of American citizenship, *Virginia Law Review* 56 (April 1970);
P. Allen Dionisopoulos, *Afroyim v Rusk:* The evolution, uncertainty and implications of a constitutional principle, *Minnesota Law Review* 55 (December 1970).

AFSCME *See* AMERICAN FEDERATION OF STATE, COUNTY AND MUNICIPAL EMPLOYEES.

Age Discrimination Act of 1975 The act barring discrimination because of age in all federally assisted programs. Structurally unrelated to the Age Discrimination in Employment Act of 1967, the 1975 act covers any enterprise or activity that receives federal monies.

Age Discrimination in Employment Act of 1967 (ADEA) The act, as amended, that prohibits employment discrimination on the basis of age and (with certain exceptions) mandatory retirement. The law applies to all public employers, private employers of twenty or more employees, employment agencies serving covered employers, and labor unions of more than twenty-five members. The ADEA prohibits help-wanted advertisements that indicate preference, limitation, specification, or discrimination based on age. For example, terms such as "girl" and "35–55" may not be used because they indicate the exclusion of qualified applicants based on age. Many states also have age discrimination laws or provisions in their fair employment practices laws. Some of these laws parallel the federal law and have no upper limit in protections against age discrimination in employment; others protect workers until they reach sixty, sixty-five, or seventy years of age. *See also* EQUAL EMPLOYMENT OPPORTUNITY COMMISSION V WYOMING.
REFERENCES
Cynthia E. Gitt, The 1978 amendments to the Age Discrimination in Employment Act—A legal overview, *Marquette Law Review* 64 (Summer 1981);
Michael H. Schuster and Christopher S. Miller, Performance appraisal and the Age Discrimination in Employment Act, *Personnel Administrator* 29 (March 1984);
Michael H. Schuster and Christopher S. Miller, An empirical assessment of the Age Discrimination in Employment Act, *Industrial and Labor Relations Review* 38 (October 1984).

agency 1 Any department, office, commission, authority, administration, board, government-owned corporation, or other independent establishment of any branch of government in the United States. **2** A formal relation whereby one person is authorized to act for another.

Agency for International Development (AID) A unit of the U.S. International Development Cooperation Agency that is authorized by the Foreign Assistance Act of 1961 to carry out assistance programs designed to help the people of certain less-developed countries develop their human and economic resources, increase their productive capacities, and improve their quality of life. AID was a part of the U.S. Department of State until 1979.

Agency for International Development
320 21st Street, N.W.
Washington, D.C. 20523
(202) 647-1850

agency mission Responsibility assigned to a specific agency and its components, in terms of the purpose served.

agency shop A union security provision, found in some collective bargaining agreements, that requires that nonunion employees of the bargaining unit must pay for the union's representational services as a condition of continuing employment. The agency shop was designed as a compromise between the union's desire to eliminate free riders by means of compulsory membership (the union shop) and management's wish that union membership be voluntary. Its constitutionality was upheld by the U.S. Supreme Court in *Abood v Detroit Board of Education,* 431 U.S. 209 (1977). Later, in *Chicago Teachers Union v Hudson,* 89 L. Ed. 2d 232 (1986), the Court held against making nonmembers of the union pay for union activities other than representation.

REFERENCES
For legal analyses, see Raymond N. Palombo, The agency shop in a public service merit system, *Labor Law Journal* 26 (July 1975);
Charles M. Rehmus and Benjamin A. Kerner, The agency shop after *Abood:* No free ride, but what's the fare? *Industrial and Labor Relations Review* 34 (October 1980).

agenda setting 1 The process of deciding what issues will be considered at a formal meeting. 2 The process by which ideas or issues bubble up through the various political processes to wind up on the agenda of a political institution, such as a legislature or court. The process makes extensive use of the mass media to take a relatively unknown or unsupported issue and, through publicity, expand the numbers who care about the issue so an institution, whether it be city hall or the U.S. Congress, is forced to take some action.

REFERENCES
2 Roger W. Cobb and Charles D. Elder, *Participation in American Politics: The Dynamics of Agenda-Building* (Boston: Allyn and Bacon, 1972);
Donald L. Shaw and Maxwell E. McCombs, *The Emergence of American Political Issues: The Agenda Setting Function of the Press* (St. Paul, MN: West, 1977);
Shanto Iyengar, Television news and issue salience: A reexamination of the agenda-setting hypothesis, *American Politics Quarterly* 7 (October 1979);
James P. Winter and Chaim H. Eyal, Agenda setting for the civil rights issue, *Public Opinion Quarterly* 45 (Fall 1981);
John Kingdon, *Agendas, Alternatives and Public Policies* (Boston: Little, Brown, 1984).

agent 1 A person authorized to act on behalf of another, such as a bargaining agent or a business agent. 2 In intelligence usage, a person who is recruited, trained, controlled, and employed to obtain and report information.

agent provocateur A French term for a person hired by an organization or country to create trouble for the opposition by inducing the members of rival organizations to do things that are contrary to their interests.

aggression The unprovoked attack by one nation on another. But what one nation may see as unprovoked another may view as justifiable retaliation. Ultimately, each nation defines aggression in its own interest.

REFERENCES
Benjamin B. Feencz, Defining aggression— The last mile, *Columbia Journal of Transnational Law* 12:3 (1973);
Vernon Cassin, Whitney Debevoise, Howard Kailes, and Terence W. Thompson, The definition of aggression, *Harvard International Law Journal* 16 (Summer 1975).

Agnew, Spiro T. (1918–   ) President Richard M. Nixon's vice president from 1969 to 1973. Agnew resigned amid charges that he accepted bribes while previously serving as Governor of Maryland. He pleaded NOLO CONTENDERE to related income tax violations and was found guilty.

REFERENCES

For Agnew's version of events, see Spiro T. Agnew, *Go Quietly . . . Or Else* (New York: Morrow, 1980).

For a more objective view, see Richard M. Cohen and Jules Witcover, *A Heartbeat Away: The Investigation and Resignation of Vice President Spiro T. Agnew* (New York: Viking, 1974).

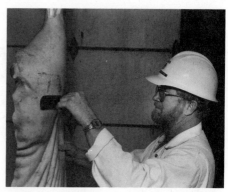

A USDA meat inspector stamps a condemned carcass.

Agricultural Adjustment Administration (AAA) The New Deal agency created in 1933 by the Agricultural Adjustment Act to stabilize farm income by providing price supports in return for limitations on crop production. The agency's enabling legislation was first held unconstitutional by the U.S. Supreme Court in *United States v Butler,* 297 U.S. 1 (1936), because it inappropriately used the federal government's power to tax. But a rewritten act in 1938 was upheld by the Court in *Mulford v Smith,* 307 U.S. 38 (1939), as a valid use of the commerce power. In 1942 the AAA was folded into the Department of Agriculture. *See also* PARITY, FARM.

REFERENCES

John L. Shover, Populism in the nineteen-thirties: The battle for the AAA, *Agricultural History* 39:1 (1965);

Van L. Perkins, *Crisis in Agriculture: The Agricultural Adjustment Administration and the New Deal, 1933* (Berkeley and Los Angeles: University of California Press, 1969).

Agricultural Trade Development and Assistance Act of 1954 *See* FOOD FOR PEACE.

Agriculture, U.S. Department of (USDA) The federal department, created in 1862, that works to improve and maintain farm income, to develop and expand markets abroad for agricultural products, to enhance the environment, and to maintain U.S. production capacity by helping landowners protect the soil, water, forests, and other natural resources. The department, through inspection and grading services,

also assures that certain standards are met in the food supply.

U.S. Department of Agriculture
14th Street and Independence Avenue, S.W.
Washington, D.C. 20250
(202) 447-2791

AID *See* AGENCY FOR INTERNATIONAL DEVELOPMENT.

aide-memoire A French term for an aid to the memory; an informal summary of a diplomatic event, such as an interview, a conversation at a social gathering, or any other matter worth retaining for the files or for sharing with colleagues.

Aid to Families with Dependent Children (AFDC) The largest federal welfare program after the Food Stamp Program. Part of the Social Security Act of 1935, the Aid to Dependent Children program was expanded by 1962 amendments to the Social Security Act and renamed. AFDC provides federal funds, administered by the states, for children living with a parent or a relative who meets state standards of need. The program has been controversial because of charges that it promotes illegitimacy and encourages fathers to abandon their families so their children can become eligible for AFDC. In 1987 about 3.8 million families were receiving AFDC.

REFERENCES

Richard J. Cebula, A note on the determinants of AFDC policies, *Public Choice* 37:2 (1981);

Larry Isaac and William R. Kelly, Developmental modernization and political class struggle theories of welfare expansion: The case of the AFDC "explosion" in the states, 1960–1970, *Journal of Political and Military Sociology* 10 (Fall 1982);

Howard Chernick, Block grants for the needy: The case of AFDC, *Journal of Policy Analysis and Management* 1 (Winter 1982);

Russell L. Hanson, The "content" of welfare policy: The states and Aid to Families with Dependent Children, *Journal of Politics* 45 (August 1983).

air traffic controllers' strike The strike of the Professional Air Traffic Controllers Organization (PATCO) in 1981, which resulted in the complete destruction of their union and the dismissal of eleven thousand controllers. On July 29, 1981, 95 percent of PATCO's thirteen thousand members went on strike. In response, the U.S. government cut back scheduled flights and reduced staff at smaller airports. Then it brought supervisors and retired controllers into service and ordered military controllers to civilian stations. Finally, President Ronald Reagan addressed the nation on television. After reminding viewers that it is illegal for federal government employees to strike and that each controller signed an oath asserting that he or she would never strike, he proclaimed: "They are in violation of the law, and if they do not report for work within forty-eight hours, they have forfeited their jobs and will be terminated." Just over one thousand controllers reported back. Most thought that the president was bluffing, but he wasn't.

REFERENCES
Bernard D. Meltzer and Cass R. Sunstein, Public employee strikes, executive discretion, and the air traffic controllers, *University of Chicago Law Review* 50 (Spring 1983);

Herbert R. Northrup, The rise and demise of PATCO, *Industrial and Labor Relations Review* 37 (January 1984).

Albany Congress A 1754 meeting of delegates from seven of the American colonies. It was there that Benjamin Franklin proposed the Albany Plan of Union, which would have united the colonies in a federation. While the colonies, fearing the loss of powers inherent in a federation, rejected the plan, the meeting helped lead to the later calling of the Continental Congresses.

Albany Regency The government of New York State from 1821 to 1850, prototype of the traditional U.S. political machine. It demonstrated the benefits of a spoils system and first gave the practice of lobbying its unsavory connotations. It was organized by Martin Van Buren (who would later be president of the United States) and the New York Democrats.

REFERENCE
Robert V. Remini, The Albany regency, *New York History* 39: 4 (1958).

Albertson v Subversive Activities Control Board 382 U.S. 70 (1965) The U.S. Supreme Court case that held that the compulsory registration of members of American communist groups was self-incrimination, in violation of the Fifth Amendment. This decision invalidated a major portion of the Internal Security (McCarran) Act of 1950. The Subversive Activities Control Board, which was created by the act to monitor communist groups, individuals, and activities, was abolished in 1973. *Compare to* APTHEKER V SECRETARY OF STATE.

alderman/alderwoman 1 Title for members of some local legislatures. It comes from the Anglo-Saxon "ealdorman,"meaning an elder person. 2 A member of the upper house of a bicameral city council.

alien 1 A legal visitor or resident in a nation of which he or she is not a citizen; a citizen of one nation living in another. A resident alien is allowed permanent residence by a nation of which he or she is not a citizen. Since no nation can demand that its nationals be allowed to visit or reside in another, the laws governing aliens are domestic matters for each nation. 2 Any creature from a planet other than Earth or any earthling on another planet. *See also* AMBACH V NORWICH; CITIZENSHIP; ESPINOZA V FARAH MANUFACTURING COMPANY; EXAMINING BOARD V FLORES DE OTERO; FOLEY V CONNELIE; HAMPTON V MOW SUN WONG; ILLEGAL ALIEN; SUGARMAN V DOUGALL.

REFERENCES
1 Richard F. Hahn, Constitutional limits on the power to exclude aliens, *Columbia Law Review* 82 (June 1982);
Scott M. Martin and Robert Kogod Goldman, International legal standards relating to the rights of aliens and refugees and United States immigration law, *Human Rights Quarterly* (August 1983).

alien and sedition laws A series of 1798 laws approved by President John Adams and passed by the last federalist-controlled Congress. These laws made it a crime to criticize the federal government, made it more difficult to become a naturalized American citizen, and gave the president the power to deport undesirable aliens. They were enacted to quiet the pro-French activities of the Jeffersonian Republicans and were repealed after Thomas Jefferson and his party took control of both the Congress and the presidency in 1801.

REFERENCES
James Morton Smith, *Freedom's Fetters: The Alien and Sedition Laws and American Civil Liberties* (Ithaca, NY: Cornell University Press, 1956, 1966);
John D. Stevens, Congressional history of the 1798 sedition law, *Journalism Quarterly* 43:2 (1966);
Alan J. Farber, Reflections on the Sedition Act of 1798, *American Bar Association Journal* 62 (March 1976).

alienation 1 Marxist term for the inevitable feeling of dissociation of industrial workers because of their lack of control over their work. (They would thus be ripe for revolution.) The word has largely lost its Marxist meaning and now refers to any feelings of estrangement from one's work, family, government, society, and the like. In the context of politics and voting behavior, alienation refers to a voluntary dropping out of the political process, to nonvoting, to feelings of contempt or indifference toward government. *Compare to* ANOMIE. 2 The legal transfer of real property.

REFERENCES
1 Murray B. Levin, *The Alienated Voter: Politics in Boston* (New York: Holt, Rinehart & Winston, 1960);
Ada W. Finifter, Dimensions of political alienation, *American Political Science Review* 64 (June 1970);
Jack Citrin, Herbert McClosky, J. Merrill Shanks, and Paul M. Sniderman, Personal and political sources of political alienation, *British Journal of Political Science* 5 (January 1974);
Loch Johnson, Political alienation among Vietnam veterans, *Western Political Quarterly* 29 (September 1976);
Paul R. Benson, Political alienation and public satisfaction with police service, *Pacific Sociological Review* 24 (January 1981);
Priscilla L. Southwell, Alienation and nonvoting in the United States: A refined operationalization, *Western Political Quarterly* 38 (December 1985).

Alien Registration Act of 1940/Smith Act The federal law that requires the annual registration of aliens and prohibits advocating the violent overthrow of the U.S. government. *See* DENNIS V UNITED STATES.

REFERENCE
Michael R. Belknap, *Cold War Political Justice: The Smith Act, The Communist Party, and American Civil Liberties* (Westport, CT: Greenwood, 1977).

alien, resident One who is not a citizen of the country in which he or she lives. Resident aliens in the United States have as a matter of right the full protection of the laws but do not have all of the privileges of citizenship, such as the right to vote, the opportunity to hold many government jobs, the right to many welfare benefits, and so on.

all deliberate speed *See* DELIBERATE SPEED.

alleged discriminatory official (ADO) An individual charged in a formal equal employment opportunity complaint with having caused or tolerated discriminatory actions. *See also* BUSH V LUCAS.

REFERENCE
For an analysis of the due process procedures to which ADOs are entitled, see Glenn E. Schweitzer, The rights of federal employees

named as alleged discriminatory officials, *Public Administration Review* 37 (January/February 1977).

allegiance 1 The loyalty and devotion that a citizen owes his or her country; the positive obligation that a citizen has to safeguard the country's interests. 2 The bond, whether emotional, coercive, or legal, that binds a subject to the nation's sovereign.

REFERENCE

James H. Kettner, The development of American citizenship in the revolutionary era: The idea of volitional allegiance, *American Journal of Legal History* 18 (July 1974).

allegiance, oath of The declaration of loyalty that people undergoing naturalization must, according to immigration law, make before they can become citizens. It reads:

I hereby declare, on oath, that I absolutely and entirely renounce and abjure all allegiance and fidelity to any foreign prince, potentate, state, or sovereignty, of whom or which I have heretofore been a subject or citizen; that I will support and defend the Constitution and laws of the United States of America against all enemies, foreign and domestic; that I will bear arms on behalf of the United States when required by the law; that I will perform noncombatant service in the armed forces of the United States when required by the law; that I will perform work of national importance under civilian direction when required by the law; and that I take this obligation freely without any mental reservation or purpose of evasion: so help me God.

allegiance, pledge of The affirmation of allegiance recited when the American flag is presented on ceremonial occasions. It reads: "I pledge allegiance to the flag of the United States of America and to the republic for which it stands, one nation under God, indivisible, with liberty and justice for all." The original version was written by Francis Bellamy in 1892 and published in the September 8 issue of *Youth's Companion,* a weekly magazine. In 1942 the Congress made the pledge officially part of the U.S. Code. In 1954 the Congress added "under God."

alliance A formal agreement between two or more nations for mutual assistance in case of war. The FOUNDING FATHERS warned against alliances. George Washington in his Farewell Address of September 17, 1796, proclaimed that "It is our true policy to steer clear of permanent alliance with any portion of the foreign world." Thomas Jefferson in his Inaugural Address of March 4, 1801, put forth the policy of "peace, commerce, and honest friendship with all nations—entangling alliances with none." Nevertheless, the modern world has forced the United States into many an entangling alliance. The main reason for peacetime alliances, such as NATO, is to deter war. By that criterion, the Western alliance, as NATO is often called, has been a resounding success because of the fact that there has been no European war since its founding in 1945.

REFERENCES

Erich Weede, Extended deterrence by superpower alliance, *Journal of Conflict Resolution* 27 (June 1983);

Stephen M. Walt, Alliance formation and the balance of world power, *International Security* 9 (Spring 1985).

Alliance for Progress President John F. Kennedy's name for his policies toward Latin America, which aimed at mutual economic cooperation.

REFERENCES

Albert L. Michaels, The Alliance for Progress and Chile's "Revolution in Liberty," 1964–1970, *Journal of the Interamerican Studies and World Affairs* 18 (February 1976);

Paul J. Dosal, Accelerating dependent development and revolution: Nicaragua and the Alliance for Progress, *Inter-American Economic Affairs* 38 (Spring 1985).

allies 1 Nations formally bound to each other by a mutual defense treaty. Thus the NATO countries refer to themselves as allies. 2 The Allies: the World War II association of nations led by the United States and the United Kingdom in the fight against the Axis powers. During World War I, the term referred to the winning coalition of the United States, the United Kingdom, France, and Italy.

Allison, Graham T., Jr. (1940–) The author of a classic study of government policy-making, *Essence of Decision: Explaining the Cuban Missile Crisis* (Boston: Little, Brown, 1971), which demonstrated the inadequacies of the view that the decisions of a government are made by a "single calculating decisionmaker" who has control over the organizations and officials within his government. Instead, as Allison showed, different bureaucratic viewpoints contend and conflict over policy.

REFERENCES

Allison first described his thesis in Conceptual models and the Cuban missile crisis, *American Political Science Review* 63 (September 1969).

Also see Graham T. Allison with Peter Szanton, *Remaking Foreign Policy: The Organizational Connection* (New York: Basic Books, 1976);

Steve Smith, Allison and the Cuban missile crisis: A review of the bureaucratic politics model of foreign policy decision-making, *Millenium: Journal of International Studies* 9 (1980).

all-volunteer force *See* ARMED FORCES, ALL VOLUNTEER.

alphabet agencies/alphabet soup Mildly pejorative terms for the New Deal agencies of the 1930s such as the AAA, CCC, SEC, TVA, WPA. Al Smith (1873–1944), governor of New York and the Democratic nominee for president of the United States in 1928, criticized the New Deal by calling it "submerged in a bowl of alphabet soup."

Ambach v Norwick 441 U.S. 68 (1979) The U.S. Supreme Court decision that held that barring aliens from permanent certification as public school teachers did not violate the Fourteenth Amendment's equal protection clause. The ruling upheld the New York education law's citizenship requirement for public (but not private) school teachers. *See also* CITIZENSHIP; FOLEY V CONNELIE; HAMPTON V MOW SUN WONG; SUGARMAN V DOUGALL.

ambassador A diplomat of the highest rank who is sent as the personal representative of

"ALPHABET SOUP"

New York politician Al Smith taunts chef Franklin Roosevelt and his pot of New Deal alphabet soup.

one head of state to another. Not all ambassadors are equal. The most powerful is an ambassador extraordinary and plenipotentiary, who has the broadest mandate of authority. Then follows an ambassador extraordinary, who has lesser powers, an ambassador plenipotentiary, who has authority of a specific nature, and an ambassador ordinary, who is the chief of a diplomatic mission without specifications as to authority. Sir Henry Wotton (1568–1639), Queen Elizabeth I's ambassador to Venice, was the first of many wits to note that "an ambassador is an honest man sent to lie abroad for the commonwealth." (Wotton has long been misjudged. He did "lie abroad" but in a sexual rather than in an ethical escapade.) Camillo Benso (1810–1861), an Italian statesman, took a different approach toward lying. "I have discovered the art of deceiving diplomats. I speak the truth, and they never believe me." *See also* COUNTRY TEAM; DIPLOMATIC PRIVILEGES AND IMMUNITIES.

REFERENCES

Elmer Plischke, American ambassadors—An obsolete species? Some alternatives to traditional diplomatic representatives, *World Affairs* 147 (Summer 1984);

amendment

Martin F. Herz, ed., *The Modern Ambassador: The Challenge and the Search* (Lanham, MD: University Press of America, 1985).
For the story of Sir Henry Wotton, see Lord Gore-Booth, *Satow's Guide to Diplomatic Practice,* 5th ed. (London: Longman, 1979), pp. 80–81.

amendment   **1** A change in a prior law by the enactment of a new law.   **2** A change in a bill during its time of consideration in a legislature.   **3** A provision of a constitution adopted since its original ratification.

REFERENCES
James M. Enelow and David H. Koehler, The amendment in legislative strategy: Sophisticated voting in the U.S. Congress, *Journal of Politics* 42 (May 1980);
Ann Stuart Diamond, A convention for proposing amendments: The Constitution's other method, *Publius* 11 (Summer 1981);
Stanley Bach, Parliamentary strategy and the amendment process: Rules and case studies of congressional action, *Polity* 15 (Summer 1983);

Four Routes to a New Amendment to the U.S. Constitution

Proposed by:

Ratified by:

A
Two-thirds vote of both houses of the Congress

B
Three-fourths of state legislatures

(usual method)

Start here

Constitution gets new amendment

C
National convention called by the Congress after a request by two-thirds of state legislatures

D
Special ratifying convention in three-fourths of states

Source: Grover Starling, *Understanding American Politics* (Chicago: Dorsey, 1982), p. 56.

Walter Dellinger, The legitimacy of constitutional change: Rethinking the amendment process, *Harvard Law Review* 97 (December 1983).

For a comparative perspective, see Walter Dellinger, The amending process in Canada and the United States: A comparative perspective, *Law and Contemporary Problems* 45 (Autumn 1982).

American Academy of Political and Social Science   A nonprofit organization formed in 1889 to promote the progress of political and social science, especially through publications and meetings. Since 1890 it has published the *Annals*.

American Academy of Political and Social Science
3937 Chestnut Street
Philadelphia, PA 19104
(215) 386-4594

American Bar Association (ABA)   Since 1878 this has been "the" professional association for lawyers. With over three hundred thousand members, it is always a major voice in the public debate over changing any aspect of the civil or criminal justice system. Its Committee on Federal Judiciary evaluates federal judicial nominations and rates the nominees according to their qualifications. These ratings may become a significant factor in the Senate confirmation or nonconfirmation of the nominees. But this is very rare. Consequently, the ABA evaluations are in reality little more than a formality. See APPOINTMENT CLAUSE.

REFERENCE

Elliot E. Slotnick, The ABA Standing Committee on Federal Judiciary: A contemporary assessment, *Judicature* 66 (March/April 1983).

American Bar Association
750 North Lake Shore Drive
Chicago, IL 60611
(312) 988-5000

American City and County   A monthly trade magazine published since 1909 (formerly *American City*) for municipal managers. Library of Congress no. HT101 .A5.

American City and County
Communication Channels, Inc.
6255 Barfield Road
Atlanta, GA 30328

American Civil Liberties Union (ACLU)
The quarter-million-strong public interest group dedicated to the promotion and protection of the civil liberties that all Americans have under the U.S. Constitution. Its main activity is the testing of civil rights issues in the courts. Thus it has played a vital role in cases on school prayer, loyalty oaths, illegal search and seizure, and the right of free speech for members of the American Nazi party and other unpopular groups. The ACLU evolved from the American Civil Liberties Bureau started by Norman Thomas (1884–1968) and Roger Baldwin (1884–1981) in 1917 to defend World War I conscientious objectors. It expanded into the ACLU in 1920 to fight the egregious violations of civil rights and due process by U.S. Attorney General A. Mitchell Palmer (1872–1936) during the postwar red scare. By taking more cases to the Supreme Court than any other private organization, the ACLU has been in the forefront of making civil rights and free speech constitutional issues.

REFERENCES

Stephen C. Halpern, Assessing the litigative role of ACLU chapters, *Policy Studies Journal* 4 (Winter 1976);

Nat Hentoff, The ACLU's trial by swastika, *Social Policy* 8 (January/February 1978);

William R. Donohue, *The Politics of the American Civil Liberties Union* (New Brunswick, NJ: Transaction, 1985).

American Civil Liberties Union
132 West 43d Street
New York, NY 10036
(212) 944-9800

American Enterprise Institute for Public Policy Research (AEI)   Independent, nonprofit, nonpartisan research and educational organization founded in 1943 whose basic purpose is to promote the competition of ideas. AEI, which tends to favor deregulation, decentralization, and a market economy, provided the Ronald Reagan administration with a fair share of both ideas and advisors.

American Enterprise Institute
1150 17th Street, N.W.
Washington, D.C. 20036
(202) 862-5800

American Federation of Government Employees (AFGE) The largest union of federal government employees. Founded in 1932, it has grown to seven hundred thousand members in 1,380 locals around the world.

REFERENCE

Richard G. Fortier, An AFGE local: An examination of factors contributing to union strength in the public sector, *Public Personnel Management* 13 (Fall 1984).

American Federation of Government
  Employees
80 F Street, N.W.
Washington, D.C. 20001
(202) 737-8700

American Federation of Government Employees v Phillips 358 F. Supp. 60 (1973) The U.S. district court case that reaffirmed the constitutional principles that the president of the United States does not have discretionary power to execute the laws, with special reference to the impoundment of congressionally appropriated funds.

American Federation of Labor–Congress of Industrial Organizations (AFL-CIO) A voluntary federation of over a hundred national and international labor unions operating in the United States and representing in total over thirteen million workers. The AFL-CIO is not itself a union; it does no bargaining. It is perhaps best thought of as a union of unions. The affiliated unions created the AFL-CIO to represent them in the creation and execution of broad national and international policies and to coordinate a wide range of joint activities. The American Federation of Labor (organized in 1881 as a federation of craft unions, the Federation of Organized Trade and Labor Unions), changed its name in 1886 after merging with those craft unions that had become disenchanted with the Knights of Labor. In 1955, the AFL merged with the Congress of Industrial Organizations to become the AFL-CIO. Each member union of the AFL-CIO remains autonomous, conducting its own affairs in the manner determined by its own members. Each has its own headquarters, officers, and staff. Each decides its own economic policies, carries on its own contract negotiations, sets its own dues, and provides its own membership services. Each is free to withdraw at any time. But through such voluntary participation, the AFL-CIO plays a role in establishing overall policies for the U.S. labor movement, which in turn advances the interests of every union.

AFL-CIO
815 16th Street, N.W.
Washington, D.C. 20006
(202) 637-5000

American Federation of State, County and Municipal Employees (AFSCME) The largest union of state and local government employees. Founded in 1936, it has grown to 1,200,000 members in three thousand locals.

American Federation of State, County, and
  Municipal Employees
1625 L Street, N.W.
Washington, D.C. 20036
(202) 452-4800

American Journal of Political Science The quarterly, published since 1957, of the Midwest Political Science Association; formerly the *Midwest Journal of Political Science*. Library of Congress no. JA1 .M5.

American Journal of Political Science
University of Texas Press Journals
P.O. Box 7819
Austin, TX 78713

American Municipal Association *See* NATIONAL LEAGUE OF CITIES.

American Party *See* KNOW-NOTHING PARTY.

American Planning Association (APA) A professional association of planning agency officials, professional planners, and planning educators formed in 1978 through a merger of the American Institute of Planners (founded in 1917 as the American City Planning Institute) and the American Society of Planning Officials (founded in 1934).

American Planning Association
1776 Massachusetts Avenue, N.W.
Washington, D.C. 20036
(202) 872-0611

American Political Science Association (APSA) Since 1903, the leading academic organization for American political scientists. APSA publishes the AMERICAN POLITICAL SCIENCE REVIEW, PS (a quarterly, which contains political analysis, articles, and news of interest to professionals in political science), directories of political scientists and college programs in political science, and a wealth of other materials relating to the teaching and practice of political science. Its annual conventions provide an opportunity for political scientists to meet and present their research findings.
American Political Science Association
1527 New Hampshire Avenue, N.W.
Washington, D.C. 20036
(202) 483-2512

American Political Science Review (APSR) A quarterly published since 1906 by the American Political Science Association; long considered the most prestigious of the academic political science journals. Library of Congress no. JA1 .A6.
American Political Science Review
1527 New Hampshire Avenue, N.W.
Washington, D.C. 20036
(202) 483-2512

American Politics Quarterly A scholarly journal published since 1972 that deals with all aspects of American governance. Library of Congress no. JK1 .A48.
American Politics Quarterly
275 South Beverly Drive
Beverly Hills, CA 90212

American Public Welfare Association (APWA) A professional association of over six thousand welfare agencies and administrators; founded in 1930.
American Public Welfare Association
1125 15th Street, N.W.
Washington, D.C. 20005
(202) 293-7550

American Public Works Association (APWA) A professional association for over twenty-three thousand city engineers and others involved in the construction, management, or maintenance of public works. Founded in 1894, until 1937 it was called the American Society of Municipal Engineers.
American Public Works Association
1313 East 60th Street
Chicago, IL 60637
(312) 667-2200

American Review of Public Administration (ARPA) A quarterly, published since 1967, "devoted to fostering a dialogue between the theoretician and the practitioner of public administration." Formerly (until 1981) *The Midwest Review of Public Administration*. Library of Congress no. JK1 .M5.
American Review of Public Administration
Park College
Parkville, MO 64152

Americans for Democratic Action (ADA) A sixty-thousand-member public interest lobby founded in 1947 to continue the domestic social welfare policies and internationalism of the New Deal. It is often considered to be the major voice of the moderate left of the Democratic Party.
REFERENCES
Hall Libros, *Hard Core Liberals: A Sociological Analysis of the Philadelphia Americans for Democratic Action* (Cambridge, MA: Schenkman, 1975);
Steven M. Gillon, *Politics and Vision: The ADA and American Liberalism, 1947–1985* (New York: Oxford, 1987).
Americans for Democratic Action
1411 K Street, N.W.
Washington, D.C. 20005
(202) 638-6447

American Society for Public Administration (ASPA) A professional organization of about twenty thousand members representative of all government levels, which, since its inception in 1939, has provided national leadership in advancing the "science, processes, and art" of public administration. It is the only organization of its kind aiming to improve administration of the public service at all levels of government and in all functional and program fields. Many of its activities are carried out through more than 117 chapters in major government and education centers.

REFERENCES

Donald C. Stone, Birth of ASPA: A collective effort in institution building, *Public Administration Review* 35 (January/February 1975);

Darrell L. Pugh, ASPA's history: Prologue! *Public Administration Review* 45 (July/August 1985).

American Society for Public Administration
1120 G Street, N.W.
Washington, D.C. 20005
(202) 393-7878

American system   **1** The essential principles of American government. Alexander Hamilton wrote in Federalist #11: "Let the thirteen states, bound together in a strict and indissoluble union, concur in erecting one great American system." Thomas Jefferson wrote in a letter of October 24, 1820, to Joseph Correa de Serra that "nothing is so important as that America shall separate herself from the systems of Europe and establish one of her own." **2** The American economic policy in the nineteenth century, which emphasized protective tariffs and public works. Henry Clay (1777–1852) as Speaker of the House of Representatives and later a leader in the Senate was the most famous advocate of an "American system" of protective domestic industries combined with internal improvements to what we now call infrastructure. **3** Eli Whitney's (1765–1825) American system of manufacturing, the first to make major use of interchangeable parts.

amicus curiae   A Latin term for friend of the court; any person or organization allowed to participate in a lawsuit who would not otherwise have a right to do so. Participation is usually limited to filing a brief on behalf of one side or the other.

REFERENCES

Samuel Krislov, The *amicus curiae* brief: From friendship to advocacy, *Yale Law Journal* (March 1963);

Karen O'Connor, The *amicus curiae* role of the U.S. solicitor general in Supreme Court litigation, *Judicature* 66 (1983).

amnesty   The act of "forgetfulness" by a government for crimes, usually political, committed by a group of people. After the U.S. Civil War, President Andrew Johnson granted amnesty to all Confederates. When the Congress tried to limit its effects, the Supreme Court ruled in *Ex parte Garland,* 4 Wallace 333 (1867), that this was an invalid interference with the president's power to pardon, given in Article II, Section 2, of the U.S. Constitution. In 1977, President Jimmy Carter granted an amnesty to all Vietnam War draft evaders (but not to military deserters). A pardon, in contrast, is usually granted to individuals. For example, in 1974 President Gerald R. Ford granted a pardon to former President Richard M. Nixon for any crimes he may have committed while in office.

REFERENCES

Wallace D. Loh, National loyalties and amnesty: A legal and social psychological analysis, *Journal of Social Issues* 31:4 (1975);

David Shichor and Donald R. Ranish, President Carter's Vietnam amnesty: An analysis of a public policy decision, *Presidential Studies Quarterly* 10 (Summer 1980).

amnesty, tax   *See* TAX AMNESTY.

Amtrak   *See* NATIONAL RAILROAD PASSENGER CORPORATION.

anarchism   The belief that government and its administrative institutions are intrinsically evil and should be abolished (typically by violence) so they can be replaced by arrangements not "corrupted" by exploitative and oppressive governments.

REFERENCES

Corinne Jacker, *The Black Flag of Anarchy: Antistatism in the United States* (New York: Scribner's, 1968);

Michael R. Dillon, The perennial appeal of anarchism, *Polity* 7 (Winter 1974);

Robert Goehlert, Anarchism: A bibliography of articles, 1900–1975, *Political Theory* 4 (February 1976);

David DeLeon, *The American as Anarchist: Reflections on Indigenous Radicalism* (Baltimore: Johns Hopkins University Press, 1978);

Kathy E. Ferguson, Toward new anarchism, *Contemporary Crises: Crime, Law and Social Policy* 7 (January 1983).

Henry David Thoreau's Defense of Anarchism

I heartily accept the motto,—"That government is best which governs least"; and I should like to see it acted up to more rapidly and systematically. Carried out, it finally amounts to this, which also I believe,—"That government is best which governs not at all"; and when men are prepared for it, that will be the kind of government which they will have. Government is at best but an expedient; but most governments are usually, and all governments are sometimes, inexpedient. The objections which have been brought against a standing army, and they are many and weighty, and deserve to prevail, may also at last be brought against a standing government. The standing army is only an arm of the standing government. The government itself, which is only the mode which the people have chosen to execute their will, is equally liable to be abused and perverted before the people can act through it.

Source: "On the Duty of Civil Disobedience" (1849).

---

anarcho-syndicalism The late-nineteenth-century movement that advocated that trade unions oppose, destroy, and replace government.

Animal Farm George Orwell's (1903–1950) 1945 novel, which has become the classic satire on Soviet communism and a warning that all revolutions eventually betray their revolutionary ideals. The revolutionary ideal was that "all animals were equal." But after the pigs took over, they decided that "some animals [pigs] were more equal than others."

Annals The bimonthly journal of the American Academy of Political and Social Science, published since 1890. Each issue focuses on a prominent social or political problem. Library of Congress no. H1 .A4.

The *Annals*
2111 West Hillcrest Drive
Newbury Park, CA 91320

Annapolis Convention A 1786 meeting at Annapolis, Maryland, called by the states to discuss interstate commerce. Its significance lies in its only recommendation: that a larger convention—which turned out to be the Constitutional Convention of 1787—be held in Philadelphia the following year.

annexation 1 The formal extension of sovereignty over new territory. For example, the United States annexed the Republic of Texas in 1845. 2 The acquisition of adjacent settlements by a city. After annexation, these settlements are part of the city. Though, in the past, most cities grew by annexation, it is difficult for most cities to annex now because the suburbs are typically incorporated entities not usually subject to involuntary annexation. Nevertheless, annexation is still a major issue in municipal politics in the western United States, where cities often have the state-legislated right to annex adjacent unincorporated areas. These unincorporated areas are often rightfully fearful that annexation will adversely affect their municipal services and tax rates, while the central city is often anxious to annex lands to expand its tax and service bases. Sometimes, however, this strategy backfires when an annexed area fails to attract significant business and industry and becomes a tax and service drain.

REFERENCES

Leo F. Schnore, Municipal annexations and the growth of metropolitan suburbs, *American Journal of Sociology* 67 (January 1962);

Alfred J. Watkins and Arnold Fleischmann, Annexation, migration, and central city population growth, *Social Science Quarterly* 61 (December 1980);

Charles K. Coe, Costs and benefits of municipal annexation, *State and Local Government Review* 15 (Winter 1983);

Eleanor Breen, Frank J. Costa, and William S. Hendon, Annexation: An economic analysis: Whether a small village or town should annex adjacent land is a cost/revenue problem, *American Journal of Economics and Sociology* 45 (April 1986).

annuit coeptis A Latin term meaning he (God) has favored our undertakings. This motto is on the Great Seal of the United States and on the back of the one-dollar bill.

anomie A social condition in which previously established norms of behavior have been dissipated or rejected; consequently, there is no effective social control of individual behavior. The concept was named and explicated by the French sociologist Emile Durkheim (1858–1917). *Compare to* ALIENATION.

REFERENCE
Stephen R. Marks, Durkheim's theory of anomie, *American Journal of Sociology* 80 (September 1974).

Antarctic Treaty The 1959 agreement that internationalized and outlawed the militarization of the continent of Antarctica. All signatories, including the United States and the U.S.S.R., have the right to inspect the facilities of other signatories to make sure the continent is used solely for peaceful purposes.

REFERENCE
Peter J. Beck, The Antarctic Treaty System after twenty-five years, *World Today* 42 (November 1986).

antiballistic missile *See* ABM.

antifederalists Those opposed to the adoption of the new U.S. Constitution in the late 1780s. They were against a strong central government and preferred the retention of powers by the state governments. Their concerns helped bring into life the BILL OF RIGHTS.

REFERENCES
Jackson Turner Main, *The Antifederalists* (Chapel Hill: University of North Carolina Press, 1961);
Alpheus T. Mason, *The States Rights Debates: Antifederalism and the Constitution* (Englewood Cliffs, NJ: Prentice-Hall, 1964);
Herbert J. Storing and Murray Dry, eds., *The Complete Anti-Federalist,* 7 vols. (Chicago: University of Chicago Press, 1981);
Gary L. McDowell, Were the anti-federalists right? Judicial activism and the problem of consolidated government, *Publius* 12 (Summer 1982).

Anti-Ku Klux Klan Act *See* CIVIL RIGHTS ACT OF 1871.

Anti-Trust Act of 1914 *See* CLAYTON ACT OF 1914.

antitrust laws Those federal and state statutes that limit the ability of businesses and unions to exercise monopoly control and to cause the restraint of trade. The Sherman Anti-Trust Act of 1890 was the first significant American break with the economic philosophy of laissez-faire. It asserted that law could create and control conditions in the marketplace and that it was sometimes in the public interest for government to exercise substantial indirect control over economic conditions. The American policy of antitrust enforcement contrasts sharply with those of most other nations, which encourage and tolerate cartels as the normal order of things. Thus commercial competitors of the United States have industries that are able, with their government's sanction and assistance, to compete as one against the fractioned industries of the United States.

REFERENCES
Suzanne Weaver, *Decision to Prosecute: Organization and Public Policy in the Antitrust Division* (Cambridge, MA: MIT Press, 1977);
Milton Handler, Reforming the antitrust laws, *Columbia Law Review* 82 (November 1982);
William M. Landes, Optimal sanctions for antitrust violations, *University of Chicago Law Review* 50 (Spring 1983).

ANZUS Pact The mutual defense treaty signed in 1951 by Australia, New Zealand, and the United States. In 1986 this treaty of mutual defense became less mutual when New Zealand decided that it could not tolerate American warships using New Zealand ports, because the ships might be carrying nuclear weapons. So both countries agreed that in the future they would both defend Australia but not each other.

REFERENCES
Joseph G. Starke, *The ANZUS Treaty Alliance* (Melbourne: Cambridge University Press, 1965);
Paul D. Wolfowitz, The ANZUS relationship: Alliance management, *Australian Outlook* 38 (December 1984);
F. A. Mediansky, ANZUS in crisis, *Australian Quarterly* 57 (Autumn/Winter 1985).

APA *See* ADMINISTRATIVE PROCEDURE ACT OF 1946; AMERICAN PLANNING ASSOCIATION.

apolitical 1 Outside of politics; not concerned with political dominance; apathetic toward voting or politics. 2 Nonpartisan; not affiliated with a political party. *Compare to* POLITICAL APATHY.

REFERENCES

Alan P. Brier and Robert E. Dowse, The politics of the apolitical, *Political Studies* 17 (September 1969);

Milton Lodge and John C. Wahlke, Politicos, apoliticals, and the processing of political information, *International Political Science Review* 3:1 (1982);

Stephen Earl Bennett, *Apathy in America, 1960–1984: Causes and Consequences of Citizen Political Indifference* (Ardsley-on-Hudson, NY: Transnational, 1986).

Appalachian Regional Commission (ARC) Federal-state compact created by the Appalachian Regional Development Act of 1965 to encourage the economic, physical, and social development of the thirteen-state Appalachian region.

Appalachian Regional Commission
1666 Connecticut Avenue, N.W.
Washington, D.C. 20035
(202) 673-7893

apparatchik A Russian word for a bureaucrat, now used colloquially to refer to any administrative functionary. The word as used in English seems to have no political connotations; it merely implies that the individual referred to mindlessly follows orders.

REFERENCE

Raymond Vernon, Apparatchiks and entrepreneurs: U.S.-Soviet economic relations, *Foreign Affairs* 52 (January 1974).

appeal 1 Any proceeding or request to a higher authority that a lower authority's decision be reviewed. 2 A formal request to a higher court that it review the actions of a lower court. *Compare to* CERTIORARI. 3 A challenge to a ruling made by a presiding officer of a legislature. If the challenge is supported by a majority vote of the legislators, the initial ruling is overridden.

REFERENCE

2 Gregory J. Rathjen, Lawyers and the appellate choice: An analysis of factors affecting the decision to appeal, *American Politics Quarterly* 6 (October 1978).

appeasement Giving in to the demands of those making explicit or implicit threats. The term is most associated with England and France's permitting Germany to occupy the Sudetenland in Czechoslovakia in 1938. Thereupon, British Prime Minister Neville Chamberlain said there would be "peace in our time," and German Chancellor Adolph Hitler declared that he had no further territorial ambitions in Europe. Because the policy of appeasement only encouraged Hitler's aggression, which led to World War II, the word appeasement (which was once merely descriptive of a policy of acceding) has taken on a decidedly negative connotation. When Chamberlain returned from appeasing Hitler in Munich, Winston Churchill told him "Prime Minister, you had the choice between war and dishonor. You have chosen dishonor, and you will get war."

REFERENCES

Paul M. Kennedy, The study of appeasement: Methodological crossroads or meeting place? *British Journal of International Studies* 6 (October 1980);

C. A. MacDonald, *The United States, Britain, and Appeasement, 1936–1939* (New York: St. Martin's, 1981);

Larry William Fuchser, *Neville Chamberlain and Appeasement* (New York: Norton, 1982);

Wolfgang J. Mommsen and Lothar Kettenacher, eds., *The Fascist Challenge and the Policy of Appeasement* (London: Allen and Unwin, 1983).

appellant One who appeals a case to a higher authority.

appellate Any court that considers appeals concerning a lower court's actions.

REFERENCES

Harold Leventhal, Appellate procedures: Design, patchwork, and managed flexibility, *UCLA Law Review* 23 (February 1976);

J. Dickson Philips, Jr., The appellate review function: Scope of review, *Law and Contemporary Problems* 47 (Spring 1984).

appellate jurisdiction   The power of a court, board, or commission to review cases previously decided by a lower authority.

appellee   The defendant in an appeal (usually the victor in a lower-court case).

Appleby, Paul H. (1891–1963)   The most influential advocate of the notion that politics and administration are intertwined. Appleby worked to destroy the myth that politics was separate from, or could somehow be taken out of, public administration. Public administrators, Appleby said, made policy; they were involved in the political process; and this political involvement acted as a check on the arbitrary exercise of bureaucratic power in a democratic state.

REFERENCES

Paul Appleby's major works are *Big Democracy* (New York: Knopf, 1945); *Policy and Administration* (University: University of Alabama Press, 1949); *Morality and Administration in Democratic Government* (Baton Rouge: Louisiana State University Press, 1952); and *Citizens as Sovereigns* (Syracuse, NY: Syracuse University Press, 1962).

For a complete review of Appleby's work and influence, see Roscoe C. Martin, ed., *Public Administration and Democracy: Essays in Honor of Paul H. Appleby* (Syracuse, NY: Syracuse University Press, 1965).

appointment   A nonelective government job. Most jurisdictions offer several kinds of appointments. For example, the federal government offers the following four varieties in its merit system: (1) *temporary appointment* does not ordinarily last more than one year; (2) *term appointment* made for work on a specific project that will last more than one year but less than four years; (3) *career-conditional appointment* leads after three years' continuous service to a career appointment; (4) *career appointment* begins with a probationary period followed by promotion, reinstatement, and transfer privileges. After probation, a career employee is in the last group to be affected by layoffs.

appointment clause   That portion of Article II, Section 2, of the U.S. Constitution that states that the president,

> by and with the advice and consent of the Senate, shall appoint ambassadors, other public ministers and consuls, judges of the Supreme Court, and all other officers of the United States whose appointments are not herein otherwise provided for, and which shall be established by law; but the Congress may by law vest the appointment of such inferior officers, as they think proper, in the President alone, in the courts of law, or in the heads of departments.

Thus offices and, by implication, departments and agencies must be provided for by law. This means that the creation of the structures of the executive branch rests largely with the Congress. The appointment clause was intended as a check on the president. Without it the president could create office after office, department after department, without congressional authorization. While the president still would have been dependent upon the Congress for the funding of such offices and departments, constitutionally, presidential authority could have been shared with these offices and departments without any effective congressional oversight or check. As it stands in the Constitution, however, the Congress creates the structure of the executive branch and obviously has the power to check up on its handiwork.

The appointment clause is also significant because it allows the Congress to vest the authority to make "inferior" appointments with the president, the courts, and the department heads. The number of such presidential appointments has varied throughout U.S. history. Today, with over 90 percent of all federal employees having a merit appointment of one type or another, presidential appointments, while not inconsequential, are decidedly limited in scope. Nevertheless, a president allowed to nominate significant numbers to federal judgeships and regulatory agencies can have a political influence extending far beyond the term of office. (*See* ADVICE AND CONSENT).

All of this adds up to what might at first seem like a startling conclusion: the Congress clearly has a great deal of authority over federal administrative processes. Not only must appropriations be granted by law, but the size, structure, mission, and authority of executive branch agencies are all solidly within the domain of congressional power. So are federal personnel administration and the oversight, or evaluation, of the bureaucracy. Having had a bad experience with a king, the founders feared executive power. This is nowhere more evident than in the constitutional clauses that bear upon public administration. While charged with the faithful execution of the laws, the president's constitutional authority over the administrative structures necessary to implement these laws is severely limited. How, then, has the president become the nation's "administrative chief"? In part through the power of dismissal and in part through congressional delegation of administrative power to him. *See also* HUMPHREY'S EXECUTOR V UNITED STATES; MYERS V UNITED STATES; PATRONAGE; PRESIDENTIAL POWER.

REFERENCES

Lois Reznick, Temporary appointment power of the president, *University of Chicago Law Review* 41 (Fall 1973);

Calvin MacKenzie, *The Politics of Presidential Appointments* (New York: Free Press, 1981);

John W. Macy and others, eds., *America's Unelected Government: Appointing the President's Team* (Cambridge, MA: Ballinger, 1983).

For analyses of appointment power at the state level, see Thad L. Beyle and Robert Dalton, Appointment power: Does it belong to the governor? *State Government* 54:1 (1981);

Diane Kincaid Blair, The gubernatorial appointment power: Too much of a good thing? *State Government* 55:3 (1982).

appointment, noncompetitive Government employment obtained without competing with others, in the sense that it is done without regard to civil service registers. The term includes reinstatements, transfers, reassignments, demotions, and some promotions.

appointment, provisional Usually, government employment without competitive examination because no appropriate eligible list is available. Most jurisdictions have a three-, six-, or twelve-month limitation on provisional appointments.

apportionment 1 A determination of how many legislators should be sent to a legislative body from a given jurisdiction. The U.S. Constitution provides that each state is entitled to two senators and at least one representative. Beyond the minimum, representatives are apportioned among the states according to population. This apportionment is adjusted after every ten-year census. Under the Apportionment Act of 1929, the Congress fixed the size of the House of Representatives at 435 seats, and after each census the Congress assigns the appropriate number of seats to each state. The states themselves carry on from there: the actual redistributing process is a matter of state law with one major exception. In 1967 Congress prohibited at-large elections in all states entitled to more than one seat in the House. For the establishment of the one man, one vote principle in legislative apportionment, *see* BAKER V CARR; REYNOLDS V SIMS. *Compare to* REDISTRICTING. 2 An executive budget function that takes place after passage of an appropriations bill when a jurisdiction's budget office creates a plan for expenditures to reconcile agency or department programs with available resources. 3 A requirement, written into the Pendleton Act of 1883, that all federal government merit system jobs in headquarters offices of agencies in metropolitan Washington, D.C., are to be distributed among the residents of the states on the basis of population. Residents of states that have not filled their allocations are considered for appointment to these apportioned positions ahead of residents of states that have exceeded their allocations. 4 The division of property and the proportionate assignment of rights and liabilities among the parties involved.

REFERENCE

1 Harvey J. Tucker, Toward consistent legal standards of state legislative apportionment, *National Civic Review* 73 (February 1984).

appropriation 1 Funds set aside by a legislature to pay for something authorized by law. 2 An act of the U.S. Congress that permits federal agencies to incur obligations and to make payments out of the Treasury for specified purposes. An appropriation usually follows the enactment of authorizing legislation and is the most common form of budget authority, but in some cases the authorizing legislation also provides the budget authority. Appropriations are categorized in a variety of ways, such as by their period of availability (one-year, multiple-year, no-year), the time of congressional action (current, permanent), and the manner of determining the amount of the appropriation (definite, indefinite). *See also* ADVANCE FUNDING; BUDGETING.

REFERENCES

2   Richard F. Fenno, Jr., The House Appropriations Committee as a political system: The problem of integration, *American Political Science Review* 61 (June 1962);

Richard F. Fenno, Jr., *The Power of the Purse: Appropriations Politics in Congress* (Boston: Little, Brown, 1966);

David Lowery, Samuel Bookheimer, and James Malachowski, Partisanship in the appropriations process: Fenno revisited, *American Politics Quarterly* 13 (April 1985);

D. Roderick Kiewiet and Mathew D. McCubbins, Appropriations decisions as a bilateral bargaining game between president and Congress, *Legislative Studies Quarterly* 10 (May 1985).

appropriation, advance An appropriation provided for use beyond the fiscal year for which the appropriation act is passed. *Compare to* ADVANCE FUNDING.

appropriation limitation A statutory restriction (or limitation amendment) in appropriation acts that establishes the maximum or minimum amount that may be obligated or expended for specified purposes.

appropriation, supplemental An appropriation enacted as an addition to a regular annual appropriation act. It provides additional budget authority beyond original estimates for programs or activities (including new programs authorized after the date of the original appropriation act) for which the need for funds is too urgent to be postponed until the next regular appropriation.

approval voting *See* VOTING, APPROVAL.

approximation of laws The process whereby governments align their laws concerning commercial transactions to facilitate international trade.

APSA *See* AMERICAN POLITICAL SCIENCE ASSOCIATION.

APSR *See* AMERICAN POLITICAL SCIENCE REVIEW.

Aptheker v Secretary of State 378 U.S. 500 (1964) The U.S. Supreme Court case that held that the passport restrictions that the Internal Security (McCarran) Act of 1950 placed on American communists were unconstitutional because the Fifth Amendment guarantees the right to travel. *Compare to* ALBERTSON V SUBVERSIVE ACTIVITIES CONTROL BOARD.

APWA *See* AMERICAN PUBLIC WELFARE ASSOCIATION; AMERICAN PUBLIC WORKS ASSOCIATION.

arbiter/arbitrator One chosen to decide a disagreement. In a formal sense, an arbiter is one who already has the power to decide, while an arbitrator is one chosen to decide by the parties to the dispute; but the words tend to be used interchangeably.

REFERENCES

Murray Greenberg and Philip Harris, The arbitrator's employment status as a factor in the decision making process, *Human Resource Management* 20 (Winter 1981);

John Smith Herrick, Labor arbitration as viewed by labor arbitrators, *Arbitration Journal* 38 (March 1983);

Orley Ashenfelter and David E. Bloom, Models of arbitrator behavior: Theory and evidence, *American Economic Review* 74 (March 1984).

arbitrary An action decided on the basis of individual judgments that do not meet commonly understood rules of procedure and hence may not appear justifiable to those seeking to explain them to others or to replicate them in similar circumstances.

REFERENCES

Raoul Berger, Administrative arbitrariness: A synthesis, *Yale Law Journal* 78 (May 1969);

Laurent Maridux, Jr., Protection from arbitrary arrest and detention under international law, *Boston College International and Comparative Law Review* 5 (Summer 1982).

arbitration The means of settling a dispute by having an impartial third party (the arbitrator) hold a formal hearing and render a decision that may or may not be binding on both sides. The arbitrator may be a single individual or a board of three, five, or more (usually an uneven number). When boards are used, they may include, in addition to impartial members, representatives from both of the disputants. In the context of labor relations, arbitrators are selected jointly by labor and management, recommended by the Federal Mediation and Conciliation Service, by a state or local agency offering similar referrals, or by the private American Arbitration Association.

REFERENCES

Henry S. Farber, Role of arbitration in dispute settlement, *Monthly Labor Review* 104 (May 1981);

Harry Graham, Arbitration results in the public sector, *Public Personnel Management* 11 (Summer 1982);

Frank Elkouri and Edna Asper Elkouri, *How Arbitration Works*, 4th ed. (Washington, D.C.: Bureau of National Affairs, 1985).

arbitration acts Laws that help (and sometimes require) the submission of certain types of problems (often labor disputes) to an arbitrator.

arbitration, compulsory A negotiating process whereby the parties are required by law to arbitrate their dispute. Some state statutes concerning collective bargaining impasses in the public sector mandate that parties who have exhausted all other means of achieving a settle-ment must submit their dispute to an arbitrator. The intent of such requirements for compulsory arbitration is to induce the parties to reach agreement by presenting them with an alternative that is certain, even though it may be unpleasant in some respects to everyone involved.

REFERENCES

Carl M. Stevens, Is compulsory arbitration compatible with bargaining? *Industrial Relations* 6 (February 1966);

Mollie H. Bowers, Legislated arbitration: Legality, enforceability, and face-saving, *Public Personnel Management* 3 (July/August 1974).

archives The records that document the daily operation of an organization. These include all internal and external communication of whatever nature, no matter how insignificant or trivial they may seem at the time. Once considered the private property of the individuals involved or the organization, and actively sought after by historians engaged in research, archives may now be subject to investigation by outside parties unless the archives are protected by specific rules governing secrecy in the case of government documents and subject to subpoena by the Congress, by the courts, or by designated review agencies. *Compare to* FREEDOM OF INFORMATION ACT OF 1966; NATIONAL ARCHIVES AND RECORDS ADMINISTRATION.

REFERENCE

Allan G. Bogue, The historian and social science data archives in the United States, *American Behavioral Scientist* 19 (March/April 1976).

aristocracy 1 Rule of a relatively small, elite group. ARISTOTLE called aristocracy rule by the most virtuous of a society. By medieval times the concept had degenerated to mean rule by the upper classes—those chosen by God to lead. Thomas Jefferson got back to the Aristotelian notion of virtue when he spoke of rule by a "natural aristocracy," whose talent entitled them to govern. Article I, Section 9, of the U.S. Constitution sought to inhibit traditional aristocracies when it proclaimed that "No Title of Nobility shall be granted by the United States." 2 Any group with great (usually hereditary) wealth and influence.

Thomas Jefferson on the True Meaning of Aristocracy

I agree with you that there is a natural aristocracy among men. The grounds of this are virtue and talents. Formerly, bodily powers gave place among the aristoi. But since the invention of gun-powder has armed the weak as well as the strong with missile death, bodily strength, like beauty, good humor, politeness, and other accomplishments, has become but an auxiliary ground for distinction. There is also an artificial aristocracy, founded on wealth and birth, without either virtue or talents; for with these it would belong to the first class. The natural aristocracy I consider as the most precious gift of nature, for the instruction, the trusts, and government of society. And indeed, it would have been inconsistent in creation to have formed man for the social state, and not to have provided virtue and wisdom enough to manage the concerns of the society. May we not even say, that that form of government is the best, which provides the most effectually for a pure selection of these natural aristoi into the offices of government? The artificial aristocracy is a mischievous ingredient in government, and provision should be made to prevent its ascendancy.

Source: Letter to John Adams, October 28, 1813.

Aristotle (384–322 BC) The Greek philosopher who originated much of the study of logic, science, and politics. For several years, Aristotle, who was a student of Plato, served as the tutor of the boy who would become Alexander the Great. In 323 BC, after Alexander the Great had died, Aristotle's close association with the Macedonians caused Athenians to indict him for "impiety." Remembering what had happened to Socrates many years earlier, Aristotle, who had no stomach for hemlock, fled from Athens, maintaining that he would not give the city a second chance to sin against philosophy.

In *Politics*, Aristotle presented the first comprehensive analysis of the nature of a state, of a polity, and of a political community. To Aristotle, the state was a natural product because "man is by nature a political animal." The state was even more important than family because, while a family exists for comfort, the state can be a vehicle for glory and the good life.

Aristotle was the ancient world's foremost authority on a CONSTITUTION, for which he had a dual definition: first, a constitution was the formally established and written rules of governance; second, a constitution also consisted of the informal processes of politics—in effect, the POLITICAL CULTURE of the community. Perhaps Aristotle's most famous analytical construct is his classification of the three basic forms of government and their perversions. He found that every political community had to be governed by either the one, the few, or the many. This corresponds to his three governing types: kingship, aristocracy, and polity (majority rule). Unfortunately, each of these had its perversions, the conditions to which it degenerated when the rulers ceased ruling in the interests of the whole community. Kingship often degenerated into tyranny; aristocracy (rule by a talented and virtuous elite) into an oligarchy (rule by a small group in its own interest); and a polity or constitutional system (where a large middle class rules for the common interest) into democracy (mob rule in the interests of the lower classes). Overall, Aristotle favored a mixed constitution (used here in the sense of political culture)—one in which all citizens "rule and are ruled by turn," where no class monopolizes power and a large middle class provides stability.

REFERENCES

Roger J. F. Chance, *Until Philosophers Are Kings: A Study of the Political Theory of Plato and Aristotle in Relation to the Modern State* (Port Washington, NY: Kennikat, 1928, 1968);

Delba Winthrop, Aristotle on participatory democracy, *Polity* 11 (Winter 1978);

Ellen Meiksins Wood, *Class Ideology and Ancient Political Theory: Socrates, Plato and Aristotle in Social Context* (New York: Oxford University Press, 1978);

George Huxley, On Aristotle's best state, *History of Political Thought* 6 (Summer 1985).

armed forces, all-volunteer The U.S. military force, now that it is totally dependent upon voluntary enlistments to fill its ranks. The last period of conscription in American history ended in 1973. Men turning eighteen years of age are required to register for the draft; but there is, in practice, no draft.

All branches of the armed forces rely on voluntary enlistments.

REFERENCES

Charles C. Moskos, How to save the all-volunteer force, *Public Interest* 61 (Fall 1980);

Morris Janowitz, Making the all-volunteer military work? *Bulletin of the Atomic Scientists* 37 (February 1981);

William P. Snyder, Officer recruitment for the all-volunteer force: Trends and prospects, *Armed Forces and Society* 10 (Spring 1984);

James Burk, Patriotism and the all-volunteer force, *Journal of Political and Military Sociology* 12 (Fall 1984).

Armed Forces of the United States A collective phrase for all components of the U.S. Army, Navy, Air Force, Marine Corps, and Coast Guard.

REFERENCES

Susan K. Kinnell, ed., *Military History of the United States: An Annotated Bibliography* (Santa Barbara, CA: ABC-Clio, 1986);

Arthur T. Hadley, *The Straw Giant, Triumph and Failure: America's Armed Forces* (New York: Random House, 1986).

arms control **1** Any international agreement governing the numbers, types, and performance characteristics of weapon systems or armed forces. **2** A general reference to any

Arms control has been a major focus of U.S.–Soviet relations since World War II.

measures taken to reduce international military instability.

REFERENCES

Michael Krepon, *Strategic Stalemate: Nuclear Weapons and Arms Control in American Politics* (New York: St. Martin's, 1984);

Strobe Talbott, *Deadly Gambits: The Reagan Administration and the Stalemate in Nuclear Arms Control* (New York: Knopf, 1984);

Charles C. Flowerree, The politics of arms control treaties: A case study, *Journal of International Affairs* 37 (Winter 1984);

John Steinbruner, Arms control: Crisis or compromise? *Foreign Affairs* 63 (Summer 1985);

Gordon Adams, Why there is no arms control, *Dissent* 32 (Spring 1985).

Arms Control and Disarmament Act of 1961 The law that created the U.S. Arms Control and Disarmament Agency to conduct research, to aid in arms control and disarmament negotiations, and to provide public information. The act specifically states that "adequate verification of compliance should be an indispensable part" of any arms control treaties.

REFERENCE

Betty G. Lall, Disarmament agency at twenty-five, *Bulletin of the Atomic Scientists* 42 (December 1986).

Aron, Raymond (1905–1983) The French sociologist and political commentator who has been the foremost European intellectual supporter of the American leadership of the Western world. His *The Imperial Republic: The United States and the World, 1945–1973*, trans. Frank Jellineck (Cambridge, MA: Winthrop, 1974), continues to serve as a response to critics of an American foreign policy that protects Western Europe from the Soviet empire.

arraignment 1 A hearing before a court having jurisdiction in a criminal case in which the identity of the defendant is established, the defendant is informed of his or her rights, and the defendant is required to enter a plea. 2 Any appearance in court prior to trial in criminal proceedings.

arrest The taking of a person into physical custody by authority of law for the purpose of charging that person with a criminal offense.

arrest, citizen's The taking of a person into physical custody by a witness to a crime other than a law enforcement officer for the purpose of delivering that person into the custody of law enforcement authorities.

REFERENCE

M. Cherif Bassiouni, *Citizen's Arrest: The Law of Arrest, Search, and Seizure for Private Citizens and Private Police* (Springfield, IL: Thomas, 1977).

arrest warrant A document issued by a judicial officer directing a law enforcement officer to arrest an identified person who has been accused of a specific crime. For an arrest warrant to be issued, there must be either a sworn complaint or evidence of probable cause that the person being arrested committed a crime. When arrest warrants do not identify a person by name, they are often called John Doe warrants or no-name warrants.

arrogance of power A phrase applied to U.S. foreign policy during the 1960s. It was mostly associated with former Senator J. William Fulbright (1905–   ) of Arkansas, Chairman of the Senate Foreign Relations Committee (1959–1975), who was a severe critic of U.S. intervention in Vietnam and the Dominican Republic.

REFERENCE

J. William Fulbright, *The Arrogance of Power* (New York: Random House, 1966).

arsenal of democracy President Franklin D. Roosevelt's phrase, first used in a 1940 speech, to describe the U.S. role in supplying arms to the nations opposed to the Axis powers in World War II. When the United States came into the war a year later, the phrase became even more significant and literal.

REFERENCE

Donald M. Nelson, *Arsenal of Democracy* (New York: Harcourt, Brace, 1946).

articles 1 The various parts of a document or law. For example, the U.S. Constitution is divided into seven Articles. **2** A system of rules, such as the articles of war. **3** A contract, as in articles of partnership.

Articles of Confederation The original framework for the government of the new United States; it went into effect in 1781 and was superseded by the U.S. Constitution in 1789. The articles provided for a weak central government, which could not compel states to respect treaties, could not regulate interstate and foreign commerce, could neither collect taxes directly from the people nor compel the states to pay for the costs of the national government, and could not create a sense of national unity and national purpose. It nonetheless provided the experience of state cooperation out of which the consciousness of the need for a stronger union could emerge.

REFERENCES
Merrill Jensen, *The New Nation: A History of the United States During the Confederation, 1781–1789* (New York: Vintage, 1950, 1965);
Jack P. Greene, The background of the Articles of Confederation, *Publius* 12 (Fall 1982);
Jack Rakove, The legacy of the Articles of Confederation, *Publius* 12 (Fall 1982).

articles of war The laws under which the U.S. military force governed itself from 1775 until 1950, when these laws were superseded by the Uniform Code of Military Justice.

art of the possible A definition of politics that implies the necessity for compromise and accommodation and suggests the limits of the application of science in the practice of politics.

REFERENCES
Robert L. Branyan and R. Alton Lee, Lyndon B. Johnson and the art of the possible, *Southwestern Social Science Quarterly* 45:3 (1964);
Martin Indyk, Reagan and the Middle East: Learning the art of the possible, *SAIS Review* 7 (Winter-Spring 1987).

arts endowment *See* NATIONAL FOUNDATION ON THE ARTS AND THE HUMANITIES.

ASEAN The Association of Southeast Asian Nations, a regional group of five noncommunist Southeast Asian countries founded in 1967 to encourage regional economic cooperation. The members are Indonesia, Malaysia, the Philippines, Singapore, and Thailand.

REFERENCES
Donald K. Crone, *The ASEAN States: Coping with Dependence* (New York: Praeger, 1983);
Michael T. Skully, *ASEAN Financial Cooperation: Developments in Banking, Finance, and Insurance* (London: Macmillan, 1985).

Ash Council President Richard M. Nixon's Advisory Council on Executive Organization, chaired by Roy Ash of Litton Industries, whose efforts led to the transformation of the Bureau of the Budget into the Office of Management and Budget.

REFERENCES
Papers Relating to the President's Departmental Reorganization Program (Washington, D.C.: Government Printing Office, 1971);
Roger G. Noll, *Reforming Regulation: An Evaluation of the Ash Council Proposals* (Washington D.C.: Brookings, 1971).

Ashwander **rules** A definition of the U.S. Supreme Court's jurisdiction put forth by Justice Louis D. Brandeis in a concurring opinion in the case of *Ashwander v TVA*, 297 U.S. 288 (1936). Brandeis asserted that the Court would not decide constitutional questions unless they were absolutely essential, would avoid a constitutional question if the case could be decided on other grounds, and would not make a constitutional ruling broader than required by a case at hand. The case also upheld the construction of dams and the selling of electric power by the federal government.

ASPA *See* AMERICAN SOCIETY FOR PUBLIC ADMINISTRATION.

assembly **1** Any large meeting. **2** The right of assembly (to meet for political or other purposes) guaranteed by the First Amendment to the U.S. Constitution. Freedom of assembly is as fundamental as the freedoms of speech and press, all three freedoms being inseparable parts of freedom of expression. While the assembly clause adds little to the protection of the rights to assemble, picket, or parade that would not already be protected by the speech clause, it does reaffirm the breadth of those rights. **3** A legislature. **4** The lower, more numerous, house of a legislature. *See also* ADDERLY V FLORIDA; HAGUE V CIO; NATIONAL ASSOCIATION FOR THE ADVANCEMENT OF COLORED PEOPLE V ALABAMA.

REFERENCE

2 For a comparative perspective, see Edward N. Muller, Pertti Pesonen, and Thomas O. Jukam, Support for the freedom of assembly in Western democracies, *European Journal of Political Research* 8 (September 1980).

assessment **1** The evaluation of property for the purposes of taxation. **2** The contributions to political parties determined according to a schedule of rates and made in order to retain a civil service patronage appointment. **3** An extra payment required by law, such as an assessment for additional taxes. **4** The financial damages charged to the loser of a lawsuit. **5** Amounts paid by labor union members in addition to their regular dues when a union needs funds urgently to support a strike or some other union-endorsed cause. The amount of these assessments are usually limited by a union's constitution or bylaws. **6** Financial contributions made by a government (such as the United States) to the regular budget of an international organization (such as the United Nations) to which it belongs.

REFERENCES

1 Jerome F. Heavey, Assessment lags and property tax impacts, *American Journal of Economics and Sociology* 37 (October 1978);
   J. Edwin Benton, Tax assessment and the role of state government, *State Government* 57:1 (1984).
2 Thomas C. Reeves, Chester A. Arthur and campaign assessments in the election of 1880, *Historian* 31:4 (1969).

assessment ratio A property tax computation; the ratio between the market value and assessed value. Assessment ratios vary tremendously, because some jurisdictions value property at or close to actual market value and others use formulas calling for assessed values to be various fractions of market value.

assessments, scale of The formula for assessing membership dues used in an international organization.

assessor **1** In ancient Rome, a legal expert who advised the governor of a province on the technical details of the law. **2** An official of a jurisdiction who determines the value of property for the purpose of taxation. **3** An expert who sits with a court to provide technical advice but has no right to decide issues. **4** An insurance investigator who determines the amount of a loss and whether the loss is genuine.

assigned counsel A lawyer, not regularly employed by government, assigned by a court to represent a person in a criminal case who cannot afford to pay for counsel. An assigned counsel may or may not be paid by a government agency. *Compare to* PUBLIC DEFENDER; RETAINED COUNSEL.

Association of Southeast Asian Nations *See* ASEAN.

asylum **1** Originally, a protected place for those fleeing authority and whose forced removal would be sacrilege. In ancient Greece, temples were inviolate, and those inside had the protection of the gods and could not be removed by force. Under Christianity, churches became places of asylum. **2** A charitable refuge for the afflicted or others unable to care for themselves. **3** Protection for those fleeing political persecution. The United States has often granted political asylum for those fleeing foreign tyrannies—especially those who would be unjustly persecuted if forced to return. In recent years the question of asylum has been caught up in a controversy over whether "economic" refugees are as worthy of asylum as "political" refugees. Normal immigration to the United States is in effect a grant of asylum. *Compare to* SANCTUARY.

Mikhail Baryshnikov—considered by many to be the greatest dancer of his time—defected from the Soviet Union and sought asylum in the West in 1974.

REFERENCES

David A. Martin, Large-scale migrations of asylum seekers, *American Journal of International Law* 76 (July 1982);

W. Scott Burke, Compassion versus self-interest: Who shall be given asylum in the United States? *Fletcher Forum* 8 (Summer 1984);

Michael S. Teitelbaum, Political asylum in theory and practice, *Public Interest* 76 (Summer 1984).

asylum, diplomatic The right to offer asylum within a diplomatic mission. Diplomatic asylum, which is not recognized as a legal right by all nations, is generally a function of local custom, humanitarian practice, and diplomatic expediency.

Atlantic Alliance An informal phrase for NATO.

REFERENCE

Jeane J. Kirkpatrick, The Atlantic Alliance and the American national interest, *World Affairs* 147 (Fall 1984).

Atlantic Charter The statement of general principles for the postwar world issued by President Franklin D. Roosevelt and British Prime Minister Winston Churchill after meeting on shipboard in the Atlantic Ocean off Newfoundland on August 14, 1941.

Atlantic Community 1 The West in general. 2 NATO. 3 The United States, Great Britain, and Canada.

at large An election in which one or more candidates for a legislature are chosen by all of the voters of a jurisdiction. This is in contrast to an election by legislative district, in which voters are limited to selecting one candidate to represent their district. Minority candidates have more difficulty gaining office in at-large elections than in district elections.

REFERENCES

John Rehfuss, Are at-large elections best for council-manager cities? *National Civic Review* 61 (May 1972);

Chandler Davidson and George Korbel, At-large elections and minority-group representation: A re-examination of historical and contemporary evidence, *Journal of Politics* 43 (November 1981).

Atomic Energy Commission *See* NUCLEAR REGULATORY COMMISSION.

atoms for peace The Dwight D. Eisenhower administration's phrase for the civilian use of nuclear power. Unlike the bomb-making aspects of atomic power, atoms for peace provided a vast field of cooperative research and development with not only allies but with non-aligned countries as well. Unfortunately, it also gave those countries much of the technical capability they needed to make nuclear weapons.

REFERENCE

Gerald E. Marsh, If "atoms for peace" are used for war, *Bulletin of the Atomic Scientists* 38 (February 1982).

attaché A French word meaning one assigned to. This person is usually a technical specialist (such as military, economic, cultural) assigned to a diplomatic mission abroad.

attack PAC   *See* TARGETING.

attainder   *See* BILL OF ATTAINDER.

attorney   **1** A lawyer; a person trained in the law, admitted to practice before the bar of a given jurisdiction, and authorized to advise, represent, and act for others in legal proceedings.   **2** Any person who formally represents another. *Compare to* ASSIGNED COUNSEL; PROSECUTOR; PUBLIC DEFENDER; RETAINED COUNSEL.

attorney general   **1** The appointed head of the U.S. Department of Justice; the chief legal advisor to the president and the federal government.   **2** The chief legal officer of a state, usually elected. While the U.S. attorney general in effect supervises the work of all of the nation's federal prosecuting attorneys and the federal prison system, a state attorney general typically has no authority over local district attorneys or state prisons.

REFERENCES

1   Luther A. Huston and others, *Role of the Attorney General of the United States* (Washington, D.C.: American Enterprise, 1968);

2   Henry J. Abraham and Robert R. Benedetti, The state attorney general: A friend of the court? *University of Pennsylvania Law Review* 117 (April 1969).

attorney general's list   A list of purportedly subversive organizations initially compiled during the Harry S Truman administration by the attorney general of the United States as part of the loyalty program. It was abolished by executive order in 1974.

audit   **1** The official examination of a financial report submitted by an individual or organization to determine whether it accurately represents expenditures, deductions, or other allowances determined by laws and regulations.   **2** The final phase of the government budgetary process, which reviews the operations of an agency, especially its financial transactions, to determine whether the agency has spent its money in accordance with the law, in the most efficient manner, and with desired results. *See also* COMPLIANCE; EVALUATION, PROGRAM.

REFERENCES

Elmer B. Staats, GAO audit standards: Development and implementation, *Public Management* 56 (February 1974);

Richard E. Brown and Ralph Craft, Auditing and public administration: The unrealized partnership, *Public Administration Review* 40 (May/June 1980).

auditing, expanded scope   Evaluating the results and effectiveness of a government activity in addition to delving into the traditional financial compliance concerns of auditing.

Australian ballot   *See* BALLOT, AUSTRALIAN.

autarchy   **1** An autocracy.   **2** A policy of national (or regional) self-sufficiency, which prevents a nation from being dependent for critical materials from any nondomestic source. This meaning of autarchy is also spelled autarky.

REFERENCE

2   Dieter Senghaas, The case for autarchy, *International Development Review* 22:1 (1980).

authoritarianism   Rule by an individual whose claim to sole power is supported by subordinates who sustain control of the system by carrying out the ruler's orders and by a public that is unwilling or unable to rebel against that control. The ruler's personality may be a significant element in maintaining the necessary balance of loyalty and fear. Authoritarianism differs from totalitarianism only in that the latter may have a specific ideology that rationalizes it, although it may require a leader who embodies that ideology to sustain public support. *Compare to* DICTATOR; TOTALITARIANISM.

REFERENCE

John H. Herz, *From Dictatorship to Democracy: Coping with the Legacies of Authoritarianism and Totalitarianism* (Westport, CT: Greenwood, 1982).

authoritative source   A journalism term applied to a public official whose particular position implies special closeness to information, even though neither the official nor the position is identified in the press. The information thus gets to the public even though the source may be "off the record."

authority 1 The feature of a leader or an institution that compels others to grant it obedience, usually because of some ascribed legitimacy. 2 A government corporation, such as the Tennessee Valley Authority or the Port of New York Authority. 3 The power inherent in a specific position or function that allows an incumbent to perform assigned duties and assume delegated responsibilities. *See also* BUREAUCRACY; POWER.

REFERENCES

1 For a classic analysis on the perceived legitimacy of authority, see Stanley Milgram, *Obedience to Authority: An Experimental View* (New York: Harper & Row, 1973).

2 William J. Quirk and Leon E. Wein, A short constitutional history of entities commonly known as authorities, *Cornell Law Review* 56 (April 1971).

3 Robert L. Peabody, *Organizational Authority: Superior-Subordinate Relationships in Three Public Service Organizations* (New York: Atherton, 1964);
   Richard Sennett, *Authority* (New York: Knopf, 1980);
   Richard E. Flathman, *The Practice of Political Authority* (Chicago: University of Chicago Press, 1980);
   Robert J. Morgan, Madison's analysis of the sources of political authority, *American Political Science Review* 75 (September 1981).

authority, backdoor Legislation enacted outside the normal appropriation process that permits the obligation of funds. The most common forms of backdoor authority are borrowing authority (authority to spend debt receipts) and contract authority. Entitlement programs may sometimes take the form of backdoor authority, since the enactment of the basic benefit legislation may, in effect, mandate the subsequent enactment of the appropriations to pay the statutory benefits.

authorization/authorizing legislation Basic substantive legislation enacted by a legislature that sets up or continues the legal operation of a government program or agency, either indefinitely or for a specific period of time, or sanctions a particular type of obligation or expenditure within a program. Such legislation is normally a prerequisite for subsequent appropriations or other kinds of budget authority to be contained in appropriation acts. It may limit the amount of budget authority to be provided subsequently or may authorize the appropriation of "such sums as may be necessary"; in a few instances, budget authority may be provided in the authorization.

authorization election Polls conducted by the National Labor Relations Board (or other administrative agency) to determine if a particular group of employees will be represented by a particular union or not. Authorization election is used interchangeably with certification election (because, if the union wins, it is certified as the representative of the workers by the administrative agency) and representative election (because a winning union becomes just that, the representative of the workers).

REFERENCES

Julius G. Getman, Stephen B. Goldberg, and Jeanne B. Herman, *Union Representation Elections: Law and Reality* (New York: Russell Sage, 1976);
John J. Lawler, The influence of management consultants on the outcome of union certification elections, *Industrial and Labor Relations Review* 38 (October 1984);
James E. Martin, Employee characteristics and representation election outcomes, *Industrial and Labor Relations Review* 38 (April 1985).

authorizing committee A STANDING committee of the U.S. House of Representatives or Senate with legislative jurisdiction over the subject matter of those laws, or parts of laws, that set up or continue the legal operations of designated federal programs or agencies. An authorizing committee also has jurisdiction in those instances where backdoor authority is provided in the substantive legislation.

autocracy A dictatorship by a single individual; a state in which one person has unlimited political power. This differs from an absolute monarchy in that a monarch claims power through lawful succession while an autocrat simply takes it without the pretense of legitimacy (which is often created after the fact).

automatic stabilizer/built-in stabilizer A government mechanism or standing policy with a COUNTERCYCLICAL effect, automatically moderating changes in incomes and outputs in the economy without specific changes in government policy. Unemployment insurance and the progressive income tax are among the most important of the automatic stabilizers in the United States.

auxiliary agency An administrative unit whose prime responsibility is to service other agencies of the greater organization. For example, in the federal government, the Office of Personnel Management and the General Services Administration are auxiliary, or overhead, agencies.

Axis **1** The World War II coalition of Germany, Italy, and Japan. It is short for Rome-Berlin Axis. **2** Any political or military alliance between two powers.

B

baby boom That age cohort born in the two decades after World War II. This group of almost seventy-four million people makes up about 30 percent of the U.S. population. The boom came about because population growth was suppressed first by the Great Depression of the 1930s and then by the prolonged absence of men for the World War II effort. With the return of prosperity and of the men in the postwar period, a baby boom commenced. As the babies in the boom continue to grow older, their sheer numbers will continue to have significant sociological, economic, and political implications. The apex of the baby boom, which began in 1946, was the year between April 1, 1959, and April 2, 1960. More living Americans were born in that year than in any other. Since then, there has been a steady decline in the birth rate. In 1972 the United States achieved theoretical zero population growth when the Census Bureau discovered that American women were, on average, only replacing, not increasing, the population. Since then, the birth rate has continued to decline. Thus the baby boom has become all the more significant because it has been followed by a birth dearth brought on by the ease of contraception and abortion, the trend toward later marriage, and the new place of women in the work force.

REFERENCES
Louise B. Russell, *The Baby Boom Generation and the Economy* (Washington, D.C.: Brookings, 1982);
Frank D. Bean, The baby boom and its explanations, *Sociological Quarterly* 24 (Summer 1983);
Ben J. Wattenberg, *The Birth Dearth* (New York: Pharas Books, 1987).

backbencher **1** Any legislator of low seniority or rank who also has no formal leadership position. **2** A member of the British House of Commons who literally sits in the back benches (there are no assigned seats) and is expected to be completely supportive of his party's leadership.

back channel Any informal method for government-to-government communications in place of normal or routine methods.

backdoor spending *See* AUTHORITY, BACK-DOOR.

backgrounder A meeting with the press by a government official in which the information can be used but attributed only to an unnamed source.

backgrounder, deep Information given to the press that can be neither quoted directly nor attributed to any source, however official the source may be.

backlash 1 A negative reaction by whites to the civil rights efforts of blacks and other protected classes when the whites feel threatened. Busing to achieve school integration and compensatory hiring practices are two situations that often create a backlash. 2 Any counterreaction by any group—sexual, ethnical, national, and so on—to preference shown toward another group.

REFERENCE
1 Lillian B. Rubin, *Busing and Backlash: White against White in a California School District* (Berkeley and Los Angeles: University of California Press, 1972).

backslider Originally, a religious believer who slipped back into sin (and hence slid back toward hell); anyone who reneges on a doctrinal commitment of any kind.

bad tendency rule *See* ABRAMS V UNITED STATES.

bagman 1 The intermediary in a political payoff; he or she carries the money in a bag from the one offering the bribe to the one accepting it. 2 The military officer who constantly attends the president, carrying the secret codes through which the president could launch an immediate retaliatory nuclear strike. *Compare to* BLACK BAG JOB.

bail 1 To arrange the release of an accused person from custody in return for a promise that the defendant will appear at a place and time specified and submit to the jurisdiction of the court, guaranteed by a pledge to pay to the court a specified sum of money or property if the defendant does not appear. The amount of bail is determined by a judge and should be appropriate to the crime. 2 The money or property pledged to a court to guarantee the appearance of a defendant at a later date. An accused who is released from custody and subsequently fails to appear for trial forfeits the bail to the court. The Eighth Amendment prohibits excessive bail—that is, any amount greater than is necessary to assure subsequent appearance in court. This amendment does not specifically provide that all citizens have a right to bail, but only that bail will not be excessive. In a few instances, as when a capital offense, such as murder, is charged, bail may be denied altogether.

REFERENCES
Donald B. Verrilli, Jr., The Eighth Amendment and the right to bail: Historical perspectives, *Columbia Law Review* 82 (March 1982);
Paul Robertshaw, The political economy of bail reform, *Contemporary Crises: Crime, Law and Social Policy* 7 (October 1983);
John S. Goldkamp and Michael R. Gottfredson, *Policy Guidelines for Bail: An Experiment in Court Reform* (Philadelphia: Temple University Press, 1985).

bail bond A document guaranteeing the appearance of a defendant in court as required and recording the pledge of money or property to be paid to the court if the defendant does not appear.

bail bondsperson A person, usually licensed, whose business it is to arrange releases on bail for persons charged with crimes by pledging to pay a sum of money if the defendant fails to appear in court as ordered. In effect, the defendant pays to borrow bail money from the bondsperson. Actually, what is usually being borrowed is not money but the bondsperson's credit with the court. The bail amount must be paid only if the defendant does not show up for trial.

bailiff 1 The court officer whose duties are to keep order in the courtroom and to maintain physical custody of the jury. A bailiff's duties might include seating witnesses, announcing the judge's entrance, or resolving disturbances in the courtroom. In some jurisdictions a bailiff may be called a court officer. Federal court bailiffs are U.S. marshalls. **2** A sheriff's aide or deputy. **3** Any low-level court official.

bailout A government-sponsored rescue (by providing loans or LOAN GUARANTEES) of a failing private-sector enterprise. The best-known government bailout of recent years was the federal government's rescue of the Chrysler Corporation in order to prevent its bankruptcy. *See* CHRYSLER CORPORATION LOAN GUARANTEE ACT OF 1979.

bail revocation The decision of a court to withdraw the status of release on bail previously given to a defendant. Bail status may be revoked if the defendant fails to appear in court when required, is arrested for another crime, or violates a condition of bail release.

Baker v Carr 369 U.S. 186 (1962) The U.S. Supreme Court case that held that under the equal protection clause of the Fourteenth Amendment the federal courts have jurisdiction in cases involving state legislative reapportionment. Apportionment thus became justiciable (*see* JUSTICIABILITY); courts then had the right to consider apportionment cases. *Baker* reversed *Colegrove v Green*, 328 U.S. 549 (1946), opened the federal courts to the problem of malapportionment, and established the basis for the one man, one vote decision in REYNOLDS V SIMS and WESBERRY V SANDERS. *See also* POLITICAL QUESTION.
REFERENCE
Gene Graham, *One Man, One Vote: Baker v. Carr and the American Levellers* (Boston: Little, Brown, 1972).

Bakke decision *See* REGENTS OF THE UNIVERSITY OF CALIFORNIA V ALLAN BAKKE.

balance **1** A state of equilibrium. **2** A condition in which the armed forces and equipment of one nation do not have an advantage or disadvantage over the military posture of another nation. **3** The internal military adjustments that a nation may make to cope with

remaining threats to its security after an arms control agreement is implemented.

balanced budget A budget in which receipts are equal to or greater than outlays. The advantages of a balanced budget, not spending more than you take in, are obvious. But there are also advantages to "unbalanced" budgets, those that require public borrowing. The "extra" spending can stimulate the economy during economic downturns (*see* JOHN MAYNARD KEYNES) and provide needed public works and public support for the less fortunate. But these considerations must be weighed against the danger that large deficits over a significant period can devalue the currency, kindle inflation, and have such a CROWDING OUT effect on capital markets that an economic depression (or recession) occurs. Note that it is only the federal government that has the option of long-term deficit spending. The states all have constitutional or statutory provisions mandating balanced budgets. *Compare to* FISCAL POLICY; MONETARY POLICY.

balanced budget amendment Any of a variety of proposals to force an end to deficit spending by the federal government by passing a constitutional amendment mandating a balanced budget. Many critics think that this is an exercise in futility because the Congress could easily create any number of mechanisms to meet the letter, but violate the spirit, of any such amendment. In 1986, the Senate was only one vote short of approving such an amendment, which read, in part, "Outlays of the United States for any fiscal year shall not exceed receipts to the United States for that year, unless three fifths of the whole number of both houses of Congress shall provide for a specific excess of outlays over receipts."
REFERENCES
Aaron Wildavsky, Why amending the Constitution is essential to achieving self-control through self-limitation of expenditure, *Bureaucrat* 9 (Spring 1980);
Rose Friedman and Milton Friedman, Constitutional amendment to limit the growth of spending, *Proceedings of the Academy of Political Science* 35:4 (1985);

William R. Keech, A theoretical analysis of the case for a balanced budget amendment, *Policy Sciences* 18 (September 1985).

balanced ticket   A slate of candidates whose characteristics mesh for maximum appeal to the voters in terms of geographic origin, race, religion, and so on.

balance of payments   A tabulation of a nation's debt and credit transactions with foreign countries and international institutions. A favorable balance, more money coming in from other countries than going out, is an economic advantage. An unfavorable balance over a significant time is one indication of problems within a nation's economy.

balance of power   1 The international relations policy on the part of rival states whose goal is to prevent any one nation or alliance of nations from gaining a preponderance of power in relation to the rival nation or alliance; thus an approximate military balance is maintained.   2 A principle of international relations that asserts that when any nation seeks to increase its military potential, neighboring or rival nations will take similar actions to maintain the military equilibrium.

REFERENCES

M. V. Naidu, *Alliances and Balance of Power: A Search for Conceptual Clarity* (New York: St. Martin's, 1975);

Edward Vose Bulick, *Europe's Classical Balance of Power: A Case History of the Theory and Practice of One of the Great Concepts of European Statecraft* (Westport, CT: Greenwood, 1955, 1982).

balance of terror   Winston Churchill's (1874–1965) phrase for the nuclear stalemate between the United States and the Soviet Union. Because the terror is in balance, neither country, in theory, would risk nuclear war because neither could win.

REFERENCES

Pierre Gallois, *The Balance of Terror: Strategy for the Nuclear Age* (Boston: Houghton Mifflin, 1961);

Edgar M. Bottome, *The Balance of Terror: A Guide to the Arms Race* (Boston: Beacon, 1971).

balance of trade   The amount by which the value of merchandise exports exceeds (trade surplus) or falls short of (trade deficit) the value of merchandise imports. The balance of trade is the visible element of a nation's balance of payments.

REFERENCE

Arthur F. Burns, The American trade deficit in perspective, *Foreign Affairs* 62 (Summer 1984).

balloon, trial   *See* TRIAL BALLOON.

ballot   1 The means by which votes are officially recorded. The word has its origins in the balls (white meaning yes and black meaning no) that the ancient Greeks anonymously put in a container to register their votes.   2 The sheet of paper on which a voter indicates preferences.   3 The array of choices presented to a voter by a voting machine.

REFERENCES

Donald S. Hecock and Henry M. Bain, *Ballot Position and Voter's Choice* (Detroit: Wayne State University Press, 1957);

Delbert A. Taebel, The effect of ballot position on electoral success, *American Journal of Political Science* 19 (August 1975);

Bruce W. Robeck and James A. Dyer, Ballot access requirements in congressional elections, *American Politics Quarterly* 10 (January 1982).

ballot, absentee   A device that allows qualified voters who anticipate being unable to appear at the polls in person on election day (because of military service, illness, and so on) to vote in advance by mail. Such ballots are then opened and integrated with the rest of the vote on election day. Absentee voting was first used during the Civil War to allow Union troops to vote. Two federal acts allow American citizens residing overseas to vote absentee: the Federal Voting Assistance Act of 1955 (FVAA) and the Overseas Citizens Voting Rights Act of 1975 (OCVRA). The FVAA applies to active duty members of the U.S. armed forces, members of the merchant marine, spouses and dependents of both categories, and other citizens temporarily residing outside the United States, who may vote absentee, wherever they are stationed, while away from their place of voting residence.

The OCVRA applies to U.S. citizens residing outside the United States and its territories on other than a temporary basis. These citizens must vote in the state in which they last resided immediately prior to departing the United States, even if many years have elapsed and the voter maintains no abode in the state and the intent to return to that state may not be certain. Most states permit those covered by OCVRA to vote only in federal elections. Other states may send complete federal and state ballots. The OCVRA provides that voting in federal elections, by any citizen outside the United States, shall not affect the determination of the voter's place of residence for purposes of any tax imposed under federal, state, or local law. Liability for state income tax, however, may be incurred in a few states by voting absentee in state elections. *See also* FEDERAL POSTCARD APPLICATION; VOTING, ABSENTEE.

REFERENCE

Samuel C. Patterson and Gregory A. Calderia, Mailing in the vote: Correlates and consequences of absentee voting, *American Journal of Political Science* 29 (November 1985)

The two major political parties in the United States (Democratic and Republican) have branches in many countries. Further information concerning their overseas political activities can be obtained by contacting

Democrats Abroad
7400 Rebecca Drive
Alexandria, VA 22307

Republicans Abroad
310 1st Street, S.E.
Washington, D.C. 20003

ballot, Australian   A ballot printed by a government (as opposed to being printed by a political party) and distributed and collected by that government's officials at a polling place. In this way, a voter's vote is secret and not known to those who collect and tabulate the votes; thus such information cannot be used to punish or reward. The ballot lists the names of all candidates lawfully nominated and provides room for write-in candidates. First used in Australia in 1858, it was introduced in the

United States in 1888. It has generally been modified by the Massachusetts or Indiana ballot format.

REFERENCES

L. E. Fredman, The introduction of the Australian ballot in the United States, *Australian Journal of Politics and History* 13:2 (1967);

Jerrold G. Rusk, The effect of the Australian ballot reform on split ticket voting: 1876–1908, *American Political Science Review* 64 (December 1970).

ballot box stuffing   **1** Putting illegal ballots into a ballot box to affect an election. Voting machines were designed in part to eliminate this practice.   **2** Any rigging of an election.

ballot, Indiana   A party-column ballot, which lists all candidates under their party designation; this makes it easy to vote for all of the candidates of one party by pulling a single lever on a voting machine. *Compare to* BALLOT, MASSACHUSETTS.

REFERENCE

Jack L. Walker, Ballot forms and voter fatigue: An analysis of the office block and party column ballots, *Midwest Journal of Political Science* 10:4 (1966).

ballot, long   Any ballot containing a large number of offices for which candidates must be selected by the voter. The longer the ballot, the more difficult it is for voters to make discriminating decisions and the easier it is for others to influence results with prepared lists of names. Jacksonian democracy favored greater numbers of elected offices to insure greater participation in government, while progressive reform and the rise of professionalism in many fields of public service favored shorter ballots and more appointments of specialists in fields like public health and educational administration. The debate over the selection of judges by ballot or appointment is still active in many parts of the country. *Compare to* BALLOT, SHORT.

ballot, Massachusetts   An office-block ballot, which lists all candidates under the office for which they are running. This ballot passively encourages ticket splitting. *Compare to* BALLOT, INDIANA.

ballot, nonpartisan A ballot not designating the political party of the candidates. The progressive movement encouraged it in order to lessen the influence of political party commitment.

REFERENCE
Carol A. Cassel, The nonpartisan ballot in the United States, *Electoral Laws and their Political Consequences,* ed. Bernard Grofman and Arend Lijphart (New York: Agathon, 1986).

ballot, preferential An advisory ballot used in an election whose results are not binding. As used in a presidential preferential primary, this ballot tells the delegates to the national nominating convention the preferences of the voters at the time of the election.

ballot, short Any ballot containing a relatively few offices for which candidates must be selected by the voter. The shorter the ballot, the more likely it is that the voters will be able to make a discriminating decision. The short ballot was advocated by the progressive reform movement so that the voters would be able to know who the rascals were when it was time to throw them out. In general, the short ballot, which presumes that competent technicians and professionals will be appointed by those who are elected, was an effort to hold elected public officials more accountable to their public. *Compare to* BALLOT, LONG.

ballyhoo 1 Noisy, sensational advertising, a carnival barker's speech, general blarney, and the like. 2 The artificial enthusiasm created by political campaigns. Ballyhoo is short for Ballyhooly, a village in Cork County, Ireland, long famous for raucous behavior.

bandwagon effect 1 The gaining of additional support by a candidate or proposal because it seems to be winning. In the days before television, a real bandwagon was popular in political campaigns. As the musically weighted wagons were pulled through the streets, sup-

This bit of ballyhoo from Jimmy Carter's 1976 presidential candidacy centered on his career as a peanut farmer.

porters of the candidate (or the music) would literally climb on or march along with the bandwagon as a gesture of enthusiasm and support. 2 Any demonstration of the herd instinct in politics.

REFERENCES
Daniel W. Fleitas, Bandwagon and underdog effects in minimal-information elections, *American Political Science Review* 65 (June 1971);
Robert Navazio, An experimental approach to bandwagon research, *Public Opinion Quarterly* 41 (Summer 1977);
Philip D. Straffin, Jr., The bandwagon curve, *American Journal of Political Science* 21 (November 1977).

banner district The electoral jurisdiction that gave a candidate the most, or greatest percentage of, votes. In the last century, such districts would literally receive a banner, which signified their enthusiastic support.

bar, the 1 The legal profession; a jurisdiction's community of lawyers. 2 The once real but now imaginary partition across a court: lawyers stood at this bar to argue their cases. Thus to be "called to the bar" meant that you were thought to be enough of a lawyer to plead a case in court. *Compare to* AMERICAN BAR ASSOCIATION.

bar examination A written test set by state bar associations that new lawyers must pass to be certified by the state to practice law. They differ from state to state.

REFERENCE

Charles B. Blackmar, Is the bar examination an anachronism? *American Bar Association Journal* 60 (October 1974).

bargaining chip 1 Anything one might be willing to trade in a negotiation; a deliberately created negotiating condition designed to provide an advantage. 2 Any military force, weapons system, or other resource, present or projected, that a nation is willing to downgrade or discard in return for a concession by a military rival. The phrase was first used in this context during the SALT talks (1969–1979) between the United States and the Soviet Union. Because the Nixon administration believed that the Soviet Union only signed SALT I because the United States had approved the development of the ABM, the Poseidon submarine, and the Minuteman III missile systems, it asked the Congress to approve, as a bargaining chip for SALT II, the development of the Trident submarine, the B-1 bomber, and the cruise missile. The bargaining chip strategy has been attacked on two fronts: first, because it is too expensive to develop weapons systems just to trade them away at the negotiating table; and second, because it is inflammatory to the arms race to develop weapons systems just as a hedge in negotiations.

REFERENCES

Robert J. Bresler and Robert C. Gray, The bargaining chip and SALT, *Political Science Quarterly* 92 (Spring 1977);

Robert C. Gray and Robert J. Bresler, Why weapons make poor bargaining chips, *Bulletin of the Atomic Scientists* 33 (September 1977).

bargaining strength The relative power each party holds during negotiation. One government has great bargaining strength vis à vis another if both sides know that it has the military power to impose its will regardless of the outcome of negotiations; management has great bargaining strength over labor if it has so much excess inventory that a short strike would be desirable. The final settlement often reflects the bargaining power of each side.

REFERENCES

Samuel B. Bacharach and Edward J. Lawler, Power and tactics in bargaining, *Industrial and Labor Relations Review* 34 (January 1981);

Christer Jonsson, Bargaining power: Notes on an elusive concept, *Cooperation and Conflict* 16 (December 1981).

barnburners Political opponents who fail to measure the ultimate or long-range cost of the tactics they are committed to using, despite the fact that these tactics may prove more costly than the benefits they may actually achieve. The term is derived from the story of a farmer who was so determined to get rid of the rats in his barn that he burned them out by burning down his barn.

barnstorm To make an election campaign trip with many brief stops, after the fashion of traveling players who would perform from barn to barn. Storm is used here in the sense of moving about to maximize coverage.

Barron v Baltimore See INCORPORATION.

Barr v Matteo 360 U.S. 564 (1959) The U.S. Supreme Court case concerning the immunity of federal administrators from civil suits for damages in connection with their official duties. The Court, without majority opinion, held that the acting director of the Office of Rent Stabilization had such an immunity. By implication, other federal employees would be immune from civil suits depending upon the nature of their responsibilities and duties. *See also* BUTZ V ECONOMOU; SPALDING V VILAS; WOOD V STRICKLAND.

Bartkus v Illinois See DOUBLE JEOPARDY.

Bay of Pigs 1 The landing site in 1961 of the American-sponsored invasion of Cuba by expatriate Cubans trained by the CIA to overthrow the government of Fidel Castro. It was a total failure and a major embarrassment to the John F. Kennedy administration. 2 Any fiasco or major flop. Just as Napoleon had his

Waterloo, Kennedy had his Bay of Pigs. But there's a major difference. Napoleon nearly won; it was an honest try. Kennedy's failure was an embarrassment because it was such an incompetent effort. The invasion was based on grossly wrong intelligence, was poorly planned and led, and lacked adequate air cover. So, if you have a Bay of Pigs, you haven't merely lost—you've disgraced yourself as well.
REFERENCES
Peter Wyden, *Bay of Pigs: The Untold Story* (New York: Simon & Schuster, 1979);
Joshua H. Sandman, Analyzing foreign policy crisis situations: The Bay of Pigs, *Presidential Studies Quarterly* 16 (Spring 1976).

bear 1 One who believes that prices on a stock market will decline, as opposed to a bull, who believes they will rise. 2 The Soviet Union, whose national symbol is the bear. 3 A series of Soviet bombers.

Beard, Charles A. See CONSTITUTION, ECONOMIC INTERPRETATION OF.

beggar-thy-neighbor policy A course of action through which a country tries to reduce unemployment and increase domestic output by raising tariffs and instituting nontariff measures that impede imports. Countries that pursued such policies in the early 1930s found that other countries retaliated by raising barriers against the first country's exports, which tended to worsen the economic difficulties that precipitated the initial protectionist action. *Compare to* PROTECTIONISM.

behavioralism 1 A philosophical disposition toward the study of the behavior of people in political situations as opposed to studying the institutional structures of politics. Thus, for example, one should not study the structure of the Congress, because what is really important is the behavior of its members. 2 The scientific study of politics that emphasizes the use of the scientific method for empirical investigations and the use of quantitative techniques.
REFERENCES
David Easton, The current meaning of "behavioralism," in *Contemporary Political Analysis,* ed. James C. Charlesworth (New York: Free Press, 1967);

Heinz Eulau, ed., *Behavioralism in Political Science* (New York: Atherton, 1969).

behavioralism, post The critical response to behavioralism that complained that, as political science adopted the orientation of behavioralism, it became less relevant to the study of politics. Because of the overemphasis on being empirical and quantitative, too much attention was being devoted to easily studied trivial issues at the expense of important topics. Postbehavioralism as a movement within political science does not advocate the end of the scientific study of politics; it mainly suggests that there is more than one way of advancing knowledge and that methodologies should be appropriate to the issue under study.
REFERENCES
George Graham and George Carey, eds., *The Post-Behavioral Era* (New York: McKay, 1972);
Thomas A. Spragens, Jr., *The Dilemma of Contemporary Political Theory: Toward a Post-Behavioral Science of Politics* (New York: Dunellen, 1973).

behavioral sciences A general term for all of the academic disciplines that study human and animal behavior by means of experimental research. The phrase was first put into wide use in the early 1950s by the Ford Foundation to describe its funding for interdisciplinary research in the social sciences; and by faculty at the University of Chicago seeking federal funding for research—and concerned in an era of MCCARTHYISM that their social science research might be confused with socialism. *Compare to* POLICY SCIENCES.

behaviorism The school of psychology that holds that only overt behavior is the proper subject matter for the entire discipline; that psychology should avoid introspection and concentrate on analyzing human behavior in the same manner that animals are objectively studied. John Broadus Watson (1878–1958) is generally considered the originator of the behaviorism movement in psychology. According to the foremost exponent of behaviorism, B. F. Skinner (1904–) in *About Behaviorism* (New York: Knopf, 1974), "behaviorism is not the science of human behavior; it is the philosophy of that science."

bellwether 1 A leading political indicator. A bellwether is literally a ram, the leader of the flock, with a bell hung about its neck. So in politics a bellwether can be a district that historically votes for the winning side, an endorsement from a political figure who has always backed winners, and so on. 2 A decoy candidate whose nomination is designed to split a vote or conceal the intentions of another candidate.

REFERENCE

1   Edward R. Tufte and Richard A. Sun, Are there bellwether electoral districts? *Public Opinion Quarterly* 39 (Spring 1975).

beltway bandits Consulting firms in the Washington, D.C., area located near the interstate beltway, Route 495, surrounding the metropolitan area.

beltway issue A political affair of little concern to the general public; mainly of concern to the Washington, D.C., national political community.

benefit district A method for financing construction of public works in which those who directly benefit are charged for the construction costs. For example, sidewalks are often financed through increases in property taxes of residents through whose property the sidewalk passes; that is, those owners are members of a sidewalk or benefit district that levies a tax, which is dissolved when the construction costs have been recovered.

benefit theory The belief that those who gain from a government action should pay for it. Thus gasoline taxes paid by drivers help pay for highway repair and construction, fees for fishing licenses help pay for restocking lakes, and so on.

benign neglect A policy of allowing a situation to improve, or at least not get worse, by leaving it alone for a while. The phrase was first used by the Earl of Durham in an 1839

report to the British Parliament, in which he observed that "through many years of benign neglect by Britain, Canada had become a nation much more prosperous than England itself." *See also* DANIEL PATRICK MOYNIHAN.

Jeremy Bentham

Bentham, Jeremy (1748–1832) A utilitarian philosopher who held that self-interest was the prime motivator and that a government should strive to do the greatest good for the greatest numbers. Bentham held that governments were created because of man's desire for happiness, not by divine intervention. Because of his beliefs, writings, and actions, Bentham is considered the major social reformer of nineteenth-century England.

REFERENCES

J. A. W. Gunn, Jeremy Bentham and the public interest, *Canadian Journal of Political Science* 1 (December 1968);

Michael James, Public interest and majority rule in Bentham's democratic theory, *Political Theory* 9 (February 1981);

Frederick Rosen, Jeremy Bentham: Recent interpretations, *Political Studies* 30 (December 1982).

Bentley, Arthur F. (1870–1957) The political scientist who was one of the pioneering voices in the behavioral analysis of politics and the intellectual creator of modern interest group theory. In *The Process of Government* (Cambridge, MA: Harvard University Press, 1908, 1967), Bentley argued that political analysis has had to shift its focus from forms of government to actions of individuals in the context of groups, because groups are the critical action mechanisms that enable numbers of individuals to achieve their political, economic, and social desires. Bentley's work was effectively "lost" until it was rediscovered and publicized by DAVID B. TRUMAN. *Compare to* INTEREST GROUP THEORY.

REFERENCES

Paul Kriese, Philosophy and method: Arthur Bentley and "transactional" political science, *Political Methodology* 5:3 (1978);

James F. Ward, Arthur F. Bentley's philosophy of social science, *American Journal of Political Science* 22 (August 1978).

Benton v Maryland   See DOUBLE JEOPARDY.

Berman v Parker   See ZONING, AESTHETIC.

Berry, Mary Frances   See WOMEN'S LIBERATION MOVEMENT.

Bertalanffy, Ludwig von (1901–1972)   Austrian-Canadian biologist considered to be the father of general systems theory.

REFERENCES

Bertalanffy's basic statement on the subject is *General System Theory: Foundations, Development, Applications,* rev. ed. (New York: Braziller, 1968).

For a biography, see Mark Davidson, *Uncommon Sense: The Life and Thought of Ludwig von Bertalanffy (1901–1972), Father of General Systems Theory* (Boston: Houghton Mifflin, 1983).

Betts v Brady   See GIDEON V WAINWRIGHT.

beyond a reasonable doubt   The criterion of proof in a criminal case. It does not amount to absolute certainty but leaves a reasonable person with the belief that the defendant has committed the alleged crime; that is, a standard of proof in which the evidence offered precludes every reasonable hypothesis except the one it supports—that of the defendant's guilt. In civil cases, judgment is supposed to rest on the weight of the evidence. This less-strict standard of proof is called "preponderance of the evidence."

REFERENCES

Rita James Simon, "Beyond a reasonable doubt": An experimental attempt at quantification, *Journal of Applied Behavioral Science* 6 (April/June 1970);

Charles R. Nesson, Reasonable doubt and permissive inferences: The value of complexity, *Harvard Law Review* 92 (April 1979).

bicameral   A legislature that consists of two separate chambers or houses. A unicameral legislature has only one. Nebraska is the only state with a unicameral legislature. Historically, bicameral legislatures arose as a means of representing both the elite and common members of a society. Thus an upper house (like the House of Lords in England) would represent the nobility, while a lower house (like the House of Commons in England) would represent the other interests including the common people. This distinction has faded somewhat in the United States, where representatives to both houses are popularly elected. But in the beginning—and until the Seventeenth Amendment in 1913 mandated the popular election of U.S. senators—the U.S. Senate represented not the people of their state, but the individual states themselves. This anecdote is often offered as an explanation and justification for a bicameral legislative system: Thomas Jefferson was in France during the Constitutional Convention. Upon returning, he met with George Washington for breakfast. The story goes that Jefferson asked Washington why the Convention, which Washington had chaired, had agreed to a second chamber, the Senate. "Why do you pour your coffee into your saucer?" Washington is supposed to have asked Jefferson. "To cool it," Jefferson replied. "Even so," concluded Washington, "we pour legislation into the senatorial saucer to cool it."

REFERENCES

Lloyd B. Omdahl, Drive for unicameralism needs national support, *National Civic Review* 63 (November 1974);

Bickel, Alexander M.

Richard F. Fenno, Jr., *The United States Senate: A Bicameral Perspective* (Washington, D.C.: American Enterprise, 1982);

Donald R. Gross, Bicameralism and the theory of voting, *Western Political Quarterly* 35 (December 1982).

Bickel, Alexander M. (1924–1974) A major analyst of the role of judicial review in American governance. Bickel asserted that, since the basis of American government was republican and majoritarian, the power of judicial review, especially that of the Supreme Court, needed considerable justification. In his *The Least Dangerous Branch* (Indianapolis: Bobbs Merrill, 1962), he wrote that "the Supreme Court's law could not in our system prevail—not merely in the very long run, but within the decade—if it ran counter to deeply felt popular needs or convictions, or even if it was opposed by a determined and substantial minority and received with indifference by the rest of the country. This, in the end, is how and why judicial review is consistent with the theory and practice of political democracy." Yet, while Bickel provided the intellectual rationale for the activism of the Warren court, he was a profound critic of its often intellectually incoherent opinions. He wrote in *The Morality of Consent* (New Haven, CT: Yale University Press, 1975) that the Warren court (as well as the court of other periods) too often made decisions that were expedient rather than principled.

REFERENCES

John Moeller, Alexander M. Bickel: Toward a theory of politics, *Journal of Politics* 47 (February 1985);

Anthony T. Kronman, Alexander Bickel's philosophy of prudence, *Yale Law Journal* 94 (June 1985).

big A term connoting threat or malevolence when used in conjunction with political terms: big government, big business, big labor. Louis Brandeis (1856–1941), as a progressive reform advocate before he became a Supreme Court justice, often used the "curse of bigness" to describe the malevolence of industrial giantism. This helped justify the antitrust policies

called for by the progressives. And former Senator Barry Goldwater (1909–) of Arizona was always fond of saying that "a government that is big enough to give you all you want is big enough to take it all away."

big brother 1 An artificial form of familial protection, as in the charitable Big Brother Association, created to offer substitutes for a missing paternal influence. 2 George Orwell's (1903–1950) symbolization, from his novel *1984* (London, 1949), of government so big and intrusive that it literally oversaw and regulated every aspect of life. The term has evolved to mean any potentially menacing power constantly looking over one's shoulder in judgment. *Compare to* ANIMAL FARM.

REFERENCES

2 For the status of big brother in today's world see Alexander J. Matejko, Canada and Poland: Two countries, two "big brothers," *Jerusalem Journal of International Relations* 4:4 (1980);

Gorman Beauchamp, Big brother in America, *Social Theory and Practice* 10 (Fall 1984);

According to six-nation survey, few of Orwell's predictions have come true, *Gallup Report*, no. 241 (October 1985).

big fix A conspiracy between a political organization and organized crime that provides for lax law enforcement in exchange for political support and bribes.

big lie 1 An untruth so great or so audacious that it is bound to have an effect on public opinion. Both Adolph Hitler (1889–1945) in Germany and Joseph R. McCarthy (1908–1957) in the United States were skillful users of this dishonorable but long-practiced political tactic. Hitler wrote in *Mein Kampf* (1927) that "the great masses of the people will more easily fall victim to a great lie than to a small one." But he was only mimicking NICCOLO MACHIAVELLI, who wrote in *The Prince* (1532) that "it is necessary that the prince should know how to color his nature well, and how to be a great hypocrite and dissembler. For men are so simple, and yield so much to immediate necessity, that the deceiver will never lack dupes." **2** PLATO's concept of the royal lie, the noble lie, the golden lie from book 3 of *Republic,* in which he asserts that the guardians of a society may put forth untruths necessary to maintain social order. Plato's noble lie was simply a poetic or allegorical way of telling ordinary people difficult truths. It is absolutely incompatible with the big lie of fascist propaganda. **3** Criticisms from a political opponent.

REFERENCES

For the theory of lying, both big and small, see Sissela Bok, *Lying: Moral Choice in Public and Private Life* (New York: Random House, 1978);

John R. Kayser, Noble lies & justice: On reading Plato, *Polity* 5 (Spring 1973).

Big MAC *See* MUNICIPAL ASSISTANCE CORPORATION.

big mo Significant momentum in an election campaign often gained by a key primary victory or a good performance in a televised debate. Ever since George Bush used the phrase in 1980, all presidential candidates have been seeking big mo on the campaign trail.

big stick President Theodore Roosevelt's foreign policy derived from the adage "speak softly and carry a big stick." The best example of his big stick policy was the dismemberment of the Isthmus of Panama from Colombia to create a government that would be more cooperative in the American effort to build a canal. When Roosevelt met with his cabinet to report what had happened, he asked Attorney General Philander C. Knox (1853–1921) to construct a defense. The attorney general is reported to have remarked, "Oh, Mr. President, do not let so great an achievement suffer from any taint of legality." Later, when Roosevelt sought to defend his heavily critized actions to the cabinet, he made a lengthy statement and then asked, "Have I defended myself?" Secretary of War Elihu Root (1845–1937) replied, "You certainly have. You have shown that you were accused of seduction, and you have conclusively proved that you were guilty of rape."

Scar, New York *Globe.*

NOW WATCH THE DIRT FLY.

Theodore Roosevelt's big stick policy furthered American interests in building the Panama Canal.

REFERENCE

David McCullough, *The Path Between the Seas: The Creation of the Panama Canal: 1870–1914* (New York: Simon & Schuster, 1977).

bilateralism **1** Joint economic policies between nations; specifically, the agreement to extend to each other privileges (usually relating to trade) that are not available to others. *Compare to* MOST-FAVORED NATION. **2** Joint security policies between nations; specifically, treaties of alliance in the event of war. **3** Joint diplomatic postures or actions by nations, whether or not in the form of a formal alliance. This is in contrast to unilateralism, in which each state goes its own way without necessarily regarding the interests of the others.

bill **1** A legislative proposal formally introduced for consideration; unfinished legislation. After a bill is passed and signed into law, it becomes an act. **2** A law passed by a legislature when it is functioning in a judicial capacity; for example, a bill of impeachment. **3** A negotiable instrument; for example, a dollar bill. **4** A statement of details in a legal proceeding; for example, a bill of indictment. 5 A petition or statement to an appellate court; for example, a bill of exceptions. 6 An important listing; for example, the Bill of Rights.

REFERENCE

1 T. R. Reid, *Congressional Odyssey: The Saga of a Senate Bill* (New York: Freeman, 1980).

The Steps by Which a Bill Becomes a Law in the U.S. Congress

1. The lawmaking process can start in either the House of Representatives or the Senate (except that Article 1, Section 7, of the Constitution, requires that "all bills for raising revenue shall originate in the House of Representatives"). This example starts in the House of Representatives with the introduction of a bill by a member of Congress who places it in the hopper, a box in the House of Representatives chamber; the bill is given a number and printed by the Government Printing Office so copies are available the next morning.
2. Referral to one or more standing committees of the House by the Speaker, on the advice of the parliamentarian.
3. Report from the committee or committees, after public hearings and mark-up meetings by subcommittee, committee, or both.
4. Placement on appropriate CALENDAR.
5. House approval of a special rule, reported by the House Rules Committee, making it in order for the House to consider the bill (in the case of major bills).
6. Consideration of the bill in Committee of the Whole, in two stages; first, general debate; second, amending the bill, one part at a time, under a rule that limits speeches to five minutes each.
7. Passage by the House after votes on amendments adopted in the Committee of the Whole.
8. Transmittal to the Senate (or to the House of Representatives if the bill originated in the Senate), by message.
9. Consideration by the Senate, usually after referral to, and report from, a Senate committee, and after debate and amendment on the Senate floor.
10. Transmission from the Senate back to the House, with or without Senate amendments.
11. Resolution of differences between the House and the Senate, either through additional amendments or the report of a conference committee.
12. Enrollment on parchment paper and signing by the Speaker of the House and the president of the Senate.
13. Transmittal to the president of the United States.
14. Approval or disapproval by the president; if the president disapproves, the bill is returned with a veto message explaining the veto.
15. House and Senate action to override the veto; each chamber must override the veto by a two-thirds vote if the bill is to become law.
16. Filing with the administrator of the General Services Administration after approval by the president or passage by the Congress over his veto.

---

bill, administration A legislative proposal that has the formal backing of the president or one of his cabinet agencies.

bill, appropriation A bill granting the moneys approved by the authorization bill, but not necessarily the total amount. Congressional appropriation bills must originate in the House, and these normally are not acted on until a corresponding authorization measure is enacted. General appropriations bills are supposed to be enacted by the seventh day after Labor Day before the start of the fiscal year to which they apply. *Compare to* APPROPRIATION.

bill, authorization A bill that authorizes a program, specifies its general aims and how they are to be achieved, and (unless open ended) puts a ceiling on moneys that can be used to finance it. *Compare to* AUTHORIZATION.

bill, by request A bill introduced by a legislator at the request of an executive branch agency or private organization. Such an introduction does not necessarily imply an endorsement by the introducing legislator.

bill, Christmas tree Any bill to which many amendments, typically conferring benefits to certain groups, have been added.

bill, clean A bill that has been revised by a legislative committee and then reintroduced as a new, or clean, bill.

bill, committee A bill introduced under the name of the chair of a committee on behalf of the entire committee which has prepared it. In the Congress, all appropriation bills are committee bills.

bill, companion A bill introduced in one house of a bicameral legislature identical to a bill submitted in the other house.

bill, deficiency A bill carrying an appropriation to supplement an appropriation that has proved insufficient. An appropriation is normally made on the basis of estimates for a year, but conditions may arise that exhaust the appropriation before the end of the fiscal year.

bill drafting The writing of legislative proposals. Most legislatures have the assistance of legislative counsel to aid with technical aspects of taking proposals and forging them into appropriate legal documents.

bill, engrossed The final copy of a bill as passed by one house of the Congress, with the text as amended by floor action and certified to by the clerk of the House or the secretary of the Senate.

bill, enrolled The final copy of a bill that has been passed in identical form by both houses of the Congress. It is certified to by an officer of the house of origin and then sent on for signatures of the House speaker, the Senate president, and the president of the United States. An enrolled bill is printed on parchment.
REFERENCES
Stephen J. Wayne and James F. C. Hyde, Jr., Presidential decision making on enrolled bills, *Presidential Studies Quarterly* 8 (Summer 1978);
Stephen J. Wayne, Richard L. Cole, and James F. C. Hyde, Jr., Advising the president on enrolled legislation: Patterns of executive influence, *Political Science Quarterly* 94 (Summer 1979).

bill, fetcher A bill introduced by a state or local legislator solely to encourage a bribe, from an adversely affected party, to withdraw the bill. Mike Royko in *Boss: Richard J. Daley*

of Chicago (New York: Dutton, 1971) discusses Mayor Daley's early years as a state legislator in Illinois: "If a day passed without profit, some legislators would dream up a 'fetcher' bill. A 'fetcher' bill would, say, require that all railroad tracks in the state be relaid six inches farther apart. It would 'fetch' a visit from a lobbyist, bearing a gift."

bill, housekeeping A bill dealing with minor legislative technicalities with no real bearing upon policy.

bill, marking up a The process of revising a bill in committee by reexamining and editing every section, phrase, word, and so on. An extensively marked-up bill is often reintroduced as a new—or clean—bill.

bill of attainder A legislative act declaring an individual guilty of a crime without a trial and sentencing him or her to death. (A punishment of less than death was called a bill of pains and penalties.) A bill of attainder has come to mean any legislatively instrumented punishment without a trial. This is forbidden by Article I, sections 9 and 10, of the Constitution. *See* UNITED STATES V LOVETT; UNITED STATES V BROWN.
REFERENCES
Raoul Berger, Bills of attainder: A study of amendment by the court, *Cornell Law Review* 63 (March 1978);
Richard D. Marsico, Jr., Linking educational benefits with draft registration: An unconstitutional bill of attainder? *Harvard Journal on Legislation* 21 (Winter 1984).

Bill of Rights The first ten amendments to the U.S. Constitution. Only a few individual rights were specified in the Constitution ratified in 1788. Shortly after its adoption, however, ten amendments—called the Bill of Rights—were added to the Constitution to guarantee basic individual liberties. The Bill of Rights originally restricted only actions of the federal government; it did not prevent state and local governments from taking action that might threaten an individual's civil liberties. States had their own constitutions, some of which contained their own bills of rights guaranteeing the same or similar rights. These rights, however, were not guaranteed by all the states; and where they did exist, they were subject to varying interpretations by state courts. In short, citizens were protected only to the extent that the states themselves recognized their rights. In 1868, the Fourteenth Amendment was added to the Constitution. In part, it provides that no state shall "deprive any person of life, liberty, or property without due process of law." It was not until 1925, in the case of *Gitlow v New York*, 268 U.S. 652, that the U.S. Supreme Court interpreted due process of law to mean, in effect, "without abridgement of certain of the rights guaranteed by the Bill of Rights." Since that decision, the Supreme Court has ruled that a denial by a state of certain of the rights contained in the Bill of Rights actually represents a denial of due process of law. While the Court has not ruled that all rights in the Bill of Rights are contained in the notion of due process, neither has it limited that notion to the rights enumerated in the Bill of Rights. It simply has found that there are concepts in the Bill of Rights so basic to a democratic society that they must be recognized as part of due process of law and made applicable to the states as well as to the federal government. *Compare to* CHARTER OF RIGHTS; INCORPORATION.

REFERENCES

Learned Hand, *The Bill of Rights* (New York: Atheneum, 1963);

Irving Brant, *The Bill of Rights: Its Origin and Meaning* (Indianapolis: Bobbs Merrill, 1965);

Bernard Schwartz, *The Great Rights of Mankind: A History of the American Bill of Rights* (New York: Oxford University Press, 1977);

Robert A. Rutland, *The Birth of the Bill of Rights: 1776–1791,* rev. ed. (Middletown, CT: Wesleyan University Press, 1983).

For a comparative perspective, see Gordon Samuels, A bill of rights for Australia? *Australian Quarterly* 51 (December 1979);

Lord Wade, A bill of rights for the United Kingdom, *Parliamentarian* 61 (April 1980);

J. Skelly Wright, The bill of rights in Britain and America: A not quite full circle, *Tulane Law Review* 55 (February 1981).

The Bill of Rights: Summarized and Grouped by Major Purpose

Freedom of Expression

First Amendment prohibits the government from establishing a religion; protects freedom of religious expression, freedom of speech and press, the right of assembly, and the right to petition the government.

Arms and Troops

Second Amendment protects the right to bear arms.

Third Amendment prohibits the government from quartering troops in citizens' homes in peacetime.

Rights of Accused Persons

Fourth Amendment protects against unreasonable search and seizure.

Fifth Amendment requires indictment by grand jury for the prosecution of a person accused of a serious crime; prohibits the government from trying a person twice for the same offense (double jeopardy); protects right of silence (one cannot be required to be a witness against oneself); prohibits the government from taking life, liberty, or property without due process; prohibits the government from taking private property for public use without fair compensation.

Sixth Amendment protects the right to a speedy and public jury trial for crimes; protects the right to be informed of accusation, to confront witnesses, to cross-examine witnesses, and to have legal counsel for defense.

Seventh Amendment protects the right to a jury trial in civil cases involving more than twenty dollars.

Eighth Amendment prohibits the government from setting excessive bail or fines and inflicting cruel and unusual punishment.

Rights of People and States

Ninth Amendment protects other, unspecified, rights.

Tenth Amendment reserves to the states those powers neither granted to the federal government nor prohibited to the states.

Source: Adapted from Samuel C. Patterson, Roger H. Davidson, and Randall B. Ripley, *A More Perfect Union: Introduction to American Government,* 3d ed. (Chicago: Dorsey, 1985), p. 32.

---

bill, omnibus A bill containing various disparate elements, although they may deal with a common theme.

bill, one-house Proposed legislation that is never intended to go beyond a single house of a legislature. Such bills are introduced so politicians or lobbyists can tell their constituents or clients that an effort was made on their behalf.

bill, private A bill that deals with individual matters (claims against the government, immigration and naturalization cases, land titles, and the like) and that becomes a private law if passed.

bill, public A bill that deals with general questions and that becomes a public law if passed.

bill, readings of The traditional parliamentary requirement that bills be read three times before they can be passed. Today in the Congress, a bill is considered to have had its first reading when it is introduced and printed in the *Congressional Record*. In the House, the second reading comes when floor consideration begins and may include an actual reading of the bill or portions of it. In the Senate, the second reading is supposed to take place on the legislative day after the bill is introduced but before it is referred to committee. The third

reading in both houses takes place when action has been completed on amendments.

bill, referral The sending of a bill to the committee whose jurisdiction it is in. In the U.S. Congress, although bills are formally referred by the Speaker of the House and by the presiding officer in the Senate, the parliamentarians of the House and Senate usually do the referrals on their behalf.

bill, true An indictment made and endorsed by a grand jury when it finds that there is sufficient evidence to bring a person to trial.

bipartisanship 1 Cooperation by political parties on political issues. Bipartisanship occurs when the leaders of interested political parties wish to assure that a given topic will not become the subject of partisan disputes. 2 Consultation and cooperation between the president and the leaders of both parties in the Congress on major foreign policy issues. The high point of this occurred after World War II when the Republicans under the leadership of Senator Arthur H. Vandenberg supported the Harry S Truman administration's efforts to re-

How a Bill Becomes a Law: A Schematic

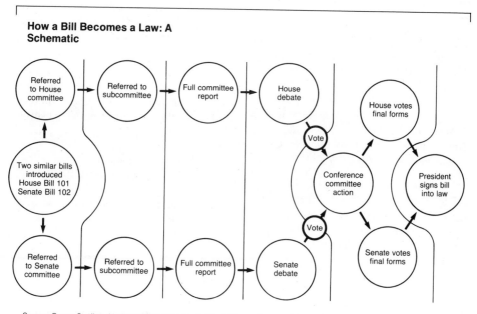

Source: Grover Starling, *Understanding American Politics* (Chicago: Dorsey, 1982), p. 274.

build Europe and contain Soviet expansionism. This bipartisan attitude—that politics ends "at the water's edge"—continued until the American foreign policy consensus broke down over the Vietnam War during the Lyndon B. Johnson administration.

REFERENCE

Thomas Michael Hill, Senator Arthur H. Vandenberg, the politics of bipartisanship, and the origins of anti-Soviet consensus, 1941–1946, *World Affairs* 138 (Winter 1975–76).

Bircher *See* JOHN BIRCH SOCIETY.

birth dearth *See* BABY BOOM.

Bivens v Six Unknown Named Federal Narcotics Agents 403 U.S. 388 (1971) The U.S. Supreme Court case establishing the principle that individuals could sue public officials for damages in connection with the violation of their constitutional rights, especially those covered by the FOURTH AMENDMENT. *See also* CARLSON V GREEN; IMMUNITY.

black bag job 1 An FBI term for illegal searches to gather intelligence. 2 The bribing of someone to obtain information. 3 A CIA nonmilitary covert operation. *Compare to* BAGMAN.

black capitalism The Richard M. Nixon administration's term for its efforts to encourage the creation of businesses owned by blacks.

REFERENCES

Theodore L. Cross, *Black Capitalism: A Strategy for Business in the Ghetto* (New York: Atheneum, 1969);

Timothy Mason Bates, *Black Capitalism: A Quantitative Analysis* (New York: Praeger, 1973).

black caucus A caucus of black legislators formed to discuss and advance issues of concern to the black community. There is a black caucus in the U.S. Congress and in some state legislatures.

REFERENCES

Charles W. Dunn, Black caucuses and political machines in legislative bodies, *American Journal of Political Science* 17 (February 1973);

Marguerite Ross Barnett, The congressional black caucus, *Proceedings of the Academy of Political Science* 32:1 (1975).

black codes Laws passed in some southern states after the Civil War that had the effect of forcing many freed blacks into a state of peonage. *Compare to* JIM CROW; *see also* PRIVILEGES AND IMMUNITIES CLAUSE.

REFERENCE

Theodore Brantner Wilson, *The Black Codes of the South* (University: University of Alabama Press, 1965).

blacklist 1 Originally, lists prepared by merchants containing the names of men who had gone bankrupt. Later, employers' "don't hire" lists of men who had joined unions. The National Labor Relations (Wagner) Act of 1935 made such blacklisting illegal. 2 The denial of employment to members of the entertainment industry for alleged un-American activities. This was a common part of the MCCARTHYISM of the 1950s.

REFERENCES

2 Victor S. Navasky, *Naming Names* (New York: Viking, 1980);

Bert Spector, The Weavers: A case history in show business blacklisting, *Journal of American Culture* 5 (Fall 1982).

Black Panthers A radical Left political party that espoused black control of the black community in America. Founded in California in the mid-1960s, it has now all but disintegrated.

REFERENCES

J. Herman Blacke, Is the Black Panther Party suicidal? *Politics and Society* 2 (Spring 1972);

Michael Tager, Looking into the whirlwind: A psychohistorical study of the Black Panthers, *Psychohistory Review* 12 (Winter 1984).

black power 1 A political slogan of militant black leaders first heard in the mid-1960s. It implied black control and self-determination of all the political and social institutions that af-

Bobby Seale (left) and Huey Newton (right) led the militant Black Panther Party in the 1960s.

fected the black community. The first usage is generally credited to Stokely Carmichael (1941–   ). **2** A general phrase for black political influence.

REFERENCES

1   Stokely Carmichael, with Charles V. Hamilton, *Black Power* (New York: Random House, 1967).
2   Joel D. Aberbach and Jack L. Walker, The meanings of black power: A comparison of white and black interpretations of a political slogan, *American Political Science Review* 64 (June 1970);
    Paul E. Peterson, Organizational imperatives and ideological change: The case of black power, *Urban Affairs Quarterly* 14 (July 1979);
    Lewis M. Killian, Black power and white reactions: The revitalization of race-thinking in the United States, *Annals of the American Academy of Political and Social Science* 454 (March 1981);
    Robert C. Smith, Black power and the transformation from protest to politics, *Political Science Quarterly* 96 (Fall 1981);
    Peter K. Eisinger, Black employment in municipal jobs: The impact of black political power, *American Political Science Review* 76 (June 1982).

Black Elected Officials

Institution	1970	1980	1985
U.S. Congress and state legislatures	182	326	407
City and county offices	715	2,832	3,522
Law enforcement	213	526	656
Education	362	1,206	1,431

Source: *Statistical Abstract of United States, 1986*

blanketing-in   A term for the large-scale importation of previously noncareer jobs into the regular civil service merit system. In the short run, blanketing-in can be (and has been) used to protect political favorites from the next administration. In the long run, blanketing-in is one of the major means through which the civil service merit system has been enlarged.

bleeding hearts   A conservative's term of invective for liberals whose hearts bleed so easily at stories of misfortune that they have an overwhelming desire to raise taxes to cure social problems.

bloc   **1** An amorphous term for any group or coalition of groups organized to promote an interest; for example, farm bloc, civil rights bloc.   **2** A temporary coalition of legislators that transcends party lines and is designed to further or to obstruct a legislative initiative.

REFERENCE

William H. Panning, The structural approach to the identification of voting blocs: The case of the House Agriculture Committee, *Political Methodology* 8:2 (1982).

block grant   *See* GRANT, BLOCK.

bloc voting   *See* VOTING, BLOC.

bloody shirt   An impassioned plea to keep alive hatreds and prejudices. "Waving the bloody shirt" was a common part of Republican oratory after the Civil War; the tactic sought to remind listeners that the Democrats started and were responsible for all of the suffering of the war. While the "bloody shirt" in

American politics has its origins in the blood-stained shirt of a Union Army veteran that was waved about in the Congress, the practice is ancient. Shakespeare best captured the spirit of a bloody appeal in *Julius Caesar* (Act III, Scene 2) when Marc Antony gives his "Friends, Romans, countrymen" speech using Caesar's blood-stained toga as a prop.

BLS *See* BUREAU OF LABOR STATISTICS.

Blue Eagle *See* NATIONAL INDUSTRIAL RECOVERY ACT OF 1933.

blue flu An informal strike by police officers, who call in sick, the blue referring to their uniforms.
REFERENCE
Casey Ichniowski, Arbitration and police bargaining: Prescriptions for the blue flu, *Industrial Relations* 21 (Spring 1982).

blue laws State and local legislation banning commercial and related activities on particular days, usually Sunday, for religious reasons; laws against anything a community considers immoral. According to David Walker's *Oxford Companion to Law* (New York: Oxford University Press, 1980), the name "may have been derived from an account purporting to list the Sabbath regulations of New Haven, Connecticut, printed on blue paper and published in 1781."

blue ribbon jury A jury specially chosen for some particular expertise.

blue ribbon panel A committee of eminent or distinguished citizens.

blue sky laws Government regulations designed to prevent fraud in the sale of land and securities by calling for full disclosure, clear title, and so on.

blue slip A letter or form from an individual senator requesting the approval of a presidential nomination. If the senator does not sign off on the blue slip, especially if he or she is of the majority party and the nominee is from the senator's state, the nomination is likely to be withdrawn.

board/commission A group charged with directing a government function. Boards or commissions are used when it is desirable to have bipartisan leadership or when their functions are of a quasi-judicial nature.

Board of Education v Allen 392 U.S. 236 (1968) The U.S. Supreme Court case that allowed tax dollars to be used for nonreligious textbooks for parochial school students, because the books benefited the students rather than the religion. *See* ESTABLISHMENT CLAUSE.

boat people **1** A term used to refer to and describe the more than one-million refugees who have fled Indochina since communist regimes rose to power there in 1975, and who have increasingly resorted to the use of small boats as a means of escape. The refugees are from Vietnam, Laos, and Kampuchea (Cambodia) and include a large proportion of ethnic Chinese families. **2** Refugees from Haiti seeking to illegally land (by boat) in the United States.
REFERENCES
1   B. Martin Tsamenyi, The "boat people": Are they refugees? *Human Rights Quarterly* 5 (August 1983).
2   Alex Stepick, Haitian boat people: A study in the conflicting forces shaping U.S. immigration policy, *Law and Contemporary Problems* 45 (Spring 1982).

Bob Jones University v United States *See* FREE EXERCISE CLAUSE.

body politic **1** A government. **2** Any collectivity organized for political purposes. **3** The citizens of a jurisdiction. *Compare to* POLITY.
REFERENCES
Anthony M. Orum, *Introduction to Political Sociology: The Social Anatomy of the Body Politic* (Englewood Cliffs, NJ: Prentice-Hall, 1978);
Joseph Kupfer, Architecture: Building the body politic, *Social Theory and Practice* 11 (Fall 1985).

Boland Amendment Any of a series of amendments beginning in 1982 that were attached to various defense related apropriations acts to prohibit U.S. funding of the CONTRAS in Nicaragua beyond what was specifically authorized by Congress. The amendments, sponsored by Edward Boland, the Chairman of the House Intelligence Committee, were intended to prevent executive branch covert support of Contra operations. Much of the controversy over the IRAN CONTRA AFFAIR was over the question of whether or not the Boland Amendment was violated when the Reagan administration used the profits or "residuals" (as they called these profits) from arms sales to Iran to fund Contra activities.

Bolling v Sharpe *See* EQUAL PROTECTION OF LAWS.

boll weevils **1** A long used term for southern Democrats in the U.S. House of Representatives who support conservative policies. **2** Southern Democrats in the U.S. House of Representatives who have supported President Ronald Reagan's economic programs. Boll weevils are insects that feed on cotton. *Compare to* GYPSY MOTHS.

bond A certificate of indebtedness issued by a borrower to a lender that constitutes a legal obligation to repay the principal of the loan plus accrued interest.

bond anticipation notes (BANs) A form of short-term borrowing commonly used to accelerate progress on approved capital construction projects. Once the revenues for a project have been realized from the sale of long-term bonds, the BANs are repaid. BANs also may be used to allow a jurisdiction to wait until the bond market becomes more favorable for the sale of long-term securities.

bond bank An arrangement whereby small units of government within a state are able to pool their long-term debt to create a larger bond issue at more advantageous rates.
REFERENCES
Martin T. Katzman, Measuring the savings from state municipal bond banking, *Governmental Finance* 9 (March 1980);

David S. Kidwell and Robert J. Rogowski, Bond banks: A state assistance program that helps reduce new issue borrowing costs, *Public Administration Review* 43 (March/April 1983).

bonds, callable Bonds that can be repaid totally or in part prior to the maturity date. For this reason, callable bonds ordinarily carry higher interest rates. Noncallable bonds, on the other hand, may not be repurchased until the date of maturation.

bonds, industrial development State or local government bonds issued to finance the building of a factory or installation that will be used by a private company. While such bonds are popular as a means of attracting new industry to a community, they are essentially fronts for private borrowing. The Congress, sensing the loss of tax revenue from these fronts, has in recent years put a variety of constraints on their use.
REFERENCES
Pearl Richardson, Industrial development bonds: High volume for small issues, or is the sky the limit? *Governmental Finance* 9 (September 1980);
James T. Bennett and Thomas J. DiLorenzo, The political economy of corporate welfare: Industrial revenue bonds, *Cato Journal* 2 (Fall 1982);
Thomas A. Pascarella and Richard D. Raymond, Buying bonds for business: An evaluation of the industrial revenue bond program, *Urban Affairs Quarterly* 18 (September 1982).

bonds, moral obligation State or local government bonds that are backed only by the jurisdiction's promise to repay; they are specifically not backed by a jurisdiction's full faith and credit. Moral obligation bonds often carry a higher interest rate than other municipal bonds, because full faith and credit bonds will always be paid first.
REFERENCE
Richard M. Jones, The future of moral obligation bonds as a method of government finance in Texas, *Texas Law Review* 54 (January 1976).

bonds, mortgage revenue State or local government bonds used to create low-interest mortgages for low-income home buyers.
REFERENCE
John A. Tuccillo and John C. Weicher, *Local Mortgage Revenue Bonds: Economic and Financial Impacts* (Washington, D.C.: Urban Institute, 1979).

bonds, municipal/tax-exempt municipal bonds The debt instruments of subnational governments; terms used interchangeably with public borrowing and debt financing. This causes some confusion because they appear to refer only to bonds issued by a local government. Yet bonds issued by states, territories, or possessions of the United States, or by any municipality, political subdivision (including cities, counties, school districts, and special districts for fire prevention, water, sewer, irrigation, and other purposes), or public agency or instrumentality (such as an authority or commission) are subsumed under the rubric municipal bonds. While the interest on municipal bonds is exempt from federal taxes, state and local exemptions may vary. Tax-exempt bonds allow jurisdictions to borrow money at lower than commercial market interest rates. The buyers of the bonds find them an attractive investment because their high marginal tax rates make a tax-free investment more advantageous than a taxable one paying even higher interest.
REFERENCES
Michael D. Joehnk and David S. Kidwell, A look at competitive and negotiated underwriting costs in the municipal bond market, *Public Administration Review* 40 (May/June 1980);
Jay H. Abrams, Financing capital expenditures: A look at the municipal bond market, *Public Administration Review* 43 (July/August 1983);
Robert B. Inzer and Walter J. Reinhart, Rethinking traditional municipal bond sales, *Governmental Finance* 13 (June 1984);
Robert L. Bland, The interest cost savings from experience in the municipal bond market, *Public Administration Review* 45 (January/February 1985).

bonds, revenue Municipal bonds whose repayment and dividends are guaranteed by revenues derived from the facility constructed from the proceeds of the sale of the bonds (e.g., stadium bonds, toll road bonds). As revenue bonds are not pledged against the tax base of the issuing jurisdiction, they are usually not regulated by the same debt limitations imposed by most states on the sale of general obligation bonds. Additionally, revenue bond questions usually do not have to be submitted to the voters for approval as they do not commit the full faith and credit of the jurisdiction.
REFERENCE
Philip J. Fischer, Ronald W. Forbes, and John E. Petersen, Risk and return in the choice of revenue bond financing, *Governmental Finance* 9 (September 1980).

bonds, serial Bonds that are sold in such a way that a certain number of them are retired each year.

bonds, term Bonds that all mature on the same date.

boom 1 The relatively sudden, short-lived, and spontaneous efforts of supporters to advance a candidate. 2 Artificially induced (via advertising and propaganda) temporary enthusiasm for a candidate. 3 A strong upturn in the economy.

boom and bust A classic but now fading description of BUSINESS CYCLES. The economic regulatory instruments of modern governments (*see* FISCAL POLICY; MONETARY POLICY) have done much to smooth out the peaks and troughs of the cycle.

boomlet 1 A boom that failed. 2 A boom never intended to succeed, undertaken for strategic purposes (such as a campaign for a favorite son at a nominating convention).

boondoggle 1 A wasteful or unproductive government program. 2 Make-work projects undertaken to stimulate the economy. Boondoggle has long been used to describe trifling but very time-consuming work such as saddle ornaments made by cowboys out of odd pieces of leather. In the 1930s it was applied to New Deal make work programs. Since then it has been synonymous with wasteful government activities.

Booth v Maryland 96 L Ed 2d 440 (1987) The U.S. Supreme Court case which held that the introduction of victim impact statements during the sentencing phase of a murder trial violated the Eighth Amendment by "impermissibly inflaming the jury."

Bordenkircher v Hayes *See* PLEA BARGAINING.

boring from within A tactic calling for one group to secretly place agents in the midst of a rival group to weaken and eventually destroy it. This is a classic technique of communist infiltration into noncommunist organizations.

boro An Americanized spelling of borough.

borough 1 A local government unit smaller than a city. New York City, for example, is divided into five boroughs: Manhattan, Brooklyn, Bronx, Queens, and Richmond (Staten Island). 2 In Alaska, a borough is similar to a county. *See also* TOWN.

REFERENCES
1 Donald G. Schlosser, *Comparison of Borough and Township Government,* 5th ed. (Harrisburg, PA: Bureau of Local Government Services, 1979).
2 Ronald C. Cease and Jerome R. Saroff, eds., *The Metropolitan Experiment in Alaska: A Study of Borough Government* (New York: Praeger, 1968).

bossism An informal system of local government in which public power is concentrated in the hands of a central figure, called a political boss, who may not have a formal government position. The power is concentrated through the use of a POLITICAL MACHINE, whereby a hierarchy is created and maintained through the use of PATRONAGE and government largesse to assure compliance with the wishes of the boss. It was a dominant system in American city government after the Civil War and was

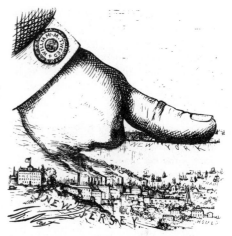

Tammany Hall boss William Tweed had New York City "under his thumb" throughout the 1850s and 1860s.

the main target of the American urban reform effort. Few authentic bosses exist today.

REFERENCES
Lee S. Greene, ed., City bosses and political machines, *Annals of the American Academy of Political and Social Science* (May 1964);
Alexander B. Callow, Jr., ed., *The City Boss in America* (New York: Oxford University Press, 1968);
Alfred Steinberg, *The Bosses* (New York: Macmillan, 1972);
Alexander B. Callow, Jr., *The Tweed Ring* (New York: Oxford University Press, 1976).

Boston Massacre The incident on March 5, 1770, in Boston, when British soldiers fired into a taunting crowd, killing five. The soldiers were tried for murder and acquitted. John Adams, later president of the United States, was their defense attorney. The incident was widely and effectively used by revolutionary agitators to generate anti-British feelings. For example, John Hancock (1737–1793), the first signer of the Declaration of Independence, told a crowd in 1774: "Let this sad tale of death never be told without a tear; let not the heaving bosom cease to burn with a manly indignation at the barbarous story through the long tracts of future time; let every parent tell the shameful story to his listening children until tears of pity glisten in their eyes, and boiling passion shake their tender frames; and whilst the anniversary of that ill-fated night is kept a jubilee in the grim court of pandemonium let all America join in one common prayer to Heaven, that the inhuman, unprovoked murders of the fifth of March, 1770 . . . may ever stand in history without parallel."

REFERENCES

L. Kinvin Wroth and Hiller B. Zobel, The Boston Massacre trials, *American Bar Association Journal* 55 (April 1969);

John Phillip Reid, A lawyer acquitted: John Adams and the Boston Massacre trials, *American Journal of Legal History* 18 (July 1974).

Boston police strike of 1919 The nation's first taste of large-scale municipal labor problems. While the patrolmen struck for a variety of reasons, including the right to form a union and affiliate with the American Federation of Labor, the strike brought chaos to the city. Samuel Gompers, the president of the AF of L, protested the police commissioner's refusal to allow the union to affiliate with the AF of L. Calvin Coolidge, then governor of Massachusetts, responded with his famous assertion that "there is no right to strike against the public safety by anybody, anywhere, anytime." These words so expressed the public's outlook that a tidal wave of support gained him the Republican vice presidential nomination in 1920 (and when President Warren G. Harding died in 1923, Coolidge became president). The failure of the Boston police strike would inhibit municipal unionization for many decades.

REFERENCES

Francis Russell, The strike that made a president, *American Heritage* 14:6 (1963);

Francis Russell, *A City in Terror—1919—The Boston Police Strike* (New York: Viking, 1975).

Boston Tea Party Perhaps the most famous act of civil disobedience in American history. On December 16, 1773, Boston colonists dressed as Indians dumped over three hundred chests of tea belonging to the British East India Company into the harbor as a protest against British taxation on tea. This was the beginning of the violence that led to the American Revolutionary War and ended with British recognition of the creation of the United States of America.

REFERENCE

Benjamin Woods Labaree, *The Boston Tea Party* (New York: Oxford University Press, 1964).

bounded rationality *See* SATISFICING.

bourgeois 1 A middle-class, ordinary citizen, as distinct from the upper class or the poor. 2 A pejorative reference by intellectuals to the cultural tastes or political judgments of the middle class. 3 In the context of Marxism, a member of the ruling class in capitalistic societies; one of the owners of the means of production. The plural is bourgeoisie. Karl Marx distinguished between the haute bourgeoisie, the real leaders of industry, and the petit bourgeoisie, the small businessmen, whom he felt really belonged with the proletariat.

Bowsher v Synar *See* GRAMM-RUDMAN-HOLLINGS ACT OF 1985.

boycott 1 Ostracize. During the mid-nineteenth century, Charles C. Boycott, a retired English army captain, managed the Irish estate of an absentee owner. His methods were so severe and oppressive that the local citizens as a group refused to deal with him in any manner. When Captain Boycott was forced to flee home to England, the first boycott, or nonviolent intimidation through ostracism, was a success. 2 In the context of labor relations, a refusal to deal with or buy the products of a business, as a means of asserting pressure in a labor dispute. 3 A tactic in diplomacy wherein one nation or group of nations pointedly ignores the diplomatic efforts of another. 4 A foreign policy of not buying the products of or doing business with a hostile country—or with a nonhostile country, as a means of influencing its domestic or foreign policies.

REFERENCE

1 Joyce Marlow, *Captain Boycott and the Irish* (New York: Saturday Review, 1973).

bracero program The legal importation, which started during World War II when the farm manpower shortage was great, of Mexican farm workers, or braceros, as seasonal workers. The practice, sanctioned by law in 1951, was long opposed by organized labor and was terminated by the Congress in 1964. Since that time, however, an informal and unofficial bracero program has evolved from the large numbers of illegal aliens coming into the United States from Mexico.

REFERENCE

Lamar B. Jones and G. Randolph Rice, Agricultural labor in the Southwest: The post-bracero years, *Social Science Quarterly* 61:1 (June 1980).

brains trust **1** Expert advisors to a candidate or office holder. **2** The professors who first advised President Franklin D. Roosevelt during the 1932 presidential campaign. **3** A sarcastic reference to any group of experts or advisors. *Compare to* CABINET, KITCHEN.

REFERENCE

2 Elliot A. Rosen, Roosevelt and the brains trust: An historiographical overview, *Political Science Quarterly* 87 (December 1972).

branches of government The three main divisions of American government at all levels: executive, legislative, and judicial.

Brandeis brief *See* BRIEF, BRANDEIS.

Branti v Finkel 445 U.S. 507 (1980) The U.S. Supreme Court case expanding on the Court's earlier ruling, in *Elrod v Burns*, that the dismissal of nonpolicymaking, nonconfidential public employees for their partisan affiliation violates the First and Fourteenth amendments. The burden is on the hiring authority to demonstrate that partisan affiliation is an appropriate requirement for effective performance in office, which could not be done in this instance involving the position of assistant public defender.

brethren The old-fashioned plural of brother. Historically, the U.S. Supreme Court has referred to its members as the brethren. This usage is all the more outdated now that the Court is no longer all male.

REFERENCE

For a gossipy account of Supreme Court decision making, see Bob Woodward and Scott Armstrong, *The Brethren: Inside the Supreme Court* (New York: Simon & Schuster, 1979).

Bretton Woods system The international monetary system devised by a conference of leading world economists in 1944 at Bretton Woods, New Hampshire. To abolish the economic ills believed to be responsible for the 1929 depression and World War II, a new international monetary system was created that established rules for an exchange rate system, balance-of-payments adjustments, and supplies of reserve assets; the conference also founded the International Monetary Fund and the International Bank for Reconstruction and Development. The Bretton Woods system is generally perceived to have collapsed in August 1971, when the United States suspended the convertibility of dollars into gold.

REFERENCES

Lawrence B. Krause, *Sequel to Bretton Woods: A Proposal to Reform the World Monetary System* (Washington, D.C.: Brookings, 1971);

Gerald M. Meier, The Bretton Woods agreement—twenty-five years after, *Stanford Law Review* 23 (January 1971);

Joanne Gowa, The past as prologue: Prospects for a new Bretton Woods, *Orbis* 28 (Summer 1984).

Brezhnev doctrine The concept that the Soviet Union has the right to protect communist regimes even if it means the use of force. This was first put forth by Leonid Brezhnev in a speech on November 12, 1968, just a few months after the Soviet Union's invasion of Czechoslovakia.

REFERENCES

R. Judson Mitchell, The Brezhnev Doctrine and communist ideology, *Review of Politics* 34 (April 1972);

Stephen M. Schwebel, The Brezhnev Doctrine repealed and peaceful co-existence enacted, *American Journal of International Law* 66 (October 1972);

bribery

R. Judson Mitchell, A new Brezhnev Doctrine: The restructuring of international relations, *World Politics* 30 (April 1978).

bribery **1** The giving or offering of anything of value with intent to unlawfully influence an official in the discharge of his or her duties. **2** A public official's receiving or asking of anything of value with the intent to be unlawfully influenced. As a crime, bribery is usually restricted to the giving or offering of bribes; the solicitation or accepting of bribes is often called corruption.

Viewed systemically, bribery is an important element in the American political system. It supplements the salaries of various public officials. Many policemen and building inspectors, for example, would be unable to maintain their standard of living if it were not for such informal salary increments. Additionally, such income supplement programs forestall the need for politically unpopular, precipitous tax hikes that would bring the legal wages of such officers up to reasonable levels. Systematic bribery allows businessmen, dependent upon the discretionary powers of public officials for their livelihood, to stabilize the relationships essential for the smooth functioning of their businesses. After all, many regulations that govern safety or conditions of business operation may not be universally applicable, reasonably enforceable, or economically feasible.

Bribery's occasional exposure by the press serves to foster the political alienation of the electorate, which in turn encourages cynicism and reduces support for the democratic processes of government. While it is possible to quibble over the particulars of any given instance or noninstance of bribery, its pervasiveness in too many American communities is generally not contested except by the most naive or the most corrupt. *Compare to* CORRUPTION, POLITICAL; FOREIGN CORRUPT PRACTICES ACT (OF 1977); POLITICAL CULTURE.

REFERENCES

Michael Johnston, *Political Corruption and Public Policy in America* (Monterey, CA: Brooks/Cole, 1982);

Michael Philips, Bribery, *Ethics* 94 (July 1984);

John Thomas Noonan, *Bribes* (New York: Macmillan, 1984);

Thomas L. Carson, Bribery, extortion, and "the Foreign Corrupt Practices Act," *Philosophy and Public Affairs* 14 (Winter 1985).

brief A written statement prepared by each side in a formal lawsuit or hearing, summarizing the facts of the situation and making arguments about how the law should be applied.

REFERENCE

For copies of briefs submitted to the U.S. Supreme Court in most of its important cases, see Philip B. Kurland and Gerhard Casper, eds., *Landmark Briefs and Arguments of the Supreme Court of the United States,* more than 100 vols. (Washington, D.C.: University Publications of America, 1975 onward).

brief, Brandeis A legal brief that takes into account not only the law but the technical data from social or scientific research that have economic and sociological implications for the law as well as society. This kind of legal argument was pioneered by Louis D. Brandeis (1856–1941), who later served on the U.S. Supreme Court (1916–1939). It was a Brandeis brief that helped win the *Brown v Board of Education* case when, with testimony from psychologists about the effects of segregation on black children, the lawyers for Brown proved that separate educational facilities were inherently unequal.

brinkmanship **1** Taking very large risks in negotiations to force the other side to back down; this tactic is always reckless and sometimes a bluff. According to Thomas C. Schelling in *The Strategy of Conflict* (New York: Oxford University Press, 1963), brinkmanship is the "deliberate creation of a recognizable risk of war, a risk that one does not completely control. It is the tactic of deliberately letting the situation get somewhat out of hand, just because its being out of hand may be intolerable to the other party and force his accommodation." **2** A critical description of the foreign policies of President Dwight D. Eisenhower's secretary of state, John Foster

Dulles, who advocated going to the brink of war as a negotiating tactic. In a famous *Life* magazine interview (January 16, 1956), he asserted that "the ability to get to the verge without getting into the war is the necessary art. If you cannot master it, you inevitably get into war. If you try to run away from it, if you are scared to go to the brink, you are lost."

REFERENCES

1 Gerald Gunther, Constitutional brinksmanship: Stumbling toward a convention, *American Bar Association Journal* 65 (July 1979);

   Richard Ned Lebow, Soviet incentives for brinkmanship? *Bulletin of the Atomic Scientists* 37 (May 1981).

Brookings Institution A research organization devoted to education and publication in economics, government, and foreign policy. While it functions as an independent analyst and critic, committed to publishing its findings for the information of the public, it has gained a reputation for being "liberal." Ironically, prior to World War II it was considered a bastion of conservatism. It was founded in 1916 as the Institute for Government Research by Robert S. Brookings (1850–1932). In 1927 it was merged with the Institute of Economics (founded 1922) to form the current Brookings Institution.

REFERENCES

For history, see Donald T. Critchlow, Robert S. Brookings: The man, the vision, and the institution, *Review of Politics* 46 (October 1984);

Donald T. Critchlow, *The Brookings Institution, 1916–1952: Expertise and the Public Interest in a Democratic Society* (Dekalb: Northern Illinois University Press, 1985).

The Brookings Institution
1775 Massachusetts Avenue, N.W.
Washington, D.C. 20036
(202) 797-6000

Brownlow Committee/President's Committee on Administrative Management A committee appointed by President Franklin D. Roosevelt in 1936 for the purpose of diagnosing the staffing needs of the president and making appropriate recommendations for the reorgani-

zation of the executive branch. The committee of three, chaired by Louis Brownlow, included CHARLES E. MERRIAM and LUTHER GULICK. The committee reported to the president in January 1937. Its proposals were simple enough; essentially, they said that the president needs help, and that he needs men around him with a passion for anonymity. This particular passion seems to have faded in recent years along with the public's belief that a modern president writes his own speeches.

Overall, the committee recommended a major reorganization of the executive branch. The president agreed, and appropriate legislation was submitted to the Congress in 1938. But the Congress, in the wake of the president's efforts to "pack" the Supreme Court and fearful of too much power in the presidency, killed the bill. The president resubmitted a considerably modified reorganization bill the following year, and the Congress passed the Reorganization Act of 1939 authorizing the president, subject to congressional veto, to redistribute and restructure executive branch agencies. President Roosevelt subsequently created the Executive Office of the President. The EOP began with six top-level assistants in 1939 but has expanded to over a hundred. *See also* EXECUTIVE OFFICE OF THE PRESIDENT.

REFERENCES

Barry D. Karl, *Executive Reorganization and Reform in the New Deal* (Cambridge, MA: Harvard University Press, 1963);

Richard Polenberg, *Reorganizing Roosevelt's Government: The Controversy over Executive Reorganization, 1936–1939* (Cambridge, MA: Harvard University Press, 1966);

John Hart, No passion for Brownlow: Models of staffing the presidency, *Politics* 17 (November 1982);

James W. Fesler, The Brownlow Committee fifty years later, *Public Administration Review* 47 (July–August 1987).

The Brownlow Committee Report

The president needs help. His immediate staff assistance is entirely inadequate. He should be given a small number of executive assistants who would be his direct aides in dealing with the managerial agencies and administrative departments of the government. These assistants, probably not exceeding six in number, would be in addition to his present secretaries, who deal with the public, with the Congress, and with the press and radio. These aides would have no power to make decisions or issue instructions in their own right. They would not be interposed between the president and the heads of his departments. They would not be assistant presidents in any sense. Their function would be, when any matter was presented to the president for action affecting any part of the administrative work of the government, to assist him in obtaining quickly and without delay all pertinent information possessed by any of the executive departments so as to guide him in making his responsible decisions; and then when decisions have been made, to assist him in seeing to it that every administrative department and agency affected is promptly informed. Their effectiveness in assisting the president will, we think, be directly proportional to their ability to discharge their functions with restraint. They would remain in the background, issue no orders, making no decisions, emit no public statements. Men for these positions should be carefully chosen by the president from within and without the government. They should be men in whom the president has personal confidence and whose character and attitude is such that they would not attempt to exercise power on their own account. They should be possessed of high competence, great physical vigor, and a passion for anonymity.

Source: President's Committee on Administrative Management, *Administrative Management in the Government of the United States, January 8, 1937* (Washington, D.C.: U.S. Government Printing Office, 1937).

Brownlow, Louis (1879–1963)   A major figure in the development of city management as a profession; best remembered as chairman of the President's Committee on Administrative Management (1936–1937).

REFERENCES

Brownlow's major works include *The President and the Presidency* (Chicago: Public Administration Service, 1949);

A Passion for Anonymity: The Autobiography of Louis Brownlow: First Half (Chicago: University of Chicago Press, 1955);

A Passion for Politics: The Autobiography of Louis Brownlow: Second Half (Chicago: University of Chicago Press, 1958).

For appreciations, see Richard Stillman II, Richard S. Childs and Louis Brownlow: Two "saints" of public administration re-

considered, pt. 1, *Midwest Review of Public Administration* 7 (January 1973);

Barry D. Karl, Louis Brownlow, *Public Administration Review* 39 (November/December 1979).

Brown v Board of Education of Topeka, Kansas 347 U.S. 483 (1954)   The landmark U.S. Supreme Court decision holding that the separation of children by race and according to law in public schools "generates a feeling of inferiority as to their [the minority group's] status in the community that may affect their hearts and minds in a way unlikely ever to be undone." Consequently, it held that "separate educational facilities are inherently unequal" and therefore violate the equal protection clause of the Fourteenth Amendment. According to Chief Justice Earl Warren, "We come then to the question presented: does segregation of children in public schools solely on the basis of race, even though the physical facilities and other 'tangible' factors may be equal, deprive the children of the minority group of equal educational opportunities? We believe that it does." This decision, one of the most significant in the century, helped create the environment that would lead to the modern Civil Rights Movement. *Also see* SEPARATE BUT EQUAL.

REFERENCES

Frank T. Read, Judicial evolution of the law of school integration since *Brown v Board of Education, Law and Contemporary Problems* 39 (Winter 1975);

Richard Kluger, *Simple Justice: The History of* Brown v Board of Education *and Black America's Struggle for Equality* (New York: Knopf, 1976);

Elbert P. Tuttle, Fall-out from *Brown v Board of Education, Emory Law Journal* 28 (Fall 1980);

Raymond Wolters, *The Burden of Brown: Thirty Years of School Desegregation* (Knoxville: University of Tennessee Press, 1984);

David L. Norman, The strange career of the Civil Rights Division's commitment to *Brown, Yale Law Journal* 93 (May 1984).

Bryce, James (1838–1922)   The British historian and ambassador to the United States

(1907–1913) who wrote a classic analysis of the American political system, *The American Commonwealth* (New York: 1888; final revised ed., 1922). Bryce was a keen observer of American political culture. He noted that civil service reform received the support of both parties, "a lip service expressed by both with equal warmth and by the average professional politician of both with equal insincerity." The most famous part of his landmark book is his chapter "Why Great Men Are Not Chosen Presidents." About most American presidents (the founders, Lincoln, and Grant excluded), Bryce concluded that "the only thing remarkable about them is that being so commonplace they should have climbed so high."

REFERENCES

Keith Robbins, History and politics: The career of James Bryce, *Journal of Contemporary History* 7 (July/October 1972);

L. E. Fredman, "Why great men are, or are not, elected president: Some British views of the presidency, *Presidential Studies Quarterly* 10 (Summer 1980);

Louis Auchincloss, Lord Bryce, *American Heritage* 32 (April/May 1981).

buck Responsibility. President Harry S Truman was famous for having a sign on his desk that read "The Buck Stops Here." Buck, a term from poker, refers to the marker put in front of the player who next had to deal. To avoid a problem or a responsibility is to pass the buck. Bureaucrats in many jurisdictions refer to the form memos that they use to direct paper from one to another as buck slips.

REFERENCE

John R. Johannes, Where does the buck stop? Congress, president, and the responsibility for legislative initiation, *Western Political Quarterly* 25 (September 1972).

Buckley v Valeo 424 U.S. 1 (1976) The U.S. Supreme Court case upholding the constitutionality of the Federal Election Campaign Act except for provisions that limited campaign spending and limited what an individual candidate could spend on his or her own campaign. The court held that the "First Amendment denies government the power to determine that spending to promote one's political views is

. . . excessive. In the free society ordained by our Constitution, it is not the government but the people . . . who must retain control over the quantity and range of debate . . . in a political campaign."

REFERENCES

Albert J. Rosenthal, The Constitution and campaign finance regulation after *Buckley v Valeo, Annals of the American Academy of Political and Social Science* 425 (May 1976);

Jonathan Bingham, Democracy or plutocracy? The case for a constitutional amendment to overturn *Buckley v Valeo, Annals of the American Academy of Political and Social Science* 486 (July 1986).

budget A financial plan serving as a pattern for and control over future operations—hence, any estimate of future costs or any systematic plan for the utilization of the work force, material, or other resources.

Budget and Accounting Act of 1921 The law which (1) mandated that the president prepare and submit to the Congress a budget for the federal government and (2) created the Bureau of the Budget (later OMB) and the General Accounting Office.

Budget, Bureau of the The central budget agency of the United States from 1921 to 1970. *See also* CONGRESSIONAL BUDGET AND IMPOUNDMENT CONTROL ACT OF 1974; OFFICE OF MANAGEMENT AND BUDGET.

REFERENCES

For histories, see Fritz Morstein Marx, The Bureau of the Budget: Its evolution and present role, *American Political Science Review* 39 (October 1945);

Allen Schick, The Budget Bureau that was: Thoughts on the rise, decline and future of a presidential agency, *Law and Contemporary Problems* 35:3 (1970).

budget, current services A budget that projects estimated budget authority and outlays for the upcoming fiscal year at the same program level (and without policy changes) as the fiscal year in progress. To the extent mandated by existing law, estimates take into account the

budget cycle

Executive Preparation and Submission of the Federal Budget

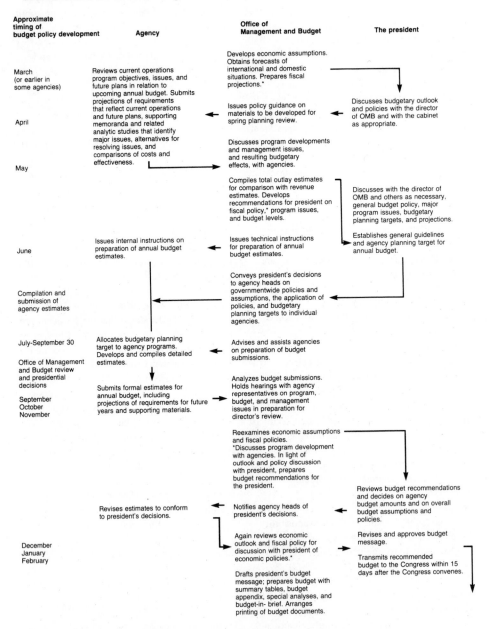

Approximate timing of budget policy development	Agency	Office of Management and Budget	The president
		Develops economic assumptions. Obtains forecasts of international and domestic situations. Prepares fiscal projections.*	
March (or earlier in some agencies)	Reviews current operations program objectives, issues, and future plans in relation to upcoming annual budget. Submits projections of requirements that reflect current operations and future plans, supporting memoranda and related analytic studies that identify major issues, alternatives for resolving issues, and comparisons of costs and effectiveness.	Issues policy guidance on materials to be developed for spring planning review.	Discusses budgetary outlook and policies with the director of OMB and with the cabinet as appropriate.
April		Discusses program developments and management issues, and resulting budgetary effects, with agencies.	
May		Compiles total outlay estimates for comparison with revenue estimates. Develops recommendations for president on fiscal policy,* program issues, and budget levels.	Discusses with the director of OMB and others as necessary, general budget policy, major program issues, budgetary planning targets, and projections.
June	Issues internal instructions on preparation of annual budget estimates.	Issues technical instructions for preparation of annual budget estimates.	Establishes general guidelines and agency planning target for annual budget.
Compilation and submission of agency estimates		Conveys president's decisions to agency heads on governmentwide policies and assumptions, the application of policies, and budgetary planning targets to individual agencies.	
July-September 30	Allocates budgetary planning target to agency programs. Develops and compiles detailed estimates.	Advises and assists agencies on preparation of budget submissions.	
Office of Management and Budget review and presidential decisions			
September October November	Submits formal estimates for annual budget, including projections of requirements for future years and supporting materials.	Analyzes budget submissions. Holds hearings with agency representatives on program, budget, and management issues in preparation for director's review.	
		Reexamines economic assumptions and fiscal policies. *Discusses program development with agencies. In light of outlook and policy discussion with president, prepares budget recommendations for the president.	Reviews budget recommendations and decides on agency budget amounts and on overall budget assumptions and policies.
	Revises estimates to conform to president's decisions.	Notifies agency heads of president's decisions.	
December January February		Again reviews economic outlook and fiscal policy for discussion with president of economic policies.*	Revises and approves budget message.
		Drafts president's budget message; prepares budget with summary tables, budget appendix, special analyses, and budget-in-brief. Arranges printing of budget documents.	Transmits recommended budget to the Congress within 15 days after the Congress convenes.

*In cooperation with the Treasury Department and Council of Economic Advisers.

Source: *A Glossary of Terms Used in the Federal Budget Process* (Washington, D.C.: U.S. General Accounting Office, 1981), pp. 8–9.

budget impact of anticipated changes in economic conditions (such as unemployment or inflation), pay increases, and benefit changes. The Congressional Budget and Impoundment Control Act of 1974 requires that the president submit a current services budget to the Congress by November 10 of each year.

budget cycle The timed steps of the budget process, which includes preparation, approval, execution, and audit.

REFERENCE

Jerry Banks and Robert F. Clark, Evaluation research and the budget cycle, *Policy Studies Journal* 8:7, special issue no. 3 (1980).

budget, executive 1 The budget document for an executive branch of government that a jurisdiction's chief executive submits to a legislature for review, modification, and enactment. 2 The process by which agency requests for appropriations are prepared and submitted to a budget bureau under the chief executive for review, alteration, and consolidation into a single budget document that can be compared to expected revenues and executive priorities before submission to the legislature.

budgeting The single most important decision-making process in U.S. public institutions today. The budget itself is also a jurisdiction's most important reference document. In their increasingly voluminous formats, budgets simultaneously record policy decision outcomes, cite policy priorities as well as program objectives, and delineate a government's total service effort.

A public budget has four basic dimensions. First, it is a political instrument that allocates scarce public resources among the social and economic needs of the jurisdiction. Second, a budget is a managerial or administrative instrument: it specifies the ways and means of providing public programs and services; it establishes the costs of programs and the criteria by which these programs are evaluated for efficiency and effectiveness; it ensures that the programs will be reviewed or evaluated at least once during each year (or cycle). Third, a budget is an economic instrument that can direct a jurisdiction's economic growth and de-

velopment. Certainly at the national level—and to a lesser extent at the state and regional levels—government budgets are primary instruments for redistributing income, stimulating economic growth, promoting full employment, combating inflation, and maintaining economic stability. Fourth, a budget is an accounting instrument that holds government officials responsible for the expenditure of the funds with which they have been entrusted. Budgets also hold governments accountable in the aggregate. The very concept of a budget implies that there is a ceiling, or a spending limitation, which literally (but theoretically) requires governments to live within their means.

REFERENCES

For texts, see Robert D. Lee and Ronald W. Johnson, *Public Budgeting Systems,* 2d ed. (Baltimore: University Park Press, 1977); Albert C. Hyde and Jay M. Shafritz, eds., *Government Budgeting Theory, Process, Politics* (Oak Park, IL: Moore, 1978); Dennis S. Ippolito, *The Budget and National Politics* (San Francisco: Freeman, 1978); John Wanat, *Introduction to Budgeting* (North Scituate, MA: Duxbury, 1978); Thomas D. Lynch, *Public Budgeting in America* (Englewood Cliffs, NJ: Prentice-Hall, 1979); Aaron Wildavsky, *The Politics of the Budgetary Process,* 4th ed. (Boston: Little, Brown, 1984).

Landmarks in Federal Budget Practices

1921   The Budget and Accounting Act established a Bureau of the Budget in the Department of the Treasury and the General Accounting Office as an audit agency of the Congress.

1939   The Reorganization Act transferred the Bureau of the Budget from the Treasury to the White House.

1950   The Budgeting and Accounting Procedures Act mandated the performance budgeting concepts called for by the Hoover Commission.

1961   The Department of Defense installed a planning programming budgeting system (PPBS).

1965   A PPBS was made mandatory for all federal agencies by the Lyndon B. Johnson administration.

1970	The Bureau of the Budget was given more responsibility for managerial oversight and renamed the Office of Management and Budget (OMB).
1971	The PPBS was formally abandoned in the federal government by the Richard M. Nixon administration.
1974	The Congressional Budget and Impoundment Control Act revised the congressional budget process and timetable and created the Congressional Budget Office.
1977	Zero-based budgeting was required of all federal agencies by the Jimmy Carter administration.
1981	Zero-based budgeting requirements were rescinded by the Ronald Reagan administration. David Stockman, director of the Office of Management and Budget, told the *Atlantic Monthly* that "none of us really understand what's going on with all these numbers."
1985	The Gramm-Rudman-Hollings Act was signed into law; it sought to balance the federal budget by mandating across-the-board cuts over a period of years.
1986	The Supreme court in *Bowsher v Synar* invalidated certain provisions of the Gramm-Rudman-Hollings Act.

budgeting, capital A budget process that deals with planning for large expenditures for capital items. Capital expenditures should be for long-term investments (such as bridges and buildings), which yield returns for years after they are completed. Capital budgets typically cover five- to ten-year periods and are updated yearly. Items included in capital budgets may be financed through borrowing (including tax-exempt municipal bonds), savings, grants, revenue sharing, special assessments, and so on. A capital budget provides for separating the financing of capital, or investment, expenditures from current, or operating, expenditures. The federal government has never had a capital budget in the sense of financing capital programs separately from current expenditures.

REFERENCES

John Matzer, Jr., ed., *Capital Financing Strategies for Local Governments* (Washington, D.C.: International City Management, 1983);

Ronald W. Chapman, Capital financing: An old approach reapplied, *Public Productivity Review* 7 (December 1983);

Raymond J. Staffeldt and Kenneth Unger, Pennsylvania's capital budgeting system, *State Government* 58 (Fall 1985).

budgeting, incremental A method of budget review that focuses on the increments of increase or decrease in the budget of existing programs. Incremental budgeting, which is often called traditional budgeting, is a counter school of thought to more rational, systems-oriented approaches, such as zero-based budgeting. But this old approach nicely takes into account the inherently political nature of the budget process and so will continue to be favored by legislative appropriations committees, if not by budget theorists.

REFERENCES

John Wanat, Bases of budgetary incrementalism, *American Political Science Review* 68 (September 1974);

Harvey J. Tucker, Incremental budgeting: Myth or model? *Western Political Quarterly* 35 (September 1982);

Allen Schick, Incremental budgeting in a decremental age, *Policy Sciences* 16 (September 1983);

Bernard T. Pitsvada and Frank D. Draper, Making sense of the federal budget the old fashioned way—incrementally, *Public Administration Review* 44 (September/October 1984).

budgeting, planning programming *See* PLANNING PROGRAMMING BUDGETING SYSTEM.

budgeting, zero-based A budgeting process that is, first and foremost, a rejection of the incremental decision-making model of budgeting. It demands a rejustification of the entire budget submission (from ground zero), whereas incremental budgeting essentially respects the outcomes of previous budgetary decisions (collectively referred to as the budget base) and focuses examination on the margin of change from year to year. In 1976, presidential candidate Jimmy Carter made the installation of zero-based budgeting (ZBB) a campaign promise, and, in 1977, as president, he ordered its adoption by the federal government. In large part, ZBB failed because the conditions that had prevailed for most of the previous budgeting systems reforms had changed. In an era of acute resource scarcity, ZBB had little utility because there was little real chance that funding could be provided for any program growth. Critics assaulted ZBB as a fraud; some called it a nonsystem of budgeting. ZBB's fate in the federal government was tied to the Carter presidency. After the inauguration of a new president in 1981, it was quietly rescinded. Still, numerous state and local governments use ZBB techniques or some adaptation of it. Now that the hype has subsided, it remains an important part of public budgeting.

REFERENCES

Peter A. Phyrr, The zero-base approach to government budgeting, *Public Administration Review* 37 (January/February 1977);

Allen Schick, The road from ZBB, *Public Administration Review* 38 (March/April 1978);

Ronald Randall, Presidential uses of management tools from PPB to ZBB, *Presidential Studies Quarterly* 12 (Spring 1982).

budget, line-item The classification of budgetary accounts according to narrow, detailed objects of expenditure (such as motor vehicles, clerical workers, or reams of paper) used within each particular agency of government, generally without reference to the ultimate purpose or objective served by the expenditure.

budget, operating A short-term plan for managing the resources necessary to carry out a program. Short term can mean anything from a few weeks to a few years. Usually an operating budget is developed for each fiscal year, with changes made as necessary.

budget, president's The executive budget for a particular fiscal year transmitted to the Congress by the president in accordance with the Budget and Accounting Act of 1921, as amended. Some elements of the budget (such as the estimates for the legislative branch and the judiciary) are required to be included without review by the Office of Management and Budget or approval by the president.

budget surplus The amount by which a government's budget receipts exceed its budget outlays for any given period.

budget, unified The present form of the budget of the federal government, in which receipts and outlays from federal funds and trust funds (such as social security) are consolidated. When these two fund groups are consolidated to display budget totals, transactions from one fund group to the other fund group (interfund transactions) are deducted to avoid double counting. The fiscal activities of off-budget federal agencies are not included in the unified budget.

budget year The fiscal year for which the budget is being considered; the fiscal year following the current year.

buffer 1 A small state between two larger powers that functions to reduce the possibility of conflict between them. 2 Organizational procedures or structures that absorb disruptive inputs and thus protect the continuity or equilibrium of some core group. For example, people in positions near the boundaries of organizations, such as receptionists, often absorb a wide variety of messages and demands. These inputs are filtered, processed, and passed to the technical core of the organization in a sequential and routine form. Because the inputs have been buffered, the central work processes are not disrupted.

REFERENCES

1 Michael Greenfield Partem, The buffer system in international relations, *Journal of Conflict Resolution* 27 (March 1983);

Mary Ellen Fischer, Eastern Europe: The unstable buffer, *Bulletin of the Atomic Scientists* 40 (December 1984).

build-down A reduction in nuclear arsenals by destroying more old warheads than new ones are built. A build-down does not necessarily change strategic relationships, because the fewer new weapons may be more accurate and powerful than the more numerous older ones.

REFERENCES

Alton Frye, Strategic build-down: A contest for restraint, *Foreign Affairs* 62 (Winter 1983–84);

Jack N. Barkenbus and Alvin M. Weinberg, Defense-protected builddown, *Bulletin of the Atomic Scientists* 40 (October 1984).

built-in stabilizers Features of the economy (such as unemployment benefits, welfare payments) that automatically act to modify the severity of economic downturns.

bull 1 One who believes that prices on a stock market will rise. *Compare to* BEAR. 2 A lame excuse or lie. 3 A slang term for a police officer or prison guard. 4 An official message from the Pope of the Roman Catholic Church, so called because bulla refers to the official seal used on such documents.

bully pulpit President THEODORE ROOSEVELT's definition of the American presidency, because the office provided its occupant an unparalled opportunity to preach to and to inspire the national congregation. Bully is an informal interjection of approval that has fallen into disuse except among those who do impersonations of Teddy Roosevelt.

buncombe/bunkum/bunk Insincere public utterings of politicians; speechmaking undertaken to please constituents; political nonsense. They have their origin in a statement by Felix Walker (1753–1828), the U.S. Representative from Buncombe County, North Carolina, who in 1820 rose in the House "to make a speech for Buncombe." It was so obviously insincere and irrelevant, his home county's name was transformed into a term for inconsequential political speech.

REFERENCE

H. L. Mencken, in *On Politics: A Carnival of Buncombe,* ed. Malcolm Moos (New York: Vintage, 1960).

Bunting v State of Oregon *See* LOCHNER V NEW YORK.

burden of proof The requirement that a party to an issue show that the weight of evidence is on his or her side to have the issue decided in his or her favor.

REFERENCES

John Calvin Jeffries, Jr., and Paul B. Stephan III, Defenses, presumptions, and burden of proof in the criminal law, *Yale Law Journal* 88 (June 1979);

Melvin R. Novick, Burden of proof/burden of remedy, *Public Personnel Management* 10 (Fall 1981).

bureau A government department, agency, or a subdivision of same.

bureaucracy 1 The totality of government offices or bureaus (a French term meaning *office*) that constitute the permanent government of a state; that is, those people and functions that continue irrespective of changes in political leadership. Modern Western-style bureaucracies originated in Europe when the governing affairs of centralized autocratic regimes became so complicated that it became necessary to delegate the king's authority to his representatives. American bureaucracy has never fully recovered from its nondemocratic European origins, and some politicians rejoice in attacking the "unresponsive" bureaucracy. At the same time, "good government" groups often contend that, once in office, politicians make the bureaucracy all too responsive to special interests instead of leaving them alone to impartially administer the programs for which they were originally established. 2 All of the public officials of a government. 3 A general invective to refer to any inefficient organization encumbered by red tape. 4 A specific set of structural arrangements.

The dominant structural definition of bureaucracy, indeed the point of departure for all further analyses on the subject, is that of the German sociologist MAX WEBER (1864–1920), who used an "ideal type" approach to extrapolate from the real world the central core of features that would characterize the most fully developed bureaucratic form of organization. This ideal type is neither a description of reality nor a statement of normative preference; it is merely an identification of the major variables or features that characterize bureaucracy. The fact that such features might not be fully present in a given organization does not necessarily imply that the organization is not bureaucratic. It may be an immature rather than a fully developed bureaucracy. At some point, however, it may be necessary to conclude that the characteristics of bureaucracy are so lacking in an organization that it could neither reasonably be termed bureaucratic nor be expected to produce patterns of bureaucratic behavior.

Weber's ideal type of bureaucracy possesses the following characteristics: (1) The bureaucrats must be personally free and subject to authority only with respect to the impersonal duties of their offices. (2) The bureaucrats are arranged in a clearly defined hierarchy of offices. (3) The functions of each office are clearly specified. (4) The bureaucrats accept and maintain their appointments freely—without duress. (5) Appointments to office are made on the basis of technical qualifications, which ideally are substantiated by examinations administered by the appointing authority, a university, or both. (6) The bureaucrats receive money salaries and pension rights, which reflect the varying levels of the hierarchy. While the bureaucrats are free to leave the organization, they can be removed from their offices only under previously stated, specific circumstances. (7) The office must be the bureaucrat's sole or at least major occupation. (8) A career system is essential; while promotion may be the result of either seniority or merit, it must be premised on the judgment of hierarchical superiors. (9) The bureaucrats do not have property rights to their office nor any personal claim to the resources that go with it. (10) The bureaucrat's conduct must be subject to systematic control and strict discipline.

While Weber's structural identification of bureaucratic organization (first published in 1922) is perhaps the most comprehensive statement on the subject in the literature of the social sciences, it is not always considered satisfactory as an intellectual construct. For example, Anthony Downs, in *Inside Bureaucracy* (Boston: Little, Brown, 1967), argued that at least two elements should be added to Weber's definition. First, the organization must be large. According to Downs, "any organization in which the highest ranking mem-

bers know less than half of the other members can be considered large." Second, most of the organization's output cannot be "directly or indirectly evaluated in any markets external to the organization by means of voluntary quid pro quo transactions." *See also* FOURTH BRANCH OF GOVERNMENT; REALPOLITIK; RED TAPE; REPRESENTATIVE BUREAUCRACY.

REFERENCES

For bureaucratic behavior, see Robert K. Merton, et al., *Reader in Bureaucracy* (New York: Free Press, 1952);

Michael Crozier, *The Bureaucratic Phenomenon* (Chicago: University of Chicago Press, 1964);

Carol H. Weiss and Allen H. Barton, eds., *Making Bureaucracies Work* (Beverly Hills, CA: Sage, 1980);

Ralph P. Hummel, *The Bureaucratic Experience*, 3d ed. (New York: St. Martin's 1987).

For the federal perspective, see Louis C. Gawthrop, *Bureaucratic Behavior in the Executive Branch: An Analysis of Organizational Change* (New York: Free Press, 1969);

Alan A. Altshuler and Norman C. Thomas, eds., *The Politics of the Federal Bureaucracy*, 2d ed. (New York: Harper & Row, 1977).

For the state and local perspective, see Douglas M. Fox, *The Politics of City and State Bureaucracy* (Pacific Palisades, CA: Goodyear, 1974);

Clarence N. Stone, Robert K. Whelan, and William J. Murin, *Urban Policy and Politics in a Bureaucratic Age* (Englewood Cliffs, NJ: Prentice-Hall, 1979).

For the historical perspective, see Michael T. Dalby and Michael S. Werthman, *Bureaucracy in Historical Perspective* (Glenview, IL: Scott, Foresman, 1971);

Henry Jacoby, *The Bureaucratization of the World* (Berkeley and Los Angeles: University of California Press, 1973);

Michael Nelson, A short, ironic history of American national bureaucracy, *Journal of Politics* 44 (August 1982);

Metin Heper, The state and public bureaucracies: A comparative and historical perspective, *Comparative Studies in Society and History* 27 (January 1985).

For the politics of bureaucracy, see Gordon Tullock, *The Politics of Bureaucracy* (Washington, D.C.: Public Affairs, 1965);

B. Guy Peters, *The Politics of Bureaucracy: A Comparative Approach* (New York: Longman, 1978);

David Nachmias and David H. Rosenbloom, *Bureaucratic Government USA* (New York: St. Martin's, 1980);

Francis E. Rourke, ed., *Bureaucratic Power in National Policy Making,* 4th ed. (Boston: Little, Brown, 1986).

For analyses of Weber's model, see Jon P. Miller, Social-psychological implications of Weber's model of bureaucracy: Relations among expertise, control, authority, and legitimacy, *Social Forces* 49 (September 1970);

Lloyd I. Rudolph and Susanne Hoeber Rudolph, Authority and power in bureaucratic and patrimonial administration: A revisionist interpretation of Weber on bureaucracy, *World Politics* 31 (January 1979);

F. G. Tenorio, The permanence of the Weberian model, *International Review of Administrative Sciences* 47:3 (1981);

Susan J. Hekman, Weber's ideal type: A contemporary reassessment, *Polity* 16 (Fall 1983).

bureaucrat A denizen of a bureaucracy. *Compare to* APPARATCHIK.

Bureaucrat The quarterly journal of the National Area Chapter of the American Society for Public Administration (ASPA) and the Federal Executive Alumni Association; published since 1972. Library of Congress no. JK1 .B86.
The *Bureaucrat*
12007 Titan Way
Potomac, MD 20854

bureaucratic risk taking An extraordinary action, generally resisted by the persons in charge, taken by a public servant who commits the government to a profitable course of action, or who blocks the execution of an illegal or immoral order, or who exposes corruption, deceit, or an unlawful act taking place within the bureaucracy.

bureaucrats, street-level Those public officials who are literally closest to the people by being in almost constant contact with the public; for example, police officers, welfare case workers, teachers.

REFERENCES

Michael Lipsky, Toward a theory of street-level bureaucracy, in *Theoretical Perspectives in Urban Politics,* ed. Willis D. Hawley et al. (Englewood Cliffs, NJ: Prentice-Hall, 1976);

Nicholas P. Lovrich, Jr., Brent S. Steel, and Mahdun Majed, The street-level bureaucrat—A useful category or a distinction without a difference? *Review of Public Personnel Administration* 6 (Spring 1986).

Bureau of Labor Statistics (BLS) The agency responsible for the economic and statistical research activities of the U.S. Department of Labor. The BLS is the federal government's principal fact-finding agency in the field of labor economics, particularly with the collection and analysis of data on work force and labor requirements, living conditions, labor-management relations, productivity and technological developments, occupational safety and health, structure and growth of the economy, urban conditions, and related socioeconomic issues. The information collected is issued in monthly press releases, in special publications, and in its official publication, the *Monthly Labor Review*. Other major BLS periodicals include: *The Consumer Price Index, Wholesale Prices and Price Index, Employment and Earnings, Current Wage Developments, Occupational Outlook Handbook,* and *Occupational Outlook Quarterly*.

REFERENCES

For histories, see Jonathan Grossman and Judson MacLaury, The creation of the Bureau of Labor Statistics, *Monthly Labor Review* 98 (February 1975);

J. P. Goldberg and W. T. Moye, The AFL and a national BLS: Labor's role is crystalized, *Monthly Labor Review* 105 (March 1982);

Edgar Weinberg, BLS and the economy; A centennial timetable, *Monthly Labor Review* 107 (November 1984).

Bureau of Labor Statistics
200 Constitution Avenue, N.W.
Washington, D.C. 20210
(202) 523-1327

Burger, Warren Earl (1907–   ) The chief justice of the United States from 1969 to 1986. He was appointed by President Richard M. Nixon in the expectation that he would lead a conservative court that would reverse many of the liberal rulings of the Warren court.

REFERENCES

For an explanation of why that reversal never happened, see V. Blasi, ed., *The Burger Court: The Counter Revolution That Wasn't* (New Haven, CT: Yale University Press, 1983);
Herman Schwartz, ed., *The Burger Years* (New York: Viking, 1987).

burgess **1** An elected member in the lower house of the legislature in colonial Virginia or Maryland. Burgess simply means a citizen of an English borough.   **2** A modern-day member of the governing board of some boroughs.

Burgess, John W. (1844–1931)   The Columbia University professor who, after studying the German university system, created the first American graduate program in political science leading to the Ph.D., in 1880. Burgess, sometimes called the father of American political science, is generally credited with the development of political science as an independent discipline.

REFERENCES

Bernard E. Brown, *American Conservatives: The Political Thought of Francis Lieber and John W. Burgess* (New York: Columbia University Press, 1951);
Albert Somit and Joseph Tanenhaus, *The Development of American Political Science: From Burgess to Behavioralism* (Boston: Allyn and Bacon, 1967);
Bert James Loewenberg, *American History in American Thought* (New York: Simon & Schuster, 1972), chapter 18.

Burke, Edmund (1729–1797)   The British political philosopher and member of parliament who is often referred to as the father of

modern conservative thought. Burke, in his 1770 pamphlet "Thoughts on the Cause of the Present Discontents," provided the first modern definition of a political party as a group united on public principle that could act as a link between the executive branch (the king) and the legislative branch (parliament), providing consistency and strength while in power and principled criticism when out of power. But Burke is best known for his 1774 "Speech to the Electors of Bristol," in which he asserted that the role of an elected member of a legislature should be that of a representative or trustee (thus free to exercise his own best judgment) rather than that of a delegate (one who is bound by prior instructions from a constituency). *Compare to* POLITICO.

REFERENCES

Heinz Eulau, John C. Wahlke, William Buchanan, and Leroy C. Ferguson, The role of the representative: Some empirical observations on the theory of Edmund Burke, *American Political Science Review* 53 (September 1959);
James Conniff, Burke, Bristol, and the concept of representation, *Western Political Quarterly* 30 (September 1977);
Michael Freeman, On revolution: Burke then and now, Edmund Burke and the theory of revolution, *Political Theory* 6 (August 1978).

Edmund Burke on the Role of a Representative

Certainly, gentlemen, it ought to be the happiness and glory of a representative to live in the strictest union, the closest correspondence, and the most unreserved communication with his constituents. Their wishes ought to have great weight with him; their opinion, high respect; their business, unremitted attention. It is his duty to sacrifice his repose, his pleasures, his satisfactions, to theirs; and above all, ever, and in all cases, to prefer their interest to his own. But his unbiased opinion, his mature judgment, his enlightened conscience, he ought not to sacrifice to you, to any man, or to any set of men living. These he does not derive from your pleasure; no, nor from the law and the constitution. They are a trust from Providence, for the abuse of which he is deeply answerable. Your representative owes you, not his industry only, but his judgment; and he betrays, instead of serving you, if he sacrifices it to your opinion.

My worthy colleague says, his will ought to be subservient to yours. If that be all, the thing is innocent. If government were a matter of will upon any side, yours, without question, ought to be superior. But government and legislation are matters of reason and judgment, and not of inclination; and what sort of reason is that, in which the determination precedes the discussion; in which one set of men deliberate, and another decide. . . .

To deliver an opinion, is the right of all men; that of constituents is a weighty and respectable opinion, which a representative ought always to rejoice to hear; and which he ought always most seriously to consider. But *authoritative* instructions; *mandates* issued, which the member is bound blindly and implicitly to obey, to vote, and to argue for, though contrary to the clearest conviction of his judgment and conscience,—these are things utterly unknown to the laws of this land, and which arise from a fundamental mistake of the whole order and tenor of our constitution.

Parliament is not a *congress* of ambassadors from different and hostile interests; which interests each must maintain, as an agent and advocate, against other agents and advocates; but parliament is a *deliberative* assembly of *one* nation, with *one* interest, that of the whole; where, not local purposes, not local prejudices, ought to guide, but the general good, resulting from the general reason of the whole. You choose a member indeed; but when you have chosen him, he is not member for Bristol, but he is a member of *parliament*.

Source: "Speech to the Electors of Bristol," November 3, 1774

Bush v Lucas 462 U.S. 367 (1983)   The U.S. Supreme Court case that held that federal employees cannot sue their supervisors for violations of their First Amendment rights because the Congress has provided an alternative remedy, namely appeals through the civil service system to the Merit Systems Protection Board.

business cycle, political   The manipulation of an economy for political purposes by means of government expenditures and monetary policy. A political business cycle would ideally seek to maintain the greatest prosperity just before elections and to suffer through the seemingly inevitable periods of economic decline just after elections. While many politicians have tried to manipulate economic activity for political advantage (increased gov-

ernment spending just before an election is an obvious example), there is no hard evidence that their success is more related to calculated policies than to luck.

REFERENCES

C. Duncan MacRae, A political model of the business cycle, *Journal of Political Economy* 85 (April 1977);

Edward R. Tufte, *Political Control of the Economy* (Princeton, NJ: Princeton University Press, 1978);

David G. Golden and James M. Poterba, The price of popularity: The political business cycle reexamined, *American Journal of Political Science* 24 (November 1980);

Kristen R. Monroe, Political manipulation of the economy: A closer look at political business cycles, *Presidential Studies Quarterly* 13 (Winter 1983);

Victor Ginsburgh and Philippe Michel, Random timing of elections and the political business cycle, *Public Choice* 40:2 (1983).

business cycles   The recurrent phases of expansion and contraction in overall business activity. Although no two business cycles are alike, they are all thought to follow a pattern of prosperity, recession (or depression), and recovery. The sophisticated analysis and measurement of business cycles was logically prior to the development of economic planning, the countercyclical concepts of fiscal and monetary policy, and the impact of Keynesianism. Wesley C. Mitchell (1874–1948), one of the founders of the National Bureau of Economic Research in 1920 and its director of research for twenty-five years (1920–1945), was the leading pioneer in business cycles analysis.

REFERENCES

Rendigs Fels, What causes business cycles? *Social Science Quarterly* 58 (June 1977);

William R. Thompson, Phases of the business cycle and the outbreak of war, *International Studies Quarterly* 26 (June 1982);

John B. Long, Jr., and Charles I. Plosser, Real business cycles, *Journal of Political Economy* 91 (February 1983).

business transfer tax *See* TAX, VALUE-ADDED.

busing   The transporting of children by bus to schools at a greater distance than those the children would otherwise attend to achieve racial desegregation. Busing has often been mandated by the federal courts as a remedy for past practices of discrimination. It has been heartily objected to by parents who want their children to attend neighborhood schools and has, in consequence, been a major factor in WHITE FLIGHT from central cities. Busing is often used as an example of government by the judiciary, because busing, one of the most controversial domestic policies in the history of the United States, has never been specifically sanctioned by the Congress. *Compare to* SWANN V CHARLOTTE-MECKLENBURG BOARD OF EDUCATION.

REFERENCES

Jonathan Kelley, The politics of school busing, *Public Opinion Quarterly* 38 (Spring 1974);

Claude H. Farrell, David N. Hyman, and Loren A. Ihnen, Forced busing and the demand for private schooling, *Journal of Legal Studies* 6 (June 1977);

David O. Sears, Carl P. Hensler, and Leslie K. Speer, Whites' opposition to "busing": Self-interest or symbolic politics? *American Political Science Review* 73 (June 1979);

John B. McConahay, Self-interest versus racial attitudes as correlates of anti-busing attitudes in Louisville: Is it the buses or the blacks? *Journal of Politics* 44 (August 1982);

Gerald W. Heaney, Busing, timetables, goals, and ratios: Touchstones of equal opportunity, *Minnesota Law Review* 69 (April 1985).

Butz v Economou 438 U.S. 478 (1978) The U.S. Supreme Court case that provided an immunity from suit for civil damages to federal administrative officials exercising adjudicatory functions.

REFERENCES

Gail M. Burgess, Official immunity and civil liability for constitutional torts committed by military commanders after *Butz v Economou, Military Law Review* 89 (Summer 1980);

Robert G. Vaughn, The personal accountability of civil servants, *Bureaucrat* 9 (Fall 1980);

Gerald J. Miller, Administrative malpractice before and after *Butz v Economou, Bureaucrat* 9 (Winter 1980–81).

buy American acts Various state and national laws that require government agencies to give a preference to American-made goods when making purchases. Similar "buy national" practices are also being used by all the major trading partners of the United States.

REFERENCE

Charles W. Trainor, The buy American act: Examination, analysis and comparison, *Military Law Review* 64 (Spring 1974).

by-election A special election. *See* ELECTION, SPECIAL.

bylaws 1 The regulations adopted by a corporation's stockholders for its internal governance. 2 The rules or regulations adopted by an organization, such as a social club or professional association. 3 The laws enacted by subordinate legislative bodies, such as municipalities.

C

Cabell v Shavez-Salido 454 U.S. 70 (1982) The U.S. Supreme Court case that held that a state statute requiring peace officers, including deputy probation officers, to be U.S. citizens did not violate the equal protection clause of the Fourteenth Amendment.

cabinet The heads of the executive departments of a jurisdiction who report to and advise its chief executive; for example, the president's cabinet, the governor's cabinet, the mayor's cabinet.

REFERENCE

Lydia Bodman and Daniel B. Garry, Innovations in state cabinet systems, *State Government* 55:3 (1982).

cabinet government 1 The British system, whereby the cabinet as a whole, rather than only the prime minister who heads it, is considered the executive, and the cabinet is collectively responsible to the parliament for its performance. In addition, whereas in the United States the cabinet secretaries are only of the executive branch, in Britain the cabinet ministers are typically drawn from among the majority party's members in parliament. 2 A concept informally applied to an American president's assertion that he and his cabinet are going to work together as a team. Such team spirit hardly lasts beyond an administration's honeymoon period.

REFERENCES

1 Ivor Jennings, *Cabinet Government,* 3d ed. (London: Cambridge University Press, 1969).

2 Peter Coaldrake, Ronald Reagan and "cabinet government": How far a collegial approach? *Politics* 16 (November 1981).

cabinet, inner Usually refers to the federal departments of State, Defense, Treasury, and Justice—because they (and their secretaries) tend to be more prominent and influential in every administration than the rest of the (or outer) cabinet. While all cabinet secretaries are equal in rank and salary, the missions of those in the inner cabinet give them an advantage in prestige, access, and visibility.

Cabinet, Kitchen The informal advisors of a chief executive. First used derisively for some of President Andrew Jackson's advisors: kitchen implying they were not respectable enough to meet in the more formal rooms of the White House. Over the years the term has lost its derisive quality. *Compare to* BRAINS TRUST.

President George Washington (left) with the first cabinet: Secretary of State Thomas Jefferson, Attorney General Edmund Randolph (back turned), Treasury Secretary Alexander Hamilton, and Secretary of War Henry Knox (seated).

cabinet, president's An institution whose existence rests upon custom rather than constitutional provision, even though its chief members, the secretaries of the federal executive departments, must be approved by the Senate. It came into being as a single body, because President George Washington found it useful to meet with the chiefs of the several executive departments. While all subsequent presidents have considered it necessary to meet with the cabinet, their attitudes toward the institution and its members have varied greatly. Some presidents have convened their cabinet only for the most formal and routine matters, while others have relied upon it for advice and support. The president's cabinet differs from the cabinet in the British parliamentary system in that, in the United States, the executive power is constitutionally vested in the president, so the cabinet members are responsible to him.

At the present time, cabinet membership consists of the secretaries of thirteen executive departments, the two newest members being the Secretary of Energy and the Secretary of Education. A substantial part of the executive branch is not represented in the cabinet. From the earliest days, presidents have accorded to others the privilege of attending and participating in cabinet meetings. In recent years, the United States ambassador to the United Nations and the director of the Office of Management and Budget, among others, have been accorded cabinet rank.

REFERENCES

Richard F. Fenno, Jr., *The President's Cabinet* (Cambridge, MA: Harvard University Press, 1959);

Nelson W. Polsby, Presidential cabinet making: Lessons for the political system, *Political Science Quarterly* 93 (Spring 1978);

James J. Best, Presidential cabinet appointments: 1953–1976, *Presidential Studies Quarterly* 11 (Winter 1981);

Dean E. Mann and Zachary A. Smith, The selection of U.S. cabinet officers and other political executives, *International Political Science Review* 2:2 (1981);

R. Gordon Hoxie, The cabinet in the American presidency, 1789–1984, *Presidential Studies Quarterly* 14 (Spring 1984);

Jeffrey E. Cohen, On the tenure of appointive political executives: The American cabinet, 1952–1984, *American Journal of Political Science* 30 (August 1986).

calendar   An agenda or list of pending business awaiting action by a legislature. The House of Representatives uses five legislative calendars: CALENDAR, CONSENT; CALENDAR, HOUSE; CALENDAR, PRIVATE; CALENDAR,

UNION; and DISCHARGE CALENDAR. In the Senate, all legislative matters reported from committee are listed in order on a single calendar, but they may be called up irregularly by the majority leader, either by motion or by obtaining the unanimous consent of the Senate. The Senate also uses one nonlegislative calendar, for presidential nominations and treaties (*see* CALENDAR, EXECUTIVE).

calendar, call of   *See* CALL OF THE CALENDAR.

calendar, consent   The calendar on which members of the House of Representatives may place any noncontroversial bill appearing on the union or house calendars. Bills on the consent calendar are normally called on the first and third Mondays of each month. On the first occasion that a bill is called in this manner, consideration may be blocked by the objection of any member. The second time, if there are three objections, the bill is stricken from the consent calendar. If fewer than three members object, the bill is given immediate consideration. A bill on the consent calendar may be postponed in another way. A member may ask that the measure be passed over "without prejudice." In that case, no objection is recorded against the bill, and its status on the consent calendar remains unchanged. A bill stricken from the consent calendar remains on the union or house calendars.

calendar, executive   A nonlegislative calendar in the Senate, on which presidential documents, such as treaties and nominations, are listed.

calendar, House   The listing of public bills, other than appropriations or revenue measures, awaiting action by the House of Representatives.

calendar, private   The calendar on which House of Representative bills dealing with individual matters—such as claims against the government, immigration, and land titles—are put. Two members may block consideration of a private bill in the chamber. If blocked, it is then recommitted to committee. An omnibus claims bill is several private bills considered as one. As with any bill, no part of an omnibus claims bill may be deleted without a vote. When a private bill goes to the floor in this form, it can be defeated only by a majority of those present. The private calendar can be called on the first and third Tuesdays of each month.

calendar, union   The calendar in the House of Representatives on which bills that directly or indirectly appropriate money or raise revenue are placed according to the date they are reported from committee.

calendar Wednesday   Certain Wednesdays when the House of Representatives is in session. On these Wednesdays, committees may be called (in the order in which they appear in House Rule 10) for the purpose of bringing up any of their bills from the House or the union calendars, except privileged bills. General debate is limited to two hours. Bills called up from the union calendar are considered in the Committee of the Whole. Calendar Wednesday is not observed during the last two weeks of a session and may be dispensed with at other times by a two-thirds vote. On the whole, it is a cumbersome and largely ineffective device for calling up a bill for floor consideration.

REFERENCE

For a description of a rare modern-day use of calendar Wednesday, see John F. Bibby and Roger H. Davidson, *On Capitol Hill: Studies in the Legislative Process*, 2d edition (Hinsdale, IL: Dryden Press, 1967).

Calhoun, John C. (1782–1850)   The leading political voice of the South in the first half of the nineteenth century and the only vice president (1825–1832) to resign over policy differences with a president (Andrew Jackson). Calhoun is most associated with the concept of nullification, which held that a state could nullify an act of the Congress within its own borders. This was later referred to as interposition, because a state might interpose its sovereignty to void a law of the United States. The whole nullification-interposition controversy was settled by the Civil War, and these concepts are now only of historical significance. In the

John C. Calhoun

1950s some southern politicians tried to revive the interposition doctrine as a way of avoiding federal court desegregation mandates. But the federal courts have rejected interposition as a violation of the supremacy clause of Article VI of the U.S. Constitution.

In his *Disquisition on Government* (1848), Calhoun, the leading states' rights and proslavery advocate of his era, ironically argued for the protection of minorities in a democratic society. He suggested that binding political decisions be made only by a "concurrent majority" representing all major elements of society. Decisions made only by a simple majority, Calhoun asserted, could not be binding on groups whose interests they violated. In effect, Calhoun was pleading for consensus government.

REFERENCES

August O. Spain, *The Political Theory of John C. Calhoun* (New York: Bookman, 1951);

Gerald Mortimer Capers, *John C. Calhoun, Opportunist: A Reappraisal* (Gainesville: University of Florida Press, 1960).

California Federal Savings and Loan Association v Guerra 93 L Ed 2d 613 (1987)   The U.S. Supreme Court case which upheld the ability of states to require special job protection for pregnant workers; in this case to require both maternity leave and later reinstatement.

California plan The method of judicial selection, often referred to as a combination compromise, in which a governor nominates a prospective judge for consideration by a review commission. If approved by the commission, the new judge serves until the next general election, when he or she then runs unopposed on a nonpartisan ballot. *Compare to* MISSOURI PLAN.

REFERENCE
John H. Culver, Politics and the California plan for choosing appellate judges: A lesson at large on judicial selection, *Judicature* 66 (September/October 1982).

callable bonds *See* BONDS, CALLABLE.

call of the calendar The means by which those Senate bills not brought up for debate by a motion or a unanimous consent agreement are brought before the Senate for action when the calendar listing them in order is "called." Bills considered in this fashion are usually noncontroversial, and debate is limited to five minutes for each Senator on a bill or on amendments to it.

Camelot King Arthur's legendary city, which became a retrospective symbol of the John F. Kennedy administration's style after Jacqueline Kennedy, the president's widow, told Theodore H. White in an interview for *Life* magazine how much the late president loved the music from the Broadway musical *Camelot* (For President Kennedy, an epilogue, *Life,* December 6, 1963). Because of some negative reassessment of Kennedy's presidency, the term is sometimes used sarcastically.

REFERENCE
James MacGregor Burns, *Edward Kennedy and the Camelot Legacy* (New York: Norton, 1976).

campaign *See* POLITICAL CAMPAIGN.

campaign, front-loaded *See* FRONT LOADED.

campaign promise What candidates say they will do "if elected." There has often been a tenuous relation between the promise and the performance. Financier Bernard Baruch (1870–1965) is usually credited with the advice to "vote for the man who promises least; he'll be the least disappointing."

REFERENCE
For an assessment of presidential campaign promises after the candidate has won, see Jeff Fishel, *Presidents and Promises: From Campaign Pledge to Presidential Performance* (Washington, D.C.: Congressional Quarterly, 1984).

Campbell, Alan K. *See* CIVIL SERVICE REFORM ACT OF 1978.

Camp David The U.S. president's private resort in the Catoctin Mountains in Maryland. Called Shangri-La by President Franklin D. Roosevelt (after James Hilton's mystical place of enchantment in his 1933 novel, *Lost Horizons),* it was changed to Camp David by Dwight D. Eisenhower in honor of his grandson.

Camp David Accords The agreements negotiated and signed by Egyptian President Anwar Sadat and Israeli Prime Minister Menachem Begin in September 1978 at Camp David. These agreements led to the formal Egyptian-Israeli peace treaty in March 1979. President Jimmy Carter sequestered the two heads of state at Camp David while he and his staff mediated an agreement.

REFERENCE
William B. Quandt, *Camp David: Peacemaking and Politics* (Washington, D.C.: Brookings, 1986).

candidate **1** One who seeks elective office. The word came from the Latin candida (white) for the white togas worn by candidati (candidates for elective office in the ancient Roman republic). Because a formal candidate for U.S. public office may have to abide by a variety of campaign spending and other limitations, many probable candidates do not announce their formal candidacy until a strategic moment, even though it is perfectly obvious to everybody that he or she is running for office. **2** An applicant for a civil service position.

REFERENCE

1 Nicole A. Gordon, The constitutional right to candidacy, *Political Science Quarterly* 91 (Fall 1976).

candidate committee A POLITICAL COMMITTEE authorized in writing by a candidate to receive campaign contributions and to make expenditures on his or her behalf.

canvassing board The state or local government agency that receives the vote counts from the various election precincts, tabulates the count, and certifies the winners.

CAP *See* COMMUNITY ACTION PROGRAMS.

capital **1** The city in which a central government is located. New York City became the first capital of the United States (1789); Philadelphia became the capital in 1790; since 1800, the capital has been Washington, D.C. *Compare to* CAPITOL. **2** Wealth; one of the three traditional factors of production, the others being land and labor.

capital budgeting *See* BUDGETING, CAPITAL.

capital gains tax *See* TAX, CAPITAL GAINS.

capitalism The private ownership of most means of production and trade, combined with a generally unrestricted marketplace of goods and services. *Compare to* MARXISM.

REFERENCES

Tibor Scitovsky, Can capitalism survive?—An old question in a new setting, *American Economic Review* 70 (May 1980);

Bruce Andrews, The political economy of world capitalism: Theory and practice, *International Organization* 36 (Winter 1982).

capital offense **1** A crime punishable by death. **2** A crime punishable by death or life imprisonment.

capital punishment The death penalty. Capital is derived from the Latin word for head, caput; thus head punishment once meant you had to give up your head—that it would be cut off. Today, most countries applying capital

In one of the first photographs of capital punishment, Mathew Brady captured the hanging of conspirators convicted of plotting Lincoln's assassination, July 7, 1865.

punishment, except those that still use the sword or guillotine, allow those who are condemned to retain their heads after all life is taken from it. While capital punishment is much talked about in the United States, it has been rarely practiced in recent years. For example, while 1,405 prisoners were legally condemned to death and awaiting execution in the various states in 1984, there were only 21 executions—all for murder. Yet polls have consistently shown great public support for capital punishment. For example, the *Gallup Report* (January/February 1986) showed that 77 percent of all Americans favored the death penalty. *Compare to* CRUEL AND UNUSUAL PUNISHMENT.

REFERENCES

Charles L. Black, Jr., *Capital Punishment: The Inevitability of Caprice and Mistake,* 2d ed. (New York: Norton, 1981);

Barbara Ann Stolz, Congress and capital punishment: An exercise in symbolic politics, *Law and Policy Quarterly* 5 (April 1983);

Nicola Lacey, Capital punishment: Objections from principle and practice, *Government and Opposition* 18 (Autumn 1983).

Means of Capital Punishment in States with the Death Penalty

Alabama, electric chair
Arizona, electric chair
Arkansas, electric chair
California, gas chamber
Colorado, electric chair
Delaware, hanging
Florida, electric chair
Georgia, electric chair
Idaho, lethal injection
Illinois, electric chair
Indiana, electric chair
Kentucky, electric chair
Louisiana, electric chair
Maryland, gas chamber
Massachusetts, electric chair
Mississippi, gas chamber
Missouri, gas chamber
Montana, hanging
Nebraska, electric chair
Nevada, gas chamber
New Hampshire, hanging
New Mexico, lethal injection
New York, electric chair
North Carolina, gas chamber
Oklahoma, lethal injection
Oregon, gas chamber
Pennsylvania, electric chair
Rhode Island, gas chamber
South Carolina, electric chair
South Dakota, electric chair
Tennessee, electric chair
Texas, lethal injection
Utah, hanging or firing squad
Vermont, electric chair
Virginia, electric chair
Washington, hanging
Wyoming, gas chamber

Capitol 1 The domed building in which the Congress of the United States meets. 2 Any building in which a state legislature meets; also called a statehouse. *Compare to* CAPITAL.

Carlson v Green 446 U.S. 14 (1980) The U.S. Supreme Court case that held that the Eighth Amendment's prohibition against cruel and unusual punishment gives federal prisoners or their survivors a direct right to bring suits

The U.S. Capitol as it appeared in 1846.

for damages against prison officials on charges of mistreatment. The decision is an expansion of the court's ruling in *Bivens v Six Unknown Named Federal Narcotics Agents*.

carpetbaggers 1 Northerners who went into the defeated South after the Civil War to seek their fortunes by taking advantage of the corrupt and unstable conditions of the times. 2 A candidate who seeks elective office in a jurisdiction of which he or she is not considered a native. When Robert Kennedy moved to New York specifically to run for U.S. senator and when Jay Rockefeller moved to West Virginia to run for secretary of state (and later governor and senator), they were carpetbaggers. But they both won, anyway, proving that the term has lost some of its negative connotations—or that enough campaign money can wash the stain away.

REFERENCE

1　For the history, see Richard N. Current, *Carpetbaggers Reconsidered* (Durham, NC: Duke University Press, 1964).

Carter Doctrine　The policy announced by President Jimmy Carter in his State of the Union address to Congress on January 23, 1980: "An attempt by any outside forces to gain control of the Persian Gulf region will be regarded as an assault on the vital interests of the United States of America, and such an assault will be repelled by any means necessary, including military force." The press labeled the statement the Carter Doctrine, and characterized it as a reversal of the Nixon Doctrine. President Ronald Reagan's 1987 military build-up in the Persian Gulf certainly supported the substance if not the title of the Carter Doctrine.

REFERENCES

Leslie Gelb, Beyond the Carter Doctrine, *New York Times Magazine,* February 10, 1980;

Bruce R. Kuniholm, The Carter Doctrine, the Reagan Corollary, and prospects for United States policy in Southwest Asia, *International Journal* 41 (Spring 1986).

Carter, Jimmy　(1924–　)　The president of the United States from 1977 to 1981. He was hard working, bright, earnest, and honest; but he brought such seeming political and decisional ineptness to the office that he became

Jimmy Carter

the first elected president to be defeated for reelection since Herbert Hoover in 1932. (Gerald Ford, who was defeated by Carter in 1976, was not running for reelection, since he was never elected president in the first place but was appointed under provisions of the Twenty-fifth Amendment.) Carter, born James Earl Carter in Plains, Georgia, graduated from the U.S. Naval Academy in 1946. After a brief career as a nuclear engineer in the U.S. Navy, he returned to Georgia to become a peanut farmer, entered local politics, and won election as governor (1971–1974). Carter was the first president to be elected from the Deep South since the Civil War (if you discount Woodrow Wilson, who was born in Virginia but elected from New Jersey, and Lyndon Johnson of Texas, who became president only when John F. Kennedy was assassinated).

REFERENCES

For Carter's memoirs, see Jimmy Carter, *Keeping Faith: Memoirs of a President* (New York: Bantam, 1982).

Also see Hamilton Jordan, *Crisis: The Last Year of the Carter Presidency* (New York: Putnam, 1982);

David D. Lee, The politics of less: The trials of Herbert Hoover and Jimmy Carter, *Presidential Studies Quarterly* 13 (Spring 1983).

The Jimmy Carter Administration

Major Accomplishments

- The Camp David Accords
- Foreign policy emphasizing worldwide human rights
- The appointment of the largest number of women and minorities to federal judgeships and policy positions
- The Panama Canal Treaties
- The Civil Service Reform Act of 1978

Major Frustrations

- Fifty-two American hostages taken in Iran
- Double-digit inflation and a poorly performing economy

Carter, Rosalynn (1927–   ) The wife of President Jimmy Carter who, as First Lady, was a strong advocate of the Equal Rights Amendment and was the most politically influential presidential wife since ELEANOR ROOSEVELT.

REFERENCE

For her autobiography, see Rosalynn Carter, *First Lady from Plains* (Boston: Houghton Mifflin, 1984).

case **1** A legal dispute, whether criminal or civil, that goes to court. **2** A judge's opinion deciding a case. **3** The evidence and arguments presented by each side in a legal dispute. **4** Any systematic presentation of arguments in favor of or in opposition to any position or circumstance.

case law All recorded judicial and administrative agency decisions.

casework **1** The services performed by legislators and their staffs at the request of and on behalf of constituents. For example, a U.S. senator may be asked to discover why a social security check has been delayed or why a veteran's claim for benefits has been denied. Casework is an important means by which legislators maintain oversight of the bureaucracy and solidify their political base with constituents. *Compare to* HOME STYLE. **2** Generally any method of providing services that proceeds on the basis of a case-by-case treatment of individuals or groups, as in social work or medicine.

REFERENCES

For casework in the U.S. Congress, see John R. Johannes, Explaining congressional casework styles, *American Journal of Political Science* 27:3 (1983);

John R. Johannes, Congress, the bureaucracy, and casework, *Administration and Society* 16 (May 1984);

John R. Johannes, *To Serve the People: Congress and Constituency Service* (Lincoln, NE: University of Nebraska Press, 1984).

For casework in state legislatures, see Richard C. Elling, The utility of state legislative casework as a means of oversight, *Legislative Studies Quarterly* 4 (August 1979);

Richard C. Elling, State legislative casework and state administrative performance, *Administration and Society* 12 (November 1980).

A Breakdown of Congressional Casework

Constituent Request	Percentage
Information on legislation	16
A government job	8
Help with social security	8
A hardship discharge from the military	7
A government publication	7
An appointment to a military academy	4
Help with unemployment assistance benefits	4
Help with a tax problem	2
Help with a legal problem	1
Help with other problems	49

Source: Adapted from U.S. House of Representatives, Commission on Administrative Review, *Final Report* (95th Cong. 1st sess. 1977), H. Doc. 95–272, p. 830.

Note: Figures total more than 100 percent because some respondents are included in more than one entry.

---

categorical grant *See* GRANT.

Cato Institute A libertarian-oriented, nonpartisan public policy research organization founded in 1977. The institute is named for the letters and pamphlets that helped lay the philosophical foundations of the American Revolution and the Constitution, which in turn were named after an ancient Roman family noted for its opposition to tyranny; it publishes the *Cato Journal*.

Cato Institute
224 2d Street, S.E.
Washington, D.C. 20003
(202) 546–0200

caucus 1 A private meeting of political party members in order to seek agreement on a common course of action, to select delegates for a state or national nominating convention, and so on. The caucus was an early method of selecting presidential candidates before its replacement by party conventions. Today's caucus method for choosing delegates to the national party conventions (and for nominating state and local candidates) rests on a series of party meetings that begin at the precinct level and extend to the state convention. The first-round caucuses are especially important, for they often establish the share of delegates awarded to each candidate. *Compare to* IOWA CAUCUS; PRIMARY, PRESIDENTIAL. 2 An organization of members of the House of Representatives or Senate. The organizations may be officially recognized, as are the House majority and minority caucuses, or they may be unofficial groups of members having shared legislative interests. *Compare to* BLACK CAUCUS; LEGISLATIVE SERVICE ORGANIZATION.
REFERENCES
1   For a classic treatment of caucuses, see E. E. Schattschneider, *Party Government* (New York: Holt, Rinehart and Winston, 1942), chapter 3;
     Also see Thomas R. Marshall, Turnout and representation: Caucuses versus primaries, *American Journal of Political Science* 22 (February 1978);
     Thomas R. Marshall, Caucuses and primaries: Measuring reform in the presidential nomination process, *American Politics Quarterly* 7 (April 1979).
2   Susan Webb Hammond, Daniel P. Mulhollan, and Arthur G. Stevens, Jr., Informal congressional caucuses and agenda setting, *Western Political Quarterly* 38 (December 1985).

cause The reason given for removing someone from an office or job (short for just cause).

The cause cited may or may not be the real reason for the removal.

CBO *See* CONGRESSIONAL BUDGET OFFICE.

CEA *See* COUNCIL OF ECONOMIC ADVISERS.

cease-and-desist order A ruling, frequently issued in unfair labor practice and regulatory cases, that requires the charged party to stop conduct held to be illegal and to take specific action to remedy the unfair or illegal practice. *Compare to* CONSENT ORDER.

census In ancient Rome, the registration of citizens and their property to determine who owed what taxes and who was entitled to vote. The modern census seeks a vast array of statistical information and is not directly concerned with taxation or suffrage. Article I, Section 2, of the U.S. Constitution requires that a census be conducted every ten years so that seats in the House of Representatives shall be appropriately apportioned among the states.
REFERENCE
Carol Steinbach, The new and improved census, *State Government* 51 (Winter 1978).

Census, Bureau of the The general-purpose statistical agency of the federal government, created as a permanent office in 1902. It collects, tabulates, and publishes a wide variety of statistical data about the people and the economy of the nation. These data are utilized by the Congress, by the executive branch, and by the public generally in the development and evaluation of economic and social programs.
REFERENCES
A. Ross Eckler, *The Bureau of the Census* (New York: Praeger, 1972);
Daniel S. Halacy, *Census: 190 Years of Counting America* (New York: Elsevier/Nelson, 1980).

Bureau of the Census
U.S. Department of Commerce
14th Street N.W., between Constitution
   Avenue and E Street
Washington, D.C. 20233
(301) 763–7662

census undercount The contention that people are missed by the census count because they move, are fearful of filling out government forms, are illiterate, or other reasons. Because the count is critical for congressional districting and for the funding level of many intergovernmental grant programs, jurisdictions are apt to make an issue of what they consider to be an undercount.

REFERENCES

Ronald B. Sann, Adjusting for the undercount: A review of census litigation, *National Civic Review* 70 (October 1981);

Abby L. Jennis, The census undercount: Issues of adjustment, *Columbia Journal of Law and Social Problems* 18:3 (1984).

Center for the Study of the Presidency A national public policy research center founded in 1965 whose primary focus is the American presidency; publishes *Presidential Studies Quarterly*.

Center for the Study of the Presidency
208 East 75th Street
New York, NY 10021
(212) 249–1200

central bank In most countries, the central monetary authority. Functions may include issuing a country's currency, carrying out a nation's monetary policy, and managing the country's foreign exchange reserves and the external value of its currency. In the United States, the Federal Reserve System functions as the nation's central bank although it is not formally a central bank and subject to only limited influences by the executive and legislative branches.

central clearance The Office of Management and Budget's (OMB) coordination and assessment of recommendations and positions taken by the various federal departments and agencies on legislative matters as they relate to a president's program. The first form of central clearance is substantive bill clearance. Drafts of bills from departments and agencies must clear the OMB before going to the Congress. Congressional committees also solicit views from interested agencies on substantive legislative bills emanating from sources other than the executive branch. However, executive agency responses are expected to be cleared by the OMB.

The second form of central clearance is financial bill clearance. Since the Budget and Accounting Act of 1921, federal agencies have not had the authority to decide for themselves what appropriations to ask of the Congress. Instead, their proposed spending measure must clear the OMB.

The third form of central clearance is enrolled bill clearance. When enrolled bill enactments come from the Congress to the president for signature or veto, the OMB solicits agency opinion on the merits of the congressionally approved legislation, evaluates these opinions, and prepares its own report to the president recommending either approval or veto and the reasons.

REFERENCES

For the accounts of the development of central clearance, see Richard E. Neustadt, Presidency and legislation: The growth of central clearance, *American Political Science Review* 48 (September 1954).

For an update, see Robert S. Gilmour, Central legislative clearance: A revised perspective, *Public Administration Review* 31 (March/April 1971);

Paul C. Light, *The President's Agenda: Domestic Policy Choice from Kennedy to Carter* (Baltimore: Johns Hopkins University Press, 1981).

Central Intelligence Agency (CIA) The federal agency created by the NATIONAL SECURITY ACT in 1947 to coordinate the various intelligence activities of the United States. The director of Central Intelligence is a member of the president's cabinet and is the principal spokesperson for the American INTELLIGENCE COMMUNITY. Both the director and the deputy director of the CIA are appointed by the president by and with the advice and consent of the Senate.

Under the direction of the president or the National Security Council, the CIA (1) correlates and evaluates intelligence relating to national security and provides for its appropriate dissemination; (2) collects, produces, and disseminates foreign intelligence and counterintelligence. The collection of foreign intelligence or counterintelligence within the United States must be coordinated with the

FBI; (3) collects, produces, and disseminates intelligence on foreign aspects of narcotics production and trafficking; (4) conducts counterintelligence activities outside the United States and, without assuming or performing any internal security functions, conducts counterintelligence activities within the United States in coordination with the FBI; (5) conducts special activities approved by the president. The CIA has no police, subpoena, or law enforcement powers, and has no internal security functions. *See also* COVERT OPERATIONS; FINDING; INTELLIGENCE; SNEPP V UNITED STATES.

REFERENCES

Victor Marchetti and John D. Marks, *The CIA and the Cult of Intelligence* (New York: Knopf, 1974);

Tom Braden, The birth of the CIA, *American Heritage* 28 (February 1977);

Loch Johnson, The U.S. Congress and the CIA: Monitoring the dark side of government, *Legislative Studies Quarterly* 5 (November 1980);

William M. Leary, ed., *The Central Intelligence Agency: History and Documents* (University: University of Alabama Press, 1984);

John Ranelagh, *The Agency: The Rise and Decline of the CIA* (New York: Simon & Schuster, 1986).

Central Intelligence Agency
Washington, D.C. 20505
(703) 482–1100

certification of eligibles The procedure whereby those who have passed competitive civil service examinations have their names ranked in order of score and placed on a list of those eligible for appointment. When a government agency has a vacancy, it requests its personnel arm to provide a list of eligibles for the class to which the vacant position has been allocated. The personnel arm then certifies to the appointing authority the names of the highest ranking eligibles. Usually, only a few of the qualified eligibles are certified. An agency requirement that three eligibles be certified to the appointing authority is called the rule of three.

REFERENCE

For an overview, see Carmen D. Saso and Earl P. Tanis, *Selection and Certification of Eligibles: A Survey of Policies and Practices* (Chicago: International Personnel Management, 1974).

certification proceeding A process by which the National Labor Relations Board or other administrative agencies determine whether a particular labor union is the majority choice, and thus the exclusive bargaining agent for a group of employees in a given bargaining unit. Decertification is the opposite process.

certify To attest to the truth or accuracy of something; to guarantee that a standard on quantity or quality has been met; to make a legal determination. Some examples of things that are certified: a certified check is a check that a bank has marked as guaranteed cashable for its customer, both on signature and amount; a certified financial statement has been examined and reported upon with an opinion expressed by an independent public accountant; certified funds are bank deposits held in suspension and awaiting claims by a certified check; certified mail is ordinary mail that provides a receipt to the sender attesting to delivery; and a certified public accountant (CPA) is an accountant certified by a state government as having met specific educational and experiential requirements.

certiorari An order or writ from a higher court demanding that a lower court send up the record of a case for review. Except for a few instances of original jurisdiction, most cases that reach the U.S. Supreme Court do so because the Court itself has issued such a writ, or has granted certiorari. If certiorari is denied by the Court, it means that the justices are content to let the lower court's decision stand. Frequently, a U.S. court of appeals case citation will include "cert. denied," meaning that certiorari has been denied by the Supreme Court, which has reviewed the case to the extent that it has made a judgment not to review the case further. It takes the votes of four justices to grant certiorari. However, at least five votes are normally needed for a majority opinion on the substance of a case. *See also* CUE THEORY.

REFERENCES

Saul Brenner, The new certiorari game, *Journal of Politics* 41 (May 1979);

Peter Linzer, The meaning of certiorari denials, *Columbia Law Review* 79 (November 1979);

Jan Palmer, An econometric analysis of the U.S. Supreme Court's certiorari decisions, *Public Choice* 39:3 (1982);

S. Sidney Ulmer, The Supreme Court's certiorari decisions: Conflict as a predictive variable, *American Political Science Review* 78 (December 1984).

CETA *See* COMPREHENSIVE EMPLOYMENT AND TRAINING ACT OF 1973.

CFR *See* CODE OF FEDERAL REGULATIONS.

Chadha **case** *See* VETO, LEGISLATIVE.

challenge 1 A formal legal objection to something. 2 An objection to a prospective jury member. 3 A charge that a person seeking to vote is ineligible or that a particular vote is invalid. 4 The assertion of opposition against an individual or a program by a challenger who believes a victory is possible. 5 A call to fight a duel over a matter of personal honor. Challenges and duels were once quite common in American politics. For example, the then vice president of the United States, Aaron Burr, killed ALEXANDER HAMILTON in a duel in 1804. And ANDREW JACKSON's many duels vastly enhanced his reputation and political career.

chamber 1 The meeting place of the total membership of a legislature, as distinguished from the respective committee rooms. 2 A house of a legislature.

chambers The private offices of a judge.

change of venue The movement of a case from the jurisdiction of one court to that of another court that has the same subject-matter jurisdiction but is in a different geographic location. The most frequent reason for a change of venue is a judicial determination that an impartial jury cannot be found in the original jurisdiction, usually because of widely publicized, prejudicial, pretrial statements.

charisma Leadership based on the compelling personality of the leader rather than upon formal position. The word charisma is derived from the Greek word for divine grace. The concept was first developed by Max Weber, who distinguished charismatic authority from both the traditional authority of a monarch and the legal authority given to someone by law. Charismatic leadership, if it is to survive, must eventually be institutionalized or routinized. Thus the founder of a movement or organization may be a charismatic spellbinder, but his or her successors are often, of necessity, comparatively dull bureaucrats.

REFERENCES

D. L. Cohen, The concept of charisma and the analysis of leadership, *Political Studies* 20 (September 1972);

Douglas Madsen and Peter G. Snow, The dispersion of charisma, *Comparative Political Studies* 16 (October 1983);

Ann Ruth Willner, *The Spellbinders: Charismatic Political Leadership* (New Haven, CT: Yale University Press, 1984);

Arthur Schweitzer, *The Age of Charisma* (Chicago: Nelson-Hall, 1985).

charter 1 Originally a document issued by a monarch granting special privileges to groups or individuals, as in the MAGNA CHARTA of 1215 or the Charter of Liberties, which preceded it. Some of the original American colonies were created by such charters granted to trading companies or to other groups to establish governments in the New World. The charters themselves ultimately came to symbolize independent powers of self-government. 2 A document that spells out the purposes and powers of a municipal corporation. To operate, a municipal corporation must have a charter like any other corporation. The municipality can perform only those functions and exercise only those powers that are in the charter. If the particular state permits home rule, a city can develop and implement its own charter. Otherwise, it is limited to statutory charters spelled out by the state legislature. 3 The constitution of an international body, such as the United Nations. **4** The government document that allows a group of people to create a corporation.

REFERENCES

2 David K. Hamilton, Lay local government charter-writing commissions, *State and Local Government Review* 14 (September 1982);
David G. Houghton and Helenan S. Robin, City charter revisions: How citizen surveys can help, *National Civic Review* 74 (June 1985).
3 Ruth B. Russell, *A History of the United Nations Charter* (Washington, D.C.: Brookings, 1958).

charter member One of the founding members of an organization. For example, the United States is a charter member of the United Nations.

Charter of Rights Canada's equivalent of the U.S. Bill of Rights.

REFERENCES

Walter S. Tarnopolsky, The new Canadian Charter of Rights and Freedoms as compared and contrasted with the American Bill of Rights, *Human Rights Quarterly* 5 (August 1983);
Peter W. Hogg, Canada's new Charter of Rights, *American Journal of Comparative Law* 32 (Spring 1984).

chauvinism An excessive, unreasoning, and unreasonable patriotism. The word comes from Nicholas Chauvin, a fanatically uncritical supporter of Napoleon Bonaparte.

REFERENCES

Horace O. Patterson, *Ethnic Chauvinism: The Reactionary Impulse* (New York: Stein and Day, 1977);
William S. Maddox and Roger Handberg, Presidential affect and chauvinism among children, *American Journal of Political Science* 23 (May 1979).

chauvinism, male The excessive and unreasoning exaltation of the virtues of one group (men) at the expense of another (women).

REFERENCE

Michael Korda, *Male Chauvinism: How It Works* (New York: Random House, 1973).

Checkers speech A speech given by a politician to exculpate himself from allegations of wrongdoing. The original Checkers speech was given by Republican vice presidential candidate RICHARD M. NIXON on September 23, 1952, in response to charges that he had a secret political slush fund. In a live televised speech, he thoroughly explained the legitimate uses of the so-called secret fund and appealed to the public to support his staying on the ticket with Dwight D. Eisenhower. The speech was a great success. It generated overwhelming support for Nixon to stay on the ticket, and he went on to become vice president under Eisenhower for eight years. But what made the speech so memorable and poignant was Nixon's reference to his dog named Checkers: "We did get something—a gift. . . . It was a little cocker spaniel dog in a crate . . . sent all the way from Texas. Black and white spotted. And our little girl, Tricia, the six-year-old, named it Checkers. And you know, the kids love that dog, and I just want to say this right now, that regardless of what they say about it, we're going to keep it."

checks and balances The notion that constitutional devices can prevent any power within a nation from becoming absolute by being balanced against, or checked by, another source of power within that same nation. First put forth by the French philosopher Charles de Montesquieu (1689–1755) in his *The Spirit of the Laws* (1734), this notion was further developed by Thomas Jefferson (1743–1826) in his *Notes on the State of Virginia* (1784), in which he asserted that "the powers of government should be so divided and balanced among several bodies of magistracy, as that none could transcend their legal limits, without being effectively checked and restrained by the others." The U.S. Constitution is often described as a system of checks and balances. *Compare to* FEDERALIST #51; SEPARATION OF POWERS.

REFERENCE

E. P. Panagopoulos, *Essays on the History and Meaning of Checks and Balances* (Lanham, MD: University Press of America, 1986).

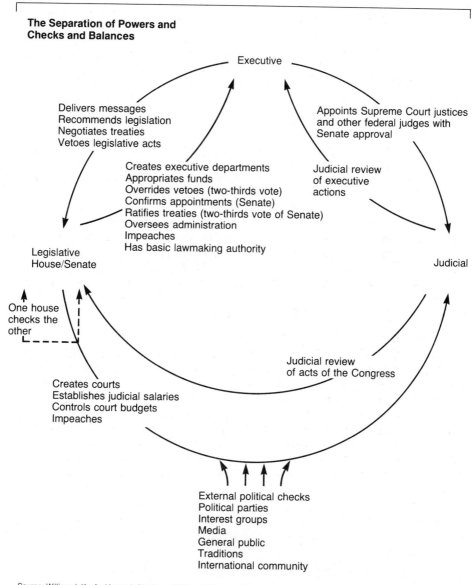

The Separation of Powers and Checks and Balances

Executive

Delivers messages
Recommends legislation
Negotiates treaties
Vetoes legislative acts

Appoints Supreme Court justices
and other federal judges with
Senate approval

Creates executive departments
Appropriates funds
Overrides vetoes (two-thirds vote)
Confirms appointments (Senate)
Ratifies treaties (two-thirds vote of Senate)
Oversees administration
Impeaches
Has basic lawmaking authority

Judicial review
of executive
actions

Legislative
House/Senate

Judicial

One house
checks the
other

Judicial review
of acts of the Congress

Creates courts
Establishes judicial salaries
Controls court budgets
Impeaches

External political checks
Political parties
Interest groups
Media
General public
Traditions
International community

Source: William J. Keefe, Henry J. Abraham, William H. Flanigan, Charles O. Jones, Morris S. Ogul, and John W. Spanier,
American Democracy: Institutions, Politics, and Policies, 2d ed. (Chicago: Dorsey, 1986), p. 21.

Chicago school 1 A loose term for those economists associated with the University of Chicago who strongly advocate a return to LAISSEZ-FAIRE capitalism. Nobel Prize-winning economists Milton Friedman (1912–   ) and George Stigler (1911–   ) are leading members of the Chicago school. The current wave of government DEREGULA-TION and government efforts at PRIVATIZATION are two examples of the school's influence. **2** A loose term for those political scientists associated with or influenced by the University of Chicago's Department of Political Science's advocacy of BEHAVIORALISM as the best approach to the study of political phenomena. **3** The style of interpretive sociology developed between the World Wars (1918–1939) at the University of Chicago. While Albion Small (1854–1926) established the first graduate Department of Sociology at Chicago in 1892, it was the interwar studies of community and urbanization that methodologically emphasized the detailed observation of the daily lives of subjects that gave the Chicago school its particular flavor.

chicken in every pot General economic prosperity; a political and economic situation in which the whole nation is well fed. The phrase is usually traced back to the French king, Henry IV (1553–1610), who was supposed to have said: "I wish that there would not be a peasant so poor in all my realm who would not have a chicken in his pot every Sunday." In the United States, the phrase is often credited to President HERBERT HOOVER, who often denied he ever said it.

chickenhawk *See* HAWK, CHICKEN.

chief judge The presiding member of a federal court of appeals.

chief justice The presiding member of a court with more than one judge. A chief justice has no more power than other judges on the same court in deciding cases. However, a chief justice can often influence the legal reasoning behind a decision if he or she has the authority, as does the chief justice of the United States, to decide which justice will write a majority opinion. The office also provides considerable mediating authority with other justices, great prestige, and a platform for leadership in the legal community.

chief justice of the United States The presiding member of the U.S. Supreme Court, who is appointed effectively for life ("during good behavior," according to Article III, Section 1, of the Constitution) by a president with the consent of the Senate. This consent must be obtained even if a president's nominee is already an associate justice on the Supreme Court.

REFERENCES

David Danelski, The influence of the chief justice in the decisional process of the Supreme Court, in *The Federal Judicial System: Readings in Process and Behavior,* ed. Thomas P. Jahnige and Sheldon Goldman (New York: Holt, Rinehart, and Winston, 1968);

Robert J. Steamer, *Chief Justice: Leadership and the Supreme Court* (Columbia: University of South Carolina Press, 1986).

Chief Justices of the United States

Chief Justice	President Who Appointed	Years Served
John Jay	Washington	1789–1795
Oliver Ellsworth	Washington	1796–1800
John Marshall	Adams	1801–1835
Roger B. Taney	Jackson	1836–1864
Salmon P. Chase	Lincoln	1864–1873
Morrison R. Waite	Grant	1874–1888
Melville W. Fuller	Cleveland	1888–1910
Edward D. White	Taft	1910–1921
William Howard Taft	Harding	1921–1930
Charles Evans Hughes	Hoover	1930–1941
Harlan Fiske Stone	Roosevelt	1941–1946
Fred M. Vinson	Truman	1946–1953
Earl Warren	Eisenhower	1953–1969
Warren E. Burger	Nixon	1969–1986
William Rehnquist	Reagan	1986–present

chief of state   The ceremonial head of a government, such as a king, queen, or president. This is in contrast to the chief executive of a government, such as a prime minister, chancellor, or president. The American presidency combines in one office, one person, the roles of chief of state and chief executive. *Compare to* COMMANDER IN CHIEF.

REFERENCES
Harold M. Barger, The prominence of the chief of state role in the American presidency, *Presidential Studies Quarterly* 8 (Spring 1978);
Merlin Gustafson, Our part-time chief of state, *Presidential Studies Quarterly* 9 (Spring 1979).

Through photographs, such as this one of a girl in a New England spinning mill, Lewis Hine mobilized public opinion against child labor.

child labor   Originally, the employment of children in a manner detrimental to their health and social development. Now that the law contains strong child labor prohibitions, the term refers to the employment of children below the legal age limit. Efforts by the labor movement and social reformers to prevent the exploitation of children in the workplace date back well into the nineteenth century. As early as 1842, some states (Connecticut and Massachusetts) legislated a maximum ten-hour workday for children. In 1848, Pennsylvania established a minimum working age of twelve years for factory jobs. But it would be twenty years more before any state had inspectors to enforce child labor laws. And it would not be until the late 1930s that federal laws would outlaw child labor (mainly through the Fair Labor Standards Act of 1938). The practice was so entrenched that earlier federal attempts to outlaw child labor were construed by the Supreme Court as being unconstitutional infringements on the power of the states to regulate conditions in the workplace.

REFERENCES
For histories of horrendous conditions that led to the passage of federal and state child labor prohibitions, see Jeremy P. Felt, *Hostages of Fortune: Child Labor Reform in New York State* (Syracuse, NY: Syracuse University Press, 1965);
Walter I. Trattner, *Crusade for the Children: A History of the National Child Labor Committee and Child Labor Reform in America* (Chicago: Quadrangle, 1970).
For present-day impact, see Daniel J. B. Mitchell and John Clapp, The impact of child-labor laws on the kinds of jobs held by young school-leavers, *Journal of Human Resources* 15 (Summer 1980);
Lee Swepston, Child labour: Its regulation by ILO standards and national legislation, *International Labour Review* 121 (September/October 1982);
Thomas A. Coens, Child labor laws: A viable legacy for the 1980s, *Labor Law Journal* 33 (October 1982).

chilling   **1** Any policies or practices that inhibit others from exercising legal rights or professional responsibilities. The first U.S. Supreme Court case mentioning this concept was *United States v Jackson* 390 U.S. 570 (1968), in which the Court asserted that: "If the provisions had no other purpose or effect than to chill the assertion of Constitutional rights by penalizing those who choose to exercise them, then it would be patently unconstitutional." **2** Employment practices, government regulations, court decisions, or legislation (or the threat of these) that inhibit the free exercise of individual employment rights. A chilling effect tends to keep minorities and women from seeking employment and advancement in an organization even in the absence of formal bars. Other chilling effects may be positive or negative, depending upon the "chillee's" perspective. For example, even discussion of proposed regulations could chill employers or unions into compliance. **3** Political activities that consciously or unconsciously inhibit judges from dealing with some cases fairly and impartially.

REFERENCES

Irving R. Kaufman, Chilling judicial independence, *Yale Law Journal* 88 (March 1979);

Raoul Berger, "Chilling judicial independence": A scarecrow, *Cornell Law Review* 64 (June 1979).

China card A policy of strengthening the relation between the United States and the People's Republic of China as a means of influencing Soviet policy and the development of U.S.–U.S.S.R. relations.

REFERENCES

Michael Y. M. Kau and Michael S. Frost, Military ties with communist China: A questionable card to play, *Asian Affairs: An American Review* 9 (May–August 1982);

Matthias Nass and Andreas Oldag, The debate within NATO and the "China Card," *Journal of Peace Research* 20 (1983).

choice, not an echo A meaningful (usually ideological) difference in what political candidates or parties stand for. In asserting that a candidate or policy is a choice, not an echo, supporters seek to refute charges of "metooism." Barry Goldwater (1909–   ) asserting that "I will offer a choice, not an echo," first used this phrase in 1963 when he announced he would be a candidate for president in 1964. Phyllis Schlafly (1924–   ) then gave the phrase wide currency when she used it as the title of her 1964 campaign polemic attacking both Republican and Democratic party leaderships and national administrations.

REFERENCES

Benjamin I. Page, *Choices and Echoes in Presidential Elections: Rational Man and Elec-* *toral Democracy* (Chicago: University of Chicago Press, 1978);

Alan I. Abramowitz, Choices and echoes in the 1978 U.S. Senate elections: A research note, *American Journal of Political Science* 25 (February 1981);

John F. Zipp, Perceived representativeness and voting: An assessment of the impact of "choices" versus "echoes," *American Political Science Review* 79 (March 1985).

Chrysler Corporation Loan Guarantee Act of 1979 The law that authorized the federal government to guarantee up to $1.5 billion in loans to the Chrysler Corporation to prevent the bankruptcy of the company, which would have had widespread negative impacts on the economy. Within four years, Chrysler became profitable again and repaid all of its federally guaranteed loans—seven years ahead of schedule. This kind of policy was long ago summed up by Will Rogers (1879–1935), who said that "the business of government is to keep the government out of business—that is, unless business needs government aid." *Compare to* BAILOUT.

REFERENCES

Gerald Turkel and David Costello, Laid-off workers, the Chrysler loan guarantee, and corporatist legitimacy: A thematic analysis, *Contemporary Crises: Crime, Law and Social Policy* 9 (July 1985);

Robert B. Reid and John O. Donahue, *New Deals: The Chrysler Revival and the American System* (New York: Times Books, 1985).

CIA *See* CENTRAL INTELLIGENCE AGENCY.

Cincinnatus, Lucius Quinctius 519–439? BC) A Roman general who has become the symbol of republican virtue and personal integrity. In 458 BC, when Rome was threatened with military defeat, Cincinnatus, a farmer, was appointed dictator by the Senate to deal with the emergency. Legend has it that he literally abandoned his plow in midfield to take command. Within sixteen days he defeated the enemy, resigned from the dictatorship, and returned to his plow. Ever since, politicians have been insincerely asserting how much they yearn to give up power and return to the farm, as Cincinnatus did. This is a very strong theme in American political history. Until recent decades, it was thought politically indecent to publicly lust after power. Politicians were expected to sit contentedly on the farm until they were called. George Washington is one of the few genuine Cincinnatus figures in world history. In an 1843 speech, Senator Daniel Webster (1792–1852) said: "America has furnished to the world the character of Washington. And if our American institutions had done nothing else, that alone would have entitled them to the respect of mankind."

REFERENCE

W. Burlie Brown, The Cincinnatus image in presidential politics, *Agricultural History* 31:1 (1957).

Circuit court of appeals *See* COURT OF APPEALS.

circuit rider A government official who travels from jurisdiction to jurisdiction providing any of a variety of technical services. The term is derived from the fact that, in the days before modern transportation, judges, preachers, and others with occupational specialties would travel a circuit, from their home base to clients in various locations and back home again.

REFERENCE

Charles P. Shannon, The circuit rider program: Lessons from a short history, *National Civic Review* 70 (April 1981).

citizen 1 A person who owes allegiance to, and in turn receives protection from, a nation. 2 A person born or naturalized in the United States. All U.S. citizens are also citizens of the state in which they permanently reside; corporations, which are artificial persons, are citizens of the state in which they were legally created. A citizen may take an active or passive role in the government process. The right to vote gives the citizen the opportunity to help select those who will determine public policy. Beyond simply voting, the citizen can assist in electoral campaigns, lobby his or her representatives, or join with others to form interest groups—all to advance personal interests or to further the citizen's conception of the public interest.

citizen participation A means of empowering individuals or groups with bargaining power to represent their own interests and to plan and implement their own programs with a view toward social, economic, and political power and control. Some government programs have enabling legislation specifically requiring that citizens affected by the program be involved in its administrative decisions. Presumably, the greater level of citizen participation in a program, the more responsive the program will be to the needs of the community and the more responsive the community will be to the needs of the program. *See also* INTEREST GROUP THEORY; LOBBY.

REFERENCES

Judy B. Rosener, Citizen participation: Can we measure its effectiveness? *Public Administration Review* 38 (September/October 1978);

Joan B. Aron, Citizen participation at government expense, *Public Administration Review* 39 (September/October 1979);

Mary Grisez Kweit and Robert W. Kweit, *Implementing Citizen Participation in a Bureaucratic Society: A Contingency Approach* (New York: Praeger, 1982);

Marcus E. Ethridge, The policy impact of citizen participation procedures, *American Politics Quarterly* 10 (October 1982);

Curtis Ventriss, Emerging perspectives on citizen participation, *Public Administration Review* 45 (May/June 1985).

citizens' councils Groups of whites who created private schools, private swimming pools, and so on, to avoid racial integration in the 1950s and 1960s.

REFERENCE

Neil R. McMillen, *The Citizens' Council: Organized Resistance to the Second Reconstruction, 1954–64* (Urbana: University of Illinois Press, 1971).

citizenship The dynamic relation between a citizen and his or her nation. The concept of citizenship involves rules of what a citizen might do (such as vote), must do (pay taxes), and can refuse to do (pledge allegiance). Increasingly, the concept involves benefits or entitlements that a citizen has a right to demand from government. In some jurisdictions, citizenship is a requirement for public employment. *See also* AFROYIM V RUSK; AMBACH V NORWICK; CABELL V SHAVEZ-SALIDO; FOLEY V CONNELIE; HAMPTON V MOW SUN WONG; SUGARMAN V DOUGALL.

REFERENCES

Morris Janowitz, Observations on the sociology of citizenship: Obligations and rights, *Social Forces* 59 (September 1980);

Mayer N. Zald, Political change, citizenship rights, and the welfare state, *Annals of the American Academy of Political and Social Science* 479 (May 1985);

Lawrence M. Mead, *Beyond Entitlement: The Social Obligations of Citizenship* (New York: Free Press, 1986).

For a discussion of recent court rulings, see Arnold L. Steigman, Public administration by litigation: The impact of court decisions concerning citizenship on public personnel management, *Public Personnel Management* 8 (March/April 1979);

Charles O. Agege, Employment discrimination against aliens: The constitutional implications, *Labor Law Journal* 36 (February 1985).

citizenship, dual **1** Having citizenship in two jurisdictions at the same time. For example, all citizens of the United States are citizens of both the United States and the state in which they reside. **2** Having citizenship in two separate nations at the same time. This is not uncommon. For example, the children of American citizens born abroad are usually considered citizens of the countries in which they were born as well as of the United States.

REFERENCE

David S. Gordon, Dual nationality and the United States citizen, *Military Law Review* 102 (Fall 1983).

citizens' ticket A slate of candidates running in opposition to the undesired offerings of the established parties.

city A municipal corporation chartered by its state. A central city is the core of a metropolitan area, while an independent city is outside of, or separate from, a metropolitan area. *Compare to* MUNICIPAL CORPORATION. A political subdivision must meet various state requirements before it can qualify for a city charter; for example, it must usually have a population above a state-established minimum level.

REFERENCES

The standard history is Lewis Mumford, *The City in History* (New York: Harcourt, Brace and World, 1961).

For other histories, see Lawrence J. R. Herson, The lost world of municipal government, *American Political Science Review* 51 (June 1957);

Ernest S. Griffith, *A History of American City Government: The Conspicuous Failure, 1870–1900* (New York: Praeger, 1974);

Ernest S. Griffith, *A History of American City Government: The Progressive Years and Their Aftermath, 1900–1920* (New York: Praeger, 1974);

Jon Teaford, *The Municipal Revolution in America: Origins of Modern Urban Government, 1630–1825* (Chicago: University of Chicago Press, 1975).

city beautiful movement The late nineteenth century and early twentieth century city-planning influence, which emphasized neoclassical architecture, parks, open spaces, monuments, boulevards, and other structures that would create a more benign urban environment.

REFERENCES

Ki Suh Park, City beautification programs: Are they still necessary? *National Civic Review* 62 (July 1973);

Jon A. Peterson, The city beautiful movement: Forgotten origins and lost meanings, *Journal of Urban History* 2 (August 1976);

William H. Wilson, J. Horace McFarland and the city beautiful movement, *Journal of Urban History* 7 (May 1981).

city charter *See* CHARTER.

city council The legislative branch, typically unicameral, of a municipal government. The duties of city council members vary greatly; but in almost all cases the most significant functions include passing ordinances (local laws) and controlling expenditures. *Compare to* COMMISSION FORM OF GOVERNMENT; COUNCIL-

MANAGER PLAN/COUNTY MANAGER PLAN;
MAYOR-COUNCIL SYSTEM.
REFERENCES
Richard A. Hughes, The role of city council,
Public Management 54 (June 1972);
Lawrence D. Landry, City councils as policy
makers: Myths that destroy effectiveness,
National Civic Review 66 (December 1977);
Delbert Taebel, Minority representation on
city councils: The impact of structure on
blacks and hispanics, *Social Science Quarterly* 59 (June 1978);
Albert K. Karnig, Black resources and city
council representation, *Journal of Politics*
41 (February 1979);
Michael S. Deeb, Municipal council members: Changing roles and functions, *National Civic Review* 68 (September 1979).

city-county consolidation The merger of several governments within a county to form one new government unit. Consolidation offers considerable cost savings by reducing overlap. Many consolidated cities and counties have the same name; for example, the City and County of Los Angeles, the City and County of Philadelphia.

REFERENCES
Brett W. Hawkins, *Nashville Metro: The Politics of City-County Consolidation* (Nashville, TN: Vanderbilt University Press, 1966);
Vincent L. Marando, The politics of city-county consolidation, *National Civic Review* 64 (February 1975);
Sharon Perlman Krefetz and Alan B. Sharaf, City-county merger attempts: The role of political factors, *National Civic Review* 66 (April 1977);
Mark Toma, The impact of institutional structures on city-county consolidation outcomes, *Public Choice* 34:1 (1979).

city manager The chief executive of the council-manager (originally commission-manager) system of local government. In contrast to the heads of other types of government, the city manager is an appointed chief executive serving at the pleasure of the council. The concept was created by Richard Childs, an urban reformer, who wanted to replace political bosses with municipal experts. To do this effectively, he created the concept of an administrative chief executive armed with critical administrative powers, such as appointment and removal of administrative officials, but denied any political powers, such as the veto. The dichotomy between administration and politics upon which the system was premised was implemented by putting all of the policymaking and political functions into the city council, essentially abolishing any separation of powers in the traditional sense at the local level. The decision-making ability of the council was assured by (1) creating a small council, typically from five to nine members, elected through at-large, nonpartisan elections; and (2) permitting the council to hire and fire the city manager, their expert in the implementation of community policies.

Present council-manager systems, found in about half of all U.S. cities, often deviate from this traditional model. Many have large councils, partisan elections, and separately elected mayors, and some if not all of the council members are elected from wards or districts. In fact, some recent federal court decisions have required ward elections in some cities. The council-manager system has been criticized by some political scientists as being unresponsive to some elements of the community and supported by public administration experts for its effective management in the public interest. In some larger cities, a variant of the system has evolved, utilizing a chief administrative officer often appointed by the mayor.

REFERENCES
John C. Bollens and John C. Ries, *The City Manager Profession, Myths and Realities* (Chicago: Public Administration Service, 1969);
Keith F. Mulrooney, ed., The American city manager: An urban administrator in a complex and evolving situation, *Public Administration Review* 31 (January/February 1971);
Ronald O. Loveridge, *City Managers in Legislative Politics* (Indianapolis: Bobbs Merrill, 1971);
Alan L. Saltzstein, City managers and city councils: Perceptions of the division of authority, *Western Political Quarterly* 27 (June 1974);

**The City Manager Form of City
Government Organization**

The city manager form of city government organization

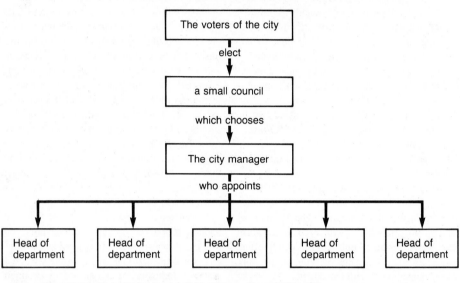

Source: Grover Starling, *Understanding American Politics* (Chicago: Dorsey, 1982), p. 355.

Richard J. Stillman II, *The Rise of the City Manager, A Public Professional in Local Government* (Albuquerque: University of New Mexico Press, 1974);

William R. Fannin and Don Hellriegel, Policy roles of city managers, *American Politics Quarterly* 13 (April 1985).

City of Los Angeles, Department of Water & Power v Manhart 435 U.S. 703 (1978) The U.S. Supreme Court case that held that a pension plan requiring female employees to contribute more from their wages to gain the same pension benefits as male employees was in violation of Title VII of the Civil Rights Act of 1964. While the actual statistics were undisputed (women live longer than men), the court reasoned that Title VII prohibits treating individuals "as simply components of a racial, religious, sexual or national class."

REFERENCES

Michael Evan Gold, Of giving and taking applications and implications of *City of Los Angeles, Department of Water and Power v.* *Manhart, Virginia Law Review* 65 (May 1979);

Linda H. Kistler and Richard C. Healy, Sex discrimination in pension plans since *Manhart, Labor Law Journal* 32 (April 1981).

City of Newport v Fact Concerts, Inc. 69 L.Ed. 2d 616 (1981) The U.S. Supreme Court case that held that municipalities are not subject to punitive damages in civil suits.

civic Belonging to citizens as a whole.

civic action 1 The use of military forces for projects useful to a local population. This has the dual effect of (1) providing needed services in areas such as education, transportation, health, sanitation, and so on, and (2) improving the standing of the military forces with the population. 2 The use of organized volunteers to provide certain community services.

REFERENCES

1 Robert L. Burke, Military civic action, *Military Review* 44 (October 1964);

Edward Bernard Glick, *Peaceful Conflict: The Non-Military Use of the Military* (Harrisburg, PA: Stackpole, 1967).
2 Irene Dabrowski, Working-class women and civic action: A case study of an innovative community role, *Policy Studies Journal* 11 (March 1983).

civic center 1 An amorphous term for the location of a city's major public buildings and cultural institutions. 2 A specific grouping of municipal and other public buildings.

civic culture A POLITICAL CULTURE.

civic duty The responsibility to vote. Angus Campbell, Philip E. Converse, Warren E. Miller, and Donald E. Stokes in their landmark study, *The American Voter* (New York: Wiley, 1960) found that "wide currency in American society is given to the idea that the individual has a civic responsibility to vote." This "sense of citizen duty," a major factor in individual turnout decisions, tends to increase with educational levels.

civic organization A formal association of local citizens that works to further its concept of the public interest. Such groups may be purely local, such as a parent-teacher association, or a chapter of a national organization, such as the Rotarians or the League of Women Voters.

civics 1 That part of political science which deals with the rights and responsibilities of citizenship. 2 The study of American government.

civic virtue A demonstrable pride in a city by its citizens, evidenced by their willingness to take responsibility for its public affairs, its physical development, its cultural activities, and so on.

Civil Aeronautics Board (CAB) The federal agency that promoted and regulated the civil air transport industry within the United States and between the United States and foreign countries. Created in 1938, it was abolished on January 1, 1985. *See* DEREGULATION.

civil affairs 1 Military government; the administrative process by which an occupying power exercises executive, legislative, and judicial authority over occupied territory. 2 A general term for all those matters concerning the relation between military forces and the surrounding civil authorities.

civil defense 1 The mobilization, organization, and direction of the civilian population, designed to minimize, by passive measures, the effects of enemy action against all aspects of civilian life. According to Robert Scheer, *With Enough Shovels: Reagan, Bush, and Nuclear War* (New York: Random House, 1982), Thomas K. "T. K." Jones, a deputy undersecretary of Defense, advised the following civil defense measures in the event of nuclear war: "Dig a hole, cover it with a couple of doors and then throw three feet of dirt on top . . . it's the dirt that does it . . . you know, dirt is just great stuff . . . if there are enough shovels to go around, everybody's going to make it." 2 The emergency repairs to, or the restoration of, vital utilities and facilities destroyed or damaged by enemy action.

REFERENCES
William H. Kincade, Repeating history: The civil defense debate renewed, *International Security* 2 (Winter 1978);
Allan M. Winkler, A forty-year history of civil defense, *Bulletin of the Atomic Scientists* 40 (June/July 1984);
Jonathan Mostow, An issue for the people: Civil defense in the nuclear age, *Fletcher Forum* 8 (Winter 1984).

civil disobedience Henry David Thoreau's (1817–1862) notion from his essay *On the Duty of Civil Disobedience* (1849) that one should not support a government (by paying taxes) if it sanctions policies (slavery) with which one disagrees. Thoreau's civil disobedience implied a willingness to publicly stand up and accept the consequences of one's disobedience such as going to jail. Now the phrase is used to refer to acts of lawbreaking designed to bring public attention to laws of questionable morality and legitimacy. The most famous practitioners of civil disobedience in this century were Mohandas K. Gandhi (1869–1948) in India and Martin Luther King, Jr. (1929–1968) in the United States. Those who practice civil disobedience often cite a HIGHER LAW as their reason. Consider the justification of Martin Luther King, Jr., from his *Why We Can't Wait* (New York: Harper & Row, 1964): "I submit that an individual who breaks a law that conscience tells him is unjust, and who willingly accepts the penalty of imprisonment in order to arouse the conscience of the community over its injustice, is in reality expressing the highest respect for the law."

REFERENCES

Paul F. Power, On civil disobedience in recent American democratic thought, *American Political Science Review* 64 (March 1970);

Menachem Marc Kellner, Democracy and civil disobedience, *Journal of Politics* 37 (November 1975);

Gregory S. Mehler, Civil disobedience in democratic society: The case of United States, *Policy Studies Review* 15 (April–December 1976);

Daniel M. Farrell, Paying the penalty: Justifiable civil disobedience and the problem of punishment, *Philosophy and Public Affairs* 6 (Winter 1977);

Brian Smart, Defining civil disobedience, *Inquiry* 21 (Autumn 1978).

civil disorder *See* RIOT.

civil law **1** That part of the law dealing with private, as opposed to criminal, actions. **2** The law that has evolved from ancient Roman law. **3** Rule by civilians as opposed to military government. **4** Codified law, such as the U.S. Code.

Civil Liberties Union *See* AMERICAN CIVIL LIBERTIES UNION.

civil liberty **1** A freedom to which an individual has a right, such as personal security, the right to own property, and the right to have children. **2** Freedom from government interference that violates the law.

REFERENCES

Robert J. Steamer, Contemporary Supreme Court directions in civil liberties, *Political Science Quarterly* 92 (Fall 1977);

Gara LaMarche, A consumer's guide to civil liberties in everyday life, *Civil Liberties Review* 5 (January/February 1979);

Richard Seltzer and Robert C. Smith, Race and civil liberties, *Social Science Quarterly* 66 (March 1985).

For a comparative perspective, see Richard J. Cummins, Constitutional protection of civil liberties in France, *American Journal of Comparative Law* 33 (Fall 1985).

civil religion **1** A belief in the "American way of life" and an acceptance of and reverence for its sacred icons (such as the flag), symbols (such as the Constitution), rituals (such as the pledge of allegiance), and secular saints (such as George Washington and Abraham Lincoln). Civil religion, which exists in parallel harmony with traditional religious beliefs, provides a society with a common set of unifying ideals that give the overarching political culture cohesiveness and form. While the concept was first used by JEAN JACQUES ROUSSEAU in *The Social Contract* (1762), it was revived by American sociologists in the late 1960s. **2** A state sponsored secular religion designed to replace the "corrupting" aspects of traditional religious practices, such as was implemented after the French Revolution of 1789 and the Russian Revolution of 1917.

REFERENCES

Robert N. Bellah, Civil religion in America, *Daedalus* 96 (Winter 1967);

Russell E. Richey and Donald G. Jones, eds., *American Civil Religion* (New York: Harper & Row, 1974);

W. Lance Bennett, Political sanctification: The civil religion and American politics, *Social Science Information* 14:6 (1975);

James David Fairbanks, The priestly functions of the presidency: A discussion of the literature on civil religion and its implications for the study of presidential leadership, *Presidential Studies Quarterly* 11 (Spring 1981).

civil rights **1** The protections and privileges given to all U.S. citizens by the Constitution; for example, freedom of assembly and freedom of religion. **2** Those positive acts of government that seek to make constitutional guarantees a reality for all citizens; for example, the

Civil Rights Act of 1964. **3** Whatever rights a citizen possesses, even if those rights are slight.

REFERENCES

Peter H. Schuck, The graying of civil rights law, *Public Interest* 60 (Summer 1980);

Charles M. Lamb, Legal foundations of civil rights and pluralism in America, *Annals of the American Academy of Political and Social Science* 454 (March 1981).

For a comparative perspective, see Drew S. Days III, Civil rights in Canada: An American perspective, *American Journal of Comparative Law* 32 (Spring 1984).

Civil Rights Act of 1866 The first civil rights law after the Civil War and the adoption of the Thirteenth Amendment, which outlawed slavery. It granted citizenship to all people (former slaves) born in the United States and granted these new citizens the same rights "as is enjoyed by white citizens."

Civil Rights Act of 1870 The reenactment of the Civil Rights Act of 1866 (with minor changes in wording), following the ratification of the Fourteenth Amendment, to allay any doubts about the act's constitutionality.

Civil Rights Act of 1871 A law enacted to enforce the Fourteenth Amendment's equal protection concerns against secret, conspiratorial, and terrorist organizations, such as the Ku Klux Klan, which were thwarting black registration, voting, jury service, and office holding after the Civil War. The act also provided civil remedies for the denial of constitutional rights and provided for damages or injunctive relief against any person who "under color of law" deprives another of any right, privilege, or immunity secured by federal law or the Constitution.

REFERENCE

Roy L. Brooks, Use of the Civil Rights Act of 1866 and 1871 to redress employment discrimination, *Cornell Law Review* 62 (January 1977).

Civil Rights Act of 1875 The civil rights law that first provided for equality in public accommodations. The U.S. Supreme Court held the act to be unconstitutional in *Civil Rights Cases,* 109 U.S. 3 (1883), and no subsequent civil rights legislation was passed until 1957. Yet the essence of the 1875 act was incorporated into the Civil Rights Act of 1964, which was later held constitutional by *Heart of Atlanta Motel v United States.*

REFERENCES

James M. McPherson, Abolitionists and the Civil Rights Act of 1875, *Journal of American History* 52:3 (1965);

Bertram Wyatt-Brown, The Civil Rights Act of 1875, *Western Political Quarterly* 18:4 (1965);

J. David Hoeveler, Jr., Reconstruction and the federal courts: The Civil Rights Act of 1875, *Historian* 31:4 (1969).

Civil Rights Act of 1957 The first federal civil rights legislation enacted since the post-Civil War Reconstruction period; significant primarily as an indication of renewed federal legislative concern with the protection of civil rights. As finally enacted (following lengthy and turbulent debate), the act accomplished essentially three things: it established the U.S. Commission on Civil Rights to investigate civil rights violations and make recommendations; it created the Civil Rights Division in the Department of Justice; and it enacted limited provisions to enforce the Fifteenth Amendment guarantee of the right to vote. The most enduring feature of the act may well be the creation of the U.S. Commission on Civil Rights. As originally enacted, the commission was only temporary and due to terminate within two years of its establishment. However, subsequent legislation in 1959, 1961, 1963, 1964, 1967, 1972, and 1978 extended the life of the commission, so its expiration was tolled until September 30, 1983. As the result of the controversy stirred by President Ronald Reagan's firing of three sitting commissioners, and his appointment of new members strongly opposed to racial quotas or entitlement programs, the Congress acted in 1983 to reconstitute the panel and extend its life for another six years. As signed by the president on November 30, 1983, P.L. 98–183 replaced the original six-member presidentially appointed commission with an eight-member panel appointed half by the president and half by the Congress. The commissioners are removable only for cause under this new legislation.

Civil Rights Act of 1960 This century's second installment of federal civil rights legislation. The act of 1960 emerged from a sharply divided Congress to reinforce certain provisions of the 1957 law, but it also included limited criminal provisions related to racially motivated bombings and burnings and to obstruction of federal court orders; a clause to enlarge the powers of the Civil Rights Commission; and a section providing for the desegregated education of children of U.S. military personnel. The most important new provision made a remedy available to those improperly denied the right to vote: a voter-referee procedure enforced by the federal courts.

REFERENCE

Daniel M. Berman, *A Bill Becomes a Law: The Civil Rights Act of 1960* (New York: Macmillan, 1962).

Civil Rights Act of 1964 By far the most significant civil rights legislation in American history, with the possible exception of the VOTING RIGHTS ACT OF 1965. Forged during the civil rights movement of the early 1960s, the act consists of eleven titles, of which the most consequential are titles II, VI, and VII. Title II bars discrimination in all places of public accommodation, whose operations affect commerce (including hotels and other places of lodging of more than five rooms, restaurants and other eating places, gasoline stations, theaters, motion picture houses, stadiums, and other places of exhibition or entertainment. In Title VI, the Congress made broad use of its spending power to prohibit racial discrimination in any program or activity receiving federal financial assistance. More important, Title VI goes on to provide that compliance with the nondiscrimination requirement is to be effected by the termination or refusal to grant federal funds to any recipient who has been found guilty of racial discrimination. Title VII makes it an unfair employment practice for any employer or labor organization engaged in commerce to refuse to hire, to fire, or to otherwise discriminate against any person because of race, religion, sex, or national origin. Title VII is enforced by the Equal Employment Opportunity Commission, which was also created by the act. *Compare to* AFFIRMATIVE ACTION; EQUAL EMPLOYMENT OPPORTUNITY.

REFERENCES

Clifford M. Lytle, The history of the Civil Rights Bill of 1964, *Journal of Negro History* 51:4 (1966);

Gary Orfield, *The Reconstruction of Southern Education: The Schools and the Civil Rights Act of 1964* (New York: Wiley-Interscience, 1969);

Richard J. Hardy and Donald J. McCrone, The impact of the Civil Rights Act of 1964 on women, *Policy Studies Journal* 7 (Winter 1978);

Augustus J. Jones, Jr., *Law, Bureaucracy, and Politics: The Implementation of Title VI of the Civil Rights Act of 1964* (Washington, D.C.: University Press of America, 1982);

Charles and Barbara Whalen, *The Longest Debate: A Legislative History of the 1964 Civil Rights Act* (Cabin John, MD: Seven Locks, 1985).

Civil Rights Act of 1968 A law that prohibited discrimination in housing rentals and sales, defined the rights of American Indians, and prescribed penalties for interfering—through violence, intimidation, or other means—with any person's enjoyment of federally protected rights.

Civil Rights Cases *See* CIVIL RIGHTS ACT OF 1875.

Civil Rights Commission *See* COMMISSION ON CIVIL RIGHTS.

civil rights movement The continuing effort of minorities and women to gain the enforcement of the rights guaranteed by the Constitution to all citizens. The modern civil rights movement is often dated from 1955, when Rosa Parks, a black seamstress, refused to sit in the back of a bus (where blacks were required by local law to sit) and was arrested. MARTIN LUTHER KING, JR., then led the Montgomery, Alabama, bus boycott, the first of a long series of nonviolent demonstrations that

Rosa Parks is fingerprinted after her arrest in 1955 in Montgomery, Alabama. Her refusal to sit in the back of a city bus marked the beginning of the civil rights movement.

eventually led to the passage of the civil rights acts of 1957, 1960, and 1964. *Compare to* SECOND RECONSTRUCTION.

REFERENCES

Maurice Jackson, The civil rights movement and social change, *American Behavioral Scientist* 12 (March/April 1969);

Barbara N. Geschwender and James A. Geschwender, Relative deprivation and participation in the civil rights movement, *Social Science Quarterly* 54 (September 1973);

James Button and Richard Scher, Impact of the civil rights movement: Perceptions of black municipal service changes, *Social Science Quarterly* 60 (December 1979);

Bruce Miroff, Presidential leverage over social movements: The Johnson White House and civil rights, *Journal of Politics* 43 (February 1981);

Lewis M. Killian, Organization, rationality, and spontaneity in the civil rights movement, *American Sociological Review* 49 (December 1984).

civil service A collective term for all nonmilitary employees of a government. Paramilitary organizations, such as police and firefighters, are always included in civil service counts in the United States. This practice may be confusing to countries where there is less distinction between the police and the military. Civil service employment is not the same as merit system employment, because all patronage positions (those not covered by merit systems) are included in civil service totals. *Compare to* MERIT SYSTEM.

civil service commission A government agency charged with the responsibility of promulgating the rules and regulations of the civilian personnel management system. Depending upon its legal mandate, a civil service commission may hear employee appeals and take an active or a passive role in the personnel management process.

REFERENCES

Donald R. Harvey, *The Civil Service Commission* (New York: Praeger, 1970);

Winston Crouch, *A Guide for Modern Personnel Commissions* (Chicago: International Personnel Management, 1973);

William M. Timmins, Conflicting roles in personnel boards: Adjudication versus policy making, *Public Personnel Management* 14 (Summer 1985).

Civil Service Commission, U.S. *See* UNITED STATES CIVIL SERVICE COMMISSION.

civil service reform 1 Efforts to improve the status, integrity, and productivity of the civil service at all levels of government by supplanting the SPOILS SYSTEM with the MERIT SYSTEM. 2 Efforts to improve the management and efficiency of the public service. 3 The historical events, the movement, leading up to the enactment of the PENDLETON ACT OF 1883. While federal civil service reform is generally dated from the post–Civil War period, the political roots of the reform effort go back much earlier—to the beginning of the republic. Thomas Jefferson was the first president to face the problem of a philosophically hostile bureaucracy. While sorely pressed by his supporters to remove Federalist officeholders and replace them with Republican partisans, Jefferson was determined not to remove officials for political reasons, alone. He maintained that only "malconduct is a just ground of removal: mere difference of political opinion is not." With occasional defections from this principle, even by Jefferson himself, this policy was the norm rather than the exception down through the administration of Andrew Jackson. President Jackson's rhetoric on the nature of public service was far more influential than his administrative example. In claiming that all men, especially the newly enfranchised who did so much to elect him, should have an equal opportunity for public office, Jackson played to his plebian constituency and put the patrician civil service on notice that they had no natural monopoly on public office. The spoils system flourished under Jackson's successors. The doctrine of rotation of office progressively prevailed over the earlier notion of stability in office.

Depending upon your point of view, the advent of modern merit systems is either an economic, political, or moral development. Economic historians would maintain that the demands of industrial expansion—a dependable postal service, a viable transportation network, and so on—necessitated a government service based upon merit. Political analysts could argue rather persuasively that it was the demands of an expanded suffrage and democratic rhetoric that sought to replace favoritism with merit. Economic and political considerations are so intertwined that it is impossible to say which factor is the true midwife of the merit system. The moral impetus behind reform is even more difficult to define. As moral impulses tend to hide economic and political motives, the weight of moral concern undiluted by other considerations is impossible to measure. Nevertheless, the cosmetic effect of moral overtones was of significant aid to the civil service reform movement, because it accentuated the social legitimacy of the reform proposals.

With the ever-present impetus of achieving maximum public services for minimum tax dollars, business interests were quite comfortable in supporting civil service reform, one of a variety of strategies they used to have power pass from the politicos to themselves: the political parties of the time were almost totally dependent for financing upon assessments made on the wages of their members in public office; with the decline of patronage, the parties had to seek new funding sources, and American business was more than willing to assume this new financial burden—and its con-

comitant influence. There is no doubt that civil service reform would have come about without the 1881 assassination of President James A. Garfield; there is also no doubt that the assassination helped. While Garfield's death was certainly instrumental in creating the appropriate climate for the passage of the Pendleton Act, historians maintain that the Republican reversals during the midterm elections of 1882 had the more immediate effect on enactment. Civil service reform had been the deciding issue in a number of congressional contests. Thus when President Chester A. Arthur signed the Pendleton Act into law on January 16, 1883, and created the UNITED STATES CIVIL SERVICE COMMISSION, it was essentially a gesture by reluctant politicians to assuage public opinion and the reform elements.

REFERENCES

Paul P. Van Riper, *History of the United States Civil Service* (Evanston, IL: Row, Peterson, 1958);

Ari Hoogenboom, *Outlawing the Spoils: A History of the Civil Service Reform Movement, 1865–1883* (Urbana: University of Illinois Press, 1961);

Frederick C. Mosher, *Democracy and the Public Service* (New York: Oxford University Press, 1968).

Civil Service Reform Act of 1978   The law that mandated that (in January of 1979) the U.S. Civil Service Commission would be divided into two agencies—an Office of Personnel Management (OPM) to serve as the personnel arm of the chief executive and an independent Merit Systems Protection Board (MSPB) to provide recourse for aggrieved employees. In addition, the act created the Federal Labor Relations Authority (FLRA) to oversee federal labor-management policies. On March 2, 1978, President Jimmy Carter, with the enthusiastic support of his Civil Service Commission leadership, submitted his civil service reform proposals to the Congress. On that same day, before the National Press Club, he further called his proposals to the attention of the Congress by charging that the present federal personnel system had become a "bureaucratic maze which neglects merit, tolerates poor performance, and permits abuse of legitimate employee rights, and mires every personnel action in red tape, delay and confusion." The reform bill faced considerable opposition from federal employee unions (which thought the bill was too management oriented) and from veterans' groups (which were aghast at the bill's curtailment of veterans' preferences). The unions lost. The veterans won. The bill passed almost intact thanks in great measure to the efforts of Alan K. "Scotty" Campbell (1923–   ), the last chairman of the U.S. Civil Service Commission, who was both the architect of the reform act and its most fervent advocate before Congress. Campbell served as the first director of the new Office of Personnel Management during 1979–1980. *See also* FEDERAL LABOR RELATIONS AUTHORITY; MERIT SYSTEMS PROTECTION BOARD; OFFICE OF PERSONNEL MANAGEMENT; SENIOR EXECUTIVE SERVICE.

REFERENCES

Mark W. Huddleston, The Carter civil service reforms: Some implications for political theory and public administration, *Political Science Quarterly* 96 (Winter 1981–82);

Kenneth W. Kramer, Seeds of success and failure: Policy development and implementation of the 1978 Civil Service Reform Act, *Review of Public Personnel Administration* 2 (Spring 1982);

Patricia W. Ingraham and Carolyn Ban, eds., *Legislating Bureaucratic Change: The Civil Service Reform Act of 1978* (Albany: State University of New York Press, 1984).

Civil War Amendments The Thirteenth, Fourteenth, and Fifteenth amendments to the U.S. Constitution providing, respectively, for the abolition of slavery, equal protection and due process of the law, and the right of all citizens to vote. These amendments were adopted immediately after the Civil War.

clandestine operations *See* COVERT OPERATIONS.

class action A search for a judicial remedy that one or more persons may undertake on behalf of themselves and all others in similar situations. Class action suits are common against manufacturers who have sold defective products that have later harmed significant

numbers of people who were unaware that there was any danger.

REFERENCES

James W. Loewen, *Social Science in the Courtroom: Statistical Techniques and Research Methods for Winning Class Action Suits* (Lexington, MA: Lexington Books, 1982);

Deborah L. Rhode, Class conflicts in class actions, *Stanford Law Review* 34 (July 1982).

classified information 1 Secrets, usually military. 2 Any matter in any form that requires protection in the interests of national security.

REFERENCE

Carol M. Barker and Matthew H. Fox, *Classified Files: The Yellowing Pages; A Report on Scholars' Access to Government Documents* (New York: Twentieth Century Fund, 1972).

classify 1 To group bureaucratic positions according to their duties and responsibilities and to assign a class title. 2 To make secret; to determine that official information requires, in the interests of national security, a certain level of protection against unauthorized disclosure.

class struggle The conflict between competing economic groups in a capitalist society. Marxists believe that the tension between the exploiting bourgeoisie and the exploited working-class masses (the proletariat) eventually leads to revolution. This has not happened in American society, in large measure because the economic system has made most working-class people middle class in both income and outlook.

REFERENCES

John Kenneth Galbraith, What happened to the class struggle? *Washington Monthly* 2 (February 1970);

Arthur Child, The concept of class interest, *Ethics* 80 (July 1970);

Adam Przeworski and Michael Wallerstein, The structure of class conflict in democratic capitalist societies, *American Political Science Review* 76 (June 1982);

Frances Fox Piven and Richard A. Cloward, *The New Class War: Reagan's Attack on the Welfare State and Its Consequences* (New York: Pantheon, 1982).

Clausewitz, Karl Maria von (1780–1831)
The Prussian general who wrote the classic
analysis of military strategy and tactics, *On
War* (1832), which is most famous for asserting
that "war is the continuation of diplomacy by
other means."
REFERENCES
Julian Lider, War and politics: Clausewitz to-
day, *Cooperation and Conflict* 12:3 (1977);
Raymond Aron, *Clausewitz, Philosopher of
War* (Englewood Cliffs, NJ: Prentice-Hall,
1985).

Clayton Act of 1914 The federal law that
extended the Sherman Act's prohibition
against monopolies and price discrimination.
It also sought to exempt labor unions from antitrust laws and to limit the jurisdiction of
courts in issuing injunctions against labor organizations. Subsequent judicial construction
limited its effectiveness in this area, and new
laws were necessary to achieve the original
intent.
REFERENCE
Steven M. Surdell, Mergers under the Reagan
Justice Department: Redefining Section 7 of
the Clayton Act, *Journal of Legislation* 11
(Summer 1984).

Clean Air Act The federal statute (passed in
1963 and amended in 1965, 1967, 1970, and
1977) intended to protect the public's health
and welfare from the effects of air pollution.
The act established national air quality stan-
dards. It specified automobile emission stan-
dards, among other things, to achieve these
goals.
REFERENCES
Charles O. Jones, *The Policies and Politics of
Pollution Control* (Pittsburgh: University of
Pittsburgh Press, 1975);
Peter Navarro, The 1977 Clean Air Act
amendments: Energy, environmental, eco-
nomic, and distributional impacts, *Public
Policy* 29 (Spring 1981);
R. Shep Melnick, *Regulation and the Courts:
The Case of the Clean Air Act* (Washington,
D.C.: Brookings, 1983).

clean bill *See* BILL, CLEAN.

clear 1 To approve or authorize or to obtain
approval or authorization. For example, a bill
may clear one house of a legislature meaning
that it has been approved by that house. *Compare to* CENTRAL CLEARANCE. 2 To be no
longer suspected of committing a crime. 3 To
pass a security clearance. 4 The final approval of a check by the bank upon which it
was drawn, 5 Free of taxes; a house may be
clear for sale after its back taxes have been
paid.

clear and present danger The U.S. Supreme Court's test on whether the exercise of
the First Amendment's right of free speech
should be restricted or punished. This was first
articulated by Associate Justice Oliver Wendell
Holmes in *Schenck v United States*, 249 U.S.
47 (1919), when he wrote that "the most strin-
gent protection of free speech would not protect a man in falsely shouting 'fire' in a theatre
and causing a panic." Holmes created the test
that has been often used in free-speech cases:
"The question in every case is whether the
words used are used in such circumstances and
are of such a nature as to create a clear and
present danger that they will bring about the
substantive evils that Congress has a right to
prevent."
REFERENCES
Hans A. Linde, "Clear and present danger"
reexamined: Dissonance in the Brandenburg
Concerto, *Stanford Law Review* 22 (June
1970);
Martin H. Redish, Advocacy of unlawful conduct and the First Amendment: In defense
of clear and present danger, *California Law
Review* 70 (September 1982).

cleared by arrest The condition of a criminal case after the suspect has been arrested but
before any trial or other legal determination of
guilt.

clerk of the House The chief administrative
officer of the U.S. House of Representatives
responsible for taking votes, certifying the passage of bills, and processing legislation. The
clerk prepares the House budget and serves as
the contracting officer of the House. *Compare
to* SECRETARY OF THE SENATE.

clientele Individuals or groups who benefit from the services provided by an agency.

REFERENCE

Joel D. Aberbach and Bert A. Rockman, Bureaucrats and clientele groups: A view from Capitol Hill, *American Journal of Political Science* 22 (November 1978).

clientele agency A loose term for any government organization whose prime mission is to promote, serve, or represent the interest of a particular group.

cloak and dagger A melodramatic phrase for the covert operations of intelligence agents. *Compare to* COVERT OPERATIONS.

REFERENCE

David Wise, Cloak and dagger operations: An overview, *Society* 12 (March/April 1975).

cloakroom A private legislative antechamber, originally used for hanging cloaks, where members may informally meet and negotiate with each other. Some cloakrooms are quite elaborate, with telephones, dining facilities, and so on. The U.S. Senate has separate Republican and Democratic cloakrooms.

closed primary *See* PRIMARY, CLOSED.

closed shop A union security provision that would require an employer to hire and retain only union members in good standing. The Labor-Management Relations (Taft-Hartley) Act of 1947 made closed shops illegal.

REFERENCE

Charles G. Goring and others, *The Closed Shop: A Comparative Study of Public Policy and Trade Union Security in Britain, the USA and West Germany* (New York: St. Martin's, 1981).

cloture The process by which a filibuster can be ended in the U.S. Senate, other than by unanimous consent. A motion for cloture can apply to any measure before the Senate, including a proposal to change the chamber's rules. It requires sixteen senators' signatures for introduction and the votes of three-fifths of the entire Senate membership (sixty, if there are no vacancies), except that to end a filibuster

against a proposal to amend the standing rules of the Senate, a two-thirds vote of senators present and voting is required. Cloture is put to a roll-call vote one hour after the Senate meets on the second day following introduction of the motion. If voted, cloture limits each senator to one hour of debate.

clout To hit someone with your fist. It has grown to be a slang term for influence or power and it implies an ability to get things done through informal, nonlegal, personal (as opposed to official) channels, whether the thing is the passage of a bill, a patronage job for a constituent, or the getting of some important person on the phone.

REFERENCES

Susan and Martin Tolchin, *Clout—Womanpower and Politics* (New York: Putnam, 1973);

Len O'Connor, *Clout: Mayor Daley and His City* (Chicago: Regnery, 1975);

Vern Bullough and Bonnie Bullough, Nurses and power: Professional power versus political clout, *Women and Politics* 4 (Winter 1984).

coalition 1 A temporary joining of political actors to advance legislation or to elect candidates. It is often the case that the actors in a coalition are poles apart on many issues but are able to put their continuing differences aside in the interest of joining to advance (or defeat) the issue at hand. Legislative coalitions tend to form around specific issues as the legislators sort themselves out, for or against a bill or policy. The leaders of a coalition may or may not occupy formal leadership positions in the legislature or their party. The best-known coalition in recent congresses has been the conservative coalition, an informal alliance of southern Democrats and Republicans. 2 An agreement between political parties in a parliamentary system to form a government. 3 A group of Supreme Court justices who tend to take the same philosophic approach to judicial decision making.

REFERENCES

William H. Riker, *The Theory of Political Coalitions* (New Haven, CT: Yale University Press, 1962);

Alan Grant, Coalition politics in the United States: President Reagan and the Ninety-seventh Congress, *Teaching Politics* 11 (September 1982);

Mack C. Shelley II, Presidents and the conservative coalition in the U.S. Congress, *Legislative Studies Quarterly* 8 (February 1983);

Thomas H. Hammond and Jane M. Fraser, Baselines for evaluating explanations of coalition behavior in Congress, *Journal of Politics* 45 (August 1983);

Lawrence C. Dodd, Coalition-building by party leaders: A case study of House democrats, *Congress and the Presidency: A Journal of Capital Studies* 10 (Autumn 1983);

Robert Axelrod, Presidential election coalitions in 1984, *American Political Science Review* 80 (March 1986).

Coastal Zone Management Act of 1972
The environmental protection legislation requiring that state coastal-area plans must meet minimal federal standards for the protection of coastal zones.

REFERENCES

Sarah Chasis, The Coastal Zone Management Act, *Journal of the American Planning Association* 46 (April 1980);

Sarah Chasis, The Coastal Zone Management Act: A protective mandate, *Natural Resources Journal* 25 (January 1985).

coattails The ability of the head of a political election ticket to help attract voters to other members of the ticket. A winning presidential candidate is said to have coattails if the election also sweeps into office a significant number of new House and Senate members from his party. Abraham Lincoln as a congressman in 1848 originally popularized this metaphor when he referred to the military coattails of generals (later presidents) Andrew Jackson and Zachary Taylor. In recent national elections, the coattail effect has been weak. Congressional incumbents (*see* INCUMBENCY EFFECT) tend to be reelected irrespective of the popularity of the presidential ticket.

REFERENCES

For presidential coattails, see George C. Edwards III, Impact of presidential coattails on outcomes of congressional elections, *American Politics Quarterly* 7 (January 1979);

Herbert M. Kritzer and Robert B. Eubank, Presidential coattails revisited: Partisanship and incumbency effects, *American Journal of Political Science* 23 (August 1979);

John A. Ferejohn and Randall L. Calvert, Presidential coattails in historical perspective, *American Journal of Political Science* 28 (February 1984);

Richard Born, Reassessing the decline of presidential coattails: U.S. House elections 1952–1980, *Journal of Politics* 46 (February 1984).

For state and local coattails, see Ronald E. Weber, Gubernatorial coattails: A vanishing phenomenon? *State Government* 53 (Summer 1980);

Susan A. MacManus, A city's first female officeholder: "Coattails" for future female officeseekers? *Western Political Quarterly* 34 (March 1981);

James E. Campbell, Presidential coattails and midterm losses in state legislative elections, *American Political Science Review* 80 (March 1986).

code A comprehensive collection of statutory laws. For example, the U.S. Code is the official compilation of federal laws. A code differs from a collection of statutes in that codes are organized by topics for easy reference rather than in the chronological order in which the various laws were passed.

code, building A usually local, legislatively enacted, regulation prescribing construction standards.

code, housing A local, legislatively enacted, regulation establishing the minimal conditions under which dwellings are fit for humans to live in.

code law Law that is to be found in law books, as opposed to equity law, which a judge makes up (based on related precedents) to deal with a new situation.

code of ethics A statement of professional standards of conduct to which the practitioners of a profession say they subscribe. Codes of ethics are usually not legally binding, so they should not be taken too seriously as constraints on behavior. They sometimes become significant factors in political campaigns when questionable behavior by one side or the other is attacked or defended as being within or without a professional code. Professional groups also hide behind codes as a way of protecting (or criticizing) a member subject to public attack.

REFERENCES

James P. Clarre, Code of ethics: Waste of time or important control? *Public Management* 49 (August 1967);

Kenneth Kernaghan, Codes of ethics and administrative responsibility, *Canadian Public Administration* 17 (Winter 1974);

Guy Benveniste, On a code of ethics for policy experts, *Journal of Policy Analysis and Management* 3 (Summer 1984).

Code of Federal Regulations (CFR) The annual accumulation of executive agency regulations published in the daily *Federal Register,* combined with regulations issued previously that are still in effect. Divided into fifty titles, each representing a broad subject area, individual volumes of the CFR are revised at least once each calendar year and issued on a staggered quarterly basis. An alphabetical listing, by agency, of subtitle and chapter assignments is provided in the back of each volume under the heading "Finding Aids" and is accurate for the revision date of that volume.

code word A word or phrase whose use in a political context alters its meaning. Code words are often used when it is not politic or respectable to address an issue directly. For example, in the early days of the civil rights movement many southern politicians emphasized that they were in favor of states rights, a code word for opposition to full civil rights for blacks. In early 1986, when world oil prices started to fall dramatically, politicians from oil-producing states started talking about the need for stable oil prices. In this context, stable became a code word for higher prices. Code words should be distinguished from buzz words, which merely refer to the technical vocabularies of various occupational specialties.

REFERENCE

Sidney Weintraub, Coping with code words, *Foreign Affairs* 51 (July 1973).

coexistence 1 An international situation wherein nations with differing social systems and conflicting ideologies refrain from war. Coexistence is less than peace, but preferable to war. It is often used to refer to strained relations between the Soviet Union and the West. **2** Any contentious relation in which genuine rivals (political, organizational, and so on) purposely refrain from a direct confrontation, which might otherwise be logically expected of them.

REFERENCES

1   Hugh Gaitskill, *The Challenge of Co-Existence* (London: Methuen, 1957);

Marshall D. Shulman, Toward a western philosophy of coexistence, *Foreign Affairs* 52 (October 1973);

Adam B. Ulam, Forty years of troubled coexistence, *Foreign Affairs* 64 (Fall 1985).

COG *See* COUNCIL OF GOVERNMENT.

Cohens v Virginia 6 Wheaton 264 (1821) The U.S. Supreme Court case that held that state court decisions involving federal questions could be appealed to a federal court. *Compare to* NATIONAL SUPREMACY.

cohort 1 One-tenth of a Roman legion.   **2** In the social sciences, a group identified as having common characteristics for the purposes of study, usually over time. Cohorts can be identified by age of the year they first had a common experience, such as graduating college, entering the military, or winning election to the Congress.

REFERENCE

K. Robert Keiser and Woodrow Jones, Jr., Congressional cohorts and voting patterns, *American Politics Quarterly* 10 (July 1982).

Coker v Georgia *See* CRUEL AND UNUSUAL PUNISHMENT.

COLA *See* COST-OF-LIVING ADJUSTMENT.

cold war 1 War by other than military means (a "hot war") and that emphasizes ideological conflict, brinksmanship, and consistently high international tension. 2 The hostile but non-lethal relations between the United States and the Soviet Union in the post–World War II period. The phrase was first used by Herbert Bayard Swope (1882–1958) in speeches he wrote for Bernard Baruch (1870–1965). After Baruch told the Senate War Investigating Committee on October 24, 1948, "Let us not be deceived—today we are in the midst of a cold war," the press picked up the phrase, and it became part of everyday speech. *Compare to* CONTAINMENT. 3 Any behind-the-scenes tension between two parties who cannot openly confront each other.

REFERENCES
2   Joseph R. Starobin, Origins of the cold war: The communist dimension, *Foreign Affairs* 47 (July 1969);
    Michael Leigh, Is there a revisionist thesis on the origins of the cold war? *Political Science Quarterly* 89 (March 1974);
    J. L. Black, *Origins, Evolution, and Nature of the Cold War: An Annotated Bibliography* (Santa Barbara, CA: ABC–Clio, 1985).

Colegrove v Green   *See* BAKER V CARR.

Coleman v Miller   *See* POLITICAL QUESTION.

Cole v Richardson 405 U.S. 676 (1971)   The U.S. Supreme Court case that upheld the right of Massachusetts to exact from its employees a promise to "oppose the overthrow of the government of the United States of America or of this Commonwealth by force, violence or by any illegal or unconstitutional method." A public employer may legitimately require employees to swear or affirm their allegiance to the Constitution of the United States and of a particular state. Beyond that, the limits of constitutional loyalty oaths are unclear. *See also* LOYALTY.

collective bargaining   Bargaining on behalf of a group of employees as opposed to individual bargaining where each worker represents only himself or herself. Collective bargaining is a comprehensive term that encompasses the negotiating process that leads to a contract between labor and management on wages, hours, and other conditions of employment as well as the subsequent administration and interpretation of the signed contract. Collective bargaining is, in effect, the continuous relation between union representatives and employers. The four basic stages of collective bargaining are: (1) the establishment of organizations for bargaining, (2) the formulation of demands, (3) the negotiation of demands, and (4) the administration of the labor agreement. *See also* ABILITY TO PAY; EXECUTIVE ORDER 10988; EXECUTIVE ORDER 11491; FEDERAL LABOR RELATIONS AUTHORITY; LABOR-MANAGEMENT RELATIONS ACT OF 1947; NATIONAL LABOR RELATIONS ACT OF 1935; NATIONAL LABOR RELATIONS BOARD; POSTAL REORGANIZATION ACT OF 1970.

REFERENCES
Clyde W. Summers, Public employee bargaining: A political perspective, *Yale Law Journal* 83 (May 1974);
Charles Feigenbaum, Civil service and collective bargaining: Conflict or compatibility? *Public Personnel Management* 3 (May/June 1974);
Alan Edward Bent and T. Zane Reeves, *Collective Bargaining in the Public Sector* (Menlo Park, CA: Benjamin/Cummings, 1978);
David Lewin, Raymond D. Horton, and James W. Kuhn, *Collective Bargaining and Manpower Utilization in Big City Governments* (Montclair, NJ: Allenheld, Osmun, 1979);
Joyce M. Najita and Helene S. Tanimoto, *Guide to Statutory Provisions in Public Sector Collective Bargaining: Characteristics, Functions and Powers of Administrative Agencies* (Honolulu: Industrial Relations Center, University of Hawaii, 1981).

collective negotiations   An alternate term for collective bargaining, which, for the public sector, may sometimes be legally or semantically unacceptable.

REFERENCE
Robert T. Woodworth and Richard B. Peterson, *Collective Negotiations for Public and Professional Employees* (Glenview, IL: Scott, Foresman, 1969).

color Having the appearance as opposed to the reality of something. For example, color of law means an action has the mere semblance of legality. An illegal act done under color of law may have the apparent authority of the law behind it but is, nevertheless, illegal.

combination compromise *See* CALIFORNIA PLAN; MISSOURI PLAN.

comity **1** The constitutional provision that "the citizens of each state shall be entitled to all privileges and immunities of citizens in the several states." **2** A courtesy by which one nation, court, house of a legislature, and so on, defers the exercise of some authority to some other nation, court, house.
REFERENCE
Walter J. Oleszek, House-Senate relationships: Comity and conflict, *Annals of the American Academy of Political and Social Science* 411 (January 1974).

commander in chief **1** The military or naval officer in charge of all allied forces in a theater of operations. **2** The authority granted under Article III, Section 2, of the U.S. Constitution that "the president shall be commander in chief of the army and the navy of the United States and of the militia of the several states when called into the actual service of the United States." The last president to exercise his authority as commander in chief to command troops in the field was James Madison during the War of 1812. At Bladensburg, Maryland, the Americans under their president met the British and were soundly defeated. The British then marched on Washington, D.C., to burn the White House and all other public buildings. No subsequent president, while in office, has sought to lead men in battle.
REFERENCES
Eberhard P. Deutsch, The president as commander in chief, *American Bar Association Journal* 57 (January 1971);
R. Gordon Hoxie, The office of the commander in chief: An historical and projective view, *Presidential Studies Quarterly* 6 (Fall 1976);
Edwin Timbers, The Supreme Court and the president as commander in chief, *Presidential Studies Quarterly* 16 (Spring 1986).

Commerce Business Daily A daily publication of the U.S. Department of Commerce that identifies upcoming federal government contracts (requests for proposals) in excess of twenty-five thousand dollars.

commerce clause The commerce power (Article I, Section 8, of the U.S. Constitution) that allows the Congress to control trade with foreign countries and among the states. If anything "affects interstate commerce" (such as labor unions and product safety) it is fair game for federal government regulation. *See* GIBBONS V OGDEN.
REFERENCES
Thomas K. Anson and P. M. Schenkkan, Federalism, the dormant commerce clause, and state-owned resources, *Texas Law Review* 59 (December 1980);
Julian N. Eule, Laying the dormant commerce clause to rest, *Yale Law Journal* 91 (January 1982).

Commerce, U.S. Department of The cabinet-level federal agency created in 1913, when the Congress split the Department of Commerce and Labor (founded in 1903) into two departments. The Department of Commerce encourages, serves, and promotes the nation's economic development and technological advancement. It offers assistance and information to domestic and international business; provides social and economic statistics and analyses for business and government planners; assists in the development and maintenance of the U.S. Merchant Marine; provides research for and promotes the increased use of science and technology in the development of the economy; provides assistance to speed the development of the economically underdeveloped areas of the nation; seeks to improve understanding of the earth's physical environment and oceanic life; promotes travel to the United States by residents of foreign countries; assists in the growth of minority businesses; and seeks to prevent the loss of life and property from fire.

U.S. Department of Commerce
14th St. N.W., between Constitution Avenue and E Street
Washington, D.C. 20230
(202) 377–2000

commercial speech Communications for business purposes; for example, advertising. Under the U.S. Constitution, commercial speech is given the same protection as political speech. However, commercial speech to propose a business transaction, such as advertising, may be subjected to regulations designed to insure that it is truthful and legitimate. *Compare to* FREE SPEECH CLAUSE.

REFERENCES

Laurence Alexander and Daniel A. Farber, Commercial speech and First Amendment, *Northwestern University Law Review* 75 (April 1980);

Fred S. McChesney, Commercial speech in the professions: The Supreme Court's unanswered questions and questionable answers, *University of Pennsylvania Law Review* 134 (December 1985).

commission 1 A group charged with directing a government function, whether on an ad hoc or a permanent basis. Commissions tend to be used (1) when it is desirable to have bipartisan leadership, (2) when their functions are of a quasi-judicial nature, or (3) when it is deemed important to have wide representation of ethnic groups, regions of the country, differing skills, and so on. 2 In the international context, a United Nations group, numbering from twenty-eight to thirty-six members, that meets once a year or every two years, and is charged with a particular subject area, such as human rights. 3 A written authorization assigning rank or authority to either a civilian or military officer. 4 To put into use, as when the navy commissions a ship. 5 A payment based on a percentage of sales or profit.

commission form of government The original reform structure of urban governance that replaced the city council. It put all the executive, legislative, and administrative powers into one commission. As a collective group, the commission is the local legislature, while each member individually serves as an administrator of a department or a set of departments. The obvious problem of coordinating administration in such a system led to its decline. It was first used in 1900 in Galveston, Texas, following a devastating hurricane; many of these commissioners were appointed by the governor. The commission form of local government has suffered a steady decline in popularity in recent decades.

REFERENCES

Bradley R. Rice, The Galveston plan of city government by commission: The birth of a

---

The Commission Form of City Government Organization

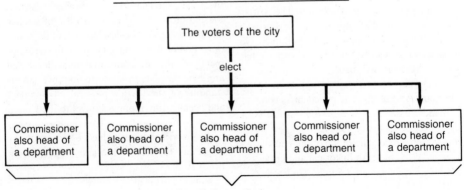

The commission form of city government operation

Source: Grover Starling, *Understanding American Politics* (Chicago: Dorsey, 1982), p. 355.

progressive idea, *Southwestern Historical Quarterly* 78 (April 1975);

Bradley R. Rice, *Progressive Cities: The Commission Government Movement in America, 1901–1920* (Austin: University of Texas Press, 1977).

Commission on Civil Rights The federal agency whose role is to encourage constructive steps toward equal opportunity for all. The commission, created by the CIVIL RIGHTS ACT OF 1957, investigates complaints, holds public hearings, and collects and studies information on denials of equal protection of the laws because of race, color, religion, sex, or national origin. The commission can make findings of fact in cases involving, for example, voting rights, administration of justice, and equality of opportunity in education, employment, and housing, but it has no enforcement authority. Its findings and recommendations are submitted to both the president and the Congress. Many of the commission's recommendations have been enacted by statute, executive order, or regulation. The commission evaluates federal laws and the effectiveness of the government's equal opportunity programs. It also serves as a national clearinghouse for civil rights information.

REFERENCE

Foster Rhea Dulles, *The Civil Rights Commission: 1957–1965* (East Lansing: Michigan State University Press, 1968).

Commission on Civil Rights
1121 Vermont Avenue, N.W.
Washington, D.C. 20425
(202) 376–8105

Commission on Intergovernmental Relations *See* KESTNBAUM COMMISSION.

Commission on the Organization of the Executive Branch *See* HOOVER COMMISSION OF 1947–1949; HOOVER COMMISSION OF 1953–1955.

commission, presidential A committee sanctioned by the president of the United States to investigate a matter of public concern

and to issue recommendations for improvement. The modern presidential commission can be traced back to the British Commission of Inquiry. Ever since the Civil War, Americans have found it a useful means of dealing with important national issues. There is great public satisfaction to be had in the bringing together of a group of responsible, respected, supposedly objective but knowledgeable citizens to examine and report upon a national problem or major disaster. Such commissions have proven to be handy devices for modern presidents who, when faced with an intractable problem, such as crime, pornography, or urban riots, can, at slight expense, appoint a commission as a gesture to indicate his awareness of constituent distress. Whether that gesture has meaning or sincerity beyond itself is inconsequential for its immediate effect. By the time a commission makes its report, six months to a year later, attention will have been diverted to other issues, and the recommendations can be safely pigeonholed or curtailed.

REFERENCES

Frank Popper, *The President's Commissions* (New York: Twentieth Century Fund, 1970);

Martha Derthick, On commissionship—Presidential variety, *Public Policy* 19 (Fall 1971);

Thomas R. Wolanin, *Presidential Advisory Commissions: Truman to Nixon* (Madison: University of Wisconsin Press, 1975);

Terrence R. Tutchings, *Rhetoric and Reality: Presidential Commissions and the Making of Public Policy* (Boulder, CO: Westview, 1979);

David Flitner, Jr., *The Politics of Presidential Commissions* (Ardsley-on-Hudson, NY: Transnational, 1986).

committee 1 A part of a larger group appointed to perform a specialized service on a one-time or continuous basis. 2 A subdivision of a legislature that prepares legislation for action by the respective house or that makes investigations as directed by the respective house. Most standing (full) committees are divided into subcommittees, which study legislation, hold hearings, and report their recommendations to the full committee. Only the full committee can report legislation for action by the entire legislature.

REFERENCES

For committees in the U.S. Congress, see
Richard F. Fenno, Jr., *Congressmen in Committees* (Boston: Little, Brown, 1973);

Walter Kravitz, Evolution of the Senate's committee system, *Annals of the American Academy of Political and Social Science* 411 (January 1974);

Roger H. Davidson, Congressional committees as moving targets, *Legislative Studies Quarterly* 11 (February 1986);

Steven S. Smith and Christopher J. Deering, *Committees in Congress* (Washington: CQ Press, 1984);

Timothy E. Cook, The policy impact of the committee assignment process in the House, *Journal of Politics* 45 (November 1983).

For committees in the state legislatures, see
Keith E. Hamm and Gary Moncrief, Effects of structural change in legislative committee systems on their performance in U.S. states, *Legislative Studies Quarterly* 7 (August 1982);

James W. Riddlesperger and Wayne L. Francis, U.S. state legislative committees: Structure, procedural efficiency, and party control, *Legislative Studies Quarterly* 7 (November 1982).

committee, ad hoc   *See* AD HOC COMMITTEE.

committee bill   *See* BILL, COMMITTEE.

committee, conference   A meeting between the representatives of the two houses of a legislature to reconcile the differences over the provisions of a bill. The most usual case is when a bill passes one house with amendments unacceptable to the other. In such a case, the house that disagrees generally asks for a conference. In the U.S. Congress, the Speaker of the House of Representatives and the vice president of the Senate appoint the managers, as the conferees are called. Generally, they are selected from the committee having charge of the bill, and they usually represent majority and minority positions on the bill. After attempting to resolve the points in disagreement, the conference committee issues a report to each house. If the report is accepted by both houses, the bill is then passed and sent to the president. If rejected by either house, the matter in disagreement comes up for disposition anew, as if there had been no conference. Unless all differences between the houses are finally adjusted, the bill fails.

REFERENCES

For analyses of conference committees in the U.S. Congress, see John Ferejohn, Who wins in conference committee? *Journal of Politics* 37 (November 1975);

Gerald S. Strom and Barry S. Rundquist, A revised theory of winning in House-Senate conferences, *American Political Science Review* 71 (June 1977);

Donald A. Gross, Conference committees, sophisticated voting, and cyclical majorities, *Legislative Studies Quarterly* 4 (February 1979);

Dennis S. Ippolito, House-Senate budget conferences: Institutional and strategic advantages, *American Politics Quarterly* 11 (January 1983).

For analyses of conference committees in state legislatures, see Donald A. Gross, House-Senate conference committees: A comparative state perspective, *American Journal of Political Science* 24 (November 1980);

Donald A. Gross, Conference committees and levels of interchamber disagreement: A comparative state perspective, *State and Local Government Review* 15 (Fall 1983).

Committee for Economic Development (CED)   A nonpartisan organization of business leaders and scholars who conduct research and formulate policy recommendations on economic and public policy issues. It was started in 1942 to prepare for the postwar economy. In 1945 it was reorganized as a permanent, independent organization with a board of directors of some two-hundred leaders from business, finance, and the universities.

Committee for Economic Development
477 Madison Avenue
New York, NY 10022
(212) 688–2063

committee, joint   A U.S. congressional committee whose members are chosen from both the House of Representatives and the Senate, generally with the chair rotating between the most senior majority party senator and representative. These committees can be created by statute or by joint or concurrent resolution. However, all existing joint committees have been established by statute, the oldest being the Joint Committee on the Library, which dates from 1800.

committeeman/committeewoman 1 The front-line workers of a political party who are assigned several city blocks or a neighborhood to recruit and service members of the party. Their single most important function is to get out the vote on election day by making sure that sympathetic voters have previously registered, by driving people to the polls, by arranging babysitters while parents vote, and so on. 2 A worker (usually) elected by co-workers to represent the union membership in the handling of grievances and the recruitment of new union members, among other duties.

Committee of the Whole The working title of what is formally the Committee of the Whole House [of Representatives] on the State of the Union. Unlike other committees, it is composed of all members of the body—now 435. It is used to debate measures that have passed through the regular committees and that are placed on the calendar, usually made "in order" by a "rule" from the Rules Committee. Because in the Committee of the Whole a quorum is only one hundred members, business is expedited. When the full House resolves itself into the Committee of the Whole, it supplants the speaker with a chair. The measure is debated or amended, with votes on amendments as needed. When the committee completes its action on the measure, it dissolves itself by "rising." The Speaker returns, and the full House hears the chair of the Committee of the Whole report that group's recommendations. The full House then acts upon the recommendations. At this time, members may demand a roll-call vote on any amendment adopted in the Committee of the Whole.

committee on committees *See* COMMITTEE, STANDING.

Committee on Political Education (COPE) A nonpartisan organization of the AFL-CIO,

made up of members of the AFL-CIO's executive council. COPE has the responsibility spelled out in the AFL-CIO constitution of "encouraging workers to register and vote, to exercise their full rights and responsibilities of citizenship, and to perform their rightful part in the political life of the city, state and national communities." COPE is not a political party, nor is it committed to the support of any particular party. From the first convention of the AFL-CIO in 1955, when COPE was founded, to the most recent, COPE has been instructed to work in support of candidates who support issues of concern to the AFL-CIO regardless of the party affiliation of the candidate. The policies of COPE are determined by its national committee in line with the policies and programs adopted by the AFL-CIO conventions.

REFERENCES

Terry Catchpole, *How to Cope with COPE: The Political Operations of Organized Labor* (New Rochelle, NY: Arlington, 1968);

Harry Holloway, Interest groups in the post-partisan era: The political machine of the AFL-CIO, *Political Science Quarterly* 94 (Spring 1979).

Committee on Political Education
815 16th Street, N.W.
Washington, D.C. 20006
(202) 637–5101

committee, recommit to A simple motion, made on the floor of the Congress after deliberation on a bill, to return it to the committee that reported it. If approved, recommittal usually is considered a death blow to the bill. A motion to recommit may include instructions to the committee to report the bill again, with specific amendments or by a certain date. Or the instructions may be to make a particular study, with no definite deadline for final action.

committee, select A committee established by the House of Representatives or the Senate, usually for a limited period and generally for a strictly temporary, usually investigative, purpose. When that function has been carried out, the select committee automatically expires. This is also known as a special committee.

committees of correspondence Citizens committees created in the American colonies after 1772 to exchange information and arouse resistance to English rule.

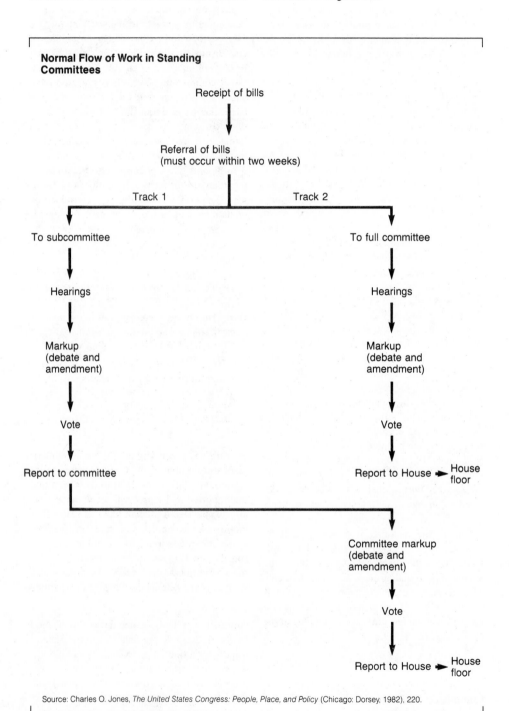

Normal Flow of Work in Standing Committees

Receipt of bills

Referral of bills
(must occur within two weeks)

Track 1   Track 2

To subcommittee   To full committee

Hearings   Hearings

Markup   Markup
(debate and   (debate and
amendment)   amendment)

Vote   Vote

Report to committee   Report to House ➤ House floor

Committee markup
(debate and
amendment)

Vote

Report to House ➤ House floor

Source: Charles O. Jones, *The United States Congress: People, Place, and Policy* (Chicago: Dorsey, 1982), 220.

Committees on Committees Take a Different Form in Each Party in Each House

Congressional House	Democrats	Republicans
House of Representatives	A Steering and Policy Committee, chaired by the Speaker, includes top party leaders plus representatives from regional House caucuses—about twenty-four members in all.	One member is appointed from each state with Republican representatives. Each member then has a number of votes equal to the number of Republican representatives from his or her state. An executive committee of about fifteen members is formed from the whole committee.
Senate	A Steering Committee of about twenty-five members is appointed by the party's floor leader, who also chairs it.	About fourteen members are appointed by the chair of the Republican caucus. The floor leader is an ex-officio member.

---

committee, standing A regular committee of a legislature that deals with bills within a specified subject area. In the U.S. Congress, each of the two principal parties has a committee on committees, which recommends committee assignments subject to caucus or conference approval. At the beginning of each Congress, members can express assignment preferences to their respective committee on committees. This committee then prepares and approves an assignment slate of members for each committee and submits it to the caucus or conference for approval. Normally, the recommendations are approved without challenge, but procedures exist by which other members can be nominated for vacant committee posts. The House, generally by strict party vote, adopts the slates presented by the two parties. The proportion of Republicans to Democrats is fixed by the majority party of the House. A similar method is used in the Senate. The influence of the standing committees of the Congress cannot be overstated. As Woodrow Wilson declared almost a hundred years ago: "I know not how better to describe our form of government in a single phrase than by calling it a government by the Chairman of the Standing Committees of Congress."

REFERENCES

Richard F. Fenno, Jr., *Congressmen in Committees* (Boston: Little, Brown, 1973);

Steven S. Smith and Christopher J. Deering, *Committees in Congress* (Washington, D.C.: Congressional Quarterly, 1984);

Heinz Eulau and Vera McCluggage, Standing committees in legislatures: Three decades of research, *Legislative Studies Quarterly* 9 (May 1984).

The Standing Committees of the Congress

House

Agriculture

Appropriations

Armed Services

Banking, Finance and Urban Affairs

Budget

District of Columbia

Education and Labor

Energy and Commerce

Foreign Affairs

Government Operations

House Administration

Interior and Insular Affairs

Judiciary

Merchant Marine and Fisheries
Post Office and Civil Service
Public Works and Transportation
Rules
Science, Space and Technology
Small Business
Standards of Official Conduct
Veterans' Affairs
Ways and Means

Senate
Agriculture, Nutrition and Forestry
Appropriations
Armed Services
Banking, Housing and Urban Affairs
Budget
Commerce, Science and Transportation
Energy and Natural Resources
Environment and Public Works
Finance
Foreign Relations
Governmental Affairs
Judiciary
Labor and Human Resources
Rules and Administration
Small Business
Veterans' Affairs

common carrier Any organization (such as a trucking company, railroad, or airline) whose transportation services for moving things or people are available to the general public.

REFERENCE

Mark A. Hall, Common carriers under the communications act, *University of Chicago Law Review* 48 (Spring 1981).

Common Cause A quarter-million-member public interest lobby founded in 1970 and devoted to making public officials more accountable to citizens and to improving government performance.

REFERENCE

Andrew S. McFarland, *Common Cause: Lobbying in the Public Interest* (Chatham, NJ: Chatham House, 1984).

Common Cause
2030 M Street, N.W.
Washington, D.C. 20036
(202) 833–1200

common law The totality of judge-made laws that initially developed in England and continued to evolve in the United States. Whenever this kind of law—which is based on custom, culture, habit, and previous judicial decisions—proved inadequate, it was supplanted by statutory laws made by legislatures. But the common law tradition, based upon PRECEDENT, is still the foundation of the American legal system, even though much of what was originally common law has converted into statutes over the years.

REFERENCES

Oliver Wendell Holmes, Jr., *The Common Law* (Boston: Little, Brown, 1881, 1964);

Arthur R. Hogue, *Origins of the Common Law* (Bloomington: Indiana University Press, 1966);

Paul H. Rubin, Why is the common law efficient? *Journal of Legal Studies* 6 (January 1977);

John C. Goodman, An economic theory of the evolution of common law, *Journal of Legal Studies* 7 (June 1978);

Thomas W. Merrill, The common law powers of federal courts, *University of Chicago Law Review* 52 (Winter 1985).

commonwealth The notion of Thomas Hobbes (1588–1679) and other philosophers of his era that the members of a social order have a common weal, which is in their collective interest to preserve and protect. Common weal evolved into commonwealth, which came to mean the state. Thus the republic established in Britain under Oliver Cromwell from 1649 to 1660 was called the Commonwealth. Four American states (Pennsylvania, Virginia, Massachusetts, and Kentucky) are formally commonwealths rather than states.

communism *See* MARXISM.

community 1 A group of people living in an identifiable area. This can range from the community of man, which occupies the planet called Earth, to the Hispanic community of San Antonio, Texas, or to the Jewish community of Miami, Florida. 2 A group having common interests, such as the medical com-

munity, the Catholic community, and so on.
3 All of the people living in a particular locality. **4** A housing development. **5** Descriptive of shared goods, such as a community swimming pool in a city, or community property in a marriage. **6** A euphemism for the vote. Thus if a candidate asks his or her campaign manager, "How is the Hispanic community today?" the question does not inquire about their general health or economic welfare; it merely asks, "How many of them plan to vote for me today?"

community action programs Local programs mandated by the Economic Opportunity Act of 1964, which provided that community action programs to alleviate poverty could be funded by the federal government but operated by community agencies exempt from political review or control at the state or local level. These programs were effectively abandoned by the Richard M. Nixon administration.

REFERENCES

Daniel P. Moynihan, *Maximum Feasible Misunderstanding: Community Action in the War on Poverty* (New York: Free Press, 1969);

Harold Wolman, Organization theory and community action agencies, *Public Administration Review* 32 (January/February 1972);

Gary English, The trouble with community action, *Public Administration Review* 32 (May/June 1972).

community control An extreme form of citizen participation in which democratically selected representatives of a neighborhood-sized government jurisdiction are given administrative and financial control over such local programs as education, land use, and police protection.

REFERENCES

Alan Altshuler, *Community Control: The Black Demand for Participation in Large American Cities* (New York: Pegasus, 1970);

Joseph F. Zimmerman, *The Federated City: Community Control in Large Cities* (New York: St. Martin's, 1972);

Norman I. Fainstein and Susan S. Fainstein, The future of community control, *American*

Political Science Review 70 (September 1976).

community development **1** An approach to the administration of social and economic development programs in which government officials are dispatched to the field to act as catalysts at the local level, encouraging local residents to form groups, to define their own needs, and to develop self-help projects. The government then provides technical and material assistance and helps the community establish institutions (such as farm cooperatives) to carry on the development programs after the officials have left. **2** Local government efforts to plan for and finance the physical development of the jurisdiction. In this context, community development block grants have been available from the U.S. Department of Housing and Urban Development for a variety of activities, such as land acquisition, new parks and playgrounds, historic preservation, and street and drainage improvements.

REFERENCES

Leanne M. Lachman, Planning for community development: A proposed approach, *Journal of Housing* 32 (February 1975);

Hayden Roberts, *Community Development: Learning and Action* (Toronto: University of Toronto Press, 1979).

community power Usually, the study or description of the political order, both formal and informal, of a segment of U.S. local governance. In the 1960s, such studies used behavioral methodologies and were considered the cutting edge of political science.

REFERENCES

Robert A. Dahl, *Who Governs? Democracy and Power in an American City* (New Haven, CT: Yale University Press, 1961);

Robert E. Agger, Daniel Goldrich, and Bert Swanson, *The Rulers and the Ruled: Political Power and Impotence in American Communities* (New York: Wiley, 1964);

Robert V. Presthus, *Men at the Top: A Study in Community Power* (New York: Oxford University Press, 1964);

Will D. Hawley and Frederick Wirt, *The Search for Community Power*, 2d ed. (Englewood Cliffs, NJ: Prentice-Hall, 1974);

Floyd Hunter, *Community Power Succession: Atlanta's Policy-Makers Revisited* (Chapel Hill: University of North Carolina Press, 1980).

community relations program   The totality of efforts by military and paramilitary organizations (such as local police) to create better understanding and acceptance of their missions in their local communities.

Company, the   A slang term for the CIA.

comparable worth   Equitable compensation for doing a job by determining its value to an organization compared to other jobs in the organization. The basic issue of comparable worth is whether Title VII of the Civil Rights Act of 1964 makes it unlawful for an employer to pay one sex at a lesser rate than the other when the job is of comparable worth or value. For example, should graduate nurses be paid less than gardeners? Or should beginning librarians with master's degrees be paid less than beginning managers with master's degrees? Historically, nurses and librarians have been paid less than occupations of comparable worth, because they were considered women's jobs. Comparable worth as a legal concept and as a social issue directly challenges traditional and market assumptions about the worth of a job.

REFERENCES
Elaine Johansen, Managing the revolution: The case for comparable worth, *Review of Public Personnel Administration* 4 (Spring 1984);
Helen Remick, ed. *Comparable Worth and Wage Discrimination: Technical Possibilities and Political Realities* (Philadelphia: Temple University Press, 1984);
Bruce Powell Majors, Comparable worth: The new feminist demand, *Journal of Social, Political and Economic Studies* 10 (Spring 1985).

comparative advantage   The position a country or a region has in the production of those goods it can produce relatively more efficiently than other goods. Modern trade theory says that, regardless of the country's productivity or labor costs relative to those of other countries, it should produce for export those goods in which it has the greatest comparative advantage and import those in which it has the greatest comparative disadvantage. The country that has few economic strengths will find it advantageous to devote its productive energies to those lines in which its disadvantage is least marked, provided the opportunity to trade with other areas is open to it. The comparative advantage theory was first proposed by the English economist David Ricardo (1772–1823) in 1817. *Compare to* ABSOLUTE ADVANTAGE.

REFERENCES
Robert W. Boatler, Comparative advantage: A division among developing countries, *Inter-American Economic Affairs* 32 (Autumn 1978);
Jon Harkness, Factor abundance and comparative advantage, *American Economic Review* 68 (December 1978);
Edward E. Leamer, *Sources of International Comparative Advantage: Theory and Evidence* (Cambridge, MA: MIT Press, 1986).

competitiveness   The ability of the United States to compete economically with the other developed nations in the Western world—especially Japan. In the late 1980s, the term became an abbreviated way of referring to the concern for a comprehensive national INDUSTRIAL POLICY, to the persistent problem of lagging productivity of American workers, and to an increasingly unfavorable U.S. BALANCE OF TRADE.

REFERENCE
Ronald W. Davis, Antitrust, the trade deficit, and U.S. international competitiveness: A time for rethinking, *New York University Journal of International Law and Politics* 18 (Summer 1986).

competitive service   A general term for those civilian positions in a government jurisdiction that are not specifically excepted from merit system regulations.

compliance   1 Acting in accordance with the law. Voluntary compliance is the basis of a civil society. No government has the resources to force all of its citizens to comply with all of the criminal and civil laws. Consequently, all governments are more dependent upon compliance than they would ever like to admit. The best single example of massive voluntary compliance is the U.S. federal income tax system, which is essentially administered by self-assessment and voluntary payment. **2** A technical term used by funding agencies as a criterion to judge whether a grantee is acting (i.e., spending their grant funds) in accordance with the granter's policies or preset guidelines.

REFERENCES

Fred S. Coombs, Bases of non-compliance with a policy, *Policy Studies Journal* 8 (Summer 1980);

Kenneth J. Meier and David R. Morgan, Citizen compliance with public policy: The national maximum speed law, *Western Political Quarterly* 35 (June 1982);

Keith Hawkins, Bargain and bluff: Compliance strategy and deterrence in the enforcement of regulation, *Law and Policy Quarterly* 5 (January 1983);

John T. Scholz, Voluntary compliance and regulatory enforcement, *Law and Policy* 6 (October 1984);

Paul Sommers and Roland J. Cole, Compliance costs of small and larger businesses, *Policy Studies Journal* 13 (June 1985).

Comprehensive Employment and Training Act of 1973 (CETA) The law that, as amended, established a program of financial assistance to state and local governments to provide job training and employment opportunities for economically disadvantaged, unemployed, and underemployed people. The CETA provided funds for state and local jurisdictions to hire unemployed and underemployed people in public service jobs. The CETA reauthorization legislation expired in September 1982. It was replaced by the Job Training Partnership Act of 1982, which provides for job-training programs to be planned and implemented under the joint control of local elected officials and private industry councils in service delivery areas designated by the governor of each state.

REFERENCES

For analyses of the CETA, see Pawan K. Sawhney, Robert H. Jantzen, and Irwin L.

Herrnstadt, The differential impact of CETA training, *Industrial and Labor Relations Review* 35 (January 1982);

Laurie J. Bassi, CETA—Did it work? *Policy Studies Journal* 12 (September 1983);

Grace A. Franklin and Randall B. Ripley, *CETA: Politics and Policy 1973–1982* (Knoxville: University of Tennessee Press, 1984).

For commentary on the Job Training Partnership Act, see Royal S. Dellinger, Implementing the Job Training Partnership Act, *Labor Law Journal* 35 (April 1984);

Camille Robinson and Relmond Van Daniker, Financial management issues in the Job Training Partnership Act, *State Government* 58 (Spring 1985);

Susan A. MacManus, Playing a new game: Governors and the Job Training Partnership Act, *American Politics Quarterly* 14 (July 1986).

Comprehensive Environmental Response, Compensation and Liability Act of 1980 The law that created a superfund to clean up hazardous waste. The fund is financed by taxes on the chemical industry and administered by the Environmental Protection Agency.

REFERENCE

Ann K. Pollock, The role of injunctive relief and settlements in superfund enforcement, *Cornell Law Review* 68 (June 1983).

comprehensive plan/master plan A local government document that establishes long-term policies for the physical development of the jurisdiction. Such documents are often required by funding agencies, such as the federal government or the states, that want to see where a proposed funding request fits into the "big picture" before they make a grant.

comptroller general of the United States *See* GENERAL ACCOUNTING OFFICE.

comptroller of the currency The officer of the U.S. Department of the Treasury responsible for monitoring the operations of all national banks. *Compare to* CONTROLLER/ COMPTROLLER.

compulsory process   *See* WITNESS.

concurrent jurisdiction   A legal situation in which two or more court systems (such as state and federal) or two or more agencies (such as the local police and the FBI) both have the power to deal with a problem or case.

concurrent majority   *See* JOHN C. CALHOUN.

concurrent power   A power held jointly by both federal and state governments. Taxation is a major example.

concurrent resolution   A congressional action, designated H. Con. Res. or S. Con. Res., which must be passed by both houses but does not require the signature of the president and does not have the force of law. Concurrent resolutions generally are used to make or amend rules applicable to both houses or to express the sentiment of the two houses. A concurrent resolution, for example, is used to fix the time for adjournment of the Congress.
REFERENCE
Doyle W. Buckwalter, The congressional concurrent resolution: A search for foreign policy influence, *Midwest Journal of Political Science* 14 (August 1970).

concurrent resolution on the budget   A resolution passed by both houses of the Congress, but not requiring the signature of the president, setting forth, reaffirming, or revising the congressional budget for the U.S. government for a fiscal year. Two such resolutions are required preceding each fiscal year. The first, due by May 15, establishes the congressional budget. The second, due by September 15, reaffirms or revises it. Other concurrent resolutions may be adopted at any time following the first required concurrent resolution.

condemn   1 To pronounce a negative judgment of an individual, an action, or an event. 2 To pronounce a negative judgment in a criminal case.   3 To impose the death penalty. 4 To exercise public domain by taking over private property with payment to the owner, who may or may not have been willing to sell. 5 To declare that a property is unfit for use or occupancy. This usually means that it must be vacated, renovated, or torn down.

confederation   A league of sovereign states that delegates powers on selected issues to a central government. In a confederation, the central government is deliberately limited and thus may be inherently weak because it has few independent powers. The United States was a confederation from 1781 to 1789. *Compare to* ARTICLES OF CONFEDERATION.

conferee   A legislator who has been appointed to a conference committee, usually a senior member on the committee that originated the bill being considered.

conference committee   *See* COMMITTEE, CONFERENCE.

conflict of interest   Any situation in which the personal interest of an officeholder may influence or appear to influence that officeholder's decision on a matter of public interest. Officeholders are wise to avoid both actual conflict and appearance of conflict. A common means of avoiding conflict is for the officeholder to abstain from voting or acting on an issue in which a personal benefit may exist. Thus a judge or an administrator may withdraw from a case or the making of a decision in a situation where his or her ownership of stock or other interest might be perceived as being benefited. The ETHICS IN GOVERNMENT ACT OF 1978 seeks to avoid conflict of interest by high-level federal employees even after they cease government employment by putting postemployment restrictions on their relations with the agencies they once worked for. The most common means of avoiding conflict—that is, by abstaining—is not practical for many elected officeholders. A major election campaign for the Congress, for example, involves so many diverse contributors and supporters that a legislator would be severely restricted in voting if the automatic criteria for abstaining was the fact that a campaign contributor would be affected.
REFERENCES
Peter Gruenstein and Daniel West, Anything you can eat, drink, or fornicate in one afternoon, *Washington Monthly* 7 (June 1975);

Common Cause, *Serving Two Masters: A Common Cause Study of Conflicts of Interest in the Executive Branch* (Washington, D.C.: Common Cause, 1976);

Robert G. Vaughn, *Conflict-of-Interest Regulation in the Federal Executive Branch* (Lexington, MA: Lexington Books, 1979);

Henry W. Chappell, Jr., Conflict of interest and congressional voting: A note, *Public Choice* 37:2 (1981);

Lloyd N. Cutler, Conflicts of interest, *Emory Law Journal* 30 (Fall 1981).

conflict of laws 1 Having the laws of more than one jurisdiction apply to a case. The judge must then choose which jurisdiction's laws are most applicable. This is a particularly thorny problem when a state law precedes federal legislation; the conflict comes after the federal legislation takes effect. 2 Having the laws of more than one nation apply to a case involving private parties (as opposed to the nations themselves); the problem then becomes one of international law.

REFERENCE

Friedrich K. Juenger, Conflict of laws: A critique of interest analysis, *American Journal of Comparative Law* 32 (Winter 1984).

confrontation clause The Sixth Amendment provision that an accused person "be confronted with the witnesses against him." This implies a right of cross-examination. The U.S. Supreme Court applied this right to state courts in *Pointer v Texas,* 380 U.S. 400 (1965), through the due process clause of the Fourteenth Amendment.

confrontation politics Political action premised on the notion that change can best be achieved by dramatic acts, such as sit-ins, demonstrations, and obstructionism. The end purpose is to alert the larger political community to the problem in order to generate a consensus for change. *Compare to* AGENDA SETTING.

REFERENCE

Jerome H. Skolnick, *The Politics of Protest: Violent Aspects of Protest and Confrontation* (Washington, D.C.: Government Printing Office, 1969).

congress 1 The legislative branch of the United States government created and defined by Article I of the Constitution. The U.S. Congress is composed of the House of Representatives and the Senate. *See* CONGRESS, UNITED STATES. 2 The two-year-long cycle of federal legislative meetings beginning on January 3 of each odd-numbered year. 3 Any large representative assembly. 4 The major political party in India.

Congress and the Presidency A scholarly quarterly subtitled A Journal of Capital Studies, published jointly by the American University's Center for Congressional and Presidential Studies and the United States Capitol Historical Society since 1982. Formerly called *Capitol Studies* (from 1972 until 1978); *Congressional Studies* (until 1981). Library of Congress no. JK1041 .C36.

Congress and the Presidency
Center for Congressional and Presidential Studies
School of Government and Public Administration
American University
Washington, D.C. 20016
(202) 885-6225

Congress, Continental The delegates from the thirteen original colonies who first met in 1774 in Philadelphia. The second Continental Congress instigated the American Revolution by adopting the DECLARATION OF INDEPENDENCE in 1776 and continued to function until the adoption of the ARTICLES OF CONFEDERATION in 1781.

REFERENCE

Jack N. Rakove, *The Beginnings of National Politics: An Interpretive History of the Continental Congress* (Baltimore: Johns Hopkins University Press, 1982).

congressional budget The U.S. budget as set forth by the Congress in a concurrent resolution on the budget. These resolutions include (1) the appropriate level of total budget outlays and of total new budget authority; (2) an estimate of budget outlays and new budget authority for each major functional category; (3) the amount, if any, of the surplus or deficit in the

Congressional Budget and Impoundment Control Act of 1974

The Congressional Budget Process

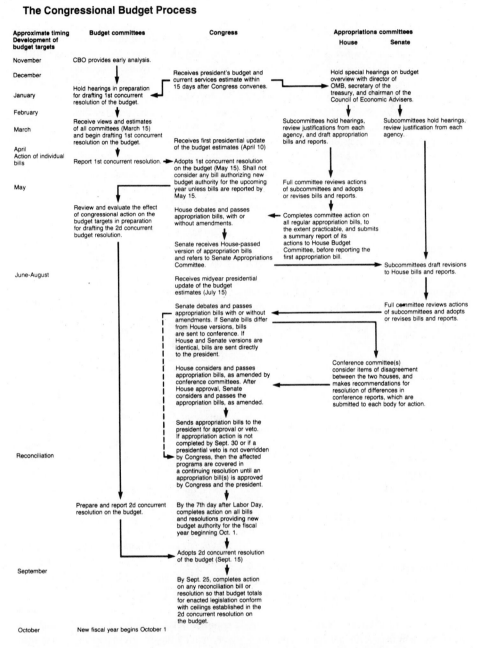

Approximate timing Development of budget targets	Budget committees	Congress	Appropriations committees — House	Appropriations committees — Senate
November	CBO provides early analysis.			
December		Receives president's budget and current services estimate within 15 days after Congress convenes.	Hold special hearings on budget overview with director of OMB, secretary of the treasury, and chairman of the Council of Economic Advisers.	
January	Hold hearings in preparation for drafting 1st concurrent resolution of the budget.			
February				
March	Receive views and estimates of all committees (March 15) and begin drafting 1st concurrent resolution on the budget.	Receives first presidential update of the budget estimates (April 10)	Subcommittees hold hearings, review justifications from each agency, and draft appropriation bills and reports.	Subcommittees hold hearings, review justification from each agency.
April Action of individual bills	Report 1st concurrent resolution.	Adopts 1st concurrent resolution on the budget (May 15). Shall not consider any bill authorizing new budget authority for the upcoming year unless bills are reported by May 15.		
May	Review and evaluate the effect of congressional action on the budget targets in preparation for drafting the 2d concurrent budget resolution.	House debates and passes appropriation bills, with or without amendments. Senate receives House-passed version of appropriation bills and refers to Senate Appropriations Committee.	Full committee reviews actions of subcommittees and adopts or revises bills and reports. Completes committee action on all regular appropriation bills, to the extent practicable, and submits a summary report of its actions to House Budget Committee, before reporting the first appropriation bill.	Subcommittees draft revisions to House bills and reports.
June-August		Receives midyear presidential update of the budget estimates (July 15) Senate debates and passes appropriation bills with or without amendments. If Senate bills differ from House versions, bills are sent to conference. If House and Senate versions are identical, bills are sent directly to the president. House considers and passes appropriation bills, as amended by conference committees. After House approval, Senate considers and passes the appropriation bills, as amended.		Full committee reviews actions of subcommittees and adopts or revises bills and reports. Conference committee(s) consider items of disagreement between the two houses, and makes recommendations for resolution of differences in conference reports, which are submitted to each body for action.
Reconciliation		Sends appropriation bills to the president for approval or veto. If appropriation action is not completed by Sept. 30 or if a presidential veto is not overridden by Congress, then the affected programs are covered in a continuing resolution until an appropriation bill(s) is approved by Congress and the president.		
	Prepare and report 2d concurrent resolution on the budget.	By the 7th day after Labor Day, completes action on all bills and resolutions providing new budget authority for the fiscal year beginning Oct. 1. Adopts 2d concurrent resolution of the budget (Sept. 15)		
September		By Sept. 25, completes action on any reconciliation bill or resolution so that budget totals for enacted legislation conform with ceilings established in the 2d concurrent resolution on the budget.		
October	New fiscal year begins October 1			

Source: William J. Keefe, Henry J. Abraham, William H. Flanigan, Charles O. Jones, Morris S. Ogul, and John W. Spanier, *American Democracy: Institutions, Politics, and Policies*, 2d ed. (Chicago: Dorsey, 1986), p. 509. Adapted from *A Glossary of Terms Used in the Federal Budget Process* (Washington, D.C.: U.S. General Accounting Office, 1981), pp. 10–11.

budget; (4) the recommended level of federal revenues; and (5) the appropriate level of the public debt.

Congressional Budget and Impoundment Control Act of 1974 A major restructuring of the congressional budgeting process. The act's Declaration of Purposes states that it is essential: (1) to assure effective congressional control over the budgetary process; (2) to provide for yearly congressional determination of the appropriate level of federal revenues and expenditures; (3) to provide a system of impoundment control; (4) to establish national budget priorities; and (5) to provide for the furnishing of information by the executive branch in a manner that will assist the Congress in discharging its duties.

The significant features of the act are: (1) the creation of the House and Senate budget committees; (2) the creation of the Congressional Budget Office to support the Congress just as the OMB serves the president; (3) the adoption of a new appropriations process for the Congress; (4) the adoption of a new budget calendar for the Congress; (5) the establishment of a new fiscal year (October 1 through September 30) to more rationally deal with the timing of the budget cycles; (6) the creation of a current services budget; and (7) the creation of two new forms of impoundments—recisions and deferrals—both of which must be submitted to the Congress. *Compare to* IMPOUNDMENT.

REFERENCES

Jerome A. Miles, The Congressional Budget and Impoundment Control Act—A departmental budget officer's view, *Bureaucrat* 5 (January 1977);

John Dumbrell, Strengthening the legislative power of the purse: The origins of the 1974 budgetary reforms in the U.S. Congress, *Public Administration* 58 (Winter 1980);

Allen Schick, *Congress and Money* (Washington, D.C.: Urban Institute, 1980);

Douglas H. Shumavon, Policy impact of the 1974 Congressional Budget Act. *Public Administration Review* 41 (May/June 1981);

Joseph J. Hogan, Ten years after: The U.S. Congressional Budget and Impoundment Control Act of 1974, *Public Administration* 63 (Summer 1985);

Mark S. Kamlet and David C. Mowery, The first decade of the Congressional Budget Act: Legislative imitation and adaptation in budgeting, *Policy Sciences* 18 (December 1985);

John W. Ellwood, The great exception: The congressional budget process in an age of decentralization, in *Congress Reconsidered,* eds. Lawrence C. Dodd and Bruce I. Oppenheimer (Washington, D.C.: Congressional Quarterly, 1985).

Congressional Budget Office (CBO) A support agency of the U.S. Congress created in 1974 by the Congressional Budget and Impoundment Act to provide the Congress with basic budget data and with analyses of alternative fiscal, budgetary, and programmatic policy issues, independent of the executive branch and of the OFFICE OF MANAGEMENT AND BUDGET.
Congressional Budget Office
2d and D streets, S.W.
Washington, D.C. 20515
(202) 226-2621

congressional committees *See* COMMITTEE, STANDING.

congressional district A division of a state, based on population, electing one member to the U.S. House of Representatives. There are 435 congressional districts in the United States. In six cases (Alaska, Delaware, North Dakota, South Dakota, Vermont, and Wyoming), the state has only one member of the House; therefore, the entire state is the congressional district.

congressional exemption The exclusion of the approximately twenty-thousand congressional staff employees from coverage of the large variety of laws regulating working conditions that the U.S. Congress has passed throughout the years. Each member of the Congress has complete autonomy over the pay and working conditions of his or her staff and need not comply with laws on labor relations, equal pay, occupational safety, and so on. *Compare to* DAVIS V PASSMAN.

congressional government 1 A government dominated by the legislature. This was the condition of American government during most of the nineteenth century (the Civil War being the major period of exception). **2** A government in which the legislature is separate from the executive and independent of it. This is in contrast to a cabinet form of government, in which an executive is chosen by, and responsible to, a legislature. Woodrow Wilson, while a college professor, published the classic account of congressional government, *Congressional Government: A Study in American Politics* (Boston: Houghton Mifflin, 1885; reprinted, Baltimore: Johns Hopkins University Press, 1981), in which he observed that authority "is perplexingly subdivided and distributed, and responsibility has to be hunted down in out-of-the-way corners." Some things haven't changed much in a hundred years!

congressional groups   *See* LEGISLATIVE SERVICE ORGANIZATIONS.

congressional immunity   *See* IMMUNITY, CONGRESSIONAL.

Congressional Index   A loose-leaf book holding reports on the status of all bills pending in the Congress.
> *Congressional Index*
> Commerce Clearing House
> 4025 W. Peterson Ave.
> Chicago, IL 60646

congressional oversight   *See* OVERSIGHT, CONGRESSIONAL.

Congressional Quarterly, Inc.   An informative service and publishing company, founded in 1945, with a reputation for publishing definitive reference works on all aspects of American government and politics. Its *Congressional Quarterly Weekly Report* (Library of Congress no. JK1 .C15), begun in 1945, is an exhaustive summary of the workings of the Congress each week. The *CQ Almanac*, an exhaustive summary of each session of the Congress, is published every spring. Its *Congress and the Nation*, a compendium of all acts of the national government for each presidential term, is published every four years. It also publishes the *Congressional Monitor*, a daily report on congressional committee actions; *Congres-*

sional Insight, a weekly analysis of congressional activities; and *Campaign Practices Reports*, a semimonthly report on election and campaign laws.
> Congressional Quarterly, Inc.
> 1414 22d Street, N.W.
> Washington, D.C. 20037

Congressional Record   The publication containing the proceedings of the Congress and issued daily when the Congress is in session. On March 4, 1873, the *Record* began to be officially reported, printed, and published directly by the federal government; prior to that time, the proceedings had been recorded by private reporters. (The *Record* superseded the privately published *Congressional Globe*, which started in 1830.)

congressional township   *See* TOWNSHIP.

congressional veto   *See* VETO, LEGISLATIVE.

congressman/congresswoman   A member of the U.S. House of Representatives. This title is preferred over representative.

Congress, member of   A person elected to either the U.S. Senate or the U.S. House of Representatives. A member of the Senate is usually referred to as senator and a member of the House of Representatives as congressman or congresswoman. The qualifications for members of the Congress are established by the Constitution (Article I, sections 2 and 3). A member of the House of Representatives must be at least twenty-five years of age, must have been a U.S. citizen for at least seven years, and must reside in the state from which he or she is elected to the Congress. When vacancies occur, special elections are held to fill them; members of the House of Representatives are never appointed—vacancies are filled only by election. *Compare to* DELEGATE. A member of the Senate must be at least thirty years of age, must have been a U.S. citizen for at least nine years, and must be a resident of the state he or she represents in the Congress. Until the Seventeenth Amendment was ratified in 1913, senators were elected by their state legislatures. The amendment required that they be popularly elected. When a vacancy occurs in the Senate for any reason, the Seventeenth Amendment directs the governor of the state to call an election to fill it and authorizes the state legislature to make provision for an immediate appointment (if lawful) pending such election. The senator appointed serves only until either the next general election or a special election. The senator chosen in a special election serves only the remainder of the original term.

REFERENCES

For an explanation of why the Congress as a whole is respected so much less than its individual members, see Glenn R. Parker and Roger H. Davidson, Why do Americans love their congressmen so much more than their Congress? *Legislative Studies Quarterly* 4 (February 1979).

For an analysis of why there are really two Congresses (the first being the national policymaking body and the second being "a collectivity of independently chosen political entrepreneurs"), see Roger H. Davidson and Walter J. Oleszek, *Congress and Its Members,* 2d ed. (Washington, D.C.: Congressional Quarterly, 1985).

For an argument that the more the Congress changes the more it remains the same, see William J. Keefe, *Congress and the American People,* 3d ed. (Englewood Cliffs, NJ: Prentice-Hall, 1987).

To find basic data on, and the voting records of, all members of the Congress, seek out the latest editions of the *Almanac of American Politics,* published by the *National Journal;* or *Politics in America: Members of Congress in Washington and at Home,* published by Congressional Quarterly.

congress, session of Each Congress is composed of two sessions. A new session of the Congress begins each January 3 at noon and continues until adjourned sine die later that year.

Congress, United States The legislative branch of the United States government. The Congress of the United States was created by Article I, Section 1, of the Constitution, which provides that "all legislative powers herein granted shall be vested in a Congress of the United States, which shall consist of a Senate and House of Representatives."

The Senate is composed of one hundred members, two from each state, who are elected to serve for a term of six years. Senators were originally chosen by the state legislatures. This procedure was changed by the Seventeenth Amendment to the Constitution, adopted in 1913, which made the election of senators a function of the people. There are three classes of senators, and a new class is elected every two years. James Madison wrote of the Senate in Federalist 62 that "such an institution may be sometimes necessary as a defense to the people against their own temporary errors and delusions."

The House of Representatives now comprises 435 representatives. The number representing each state is determined by population, but every state is entitled to at least one representative. Members are elected by the people for two-year terms, all terms running for the same period. James Madison wrote of the importance of the House in Federalist 52:

> As it is essential to liberty that the government in general should have a common interest with the people, so it is particularly essential that the [House of Representatives] should have an immediate dependence on, and an intimate sympathy with, the people. Frequent elections are unquestionably the only policy by which this dependence and sympathy can be effectually secured.

A resident commissioner from Puerto Rico (elected for a four-year term) and delegates (elected for a term of two years) from American Samoa, the District of Columbia, Guam, and the Virgin Islands complete the composition of the Congress. The resident commissioner and delegates may take part in committee and floor discussions and vote in committees but cannot vote on the floor.

REFERENCES

For histories of the Congress, see Congressional Quarterly, Inc., *Origins and Development of Congress,* 2d ed. (Washington, D.C.: Congressional Quarterly, 1982);

Robert U. Goehlert and John R. Sayre, *The United States Congress: A Bibliography* (New York: Free Press, 1982).

U.S. Senate
The Capitol
Washington, D.C. 20510
(202) 224–3121

U.S. House of Representatives
The Capitol
Washington, D.C. 20515
(202) 224–3121

Major Differences Between House and Senate

House	Senate
Larger (435 members)	Smaller (100 members)
Shorter term (two years)	Longer term (six years)
More hierarchical	Less hierarchical
Quicker to act	Slower to act
More rigid rules	Less rigid rules
Limited debate	Unlimited debate
Less evenly distributed power	More evenly distributed power
More policy specialization	Less policy specialization
Less personal	More personal
Less-"important" constituencies	More-"important" constituencies
Less prestige	More prestige

Source: Adapted from William J. Keefe, Henry J. Abraham, William H. Flanigan, Charles O. Jones, Morris S. Ogul, and John W. Spanier, *American Democracy: Institutions, Politics, and Policies,* 2d ed. (Chicago: Dorsey, 1986); and Lewis A. Froman, Jr., *The Congressional Process* (Boston: Little, Brown, 1967).

Connecticut compromise   The proposal put forth by the Connecticut delegation to the Constitutional Convention of 1787 that melded elements of the Virginia plan and the New Jersey plan into the present arrangement of the U.S. Congress: one house in which each state has an equal vote (the Senate) and one house in which representation is based on population (the House).

Connecticut, Fundamental Orders of   *See* FUNDAMENTAL ORDERS OF CONNECTICUT.

Connell v Higginbotham 403 U.S. 207 (1971) The U.S. Supreme Court case that held that it was unconstitutional to require public employees to swear that they "do not believe in the overthrow of the Government of the United States or of the State of Florida by force or violence." The Court reasoned that, at the very least, the Constitution required that a hearing or inquiry be held to determine the reasons for refusal. *Compare to* LOYALTY.

conscientious objector   A person who will not accept military service because of religious or personal beliefs. Whether a person is a true conscientious objector or merely seeking to avoid military service is a question that has been decided on an individual basis by local draft boards and the courts. Once conscientious objector status has been granted, the potential draftee does not have the right to refuse military or alternative service, only the right not to participate in combat. The U.S. Supreme Court has held in *United States v Seeger,* 380 U.S. 128 (1965), and in *Welsh v United States,* 398 U.S. 333 (1970), that people without "traditional" religious beliefs can be conscientious objectors. But the Court, in *Gillette v United States,* 401 U.S. 437 (1971), held that one cannot be a conscientious objector just for a specific war (the Vietnam War, in this case).

REFERENCE
John T. Hansen, Judicial review of in-service conscientious objector claims, *UCLA Law Review* 17 (May 1970).

conscription   The authority of the U.S. Congress to demand the enrollment of men in military service. The U.S. Supreme Court held in *Selective Draft Law Cases,* 245 U.S. 366 (1918), that the power of conscription is implied by the constitutional power to raise armies. When the Constitution was written it was understood that the assembling of state militias was to be the basis of any significant military forces; therefore, conscription was never directly addressed in the document. The founders were very concerned that a national army raised the threat of "royal" forces under the command of a "king." The story goes that at the Constitutional Convention it was moved by one of the delegates that "the standing army be restricted to five thousand men at any one time." George Washington, as chairman of the convention, could not offer an amending motion himself, so he asked another delegate to suggest the amendment that "no foreign army should invade the United States at any time with more than three thousand troops."

REFERENCES

Leon Friedman, Conscription and the Constitution: The original understanding, *Michigan Law Review* 67 (June 1969);

Michael J. Malbin, Conscription, the Constitution and the framers: An historical analysis, *Fordham Law Review* 40 (May 1972);

M. Mushkat, Jr., Military manpower procurement: From conscription to a voluntary service, *Political Science* 31 (December 1979);

Robert K. Griffith, Jr., Conscription and the all-volunteer army in historical perspective, *Parameters: Journal of the US Army War College* 10 (September 1980);

Michael Useem, Conscription and class, *Society* 18 (March/April 1981).

consensual encounter *See* IMMIGRATION AND NATURALIZATION SERVICE V HERMAN DELGATO.

consensus Agreement; a convergence of public opinion; a time of temporary truce between normally hostile political parties and factions. A political consensus is not necessarily total agreement and harmony; but it does represent agreement enough that action can be taken knowing that there is far more than majority support behind it. The concept of consensus was first analyzed by Marcus Tullius Cicero (106–43 BC), the Roman politician and philosopher who wrote that a consensus was a prerequisite for the creation and endurance of a republican form of government. Since the 1950s, some historians and political scientists have argued from various perspectives that the American polity did not need either an IDEOLOGY or ideological confrontation because the nation, fortunately, possessed a common set of values and beliefs (a consensus) that obviated the need for such conflict.

REFERENCES

Herbert McClosky, Consensus and ideology in American politics, *American Political Science Review* 58 (June 1964);

Robert E. Lane, The politics of consensus in an age of affluence, *American Political Science Review* 59 (December 1965);

Murray Clark Havens, *The Challenges to Democracy: Consensus and Extremism in American Politics* (Austin: University of Texas Press, 1965);

Sidney Hyman, *The Politics of Consensus* (New York: Random House, 1968).

Thomas Jefferson Pleads for a Consensus

All will of course arrange themselves under the will of the law, and unite in common efforts for the common good. All too will bear in mind this sacred principle, that though the will of the majority is in all cases to prevail, that will, to be rightful, must be reasonable; that the minority possess their equal rights, which equal laws must protect, and to violate which would be oppression.

Let us then, fellow-citizens, unite with one heart and one mind, let us restore to social intercourse that harmony and affection without which liberty and even life itself are but dreary things. And let us reflect, that having banished from our land that religious intolerance under which mankind so long bled and suffered, we have yet gained little, if we countenance a political intolerance, as despotic as wicked and as capable of as bitter and bloody persecutions . . . . Every difference of opinion is not a difference of principle. We have called by different names brethren of the same principle. We are all Republicans; we are all Federalists.

Source: First Inaugural Address, March 4, 1801.

---

consent calendar *See* CALENDAR, CONSENT.

consent of the governed The notion that the institutions of government must be based on the will of the people. The Declaration of Independence asserts that "governments are instituted among men, deriving their just powers from the consent of the governed, that whenever any form of government becomes destructive of these ends, it is the right of the people to alter or abolish it." While this theme can be traced back to PLATO, it was JOHN LOCKE's development of the idea that most influenced the Founding Fathers.

consent order A regulatory agency procedure to induce voluntary compliance with its policies. A consent order usually takes the form of a formal agreement whereby an industry or company agrees to stop a practice in conservation

exchange for the agency's cessation of legal action against it. *Compare to* CEASE-AND-DESIST ORDER.

conservation The protection, preservation, replenishment, and prudent use of natural resources, which indicates the planned use of public lands, forests, wildlife, water, and minerals. Federal conservation programs and policies have a long history: the greatest efforts at conservation in the continental United States were made during the administrations of Theodore Roosevelt (1901–1909) and Franklin D. Roosevelt (1933–1945). The Department of the Interior, established in 1849, is the custodian of the national government's natural resources. Conservation policy over the years has tended to be a fight for the soul—or control—of that department. Since the 1970s, conservation groups, such as the Sierra Club and the National Audubon Society, have joined with other groups interested in environmental policy to take a more active role in lobbying for conservation issues. The basic policy issue in conservation has always been whether preservation or controlled use would win out over industrial exploitation or vice versa. *Compare to* ENVIRONMENTAL POLICY; NATIONAL ENVIRONMENTAL POLICY ACT OF 1969.

REFERENCES
Samuel P. Hays, *Conservation and the Gospel of Efficiency: The Progressive Conservation Movement, 1890–1920* (Cambridge, MA: Harvard University Press, 1959);
Frank Ellis Smith, *The Politics of Conservation* (New York: Pantheon, 1966);
Joseph M. Petulla, *American Environmental History: The Exploitation and Conservation of Natural Resources* (San Francisco: Boyd and Fraser, 1977);
A. L. Riesch Owen, *Conservation under F.D.R.* (New York: Praeger, 1983).

conservatism Adherence to a political disposition that tends to prefer the status quo and accepts change only in moderation. Both major parties have historically had a substantial number of conservatives, but since the 1960s many of the conservatives in the Democratic party (especially from the South) have been shifting to the Republicans. Conservatives are most often found among those who have, or have the potential to have, wealth and property. They naturally resist change, because they have something to lose. As John Kenneth Galbraith wrote in *American Capitalism* (Boston: Houghton Mifflin, 1956): "It is a simple matter of arithmetic that change *may* be costly to the man who has something: it cannot be so to the man who has nothing." If modern conservatism can be said to have a founding father, that person would be Edmund Burke (1729–1797), the British politician who asserted that a political community should conserve the best policies of the past by carefully, slowly, blending them into the ever-evolving future. Conservatism's founding document is often held to be Burke's *Reflections on the Revolution in France* (1790), in which he said that "it is with infinite caution that any man ought to venture upon pulling down an edifice which has answered in any tolerable degree for ages the common purposes of society." *Compare to* REACTIONARY; RIGHT.

REFERENCES
Clinton Rossiter, *Conservatism in America* (New York: Knopf, 1955);
Alan L. Clem, Do representatives increase in conservatism as they increase in seniority? *Journal of Politics* 39 (February 1977);
David Noble, Conservatism in the U.S.A., *Journal of Contemporary History* 13 (October 1978);
David Y. Allen, Modern conservatism: The problem of definition, *Review of Politics* 43 (October 1981);
A. James Reichley, The conservative roots of the Nixon, Ford, and Reagan administrations, *Political Science Quarterly* 96 (Winter 1981–82);
Karen O'Connor and Lee Epstein, The rise of conservative interest group litigation, *Journal of Politics* 45 (May 1983).

conservatism, new 1 Peter Viereck's conception of a "non-Republican, non-commercialist, non-conformist" conservatism that would synthesize the "ethical New Deal social reforms with the more pessimistic, anti-mass insights of America's Burkean founders" (see his 1949 *Conservatism Revisited*). Unfortunately, in an author's note to the 1962 edition

(New York: Collier Books), Viereck found that "the new conservatism has at least halfway degenerated into a facade for either plutocratic profiteering or fascist-style thought-control nationalism." **2** The resurgence of the Republican party under the leadership of Ronald Reagan in the 1970s and 1980s. This built upon the foundation established by Barry Goldwater in his 1964 presidential bid. *Compare to* RIGHT, NEW.

conservative coalition *See* COALITION.

conservative, neo *See* NEOCONSERVATISM.

consolidated government *See* METROPOLITAN GOVERNMENT.

constable A law enforcement officer in a town or township. The word comes from the Latin *comes*, meaning a companion, and *stabulum*, meaning stable. So the first constables were stable attendants. Over the centuries, they worked themselves up to be guards; thus the modern meaning.

constant dollar A dollar value adjusted for changes in prices. Constant dollars are derived by dividing current dollar amounts by an appropriate price index, a process generally known as deflating. The result is a constant-dollar series as it would presumably exist if prices and transactions were the same in all subsequent years as in the base year. Any changes in such a series would reflect only changes in the real volume of goods and services. Constant dollar figures are commonly used for computing the gross national product and its components and for estimating total budget outlays. *Compare to* CURRENT DOLLAR.

constituency **1** A legislator's geographical district. **2** The voters to whom an elected official is responsible. The constituency for a U.S. congressman is a district; for a U.S. senator, a state; and for the president, the entire nation. *See also* HOME STYLE.
REFERENCES
Warren E. Miller and Donald E. Stokes, Constituency influence in Congress, *American Political Science Review* 57 (March 1963);

Malcolm E. Jewell, Legislator-constituency relations and the representative process, *Legislative Studies Quarterly* 8 (August 1983);
Amoz Kats, Can a party represent its constituency? *Public Choice* 44:3 (1984).

constituent **1** One who lives in a legislator's district. **2** One of a group that an elected representative or elected political executive represents.
REFERENCES
Sam Peltzman, Constituent interest and congressional voting, *Journal of Law & Economics* 27 (April 1984);
Michael W. Combs, John R. Hibbing, and Susan Welch, Black constituents and congressional roll call votes, *Western Political Quarterly* 37 (September 1984).

constituent power **1** The right of the people as the ultimate sovereign to amend a constitution as exercised by their representatives in a legislature. **2** The authority of a constitutional convention.
REFERENCE
Murray Forsyth, Thomas Hobbes and the constituent power of the people, *Political Studies* 29:2 (1981).

constitution **1** The basic political and legal structures prescribing the rules by which a government operates. There are three kinds of constitutions: (1) written, which are based upon a specific document supplemented by judicial interpretations and traditional practices; (2) unwritten, where there is no specific document but many laws, judicial decisions, and accepted practices that in their totality establish the principles of governance; and (3) autocratic, where all power is in the hands of a dictator or elite, which defines governance as it wills—even though the state may have a legal document called a constitution calling for democratic governance. James Madison wrote in Federalist #57 that "the aim of every political constitution is, or ought to be, first to obtain for rulers men who possess most wisdom to discern, and most virtue to pursue, the common good of the society; and in the next place, to take the most effectual precautions for keeping them virtuous whilst they continue to hold their public trust." **2** The Constitution of the United States (see appendix A). It is the oldest written constitution continuously in force and a constant example to the rest of the world of the benefits and effectiveness of such a well-crafted document. But the U.S. Constitution is more than just a piece of fading parchment—it is the national icon, the premier symbol of American freedom and governance; above all, it represents the collective political will of the American people over two centuries to maintain their republican form of government. **3** A constitution of an American state. **4** The political culture of a community or nation. *Compare to* ARISTOTLE. **5** The formal rules prescribing the governance practices of a club, an association, a union, a political party, and so on, even though the rules may be called charters, by-laws, articles of association, and the like.

REFERENCES

1   Graham Maddox, A note on the meaning of "constitution," *American Political Science Review* 76 (December 1982).
2   Leonard W. Levy, ed., *Encyclopedia of the American Constitution,* 4 vols. (New York: Macmillan, 1986);
    Suzanne Robitaille Ontiveros, ed., *The Dynamic Constitution: A Historical Bibliography* (Santa Barbara, CA: ABC-Clio, 1986).
3   Daniel J. Elazar, The principles and traditions underlying American state constitutions, *Publius* 12 (Winter 1982).
4   Michael Kammen, *A Machine That Would Go of Itself: The Constitution in American Culture* (New York: Knopf, 1986).

constitutional   Consistent with and reflective of the U.S. Constitution, which lies at the very heart of the American political system and establishes the framework and rules of the game within which that system operates. It defines the roles and powers of the legislative, judicial, and executive branches, delineates the extent of federal political power, and places limitations on the authority of the states. Moreover, American politics have grown up around the Constitution and have been, thereby, "constitutionalized." Many domestic political issues are eventually treated in constitutional terms; for example, civil rights, crime, pornography, abortion, women's rights, and impeachment, to name but some of the more obvious cases. Only the realm of foreign affairs has substantially escaped this tendency. In addressing matters of government and politics, Americans are likely to pose as the first question, "Is it constitutional?" Only afterward are the desirabilities of policies and government arrangements considered on their own merits.

But what is constitutional is often a matter of political debate and considerable conflict. In October 1986, U.S. Attorney General Edwin Meese renewed the debate on what is constitutional when he proclaimed in a speech at Tulane University that the rulings of the Supreme Court were not "the supreme law of the land." The Constitution was. Therefore, Meese argued, citizens might be obligated to obey only the "original intent" and not the intent as the Court interprets it. After all, Court rulings are not definitive; it has reversed itself several hundred times. But if the Court is not the national referee of what is or is not constitutional, who or what will be? In spite of Meese's attack on the Court, it remains solidly ensconced as the referee in the constant battle over what is constitutional. *See also* BILL OF RIGHTS.

constitutional amendment   **1** An addition to a constitution. **2** A proposed change to the U.S. Constitution or to a state constitution. *See* AMENDMENT.

constitutional convention   A group chosen either by popular vote or legislative appointment to create or revise a constitution. After a new or revised constitution has been produced by the constitutional convention, it must be ratified either by the people or their legislature. The various states have had more than two hundred constitutional conventions in the last two centuries; the United States has had only one, the Constitutional Convention of 1787, even though the U.S. Constitution in Article V provides for the calling of a convention at the request of two-thirds of the states.

A constitutional convention is one way of amending the constitution. In recent years, political conservatives have been urging a convention to enact a BALANCED BUDGET AMENDMENT, and by 1985 over half the states had passed bills requesting such a convention. However, no convention could be limited to one amendment: it might open up a Pandora's box of new troubles, or it might be the means of fine tuning one of the greatest political instruments in world history—if the delegates collectively have the same political acumen as the founders.

REFERENCES

Elmer E. Cornell, Jr., Jay S. Goodman, and Wayne R. Swanson, *State Constitutional Conventions: The Politics of the Revision Process in Seven States* (New York: Praeger, 1975);

Wilbur Edel, Amending the Constitution by convention: Myths and realities, *State Government* 55:2 (1982);

Geoffrey Marshall, What are constitutional conventions? *Parliamentary Affairs* 38 (Winter 1985).

Constitutional Convention of 1787 The meeting in Philadelphia, May 25 to September 18, at which fifty-five delegates from the various states designed the U.S. Constitution. The convention was called to revise the Articles of Confederation. Instead, the convention, presided over by George Washington, discarded the articles and designed an entirely new framework for American governance. Benjamin Franklin, a delegate from Pennsylvania, told his fellow delegates on the next to the last day of the convention:

I agree to this Constitution with all its faults— if they are such—because I think a general government necessary for us, and there is no form of government but what may be a blessing to the people if well administered; and I believe, further, that this is likely to be well administered for a course of years, and can only end in despotism, as other forms have done before it, when the people shall become so corrupted as to need despotic government, being incapable of any other. I doubt, too, whether any other convention we can obtain may be able to make a better Constitution; for, when you assemble a number of men, to have the advantage of their joint wisdom, you inevitably assemble with those men all their prejudices, their passions, their errors of opinion, their local interests, and their selfish views. From such an assembly can a perfect production be expected? It therefore astonishes me, sir, to find this system approaching so near to perfection as it does; and I think it will astonish our enemies, who are waiting with confidence to hear that our counsels are confounded.

See also CONNECTICUT COMPROMISE; FEDERALIST PAPERS; JAMES MADISON; NEW JERSEY PLAN; VIRGINIA PLAN.

REFERENCES

Catherine Drinker Bowen, *Miracle at Philadelphia: The Story of the Constitutional Convention, May to September 1787* (Boston: Little, Brown, 1966, 1987);

Ratification of the Constitution

State	Date	Vote
1. Delaware	December 7, 1787	Unanimous
2. Pennsylvania	December 12, 1787	46–32
3. New Jersey	December 19, 1787	Unanimous
4. Georgia	January 2, 1788	Unanimous
5. Connecticut	January 9, 1788	128–40
6. Massachusetts	February 6, 1788	187–168
7. Maryland	April 28, 1788	63–11
8. South Carolina	May 23, 1788	149–73
9. New Hampshire	June 21, 1788	57–47
10. Virginia	June 25, 1788	89–79
11. New York	July 26, 1788	30–27
12. North Carolina	November 21, 1789	194–77
13. Rhode Island	May 29, 1790	34–32

Clinton Rossiter, *1787: The Grand Convention* (New York: Macmillan, 1976);

Christopher Wolfe, On understanding the Constitutional Convention of 1787, *Journal of Politics* 39 (February 1977);

Ann Stuart Diamond, The zenith of separation of powers theory: The Federal Convention of 1787, *Publius* 8 (Summer 1978);

Calvin C. Jillson and Cecil L. Eubanks, The political structure of constitution making: The Federal Convention of 1787, *American Journal of Political Science* 28 (August 1984);

Wilbourn E. Benton, ed., *1787: Drafting the U.S. Constitution* (College Station: Texas A&M University Press, 1986).

constitutional court Any court specifically authorized by a constitution; for example, the U.S. Supreme Court, which is authorized by Article III of the Constitution. This is in contrast to a legislative court, which is created by statute without specific constitutional authorization, such as the U.S. Court of Military Appeals.

constitutional government A form of limited government in which a constitution, whether written, as is the case in the United States, or unwritten, as is the case in England, establishes who has the right to what powers; and in which any officer who violates constitutional provisions ceases to hold power legitimately and thus is removable from office by constitutional provisions for IMPEACHMENT or the people's right of REVOLUTION.

constitutional initiative *See* INITIATIVE, CONSTITUTIONAL.

constitutionalism The evolution of constitutional thinking through the ages. While theorizing on constitutions goes back to ARISTOTLE, modern theory stems from the seventeenth-century social contract theorists. The hallmark of modern thinking on constitutions is the notion of a limited government whose ultimate authority is the consent of the governed.

REFERENCES

Francis D. Wormuth, *The Origins of Modern Constitutionalism* (New York: Harper & Row, 1949);

A. E. Dick Howard, *The Road from Runnymede: Magna Carta and Constitutionalism in America* (Charlottesville: University of Virginia Press, 1968);

Charles H. McIlwain, *Constitutionalism and the Changing World* (New York: Cambridge University Press, 1969).

constitutionalist One who believes that the U.S. Constitution, more than anything else, has guided the development of American politics and culture; that the existence of the document and its revered place in the American consciousness largely differentiates the United States from other nations. What better example is there of the constitutionalist view of American society than the discussions of public policy innovations that start or end with the question: "Is it constitutional?"

constitutional law That area of the law concerned with the interpretation and application of the nation's highest law—the Constitution of the United States.

constitutional officers Those positions in a government specifically established by its constitution (such as president or governor) as opposed to positions created by subsequent legislation or executive order.

constitutional right A prerogative guaranteed to the people by a constitution. For example, the Fourth Amendment of the U.S. Constitution guarantees "the right of the people to be secure in their persons, houses, papers, and effects, against unreasonable searches and seizures," and the Eighth Amendment guarantees that "excessive bail shall not be required."

REFERENCES

David Fellman, *The Constitutional Right of Association* (Chicago: University of Chicago Press, 1963);

Stephen P. Halbrook, *That Every Man Be Armed: The Evolution of a Constitutional Right* (Albuquerque: University of New Mexico Press, 1984).

constitution, economic interpretation of A reference to Charles A. Beard's (1874–1948) contention, in *An Economic Interpretation of the Constitution of the United States* (New York:

Macmillan, 1913), that the founders wrote the U.S. Constitution in large measure to protect their economic interests and that it is "an economic document drawn with superb skill by men whose property interests were immediately at stake." While best known for explaining how the founders developed a political system to protect their economic interests, Beard was one of the most influential of all American historians in part because of the sheer number of his books (more than fifty), often written with his wife, Mary (1876–1958), and which in their totality sold many millions. In addition to being both a major scholar and popular historian, Beard was also a major figure in the early evolution of public administration.

REFERENCES

Ellen Nore, *Charles A. Beard: An Intellectual Biography* (Carbondale: Southern Illinois University Press, 1983);

Charles T. Goodsell, Charles A. Beard, prophet for public administration, *Public Administration Review* 46 (March/April 1986).

For modest support of Beard's thesis, see James E. Ferguson, The nationalists of 1781–1783 and the economic interpretation of the Constitution, *Journal of American History* 56:2 (1969);

Pope McCorkle, The historian as intellectual: Charles Beard and the constitution reconsidered, *American Journal of Legal History* 28 (October 1984).

For rebuttals, see Robert E. Brown, *Charles Beard and the Constitution* (Princeton, NJ: Princeton University Press, 1956);

Forest McDonald, *We The People: The Economic Origin of the Constitution* (Chicago: University of Chicago Press, 1963).

Constitution, living The governing document of the United States whose meaning changes and evolves over time in response to new circumstances. This evolution takes place mainly in the minds of the justices of the U.S. Supreme Court, not to mention other officials, whose actions and decisions constantly forge the written Constitution into directions never imagined by the framers. Yet this is in accord with their intent. In 1789 Thomas Jefferson wrote to James Madison that "no society can make a perpetual constitution, or even a perpetual law. The earth belongs always to the living generation." Ultimately, the Constitution is whatever each succeeding Supreme Court says it is.

REFERENCES

Saul K. Padover, *The Living U.S. Constitution,* rev. ed. (New York: World, 1968);

William H. Rehnquist, The notion of a living Constitution, *Texas Law Review* 54 (May 1976).

constructive engagement A diplomatic phrase for maintaining political and economic ties with regimes with whom a nation has many disagreements in the hope that the ties will gradually lead to changes in the regime's objectionable policies and practices. It has often been used to describe the relations of the United States with South Africa.

REFERENCES

John Seiler, Has constructive engagement died? *Orbis* 25 (Winter 1982);

Sanford J. Ungar and Peter Vale, South Africa: Why constructive engagement failed, *Foreign Affairs* 64 (Winter 1985–86);

Michael Clough, Beyond constructive engagement, *Foreign Policy* 61 (Winter 1985).

consumer movement The continuous efforts of citizen pressure and government action for such things as the wholesomeness and safety of consumer products, consumer representation on government boards, truth in labeling, and hospital cost containment. While the movement has its roots in the progressive movement, its modern impetus is usually traced to the 1960s auto safety efforts of RALPH NADER.

REFERENCE

Michael Pertschuk, *Revolt Against Regulation: The Rise and Pause of the Consumer Movement* (Berkeley and Los Angeles: University of California Press, 1982).

Landmark Consumer Legislation

1906 **Pure Food and Drug Act** outlawed adulterated food and drugs.

1914 **Federal Trade Commission Act** inhibited deceptive advertising of food, drugs, and cosmetics.

1938	**Food, Drug and Cosmetics Act** made manufacturers prove the safety of drugs.
1958	**Food, Drug and Cosmetics Act amendments** made manufacturers prove the safety of food additives and banned additives that cause cancer in humans or animals.
1962	**Food, Drug and Cosmetics Act amendments** made manufacturers prove the effectiveness of drugs.
1966	**Fair Packaging and Labeling Act** prohibited deceptive packaging and labeling.
1966	**National Traffic and Motor Vehicle Safety Act** established safety standards for tires and motor vehicles.
1968	**Truth-in-Lending Act** made lenders inform consumers of total cost of loans.
1970	**Highway Safety Act** created the National Highway Traffic Safety Administration.
1972	**Consumer Product Safety Act** created the Consumer Product Safety Commission.

consumer price index (CPI) The Bureau of Labor Statistics' cost-of-living index, the monthly statistical measure of the average change in prices over time in a fixed market basket of goods and services. The CPI is one of the nation's most important measures of IN-FLATION/DEFLATION. Many employment and labor union contracts relate wage increases directly to changes in the CPI.

REFERENCES

Robert J. Gordon, The consumer price index: Measuring inflation and causing it, *Public Interest* 63 (Spring 1981);

Richard W. Wahl, Is the consumer price index a fair measure of inflation? *Journal of Policy Analysis and Management* 1 (Summer 1982);

John L. Marcoot, Revisions of the consumer price index now under way, *Monthly Labor Review* 108 (April 1985).

Consumer Product Safety Commission (CPSC) The federal commission created by the Consumer Product Safety Act of 1972 to protect the public against unreasonable risks of injury from consumer products; to assist consumers to evaluate the comparative safety of consumer products; to develop uniform safety standards for consumer products and minimize conflicting state and local regulations; and to promote research and investigation into the causes and prevention of product-related deaths, illnesses, and injuries.

REFERENCE

R. David Pittle, The Consumer Product Safety Commission, *California Management Review* 18 (Summer 1976).

Consumer Product Safety Commission
5401 Westbard Ave.
Bethesda, MD 20207
(301) 492-6580

containment The underlying basis of U.S. foreign and military policy since World War II, to contain the expansion of communist influence. It was first espoused by George F. Kennan in a June 1947 *Foreign Affairs* article, The sources of soviet conduct, in which he asserted that "Soviet pressure against the free institutions of the Western World is something that can be contained by the adroit and vigilant application of counterforce." (The official author of this article was X because Kennan wrote it while serving as a Foreign Service officer; but it was never a secret who the actual author was.)

REFERENCES

Charles Gati, What containment meant, *Foreign Policy* 7 (Summer 1972);

Samuel P. Huntington, After containment: The functions of the military establishment, *Annals of the American Academy of Political and Social Science* 406 (March 1973);

William Welch, Containment: American and soviet versions, *Studies in Comparative Communism* 6 (Autumn 1973);

Robert E. Osgood, The revitalization of containment, *Foreign Affairs* 60:3 (1982).

contempt of court The intentional obstruction of a court in the administration of justice; or an action calculated to lessen a court's authority or dignity; or the failure to obey a court's lawful orders. Flight to avoid prosecution or to avoid prison following conviction is usually prosecuted as contempt of court.

REFERENCE

Ronald L. Goldfarb, *The Contempt Power* (Garden City, NY: Anchor, 1971).

continuing appropriations The means by which the U.S. Congress allows federal agencies to continue operations when their annual budget appropriations has been delayed because of the usual political crisis over the budget. When a fiscal year begins and the Congress has not yet enacted all the regular appropriation bills for that year, it passes a joint resolution continuing appropriations at rates generally based on the previous year's appropriations for government agencies not yet funded.

continuing resolution Legislation that provides budget authority for specific ongoing activities when the regular fiscal-year appropriation for such activities has not been enacted by the beginning of the fiscal year. The continuing resolution usually specifies a maximum rate at which the agency may incur an obligation based on the rate of the prior year, the president's budget request, or an appropriation bill passed by either or both houses of the Congress.

contract authorizations Stopgap provisions, found in both authorization and appropriation bills, that permit the federal government to let contracts or to obligate itself for future payments from funds not yet appropriated. The assumption is that funds will be available for payment when contracted debts come due.

contracting out Having work performed outside an organization's own work force. Contracting out is often an area of union-management disagreement, especially in the public sector. While many unions recognize management's right to occasionally subcontract a job requiring specialized skills and equipment not possessed by the organization or its employees, they oppose the letting of work that could be done by the organization's own work force. In particular, unions are concerned if work normally performed by its members is contracted out to firms having inferior wages or working conditions or if such action may result in reduced earnings or layoffs of regular employees. Contracting out is one of the major means of privatizing and thus reducing the size of the public sector.

REFERENCES

Charles Hoch, Municipal contracting in California: Privatizing with class, *Urban Affairs Quarterly* 20 (March 1985);

James Ferris and Elizabeth Graddy, Contracting out: For what? With whom? *Public Administration Review* 46 (July/August 1986).

contras The U.S.-backed "democratic resistance movement" in Nicaragua. The contras oppose the communist Sandinista government. They are called contras by their government because they are contra (counter) revolutionaries (against the revolution). President Ronald Reagan has preferred to call them "freedom fighters" and has had consistent problems getting funding for their guerrilla operations from the Congress. *See* IRAN-CONTRA AFFAIR.

REFERENCES

Christopher Dickey, *With the Contras: A Reporter in the Wilds of Nicaragua* (New York: Simon & Schuster, 1985);

D. Brent Hardt, The Reagan administration's battle for contra aid, *Fletcher Forum* 10 (Summer 1986).

controllability The ability of the U.S. Congress or the president under existing law to control spending during a given fiscal year. Uncontrollable spending—spending that cannot be increased or decreased without changes in existing substantive law—is usually the result of open-ended programs and fixed costs, such as social security and veterans' benefits (sometimes called entitlements), but also includes payments due under obligations incurred during prior years.

controller/comptroller The financial officer of a company or a government agency. For example, the comptroller general of the United States heads the GENERAL ACCOUNTING OFFICE, which audits government agencies. Normally, a controller has the technical skills of an accountant. The basic functions of the office are to supervise accounting and to make sure that funds are spent for acceptable purposes. The AUDIT function comes afterward; it is a review to see that funds were expended correctly.

REFERENCE

Fred Thompson and L. R. Jones, Controllership in the public sector, *Journal of Policy Analysis and Management* 5 (Spring 1986).

convention 1 A political meeting of the members of one party (*see* NATIONAL CONVENTION). 2 A CONSTITUTIONAL CONVENTION. 3 An international agreement on matters less significant than those regulated by treaty. The best-known conventions are probably the Geneva conventions of 1864, 1906, and 1949, which concern the treatment of prisoners of war.

conventional war A conflict fought by regular (and sometimes irregular) military forces using any weapons short of nuclear weapons. Thus conventional forces are military units capable of undertaking operations using only nonnuclear weapons. And a conventional weapon is anything capable of inflicting damage to an enemy so long as that weapon is not nuclear, biological, or chemical.

REFERENCES

Myra Struck McKitrick, A conventional deterrent for NATO: An alternative to the nuclear balance of terror, *Parameters: Journal of the US Army War College* 13 (March 1983);
Samuel F. Wells, Jr., Constraints in conventional war: The American experience, *Jerusalem Journal of International Relations* 7:1, 2 (1984);
Richard K. Betts, Conventional deterrence: Predictive uncertainty and policy confidence, *World Politics* 37 (January 1985);
William M. Arkin, Conventional buildup—A deliberate delusion, *Bulletin of the Atomic Scientists* 41 (February 1985).

conventional wisdom That which is generally believed to be true. However, any writer who uses the phrase is setting something up to be knocked down; so conventional wisdom really means that which most people believe to be true, but really isn't. The phrase first gained currency after John Kenneth Galbraith used it in his *The Affluent Society* (Boston: Houghton Mifflin, 1958). Galbraith observed: "Only posterity is unkind to the man of conventional wisdom, and all posterity does is bury him in a blanket of neglect."

REFERENCES

R. James Woolsey, Planning a navy: The risks of conventional wisdom, *International Security* 3 (Summer 1978);
Aaron D. Rosenbaum, Discard conventional wisdom, *Foreign Policy* 49 (Winter 1982–83);
Walter J. Petersen, Deterrence and compellence: A critical assessment of conventional wisdom, *International Studies Quarterly* 30 (September 1986).

cookie pushers A derogatory term for professional diplomats, implying that they spend their time at social functions (eating cookies) and thus are overly concerned with diplomatic niceties.

cooking the books 1 Creating financial records that do not reflect the truth. 2 Preparing the federal budget. President Ronald Reagan's former director of the Office of Management and Budget, David Stockman, said of the federal budget: "We have increasingly resorted to squaring the circle with accounting gimmicks, evasions, half-truths and downright dishonesty in our budget numbers, debate and advocacy. Indeed, if the SEC had jurisdiction over the Executive and Legislative branches, many of us would be in jail" (*Time,* July 22, 1985).

Cooley v Board of Wardens 12 Howard 299 (1851) The U.S. Supreme Court case that established the Cooley Doctrine—that the states had the right to regulate foreign and interstate commerce if the Congress hadn't dealt with the area of concern. However, once the Congress took action, state legislation could not validly contradict federal law.

REFERENCE

Edwin A. Gere, Jr., Dillon's rule and the Cooley doctrine: Reflections of the political culture, *Journal of Urban History* 8 (May 1982).

Coolidge, Calvin (1872–1933) The vice president who became president (1923–1929)

Calvin Coolidge

cooling-off period Any legal provision that postpones a labor strike or lockout for a specific time to give the parties an additional opportunity to mediate their differences. While the device has great popular appeal, it has proven to be of doubtful value because more time will not necessarily resolve a labor dispute. The first federal requirements for a cooling-off period were set forth in the War Labor Disputes Act of 1943. This was superseded by the national emergency provisions of the Labor-Management Relations (Taft-Hartley) Act of 1947, which called for an eighty-day cooling-off period in the event of a national emergency.

cooperative federalism *See* FEDERALISM, COOPERATIVE.

cooptation The inclusion of new potentially dissident group members into an organization's policy-making process to prevent such elements from being a threat to the organization or its mission.

REFERENCES
The classic analysis of cooptation is found in Philip Selznick's *TVA and the Grass Roots* (Berkeley and Los Angeles: University of California Press, 1949); also see Frederick J. Fleron, Jr., Cooptation as a mechanism of adaptation to change, *Polity* 2 (Winter 1969);
Susan Rose-Ackerman, Cooperative federalism and cooptation, *Yale Law Journal* 92:7 (1983).

upon the death of President Warren G. Harding. Coolidge was a traditional conservative who believed that "the business of America is business." Known as Silent Cal, Coolidge would often sit through entire dinner parties without saying a word. Legend has it that a woman dinner companion told him she made a large bet with her friends that she could get him to say more than three words. Coolidge responded, "You lose." *Compare to:* BOSTON POLICE STRIKE OF 1919.

REFERENCES
Donald R. McCoy, *Calvin Coolidge: The Quiet President* (New York: Macmillan, 1967);
Robert K. Murray, *The Politics of Normalcy: Governmental Theory and Practice in the Harding-Coolidge Era* (New York: Norton, 1973).

The Calvin Coolidge Administration

Major Accomplishments
• The Briand-Kellogg Pact, in which sixty-three nations outlawed war.
• The Rogers Act, which consolidated the U.S. diplomatic and consular service.
• Economic prosperity and an unregulated boom (which, however, led to the biggest bust in history—the Great Depression).

---

copayment A type of cost sharing whereby insured or covered people pay a specified flat amount per unit of service or unit of time (for example, in health insurance, two dollars per office visit and ten dollars per inpatient hospital day), their insurer paying the rest of the cost. The copayment is incurred at the time the service is used. The amount paid does not vary with the cost of the service (unlike coinsurance, which is payment of some percentage of the cost).

REFERENCE

Terry M. Kinney, Medicaid copayments: A bitter pill for the poor, *Journal of Legislation* 10 (Winter 1983).

COPE *See* COMMITTEE ON POLITICAL EDUCATION.

copperhead A term of contempt for supporters of the South who lived in the North during the U.S. Civil War; named for a reddish-brown poisonous snake, sometimes undetectable before it strikes because of its natural camouflage. Now the term can refer to citizens who support the policies of adversary governments.

copyright An author's exclusive right to control the copying of books, articles, movies, and so on. Article I, Section 8, of the U.S. Constitution provides that the Congress shall "promote the progress of science and useful arts, by securing for limited times to authors and inventors the exclusive right to their respective writings and discoveries." According to the Copyright Act of 1976, the legal life of a copyright is the author's life plus fifty years and a flat seventy-five years for one held by a company. The symbol for copyright is ©. Copyrights are registered in the copyright office of the Library of Congress.

REFERENCES

Nicholas Henry, *Copyright, Information Technology, Public Policy* (New York: Dekker, 1975);

Melville B. Nimmer, *A Preliminary View of the Copyright Act of 1976: Analysis and Text* (New York: Bender, 1977).

coroner The county official responsible for determining the causes of deaths occurring under violent, unusual, or suspicious circumstances. Ideally, a coroner (whose title comes from the fact that such officers originally represented the crown) should be both a medical examiner (who performs autopsies) and a trained criminal investigator. Unfortunately, many jurisdictions have no particular qualifications for the office, and it is often a political

plum. Coroners usually have the power to hold a formal hearing or inquest into suspicious deaths. If evidence of wrongdoing is discovered, the case is then turned over to an appropriate prosecutor or grand jury.

REFERENCES

Robert C. Hendrix, *Investigation of Violent and Sudden Death: A Manual for Medical Examiners* (Springfield, IL: Thomas, 1972);

Thomas T. Noguchi, *Coroner at Large* (New York: Simon & Schuster, 1985).

corporate income tax *See* TAX, CORPORATE INCOME.

corporation counsel An attorney for a municipal corporation (a city).

correcting the record The method by which members of the U.S. Congress may change recorded votes. Rules prohibit members from changing their votes after the result has been announced, but frequently, hours, days, or months after a vote has been taken, a member might announce that he or she was incorrectly recorded. In the Senate, a request to change one's vote almost always receives unanimous consent. In the House of Representatives, members are prohibited from changing their votes if the votes were tallied by the electronic voting system. If they were taken by a roll call, a vote may be changed if consent is granted. "Errors" in the text of the *Congressional Record* may be corrected by unanimous consent.

correctional institution A prison, reformatory, house of correction, or other institution for the confinement and possible correction of adults or juveniles convicted of crimes.

corrections A generic term that refers to all government agencies, facilities, programs, procedures, personnel, and techniques concerned with the investigation, intake, custody, confinement, supervision, or treatment of alleged or adjudicated adult offenders, delinquents, or status offenders.

corrupt and contented MUCKRAKER Lincoln Steffens' (1866–1936) famous description of BOSSISM in Philadelphia at the turn of the century.

In 1986, U.S. federal and state correctional institutions housed over 500,000 people.

REFERENCE
Lincoln Steffens, *The Shame of the Cities* (New York: Hill and Wang, 1904).

corruption of blood A medieval legal doctrine that held that people convicted of treason or other major crimes had corrupt blood, which necessarily would be passed on to their children. Consequently, when they were punished, so were their children. Article III, Section 3, of the U.S. Constitution forbids such biblical visiting of "the iniquity of the fathers upon the children" (*Exodus,* chapter 20, verse 5).

corruption, political The unauthorized use of public office for private gain. The most common forms of corruption are bribery, extortion, and the misuse of inside information. While there are isolated pockets of rectitude, just as there are instances of abject venality, most communities come to tolerate the systematic corruption of their officials through one of three patterns:

1. *Nonenforcement policies for officials high in an organization.* For obvious reasons, police departments tend to be the bellwethers of systematic corruption, the only surprise being the shock of political leaders when confronted with the evidence. The most publicized police exposés of recent years were the Knapp Commission hearings in New York City, yet the hearings turned up nothing that had not been well documented about big city police operations since the Wickersham Commission in the early 1930s. While it is more comforting to dwell upon just justices and honest police, thoughtful citizens do not have to be cynics to support Senator Daniel P. Moynihan's contention, made during his youth, that "corruption by organized crime is a normal condition of American local government and politics."

2. *Community indifference.* This sort of toleration of corruption amounts to consent, and a community unwilling to devote the necessary resources to weed out corrupting influences deserves the conditions it tacitly supports.

3. *Encouragement by "leading citizens."* A society cannot reasonably maintain moral standards for its public officials that grossly differ from those of the leaders of the community. While it is not illegal for a businessman to tip a truck driver to insure that a valuable shipment arrives on time, it is quite illegal to tip a municipal construction inspector to insure that he arrives at the construction site at an agreed-upon time. If a plumbing inspector arrives two hours later than his appointment, this could cost the contractor thousands of dollars in unnecessary payroll, since the brickmasons, carpenters, and plasterers, for example, cannot begin their work until the plumbing has been inspected. It is simply good business sense for the contractor to tip the plumbing inspector twenty dollars to show up on time, rather than risk having a variety of skilled workers idle for several expensive hours. But, once started, this tipping of government officials frequently has no end: building plans must be expedited through city architectural reviewers; police must allow construction equipment to be illegally parked on side streets. It

is estimated that about 5 percent of the cost of construction in New York City goes for bribes of public officials. *Compare to* BRIBERY; HONEST GRAFT/DISHONEST GRAFT.

REFERENCES

Edward C. Banfield, Corruption as a feature of government organization, *Journal of Law & Economics* 18 (December 1975);

Barry S. Rundquist, Gerald S. Strom, and John G. Peters, Corrupt politicians and their electoral support: Some experimental observations, *American Political Science Review* 71 (September 1977);

Susan Welch and John G. Peters, Attitudes of U.S. state legislators toward political corruption: Some preliminary findings, *Legislative Studies Quarterly* 2 (November 1977);

John G. Peters and Susan Welch, Political corruption in America: A search for definitions and a theory—Or, if political corruption is in the mainstream of American politics, why is it not in the mainstream of American politics research? *American Political Science Review* 72 (September 1978);

John G. Peters and Susan Welch, The effects of charges of corruption on voting behavior in congressional elections, *American Political Science Review* 74 (September 1980);

David C. Nice, Political corruption in the American states, *American Politics Quarterly* 11 (October 1983);

Michael Johnson, Corruption and political culture in America: An empirical perspective, *Publius* 13 (Winter 1983).

Corwin, Edward S. (1878–1963) A major constitutional law scholar who sought to integrate legal doctrine with societal, political, economic, and larger philosophic issues. He was the leading academic who advocated President Franklin D. Roosevelt's 1937 court-packing plan. Indeed, he was the first witness who was not a member of the administration to testify in favor of it. Corwin would later become the leading academic opponent of a strengthened national executive.

REFERENCES

Edward S. Corwin, *The President: Office and Powers* (New York: New York University Press, 1940; 4th ed., 1957);

Kenneth D. Crews, *Edward S. Corwin and the American Constitution: A Bibliographical Analysis* (Westport, CT: Greenwood, 1985).

cosmopolitanism 1 The concept of an intellectual understanding of a variety of cultures outside one's own, as opposed to parochialism. This later became a term of abuse in the Soviet Union for internal expressions of admiration for any aspect of external bourgeois capitalistic culture. 2 The belief in the ancient ideal of a world state, to which all human beings would belong.

REFERENCE

Frederick Meinecke, *Cosmopolitanism and the National State* (Princeton, NJ: Princeton University Press, 1970).

cosponsor To jointly submit a bill for legislative consideration. In the U.S. Congress there is no limit to the number of cosponsors a bill may have; a very popular bill may even have more cosponsors than is needed for eventual passage. The first senator or representative listed on a bill is the sponsor; all that follow are cosponsors.

REFERENCE

James E. Campbell, Cosponsoring legislation in the U.S. Congress, *Legislative Studies Quarterly* 7 (August 1982).

cost-of-living adjustment (COLA) An increase in compensation in response to increasing inflation. Some labor union contracts and some entitlement programs (such as social security) provide for automatic COLAs if inflation reaches predetermined levels.

cost-of-living index *See* CONSUMER PRICE INDEX.

cost-push inflation *See* INFLATION, COST-PUSH.

council-manager plan/county-manager system A form of municipal government in which an elected city council appoints a professional city manager to administer the city government. A county-manager system offers the same essential structure at the county level. *Compare to* CITY MANAGER.

REFERENCES

Richard S. Childs, *The First Fifty Years of the Council-Manager Plan of Municipal Government* (New York: National Municipal League, 1965);

John Porter East, *Council-Manager Government: The Political Thought of Its Founder, Richard S. Childs* (Chapel Hill: University of North Carolina Press, 1965);

David A. Booth, comp., *Council-Manager Government 1940–1964: An Annotated Bibliography* (Chicago: International City Management, 1965);

Robert Boynton and Deil Wright, Mayor-manager relationships in large council-manager cities: A re-interpretation, *Public Administration Review* 31 (January/February 1971).

Council of Economic Advisers (CEA) The U.S. president's primary source of economic advice. It assists the president in preparing various economic reports, including the annual *Economic Report of the President*. Established in the Executive Office of the President by the Employment Act of 1946, the CEA consists of three economists (one designated chair) appointed by the president, with the advice and consent of the Senate, who formulate proposals to "maintain employment, production and purchasing power." While council members are now usually professional economists, the Congress initially objected to them and preferred practical businessmen.

REFERENCES

For histories, see Stephen K. Bailey, *Congress Makes a Law: The Story Behind the Employment Act of 1946* (New York: Columbia University Press, 1950);

Edward S. Flash, *Economic Advice and Presidential Leadership: The Council of Economic Advisers* (New York: Columbia University Press, 1965);

David Naveh, The political role of academic advisers: The case of the U.S. president's Council of Economic Advisers, 1946–1976, *Presidential Studies Quarterly* 11 (Fall 1981);

Roger B. Porter, Economic advice to the president: From Eisenhower to Reagan, *Political Science Quarterly* 98 (Fall 1983);

Murray L. Weidenbaum, The role of the president's Council of Economic Advisers: Theory and reality, *Presidential Studies Quarterly* 16 (Summer 1986).

Council of Economic Advisers
Executive Office Building
Washington, D.C. 20500
(202) 395–5084

council of government (COG) A multijurisdictional cooperative arrangement to permit a regional approach to planning, development, transportation, environment, and other problems that affect a region as a whole. The COGs are substate regional planning agencies established by states and are responsible for areawide review of projects applying for federal funds and for development of regional plans and other areawide special purpose arrangements. They are composed of designated policymaking representatives from each participating government within the region. Some COGs have assumed a more enterprising role in the 1980s by acting as contractors for and service providers to their local governments.

REFERENCES

William J. Pitstick, COGs—Strategies for legislative lobbying, *Public Management* 56 (November 1974);

Charles W. Harris, COGs: A regional response to metro-urban problems, *Growth and Change* 6 (July 1975);

Harry West, The unique role of the regional council administrator, *Municipal Year Book, 1981* (Washington, D.C.: International City Management, 1981);

George Scarborough, A council of governments approach, *National Civic Review* 71 (July/August 1982);

Nelson Wikstrom, *Councils of Governments: A Study of Political Incrementalism* (Chicago: Nelson-Hall, 1985).

Council of State Governments (CSG) The joint agency of all state governments—created, supported, and directed by them. The purpose of the CSG is to strengthen all branches of state government and preserve the state government role in the federal system through catalyzing the expression of states' views on major issues; to conduct research on state programs and problems, assisting in federal-state liaison and state-regional-local cooperation; to offer training, reference, and consultation services to state agencies, officials, and legislators; and to serve as a broad instrument for bringing together all elements of state government. Originally created as the American Legislators Association in 1925, it took its present name in 1933. *See* PUBLIC INTEREST GROUPS.

Council of State Governments
Ironworks Pike
P.O. Box 11910
Lexington, KY 40578
(606) 252-2291

Council on Environmental Quality The federal advisory council that develops and recommends to the president national policies to further environmental quality; continually analyzes changes or trends in the national environment; administers the environmental impact statement process; provides an ongoing assessment of the nation's energy research and development from an environmental and conservation standpoint; and assists the president in the preparation of the annual environmental quality report to the Congress. It was established by the National Environmental Policy Act of 1969 within the Executive Office of the President.

Council on Environmental Quality
722 Jackson Place, N.W.
Washington, D.C. 20503
(202) 395-5750

council ward A legislative district from which a person is elected to a city council.

countercyclical Descriptive of government actions aimed at smoothing out swings in economic activity. Countercyclical actions may take the form of monetary and fiscal policy (such as countercyclical revenue sharing or jobs programs). Automatic (built-in) stabilizers have a countercyclical effect without necessitating changes in government policy.

countervailing duty A retaliatory extra charge that a country places on imported goods to counter the subsidies or bounties granted to the exporters of the goods by their home governments.

REFERENCE
Steven R. Berger, Judicial review of countervailing duty determinations, *Harvard Law International Journal* 19 (Summer 1978).

country desk The unit within the U.S. Department of State that has the daily responsibility of monitoring and analyzing the activities of a given foreign country.

country team In a foreign country, the coordinating and supervisory body headed by the chief of the U.S. diplomatic mission, usually an ambassador, and composed of the senior member of each represented U.S. department or agency.

county The basic unit for administrative decentralization of state government. Although it is typically governed by an elected board or commission, there is a movement at present toward a county administrator or executive (sometimes elected). In Louisiana, the comparable unit is called a parish; in Alaska, it is a borough. In 1982, the United States had 3,041 county governments. Each state determines for itself how many counties it will have. Two states, Connecticut and Rhode Island, have no counties at all.

REFERENCES
John C. Bollens, *American County Government, with an Annotated Bibliography* (Beverly Hills, CA: Sage, 1969);
Susan Walker Torrence, *Grass Roots Government: The County in American Politics* (Washington, D.C.: Luce, 1974);
Herbert Sydney Duncombe, *Modern County Government* (Washington, D.C.: National Association of Counties, 1977).

county agent A field officer of the U.S. Department of Agriculture and one of over three thousand county government officials who is responsible for disseminating information about new agricultural techniques developed by research funded by the U.S. Department of Agriculture and state land-grant universities. The county agent is the grass-roots officer of the Cooperative Extension Service, a partnership of all three levels of government authorized by the Smith-Lever Act of 1914.

REFERENCE

H. C. Sanders, ed., *The Cooperative Extension Service* (Englewood Cliffs, NJ: Prentice-Hall, 1966).

county chairman/county chairwoman The head of a political party organization at the county level who supervises the activities of the party precinct leaders and who helps select (along with other chairs in the state) the state party officials.

REFERENCE

Michael A. Maggiotto and Ronald E. Weber, The impact of organizational incentives on county party chairpersons, *American Politics Quarterly* 14 (July 1986).

county commissioner An elected member of the governing body of a county government, often called a county board or board of supervisors. In some southern states, the elected county commissioners are formally called judges, even though their judicial duties are minimal.

REFERENCES

Vincent L. Marando and Robert D. Thomas, *The Forgotten Governments: County Commissioners as Policy Makers* (Gainesville: University of Florida Press, 1977);
Vincent L. Marando and Robert D. Thomas, County commissioners' attitudes toward growth: A two-state comparison, *Social Science Quarterly* 58 (June 1977).

county-manager system *See* COUNCIL-MANAGER PLAN/COUNTY-MANAGER SYSTEM.

county seat The capital of a county, where the courts and administrative offices are located. In much of the United States, the county seat was so located in the geographical center of the county that it would not be more than one day's ride on horseback from the farthest part of the county.

coup d'état A French phrase meaning a stroke or sharp blow to the state; a change in the leadership of a government brought on by force by people who already hold some form of power (either military or political). A coup d'état technically differs from a revolution in that revolutions are usually brought about by those who are not in power. There has never been a coup d'état in the United States. The closest we may have come to one was in 1783, when a group of unpaid Revolutionary War officers meeting in Newburgh, New York, asked George Washington to help them oust the Congress and take over the government. Washington defused the situation, and the Congress, sensing the danger to its position, quickly paid the officers in one lump sum the five-years' back pay they were each due. *Compare to* DICTATOR.

REFERENCES

James W. Wensyel, The Newburgh conspiracy, *American Heritage* 32 (April/May 1981);
For theoretical analyses of coups d'état, see P. A. J. Waddington, The coup d'état—An application of a systems framework, *Political Studies* 22 (September 1974);
Ekkart Zimmermann, Toward a causal model of military coups d'état, *Armed Forces and Society* 5 (Spring 1979);
Rosemary H. T. O'Kane, A probabilistic approach to the causes of coups d'état, *British Journal of Political Science* 11 (July 1981);
Rosemary H. T. O'Kane, Towards an examination of the general causes of coups d'état, *European Journal of Political Research* 11 (March 1983).

court An agency of the judicial branch of government authorized or established by statute or constitution that consists of one or more judicial officers and that has the authority to decide upon controversies in law and disputed matters of fact brought before it. There are two basic types of courts: those having original jurisdiction to make decisions regarding matters of fact and law (trial courts), and those having appellate jurisdiction to review issues of law in connection with decisions made in specific cases previously adjudicated by other courts and administrative agencies (appeals courts).

Article III of the U.S. Constitution outlines the structure and power of the federal court system and establishes a federal judiciary, which helps maintain and define the rights of American citizens. Article III, Section 2, also contains a guarantee that the trial of all federal crimes, except cases of impeachment, shall be by jury. The Supreme Court has interpreted this guarantee as containing exceptions for "trials of petty offenses," cases rightfully tried before court-martial or other military tribunal, and some cases in which the defendant has voluntarily relinquished his or her right to a jury. This section also requires that a federal criminal trial be held in a federal court sitting in the state where the crime was committed. Thus citizens are protected against being tried without their consent in a place distant from where their alleged violation of federal laws occurred. State constitutions establish parallel court systems at the state level.

court, appellate A court whose primary function is to review the judgments of other courts and of administrative agencies.

court, divided An appeals court, such as the U.S. Supreme Court, whose judges have reached a decision by a narrow majority, say five to four. "Divided" applies only to the case at hand, not to the court in general. Any opinion by a divided court is subject to continued legal debate; but it is just as legally binding as if the court had been unanimous. An equally divided court results in the affirmation of the lower court's decision.

courthouse gang A derisive phrase for the dominant political figures in rural county politics; the political machine of county government.

court-martial 1 A military court that tries members of the armed forces for violations of military law. 2 To force someone to be tried by a military court. The U.S. Supreme Court held in *Ex parte Milligan,* 4 Wallace 2 (1866), that in the United States it is illegal to try civilians by military court when regular courts are available. *See* WRIT OF HABEAS CORPUS.
REFERENCE
David A. Schlueter, The court-martial: An historical survey, *Military Law Review* 87 (Winter 1980).

court of appeals 1 A court that hears appeals from a trial court. In most states, it is the midlevel court, between the trial courts and the state supreme court. However, in some states, where the supreme court is the midlevel court, the appeals court is the highest (in effect the supreme) state court. 2 One of twelve U.S. courts of appeals, the appellate courts below the U.S. Supreme Court, which hear appeals from cases tried in federal district courts. In most cases, a decision by a court of appeals is final, since only a small fraction of its decisions are ever reviewed by the U.S. Supreme Court. Before 1948, these courts were called circuit courts of appeals. They were created in 1891 to relieve the Supreme Court of considering all appeals in cases originally decided by the federal trial courts. The United States is divided into twelve judicial circuits, each of which has a court of appeals. At present, each court of appeals has from four to twenty-three permanent judgeships, depending upon the amount of judicial work in that circuit. The judge senior in commission who has not reached his or her seventieth birthday is the chief judge. One of the justices of the Supreme Court serves as circuit justice for each circuit. Divisions of three judges usually hear cases, but all the judges of the circuit may sit en banc.
REFERENCE
J. Woodford Howard, Jr., *Courts of Appeals in the Federal Judicial System* (Princeton, NJ: Princeton University Press, 1981).

court of general jurisdiction A trial court having original jurisdiction over all subject areas not specifically assigned to a court of limited jurisdiction. These are often called superior or district courts.

court of last resort 1 An appellate court having final jurisdiction over appeals in a given state. 2 The Supreme Court of the United States. 3 The last authority from whom one can hope for a reversal of judgment or opinion. Thus public opinion or history may be perceived as a court of last resort.

court of limited jurisdiction A trial court having original jurisdiction over only that subject area specifically assigned to it by law; for examples: traffic court, small claims court, and probate court.

REFERENCE

Karen M. Knab, ed., *Court of Limited Jurisdiction: National Survey* (Washington, D.C.: Government Printing Office, 1977).

Franklin Roosevelt consults with Harold Ickes, administrator of public works, about his court-packing plan.

court packing 1 President Franklin D. Roosevelt's unsuccessful 1937 attempt to enlarge the U.S. Supreme Court by appointing additional justices who would be more sympathetic to New Deal legislation. Roosevelt sought congressional approval to appoint one new Supreme Court justice for each sitting justice over the age of seventy years. This would have allowed him to immediately put six new justices on the Court for a total of fifteen. The Congress would not approve, but the issue soon became moot because the court suddenly started approving New Deal legislation, a change often referred to as "the switch in time that saved nine." *See also* EDWARD S. CORWIN. 2 Any administration's efforts to fill judicial vacancies with appointees philosophically sympathetic to the administration, rather than with the best qualified candidates, regardless of party affiliation. President Ronald Reagan has been accused of court packing, because his administration has been said to impose an ideological LITMUS TEST for potential judicial appointments.

REFERENCES

1   William E. Leuchtenburg, The origins of Franklin D. Roosevelt's "court-packing" plan, *The Supreme Court Review,* 1966, ed., Philip B. Kurland (Chicago: University of Chicago Press, 1966); Gerald Garvey, Scholar in politics; Edward S. Corwin and the court packing battle, *Princeton University Library Chronicle* 31:1 (1969).

2   Sheldon Goldman, Reaganizing the judiciary: The first term appointments, *Judicature* 68 (April/May 1985).

court, small claims A court that handles civil cases with a value under a specified limit (usually five hundred to a thousand dollars). Such courts are designed to allow the "little person" to take even a large corporation to court. Sessions are often at night, and plaintiffs do not need to be represented by a lawyer—(although corporations usually are).

REFERENCES

Virginia P. Sikes, Small claims arbitration: The need for appeal, *Columbia Journal of Law and Social Problems* 16:3 (1981);

Craig A. McEwen and Richard J. Maiman, Mediation in small claims court: Achieving compliance through consent, *Law and Society Review* 18:1 (1984);

Neil Vidmar, The small claims court: A reconceptualization of disputes and an empirical investigation, *Law and Society Review* 18:4 (1984).

court, special Specialized federal courts created by the U.S. Congress to deal with special classes of cases: (1) the U.S. Tax Court handles disputes between citizens and the Internal Revenue Service; (2) the U.S. Court of Military Appeals is the final appellate tribunal to review court-martial convictions in all the military services; (3) the U.S. Court of International Trade has jurisdiction over any civil action against the United States arising from federal laws governing import transactions; (4) the U.S. Claims Court has original jurisdiction to render judgment on a claim against the United States, an act of the Congress, and expressed or implied contracts with the United States; (5) a bankruptcy court system operates under the supervision of the U.S. district courts. All decisions of these courts are appealable to a court of appeals or directly to the Supreme Court.

court, supreme **1** The highest United States court. *See* SUPREME COURT, UNITED STATES. **2** The highest state court. **3** A midlevel state court of appeals in states such as New York, where the highest state court is a court of appeals.

court, trial A court whose primary function is to initially hear and decide cases. All U.S. district courts are trial courts.

covenant **1** The religious belief that God has promised salvation to man. **2** The biblical tradition of a promise sanctioned by an oath with an appeal to the deity to punish any violation of the covenant. **3** A legally binding instrument, such as a restriction in a deed. While covenants as legal tools are neutral devices, they were once widely used to prevent land and houses from being sold to blacks and Jews. Such restrictive covenants are now illegal through a variety of federal and state civil rights and equal housing laws. **4** An international treaty, such as the Covenant of the League of Nations, the first part of the Treaty of Versailles of 1919, which formally ended World War I. **5** A political compact.

REFERENCES

1   David C. Rapoport, Moses, charisma and covenant, *Western Political Quarterly* 32 (June 1979);
    Daniel J. Elazar, The political theory of covenant: Biblical origins and modern developments, *Publius* 10 (Fall 1980);
    Brian T. Trainor, The politics of peace: The role of the political covenant in Hobbes' *Leviathan, Review of Politics* 47 (July 1985).

2   Clement E. Vose, *Caucasians Only: The Supreme Court, the NAACP, and the Restrictive Covenant Cases* (Berkeley and Los Angeles: University of California Press, 1959);
    Robert C. Elickson, Alternatives to zoning: Covenants, nuisance rules, and fines as land use controls, *University of Chicago Law Review* 40 (Summer 1973).

covert operations Military, police, or intelligence activities that are planned and executed to conceal the identity of, or permit plausible denial by, the sponsor. They differ from clandestine operations in that emphasis is placed on concealment of the identity of the sponsor, rather than on concealment of the operation. *Compare to* OVERT OPERATIONS.

REFERENCES

Richard A. Falk, CIA covert action and international law. *Society* 12 (March/April 1975);

Stephen D. Wrage, A moral framework for covert action, *Fletcher Forum* 4 (Summer 1980);

John Prados, *Presidents' Secret Wars: CIA and Pentagon Covert Operations Since World War II* (New York: Morrow, 1986).

cozy triangles/iron triangles The mutually supportive relations among government agencies, interest groups, and the legislative committee or subcommittee with jurisdiction over their areas of common concern. Such coalitions constantly exchange information, services, and money (in the form of campaign contributions from the interest groups to the members of the legislative committee and budget approval from the committee to the agency). As a whole, they tend to dominate policymaking in their areas of concern. The triangles are considered to be as strong as iron, because the supportive relations are so strong that others elected or appointed to control administrative policy as representatives of the public's interest are effectively prohibited from interfering on behalf of the public. *Compare to* ISSUE NETWORKS.

JOHN W. GARDNER, founder of Common Cause, testified about the operations of cozy triangles before a 1971 meeting of the Senate Government Operations Committee:

As everyone in this room knows but few outside Washington understand, questions of public policy . . . are often decided by a trinity consisting of (1) representatives of an outside body, (2) middle level bureaucrats, and (3) selected members of Congress, particularly those concerned with appropriations. In a given field, these people may have collaborated for years. They have a durable alliance that cranks out legislation and appropriations on behalf of their special interests. Participants in such durable alliances do not want the department secretaries strengthened. The outside special interests are particularly resistant to such change. It took them years to dig their particular tunnel into the public vault, and they don't want the vaults moved.

REFERENCES

Barry M. Casper, Congress and the cozy triangles: The case of energy, *Bulletin of the Atomic Scientists* 33 (May 1977);

Roger H. Davidson, Breaking up those "cozy triangles": An impossible dream? in *Legislative Reform and Public Policy,* eds. Susan Welch and John G. Peters (New York: Praeger, 1977);

Keith E. Hamm, Patterns of influence among committees, agencies, and interest groups, *Legislative Studies Quarterly* 8 (August 1983);

Thomas L. Gais, Mark A. Peterson, and Jack L. Walker, Interest groups, iron triangles, and representative institutions in American national government, *British Journal of Political Science* 14 (April 1984).

Cozy Triangles

Government agency (that administers policy)

Congressional subcommittee (that enacts policy)

Lobbying organization (that lobbies for the policy)

Source: Samuel C. Patterson, Roger H. Davidson, and Randall B. Ripley, *A More Perfect Union: Introduction to American Government,* 3d ed. (Chicago: Dorsey, 1985), p. 249.

CPI *See* CONSUMER PRICE INDEX.

CPSC *See* CONSUMER PRODUCT SAFETY COMMISSION.

cradle to the grave/womb to tomb Slang phrases that refer to the total security offered citizens in the fully realized welfare state. Historically, the term was applied to the postwar program President Franklin D. Roosevelt an-nounced in 1943, intended as a promise of an expanded postwar New Deal. President Harry S Truman attempted to pick up the pieces of it in his Fair Deal program.

creation science *See* EDWARDS V AGUILLARD.

creative federalism *See* FEDERALISM, CREATIVE.

credibility **1** In diplomacy, the belief in the mind of the opposition that a threat or promise will be fulfilled if specific contingencies arise. One side in a negotiation can be said to have credibility if the other side believes it is not bluffing—even if it is bluffing. **2** A military posture that would allow one side to do unacceptable damage to an aggressor even after absorbing a first strike. Thus credibility functions as a deterrent.

credibility gap The difference between official description of events and the public's understanding of those events from other sources, chiefly the news media and political critics. A credibility gap engenders public mistrust and disbelief of elected officials. Credibility was an especially acute problem for the Lyndon B. Johnson and Richard M. Nixon administrations, the first for lies about the Vietnam War, the second for lies over Watergate. Public trust tended to increase during the Ronald Reagan administration; at least until the IRAN-CONTRA AFFAIR.

REFERENCES

David Wise, *The Politics of Lying: Government Deception, Secrecy, and Power* (New York: Random House, 1973);

Seymour Martin Lipset and William Schneider, *The Confidence Gap: Business, Labor, and Government in the Public Mind* (New York: Free Press, 1983).

creeping socialism *See* SOCIALISM, CREEPING.

critical election *See* ELECTION, CRITICAL.

crony *See* GOVERNMENT BY CRONY.

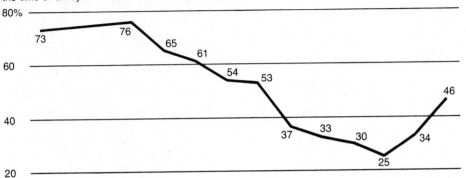

Trust in Government: 1958–1984

Percentage of the public agreeing that the government in Washington can be trusted to do the right thing most of the time or always

Source: CBS News/*New York Times* poll of November 18, 1984, as reported in William J. Keefe, Henry J. Abraham, William H. Flanigan, Charles O. Jones, Morris S. Ogul, and John W. Spanier, *American Democracy: Institutions, Politics, and Policies,* 2d ed. (Chicago: Dorsey, 1986), p. 138.

cross-examination The questioning of witnesses by opposition counsel during a trial or formal hearing.

REFERENCE

For the classic analysis of cross-examination, see Francis L. Wellman, *The Art of Cross Examination,* 4th ed. (New York: Macmillan, 1936).

cross-filing Formally becoming a candidate for elective office in the primary elections of more than one party, as permitted in some states, particularly for judicial offices.

crowding out The displacement of private investment expenditures by increases in public expenditures financed by the sale of government securities. It is often suggested that, as the federal deficit increases, the money borrowed from the public to pay for it is therefore unavailable for private investment. Such crowding out could thus lead to a recession or worse.

REFERENCES

Richard J. Cebula, Christopher Carlos, and James V. Koch, The "crowding out" effect of federal government outlay decisions: An empirical note, *Public Choice* 36:2 (1981); Richard J. Cebula, New evidence on financial crowding out, *Public Choice* 46:3 (1985).

cruel and unusual punishment Criminal penalties not considered appropriate by a society; inhumane punishment involving torture; any punishment that could result in death when the death penalty had not been ordered. This is the criminal penalty prohibited by the Eighth Amendment, which not only bars government from imposing punishment that is barbarous but, as the U.S. Supreme Court has announced, forbids punishment that society's "evolving standards of decency" would mark as excessive. It also bars punishment disproportionate to the offense committed, based on the facts of the particular case.

In *Gregg v Georgia,* 428 U.S. 153 (1976), the Court ruled that the death penalty as a punishment for murder does not necessarily constitute cruel and unusual punishment. But the Court held in *Woodson v North Carolina* 428

U.S. 280 (1976), that the death penalty may not be made mandatory. The jury or the judge must be given discretion, structured by legislative determination of the factors looking toward imposition of death, to consider the individual defendant, the particular crime, mitigating circumstances, and the treatment of similarly situated defendants. The Court has closely reviewed the substantive and procedural rules and practices associated with the determination of whether to put a convicted murderer to death. The most recent trend appears to be to enlarge the discretion of the jury, which many find to be inconsistent with the 1972 decision of *Furman v Georgia,* 408 U.S. 238, which temporarily struck down the death penalty because of the arbitrary, capricious, and racist manner in which it was usually applied by juries and judges.

Death as a penalty for any crime other than the actual commission of murder is of doubtful status. For example, it was held to be disproportionate, and thus not permitted, for the crime of rape of an adult woman in *Coker v Georgia,* 433 U.S. 584 (1977). Finally, punishment for narcotics addiction has been held to be cruel and unusual in *Robinson v California,* 370 U.S. 660 (1962), on the grounds that addiction is an illness and therefore cannot be properly categorized as a crime.

REFERENCES

Anthony F. Granucci, "Nor cruel and unusual punishments inflicted": The original meaning, *California Law Review* 57 (October 1969);

Maria Foscarinis, Toward a constitutional definition of punishment, *Columbia Law Review* 80 (December 1980).

CSG   *See* COUNCIL OF STATE GOVERNMENTS.

C-SPAN   The Cable-Satellite Public Affairs Network, the cable television channel that broadcasts live sessions of the U.S. House of Representatives and Senate, press conferences of the National Press Club, and a wide variety of other political presentations, such as panels at the annual meetings of the American Political Science Association.

Cuban missile crisis   The 1962 confrontation between the United States and the Soviet Union over the Soviet placement of nuclear missiles in Cuba. President John F. Kennedy demanded the removal of the missiles, imposed a naval blockade on Cuba, and waited for the Soviet response. In the end, the Soviets removed their missiles in exchange for a U.S. promise not to invade Cuba and an understanding that the United States would also remove its nuclear missiles in Turkey.

REFERENCES

Graham T. Allison, Jr., *Essence of Decision: Explaining the Cuban Missile Crisis* (Boston: Little, Brown, 1971);

Richard Ned Lebow, The Cuban missile crisis: Reading the lessons correctly, *Political Science Quarterly* 98 (Fall 1983);

Thomas G. Peterson and William J. Brophy, October missiles and November elections: The Cuban missile crisis and American politics, 1962, *Journal of American History* 73 (June 1986).

cue theory   In the context of the Supreme Court decisions on whether to grant certiorari, a methodological approach that uses case characteristics, such as whether the federal government is an appellant, whether civil liberties is an issue, whether the lower court was narrowly divided, and so on, to explain the Court's CERTIORARI decisions.

REFERENCES

Stuart H. Teger and Douglas Kosinski, The cue theory of Supreme Court certiorari jurisdiction: A reconsideration, *Journal of Politics* 42 (August 1980);

Virginia Armstrong and Charles A. Johnson, Certiorari decisions by the Warren and Burger courts: Is cue theory time bound? *Polity* 15 (Fall 1982).

cult of personality   A concentration of political power and authority in one individual, rather than in the office. The phrase came from the 1956 meeting of the Russian Communist party, where Joseph Stalin (1879–1953), the Soviet dictator from 1924 until his death, was denounced for his excesses in office.

REFERENCE

Jeremy T. Paltiel, The cult of personality: Some comparative reflections on political culture in Leninist regimes, *Studies in Com-*

parative Communism 16 (Spring–Summer 1983).

cultural pluralism   *See* PLURALISM, CULTURAL.

current dollar   The dollar value of a good or service in terms of prices current at the time the good or service was sold. This is in contrast to the value of the good or service in constant dollars.

***Curtiss-Wright* case**   *See* UNITED STATES V CURTISS-WRIGHT EXPORT CORPORATION.

custom duties   Taxes on imports or exports. *See also* DUTY.

Customs Service, U.S.   The agency of the Department of the Treasury that collects revenue from imports and enforces customs and related laws. The service was established in 1973; its forerunner was the Bureau of Customs, created in 1789 and placed in the Treasury Department in 1927.

U.S. Customs Service
1301 Constitution Avenue, N.W.
Washington, D.C. 20229
(202) 566–8195

Nineteenth-century customs officials examine the baggage of well-to-do New Yorkers returning from their European holiday.

customs union   A group of nations that has eliminated trade barriers among themselves and imposed a common tariff on all goods imported from all other countries. The European Common Market is a customs union, as are the United States in themselves.

czar   **1** A former Russian absolute monarch; also anglicized as tzar.   **2** A nickname for any high-ranking administrator who is given great authority over something; for example, an energy czar, a housing czar.

D

Dahl, Robert A. (1915–   )   One of the most influential U.S. political scientists, who, in "The Science of Public Administration: Three Problems," *Public Administration Review* 7 (Winter 1947), was an early advocate of a science of public administration; whose *Politics, Economics and Welfare,* with Charles E. Lindblom (New York: Harper, 1953) was one of the pioneering works on incrementalism; who, in *A Preface to Democratic Theory* (Chicago: University of Chicago Press, 1956), sought to integrate traditional thinking about democracy with the reality of American politics; and whose *Who Governs? Democracy and Power in an American City* (New Haven, CT: Yale University Press, 1961) has become a classic analysis of pluralistic governance, in which local political power was seen as dispersed only to coalesce about different issues.

REFERENCES

Dahl's other major works include *After the Revolution? Authority in a Good Society*

(New Haven, CT: Yale University Press, 1970);

Polyarchy: Participation and Opposition (New Haven, CT: Yale University Press, 1971);

Modern Political Analysis (Englewood Cliffs, NJ: Prentice-Hall, 1963, 4th ed., 1984).

For analyses of Dahl's influence, see Peter Morriss, Power in New Haven: A reassessment of "Who Governs?" *British Journal of Political Science* 2 (October 1972);

George Von der Muhll, Robert A. Dahl and the study of contemporary democracy: A review essay, *American Political Science Review* 71 (September 1977);

Richard W. Krouse, Polyarchy and participation: The changing democratic theory of Robert Dahl, *Polity* 14 (Spring 1982).

dark horse 1 A relatively unknown candidate nominated for political office. 2 A long-shot candidate who is not given much chance to win a party's nomination for office. 3 A compromise candidate, being the first choice of few but the final choice of the majority. The phrase came from and is still used in racing, where it refers to a horse about whom little is known but who has a reasonable chance to win. Under the democratizing reforms of the major parties in recent years, it has become increasingly unlikely that a dark horse can be nominated for president.

REFERENCES

Mark Bisnow, *Diary of a Dark Horse: The 1980 Anderson Presidential Campaign* (Carbondale: Southern Illinois University Press, 1983);

Steve Neal, *Dark Horse: A Biography of Wendell Willkie* (Garden City, NY: Doubleday, 1984).

Dartmouth College v Woodward 4 Wheaton 518 (1819) The U.S. Supreme Court case that upheld the legal sanctity of contracts under the Constitution. The State of New Hampshire wanted to change unilaterally Dartmouth College's 1769 charter, but the Court held that the charter was a contract and could be changed only by the mutual consent of the parties. Daniel Webster (1782–1852), who argued the case for the college before the Court, summarized his case with the words: "It is, sir . . . a small

college, and yet there are those that love it." *Compare to* FLETCHER V PECK.

REFERENCES

Francis N. Stites, *Private Interest and Public Gain: The Dartmouth College Case, 1819* (Amherst, MA: University of Massachusetts Press, 1972);

Bruce A. Campbell, John Marshall, the Virginia political economy, and the *Dartmouth College* decisions, *American Journal of Legal History* 19 (January 1975);

Eldon L. Johnson, The Dartmouth College case: The neglected educational meaning, *Journal of the Early Republic* 3 (Spring 1983).

Davis-Bacon Act of 1931 The federal prevailing wage law, which requires federal contractors on construction projects to pay the rates of pay and fringe benefits that prevail in the geographic area. In recent years, it has been heavily criticized for unnecessarily raising the cost of federal construction.

REFERENCE

Steven G. Allen, Much ado about Davis-Bacon: A critical review and new evidence, *Journal of Law and Economics* 26 (October 1983).

Davis v Bandemer *See* GERRYMANDER.

Davis v Passman 442 U.S. 229 (1979) The U.S. Supreme Court case that held that a woman discharged from employment by a U.S. congressman had the Fifth Amendment right to seek to recover damages from the congressman for alleged sex discrimination. *See* CONGRESSIONAL EXEMPTION.

dealignment A decline in political party loyalty and a rise in political independence. In a period of party dealignment, group ties to parties are weakened, and the electorate becomes more volatile in its behavior. *Compare to* REALIGNMENT.

REFERENCE

Helmut Norpoth and Jerrold Rusk, Partisan dealignment in the American electorate: Itemizing the deductions since 1964, *American Political Science Review* 76 (September 1982).

death penalty *See* CAPITAL PUNISHMENT;
CRUEL AND UNUSUAL PUNISHMENT.

Eugene V. Debs

Debs, Eugene V. (1855–1926) The most famous labor organizer of his time, who founded the Socialist Party of the United States in 1898 and was its candidate for president five times between 1900 and 1920.
REFERENCE
Nick Salvatore, *Eugene V. Debs: Citizen and Socialist* (Urbana: University of Illinois Press, 1982).

Debs, In re 158 U.S. 564 (1895) The U.S. Supreme Court case that arose out of the May 1894 strike by workers at the Pullman Palace Car Company in response to an arbitrary wage cut by the company. The strike was so effective—no member of the American Railway Union would, in sympathy, handle trains with Pullman (sleeper) cars—that it spread to twenty-seven states and territories. Because the American Railway Union, led by Eugene V. Debs, interfered with interstate commerce and supposedly prevented the U.S. mail from moving, the company got an injunction against the union. When Debs and his associates refused to comply, they were convicted of contempt.

The strike was finally broken in July, when President Grover Cleveland sent federal troops to Chicago to enforce the federal court injunction, citing "interference with interstate commerce and the postal service" as the justification. Governor John P. Altgeld and many others protested this first use of the army to break a strike. In December, Debs was sentenced to six months imprisonment for failing to comply with the injunction. In *In re Debs*, the Supreme Court upheld Debs's conviction and upheld the right of a president to send federal troops into a state. The Court wrote that "The strong arm of the national government may be put forth to brush away all obstructions to the freedom of interstate commerce or the transportation of the mails. If the emergency arises, the army of the Nation, and all its militia, are at the service of the Nation to compel obedience to its laws."
REFERENCES
Colston Estey Warne, *The Pullman Boycott of 1894: The Problem of Federal Intervention* (Boston: Heath, 1955);
Almont Lindsey, *The Pullman Strike: The Story of a Unique Experiment and of a Great Labor Upheaval* (Chicago: University of Chicago Press, 1964);
Stanley Buder, *Pullman: An Experiment in Industrial Order and Community Planning, 1880–1930* (New York: Oxford, 1967);
Ernst Freund, The *Debs* case and freedom of speech, *University of Chicago Law Review* 40 (Winter 1973).

debt crisis The recurrent problem of Third World nations to repay their loans from, and service the interest owed to, free world commercial banks and international financial institutions.
REFERENCES
Peter Nunerkamp, *The International Debt Crisis of the Third World* (London: Wheatsheaf, 1986);
David F. Lomax, *The Developing Country Debt Crisis* (London: Macmillan, 1986).

debt financing Paying for government programs or capital improvements by borrowing.

debt, general obligation A long-term full-faith-and-credit obligation other than one payable initially from nontax revenue. It includes a debt payable in the first instance from earmarked taxes, such as motor fuel sales taxes or property taxes.

debt, nonguaranteed Long-term debt payable solely from pledged specific sources; for example, from earnings of revenue-producing activities (such as university and college dormitories, toll highways and bridges, electric power projects, and public building authorities) or from specific nonproperty taxes. It includes only debt that does not constitute an obligation against any other resources if the pledged sources are insufficient.

debtor nation **1** A nation that borrows more from other nations than it loans them. **2** A nation that receives more investments from foreign sources than from its own internal sources.

debt service The regular payment of principal, interest, and other costs (such as insurance) to pay off a financial obligation.

DeCanas v Bica 424 U.S. 351 (1976) The U.S. Supreme Court case that upheld a California statute penalizing those who employed illegal aliens when such employment decreased the employment of citizens and legal aliens.

decision theory A body of knowledge concerned with the nature and process of decision making. Decision theory abstracts given situations into a structured problem, which calls for the decision maker to make an objective judgment. Frequently, dependent upon quantitative analysis, decision theory is also called statistical decision theory and Bayesian decision theory. Bayesian refers to Thomas Bayes (1702–1761), who provided a mathematical basis for probability inference.

declaration **1** A document stating a course of action and usually the reasons for it to which the signatories (either individuals or nations) bind themselves. Perhaps the most famous of all political declarations is the American Declaration of Independence of 1776. **2** A declaration of war (or neutrality), which expresses to the world a nation's intentions on a matter. **3** A statement of intention by a political leader. The leader can be either in power, speaking for

the government, or out of power, speaking for an opposition party. For example, in 1986 the British Labour Party opposition (to the "in power" Conservative Party) declared that it would dismantle all British nuclear weapons should Labour regain power. **4** A customs form on which, upon entering a country, one must declare items for which duty should be paid.

Declaration of Independence The document that heralded the birth of the United States of America. In 1776, during the Second Continental Congress, Richard Henry Lee (1732–1794) of Virginia made the motion that "these United Colonies are, and of right ought to be, free and independent states." In response, a committee of five was appointed to write a Declaration of Independence. But one member of the committee, Thomas Jefferson, drafted almost all of it. The Declaration starts off with a philosophic discussion of the nature of law and the rights of men. Then the influence of John Locke and other social contract theorists is seen, as Jefferson provides the philosophic justification for breaking with a tyrannical king. This is followed by a long list of the king's abuses and a statement of how the colonists constantly petitioned for redress with no effect. The attack on the king was thought necessary to justify breaking with the long-held notion that it was a citizen's responsibility to be loyal to his king. Then the "Representatives of the United States of America" declare their independence and "mutually pledge to each other our lives, our fortunes and our sacred honor." The Declaration, which was approved by the convention in July 1776, was the first significant political—as opposed to philosophical—statement that the people of a nation had a right to choose their own government. It was the beginning of the independence of the United States and has been a significant influence on revolutionary movements ever since.

REFERENCES

Carl L. Becker, *The Declaration of Independence: A Study of the History of Political Ideas* (New York: Random House, 1942);

David Hawke, *A Transaction of Free Men: The Birth and Course of the Declaration of Independence* (New York: Scribner's, 1964);

Declaration of Independence

Alan P. Grimes, Conservative revolution and liberal rhetoric: The Declaration of Independence, *Journal of Politics* 38 (August 1976);

Walter Nicgorski, The significance of the non-Lockean heritage of the Declaration of Independence, *American Journal of Jurisprudence* 21 (1976);

Gary Wills, *Inventing America: Jefferson's Declaration of Independence* (New York: Random House, 1978).

Declaration of Independence

The Declaration of Independence in Congress, July 4, 1776.

The unanimous Declaration of the thirteen united States of America,

When in the course of human events, it becomes necessary for one people to dissolve the political bands which have connected them with another, and to assume among the Powers of the earth, the separate and equal station to which the Laws of Nature and of Nature's God entitle them, a decent respect to the opinions of mankind requires that they should declare the causes which impel them to the separation.

We hold these truths to be self-evident, that all men are created equal, that they are endowed by their Creator with certain unalienable Rights, that among these are Life, Liberty and the pursuit of Happiness. That to secure these rights, Governments are instituted among Men, deriving their just powers from the consent of the governed. That whenever any Form of Government becomes destructive of these ends, it is the Right of the People to alter or abolish it, and to institute new government, laying its foundation on such principles and organizing its powers in such form, as to them shall seem most likely to effect their Safety and Happiness. Prudence, indeed, will dictate that Governments long established should not be changed for light and transient causes; and accordingly all experience hath shown, that mankind are more disposed to suffer, while evils are sufferable, than to right themselves by abolishing the forms to which they are accustomed. But when a long train of abuses and usurpations, pursuing invariably the same Object evinces a design to reduce them under absolute Despotism, it is their right, it is their duty, to throw off such Government, and to provide new Guards for their future security.—Such has been the patient sufferance of these Colonies; and such is now the necessity which constrains them to alter their former Systems of Government. The history of the present King of Great Britain is a history of repeated injuries and usurpations, all having in direct object the establishment of an absolute tyranny over these States. To prove this, let Facts be submitted to a candid world.

He has refused his Assent to Laws, the most wholesome and necessary for the public good.

He has forbidden his Governors to pass Laws of immediate and pressing importance, unless suspended in their operation till his Assent should be obtained; and when so suspended, he has utterly neglected to attend to them.

He has refused to pass other Laws for the accommodation of large districts of people, unless those people would relinquish the right of Representation in the Legislature, a right inestimable to them and formidable to tyrants only.

He has called together legislative bodies at places unusual, uncomfortable, and distant from the depository of their Public Records, for the sole purpose of fatiguing them into compliance with his measures.

He has dissolved Representative Houses repeatedly, for opposing with manly firmness his invasions on the rights of the people.

He has refused for a long time, after such dissolutions, to cause others to be elected; whereby the Legislative Powers, incapable of Annihilation, have returned to the People at large for their exercise; the State remaining in the meantime exposed to all the dangers of invasion from without, and convulsions within.

He has endeavoured to prevent the population of these States; for that purpose obstructing the Laws of Naturalization of Foreigners; refusing to pass others to encourage their migrations hither, and raising the conditions of new Appropriations of Lands.

He has obstructed the Administration of Justice, by refusing his Assent to Laws for establishing Judiciary Powers.

He has made Judges dependent on his Will alone, for the tenure of their offices, and the amount and payment of their salaries.

He has erected a multitude of New Offices, and sent hither swarms of Officers to harass our people, and eat out their substance.

He has kept among us, in times of peace, Standing Armies without the Consent of our legislatures.

He has affected to render the Military independent of and superior to the Civil Power.

He has combined with others to subject us to a jurisdiction foreign to our constitution, and unacknowledged by our laws; giving his Assent to their acts of pretended Legislation:

For quartering large bodies of armed troops among us:

For protecting them, by a mock Trial, from Punishment for any Murders which they should commit on the inhabitants of these States:

For cutting off our Trade with all parts of the world:

For imposing taxes on us without our Consent:

For depriving us in many cases, of the benefits of Trial by Jury:

For transporting us beyond Seas to be tried for pretended offences:

For abolishing the free System of English Laws in a neighbouring Province, establishing therein an Arbitrary government, and enlarging its Boundaries so as to render it at once an example and fit instrument for introducing the same absolute rule into these Colonies:

For taking away our Charters, abolishing our most valuable Laws, and altering fundamentally the Forms of our Governments:

For suspending our own Legislatures, and declaring themselves invested with Power to legislate for us in all cases whatsoever.

He has abdicated Government here, by declaring us out of his Protection and waging War against us.

He has plundered our seas, ravaged our Coasts, burnt our towns, and destroyed the lives of our people.

He is at this time transporting large armies of foreign mercenaries to compleat the works of death, desolation and tyranny, already begun with circumstances of Cruelty & perfidy scarcely paralleled in the most barbarous ages, and totally unworthy the Head of a civilized nation.

He has constrained our fellow Citizens taken Captive on the high Seas to bear Arms against their Country, to become the executioners of their friends and Brethren, or to fall themselves by their Hands.

He has excited domestic insurrections amongst us, and has endeavoured to bring on the inhabitants of our frontiers, the merciless Indian Savages, whose known rule of warfare, is an undistinguished destruction of all ages, sexes and conditions.

In every stage of these Oppressions We have Petitioned for Redress in the most humble terms: Our repeated Petitions have been answered only by repeated injury. A Prince, whose character is thus marked by every act which may define a Tyrant, is unfit to be the ruler of a free people.

Nor have We been wanting in attentions to our British brethren. We have warned them from time to time of attempts by their legislature to extend an unwarrantable jurisdiction over us. We have reminded them of the circumstances of our emigration and settlement here. We have appealed to their native justice and magnanimity, and we have conjured them by the ties of our common kindred to disavow these usurpations which, would inevitably interrupt our connections and correspondence. They too have been deaf to the voice of justice and of consanguinity. We must, therefore, acquiesce in the necessity, which denounces our Separation, and hold

them, as we hold the rest of mankind, Enemies in War, in Peace Friends.

We, therefore, the Representatives of the united States of America, in General Congress, Assembled, appealing to the Supreme Judge of the world for the rectitude of our intentions, do, in the Name, and by authority of the good People of these Colonies, solemnly publish and declare, That these United Colonies are, and of Right ought to be Free and Independent States; that they are Absolved from all Allegiance to the British Crown, and that all political connection between them and the State of Great Britain, is and ought to be totally dissolved; and that as Free and Independent States, they have full power to levy War, conclude Peace, contract Alliances, establish Commerce, and to do all other Acts and Things which Independent States may of right do. And for the support of this Declaration, with a firm reliance on the Protection of Divine Providence, we mutually pledge to each other our Lives, our Fortunes and our sacred Honor.

John Hancock
(Massachusetts)

New Hampshire
Josiah Bartlett
William Whipple
Matthew Thornton

Massachusetts
Samuel Adams
John Adams
Robert Treat Paine
Elbridge Gerry

Delaware
Caesar Rodney
George Read
Thomas McKean

New York
William Floyd
Philip Livingston
Francis Lewis
Lewis Morris

New Jersey
Richard Stockton
John Witherspoon
Francis Hopkinson
John Hart
Abraham Clark

North Carolina
William Hooper
Joseph Hewes
John Penn

Maryland
Samuel Chase
William Paca
Thomas Stone
Charles Carroll of
  Carrollton

South Carolina
Edward Rutledge
Thomas Heywood, Jr.
Thomas Lynch, Jr.
Arthur Middleton

Rhode Island
Stephen Hopkins
William Ellery

Connecticut
Roger Sherman
Samuel Huntington
William Williams
Oliver Wolcott

Pennsylvania
Robert Morris
Benjamin Rush
Benjamin Franklin
John Morton
George Clymer
James Smith
George Taylor
James Wilson
George Ross

Virginia
George Wythe
Richard Henry Lee
Thomas Jefferson
Benjamin Harrison
Thomas Nelson, Jr.
Francis Lightfoot Lee
Carter Braxton

Georgia
Button Gwinnett
Lyman Hall
George Walton

declaration of war   The legal obligation (under international law) on the part of a nation to formally notify another sovereign nation that a "state of war" exists between them if the first nation intends to commence hostilities. The last time the United States declared war was during World War II, when President Franklin D. Roosevelt called December 7, 1941 "a date which will live in infamy" and asked "that the Congress declare that since the unprovoked and dastardly attack on Sunday, December 7th, 1941, a state of war has existed between the United States and the Japanese empire." The United States was then at war with both Japan and Germany, because Germany, as an ally of Japan, promptly declared war on the United States. Formal declarations of war seem to be rapidly becoming quaint relics of diplomatic history. The phrase "undeclared war" was used by American policymakers in the 1930s to define the illegality of the Japanese action against China. President Harry S Truman's actions in Korea (*see* KOREAN WAR) told the world that, when a war was not a war, it was a "police action." President Dwight D. Eisenhower's request for a congressional resolution empowering action in defense of Formosa set the stage for President Lyndon B. Johnson's GULF OF TONKIN RESOLUTION, that is, the prior approval by the Congress for a war action. There has been a real transformation of the concept of war power, which has led to the War Powers Resolution (*see* WAR POWERS) through a series of transforming stages. Consequently, today the American president as commander in chief can commit American forces without congressional approval until after the fact.

declaratory judgment   **1** A court ruling on the rights of parties in a particular case, without a judicial order that any particular action be taken in sequence. Thus the legal issues of a dispute can be examined and ruled in an effort to forestall more complicated lawsuits. It differs from an advisory opinion in that there exists a real controversy, even though no actual injuries have yet to occur. The Declaratory Judgments Act of 1934 empowers the federal courts to issue declaratory judgments.   **2** A judicial decision in a case or controversy in which no party has yet suffered specific harm

or injury through the enforcement of a law or administration regulation. However, such harm or injury is considered sufficiently likely to make a court decision on the issue reasonable before any harm or injury occurs. *Compare to* OPINION, ADVISORY.

DeConcini reservation   A reservation sponsored by Dennis DeConcini, Democratic senator from Arizona, and attached to the Panama Canal Neutrality Treaty, which was ratified by the U.S. Senate on March 16, 1978. The DeConcini reservation specifies that the United States and the Republic of Panama each has the independent right to take military steps if necessary to prevent the canal from being closed or otherwise interfered with. This means that, if a future government of Panama or any other power tries to interfere with the normal operations of the Panama Canal, the United States has the right, according to the treaty, to militarily intervene.

de facto   **1** A Latin phrase meaning in fact; actual. For example, de facto segregation has occurred without the formal assistance of government; it evolved from social and economic conditions. In contrast, de jure (by law) segregation in schools was once a legal requirement in many states. While segregation practices are no longer sanctioned by government (are no longer de jure), they often remain de facto. According to Shirley Chisholm, *Unbought and Unbossed* (Boston: Houghton Mifflin, 1970), "The difference between *de jure* and *de facto* segregation is the difference between open, forthright bigotry and the shamefaced kind that works through unwritten agreements between real estate dealers, school officials, and local politicians."   **2** Diplomatic recognition that implies acceptance but falls short of formal, legal (de jure) recognition.

defamation of character   The injuring of the good name or reputation of another. When this is done in writing, it is LIBEL. When done orally, it is SLANDER.

defendant   Someone formally accused of a crime. A person becomes a defendant when a formal accusation is entered into the record of a court and remains so until the charge is dropped, the case is dismissed, or the court pronounces judgment (acquittal or conviction).

Defense, U.S. Department of (DOD) The federal agency, created by the NATIONAL SECURITY ACT amendments of 1949, responsible for providing the military forces needed to deter war and protect U.S. security. The major elements of these forces are the army, navy, marine corps, and air force, consisting of over a million men and women on active duty. Of these, almost half, including about fifty thousand on ships at sea, serve outside the United States. They are backed, in case of emergency, by the two and a half million members of the reserve components. In addition, there are over a million civilian employees in the Defense Department. The creation of a single Department of Defense to replace the separate departments of the War and Navy was a major effort to consolidate and integrate the military services and to obviate interservice rivalry. Critics of the Defense Department argue that interservice consolidation has not been achieved in any meaningful way because the department tends to function as a holding company for the individual services. One illustration of this is the fact that the individual service secretaries (army, navy, air force) are still retained.

REFERENCES

C. W. Borklund, *The Department of Defense* (New York: Praeger, 1968);

Ralph Sanders, Bureaucratic ploys and strategems: The case of the U.S. Department of Defense, *Jerusalem Journal of International Relations* 4 (1979);

Laurence E. Lynn, Jr. and Richard I. Smith, Can the Secretary of Defense make a difference? *International Security* 7 (Summer 1982).

U.S. Department of Defense
The Pentagon
Washington, D.C. 20310
(202) 545-6700

deficiency bill *See* BILL, DEFICIENCY.

deficit The amount by which a government's expenditures exceed its revenues.

Federal Budget Deficits Since 1970

Year	President	Deficit in Billions	Percentage of GNP
1970	Nixon	2.8	0.3
1971	Nixon	23.0	2.2
1972	Nixon	23.4	2.0
1973	Nixon	14.9	1.2
1974	Nixon	6.1	0.4
1975	Ford	53.2	3.5
1976	Ford	73.7	4.3
1977	Carter	53.6	2.8
1978	Carter	59.2	2.7
1979	Carter	40.2	1.6
1980	Carter	73.8	2.8
1981	Reagan	78.9	2.6
1982	Reagan	127.9	4.1
1983	Reagan	207.8	6.3
1984	Reagan	185.3	5.0
1985	Reagan	212.3	5.4
1986	Reagan	220.7	5.3

Source: U.S. Office of Management and Budget, *The United States Budget in Brief, Fiscal Year 1988.*
Note: 1985 deficit is estimated.

deficit financing A situation in which a government's excess of outlays over receipts for a given period is financed primarily by borrowing from the public. Deficit financing, and especially the general acceptance of it by economic theorists, is largely a twentieth-century phenomenon. Depending on the economist you listen to, a large deficit is either considered a major drag on the economy (*see* CROWDING OUT) or a significant stimulus (*see* JOHN MAYNARD KEYNES). The national debt is the sum total of all federal deficits and interest currently owed to holders of federal government securities, such as Treasury bills and savings bonds.

REFERENCES

Robert H. Rasche, Financing the government deficit, *Policy Studies Journal* 9 (Autumn 1980);

Robert Eisner and Paul J. Pieper, How to make sense of the deficit, *Public Interest* 78 (Winter 1985);

Ali F. Darrat, Inflation and the federal budget deficits: Some empirical results, *Public Finance Quarterly* 13 (April 1985);

Paul E. Peterson, The new politics of deficits, *Political Science Quarterly* 100 (Winter 1985–86).

deficit reduction act *See* GRAMM-RUDMAN-HOLLINGS ACT OF 1985.

DeFunis v Odegaard 416 U.S. 312 (1974) The U.S. Supreme Court case concerning a white male denied admission to law school at the same time minority applicants with lesser academic credentials were accepted. DeFunis challenged the school's action on the grounds that it denied him equal protection of the laws in violation of the Fourteenth Amendment. He was successful in state court and was admitted to the school. On appeal, the school won a reversal. Nevertheless, DeFunis remained in school pending further action by the Supreme Court. As the nation awaited a definitive resolution of the issue of reverse discrimination, the Court sought to avoid the problem. Since DeFunis had completed all but his last quarter of law school and was not in danger of being denied his diploma, a majority of the justices seized upon this fact and declared that the case was moot—beyond the Court's power to render a decision on a hypothetical matter of only potential constitutional substance. *See also* REGENTS OF THE UNIVERSITY OF CALIFORNIA V ALLEN BAKKE; REVERSE DISCRIMINATION; UNITED STEELWORKERS OF AMERICA V WEBER, ET AL.
REFERENCES
Larry M. Lavinsky, *DeFunis v Odegaard:* The non-decision with a message, *Columbia Law Review* 75 (April 1975);
Allan P. Sindler, *Bakke, DeFunis, and Minority Admissions: The Quest for Equal Opportunity* (New York: Longman, 1978).

de jure A Latin phrase meaning by right; by law. *See* DE FACTO.

delegate 1 An accredited representative to a national nominating convention. 2 A member of the lower house of the legislature in Maryland, Virginia, and West Virginia. 3 A representative to the U.S. House of Representatives from the District of Columbia (since 1971), Guam (since 1973), the Virgin Islands (since 1973), and American Samoa (since 1981). Delegates can participate in House debates but are not permitted to vote on the floor. They can serve on committees, and they possess the powers and privileges of committee members. Puerto Rico has had similar representation in the House since 1946, but its representative is called a resident commissioner. 4 A legislator who assumes the role of a conduit for constituency opinions as opposed to a Burkean TRUSTEE. *See* EDMUND BURKE; FIDUCIARY.
REFERENCES
1 John W. Soule and James W. Clarke, Amateurs and professionals: A study of delegates to the 1968 Democratic National Convention, *American Political Science Review* 64 (September 1970);
Warren J. Mitofsky and Martin Plissner, The making of the delegates, 1968–1980, *Public Opinion* 3 (October/November 1980).

delegate, super A new category of national convention delegate created by the Democrats in 1984 to make sure that elected public officials as well as party officials are able to attend the convention as delegates. Super delegates are chosen by congressional caucuses and state conventions and are intended to give the party leadership a greater voice at the convention.
REFERENCE
Priscilla L. Southwell, The 1984 Democratic nomination process: The significance of unpledged superdelegates, *American Politics Quarterly* 14 (January-April 1986).

delegation of power The empowering of one to act for another. The delegation of power from one part of government to another and from one official to another is fundamental to American government. Article I, Section 8, of the U.S. Constitution enumerates the powers of the Congress and then grants to the Congress the power "to make all laws which shall be necessary and proper for carrying into execution the foregoing powers, and all other powers vested by this Constitution in the government of the United States, or in any department or officer thereof." But how explicit must such laws be? If the Congress were to attempt to legislate in such a fashion to give complete direction to administrative officials, it would result in an unworkable government. Every contingency would have to be anticipated in advance; the legislature would have to be expert in all phases of all policy areas. Moreover, changes in the nature of implementing statutes would have to be accomplished by new laws; the congressional work load would be crushing. Consequently, the Congress typically avoids writing highly detailed legislation, preferring to state broad policy objectives and allowing administrators to choose the means of attaining them.

While administrative discretion is clearly necessary, it can raise important constitutional questions. If the delegation is so broad as to allow administrators to exercise legislative power without congressional guidance or standards, then the requirements of the separation of powers may be breached. This issue is of great importance, because the Congress does tend to delegate important questions of public policy to administrative officials, rather than come to grips with the questions itself. Excellent examples of this can be found in the areas of equal opportunity for minorities, women, and the handicapped. Certainly, the administratively chosen means of affirmative action have been more controversial and politicized than the legislatively enacted end of equal opportunity. *See also* GRAMM-RUDMAN-HOLLINGS ACT; NECESSARY AND PROPER CLAUSE; PANAMA REFINING CO. V RYAN; REGULATION; SCHECHTER POULTRY CORPORATION V UNITED STATES; UNITED STATES V CURTISS-WRIGHT EXPORT CORPORATION.

REFERENCES

Sotirios A. Barber, *The Constitution and the Delegation of Congressional Power* (Chicago: University of Chicago Press, 1975);

Carl McGowan, Congress, court, and control of delegated power, *Columbia Law Review* 77 (December 1977);

Benjamin Jones, Public employee labor arbitration and the delegation of governmental powers, *State Government* 51 (Spring 1978);

Peter H. Aranson, Ernest Gellhorn, and Glen O. Robinson, A theory of legislative delegation, *Cornell Law Review* 68 (November 1982).

deliberate speed   The pace of school integration. The U.S. Supreme Court held in *Brown v Board of Education of Topeka, Kansas* that school integration should proceed "with all deliberate speed." This is a good example of the Court's use of a vague word to avoid dealing head on with a difficult policy problem.

REFERENCE

John H. McCord, ed., *With All Deliberate Speed: Civil Rights Theory and Reality* (Urbana: University of Illinois Press, 1967).

Among American politicians, few have exemplified the demagogue as well as the fiery orator Huey Long, who propounded his programs as a U.S. senator and as governor of Louisiana.

demagogue   1 A political leader accused of seeking or gaining power through the use of arguments designed to appeal to a mass public's sentiments, even though critics may consider those arguments exaggerated or spurious. The term is loaded and is never considered a compliment except as an indirect way of referring to a politician's rhetorical powers. The term, derived from the Greek *demagogos*, meaning a leader of the people, is one of the most time-honored epithets thrown at successful opposition politicians.   2 The archetypal ruthless but charismatic politician who longs for power for its own sake and is loose with the truth, the law, and the public's purse. Well-known American demagogues include Huey R. Long (1893–1935) of Louisiana and Joseph McCarthy (1903–1957) of Wisconsin (see MCCARTHYISM). Of course, one person's demagogue may be another's honorable advocate of good government. Dead demagogues often make good subjects for writers. Robert Penn Warren (1905–   ) won the Pulitzer Prize for fiction for his 1946 novelization of Huey Long's life, *All the King's Men*. And when it was made into a movie, it won an Academy Award for best picture of 1949. More than twenty years later, T. Harry Williams (1909–   ) won the Pulitzer Prize in biography for his definitive account of Long's life, *Huey Long* (New York: Knopf, 1969).

REFERENCE

Dean Jards and Gene L. Mason, Party choice and support for demagogues: An experimental examination, *American Political Science Review* 63:1 (1969).

de minimus   Short form of *de minimus non curat lex*, Latin for the law does not bother with trifles. This means that a court will not waste its time on a matter it considers ridiculously trivial.

democracy   The Greek word for rule by the ordinary populace, the plebian public, whose well-being was necessary for the stability of the state but whose judgment could not necessarily be trusted in the management of the state. The growth of democracy as an ideal thus depended upon the slow evolution of classes of educated and experienced citizens, whose capacity to govern themselves and others depended on the transformation of ways of understanding and interpreting the will of the people—although not necessarily giving the people the power to exercise that will for themselves.

The development of concepts of popular or universal democracy in the nineteenth century, known in various parts of the world as POPULISM, rested on a much stronger faith in individual intuition and universal rights, regardless of education or social status, and led in turn to new revolutionary conceptions of democracy

that called for the placing of all power in the people. The problem of constructing a state that could exercise that power resulted in debates over the definition of the state that ranged from anarchy, or total absence of the state, through socialism and various forms of state control of industrial production and public welfare, to totalitarianism, or total control of all the people by an all-powerful state acting on behalf of all the people. Thus the term democracy is often used by totalitarian regimes and their people's democracies. So one person's democratic regime is another's totalitarian despotism. Democracy, like beauty, is in the eye of the beholder.

By becoming a term that could be used to describe so broad a range of institutional possibilities, democracy has thus tended to lose its meaning in political debate—but not its vitality. It continues to serve as an ideal over which political debate can take place. Like the Cheshire cat, perhaps everything has disappeared but the smile.

The founders of the United States were rightly suspicious of the pure democracy available to the free male citizens of ancient Athens. As Artistotle had warned, time and again throughout history pure democracies had degenerated into dictatorial tyrannies. John Adams wrote: "Remember, democracy never lasts long. It soon wastes, exhausts, and murders itself. There never was a democracy yet that did not commit suicide." This well-justified fear of the mob led the founders to create a REPUBLIC, a form of government one step removed from democracy, that presumably protects the people from their own passions. The frustration of coming to grips with the concept and the reality of democracy is illustrated by Winston Churchill's remark, that "no one pretends that democracy is perfect or all-wise. Indeed, it has been said that democracy is the worst form of government except all those other forms that have been tried from time to time."

REFERENCES

Charles S. Hyneman, *Bureaucracy in a Democracy* (New York: Harper & Row, 1950);
John D. May, Defining democracy: A bid for coherence and consensus, *Political Studies* 26 (March 1978);

Raymond Duncan Gastil, The past, present, and future of democracy, *Journal of International Affairs* 38 (Winter 1985);

Jean-Francois Revel, *How Democracies Perish* (New York: Harper & Row, 1985);

Giovanni Sartori, *The Theory of Democracy Revisited,* 2 vols. (Chatham, NJ: Chatham House, 1986).

James Madison Denounces "Pure Democracy"

It may be concluded that a pure democracy, by which I mean a society consisting of a small number of citizens, who assemble and administer the government in person, can admit of no cure for the mischiefs of faction. A common passion or interest will, in almost every case, be felt by a majority of the whole; a communication and concert results from the form of government itself; and there is nothing to check the inducements to sacrifice the weaker party or an obnoxious individual. Hence it is that such democracies have ever been spectacles of turbulence and contention; have ever been found incompatible with personal security or the rights of property; and have in general been as short in their lives as they have been violent in their deaths. Theoretic politicians, who have patronized this species of government, have erroneously supposed that by reducing mankind to a perfect equality in their political rights, they would at the same time be perfectly equalized and assimilated in their possessions, their opinions and their passions.

Source: Federalist #10

---

democracy, constitutional Any system of democratic governance that places formal limits, by means of a constitution, on what government can do. The United States, while a REPUBLIC in structure, is a constitutional democracy in concept. Thomas Jefferson wrote in 1798: "In questions of power, then, let no more be heard of confidence in man, but bind him down from mischief by the chains of the Constitution." *Compare to* CONSTITUTIONALISM.

democracy, direct Any governing system in which decisions are made directly by the people, as opposed to being made by elected representatives. Examples of direct democracy include the political meetings of male citizens in the ancient Greek city-states and the New England town meeting. More modern forms of direct democracy include such processes as the initiative, the referendum, and the recall, which allow citizens to directly enact laws or to remove officials by voting.

REFERENCE

Eli M. Noam, The efficiency of direct democracy, *Journal of Political Economy* 88 (August 1980).

democracy, economic An equality of economic rights, which parallels the equality of political rights possessed by all citizens. In an economic democracy, citizens would have a right to a job, decent housing, and so on.

REFERENCES

Martin Carnoy and Derek Shearer, *Economic Democracy* (White Plains, NY: Sharpe, 1980);

Allen Graubard, Ideas of economic democracy, *Dissent* 31 (Fall 1984).

Democracy in America *See* TOCQUEVILLE, ALEXIS DE.

democracy, industrial Any of a variety of efforts designed to encourage employees to participate in an organization's decision-making processes by identifying problems and suggesting solutions to them in a formal manner. While the terms industrial democracy and participative management tend to be used almost interchangeably, there is a distinction. Industrial democracy was used as far back as 1897 by the English economists Beatrice Webb (1858–1943) and Sidney Webb (1859–1947) to describe democratic practices within the British trade union movement. The term's modern usage to cover innumerable types of joint or cooperative management programs dates from World War I. Then it connoted a scheme to avoid labor-management disputes that might adversely affect war production. Today, industrial democracy connotes joint action by management and workers' representatives. Participative management, in contrast, connotes cooperative programs that are unilaterally implemented from on high. Nevertheless, both terms seem to be rapidly losing their distinctive connotations.

REFERENCES
Edward S. Greenberg, Industrial democracy and the democratic citizen, *Journal of Politics* 43 (November 1981);
Henry P. Guzda, Industrial democracy: Made in the U.S.A., *Monthly Labor Review* 107 (May 1984);
Robert E. Lane, From political to industrial democracy? *Polity* 17 (Summer 1985).

democracy, Jacksonian The move toward equalitarianism in American politics and social life, dating from ANDREW JACKSON's election as president in 1828. It signaled the disappearance of the aristocratic tradition in politics by rejecting Thomas Jefferson's notion of a natural aristocracy and upheld in its place the notion that the desires of the common man should rule in all things.

REFERENCES
Marvin Meyers, *The Jacksonian Persuasion: Politics and Belief* (Stanford, CA: Stanford University Press, 1957);
Lee Benson, *The Concept of Jacksonian Democracy* (Princeton, NJ: Princeton University Press, 1961).

democracy, Jeffersonian Thomas Jefferson's ideals of a limited government for an agrarian society: freedom of religion, speech, and the press; a natural aristocracy, who ought to rule; laissez-faire economic policies; and strong state governments allied with a relatively weak constitutional government at the national level.

REFERENCES
Charles A. Beard, *The Economic Origins of Jeffersonian Democracy* (New York: Free Press, 1943, 1965);
Charles M. Wiltse, *The Jeffersonian Tradition in American Democracy* (New York: Hill and Wang, 1960);
James MacGregor Burns, *The Deadlock of Democracy; Four Party Politics in America* (Englewood Cliffs, NJ: Prentice-Hall, 1963), chapter 2.

democracy, participatory The direct involvement of individuals and groups in the decision-making processes of government. This is often manifest by citizen participation in the planning and implementation activities of the various government agencies by interest groups and individuals. Many laws have built-in features of participatory democracy, such as hearings (where the public may testify) preliminary to changes, such as in rules, regulations, and tax rates. The new Left picked up on this theme when, in the 1960s, it called for citizen control of local public services. The main problem with participatory democracy is that self-appointed spokespersons for the people often have a disproportionate impact on public policy; so the situation may all too quickly turn oligarchic, rather than democratic.

REFERENCES
Daniel C. Kramer, *Participatory Democracy: Developing Ideals of the Political Left* (Cambridge, MA: Schenkman, 1972);
Frank MacKinnon, *Postures and Politics: Some Observations on Participatory Democracy* (Toronto: University of Toronto Press, 1973).

democracy, people's A communist regime. This is in no way comparable to democracy as practiced in the Western world.

democracy, pluralistic A governing system in which real power is held by various groups and institutions that, from time to time, combine to advance the interests, the causes, and the people they represent. American government is often analyzed as a pluralistic democracy. *Compare to* PLURALISM.

REFERENCE
Robert A. Dahl, *Pluralist Democracy in the United States* (Chicago: Rand McNally, 1967).

democracy, procedural The elective process whereby citizens reaffirm their commitment to popular government and confer legitimacy on elected political leaders.

democracy, representative A form of governance in which the citizens rule through representatives, who are periodically elected in order to keep them accountable. The United States, as a republic, is a representative democracy.

democrat A person who espouses belief in the core principles of democracy—that all power in government is ultimately derived from the will of the people. *Compare to* REPUBLICAN.

Democrat A member of the Democratic party. The humorist Will Rogers (1879–1935) said, "I belong to no organized party. I am a Democrat."

Democratic party One of the two main parties in American politics. The Democratic party traces its origins to the Democratic-Republican party of Thomas Jefferson. In 1828, under Andrew Jackson, the party took its current name. The ideals of the party have from the beginning tended toward greater egalitarianism and the abolition of special privilege, but it had difficulty living up to its ideals so long as the party favored slavery. Once that issue was decided by the Civil War, the party in the South took a "whites only" orientation. The first major change in this attitude came about when, under the leadership of Hubert Humphrey (1911–1978) and President Harry S Truman, the party accepted a civil rights plank in its platform approved at the 1948 national convention. This was the first major split in the traditionally SOLID SOUTH, which defected and formed its own third party that year, the DIXIECRATS. But the Democratic party was able to win the White House without them. The party's appeal to blacks was solidified when the Democrats under Lyndon B. Johnson sponsored the Civil Rights Act of 1964 and the Voting Rights Act of 1965. Now, most black Americans are solidly and influentially in the Democratic camp. Since the New Deal coalition of Franklin D. Roosevelt, the Democrats have been the leading party (*see* PARTY IDENTIFICATION) in terms of sheer numbers; but with the election of Ronald Reagan in 1980, their lead has grown much smaller. Ever since the New Deal, the Democratic party has had a reputation for being liberal, for appealing to low-income groups, for expanding civil rights protection, and for believing that government is a legitimate vehicle for solving social problems.

REFERENCES
William J. Crotty, *Decision for the Democrats: Reforming the Party Structure* (Baltimore: Johns Hopkins University Press, 1978);
Walter Dean Burnham, The Eclipse of the Democratic Party, *Society* 21 (July/August 1984);
Alan Ware, *The Breakdown of Democratic Party Organization, 1940–1980* (New York: Oxford University Press, 1985).

Democratic Party National Headquarters
430 South Capitol Street, S.E.
Washington, D.C. 20003
(202) 863-1500

How to Tell Democrats from Republicans

A few years ago, an anonymous wit drew up a list of the main differences between Democrats and Republicans. A Republican congressman from California, Craig Hosmer, included this anonymous author's formulation in the *Congressional Record*. It reads as follows:

- Democrats buy most of the books that have been banned somewhere. Republicans form censorship committees and read them as a group.
- Democrats give their worn-out clothes to those less fortunate. Republicans wear theirs.
- Republicans employ exterminators. Democrats step on the bugs.
- Democrats name their children after currently popular sports figures, politicians, and entertainers. Republican children are named after their parents or grandparents, according to where the most money is.
- Democrats keep trying to cut down on smoking but are not successful. Neither are Republicans.
- Republicans tend to keep their shades drawn, although there is seldom any reason why they should. Democrats ought to, but don't.
- Republicans study the financial pages of the newspaper. Democrats put them in the bottom of the bird cage.
- Republicans raise dahlias, Dalmatians, and eyebrows. Democrats raise Airedales, kids, and taxes.
- Democrats eat the fish they catch. Republicans hang them on the wall.
- Republican boys date Democratic girls. They plan to marry Republican girls but feel they're entitled to a little fun first.
- Democrats make up plans and then do something else. Republicans follow the plans their grandfathers made.

- Republicans sleep in twin beds—some even in separate rooms. That is why there are more Democrats.

  Source: Adapted from Samuel C. Patterson, Roger H. Davidson, and Randall B. Ripley, *A More Perfect Union: Introduction to American Government*, 3d ed. (Chicago: Dorsey, 1985), p. 153.

democratic socialism Socialism achieved by democratic means (through honest elections), as opposed to socialism imposed by force. *Compare to* SOCIAL DEMOCRACY.

REFERENCES

Bogdan Denitch, ed., *Democratic Socialism: The Mass Left in Advanced Industrial Societies* (Montclair, NJ: Allanheld, Osmun, 1981);

Anton Pelinka, *Social Democratic Parties in Europe* (New York: Praeger, 1983).

Democratic Study Group *See* LEGISLATIVE SERVICE ORGANIZATIONS.

democratization The gradual installation of collective choice and majority rule in social institutions (schools, churches, factories), not just in the government institutions.

REFERENCE

Paul Bernstein, *Workplace Democratization— Its Internal Dynamics* (Kent, OH: Kent State University Press, 1976).

Democrat party A mildly offensive Republican term for the Democratic party, a way of reminding the Democrats that they may not be the only democratic party.

Demonstration Cities and Metropolitan Development Act of 1966 *See* MODEL CITIES PROGRAM.

deniability The prearranged insulation of a political executive from a decision that he or she actually made, but is later able to plausibly deny, because there is no paper or other trail that would lead to the top. Arrangements for deniability are important parts of covert actions and diplomacy.

Dennis v United States 341 U.S. 494 (1951) The U.S. Supreme Court case that upheld the Smith Act of 1940 by allowing the conviction of American communists who advocated and taught the violent overthrow of the government of the United States. The Court found that the defendants posed a "clear and present danger" to the government and that it was not essential for the government to wait to take action until after the violence began. In a later case, *Yates v United States*, 354 U.S. 298 (1957), the *Dennis* decision was effectively negated when the Court ruled that a distinction had to be drawn between "conduct" and "advocacy." Now, for a conviction under the Smith Act, the government must prove that specific illegal acts were committed. Mere membership in the Communist party is not enough.

department 1 A CABINET-level agency of the U.S. government. 2 One of the three branches of government: executive, legislative, or judicial. 3 A general term for any administrative subdivision. 4 Usually the largest and most important administrative agencies at all levels of government. 5 A ministry in a country using a PARLIAMENTARY SYSTEM of government.

U.S. Cabinet Departments

Department	Year Created
State	1789
Treasury	1789
Defense	1949 (War, 1789; Navy, 1798)
Justice	1870 (attorney general, 1789)
Interior	1849
Agriculture	1862
Post Office	1872 (became independent, 1970)
Commerce	1913 (Commerce and Labor, 1903)
Labor	1913 (Commerce and Labor, 1903)
Health and Human Services	1979 (Health, Education, and Welfare, 1953)
Housing and Urban Development	1965
Transportation	1966
Energy	1977
Education	1979

department head The chief executive officer of a government department; sometimes called a secretary, as in secretary of State.

Depression, Great *See* GREAT DEPRESSION.

deregulation The lifting of restrictions on business, industry, and other professional activities for which government rules were established and bureaucracies created to administer. The modern movement toward deregulation, which really began during the Jimmy Carter administration under the leadership of Alfred Kahn at the Civil Aeronautics Board, was supported by both parties, but for different reasons. Republicans tended to support it because they were inclined to be philosophically hostile toward government interference with business in the first place. Democrats tended to support it because they felt that greater market competition would bring down prices for the consumer. *See also* REGULATION.

REFERENCES
Susan J. Tolchin and Martin Tolchin, *Dismantling America: The Rush to Deregulate* (Boston: Houghton Mifflin, 1983);
Martha Derthick and Paul J. Quirk, *The Politics of Reregulation* (Washington, D.C.: Brookings, 1985).

Deregulation: A Chronology

1976   Railroad Revitalization and Regulatory Reform Act gave railroads limited rate-setting authority.

1978   Airline Deregulation Act provided for the abolition of the Civil Aeronautics Board in 1985 and ended government authority over fares and mergers.

1980   Staggers Rail Act put further limits on the Interstate Commerce Commission's ability to set rates.

1980   Motor Carrier Act eased restrictions on the trucking industry.

1980   Depository Institution Deregulation and Monetary Control Act took some restrictions off mutual savings banks, allowed for interest on checking accounts, and removed interest rate ceilings.

1982   Bus Deregulatory Reform Act allowed bus companies to operate without applying to the ICC.

1982   Thrift Institutions Restructuring Act allowed savings and loan institutions to make commercial loans and nonresidential investments.

---

détente 1 A French word meaning the easing of strained relations. In diplomatic usage, this refers to the lessening of military and diplomatic tensions between two countries. *Compare to* ENTENTE. 2 The ongoing process of Soviet-American relations in the 1970s, which included political summit conferences, economic agreements leading to increased trade, and strategic arms limitations (SALT) agreements. *Compare to* COLD WAR; CONTAINMENT.

REFERENCES
Raymond L. Garthoff, *Détente and Confrontation: American-Soviet Relations from Nixon to Reagan* (Washington, D.C.: Brookings, 1985);
Peter Wallensteen, American-Soviet détente: What went wrong? *Journal of Peace Research* 22:1 (1985);
Norman Podhoretz, The Reagan road to détente, *Foreign Affairs* 63:3 (1985).

deterrence The prevention of an action by fear of the consequences. Deterrence is a state of mind brought about by the existence of a credible threat of unacceptable counteraction; it is the foundation of American defense policy. The basic argument is that, as long as a potential enemy believes that the United States is capable of responding to an attack with a devastating counterattack, there will be no war. Therefore a massive defense establishment is essential to maintain the peace.

REFERENCES
For analyses of nuclear deterrence, see Bruce M. Russett, *The Prisoners of Insecurity: Nuclear Deterrence, the Arms Race, and Arms Control* (San Francisco: Freeman, 1983);
Richard Wasserstrom, War, nuclear war, and nuclear deterrence: Some conceptual and moral issues, *Ethics* 95 (April 1985);
Robert Powell, The theoretical foundations of strategic nuclear deterrence, *Political Science Quarterly* 100 (Spring 1985).

deterrent effect Discouraging people from doing something by having policies or laws designed to prevent the unwanted behavior. Deterrence, which seems to have worked well as a matter of defense policy, has had a poorer record of success in the domestic arena: some people will violate the law no matter how severe the penalties.

REFERENCES

For the deterrent effect of capital punishment, see David P. Phillips, The deterrent effect of capital punishment: New evidence on an old controversy, *American Journal of Sociology* 86 (July 1980);

Brian Forst, Capital punishment and deterrence: Conflicting evidence? *Journal of Criminal Law & Criminology* 74 (Fall 1983).

For a comparative perspective, see Dane Archer, Rosemary Gartner, and Marc Beittel, Homicide and the death penalty: A cross-national test of a deterrence hypothesis, *Journal of Criminal Law & Criminology* 74 (Fall 1983).

For analyses of the deterrent effect of other law enforcement policies, see Stephen L. Mehay, The deterrent effect of urban police services: Further results, *Annals of Regional Science* 13 (March 1979);

Colin Loftin and David McDowall, The deterrent effects of the Florida Felony Firearm Law, *Journal of Criminal Law & Criminology* 75 (Spring 1984);

Lawrence W. Sherman and Richard A. Berk, The specific deterrent effects of arrest for domestic assault, *American Sociological Review* 49 (April 1984).

de Tocqueville, Alexis *See* TOCQUEVILLE, ALEXIS DE.

devaluation The lowering of the value of a nation's currency in relation to gold, or to the currency of other countries, when this value is set by government intervention in the exchange market. Devaluation normally refers to fixed exchange rates. In a system of flexible rates, if the value of the currency falls, it is referred to as depreciation; if the value of the currency rises, it is referred to as appreciation.

REFERENCE

Mark A. Miles, *Devaluation, the Trade Balance, and the Balance of Payments* (New York: Dekker, 1978).

developed countries Industrialized countries with per capita incomes of over two thousand dollars a year and with high standards of living in comparison to the nonindustrialized world. Whether a country is termed developed or developing is determined by such factors as GROSS NATIONAL PRODUCT, education, level of industrial development and production, health and welfare, and agricultural productivity. In general, the developed market economies of the FIRST WORLD together with the developed centrally planned economies of the SECOND WORLD are considered the developed countries.

developing countries Used interchangeably with THIRD WORLD, less-developed countries, underdeveloped countries, and the South, to refer to those countries with per capita incomes of under two thousand dollars and with comparatively low standards of living. Very low-income developing countries are often referred to as the FOURTH WORLD.

REFERENCE

George Dellaportas, Classification of nations as developed and less developed: An arrangement by discriminant analysis of socioeconomic data, *American Journal of Economics and Sociology* 42 (April 1983).

DHHS *See* HEALTH AND HUMAN SERVICES, DEPARTMENT OF.

dicta 1 OBITER DICTUM. 2 In the context of arbitration, an opinion or recommendation an arbitrator expresses in making an award that is not essential to the resolution of the dispute.

dictator The ancient Roman republic's term for the leader to whom was given extraordinary powers in times of crisis. Under the republic, the office was inherently temporary, but Julius Caesar and the Caesars who followed him gave the term its modern definition as a government in which one person or party controls all political action. In this century, the classic dictators, Adolph Hitler (1889–1945) of Germany and Benito Mussolini (1883–1945) of Italy, came to power as the leaders of mass movements. Others, such as Joseph Stalin (1879–1953) of the Soviet Union, rose to power by taking over a party that was already in control of a government. One should also differentiate between the dictators mentioned above, whose power was based on their personalities and control of force, and many modern dictators, such as the current leaders of China and the Soviet Union, who tend to be just the "first among equals" within a ruling elite.

The United States has never had a dictator, although some political bosses have sometimes approached such powers at the local level and some presidents, most notably Franklin D. Roosevelt, have been accused of seeking to become a dictator. The only president who had to face the real possibility of a dictatorship was Abraham Lincoln. During the middle of the Civil War, General Joseph Hooker (1814–1878) publicly stated that the country needed a dictator. Lincoln responded by writing to him on January 26, 1863, that "I have heard, in such a way as to believe it, of your recently saying that both the army and the government needed a dictator. Of course it was not for this, but in spite of it, that I have given you the command. Only those generals who gain successes can set up dictators. What I now ask of you is a military success, and I will risk the dictatorship." Because Hooker wasn't a very successful general, the question never came up again. However, Hooker's other wartime activities were so notorious that his name quickly became and remains synonymous with prostitute.

REFERENCE
William P. Bundy, Dictatorships and American foreign policy, *Foreign Affairs* 54 (October 1975).

diffusion theory of taxation The assertion that the real burden of an increase in taxes of any kind is eventually distributed throughout the population because of price changes.

dilatory motion A legislative motion, usually made upon a technical point, for the purpose of killing time and preventing action on a bill. Legislative rules usually outlaw dilatory motions, but enforcement is largely within the discretion of the presiding officer.

Dillon's rule The criteria developed by state courts to determine the nature and extent of powers granted to municipal corporations. It is a very strict and limiting rule, stating that municipal corporations have only those powers (1) expressly granted in the city charter, (2) necessarily or fairly implied by or incidental to formally expressed powers, and (3) essential to the declared purposes of the corporation. "Any fair, reasonable, substantial doubt" about a power is to result in denying that power to the corporation. The rule was formulated by John F. Dillon in his *Commentaries on the Law of Municipal Corporations,* 5th ed. (Boston: Little, Brown, 1911). In some states, the rule has been relaxed, especially in dealing with home rule cities. *See also* HOME RULE; MUNICIPAL CORPORATION.

REFERENCES
John G. Grumm and Russell D. Murphy, Dillon's rule reconsidered, *Annals of the American Academy of Political and Social Science* 416 (November 1974);

Doyle W. Buckwalter, Dillon's rule in the 1980s: Who's in charge of local affairs? *National Civic Review* 71 (September 1982).

diminishing marginal utility of income The principle that the marginal value of an additional dollar of income to a rich person is less than to a poor person. This concept underlies progressive taxation: proportionally larger tax payments by those with higher incomes recognizes the diminishing marginal utility of income. *Compare to* ABILITY TO PAY.

diplomacy 1 A state's foreign policy. While this is the most popular usage of the term, a policy in itself is not diplomacy. Foreign policies, made by governments or heads of state, represent the ends or goals of a nation's diplomacy. The word comes from the Greek *diploma,* which means a document that has been folded twice. This was a reference to the format of state papers and letters historically carried by diplomats. **2** The formal relations that independent nations maintain with each other; in effect, all of the normal and idiosyncratic intentional communications that nations have with each other short of war. Indeed, it is often said that diplomacy has failed when war begins. On the other hand, many nations throughout history have taken CLAUSEWITZ's attitude that war is only the continuation of diplomacy "by other means." **3** The art of maintaining and conducting international relations and negotiations. **4** According to Ambrose Bierce's *The Devil's Dictionary* (1911), "The patriotic art of lying for one's country." *Compare to* AMBASSADOR. **5** Skillful negotiations in any area.

REFERENCES

Harold Nicolson, *Diplomacy,* 3d ed. (New York: Oxford University Press, 1939, 1964);

Warren F. Ilchman, *Professional Diplomacy in the United States, 1770–1939: A Study in Administrative History* (Chicago: University of Chicago Press, 1961);

William Hayter, *The Diplomacy of the Great Powers* (New York: Macmillan, 1961);

Michael Donelan, The trade of diplomacy, *International Affairs* 45 (October 1969);

William H. Sullivan, The transformation of diplomacy, *Fletcher Forum* 8 (Summer 1984);

Kenneth W. Thompson, The ethical dimensions of diplomacy, *Review of Politics* 46 (July 1984);

Howard Jones, *The Course of American Diplomacy: From the Revolution to the Present* (New York: Watts, 1985).

diplomacy, dollar **1** The expansion of American business overseas. **2** A pejorative term for those diplomatic and military efforts that seek to help American business penetrate into foreign markets. **3** The foreign policy of the William Howard Taft administration (1909–1913), which actively sought to expand American trade in Latin America.

REFERENCES

Herbert Feis, *The Diplomacy of the Dollar* (New York: Norton, 1950);

Dana Gardner Munro, *Intervention and Dollar Diplomacy in the Caribbean, 1900–1921* (Princeton, NJ: Princeton University Press, 1964);

Louis A. Perez, Jr., Dollar diplomacy, preventive intervention, and the Platt amendment in Cuba, 1909–1912, *Inter-American Economic Affairs* 38 (Autumn 1984).

diplomacy, gunboat *See* GUNBOAT.

diplomacy, media Diplomatic activities conducted not through established diplomatic channels but through statements made through the mass media. Such wars by press release are inherent parts of propaganda and disinformation campaigns, but sometimes yield positive results. For example, in 1977 when President Anwar Sadat (1918–1981) of Egypt used the media to announce that he would go anywhere for peace, President Menachem Begin (1913–   ) of Israel used this statement as the "excuse" to invite Sadat to Jerusalem, a visit that eventually led to a peace treaty between the two nations.

REFERENCES

Patricia A. Karl, Media diplomacy, *Proceedings of the Academy of Political Science* 34 (1982);

Yoel Cohen, *Media Diplomacy: The Foreign Office in the Mass Communications Age* (London: Cass, 1986).

diplomacy, personal International negotiations conducted by a high-profile political actor, such as a head of government or foreign minister, as opposed to negotiations undertaken solely by professional diplomats. President Theodore Roosevelt's personal diplomacy earned him the Nobel Prize for Peace when he brokered the end of war between Russia and Japan in 1905. President Jimmy Carter's personal diplomacy led to the CAMP DAVID ACCORD, which preceded the peace treaty between Egypt and Israel.

diplomacy, shuttle International negotiations dependent upon a third-party neutral shuttling by airplane back and forth between the capitals of the countries involved. Henry Kissinger (1923–   ), secretary of state (1973–1977) under presidents Richard M. Nixon and Gerald R. Ford became the archetypal shuttle diplomat, flying between Middle Eastern capitals during the 1970s.

diplomatic agent A representative sent by one nation to another. The four categories of diplomatic rank were established at the Congress of Vienna in 1815. Ranks are important, because diplomatic precedence is based on rank and seniority. The ranks in order are

(1) ambassadors, papal legates, and nuncios; (2) envoys extraordinary and ministers plenipotentiary; (3) ministers resident; and (4) charges d'affaires (who act in the absence of the ambassador or minister).

diplomatic channels The normal, regularly established means by which governments collect and exchange information. A nation's most formal diplomatic channel to another nation is its diplomatic mission located in that nation.

diplomatic corps The totality of foreign diplomats residing in a capital city. The dean of the diplomatic corps is an honorary title given to the senior foreign ambassador, the one who has been in residence the longest.

diplomatic privileges and immunities The special rights that formally accredited diplomatic officials have, to be immune from the civil and criminal laws of the nation to which they are assigned. This immunity also applies to the physical grounds of an embassy, which is technically considered the soil of the foreign government. Abuses of diplomatic immunity often receive widespread publicity. They range from excessive parking tickets received by United Nations diplomats in New York City to using diplomatic offices as centers for terrorism against the host country. The most outrageous abuse of diplomatic immunity by a host government in recent times was the IRANIAN HOSTAGE CRISIS.

REFERENCES

Terry A. O'Neill, A new regime of diplomatic immunity: The Diplomatic Relations Act of 1978, *Tulane Law Review* 54 (April 1980);

L. C. Green, Niceties and necessities—The case for diplomatic immunity, *International Perspectives* (March/April 1980);

M. Cherif Bassiouni, Protection of diplomats under Islamic law, *American Journal of International Law* 74 (July 1980);

James D. Ross, Diplomatic immunity, territorial asylum and child rights, *Harvard International Law Journal* 25 (Winter 1984);

Rosalyn Higgins, The abuse of diplomatic privileges and immunities: Recent United Kingdom experience, *American Journal of International Law* 79 (July 1985).

diplomatic summit What occurs when heads of state, as opposed to just their representatives, meet to confer on international issues.

REFERENCES

Coit D. Blacker, Lessons from U.S.–Soviet summits, *Bulletin of the Atomic Scientists* 41 (November 1985);

Kenneth L. Adelman, Summitry: The historical perspectives, *Presidential Studies Quarterly* 16 (Summer 1986).

diplomat in chief The head of a government, such as a president or chief of state, to whom a country's diplomats ultimately report.

REFERENCES

Elmer Plischke, The President's image as diplomat in chief, *Review of Politics* 47 (October 1985);

Elmer Plischke, *Diplomat in Chief: The President at the Summit* (New York: Praeger, 1986).

direct action 1 Politically inspired violence. 2 Obstructing the political process to within the limits of the law.

direct democracy *See* DEMOCRACY, DIRECT.

directive An order, whether oral or written, issued by one civilian government official commanding action from lower-rank officials who might be affected.

REFERENCES

Raymond L. Chambers, The executive power: A preliminary study of the concept and of the efficacy of presidential directives, *Presidential Studies Quarterly* 7 (Winter 1977);

James C. Garand and Donald A. Gross, Toward a theory of bureaucratic compliance with presidential directives, *Presidential Studies Quarterly* 12 (Spring 1982).

direct legislation The use of direct democratic techniques, such as the INITIATIVE, the REFERENDUM, or the RECALL.

REFERENCE

Howard D. Hamilton, Direct legislation: Some implications of open housing referenda, *American Political Science Review* 64 (March 1970).

direct mail 1 Selling a product directly to a customer, using the mail as the vehicle for both advertising and solicitation. 2 An increasingly popular way to solicit political campaign contributions. It is often thought that large donors are the prime financial supporters of candidates for major offices. Not so. The reality is that the small donor is the backbone of most modern campaign finances—and the best, most economical, most efficient, and most cost effective way to reach them is through direct mail.

REFERENCE

2 R. Kenneth Godwin and Robert Cameron Mitchell, The implications of direct mail for political organizations, *Social Science Quarterly* 65 (September 1984).

direct primary *See* PRIMARY, DIRECT.

direct tax *See* TAX, DIRECT/INDIRECT TAX.

dirty tricks 1 The covert operations of an intelligence agency. 2 Dishonorable acts during a political campaign by the opposition or by pranksters. Examples include starting false rumors, creating scandals with forged evidence, and disrupting campaign schedules.

REFERENCES

1 Richard J. Barnet, Dirty tricks and the intelligence underworld, *Society* 12 (March/April 1975);
   Philip Agee and Louis Wolf, eds., *Dirty Work: The CIA in Western Europe* (Secaucus, NJ: Stuart, 1978).

2 Bruce L. Felknor, *Dirty Politics* (Westport, CT: Greenwood, 1966).

disarmament The recurring efforts of the major powers to put limits on their war-making capabilities. *Compare to* ARMS CONTROL.

REFERENCE

James Clotfelter, Disarmament movements in the United States, *Journal of Peace Research* 23 (June 1986).

discharge a committee To relieve a legislative committee from jurisdiction over a measure that is before it. In the U.S. House of Representatives, if a committee does not report a bill within thirty days after the bill is referred to it, any member may file a discharge motion to bring the bill to the floor for consideration. This motion, treated as a petition, needs the signatures of 218 members (a majority of the House). If a resolution to consider a bill is held up in the Rules Committee for more than seven legislative days, any member may enter a motion to discharge the committee. The motion is handled like any other discharge motion in the House. Occasionally, to expedite noncontroversial legislative business, a committee is discharged upon unanimous consent of the House, and a petition is not required. Discharge motions are rarely successful.

discharge calendar The U.S. House of Representatives calendar to which motions to discharge committees are referred when the necessary 218 signatures have been obtained.

discharge resolution In the U.S. Senate, a special motion that any senator may introduce to relieve a committee from consideration of a bill that is before it. The resolution can be called up on motion for approval or disapproval, in the same manner as other matters of Senate business. *Compare to* DISCHARGE A COMMITTEE.

discount rate The interest rate paid by a commercial bank when it borrows from a Federal Reserve Bank. The discount rate is one of the tools of monetary policy used by the Federal Reserve System. The Federal Reserve customarily raises or lowers the discount rate to signal a shift toward restraining or toward easing its money and credit policy.

discrimination In employment, the failure to treat equals equally. Whether deliberate or unintentional, any action that has the effect of limiting employment and advancement opportunities because of an individual's sex, race, color, age, national origin, religion, physical handicap, or other irrelevant criteria, is discrimination. Because of the EEO and civil rights legislation of recent years, people aggrieved by unlawful discrimination now have a variety of administrative and judicial remedies open to them. Employment discrimination has its origins in the less-genteel concept of bigotry. *See also* CIVIL RIGHTS ACT OF 1964;

EQUAL EMPLOYMENT OPPORTUNITY; EQUAL EMPLOYMENT OPPORTUNITY ACT OF 1972; REVERSE DISCRIMINATION; RIGHTFUL PLACE; WASHINGTON V DAVIS.

REFERENCES

For the standard history, see Gustavus Myers, *History of Bigotry in the United States,* ed. and rev. Henry M. Christman, (New York: Capricorn, 1943, 1960).

Also see Frank P. Samford III, Toward a constitutional definition of racial discrimination, *Emory Law Journal* 25 (Summer 1976);

William P. Murphy, Julius G. Getman, and James E. Jones, Jr., *Discrimination in Employment,* 4th ed. (Washington, D.C.: Bureau of National Affairs, 1979).

dishonest graft *See* HONEST GRAFT/DISHONEST GRAFT.

disinformation A term used in intelligence work to refer to (1) the purposeful lies a government overtly or covertly releases to the international mass media to mislead adversary nations; (2) false information secretly transmitted to rival intelligence agencies; or (3) the purposeful lies a government tells its own people to hide actions that would be considered unacceptable and possibly be checked by another branch of government if known. *Compare to* PROPAGANDA.

REFERENCES

Arnaud de Borchgrave, Disseminating disinformation, *Society* 19 (March/April 1982);

L. John Martin, Disinformation: An instrumentality in the propaganda arsenal, *Political Communication and Persuasion* 2:1 (1982);

Dennis Kux, Soviet Active measures and disinformation: Overview and assessment, *Parameters: Journal of the U.S. Army War College* 15 (Winter 1985).

dissent *See* OPINION, MINORITY.

district A subdivision of many different types of areas (such as countries, states, or counties) for judicial, political, or administrative purposes. Districting is the process of drawing a district's boundary lines for purposes of APPORTIONMENT.

REFERENCES

Richard G. Niemi and John Deegan, Jr., A theory of political districting, *American Political Science Review* 72 (December 1978);

Robert G. Dixon, Jr., Fair criteria and procedures for establishing legislative districts, *Policy Studies Journal* 9 (Special Issue no. 3, 1980–81).

district council A level of labor organization below the national union but above the locals. The district council is composed of local unions in a particular industry within a limited geographic area. The district councils of local government employee unions are often major influences in municipal affairs.

REFERENCES

Edward Handman and Norman Adler, District Council 37 (AFSCME) and the community, *Social Policy* 13 (Spring 1983);

Bernard Bellush and Jewel Bellush, Participation in local politics: District Council 37 in New York, *National Civic Review* 74 (May 1985).

district court/federal district court/U.S. district court The court of original jurisdiction for most federal cases. This is the only federal court that holds trials in which juries and witnesses are used. Each state has at least one district court. Altogether, there are eighty-nine district courts in the fifty states, plus one in the District of Columbia. In addition, the Commonwealth of Puerto Rico has a U.S. district court with jurisdiction corresponding to that of district courts in the various states. At present, each district court has from one to twenty-seven federal district judgeships, depending upon the amount of judicial work within its territory. In districts with more than one judge, the judge senior in commission who has not reached his or her seventieth birthday acts as chief judge. There are altogether 485 permanent district judgeships in the fifty states and fifteen in the District of Columbia. There are seven district judgeships in Puerto Rico. *Compare to* COURT OF APPEALS.

REFERENCES

Frank M. Johnson, The Constitution and the federal district judge, *Texas Law Review* 54 (June 1976);

Wolf V. Heydebrand, The context of public bureaucracies: An organizational analysis for federal district courts, *Law and Society Review* 11 (Summer 1977);

Ronald Stidham, Robert A. Carp, and C. K. Rowland, Patterns of presidential influence on the federal district courts: An analysis of the appointment process, *Presidential Studies Quarterly* 14 (Fall 1984).

district, floterial Defined by the U.S. Supreme Court in *Davis v Mann,* 377 U.S. 678 (1964), as "a legislative district which includes within its boundaries several separate districts or political subdivisions which independently would not be entitled to additional representation, but whose conglomerate population entitles the entire area to another seat in a particular legislative body being apportioned."
REFERENCE
Sidney Duncombe and Tony Stewart, Idaho's unique approach to state legislative apportionment: Statewide floterial districts, *State Government* 58 (Fall 1985).

district, multimember Any electoral district that elects more than one candidate to a legislature at the same time. This is often the case with AT-LARGE seats on a city council. The U.S. Supreme Court has held in *White v Regester,* 412 U.S. 755 (1973), that it is unconstitutional for a multimember district to deprive a racial minority within the district of meaningful access to political representation. But multimember districts, according to *Whitcomb v Chavis,* 403 U.S. 124 (1971), are not automatically unconstitutional simply because minorities would do better politically under a single-member district system.
REFERENCES
Manning J. Dauer and Michael A. Maggiotto, The status of multi-member districts in state and local government, *National Civic Review* 68 (January 1979);
Alan L. Clem and W. O. Farber, Manipulated democracy: The multi-member district, *National Civic Review* 68 (May 1979);
Richard G. Niemi, Jeffrey S. Hill, and Bernard Grofman, The impact of multimember districts on party representation in U.S.

state legislatures, *Legislative Studies Quarterly* 10 (November 1985).

district, open A legislative district in which the incumbent legislator is not running for reelection. This means that none of the challengers will have the advantage of the INCUMBENCY EFFECT.

district, single-member Any electoral district that elects only one candidate (chosen by a plurality) to a legislature such as a city council, state assembly, or the U.S. House of Representatives.
REFERENCE
Joseph F. Zimmerman, The single-member district system: Can it be reformed? *National Civic Review* 70 (May 1981).

diversity of citizenship The situation that exists when the parties in a lawsuit come from different states. Article III, Section 2, of the U.S. Constitution gives jurisdiction in such cases to the federal courts. But the Congress has since given exclusive jurisdiction for these cases to state courts if no federal question is involved and any amount in question is less than ten thousand dollars. Above that, there is CONCURRENT JURISDICTION.

divestiture 1 The removing of something from one's possession; to be legally deprived of an asset; a stripping off. 2 A court order to a corporation that it get rid of something (another company, stock, property) because of ANTITRUST LAWS. Also, carrying out of the court's order. 3 A policy calling for companies or for administrators of pension funds, endowment funds, and so on, to sell off all assets of or stock in companies with assets in South Africa, in an effort to encourage that country to change its domestic civil rights policies. *Compare to* BOYCOTT.
REFERENCES
2 Harry M. Shooshan, ed., *Disconnecting Bell: The Impact of the AT&T Divestiture* (New York: Pergamon, 1984).
3 Mary C. Gosiger, Strategies for divestment from United States companies and financial institutions doing business with or in South Africa, *Human Rights Quarterly* 8 (August 1986).

divine right of kings The notion that monarchs rule by the will of, indeed in place of, God. Since God created this situation, any effort to change it would be considered sinful, because it is through kings that God works his will on men. Because it was, as Alexander Pope (1688–1744) wrote, "the right divine of Kings to govern wrong," the founding fathers thoroughly rejected this doctrine in the U.S. Declaration of Independence.

division vote *See* VOTE, STANDING.

Dixiecrats Southern Democrats who opposed their party's presidential nomination of Harry S Truman in 1948 because of his civil rights policies. They subsequently ran their own candidate for president (J. Strom Thurmond, now a Republican senator from South Carolina) and lost.
REFERENCE
William D. Barnard, *Dixiecrats and Democrats: Alabama Politics, 1942–1950* (University: University of Alabama Press, 1974).

doctrine 1 A legal principle or rule, such as the FAIRNESS DOCTRINE. 2 A foreign policy, such as the MONROE DOCTRINE or TRUMAN DOCTRINE. 3 The principles by which military forces guide their actions in support of objectives. *See also* BREZHNEV DOCTRINE; CARTER DOCTRINE; EISENHOWER DOCTRINE; NIXON DOCTRINE; REAGAN DOCTRINE.

DOD *See* DEFENSE, U.S. DEPARTMENT OF.

DOE *See* EDUCATION, U.S. DEPARTMENT OF; ENERGY, U.S. DEPARTMENT OF.

do gooders A derisive term for social and political reformers. Do gooders are often joined by goo-goos, who stand for good government.

DOI *See* INTERIOR, U.S. DEPARTMENT OF THE.

DOL *See* LABOR, U.S. DEPARTMENT OF.

dollar diplomacy *See* DIPLOMACY, DOLLAR.

Domestic Council *See* OFFICE OF POLICY DEVELOPMENT.

domicile A person's permanent legal residence. While a person can legally have many residences, he or she can have only one domicile. Some government jurisdictions require their employees to be domiciled within the bounds of that jurisdiction. *Compare to* VOTING RESIDENCE; *see also* MCCARTHY V PHILADELPHIA CIVIL SERVICE COMMISSION.
REFERENCE
Stephen L. Hayford, Local government residency requirements and labor relations: Implications and choices for public administrators, *Public Administration Review* 38 (September/October 1978).

domino theory The notion that if a critically situated country falls to communism, its neighbors will soon follow. This was a major element in the rationale for American involvement in the Vietnam War. The domino metaphor was first popularized by President Dwight D. Eisenhower in a press conference on April 7, 1954, with reference to the strategic importance of Indochina. He said: "You have a row of dominoes set up. You knock over the first one, and what will happen to the last one is a certainty that it will go over very quickly." The domino theory has not proved very useful as a predictor of communist expansion, because it is sometimes true and sometimes not. Nevertheless, the domino theory remains a general justification for taking action in a given instance, because failure to do so would produce effects on neighboring nations.
REFERENCE
Jerry Mark Silverman, The domino theory: Alternatives to a self-fulfilling prophecy, *Asian Survey* XV (November 1975).

donkey The symbol of the Democratic party, first used by Thomas Nast (1840–1902) in 1874 in a series of cartoons that expounded upon Ignatius Donnelly's (1831–1901) critical comment that "the Democratic party is like a

Cartoonists popularized the donkey as the symbol of the Democratic Party as early as 1874.

mule—without pride of ancestry nor hope of posterity." *Compare to* ELEPHANT.

Dooley, Mr. *See* FINLEY PETER DUNNE.

doomsday machine **1** Herman Kahn's concept from *On Thermonuclear War* (Princeton, NJ: Princeton University Press, 1961) of a theoretical device that would automatically destroy the entire world if the nation that built it suffered unacceptable nuclear damage from an aggressor. Thus the doomsday machine, with its capability for total thermonuclear destruction, would function as a deterrent. **2** A full nuclear exchange by the superpowers, because it would virtually destroy the entire world.

Dothard v Rawlinson 433 U.S. 321 (1977) The U.S. Supreme Court case that upheld an Alabama regulation prohibiting the employment of women as prison guards in "contact positions" (those requiring continual close physical proximity to inmates) within the state's correctional facilities.

double dippers **1** Retired military personnel, drawing their military pensions and also employed by the federal government as civilian workers. **2** State and local government employees, even elected officials, who hold private-sector jobs while occupying what are thought of as full-time government positions.

3 Federal civil service pensioners who also become eligible for social security retirement benefits and thus, quite legitimately, collect two federal pensions.

double jeopardy The Fifth Amendment requirement that no person "be subject for the same offense to be twice put in jeopardy of life or limb." This clause prevents retrials in either state or federal court of those already tried once—and thus placed in "jeopardy" once. Jeopardy attaches not only after a prior conviction or acquittal but also in jury trials once the jury is sworn and, in trials without juries, once the introduction of evidence has begun. Thereafter, if for some reason the trial is terminated, a second trial is barred, except in limited circumstances. Such circumstances include those cases in which mistrials are declared at the request or with the consent of the defendant or in cases of manifest necessity, such as when the jury deadlocks or when illness or death prevents continuation of a trial. A second trial also is permissible when an appellate court sets aside a guilty verdict and orders a new trial.

The double jeopardy clause offers no protection when conduct violates both federal and state law; the Supreme Court has held in *Bartkus v Illinois,* 355 U.S. 281 (1958), that an offender may be prosecuted in the courts of both jurisdictions. Neither does the clause prevent the multiple prosecutions of a suspect for conduct that constitutes more than one offense, though factual issues decided by one jury may prevent relitigation of those factual issues in a subsequent trial. Furthermore, if a defendant obtains a reversal of a conviction and is retried, the clause does not prevent an increase of penalty in the event that the defendant is reconvicted, although due process requires the sentencing judge to demonstrate that the penalty was not increased to penalize the defendant for exercising the right to appeal. The Supreme Court held in *Benton v Maryland,* 395 U.S. 784 (1969), that the Fifth Amendment prohibition on double jeopardy applies to the states through the Fourteenth Amendment.

REFERENCES

Jay A. Sigler, *Double Jeopardy: The Development of a Legal and Social Policy* (Ithaca, NY: Cornell University Press, 1969);

James E. King, The problems of double jeopardy in successive federal-state prosecutions: A Fifth Amendment solution, *Stanford Law Review* 31 (February 1979);

Michael J. Klarman, Mistrials arising from prosecutorial error: Double jeopardy protection, *Stanford Law Review* 34 (May 1982).

double taxation **1** The illegal imposition of two taxes on the same property by the same government during the same time period for the same purpose. **2** Taxing the same money twice. One legal form of double taxation is taxing a corporation on its profits, then taxing its stockholders on dividends from the corporation. Another is the taxation of the income of foreign nationals who will be taxed on the same income when they return home.

REFERENCES
1   Charles K. Coe, Double taxation: Identifying the hidden tax burden in America's cities, *Urban Affairs Quarterly* 19 (December 1983).
2   Charles R. Irish, International double taxation agreements and income taxation at source, *International and Comparative Law Quarterly* 23, Part 2 (April 1974).

doubt, beyond a reasonable *See* BEYOND A REASONABLE DOUBT.

dove *See* HAWK.

Downs, Anthony (1930–   ) The economist and policy analyst who is generally credited with establishing the intellectual framework for public choice economics in his *An Economic Theory of Democracy* (New York: Harper & Row, 1957). His classic book on bureaucracy, *Inside Bureaucracy* (Boston: Little, Brown, 1967), sought to justify bureaucratic government on economic grounds and to develop laws and propositions that would aid in predicting the behavior of bureaus and bureaucrats. *See also* BUREAUCRACY; ISSUE-ATTENTION CYCLE.

draft **1** The CONSCRIPTION of citizens into the armed services. *Compare to* SELECTIVE SERVICE. **2** The nomination of a political candidate who has claimed disinterest by refusing to announce his or her candidacy or to go through the normal procedures that involve announced candidacy. It is a device that can be used to suggest vast popular support and an unwillingness to incur political indebtedness to obtain support. Only in the rarest of cases is someone drafted who was not encouraging the process from behind the scenes. One such rare person was William Tecumseh Sherman (1820–1891), the Civil War general who, upon being asked to be the Republican presidential nominee in 1884, said: "I will not accept if nominated, and I will not serve if elected." The Shermanesque refusal is now the classic manner in which to genuinely refuse a draft.

REFERENCES
1   Patricia M. Shields, The burden of the draft: The Vietnam Years, *Journal of Political and Military Sociology* 9 (Fall 1981).
2   Daniel Zenkel, Presidential "draft" committees and the Federal Election Campaign Act, *Columbia Law Review* 84 (January 1984).

Drago Doctrine The policy that nations should not use their armed forces in foreign countries to force the payments of debts owed by the citizens of the second country to citizens of the first. This doctrine, which has since been widely endorsed, was formulated by Luis M. Drago (1859–1921) while foreign minister of Argentina in 1902.

dramaturgy The manner in which a person acts out or theatrically stages his or her organizational or political role. Political candidates who make an effort to look or sound senatorial or presidential are engaging in dramaturgy. Of course, if they have to make an effort to look it or sound it, they may not have it. One is reminded of the traditional advice to actors: "Always be sincere. If you can fake that, you've got it made."

REFERENCE
Bruce E. Gronbeck, Functional and dramaturgical themes of presidential campaigning, *Presidential Studies Quarterly* 14 (Fall 1984).

Draper v United States *See* PROBABLE CAUSE.

Dred Scott v Sandford 19 Howard 393 (1857) The second case in which the U.S. Supreme Court declared an act of the Congress to be unconstitutional (the first was *Marbury v Madison* in 1803). While it helped to further entrench the Court's right to judicial review, its holdings—that blacks could not become citizens and that the United States could not prohibit slavery in unsettled territories—did much to make the Civil War inevitable, especially because the decision made a legislative solution to the slavery issue virtually impossible. The Dred Scott decision was overturned by the Thirteenth and Fourteenth amendments.

REFERENCES

Stanley I. Kutler, ed., *The Dred Scott Decision: Law or Politics?* (Boston: Houghton Mifflin, 1967);

Don E. Fehrenbacher, *The Dred Scott Case: Its Significance in American Law and Politics* (New York: Oxford University Press, 1978).

Dror, Yehezkel (1928–   ) A leading proponent of a more rational approach to policy formulation and evaluation. Dror advocates an optimal approach to policymaking that seeks out the best possible policy, regardless of the past. As such, he is a major critic of incremental approaches to policymaking.

REFERENCES

Dror's major works include Policy analysts: A new professional role in government service, *Public Administration Review* 27 (September 1967);

Public Policymaking Reexamined (Scranton, PA: Chandler, 1968);

Design for Policy Sciences (New York: American Elsevier, 1971);

Ventures in Policy Sciences (New York: American Elsevier, 1971).

dual federalism *See* FEDERALISM, DUAL.

due process The constitutional requirement that "no person shall be deprived of life, liberty, or property without due process of law." While the specific requirements of due process vary with U.S. Supreme Court decisions, the essence of the idea is that people must be given adequate notice and a fair opportunity to present their side in a legal dispute and that no law or government procedure should be arbitrary or unfair.

REFERENCES

Deborah D. Goldman, Due process and public personnel management, *Review of Public Personnel Administration* 2 (Fall 1981);

David L. Kirp and Donald N. Jensen, What does due process do? *Public Interest* 73 (Fall 1983);

J. S. Fuerst and Roy Petty, Due process—How much is enough? *Public Interest* 79 (Spring 1985).

due process of law A right guaranteed by the Fifth, Sixth, and Fourteenth amendments and generally understood to mean that legal proceedings will follow rules and forms established for the protection of private rights. The Fourteenth Amendment's provision that "no person shall be deprived of life, liberty, or property without due process of law" is considered to be a powerful restraint on government interference in the rights or property interests of citizens. However, the concept raises considerable questions regarding both the procedures deemed fair and the kinds of rights and interests protected by it. For the most part, these two elements are related, in that the more fundamental the right or interest, the greater the procedural protections. The degree of protection ranges from a jury trial and appellate processes to a hearing, perhaps including a right to counsel, confrontation, and cross-examination of adverse witnesses before an impartial examiner. Of course, there are instances in which citizens are adversely affected by administrative decisions but have no right or opportunity to be heard. In recent years, the most interesting developments in this area of constitutional law have been (1) the extension of the procedural safeguards afforded citizens at the hearing stage and (2) the extension of the right to have a hearing in situations previously not deemed sufficiently important to warrant such protections. Consider the procedural protections afforded public employees in dismissals; it has now been found that where constitutionally protected rights and interests are at stake, there may be a right to an open hearing, including counsel, confrontation, and cross-examination.

REFERENCES

William Cohen, Congressional power to interpret due process and equal protection, *Stanford Law Review* 27 (February 1975);

Keith Jurow, Untimely thoughts: A reconsideration of the origins of due process of law, *American Journal of Legal History* 19 (October 1975);

Daniel J. Leffell, Congressional power to enforce due process rights, *Columbia Law Review* 80 (October 1980);

M. A. McGhehey, The overextension of due process, *Education and Urban Society* 14 (February 1982);

Jerry L. Mashaw, *Due Process in the Administrative State* (New Haven, CT: Yale University Press, 1985).

due process, procedural The legal process and machinery that ensures due process. Daniel Webster (1782–1852) gave the classic description of due process as that "which hears before it condemns, which proceeds upon inquiry, and renders judgment only after trial." Procedural due process thus requires the legal system to follow the rules.

due process, substantive The formal legal requirement that due process requirements be observed by government or its agents. Thomas M. Cooley's *Constitutional Limitations* (Boston: Little, Brown, 1868) is considered the doctrinal foundation of substantive due process in the United States. According to Bernard Schwartz in *The Law in America: A History* (New York: McGraw-Hill, 1974), "Cooley identified due process with the doctrine of vested rights drawn from natural law, which had been developed to protect property rights. This meant that due process itself was the great substantive safeguard of property." It was "Cooley's analysis which prepared the way for the virtual takeover of American public law by the Due Process Clause of the Fourteenth Amendment." Thus, the threads of Cooley's analysis can be found whenever an American court strikes down an executive or legislative act for being arbitrary or unreasonable and thus lacking in substantive due process.

dumping 1 Getting rid of a political candidate or supporter who has proven useless, unpopular, or embarrassing. 2 Selling a product in export markets below that product's selling price in domestic markets. Rules created by countries to protect themselves from this practice are called antidumping laws. Additional tariffs that may be imposed on imports that have been dumped are called dumping duties.

REFERENCES

Wilfred J. Ethier, Dumping, *Journal of Political Economy* 90 (June 1982);

Clyde Stoltenberg, United States antidumping laws and Chinese exports to the United States, *Hastings International and Comparative Law Review* 7 (Fall 1983).

Duncan v Louisiana *See* JURY, TRIAL.

Dunne, Finley Peter (1867–1936) The political satirist and journalist who created Mr. Dooley, the worldly philosopher and saloon-keeper who spouted political commentary and irreverence. For example, it was Mr. Dooley who first observed—as always, in a rich Irish brogue—that "no matter whether th' Constitution follows th' flag or not, th' Supreme Court follows th' illiction returns." And it was Mr. Dooley who first made the empirical observation that "I niver knew a pollytician to go wrong ontil he's been contaminated by contact with a business man." And finally, it was Mr. Dooley who defined an appeal as "where ye ask wan coort to show its contempt f'r another coort." *Compare to* HONEST GRAFT/DISHONEST GRAFT.

REFERENCES

John M. Harrison, Finley Peter Dunne and the progressive movement, *Journalism Quarterly* 44:3 (1967);

Charles Fanning, *Finley Peter Dunne and Mr. Dooley: The Chicago Years* (Lexington: University Press of Kentucky, 1978);

Grace Eckley, *Finley Peter Dunne* (Boston: Twayne, 1981).

Dunn v Blumstein *See* RESIDENCY REQUIREMENT.

Durkheim, Emile *See* ANOMIE.

duty 1 A tax imposed on imported products. A duty is distinguished from a tariff solely by the fact that the duty is the actual tax imposed or collected, while the tariff, technically speaking, is the schedule of duties. However, in practice the words are often used interchangeably. **2** A legal obligation to do something because of an office one holds, a profession one practices, and so on. **3** A moral obligation that, if left unfulfilled, would cause only a bruised conscience.

REFERENCES

1 William A. Brock and Stephen P. Magee, The economics of special interest politics: The case of the tariff, *American Economic Review* 68 (May 1978);

Jagdish N. Bhagwati and T. N. Srinivasan, Revenue seeking: A generalization of the theory of tariffs, *Journal of Political Economy* 88 (December 1980);

Edward John Ray, The determinants of tariff and nontariff trade restrictions in the United States, *Journal of Political Economy* 89 (February 1981).

3 R. W. M. Dias, The unenforceable duty, *Tulane Law Review* 33 (1959);

Amitai Etzioni, Duty: The forgotten virtue, *Bureaucrat* 15 (Summer 1986).

duty, ad valorem A tax imposed on goods on the basis of value. The advantage of ad valorem duties is that they fluctuate with economic conditions—that is, the duty rises and falls in relation to prices. The disadvantages of the ad valorem system are that it presents a valuation problem, is an expensive system to maintain, and opens the doors to corruption.

duty, antidumping A tax calculated to offset the advantage gained by exporters when they sell their products in a foreign country at a price lower than that at which the same article sells at home or at a price even lower than the cost of production.

REFERENCE

Greyson Bryan, *Taxing Unfair International Trade Practices: A Study of U.S. Antidumping and Countervailing Duty Laws* (Lexington, MA: Lexington Books, 1980).

duty, civic *See* CIVIC DUTY.

duty, compound A tax with the combined attributes of ad valorem and specific duties.

Fifty cents per pound plus 10 percent ad valorem is an example of how a combined duty would be imposed.

duty, countervailing A tax imposed in addition to the regular duty for the purpose of counteracting the effect of a bounty or subsidy in another country.

REFERENCE

A. Paul Victor, Injury determinations by the United States International Trade Commission in antidumping and countervailing duty proceedings, *New York University Journal of International Law and Politics* 16 (Spring 1984).

duty, export A tax imposed on goods leaving a nation or political unit. Export duties are expressly forbidden in the United States by the U.S. Constitution, which provides that "no tax or duty shall be laid on articles exported from any state." Other countries, however, lay export duties even on their chief exports—for revenue purposes, to bolster domestic manufacture of some article, or to encourage keeping scarce raw materials within the country for home use.

duty, specific A tax imposed on the basis of some unit of measurement—so much per pound, per bushel, per dozen. Specific duties avoid the problems of appraisement involved in the collection of ad valorem taxes. The disadvantages of specific duties are that they require a minute detailing of rates for the many products imported and that they do not reflect changes in economic conditions.

duty, transit A tax imposed by a country simply for allowing goods to pass through its territory en route from one country to another. The United States does not levy transit duties.

Duverger's law French political scientist Maurice Duverger's (1917–   ) assertion, from his *Political Parties: Their Organization and Activity in the Modern State* (New York: Wiley, 1951, 1963), that "the simple-majority single-ballot system favours the two-party system. Of all the hypotheses that have been defined in this book, this approaches the most nearly perhaps to a true sociological law. An almost complete correlation is observable between the simple-majority single-ballot system and the two-party system: dualist countries use the simple-majority vote, and simple-majority vote countries are dualist. The exceptions are very rare and can generally be explained as the result of special conditions." Thus, according to Duverger's law, the strong American two-party system is very much a product of the simple-majority winner-take-all voting system, the norm in American elections. Any newly installed system of proportional representation in American politics would necessarily weaken the two-party system. *Compare to* TWO-PARTY SYSTEM.

REFERENCES

Kenneth Janda and Desmond S. King, Formalizing and testing Duverger's theories on political parties, *Comparative Political Studies* 18 (July 1985);

Rein Taagepera and Bernard Grofman, Rethinking Duverger's law, *European Journal of Political Research* 13 (December 1985);

William H. Riker, Duverger's law revisited, *Electoral Laws and Their Political Consequences* ed. Bernard Grofman and Arend Lijphart (New York: Agathon, 1986).

dyed in the wool   The most partisan of the partisans; one who cannot be converted; one who goes all out for his or her party. The phrase comes from the fact that wool dyed while still raw retains its color better than wool dyed after processing.

Dyer Act of 1919   The federal law that makes it a federal crime to transport stolen motor vehicles across state lines. This is the law that so often brings the FBI into a crime that would otherwise be solely the concern of state and local police.

The Kennedy family exemplified political dynasties in the mid- to late-twentieth century. (Left to right: Edward, John, and Robert Kennedy in 1958.)

dynasty   **1** The passing of political power through a succession of rulers directly related by blood.   **2** An American political family, such as Adams, Roosevelt, or Kennedy, whose various members seek and gain political office over a long period of time.

REFERENCES

Stephen Hess, *American Political Dynasties from Adams to Kennedy* (Garden City, NY: Doubleday, 1966);

Sandra L. Quinn and Sanford Kanter, *America's Royalty: All the Presidents' Children* (Westport, CT: Greenwood, 1983).

E

earmarked tax *See* TAX, EARMARKED.

easement *See* RIGHT-OF-WAY/EASEMENT.

Easton, David (1917–   ) The political scientist who wrote the most influential applications of systems analysis to the political process. Easton sought, in his own words, "in some small way to win back for theory its proper and necessary place" in political science. He succeeded admirably. Most modern theorizing about the workings of the American political system can be traced back to his direct or indirect influence. Heinz Eulau, in the introduction to his edited *Behavioralism in Political Science* (New York: Atherton, 1969), writes that Easton's 1953 *The Political System* (New York: Knopf) "thoroughly castigated the discipline for its theoretical antiquarianism, its methodological backwardness, its failure to march at the frontiers of inquiry alongside the behavioral sciences. Easton's view of the state of the discipline was widely shared by the generation for which he spoke." Easton was a major factor in advancing political science into BEHAVIORALISM, a position from which the profession has yet to retreat.

REFERENCES

David Easton, *A Systems Analysis of Political Life* (New York: Wiley, 1965).

For accounts of Easton's influences, see Michael Evans, Notes on David Easton's model of the political system, *Journal of Commonwealth Political Studies* 8 (July 1970);

Peter Leslie, General theory in political science: A critique of Easton's system analysis, *British Journal of Political Science* 2 (April 1972).

East-West **1** East: the Soviet Union and its Eastern European satellites; West: the United States and its Western European allies (plus Japan). **2** A linguistic symbol of the traditional and perhaps irreconcilable difference between cultures. The most famous expression of

this is that portion of Rudyard Kipling's (1865–1936) *The Ballad of East and West* (1889), which says: "Oh, East is East, and West is West, and never the twain shall meet." This vestigial racism will continue to recede— but will also continue to exist.

REFERENCES

1 Klaus von Beyme, Detente and East-West economic relations, *Journal of Politics* 43 (November 1981);

Hans-Georg Wieck, The future of East-West relations, *NATO Review* 29 (December 1981).

econometric model A set of related equations used to analyze economic data through mathematical and statistical techniques. Such models are devised to depict the essential quantitative relations that determine the behavior of output, income, employment, and prices. Econometric models are used for forecasting, for estimating the likely quantitative impact of alternative assumptions, including those pertaining to government policies, and for testing various propositions about the way the economy works.

REFERENCE

W. Patrick Beaton, ed., *Municipal Expenditures, Revenues, and Services: Economic Models and Their Use by Planners* (New Brunswick, NJ: Center for Urban Policy Research/Rutgers University, 1983).

econometrics A subdiscipline of economics known by its use of mathematical techniques, such as regression analysis and modeling, to test economic theories and to forecast economic activity.

REFERENCE

Gregory C. Chow and Sharon Bernstein Megdal, An econometric definition of the inflation-unemployment tradeoff, *American Economic Review* 68 (June 1978).

economic action The planned use of economic measures (as opposed to political or military) designed to influence the policies or actions of another state in order (1) to hurt the economy of a real or potential enemy, as with a trade embargo or (2) to help the economy of a friendly power, as with loans or favorable terms of trade.

REFERENCE

David A. Baldwin, *Economic Statecraft* (Princeton, NJ: Princeton University Press, 1985).

Economic Advisers, Council of *See* COUNCIL OF ECONOMIC ADVISERS.

economic analysis A systematic approach to the problem of choosing how to employ scarce resources and an investigation of the full implications of achieving a given economic objective in the most efficient and effective manner. The determination of efficiency and effectiveness is implicit in the assessment of the cost effectiveness of alternative approaches.

economic democracy *see* DEMOCRACY, ECONOMIC.

economic determinism The doctrine holding that economic concerns are the primary motivating factors of human behavior and historical development, and that all social, political, or moral justifications for action can be traced to conscious or unconscious economic motives.

economic growth The increase in a nation's productive capacity, leading to an increase in the production of goods and services. Economic growth usually is measured by the annual rate of increase in real (constant dollars) gross national product.

economic indicators Measurements of various economic and business movements and activities in a community, such as employment, unemployment, hours worked, income, savings, volume of building permits, and volume of sales, whose fluctuations affect and may be used to determine overall economic trends. The various economic time series can be segregated into leaders, laggers, and coinciders in relation to movements in aggregate economic activity. *Compare to* LEADING INDICATORS.

economic mobilization The organizing of a domestic economy in response to a wartime emergency.

Economic Opportunity Act of 1964 The keystone of the Lyndon B. Johnson administration's war on poverty. The act created the Job Corps, community action programs, and other work incentive programs. *See also* GREAT SOCIETY.

REFERENCES

For histories, see Robert H. Haveman, ed., *A Decade of Federal Anti-Poverty Programs: Achievements, Failures, and Lessons* (New York: Academic, 1977);

Sar A. Levitan and Robert Taggart, The Great Society did succeed, *Political Science Quarterly* 91 (Winter 1976–77);

James T. Patterson, *America's Struggle Against Poverty, 1900–1980* (Cambridge, MA: Harvard University Press, 1981).

economic policy The processes by which a government manages its economy. Economic policy generally consists of three dimensions— fiscal policy, monetary policy, and those other facets of public policy with economic implications, such as energy policy, farm policy, and labor union policy. The interaction of these dimensions of economic policy is crucial, since none operate in a vacuum. While monetary policy basically exercises control over the quantity and cost (interest rates) of money and credit in the economy, fiscal policy deals with the sizes of budgets, deficits, and taxes. Other policy areas, such as housing policy (also dependent upon interest rates) and programs dependent upon deficit spending, involve aspects of both monetary and fiscal policy, and vice versa. However, their interrelationship does not exist with regard to implementation. Monetary policy, while receiving major inputs from the president and other executive agencies, is the responsibility of the Federal Reserve Board, an independent agency. Fiscal policy, while receiving similar inputs from the Federal Reserve Board, is primarily the responsibility of the president and the Congress. The degree of equality and subsequent share of responsibility varies within a stable range. While a president may wish to spend this or that amount, only the Congress has the constitutional ability to levy taxes (although tax laws, like any others, must be signed or vetoed by the president). Also limiting a president's discretion over economic policy is the fact that so much of it is controlled by prior decisions to fund, for example, welfare, entitlement, and pension programs, which are not easily changed. *See also* FISCAL POLICY; MONETARY POLICY; POLITICAL ECONOMY.

REFERENCES

Edward R. Tufte, *Political Control of the Economy* (Princeton, NJ: Princeton University Press, 1979);

Robin W. Boadway, *Public Sector Economics*, 2nd ed. (Boston: Little, Brown, 1984);

Mark Peffley and John T. Williams, Attributing presidential responsibility for national economic problems, *American Politics Quarterly* 13 (October 1985).

Economic Report of the President   The economic assessment and forecast prepared by the COUNCIL OF ECONOMIC ADVISERS on behalf of the president for presentation to the Congress each January.

REFERENCE

Stephen J. Cimbala and Robert L. Stout, The Economic Report of the President: Before and after the Full Employment and Balanced Growth Act of 1978, *Presidential Studies Quarterly* 13 (Winter 1983).

economics voodoo   *See* VOODOO ECONOMICS.

economic warfare   An aggressive use of economic means to achieve national objectives.

REFERENCE

Thomas A. Wolf, *U.S. East-West Trade Policy: Economic Warfare versus Economic Welfare* (Lexington, MA: Lexington Books, 1973).

economy and efficiency audits   Audits that seek to determine (1) whether an organizational entity is managing and utilizing its resources (such as personnel, property, and space) economically and efficiently; (2) the causes of inefficiencies or uneconomical practices; and (3) whether the entity has complied with laws and regulations concerning matters of economy and efficiency.

economy, underground   *See* UNDERGROUND ECONOMY.

Education, U.S. Department of (ED)
The cabinet-level department that establishes policy for, administers, and coordinates most federal assistance to education; created on October 17, 1979, by the Department of Education Organization Act, when the Department of Health, Education, and Welfare was divided in two. The Ronald Reagan administration pledged to eliminate ED but has bowed to political pressures and retained it as a platform for conservative stands on education policy.

REFERENCES

David Stephens, President Carter, the Congress, and NEA: Creating the Department of Education, *Political Science Quarterly* 98 (Winter 1983–84);

Beryl A. Radin and Willis D. Hawley, *The Politics of Federal Reorganization: Creating the Department of Education* (Elmsford, NY: Pergamon, 1987).

U.S. Department of Education
400 Maryland Avenue, S.W.
Washington, D.C. 20202
(202) 245–3192

Edwards v Aguillard 96 L Ed 2d 510 (1987)
The U.S. Supreme Court case which held that a Louisiana statute requiring public schools that teach evolution to also teach "creation science" advanced religious doctrine in violation of the First Amendment establishment clause.

EEO   *See* EQUAL EMPLOYMENT OPPORTUNITY.

EEOC   *See* EQUAL EMPLOYMENT OPPORTUNITY COMMISSION.

egalitarianism   *See* EQUALITY/ EGALITARIANISM.

egghead   An intellectual; a politician with a highbrow image; someone who reads serious books on a regular basis—when he or she doesn't have to for school. The term was first used in American politics to derisively refer to Adlai Stevenson (1900–1965) when he was the Democratic nominee for president in 1952. The term fit Stevenson because he was all that the word implied, and worse—he had a balding, egg-shaped head. Stevenson responded in good humor by paraphrasing Marx: "Eggheads of the world unite; you have nothing to lose but your yolks."

Eighteenth Amendment *See* PROHIBITION.

Eighth Amendment The amendment to the U.S. Constitution that prohibits excessive bail, excessive fines, and cruel and unusual punishments. *See* BAIL; BOOTH V MARYLAND; CRUEL AND UNUSUAL PUNISHMENT.

Eisenhower Doctrine The 1957 statement of U.S. policy in the Middle East, which asserted that the United States would use force "to safeguard the independence of any country or group of countries in the Middle East requesting aid against aggression" from a communist country. This differs from other presidential doctrines in that it was adopted as a joint resolution of the Congress.

REFERENCE

Harry N. Howard, The regional pacts and the Eisenhower Doctrine, *Annals of the American Academy of Political and Social Science* 401 (May 1972).

Eisenhower, Dwight David "Ike" (1890–1969) The president of the United States (1953–1961) who, while commander of allied forces in Europe, orchestrated the defeat of Germany in World War II. The returning war hero could have had the nomination of either major party. While he won the Republican nomination narrowly, he won the 1952 election overwhelmingly. In the midst of the frustrating "limited war" of Korea (*see* KOREAN WAR) Americans flocked to support a winning general who pledged: "I will go to Korea." With the war over within six months (through a negotiated armistice), the rest of the Eisenhower years were noted for cold war diplomacy and the lack of domestic initiatives. Yet this belies the fact that the Eisenhower administration was basically one of peace abroad and prosperity at home. In recent years, Eisenhower's reputation as a president has risen sharply, as his decade of the 1950s is compared to what followed. Analysts, such as Fred Greenstein in *The Hidden-Hand Presidency: Eisenhower as Leader*

Dwight D. Eisenhower

(New York: Basic Books, 1982) have looked anew at Eisenhower's "hidden hand" style of leadership, which entailed deft behind-the-scenes maneuvering with a public posture of a leader who was above the political fray. One innovation of the Eisenhower years that is still with us was a new candor about the president's health. After a heart attack in his first term, the president's bodily functions (or nonfunctions) became news. Now, any president's physical maladies are as legitimate a news story as a major foreign policy decision.

REFERENCES

Stephen E. Ambrose, *Eisenhower: Soldier, General of the Army, President-Elect, 1890–1952* (New York: Simon & Schuster, 1983);

Stephen E. Ambrose, *Eisenhower: President and Elder Statesman, 1952–1969* (New York: Simon & Schuster, 1984).

The Dwight D. Eisenhower Administration

Major Accomplishments

- The Korean War ended; a general climate of peace.
- U.S. military force sent into Little Rock, Arkansas, to enforce integration of schools.

- The appointment of Earl Warren as chief justice of the Supreme Court.
- Launching of the interstate highway program.

Major Frustrations
- The continued cold war with the Soviet Union.
- The crash of an American spy plane, the U-2, in the Soviet Union, forcing the cancellation of a summit meeting.
- Senator Joseph McCarthy.

elastic clause *See* NECESSARY AND PROPER CLAUSE.

election **1** A process of selecting one person or more for an office, public or private, from a wider field of candidates. Thus the public of a jurisdiction elects its highest officials, a corporation's stockholders elects its board of directors, and the members of a club or honorary society elect new members. In essence, an election is the aggregating of individual preferences and occurs whenever selection is not the will of a single decision maker. **2** The government-administered process by which people, whether opposed or unopposed, seek a political party's nomination for, or election to, public office. In most of today's world, elections are the only legitimate way by which governments can claim the right to power. Consequently, even totalitarian regimes and military dictatorships use elections (though fraught with fraud and hardly free) to justify their remaining in power. Thus there are two basic kinds of elections: (1) *free*, where parties of competing philosophies compete for power in a fair contest; and (2) *sham*, where rulers hold cynically staged elections in order to justify their rule.

Gerald M. Pomper, in *Elections in America* 2d ed. (New York: Dodd, Mead, 1980), has classified U.S. presidential elections into the following four categories. (1) *Maintaining:* party loyalties remain stable and the majority party wins. (2) *Deviating:* the majority party loses. (3) *Converting:* the majority party wins, but there are basic changes in the distribution of party membership. (4) *Realigning:* the majority party may lose because of changing party loyalties (*see* REALIGNMENT).

election, authorization *See* AUTHORIZATION ELECTION.

election, certification *See* AUTHORIZATION ELECTION.

election, contested An election in which more than one person claims to have won. In such cases, a recount is often undertaken, and if there is still ambiguity as to the winner, the disputes may be settled in court or by a legislature.

election, contesting An election in which there is more than one candidate on the ballot from which to choose.

election, critical An election that heralds a new political alignment, that produces a new political majority, or that indicates a long-term shift in electoral behavior.

REFERENCES
V. O. Key, Jr., A theory of critical elections, *Journal of Politics* 17:1 (1955);
Walter D. Burnham, *Critical Elections and the Mainsprings of American Politics* (New York: Norton, 1975).

election day The first Tuesday after the first Monday in November in an election year. The U.S. Constitution provides in Article II, Section 1, that the Congress may determine the time of choosing the electors and the day on which they shall give their votes, "which day shall be the same throughout the United States." In 1792, the Congress by law designated the first Wednesday in December as the date for presidential electors to meet and cast their vote for president and vice president. This same act required the states to "appoint" their electors within thirty-four days of the date set for the electors to vote. Following this act, until 1845, there was no national election day, and each state fixed its own date, usually in November, for the selection of presidential electors. The decision to create a single national day for the selection of presidential electors grew out of the need to prevent election abuses resulting from electors being selected on separate days in neighboring states. Thus in 1845, the Congress established by law that in each state the electors were to be selected on the "Tuesday next after the first Monday in the month of November of the year in which they are to be appointed." In 1872, the Congress adopted legislation requiring states to hold their elections for members and delegates to the U.S. House of Representatives on this same day. After the adoption of the Seventeenth Amendment, providing for the direct popular election of U.S. senators, the Congress enacted legislation in 1914 to require that U.S. senators also be elected on the same Tuesday in November.

Tuesday was selected to protect the rights of persons opposed for religious reasons to holding elections on Sunday or to traveling to the polls on that day. Therefore, it was desirable to have at least one day intervening between Sunday and election day. The first Tuesday of the month was eliminated, because it might fall on the first day of the month and cause inconvenience to business. But Tuesday has proved inconvenient for many, in that it is a working day, not a holiday. Many advocate Sunday elections for that reason.

election, deviating An election in which a new party wins, not because there has been a realignment in political party preferences but because the winning party just happened to have an attractive candidate or some other factor in its favor (such as a scandal in the other party). In a deviating election, existing party loyalties are temporarily displaced by short-term forces.

electioneering Campaigning actively on behalf of a candidate; the total efforts made to win an election. Many polling places have signs reminding political workers that electioneering is prohibited within a specified distance from the polls.

REFERENCE

David Leuthold, *Electioneering in a Democracy: Campaigns for Congress* (New York: Wiley, 1968).

election, general An election held to choose among candidates nominated in a primary (or by convention or caucus) for federal, state, and local office.

REFERENCE

David J. Maurer, *U.S. Politics and Elections: A Guide to Information Sources* (Detroit: Gale Research, 1978).

election, maintaining An election that reaffirms the existing patterns of political party support. In other words, the party dominant in the electorate wins.

election, midterm The U.S. congressional election that occurs in the middle of a president's four-year term. It is usually the case that the party of the president in power loses seats in the House of Representatives and Senate. This has so often been the case that the president's party now declares it a victory when they lose only a few seats. While the pattern of midterm elections is clear, one can only speculate on the reasons for it. Some analysts contend that many voters who turn out to vote only in presidential contests tend to vote also for congressional nominees from the president's party. These voters are absent at midterm elections. Other analysts suggest that voters exercise rational judgment on individual candidates and turn out of office those whom they perceive as not having delivered on their promises; thus a decline in the party in the White House. Still others contend that a midterm congressional election is a de facto referendum on a president's performance for the previous two years.

REFERENCES

James E. Piereson, Presidential popularity and midterm voting at different electoral levels, *American Journal of Political Science* 19 (November 1975);

Randall L. Calvert and R. Mark Isaac, The inherent disadvantage of the presidential party in midterm congressional elections, *Public Choice* 36:1 (1981);

M. Margaret Conway, Political participation in midterm congressional elections: Attitudinal and social characteristics during the 1970s, *American Politics Quarterly* 9 (April 1981);

Alan I. Abramowitz, Economic conditions, presidential popularity, and voting behavior in midterm congressional elections, *Journal of Politics* 47 (February 1985);

Congressional Midterm Election Results

Year	President	Party	Gains or Losses of President's Party	
			House	Senate
1934	Roosevelt	Democratic	+9	+9
1938	Roosevelt	Democratic	−70	−7
1942	Roosevelt	Democratic	−50	−8
1946	Truman	Democratic	−54	−11
1950	Truman	Democratic	−29	−5
1954	Eisenhower	Republican	−18	−1
1958	Eisenhower	Republican	−47	−13
1962	Kennedy	Democratic	−5	+2
1966	Johnson	Democratic	−48	−4
1970	Nixon	Republican	−12	+1
1974	Ford	Republican	−48	−5
1978	Carter	Democratic	−12	−3
1982	Reagan	Republican	−26	0
1986	Reagan	Republican	−5	−8

James E. Campbell, Explaining presidential losses in midterm congressional elections, *Journal of Politics* 47 (November 1985).

election, nonpartisan A local election in which a candidate runs for office without formally indicating political party affiliation. Judges and members of school boards, for example, are often elected in nonpartisan elections.

REFERENCES

Owen E. Newcomer, Nonpartisan elections: A look at their effect, *National Civic Review* 66 (October 1977);

Susan Welch and Timothy Bledsoe, The partisan consequences of nonpartisan elections and the changing nature of urban politics, *American Journal of Political Science* 30 (February 1986).

election, representation *See* AUTHORIZATION ELECTION.

election, runoff A second election held in some states if no one candidate for an office receives a majority (or a specified percentage) of votes. Voters then choose in a runoff election between the two candidates who received the most votes in the first election.

election, special An election specially scheduled to fill an office that has become vacant before the term of its expiration.

REFERENCE

Lee Sigelman, Special elections to the U.S. House: Some descriptive generalizations, *Legislative Studies Quarterly* 6 (November 1981).

election, uncontested An election in which a candidate has no opposition.

elector 1 A qualified voter. 2 One of the 538 members of the electoral college.

electoral college The 538 electors who, on the first Monday after the second Wednesday in December of a presidential election year, officially elect the president and vice president of the United States. Each state chooses in the November general election—in a manner determined by its legislature—a number of electors equal to the total of its senators and representatives in the Congress. The District of Columbia, under the Twenty-third Amendment, chooses a number of electors equal to the number chosen by the least populous states. All fifty-one jurisdictions provide that presidential electors be elected by popular vote.

The electoral college never meets as one body, but state electors usually meet in their state's capital and the District of Columbia. Once the electors have voted and the results have been certified by the chief executive of each state, the results are sent to Washington, D.C., to be counted before a joint session of the newly elected Congress, meeting the first week in January. If no candidate for president or vice president has received a majority, the House, voting by states, elects the president; and the Senate, voting as individuals, elects the vice president.

It was originally thought that electors would exercise their own judgment in selecting the president and vice president; nobody expected that political parties would arise and create the situation whereby electors were no longer independent voters but the representatives of a party. (In six of the last nine elections, however, one elector has cast his electoral vote for some-

one other than the person he was pledged to.) The election of 1800 resulted in a tie for president and vice president, because party discipline was so complete that each Republican elector cast his two votes for Thomas Jefferson and Aaron Burr. Ironically, the new president was then determined by the lame duck Federalist-controlled Congress. To prevent this from ever happening again, the Twelfth Amendment was ratified in 1804, which requires electors to vote separately for president and vice president.

Supporters of the electoral college argue that it should be kept—because it works. Even though it has failed in three instances to elect a president (1800, 1824, and 1876), the Congress was able to resolve the disputes peaceably. Critics of the electoral college have charged it with being undemocratic, because it permits candidates to win the presidency without having most of the popular votes, and dangerous, because whenever the election is

The Electoral Map for the 1980s

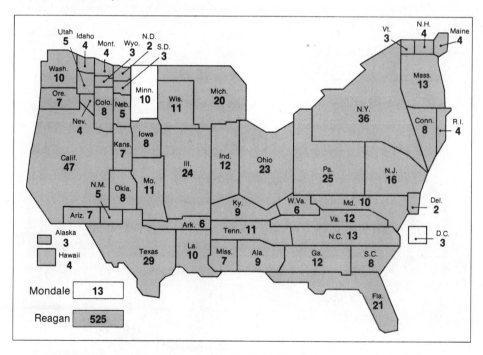

Source: Samuel C. Patterson, Roger H. Davidson, and Randall B. Ripley, *A More Perfect Union: Introduction to American Government*, 3d ed. (Chicago: Dorsey, 1985), p. 165.

thrown into the House of Representatives the choice must be made from among the three top candidates. Critics believe it is a threat to the legitimacy of the American political system, and they periodically demand its abolition and a system of direct election put in its place.

REFERENCES

Michael C. Nelson, Partisan bias in the electoral college, *Journal of Politics* 36 (November 1974);

Martin Diamond, The electoral college and the ideal of federal democracy, *Publius* 8 (Winter 1978);

Douglas H. Blair, Electoral college reform and the distribution of voting power, *Public Choice* 34:2 (1979);

Thomas E. Cronin, The direct vote and the electoral college: The case for meshing things up! *Presidential Studies Quarterly* 9 (Spring 1979);

Eric M. Uslaner, The electoral college's alma mater should be a swan song, *Presidential Studies Quarterly* 10 (Summer 1980);

Neal R. Peirce and Lawrence D. Longley, *The People's President: The Electoral College in American History and the Direct Vote Alternative* (New Haven, CT: Yale University Press, 1981).

electoral vote The votes cast for president and vice president by presidential electors in what is known popularly as the electoral college. The total electoral vote is 538, with 270 needed to win the election. The candidate who wins the most popular votes in a state wins all of that state's electoral votes. In 1984, Ronald Reagan won 525 electoral votes to Walter Mondale's 13.

elephant The symbol of the Republican Party, first used by Thomas Nast (1840–1902) in a *Harper's Weekly* cartoon on November 7, 1874.

Eleventh Amendment The 1798 amendment to the U.S. Constitution that prohibits the federal courts from hearing cases brought against a state by citizens of other states or of foreign countries. This reversed the Supreme Court's decision in *Chisholm v Georgia*, 2 Dallas 419 (1793), which held that citizens of one

The Republican party elephant appears in an 1875 Thomas Nast cartoon.

state could sue the citizens of other states in federal court.

REFERENCES

William A. Fletcher, A historical interpretation of the Eleventh Amendment: A narrow construction of an affirmative grant of jurisdiction rather than a prohibition against jurisdiction, *Stanford Law Review* 35 (July 1983);

John J. Gibbons, The Eleventh Amendment and state sovereign immunity: A reinterpretation, *Columbia Law Review* 83 (December 1983).

Elfbrandt v Russell 384 U.S. 11 (1966)   The U.S. Supreme Court case that held an Arizona loyalty oath unconstitutional by being in violation of freedom of association, since, coupled with a perjury statute, it proscribed membership in any organization having for only one of its purposes the overthrow of the government of the State of Arizona. The Court reasoned that one might join such an organization without supporting its illegal purposes. *See also* LOYALTY.

elite party   *See* MASS PARTY.

Elrod v Burns 427 U.S. 347 (1976)   The U.S. Supreme Court case that held that the First Amendment, which safeguards the rights of political beliefs and association, prevents political firing of state, county, and local workers who are below the policymaking level. *Compare to* BRANTI V FINKEL; PATRONAGE.

Emancipation Proclamation   President Abraham Lincoln's formal declaration that all slaves residing in the states still in rebellion against the United States on January 1, 1863, would be free once those states came under the military control of the Union army. It did not abolish slavery (that was done by the Thirteenth Amendment in 1865); but it did ensure that slavery would be abolished once the war concluded with a Northern victory. Lincoln showed his cabinet the draft of the proclamation about half a year earlier, on July 22, 1862, but felt that he had to keep it secret until the military situation improved for the North. While the battle of Antietam of September 17,

1862, was essentially a draw, Lincoln considered it enough of a victory to announce the proclamation.

REFERENCES

Mark M. Krug, The Republican party and the Emancipation Proclamation, *Journal of Negro History* 48:2 (1963);

John Hope Franklin, *The Emancipation Proclamation* (Garden City, NY: Anchor, 1963).

embargo   A government prohibition of the import or export of commodities or of the vessels of specific nations. An embargo is a mildly hostile act, more related to foreign policy than to trade policy. For example, shortly after the communists came to power in Cuba, the United States embargoed sugar from Cuba in an effort to disrupt the Cuban economy. And after the Soviet Union invaded Afghanistan, the United States embargoed grain shipments to the Soviets in an effort to make them aware of American displeasure with their aggressive actions. The Cuban sugar embargo is still in effect; but the Soviet grain embargo was lifted by the Reagan Administration.

REFERENCES

Alan Abouchar, The case for the U.S. grain embargo, *World Today* 37 (July/August 1981);

Clas Bergstrom, Glenn C. Loury, and Mats Persson, Embargo threats and the management of emergency reserves, *Journal of Political Economy* 93 (February 1985).

embassy   1 The highest class of diplomatic mission, headed by an AMBASSADOR. In this context, the embassy refers to all of the diplomatic staff as well as to all of their support personnel.   2 The physical building or buildings (also called the mission) used to house the office (the chancery) and personal quarters of the embassy staff, including the ambassador. 3 The job (also called the mission) of an ambassador. Thus an ambassador's mission (the job) might be to negotiate a treaty, which might be signed in the mission (a building), which is also known as the embassy.

Emergency Employment Act of 1971   The federal statute that authorized federal funds for state and local government public service jobs during times of high unemployment. It was superseded by the Comprehensive Employment and Training Act of 1973.

REFERENCES

Roger H. Davidson, *The Politics of Comprehensive Manpower Legislation* (Baltimore: Johns Hopkins University Press, 1972);

Howard W. Hallman, *Emergency Employment: A Study in Federalism* (University: University of Alabama Press, 1977).

emergency powers The enlarged authority that the president of the United States is deeded to have, either by statute, from the U.S. Constitution, or because of the nature of the emergency, to deal with the problem at hand. An exercise of emergency powers may or may not be later upheld by the Supreme Court. In the case of *Korematsu v United States*, 323 U.S. 214 (1944), the Court affirmed President Franklin D. Roosevelt's World War II decision to forcibly relocate American citizens of Japanese origin. Yet in the case of *Youngstown Sheet and Tube v Sawyer*, the Court denied President Harry S Truman's assertion that he had inherent emergency powers to seize civilian steel mills to maintain wartime production. The president can pretty much do what he wants under the rubric of emergency powers until he is checked by one of the other branches of government. The fact that such checks exist goes a long way in keeping a president's emergency powers "in the closet" until there is substantial agreement that they are needed. *Compare to* NATIONAL EMERGENCY ACT OF 1976.

REFERENCES

Harold C. Relyea, National emergency powers: A brief overview of presidential suspensions of the habeas corpus privilege and invocations of martial law, *Presidential Studies Quarterly* 7 (Fall 1977);

A. S. Klieman, Preparing for the hour of need: Emergency powers in the United States, *Review of Politics* 41 (April 1979);

Michael A. Genovese, Democratic theory and the emergency powers of the president, *Presidential Studies Quarterly* 9 (Summer 1979).

éminence grise A French term meaning gray eminence, or the power behind the throne.

Staff officers are sometimes accused of exercising such power.

eminent domain A government's right to take private property for the public's use. The Fifth Amendment requires that, whenever a government takes an individual's property, the property acquired must be taken for public use, and the full value thereof paid to the owner. Thus a government cannot take property from one person simply to give it to another. However, the U.S. Supreme Court has held that it is permissible to take private property for such purposes as urban renewal, even though ultimately the property taken will be returned to private ownership, since the taking is really for the benefit of the community as a whole. Property does not have to be physically taken from the owner to acquire Fifth Amendment protection. If government action leads to a lower value of private property, that may also constitute a "taking" and therefore require payment of compensation. Thus the Supreme Court has held that the disturbance of chickens' egg laying on a man's poultry farm, caused by the noise of low-level flights by military aircraft from a nearby airbase, lessened the value of the farm and that, accordingly, the landowner was entitled to receive compensation equal to his loss.

REFERENCE

James Geoffrey Durham, Efficient just compensation as a limit on eminent domain, *Minnesota Law Review* 69 (June 1985).

Employment Act of 1946 The federal statute that created the Council of Economic Advisers in the Executive Office of the President and asserted that it was the federal government's responsibility to maintain economic stability and promote full employment.

REFERENCES

For legislative histories of the act see Stephen K. Bailey, *Congress Makes a Law* (New York: Columbia University Press, 1950);

Hugh S. Norton, *The Employment Act and the Council of Economic Advisers, 1946–1976* (Columbia: University of South Carolina Press, 1977).

enabling act   Legislation permitting cities or districts to engage in particular programs. Enabling acts prescribe some of the administrative details of implementation. As cities are the creatures of their state, their ability to participate in particular types of programs, especially those of the national government, depends upon state enabling acts.

en banc   A French term meaning on the bench; a case heard and decided by all of the judges of a court as opposed to judges acting indivdually. The U.S. Supreme Court always sits en banc.

Energy Act of 1976   An omnibus federal law containing provisions for conservation, production, and allocation of energy supplies. Its parts include (1) executive branch authority to order major fuel-burning plants to switch from oil to coal, (2) fuel economy standards for automobiles and efficiency measures for major appliances, (3) standby presidential power to allocate supplies in a crisis and the creation of an oil reserve, (4) presidential authority to adjust oil prices, and (5) congressional review of presidential actions and General Accounting Office audits of energy producers and consumers. *See also* NATIONAL ENERGY ACT OF 1978.

REFERENCE
Edward J. Mitchell, The basis of congressional energy policy, *Texas Law Review* 57 (March 1979).

Energy, U.S. Department of (DOE)   The cabinet-level department created by the Department of Energy Organization Act of 1977 that provides the framework for a national energy plan through the coordination and administration of the energy functions of the federal government. The DOE is responsible for the research, development, and demonstration of energy technology; for marketing of federal power; for energy conservation; for regulation of energy production and use; for pricing and allocation; and for a data collection and analysis program. The DOE absorbed the Atomic Energy Commission (now known as the NU-CLEAR REGULATORY commission) and has major responsibilities for both military and nonmilitary uses of nuclear power.

The DOE is responsible for the development of energy technology. Here, a wind turbine at Sandia Lab in Albuquerque, NM.

REFERENCE
David Howard Davis, Establishing the Department of Energy, *Journal of Energy and Development* 4 (Autumn 1978).

U.S. Department of Energy
1000 Independence Avenue, S.W.
Washington, D.C. 20585
(202) 586–5000

energy policy   Efforts that encourage energy development, protect against energy shortages, conserve energy resources, and safeguard the environment from damage caused by expansion of energy supplies. Although most observers predict that by the year 2000 Americans will use twice as much energy as they did in 1980, the United States does not have a comprehensive energy policy.

REFERENCES
Robert Stobaugh and Daniel Yergin, eds., *Energy Future* (New York: Random House, 1979);

Richard H. K. Vietor, *Energy Policy in America Since 1945: A Study of Business-Government Relations* (New York: Cambridge University Press, 1984);

Don E. Kash and Robert W. Rycroft, Energy policy: How failure was snatched from the jaws of success, *Policy Studies Review* 4 (February 1985).

engrossed bill   *See* BILL, ENGROSSED.

enjoin To require or command. A court's injunction directs (enjoins) a person or persons to do or not do certain acts.

enrolled bill *See* BILL, ENROLLED.

entente A French word meaning an understanding. In diplomatic usage, it is more than a DÉTENTE but less than a formal treaty; however it may imply a tacit alliance.
REFERENCES
Richard Rosecrance, Détente or entente? *Foreign Affairs* 53 (April 1975);
Robert A. Kann, Alliances versus ententes, *World Politics* 28 (July 1976).

enterprise zone/urban enterprise zone An area of high unemployment and poverty that is granted business tax reductions by a state to lure industry and concomitant prosperity.
REFERENCES
Abe L. Frank, Federal enterprise zone proposals: Incentives to revive our decaying inner cities, *Journal of Legislation* 10 (Summer 1983);
Lawrence Revzan, Enterprise zones: Present status and potential impact, *Governmental Finance* 12 (December 1983).
For a comparative perspective, see Janet H. Malone, The questionable promise of enterprise zones: Lessons from England and Italy, *Urban Affairs Quarterly* 18 (September 1982).

entitlement authority Legislation that requires the payment of benefits to any person or government meeting the requirements established by such law (such as social security benefits and veterans' pensions). Section 401 of the Congressional Budget and Impoundment Control Act of 1974 places certain restrictions on the enactment of new entitlement authority. *See also* AUTHORITY, BACKDOOR.

entitlement program Any government program that pays benefits to individuals, organizations, or other governments that meet eligibility requirements set by law. Social security is the largest federal entitlement program for individuals. Others include farm price supports, Medicare, Medicaid, unemployment insurance, and food stamps. Entitlement programs have great budgetary significance, in that they lock in such a great percentage of the total federal budget each year that changes in the budget can only be made at the margin.
REFERENCES
Eleanor Chelimsky, Reducing fraud and abuse in entitlement programs: An evaluative perspective, *The GAO Review* (Summer 1981);
Edward J. Green, Equilibrium and efficiency under pure entitlement systems, *Public Choice* 39:1 (1982).

entrapment Inducing a person to commit a crime that the person would not have committed without such inducement. When done by government agents, usually police, for the purposes of prosecuting a person, it is generally unlawful. In most cases, a criminal charge based on entrapment will fail. *Compare to* ABSCAM.
REFERENCES
Roger Park, The entrapment controversy, *Minnesota Law Review* 60 (January 1976);
Bennett L. Gershman, Entrapment, shocked consciences, and the staged arrest, *Minnesota Law Review* 66 (April 1982);
Andrew Altman and Steven Lee, Legal entrapment, *Philosophy and Public Affairs* 12 (Winter 1983);
Molly K. Nichols, Entrapment and due process: How far is too far? *Tulane Law Review* 58 (May 1984).

enumerated powers Those powers of the U.S. government specifically provided for and listed in the Constitution. *Compare to* IMPLIED POWER.

environmental impact statement (EIS) *See* ENVIRONMENTAL POLICY/NATIONAL ENVIRONMENTAL POLICY ACT OF 1969.

environmental movement A spontaneous grassroots mobilization of citizens that grew out of the earlier conservation movement and that is concerned with the quality of natural and human environment. Earth Day, April 22, 1970, which had nationwide parades, teach-ins, and demonstrations, was a high point in the environmental movement. The movement receives its organizational expression through interest groups that engage in lobbying, court litigation, and public information activities.

environmental policy/National Environmental Policy Act of 1969 The National Environmental Policy Act of 1969 declared that the federal government had responsibility for the protection of the environment. The act, which created the President's Council on Environmental Quality, provides for the preparation of an environmental impact statement (a document assessing the impact of a new program upon the environment) for all major federal actions significantly affecting the quality of the human environment. *Compare to* CONSERVATION.

REFERENCES

For year-end summaries of the state of the environment, see Council on Environmental Quality, *Annual Report* (Washington, D.C.: Government Printing Office; annual, beginning 1970).

Also see Eugene Bardach and Lucian Pugliaresi, The environmental-impact statement vs. the real world, *Public Interest*, 49 (Fall 1977);

Bernard J. Frieden, *The Environmental Protection Hustle* (Cambridge, MA: MIT Press, 1979);

Lynton K. Caldwell, *Science and the National Environmental Policy Act* (University: University of Alabama Press, 1982);

Norman J. Vig and Michael E. Kraft, eds., *Environmental Policy in the 1980s: Reagan's New Agenda* (Washington, D.C.: Congressional Quarterly, 1984).

Environmental Protection Agency, U.S. (EPA) The federal agency created by Reorganization Plan no. 3 of 1970 to permit coordinated and effective government action on behalf of the environment. The EPA endeavors to abate and control pollution systematically, by proper integration of research, monitoring, standard setting, and enforcement activities. As a complement to its other activities, the EPA coordinates and supports research and antipollution activities by state and local governments, private and public groups, individuals, and educational institutions.

U.S. Environmental Protection Agency
401 M. Street, S.W.
Washington, D.C. 20460
(202) 382-2090

Landmark Federal Environmental Laws

1899 **Refuse Act** restricted dumping of hazardous wastes.

1948 **Water Pollution Control Act** provided for federal assistance to state water quality programs.

1955 **Air Pollution Control Act** provided for federal assistance to state air quality programs.

1963 **Clean Air Act** authorized federal aid to develop air pollution prevention programs.

1970 **National Environmental Protection Act** created the U.S. Environmental Protection Agency and mandated environmental impact statements for major federal projects.

1970 **Water Quality Improvement Act** made oil companies liable for oil spills.

1970 **Clean Air Act amendments** created auto pollution emission standards.

1972 **Federal Water Pollution Control Act amendments** required permits to discharge pollutants into rivers and lakes.

1974 **Safe Drinking Water Act** created standards for safe public drinking water.

1976 **Toxic Substances Control Act** banned PCBs and required testing of toxic substances.

1977 **Federal Water Pollution Control Act amendments** authorized "best conventional technology" standards.

1977 **Clean Air Act amendments** strengthened auto emission and air quality standards.

EOP *See* EXECUTIVE OFFICE OF THE PRESIDENT.

EPA *See* ENVIRONMENTAL PROTECTION AGENCY, U.S.

e pluribus unum A Latin phrase meaning one out of many; the motto on the Great Seal of the United States.

equal employment opportunity (EEO) A concept fraught with political, cultural, and emotional overtones. Generally, it applies to a set of employment procedures and practices that effectively prevent any individual from being adversely excluded from employment opportunities on the basis of race, color, sex, religion, age, national origin, or other factors that cannot lawfully be used in employing people. While the ideal of EEO is an employment system devoid of both intentional and unintentional discrimination, achieving this ideal may be a political impossibility because of the problem of definition. One man's equal opportunity may be another's institutional racism or a woman's institutional sexism. Because of this problem of definition, only the courts have been able to say if, when, and where EEO exists.

See also AFFIRMATIVE ACTION; CHILLING; DISCRIMINATION; FAIR EMPLOYMENT PRACTICE COMMISSION; FAIR EMPLOYMENT PRACTICE COMMITTEE; GOALS; MAKE WHOLE; NATIONAL ASSOCIATION FOR THE ADVANCEMENT OF COLORED PEOPLE V FEDERAL POWER COMMISSION; REPRESENTATIVE BUREAUCRACY; REVERSE DISCRIMINATION; RIGHTFUL PLACE; TITLE VII; TOKENISM.

REFERENCES
For the law of EEO, see Charles A. Sullivan, Michael J. Zimmer, and Richard F. Richards, *Federal Statutory Law of Employment Discrimination* (Indianapolis: Michie Bobbs-Merrill, 1980);
Arthur B. Smith, Jr., The law and equal employment opportunity: What's past should not be prologue, *Industrial and Labor Relations Review* 33 (July 1980);
Daniel B. Edelman, *EEO in the Judicial Branch: An Outline of Policy and Law* (Williamsburg, VA: National Center for State Courts, 1981);
Barbara Lindemann Schlei and Paul Frossman, *Employment Discrimination Law*, 2d ed. (Washington, D.C.: Bureau of National Affairs, 1983).
For the history of EEO in the federal government, see David H. Rosenbloom, *Federal Equal Employment Opportunity: Politics and Public Personnel Administration* (New York: Praeger, 1977).

Equal Employment Opportunity Act of 1972 An amendment to Title VII of the 1964 Civil Rights Act strengthening the authority of the Equal Employment Opportunity Commission and extending antidiscrimination provisions to state and local governments and labor organizations with fifteen or more employees, and to public and private employment agencies.

REFERENCES
William Brown III, The Equal Employment Opportunity Act of 1972—The light at the top of the stairs, *Personnel Administration* 35 (June 1972);
Harry Grossman, The Equal Employment Opportunity Act of 1972: Its implications for the state and local government manager, *Public Personnel Management* 2 (September/October 1973).

Equal Employment Opportunity Commission (EEOC) A five-member commission created by Title VII of the Civil Rights Act of 1964. The EEOC members (one designated chair) are appointed for five-year terms by the president, subject to the advice and consent of the Senate. The EEOC's mission is to end discrimination based on race, color, religion, sex, or national origin in hiring, promotion, firing, wages, testing, training, apprenticeship, and all other conditions of employment, and to promote voluntary action programs by employers, unions, and community organizations to make equal employment opportunity an actuality.

REFERENCES
William A. Webb, The mission of the Equal Employment Opportunity Commission, *Labor Law Journal* 34 (July 1983);
Frank J. Thompson, Deregulation at the EEOC: Prospects and implications, *Review of Public Personnel Administration* 4 (Summer 1984);
Donald W. Crowley, Selection tests and equal opportunity: The Court and the EEOC, *Administration and Society* 17 (November 1985).

Equal Employment Opportunity Commission
2401 E Street, N.W.
Washington, D.C. 20507
(202) 634–6922
(800) USA–EEOC (toll free)

Equal Employment Opportunity Commission v Wyoming 75 L. Ed. 2d 18 (1983)   The U.S. Supreme Court case that upheld the federal government's 1974 extension of the Age Discrimination in Employment Act to cover state and local government workers.

equality/egalitarianism   A philosophic disposition toward the greater political and social equality of the citizens within a nation; that is, all citizens would have an equal claim on the political and economic rewards of the society. However, such economists as Arthur Okun have warned that "any insistence on carving the pie into equal slices would shrink the size of the pie."
REFERENCES
Arthur M. Okun, *Equality and Efficiency: The Big Tradeoff* (Washington, D.C.: Brookings, 1975);
Martin Diamond, The American idea of equality: The view from the founding, *Review of Politics* 38 (July 1976);
Kai Nielsen, A rationale for egalitarianism, *Social Research* 48 (Summer 1981);
Timothy J. O'Neill, The language of equality in a constitutional order, *American Political Science Review* 75 (September 1981);
Peter Westen, The empty idea of equality, *Harvard Law Review* 95 (January 1982);
Lyle A. Dowling and Robert B. Thigpen, Equality: The embattled status of a concept, *Polity* 15 (Summer 1983).

equalization   The adjustment of assessments and taxes on real estate to make sure that properties are properly valued and are fairly taxed according to value.

Equal Pay Act of 1963   An amendment to the Fair Labor Standards Act of 1938 prohibiting pay discrimination because of sex and providing that men and women working in the same establishment under similar conditions must receive the same pay if their jobs require equal (similar) skill, effort, and responsibility.
REFERENCES
John E. Burns and Catherine G. Burns, An analysis of the Equal Pay Act, *Labor Law Journal* 24 (February 1973);

P. Andiappan, Public policy and equal pay: A comparative study of equal pay laws in Canada, U.S.A., and U.K., *International Review of Administrative Sciences* 51:1 (1985).

equal protection of laws   The constitutional requirement that a government will not treat people unequally, nor set up illegal categories to justify treating people unequally, nor give unfair or unequal treatment to a person based on that person's race or religion. The Fourteenth Amendment prohibits states from denying their residents the equal protection of the law. The due process clause of the Fifth Amendment has also been held, in *Bolling v Sharpe*, 347 U.S. 497 (1954), to include a requirement of equal protection. *Compare to* REVERSE DISCRIMINATION.

While equal protection has been the law since the ratification of the Fourteenth Amendment in 1868, it was largely a dormant concept until awakened by the Warren Court in the 1950s. It can truly be said that landmark decisions, such as BROWN V BOARD OF EDUCATION OF TOPEKA, KANSAS and BAKER V CARR, used the equal protection clause of the Fourteenth Amendment to revolutionize American society. The United States is an increasingly more equal nation because of it. Without it, the peaceful changes that have come about in race relations might not have been possible.
REFERENCE
Polyvios G. Polyviou, *The Equal Protection of the Laws* (London: Duckworth, 1980).

Equal Rights Amendment (ERA)   A proposed amendment to the U.S. Constitution passed by the Congress in 1972 that never became law because too few states ratified it. The proposed Twenty-seventh Amendment read in part: "Equality of rights under the law shall not be denied or abridged by the United States or any state on account of sex." At first, the ERA seemed headed for quick passage. It was approved in both houses of the Congress with overwhelming majorities; both major party platforms endorsed it. By the end of 1972, over twenty-two states had ratified it. But when it became apparent that ERA would eventually become law, a conservative opposition organized. It argued that the ERA would not only subject women to a potential military draft, but also to combat duty. And that women would lose the legal advantages they hold under many state domestic relations laws and labor codes. As ERA became more controversial, fewer states moved to ratify it. In 1980 the Republican party platform became officially neutral on it. As the issue became more and more controversial, the states that had not acted on it held hearings and encountered delay after delay. On March 27, 1982, the final deadline, three states were still needed for ratification, and the ERA was dead—for now. *See* WOMEN'S LIBERATION MOVEMENT.

REFERENCES

Val Burris, Who opposed the ERA? An analysis of the social bases of antifeminism, *Social Science Quarterly* 64 (June 1983);

Gilbert Y. Steiner, *Constitutional Inequality: The Political Fortunes of the Equal Rights Amendment* (Washington, D.C.: Brookings, 1985);

Mary F. Berry, *Why ERA Failed: Politics, Women's Rights, and the Amending Process to the Constitution* (Bloomington: Indiana University Press, 1986);

Joan Huff-Wilson, *Rights of Passage: The Past and Future of the ERA* (Bloomington: Indiana University Press, 1986);

Jane J. Mansbridge, *Why We Lost the E.R.A.* (Chicago: University of Chicago Press, 1986).

Equal Rights Amendment, State An amendment to a state constitution paralleling the proposed federal Equal Rights Amendment.

REFERENCE

Bruce E. Altshuler, State ERAs: What have they done? *State Government* 56:4 (1983).

equal-time doctrine *See* FAIRNESS DOCTRINE.

equity jurisdiction The authority of a court to administer justice when no specific laws exist to cover the case at hand.

equity law *See* CODE LAW.

era of good feeling **1** The time of supposed political tranquility during the administration of President James Monroe, when, because of the demise of the Federalist party, no effective political opposition disturbed the supremacy of the Democratic-Republican party. **2** A time of consensus for presidential policies.

REFERENCES

1 George Dangerfield, *The Era of Good Feelings* (New York: Harcourt, Brace, Jovanovich, 1952, 1963).

Joel H. Silbey, The incomplete world of American politics, 1815–1829: Presidents, parties, and politics in the "era of good feelings," *Congress and the Presidency: A Journal of Capital Studies* 11 (Spring 1984).

Escobedo v Illinois 378 U.S. 478 (1964) The U.S. Supreme Court case that held that a criminal defendant must be allowed to consult an attorney if he or she requests to do so. Denying this is a violation of the "assistance to counsel" provision of the Sixth Amendment.

Espinoza v Farah Manufacturing Company 414 U.S. 86 (1973) The U.S. Supreme Court case that held that an employer who refused to hire a legal resident alien because of a long-standing policy against the employment of aliens could not be held liable under Title VII of the Civil Rights Act of 1964 if the company already employed a significant percentage of people of the same national origin who were U.S. citizens.

espionage Actions designed to obtain secrets, usually diplomatic or military, of a government through clandestine operations. *Compare to* INTELLIGENCE.

REFERENCES

Herbert Scoville, Jr., Is espionage necessary for our security? *Foreign Affairs* 54 (April 1976);

Henry S. A. Becket, *The Dictionary of Espionage: Spookspeak into English* (New York: Stein and Day, 1986).

establishment The collective holders of power in all segments of society: political, military, social, academic, religious, literary. It is always the establishment that revolutionaries—

whether political, organizational, or otherwise—wish to overthrow, so they and their ideas can become the new establishment.

REFERENCES

Richard H. Rovere, *The American Establishment* (New York: Harcourt, Brace, Jovanovich, 1962);

Adam Yarmolinsky, *The Military Establishment* (New York: Harper & Row, 1971);

Leonard Silk and Mark Silk, *The American Establishment* (New York: Basic Books, 1980).

establishment clause The first part of the First Amendment that asserts that "Congress shall make no law respecting an establishment of religion." The clause is the basis for the separation of church and state in the United States. Yet the Supreme Court has held in *Everson v Board of Education*, 330 U.S. 1 (1947), that it is not a violation of the establishment clause for the government to pay for the cost of busing children to religious schools; nor was the tax-exempt status of religious property—at issue in *Walz v Tax Commission of the City of New York*, 397 U.S. 664 (1970)—a violation. Increasingly, the Court is taking an attitude of "benevolent neutrality" toward religion. Government activity that has the purpose or primary effect of advancing or inhibiting religion or that results in excessive government entanglement with religion is proscribed. Moreover, the establishment clause guards against measures that would foster political divisiveness on religious grounds in the general community. One continuing problem with the establishment clause is that, traditionally, many welfare and educational services in local communities have been provided by privately funded religious groups. This has posed a problem as far back as the New Deal. A significant part of the public-private controversy in the United States rests on the problem raised by the religious interests in such services and what happens when the federal government begins funding them. *Compare to* FREE EXERCISE CLAUSE; *see also* BOARD OF EDUCATION V ALLEN; EDWARDS V AGUILLARD; ZORACH V CLAUSON.

REFERENCES

Frank Sorauf, *Wall of Separation: The Constitutional Politics of Church and State*

(Princeton, NJ: Princeton University Press, 1976);

Leonard W. Levy, *The Establishment Clause: Religion and the First Amendment* (New York: Macmillan, 1986).

estate tax *See* TAX, ESTATE.

ethics A set of moral principles or values that can be applied to societies or social groups as a whole but that may also involve standards of behavior that constitute implied responsibilities for any professional activity. There are many ethical people in government, as there are in each of the professions. However, their ethical standards tend to reflect their personal background, rather than some abstract standard of professional conduct. Analyses of the ethical issues in public life range from the always-plead-innocent school of venality to the philosophic concerns of providing equitable public services to each member of the community. *See also* CODE OF ETHICS; WHISTLE BLOWER.

REFERENCES

Paul H. Douglas, *Ethics in Government* (Cambridge, MA: Harvard University Press, 1957);

Abraham Kaplan, *American Ethics and Public Policy* (New York: Oxford University Press, 1963);

George A. Graham, Ethical guidelines for public administrators: Observations on rules of the game, *Public Administration Review* 34 (January/February 1974);

John Rohr, *Ethics for Bureaucrats* (New York: Dekker, 1978);

Lee C. McDonald, Three forms of political ethics, *Western Political Quarterly* 31 (March 1978);

John A. Worthley and Barbara R. Grumet, Ethics and public administration: Teaching what "can't be taught," *American Review of Public Administration* 17 (Spring 1983);

Bruce Jennings and Daniel Callahan, eds., *Representation and Responsibility: Exploring Legislative Ethics* (New York: Plenum, 1985).

Ethics in Government Act of 1978 The federal statute that seeks to deal with possible conflicts of interest by former federal executive branch employees by imposing postemployment prohibitions on their activities. The restrictions in the law are concerned with former government employees' representation or attempts to influence federal agencies, not with their employment by others. What is prohibited depends on how involved a former employee was with a matter while with the government and whether he or she was one of a specified group of senior employees.

REFERENCE

J. Jackson Walter, The Ethics in Government Act, conflict of interest laws and presidential recruiting, *Public Administration Review* 41 (November/December 1981).

ethnic group Social, biological, or (sometimes) political division of humankind when the latter refers to national origins and religious beliefs in combination with one another. The United States used to be referred to as a MELTING POT for ethnic groups. *Compare to* RACE.

REFERENCES

Thomas Sowell, *Ethnic America: A History* (New York: Basic Books, 1981);

Stephen Steinberg, *The Ethnic Myth: Race, Ethnicity, and Class in America* (New York: Atheneum, 1981).

ethnic politics 1 The politics of FACTIONS when those factions are ethnic groups. 2 The politics within a minority ethnic community of a larger polity. 3 Specific political appeals to ethnic group members. A politician may be said to be practicing ethnic politics when he tells his Irish constituents of his support for a united Ireland, his Jewish constituents of his support for a strong State of Israel, and his Hispanic constituents of his strong support for bilingual education. Ethnic politics does not have to be substantive; sometimes it is nothing more than a "photo opportunity" of the politician eating ethnic food or attending an ethnic cultural festival or wedding. 4 Any appeal to racism. It is racism for candidates to imply that people should vote for them because of their ethnic background. 5 The resurging pride in ethnicity that came about since the civil rights movement of the 1960s. This has radically affected how minorities view themselves and

their roles in the polity. 6 Laying claim to a significant ethnic constituency largely because of one's ethnic origins. In this sense, JESSE JACKSON is an ethnic politician.

Ethnic politics aren't what they used to be. Originally, the term applied only to European ethnics. The term is now more likely to refer to the new ethnics, both those that have long been here and those that are more recent arrivals, for example, the blacks, the Hispanics, the Vietnamese. Technically, every American is a member of an ethnic group except for white Anglo-Saxon Protestants. And now that they are in the minority, many of them have begun to claim that they are an ethnic group, too.

REFERENCES

Harry A. Bailey, Jr., and Ellis Katz, eds., *Ethnic Group Politic* (Columbus, OH: Charles E. Merrill, 1969);

R. Robert Huckfeldt, The social contexts of ethnic politics: Ethnic loyalties, political loyalties, and social support, *American Politics Quarterly* 11 (January 1983).

evaluation, policy The analysis of policy alternatives in advance of a decision.

REFERENCES

David Nachmias, *Public Policy Evaluation* (New York: St. Martin's, 1979);

Richard C. Larson and Leni Berliner, On evaluating evaluations, *Policy Sciences* 16 (November 1983).

evaluation, program 1 The systematic examination of any activity or group of activities undertaken by government to make a determination about their effects, both short and long range. Program evaluation is distinguished from management evaluation (also called organization evaluation), because the latter is limited to a program's internal administrative procedures. While program evaluations use management and organizational data, the main thrust is necessarily on overall program objectives and impact. 2 An assessment of the effectiveness of a program or grant project after it has been completed. It is undertaken by the granting agency to determine if its funds were spent effectively, legally, and according to the original grant application.

REFERENCES

A. C. Hyde and J. M. Shafritz, eds. *Program Evaluation in the Public Sector* (New York: Praeger, 1979);

Theodore H. Poister, James C. McDavid, and Anne H. Magoun, *Applied Program Evaluation in Local Government* (Lexington, MA: Lexington Books, 1979);

Judith R. Brown, Legislative program evaluation: Defining a legislative service and a profession, *Public Administration Review* 44 (May/June 1984);

Eleanor Chelimsky, ed., *Program Evaluation: Patterns and Directions* (Washington, D.C.: American Society for Public Administration, 1984).

evaluation research An attempt to assess specific policy options by conducting experiments, assessing their outcomes, and recommending whether the new concept should be broadly applied.

REFERENCES

Carol H. Weiss, *Evaluation Research* (Englewook Cliffs, NJ: Prentice-Hall, 1972);

Joseph S. Wholey, The role of evaluation in improving public programs, *Public Administration Review* 36 (November/December 1976);

Erwin C. Hargrove, The bureaucratic politics of evaluation: A case study of the Department of Labor, *Public Administration Review* 40 (March/April 1980).

Everson v Board of Education See ESTABLISHMENT CLAUSE.

Examining Board v Flores de Otero 426 U.S. 572 (1976) The U.S. Supreme Court case that held that a Puerto Rican statute permitting only U.S. citizens to practice privately as civil engineers was unconstitutional and that resident aliens could not be denied the same opportunity.

excepted positions/exempted positions U.S. civil service positions that have been excepted or exempted from merit system requirements. Most of these positions are excluded by statute and are under merit systems adminis-

tered by agencies, such as the Tennessee Valley Authority, the Federal Bureau of Investigation, the U.S. Foreign Service, and the U.S. Postal Service. They are in the same category as unclassified positions, positions excepted by law, positions excepted by executive order, positions excepted by civil service rule, or positions outside the competitive service. *Compare to* EXEMPT EMPLOYEES.

excess profits tax *See* TAX, EXCESS PROFITS.

excise tax *See* TAX, EXCISE.

exclusionary clause That part of a contract that tries to restrict the legal remedies available to one side if the contract is broken.

exclusionary rule The constitutional ruling that evidence obtained through an illegal search or seizure may not be used in a criminal trial. The exclusionary rule, which is premised upon the Fourth Amendment prohibition against unreasonable searches and seizures, was established for the federal courts in the Supreme Court case of *Weeks v United States*, 232 U.S. 383 (1914). It was extended to state courts in *Mapp v Ohio*. In recent years, the exclusionary rule has been increasingly refined and limited by the Supreme Court. In *United States v Calandra*, 414 U.S. 338 (1974), the Court held that the rule does not extend to grand jury proceedings where witnesses might be required to answer questions about illegally obtained evidence. *United States v Havens*, 446 U.S. 620 (1980), allowed the use of illegally obtained evidence to contradict a defendant's testimony. And in *United States v Salvucci*, 448 U.S. 83 (1980), the Court restricted a defendant's "automatic standing" to challenge searches and seizures. The trend continues.

REFERENCES

Bradley C. Canon, Testing the effectiveness of civil liberties policies at the state and federal levels: The case of the exclusionary rule, *American Politics Quarterly* 5 (January 1977);

Morris D. Forkosch, In defense of the exclusionary rule: What it protects are the constitutional rights of citizens threatened by the court, the executive, and the congress, *American Journal of Economics and Sociology* 41 (April 1982);

Steven D. Clymer, Warrantless vehicle searches and the Fourth Amendment: The Burger Court attacks the exclusionary rule, *Cornell Law Review* 68 (November 1982).

exclusive economic zone (EEZ) An international law concept, which has evolved since World War II, meaning a nation has unilaterally extended its sovereignty over its adjacent waters. The zone is declared to control economic resources, mainly fishing and mining. The 1982 United Nations Convention on the Law of the Sea formally codified the EEZ concept to allow coastal nations to have exclusive jurisdiction to the seabed and waters up to two hundred miles from their shores. However, not all nations, most notably the United States, accept the U.N. Convention or recognize the EEZs of other nations.

REFERENCE

David Attard, *The Exclusive Economic Zone in International Law* (Oxford, U.K.: Oxford University Press, 1986).

executive 1 Any of the highest managers in an organization. 2 That branch of government concerned with the implementation of the policies and laws created by a legislature.

executive action 1 The last stage of the policymaking process. 2 An intelligence community term for assassination.

executive agreement A term that covers a wide variety of international agreements and understandings that are reached by the governments concerned in the course of administering their relations. The executive agreement device permits a U.S. president to enter into open or secret arrangements with a foreign government without the advice and consent of the Senate. There are two broad categories of executive agreements: presidential agreements and congressional-executive agreements. Presidential agreements are those made solely on the basis of the constitutional authority of the president; congressional-executive agreements cover all international agreements entered into under the combined authority of the president and the Congress. The executive agreement is used for significant political agreements, such as an aid-for-naval-bases agreement with Spain, as well as routine, nonpolitical agreements, such as reciprocal postal arrangements with England. The former are usually made under the president's sole power to faithfully execute the laws or under his diplomatic or commander-in-chief powers. The latter are usually made under authority of the Congress and the president. The vast majority of executive agreements are entered into in pursuit of specific congressional authority.

The Supreme Court in *U.S. v Belmont,* 301 U.S. 324 (1937), unanimously held an executive agreement to be a valid international compact, state policy notwithstanding. The Court said in part: "In respect of all international negotiations and compacts, and in respect of our foreign relations generally, state lines disappear." The Court has ruled, however, that the president is not free to enter into executive agreements that violate constitutional provisions. See *U.S. v Guy W. Capps, Inc.,* 204 F. 2d 655 (4th Cir. 1953) aff'd on other grounds, 348 U.S. 296 (1955); and *Reid v Covert,* 354 U.S. 1 (1957).

By the Case Act of 1972, Congress required that the U.S. Secretary of State transmit to the Congress all executive agreements to which the United States is a party no later than sixty days after such agreement has entered into force. The president need report secret agreements only to the Foreign Relations committees of the two houses. The act did not give the Congress the authority to disapprove an executive agreement. Because there is often a thin line between what constitutes an executive agreement a president can make on his own and a treaty that must be ratified by the Senate, there is often considerable concern that a president might be using executive agreements to avoid the Senate's constitutional role in the foreign relations process.

REFERENCES

Executive agreements have been published since 1950 in a series entitled *United States Treaties and Other International Agreements.* Also see Charles J. Stevens, The use and control of executive agreements: Recent congressional initiatives, *Orbis* 20 (Winter 1977);

David J. Kuchenbecker, Agency-level executive agreements: A new era in U.S. treaty practice, *Columbia Journal of Transactional Law* 18:1 (1979);

Gary J. Schmitt, Separation of powers: Introduction to the study of executive agreements, *American Journal of Jurisprudence* 27 (1982);

Gary J. Schmitt, Executive agreements and separation of powers; A reconsideration, *American Journal of Jurisprudence* 28 (1983).

executive branch   In a government with SEP-ARATION OF POWERS, that part which is responsible for applying or administering the law. Thus a president, governor or mayor and their respective supporting bureaucracies are the executive branches of their respective jurisdictions. But not all of the federal bureaucracy is part of the executive branch. Some agencies such as the General Accounting Office are directly responsible to Congress. Others, such as the Federal Trade Commission (and other regulatory agencies) have been held by the Supreme Court not to be part of the executive branch. *See* HUMPHREY'S EXECUTOR V UNITED STATES.

executive budget   *See* BUDGET, EXECUTIVE.

executive calendar   *See* CALENDAR, EXECUTIVE.

executive, chief   The highest elected office in a jurisdiction, whether it be the mayor of a city, the governor of a state, or the president of the United States.
REFERENCES
The classic analysis of the qualities of leadership needed in the highest-level corporate executive is Chester I. Barnard's *The Functions of the Executive* (Cambridge, MA: Harvard University Press, 1938).
For an application of Barnard's theories to the office of chief executive of the United States, see Jacqueline Vaughn, The functions of the (chief) executive: How Chester

Barnard might view the presidency, *Presidential Studies Quarterly* 8 (Winter 1978).

executive communication   A message from the president of the United States to the Speaker of the House of Representatives and the president of the Senate, usually to request legislation, to make a report, or to express a view on problems and policies.

executive department   A cabinet-level agency in the federal government.

executive document   A document, usually a treaty, sent to the Senate by the president of the United States for consideration or approval. These are identified for each session of Congress as Executive A, 97th Congress, 1st Session; Executive B, and so on. They are referred to committee in the same manner as other measures. Unlike legislative documents, however, treaties do not die at the end of a Congress but remain live proposals until acted on by the Senate or withdrawn by the president.

Executive Office of the President (EOP)
The umbrella office consisting of the top presidential staff agencies that provide the president help and advice in carrying out his major responsibilities. The EOP was created by President Franklin D. Roosevelt under the authority of the Reorganization Act of 1939. Since then, presidents have used executive orders, reorganization plans, and legislative initiatives to reorganize, expand, or contract the EOP. *See also* BROWNLOW COMMITTEE/PRESIDENT'S COMMITTEE ON ADMINISTRATIVE MANAGEMENT; PRESIDENCY, AMERICAN; PRESIDENTIAL POWER.
REFERENCES
For studies on the growth of the EOP, see Thomas E. Cronin, The swelling of the presidency, *Saturday Review* (February 1973);
Emmette S. Redford and Marlan Blisset, *Organizing the Executive Branch: The Johnson Presidency* (Chicago: University of Chicago Press, 1981).

Executive Office of the President
1600 Pennsylvania Avenue, N.W.
Washington, D.C. 20500
(202) 456–1414

The Executive Office of the President

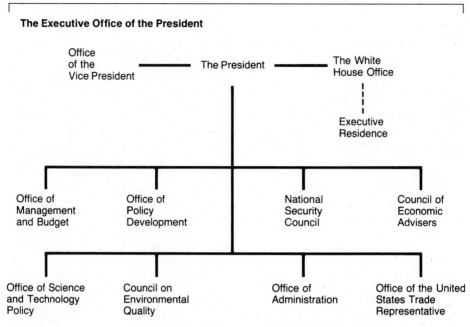

Source: William J. Keefe, Henry J. Abraham, William H. Flanigan, Charles O. Jones, Morris S. Ogul, and John W. Spanier, *American Democracy: Institutions, Politics, and Policies*, 2d ed. (Chicago: Dorsey, 1986), p. 397.

executive order **1** Any rule or regulation issued by a chief administrative authority that, because of precedent and existing legislative authorization, has the effect of law. **2** The principal mode of administrative action on the part of the president of the United States. The power of a president to issue executive orders emanates from the constitutional provision requiring him to "take care that the laws be faithfully executed," the commander-in-chief clause, and express powers vested in him by congressional statutes.

REFERENCES

For presidential executive orders, see John E. Noyes, Executive orders, presidential intent, and private rights of action, *Texas Law Review* 59 (May 1981);

Robert A. Shanley, Presidential executive orders and environmental policy, *Presidential Studies Quarterly* 13 (Summer 1983);

Phillip J. Cooper, By order of the president: Administration by executive order and proclamation, *Administration and Society* 18 (August 1986).

For executive orders by state governors, see

E. Lee Bernick, Discovering a governor's powers: The executive order, *State Government* 57:3 (1984);

E. Lee Bernick and Charles W. Wiggins, The governor's executive order: An unknown power, *State and Local Government Review* 16 (Winter 1984).

Executive Order 8802 The presidential executive order of June 25, 1941, that (1) required that defense contractors not discriminate against any worker because of race, creed, or national origin, and (2) established a Committee on Fair Employment Practice to investigate and remedy violations.

Executive Order 9981 The presidential executive order of July 26, 1948, by which President Harry S Truman mandated the racial integration in the military and naval forces of the United States and called for an end to racial discrimination in all federal employment.

Executive Order 10925 The presidential executive order of March 6, 1961, that for the first time required that "affirmative action" be used to implement the policy of nondiscrimination in employment by the federal government and its contractors.

Executive Order 10988 The presidential executive order of January 17, 1962, that established the right of federal employees to bargain with management over certain limited issues. Considered the "magna carta" of labor relations in the federal government, it was superseded by Executive Order 11491.

Executive Order 11246 The presidential executive order of September 24, 1965, that required federal government contractors to have affirmative action programs. There has been much debate within the Ronald Reagan administration about whether to rescind or modify this order.

Executive Order 11491 The presidential executive order of October 29, 1969, that granted each federal employee the right to join or not join a labor organization, that created the Federal Labor Relations Council (which was superseded by the Federal Labor Relations Authority), and that generally expanded the scope of bargaining for federal employees.

REFERENCE

Ed D. Roach and Frank W. McClain, Executive Order 11491: Prospects and problems, *Public Personnel Review* 31 (July 1970).

executive oversight The total process by which executives attempt to control their organization and to hold individual managers responsible for the implementation of their programs.

REFERENCES

Lance T. LeLoup and William B. Moreland, Agency strategies and executive review: The hidden politics of budgeting, *Public Administration Review* 31 (May/June 1978);

W. Kip Viscusi, Presidential oversight: Controlling the regulators, *Journal of Policy Analysis and Management* 2 (Winter 1983).

executive, plural *See* PLURAL EXECUTIVE.

executive privilege The presidential claim that the executive branch may withhold information from the Congress or its committees and the courts to preserve confidential communications within the executive branch or to secure the national interest. Although the Constitution does not explicitly grant the executive a privilege to withhold information from the Congress, presidents have from the beginning of the Republic claimed it. President George Washington withheld from the House of Representatives papers and documents connected with the Jay Treaty because, he argued, the House had no constitutional role in the treaty-making process. The presidential claim of executive privilege was not seriously challenged until President Richard M. Nixon sought to use executive privilege to sustain immunity from the judicial process. In 1974, the U.S. Supreme Court restricted the privilege when it held that, in a criminal case before a court, a concrete need for evidence takes precedence over a generalized assertion of executive privilege unrelated to defense or diplomacy. The Court did acknowledge a constitutional protection for the "president's need for complete candor and objectivity from [his] advisors" and for "military, diplomatic, or sensitive national security secrets." *See* UNITED STATES V NIXON.

REFERENCES

For a listing of previous presidential uses of the executive privilege, see *The Power of the President to Withhold Information from the Congress,* compiled by the Subcommittee on Constitutional Rights of the Senate Committee on the Judiciary, 85th Cong., 2d sess. (1958).

For the view that the presidential claim of executive privilege is without historical foundation, see Raoul Berger, *Executive Privilege: A Constitutional Myth* (Cambridge, MA: Harvard University Press, 1974).

Also see Adam C. Breckenridge, *The Executive Privilege: Presidential Control Over Information* (Lincoln: University of Nebraska Press, 1974);

Archibald Cox, Executive privilege, *University of Pennsylvania Law Review* 122 (June 1974);

Louis Henkin, Executive privilege: Mr. Nixon loses but the presidency largely prevails, *UCLA Law Review* 22 (October 1974);

James Hamilton and John C. Grabow, A legislative proposal for resolving executive privilege disputes precipitated by congressional subpoenas, *Harvard Journal on Legislation* 21 (Winter 1984).

executive session   1 A secret meeting.   2 A confidential meeting of any governing body. 3 A meeting of a U.S. Senate or a House of Representatives committee (or, occasionally, of the entire membership) that only the group's members are privileged to attend. Frequently, witnesses appear before committees meeting in executive session and other members of the Congress may be invited, but the public and press are not allowed to attend. As a result of SUNSHINE RULES, most committee meetings in the Congress are now open to the public.   4 A meeting of the U.S. Senate when it is dealing with executive functions, such as the confirmation of presidential nominations and the ratification of treaties. In this context, an executive session is distinguished from a legislative session.

exempt employees   Employees who, because of their administrative, professional, or executive status, are not covered by the overtime provisions of the Fair Labor Standards Act. In consequence, their employers are not legally required to pay them for overtime work. *Compare to* EXCEPTED POSITIONS/EXEMPTED POSITIONS.

exemption   A deduction from gross income for income tax purposes allowed for the support of one's self and dependents.

exit polls   *See* POLLS, EXIT.

ex officio   A Latin phrase meaning by virtue of the office. Many people hold positions on boards, commissions, councils, and so on because of another office they occupy. For example, the mayor of a city may be an ex officio member of the board of trustees of a university in that city.

ex parte   A Latin phrase meaning with only one side present. It usually refers to a hearing or trial in which only one side is present because the other side failed to show up, was not given notice, and so on.

Ex parte McCardle 7 Wallace 506 (1869) The U.S. Supreme Court case that held that the Congress could regulate the appellate jurisdiction of the Court by passing legislation even if the legislation affected a case under active consideration. Article III, Section 2, of the U.S. Constitution gives appellate jurisdiction to the Supreme Court with "such exceptions and under such regulations, as the Congress shall make."

REFERENCE
Stanley Kutler, *Ex Parte McCardle:* Judicial impotency? The Supreme Court and reconstruction reconsidered, *American Historical Review* 72:3 (1967).

Ex parte Milligan   *See* WRIT OF HABEAS CORPUS.

expenditures   The actual spending of money as distinguished from its appropriation. Expenditures are made by the disbursing officers of a government; appropriations are made by a legislature. The two are rarely identical: in any fiscal year, expenditures may represent money appropriated one, two, or more years previously.

exported tax   *See* TAX, EXPORTED.

Export-Import Bank (Eximbank)   An autonomous agency of the U.S. government created by the Export-Import Bank Act of 1945 to facilitate export-import trade. Under various programs, the Eximbank provides export credits and direct loans to foreign buyers and sells insurance and export guarantees to U.S. manufacturers.

REFERENCE
John A. Bohn, Jr., Governmental response to Third World debt: The role of the Export-Import Bank, *Stanford Journal of International Law* 21 (Fall 1985).

Eximbank
811 Vermont Avenue, N.W.
Washington, D.C. 20571
(202) 566–8990

ex post facto law   A law that makes something retroactively illegal—makes unlawful any act that was not a crime when it was committed. The U.S. Constitution prohibits ex post facto laws by the federal government (Article I, Section 9) and by the states (Article I, Section 10). These prohibitions have been interpreted to prevent the imposition of a greater penalty for a crime than that in effect when the crime was committed. However, laws that retroactively determine how a person is to be tried for a crime may be changed, as long as no important rights are lost. Laws are not considered ex post facto if they make the punishment less severe than it was when the crime was committed.

expropriation The confiscation of private property by a government, which may or may not pay a portion of its value in return. *Compare to* NATIONALIZATION.

REFERENCES
Rudolf Dolzer, New foundations of the law of expropriation of alien property, *American Journal of International Law* 75 (July 1981);
Pamela B. Gann, Compensation standard for expropriation, *Columbia Journal of Transnational Law* 23:3 (1985).

extension of remarks That portion of the *Congressional Record* that contains speeches and other material not immediately germane to the current debate but that a member of the Congress wants printed as part of the *Record*.

extradition The surrender by one nation or state to another of a person accused or convicted of an offense in the second nation or state.

REFERENCES
Christopher L. Blakesley, The practice of extradition from antiquity to modern France and the United States: A brief history, *Boston College International and Comparative Law Review* 4 (Spring 1981);
Barbara Ann Anoff and Christopher H. Pyle, "To surrender political offenders": The political offense exception to extradition in United States law, *New York University Journal of International Law and Politics* 16 (Winter 1984).

extraordinary majority Any vote that is required to be more than a simple majority, more than half plus one. The ratification of constitutional amendments requires extraordinary majorities.

extraterritoriality A nation's exercise of its authority and laws outside of its physical limits, such as on its ship at sea, over its own soldiers in foreign countries, and in the residences of its diplomats stationed abroad.

REFERENCES
David Leyton-Brown, Extraterritoriality in Canadian-American relations, *International Journal* 36, (Winter 1980–81);
Harold G. Maier, Interest balancing and extraterritorial jurisdiction, *American Journal of Comparative Law* 31 (Fall 1983).

F

faction 1 In English political history, any group whose motives for supporting a given action were inherently suspect because of the assumption of selfish interest, as opposed to the welfare of the community as a whole. 2 The term used by James Madison in *Federalist* 10 to describe "a number of citizens, whether amounting to a majority or minority of the whole, who are united and actuated by some common impulse of passion or of interest, adverse to the rights of other citizens, or to the permanent and aggregate interests of the community." 3 Any subgroup within a larger organization; for example, the moderate faction of the Republican party, the conservative faction of the Democratic party.

REFERENCES

3   Austin Ranney, *Curing the Mischiefs of Faction: Party Reform in America* (Berkeley and Los Angeles: University of California Press, 1975);

Glenn R. Parker and Suzanne L. Parker, Factions in committees: The U.S. House of Representatives, *American Political Science Review* 73 (March 1979).

factory survey   See IMMIGRATION AND NATURALIZATION SERVICE V HERMAN DELGATO.

Fair Credit Reporting Act of 1971   The federal law that gives citizens the right to learn of the contents of files on them created and maintained by commercial credit bureaus.

REFERENCE

Robert M. McNamara, Jr., The Fair Credit Reporting Act: A legislative overview, *Journal of Public Law* 22:1 (1973).

Fair Deal   President Harry S Truman's domestic programs. He first used the phrase in an address to the Congress in 1949. The Fair Deal was in essence an effort on the part of the Truman administration to sustain and extend the New Deal.

REFERENCE

Alonzo L. Hamby, ed., *Harry S Truman and the Fair Deal* (Lexington, MA: Heath, 1974).

fair employment practice commission   A generic title for any state or local government agency responsible for administering or enforcing laws prohibiting employment discrimination because of race, color, sex, religion, national origin, or other factors.

Fair Employment Practice Committee   A federal committee created in 1941 by President Franklin D. Roosevelt in Executive Order 8802, calling for the elimination of discrimination based on race, color, religion, or national origin within the defense production industries and the federal service. By almost all accounts, however, the committee was weak and even somewhat uninterested in combating discrimination in the federal service. In 1946, it met its demise through an amendment to an appropriations bill.

REFERENCES

For its history, see Will Maslow, FEPC—A case history in parliamentary maneuver, *University of Chicago Law Review* 13 (June 1946);

Louis C. Kesselman, *The Social Politics of FEPC* (Chapel Hill: University of North Carolina Press, 1948).

fair employment practice laws   All government requirements designed to prohibit discrimination in the various aspects of employment.

REFERENCE

James S. Russell, A review of fair employment cases in the field of training, *Personnel Psychology* 37 (Summer 1984).

fair housing laws   State, local, and federal statutes prohibiting discrimination in the sale, rental, or financing of housing.

Fair Labor Standards Act of 1938 (FLSA)   The federal statute, also called Wages and Hours Act, that, as amended, established standards for minimum wages, overtime pay, equal pay, recordkeeping, and child labor. It affected more than sixty-million full-time and part-time workers. The U.S. Supreme Court's 1985 decision in GARCIA V SAN ANTONIO METROPOLITAN TRANSIT AUTHORITY extended coverage of the FLSA to state and local government employees. *See also* CHILD LABOR; NATIONAL LEAGUE OF CITIES V USERY; UNITED STATES V DARBY LUMBER.

REFERENCES

For histories of FLSA, see Jonathan Grossman, Fair Labor Standards Act of 1938: Maximum struggle for a minimum wage, *Monthly Labor Review* 101 (June 1978);

P. K. Elder and H. D. Miller, The Fair Labor Standards Act: Changes of four decades, *Monthly Labor Review* 102 (July 1979);

Ronald G. Ehrenberg and Paul L. Schumann, Compliance with the overtime pay provisions of the Fair Labor Standards Act, *Journal of Law & Economics* 25 (April 1982);

Horst Brand, The evolution of fair labor standards: A study in class conflict, *Monthly Labor Review* 106 (August 1983).

fairness doctrine   The now abandoned policy of the Federal Communications Commission that radio and television stations must allow all sides on public issues equal access to the airwaves. This meant that all candidates for political office had to have an equal opportunity to present their views; thus a station or network had to offer airtime on the same basis to all candidates. The fairness or equal-time doctrine was upheld by the U.S. Supreme Court in *Red Lion Broadcasting v FCC*, 395 U.S. 367 (1969). But in 1986 a federal court of appeals ruled that the doctrine was not law and thus could be repealed without congressional approval. In response, Congress passed a bill in 1987 which would have made the fairness doctrine permanent. President Ronald Reagan vetoed the bill citing the first amendment's requirement for freedom of the press and observing that: "In any other medium besides broadcasting, such federal policing of the editorial judgment of journalists would be unthinkable." When the veto was not overridden, the FCC promptly negated the fairness doctrine which it had first enunciated in 1949.

REFERENCES

Steven J. Simmons, *The Fairness Doctrine and the Media* (Berkeley and Los Angeles: University of California Press, 1978);

Ford Rowan, *Broadcast Fairness: Doctrine, Practice, Prospects: A Reappraisal of the Fairness Doctrine and Equal Time Rule* (New York: Longman, 1984);

Anna C. Goldoff, The Federal Communications Commission's "fairness" doctrine: Broadcaster attitudes and compliance, *Administration & Society* 15 (February 1984).

fairness question   An abbreviated way of referring to concerns over the fairness of the domestic budget cuts made by the Ronald Reagan administration. This concern, which has been expressed mainly by Democrats, basically asks the question of whether it is fair to cut funds from welfare programs to pay for a peacetime defense buildup. And, additionally, whether the cutbacks in social programs combined with benefits for middle and upperclass citizens resulted in a "fair" distribution of benefits.

Falwell, Jerry   *See* MORAL MAJORITY.

family allowances   Payments to workers in addition to regular wages, based on the number of dependent children that a worker has. Almost all of the major industrial countries except the United States have family allowance programs financed by their governments.

REFERENCES

George E. Rejda, Family allowances as a program for reducing poverty, *Journal of Risk and Insurance* 37 (December 1970);

John Macnicol, *The Movement for Family Allowances, 1918–45; A Study in Social Policy Development* (London: Heinemann, 1980).

family policy   A vague term for the totality of current or future legislation (or corporate policies) aimed at reconciling the role of women as both mothers and members of the work force. Family policies seek to help working mothers better cope with their family responsibilities through paid maternity leave, subsidized or free day-care programs for children, and so on. A main difference in attitudes toward family policy is that liberals, as opposed to conservatives, seek policies that call for additional government spending; while conservatives, as opposed to liberals, seek policies that emphasize traditional religious values and the enforcement of their standards of morality (for example, in regard to abortion and pornography) for the entire society.

REFERENCES

Burton Mindick, *Social Engineering in Family Matters* (New York: Praeger, 1985);

Daniel P. Moynihan, *Family and Nation* (San Diego, CA: Harcourt Brace Jovanovich, 1986);

Robert Moroney, *Shared Responsibility: Family and Social Policy* (New York: Aldine, 1986).

farewell address   A political leader's last major speech while in high office and made in anticipation of retirement from public life. Just as deathbed confessions are given special credence, farewell addresses have a similar poignancy. Many presidents of the United States have made farewell addresses: George Washington used his to urge the nation "to steer clear of permanent alliance with any portion of the foreign world"; Dwight D. Eisenhower used his to warn the nation of the MILITARY-INDUSTRIAL COMPLEX.

The fasces symbol as it appears on the wall of the House of Representatives in Washington, D.C.

fascism **1** A political philosophy that advocates governance by a dictator, assisted by a hierarchically organized, strongly ideological party, in maintaining a totalitarian and regimented society through violence, intimidation, and the arbitrary use of power. **2** A mass-based REACTIONARY political movement in an industrialized nation that, through the means of a charismatic leader, espouses nationalism in the extreme. The main difference between totalitarian fascism and totalitarian communism is that fascism professes sympathy toward many aspects of private capitalism and would resolve the conflict between capital and labor by using the government to enforce their relations to one another in the interest of full employment and high productivity. Charismatic leadership is believed to appeal to the irrational and would cement the loyalty of the mass public to the nation through its emotional commitment to an individual. Italy's Benito Mussolini (1883–1945) created the prototype of the modern fascist state in the 1920s. According to Mussolini, in *The Doctrine of Fascism* (1932), "The key-stone of the Fascist doctrine is the conception of the State, of its essence, of its functions, its aims. For Fascism the State is

absolute, individuals and groups relative." In the early 1930s, Huey P. Long (1893–1935), the political boss of Louisiana, predicted that "if fascism came to America, it would be on a program of Americanism." Sinclair Lewis (1885–1951), the first American to win the Nobel Prize for literature, showed exactly how this could happen in his 1935 novel *It Can't Happen Here*. The word fascism is derived from the official symbol of power and justice of ancient Roman magistrates: a bundle of sticks (fascis) with an ax protruding. This symbol can be seen on the back of a dime, on the wall of the U.S. House of Representatives, and on the stairs of the Lincoln Memorial. Mussolini used this ancient symbol of justice to represent his modern style of tyranny.

REFERENCES

A. James Gregor, *The Ideology of Fascism: The Rationale of Totalitarianism* (New York: Free Press, 1969);

Walter Laqueur, ed., *Fascism: A Reader's Guide* (Berkeley and Los Angeles: University of California Press, 1976);

Stanley G. Payne, *Fascism: Comparison and Definition* (Madison: University of Wisconsin Press, 1980);

Geoff Eley, What produces fascism: Preindustrial traditions or a crisis of the capitalist state, *Politics and Society* 12:1 (1983).

favorite son/favorite daughter A presidential aspirant at a national nominating convention who seeks to keep the votes of his or her state's delegation together behind his or her candidacy to maintain a strong political bargaining position. Such candidates seldom have any real support beyond their own states. They are also of lessening significance since the adoption of party democratizing rules in the 1970s.

FBI *See* FEDERAL BUREAU OF INVESTIGATION.

FCC *See* FEDERAL COMMUNICATIONS COMMISSION.

FDIC *See* FEDERAL DEPOSIT INSURANCE CORPORATION.

FECA *See* FEDERAL ELECTION CAMPAIGN ACT OF 1971.

Fed *See* FEDERAL RESERVE SYSTEM.

federal assistance programs The totality of federal financial aid programs available to state and local governments, including counties, cities, and metropolitan and regional governments; schools, colleges, and universities; health institutions; nonprofit and for-profit organizations; and individuals and families. Current federal assistance programs are listed in the annual *Catalogue of Federal Domestic Assistance*.

Federal Bureau of Investigation (FBI) The principal investigative arm of the U.S. Department of Justice, established in 1908 as the Bureau of Investigation. It is charged with gathering and reporting facts, locating witnesses, and compiling evidence in matters in which the federal government is, or may be, a party in interest. Cooperative services of the FBI for other duly authorized law enforcement agencies include fingerprint identification, laboratory services, police training, and the National Crime Information Center. J. Edgar Hoover (1895–1972), as director of the FBI from 1924 to his death, created the modern identity and functions of the FBI: the FBI achieved its greatest prestige and public support under Hoover, and the FBI agent became a national symbol of incorruptible law enforcement. But toward the end of his reign, Hoover's reputation and that of the FBI were hurt when a variety of scandals came to light about illegal wiretapping, burglaries, and violations of the civil rights of citizens. Since then, the FBI has been kept on a tighter rein by the Justice Department. *Compare to* G-MEN.

REFERENCES

Sanford J. Ungar, *FBI* (Boston: Atlantic–Little, Brown, 1976);

Andrew Tully, *Inside the FBI* (New York: McGraw-Hill, 1980);

Tony G. Poveda, The rise and fall of FBI domestic intelligence operations, *Contemporary Crises: Crime, Law and Social Policy* 6 (April 1982).

Federal Bureau of Investigation
9th Street and Pennsylvania Avenue, N.W.
Washington, D.C. 20535
(202) 324-3000

Federal Communications Commission (FCC) The independent federal agency created by the Communications Act of 1934 that regulates interstate and foreign communications by radio, television, wire, and cable. It is responsible for the orderly development and operation of broadcast services and the provision of nationwide and worldwide communications services at reasonable rates. The FCC also has the responsibility for establishing and monitoring moral standards in broadcasting. *See* FAIRNESS DOCTRINE.

Federal Communications Commission
1919 M Street, N.W.
Washington, D.C. 20554
(202) 632-7000

Federal Council on the Arts and Humanities *See* NATIONAL FOUNDATION ON THE ARTS AND THE HUMANITIES.

Federal Court of Appeals *See* COURT OF APPEALS.

Federal Deposit Insurance Corporation (FDIC) The federal agency established in 1933 to promote and preserve public confidence in banks and to protect the money supply through provision of insurance coverage for bank deposits. Created by an amendment to the Federal Reserve Act, it was reauthorized by the Federal Deposit Insurance Act of 1950.

REFERENCES

Federal Deposit Insurance Corporation, *Federal Deposit Insurance Corporation, the First Fifty Years: A History of the FDIC, 1933–1983* (Washington, D.C.: FDIC, 1984);

Edward J. Kane, *The Gathering Crisis in Federal Deposit Insurance* (Cambridge, MA: MIT Press, 1985).

Federal Deposit Insurance Corporation
550 17th Street, N.W.
Washington, D.C. 20429
(202) 393-8400

federal district court *See* DISTRICT COURT/ FEDERAL DISTRICT COURT/U.S. DISTRICT COURT.

Federal Election Campaign Act of 1972 (FECA) The basic law that, as amended in

1974, 1976, and 1979, regulates the federal election process, including primaries, general elections, special elections, caucuses, and conventions. The FECA and its amendments establishes strict reporting requirements for all candidates for federal office, their campaign committees, and others spending money to influence federal elections. Contributions are limited but expenditures, in general, are not. Furthermore, full—though optional—public financing is provided for major-party presidential candidates in the general election and major-party national nominating conventions, and matching public funding is provided in presidential primary elections. Minor-party presidential candidates may receive partial public funding in the general election. Expenditures by candidates accepting federal funds are limited, as are the personal funds such a candidate may spend on his or her own campaign. *See* BUCKLEY V VALEO.

REFERENCES

Elmer B. Staats, Impact of the Federal Election Campaign Act of 1971, *Annals of the American Academy of Political and Social Science* 425 (May 1976);

Thomas E. Harris, Implementing the federal campaign finance laws, *National Civic Review* 67 (May 1978);

Michael S. Berman, Living with the FECA: Confessions of a sometime campaign treasurer, *Annals of the American Academy of Political and Social Science* 486 (July 1986).

candidate could spend up to $20.2 million in all presidential primaries. The amount that can be spent within each state is also limited.

Expenditures in general elections are governed by public financing provisions. Each national party may make certain expenditures on behalf of its presidential and congressional candidates (for example, two cents per voter on behalf of its presidential candidate). There are no limits on how much candidates for the U.S. Senate and House of Representatives may collect and spend in their campaigns or on the amount that individuals and groups may spend on behalf of any presidential or congressional candidate, so long as these expenditures are independent.

Public Financing

Major party candidates for the presidency qualify for full funding prior to the campaign. In 1984, the Democratic and Republican nominees each received $40.4 million in campaign funds. These funds are derived from the federal income tax dollar checkoff. Minor party and independent candidates qualify for public funds (after the election) if they receive 5 percent of the vote. Matching federal funds are available for presidential primary candidates after they have first raised $100 thousand in private funds ($5 thousand in contributions of no more than $250 in each of twenty states). Once the $100 thousand threshold is reached, the candidate receives matching funds up to $250 per contribution. The maximum amount of matching funds available to any candidate in 1984 was $10.1 million; only Ronald Reagan qualified for this sum.

Source: William J. Keefe, Henry J. Abraham, William H. Flanigan, Charles O. Jones, Morris S. Ogul, and John W. Spanier, *American Democracy: Institutions, Politics, and Policies,* 2d ed. (Chicago: Dorsey, 1986), p. 232.

Key Provisions of the Federal Elections Campaign Act of 1974

Contributions Limits

Campaign contributions by individuals to any candidate or candidate committees are limited to a thousand dollars per election. Total contributions by an individual to all federal candidates in one year cannot exceed twenty-five thousand dollars. Political action committees formed by businesses, trade associations, or unions are limited to contributions of not more than five thousand dollars to any candidate in any election. There are no limits on their aggregate contributions.

Expenditure Limits

Expenditures in presidential primaries and general elections are limited. In 1984, each

Federal Election Commission The principal enforcement agency for the Federal Election Campaign Act established by the Federal Election Campaign Act of 1971. This six-member commission has the power to prescribe regulations to implement and clarify campaign laws and to issue advisory opinions to guide compliance with the federal election laws. Naturally beset by intense political pressures, it is often in the middle of a storm of controversy.

REFERENCE

Paul T. David, The Federal Election Commission: Origins and early activities, *National Civic Review* 65 (June 1976).

Federal Election Commission
999 E Street, N.W.
Washington, D.C. 20463
(202) 376-3120
(800) 424-9530 (toll free)

Federal Emergency Management Agency (FEMA) The agency, established by Reorganization Plan no. 3 of 1978, that plans for and coordinates emergency preparedness and response for all levels of government and for all kinds of emergencies—natural, man made, and nuclear. This is the organization that decides what the various governments should be doing after such a catastrophe.

REFERENCE

Peter J. May, FEMA's role in emergency management: Examining recent experience, *Public Administration Review* 45 (January 1985).

Federal Emergency Management Agency
500 C Street, S.W.
Washington, D.C. 20472
(202) 646-4600

federalese *See* GOBBLEDY GOOK/OFFICIALESE/ FEDERALESE/BAFFLEGAB.

Federal Executive Institute (FEI) The federal government's primary in-residence training facility for executive development; established by Executive Order in 1968.

REFERENCE

Paul Lorentzen, Role of the Federal Executive Institute, *Bureaucrat* (Summer 1981).

Federal Executive Institute
1301 Emmit Street
Charlottesville, VA 22901
(804) 296-0181

federal funds rate The interest rate at which depository institutions, such as banks, lend each other reserve funds on an overnight or temporary basis.

Federal Home Loan Bank Board The federal agency, created by the Federal Home Loan Bank Act of 1932, that supervises and regulates savings and loan associations, which are the country's major private source of funds for building and buying homes. The board operates the Federal Savings and Loan Insurance

Corporation, which protects savings of the more than seventy-five million Americans with savings accounts in FSLIC-insured savings and loan associations. The board also directs the Federal Home Loan Bank System, which, like the Federal Reserve System for banks, provides reserve credit and the assurance that member savings and loan associations will continue to be a source of financing for homes.

REFERENCES

Thomas B. Marvell, *The Federal Home Loan Bank Board* (New York: Praeger, 1969);

H. Glenn Boggs II and Claude C. Lilly III, FSLIC: A financial buffer? *California Management Review* 25 (January 1983).

Federal Home Loan Bank Board
1700 G Street, N.W.
Washington, D.C. 20552
(202) 377-6000

federalism A system of governance in which a national, overarching government shares power with subnational or state governments. History indicates clearly that the principal factor in the formation of federal systems of government has been a common external threat. Tribes, cities, colonies, or states have joined together in voluntary unions to defend themselves. However, not all systems so formed have been federal. A federal system has the following features: (1) a written constitution that divides government powers between the central government and the constituent governments, giving substantial powers and sovereignty to each; (2) levels of government, through their own instrumentalities, exercising power directly over citizens (unlike a confederation, in which only subnational units act directly on citizens while the central government acts only on the subnational governments); and (3) a constitutional distribution of powers that cannot be changed unilaterally by any level of government or by the ordinary process of legislation.

REFERENCES

William H. Riker, *Federalism: Origin, Operation, Significance* (Boston: Little, Brown, 1964);

James T. Patterson, *The New Deal and the States: Federalism in Transition* (Princeton, NJ: Princeton University Press, 1969);

Richard H. Leach, *American Federalism: A View from the States,* 2d ed. (New York: Crowell, 1972);

Parris N. Glendening and Mavis M. Reeves, *Pragmatic Federalism: An Intergovernmental View of the American Government* (Pacific Palisades, CA: Palisades, 1977);

David B. Walker, *Toward a Functioning Federalism* (Cambridge, MA: Winthrop, 1981);

Deil S. Wright and Harvey L. White, eds., *Federalism and Intergovernmental Relations* (Washington, D.C.: American Society for Public Administration, 1984).

federalism, cooperative The notion that the national, state, and local governments are co-operating, interacting agents, jointly working to solve common problems, rather than conflicting, sometimes hostile competitors, pursuing similar or, more likely, conflicting ends. While some cooperation has always been evident in spite of the conflict, competition, and complexity of intergovernmental relations, cooperation was most prominent between the 1930s and the 1950s. The emergency funding arrangements of the depression years known collectively as the New Deal and the cooperation among federal, state, and local authorities during World War II to administer civilian defense, rationing, and other wartime programs are noteworthy examples of cooperative federalism in the United States.

REFERENCE

Daniel J. Elazar, *The American Partnership: Intergovernmental Cooperation in the 19th Century United States* (Chicago: University of Chicago Press, 1962).

federalism, creative The Lyndon B. Johnson administration's term for its approach to intergovernmental relations, which was characterized by joint planning and decision making among all levels of government (as well as the private sector) in the management of intergovernmental programs. Many new programs of this period had an urban-metropolitan focus, and much attention was given to antipoverty issues. Creative federalism sought to foster the development of a singular Great Society by integrating the poor into mainstream America. Its expansive efforts were marked by the rapid development of categorical grant programs to state and local governments and direct federal grants to cities, frequently bypassing state governments entirely.

REFERENCES

James L. Sundquist, *Making Federalism Work* (Washington, D.C.: Brookings, 1969);

Edmond F. Ricketts and Herbert Waltzer, American federalism: Creative or stifling? *Midwest Review of Public Administration* 4 (August 1970).

federalism, dual The nineteenth-century concept, now no longer operational, that the functions and responsibilities of the federal and state governments were theoretically distinguished and functionally separate from each other. Some analysts suggest that this kind of federalism, which went out when the New Deal of 1933 came in, is what the Ronald Reagan administration sought, at least rhetorically, to eventually get back to. The basic idea of dual federalism was expressed succinctly by JAMES BRYCE, a British scholar who visited the United States in the 1880s to observe its political system:

> The characteristic feature and special interest of the American Union is that it shows us two governments covering the same ground yet distinct and separate in their action. It is like a great factory wherein two sets of machinery are at work, their revolving wheels apparently intermixed, their bands crossing one another, yet each doing its own work without touching or hampering the other. (*The American Commonwealth,* vol. 1, 2d ed. London: Macmillan, 1891.)

federalism, fiscal The fiscal relations between and among units of government in a federal system. The theory of fiscal federalism, or multiunit government finance, is one part of the branch of applied economics known as public finance.

REFERENCES

Richard Musgrave, *Essays on Fiscal Federalism* (Washington, D.C.: Brookings, 1965);

Richard E. Wagner, *The Fiscal Organization of American Federalism* (Chicago: Markam, 1971);

Wallace E. Oates, *Fiscal Federalism* (New York: Harcourt Brace Jovanovich, 1972);

Wallace E. Oates, ed., *The Political Economy of Fiscal Federalism* (Lexington, MA: Lexington Books, 1977).

federalism, horizontal State-to-state interactions and relations. Interstate relations take many forms, including compacts and commissions established for specific purposes: river basin management, transportation, extradition of criminals, conservation of forests and wildlife, and administration of parks and recreation. Horizontal relations between local governments also are numerous. Cities frequently contract for services from various neighboring local governments (and even from private providers). The Lakewood plan (*see* SERVICE CONTRACT), established in southern California in 1954, has been the most comprehensive example of interlocal contracting for services to date. Under this plan, the City of Lakewood contracted for a rather comprehensive package of services from Los Angeles County, where Lakewood is located.

federalism, marble-cake The concept that the cooperative relations among the varying levels of government result in an intermingling of activities; in contrast to the more traditional view of layer-cake federalism, which holds that the three levels of government are totally or almost totally separate. Marble-cake federalism is usually associated with Morton Grodzins (1917–1964), who pointed out the case of rural county health officials called sanitarians: sanitarians are appointed by the state government under merit standards established by the federal government, and while their base salaries come from state and federal funds, the county provides them with offices and office amenities and pays a portion of their expenses.
REFERENCE
Morton Grodzins, *The American System,* ed. Daniel J. Elazar (Chicago: Rand McNally, 1966).

federalism, new 1 The reconceptualization of federalism as INTERGOVERNMENTAL RELATIONS. 2 The actual relations between the levels of government as they shared in the performance of expanding government functions in the early 1970s. The term has its origins in the liberal Republican effort to find an alternative to the centralized state perceived as having been set up by the New Deal, but an alternative that nonetheless recognized the need for effective national government. During the Richard M. Nixon administration, new federalism referred to the style of decentralized management at the federal level symbolized by such programs as Federal Assistance Review, General Revenue Sharing, and the decentralization of federal regional management to ten coterminous regions, each with a common regional center. New federalism as developed by the Ronald Reagan administration disregarded the Nixon approach of decentralized federal regional management and turned to development of direct relations between the federal government and the state governments. The intent was to return power and responsibility to the states and to dramatically reduce the role of the federal government in domestic programs, reminiscent of the DUAL FEDERALISM that prevailed in the United States in the last century. Reagan's new federalism had two phases: phase one consisted of the president's economic recovery program, which included reductions in the federal budget, the use of new block grant programs to give states greater flexibility in using federal monies, the reduction of the volume of new federal regulations, and tax reductions to stimulate the economy; phase two was the return from the federal to state governments of some authority to tax, thereby increasing the revenue capacity of state governments. These goals have had a mixed success.
REFERENCES
For new federalism under Nixon, see Michael D. Reagan, *The New Federalism* (New York: Oxford University Press, 1972);
Leigh E. Grosnick, ed., *The Administration of the New Federalism: Objectives and Issues* (Washington, D.C.: American Society for Public Administration, 1973);
Carl E. Van Horn, Evaluating the new federalism: National goals and local implementors, *Public Administration Review* 39 (January/ February 1979).
For new federalism under Reagan, see Irving Louis Horowitz, From the New Deal to the new federalism: Presidential ideology in the

U.S. from 1932 to 1982, *American Journal of Economics and Sociology* 42 (April 1983);

Terry Nichols Clark, Local fiscal dynamics under old and new federalism, *Urban Affairs Quarterly* 19 (September 1983);

Thomas Luce and Janet Rothenberg Pack, State support under the new federalism, *Journal of Policy Analysis and Management* 3 (Spring 1984);

Richard P. Nathan and Fred C. Doolittle, The untold story of Reagan's "new federalism," *Public Interest* 77 (Fall 1984);

J. Edwin Benton, American federalism's first principles and Reagan's new federalism policies, *Policy Studies Journal* 13 (March 1985).

federalism, picket fence The concept that implies that bureaucratic specialists at the various levels of government (along with clientele groups) exercise considerable power over the nature of intergovernmental programs. Bureaucratic or program specialists at national, state, and local government levels for such fields as public housing, vocational education, health and hospitals, and higher education represent the pickets in the picket fence. They communicate with each other in daily work, belong to the same professional organizations, and have similar professional training. They are likely to be in conflict with general-purpose government officials (mayors, governors, the president), who attempt to coordinate the vertical power structures, or pickets. The general-purpose officials are the cross pieces of the fence. The metaphor is credited to Terry Sanford, when he was governor of the state of North Carolina.

REFERENCE

Terry Sanford, *Storm Over the States* (New York: McGraw-Hill, 1967).

federalism, vertical State-national government interactions. Such interactions are not limited to the executive branches of the national and state governments; close coordination also exists between the federal and state court systems. Crisscrossing vertical relations also have become more common. For example, the executive branch of the national government embarked upon several programs for assistance to state courts and state legislatures in the 1970s.

Federalist Papers The commentary on the U.S. Constitution and the theories behind it, published in 1787–88, and considered by many political scientists to be the most important work of political theory written in the United States—the one product of the American mind counted among the classics of political philosophy. The papers were originally newspaper articles written by Alexander Hamilton, James Madison, and John Jay (under the name Publius) to encourage New York to ratify the new Constitution. The papers reflect the genius of the balance achieved in the American system between the views of Madison, an exponent of limited government, and Hamilton, an admirer of an energetic national government. It has been suggested that the papers reflected the thinking of the minority of Americans, who wanted a more nationalist government than most of the postrevolutionary generation wanted. They succeeded in getting it, in part, through JOHN MARSHALL's influence on the U.S. Supreme Court. *Compare to* ANTI-FEDERALISTS.

REFERENCES

George Mace, *Locke, Hobbes, and the Federalist Papers: An Essay on the Genesis of the American Political Heritage* (Carbondale: Southern Illinois University Press, 1979);

Garry Wills, *Explaining America: The Federalist* (Garden City, NY: Doubleday, 1981);

Albert Furtwangler, *The Authority of Publius: A Reading of the Federalist Papers* (Ithaca, NY: Cornell University Press, 1984);

David F. Epstein, *The Political Theory of the Federalist* (Chicago: University of Chicago Press, 1984).

Federalist 10 The Federalist paper in which James Madison discusses the problem of FACTIONS and the danger they pose to a political system. Madison feared that the interests of parties and pressure groups could destabilize a government; but he believed that an overarching representative government, with a functional as well as territorial separation of powers, could prevent this. Madison's brief essay, a defense of a pluralistic society, is the best known of the *Federalist Papers*. In the federal union he advocated, Madison envisioned "a republican remedy for the diseases most incident to republican government." The essay is one of the first attempts by an American to explain the political nature of man. Madison found the causes of political differences and the creation of factions to be "sown in the nature of man." The essay is the classic explanation of why it is not easy to achieve change in the American political system. The constitutional structure is purposely designed to protect minorities from the possible tyranny of 50 percent plus one. The essay was more or less rediscovered by Charles A. Beard and other political analysts early in this century, when they sought to build an historical justification for modern interest group theory. Beard wrote in his *An Economic Interpretation of the Constitution* (*see* CONSTITUTION, ECONOMIC INTERPRETATION OF) that "The most philosophical examination of the foundations of political science is made by Madison in the tenth number."

REFERENCES

Robert J. Morgan, Madison's theory of representation in the tenth Federalist, *Journal of Politics* 36 (November 1974);

James Conniff, The enlightenment and American political thought: A study of the origins of Madison's *Federalist Number 10, Political Theory* 8 (August 1980).

Federalist 35   The Federalist paper in which James Madison discusses the nature and advantages of a legislature representing all classes of society, something he considered "altogether visionary." Madison concluded that, as long as the votes of the people are free, "the representative body . . . will be composed of landholders, merchants, and men of the learned professions," who out of their own self-interest would look after the interests of those not directly represented.

REFERENCES

William B. Allen, Federal representation: The design of the thirty fifth *Federalist Paper, Publius* 6 (Summer 1976);

Jean Yarbrough, Thoughts on the *Federalist*'s view of representation, *Polity* 12 (Fall 1979).

Federalist 51   The Federalist paper in which James Madison explains how the federal constitution provides for a SEPARATION OF POWERS whereby "those who administer each department [have] the necessary constitutional means and personal motives to resist encroachments of the others." This is achieved by "contriving the interior structure of the government as that its several constituent parts may, by their mutual relations, be the means of keeping each other in their proper places." *Compare to* CHECKS AND BALANCES.

Federalist 78   *See* JUDICIAL REVIEW, LEAST DANGEROUS BRANCH.

federalists   **1** Those who supported the U.S. Constitution before its ratification. *Compare to* ANTIFEDERALISTS.   **2** After ratification of the Constitution, the term was applied to members of the Federalist political party of George Washington, John Adams, and Alexander Hamilton. The party disappeared from national politics in 1816.

REFERENCE

2   Leonard D. White, *The Federalists* (New York: Macmillan, 1948).

federalists, anti   *See* ANTIFEDERALISTS.

Federal Judicial Center   The judicial branch's agency created in 1967 for policy research, systems development, and continuing education.

Federal Judicial Center
Dolly Madison House
1520 H Street, N.W.
Washington, D.C. 20005
(202) 633-6011

Federal Labor Relations Authority (FLRA)   The agency created by the Civil Service Reform Act of 1978 to oversee the creation of bargaining units, to supervise elections, and to otherwise deal with labor-management issues in federal agencies. The FLRA is headed by a three-member panel—a chair and two members—who are appointed on a bipartisan basis to staggered five-year terms. The FLRA replaced the Federal Labor Relations Council (FLRC). A general counsel, also appointed to a five-year term, investigates alleged unfair labor practices and prosecutes them before the FLRA. Also within the FLRA and acting as a separate body, the Federal Service Impasses Panel (FSIP) acts to resolve negotiation impasses.

REFERENCE

Kenneth A. Kovach, The F.L.R.A. and federal employee unionism, *Public Personnel Management* 9 (January/February 1980).

Federal Labor Relations Authority
500 C Street, S.W.
Washington, D.C. 20424
(202) 382-0711

Federal Maritime Commission (FMC) The independent agency, created by Reorganization Plan no. 7 of 1961, that regulates the waterborne foreign and domestic offshore commerce of the United States, assures that U.S. international trade is open to all nations on fair and equitable terms, and guards against unauthorized monopoly in the waterborne commerce of the United States.

Federal Maritime Commission
1100 L Street, N.W.
Washington, D.C. 20573
(202) 523-5773

Federal Mediation and Conciliation Service (FMCS) The labor-management mediation agency created by the Labor-Management Relations (Taft-Hartley) Act of 1947 as an independent agency of the federal government. The FMCS helps prevent disruptions in the flow of interstate commerce caused by labor-management disputes by providing mediators to assist disputing parties in the resolution of their differences. The FMCS can intervene on its own motion or by invitation of either side in a dispute. Mediators have no law enforcement authority and rely wholly on persuasive techniques. The FMCS also helps provide qualified third-party neutrals as factfinders or arbitrators.

REFERENCES

Jerome T. Barrett and Lucretia Dewey Tanner, The FMCS role in age discrimination complaints: New uses of mediation, *Labor Law Journal* 32 (November 1981);

Kay McMurray, The Federal Mediation and Conciliation Service: Serving labor-management relations in the eighties, *Labor Law Journal* 34 (February 1983).

Federal Mediation and Conciliation Service
2100 K Street, N.W.
Washington, D.C. 20427
(202) 653-5290

federal office The offices of vice president or president of the United States, or of senator or representative in, or delegate or resident commissioner to, the United States Congress.

Federal Open Market Committee The seven members of the Federal Reserve Board plus five of the twelve Federal Reserve Bank presidents. The committee meets every four to six weeks to set Federal Reserve guidelines regarding purchases and sales of government securities in the open market as a means of influencing the volume of credit and money. It also sets Federal Reserve policy relating to foreign exchange markets.

federal postcard application (FPCA) A postage-free postcard printed and distributed by the federal government for use by absentee voters covered by the Federal Voting Assistance Act of 1955 (FVAA) and the Overseas Citizens Voting Rights Act of 1975 (OCVRA). Federal law requires that a single form of postcard application serve all states as a simultaneous registration form and application for an absentee ballot. The extent and manner of its use, however, is controlled by state law and sometimes by local procedure. In most states, the FPCA serves as a valid ballot request for those voters entitled to use it, regardless of whether they have registered prior to its submission. For such voters, registration is either waived or considered accomplished upon submission of the FPCA requesting a ballot. A few states do require their own registration form be used, but the local election official will send it out along with the ballot. Only in West Virginia must the voter register (by FPCA) prior to submitting an FPCA (a second one) requesting a ballot.

federal question An aspect of a legal case that involves rights or privileges guaranteed by the U.S. Constitution or federal laws. A legal matter must involve a federal question if it is to be heard in a federal court.

Federal Register   The daily publication, begun in 1935, that is the medium for making available to the public federal agency regulations and other legal documents of the executive branch. These documents cover a wide range of government activities—environmental protection, consumer product safety, food and drug standards, occupational health and safety, and many more areas of concern to the public. Perhaps more important, the *Federal Register* includes proposed changes in regulated areas. Each proposed change published carries an invitation for any citizen or group to participate in the consideration of the proposed regulation through the submission of written data, views, or arguments, and sometimes by oral presentations.

Office of the *Federal Register*
National Archives and Records Service
Washington, D.C. 20408

Federal Register System   The system established in 1935 by the Federal Register Act. Administrative rules and regulations issued by executive departments and agencies under authority of law are codified and made known to the public through the system. It consists of the *Federal Register,* published daily Tuesday through Saturday except for the day following a legal holiday; the *Code of Federal Regulations,* an annually issued multivolume cumulation of administrative regulations in force; and the annually published *United States Government Manual.* The system is administered by the National Archives and Records Service of the General Services Administration. There are four basic kinds of documents that must be published in the *Federal Register* before they are considered legally binding: (1) presidential proclamations, executive orders of general interest, and any other document the president submits or orders to be published; (2) every document issued under proper authority that prescribes a penalty or course of conduct; confers a right, privilege, authority, or immunity; or imposes an obligation; and is relevant or applicable to the general public, members of a class of people, or persons of a locality;

(3) documents or classes of documents required by an act of the Congress to be filed and published; and (4) other documents deemed by the director of the *Federal Register* to be of sufficient interest. Although the *Federal Register* is unknown to many citizens, it constitutes a major means of regulating and governing in the United States.

Federal Regulation of Lobbying Act of 1946
See LOBBYING ACT OF 1946.

Federal Reserve notes   Paper money; obligations of the Federal Reserve backed by the full faith and credit of the U.S. government. Nearly all of the nation's circulating paper currency consists of Federal Reserve notes printed by the Treasury Department and issued to the Federal Reserve banks, which place them in circulation through depository institutions. The Federal Reserve notes contrast with paper money backed by gold or silver payable on demand. While some silver certificate dollar (or higher) notes are still in circulation, the Congress revoked the right to redeem them for silver in 1968.

Federal Reserve System   Colloquially known as the Fed, this is in effect the central bank of the United States, created by the Federal Reserve Act of 1913 and charged with administering and making policy for the nation's credit and monetary affairs. Run by a seven-member board of governors appointed by the president (who also appoints their chairman), the system includes twelve Federal Reserve banks, twenty-four branches, all national banks, and many state banking institutions. Three major monetary tools are available to the Federal Reserve System to control the economy's supply of money and credit: (1) Open-market operations, which, through the purchase or sale of government bonds, increase or decrease the availability of dollars to member banks. (2) Discount-rate adjustments, which increase or decrease the interest rate charged to member banks for the money they borrow. (3) Reserve requirements, which, through changes in levels of reserve, increase or decrease the number of dollars a bank may make available for loan. Two less significant tools, moral suasion and selective controls over stock purchase margin requirements, are also used to help manage the economy. *See* FISCAL POLICY; MONETARY POLICY.

REFERENCES

Nathaniel Beck, Presidential influence on the Federal Reserve in the 1970s, *American Journal of Political Science* 26 (August 1982);

Robert J. Shapiro, Politics and the Federal Reserve, *Public Interest* 66 (Winter 1982);

Ralph C. Bryant, *Controlling Money: The Federal Reserve and Its Critics* (Washington, D.C.: Brookings, 1983);

Neil T. Skaggs, The Federal Reserve System and congressional demands for information, *Social Science Quarterly* 64 (September 1983);

Donald J. Hubbard, Should the Federal Reserve be preserved? *Journal of Legislation* 11 (Winter 1984).

Federal Reserve System
20th Street and Constitution Avenue, N.W.
Washington, D.C. 20551
(202) 452-3000

Federal Savings and Loan Insurance Corporation *See* FEDERAL HOME LOAN BANK BOARD.

Federal Service Impasses Panel (FSIP) *See* FEDERAL LABOR RELATIONS AUTHORITY.

Federal Trade Commission (FTC) The independent regulatory agency, created by the Federal Trade Commission Act of 1914, whose objective is to prevent the free enterprise system from being stifled, substantially lessened, fettered by monopoly or restraints on trade, or corrupted by unfair or deceptive trade practices. The commission deals with trade practices on a continuing and corrective basis. It has no authority to punish; its function is to prevent, through cease-and-desist orders and other means, those practices condemned by the law of federal trade regulation. However, court-ordered civil penalties up to ten thousand dollars may be obtained for each violation of a commission order. *See* HUMPHREY'S EXECUTOR V UNITED STATES.

REFERENCES

Edward F. Cox, Robert C. Fellmuth, and John E. Schulz, *The Nader Report on the Federal Trade Commission* (New York: Grove, 1969);

Thomas G. Krattenmaker, The Federal Trade Commission and consumer protection, *California Management Review* 18 (Summer 1976);

Kenneth W. Clarkson and Timothy J. Muris, *The Federal Trade Commission Since 1970: Economic Regulation and Consumer Welfare* (New York: Cambridge University Press, 1981);

Barry B. Boyer, "Too many lawyers, not enough practical people": The policy-making discretion of the Federal Trade Commission, *Law and Policy Quarterly* 5 (January 1983);

Barry R. Weingast and Mark J. Moran, Bureaucratic discretion or congressional control? Regulatory policymaking by the Federal Trade Commission, *Journal of Political Economy* 91 (October 1983).

Federal Trade Commission
Pennsylvania Avenue at 6th Street, N.W.
Washington, D.C. 20580
(202) 326–2000

Federal Trade Commission v Sperry Hutchinson Co. 405, U.S. 233 (1972) The U.S. Supreme Court case that stated the principle that the adjudicatory decisions of administrative agencies show a "rational connection between the facts found and the choice made." The case signaled a wider scope of judicial review of the substance of such adjudicatory decisions.

Federal Voting Assistance Act of 1955 *See* BALLOT, ABSENTEE.

federated governments *See* METROPOLITAN GOVERNMENT.

fellow traveler 1 A person sympathetic to communist thinking but not formally a Communist party member. 2 A person passively in agreement with any cause or group.

REFERENCE

Lewis S. Feuer, The fellow-travellers, *Survey* 20 (Spring/Summer 1974).

felony A serious crime. In most jurisdictions, felonies are one of two major classes of crimes, the other being misdemeanors. With felonies, the upper limit of potential penalties depends upon the particular crime and ranges from a few years in prison to death. One year in prison is almost always the minimum scheduled penalty for a felony conviction. *Compare to* MISDEMEANOR.

FEMA *See* FEDERAL EMERGENCY MANAGEMENT AGENCY.

Fenno, Richard F., Jr. (1926–   ) The American political scientist who wrote the classic analysis of the evolution of the modern president's cabinet, who produced landmark analyses of the congressional APPROPRIATIONS process, whose book *Congressmen in Committees* (Boston: Little, Brown, 1973) is the point of departure for the study of the subject, and who used the term HOME STYLE to describe the political activities of members of the Congress when they return to their home districts.

REFERENCE

Steven S. Smith, The central concepts in Fenno's committee studies, *Legislative Studies Quarterly* 11 (February 1986).

Ferraro, Geraldine (1935–   ) A New York congresswoman who was the first female nominee for the vice presidency on the 1984 Democratic party ballot with Walter Mondale. *See* WOMEN'S LIBERATION MOVEMENT.

fetcher bill *See* BILL, FETCHER.

fiduciary 1 A person who manages money or property for others. Anyone who has discretionary authority or responsibility for the administration of a pension plan is a fiduciary. 2 A concept in the theory of representation. A "fiduciary" is a representative who votes as the voters he or she represents would vote if they were present to vote for themselves; that is, the representative acts as a fiduciary for constituents. *Compare to* DELEGATE, TRUSTEE.

REFERENCES

1 Tamar Frankel, Fiduciary law, *California Law Review* 71 (May 1983).
2 William H. Riker, *The Theory of Political Coalitions* (New Haven, CT: Yale University Press, 1962).

Fifteenth Amendment The amendment to the U.S. Constitution that guarantees to all citizens the right to vote regardless of "race, color, or previous condition of servitude." This is the legal source of federal voting rights legislation. *See* VOTING RIGHTS ACT OF 1965.

Fifth Amendment The amendment to the U.S. Constitution that provides for the grand jury, prohibits double jeopardy and the compelling of self-incrimination, requires that citizens will not "be deprived of life, liberty, or property, without due process of law," and mandates that private property shall be taken only for public use (eminent domain) with "just compensation." While the guarantees of the Fifth Amendment originally applied only to the federal government, they have been extended to the states through the due process clause of the Fourteenth Amendment. A person who "takes the Fifth Amendment" before a congressional committee or court is exercising his or her privilege against compulsory self-incrimination. *See* GARRITY V NEW JERSEY.

REFERENCE

Leonard W. Levy, *Origin of the Fifth Amendment: The Right Against Self-Incrimination* (New York: Oxford University Press, 1968).

fifth column Those traitors within a country who wait to join the forces of invading enemy soldiers. The term dates from the Spanish Civil War of the 1930s, when a general advanced on Madrid with four columns of troops and boasted that a fifth column awaited him within the city. During World War II, the term came to be used for anyone secretly sympathetic with the Germans.

filibuster A time-delaying tactic used by a legislative minority in an effort to prevent a vote on a bill. The most common method is unlimited debate, but other forms of parliamentary maneuvering may be used. The stricter rules in the U.S. House of Representatives make filibusters most difficult, but they may be attempted through various delaying tactics. True filibusters are not possible in the House, because no member is permitted to speak for longer than one hour without unanimous consent. Moreover, a majority can call for the "previous question" and bring a bill to an immediate vote. In the Senate a member can filibuster without speaking continuously; he or she may yield to a colleague for a question or call for a quorum without losing the floor. In the event a recess is called, he or she is entitled to regain the floor when the Senate reassembles. A filibuster is a kind of guerrilla warfare on the part of a minority to prevent a majority from exercising its will. In this sense, it is antidemocratic, especially as it was once notoriously used by U.S. senators from the South to delay or defeat civil rights bills. But it is in reality no more antidemocratic than any other parliamentary delaying tactic. The word originally meant a kind of pirate who waged irregular warfare for private gain. In 1917, the Senate adopted the first cloture rule. As amended in 1975, it provides that the Senate may end debate—may end a filibuster—on a pending bill by a three-fifths vote of the entire Senate membership. In the modern Senate, filibusters—and cloture—are more common than ever. *See also* CLOTURE.

REFERENCES

Franklin L. Burdette, *Filibustering in the Senate* (Princeton, NJ: Princeton University Press, 1940);

Raymond E. Wolfinger, Filibusters: Majority rule, presidential leadership, and Senate norms, *Readings on Congress*, ed. Raymond E. Wolfinger (Englewood Cliffs, NJ: Prentice-Hall, 1971);

Allan L. Damon, Filibuster, *American Heritage* 27 (December 1975).

financial bill clearance   *See* CENTRAL CLEARANCE.

finding   1 A decision (by a judge or jury) on a question of fact or law.   2 A formal, written, signed-off-on, presidential determination that a covert operation of the CIA is legal, important to national security, and (according to law) will be reported to the appropriate congressional committee in a timely fashion. Title XXII of the Intelligence Oversight Act of 1980 mandates "a report to the Congress concerning any finding or determination under any section of this chapter. That finding shall be reduced to writing and signed by the president."

Finlandization   The limitation of a smaller country's sovereignty by the practical consequences of establishing a modus vivendi with a larger and stronger close neighbor. The term originated in the relation between Finland and the Soviet Union, in which Finland retains its independence but is tied to the Soviet Union by a 1948 treaty that requires Finnish neutrality, limits Finnish foreign policy initiatives, and inhibits domestic political behavior. The potential Finlandization of other close neighbors of the Soviet Union is frequently the subject of international speculation.

REFERENCES

William Pfaff, Finlandization, *Atlantic Community Quarterly* 18 (Winter 1980–81);

Fred Singleton, The myth of "Finlandisation," *International Affairs* (Great Britain) 57 (Spring 1981);

Paul Malone, "Finlandization" as a method of living next door to Russia, *International Perspectives* (July/August 1981).

Fire Fighters Local Union No. 1784 v Stotts 81 L.Ed. 483 (1984)   The U.S. Supreme Court case that held that courts may not interfere with bona fide seniority systems to protect newly hired black employees from layoff. Writing for the majority, Justice Byron R. White said that the law permits remedies only for individuals who can prove they are "actual victims" of job discrimination, rather than for groups of disadvantaged minorities who may not have suffered specific wrongs in a specific job situation. To back this holding, he cited a 1964 memorandum, issued by sponsors of Title VII, that said "Title VII does not permit the ordering of racial quotas in business or unions." Justice White also said that it is "inappropriate to deny an innocent employee the benefit of seniority."

REFERENCES
Louis P. Britt III, Affirmative action: Is there life after *Stotts? Personnel Administrator* 29 (September 1984);
Robert N. Roberts, The public law litigation model and *Memphis v Stotts, Public Administration Review* 45 (July/August 1985).

"Freedom of the Seas" was the subject of Franklin Roosevelt's fireside chat on September 11, 1941.

fireside chat **1** President Franklin D. Roosevelt's radio talks to the nation. Part of the effectiveness of FDR's fireside chats was in their novelty; for the first time, the president could visit every home (via the radio) and in a very real sense "chat" with each citizen. **2** Any informal address by a political leader to constituents via radio or television.

First Amendment The amendment to the U.S. Constitution that asserts that the "Congress shall make no law respecting an establishment of religion, or prohibiting the free exercise thereof; or abridging the freedom of speech, or of the press; or the right of the people peaceably to assemble, and to petition the government for a redress of grievances." This, the first part of—and the backbone of—the Bill of Rights, originally applied only to the federal government but has been extended to the states through the due process and equal protection clauses of the Fourteenth Amendment. *See also* ASSEMBLY; ESTABLISHMENT CLAUSE; FREE EXERCISE CLAUSE; FREE PRESS CLAUSE; FREE SPEECH CLAUSE; GRISWOLD V CONNECTICUT; INCORPORATION.

REFERENCES
Gerald Gunther, Learned Hand and the origins of modern First Amendment doctrine: Some fragments of history, *Stanford Law Review* 27 (February 1975);
Kenneth L. Karst, Equality as a central principle in the First Amendment, *University of Chicago Law Review* 43 (Fall 1975);
Thomas I. Emerson, Colonial intentions and current realities of the First Amendment, *University of Pennsylvania Law Review* 125 (April 1977);
Alexis J. Anderson, The formative period of First Amendment theory, 1870–1915, *American Journal of Legal History* 24 (January 1980);
Thomas I. Emerson, First Amendment doctrine and the Burger Court, *California Law Review* 68 (May 1980);
David M. Rabban, The emergence of modern First Amendment doctrine, *University of Chicago Law Review* 50 (Fall 1983);
Stephen L. Hayford, First Amendment rights of government employees: A primer for public officials, *Public Administration Review* 45 (January/February 1985).

first branch **1** The U.S. Congress, established by Article I of the Constitution. **2** A legislature in any government with separation of powers. The legislature is first because it is the branch most representative of and closest to the people.

REFERENCES
Alfred de Grazia, ed., *Congress, The First Branch of Government* (Washington, D.C.: American Enterprise Institute, 1966);
Marcia Whicker Taylor, Daniel R. Sabia, Jr., and Alfred Mauet, Making "the first branch" first: A radical structural proposal, *Journal of Political Science* 9 (Spring 1982).

First Lady **1** The wife of the president of the United States. **2** The wife of a state governor.
REFERENCE
1 Betty Boyd Caroli, *First Ladies* (New York: Oxford, 1987).

first-strike capability The ability of one nuclear power to destroy so much of another's nuclear retaliatory forces with a surprise nuclear attack that the other side is unable to retaliate effectively. The strategic nuclear policy of the United States is to maintain a second-strike capability to encourage deterrence; that is, to maintain nuclear forces in such numbers and variety that no first strike by the other side could prevent America from then inflicting unacceptable damage to the other side.

REFERENCES

Keith B. Payne, What if we "ride out" a Soviet first strike? *Washington Quarterly* 7 (Fall 1984);

William M. Arkin, The drift toward first strike, *Bulletin of the Atomic Scientists* 41 (January 1985).

First World The rich, industrialized Western democracies: the United States, Canada, Western Europe, Australia, New Zealand, and Japan. These countries are also referred to as the North, the OECD countries, or the developed countries. *See* SECOND WORLD; THIRD WORLD; FOURTH WORLD.

fiscal Having to do with taxation, public revenues, or public debt.

fiscal federalism *See* FEDERALISM, FISCAL.

fiscal integrity 1 A characteristic of a government budget that spends no more than anticipated revenues. A balanced budget has fiscal integrity; a budget with a significant deficit does not. 2 Agreement on fiscal matters. You will be deemed to have fiscal integrity when the person so deeming agrees with your fiscal policies. If that same person disagrees with your policies, you may be deemed so lacking in fiscal responsibility as to be considered fiscally irresponsible.

fiscal policy The manipulation of government finances by raising or lowering taxes or levels of spending to promote economic stability and growth. Stability and growth must be combined, since stability without growth is stagnation. The use of fiscal policy for economic objectives is a decidedly recent phenomenon. For the greater part of the two-hundred-year history of the United States, fiscal policy was not a factor. The national budgetary policy

was premised upon expenditures equaling revenues (a balanced budget). In fact, with the exception of war years, budgeting before the 1900s was primarily an exercise in deciding how to get rid of excess revenues, generated primarily by tariffs. This is not to say that modern fiscal policies would not have saved the nation considerable distress from assorted recessions and depressions, but the nineteenth century held that the economy followed a natural order. The first major tampering with the natural order of things came in 1913, with the advent of the federal income tax and the establishment of the FEDERAL RESERVE SYSTEM. In 1921, the Budget and Accounting Act provided for a unified federal executive budget. The Great Depression of the 1930s, along with the initiation of social security and unemployment compensation programs, provided the first recognitions of the need for a national economic policy. However, legitimization of the goal of a national economic policy came with the passage of the Full Employment Act of 1946. The act not only created a Council of Economic Advisers for the president, but it prescribed objectives for economic prosperity and charged the president with insuring their achievement.

Basically, fiscal policy offers two courses of action, discretionary and built in. The first involves changing policy decisions. Discretionary fiscal policy has two major facets—the level of receipts and the level of expenditures. The major fiscal policy actions of recent years are replete with tax cuts and temporary reductions. Given the time lags involved in legislating tax changes, it is easy to see why presidents have preferred to wage fiscal policy battles in terms of government spending. The second dimension involves built-in fiscal stabilizers—that is, preset or automatic policy. These are the transfer payments, the progressive tax rates, and the changing federal budget deficits and surpluses that move automatically to counter economic downturns or to control excessive periods of demand and business activity. For example, as people are laid off from work in a recessionary period, payments for unemployment compensation mount automatically. This increases the federal budget deficit, which in turn stimulates the economy and moves to offset the economic downswing. If the economy heats up, both regular and overtime wages increase, fueling demand for goods and services and creating inflation. As personal income increases, however, more and more people move into higher tax brackets; the tax structure thus functions as an automatic stabilizer by absorbing more personal income and thus restraining demand for goods and services. *See also* BUDGETING; ECONOMIC POLICY; MONETARY POLICY; POLITICAL ECONOMY.

REFERENCES

Lawrence C. Pierce, *The Politics of Fiscal Policy Formation* (Pacific Palisades, CA: Goodyear, 1971);

James C. Snyder, *Fiscal Management and Planning in Local Government* (Lexington, MA: Lexington Books, 1977);

David C. Mowery, Mark S. Kamlet, and John P. Crecine, Presidential management of budgetary and fiscal policymaking, *Political Science Quarterly* 95 (Fall 1980);

Henry C. Wallich, The interface of fiscal and monetary policy, *Policy Studies Journal* 9 (Autumn 1980);

David Lowery, The Keynesian and political determinants of unbalanced budgets: U.S. fiscal policy from Eisenhower to Reagan, *American Journal of Political Science* 29 (August 1985).

fiscal responsibility *See* FISCAL INTEGRITY.

fiscal year Any yearly accounting period without regard to a calendar year. The fiscal year for the federal government through fiscal year 1976 began on July 1 and ended on June 30. Since fiscal year 1977, fiscal years for the federal government begin on October 1 and end on September 30. The fiscal year is designated by the calendar year in which it ends (e.g., fiscal year 1988 was the fiscal year ending September 30, 1988).

Fisher v City of Berkeley *See* RENT CONTROL.

Fitzgerald, A. Ernest (1926–   ) Famous U.S. government WHISTLE BLOWER. Fitzgerald was the GS-17 deputy for Management Systems in the Office of the Assistant Secretary of the Air Force who in 1968 testified about cost overruns on the Air Force's giant C-5A mili-

tary cargo plane. The Air Force, which had not acknowledged the cost overruns, stripped him of his primary duties of overseeing cost reports on the major weapons systems and assigned him to essentially clerical tasks. A year later, the Air Force reorganized Fitzgerald's office and abolished his job. Fitzgerald appealed the Air Force action. After almost four years of litigation, Fitzgerald was reinstated to his original civil service position and given back pay. The Fitzgerald affair triggered a great deal of discussion in the media and the government about the need to protect whistle blowers.

REFERENCE

For Fitzgerald's own account, see A. Ernest Fitzgerald, *The High Priests of Waste* (New York: Norton, 1972).

Fitzpatrick v Bitzer 424 U.S. 953 (1976) The U.S. Supreme Court case that ruled that the Equal Employment Opportunity Act of 1972 amendments to Title VII of the Civil Rights Act of 1964 created an exception to the immunity of states to back-pay suits. The Court held that this exception was authorized by the Fourteenth Amendment's grant of power to the Congress to enforce that amendment's ban on state denials of equal protection.

flag of convenience The registration of a merchant ship in a foreign country, rather than in the country where it is owned or does business, to avoid high fees, high safety requirements, and so on; the ship then must legally fly the flag (the flag of convenience) of the country in which it is registered. This is different from reflagging which is a diplomatic undertaking designed to qualify previously ineligible merchant ships for naval protection from friendly powers—whose flag they then fly.

REFERENCES

Adam Bozcek, *Flags of Convenience* (Cambridge, MA: Harvard University Press, 1962);

Rodney Carlisle, *Sovereignty for Sale: The Origins and Evolution of the Panamanian and Liberian Flags of Convenience* (Annapolis, MD: Naval Institute Press, 1981).

Flast v Cohen 392 U.S. 83 (1968) The U.S. Supreme Court case concerning the expenditure of federal funds for instructional purposes in religious schools under the Elementary and Secondary Education Act of 1965. The Court found that parties had standing to challenge these expenditures if they could show that (1) they were taxpayers and (2) the challenged enactment exceeded specific constitutional limitations imposed on the exercise of the congressional power to tax and spend.

REFERENCE

Boris I. Bittker, The case of the fictitious tax-payer: The federal taxpayer's suit twenty years after *Flast v. Cohen, University of Chicago Law Review* 36 (Winter 1969).

Fletcher v Peck 6 Cranch 87 (1810)   The first case in which the U.S. Supreme Court declared a state law to be unconstitutional. It held that a state's legislatively conferred charter (in effect, a contract) could not be unilaterally rescinded by a subsequent session of the legislature. *Compare to* DARTMOUTH COLLEGE V WOODWARD.

The Opinion of Chief Justice John Marshall in *Fletcher v Peck*

The principle asserted is that one legislature is competent to repeal any act which a former legislature was competent to pass; and that one legislature cannot abridge the powers of a succeeding legislature. The correctness of this principle, so far as respects general legislation, can never be controverted. But if an act be done under a law, a succeeding legislature cannot undo it. The past cannot be recalled by the most absolute power.

Conveyances have been made, those conveyances have vested legal estates, and, if those estates may be seized by the sovereign authority, still, that they originally vested is a fact, and cannot cease to be a fact. When, then, a law is in its nature a contract, when absolute rights have vested under that contract, a repeal of the law cannot divest those rights.

---

flexible response   The capability of military forces to make an effective reaction to an enemy threat or attack; to meet an enemy threat with a commensurate level of counterthreat. This implies that there is an option to use a variety of conventional forces as well as nuclear weapons as the circumstances warrant.

REFERENCES

Phillip A. Karber, Nuclear weapons and "flexible response," *Orbis* 14 (Summer 1970);

David Dessler, "Just in case"—The danger of flexible response, *Bulletin of the Atomic Scientists* 38 (November 1982).

floor   1 The main part of a legislative chamber; that portion of a legislative chamber reserved for members; the place where legislators vote.   2 The exclusive right to speak; a legislator who "has the floor" may usually continue to speak until willing to "yield the floor."

REFERENCES

1   Joseph K. Unekis, From committee to the floor: Consistency in congressional voting, *Journal of Politics* 40 (August 1978);

Richard Fleisher and Jon R. Bond, Beyond committee control: Committee and party leader influence on floor amendments in Congress, *American Politics Quarterly* 11 (April 1983).

floor fight   Disputes at a national nominating convention, often concerning the party platform or delegate credentials, that cannot be resolved in committee and must be taken to the floor of the full convention for resolution.

floor manager   A legislator, usually representing sponsors of a bill, who attempts to steer the bill through debate and revision to a final vote in the chamber. Floor managers in the U.S. Congress are frequently chairs or ranking members of the committee that reported the bill. Increasingly, subcommittee chairs are being selected to manage legislation on the floor. Floor managers are responsible for apportioning the time granted to supporters of the bill for debating it. The minority leader or the ranking minority member of the committee often apportions time for the opposition.

REFERENCE

For the parliamentary procedures used by floor managers, see Terry Sullivan, *Procedural Structure: Success and Influence in Congress* (New York: Praeger, 1984).

floterial district   *See* DISTRICT, FLOTERIAL.

FLRA *See* FEDERAL LABOR RELATIONS AUTHORITY.

FLSA *See* FAIR LABOR STANDARDS ACT OF 1938.

FMC *See* FEDERAL MARITIME COMMISSION.

FMCS *See* FEDERAL MEDIATION AND CONCILIATION SERVICE.

foggy bottom A slang phrase for the U.S. State Department, because its present building is located on a site that was once considered a swamp (now drained). The term continues in use, because foggy aptly describes the kinds of pronouncements so often necessitated by diplomacy.

REFERENCES

Charles Frankel, *High on Foggy Bottom* (New York: Harper & Row, 1968);

John Franklin Campbell, Clearing foggy bottom, *Interplay* 3 (April 1970).

Foley v Connelie 435 U.S. 291 (1978) The U.S. Supreme Court case that upheld a New York law requiring state police to be U.S. citizens. The court reasoned that, because state police exercise considerable discretion in executing the laws, a state may exclude aliens from such positions without unconstitutionally denying them equal protection of the laws. *See also* AMBACH V NORWICK; CITIZENSHIP; HAMPTON V MOW SUN WONG; SUGARMAN V DOUGALL.

Food for Peace (FFP) The overseas food donation program authorized by the Agricultural Trade Development and Assistance Act of 1954. Under this program, U.S. agricultural surpluses are donated to "friendly governments" through nonprofit relief organizations or voluntary agencies, such as CARE or the Catholic Relief Services. The program is administered jointly by the Agency for International Development and the U.S. Department of Agriculture.

REFERENCES

Peter A. Toma, *The Politics of Food for Peace* (Tucson: University of Arizona Press, 1967);

Mitchell B. Wallerstein, *Food for War—Food for Peace: United States Food Aid in a Global Context* (Cambridge, MA: MIT Press, 1980).

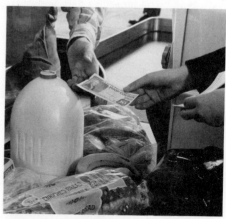

The food stamp program is the single largest welfare program in the United States.

food stamps A welfare program designed to improve the nutrition of the poor. Administered by the Department of Agriculture and state and local welfare organizations, the program provides coupons (stamps) that can be exchanged for food at many grocery stores. This is the nation's single largest welfare program. It is a good example of an ENTITLEMENT PROGRAM. The idea of food stamps originated in the late New Deal as a way of providing food to the poor from surpluses held by the government.

REFERENCES

J. Fred Giertz and Dennis H. Sullivan, On the political economy of food stamps, *Public Choice* 33:3 (1978);

Matthew D. Slater, Going hungry on food stamps, *Social Policy* 11 (January/February 1981);

Barbara A. Claffey and Thomas A. Stucker, The food stamp program, *Proceedings of the Academy of Political Science* 34:3 (1982);

Daniel S. Hamermesh and James M. Johannes, Food stamps as money: The Macroeconomics of a transfer program, *Journal of Political Economy* 93 (February 1985).

forced savings Tax refunds. This is the money that people are forced to save because of federal and state income tax withholding requirements.

force majeure 1 A French phrase for superior force. 2 Compelling circumstances. Force majeure is the means by which things are often accomplished in international relations; it is an underlying factor in all negotiations.

REFERENCE

Barry Nicholas, Force majeure and frustration, *American Journal of Comparative Law* 27 (Spring/Summer 1979).

Ford, Betty *See* WOMEN'S LIBERATION MOVEMENT.

Gerald R. Ford

Ford, Gerald R. (1913–   ) The president of the United States (1974–1977) after Richard M. Nixon was forced to resign because of the Watergate scandals. Ford was appointed vice president by Nixon in 1973, with the consent of the Congress, to replace Spiro Agnew, who had resigned in disgrace. Ford was narrowly defeated for election in his own right when he ran against Jimmy Carter in 1976. Ford is the only person to have served as president without election to that office by the people. Ford, who had served in the U.S. House of Representa-

tives since 1948, was the personally popular leader of the House Republicans when Nixon appointed him to the vice presidency. This meant that his confirmation would go smoothly and quickly and that Ford might prove useful to Nixon in the then-surfacing call for Nixon's impeachment over Watergate. Many analysts feel that Ford might have won election to the presidency in his own right if he had not pardoned Nixon for "all crimes he may have committed while in office."

REFERENCE

For his memoirs, see Gerald Ford, *A Time to Heal: The Autobiography of Gerald R. Ford* (New York: Harper & Row, 1979).

The Gerald R. Ford Administration

Major Accomplishments
- The restoration of public confidence in and integrity to the White House after Watergate.

Major Frustrations
- Double-digit inflation and a deep recession.
- The fall of South Vietnam.

Foreign Agents Registration Act of 1938 The federal law that requires all lobbyists, public relations consultants, political consultants, and so on, working for foreign governments, to register with the U.S. attorney general. Exempted from the registration requirement are foreign diplomats, attorneys, and those engaged in international trade and humanitarian, religious, academic, and cultural activities.

foreign aid All official grants and concessional loans (i.e., loans made on softer than commercial terms), in currency or in kind, broadly aimed at transferring resources from developed to less-developed countries for the purposes of economic development or income distribution. Foreign aid may be bilateral (from one country to another) or multilateral (distributed through international financial institutions, such as the World Bank or the International Monetary Fund). Foreign aid, also referred to as economic assistance, may be given as project aid (where the donor provides money for a specific project, such as a dam or a school) or as program aid (where the donor does not know what projects the money will be spent on). Economic assistance consists of both hard loans (i.e., at commercial bank interest rates) and soft loans (concessional, or at low interest rates). Aid may be tied to multilateral aid agencies (i.e., the loans may be partially financed by the recipient country), or aid may be tied in bilateral arrangements (i.e., the money must be spent on procurement in the donor country or must be transported by the donor country's shipping).

Countries give foreign aid for various reasons: to give humanitarian assistance after wars or natural disasters; to militarily strengthen allies against external or internal threats; to promote the economic development of the recipient country; or to simply meet the basic human needs of the poor citizens of the recipient country. The first significant instance of foreign aid was that given by the United States to its allies during and right after World War I. But this was ad hoc. Not until the Harry S Truman administration did foreign aid become institutionalized and a continuous part of American foreign policy (*see* MARSHALL PLAN). It was and remains motivated both by humanitarian concerns and a desire to allow grantees to achieve the kind of economic and social growth that would allow their governments to withstand the efforts of communists to take them over.

REFERENCES

Peter Bauer and Basil Yamey, Foreign aid: What is at stake? *Public Interest* 68 (Summer 1982);

Manual F. Ayau, The impoverishing effects of foreign aid, *Cato Journal* 4 (Spring/Summer 1984).

Foreign Corrupt Practices Act of 1977 The federal law that prohibits American corporations from making improper payments (bribes) in other countries. The law was passed in response to journalistic exposure of American defense contractors paying off foreign nationals to gain large orders for military equipment.

REFERENCES

Mark Romaneski, The Foreign Corrupt Practices Act of 1977: An analysis of its impact

and future, *Boston College International and Comparative Law Review* 5 (Summer 1982);

Mark B. Bader and Bill Shaw, Amendment of the Foreign Corrupt Practices Act, *New York University Journal of International Law and Politics* 15 (Spring 1983);

Bartley A. Brennan, Amending the Foreign Corrupt Practices Act of 1977: "Clarifying" or "gutting" a law? *Journal of Legislation* 11 (Winter 1984).

foreign ministry/foreign office That agency in most parliamentary governments that corresponds to the U.S. Department of State.

REFERENCE

Zara Steiner, Foreign ministries old and new, *International Journal* 37 (Summer 1982).

foreign service A corps of professional diplomats. The Rogers Act of 1924 combined U.S. diplomatic and consular services into the present U.S. Foreign Service, the diplomatic corps responsible for administering U.S. foreign policies. While most American ambassadors gain their positions through a long career in the Foreign Service, historically a significant number of them are patronage appointees whose only outward qualification for the job is a demonstrated ability to make large campaign contributions to the party in power. While many distinguished outsiders have been appointed to ambassadorships, the de facto selling of these offices is a continuous, if quiet, bipartisan national scandal.

REFERENCES

Ralph Hilton, *Worldwide Mission: The Story of the United States Foreign Service* (New York: World, 1970);

David Garnham, Attitude and personality patterns of United States Foreign Service officers, *American Journal of Political Science* 18 (August 1974);

Andrew L. Steigman, *The Foreign Service of the United States: First Line of Defense* (Boulder, CO: Westview, 1985).

foreign trade zones (FTZs) Designated areas in the United States, usually near ports of entry, outside the customs territory of the United States. Foreign and domestic merchandise may be moved into these areas for storage, exhibition, assembly, manufacturing, or processing without incurring state or federal duties and without involving quota restrictions. If the finished product is exported, no U.S. duty is paid; if the product is to be sold in the United States, no duty is paid until the product is ready to leave the zone. Typically, FTZs are fenced-in areas with warehouse facilities and easy access to transportation. Outside the United States, such areas are called free trade zones.

Forest Service, U.S. The agency within the U.S. Department of Agriculture, created in 1905, that has the federal responsibility for national leadership in forestry. The Forest Service manages 154 national forests and 19 national grasslands, totalling 187 million acres in forty-one states and Puerto Rico, under the principles of multiple use and sustained yield. The Forest Service has continually been in the forefront of the development of professional forestry. While inexorably associated with the CONSERVATION movement, it has also at times been at odds with conservationists over the commercial use of national forests.

REFERENCES

Herbert Kaufman, *The Forest Ranger: A Study in Administrative Behavior* (Baltimore: Johns Hopkins University Press, 1960);

Dennis C. LeMaster, *Decade of Change: The Remaking of Forest Service Statutory Author-*

A Forest Service official examines seedling growth on Mount St. Helens, Washington, shortly after the volcano's eruption on May 18, 1980.

ity During the 1970s (Westport, CT: Greenwood, 1984).

U.S. Forest Service
P.O. Box 96090
Washington, D.C. 20090
(202) 447-3760

forgotten man   President Franklin D. Roosevelt's term for the ordinary citizen who had not been served well by the previous, Republican, administrations and for the millions left in desperate destitution by the Great Depression. While the forgotten man was first mentioned by Yale University professor William Graham Sumner (1840–1910) in 1883, Roosevelt made it one of the most potent political symbols of the twentieth century.

REFERENCES
William Graham Sumner, *The Forgotten Man and Other Essays* ed. by Albert Galloway Keller (New Haven, CT: Yale University Press, 1919);
Mark H. Leff, Taxing the "forgotten man": The politics of social security finance in the New Deal, *Journal of American History* 70 (September 1983);
Robert S. McEluaine, ed., *Down and Out in the Great Depression: Letters from the "Forgotten Man"* (Chapel Hill: University of North Carolina Press, 1983).

Forrestal, James V. (1892–1949)   The secretary of the Navy during the latter part of World War II and the first secretary of the new Department of Defense from 1947 to 1949. Although he personally opposed service unification, he was a major participant in the development of the National Security Act of 1947 (which combined the services into one agency) and subsequently did much to strengthen the office of the secretary of Defense at a time when it was considered weak vis-à-vis the military.

REFERENCES
Walter Millis, ed., *The Forrestal Diaries* (New York: Viking, 1951);
Robert Greenhaigh Albion, *Forrestal and the Navy* (New York: Columbia University Press, 1962);
Arnold A. Rogow, *James Forrestal: A Study of Personality, Politics, and Policy* (New York: Macmillan, 1963).

forward funding   The practice of obligating funds in one fiscal year for programs that are to operate in a subsequent year.

Founding Fathers/the founders   1 An imprecise phrase for all of those individuals who played a major role in declaring U.S. independence, fighting the Revolutionary War, and writing and adopting the U.S. Constitution. 2 Those who framed and signed the U.S. Constitution.

REFERENCES
David G. Smith, *The Convention and the Constitution: The Political Ideas of the Founding Fathers* (New York: St. Martin's, 1965);
Hans J. Morgenthau, The Founding Fathers and foreign policy: Implications for the late twentieth century, *Orbis* 20 (Spring 1976).

Fourteenth Amendment   The post–Civil War amendment to the U.S. Constitution that defines citizenship and mandates due process as well as equal protection of the laws for all citizens. Through the due process and equal protection clause of the Fourteenth Amendment, the U.S. Supreme Court has gradually applied (incorporated) most of the protections of the Bill of Rights to the states. The Fourteenth Amendment, which has produced more litigation and court interpretation than any other part of the Constitution, was enacted originally to protect the freed slaves from abrogations of their rights by the southern states.

When the Congress met in 1866, it faced several unprecedented circumstances: the Confederacy had recently surrendered, President Abraham Lincoln had been assassinated, and Andrew Johnson had taken over the presidency and had moved to begin the reconstruction of the South. These conditions contributed, either directly or indirectly, to the eventual framing of the Fourteenth Amendment. The Congress was dominated by a strong coalition of pro-civil rights and anti-Confederate congressmen. This coalition, termed the Radical Republicans, differed on almost every point of President Johnson's reconstruction program. They felt that Johnson's plan did not provide for adequate protection against state infringements of the former slaves' civil rights. In addition, they protested that the Johnson plan

231

was not severe enough in reprimanding former Confederates. Finally, the Radicals feared that the president's plan would allow the southern states to regain their congressional seats too quickly, enabling the former Confederates to block the Radicals' own plan for reconstruction. Ultimately, the Radicals turned to amending the Constitution as a means of implementing their reconstruction program, without fear of veto by the president or opposition by former Confederate states.

REFERENCES

Joseph B. James, *The Framing of the Fourteenth Amendment* (Urbana: University of Illinois Press, 1956);

Kenneth L. Karst, Equal citizenship under the Fourteenth Amendment, *Harvard Law Review* 91 (November 1977);

Raoul Berger, *Government by Judiciary: The Transformation of the Fourteenth Amendment* (Cambridge, MA: Harvard University Press, 1977);

Richard C. Cortner, *The Supreme Court and the Second Bill of Rights: The Fourteenth Amendment and the Nationalization of Civil Liberties* (Madison: University of Wisconsin Press, 1981);

Judith A. Baer, *Equality Under the Constitution: Reclaiming the Fourteenth Amendment* (Ithaca, NY: Cornell University Press, 1983).

Fourth Amendment   The amendment to the U.S. Constitution that protects individuals and their properties from unreasonable searches and seizures by generally prohibiting state acts that invade one's reasonable expectation of privacy. This provision applies both to arrests of persons and to searches of their person or properties for evidence. *See* EXCLUSIONARY RULE; MAPP V OHIO.

REFERENCE

J. David Herschel, *Fourth Amendment Rights* (Lexington, MA: Lexington Books, 1979).

fourth branch of government   1 The press; the mass media in general. *Compare to* FOURTH ESTATE.   2 The bureaucracy. While technically under the control of the executive branch, it sometimes seems to function as if it had a will, power, and legal authority all its own.   3 The independent regulatory agencies.

REFERENCES

1 Douglass Cater, *The Fourth Branch of Government* (Boston: Houghton Mifflin, 1959).

2 Kenneth J. Meier, *Politics and Bureaucracy: Policymaking in the Fourth Branch of Government* (North Scituate, MA: Duxbury, 1979).

3 Peter L. Strauss, The place of agencies in government: Separation of powers and the fourth branch, *Columbia Law Review* 84 (April 1984).

fourth estate   The press; the media in general; the journalistic profession. The term is usually credited to Edmund Burke (1729–1797), who observed that in the reporters' gallery in the British Parliament "there sat a Fourth Estate more important by far than them all." The word estate is used here to mean class—the other three estates being the nobility, the commons, and the clergy.

REFERENCES

John L. Hulteng and Roy Paul Nelson, *The Fourth Estate: An Informal Appraisal of the News and Opinion Media*, 2d ed. (New York: Harper & Row, 1983);

Louis E. Ingelhart, *Freedom for the College Student Press: Court Cases and Related Decisions Defining the Campus Fourth Estate Boundaries* (Westport, CT: Greenwood, 1985).

For a comparative perspective, see Joanmarie Kalter, The fourth estate in the Third World, *Bulletin of the Atomic Scientists* 39 (November 1983).

Fourth World   Those developing countries with per capita annual incomes below two hundred dollars, no financial reserves, little expectation of economic growth, and few natural resources—in effect, the poorest of the poor. Compare to FIRST WORLD; SECOND WORLD; THIRD WORLD.

REFERENCE

Richard E. Bissell, The "fourth world" at the United Nations, *World Today* 31 (September 1975).

frank   The facsimile signature of a member of the U.S. Congress used on envelopes in lieu of stamps on official outgoing mail. The franking privilege is a major political advantage for congressional incumbents. While designed to allow members of the Congress to freely communicate with their constituents, it has grown to be a significant element in most members' reelection campaigns. While it is illegal to use the frank for other than official business or to solicit political support or campaign contributions, it is perfectly legal for members to communicate with their constituents on a massive basis. COMMON CAUSE once estimated that, during an election year, about forty million pieces of franked mail is sent out each month by the House of Representatives alone.

REFERENCE

Albert D. Cover, The electoral impact of franked congressional mail, *Polity* 17 (Summer 1985).

frank and candid exchange of views A phrase usually used to signify diplomatic negotiations that have reached an impasse over differences neither side is prepared to publicize in the hope that future negotiations may resolve some of them. In short, negotiations that go nowhere.

fraud *See* ABUSE.

freedom 1 The liberty to do or not do something, for example, to speak or to practice religion. 2 The condition of not being in the power of others. 3 The capacity to perform legal acts, for example, to vote or to buy property. In this sense, children in the United States under eighteen years of age are generally not free; they are still in the power of others. Freedom is one of the most important of America's intellectual icons. It implies the political independence of the nation and of each of its individual citizens. Yet there are those who would argue that political freedom is only one side of the issue; the other being economic freedom. What good are political rights if one must go to sleep hungry in a public park? A society must provide the conditions for both kinds of freedom, political and economic, if it is to survive and thrive over the long term.

REFERENCES

Sidney Hook, *The Pardoxes of Freedom* (Berkeley and Los Angeles: University of California Press, 1962);

Herbert J. Muller, *Freedom in the Modern World* (New York: Harper & Row, 1966);

John G. Gill, The definition of freedom, *Ethics* 82 (October 1971);

Constance Baker Motley, The quest for freedom: The continuing American revolution, *Journal of Negro History* 61 (January 1976);

George F. Will, The meaning of freedom, *Parameters: Journal of the US Army War College* 13 (June 1983).

Freedom of Information Act of 1966 The law that provides for making information held by federal agencies available to the public unless the information falls within one of the specific categories exempt from public disclosure. Exempt records are those whose disclosure would impair rights of privacy or national security. Virtually all agencies of the executive branch of the federal government have issued regulations to implement the Freedom of Information Act. These regulations inform the public where certain types of information may be readily obtained, how other information may be obtained on request, and what internal agency appeals are available if the request for information is refused. *See also* PRIVACY ACT OF 1974.

REFERENCES

To locate specific agency regulations pertaining to freedom of information, consult the *Code of Federal Regulations* index under Information Availability.

Also see Robert L. Saloschin, The Freedom of Information Act: A governmental perspective, *Public Administration Review* 35 (January/February 1975);

Harold C. Relyea, ed., The Freedom of Information Act a decade later, *Public Administration Review* 39 (July/August 1979);

Ann H. Wion, The definition of "agency records" under the Freedom of Information Act, *Stanford Law Review* 31 (July 1979);

Patricia M. Wald, The Freedom of Information Act: A short case study in the perils and paybacks of legislating democratic values, *Emory Law Journal* 33 (Summer 1984).

For a comparative perspective, see Donald C. Rowat, ed., *Administrative Secrecy in Devel-*

oped Countries (New York: Columbia University Press, 1979).

freedom of religion *See* ESTABLISHMENT CLAUSE.

free exercise clause That portion of the First Amendment to the U.S. Constitution that prevents the Congress from "prohibiting the free exercise of" religion. However, the Supreme Court held in *Reynolds v United States*, 98 U.S. 145 (1879), that this freedom does not extend to "religious acts which are crimes or contrary to generally accepted public morals" (in this case the polygamous practices of some Mormons). In another case, *Bob Jones University v United States*, 76 L.Ed. 2d 157 (1983), the Court denied tax-exempt status to a private school because it practiced racial discrimination that was grounded in religious doctrine. In interpreting the free exercise clause, the Court has held that if the purpose or effect of a statute is to impede the observance of religion, or to discriminate invidiously among religions, then the free exercise of religion is abridged. Indeed, only a compelling government interest, such as nondiscrimination in higher education, can legitimize a statute restrictive of the free exercise of religion. In this regard, it is clear that no statute can validly impinge upon religious thought—that is, religious belief devoid of conduct. Moreover, by applying the compelling interest test, the Court has assured that forms of conduct based on religious belief are to receive increasing protection. Thus when a Seventh-Day Adventist was fired for refusing to work on Saturdays (her sabbath), the Supreme Court in *Thomas v Review Board of the Indiana Employment Security Division*, 67 L.Ed. 2d 624 (1981), ruled that she was fully entitled to unemployment benefits.

REFERENCE

Timothy L. Hall, The sacred and the profane: A First Amendment definition of religion, *Texas Law Review* 61 (August 1982).

free list A listing of things exempt from import duty.

free press clause That portion of the First Amendment to the U.S. Constitution that protects press freedom from being abridged by government. Thomas Jefferson wrote on the subject to Edward Carrington on January 16, 1787, "Were it left to me to decide whether we should have a government without newspapers, or newspapers without a government, I should not hesitate a moment to prefer the latter." The Supreme Court has also interpreted the amendment to prohibit prior restraint, that is, prepublication censorship. In the leading case on prior restraint, *Near v Minnesota*, 283 U.S. 697 (1931), the Court declared unconstitutional a State of Minnesota gag law, which allowed judges to bar publication of newspapers considered "malicious, scandalous or defamatory." This ruling was reinforced by *New York Times v United States*, 403 U.S. 317 (1971), when the Court dissolved an injunction against the *New York Times* that had halted publication of the Pentagon Papers.

The concept of a free press is often confused with the notion of free access. While government in the United States cannot prevent the press from printing (or broadcasting) the information it has, it can and often does deny the press access to information. The best recent example of this occurred when the Ronald Reagan administration, as a matter of policy, refused to allow reporters to accompany American forces in the INVASION OF GRENADA. Nor does freedom of the press insulate the press, as corporations, from those economic regulations applied to all business—such as taxation, equal employment opportunity, labor management, and antitrust laws. Because television and radio station owners are licensees of scarce frequencies, they have been held subject to additional government regulation in a number of areas. *Compare to* FAIRNESS DOCTRINE; *see also* SNEPP V UNITED STATES.

REFERENCES

Robert F. Ladenson, Freedom of the press: A jurisprudential inquiry, *Social Theory and Practice* 6 (Summer 1980);

Fred W. Friendly, *Minnesota Rag: The Dramatic Story of the Landmark Supreme Court Case that Gave New Meaning to Freedom of the Press* (New York: Random House, 1981);

Paul L. Murphy, *Near v. Minnesota* in the context of historical developments, *Minnesota Law Review* 66 (November 1981);

John Immerwahr and John Doble, Public attitudes toward freedom of the press, *Public Opinion Quarterly* 46 (Summer 1982);

Robert Friedman, Freedom of the press: How far can they go? *American Heritage* 33 (October/November 1982);

Howard B. Homonoff, The First Amendment and national security: The constitutionality of press censorship and access denial in military operations, *New York University Journal of International Law and Politics* 17 (Winter 1984).

free ride The seeking of office by an incumbent officeholder who campaigns for a higher office without giving up his or her present one. For example, an incumbent governor who runs for president in a year when he or she is not up for reelection as governor is getting a free ride.

free rider One who does not belong to an organized group, such as a union or a political party, but who nevertheless benefits from its activities. For example, a worker in a given organization who does not belong to a union, when most of the other workers do, may receive all of the wage increases and fringe benefits bargained for by the union without paying dues to the union. *See* AGENCY SHOP.

REFERENCES

Mancur Olson, *The Logic of Collective Action: Public Goods and the Theory of Groups* (Cambridge, MA: Harvard University Press, 1965); pp. 76–91;

Thomas S. McCaleb and Richard E. Wagner, The experimental search for free riders: Some reflections and observations, *Public Choice* 47:3 (1985).

free speech clause That portion of the First Amendment to the U.S. Constitution that prevents the Congress from passing any law that would inhibit free speech. While the English common law concept of freedom of speech meant freedom from prior restraint only, the present American theory of freedom of speech generally establishes both freedom from prior restraint and freedom from subsequent punishment for the exercise of these rights. Some U.S. Supreme Court justices have, in fact, suggested that freedom of speech is absolute; but a majority of the Court always has maintained

that it must be balanced against other legitimate interests: in short, the Court has attempted to preserve the greatest degree of expression consistent with the protection of overriding and compelling government interests. *Compare to* CLEAR AND PRESENT DANGER; COMMERCIAL SPEECH.

REFERENCES

C. Edwin Baker, Scope of the First Amendment freedom of speech, *UCLA Law Review* 25 (June 1978);

John W. Patterson, Moral development and political thinking: The case of freedom of speech, *Western Political Quarterly* 32 (March 1979);

Nat Hentoff, *The First Freedom: The Tumultuous History of Free Speech in America* (New York: Delacorte, 1980);

Thomas M. Franck and James J. Eisen, Balancing national security and free speech, *New York University Journal of International Law and Politics* 14 (Winter 1982);

Robert F. Nagel, How useful is judicial review in free speech cases? *Cornell Law Review* 69 (January 1984).

free trade A theoretical concept that refers to international trade unhampered by government restrictions or tariffs. Since World War II, American policy has been in favor of free trade—with a variety of politically expedient limitations. In 1924, English historian Lord Macaulay (1800–1859) wrote that "free trade, one of the greatest blessings which a government can confer on a people, is in almost every country unpopular." This is still true today. *Compare to* PROTECTIONISM.

REFERENCES

Harry Shutt, *The Myth of Free Trade: Patterns of Protectionism Since 1945* (New York: Blackwell, 1985);

Robert Z. Lawrence and Robert E. Litan, *Saving Free Trade: A Pragmatic Approach* (Washington, D.C.: Brookings, 1986).

free trade protectionist A member of the U.S. Congress who believes in free trade "in principle" but seeks protectionist legislation on a "temporary" basis for industries in his or her district that are adversely affected by foreign imports.

free trade zones *See* FOREIGN TRADE ZONES.

free world 1 The Western European and North American democracies plus Japan. 2 Those portions of the world not under communist control.

freeze *See* NUCLEAR FREEZE.

Friedan, Betty *See* WOMEN'S LIBERATION MOVEMENT.

Milton Friedman

Friedman, Milton (1912–) A conservative economist of the Chicago school, generally considered the leading proponent of a return to laissez-faire economics. A 1976 Nobel Prize winner, he has been a major influence on thinking about monetary policy, consumption, and government regulation. Friedman is generally considered to be the intellectual godfather to the movement toward government deregulation. His most important work, *A Monetary History of the United States, 1867–1960* (Princeton, NJ: Princeton University Press, 1963), with Anna Schwartz, is a major reconstruction of the history of money and banking. In it, he argues that the Great Depression was caused not by a failure of free markets but by a sharp and continuous decline in the money supply for which the government was responsible. Consequently, Friedman is the leading advocate for a monetary policy that calls for a constant and predictable money growth.

REFERENCES
Friedman's other works include *A Theory of the Consumption Function* (Princeton, NJ: Princeton University Press, 1957);
Capitalism and Freedom (Chicago: University of Chicago Press, 1962);
Essays in Positive Economics (Chicago: University of Chicago Press, 1966);
Free to Choose: A Personal Statement, with Rose Friedman (New York: Harcourt Brace Jovanovich, 1980).
For analyses of Friedman's influence, see David Ignatius, Milton Friedman: The ambiguous achievement of a positive economist, *Washington Monthly* 7 (December 1975);
Rick Tilman, Ideology and utopia in the political economy of Milton Friedman, *Polity* 8 (Spring 1976);
J. R. Shackleton, Milton Friedman, superstar? *Political Quarterly* 51 (July/September 1980).

Friedrich, Carl J. *See* ADMINISTRATIVE ACCOUNTABILITY.

friend of the court *See* AMICUS CURIAE.

friends and neighbors effect V. O. Key's description from his *Southern Politics in State and Nation* (New York: Knopf, 1949) of a local voting pattern in which candidates for statewide offices gain large majorities in their home counties, heavy support in nearby counties, and slight support in the rest of the state. To Key, this points out the "absence of stable, well-organized, statewide factions of like-minded citizens formed to advocate measures of common concern."

REFERENCES
Alexander Heard, *A Two-Party South?* (Chapel Hill: University of North Carolina Press, 1952);
Raymond Tatalovich, "Friends and neighbors" voting: Mississippi, 1943–73, *Journal of Politics* 37 (August 1975).

frontage assessment A tax to pay for improvements (such as sidewalks or sewer lines) charged in proportion to the frontage (number of feet bordering the road) of each property.

front loaded **1** Presidential primaries that are scheduled disportionately early in the primary season, presumably increasing the influence of these early states in the selection process and making it more difficult for new candidates to emerge later in the season. **2** A labor agreement that provides for a greater wage increase in its first year of effect than in subsequent years.

front runner The candidate who seems to be leading in a major race for a political party's nomination. Because early front runners have so often stumbled and fallen out of the political race, no candidate wants to be called a front runner; they prefer the underdog label. Indeed, candidates nowadays spend considerable time accusing each other of being the front runner. It's what all candidates want to be but don't want to be called.

frostbelt *See* SUNBELT-SNOWBELT TENSION; RUSTBELT.

Fry v United States 421 U.S. 542 (1975) The U.S. Supreme Court case that held that state governments had to abide by federal wage and salary controls even though the enabling legislation did not expressly refer to the states. Such legislation was ruled constitutional because general raises to state employees, even though purely intrastate in character, could significantly affect interstate commerce, and thus could be validly regulated by Congress under the Constitution's COMMERCE CLAUSE.

FTC *See* FEDERAL TRADE COMMISSION.

full employment An economic situation in which all those who want to work have jobs available. Whether government should provide such jobs when the private sector is unable to has been a subject of debate since the New Deal. In recent years, economists have been forced to accept unemployment of 3 to 6 per-

cent as full employment, as they have adjusted their theories and statements to include elements of the population that may for various reasons be unable to find work for which they are physically or educationally capable, as well as to include the effects of public support programs that may be preferable to private employment.

REFERENCE

Richard D. DuBoff, Full employment: The history of a receding target, *Politics and Society* 7:1 (1976).

Full Employment and Balanced Growth Act of 1977 *See* HUMPHREY-HAWKINS ACT OF 1977/FULL EMPLOYMENT AND BALANCED GROWTH ACT OF 1977.

full faith and credit **1** The clause in Article IV, Section 1, of the U.S. Constitution that requires states to legally recognize (i.e., to give full faith and credit to) the official acts of other states. This ensures that property rights, wills, deeds, and so on, will be honored for all citizens in all states. However, the clause is limited to civil judicial proceedings. **2** The descriptive term for those debt obligations, such as certain bonds, that have first claim upon the resources of the state.

Fullilove v Klutznick 448 U.S. 448 (1980) The U.S. Supreme Court case that held that the Congress has the authority to use quotas to remedy past discrimination in government public works programs, reasoning that the Fourteenth Amendment's requirement of equal protection means that groups historically denied this right may be given special treatment. *See* SET ASIDES.

REFERENCE

Peter G. Kilgore, Racial preferences in the federal grant programs: Is there a basis for challenge after *Fullilove v Klutznick*? *Labor Law Journal* 32 (May 1981).

full responsibility In administrative theory, the principle that an executive bears responsibility for the actions of the subordinates he or she has selected, whether or not the executive had actual knowledge of the actions. It is based, again in principle, on the belief that the selection of subordinates and the monitoring of their behavior is an executive responsibility. When the chief executive is an elected official and the subordinates are appointees, the concept of responsibility becomes more complex. Nowhere is primitive ritual or Machiavellian feigning more apparent than in the periodic assumption of full responsibility by an organization's chief executive. Although one of the advantages of delegating a problem is the ease with which the cunning leader can shift the blame for the situation if it sours, modern executives are seldom so crude as to lay blame. The appropriate tactic is to assume full responsibility for the situation. Paradoxically, in assuming full responsibility, the executive is seemingly relieved of it. Murray Edelman observed in *The Symbolic Uses of Politics* (Urbana: University of Illinois Press, 1967) that whenever this ritual is enacted, all of the participants tend to experience "a warm glow of satisfaction and relief that responsibility has been assumed and can be pinpointed. It once again conveys the message that the incumbent is the leader, that he knows he is able to cope, and that he should be followed." In reality, however, this ritual proves to have no substance. It "emphatically does not mean that the chief executive will be penalized for the mistakes of subordinates or that the latter will not be penalized." This is the tactic that President Richard M. Nixon employed when he first addressed the nation concerning the Watergate scandals in the spring of 1973. He boldly proclaimed that all of the possibly illegal actions of the White House officials were his responsibility and that he fully accepted that responsibility. Certainly Nixon did not mean to imply—at that point in time—that he should be punished for the transgressions of his underlings. Nor did Ronald Reagan in 1987 when he took full responsibility for the Iran–Contra Affair. Government officials of lesser rank are no less sophisticated with their manipulations of rituals and symbols. *See also* SYMBOLS.

functus officio   A Latin phrase for one who has fulfilled the duties of an office that has expired and who, in consequence, has no further formal authority. Arbitrators and judges are said to be functus officio concerning a particular case after they have made their decisions about it.

REFERENCE
Israel Ben Scheiber, The doctrine of functus officio with particular relation to labor arbitration, *Labor Law Journal* 23 (October 1972).

Fundamental Orders of Connecticut   A document for self-government adopted by the citizens of Connecticut in 1639. The first written constitution in the American colonies, it consisted of a preamble and eleven orders, which provided for the calling of general assemblies, the qualifications of voters, the organization of courts, the apportionment of taxes, and so on. This is generally conceded to be the world's first written constitution—for a general government.

Furman v Georgia   *See* CRUEL AND UNUSUAL PUNISHMENT.

fusion   1 The temporary joining of two or more political parties to support a common candidate or ticket.   2 The process underlying thermonuclear weapons.

G

gag rule/gag order **1** Any formal instruction from a competent authority, usually a judge, to refrain from discussing or advocating something, or both. The Supreme Court held in *Nebraska Press Association v Stuart,* 427 U.S. 539 (1976), that a judge could not gag the press about what could be reported prior to a trial. Perhaps the most famous gag rules are President Theodore Roosevelt's executive orders in 1902 and 1904 that forbade federal employees, on pain of dismissal, to seek pay increases or to attempt to influence legislation before the Congress, either as individuals or as members of organizations, except through the heads of their departments. Roosevelt's gag orders were repealed by the Lloyd-LaFollette Act of 1912, which also granted federal employees the right to organize unions. **2** A judge's order that a disruptive defendant literally be gagged. This was upheld in the case of *Illinois v Allen,* 397 U.S. 337 (1970). **3** A judge's order to witnesses and lawyers that they not discuss a case with people who are not directly involved with it. **4** A legislative rule that limits debate on a bill. *Compare to* CLOTURE, RULE. **5** The rule adopted by Congress in 1836 which provided that all antislavery measures be "laid upon the table"; and ignored. This unconstitutional denial of the First Amendment right "to petition the government for a redress of grievances" was repealed in 1844.

REFERENCE
Robert T. Roper, The gag order: Asphyxiating the First Amendment, *Western Political Quarterly* 34 (September 1981).

Gallup, George Horace (1901–1984) The best known of American pollsters, whose Gallup poll has become synonymous with the measurement of public opinion. He was a pioneer of scientific polling techniques that use a small sample of respondents from a large population. Because the Gallup poll (the American Institute of Public Opinion located in Princeton, NJ), which covers all aspects of public opinion, not just politics, has been published con-

tinuously since the mid-1930s, it contains a wealth of baseline data about American social attitudes. For example, in 1939 a survey asked about topless bathing suits—for men; over one third of all Americans found them objectionable. Many serious studies of changing American social and political attitudes during the last half-century necessarily start with historical data from the Gallup poll. *Compare to* SAMPLE.

REFERENCES
George H. Gallup, *The Sophisticated Poll Watcher's Guide* (Princeton, NJ: Princeton Opinion Press, 1972);
George H. Gallup, Jr., The Gallup poll—An American institution, *The Gallup Report* 241 (October 1985).

Gallup Report The report of the Gallup poll's findings on American public opinion, published monthly since 1965. Library of Congress no. HM261 A1 G34.
Gallup Report
53 Bank Street
Princeton, NJ 80540

GAO *See* GENERAL ACCOUNTING OFFICE.

Garcia v San Antonio Metropolitan Transit Authority 83 L. Ed. 2d 1016 (1985) The U.S. Supreme Court case that held that the application of the minimum wage and overtime requirements of the Fair Labor Standards Act to state public employment does not violate any constitutional provision. This reversed *National League of Cities v Usery,* which held that the Tenth Amendment prohibited the federal government from establishing wages and hours for state employees. In *Garcia,* the Court held that the states would have to ask the Congress for new legislation if they wanted to avoid having federal wage and overtime standards applied to them.

REFERENCES
Martha A. Field, *Garcia v San Antonio Metropolitan Transit Authority:* The demise of a misguided doctrine, *Harvard Law Review* 99 (November 1985);

S. Kenneth Howard, A message from *Garcia,
Public Administration Review* 45, special issue (November 1985);

A. E. Dick Howard, *Garcia*: Of federalism
and constitutional values, *Publius* 16 (Summer 1986).

garden city   An urban residential area that includes gardens and that is surrounded by a
greenbelt. Around the turn of the century, the
general belief in the efficacy of science and the
growing awareness of the consequences of urbanization led to a series of movements based
on ideal cities: residential areas that fulfilled
citizens' needs through technology combined
with the physical, social, and healthful amenities of rural life.

REFERENCES

Ebenezer Howard, *Garden Cities of Tomorrow*
(Cambridge, MA: MIT Press, 1965);

Daniel Schaffer, *Garden Cities for America:
The Radburn Experience* (Philadelphia:
Temple University Press, 1982);

Carol A. Christensen, *The American Garden
City and the New Town Movement* (Ann Arbor, MI: UMI Research Press, 1985).

Gardner, John W. (1912–   ) Former
president of the Carnegie Corporation (1955–
1965); former secretary of Health, Education,
and Welfare (1965–1968); former chairman of
the National Urban Coalition (1968–1970);
founder of Common Cause (1970); founder of
the Independent Sector, a national coalition of
voluntary organizations (1980). Gardner is the
author of a variety of books, criticized for their
sermonizing qualities by some but praised for
their sincere moral tone by others.

REFERENCES

Gardner's major works include *Excellence:
Can We Be Equal and Excellent Too?* (New
York: Harper & Row, 1964);

No Easy Victories (New York: Harper & Row,
1968);

The Recovery of Confidence (New York: Norton, 1970);

In Common Cause (New York: Norton, 1972).

Gardner v Broderick 392 U.S. 273 (1968);
*Uniformed Sanitation Men's Association v Com-
missioner of Sanitation of the City of New York*
392 U.S. 280 (1968)   The U.S. Supreme
Court decisions holding the dismissals of public employees for refusing to waive immunity
from prosecution or refusing to testify at grand
jury hearings to be unconstitutional.

James A. Garfield

Garfield, James A. (1831–1881)   Twentieth
president of the United States, assassinated on
July 2, 1881, by Charles Guiteau, an insane
attorney who had worked for Garfield's election and was angry about not receiving a patronage appointment. Garfield's death gave
new life to the civil service reform movement,
culminating in the passage of the Pendleton or
Civil Service Act of 1883.

*Garner v Board of Public Works of Los An-
geles* 341 U.S. 716 (1951)   The U.S. Supreme Court case upholding the constitutionality of a municipal loyalty oath requiring
employees to disclose whether they were or
ever had been a member of the Communist
party and to take an oath to the effect that for
five years prior to the effective date of the ordinance they had not advocated the overthrow
of the U.S. government by force or belonged to
any organization so advocating. *See also*
LOYALTY.

garrison state Harold Lasswell's conceptualization of a society organized primarily for violence as opposed to other purposes. A garrison state is inclusive of military state and police state. Lasswell wrote that "the master challenge of modern politics . . . is to civilianize a garrisoning world, thereby cultivating the conditions for its eventual dissolution."

REFERENCES

Harold Lasswell, The garrison state hypothesis today, in *Changing Patterns of Military Politics,* ed. Samuel P. Huntington (New York: Free Press, 1962);

Raymond Aron, Remarks on Lasswell's "the garrison state," *Armed Forces and Society* 5 (Spring 1979);

J. Samuel Fitch, The garrison state in America: A content analysis of trends in the expectation of violence, *Journal of Peace Research* 22:1 (1985).

Garrity v New Jersey 385 U.S. 493 (1967) The U.S. Supreme Court case holding that a New Jersey practice of dismissing public employees who relied upon the Fifth Amendment privilege against self-incrimination was unconstitutional.

gatekeeper **1** A critical decision maker in a political system. Such a person or institution decides who shall and who shall not get political rewards and can effectively veto a person's advance in a political or social system. For example, a local political leader may be the gatekeeper for nominations for city council membership, a legislative committee chair may be a gatekeeper for certain kinds of bills. **2** A mass media decision maker who decides what stories will be printed or broadcast; in effect, what will become news. *Compare to* AGENDA SETTING.

REFERENCES

1 A. Lee Hunt, Jr. and Robert E. Pendley, Community gatekeepers: An examination of political recruiters, *Midwest Journal of Political Science* 16 (August 1972);

Charles H. Williams, The "gatekeeper" function on the governor's staff, *Western Political Quarterly* 33 (March 1980);

Arthur T. Denzau and Robert J. Mackay, Gatekeeping and monopoly power of committees: An analysis of sincere and sophisticated behavior, *American Journal of Political Science* 27 (November 1983).

2 Lewis A. Coser, Publishers as gatekeepers of ideas, *Annals of the American Academy of Political and Social Science* 421 (September 1975);

Donald Shaw and Maxwell McCombs, *The Emergence of the American Political Issue: The Agenda Setting Function of the Press* (St. Paul, MN: West, 1977).

gay rights movement The total efforts to achieve full civil rights for homosexuals, to repeal laws that hold that homosexual acts are illegal, and to create a more positive image of homosexuals. A landmark in the gay rights movement was the 1975 decision of the American Psychiatric Association to remove homosexuality from its list of mental disorders. Some jurisdictions, such as San Francisco and New York City, have enacted laws making it illegal to discriminate against someone because of sexual orientation. The increasing demands for acceptance of homosexual lifestyles is a direct result of the civil rights movement, which made it possible for all minorities to insist upon their full rights as citizens.

REFERENCES

Joshua Dressler, Judicial homophobia: The gay rights movement's biggest roadblock, *Civil Liberties Review* 5 (January/February 1979);

A. S. Cohan, Obstacles to equality: Government responses to the gay rights movement in the United States, *Political Studies* 30 (March 1982).

gender gap The difference in political opinions between men and women. During the 1984 presidential election, the gender gap was a big issue—which turned out in the end to be a nonissue, in that men and women voted pretty much alike. For example, in the 1984 election, 57 percent of the women and 61 percent of the men voted for Ronald Reagan. Nevertheless, there are significant differences:

women are more likely to be registered voters and more likely to be Democrats.

REFERENCES

Robert Y. Shapiro and Harpreet Mahajan, Gender differences in policy preferences: A summary of trends from the 1960s to the 1980s, *Public Opinion Quarterly* 50 (Spring 1980);

Ethel Klein, *Gender Politics* (Cambridge, MA: Harvard University Press, 1984);

Daniel Wirls, Reinterpreting the gender gap, *Public Opinion Quarterly* 50 (Fall 1986).

General Accounting Office (GAO) A support agency created by the Budget and Accounting Act of 1921 to audit federal government expenditures and to assist the Congress with its legislative oversight responsibilities. The GAO is directed by the comptroller general of the United States, who is appointed by the president with the advice and consent of the Senate for a term of fifteen years. While the GAO originally confined itself to auditing financial records to see that funds were properly spent, since the 1960s it has redefined its mission to include overall program evaluation (*see* EVALUATION, PROGRAM).

REFERENCES

Keith E. Marvin and James L. Hedrick, GAO helps Congress evaluate programs, *Public Administration Review* 34 (July/August 1974);

John T. Rourke, The GAO: An evolving role, *Public Administration Review* 38 (September/October 1978);

Erasmus H. Kloman, ed., *Cases in Accountability: The Work of the GAO* (Boulder, CO: Westview, 1979);

Frederick C. Mosher, *The GAO: The Quest for Accountability* (Boulder, CO: Westview, 1979).

General Accounting Office
441 G Street, N.W.
Washington, D.C. 20548
(202) 275-5067

General Agreement on Tariffs and Trade (GATT) A multilateral trade agreement containing guidelines for conduct of international trade based on three basic principles: nondiscriminatory treatment of all signatories in trade matters; eventual elimination of tariff and nontariff barriers to trade, mostly through negotiations; and resolution of conflicts or damages arising from trade actions of another signatory through consultation. The agreement, however, contains many practical exceptions to these principles and no sanctions for their violation. The GATT has sponsored multilateral trade negotiations at various times.

REFERENCES

D. M. McRae and J. C. Thomas, The GATT and multilateral treaty making: The Tokyo round, *American Journal of International Law* 77 (January 1983);

Kim Jae-Ik, Need for the developing countries to play their part in the GATT, *World Economy* 6 (September 1983);

Robert Kuttner, Guide to the GATT, *The New Republic* 195 (September 15 and 22, 1986).

General Assembly 1 The largest unit of the United Nations, in which all member nations are represented and each has a single vote. While the General Assembly, which meets annually each fall, is a continuing international conference that has many U.N. housekeeping responsibilities and generates a goodly number of resolutions, it has no real power to affect the behavior of sovereign states. It functions mainly as a forum for international propaganda and debate. 2 A legislature in some state governments. *Compare to* SECURITY COUNCIL.

general election *See* ELECTION, GENERAL.

General Electric Co v Gilbert 429 U.S. 125 (1976) The U.S. Supreme Court case that held that excluding pregnancy from sick leave and disability benefit programs is not "discrimination based on sex" and so is not a violation of Title VII of the Civil Rights Act of 1964. This decision led to a Title VII amendment (the Pregnancy Discrimination Act of 1978), which reversed the impact of the Court's decision.

general manager/city administrator/chief administrative officer The administrative official appointed in a council-mayor system of government. He or she is typically appointed by the mayor and shares powers with that office. *Compare to* CITY MANAGER.

general revenue sharing *See* REVENUE SHARING.

general schedule The basic pay system for federal white-collar employees. It is the largest of the civilian pay systems, covering approximately half of the almost three-million civilian employees.

Claes Oldenburg's Batcolumn *in Chicago was commissioned by the GSA's art-in-architecture program in 1977.*

General Services Administration The federal agency, created by the Federal Property and Administrative Services Act of 1949, which establishes policy and provides for the management of the federal government's property and records, including construction and operation of buildings, procurement and distribution of supplies, utilization and disposal of property, transportation, traffic and communications management, stockpiling of strategic materials, and the management of a governmentwide automatic data-processing resources program.

General Services Administration
General Services Building
18th and F Streets, N.W.
Washington, D.C. 20405
(202) 472–1082

general strike A work stoppage by a substantial portion of the total work force of a locality or country. Because general strikes have tended to be more political and ideological than pragmatic and economically oriented in their goals, they have historically been more popular in Europe than in the United States. European unions have often acted in unison against their governments, while American unions have been more interested in bread and butter issues than political confrontation. General strikes have been decidedly infrequent since World War II.

REFERENCES

David Jay Bercuson, *Confrontation at Winnipeg: Labour, Industrial Relations and the General Strike* (Montreal: McGill-Queen's University Press, 1974);

Gordon Ashton Phillips, *The General Strike: The Politics of Industrial Conflict* (London: Weidenfeld and Nicolson, 1976).

general welfare clause That part of Article I, Section 8, of the U.S. Constitution that authorizes the Congress to "provide for the common Defense and general Welfare of the United States." It has long been argued whether this is an unlimited grant of power to spend or whether its power is limited to spending on those activities specifically mentioned in other parts of the Constitution. A liberal interpretation has prevailed, and the spending power of the Congress has never been successfully challenged in the courts.

general will Jean Jacques Rousseau's ideal from *The Social Contract* (1761) that there is a collective will or consensus among the people, which is the ultimate locus of all political power. Only majority rule can define the general will. However, there are instances when politicians pointedly ignore the general will, such as when the Congress grants itself a pay increase. When then Speaker of the House Thomas P. "Tip" O'Neill was asked why the Congress authorized a pay raise for itself without a formal vote, he said "There are instances where it is in the best interests of the nation not to vote the will of the people."

REFERENCES

James Conniff, On the obsolescence of the general will: Rousseau, Madison, and the evolution of republican political thought, *Western Political Quarterly* 28 (March 1975);

Patrick Riley, The general will before Rousseau, *Political Theory* 6 (November 1978);

Richard K. Dagger, Understanding the general will, *Western Political Quarterly* 34 (September 1981).

Geneva conventions *See* CONVENTION.

Gentrification is usually manifested in upgraded urban neighborhoods.

gentrification The gradual replacement of the poor of a neighborhood by people with middle and upper incomes; the upgrading of inner-city neighborhoods when well-to-do families refurbish vacant or abandoned properties to move into them. Gentrification can have many social and political implications. The most intractable problem is that, once gentrification starts, poorer residents are forced out because they cannot pay increased rents or property taxes.

REFERENCES

Jeffrey R. Henig, Gentrification and displacement within cities: A comparative analysis, *Social Science Quarterly* 61 (December 1980);

Jeffrey R. Henig, Neighborhood response to gentrification: Conditions of mobilization, *Urban Affairs Quarterly* 17 (March 1982);

J. John Palen and Bruce London, eds., *Gentrification, Displacement and Neighborhood Revitalization* (Albany: State University of New York Press, 1983).

George, Henry (1839–1897) An American economist whose *Progress and Poverty* (1879)

advocated a single tax on land to replace all other taxes. George argued that a single tax on the unearned increases in the value of land, as opposed to income from the use of land or its improvements, would more than pay for the total cost of government. While George was one of the most significant voices of the progressive era, his simplistic tax proposal would not fit an industrial society.

REFERENCES

George W. Bishop, Jr., The message of Henry George: A social philosopher's indictment of monopoly and privilege as causes of poverty, *American Journal of Economics and Sociology* 34 (April 1975);

Will Lissner, On the centenary of *Progress and Poverty, American Journal of Economics and Sociology* 38 (January 1979);

Dominic Candeloro, The single tax movement and progressivism, 1880–1920, *American Journal of Economics and Sociology* 38 (April 1979);

Terence M. Dwyer, Henry George's thought in relation to modern economics, *American Journal of Economics and Sociology* 41 (October 1982).

germane Pertaining to the subject matter of the measure at hand. All U.S. House of Representatives amendments must be germane to the bill. The Senate requires that amendments be germane only when they are proposed to general appropriation bills, bills being considered under cloture, or, often, when proceeding under an agreement to limit debate.

REFERENCE

Stanley Bach, Germaneness rules and bicameral relations in the U.S. Congress, *Legislative Studies Quarterly* 7 (August 1982).

germ theory of politics *See* HERBERT BAXTER ADAMS.

gerrymander To reshape an electoral district to enhance the political fortunes of the party in power (or incumbents), as opposed to creating a district with geographic compactness. The term first arose in 1811, when Massachusetts Governor Elbridge Gerry (1744–1814) reluctantly signed a redistricting bill, creating a district shaped like a salamander. Gerryman-

Gerrymandering—Old and New

The Original Gerrymander—
Massachusetts 1812

California Congressional
Districts—Los Angeles
Area 1984

Source: Samuel C. Patterson, Roger H. Davidson, and Randall B. Ripley, *A More Perfect Union: Introduction to American Government*, 3d ed. (Chicago: Dorsey, 1985), p. 147.

dering is often called an abuse of political power by the party out of power. Actually, it is simply the use of political power by the party in control of the redistricting process. The only thing abused is geography. But in 1986, the Supreme Court ruled in *Davis v Bandemer*, 92 L.Ed. 2d 85, that partisan gerrymandering is unconstitutional "when the electoral system is arranged in a manner that will consistently degrade a voter's or a group of voters' influence on the political process as a whole." *Compare to* REDISTRICTING.

REFERENCES

Robert S. Erikson, Malapportionment, gerrymandering, and party fortunes in congressional elections, *American Political Science Review* 66 (December 1972);

Richard L. Engstrom and John K. Wildgen, Pruning thorns from the thicket: An empiri-

cal test of the existence of racial gerrymandering, *Legislative Studies Quarterly* 2 (November 1977);

Joseph C. Markowitz, Constitutional challenges to gerrymanders, *University of Chicago Law Review* 45 (Summer 1978).

gerrymandering, affirmative Redistricting to consolidate minority votes so that a minority group member will most likely win the next election.

REFERENCES

David I. Wells, Affirmative gerrymandering compounds districting problems, *National Civic Review* 67 (January 1978);

Kenneth Eshleman, Affirmative gerrymandering is a matter of justice, *National Civic Review* 69 (December 1980);

Gettysburg Address

David Wells, Con affirmative gerrymandering, *Policy Studies Journal* 9, special issue no. 3 (1980–81);

David C. Saffell, Affirmative gerrymandering: Rationale and application, *State Government* 56:4 (1983).

Gettysburg Address   President Abraham Lincoln's brief remarks at the dedication of an 1863 Civil War battlefield cemetery in Gettysburg, Pennsylvania. Over time, the address has become sanctified as one of the great political statements of all time. The story that Lincoln jotted it down on the back of an envelope en route to Gettysburg is totally false. It was complete except for minor revisions before he left Washington.

REFERENCES

Florence Jean Goodman, Pericles at Gettysburg, *Midwest Quarterly* 6:3 (1965);

H. Mark Roelofs, The Gettysburg Address: An exercise in presidential legitimation, *Presidential Studies Quarterly* 8 (Summer 1978).

The Gettysburg Address

Fourscore and seven years ago our fathers brought forth upon this continent, a new nation, conceived in Liberty, and dedicated to the proposition that all men are created equal.

Now, we are engaged in a great civil war, testing whether that nation, or any nation so conceived, and so dedicated, can long endure. We are met on a great battlefield of that war. We have come to dedicate a portion of it as a final resting place for those who here gave their lives that that nation might live. It is altogether fitting and proper that we should do this.

But in a larger sense we can not dedicate—we can not consecrate—we can not hallow—this ground. The brave men, living and dead, who struggled here have consecrated it far above our poor power to add or detract. The world will little note nor long remember what we say here, but it can never forget what they did here. It is for us the living, rather, to be dedicated here to the unfinished work which they have, thus far, so nobly carried on. It is rather for us to be here dedicated to the great task remaining before us—that from these honored dead we take increased devotion to that cause for which they gave the last full measure of devotion—that we here highly resolve that these dead shall not have died in vain—that this nation, under God, shall have a new birth of freedom—and that this government of the people, by the people, for the people, shall not perish from the earth.

---

ghetto   **1** Those areas of European or Middle Eastern cities where Jews were once legally forced to live.   **2** An area of a city inhabited almost exclusively by members of an ethnic, racial, religious, or social group. It often carries connotations of low income. The black urban ghettos of the nation have long been centers of social unrest and sometimes of disorder. After a series of urban riots during the mid-1960s, President Lyndon B. Johnson appointed an Advisory Commission on Civil Disorders (the Kerner Commission) to investigate the problem. It reported that "what white Americans have never fully understood—but what the Negro can never forget—is that white society is deeply implicated in the ghetto. White institutions created it, white institutions maintain it, and white society condones it."

REFERENCES

William K. Tabb, *The Political Economy of the Ghetto* (New York: Norton, 1970);

David A. Snow and Peter J. Leahy, The making of a black slum-ghetto: A case study of neighborhood transition, *Journal of Applied Behavioral Science* 14 (October/November/December 1980);

Daniel R. Fusfeld and Timothy Bates, *The Economics of the Urban Ghetto* (Middletown, CT: Wesleyan University Press, 1984).

Gibbons v Ogden 9 Wheaton 1 (1924)   The U.S. Supreme Court case in which Chief Justice JOHN MARSHALL first put forth a broad interpretation of the COMMERCE CLAUSE by defining interstate commerce to include all navigable waters—even those within a state.

Gideon v Wainwright 372 U.S. 335 (1963)   The U.S. Supreme Court case that held that the due process clause of the Fourteenth Amendment required that persons brought to trial in state courts on felony charges are entitled to have a court-appointed lawyer if they cannot afford to pay for one of their own. Previously, state courts were required to provide legal counsel to indigent defendants only in cases where the death penalty was at issue (*Powell v Alabama*, 287 U.S. 45 [1932]) or when the defendant was young or mentally incompetent (*Betts v Brady*, 316 U.S. 455 [1942]). *Gideon v Wainwright* extended the right to legal assistance to all felony defendants in all state criminal trials. Justice Hugo Black wrote that "reason and reflection require us to recognize that, in our adversary system of criminal justice, any person hauled into court, who is too poor to hire a lawyer, cannot be assured a fair trial unless counsel is provided for him. This seems to be an obvious truth."

REFERENCES

For the classic account of this case, see Anthony Lewis, *Gideon's Trumpet* (New York: Random House, 1964).

Also see James P. Levine, The impact of "Gideon": The performance of public and private criminal defense lawyers, *Polity* 8 (Winter 1975).

Gillette v United States   *See* CONSCIENTIOUS OBJECTOR.

Gitlow v New York 268 U.S. 652 (1925) The U.S. Supreme Court case that held that the freedom of speech and press as guaranteed by the First Amendment "are among the fundamental personal rights and 'liberties' protected by the due process clause of the Fourteenth Amendment from impairment by the states." This case is a landmark because it was the first time that the Court said that a portion of the Bill of Rights was applicable to the states by means of the Fourteenth Amendment.

Givhan v Western Line Consolidated School District 435 U.S. 950 (1979)   The U.S. Supreme Court decision upholding the constitutional right of an employee (here a teacher) to express his or her views privately on matters of public concern to a supervisor (here a principal).

globalism   A description of a U.S. foreign policy of active involvement, both politically and militarily, in all parts of the world; the

polar opposite of ISOLATIONISM. American globalism has been more restrained since the VIETNAM WAR.

REFERENCE

Stephen E. Ambrose, *Rise to Globalism: American Foreign Policy Since 1938*, 4th ed. (New York: Penguin, 1985).

James Cagney in a scene from Warner Brothers' G-Men (1935).

G-men   **1** FBI agents. Legend has it that the term originated in 1933 when public enemy George "Machine Gun" Kelly (1895–1954), upon being surrounded by FBI agents in a Memphis, Tennessee, boarding house, screamed, "It's the government men—don't shoot, G-men, don't shoot!" Well, don't believe it. First, the FBI didn't capture Kelly; local Memphis police did. Second, the term was long in use as slang to describe government workers and agents. Nevertheless, in the public's mind G-men became synonymous with the FBI, especially after the 1935 James Cagney movie, *G-Men*.   **2** Secret Service agents (*see* SECRET SERVICE, UNITED STATES). Interestingly, the U.S. Secret Service is today located on G Street in Washington, D.C.   **3** Relatively low-level civil servants who are members of the FBI's special support group. These G's, as they are known, relieve the higher-paid FBI agents of the drudgery of routine surveillance work.

REFERENCE

1   Richard Gid Powers, *G-Men: Hoover's FBI in American Popular Culture* (Carbondale: Southern Illinois University Press, 1983).

GNP *See* GROSS NATIONAL PRODUCT.

goals Within the context of equal employment opportunity, realistic objectives that an organization endeavors to achieve through affirmative action. Quotas, in contrast, restrict employment or development opportunities to members of particular groups by establishing a required number or proportionate representation, which managers are obligated to attain, without regard to equal employment opportunity. To be meaningful, any program of goals or quotas must be associated with a specific timetable—a schedule of when the goals or quotas are to be achieved. *See also* FULLILOVE V KLUTZNICK; UNITED STATES V PARADISE.

REFERENCE

David H. Rosenbloom, The Civil Service Commission's decision to authorize the use of goals and timetables in the Federal Equal Employment Opportunity Program, *Western Political Quarterly* 26 (June 1973).

gobbledygook / officialese / federalese / bafflegab Slang terms for the obtuse language so frequently used by bureaucrats.

REFERENCES

John O'Hayre, *Gobbledygook Has Gotta Go* (Washington, D.C.: Government Printing Office, 1966);

Alan Siegel, Fighting business gobbledygook: How to say it in plain English, *Management Review* 25 (November 1979).

Goesaert v Cleary 335 U.S. 464 (1948) The U.S. Supreme Court case that found state laws denying women the right to practice certain occupations (in this case bartending) to be unconstitutional under the Fourteenth Amendment's equal protection clause.

Goldberg v Kelly 397 U.S. 254 (1970) The U.S. Supreme Court case that held that the due process clause of the Fourteenth Amendment requires government agencies to provide welfare recipients with an opportunity for an evidentiary hearing before terminating their benefits.

REFERENCE

Albert H. Meyerhoff and Jeffrey A. Mishkin, Application of *Goldberg v. Kelly* hearing requirements to termination of social security benefits, *Stanford Law Review* 26 (January 1974).

gold standard A monetary system in which all forms of money, paper and otherwise, are held at a parity with a coined monetary unit defined by its gold content and are convertible into this gold coin on demand. This monetary unit is coined freely, without an appreciable charge for the process; gold coins circulate freely and may be freely exported, imported, or melted down; gold is unlimited legal tender; and gold constitutes a large part of the nation's reserve. Because of the first two conditions, this is sometimes referred to as the gold coin standard. A close cousin is the gold bullion standard, which differs only in that a special condition of convertibility is imposed: a stipulated minimum of bullion must be purchased with paper money for redemption to take place. On March 10, 1933, President Franklin D. Roosevelt, relying on the Emergency Banking Act, prohibited by executive order the export of gold and gold certificates as well as payments in gold by banks. A few days earlier, he used provisions of the World War I Trading with the Enemy Act to control the export of gold. The United States was then off the gold standard. The Emergency Banking Act of 1933 authorized the secretary of the Treasury to call in all gold coins or currency in gold certificates. The Richard M. Nixon administration ended this government monopoly on the holding of gold: Public Law 93–373 allowed Americans, beginning January 1, 1975, to legally buy, hold, and sell gold.

REFERENCE

Roger W. Garrison, Gold: A standard and an institution, *Cato Journal* 3 (Spring 1983).

Goldwater v Carter *See* TREATY.

good neighbor policy A phrase first used by President Herbert Hoover but best known for describing President Franklin D. Roosevelt's policies toward Central and South America. Roosevelt said, in his inaugural address of March 4, 1933: "I would dedicate this nation to the policy of the good neighbor—the neighbor who resolutely respects himself and, because he does so, respects the rights of others—the neighbor who respects his obligations and respects the sanctity of his agreements in and with a world of neighbors."

REFERENCES

David Green, *The Containment of Latin America: A History of the Myths and Realities of the Good Neighbor Policy* (Chicago: Quadrangle, 1971);

Bryce Wood, *The Dismantling of the Good Neighbor Policy* (Austin: University of Texas Press, 1985).

Goodnow, Frank J. (1859–1939) A leader of the progressive reform movement and one of the founders and first president (in 1903) of the American Political Science Association. Goodnow is now best known as one of the principal exponents, along with Woodrow Wilson, of public administration's POLITICS-ADMINISTRATION DICHOTOMY.

REFERENCES

Goodnow's most enduring work is *Politics and Administration: A Study in Government* (New York: Macmillan, 1900).

For appreciations, see Charles G. Haines and Marshall E. Dimock, eds., *Essays on the Law and Practice of Governmental Administration: A Volume in Honor of Frank J. Goodnow* (Baltimore: Johns Hopkins University Press, 1935);

Austin Ranney, *The Doctrine of Responsible Party Government, Its Origins and Present State* (Urbana, IL: University of Illinois Press, 1954), Chapter 6 "Frank J. Goodnow";

Lurton W. Blassingame, Frank J. Goodnow: Progressive urban reformer, *North Dakota Quarterly* 40 (Summer 1972).

good offices The disinterested use of one's official position, one's office, to help others settle their differences; an offer to mediate a dispute.

REFERENCE

B. G. Ramcharan, The good offices of the United Nations secretary-general in the field of human rights, *American Journal of International Law* 76 (January 1982).

GOP Grand Old Party; the REPUBLICAN PARTY.

governance 1 The process of government; the exercise of government power; government action. 2 PUBLIC ADMINISTRATION. 3 The system or method of government, for example, democracy or fascism. 4 The state of being under the control of a higher legal or political authority. Thus citizens are under the governance of their national government, agencies are under the governance of their jurisdictions, and police officers are under the governance of their department. 5 The collective actions of a board of directors, board of trustees, or a board of governors in providing policy guidance to the organization that the board was established to manage.

government 1 The formal institutions and processes through which binding decisions are made for a society. Henry David Thoreau (1817–1862) wrote in *Civil Disobedience* (1849) that "that government is best which governs least." This statement is often attributed to Thomas Jefferson; but while it certainly reflects his philosophic sentiments, it has never been found in any of Jefferson's writings. 2 The apparatus of a state, consisting of executive, legislative, and judicial branches. 3 A political entity that has taxing authority and jurisdiction over a defined geographic area for some specified purpose, such as fire protection or schools. 4 The individuals who temporarily control the institutions of a state or subnational jurisdiction. 5 The United States government, especially as in "the government." *Compare to* BODY POLITIC.

Governments in the United States

Type	Number
National	1
State	50
County	3,041
Municipal	19,076
Townships	16,734
School districts	14,851
Other special districts	28,588

Source: *Statistical Abstract of the United States, 1986.*

Governmental Finance   The quarterly journal, published since 1926, of the Municipal Finance Officers Association and devoted to budgetary and financial management policies and procedures. Library of Congress no. HJ9103 .M782.

> *Governmental Finance*
> 180 North Michigan Avenue
> Chicago, IL 60601

government by crony   Rule by people who are appointed to office, not because of their qualifications for the job but because of their personal relationship to those in power. The phrase first gained currency in 1946 when Harold L. Ickes (1874–1952), then secretary of the Interior, resigned from President Harry S Truman's cabinet with the blast to the press that "I am against government by crony."

government corporation   A government-owned corporation or an agency of government that administers a self-supporting enterprise. Such a structure is used (1) when an agency's business is essentially commercial, (2) when an agency can generate its own revenue, and (3) when the agency's mission requires greater flexibility than government agencies normally have. Examples of federal government corporations include the Saint Lawrence Seaway Development Corporation, the Federal Deposit Insurance Corporation, the National Railroad Passenger Corporation (AMTRAK), and the Tennessee Valley Authority. At the state and municipal levels, corporations (often bearing different names, such as authorities) operate such enterprises as turnpikes, airports, and harbors.

REFERENCES

Annmarie Hauck Walsh, *The Public's Business: The Politics and Practices of Government Corporations* (Cambridge, MA: MIT Press, 1980);

Lloyd Musolf, *Uncle Sam's Private, Profit-Seeking Corporations: Comsat, Fannie Mae, Amtrak and Conrail* (Lexington, MA: Lexington Books, 1983).

government, limited   *See* LIMITED GOVERNMENT.

government of laws, not of men   *See* RULE OF LAW.

Government Printing Office (GPO)   The federal agency that executes orders for printing and binding placed by the Congress and the departments and establishments of the federal government. It sells through mail orders and government bookstores over twenty-five thousand different publications that originate in various government agencies. The GPO publications include information designed to keep citizens informed about everything from agricultural and scientific research to legislation, regulatory policies, and foreign affairs. It also administers the depository library program, through which selected government publications are made available in libraries throughout the country. These collections are essential sources of information for research on all aspects of government.

> Government Printing Office
> North Capitol and H Streets, N.W.
> Washington, D.C. 20401
> (202) 275–2051

government, unitary   A system of governance in which all authority is derived from a central authority, such as a parliament, an absolute monarch, or a dictator. The United States is not a unitary government. *Compare to* CONFEDERATION; FEDERALISM; LIMITED GOVERNMENT.

governor   The elected chief executive of a state government. A governor's responsibilities sometimes parallel those of a U.S. president, on a smaller scale, but each governor has only the powers granted to the office by the state constitution. Some states severely limit executive powers, while others give their governors powers such as the item veto (see VETO, ITEM) that are greater than those possessed by the president of the United States. The term of office for a governor is four years, except in four states (Arkansas, New Hampshire, Rhode Island, and Vermont), where it is two. In one sense, it is a misnomer to call a governor the chief executive of a state. The reality is that most state constitutions provide for what amounts to a plural executive, because governors, in marked contrast to the U.S. president, typically must share powers with a variety of other independently elected executive branch officers, such as a secretary of state, an attorney general, a treasurer, and an auditor (or controller). Consequently, a governor's informal powers as a lobbyist for his or her initiatives and as head of his or her party may often be far more useful than the formal authority that comes with the office. *Compare to* GUBERNATORIAL.

REFERENCES

Larry J. Sabato, The governorship as pathway to the presidency, *National Civic Review* 67 (December 1978);

Nelson C. Dometrius, The efficacy of a governor's formal powers, *State Government* 52 (Summer 1979);

Coleman B. Ransome, Jr., *The American Governorship* (Westport, CT: Greenwood, 1982);

Theodore J. Eismeier, Votes and taxes: The political economy of the American governorship, *Polity* 15 (Spring 1983);

Larry J. Sabato, *Goodbye to Good-time Charlie: The American Governorship Transformed,* 2d ed. (Washington, D.C.: Congressional Quarterly, 1983).

For facts on specific governors, see Robert Sobel and John W. Ralmo, eds., *Biographical Directory of the Governors of the United States, 1789–1978* (New York: Meckler, 1978);

John W. Ralmo, *Biographical Directory of the Governors of the United States, 1978–1982* (New York: Meckler, 1983).

governor, lieutenant The elected state official who would replace the governor should he or she be unable to complete a term of office. The lieutenant governor in a state government parallels the position of the vice president in the national government but differs in that in many states the lieutenant governor is separately elected and thus may be of a different party from the governor. This can sometimes cause considerable friction when the two officeholders are political rivals—and especially when, as in California, the lieutenant governor has some of the governor's powers to act whenever the governor is out of the state. Seven

states have felt no need for a lieutenant governor: Arizona, Maine, New Hampshire, New Jersey, Oregon, West Virginia, and Wyoming. In four of these states, the president of the state senate would succeed to the governorship; in the other three, the secretary of state succeeds.

REFERENCE

Thad L. Beyle and Nelson C. Dometrius, Governors and lieutenant governors, *State Government* 52 (Autumn 1979).

GPO *See* GOVERNMENT PRINTING OFFICE.

Grace Commission Formally, the President's Private Sector Survey on Cost Control. Chaired by J. Peter Grace, it was created in 1982 to examine the federal government's operations and policies from a business perspective. Its final report, prepared by over two-thousand volunteer, private-sector executives, contained over two-thousand recommendations for improving the efficiency of the federal government.

REFERENCES

Charles T. Goodsell, The Grace commission: Seeking efficiency for the whole people? *Public Administration Review* 44 (May/June 1984);

J. Peter Grace, *Burning Money: The Waste of Your Tax Dollars* (New York: Macmillan, 1984);

C. Lowell Harriss, Blueprints for cost control: Recommendations of the Grace Commission, *Proceedings of the Academy of Political Science* 35:4 (1985);

Steven Kelman, The Grace Commission: How much waste in government? *Public Interest* 79 (Winter 1985).

graft *See* HONEST GRAFT/DISHONEST GRAFT.

Gramm-Rudman-Hollings Act of 1985 The Balanced Budget and Emergency Deficit Control Act of 1985, which sets a maximum deficit amount for federal spending for each of the fiscal years 1986 through 1991 (progressively reducing the deficit amount to zero in 1991). If in any fiscal year the budget deficit exceeds the prescribed maximum by more than a specified sum, the act requires basically across-the-board cuts in federal spending to reach the targeted deficit level. These reductions are accomplished under the "reporting provisions" spelled out in the act, which require the directors of the Office of Management and Budget and the Congressional Budget Office to submit their deficit estimates and program-by-program budget reduction calculations to the comptroller general, who, after reviewing the directors' joint report, then reports his conclusions to the president. The president in turn must issue a "sequestration" order, mandating the spending reductions specified by the comptroller general, and the sequestration order becomes effective unless, within a specified time, the Congress legislates reductions to obviate the need for the sequestration order. In 1986 the U.S. Supreme Court ruled in *Bowsher v Synar,* 106 S. Ct. 3181 (1986), that the comptroller general's role in exercising executive functions under the act's deficit reduction process violated the constitutionally imposed doctrine of SEPARATION OF POWERS, because the comptroller general is removable only by a congressional joint resolution or by impeachment, and the Congress may not retain the power of removal over an officer performing executive powers. However, in anticipation of this possibility, the act contains a fallback deficit reduction process, which eliminates the comptroller general's role. *See* BALANCED BUDGET AMENDMENT.

REFERENCES

Jack Brooks, Gramm-Rudman: Can Congress and the president pass this buck? *Texas Law Review* 64 (August 1985);

John F. Hoadley, Easy riders: Gramm-Rudman-Hollings and the legislative fast track, *PS* 19 (Winter 1986);

Ronald S. Boster, The simple politics of Gramm-Rudman, *Bureaucrat* 15 (Summer 1986).

grandfather clause Originally, a device used by some states of the Old South to disenfranchise black voters. Grandfather clauses, written into seven state constitutions during the Reconstruction Era, granted the right to vote only to persons whose ancestors—"grandfathers"—had voted prior to 1867. The U.S. Supreme Court ruled in *Guinn v United States,* 238 U.S. 347 (1915), that all grandfather clauses were

unconstitutional because of the Fifteenth Amendment. Today, a grandfather clause is a colloquial expression for any provision or policy that exempts a category of individuals from meeting new standards. For example, if a jurisdiction were to establish a policy that all managers had to have a master's degree in public administration as of a certain date, it would probably exempt managers without such degrees who were hired prior to that date. This statement of exemption would be a grandfather clause.

REFERENCES

Christopher Leman, How to get there from here: The grandfather effect and public policy, *Policy Analysis* 61 (Winter 1980);

Benno C. Schmidt, Jr., Principle and prejudice: The Supreme Court and race in the progressive era, part III: Black disfranchisement from the KKK to the grandfather clause, *Columbia Law Review* 82 (June 1982).

grand jury *See* JURY, GRAND.

grant 1 A form of gift that entails certain obligations on the part of the grantee and expectations on the part of the grantor; for example, grants from a king or a tax-exempt charitable foundation. 2 An intergovernmental transfer of funds (or other assets). Since the New Deal, state and local governments have become increasingly dependent upon federal grants for an almost infinite variety of programs, growing to over 21 percent of all state and local expenditures in 1985. From the era of land grant colleges to the present, a grant by the federal government has been a continuing means of providing states, localities, public (and private) educational or research institutions, and individuals with funds to support projects the national government considered useful for a wide range of purposes. In recent years, grants have been made to support the arts as well as the sciences. All such grants are capable of generating debate over what the public as a whole, acting through the grant-making agencies of the federal government, considers useful and in the national interest.

REFERENCES

J. Theodore Anagnoson, Federal grant agencies and congressional election campaigns,

American Journal of Political Science 26 (August 1982);

Lawrence D. Brown, James W. Fossett, and Kenneth T. Palmer, *The Changing Politics of Federal Grants* (Washington, D.C.: Brookings, 1984);

Richard P. Nathan and Fred C. Doolittle, Federal grants: Giving and taking away, *Political Science Quarterly* 100 (Spring 1985).

grant, block A grant distributed in accordance with a statutory formula for use in a variety of activities within a broad functional area, largely at the recipient's discretion. For example, the community development block grant program, administered by the Department of Housing and Urban Development, funds community and economic development programs in cities, in counties, on Indian reservations, and in U.S. territories. The nature of the block grant allows these jurisdictions to allocate the funds to supplement other resources in ways they choose.

REFERENCES

Harold L. Bunce, The community development block grant formula: An evaluation, *Urban Affairs Quarterly* 14 (July 1979);

Richard S. Williamson, Block grants—A federalist tool, *State Government* 54:4 (1981);

Catherine Lovell, Community development block grant: The role of federal requirements, *Publius* 13 (Summer 1983);

Timothy J. Conlan, The politics of federal block grants: From Nixon to Reagan, *Political Science Quarterly* 99 (Summer 1984).

grant, categorical A grant that can be used only for specific, narrowly defined, activities, such as for the construction of interstate highways. The authorizing legislation usually details the parameters of the program and specifies the types of eligible activities, but sometimes these may be determined by administrators. At least 75 percent of all federal aid to states and localities comes in the form of categorical grants.

REFERENCES

Alan L. Saltzstein, Federal categorical aid to cities; Who needs it versus who wants it, *Western Political Quarterly* 30 (September 1977);

George J. Gordon and Irene Fraser Rothenberg, Regional coordination of federal categorical grants: Change and continuity under the new federalism, *Journal of the American Planning Association* 51 (Spring 1985).

grant, conditional A grant awarded with limitations (conditions) attached to use of the funds. Both categorical and block grants are conditional, although the categorical grant generally has a greater number and severity of conditions.

grant, discretionary A grant awarded at the discretion of a federal administrator and subject to conditions specified by legislation—the term is used interchangeably with project grant.

grant, formula-based categorical A categorical grant under which funds are allocated among recipients according to factors specified in legislation or in administrative regulations.

grant, formula project categorical A project categorical grant for which a formula specified in statutes or regulations is used to determine the amount available for a state. Funds then are distributed at the discretion of the administrator in reponse to project applications submitted by substate entities.

grant-in-aid Federal payments to states; or federal or state payments to local governments for specified purposes and usually subject to supervision and review by the granting government or agency in accordance with prescribed standards and requirements. One function of a federal grant-in-aid is to direct state or local funding to a purpose considered nationally useful by providing federal money, on condition that the jurisdiction receiving it match a certain percentage of it. The federal government actively monitors the grantee's spending of the funds to insure compliance with the spirit and letter of federal intent. Grants-in-aid have other public policy implications as well, because a jurisdiction that accepts federal money must also accept the federal "strings," or guidelines, that come with it. All federal grantees must comply with federal standards on equal employment opportunity in the selection of personnel and contractors, for example.

REFERENCES

Deil S. Wright, *Federal Grants-in-Aid: Perspectives and Alternatives* (Washington, D.C.: American Enterprise, 1968);

Helen Ingram, Policy implementation through bargaining: The case of federal grants-in-aid, *Public Policy* 25 (Fall 1977);

Charles L. Vehorn, *The Regional Distribution of Federal Grants-in-Aid* (Washington, D.C.: Academy for Contemporary Problems, 1978);

Joseph P. Magaddino and Roger E. Meiners, Bureaucracy and grants-in-aid, *Public Choice* 34:3, 4 (1979).

grant, open-end reimbursement A grant often regarded as a formula grant, but characterized by an arrangement wherein the federal government commits itself to reimbursing a specified portion of state and local program expenditures with no limit on the amount of such expenditures. Examples include AID TO FAMILIES WITH DEPENDENT CHILDREN, FOOD STAMPS and MEDICAID.

grant, project categorical Nonformula categorical grants awarded on a competitive basis to recipients who submit specific, individual applications in the form and at the times indicated by the grantor agency.

grants-in-kind Donations of surplus property or commodities.

grant, target A grant that packages and co-ordinates funds for wide-ranging public services directed at a specific clientele group or geographic area. Major examples include the Appalachian Regional Development Program (*see* APPALACHIAN REGIONAL COMMISSION), the COMMUNITY ACTION PROGRAMS, and the MODEL CITIES PROGRAM.

grassroots 1 The rank and file of a political party. 2 The voters in general. 3 Decentralized. 4 A patronizing way of referring to the origin of political power.

REFERENCES

1 John M. Orbell, Robyn M. Dawes, and Nancy J. Collins, Grass roots enthusiasm and the primary vote, *Western Political Quarterly* 25 (June 1972);

Thomas R. Marshall, Party responsibility revisited: A case of policy discussion at the grass roots, *Western Political Quarterly* 32 (March 1979).

2 John Osgood Field, Development at the grassroots: The organizational imperative, *Fletcher Forum* 4 (Summer 1980);

Chadwick F. Alger and Saul Mendlovita, Grass-roots activism in the United States: Global implications? *Alternatives: A Journal of World Policy* 9 (Spring 1984).

3 Janice Perlman, Grassroots empowerment and government response, *Social Policy* 10 (September/October 1979);

Erwin C. Hargrove and Gillian Dean, Federal authority and grassroots accountability: The case of CETA, *Policy Analysis* 6 (Spring 1980).

gray power A general phrase for the political efforts of "older" Americans to achieve better government benefits and services for people in their age group. As the aging population continues to increase as a percentage of the overall population, its political influence will keep pace. Until the New Deal, those who were old and in need of assistance were considered solely a local or family responsibility. The Social Security Act of 1935 changed that forever. As the BABY BOOM babies age, the influence of the aged on legislation and entitlement programs affecting them will be more pronounced than ever.

Great Depression The period between the stock market crash of October 29, 1929, and World War II, when the United States and the rest of the Western world experienced the most severe economic decline in this century. The main focus of the NEW DEAL was to lessen privations caused by the depression and to create regulatory structures and economic policies that would modify the severity of the normal business cycle.

REFERENCE

Robert Goldston, *The Great Depression: The United States in the Thirties* (Indianapolis: Bobbs Merrill, 1968).

"I'm sure that people we know wouldn't want to belong to the Great Society."

Great Society   The label for the 1960s domestic policies of the Lyndon B. Johnson administration, which were premised on the belief that social and economic problems could be solved by new federal programs. This was Johnson's effort to revive the federal reform presence in social change represented in the Progressive movement, the New Deal, and the Fair Deal. According to a May 23, 1964, speech of President Johnson, "we have the opportunity to move not only toward the rich society and the powerful society, but upward to the Great Society. The Great Society rests on abundance and liberty for all. It demands an end to poverty and racial injustice." While Richard Goodwin (1931–   ), then a Johnson speechwriter, is generally credited with coming up with the phrase, earlier authors had also used it. William Blackstone (1723–1780) in his *Commentaries on the Laws of England* (1765–69) wrote how it was "impossible for the whole race of mankind to be united in one great society." Graham Wallas (1858–1932) wrote of the utopian aims of an industrial society in his 1914 *The Great Society*. Even Harold Laski (1893–1950) in his 1931 *Introduction to Politics* wrote of the "place of the state in the great society." In recent years Johnson's Great Society has been subject to considerable analysis. Contending authorities (such as Charles Murray and John Schwartz) with equal statistical sophistication have asserted that the great society was either a considerable success or a considerable failure.

REFERENCES

See Sar A. Levitan and Robert Taggart, The Great Society did succeed, *Political Science Quarterly* 91 (Winter 1976–77);

Michael K. Brown and Stephen P. Erie, Blacks and the legacy of the Great Society: The economic and political impact of federal social policy, *Public Policy* 29 (Summer 1981);

John E. Schwartz, *America's Hidden Success: A Reassessment of Twenty Years of Public Policy* (New York: Norton, 1983);

Charles Murray, *Losing Ground: American Social Policy 1950–1980* (New York: Basic Books, 1984);

Marshall Kaplan and Peggy Cuciti, eds., *The Great Society Revisited* (Durham, NC: Duke University Press, 1986).

Major Great Society Legislation

1964

The *Civil Rights Act* was the most comprehensive civil rights legislation since Reconstruction.

The *Revenue Act* brought about a major reduction in taxes.

The *Food Stamp Act*, begun in the late New Deal era as an agricultural surplus disposal program, became in the Great Society a program to improve the nutrition of the poor.

The *Economic Opportunity Act*, also called the war on povery, was a major Johnson initiative.

The extension of the *Hill-Burton Act* provided grants for hospital construction and modernization.

The *Nurse Training Act* gave grants for training nurses and constructing nursing schools.

The *Omnibus Housing Act* extended current programs and added four more.

The *National Wilderness Preservation System* designated land for the system and established regulations.

1965

Medicare provided health benefits for the aged.

Medicaid provided health benefits for the poor.

The *Elementary and Secondary Education Act* was the most sweeping federal education act in history.

The *Higher Education Act* provided aid for students and colleges.

The *Department of Housing and Urban Development* was created.

The *Older Americans Act* created an Administration on Aging and authorized grants to states.

The *Voting Rights Act* enforced registration of voters in areas of discrimination.

1968

The *Housing and Urban Development Act* was the most far reaching since the 1949 act.

The *Community Mental Health Centers Act* amendments provided grants for staffing.

The *Omnibus Crime Control and Safe Streets Act* provided aid for local law enforcement officials.

Source: Adapted from William J. Keefe, Henry J. Abraham, William H. Flanigan, Charles O. Jones, Morris S. Ogul, and John W. Spanier, *American Democracy: Institutions, Politics, and Policies*, 2d ed. (Chicago: Dorsey, 1986), p. 463.

green card   A small document identifying an alien as a permanent resident of the United States entitled to legally find employment.

green revolution   The phrase that refers to the development of new hybrid grain seeds and the application of scientific methods to agriculture in developing countries to achieve higher food production. After the new seed varieties (which are highly responsive to fertilizer, less sensitive to growing conditions, and produce a grain that matures early) were introduced in the mid-1960s, grain production in many developing countries approached self-sufficiency for the first time. However, the green revolution has also had the unfortunate dysfunction of requiring fertilizers and other inputs that Third World farmers sometimes find difficult to acquire.

REFERENCES

Kenneth A. Dahlberg, *Beyond the Green Revolution* (New York: Plenum, 1979);

Andrew C. Pearse, *Seeds of Plenty, Seeds of Want: A Critical Analysis of the Green Revolution* (New York: Oxford University Press, 1980).

Gregg v Georgia   *See* CRUEL AND UNUSUAL PUNISHMENT.

Grenada, invasion of   The American military action of October 25, 1983, that took control of the Caribbean island nation of Grenada away from a Marxist military government, which had seized power six days earlier. The Ronald Reagan administration acted in response to requests for military intervention from the Grenada governor-general and from the Organization of Eastern Caribbean States; and to guarantee the safety of the approximately one-thousand American citizens (mostly medical students) on the island. Within sixty days, all U.S. combat units were gone and the island was left in the control of a civilian council, which would govern pending elections.

REFERENCES

Isaak I. Dore, The U.S. invasion of Grenada: Resurrection of the "Johnson Doctrine"? *Stanford Journal of International Law* 20 (Spring 1984);

Ronald M. Riggs, The Grenada Intervention: A legal analysis, *Military Law Review* 109 (Summer 1985);

Laura K. Wheeler, The Grenada Invasion: Expanding the scope of humanitarian intervention, *Boston College International and Comparative Law Review* 8 (Summer 1985);

Michael Rubner, The Reagan administration, the 1973 War Powers Resolution, and the invasion of Grenada, *Political Science Quarterly* 100 (Winter 1985–86).

Griggs et al. v Duke Power Company 401 U.S. 424 (1971)   The most significant single U.S. Supreme Court decision concerning the validity of employment examinations. The Court unanimously ruled that Title VII of the Civil Rights Act of 1964 "proscribes not only overt discrimination but also practices that are discriminatory in operation." Thus if employment practices operating to exclude minorities "cannot be shown to be related to job performance, the practice is prohibited." The ruling dealt a blow to restrictive credentialism, stating that, while diplomas and tests are useful, the "Congress has mandated the commonsense proposition that they are not to become masters of reality." In essence, the court held that the law requires that tests used for employment purposes "must measure the person for the job and not the person in the abstract." The *Griggs* decision applied only to the private sector until the Equal Employment Opportunity Act of 1972 extended the provisions of Title VII to cover public employees.

REFERENCE

Herbert N. Bernhardt, *Griggs v. Duke Power Co.:* The implications for private and public employers, *Texas Law Review* 50 (May 1972).

Griswold v Connecticut 381 U.S. 479 (1965) The U.S. Supreme Court case that, in holding that the state regulation of birth control devices was an impermissible invasion of privacy, helped to establish privacy as a constitutionally protected right under the Ninth and Fourteenth amendments. Justice William O. Douglas wrote, in this case: "The First Amendment has a penumbra where privacy is protected from governmental intrusion."

gross national product (GNP) The monetary value of all of the goods and services produced in a nation in a given year, one of the most important tools for measuring the health of a nation's economy. The U.S. Department of Commerce is responsible for gathering GNP data. All GNP figures must be adjusted for inflation or deflation if they are to accurately reflect the growth (or nongrowth) of the economy.

groupthink The psychological drive for consensus at any cost, which tends to suppress both dissent and the appraisal of alternatives in small decision-making groups. Groupthink, because it refers to a deterioration of mental efficiency and moral judgment due to in-group pressures, has an invidious connotation.

REFERENCES

Irving L. Janis, *Victims of Groupthink: A Psychological Study of Foreign Policy Decisions and Fiascoes* (Boston: Houghton Mifflin, 1972; 2nd ed., 1982);

Irving L. Janis, Groupthink and group dynamics: A social psychological analysis of defective policy decisions, *Policy Studies Journal* 2 (Autumn, 1973);

Steve Smith, Groupthink and the hostage rescue mission, *British Journal of Political Science* 15 (January 1985).

GS *See* GENERAL SCHEDULE.

GSA *See* GENERAL SERVICES ADMINISTRATION.

gubernatorial Pertaining to the office of governor, which comes from the Greek *kybernan*, meaning to direct a ship. The Romans borrowed the word from the Greeks as *guberno*. Then the French took it and sent it across the English channel as governor. When the word is used as an adjective, it goes back to its Latin roots; thus gubernatorial.

REFERENCES

Nelson C. Dometrius, Measuring gubernatorial power, *Journal of Politics* 41 (May 1979);

F. Ted Hebert, Jeffrey L. Brudney, and Deil S. Wright, Gubernatorial influence and state bureaucracy, *American Politics Quarterly* 11 (April 1983).

guerrilla warfare Military operations conducted by irregular troops in enemy controlled territory. The term was first used to refer to the Spanish partisans who fought against Napoleon's troops in the early 1800s, but today any armed uprising by the people of a nation against their oppressors is considered guerrilla warfare. Since guerrilla troops do not follow normal battle tactics or use standard weapons in open combat, they are much more difficult for official battle troops to control. Chairman Mao Tse-tung (1893–1976), leader of the People's Republic of China (1949–1976), summed up the essence of guerrilla strategy: "The enemy advances, we retreat; the enemy camps, we harass; the enemy tires, we attack; the enemy retreats, we pursue." Henry Kissinger (1923–), secretary of State under presidents Richard M. Nixon and Gerald R. Ford, summed up its result: "The conventional army loses if it does not win. The guerrilla wins if he does not lose." (*Foreign Affairs* 13 [January 1969].)

REFERENCES

Walter Laqueur, The origins of guerrilla doctrine, *Journal of Contemporary History* 10 (July 1975);

John J. Tierney, Jr., America's forgotten wars: Guerrilla campaigns in U.S. history, *Con-*

flict: An International Journal for Conflict and Policy Studies 2:3 (1980).

John F. Kennedy on Guerrilla Warfare

There is another type of warfare—new in its intensity, ancient in its origin—war by guerrillas, subversives, insurgents, assassins; war by ambush instead of by combat, by infiltration instead of aggression, seeking victory by eroding and exhausting the enemy instead of engaging him. It is a form of warfare uniquely adapted to what have been strangely called "wars of liberation," to undermine the efforts of new and poor countries to maintain the freedom that they have finally achieved. It preys on unrest and ethnic conflicts.

Source: Speech to U.S. Naval Academy graduating class, June 6, 1962.

Guinn v United States *See* GRANDFATHER CLAUSE.

Gulf of Tonkin Resolution The joint resolution of the U.S. Congress that sanctioned the use of great numbers of American forces in the VIETNAM WAR. It was premised upon a presumed 1965 attack on U.S. ships in the Gulf of Tonkin by North Vietnamese naval units. Subsequent investigations have conclusively shown that the information about the "attack" given to the Congress by the Lyndon B. Johnson administration to encourage the passage of the resolution was false. *Compare to* CREDIBILITY GAP.

REFERENCE

Joseph C. Goulden, *Truth Is the First Casualty: The Gulf of Tonkin Affair—Illusion and Reality* (Chicago: Rand McNally, 1969).

Gulick, Luther (1892–) Perhaps the most highly honored reformer, researcher, and practitioner of public administration in the United States. Often called the dean of American public administration, Gulick was intimately involved with the pioneering development and installation of new budget, personnel, and management systems at all levels of government. He was a member of the BROWNLOW COMMITTEE/PRESIDENT'S COMMITTEE ON ADMINISTRATIVE MANAGEMENT and a close advisor to President Franklin D. Roosevelt. Gul-

ick was also a founder of the Institute of Public Administration, the American Society for Public Administration, and the National Academy of Public Administration.

REFERENCE

For an appreciation of Gulick's career, see Stephen K. Blumberg, Seven decades of public administration: A tribute to Luther Gulick, *Public Administration Review* 41 (March/April 1981).

gunboat A small warship. References to gunboat "this" or gunboat "that" in the context of international relations imply that a great power is seeking to have its way with a small power through the threat of force. Gunboat diplomacy follows the recommendation of Oliver Cromwell (1599–1658) who said that: "A Man-of-war is the best ambassador."

REFERENCES

James Cable, *Gunboat Diplomacy 1919–1979: Political Applications of Limited Naval Force*, rev. ed. (New York: St. Martin's, 1981);

Jeffrey E. Garten, Gunboat economics, *Foreign Affairs* 63:3 (1985);

Robert Mandel, The effectiveness of gunboat diplomacy, *International Studies Quarterly* 30 (March 1986).

gun control Any government effort to regulate the use of firearms by the civilian population. While there are minor laws dealing with the registration of guns and the prohibition of their sale to criminals, there is no effective gun control in the United States. Proponents of free access to all kinds of weapons point to the Second Amendment of the U.S. Constitution: "A well-regulated militia, being necessary to the security of a free state, the right of the people to keep and bear arms, shall not be infringed." Opponents of easy access to guns point out that the "right" referred to in the amendment logically belongs only to members of the militia; not to all citizens. Right or wrong about the "right," gun control advocates have been consistently overwhelmed by the political strength of those who advocate free access. The basic federal law on gun control is the Gun Control Act of 1968. In 1986, the Congress significantly weakened this act and made it much easier to buy and sell rifles and shotguns and to transport them across state lines. The amending legislature was passed with the support of Republicans and Southern Democrats—the conservative coalition.

REFERENCES

Don B. Kates, Jr., Why a civil libertarian opposes gun control, *Civil Liberties Review* 3 (June/July 1976);

John Kaplan, The wisdom of gun prohibition, *Annals of the American Academy of Political and Social Science* 455 (May 1981);

Colin Loftin, Milton Heumann, and David McDowall, Mandatory sentencing and firearms violence: Evaluating an alternative to gun control, *Law and Society Review* 17:2 (1983);

Mark H. Moore, The bird in hand: A feasible strategy for gun control, *Journal of Policy Analysis and Management* 2 (Winter 1983);

John J. Hasko, Gun control: A selective bibliography, *Law and Contemporary Problems* 49 (Winter 1986).

gypsy moths Those liberal and moderate Republicans in the U.S. House of Representatives who tend to deny support to President Ronald Reagan's domestic and foreign policies. They are called gypsy moths, in contrast to BOLL WEEVILS, after a leaf-eating moth found in the north, because most of these House members represent congressional districts from the Northeast and Midwest.

H

habeas corpus *See* WRIT OF HABEAS CORPUS.

hack A drudge; a petty officeholder; an inferior politician. Hack is short for a hackney horse—a worn-out horse available for hire. While the political use of the term started in the last century, party hacks of one kind or another still abound.

Hague v CIO 307 U.S. 496 (1939) The U.S. Supreme Court case that struck down a Jersey City, N.J., ordinance requiring the permission of the local municipality for individuals (in this case, a union) to hold a meeting in a public place. This ruling established that the right of freedom of assembly applies not only to meetings in private but to public meetings (in streets and parks) as well. Compare to ADDERLY V FLORIDA.

Hamilton, Alexander (1755–1804) George Washington's aide and secretary during the Revolutionary War (he led the American charge at the Battle of Trenton in 1776 and commanded a regiment at the Battle of Yorktown in 1781) who went on to become a Wall Street lawyer. Hamilton was a prime sponsor of the Annapolis Convention, which called for the Constitutional Convention. A strong supporter of a strong national government, he signed the U.S. Constitution and coauthored the *Federalist Papers* to help get it ratified in his native New York. When Washington became president, he made Hamilton first secretary of the Treasury. As such, Hamilton is credited with putting the new nation on sound financial footing by having the new government, with the approval of the Congress, assume the Revolutionary War debt. Even though paying off the war debts mostly benefited financial speculators, that one act of honoring the debt of the Continental Congress established the United States internationally as a nation capable of paying its bills and managing its finances. Hamilton was also a strong advocate of a national bank and national currency. He was killed in 1804 by a political enemy, the vice president of the United States, Aaron Burr, in a duel.

REFERENCES

Clinton Rossiter, *Alexander Hamilton and the Constitution* (New York: Harcourt Brace Jovanovich, 1964);

James Willard Hurst, Alexander Hamilton, law maker, *Columbia Law Review* 78 (March 1978);

Richard Loss, Alexander Hamilton and the modern presidency: Continuity or discontinuity? *Presidential Studies Quarterly* 12 (Winter 1982).

Hamilton versus Jefferson

President George Washington's first cabinet contained Thomas Jefferson as secretary of State and Alexander Hamilton as secretary of the Treasury. Their conflicting attitudes illustrate the continuous tension in American politics between those who would interpret the Constitution strictly and those who take a more expansive view. Jefferson favored a strict interpretation of the Constitution, which held that the government had only those powers explicitly stated in the Constitution. Hamilton, in contrast, felt that "if the end be clearly comprehended within any of the specified powers, and if the measure is not forbidden by any particular provision of the Constitution, it may safely be deemed to come within the compass of national authority." Hamilton's loose interpretation is based upon the "elastic" clause of the Constitution, which allows Congress to make "all laws which shall be necessary and proper." Hamilton and Jefferson's acrimonious relationship set the tone for the argument over loose versus strict construction of the Constitution that continues today without any diminution.

Source: Adapted from James A. Henretta, W. Elliot Brownlee, David Brody, and Susan Ware, *America's History* (Chicago: Dorsey, 1987), pp. 210–13.

Hamilton's *Report on Manufactures* Alexander Hamilton's 1791 analysis, written while he was secretary of the Treasury (1789–1795), of why government intervention in the economy is desirable. The *Report*, which calls for a tariff system to protect American industry and for federal public works for roads and canals, was to influence American economic policy for generations. Hamilton felt that the general welfare required that government encourage infant industries to avoid overdependence on other countries for essential supplies.

REFERENCE

Morton J. Frisch, Hamilton's *Report on Manufactures* and political philosophy, *Publius* 8 (Summer 1978).

Hammer v Dagenhart 247 U.S. 251 (1918) The Supreme Court case that held unconstitutional a federal statute barring goods made by child labor from interstate commerce. The Court would not concede that the federal government could regulate child labor in interstate commerce until 1941, when it upheld the Fair Labor Standards Act of 1938, which put restrictions on the use of child labor. The landmark case was *United States v Darby Lumber Company*.

Hampton v Mow Sun Wong 426 U.S. 88 (1976) The U.S. Supreme Court case that held that a U.S. Civil Service Commission regulation excluding resident aliens from the federal competitive service had been adopted in violation of the due process clause of the Fifth Amendment. Because the Court expressly decided only the validity of the regulations promulgated by the Civil Service Commission and reserved comment on the appropriateness of a citizenship requirement instituted by the president, on September 2, 1976, President Gerald Ford issued Executive Order 11935, which provides that only U.S. citizens and nationals may hold permanent positions in the federal competitive service except when necessary to promote the efficiency of the serivce. *See also* SUGARMAN V DOUGALL.

REFERENCE

For a legal analysis, see Eric C. Scoones, Procedural due process and the exercise of delegated power: The federal civil service employment restriction on aliens, *Georgetown Law Journal* 66 (October 1977).

hard cases Cases in which fairness may require judges to be loose with legal principles. "Hard cases make bad law," because the specific complexity of the issues may force judges to take positions that, while appropriate to the circumstances presented to them, may suggest future legal applications that are likely to be considered unjust.

REFERENCE

Robert W. Bennett, Abortion and judicial review: Of burdens and benefits, hard cases and some bad law, *Northwestern University Law Review* 75 (February 1981).

hard funds *See* SOFT MONEY.

Warren G. Harding.

Harding, Warren Gamaliel (1865–1923) The DARK HORSE compromise candidate at the 1920 Republican National Convention who won election as the 29th President with a call to a "return to normalcy" after the tumult of World War I. He died suddenly in office in August of 1923, leaving to his successor a series of government scandals for which he himself was not personally responsible but which gave his administration a reputation for corruption that became representative of political attitudes in the 1920s.

REFERENCES

Francis Russell, *The Shadow of Blooming Grove: Warren G. Harding in His Times* (New York: McGraw-Hill, 1968);

Robert K. Murray, *The Harding Era: Warren G. Harding and His Administration* (Minneapolis: University of Minnesota Press, 1969).

The Warren G. Harding Administration

Major Accomplishments
- The Washington Conference of 1921–1922 on naval disarmament.
- The Appointment of William Howard Taft as chief justice of the Supreme Court.
- The Budget and Accounting Act of 1921.

Major Frustrations
- The Teapot Dome scandals.

---

hard line 1 A policy of taking a strong stand against Communist expansionism. 2 Any policy that is unyielding to compromise.

Hare voting system *See* VOTING, HARE SYSTEM.

Harper v Virginia State Board of Elections *See* TAX, POLL.

Hatch Act The collective, popular name for two federal statutes, restricting the political activities of federal employees. The 1939 act restricted almost all federal employees, whether in the competitive service or not. The impetus for this legislation came primarily from a decrease in the proportion of federal employees in the competitive service, a result of the creation of several score New Deal agencies outside the merit system. Senator Carl Hatch (1889–1963), a Democrat from New Mexico, had worked for several years to have legislation enacted that would prevent federal employees from being active at political conventions. He feared that their involvement and direction by politicians could lead to the development of a giant national political machine.

A second Hatch Act, in 1940, extended these restrictions to positions in state employment having federal financing. Penalties for violation of the Hatch Act by federal employees have been softened considerably over time. Originally, removal was mandatory, but, by 1962, the minimum punishment was suspension for thirty days.

It has never been possible to define completely the political activities prohibited by the Hatch Act. However, the following are among the major limitations: (1) serving as a delegate or alternate to a political party convention; (2) soliciting or handling political contibutions; (3) being an officer or organizer of a political club; (4) engaging in electioneering; (5) being, with some exceptions, a candidate for elective political office; and (6) speaking to or leading partisan political meetings or rallies. The constitutionality of these regulations was first upheld by the U.S. Supreme Court in *United Public Workers v Mitchell*, 330 U.S. 75 (1947), and reaffirmed in *Civil Service Commission v National Association of Letter Carriers*, 413 U.S. 548 (1973). Repeal of the Hatch Act (or relaxation of some of its provisions) has been high on the legislative agenda of unions, especially since union legal challenges to the act have been unsuccessful.

REFERENCES

Dorothy Ganfield Fowler, Precursors of the Hatch Act, *Mississippi Valley Historical Review* 47:2 (1960);

Philip L. Martin, The Hatch Act: The current movement for reform, *Public Personnel Management* 3 (May/June 1974);

David R. Morgan and James L. Regens, Political participation among federal employees: The Hatch Act and political equality, *Midwest Review of Public Administration* 10 (December 1976);

Marick F. Masters and Leonard Bierman, The Hatch Act and the political activities of federal employee unions: A need for policy reform, *Public Administration Review* 45 (July/August 1985);

William L. Magness, "Un-Hatching" federal employee political endorsements, *University of Pennsylvania Law Review* 134 (July 1986).

hatch acts, little State laws that parallel the federal government's prohibition on partisan political activities by employees paid with federal funds.

REFERENCE

Melvin Hill, Jr., The "littler hatch acts": State laws regulating political activities of local government employees, *State Government* 52 (Autumn 1979).

hat in the ring Active political candidacy. It's a term from boxing and was first applied to

politics by President Theodore Roosevelt; when someone was willing to box all comers, he threw his hat in the boxing ring.

hawk Inclined toward military action. Its antithetical term is dove. A dove, a far more peaceful bird in metaphor and a symbol of peace since ancient times, is not. The terms were used during the Vietnam War as a quick way of describing someone's attitude toward American participation in the war. Thomas Jefferson in a letter to James Madison on April 26, 1798, used "war hawks" to describe those Federalists who wanted to bring on war with France. Later, the term was applied to those who brought on the War of 1812 with England. Dove is of more recent vintage in American national politics; it was first used during the John F. Kennedy administration to describe those presidential advisors who advocated a policy of accommodation with the Soviet Union. The hardliners were, of course, hawks; and the metaphors carried on to the Vietnam period.

REFERENCES

Richard A. Brody and Sidney Verba, Hawk and dove: The search for an explanation of Vietnam policy preferences, *Acta Politica* 7 (July 1972);

Andre Modigliani, Hawks and doves, isolationism and political distrust: An analysis of public opinion on military policy, *American Political Science Review* 66 (September 1972);

Colin S. Gray, Hawks and doves: Values and policy, *Journal of Political & Military Sociology* 3 (Spring 1975);

Paul Burstein, Senate voting on the Vietnam War, 1964–1973: From hawk to dove, *Journal of Political and Military Sociology* 7 (Fall 1979).

hawk, chicken 1 A public figure, whether congressman or movie star, of the right age and eligible for military service during the Vietnam War, but who legally avoided it, and who now advocates a hard line foreign policy that might lead to American troops being sent into combat. 2 Birds with a reputation for preying on young chickens; by extension, prison slang for older homosexuals who seek sex with younger inmates. **3** A combat helicopter pilot. Robert Mason, in his Vietnam War novel, *Chickenhawk* (New York: Viking, 1983) explains how pilots often felt "chicken" or fearful about combat missions until they were airborne, soaring like seemingly invincible hawks over the enemy.

Hawkins v Bleakly 243 U.S. 210 (1917) The U.S. Supreme Court case that upheld the constitutionality of state workmen's compensation laws.

Health and Human Services covers many departments. Here a scientist from the National Institutes of Health checks test results for herpes infections.

Health and Human Services, U.S. Department of (DHHS) The cabinet-level department of the federal government most concerned with health, welfare, and income security plans, policies, and programs. Its largest single agency is the Social Security Administration. It was created on October 17, 1979, when the Department of Education Organization Act divided the Department of Health, Education, and Welfare in two.

U.S. Department of Health and Human Services
200 Independence Avenue, S.W.
Washington, D.C. 20201
(202) 475–0257

Health, Education, and Welfare, U.S. Department of (HEW) A former cabinet-level department of the federal government. Created in 1953, HEW was reorganized into the Department of Education and the Department of Health and Human Services in 1979. *See* EDU-

CATION, U.S. DEPARTMENT OF; HEALTH AND HUMAN SERVICES, U.S. DEPARTMENT OF.

hearing **1** A legal or quasi-legal proceeding in which arguments, witnesses, or evidence are heard by a judicial officer or administrative body. **2** A legislative committee session for hearing witnesses. At hearings on legislation, witnesses usually include specialists, government officials, and representatives of those affected by the bills under study. Subpoena power may be used to summon reluctant witnesses. The public and press may attend open hearings but are barred from closed (executive) hearings.

hearing examiner *See* ADMINISTRATIVE LAW JUDGE/HEARING EXAMINER/HEARING OFFICER.

hearsay A statement of a witness based not on direct knowledge but on what the witness heard someone else say. Hearsay evidence is generally not accepted in court.
REFERENCE
Olin Guy Wellborn III, The definition of hearsay in the federal rules of evidence, *Texas Law Review* 61 (August 1982).

Heart of Atlanta Motel v United States 379 U.S. 41 (1964) The U.S. Supreme Court case that upheld the constitutionality of Title II of the Civil Rights Act of 1964, which prohibited discrimination because of race, color, sex, religion, or national origin in restaurants, hotels, and other places of public accommodation engaged in interstate commerce.

Helsinki Agreement The final act of the Conference on Security and Cooperation in Europe, signed on August 1, 1975, by the United States, Canada, and thirty-three European countries (including the Soviet Union) in Helsinki, Finland. The final act is not a treaty and is not legally binding, yet it carries considerable moral weight because it was signed at the highest level. The agreement included an endorsement of human rights, which has become controversial because of its "observance in the breach" by Soviet bloc countries.
REFERENCES
Arthur J. Goldberg and James S. Fay, Human rights in the wake of the Helsinki Accords,

Hastings International and Comparative Law Review 3 (Fall 1979);

Max M. Kampelman, The Helsinki process is in danger, *Atlantic Community Quarterly* 20 (Summer 1982).

Helvering v Davis 301 U.S. 619 (1937) The U.S. Supreme Court case that held constitutional the Social Security Act of 1935.

Heritage Foundation A conservatively oriented public policy research institution and think tank; founded 1973. Publishes *Policy Review*.

Heritage Foundation
214 Massachusetts Ave., NE
Washington, D.C. 20002
(202) 546–4400

Herring, E. Pendleton (1903–   ) One of the most influential of the pre-World War II scholars of public administration who later served as president (1948–1968) of the Social Science Research Council.

REFERENCES

Herring's *Group Representation before Congress* (New York: Russell and Russell, 1929, 1967) was one of the pioneering works in the study of pressure groups. His *Federal Commissioners: A Study of Their Careers and Qualifications* (Cambridge, MA: Harvard University Press, 1936) was one of the first studies of the relation between a manager's background and behavior in office. His *Public Administration and the Public Interest* (New York: Russell and Russell, 1936) remains a major analysis of the relations between government agencies and their formal and informal constituencies.

Hicklin v Orbeck 434 U.S. 919 (1978) The U.S. Supreme Court case that held unconstitutional an Alaska law granting employment preferences to Alaskan residents. The law violated the constitutional requirement that states grant all U.S. citizens the same "privileges and immunities" granted to their own citizens.

hidden agenda The unannounced or unconscious goals, personal needs, expectations, and strategies that each individual or group possesses. Parallel to a group's open agenda are the private or hidden agendas of each of its members.

REFERENCES

Stephen C. Halpern, The hidden agenda of environmental reform, *Society* 18 (July/August 1981);

Priscilla Elfrey, *The Hidden Agenda: Recognizing What Really Matters at Work* (New York: Wiley, 1982);

David I. Meiselman, Hoaxes, hidden agendas, and hokum, *Society* 20 (January/February 1983).

high crimes and misdemeanors In addition to treason and bribery, grounds for impeachment and removal from office of "the president, vice president and all civil officers of the United States," as stated in Article II, Section 4, of the U.S. Constitution.

higher law The notion that no matter what the laws of a state are, there remains a higher law, to which a person has an even greater obligation. A higher law is often appealed to by those who wish to attack an existing law or practice that courts or legislators are unlikely or unwillng to change. Martyrs throughout the ages have asserted a higher law in defiance of the state, thus earning their martyrdom. The classic presentation of this concept is in Sophocles' (496–406 BC) play *Antigone*, in which the heroine defies the king, asserts a higher law as her justification, and forces the king to have her killed. Because the courts of any state will only enforce the law of the land, appealing to a higher law is always chancy business. Examples of Americans who have appealed to a higher law and wound up in jail as a result are Henry David Thoreau (see CIVIL DISOBEDIENCE), MARTIN LUTHER KING, JR., and Vietnam War resisters.

REFERENCE

Edward S. Corwin, *The "Higher Law" Background of American Constitutional Law* (Ithaca, NY: Great Seal, 1929, 1961), first published in the *Harvard Law Review*, 42 (1928–29).

hill, the The U.S. Congress, because it is literally situated on a hill; it is eighty-eight feet above sea level; the White House is fifty-five feet above sea level. Now there can be no doubt about which is the higher branch of government.

REFERENCES

Alvin M. Josephy, Jr., *On the Hill: A History of the American Congress* (New York: Simon & Schuster, 1979);

Alvin P. Drischler, Foreign policy making on the hill, *Washington Quarterly* 8 (Summer 1985).

hippies The flower children of the late 1960s, who advocated love and peace, protested the Vietnam War, tended to drop out of conventional schools or careers, and had lifestyles that deviated from community norms. The name originated from a San Francisco political group, the Haight-Ashbury Independent Proprietors, known as HIP. *Compare to* YIPPIES.

Hishon v King and Spalding 81 L. Ed. 2d 59 (1984) The U.S. Supreme Court case that held that a law firm must comply with federal antidiscrimination laws when deciding which members of the firm should be elevated to partners.

Hobbes, Thomas (1588–1679) The English political philosopher and social contract theorist who wrote *Leviathan* (1651), a highly influential and comprehensive theory of government. Hobbes asserted that, in a state of nature, man is in a chaotic condition "of war of everyone against everyone." For safety's sake, men formed governments to which they surrendered their freedom but from which they got security and order. Hobbes's government is an absolute monarch. While Hobbes preferred monarchs who were not tyrants, his theorizing offered no recourse to those finding themselves under one. His greatest significance to students of American government is that he, as the first of the major social contract theorists (see JOHN LOCKE and JEAN-JACQUES ROUSSEAU), provided the foundation upon which the others would build and ultimately influence the American Revolution.

REFERENCES

Frank M. Coleman, The Hobbesian basis of American constitutionalism, *Polity* 7 (Fall 1974);

Robert R. Albritton, Hobbes on political science and political order, *Canadian Journal of Political Science* 9 (September 1976);

Robert Ladenson, In defense of a Hobbesian conception of law, *Philosophy and Public Affairs* 9 (Winter 1980);

J. H. Hexter, Thomas Hobbes and the law, *Cornell Law Review* 65 (April 1980);

Mark A. Heller, The use and abuse of Hobbes: The state of nature in international relations, *Polity* 13 (Fall 1980).

Holden v Hardy 169 U.S. 336 (1898) The U.S. Supreme Court case that held that a state, in exercising its police power to protect the public health, had the right to legislate hours of work.

home rule The ability of a municipal corporation to develop and implement its own charter. It resulted from the urban reform movement of the turn of the century, which hoped to remove urban politics from the harmful influence of state politics. Home rule can be either a statutory or a constitutional system and varies in its details from state to state.

REFERENCES

Frank J. Goodnow, *Municipal Home Rule* (New York: Macmillan, 1895);

J. D. McGoldrick, *Law and Practice of Municipal Home Rule, 1916–1930* (New York: Columbia University Press, 1933);

Leon Ovsiew, Home rule is no longer enough, *Education and Urban Society* 12 (August 1980);

Jon A. Baer, Municipal debt and tax limits: Constraints on home rule, *National Civic Review* 70 (April 1981);

Leslie Bender, Home rule, revisited, *Journal of Legislation* 10 (Winter 1983).

home style The manner in which members of the U.S. Congress project themselves to their home constituencies so they can retain constituent support and get reelected. The significant elements of home style include the personal style by which legislators present themselves, how they explain their legislative records, and how they allocate scarce resources, such as time for this or that issue or attention to this or that constituent. *Compare to* CASEWORK.

265

REFERENCES
The term comes from Richard F. Fenno, Jr., *Home Style: House Members in their Districts* (Boston: Little, Brown, 1978).
Also see William A. Taggart and Robert F. Durant, Home style of a U.S. senator: A longitudinal analysis, *Legislative Studies Quarterly* 10 (November 1985);
Arthur Denzau, William Riker, and Kenneth Shepsle, Farquharson and Fenno: Sophisticated voting and home style, *American Political Science Review* 79 (December 1985).

honest graft/dishonest graft The classic distinction between the two genres of graft, made by George Washington Plunkitt, a politico associated with New York's Tammany Hall early in this century. Dishonest graft, as the name implies, involves bribery, blackmailing, extortion, and other obviously illegal activities. As for honest graft, let Plunkitt speak:

> Just let me explain by examples. My party's in power in the city, and its goin' to undertake a lot of public improvements. Well, I'm tipped off, say, that they're goin' to lay out a new park at a certain place.
>
> I see my opportunity and I take it, I go to that place and I buy up all the land I can in the neighborhood. Then the board of this or that makes its plan public, and there is a rush to get my land, which nobody cared particular for before.
>
> Ain't it perfectly honest to charge a good price and make a profit on my investment and foresight? Of course, it is. Well, that's honest graft.

Compare to PREFERMENTS.

REFERENCE
For more of Plunkitt's wisdom, see William Riordon, *Plunkitt of Tammany Hall* (New York: Dutton, 1963).

honeymoon period The relatively short time after taking office that an elected executive may have harmonious relations with the press, with the legislature, and with the public. Honeymoons, which may last from a few hours to a few months, tend to end once the executive (whether a president, governor, or mayor) starts to make the hard decisions that alienate one constituency or another.

honorable A form of address used for many public officials, such as judges, mayors, and members of the U.S. Congress. Honorable does not necessarily imply personal honor or integrity; it merely signifies incumbency.

Hoover Commission of 1947–1949 The first Hoover Commission, formally known as the Commission on the Organization of the Executive Branch of the Government, created by the Congress via the Lodge-Brown Act of 1947 for the ostensible purpose of integrating and reducing the number of government agencies generated by World War II. Former President Herbert Hoover was chosen by the commission to be its chairman. Instead of calling for a reduction of government agencies, the commission made a vigorous call for increased managerial capacity in the Executive Office of the President (EOP) through: (1) unlimited discretion over presidential organization and staff, (2) a strengthened Bureau of the Budget, (3) an office of personnel located in the EOP, and (4) the creation of a staff secretary to provide liaison between the president and his subordinates. In addition, the commission recommended that executive branch agencies be reorganized to permit a coherent purpose for each department and better control by the president. Many of its recommendations were adopted, including passage of the Reorganization Act of 1949 and the establishment of the Department of Health, Education and Welfare in 1953.

REFERENCES
Peri E. Arnold, The first Hoover Commission and the managerial presidency, *Journal of Politics* 38 (February 1976);
Ronald C. Moe, A new Hoover Commission: A timely idea or misdirected nostalgia? *Public Administration Review* 42 (May/June 1982).

Hoover Commission of 1953–1955 The second Hoover Commission, formally known as the Commission on the Organization of the Executive Branch of the Government, was created by Congress via the Ferguson-Brown Act of 1953 for three ostensible purposes: (1) the promoting of economy, efficiency, and improved service in the transaction of the public business; (2) the defining and limiting of executive functions; and (3) the curtailment and abolition of government functions and activities competitive with private enterprise. A major recommendation was the elimination of nonessential government services and activities competitive with private enterprise, based on the assumptions that the federal government had grown beyond appropriate limits and that such growth should be reversed. In contrast to the earlier commission, the second commission's recommendations accomplished little.

REFERENCES

William R. Devine, The second Hoover Commission reports: An analysis, *Public Administration Review* 15 (Autumn 1955);

James W. Fesler, Administrative literature and the second Hoover Commission reports, *American Political Science Review* 61 (March 1967).

Herbert Hoover.

Hoover, Herbert (1874–1964) The Republican president of the United States from 1929 to 1933. Hoover had the great misfortune to become president just when the Great Depression almost destroyed the American economy. He believed that the depression was the result of the international consequences of the Ver-

sailles Treaty, rather than of any fundamental internal economic condition of the United States. A whole generation of Americans grew up holding him personally responsible for economic events that no president of that time could have controlled. Ironically, Hoover, who made a fortune early in life as an engineer, headed allied relief operations during and after World War I, served as secretary of Commerce under presidents Warren G. Harding and Calvin Coolidge, had a worldwide reputation as a preeminent administrator, and in later life was respected as an "elder statesman."

REFERENCES

Joan Hoff Wilson, *Herbert Hoover, Forgotten Progressive* (Boston: Little, Brown, 1975);

Peri E. Arnold, The "great engineer" as administrator: Herbert Hoover and modern bureacracy, *Review of Politics* 42 (July 1980);

Carl E. Krog and William R. Tanner, eds., *Herbert Hoover and the Republican Era; A Reconsideration* (Lanham, MD: University Press of America, 1984).

The Herbert Hoover Administration

Major Accomplishments
- The Smoot-Hawley Tariff of 1930, which raised import duties to an all-time high.
- The Reconstruction Finance Corporation, which made emergency loans to institutions hurt by the Great Depression.
- The all-nation debt moratorium on World War I loans and reparations (which, however, only temporarily helped the world's financial communities).

Major Frustrations
- The stock market crash of 1929.
- The Great Depression.

---

hopper The box in a legislature where bills are deposited on introduction.

horizontal federalism *See* FEDERALISM, HORIZONTAL.

hot line 1 The telephone and teletype links between the White House and the Kremlin established for instant communications should a crisis occur. 2 Any communications system that links chief executives of governments with each other.   **3** The communications that link a chief executive with his or her military commanders.

hot pursuit   1 The legal doctrine that allows a law enforcement officer to arrest a fleeing suspect who has fled into another jurisdiction. **2** The doctrine of international maritime law that allows a state to seize a foreign vessel that has initiated an act of war on the territory of the invaded state and is pursued into international waters.

REFERENCE

2   Eugene R. Fidell, Hot pursuit from a fisheries zone, *American Journal of International Law* 70 (January 1976).

house   1 One of the two divisions of a bicameral legislature.   **2** The lower branch of a bicameral legislature.   **3** The U.S. House of Representatives, as distinct from the Senate, although each body is a house of the U.S. Congress.

house calendar   *See* CALENDAR, HOUSE.

House of Representatives   See CONGRESS, UNITED STATES.

housing allowance   1 A special compensation, consisting of a flat rate or a salary percentage, to subsidize the living expenses of an employee, usually paid only to those sent overseas.   **2** A subsidy paid directly or indirectly to citizens whose incomes are below a certain standard to enable them to live in conventional, nonpublic housing.

REFERENCES

2   Bernard J. Frieden, Housing allowances: An experiment that worked, *Public Interest* 59 (Spring 1980);

Katharine L. Bradbury and Anthony Downs, eds., *Do Housing Allowances*

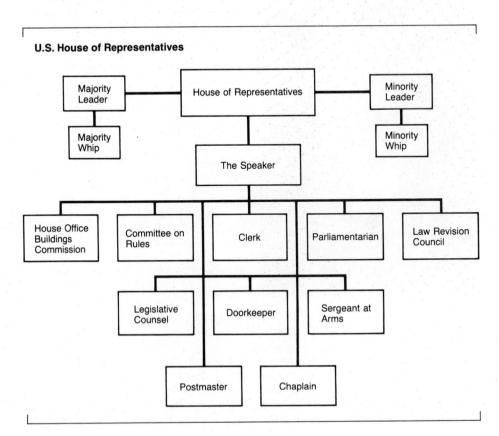

U.S. House of Representatives

Work? (Washington, D.C.: Brookings, 1981);

Jill Khadduri and Raymond J. Struyk, Housing vouchers for the poor, *Journal of Policy Analysis and Management* 1 (Winter 1982).

Housing and Community Development Act of 1974 *See* URBAN RENEWAL.

The recent restoration of the Chicago Theater was underwritten by HUD loans.

Housing and Urban Development, U.S. Department of (HUD) The principal cabinet-level federal agency responsible for programs concerned with housing needs and with improving and developing the nation's communities. The Department of Housing and Urban Development Act of 1965 created HUD by transferring to it all of the functions, powers, and duties of the Housing and Home Finance Agency, the Federal Housing Administration, and the Public Housing Administration. *Compare to* URBAN RENEWAL.

REFERENCES

For histories, see Dwight A. Ink, Establishing the new Department of Housing and Urban Development, *Public Administration Review* 27 (September 1967);

Moon Landrieu and Jane Lang McGrew, HUD: The federal catalyst for urban revitalization, *Tulane Law Review* 55 (April 1981);

Robert C. Weaver, The first twenty years of HUD, *Journal of the American Planning Association* 51 (Autumn 1985).

U.S. Department of Housing and Urban Development
451 7th Street, S.W.
Washington, D.C. 20410
(202) 755–6422

HUD *See* HOUSING AND URBAN DEVELOPMENT, U.S. DEPARTMENT OF.

human resources administration An increasingly popular euphemism for the management of social welfare programs. Many jurisdictions that had departments of public or social welfare have replaced them with departments of human resources.

human rights **1** The minimal rights to which all people are entitled as human beings. **2** Whatever rights and privileges are given or guaranteed to a people by its government. **3** A foreign policy initiative of the Jimmy Carter administration, which called for all people (1) to be free from government-sponsored physical violence; (2) to have such vital needs as food, shelter, health care, and education; and (3) to enjoy civil and political liberties. *Compare to* HELSINKI AGREEMENT.

REFERENCES

Lincoln P. Bloomfield, From ideology to program to policy: Tracking the Carter human rights policy, *Journal of Policy Analysis and Management* 2 (Fall 1982);

Paul Gorden Lauren, First principles of racial equality: History and the politics and diplomacy of human rights provisions in the United Nations Charter, *Human Rights Quarterly* 5 (Winter 1983);

David Carleton and Michael Stohl, The foreign policy of human rights: Rhetoric and reality from Jimmy Carter to Ronald Reagan, *Human Rights Quarterly* 7 (May 1985);

David P. Forsythe, The United Nations and human rights, 1945–1985, *Political Science Quarterly* 100 (Summer 1985).

human services General term for organizations that seek to improve the quality of their client's lives by providing such services as counseling, rehabilitation, and nutritional help. *See also* PENNHURST STATE SCHOOL V HALDERMAN; YOUNGBERG V ROMEO.

269

REFERENCES

Wayne F. Anderson, Bernard J. Frieden, and Michael J. Murphy, eds., *Managing Human Services* (Washington, D.C.: International City Management, 1977);

Laurence E. Lynn, Jr., *The State and Human Services: Organizational Change in a Political Context* (Cambridge, MA: MIT Press, 1980);

Yeheskel Hasenfeld, The administration of human services, *Annals of the American Academy of Political and Social Science* 479 (May 1985).

Humphrey-Hawkins Act of 1977/Full Employment and Balanced Growth Act of 1977   The federal statute that asserts it is the policy of the federal government to reduce overall unemployment to a rate of 4 percent by 1983, while reducing inflation to an annual rate of 3 percent. The act explicitly states that it is the "right of all Americans able, willing and seeking to work" to have "full opportunities for useful paid employment." However, the discussion of the act in the *Congressional Record* of December 6, 1977, states that "there is clearly no right to sue for legal protection of the right to a job." The popular name of the act comes from its cosponsors, Senator Hubert H. Humphrey (1911–1978) and Congressman Augustus F. Hawkins (1907–   ).

REFERENCE

Harvey L. Schantz and Richard H. Schmidt, The evolution of Humphrey-Hawkins, *Policy Studies Journal* 8 (Winter 1979).

Humphrey's Executor v United States 295 U.S. 602 (1935)   The U.S. Supreme Court case prohibiting the dismissal of commissioners of the Federal Trade Commission by the president for reasons of disagreement over policy. The Court reasoned that an FTC commissioner "occupies no place in the executive department and . . . exercises no part of the executive power," thereby distinguishing the case from MYERS V UNITED STATES. By implication, the decision applied to positions in any federal agency exercising predominantly quasi-judicial or quasi-legislative functions. *See also* WIENER V UNITED STATES.

REFERENCE

John R. Hibbing, The independent regulatory commissions fifty years after *Humphrey's Executor v. U.S., Congress and the Presidency: A Journal of Capital Studies* 12 (Spring 1985).

hundred days   The first one-hundred days of Franklin D. Roosevelt's administration in 1933, when a great deal of landmark legislation was enacted to cope with the Great Depression. The term initially came from the period between Napoleon's 1815 triumphant return from Elba and his defeat at Waterloo. The first hundred days of all new administrations since FDR's have been unfavorably compared to his in terms of legislative productivity. Nevertheless, all newly inaugurated presidents seek to use the leftover energy of their successful campaign, their honeymoon era with press and public, and the inexperience of a new Congress to generate and see passed a program of legislation that almost certainly will be more difficult to get through at a later time.

REFERENCE

James E. Sargent, *Roosevelt and the Hundred Days: Struggle for the Early New Deal* (New York: Garland, 1981).

Major Legislative Accomplishments of the First Hundred Days of the Administration of President Franklin D. Roosevelt in 1933

March 9	The **Emergency Banking Relief Act** was introduced, passed, and signed in less than eight hours.
March 20	The **Economy Act** cut pensions and salaries and reorganized agencies.
March 22	The **Beer and Wine Revenue Act** legalized the sale of wine and beer.
March 31	The **Civilian Conservation Corps Reconstruction Relief Act** provided jobs for young men.
April 19	The **gold standard** was abandoned.
May 12	The **Federal Emergency Relief Act** enacted.
May 13	The **Agricultural Adjustment Act** created the Agricultural Adjustment Administration to raise farm prices.

May 18	The **Tennessee Valley Authority Act** authorized construction of dams and power plants on the Tennessee River.
May 27	The **Federal Securities Act** provided for the registration of new securities with the Federal Trade Commission.
June 13	The **Home Owners Refinancing Act** authorized the refinancing of nonfarm mortgage debts.
June 16	The **National Industrial Recovery Act** established regulatory codes for industries and a public works administration to reduce unemployment.
June 16	The **Banking Act of 1933** created the Federal Deposit Insurance Corporation (FDIC) to guarantee bank deposits.
June 16	The **Emergency Railroad Transportation Act** established greater coordination of railroads.

| June 16 | The **Farm Credit Act** reorganized agricultural credit programs. |

Source: Adapted from William J. Keefe, Henry J. Abraham, William H. Flanigan, Charles O. Jones, Morris S. Ogul, and John W. Spanier, *American Democracy: Institutions, Politics, and Policies,* 2d ed. (Chicago: Dorsey, 1986), p. 458.

hustings Any place in which a political speech is made. A candidate on the campaign trail may be said to be on the hustings. The word is derived from an old Norse word meaning a house assembly or meeting. In British usage, the hustings is also the literal platform from which a speech is given.

I

ICBM Intercontinental ballistic missile; a land-based long-range nuclear rocket. The ICBMs are a major element of the U.S. strategic nuclear triad.

REFERENCES
Albert Carnesale and Charles Glaser, ICBM vulnerability: The cures are worse than the disease, *International Security* 7 (Summer 1982);
David C. Morrison, ICBM vulnerability, *Bulletin of the Atomic Scientists* 40 (November 1984).

ICC *See* INTERSTATE COMMERCE COMMISSION.

ICMA *See* INTERNATIONAL CITY MANAGEMENT ASSOCIATION.

ideologues Those who believe intensely in a political ideology; those who believe in abstract principles without due regard to the realities of

a situation. Such true believers tend to interpret all acts, whether political or apolitical, from the perspective of their ideology.
REFERENCE
Eric Hoffer, *The True Believer: Thoughts on the Nature of Mass Movements* (New York: Harper & Row, 1951).

ideology **1** A comprehensive system of political beliefs about the nature of people and society; an organized collection of ideas about the best way to live and about the most appropriate institutional arrangements for society. The term first arose during the French Revolution to refer to a school of thought, separate from religion, about how a society should be organized. But the term has evolved to mean the philosophic bent of true believers of whatever belief. The mainstreams of American politics have never been rigidly ideological; only the extremes of both major parties—on the far Right and far Left—are much concerned with

271

correct rules of thought for the party's most faithful. One major writer, Daniel Bell, even discovered an "end of ideology" in America in his 1960 book *End of Ideology: On the Exhaustion of Political Ideas in the Fifties* (Glencoe, IL: Free Press). Many post–World War II historians and political scientists saw and still see pragmatism (a problem-by-problem approach to the solution of problems without regard to theoretically determined ends) as the American alternative to ideology. But ideology seems to be making a comeback, especially with the new Right (*see* RIGHT, NEW), and, of course, it has never left the old Left (*see* LEFT, OLD). **2** Whatever one believes about the political process, whether it is articulated or not. **3** An interrelated set of ideas or a worldview that explains complex social phenomena in a relatively simple way. **4** The selected and often distorted notions about how a society operates. A group may adhere to such notions as a means of retaining group solidarity and of interpreting a world from which they have become alienated.

REFERENCES

Robert E. Lane, *Political Ideology: Why the American Common Man Believes What He Does* (New York: Free Press, 1962);

Willard A. Mullins, On the concept of ideology in political science, *American Political Science Review* 66 (June 1972);

David C. Nice, Party ideology and policy outcomes in the American states, *Social Science Quarterly* 63 (September 1982);

Roy C. Macridis, *Contemporary Political Ideologies: Movements and Regimes*, 2d ed. (Boston: Little, Brown, 1983);

John P. Robinson and John A. Fleishman, Ideological trends in American public opinion, *Annals of the American Academy of Political and Social Science* 472 (March 1984);

Everett Carll Ladd, Jr., *Ideology in America: Change and Response in a City, a Suburb, and a Small Town* (Lanham, MD: University Press of America, 1986).

illegal alien   A person from another country who is living or working in the United States unlawfully. The U.S. Department of Labor prefers to refer to these people as undocumented workers, a term that preserves the presumption of innocence and sounds less criminal. *See also* ALIEN; DECANAS V BICA; IMMIGRATION AND NATURALIZATION SERVICE V HERMAN DELGATO; SIMPSON-MAZZOLI BILL.

REFERENCES

Alison A. Clarke, State legislation denying subsistence benefits to undocumented aliens: An equal protection approach, *Texas Law Review* 61 (February 1983);

Jean Baldwin Grossman, Illegal immigrants and domestic employment, *Industrial and Labor Relations Review* 37 (January 1984);

Lawrence W. Miller, Jerry L. Polinard, and Robert D. Wrinkle, Attitudes toward undocumented workers: The Mexican American perspective, *Social Science Quarterly* 65 (June 1984).

Illinois v Allen   *See* GAG RULE/GAG ORDER.

ILO   *See* INTERNATIONAL LABOR ORGANIZATION.

In the 1972 film The Candidate, *image makers packaged a senatorial nominee (played by Robert Redford) into a slick, winning product.*

image makers   Political consultants who take on the publicizing of a candidate much like an advertising agency takes on the publicizing of a product. The resulting public image of the candidate is intended as a clear, simple, portrait-like characterization, acceptable to all groups. The end result can be (1) a fairly accurate image of the candidate achieved through paid advertising and unpaid advertising, known as media events; (2) a made-over image—a candidate inaccurately presented in paid advertising and allowed only controlled access to the news media; or (3) something in between. *Compare to* POLITICAL CONSULTANTS.

REFERENCES

Dan Nimmo and Robert L. Savage, *Candidates and their Images: Concepts, Methods, and Findings* (Glenview, IL: Scott, Foresman, 1976);

Dan Nimmo, Political image makers and the mass media, *Annals of the American Academy of Political and Social Science* 427 (September 1976).

Immigration and Naturalization Service (INS) The federal agency created in 1891 responsible for administering the immigration and naturalization laws relating to the admission, exclusion, deportation, and naturalization of aliens. Specifically, the INS inspects aliens to determine their admissibility into the United States; adjudicates requests of aliens for benefits under the law; guards against illegal entry into the United States; investigates, apprehends, and removes aliens who are in violation of the law; and examines applications of aliens wishing to become citizens. The INS was originally in the Department of Labor; but after more restrictive immigration laws made it necessary to more carefully monitor prospective new citizens, the INS was relocated into the Department of Justice.

REFERENCES

Franklin Abrams, American immigration policy: How strait the gate? *Law and Contemporary Problems* 45 (Spring 1982);

Elsa Banuelos, Justice and the undocumented immigrant: Authority and practices of the Immigration and Naturalization Service, *Stanford Journal of International Law* 19 (Summer 1983);

Edwin Harwood, Can immigration laws be enforced? *Public Interest* 12 (Summer 1983);

Milton D. Morris, *Immigration—The Beleaguered Bureaucracy* (Washington, D.C.: Brookings, 1985);

Leslie R. Prepon, Immigration reform and control: A selective bibliography, *New York University Journal of International Law and Politics* 17 (Summer 1985).

Immigration and Naturalization Service
425 I Street, N.W.
Washington, D.C. 20536
(202) 633–4316

Immigration and Naturalization Service v Chadha *See* VETO, LEGISLATIVE.

Immigration and Naturalization Service v Herman Delgato 80 L.Ed. 247 (1984) The U.S. Supreme Court case that held that it is constitutional for federal agents to conduct "factory surveys" to enforce immigration laws. Such a practice had agents move systematically through a factory, approaching employees and questioning them about their citizenship. If an employee gave a credible reply, the agent moved to another employee. The Court held that the surveys did not result in the seizure of the entire work force and that the individual questioning of the employees did not amount to a detention or seizure under the Fourth Amendment. Justice William Rehnquist said that a "consensual encounter" between a police officer and a citizen could be transformed into a violation of the Fourth Amendment if, in view of all the circumstances surrounding the incident, a reasonable person would have believed that he was not free to leave. This did not happen here, because employees were free to move about in the normal course of their duties. Finally, the Court said that, because there was no seizure of the entire work force, the respondents could litigate only what happened to them, which, based on their own descriptions, were "classic consensual encounters," rather than violations of the Fourth Amendment. This decision means that factory surveys as a standard means of locating illegal aliens can continue, even though critics contend that they have a CHILLING effect on the employment of Hispanics.

REFERENCE

David K. Chan, INS factory raid as nondetentive seizures, *Yale Law Journal* 95 (March 1986).

Immigration Reform and Control Act of 1986 *See* SIMPSON-MAZZOLI BILL.

immunity 1 An exemption from a duty or obligation. For example, foreigners with diplomatic immunity cannot be prosecuted for breaking the laws of their host country; they can only be expelled. 2 An exemption from prosecution granted to persons to force them to testify in a criminal matter without violating their Fifth Amendment protections against self-incrimination. Anyone who refuses to testify to a grand jury or a court after being granted immunity can be held in contempt and be sent to jail until he or she reconsiders. **3** The freedom of governments in the American federal system from being taxed by other governments. **4** An exemption from ordinary legal culpability while holding public office. Government officials generally need some protection against law suits, whether frivolous or not, which might be brought against them by people dissatisfied with their actions or adversely affected by them. Otherwise, government could be brought to a standstill by such suits or be crippled by the threat of them. In general, judges and legislators are well protected by judicial doctrines concerning immunities, whereas police officers, sheriffs, and most public administrators are not. *See also* BARR V MATTEO; BUTZ V ECONOMOU; CITY OF NEWPORT V FACT CONCERTS, INC.; FITZPATRICK V BITZER; GARDNER V BRODERICK; OWEN V CITY OF INDEPENDENCE; SCHEUER V RHODES; SMITH V WADE; SOVEREIGN IMMUNITY; SPALDING V VILAS; WOOD V STRICKLAND.

REFERENCES

3 Maureen Mahoney, Federal immunity from state taxation: A reassessment, *University of Chicago Law Review* 45 (Spring 1978).

4 David H. Rosenbloom, Public administrators' official immunity and the Supreme Court developments during the 1970s, *Public Administration Review* 40 (March/April 1980);

Walter S. Groszyk, Jr., and Thomas J. Madden, Managing without immunity: The challenge for state and local government officials in the 1980s. *Public Administration Review* 41 (March/April 1981);

Janell M. Byrd, Rejecting absolute immunity for federal officials, *California Law Review* 71 (December 1983);

Phillip J. Cooper, The Supreme Court on governmental liability: The nature and origins of sovereign and official immunity, *Administration and Society* 16 (November 1984).

Immunity Act of 1954 The federal law authorizing immunity from criminal prosecution for testimony in criminal cases concerned with national security issues. It was upheld by the U.S. Supreme Court in ULLMAN V UNITED STATES.

immunity bath The granting of immunity from prosecution to a large number of witnesses.

immunity, congressional The immunity of members of the U.S. House of Representatives and the Senate from lawsuits derived from what they say on the floors of the Congress. This limited immunity is established by the "speech and debate" portion of the Constitution, Article I, Section 6, which also holds that they may not be arrested except for "treason, felony and breach of the peace." So they are clearly subject to criminal prosecution, just as any other citizen. Furthermore, what they say in newsletters and press releases is also prosecutable. *Compare to* PRIVILEGE.

immunity, presidential The immunity of the president of the United States from judicial action. There are many reasons for this: case law (*Kendall v U.S.*, 12 Peters 524 [1838]); the futility of prosecuting a person who has the power of pardon; the separation of powers, which asserts that one branch of government is not answerable to another; and the need for the undisturbed exercise of the office of the president. Consequently, the only way to bring a president to account is by impeachment.

REFERENCE

Aviva A. Orenstein, Presidential immunity from civil liability: *Nixon v. Fitzgerald, Cornell Law Review* 68 (January 1983).

immunity, transactional The immunity that prevents a witness from being prosecuted only for the crime about which he or she is specifically being questioned.

immunity, use The immunity that prevents a witness from being prosecuted for any crimes revealed through compelled testimony or leads derived from the testimony. This is the most common form of immunity.

Murray Clark Havens and Dixie Mercer Mc-Neil, Presidents, impeachment, and political accountability, *Presidential Studies Quarterly* 8 (Winter 1978);

Lonnie E. Maness and Richard M. Chestlee, The first attempt at presidential impeachment: Partisan politics and intra-party conflict at loose, *Presidential Studies Quarterly* 10 (Winter 1980);

Brian R. Fry and John S. Stolarek, The impeachment process: Predispositions and votes, *Journal of Politics* 42 (November 1980);

Brian R. Fry and John S. Stolarek, The Nixon impeachment vote: A speculative analysis, *Presidential Studies Quarterly* 11 (Summer 1981).

impeachment A quasi-judicial process for removing public officials from office. Impeachment is the beginning of the process by which the president, vice president, federal judges, and all civil officials of the United States may be removed from office if convicted of the charges brought against them. Officials may be impeached for treason, bribery, and other high crimes and misdemeanors. The U.S. House of Representatives has the sole authority to bring charges of impeachment (by a simple majority vote), and the Senate has the sole authority to try impeachment charges. An official may be removed from office only upon conviction, which requires a two-thirds vote of the Senate. The Constitution provides that the chief justice shall preside when the president is being tried for impeachment. Only two presidents have ever been charged with impeachable offenses by the House: Andrew Johnson in 1868 (he was acquitted by the Senate) and Richard Nixon in 1974 (his resignation stopped the impeachment process).

REFERENCES

Raoul Berger, *Impeachment: The Constitutional Problems* (Cambridge, MA: Harvard University Press, 1973);

Michael Les Benedict, A new look at the impeachment of Andrew Johnson, *Political Science Quarterly* 88 (September 1973);

The Impeachment of President Andrew Johnson

[In 1867] Congress passed the Tenure of Office Act, which required congressional consent for the removal of any government officer whose appointment required congressional approval. The Republicans chiefly wanted to protect Secretary of War Edwin Stanton, a Lincoln appointee and the only member of Johnson's cabinet to support congressional Reconstruction. As commander of the armed forces in the South, Stanton could do much to prevent Johnson from frustrating congressional Reconstruction. The Congress also required the president to issue orders to the army through General Ulysses S. Grant, who also supported a more radical reconstruction. In effect, the Congress was attempting to reconstruct the presidency as well as the South. A crisis was clearly at hand.

In August 1867, after the Congress adjourned, Johnson made his move. He fired Stanton and replaced him with Grant on a temporary basis, hoping Grant would be more cooperative. He next placed four Republican generals—who commanded Southern districts, including Philip H. Sheridan, Grant's favorite cavalry general.

Johnson had misjudged Grant, who wrote a letter protesting the president's thwarting of the Congress and leaked it to the press. After the Congress overruled Stanton's suspension, Grant resigned, allowing Stanton to resume his office. Johnson's public protests against Grant's resignation led Grant to emerge openly as an enemy of the president.

Johnson decided to test, unequivocally, the constitutionality of the power granted to the Congress by the Tenure of Office Act. In February 1868, he again dismissed Stanton.

Stanton barricaded the door of his office, refusing to admit the replacement whom Johnson had appointed. Republicans in the Congress responded by charging the president with criminal misconduct in office. The Constitution gave the House the power to impeach—to charge formally—federal officials for "Treason, Bribery, or other high Crimes and Misdemeanors," and the Senate the power to convict them, with a two-thirds majority needed in each house. But impeachment and conviction were drastic steps; the Congress had removed federal judges from office, but never before had it seriously considered removing a president. After a year of political struggle, on February 24, 1868, radicals and moderates in the House joined to impeach the president. A radical-dominated committee was appointed to bring to the Senate charges of "high crimes and misdemeanors" against Johnson; it concentrated on alleged violations of the Tenure of Office Act.

The Senate, acting as a court, failed to convict Johnson. On May 26, after deliberating for eleven weeks, thirty-five senators voted for conviction—one vote short of the two-thirds required. Seven moderate Republicans had broken ranks, voting with 12 Democrats in support of Johnson. These Republicans reached their decision partly because they feared Benjamin Wade, the radical Republican who, as president pro tempore of the Senate, was next in the line of succession. Primarily, they worried about the precedent of the Congress deposing a president over an issue of policy. They believed that the Civil War had demonstrated the need for a strong federal government administered by a powerful executive. Without a strong presidency, the moderate Republicans doubted whether the nation could preserve internal unity, advance the Republican economic program, and defend itself against foreign enemies. The radical Republicans had failed to convict Johnson, but they had defeated him. For the remainder of his term, Johnson let Reconstruction proceed under congressional direction.

Source: James A. Henretta, W. Elliot Brownlee, David Brody, and Susan Ware, *America's History* (Chicago: Dorsey, 1987), pp. 488–89.

imperial presidency   *See* PRESIDENCY, IMPERIAL.

implied power   That authority not explicitly granted by the U.S. Constitution but inferred, based on a broad interpretation of other expressed or enumerated powers. The notion of implied power was first given voice in the case of *McCulloch v Maryland*, 4 Wheaton 316 (1819), when Chief Justice John Marshall wrote: "Let the end be legitimate, let it be within the scope of the Constitution, and all means which are appropriate, which are plainly adapted to that end, which are not prohibited, but consist with the letter and the spirit of the Constitution are constitutional."

import duty   *See* DUTY.

impoundment   A tactic available to fiscal strategists—the withholding by the executive branch of funds authorized and appropriated by law. There are several types of impoundment decisions. The earliest example traces back to Thomas Jefferson, who impounded funds designed to finance gunboats for the Mississippi River. A primary and accepted mode of impoundment is for emergencies, as in the case of war. President Franklin D. Roosevelt impounded funds slated for numerous programs that were "superseded" by the events of late 1941. Another mode of impoundment is to confiscate funds when the program objective has been accomplished. Presidents Dwight D. Eisenhower and Harry S Truman both made use of impoundment to take back "extra" funds from programs whose objectives had been met or were clearly not in need of funds. Another mode of impoundment is for legal compliance. President Lyndon B. Johnson impounded funds and threatened to impound other funds for local governments and school districts in violation of the Civil Rights Act or federal court orders.

The case for fiscal impoundment was made by the Richard M. Nixon administration as being necessary for economic stabilization and to enable the president to accomplish his legal responsibilities under the Employment Act of 1946. However, fiscal impoundment really amounts to a form of line-item veto. Several state governments empower their governors with the right to specify a budgetary figure for each program in the budget; if the legislature exceeds the recommended sum, the governor may veto any legislatively added sum above the original recommendation. Of course, any cuts made by the legislature are binding. However, the line-item veto is not an executive power granted by either the U.S. Constitution or by subsequent legislation.

The arguments in favor of impoundment made by the Nixon administration focused on the difficulties that the executive had in planning a budget (based on the revenue estimates) and then having the Congress essentially tack on twenty to thirty billion dollars more for "favorite programs." As a direct result of the impoundment controversy, the Congress set up its own parallel budget machinery in 1974 under the Congressional Budget and Impoundment Control Act. Significant for fiscal policy is the fact that the act established a new congressional budget process requiring the Congress to set a maximum limit (recognizing the fiscal implications) and to make the various subcommittees keep the total final budget under that ceiling. Of course, this doesn't prevent the Congress from establishing a very high ceiling, but it does force it to face the total fiscal issue directly.

The ad hoc impoundments of the Nixon administration were repeatedly rejected by the federal courts when they were challenged. Now Title X of the Congressional Budget and Impoundment Control Act provides for two kinds of legal impoundments: (1) deferrals which are presidential decisions not to spend funds until a later date and (2) rescissions which are presidential decisions not to spend funds at all. Both deferrals and rescissions must also be approved by Congress. *See also* AMERICAN FEDERATION OF GOVERNMENT EMPLOYEES V PHILLIPS.

REFERENCES
Louis Fisher, Funds impounded by the president: The constitutional issue, *George Washington Law Review* 38 (July 1970);
Louis Fisher, The politics of impounded funds, *Administrative Science Quarterly* 15 (September 1970);
Vivian Vale, The obligation to spend: Presidential impoundment of congressional appropriations, *Political Studies* 25 (December 1977).

impoundment resolution A resolution by either the U.S. House of Representatives or the Senate that expresses disapproval of a proposed rescission or deferral of budget authority. Whenever all or part of any budget authority provided by the Congress is deferred, the president is required to transmit a special message to the Congress describing the deferrals. Either house may, at any time, pass a resolution disapproving this deferral of budget authority, thus requiring that the funds be made available for obligation. When no congressional action is taken, deferrals may remain in effect until, but not beyond, the end of the fiscal year.

inalienable rights Rights derived from natural law, which all people have and which cannot be taken away or transferred. Thomas Jefferson, influenced by John Locke, asserted in the Declaration of Independence "that all men are created equal, that they are endowed by their Creator with certain inalienable rights, that among them are life, liberty, and the pursuit of happiness."
REFERENCES
Gary D. Glenn, Inalienable rights and positive government in the modern world, *Journal of Politics* 41 (November 1979);
A. John Simmons, Inalienable rights and Locke's *Treatises, Philosophy and Public Affairs* 12 (Summer 1983);
Gary D. Glenn, Inalienable rights and Locke's argument for limited government: Political implications of a right to suicide, *Journal of Politics* 46 (February 1984);
Diana T. Meyers, *Inalienable Rights: A Defense* (New York: Columbia University Press, 1985).

inaugural address The speech that a political executive makes upon being sworn into office. These speeches are often used to set a tone for an administration. President Abraham Lincoln used his in 1861 to appeal to "the better angels of our nature." President Franklin D. Roosevelt used his in 1933 to remind the nation that " the only thing we have to fear is fear itself." President John F. Kennedy used his in 1961 to tell Americans to "ask what you can do for your country." All new executives, presidents, governors, and mayors try to make their inaugural addresses memorable. Few succeed.
REFERENCES
Edward W. Chester, Beyond the rhetoric: A new look at presidential inaugural addresses, *Presidential Studies Quarterly* 10 (Fall 1980);

Edward W. Chester, Shadow or substance?
Critiquing Reagan's inaugural address,
Presidential Studies Quarterly 11 (Spring
1981);

Dante Germino, *Inaugural Addresses of American Presidents: The Public Philosophy of
Rhetoric* (Lanham, MD: University Press of
America, 1984).

inauguration   The heralding into office of a
chief executive with a formal ceremony, which
includes taking an oath of office. The word is
derived from an ancient Roman practice before
a new governor took office: the augurs (the diviners and prophets) would study the movements of birds to foretell the future of the
administration. Today, this function is performed by political columnists and television
commentators—and the birds are left alone.

in camera   1 A Latin phrase meaning in
chambers; in a judge's office.   2 Any judicial
proceeding conducted in private.

income tax   *See* TAX, PERSONAL INCOME.

Income Tax Amendment   *See* SIXTEENTH
AMENDMENT.

incompetence   The demonstrated failure of
an employee or policy maker to meet minimum standards of job performance. Unless incompetence is gross, it is difficult to prove,
especially when it involves judgments by
professional organizations that may have to follow established procedures. Barbara W. Tuchman in a September 20, 1987 *New York Times
Magazine* article, "A Nation in Decline?" defines incompetence as "sloppy and ragged performance that ends in unwanted result." She
further classifies incompetence into two categories: (1) "the inability to accomplish a given
task without making a mess of it," and
(2) "poor thinking—also known as stupidity."

REFERENCES

For the classic analysis of why such people
manage to hang in there despite their poor
performance, see William J. Goode, The
protection of the inept, *American Sociological Review* 32 (February 1967).

For how to remove incompetents in the federal
service, see *The Other Side of the Merit
Coin: Removals for Incompetence in the Federal Service* (Washington, D.C.: U.S. Merit
Systems Protection Board, 1982).

For dealing with incompetent lawyers, see
William W. Schwarzer, Dealing with incompetent counsel: The trial judge's role,
Harvard Law Review 93 (February 1980).

incorporation   1 The creation of a government corporation by a legislature.   2 The creation of a private corporate entity by following
procedures called for in applicable state law.
The corporation then created becomes a legal
entity, an artificial person, subject to legal
action.   3 The selective application of the protections of the federal Bill of Rights to the
states. This nationalization of many of the provisions of the Bill of Rights was accomplished
mostly through the due process clause of the
Fourteenth Amendment. The incorporation
doctrine overcame the U.S. Supreme Court's
ruling in *Barron v Baltimore,* 7 Peters 243
(1833), that the Bill of Rights limited only the
actions of the federal government, not those of
individual state governments.

**Chronological Record of the
Incorporation of the Bill of Rights**

Year	Issue: Amendment	Case
1897	Eminent Domain: Fifth	*Chicago, Burlington and Quincy RR v Chicago,* 166 U.S. 226
1925	Speech and press: First	*Gitlow v New York,* 268 U.S. 652
1927	Speech: First	*Fiske v Kansas,* 274 U.S. 380
1931	Press: First	*Near v Minnesota,* 283 U.S. 687

Year	Issue: Amendment	Case
1932	Counsel in capital criminal cases: Sixth	*Powell v Alabama*, 287 U.S. 45
1934	Free exercise of religions: First	*Hamilton v Regents of the University of California*, 293 U.S. 245
1937	Assembly and petition: First	*De Jonge v Oregon*, 299 U.S. 253
1947	Separation of church and state: First	*Everson v Board of Education of Ewing Township, New Jersey*, 330 U.S. 1
1948	Public trial: Sixth	*In re Oliver*, 333 U.S. 257
1961	Unreasonable searches and seizures: Fourth (exclusionary rule)*	*Mapp v Ohio*, 367 U.S. 643
1962	Cruel and unusual punishment: Eighth	*Robinson v California*, 370 U.S. 660
1963	Counsel in all criminal cases: Sixth†	*Gideon v Wainwright*, 372 U.S. 335
1964	Compulsory self-incrimination: Fifth	*Malloy v Hogan*, 378 U.S. 1; *Murphy v Waterfront Commission of New York Harbor*, 378 U.S. 52
1965	Confrontation of hostile witnesses: Sixth	*Pointer v Texas*, 380 U.S. 400
1966	Impartial jury: Sixth	*Parker v Gladden*, 385 U.S. 363
1967	Confrontation of favorable witnesses: Sixth	*Washington v Texas*, 388 U.S. 14
1967	Speedy trial: Sixth	*Klopfer v North Carolina*, 386 U.S. 213
1968	Jury trial in nonpetty criminal cases: Sixth	*Duncan v Louisiana*, 391 U.S. 145
1969	Double jeopardy: Fifth	*Colgrove v Battin*, 413 U.S. 149

*In theory, the Fourth had been incorporated earlier in *Wolf v Colorado*, 338 U.S. 25 (1949)—but not in reality. It took *Mapp* to do it.

†Extended even to incarcerable offenses in petty criminal cases in a nine to zero holding in *Argersinger v Hamlin*, 407 U.S. 25 (1972).

Source: Adapted from William J. Keefe, Henry J. Abraham, William H. Flanigan, Charles O. Jones, Morris S. Ogul, and John W. Spanier, *American Democracy: Institutions, Politics, and Policies*, 2d ed. (Chicago: Dorsey, 1986), p. 72.

incrementalism **1** An approach to decision making in government in which policymakers begin with the current situation, consider a limited number of changes in that situation based upon a restricted range of alternatives, and test those changes by instituting them one at a time. The contrast to incrementalism is a more radically oriented decision-making process (*see, for example*, BUDGETING, ZERO-BASED). Incrementalism is an especially important aspect of BUDGETING. **2** A normative theory of government that views policymaking as a process of bargaining and competition involving the participation of people with conflicting points of view. *See also* CHARLES E. LINDBLOM.

REFERENCES

John J. Bailey and Robert J. O'Connor, Operationalizing incrementalism: Measuring the muddles, *Public Administration Review* 35 (January/February 1975);

Bruce Adams, The limitations of muddling through: Does anyone in Washington really think anymore? *Public Administration Review* 39 (November/December 1979).

incumbency effect The overwhelming advantage of political incumbents in a contest for reelection. Short of a major scandal, voters tend to be more comfortable supporting a familiar name. This is all the more true for legislators of long standing who have had the opportunity to do considerable casework for their constituents.

REFERENCES

Jim Seroka, Incumbency and reelection: Governors versus U.S. Senators, *State Government* 53 (Summer 1980);

John R. Alford and John R. Hibbing, Increased incumbency advantage in the House, *Journal of Politics* 43 (November 1981);

Keith Krehbiel and John R. Wright, The incumbency effect in congressional elections: A test of two explanations, *American Journal of Political Science* 27 (February 1983);

Peter Tuckel, Length of incumbency and the reelection chances of U.S. senators, *Legislative Studies Quarterly* 8 (May 1983);

James E. Campbell, The return of the incumbents: The nature of the incumbency advantage, *Western Political Quarterly* 36 (September 1983);

Keith S. Henry and Michael J. Scicchitano, Congressional perquisites and incumbent safety, *Journal of Political Science* 12 (Spring 1985).

Advantages of the Incumbent in U.S. House Elections: A Comparison of Incumbents with Their Challengers

- Three times as many voters recall the incumbent's name.
- Twice as many voters recognize the incumbent's name.
- Twice as many voters have had some contact with the incumbent.
- Five times as many voters have met the incumbent personally.
- Six times as many voters have attended a meeting where the incumbent spoke.
- Four times as many voters have received mail from the incumbent.
- Twice as many voters have read about the incumbent.
- Twice as many voters have heard the incumbent on radio or seen him or her on television.
- Five times as many voters report liking something about the incumbent.

Source: Adapted from William J. Keefe, Henry J. Abraham, William H. Flanigan, Charles O. Jones, Morris S. Ogul, and John W. Spanier, *American Democracy: Institutions, Politics, and Policies*, 2d ed. (Chicago: Dorsey, 1986), p. 207.

---

incumbent The person serving in a position at present. John Kenneth Galbraith observed in *The New Industrial State* (Boston: Houghton Mifflin, 1967) that "between being in and out of political office the difference is not slight. It is total."

independent A registered voter who does not declare an affiliation with a political party. Since the overwhelming majority of a party's members will vote for the party's candidate in the general election, many a political contest is a fight for the support of the independent voters. About one third of all voters describe themselves as independents; some, of course, are undercover partisans.

REFERENCE

Hugh L. Leblanc and Mary Beth Merrin, Independents, issue partisanship and the decline of party, *American Politics Quarterly* 7 (April 1979).

independent agency/regulatory commission A federal executive agency not included in an executive department or within the Executive Office of the President. Some, such as the Smithsonian Institution, are of long standing. Many others have been created in this century, as the responsibilities of government have increased. A regulatory commission is an independent agency established by the U.S. Congress to regulate some aspect of U.S. economic life. Among these are the Securities and

Exchange Commission and the Interstate Commerce Commission. Such agencies are, of course, not independent of the U.S. government. They are subject to the laws under which they operate as these laws are enacted and amended by the Congress. Independent agencies and regulatory commissions can be divided into those units under the direct supervision and guidance of the president, and therefore responsible to him, and those not under such supervision and guidance, and therefore not responsible to him. The units in the first group can be categorized as independent executive agencies, while those in the second group can be subdivided into independent regulatory commissions and government-sponsored enterprises.

Independent executive agencies, with rare exceptions, are headed by single administrators appointed by the president and confirmed by the Senate. These administrators serve at the pleasure of the president and can be removed by him at any time. In addition, they must submit their budget requests to the Office of Management and Budget (OMB), which is located within the Executive Office of the President, for review and clearance. Examples of independent executive agencies include the Environmental Protection Agency, the General Services Administration, the Small Business Administration, and the Veterans Administration.

Independent regulatory commissions (such as the ICC) and government-sponsored enterprises (such as the TVA) are bodies headed by several commissioners, directors, or governors, also appointed by the president and confirmed by the Senate. Unlike administrators of independent executive agencies, they serve for fixed terms and cannot be removed at the pleasure of the president. While all of the independent regulatory commissions and most of the government-sponsored enterprises submit their budget requests to the OMB for review and clearance, the degree of dependence on these budgets varies considerably. Nearly all of the government-sponsored enterprises generate a considerable part of their financial resources from outside sources, while the independent regulatory commissions (except for the Federal Reserve Board and the Federal Home Loan Bank Board) rely on the government for their funding. Those units subject to periodic authorization and appropriations hearings (all of the independent executive agencies and independent regulatory commissions and most of the government-sponsored enterprises) must undergo a review of their activities at those congressional hearings. Note that many regulatory functions are also performed by regular cabinet departments. For example, the Food and Drug Administration is located within the Department of Health and Human Services and there is a Food Safety and Inspection Service within the Department of Agriculture. *Compare to* REGULATION.

REFERENCES

Marver Bernstein, *Regulating Business by Independent Commissions* (Princeton, NJ: Princeton University Press, 1955);

Louis M. Kohlmeier, Jr., *The Regulators, Watchdog Agencies and the Public Interest* (New York: Harper & Row, 1969);

William L. Cary, *Politics and the Regulatory Agencies* (New York: McGraw-Hill, 1967);

Roger G. Noll, *Reforming Regulation* (Washington, D.C.: Brookings, 1971);

David M. Welborn and Anthony E. Brown, Power and politics in federal regulatory commissions, *Administration and Society* 12 (May 1980);

William E. Brigman, The executive branch and the independent regulatory agencies, *Presidential Studies Quarterly* 11 (Spring 1981);

Joseph Stewart, Jr., James E. Anderson, and Zona Taylor, Presidential and congressional support for "independent" regulatory commissions: Implications of the budgetary process, *Western Political Quarterly* 35 (September 1982);

Jeffrey E. Cohen, Presidential control of independent regulatory commissions through appointment: The case of the ICC, *Administration and Society* 17 (May 1985).

independent candidate An aspirant for political office who is not affiliated with a political party.

independent counsel A euphemism for a special prosecutor. *See* PROSECUTOR, SPECIAL.

independent expenditure Payment for political advertising expressly advocating the election or defeat of a clearly identified candidate for federal office and which expenditure is not made with the cooperation of, or in consultation with, the supported candidate or his or her agents. Individuals, groups, and political action committees may support candidates by making independent expenditures on their behalf without limit, according to the FEDERAL ELECTION CAMPAIGN ACT.

indexing A system by which salaries, pensions, welfare payments, and other kinds of income are automatically adjusted to account for inflation.
REFERENCES
Robert S. Kaplan, *Indexing Social Security: An Analysis of the Issues* (Washington, D.C.: American Enterprise, 1977);
Geoffrey Brennan, Inflation, taxation, and indexation, *Policy Studies Journal* 5 (Spring 1977);
John L. Knapp and Philip J. Grossman, Indexation of state income taxes, *State Government* 54:2 (1981).

Indiana ballot *See* BALLOT, INDIANA.

indictment 1 A formal written accusation submitted to a court by a grand jury, alleging that a specified person has committed a specified crime, usually a felony. 2 Any accusation of wrongdoing.

indirect tax *See* TAX, DIRECT/INDIRECT TAX.

industrial democracy *See* DEMOCRACY, INDUSTRIAL.

industrial policy Government regulation of industrial planning and production through law, tax incentives, and subsidies. The United States does not have a comprehensive industrial policy, compared to other nations, especially Japan, whose government exercises considerable control over industrial planning and decision making. This is because of traditional American abhorrence of central planning, which is associated with communism and considered the antithesis of the free enterprise system. But because of increasing economic competition from Japan and other nations, where government and business work cooperatively to advance industrial interests, there is now a considerable debate in the United States over whether the national government should develop a more cohesive and comprehensive industrial policy. *Compare to* COMPETITIVENESS.
REFERENCES
Richard P. Nielsen, Industrial policy: Review and historical perspective, *Public Administration Review* 43 (September/October 1983);
Mel Dubnick and Lynne Holt, Industrial policy and the states, *Publius* 15 (Winter 1985);
William E. Hudson, The feasibility of a comprehensive U.S. industrial policy, *Political Science Quarterly* 100 (Fall 1985).

industrial revolution A very general term that refers to a society's change from an agrarian to an industrial economy. The Industrial Revolution of the Western world is considered to have begun in England in the eighteenth century. The American industrial revolution began in the nineteenth century and is now so complete that many analysts see aspects of the American economy indicative of a POSTINDUSTRIAL SOCIETY. Industrialization means urbanization and a shift in political power from rural to urban interests. This has had innumerable and revolutionary effects on the nature and dimensions of American governance.
REFERENCE
For the case that the industrial revolution actually began much earlier, see Jean Gimpel, *The Industrial Revolution of the Middle Ages* (New York: Holt, Rinehart & Winston, 1976).

industrial union *See* TRADE UNION.

inferior federal courts All federal courts below the U.S. Supreme Court.

inflation, cost-push Inflation caused by increases in the costs of production independent of demand.

inflation/deflation Inflation is a rise in the costs of goods and services equated to a fall in the value of a nation's currency. Deflation is the reverse—a fall in costs and a rise in the value of money. Milton Friedman has observed that "inflation is one form of taxation that can be imposed without legislation."

REFERENCES

Robert J. Gordon, The theory of domestic inflation, *American Economic Review* 67 (February 1977);

Stahrl W. Edmunds, Who pays the costs of inflation? *Policy Studies Journal* 7 (Spring 1979);

Kristen R. Monroe, Inflation and presidential popularity, *Presidential Studies Quarterly* 9 (Summer 1979);

Laurence Whitehead, The political causes of inflation, *Political Studies* 27 (December 1979);

John Case, *Understanding Inflation* (New York: Morrow, 1981);

T. Kristensen, *Inflation and Unemployment in Modern Society* (New York: Praeger, 1981);

Arthur F. Burns, Our inflation in historical perspective, *Atlantic Community Quarterly* 19 (Spring 1981).

Comparative Inflation

Country	Percentage Annual Inflation	
	1983	1985
Argentina	344.0	851.0
Israel	146.0	407.0
Brazil	142.0	220.0
Mexico	102.0	65.0
Italy	14.7	9.3
Britain	4.6	6.1
Canada	5.8	3.7
United States	3.2	3.7
West Germany	3.3	2.5
Japan	1.8	1.6

Source: International Monetary Fund

---

inflation, demand-pull Inflation caused by increased demand, rather than by increases in the cost of production.

inflation, hidden A price increase achieved by selling smaller quantities (or a poorer quality) of a product for the same price as before.

inflation, hyper Inflation so extreme that it practically destroys the value of paper money.

influence industry According to George F. Will, "the expensive, sophisticated, Washington-based lawyer-lobbyist complex that works to make government a servant of the strong."

influence peddler 1 One who claims to have special access to people in power and for a fee will use that access on your behalf. 2 One who offers bribes to public officials on behalf of a third party.

informal congressional groups *See* LEGISLATIVE SERVICE ORGANIZATIONS.

infrastructure 1 A general term for a jurisdiction's fixed assets, such as bridges, highways, tunnels, and water treatment plants. 2 A political party's or a government's administrative structure, the people and processes that make it work. 3 The institutional framework of a society that supports the educational, religious, and social ideology, which in turn supports the political order. 4 The permanent installations and facilities for the support, maintenance, and control of naval, land, or air forces.

REFERENCE

1 David A. Grossman, The infrastructure blues: A tale of New York and other cities, *Governmental Finance* 9 (June 1980).

inherent power *See* POWER, INHERENT.

initiative A procedure that allows citizens, as opposed to legislators, to propose the enactment of state and local laws. An initiative, the proposed new law, is placed on the ballot (often as a proposition) only after the proper filing of a petition containing signatures from 5 to 15 percent of the voters. Fewer than half of the states provide for the initiative. Initiatives are not possible with federal legislation because Article I of the U.S. Constitution prevents the Congress from delegating its legislative responsibilities. *Compare to* REFERENDUM.

REFERENCES

Craig N. Oren, The initiative and referendum's use in zoning, *California Law Review* 64 (January 1976);

initiative, constitutional

Eugene C. Lee, The initiative and referendum: How California has fared, *National Civic Review* 68 (February 1979);

David H. Everson, The effects of initiatives on voter turnout: A comparative state analysis, *Western Political Quarterly* 34 (September 1981).

initiative, constitutional　An initiative proposing to amend a state constitution.

States that Allow for Constitutional Initiatives

- Arizona
- Arkansas
- California
- Colorado
- Florida
- Illinois
- Massachusetts
- Michigan
- Missouri
- Montana
- Nebraska
- Nevada
- North Dakota
- Ohio
- Oklahoma
- Oregon
- South Dakota

---

initiative, direct　A citizen-initiated proposal that must be submitted directly to the voters at a special election or the next general election.

initiative, indirect　A citizen-initiated proposal that must first be submitted to the legislature. It is submitted to the voters only if the legislature rejects it or proposes a substitute measure.

injunction　A court order forbidding specific individuals or groups to perform acts the court considers injurious to the property or other rights of a person or community. There are two basic types of injunctions: (1) a temporary restraining order, which is issued for a limited time prior to a formal hearing; and (2) a permanent injunction, which is issued after a full formal hearing. Once an injunction is in effect, the court has contempt power to enforce its ruling through fines or imprisonment, or both.

REFERENCE
John Leubsdorf, The standard for preliminary injunctions, *Harvard Law Review* 91 (January 1978).

in-kind transfers　A welfare benefit other than cash, such as clothing, food, or food stamps.
REFERENCE
Judith A. Barmack, The case against in-kind transfers: The food stamp program, *Policy Analysis* 3 (Fall 1977).

inner club　*See* SENATE ESTABLISHMENT.

inoperative　Descriptive of a piece of machinery that no longer works and applied to a lie (or possibly a "truth") retracted because it is no longer effective. The word in this context was first used by President Richard M. Nixon's press secretary, Ronald Ziegler, in a 1973 press conference about Watergate, when he said that previous statements about Watergate were inoperative.

in re　A Latin phrase meaning in the matter of; regarding.

In re Debs　*See* DEBS, IN RE.

In re Neagle　*See* NEAGLE, IN RE.

INS　*See* IMMIGRATION AND NATURALIZATION SERVICE.

inspector general　The job title (of military origin) for the administrative head of an inspection or investigative unit of a larger agency.
REFERENCES
Jarold L. Kieffer, The case for an inspector general of the United States, *Bureaucrat* 9 (Summer 1980);

Dan W. Reicher, Conflicts of interest in inspector general, Justice Department, and special prosecutor investigations of agency heads, *Stanford Law Review* 35 (May 1983).

Institute for Social Research (ISR)　An institute established at the University of Michigan in 1946. The ISR conducts research on a broad range of subjects within its four constituent research centers. (1) The Survey Research Center studies primarily large populations, organizations, and special segments of society, and generally uses interview surveys. (2) The Research Center for Group Dynamics seeks to explain the nature of the social forces that affect group behavior, the relations among members, and the activities of the group as a whole. (3) The Center for Research on Utilization of Scientific Knowledge studies the processes required for the full use of research findings and new knowledge. (4) The Center for Political Studies investigates political behavior, focusing on national politics in many countries and maintaining a rich collection of election data.

Institute for Social Research
University of Michigan
426 Thompson Street
Ann Arbor, MI 48109
(313) 764–8363

Institute of Public Administration A private research organization founded in 1906 as the New York Bureau of Municipal Research, it is one of the most influential forces for urban reform and technical innovation in public administration. It provides consultation, technical services, and training in many areas of public administration.

REFERENCE

For a history, see Jane S. Dahlberg, *The New York Bureau of Municipal Research* (New York: New York University Press, 1966).

Institute of Public Administration
55 West 44th Street
New York, NY 10036
(212) 730–5480

institutional discrimination Practices contrary to equal employment opportunity policies, without intent to discriminate. Institutional discrimination (also known as institutional racism) exists whenever a practice or procedure has the effect of treating one group of employees differently from another.

REFERENCES

Neil Gilbert and Harry Specht, Institutional racism, *Urban and Social Change Review* 6 (Fall 1972);

Jenny Williams, Redefining institutional racism, *Ethnic and Racial Studies* 8 (July 1985).

intelligence 1 A person's ability to cope with his or her environment and to deal with mental abstractions. 2 Information. The military, as well as other organizations concerned with national security, use the word thus in its original Latin sense. But intelligence in this context also implies secret or protected information. Courtney Whitney in *MacArthur: His Rendezvous* (New York: Knopf, 1956) quotes General Douglas MacArthur (1880–1964) as saying: "Expect only five per cent of an intelligence report to be accurate. The trick of a good commander is to isolate the five percent."

REFERENCES

Steve Chan, The intelligence of stupidity: Understanding failures in strategic warning, *American Political Science Review* 73 (March 1979);

Stansfield Turner and George Thibault, Intelligence: The right rules, *Foreign Policy* 48 (Fall 1982);

Michael I. Handel, The study of intelligence, *Orbis* 26 (Winter 1983).

intelligence community 1 All the spies in the world; the totality of the employees of the world's civilian and military intelligence agencies. 2 All of a single nation's military and civilian intelligence-gathering agencies. More than forty federal agencies do intelligence work of one kind or another. The leading members of the American intelligence community include the Central Intelligence Agency, the National Security Agency, the Defense Intelligence Agency, the State Department, and the FBI.

REFERENCES

1 Ronald Payne and Christoper Dobson, *Who's Who in Espionage* (New York: St. Martin's, 1984).

2 William J. Casey, The American intelligence community, *Presidential Studies Quarterly* 12 (Spring 1982);

Stephen J. Flanagan, Managing the intelligence community, *International Security* 10 (Summer 1985).

intelligence oversight The review of the policies and activities of intelligence agencies, such as the CIA, by the appropriate congressional committees. This was not formally done by the Congress until the 1970s, when reports of FBI and CIA abuses of their operating mandates encouraged the Congress to move carefully, systematically, and formally to watch over them.

REFERENCES

Barry Goldwater, Congress and intelligence oversight, *Washington Quarterly* 6 (Summer 1983);

Loch K. Johnson, Legislative reform of intelligence policy, *Polity* 17 (Spring 1985);

Loch K. Johnson, *A Season of Inquiry: Congress and Intelligence* (Chicago, IL: The Dorsey Press, 1988).

intelligence, strategic   Information gathered by intelligence agencies that can be used for formulating a nation's diplomatic and military policies; it is long range and widely focused, as opposed to tactical intelligence, which is short range and narrowly focused.

REFERENCES

Harry Howe Ransom, Strategic intelligence, *Proceedings of the Academy of Political Science* 34:4 (1982);

Loch Johnson, Seven sins of strategic intelligence, *World Affairs* 146 (Fall 1983).

interest   **1** A benefit or advantage that one seeks to gain through the political process. **2** The extra money a person or institution receives in return for lending money to another person; money paid for the use of money. **3** Engagement in an occupation or profession that influences one's attitudes toward other social, economic, or political actions.   **4** A right to something, whether it's an intangible, such as freedom, or concrete, such as half ownership in a cement factory.   **5** A group of persons who share a common cause, which puts them into political competition with other groups or interests. Thus the oil interests want better tax breaks for the oil industry; and the consumer interests want new laws protecting consumer rights vis-à-vis the business interests, who want fewer laws protecting consumer rights.

REFERENCES

Theodore M. Benditt, The concept of interest in political theory, *Political Theory* 3 (August 1975);

Grenville Wall, The concept of interest in politics, *Politics and Society* 5:4 (1975).

interest group liberalism   A theory of policymaking (most associated with Theodore J. Lowi) maintaining that public authority is parceled out to private interest groups and results in a weak, decentralized government incapable of long-range planning. Powerful interest groups operate to promote private goals but do not compete to promote the public interest. Government becomes, not an institution that makes hard choices among conflicting values, but a holding company for interests. These interests are promoted by alliances of interest groups, relevant government agencies, and the appropriate congressional committees in each issue area. *See also* COZY TRIANGLES/IRON TRIANGLES; PLURALISM.

REFERENCES

Major works expounding this view are Grant McConnell, *Private Power and American Democracy* (New York: Knopf, 1966);

Theodore J. Lowi, *The End of Liberalism*, 2d ed. (New York: Norton, 1979).

interest group theory   A theory based on the premise that individuals function primarily through groups and that these groups act as appropriate and necessary to further group goals (based on common interests). The group process, including formulation of group objectives and development of specific group actions and response, is seen as a fundamental characteristic of the political process.

The significance of groups in the political process has been recognized for over two-thousand years: Aristotle noted that political associations were both significant and commonplace because of the "general advantages" members obtained. One of the first specific references to groups in the American political process was James Madison's famous discussion of factions in Federalist #10. In Madison's view, the group was inherent in the nature of people, and its causes were unremovable. The only choice then was to control the effects of group pressure and power. A more elaborate discussion of group theory can be traced to John C. Calhoun's treatise on governance, *A Disquisition on Government* (1853). While essentially an argument for the protection of minority interests, the treatise suggested that ideal governance must deal with all interest groups, since they represent the legitimate interests of the citizens. If all groups participated on some level of parity within the policymaking process, then all individual interests would be recognized by the policymakers.

While the work of Calhoun represents the development of early group theory, modern political science group theory has taken greater impetus from the work of ARTHUR F. BENTLEY. But it remained for DAVID B. TRUMAN and Earl Latham (1907–1977) to conceptualize the theoretical implications of group action and to begin assembling a theory of the group process. Truman's principal work—*The Governmental Process* (New York: Knopf, 1951)—viewed group interaction as the real determinant of public policy, the primary focal point of study, in his view.

Earl Latham's *The Group Basis of Politics* (Ithaca, NY: Cornell University Press, 1952) was particularly significant, because of his conceptualization that government itself is a group just like the various private groups attempting to access the policy process. Latham ascribed to government the same characteristics and concern for power associated with all organized private groups. He contended that the basic structure of the political community is associational. The state or political community will establish "norms of permissible behavior in group relations and enforce these norms." In essence, the state becomes more than a referee between groups in conflict, because it is also developing goals as well as overseeing activity.

Latham viewed the legislature as the referee of the group struggle, responsible for "ratifying the victories of the successful coalitions and recording the terms of the surrenders, compromises, and conquests in the form of statutes." The function of the bureaucrat is quite different, however. They are like "armies of occupation left in the field to police the rule won by the victorious coalition." Although Latham's description was aimed primarily at regulatory agencies, he saw the bureaucrat being deluged by the losing coalitions of groups for more favorable actions despite the general rules established. The result is that "regulatory agen-

cies are constantly besought and importuned to interpret their authorities in favor of the very groups for the regulation of which they were originally granted." (E. E. Schattschneider in *The Semisovereign People* [New York: Holt, Rinehart & Winston, 1960] challenged Latham's assumption that the results of political conflict can be analyzed so facilely: "To assume that the forces in a political situation could be diagrammed as a physicist might diagram the resultant of opposing physical forces is to wipe the slate clean of all remote, general and public considerations for the protection of which civil societies have been instituted.")

Latham distinguished three types of groups, based on phases of development: incipient, conscious, and organized. An incipient group is one "where the interest exists but is not recognized" by the potential members; a conscious group is one "in which the community sense exists but which has not become organized"; and finally an organized group is "a conscious group which has established an objective and formal apparatus to promote the common interest." Latham's incipient and conscious groups are essentially the same as David B. Truman's potential groups, which always exist but don't come together until there is a felt need for action on an issue.

The concept of potential groups keeps the bureaucratic policymaking process honest (or perhaps balanced), given the possibility that new groups might surface or some issues may influence decision making. The potential groups concept also serves as a counterargument to the claim that group theory is undemocratic. Once the concept of potential group is married to the active role of organized groups, the claim can be made, in David Truman's words, that "all interests of society by definition are taken into account in one form or another by the institutions of government." *See also* PRESSURE GROUP; LOBBY.

REFERENCES

G. David Garson, On the origins of interest-group theory: A critique of the process, *American Political Science Review* 68 (December 1974);

Terry M. Moe, Toward a broader view of interest groups, *Journal of Politics* 43 (May 1981);

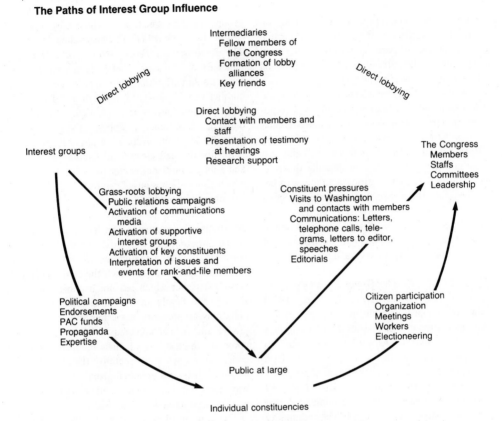

The Paths of Interest Group Influence

Intermediaries
Fellow members of
the Congress
Formation of lobby
alliances
Key friends

Direct lobbying

Direct lobbying

Direct lobbying
Contact with members and
staff
Presentation of testimony
at hearings
Research support

Interest groups

The Congress
Members
Staffs
Committees
Leadership

Grass-roots lobbying
Public relations campaigns
Activation of communications
media
Activation of supportive
interest groups
Activation of key constituents
Interpretation of issues and
events for rank-and-file members

Constituent pressures
Visits to Washington
and contacts with members
Communications: Letters,
telephone calls, tele-
grams, letters to editor,
speeches
Editorials

Political campaigns
Endorsements
PAC funds
Propaganda
Expertise

Citizen participation
Organization
Meetings
Workers
Electioneering

Public at large

Individual constituencies

Source: William J. Keefe, Henry J. Abraham, William H. Flanigan, Charles O. Jones, Morris S. Ogul, and John W. Spanier, *American Democracy: Institutions, Politics, and Policies*, 2d ed. (Chicago: Dorsey, 1986), p. 286.

W. Douglas Costain and Anne N. Costain, Interest groups as policy aggregators in the legislative process, *Polity* 14 (Winter 1981);

Michael T. Hayes, *Lobbyists and Legislators* (New Brunswick, NJ: Rutgers University Press, 1981);

Charles W. Wiggins and William P. Browne, Interest groups and public policy within a state legislative setting, *Polity* 14 (Spring 1982);

Jack L. Walker, The origins and maintenance of interest groups in America, *American Political Science Review* 77 (June 1983);

Jeffrey M. Berry, *The Interest Group Society* (Boston: Little, Brown, 1984);

Glenn Abney and Thomas P. Lauth, Interest group influence in city policymaking: The

views of administrators, *Western Political Quarterly* 38 (March 1985);

James L. Franke and Douglas Dobson, Interest groups: The problem of representation, *Western Political Quarterly* 38 (June 1985);

Allan J. Cigler and Burdett A. Loomis, eds., *Interest Group Politics*, 2d ed. (Washington, D.C.: Congressional Quarterly, 1986).

interface 1 Any common boundary between things. For example, in tailoring it refers to a fabric that is placed between two other fabrics to give them body and shape. 2 The point of contact, or the boundary between organizations, people, jobs, or systems. Nowadays, the verbose politician does not mix with or visit with constituents; he or she has the pleasure of interfacing with them. During the Jimmy Carter administration, Vice President Walter Mondale observed: "In the Senate, you have friends; in the executive, you interface."

REFERENCE

Josef C. Brada, The interface of different systems: The United States and communist countries, *Annals of the American Academy of Political and Social Science* 460 (March 1982).

intergovernmental expenditure An amount paid to other governments as political, fiscal, or programmatic aid in the form of shared revenues and grants-in-aid, as reimbursements for performance of general government activities, and for specific services for the paying government (e.g., care of prisoners and contractual research), or in lieu of taxes. *See also* FEDERALISM, FISCAL.

intergovernmental relations (IGR) The political, fiscal, programmatic, and administrative processes by which higher units of government share revenues and other resources with lower units of government, generally accompanied by special conditions that the lower units must satisfy as prerequisites to receiving the assistance. *See also* ADVISORY COMMISSION ON INTERGOVERNMENTAL RELATIONS; FEDERALISM.

REFERENCES

W. Brook Graves, *American Intergovernmental Relations: Their Origins, Historical Development and Current Status* (New York: Scribner, 1964);

David J. Kennedy, The law of appropriateness: An approach to a general theory of intergovernmental relations, *Public Administration Review* 32 (March/April 1972);

Donald H. Haider, *When Governments Come to Washington: Governors, Mayors and Intergovernmental Lobbying* (New York: Free Press, 1974);

Deil S. Wright, *Understanding Intergovernmental Relations*, 2d ed. (Monterey, CA: Brooks/Cole, 1982);

Richard H. Leach, ed., *Intergovernmental Relations in the 1980s* (New York: Dekker, 1983).

intergovernmental revenue Amounts received from other governments as fiscal aid in the form of shared revenues and grants-in-aid, as reimbursements for performance of general government functions, and specific services for the paying government (e.g., care of prisoners and contractual research), or in lieu of taxes.

The U.S. Geological Survey, part of DOI, produces topographic maps of the entire country. Here, a detail of Acadia National Park.

Interior, U.S. Department of the (DOI) The cabinet-level federal agency created in 1849. It was chiefly responsible for the westward expansion of the nation and the control of the distribution of public lands and resources. For much of its history, it was a center of controversy over corruption and opportunism, as well as, with the War Department, the sometimes brutal control of the Indian inhabitants and their various removals from opening territories. As the nation's principal conservation agency, Interior has responsibility for most of our nationally owned public lands and natural resources; it also has a major responsibility for American Indian reservation communities and for people who live in island territories under U.S. administration. *Compare to* CONSERVATION.

U.S. Department of the Interior
C Street between 18th and 19th streets, N.W.
Washington, D.C. 20240
(202) 343–3171

interlocking directorate 1 Several people serving as directors of the same companies. Federal and state laws limit the extent of interlocking in certain industries and between certain types of businesses. Also, courts look more closely at deals between companies with common directors than at other deals. 2 A pejorative reference to a managerial elite that exercises more power than it should. Abusive interlocking directorates, the systems for assuring common interests and control among managers of related firms, led to the antitrust movement.

REFERENCES

Beth Mintz and Michael Schwartz, Interlocking directorates and interest group formation, *American Sociological Review* 46 (December 1981);

Floyd David Russell III, Interlocking directorates among banks and nonbanking institutions, *Journal of Legislation* 9 (Summer 1982);

William G. Roy, The unfolding of the interlocking directorate structure of the United States, *American Sociological Review* 48 (April 1983).

Internal Revenue Service (IRS) The federal agency, established in 1862 within the Treasury Department, responsible for administering and enforcing the internal revenue laws, except those relating to alcohol, tobacco, firearms, and explosives (which are the responsibility of the Bureau of Alcohol, Tobacco and Firearms). The IRS mission is to encourage and to achieve the highest possible degree of voluntary COMPLIANCE with the tax laws and regulations. Basic IRS activities include taxpayer service and education; determination, assessment, and collection of taxes; determination of pension plan qualifications and exempt organization status; and preparation and issuance of rulings and regulations to supplement the provisions of the Internal Revenue Code. The IRS is the largest controller of information about financial information on private citizens. The potential for abuse of this data and of the tax system is ever present. For example, there were major scandals about using the IRS for political purposes in both the Harry S Truman and Richard M. Nixon administrations.

Internal Revenue Service
111 Constitution Avenue, N.W.
Washington, D.C. 20224
(202) 566–5000

Internal Security Act of 1950 *See* ALBERTSON V SUBVERSIVE ACTIVITIES CONTROL BOARD.

International Bank for Reconstruction and Development (IBRD)/World Bank A sister organization to the INTERNATIONAL MONETARY FUND. Created as a result of the 1944 Bretton Woods Conference, the World Bank began its operations in 1946. Its purpose, after initially emphasizing the reconstruction of Europe after World War II, has been both to lend funds at commercial rates and to provide technical assistance to facilitate economic development in the developing countries.

REFERENCES

William Ascher, New development approaches and the adaptability of international agencies: The case of the World Bank, *International Organization* 37 (Summer 1983);

Richard Swedberg, The doctrine of economic neutrality of the IMF and the World Bank, *Journal of Peace Research* 23 (December 1986).

World Bank
1818 H Street, N. W.
Washington, D.C. 20043
(202) 477–1234

International City Management Association (ICMA) A professional organization, formed as the City Managers' Association in 1914, for appointed chief executives of cities, counties, towns, and other local governments. Its primary goals include strengthening the quality of urban government through professional management, and developing and disseminating new concepts and approaches to management through information services training programs and publications. *See also* PUBLIC INTEREST GROUPS.

International City Management Association
1120 G Street, N.W.
Washington, D.C. 20005
(202) 626–4600

International Court of Justice *See* WORLD COURT.

International Labor Organization (ILO) A specialized agency associated with the United Nations, created by the Treaty of Versailles in 1919 as a part of the League of Nations. The United States joined this autonomous intergovernmental agency in 1934 and is currently one of 132 member countries that finance ILO operations. The purpose of the ILO is to improve labor conditions, to raise living standards, and to promote economic and social stability as the foundation for lasting peace. The standards developed by the annual ILO conference form an international labor code that covers such questions as employment, freedom of association, and hours of work. The only obligation on any country is to consider these standards; no country is obligated to adopt, accept, or ratify them.

REFERENCES

Antony Alcock, *History of the International Labor Organization* (New York: Octagon, 1972);

Walter Galenson, *The International Labor Organization: An American View* (Madison: University of Wisconsin Press, 1981).

International Labor Organization
International Labor Office
Geneva, Switzerland

International Labor Organization
Washington Branch
1750 New York Avenue, N.W.
Washington, D.C. 20006
(202) 376–2315

international law The totality of treaties, customs, and agreements among nations. Jeremy Bentham (1748–1832) is credited with coining the phrase in 1780 in *Principles of Morals and Legislation*, but many others before and since him have tried to give substance and theoretical cohesiveness to practices that are often chaotic and frequently break down into war. When the international concerns that are at issue apply to individuals, it becomes a matter of CONFLICT OF LAWS. Hugo Grotius (1583–1645) is often called the father of international law, because his 1625 *De Jure Belli Ac Pacis* (The Law of War and Peace), which asserted that it was possible to create a code of international law suitable for every time and place, has influenced all subsequent thinking on the subject.

REFERENCES

F. S. Ruddy, The origin and development of the concept of international law, *Columbia Journal of Transnational Law* 7 (Fall 1968);

M. W. Janis, Jeremy Bentham and the fashioning of "international law," *American Journal of International Law* 78 (April 1984);

Marian Nash Leich, Contemporary practice of the United States relating to international law, *American Journal of International Law* 79 (October 1985);

Anthony D'Amato, *International Law: Prospect and Process* (Ardsley-on-Hudson, NY: Transnational, 1986).

International Monetary Fund (IMF) A banking organization created at the end of World War II as a specialized agency of the United Nations to maintain international monetary stability. The IMF lends funds to member countries to finance temporary balance-of-payments problems, facilitates the expansion and balanced growth of international trade, and promotes international monetary cooperation.

REFERENCES

E. Walter Robichek, The International Monetary Fund: An arbiter in the debt restructuring process, *Columbia Journal of Transnational Law* 23:1 (1984);

Jeanne Asherman, The International Monetary Fund: A history of compromise, *New York University Journal of International Law and Politics* 16 (Winter 1984);

Blanka Kudej and Victor Essien, International Monetary Fund and debt crisis: A selective bibliography, *New York University Journal of International Law and Politics* 17 (Spring 1985);

Richard Good, *Economic Assistance to Developing Countries Through the IMF* (Washington, D.C.: Brookings, 1986).

International Monetary Fund
700 19th Street, N.W.
Washington, D.C. 20431
(202) 477–2963

international relations 1 The academic field of study that examines the political, military, and economic interactions among nations; the analysis of who gets what, when, and how on the world's political stage; international politics. **2** The totality of private interactions among citizens of differing countries. **3** The practice of diplomacy.

REFERENCES

Norman D. Palmer, The study of international relations in the United States: Perspectives of half a century, *International Studies Quarterly* 24 (September 1980);

Margot Light and A. J. R. Groom, *International Relations: A Handbook of Current Theory* (London: Pinter, 1985);

John A. Vasquez, ed., *Classics of International Relations* (Englewood Cliffs, NJ: Prentice-Hall, 1986).

International Trade Commission, United States (ITC) The federal agency that furnishes and studies reports and makes recommendations involving international trade and tariffs to the president, the Congress, and other government agencies. It was created in 1916 as the United States Tariff Commission and changed to its present name in 1974 under provisions of the Trade Act of 1974.

REFERENCES

Will E. Leonard and F. David Foster, The metamorphosis of the U.S. international trade commission under the Trade Act of 1974, *Virginia Journal of International Law* 16 (Summer 1976);

John M. Dobson, Six decades of stalemate: The changing mandate of the U.S. Tariff Commission, *Midwest Review of Public Administration* 14 (December 1980).

U.S. International Trade Commission
701 E Street, N.W.
Washington, D.C. 20436
(202) 523–0161

interposition *See* JOHN C. CALHOUN.

Interstate Commerce Commission (ICC) The federal commission that regulates interstate surface transportation, including trains, trucks, buses, inland waterway and coastal shipping, freight forwarders, and express companies. The regulatory laws vary with the type of transportation; however, they generally in-

volve (1) certification of carriers seeking to provide transportation for the public, (2) rates, (3) adequacy of service, and (4) purchases and mergers. The ICC, established in 1887, is considered the prototype for independent federal regulatory commissions.

REFERENCES

Robert Fellmeth, *The Interstate Commerce Omission* (New York: Grossman, 1970);

John Guandolo, The role of the Interstate Commerce Commission in the 1980s, *American Economic Review* 71 (May 1981);

Marcus Alexis, The applied theory of regulation: Political economy at the Interstate Commerce Commission, *Public Choice* 39:1 (1982).

Interstate Commerce Commission
12th Street and Constitution Avenue, N.W.
Washington, D.C. 20423
(202) 275–7119

interstate compacts Formal arrangements entered into by two or more states, generally with the approval of the U.S. Congress, to operate joint programs. While Article I, Section 10, of the Constitution requires that interstate compacts be approved by the Congress, as a practical matter many agreements on minor matters ignore this requirement. The initial intent was to prevent states from forming regional alliances that might threaten national unity.

REFERENCES

Weldon V. Barton, *Interstate Compacts in the Political Process* (Chapel Hill: University of North Carolina Press, 1967);

David E. Engdahl, Interstate urban areas and interstate "agreements" and "compacts": Unclear possibilities, *Georgetown Law Journal* 58 (March–May 1970);

Susan Welch and Cal Clark, Interstate compacts and national integration: An empirical assessment of some trends, *Western Political Quarterly* 26 (September 1973);

Paul Hardy, *Interstate Compacts: The Ties That Bind* (Athens: Institute of Government, University of Georgia, 1982).

invisible government **1** Any powerful organization, whether public or private, that wields secret, extensive, unwarranted, and unaccountable power. The CIA has often been called an invisible government. **2** Rule by political party bosses (*see* BOSSISM), the real, although unseen, powers behind the elected representatives of the people.

REFERENCE

David Wise and Thomas B. Ross, *Invisible Government* (New York: Random House, 1964).

invisible hand Adam Smith's description from *The Wealth of Nations* (1776) of the capitalistic market mechanism that invisibly and automatically promotes the general welfare as long as individuals are allowed to pursue their self-interest.

REFERENCES

J. S. Sorzano, David Easton and the invisible hand, *American Political Science Review* 69 (March 1975);

Samuel Bowles and Herbert Gintis, The invisible fist: Have capitalism and democracy reached a parting of the ways? *American Economic Review* 68 (May 1978).

Iowa caucus The earliest caucus in a presidential election year, in which delegates to the national political party nominating conventions are selected. A good showing in the Iowa caucus is often critical for a candidate if he or she is to establish the needed momentum to be taken seriously as a candidate.

REFERENCE

Hugh Winebrenner, *The Iowa Caucuses* (Ames, Iowa: Iowa State University Press, 1987).

Iran-contra affair The controversy arising in the fall of 1986, when it was revealed that the Ronald Reagan administration had secretly

In the early stages of the Iran-contra Affair, administration officials maintained that President Reagan had little knowledge of the actions of his subordinates.

sold arms to the government of Iran (so Iran would use its good offices to gain the release of American hostages in Lebanon) at higher than normal prices and used the "profits" to fund the CONTRAS in Nicaragua. The controversy grew into a scandal because it was illegal to sell arms to Iran, illegal to fund the contras beyond limits set by the Congress (see BOLAND AMENDMENT), and against the expressed policy of the United States to negotiate for, let alone trade arms for, the release of hostages. Because the Iran-contra operation was undertaken primarily by the National Security Council without the formal approval of the departments of Defense and State, the affair called into question the coherence of the Reagan administration's foreign policy. See TOWER COMMISSION.

REFERENCE

Oliver Trager, ed., *The Iran Arms Scandal: Foreign Policy Disaster* (New York: Facts On File, 1988).

Iranian hostage crisis The wholesale violation of diplomatic privileges and immunities that occurred when the Iranian government-backed "students" captured the American Embassy complex of buildings in Teheran on November 4, 1979, and held fifty-three Americans hostage for 444 days, until January 20, 1981. The crisis so dominated the last year of the Jimmy Carter administration that it badly damaged Carter's reelection prospects, especially after an unsuccessful rescue effort on April 24, 1980. The Iranians agreed to free the hostages only after the Carter administration agreed to some of the Iranian demands "in principle." As one last insult to the Carter administration, the hostages were freed on the day Ronald Reagan succeeded Jimmy Carter as president.

REFERENCE

Warren Christopher and others, *American Hostages in Iran: The Conduct of a Crisis* (New Haven, CT: Yale University Press, 1985).

iron curtain The political, social, and economic schism between the countries of Eastern and Western Europe. The phrase was popularized by Winston Churchill in a March 5, 1946, speech at Westminster College, Fulton,

Missouri, in which he said: "From Stettin in the Baltic to Trieste in the Adriatic, an iron curtain has descended across the continent." Now the phrase is also used to refer to any hostile and seemingly permanent political division.

iron law of oligarchy "Who says organization says oligarchy." This is Robert Michels's theory, stated in *Political Parties* (Glencoe, IL: Free Press, 1915, 1949), that organizations are by their nature oligarchic because majorities within an organization are not capable of ruling themselves:

Organization implies the tendency to oligarchy. In every organization, whether it be a political party, a professional union, or any other association of the kind, the aristocratic tendency manifests itself very clearly. The mechanism of the organization, while conferring a solidity of structure, induces serious changes in the organized mass, completely inverting the respective position of the leaders and the led. As a result of organization, every party or professional union becomes divided into a minority of directors and a majority of the directed.

REFERENCE

C. Fred Alford, The "iron law of oligarchy" in the Athenian polis . . . and today, *Canadian Journal of Political Science* 18 (June 1985).

iron triangles See COZY TRIANGLES/IRON TRIANGLES.

IRS *See* INTERNAL REVENUE SERVICE.

isolationism The policy of curtailing as much as possible a nation's international relations so one's country can exist in peace and harmony by itself in the world. Isolationism was the dominant U.S. foreign policy for many periods in its history, particularly during most of the nineteenth century and the two decades between the World Wars. But modern trade, communications, and military weapons make isolationism virtually impossible for any nation today, even though such wishful thinking will continue to be a significant factor in domestic politics. *Compare to* GLOBALISM.

REFERENCES

Thomas N. Guinsburg, *The Pursuit of Isolationism in the United States Senate from Ver-*

sailles to Pearl Harbor (New York: Garland, 1982);

Charles Krauthammer, Isolationism, Left and Right, *New Republic* 192 (March 4, 1985).

ISR *See* INSTITUTE FOR SOCIAL RESEARCH.

issue-attention cycle A model developed by Anthony Downs that attempts to explain how many policy problems evolve onto the political agenda. The cycle is premised on the proposition that the public's attention rarely remains focused on any one issue for a very long time, regardless of the objective nature of the problem. The cycle consists of five steps: (1) the preproblem stage (an undesirable social condition exists, but has not captured public attention); (2) alarmed discovery and euphoric enthusiasm (a dramatic event catalyzes the public attention, accompanied by an enthusiasm to solve the problem); (3) recognition of the cost of change (the public gradually realizes the difficulty of implementing meaningful change); (4) decline of public interest (people become discouraged or bored or a new issue claims attention); and (5) the postproblem stage (although the issue has not been solved, it has been dropped from the nation's agenda).
REFERENCES
Anthony Downs, Up and down with ecology—The "issue-attention cycle," *Public Interest* 28 (Summer 1972);

B. Guy Peters and Brian W. Hogwood, In search of the issue-attention cycle, *Journal of Politics* 47 (February 1985).

issue group A politically active organization created in response to a specific issue. For example, the Right to Life Association was created as a response to the U.S. Supreme Court's 1973 *Roe v Wade* decision legalizing abortion.

issue networks **1** The totality of public and private actors who interact and combine either to put forth and enact into law or to oppose public policy initiatives. This is an inherently chaotic process with little neatness or definition. The concept is mainly used after the fact by policy analysts to explain how a policy or issue came into being. **2** The bureaucratic experts, professional associations, and private sector practitioners of a technical specialty that both formally and informally define standards of practice and development consensus on public policy issues affecting their profession. *Compare to* COZY TRIANGLES/IRON TRIANGLES.
REFERENCES
Hugh Heclo, Issue networks and the executive establishment, *The New American Political System*, ed. Anthony King (Washington, D.C.: American Enterprise, 1978);
Michael W. Kirst, Gail Meister, and Stephen R. Rowley, Policy issue networks: Their influence on state policymaking, *Policy Studies Journal* 13 (December 1984).

Characteristics of Issue Networks

Network Type	Number of Participants	Access	Function
Cozy little connection (micropolitics)	Very few (one-on-one)	Restricted (on demand)	Provides favors
Cozy little triangle (intermediary politics)	Few (legislators, administrators)	Less restricted (interest/expertise)	Stabilizes policy
Sloppy large hexagon (macropolitics)	Many (legislators, administrators, leaders, clientele, publics)	Unrestricted (demand involvement)	Acknowledges issue, initiates action

Source: Adapted from Charles O. Jones, *The United States Congress: People, Place, and Policy* (Chicago: Dorsey, 1982), p. 362.

issue voting 1 The casting of a vote for a candidate on the basis of one issue alone, such as the candidate's support for or against legal abortion. 2 Voting for a candidate because of his or her stand on issues, rather than because of the candidate's party affiliation.

REFERENCES

Edward G. Carmines and James A. Stimson, The two faces of issue voting, *American Political Science Review* 74 (March 1980); Patricia A. Hurley and Kim Quaile Hill, The prospects for issue-voting in contemporary congressional elections: An assessment of citizen awareness and representation, *American Politics Quarterly* 8 (October 1980); Linda L. Fowler, How interest groups select issues for rating voting records of members of the U.S. Congress, *Legislative Studies Quarterly* 7 (August 1982).

item veto *See* VETO, ITEM.

J

Jackson, Andrew (1767–1845) The commanding general at the 1815 Battle of New Orleans where the Americans, in the last engagement of the War of 1812, literally killed half of the attacking British force of five thousand, with less than a dozen casualties of their own. Elected U.S. president in 1828, he was the first westerner (being from Tennessee) to occupy the White House (1829–1837) and the first president elected by the Democratic party. Jackson opposed state nullification of federal laws and advocated a strong national government, an expanded suffrage (through the removal of property requirements for white males), and a strengthened party system. His contributions to the conduct of the presidency included vigorous use of patronage, transformation of the cabinet into a group of loyal advisors and allies, reliance on informal advisors (his "kitchen cabinet"), and highly publicized resort to the veto to enforce his policy positions. Compare to JOHN C. CALHOUN.

REFERENCES

Arthur M. Schlesinger, Jr., *The Age of Jackson* (Boston: Little, Brown, 1945);

Leonard D. White, *The Jacksonians* (New York: Macmillan, 1954);

Matthew A. Crenson, *The Federal Machine: Beginnings of Bureaucracy in Jacksonian America* (Baltimore: Johns Hopkins University Press, 1975);

James Roger Sharp, Andrew Jackson and the limits of presidential power, *Congressional Studies* 7 (Winter 1980).

Andrew Jackson.

Andrew Jackson and the Spoils System

During his two terms of office (1829–1837), Andrew Jackson was blamed for inventing the spoils system. Prior to Jackson, the federal service was a stable, long-tenured, corps of officials decidedly elitist in character and remarkably free of corruption. Jackson, for the most part, continued with this tradition in practice, turning out of office about as many appointees as had Jefferson. But in his most famous statement on the character of public office, Jackson asserted that the duties of public office are "so plain and simple that men of intelligence may readily qualify themselves for their performance; and I cannot but believe that more is lost by the long continuance of men in office than is generally to be gained by their experience." Jackson was claiming that all men, especially the newly enfranchised who did so much to elect him, should have an equal opportunity for public office. In playing to his plebeian constituency, Jackson put the patrician civil service on notice that they had no natural monopoly on public office. His rhetoric on the nature of the public service was to be far more influential than his administrative example. While Jackson's personal indulgence in spoils was more limited than popularly thought, he did establish the intellectual and political rationale for the unmitigated spoils system that was to follow.

Source: Adapted from Jay M. Shafritz, *Public Personnel Management: The Heritage of Civil Service Reform* (New York: Praeger, 1975), pp. 11–14.

Jesse Jackson.

Bob Faw and Nancy Skelton, *Thunder in America: The Improbably Presidential Campaign of Jesse Jackson* (Austin: Texas Monthly, 1986);

Adolph L. Reed, Jr., *The Jesse Jackson Phenomenon* (New Haven, CT: Yale University Press, 1986).

Jacksonian democracy *See* DEMOCRACY, JACKSONIAN.

Jackson, Jesse (1941–   )   The civil rights activist who in 1984 became the first black to mount a major national campaign for the Democratic nomination for president. Shirley Chisolm (1924–   ), as a black congresswoman from New York, sought the nomination in 1972; but her candidacy was more symbolic than real. Jackson is president of the National Rainbow Coalition, a decidedly left-of-center splinter group within the Democratic party for those, in Jackson's words, "who are being locked out of their party."

REFERENCES

Thomas Landess and Richard Quinn, *Jesse Jackson and the Politics of Race* (Ottawa, IL: Jameson, 1985);

Jarvis-Gann Initiative *See* PROPOSITION 13/ JARVIS-GANN INITIATIVE.

jar wars   President Ronald Reagan's antidrug program, in which the main weapon is drug testing through urinalysis. It is called jar wars because urine samples are deposited in small jars, because it is a war (on drugs), and because the combination rhymes with another favored Reagan program, star wars (*see* STRATEGIC DEFENSE INITIATIVE). The jar wars initiative became controversial because it is asserted that mandatory testing of all of a group of employees might violate the Fourteenth Amendment prohibition against unreasonable searches and seizures.

jawboning   Any presidential pressure on labor, management, or other groups to make their behavior more compatible with the national interest. The jawbone in jawboning refers to the biblical "jawbone of an ass," with which Samson slew a "thousand men" (Judges 15:16). According to Theodore C. Sorenson, in *Kennedy* (New York: Harper & Row, 1965), the term was first used by Walter Heller (then chairman of the Council of Economic Advisers) in reference to President John F. Kennedy's efforts to impose his economic guidelines on price setting and collective bargaining. While President Kennedy never used the term itself, his successor, President Lyndon B. Johnson, used jawboning extensively, because it neatly complemented both his policies and personality. Subsequent presidents have tried to avoid the term but have stuck with the practice.

REFERENCE

Paul R. Verkuil, Jawboning administrative agencies: Ex parte contacts by the White House, *Columbia Law Review* 80 (June 1980).

Jay, John (1745–1826)   One of the authors of the *Federalist Papers* and in 1789 the first chief justice of the United States. But he found the office so insignificant that in 1795 he resigned to become governor of New York.

REFERENCE

Richard B. Morris, *John Jay, The Nation and the Court* (Brookline, MA: Boston University Press, 1967).

Jefferson, Thomas (1743–1826)   The primary author of the Declaration of Independence, the first secretary of State (under President George Washington), the second vice president (under President John Adams), the third president of the United States (1801–1809), and the founder of the University of Virginia (1819). Jefferson is universally acknowledged as one of the major forces in the creation of the American political party system, and both of today's major parties trace their philosophic origins to him. Jefferson was the leader of the Republican party, which originated in 1791 (see Noble E. Cunningham, Jr., *The Jeffersonian Republicans* [Chapel Hill: University of North Carolina Press, 1957]). This evolved into the Democratic-Republican party, which changed its name to the Democratic party in 1828. Many disaffected Demo-

Thomas Jefferson.

cratic-Republicans, who called themselves National Republicans, united with other splinter groups in 1834 to form the Whig party, which disintegrated in 1852. A coalition of disaffected Democrats and former Whigs formed the modern Republican party in 1856.

Jefferson was the first president to face the problem of a philosophically hostile bureaucracy. Although sorely pressed by his supporters to remove Federalist officeholders and replace them with Republican partisans, Jefferson was determined not to remove officials for political reasons alone. Jefferson rather courageously maintained that only "malconduct is a just ground of removal: mere difference of political opinion is not." With occasional defections from this principle, even by Jefferson himself, this policy became the norm rather than the exception down through the administration of Andrew Jackson.

Jefferson was so talented and so influential in so many areas that in 1962, when President John F. Kennedy invited all of the Nobel Prize winners to dine at the White House, he told them: "I think this is the most extraordinary collection of talent, of human knowledge, that has ever been gathered together at the White House—with the possible exception of when

Thomas Jefferson dined here alone." Compare to ALEXANDER HAMILTON.

REFERENCES

For the definitive biography of Jefferson, see Dumas Malone, *Jefferson and His Time*, 6 vols. (Boston: Little, Brown, 1948–1981).

For historical gossip, see Fawn M. Brodie, *Thomas Jefferson: An Intimate History* (New York: Norton, 1974).

For a bibliography, see Frank Shuffelton, *Thomas Jefferson: A Comprehensive, Annotated Bibliography of Writings About Him (1826–1880)* (New York: Garland, 1983).

Jeffersonian democracy *See* DEMOCRACY, JEFFERSONIAN.

Jim Crow A name given to any law requiring the segregation of the races. All such statutes are now unconstitutional.

REFERENCE

C. Vann Woodward, *The Strange Career of Jim Crow*, 3d ed. (New York: Oxford University Press, 1974).

jingoism Strong nationalist sentiment characterized by a proclivity for a belligerent foreign policy. The term first became current in England in the mid-1870s, when the British seemed on the verge of war with Russia. A popular song went:

> We don't want to fight,
> But by Jingo, if we do,
> We've got the ships, we've got the men,
> We've got the money too.

Jingo was a euphemism for by God or by Jesus. It soon crossed the Atlantic and became increasingly popular in the United States.

Job Corps The federal training program created by the COMPREHENSIVE EMPLOYMENT AND TRAINING ACT OF 1973, which offers social and occupational development for disadvantaged youths through centers with the unique feature of residential facilities for all or most enrollees. Its purpose is to prepare them for the responsibilities of citizenship and to increase their employability by providing them with education, vocational training, and useful work experience in rural, urban, or inner-city centers. En-

All Jim Crow laws are now unconstitutional.

rollees may spend a maximum of two years in the Job Corps. However, a period of enrollment from six months to a year is usually sufficient to provide adequate training and education to improve employability to a substantial degree. Job Corps recruiting is accomplished primarily through state employment services.

REFERENCES

Christopher Weeks, *Job Corps: Dollars and Dropouts* (Boston: Little, Brown, 1967);

Sar A. Levitan, Job Corps experience with Manpower Training, *Monthly Labor Review* 98 (October 1975);

David A. Long, Charles D. Mallar, and Craig V. D. Thornton, Evaluating the benefits and costs of the Job Corps, *Journal of Policy Analysis and Management* 1 (Fall 1981).

Job Training Partnership Act of 1983 *See* COMPREHENSIVE EMPLOYMENT AND TRAINING ACT OF 1973.

John Birch Society A secretive, far-right, ultraconservative organization founded in 1959 to fight communism and communist influences in American life. It was named after John Birch, a U.S. army captain killed by the Chinese communists in 1945. His namesake society honors him as the first victim of the cold war. Under the leadership of its founder, Robert H. Welch, Jr. (1899–1985), the society sought (1) to impeach then Chief Justice EARL WARREN, (2) to withdraw the United States from the United Nations, (3) to end U.S. participation in NATO, and (4) to eliminate all federal welfare programs. At the local level it sought to place its members on school boards, city councils, and so on. Because of the society's paranoid anticommunism (it considered the fluoridation of drinking water to be a Communist plot), a Bircher has become synonymous with a right-wing extremist. At its height, the society had about eight hundred local chapters and more than a hundred thousand members. These figures are much, much lower now.

REFERENCES

Fred W. Grupp, Jr., Personal satisfaction derived from membership in the John Birch Society, *Western Political Quarterly* 24 (March 1971);

Barbara S. Stone, The John Birch Society: A profile, *Journal of Politics* 36 (February 1974).

Andrew Johnson.

Johnson, Andrew (1808–1875) The border state (Tennessee) vice president who succeeded to the presidency in 1865 after Abraham Lincoln was assassinated. He was the only president to be impeached by the U.S. House of Representatives and to be tried for "high crimes and misdemeanors" by the Senate. The Radical Republicans wanted to get rid of him because of his compassionate policies toward the defeated South. He was acquitted by one vote, a narrow win for himself and the institution of the presidency. Compare to IMPEACHMENT.

REFERENCES

Michael Les Benedict, *The Impeachment and Trial of Andrew Johnson* (New York: Norton, 1973);

Gene Smith, *High Crimes and Misdemeanors: The Impeachment and Trial of Andrew Johnson* (New York: Morrow, 1977).

Johnson, Lyndon B. (1908–1973) The U.S. vice president who became president when President John F. Kennedy was assassinated on

Lyndon B. Johnson.

November 22, 1963. A member of the Congress since 1937 and the leader of the Democrats in the Senate since 1953 (majority leader from 1955 to 1961), Johnson proved extremely skillful in getting liberal legislation through a Congress still dominated by southern conservative Democrats. He won election to the presidency in his own right in 1964 by such an overwhelming landslide and carried such significant numbers of new Democratic congressmen in on his COATTAILS that there was much talk of the total disintegration of the Republican party. Yet in spite of an excellent record on civil rights and domestic programs, his questionable and ineffective tactics in pursuing the Vietnam War divided the country considerably, and, after Johnson declined to run for a second full term, gave the Republicans and Richard M. Nixon the presidency in 1968. It was sarcastically said at the time: "Roosevelt gave us the New Deal, Truman gave us the Fair Deal, but Johnson gave us the Ordeal."

According to Doris Kearns, in *Lyndon Johnson and the American Dream* (New York: Harper & Row, 1976), Johnson said:

I knew from the start that I was bound to be crucified either way I moved. If I left the woman I really loved—the Great Society—in order to get involved with that bitch of a war on the other side of the world, then I would lose everything at home. . . . But if I let the Communists take over South Vietnam, then I would be seen as a coward and my nation would be seen as an appeaser. . . . Oh, I could see it coming all right. History provided too many cases where the sound of the bugle put an immediate end to the hopes and dreams of the best reformers.

REFERENCES

For Johnson's memoirs, see *The Vantage Point: Perspective on the Presidency, 1963–1969* (New York: Holt, Rinehart & Winston, 1971).

For more objective treatments, see Herbert Y. Schandler, *The Unmaking of a President: Lyndon Johnson and Vietnam* (Princeton, NJ: Princeton University Press, 1977);

Merle Miller, *Lyndon: An Oral Biography* (New York: G. P. Putnam's Sons, 1980);

Robert A. Caro, *The Years of Lyndon Johnson: The Path to Power* (New York: Knopf, 1982);

Ronnie Dugger, *The Politician: The Life and Times of Lyndon Johnson* (New York: Norton, 1982).

The Lyndon Johnson Administration

Major Accomplishments

- The Civil Rights Act of 1964.
- Department of Housing and Urban Development created.
- The Economic Opportunity Act of 1964.
- Medicare.
- Medicaid.
- The Elementary and Secondary Education Act of 1965.
- The Higher Education Act of 1965.
- The Voting Rights Act of 1965.

Major Frustrations

- The Vietnam War.
- Urban Riots.
- Antiwar demonstrations.

Johnson v Santa Clara County   See REVERSE DISCRIMINATION.

Joint Chiefs of Staff   The primary military advisors to the secretary of Defense and to the president of the United States. It consists of the chiefs of staff of the U.S. army and air force, the chief of naval operations, the commandant of the marine corps (but only when marine corps matters are at issue), and a chairman, who is generally considered the spokesman for the nation's military establishment. The Joint Chiefs has been heavily criticized because it does not operate as a unified command but works mainly to perpetuate interservice rivalries and identities. While an organization known as the Joint Chiefs of Staff operated during World War II, the present organization was created by the National Security Act of 1947.

The Pentagon Reorganization Act of 1986 sought to strengthen the role of the Chairman of the Joint Chiefs of Staff by making him personally the president's "principal military adviser," instead of, as before, the representative of the collective opinion of all of the service chiefs.

REFERENCES

Lawrence J. Korb, The Joint Chiefs of Staff: Access and impact in foreign policy, *Policy Studies Journal* 3 (Winter 1974);

F. Whitney Hall, Understanding the Joint Chiefs of Staff, *Armed Forces and Society* 5 (Winter 1979);

David C. Jones, Why the Joint Chiefs of Staff must change, *Presidential Studies Quarterly* 12 (Spring 1982);

William J. Lynn and Barry R. Posen, The case for JCS reform, *International Security* 10 (Winter 1985–86).

joint committee *See* COMMITTEE, JOINT.

joint resolution *See* RESOLUTION, JOINT.

Jones Act **1** The 1916 law that promised independence to the Philippines "as soon as a stable government can be established therein." It was superseded by the Tydings-McDuffie Act of 1934, which promised absolute independence (granted in 1946). **2** The 1917 law that granted political autonomy to Puerto Rico and American citizenship to all its people.

REFERENCE

1 Wong Kwok Chu, The Jones bills, 1912–1916: A reappraisal of Filipino views on independence, *Journal of Southeast Asian Studies* 13 (September 1982).

Journal The official record of the proceedings of the U.S. House of Representatives and the Senate. The *Journal* records the actions taken in each chamber but, unlike the *Congressional Record*, it does not include the verbatim report of speeches and debate.

Journal of Policy Analysis and Management A scholarly quarterly, the official publication of the Association for Public Policy and Management, which became in 1981 the successor journal to both *Public Policy* and *Policy Analysis*. Library of Congress no. H97 .J68.

> *Journal of Policy Analysis and Management*
> 605 Third Avenue
> New York, NY 10158

Journal of Political Economy The bimonthly journal of the Department of Economics and the Graduate School of Business of the University of Chicago; published since 1892. Library of Congress no. HB1 .J7.

> *Journal of Political Economy*
> University of Chicago Press
> Journals Division
> P.O. Box 37005
> Chicago, IL 60637

Journal of Politics The political science quarterly published by the Southern Political Science Association since 1939. Articles deal with domestic as well as international issues. Library of Congress no. JA1 .J6.

> *Journal of Politics*
> Department of Political Science
> University of Florida
> Gainesville, FL 32611

Journal of Public Policy A quarterly of public policy analysis that offers an international, interdisciplinary perspective; published since 1981. Library of Congress no. H96 .J68.

> *Journal of Public Policy*
> Cambridge University Press
> 32 East 47th Street
> New York, NY 10022

journals *See individual entries for the following:* ADMINISTRATION AND SOCIETY; AMERICAN CITY AND COUNTY; AMERICAN JOURNAL OF POLITICAL SCIENCE; AMERICAN POLITICAL SCIENCE REVIEW; AMERICAN POLITICS QUAR-

TERLY; AMERICAN REVIEW OF PUBLIC ADMIN-
ISTRATION; ANNALS; BUREAUCRAT; CONGRESS
AND THE PRESIDENCY; CONGRESSIONAL QUAR-
TERLY WEEKLY REPORT; FEDERAL REGISTER.

GALLUP REPORT; GOVERNMENTAL FINANCE;
JOURNAL OF POLICY ANALYSIS AND MANAGE-
MENT; JOURNAL OF POLITICAL ECONOMY;
JOURNAL OF POLITICS; JOURNAL OF PUBLIC
POLICY; MONTHLY LABOR REVIEW; NATIONAL
CIVIC REVIEW; NATIONAL JOURNAL; NATION'S
CITIES.

POLICY REVIEW; POLICY SCIENCES; POLICY
STUDIES JOURNAL/POLICY STUDIES REVIEW;
POLITICAL SCIENCE QUARTERLY; POLITY;
PRESIDENTIAL STUDIES QUARTERLY; PUBLIC
ADMINISTRATION; PUBLIC ADMINISTRATION RE-
VIEW; PUBLIC INTEREST; PUBLIC MANAGEMENT;
PUBLIC OPINION QUARTERLY; PUBLIUS.

REVIEW OF POLITICS; STATE AND LOCAL
GOVERNMENT REVIEW; STATE GOVERNMENT;
URBAN AFFAIRS QUARTERLY; WASHINGTON
MONTHLY; WESTERN POLITICAL QUARTERLY.

judge A judicial officer elected or appointed
to preside over a court of law, whose position
has been created by statute or by constitution,
and whose decisions may be reviewed only by
a judge of a higher court. Thomas Jefferson
realized that "our judges are as honest as most
men, and not more so."

REFERENCES
Elliott E. Slotnick, Federal trial and appellate
judges: How do they differ? *Western Political Quarterly* 36 (December 1983);
Sheldon Goldman, Judicial selection and the
qualities that make a "good" judge, *Annals
of the American Academy of Political and
Social Science* 462 (July 1982).

Federal Judges

Court	Number	Salary
Supreme		
Chief justice	1	$104,700
Associate justices	8	100,000
Courts of appeals	168	80,400
District courts	576	76,000

Note: 1985 data.

---

judicial activism The making of new public
policies through the decisions of judges. This
may take the form of a reversal or modification
of a prior court decision, the nullification of a
law passed by the legislature, or the overturning
of some action of the executive branch. The
concept of judicial activism is most associated
with the U.S. Supreme Court, which from time
to time has found new laws when none were
there before. However, judges at any level can
be said to engage in judicial activism when
their judicial positions are used to promote
what they consider to be desirable social goals.
The main argument against judicial activism is
that it tends to usurp the power of the legislature. The counterargument holds that, because
laws—being products of compromise—tend to
be vague on "hot" issues, the courts are in
effect forced by the nature of the cases they
receive to sort things out in a manner that
seems "activist" to critics. In a larger historical
sense, John Marshall's introduction of JUDI-
CIAL REVIEW began judicial activism by claiming a special constitutional authority for the
Court over the actions of other branches of government. Compare to JUDICIAL SELF-
RESTRAINT.

REFERENCES
Alpheus Thomas Mason, Judicial activism:
Old and new, *Virginia Law Review* 55
(April 1969);
Wallace Mendelson, The politics of judicial
activism, *Emory Law Journal* 24 (Winter
1975);
Richard Lehne and John Reynolds, The im-
pact of judicial activism on public opinion,
American Journal of Political Science 22
(November 1978);
Frank M. Johnson, Jr., In defense of judicial
activism, *Emory Law Journal* 28 (Fall
1980);
Gary L. McDowell, A modest remedy for ju-
dicial activism, *Public Interest* 67 (Spring
1982);
Robert M. Cover, The origins of judicial activism in the protection of minorities, *Yale
Law Journal* 91 (June 1982);
Maxwell A. Miller and Nancie George, Judicial activism and the constitutional amendment process, *Journal of Social, Political
and Economic Studies* 9 (Fall 1984);

P. N. Bhagwati, Judicial activism and public interest litigation, *Columbia Journal of Transnational Law* 23:3 (1985).

Judicial Conference of the United States The group of federal judges, chaired by the chief justice of the United States, which provides for administrative policymaking for the federal court system.

REFERENCE

David S. Myers, Origin of the judicial conference, *American Bar Association Journal* 57 (June 1971).

judicial officer Any person exercising judicial powers in a court of law; a judge.

judicial review 1 The power of the U.S. Supreme Court to declare actions of the president, the Congress, or other agencies of government at any level to be invalid or unconstitutional. While it was first asserted by the Supreme Court in *Marbury v Madison*, the theoretical basis for judicial review was earlier presented by Alexander Hamilton in Federalist 78:

The complete independence of the courts of justice is peculiarly essential in a limited Constitution. By a limited Constitution I understand one which contains certain specified exceptions to the legislative authority; such, for instance, as that it shall pass no bills of attainder, no *ex post facto* laws, and the like. Limitations of this kind can be preserved in practice no other way than through the medium of courts of justice, whose duty it must be to declare all acts contrary to the manifest tenor of the Constitution void. . . .

The interpretation of the laws is the proper and peculiar province of the courts. A constitution is, in fact, and must be regarded by the judges, as a fundamental law. It therefore belongs to them to ascertain its meaning, as well as the meaning of any particular act proceeding from the legislative body. If there should happen to be an irreconcilable variance between the two, that which has the superior obligation and validity ought, of course, to be preferred; or, in other words, the Constitution ought to be preferred to the statute, the intention of the people to the intention of their agents.

2 Any court's power to review executive actions, legislative acts, or decisions of lower courts (or quasi-judicial entities, such as arbitration panels) to either confirm or overturn them. *See also* ALEXANDER M. BICKEL, LEAST DANGEROUS BRANCH.

REFERENCES

For classic commentaries on judicial review, see Edward Samuel Corwin, *The Doctrine of Judicial Review, Its Legal and Historical Basis, and Other Essays* (Princeton, NJ: Princeton University Press, 1914);

Charles G. Haines, *The American Doctrine of Judicial Supremacy*, 2d ed. (Berkeley, CA: University of California Press, 1932);

Henry Steele Commager, Judicial review and democracy, *The Virginia Quarterly Review* 19 (Summer 1943).

For contemporary analyses, see Jesse H. Chopper, *Judicial Review and the National Political Process* (Chicago: University of Chicago Press, 1980);

Harry H. Wellington, The nature of judicial review, *Yale Law Journal* 91 (January 1982);

Christopher Wolfe, *The Rise of Modern Judicial Review: From Constitutional Interpretation to Judge-Made Law* (New York: Basic Books, 1985).

judicial self-restraint A self-imposed limitation on judicial decision making; the tendency on the part of judges to favor a narrow interpretation of the laws and to defer to the policy judgment of the legislative and executive branches. Justice Harlan Fiske Stone wrote in *United States v Butler*, 297 U.S. 1 (1936), that "while unconstitutional exercise by the executive and legislative branches is subject to judicial restraint, the only check on our own exercise of power is our own sense of self-restraint." *Compare to* JUDICIAL ACTIVISM; POLITICAL QUESTION.

REFERENCE

John P. Roche, Judicial self-restraint, *American Political Science Review* 49 (September 1955).

judiciary 1 The courts in general; the judicial branch of government. It is the judiciary that protects citizens from real and potential abuses by the other branches. Chief Justice John Marshall said: "To what quarter will you look for protection from an infringement on the

Constitution, if you will not give that power to the judiciary? There is no other body that can afford such a protection." **2** The courts of a specific jurisdiction such as the federal judiciary.

REFERENCES

1 Jeremy Rabkin, The judiciary in the administrative state, *Public Interest* 71 (Spring 1983).

2 Daniel J. Meador, The federal judiciary and its future administration, *Virginia Law Review* 65 (October 1979).

junket *See* OVERSIGHT, CONGRESSIONAL.

juridical democracy An alternative to interest group liberalism offered by THEODORE J. LOWI in *The End of Liberalism* (New York: Norton, 1969), which calls for the federal courts to take a stronger role in achieving democratic ideals by forcing the Congress into a greater "rule of law" posture. Such force would come about by increasingly declaring statutes unconstitutional if they continue to be so vague that significant policy powers are delegated to government agencies who use this discretion to play the interest group game. Lowi views the competition of interest groups for influence over program implementation as inherently undemocratic, because these decisions should be made in great detail in the legislation itself. And only the courts can force the Congress to do this.

REFERENCES

Robert C. Grady, Interest-group liberalism and juridical democracy: Two theses in search of legitimacy, *American Politics Quarterly* 6 (April 1978);

Robert C. Grady, Juridical democracy and democratic values: An evaluation of Lowi's alternative to interest-group liberalism, *Polity* 16 (Spring 1984).

jurisdiction **1** A territory, subject matter, or person over which lawful authority may be exercised. **2** A union's exclusive right to represent particular workers within specified industrial, occupational, or geographical boundaries. **3** The power of a court to act on a case.

jurisdictional dispute **1** A disagreement between two government entities over which should provide services to a disputed area, over who has the authority to tax a disputed source, who has the prior right to initiate prosecution in a criminal or noncompliance case, and so on. **2** A disagreement between two unions over which should control a particular job or activity.

REFERENCE

F. Bruce Simmons III, Jurisdictional disputes: Does the board really snub the Supreme Court? *Labor Law Journal* 36 (March 1985).

jurisdictional strike A strike that results when two unions have a dispute over whose members should perform a particular task, and one or the other strikes to gain its way. For example, both electricians and carpenters may claim the right to do the same task at a construction site. Because the employer is caught in the middle, the Labor-Management Relations (Taft-Hartley) Act of 1947 makes jurisdictional strikes illegal.

jurisdiction, original The power of a court to hear a case first. This is in contrast to appellate jurisdiction, which means that the court reviews cases only after they have been tried elsewhere. Article III, Section 2, of the U.S. Constitution gives the Supreme Court original jurisdiction in cases involving foreign ambassadors and disputes between the states.

jurisprudence **1** The art and science of the law; not the laws of any given jurisdiction but the origin, form, and nature of the law in general; the structure of legal systems. **2** The study of legal philosophy and its underlying concepts. **3** A trend in case law; the collective course of judicial decision making on a given issue over time.

REFERENCES

Owen M. Fiss, The jurisprudence of busing, *Law and Contemporary Problems* 39 (Winter 1975);

Philip Selznick, Jurisprudence and social policy: Aspirations and perspectives, *California Law Review* 68 (March 1980);

E. Donald Elliott, The Evolutionary tradition in jurisprudence, *Columbia Law Review* 85 (January 1985).

jury, death qualified *See* LOCKHART V MCCREE.

jury, grand A group of citizens selected to review evidence against accused persons to determine whether there is sufficient evidence to bring the accused to trial—to indict or not to indict. A grand jury usually has from twelve to twenty-three members and operates in secrecy to protect the reputation of those not indicted. Grand juries have been both criticized for being easily manipulated tools in the hands of prosecutors and praised for protecting the rights of those falsely accused.

REFERENCES

Seymour Gelber, A reappraisal of the grand jury concept, *Journal of Criminal Law, Criminology and Police Science* 60 (March 1969);

Robert Gilbert Johnston, The grand jury—Prosecutorial abuse of the indictment process, *Journal of Criminal Law & Criminology* 65 (June 1974);

Robert Carp, The behavior of grand juries: Acquiescence or justice, *Social Science Quarterly* 55 (March 1975);

William H. Diamond, Federal remedies for racial discrimination in grand juror selection, *Columbia Journal of Law and Social Problems* 16 (1980);

Symposium on the grand jury, *Journal of Criminal Law & Criminology* 75 (Winter 1984).

jury, hung A jury that is so irreconcilably divided in opinion that it is unable to reach a verdict.

REFERENCE

Janet E. Findlater, Retrial after a hung jury: The double jeopardy, *University of Pennsylvania Law Review* 129 (January 1981).

jury panel The group of persons summoned to appear in court as potential jurors, from among whom the actual jurors are selected.

jury, trial A statutorily defined number of persons (usually at least six and no more than twelve) selected to determine matters of fact based on evidence presented at a trial and to render a verdict. The right of a public trial by an impartial jury in all criminal prosecutions is guaranteed by the Sixth Amendment. However, most defendants waive this right and accept a plea bargain. In *Duncan v Louisiana*, 391 U.S. 145 (1968), the U.S. Supreme Court held

> that trial by jury in criminal cases is fundamental to the American scheme of justice. We hold that the Fourteenth Amendment guarantees a right of jury trial in all criminal cases which—were they to be tried in a federal court—would come within the Sixth Amendment's guarantee. . . . The nation has a deep commitment to the right of jury trial and is reluctant to entrust plenary powers over the life and liberty of the citizen to one judge or to a group of judges.

The pros and cons of jury trial have often been debated. Arguments in favor include (1) the value of citizen participation in the criminal justice system; (2) the obvious advantage of twelve (or six) minds over one; (3) the likelihood that, if a jury is convinced, a case has been established; (4) the protection of civil liberties and commonsense application of the law by choosing a group at random from the lists of registered voters; and (5) the great difficulty in intimidating or bribing a group that does not come together until the beginning of a trial. Arguments against juries are (1) the sheer expense of so cumbersome a process; (2) the uncertainty of whether the jurors will understand the issues at hand; (3) the almost inevitable delays associated with jury trials; and (4) the fact that a jury does not give reasons for its decision, making it more difficult to appeal.

REFERENCES

David Kairys, Joseph B. Kadane, and John P. Lehoczky, Jury representativeness: A mandate for multiple source lists, *California Law Review* 65 (July 1977);

Rita James Simon, The American jury: Instrument of justice or of prejudice and conformity? *Sociological Inquiry* 47:3–4 (1977);

Robert T. Roper, Jury size: Impact on verdict's correctness, *American Politics Quarterly* 7 (October 1979);

Marjorie S. Schultz, The jury redefined: A review of Burger Court decisions, *Law and Contemporary Problems* 43 (Autumn 1980);

Valerie P. Hans and Neil Vidmar, *Judging the Jury* (New York: Plenum, 1986).

justice 1 The title of a judge; for example, an associate justice of the U.S. Supreme Court. *Compare to* CHIEF JUSTICE. 2 An elusive quality of treatment by one's nation that is perceived by the overwhelming majority of the citizens to be fair and appropriate. 3 The philosophic search for perfection in governance. James Madison wrote in Federalist 51 that "justice is the end of government. It is the end of civil society." 4 The ideal that each nation's laws seek to achieve for each of its citizens. According to Alexis de Tocqueville in *Democracy in America* (1835): "There is one universal law that has been formed or at least adopted . . . by the majority of mankind. That law is justice. Justice forms the cornerstone of each nation's law." 5 A cynical justification for tyranny. Plato in *Republic* (370 BC) wrote that "justice is but the interest of the stronger."

REFERENCES
Nancy Eisenberg Berg and Paul Mussen, The origins and development of concepts of justice, *Journal of Social Issues* 31:3 (1975);
Joseph F. Fletcher and Patrick Neal, Hercules and the legislator: The problem of justice in contemporary political philosophy, *Canadian Journal of Political Science* 18 (March 1985).

Justice, U.S. Department of A cabinet-level department of the federal government. As the largest law firm in the nation, the Department of Justice is supposed to represent the citizens of the United States in enforcing the law in the public interest. The department conducts all suits in the U.S. Supreme Court in which the United States is concerned. It represents the government in legal matters generally, rendering legal advice and opinions, upon request, to the president and to the heads of the executive departments. The U.S. ATTORNEY GENERAL supervises and directs these activities, as well as those of the U.S. attorneys and U.S. marshals in the various judicial districts around the country. While the attorney general was placed in the president's cabinet in 1789, it wasn't until 1870 that the Congress created a Department of Justice to assist him.

REFERENCE
Daniel J. Meador, Role of the Justice Department in maintaining an effective judiciary, *Annals of the American Academy of Political and Social Science* 462 (July 1982).

U.S. Department of Justice
Constitution Avenue and 10th Street, N.W.
Washington, D.C. 20530
(202) 633-2000

justice of the peace A minor judicial official, not necessarily a lawyer, who has the authority to deal with petty civil and criminal cases, fix bail, perform marriages, and so on. In most urban areas, the justice of the peace has been replaced by a municipal court.

justiciability Appropriate for a court decision; the question of whether an issue should properly come to a court; whether a law exists that has been violated. Justiciability assures that a court has jurisdiction (the power) to hear a case; thus the concern is whether hearing the case at hand would be a proper exercise of judicial power. In *Baker v Carr,* for example, the Supreme Court held that apportionment was a justiciable issue.

REFERENCE
Jonathan D. Varat, Variable justiciability and the *Duke Power* case, *Texas Law Review* 58 (February 1980).

K

Kafkaesque A reference to Franz Kafka's (1883–1924) novels and short stories, most particularly *The Trial* (posthumously published in 1937), which detailed the experiences of characters accused of crimes that are never explained to them and punished by agents whose authority they cannot understand for actions they have no clear sense of having committed. Kafka's name has come to stand for bureaucratic behavior that is threatening to the individual without being intelligible, behavior not based on any rules the individual can be expected to know, or behavior not subject to any redress to which the individual has access.

Kaiser Aluminum & Chemical Corporation v Weber, et al. *See* UNITED STEELWORKERS OF AMERICA V WEBER, ET AL.

Kelley v Johnson 425 U.S. 238 (1976) The U.S. Supreme Court case that upheld a municipal regulation limiting the hair length of police.

Kennedy, Edward Moore "Ted" (1932–   )
The youngest brother of President John F. Kennedy and a U.S. senator from Massachusetts since 1963. Kennedy, who is often mentioned as a possible Democratic nominee for president (he actively sought but lost the nomination to President Jimmy Carter in 1980), is a major voice for traditionally liberal legislation in the Senate.

REFERENCES
James MacGregor Burns, *Edward Kennedy and the Camelot Legacy* (New York: Norton, 1976);
Stephen J. Wayne, Cheryl Beil, and Joy Falk, Public perceptions about Ted Kennedy and the presidency, *Presidential Studies Quarterly* 12 (Winter 1982).

Kennedy, John Fitzgerald (1917–1963)
The first Roman Catholic to be elected president of the United States. His administration (1961–1963) is now more noted for its style

John F. Kennedy.

(*see* CAMELOT) than substance. His charming and charismatic personality tended to overshadow his failure to get any major legislation through a conservative-dominated Congress and his foreign policy frustrations with Cuba (*see* BAY OF PIGS), the Soviet Union (*see* CUBAN MISSILE CRISIS), and Vietnam, where he had placed sixteen thousand American military "advisors." (*See also* ALLIANCE FOR PROGRESS.) But in spite of all this, Kennedy will always be remembered as the president who brought a sense of youthful vigor to the White House and launched the space age with his decision to put Americans on the moon within a decade. Just as President Franklin D. Roosevelt used radio to create a personal relationship with the American public, Kennedy became the first president to effectively use live television on a regular basis (*see* PRESIDENTIAL PRESS CONFERENCE). Perhaps Kennedy's most significant decision for the future of the nation was his selection of LYNDON B. JOHNSON to be his vice president—with all the good and ill that implied for the 1960s. Kennedy was assassinated in Dallas, Texas, on November 22, 1963 (*see* WARREN COMMISSION).

REFERENCES

For adoring biographies by former aides, see Arthur M. Schlesinger, Jr., *A Thousand Days: John F. Kennedy in the White House* (Boston: Houghton Mifflin, 1965); Theodore C. Sorensen, *Kennedy* (New York: Harper & Row, 1965).

For more objective accounts, see Lewis J. Paper, *The Promise and the Performance: The Leadership of John F. Kennedy* (New York: Crown, 1975); Herbert S. Parmet, *The Presidency of John F. Kennedy* (New York: Dial, 1983); Allen J. Matusow, *The Unravelling of America: The History of Liberalism in the 1960s* (New York: Harper & Row, 1984).

For how he became president, see Theodore H. White, *The Making of the President 1960* (New York: Atheneum, 1961).

The John F. Kennedy Administration

Major Accomplishments

- The Cuban missile crisis (nuclear war was avoided).
- A vastly expanded space program.
- A policy framework for the civil rights and Great Society legislation of the Lyndon B. Johnson administration.
- Tax cuts to stimulate the economy.
- The Peace Corps.

Major Frustrations

- Inability to get domestic proposals past the conservative coalition in the Congress.
- The Bay of Pigs.
- The continuing cold war with the Soviet Union.

Kennedy, Robert Francis (1925–1968) The younger brother of President John F. Kennedy, his campaign manager in 1960, then his attorney general. In 1964 he was elected to the U.S. Senate from New York. He was assassinated while campaigning for the Democratic party's presidential nomination on June 6, 1968.

REFERENCE

For a biography, see Arthur M. Schlesinger, Jr., *Robert F. Kennedy and His Times* (Boston: Houghton Mifflin, 1978).

Keogh Plan/H.R. 10 Plan The Self-Employed Individuals Tax Retirement Act of 1962, which encourages the establishment of voluntary pension plans by self-employed individuals. Congressman Eugene J. Keogh was the prime sponsor of the act; H.R. 10 was the number assigned to the bill prior to its passage.

Kerner Commission The National Advisory Commission on Civil Disorders, chaired by Governor Otto Kerner (1908–1976) of Illinois, which reported in 1968 that the "nation is rapidly moving toward two increasingly separate Americas; one black and one white."

Kerr-Mills Act The popular name for the Social Security amendments of 1960, which expanded and modified the federal government's existing responsibility for assisting the states in paying for medical care for the poor.

Kestnbaum Commission The Commission on Intergovernmental Relations, created (in 1953) by President Dwight D. Eisenhower and chaired by Meyer Kestnbaum, whose report (submitted in 1955) led to the creation of the permanent Advisory Commission on Intergovernmental Relations in 1959.

Keyishian v Board of Regents 385 U.S. 589 (1967) The U.S. Supreme Court case that held that laws "which make Communist Party membership, as such, prima facie evidence of disqualification for employment in the public school system are overbroad and therefore unconstitutional."

Keynes, John Maynard (1883–1946) The English economist who wrote the most influential book on economics of this century, *The General Theory of Employment, Interest and Money* (London: Macmillan, 1936). Keynes founded a school of thought known as Keynesian economics, which called for using a government's fiscal and monetary policies to positively influence a capitalistic economy, and developed the framework of modern macroeconomic theory. All U.S. presidents since Franklin D. Roosevelt have used Keynes' theories to, admittedly or unadmittedly, justify def-

John Maynard Keynes.

icit spending to stimulate the economy. Even President Richard M. Nixon admitted, "We're all Keynesians now." Keynes observed that "practical men, who believe themselves to be quite exempt from any intellectual influences, are usually the slaves of some defunct economist." He provided the definitive economic forecast when he asserted that "in the long run we are all dead."

REFERENCES

For biographies, see Robert Lekachman, *The Age of Keynes* (New York: Random, 1975);

John Fender, *Understanding Keynes: An Analysis of "The General Theory"* (New York: Wiley, 1981);

Charles H. Hession, *John Maynard Keynes: A Personal Biography of the Man Who Revolutionized Capitalism and the Way We Lived* (New York: Macmillan, 1984).

Also see Elizabeth Johnson, John Maynard Keynes: Scientist or politician? *Journal of Political Economy* 82 (January/February 1974);

Robert Eisner, The Keynesian revolution reconsidered, *American Economic Review* 65 (May 1975);

Martin Feldstein, The retreat from Keynesian economics, *Public Interest* 64 (Summer 1981);

Roberta Schaefer and David Schaefer, The political philosophy of J. M. Keynes, *Public Interest* 71 (Spring 1983);

James Tobin, A Keynesian view of the budget deficit, *California Management Review* 26 (Winter 1984).

keynote address   The major political speech (other than the candidate's acceptance speech) at a national nominating convention that is supposed to set the tone for the campaign to come. It is an opportunity to make the party's case on prime-time television to the people and is usually given by one of the party's most gifted orators.

Key, V. O., Jr. (1908–1963)   The political scientist who did pioneering work in developing empirical methods to explore political and administrative behavior. His article "The Lack of a Budgetary Theory," *American Political Science Review* 34 (December 1940), posed what was soon acknowledged as the central question of budgeting—"on what basis shall it be decided to allocate X dollars to activity A instead of activity B?" His *Politics, Parties and Pressure Groups* (New York: Crowell, 1942, 5th ed., 1964) was the pioneering text in the functional analysis of the various elements in the political process. His *Southern Politics in State and Nation* (New York: Knopf, 1949) was the classic study of why the Democratic party dominated the South for so long after the Civil War.

REFERENCES

Other major works include *A Primer of Statistics for Political Scientists* (New York: Crowell, 1954);

American State Politics: An Introduction (New York: Knopf, 1956);

Public Opinion and American Democracy (New York: Knopf, 1961);

The Responsible Electorate, ed. Milton C. Cummings, Jr. (Cambridge, MA: Harvard University Press, 1966). This last work was published posthumously.

KGB   *Komitet Gosudarstuennoe Bezopasnosti* (Committee for State Security), the internal security police and international espionage organization of the Soviet Union.

REFERENCE

Amy W. Knight, The KGB's special departments in the Soviet armed forces, *Orbis* 28 (Summer 1984).

Martin Luther King, Jr.

King, Martin Luther, Jr. (1929–1968) The black southern Baptist minister who became the preeminent leader of the civil rights movement. His tactics of nonviolent confrontation with southern segregational policies aroused enough sympathy and support in the rest of the nation that they led to landmark civil rights legislation. King was assassinated in Memphis, Tennessee, on April 4, 1968. His influence as the "saint" of civil rights was so strong that his birthday was made a national holiday in 1983.

REFERENCES

David J. Garrow, *Protest at Selma: Martin Luther King, Jr., and the Voting Rights Act of 1965* (New Haven, CT: Yale University Press, 1978);

Stephen B. Oates, *Let the Trumpets Sound! The Life of Martin Luther King, Jr.* (New York: Harper & Row, 1982);

David J. Garrow, *Bearing the Cross: Martin Luther King, Jr., and the Southern Christian Leadership Conference* (New York: Morrow, 1986).

Martin Luther King, Jr., and the Civil Rights Movement: A Chronology

1954   U.S. Supreme Court in *Brown v Board of Education* declared that racial segregation in public schools was unconstitutional.

1954   King became pastor of the Dexter Avenue Church in Montgomery, Alabama.

1955   King earned a Ph.D. in Systematic Theology from Boston University.

1955   Rosa Parks, a forty-two-year-old black woman, refused to give up her seat on a Montgomery bus to a white man and was arrested.

1955   King led the Montgomery bus boycott.

1956   Montgomery buses were integrated. The success of the boycott under King's leadership made him a national spokesman for civil rights.

1957   The Southern Christian Leadership Conference was formed, with King as president.

1957   The Civil Rights Act of 1957 created the Civil Rights Commission.

1959   King went to India to study Gandhi's techniques of nonviolence.

1960   King moved to Atlanta, Georgia, to become copastor with his father, Martin Luther King, Sr., of the Ebenezer Baptist Church.

1960   Students in Greensboro, North Carolina, initiated a nationwide wave of sit-in protests.

1963   King was arrested in Birmingham, Alabama, while participating in a sit-in to protest segregated eating facilities. While imprisoned, King wrote his "Letter from a Birmingham Jail."

1963   The March on Washington was held on August 28. King spoke to 250,000 people gathered at the Lincoln Memorial. He said, in part:

> I have a dream that one day this nation will rise up and live out the true meaning of its creed: "We hold these truths to be self-evident; that all men are created equal."
>
> I have a dream that one day on the red hills of Georgia the sons of former slaves and the sons of former slaveowners will be able to sit down together at the table of brotherhood.
>
> I have a dream that one day even the state of Mississippi, a desert state sweltering with the heat of injustice and oppression, will be transformed into an oasis of freedom and justice.

> I have a dream that my four little children will one day live in a nation where they will not be judged by the color of their skin but by the content of their character.

1964	The Civil Rights Act of 1964 was passed.
1964	King received the Nobel Peace Prize.
1965	The Voting Rights Act of 1965 was passed.
1966	The U.S. Supreme Court ruled that the poll tax was unconstitutional.
1967	King denounced the Vietnam War.
1968	King was assassinated in Memphis, Tennessee, on April 4.
1983	King's birthday was made national holiday.

Kingsley, J. Donald (1908–1972) The former director-general of the United Nations' International Refugee Organization, coauthor of the first full-scale text on public personnel administration, and creator of the concept of representative bureaucracy. *Compare to* SAMUEL KRISLOV.

REFERENCES
Kingsley's major works include *Public Personnel Administration,* with William E. Mosher (New York: Harper & Row, 1936);
Representative Bureaucracy: An Interpretation of the British Civil Service (Yellow Springs, OH: Antioch, 1944).

Kitchen Cabinet *See* CABINET, KITCHEN.

Know-Nothing party The Supreme Order of the Star Spangled Banner, formed by secret far-right patriotic societies in the late 1840s. The order wanted to restrict immigration, increase the residency requirement for citizenship to twenty-one years, and prohibit Catholics and the foreign born from holding elected office. Since it was a secret society, members were bound to reply "I know nothing" when asked about their organization's activities. In the early 1850s, they became the American party and won some state elections in New England. In 1856 Millard Fillmore (1800–1874), the former president (1850–1853), was the party's candidate for president. His loss was so great (he carried only one

state, Maryland), that the party disintegrated. Know-nothing was an informal title given to them by the press; but the term is still used to describe anyone who is a bigot and political reactionary.

REFERENCE
Ray Allen Billington, The Know-Nothing uproar, *American Heritage* 10:2 (1959).

Kolender v Lawson 461 U.S. 352 (1983) The U.S. Supreme Court case that held that a California statute that required people who loiter or wander to provide "credible and reliable" identification and an account for their presence when requested by a "peace officer" was unconstitutionally vague and vested too much discretion in police officers.

Korean War The war between communist North Korea and noncommunist South Korea, which began on June 25, 1950, when the North invaded the South. The decision on the part of President Harry S Truman and his advisors to promote intervention was a reversal of a policy previously announced by Secretary of State Dean Acheson, that Korea lay outside the defense perimeter of the United States. The decision was based on the belief that the actions of North Korea reflected larger policy interests promoted by the Soviet Union and Communist China and therefore required a strong American response. With the encouragement of the United States, the United Nations Security Council (with the Soviet Union temporarily absent) asked member nations to aid the South in resisting the invasion. Thus the war, called a police action, was fought under the flag of the United Nations by U.S. forces with small contingents from over a dozen other nations. The North Koreans, in turn, soon got help from Chinese Communist "volunteer" forces. After three years, an armistice was signed (July 27, 1953), which maintained the division of the Koreas almost exactly where it was before the war started. No peace treaty has ever been signed. The Korean War is an example of a LIMITED WAR with ambiguous objectives. When the commander of all U.N. and U.S. forces during the first part of the war, General Douglas MacArthur (1880–1964), publicly disagreed with President Truman's limited war policies, he was publicly dismissed from command in April 1951. More than fifty thousand Americans died in the Korean War; another hundred thousand were wounded.

REFERENCE

Keith D. McFarland, *The Korean War: An Annotated Bibliography* (New York: Garland, 1986).

Korematsu v United States *See* EMERGENCY POWERS.

Krislov, Samuel (1929–   ) A constitutional law scholar best known for his development of the concept of representative bureaucracy. In *The Negro in Federal Employment* (Minneapolis: University of Minnesota Press, 1967), Krislov examined the advantages of "representation in the sense of personification," and thereby gave a name to the goal for the movement for the fullest expression of civil rights in government employment—representa-

tative bureaucracy. In a subsequent work in 1974, *Representative Bureaucracy* (Englewood Cliffs, NJ: Prentice-Hall), Krislov asked how any bureaucracy could have legitimacy and public credibility if it didn't represent all sectors of its society. So, thanks in large part to Krislov, the phrase representative bureaucracy grew to mean that all social groups have a right to participation in their governing institutions. In recent years, the phrase has even developed a normative overlay—that all social groups should occupy bureaucratic positions in direct proportion to their number in the general population. *Compare to* J. DONALD KINGSLEY.

REFERENCES

Krislov's other major works include *The Supreme Court and Political Freedom* (New York: Free Press, 1968);

The Judicial Process and Constitutional Law (Boston: Little, Brown, 1972);

Representative Bureaucracy and the American Political System, with David H. Rosenbloom (New York: Praeger, 1981).

L

Labor, U.S. Department of (DOL) The cabinet-level federal agency created in 1913 to foster, promote, and develop the welfare of the wage earners of the United States, to improve their working conditions, and to advance their opportunities for profitable employment. In carrying out this mission, the DOL administers more than 130 federal labor laws guaranteeing workers' rights to safe and healthful working conditions, a minimum hourly wage and overtime pay, unemployment insurance, workers' compensation, and freedom from employment discrimination. The DOL also protects workers' pension rights, sponsors job training programs, helps workers find jobs, works to strengthen free collective bargaining, and

keeps track of changes in employment, prices, and other national economic measurements.

U.S. Department of Labor
200 Constitution Avenue, N.W.
Washington, D.C. 20210
(202) 523–4000

Labor-Management Relations Act of 1947/ Taft-Hartley Act The federal statute that modified what the Congress thought was a prounion bias in the National Labor Relations (Wagner) Act of 1935. Essentially a series of amendments to the National Labor Relations Act, Taft-Hartley (1) allowed national emergency strikes to be put off for an eighty-day cooling-off period, during which the president might make recommendations to the Congress for legislation; (2) delineated unfair labor practices by unions to balance the unfair labor practices by employers delineated in the Wagner Act; (3) made the closed shop illegal, allowing states to pass right-to-work laws; (4) excluded supervisory employees from coverage under the act; (5) allowed suits against unions for contract violations (judgments enforceable only against union assets); (6) required a party seeking to cancel an existing collective bargaining agreement to give sixty days' notice; (7) gave employers the right to seek a representation election if a union claimed recognition as a bargaining agent; (8) allowed the National Labor Relations Board to be reorganized and enlarged, from three to five members; and (9) provided for the creation of the Federal Mediation and Conciliation Service to mediate labor disputes. The act was passed over the veto of President Harry S Truman.

REFERENCE

Anil Baran Ray, President Truman and Taft-Hartley Act: A psycho-political inquiry, *Journal of Constitution and Parliamentary Studies* 14 (October/December 1980).

Labor-Management Reporting and Disclosure Act of 1959/Landrum-Griffin Act The federal statute enacted in response to findings of corruption in the management of some unions. The act provided for the reporting and disclosure of certain financial transactions and administrative practices of labor organizations and employers and created standards for the election of officers of labor organizations. The Congress determined that certain basic rights should be assured to members of labor unions, and these are listed in Title I of the act—as a "bill of rights." Existing rights and remedies of union members under other federal or state laws, before any court or tribunal, or under the constitution and bylaws of their unions are not limited by the provisions of Title I. Executive Order 11491 applied these rights to members of unions representing employees of the executive branch of the federal government.

REFERENCES

Doris B. McLaughlin and Anita L. W. Schoomaker, *The Landrum-Griffin Act and Union*

Democracy (Ann Arbor: University of Michigan Press, 1978);

Janice R. Bellace and Alan D. Berkowitz, *The Landrum-Griffin Act: Twenty Years of Federal Protection of Union Members' Rights* (Philadelphia: Wharton School, University of Pennsylvania, 1979).

labor movement 1 An inclusive phrase for the progressive history of unionism in the United States. Sometimes it is used in a broader sense to encompass the fate of the workers. The political influence of American unions has been declining precipitously in recent decades. In 1955, close to 40 percent of all nonfarm workers belonged to unions. By the late 1980s, that number had dropped to less than 18 percent. **2** The political organization of working class interests.

REFERENCES

For histories, see Leon Litwack, *The American Labor Movement* (Englewood Cliffs, NJ: Prentice-Hall, 1962);

Jack Barbash, Labor movement theory and the institutional setting, *Monthly Labor Review* 104 (September 1981).

The Labor Movement in Action

When Lane Kirkland succeeded George Meany as president of the AFL-CIO in 1979, he inherited an organization that had lost much of its former political muscle. In 1980, Ronald Reagan won about 40 percent of the labor vote, although the AFL-CIO had formally endorsed Jimmy Carter for reelection. In an effort to revitalize labor's sagging political influence, Kirkland developed a strategy, and in 1981 he started floating the idea of a preprimary endorsement. After Senator Edward M. Kennedy announced his noncandidacy, former vice-president Walter F. Mondale became the obvious choice. Kirkland reasoned that, with the unions' combined financial and organizational strength, their candidate for the Democratic party's presidential nomination would win. The trick was for labor to stick together. In years past, individual unions had endorsed and financially supported a variety of candidates. Some unions have even supported the Republican candidate in the general election. Labor's faltering political clout had to be mended. The only question was how. As Kirkland told one AFL-CIO executive council session, "We've tried everything else, why don't we try unity?"

The key to the strategy was the commitment of the heads of the individual unions to unite behind one candidate in advance of the primaries. This would mean that they would have to give up the usual courting by candidates and concomitant media attention—attention that significantly contributed to their own job security by making them appear to be influential in the eyes of their membership. Kirkland was able to form the needed consensus, and the AFL-CIO became more actively involved in Democratic party politics than it had ever been before. In October 1983, more than a year before the 1984 presidential election, the general board of the AFL-CIO met to endorse Mondale for president of the United States.

In a sense, the policy of preprimary endorsement was a sure winner for labor. If their candidate won the nomination, his debt to labor would be obvious. If the convention contest was close, a unified group of labor delegates could have a great influence on the outcome. But what if labor's candidate lost and there was no opportunity to play kingmaker at the convention? Then labor was graciously prepared to support the winner who, no doubt, would be delighted to have the enthusiastic support of labor in the general election. In possible anticipation of this, AFL-CIO political operatives were told not to openly criticize the other Democratic candidates. In the end, there had to be unity. The goal of defeating Ronald Reagan, the former union leader who turned out to be the most antilabor president of modern times, was paramount. But what if the Democrats lost the presidential election in 1984? They did; but labor still won, because it emerged as the most influential and unified force within the Democratic party—the group that is the most experienced, most determined, and most ready for 1988.

As Kirkland explained his strategy to the AFL-CIO convention in 1983: "If we do not do what we propose to do, we shall be reviled as toothless and irrelevant. If we succeed, we shall be condemned for daring to aspire to a share of power in our society. Given that choice of slurs, I assure you that I much prefer the latter."

Source: Adapted from David H. Rosenbloom and Jay M. Shafritz, *Essentials of Labor Relations* (Reston, VA: Reston/Prentice-Hall, 1985).

labor union *See* TRADE UNION.

Laffer curve The purported relation between tax rates and government revenues publicized by economist Arthur B. Laffer. According to Laffer, higher taxes reduce government revenues because high tax rates discourage taxable activity. Following this logic, a government can raise its total revenues by cutting taxes. This should stimulate new taxable activity, and the revenue from this should more than offset the loss from lower tax rates. While Laffer may have been the first to draw his curve, many others had earlier expressed the ideas behind it. For example, JOHN MAYNARD KEYNES wrote: "Taxation may be so high as to defeat its object. . . . Given sufficient time to gather the fruits, a reduction of taxation will run a better chance, than an increasing, of balancing the budget." Even President John F. Kennedy observed in a speech of December 14, 1962, that "it is a paradoxical truth that tax rates are too high today and tax revenues are too low—and the soundest way to raise revenues in the long run is to cut tax rates now." *Compare to* SUPPLY-SIDE ECONOMICS.

REFERENCES

Jude Wanniski, Taxes, revenues, and the "Laffer curve," *Public Interest* 50 (Winter 1978);

David Henderson, Limitations on the Laffer curve as a justification for tax cuts, *Cato Journal* 1 (Spring 1981);

James M. Buchanan and Dwight R. Lee, Politics, time, and the Laffer curve, *Journal of Political Economy* 90 (August 1982);

Roger N. Waud, Politics, deficits, and the Laffer curve, *Public Choice* 47:2 (1985).

laissez-faire A hands-off style of governance that emphasizes economic freedom so the capitalist invisible hand can work its will. The concept is most associated with ADAM SMITH and his *Wealth of Nations* (1776).

REFERENCE

Benjamin R. Twiss, *Lawyers and the Constitution: How Laissez-Faire Came to the Supreme Court* (Princeton, NJ: Princeton University Press, 1942).

Lakewood plan *See* SERVICE CONTRACT.

lame duck 1 Any officeholder who is serving out the remainder of a fixed term after declining to run or being defeated or ineligible for reelection. The authority of such an officeholder is considered impaired, or lame. The phrase originated in the early days of the London stock market (known as Exchange Alley

315

until 1773). A broker who went bankrupt would "waddle out of the Alley" like a lame duck. By the time of the American Civil War, the phrase had crossed the Atlantic to refer to a bankrupt politician. **2** Anyone in an organization whose leaving has been announced, whether for retirement, promotion, or transfer.

lame duck amendment   The Twentieth Amendment to the U.S. Constitution, ratified in 1933, which provides that the terms of the president and vice president shall end at noon on January 20 instead of March 4, the terms of senators and representatives shall end at noon on January 3 instead of March 4, and the terms of their successors shall then begin. Prior to this amendment, the annual session of the Congress began on the first Monday in December (Article I, Section 4). Since the terms of new members formerly began on March 4, members who had not been reelected in November continued to serve during the lame duck session, December through March 4. Thus the lame duck amendment is in reality an antilame duck amendment.

lame duck appointment   A political appointment made by a lame duck or outgoing executive. A lame duck appointment was one of the major questions at issue in *Marbury v Madison*.

lame duck president   **1** Any president who has not been reelected. Jimmy Carter was a lame duck president after he lost to Ronald Reagan in 1980.   **2** Any president in his second term, even though the Twenty-second Amendment, making the president ineligible to run for a third term, was not intended to create an automatic lame duck president. But no matter how large a second term victory is, it (the amendment) appears in effect to have done so. One must also remember that two terms were an accepted limit until Franklin D. Roosevelt's unprecedented four elections, and the American experiences with two-term presidencies since passage of the amendment has been very limited.

REFERENCE

Karen S. Johnson, The portrayal of lame-duck presidents by the national print media, *Presidential Studies Quarterly* 16 (Winter 1986).

Landrum-Griffin Act   *See* LABOR-MANAGEMENT REPORTING AND DISCLOSURE ACT OF 1959/LANDRUM-GRIFFIN ACT.

landslide   A decidedly lopsided political victory, one in which the opponent is metaphorically buried in a landslide. Both of President Ronald Reagan's electoral victories in 1980 and 1984 were landslides, because the opposition (Jimmy Carter in 1980; Walter F. Mondale in 1984) carried so few states. A landslide victory is not synonymous with an unspecified MANDATE for action. There are a significant number of instances where presidents won reelection by overwhelming landslides only to find their effectiveness seriously curtailed shortly thereafter (Franklin D. Roosevelt after 1936, Lyndon B. Johnson after 1964, Richard M. Nixon after 1972, and Ronald Reagan after 1984). In contrast, a very narrow victory may generate too much caution. For example, John F. Kennedy won by such a narrow margin in 1960 that he felt he had to wait until a hoped-for more decisive victory in 1964 before he could act boldly on critical issues.

Sometimes the word landslide is used sarcastically, as in 1948 when Lyndon B. Johnson was elected as a U.S. senator from Texas by a majority of eighty-seven votes out of a million cast. Johnson earned the nickname "Landslide Lyndon," which was all the more sarcastic because of the general belief (since then supported by historians) that the votes were fraudulently obtained.

Lane v Wilson   *See* VOTING, COMPULSORY.

Lasswell, Harold D.   (1902–1978)   One of the most influential and prolific of social scientists. While he made major contributions to the fields of communications, psychology (he pioneered the application of Freudian theory to politics), political science (as a major voice in the CHICAGO SCHOOL), sociology, and law, his most lasting legacy is probably his pioneering work in developing the concept and methodology of the POLICY SCIENCES.

REFERENCES

Lasswell's major works include *Propaganda Technique in World War I* (Cambridge, MA: MIT Press, 1927, 1971);

Psychopathology and Politics (New York: Viking, 1930, 1960);

Politics: Who Gets What, When, How (New York: Smith, 1936, 1950);

Power and Society, with Abraham Kaplan (New Haven, CT: Yale University Press, 1950, 1963);

The Policy Sciences, ed. with David Lerner (Stanford, CA: Stanford University Press, 1951, 1968);

Pre-view of Policy Sciences (New York: American Elsevier, 1971).

For appreciations, see Arnold A. Rogow, *Politics, Personality, and Social Science in the Twentieth Century: Essays in Honor of Harold D. Lasswell* (Chicago: University of Chicago Press, 1969);

Kuo-Wei Lee, Harold Lasswell's psychoanalytical approach, *Political Science Review* 14 (January–June 1975);

Douglas Torgerson, Contextual orientation in policy analysis: The contribution of Harold D. Lasswell, *Policy Sciences* 18 (November 1985).

Latham, Earl   *See* INTEREST GROUP THEORY.

law   1 A generalization about nature that posits an order of behavior that will be the same in every instance where the same factors are involved.   **2** Enforceable rules.   **3** A statute passed by a legislature and signed by an executive or passed over a veto.   **4** The totality of the rules and principles promulgated by a government.   *Compare to* ACT; ORDINANCE; STATUTE.

REFERENCE

H. L. A. Hart, *The Concept of Law* (New York: Oxford University Press, 1961).

law, administrative   *See* ADMINISTRATIVE LAW.

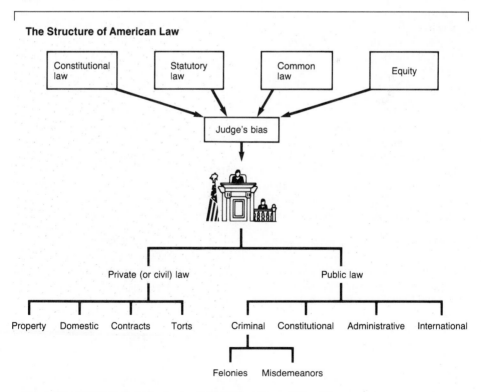

The Structure of American Law

Source: Grover Starling, *Understanding American Politics* (Chicago: Dorsey, 1982), p. 302.

law, admiralty *See* ADMIRALTY LAW.

law, blue *See* BLUE LAWS.

law, civil *See* CIVIL LAW.

law, common *See* COMMON LAW.

law, constitutional *See* CONSTITUTIONAL LAW.

law enforcement agency A federal, state, or local criminal justice agency of which the principal functions are the prevention, detection, and investigation of crime and the apprehension of alleged offenders.

law, ex post facto *See* EX POST FACTO LAW.

law, Jim Crow *See* JIM CROW.

law, natural The rules that would govern human kind in a STATE OF NATURE, before governments or positive law existed. Correspondingly, natural rights are the rights that all people have irrespective of the governing system under which they live. *Compare to* IN-ALIENABLE RIGHTS.

REFERENCE
Paul E. Sigmund, *Natural Law in Political Thought* (Lanham, MD: University Press of America, 1982).

law of the land 1 The U.S. Constitution. Article VI states that "this Constitution . . . shall be the supreme law of the land." 2 Laws enforced throughout a geographical area. 3 A nation's customs, which over time are incorporated into the common law.

law, Parkinson's *See* PARKINSON'S LAW.

law, positive Law that has been created by a recognized authority, such as a legislature, as opposed to natural or common law.

law, private *See* PRIVATE LAW.

law, public *See* PUBLIC LAW.

law, Roman The body of law codified by the Romans under the Emperor Justinian in 530 AD, which provides the underlying basis for civil law in much of the Western world. Why else are so many legal phrases and concepts in Latin? Roman law, a major example of a CODE LAW, which seeks to cover all instances of behavior, is contrasted with COMMON LAW, which evolves over long periods through court action and custom.

REFERENCES
Franz Wieacker, The importance of Roman law for Western civilization and Western legal thought, *Boston College International and Comparative Law Review* 4 (Fall 1981);
Shael Herman, The uses and abuses of Roman law texts, *American Journal of Comparative Law* 29 (Fall 1981);
W. Hamilton Bryson, The use of Roman law in Virginia courts, *American Journal of Legal History* 28 (April 1984).

laws, fair employment practice *See* FAIR EMPLOYMENT PRACTICE LAWS.

law, slip *See* SLIP LAWS.

laws, right-to-work *See* RIGHT-TO-WORK LAWS.

leadership The exercise of authority, whether formal or informal, in directing and coordinating the work of others. The best leaders are those who can simultaneously exercise both kinds of leadership: the formal, based on the authority of rank or office, and the informal, based on the willingness of others to give service to a person whose special qualities of authority they admire. It has long been known that leaders who must rely only upon formal authority are at a disadvantage when compared to those who can also mobilize the informal strength of an organization or nation. Shakespeare observed this when in *Macbeth* (Act 5, Scene 2) he has Angus describe Macbeth's waning ability to command the loyalty of his troops:

Those he commands move only in command,
Nothing in love: now does he feel his title
Hange loose about him, like a giant's robe
Upon a dwarfish thief.

Perhaps the most succinct analysis on the problems of leadership comes from Harry S Truman, who said, while discoursing on his job as president of the United States: "I sit here all day trying to persuade people to do the things they ought to have sense enough to do without my persuading them." *See also* CHARISMA; FULL RESPONSIBILITY; POWER.

REFERENCES

The best one-volume summary of the literature on leadership is Ralph M. Stogdill, *Handbook of Leadership: A Survey of Theory and Research,* rev. ed. (New York: Free Press, 1981).

Also see Robert L. Peabody, *Leadership in Congress* (Boston: Little, Brown, 1976);

James M. Burns, *Leadership* (New York: Harper & Row, 1978);

Valerie Bunce, *Do New Leaders Make a Difference: Executive Succession and Public Policy under Capitalism and Socialism* (Princeton, NJ: Princeton University Press, 1981);

John B. Miner, The uncertain future of the leadership concept; Revisions and clarifications, *Journal of Applied Behavioral Science* 18:3 (1982).

leadership, transformational Leadership that strives to change organizational culture and directions, rather than continuing along traditional paths. It reflects the ability of a leader to develop a values-based vision for the organization, to convert the vision into reality, and to maintain it over time. Transformational leadership is a 1980s concept, closely identified with the concepts of symbolic management and organizational culture.

REFERENCES

W. G. Bennis, Transformative power and leadership, in *Leadership and Organizational Culture*, ed. T. J. Sergiovanni and J. E. Corbally (Urbana: University of Illinois Press, 1984);

N. M. Tichy and D. O. Ulrich, The leadership challenge—A call for the transformational leader, *Sloan Management Review 26* (Fall 1984).

leading indicators Statistics that generally precede a change in a situation. For example, an increase in economic activity is typically preceded by a rise in the prices of stocks. Each month, the Bureau of Economic Analysis of the Department of Commerce publishes data on hundreds of economic indicators in its *Business Conditions Digest*. Several dozen of these are classified as leading. The bureau's composite index of twelve leading indicators is a popular means of assessing the general state of the economy. Typical leading indicators include average work week of production workers in manufacturing, average weekly claims for state unemployment insurance, new factory orders for consumer goods, and new building permits issued.

The League of Women Voters is the most respected private source of information on elections.

League of Women Voters A national, nonpartisan, public interest organization. Founded in 1920 by the delegates to the last convention of the National American Woman Suffrage Association to educate newly enfranchised women in public affairs, it has grown to be the most respected private source of nonbiased information on elections at all jurisdictional levels.

REFERENCE

Naomi Black, The politics of the League of Women Voters, *International Social Science Journal* 35:4 (1983).

League of Women Voters
1730 M Street, N.W.
Washington, D.C. 20036
(202) 429–1965

leak 1 The deliberate disclosure of confidential or classified information by someone in government who wants to advance the public interest, embarrass a bureaucratic rival, or help a reporter disclose incompetence or skulduggery to the public. As James Reston (1909–   ) has written, "the government is the only known vessel that leaks from the top." **2** The inadvertent disclosure of secret information.

REFERENCES

1 Alan M. Katz, Government information leaks and the First Amendment, *California Law Review* 64 (January 1976);

Bruce Catton, The inspired leak, *American Heritage* 28 (February 1977);

Stephen Hess, *The Government/Press Connection: Press Officers and the Offices* (Washington, D.C.: Brookings, 1984).

least dangerous branch The federal judiciary; the U.S. Supreme Court; the judicial branch in general. This is Alexander Hamilton's description of the judicial department of government in Federalist 78:

> Whoever attentively considers the different departments of power must perceive that, in a government in which they are separated from each other, the judiciary, from the nature of its functions, will always be the least dangerous to the political rights of the Constitution; because it will be least in a capacity to annoy or injure them. The Executive not only dispenses the honours, but holds the sword of the community. The legislature not only commands the purse, but prescribes the rules by which the duties and rights of every citizen are to be regulated. The judiciary, on the contrary, has no influence over either the sword or the purse; no direction either of the strength or of the wealth of the society; and can take no active resolution whatever. It may truly be said to have neither force nor will, but merely judgment; and must ultimately depend upon the aid of the executive arm even for the efficacy of its judgments.

Also see ALEXANDER M. BICKEL.

REFERENCE

Henry J. Abraham, The "least dangerous branch" revisited: Reflections on a half-truth two centuries later, *Teaching Political Science* 14 (Fall 1986).

least-developed countries Those countries identified by the U.N. General Assembly in 1971 as without significant economic growth, with very low per capita incomes, and with low literacy rates. These countries plus those the United Nations designated as most seriously affected by the oil price increases of 1973–74 compose the Fourth World.

L. Ed. The abbreviation for *Lawyer's Edition* of the *U.S. Supreme Court Reports*.

Left The liberal, sometimes socialistic, elements of the political spectrum. The political Left in all free countries tends to favor a highly regulated capitalism, socially responsible free enterprise, and a strong welfare state. In contrast to the Right, which tends to be conservative, the Left has historically been an enthusiastic advocate of change (though in welfare states, the Left has assumed a conservative position aimed at preserving the structure and benefits of that state). The extreme Left tends to consist of those radicals who would take their nation all the way to communism. The terms Left and Right have come down to us from the fact that nineteenth-century European parliaments had the nobility sit on the king's right, the place of honor; that left the left side for the ignoble masses. *Compare to* LIBERALISM; SOCIALISM.

REFERENCES

Christopher Lasch, *The Agony of the American Left* (New York: Knopf, 1969);

Peter Clecak, Dilemmas of the American Left, *Social Research* 41 (Autumn 1974);

Bogdan Denitch, ed., *Democratic Socialism: The Mass Left in Advanced Industrial Societies* (Montclair, NJ: Allanheld, Osmun, 1981);

Asher Arian and Michal Shamir, The Primarily political functions of the Left-Right continuum, *Comparative Politics* 15 (January 1983).

leftist Someone who philosophically leans to the political Left. However, the word should be used cautiously, because it has taken on a taint that suggests the person being so called is a radical, a Communist, or worse.

Left, new The political reformers of the 1960s and 1970s who fought for civil rights for all, cheered on the war on poverty, opposed the war in Vietnam, and sought radical change in the American political and economic systems. Their influence dissipated as the war ended and the nation turned away from social reform and toward conservatism. While the term was first used to refer to those associated with the *New Left Review* journal in 1959, it was soon adopted by the mass media and the student movement of the 1960s.

REFERENCES

Irwin Unger, *The Movement: A History of the American New Left, 1959–1972* (New York: Dodd, Mead, 1974);

Sara Evans, *Personal Politics: The Roots of the Women's Liberation in the Civil Rights Movement and the New Left* (New York: Vintage, 1980);

Philip Abbott, The enlightenment legacy of the new Left, *Polity* 15 (Summer 1983).

Left, noncommunist The post–World War II New Deal liberals who sought to sustain a leftward movement in American politics that was not associated either with Marxism or with traditional Democratic party compromises with the conservative South. Many were associated with AMERICANS FOR DEMOCRATIC ACTION.

Left, old The between-the-World-Wars American leftists who were heavily influenced by communist ideology, were often members of the Communist party, and who felt themselves very much engaged in the Marxist class struggle.

REFERENCE

Armand L. Mauss, The lost promise of reconciliation: New Left vs. old Left, *Journal of Social Issues* 27 (Winter 1971).

legislation The end product of legislative action: laws, statutes, ordinances, and so on. There may not always be an end product. Depending on one's attitude toward a bill, the best legislation may be no legislation. Woodrow Wilson poetically wrote in his landmark study, *Congressional Government* (New York: Meridian, 1885, 1956), that "once begin the dance of legislation, and you must struggle through its mazes as best you can to its breathless end,—if any end there be." The legislative process is inherently messy. It is so full of compromise, hypocrisy, and self-interest that its end product, legislation, is sometimes compared to sausage, in that a wise person will avoid watching either of them being made.

REFERENCE

Eric Redman, *The Dance of Legislation* (New York: Simon & Schuster, 1973).

legislation, direct Laws enacted by a jurisdiction's population via an INITIATIVE, a REFERENDUM, or a TOWN MEETING, in contrast to laws enacted by an elected legislature.

REFERENCE

David B. Magleby, *Direct Legislation: Voting on Ballot Propositions in the United States* (Baltimore: Johns Hopkins University Press, 1984).

legislative branch 1 Members of the Congress, supporting staffs, plus the General Accounting Office (GAO), the Government Printing Office, and the Library of Congress. Several organizations in addition to the GAO are considered support agencies of the Congress: the Congressional Research Service, a division of the Library of Congress; the Office of Technology Assessment; and the Congressional Budget Office. 2 The representative lawmaking assembly of any level of government.

legislative clearance *See* CENTRAL CLEARANCE.

legislative council A group of state legislators, sometimes joined by administrative officers, who meet between legislative sessions to develop a legislative agenda, engage in research on policy issues, and so on.

legislative counsel The lawyer (or office) who aids legislators and legislative committees in the legal research necessary for such work as writing bills and holding hearings.

legislative court *See* CONSTITUTIONAL COURT.

legislative day The "day" extending from the time either house of the U.S. Congress meets after an adjournment until the time it next adjourns. Because the House of Representatives normally adjourns from day to day, legislative days and calendar days usually coincide. But in the Senate, a legislative day may, and frequently does, extend over several calendar days.

legislative history The written record of the writing of an act of the U.S. Congress. It may be used in writing rules, or by courts in interpreting the law, to ascertain the intent of the Congress if the act is ambiguous or lacking in detail. The legislative history is listed in the SLIP LAWS and consists of House, Senate, and conference committee reports (if any) and the House and Senate floor debates on the law. The history, particularly the committee reports, often contains the only complete explanation of the meaning and intent of the law. Members of the Congress, their staffs, and other interested parties often try to influence a legislative history to help shape the way the law is eventually administered by agencies and interpreted by the courts.

REFERENCES

Jorge L. Carro and Andrew R. Brann, Use of legislative histories by the U.S. Supreme Court; A statistical analysis, *Journal of Legislation* 9 (Summer 1982);

Beth M. Henschen, Judicial use of legislative history and intent in statutory interpretation, *Legislative Studies Quarterly* 10 (August 1985).

legislative immunity   *See* IMMUNITY, CONGRESSIONAL.

legislative intent   The supposed real meaning of a statute as interpreted from its legislative history. Sometimes, during the legislative debate on a bill, a member of the legislature will specifically talk about what is intended or not intended by the bill so that the ensuing legislative history will be a better guide to future interpretations of what really was meant by the law. *Compare to* ORIGINAL INTENT.

REFERENCE

Richard Marvel, Robert J. Parsons, Winn Sanderson, and N. Dale Wright, Legislative intent and oversight, *State Government* 49 (Winter 1976).

legislative liaison   The coordination of executive branch communications to the legislature. Liaison is a critical activity if an executive, whether president, governor, mayor, or executive agency, is to see his, her, or its legislative proposals enacted into law. In effect, the legislative liaison is a chief executive's or an agency's lobbyist.

REFERENCES

Abraham Holtzman, *Legislative Liaison: Executive Leadership in Congress* (Chicago: Rand McNally, 1970);

Eric L. Davis, Legislative liaison in the Carter administration, *Political Science Quarterly* 94 (Summer 1979).

legislative oversight   *See* OVERSIGHT, CONGRESSIONAL.

legislative service organizations   Informal groups of members of the U.S. Congress who meet to discuss policy issues of mutual concern. While such organizations have always existed, only in the last few decades have they become institutionalized and given formal staff assistance to do in-depth policy research analyses of major issues. The oldest such organization is the Democratic Study Group (DSG), organized in 1958. The success of the DSG in providing its members with information on pending legislation led other House and Senate members to organize informal groups around other issues. There are now about a hundred such groups in the Congress, among them the Republican Study Committee, the Congressional Black Caucus, the Northeast-Midwest Congressional Coalition, the Congressional Steel Caucus, the Congressional Rural Caucus, and the Congressional Hispanic Caucus.

Informal groups have traditionally been financed by members donating a portion of their staffing and equipment allowances to the group. In 1979, the House established new accounting procedures for informal groups (which the House officially calls legislative service organizations). A group above a certain size can be designated a legislative service organization and, in return for streamlined congressional funding and accounting procedures, is required to make regular public disclosure of its finances and to refrain from accepting noncongressional funds in support of legislative activities. *Compare to* CAUCUS.

REFERENCES

Arthur G. Stevens, Jr., Arthur H. Miller, and Thomas E. Mann, Mobilization of liberal strength in the House, 1955–1970: The Democratic Study Group, *American Political Science Review* 68 (June 1974);

Susan Webb Hammond, Arthur G. Stevens, Jr., and Daniel P. Mulhollan, Congressional caucuses: Legislators as lobbyists, *Interest Group Politics*, eds. Allan J. Cigler and Burdett A. Loomis (Washington, D.C.: Congressional Quarterly, 1983).

Informal Organizations in the U.S. Congress, 1984

House

Democratic

California Democratic Congressional Delegation (28)

Congressional Populist Caucus (15)

Conservative Democratic Forum—"boll weevils" (38)

Democratic Study Group (228)

House Democratic Research Organization (100)

Ninety-fifth Democratic Caucus (35)

Ninety-sixth Democratic Caucus (20)

Ninety-seventh New Members Caucus (24)

Ninety-eighth New Members Caucus (52)

United Democrats of Congress (125)

Republican

Conservative Opportunity Society

House Republican Study Committee (130)

House Wednesday Group (32)

Ninety-fifth Republican Club (14)

Northeast-Midwest Republican Coalition— "gypsy moths"

Republican Freshman Class of the Ninety-sixth Congress

Republican Freshman Class of the Ninety-seventh Congress

Republican Freshman Class of the Ninety-eighth Congress

Bipartisan

Ad Hoc Congressional Committee on Irish Affairs (110)

Budget Study Group (60)

Conference of Great Lakes Congressmen (100)

Congressional Agricultural Forum

Congressional Arts Caucus (186)

Congressional Automotive Caucus

Congressional Black Caucus (21)

Congressional Border Caucus (12)

Congressional Caucus for Science and Technology (15)

Congressional Coal Group (55)

Congressional Emergency Housing Caucus

Congressional Hispanic Caucus (11)

Congressional Human Rights Caucus (150)

Congressional Metropolitan Caucus (8)

Congressional Mushroom Caucus (60)

Congressional Port Caucus (150)

Congressional Rural Caucus (100)

Congressional Space Caucus (161)

Congressional Steel Caucus (120)

Congressional Sunbelt Council

Congressional Territorial Caucus (4)

Congressional Textile Caucus (42)

Congressional Travel and Tourism Caucus (154)

Export Task Force (102)

Federal Government Service Task Force (38)

House Caucus on North American Trade

House Fair Employment Practices Committee

House Footwear Caucus

Local Government Caucus (22)

New England Congressional Caucus (24)

Northeast-Midwest Congressional Coalition (196)

Pennsylvania Congressional Delegation Steering Committee (5)

Task Force on Devaluation of the Peso

Task Force on Industrial Innovation and Productivity

Tennessee Valley Authority Caucus (23)

Senate

Democratic

Moderate/Conservative Senate Democrats (15)

Republican

Senate Steering Committee

Bipartisan

Border Caucus

Concerned Senators for the Arts (35)

Northeast-Midwest Senate Coalition (40)

Senate Caucus on North American Trade

Senate Caucus on the Family (31)

Senate Children's Caucus (18)

Senate Coal Caucus (39)

Senate Copper Caucus (18)

Senate Drug Enforcement Caucus (44)

Senate Export Caucus

Senate Footwear Caucus

Senate Rail Caucus

Senate Steel Caucus (46)

Senate Tourism Caucus (60)

Senate Wine Caucus

Western State Coalition (30)

Bicameral

Ad Hoc Congressional Committee on the Baltic States and the Ukraine (75)

Arms Control and Foreign Policy Caucus
(129)
Coalition for Peace through Strength (232)
Congressional Alcohol Fuels Caucus (90)
Congressional Caucus for Women's Issues
(129)
Congressional Clearinghouse on the Future
(84)
Congressional Jewelry Manufacturing
Coalition
Congressional Senior Citizens Caucus
Congressional Wood Energy Caucus
Environmental and Energy Study Conference
(37)
Friends of Ireland (80)
Long Island Congressional Caucus
Military Reform Caucus
New York State Congressional Delegation
(36)
Pacific Northwest Trade Task Force
Pennsylvania Congressional Delegation (27)
Pro-Life Caucus (60)
Renewable Energy Congressional Staff
Group (50)
Senate/House Ad Hoc Monitoring Group on
Southern Africa (53)
Vietnam Veterans in Congress (38)

Note: Number of members, if known, in parentheses.

Source: Samuel C. Patterson, Roger H. Davidson, and
Randall B. Ripley, *A More Perfect Union: Introduction to
American Government*, 3d ed. (Chicago: Dorsey, 1985),
p. 347.

legislative veto *See* VETO, LEGISLATIVE.

legislator A member of a legislature elected to represent the interests or the voters of a specific constituency. But interests as used here go far beyond legislation. According to Congressman Morris K. Udall (1922–   ) of Arizona:

A congressman's primary job is to legislate. Yet our society and government are so complex that we spend less than a third of our time on legislative matters. A congressman is not only a legislator; he is also an employment agent, passport finder, constituent greeter, tourist agent, getter-outer of the armed services, veterans' affairs adjuster, public buildings dedicator, industrial development specialist, party leader, bill finder, newsletter writer, etc. His typical day will be far more concerned with these problems than with national defense, foreign aid, or appropriations for public works.

Compare to EDMUND BURKE; POLITICO.

REFERENCE

Donald G. Tacheron and Morris K. Udall, *The Job of the Congressman: An Introduction to Service in the U.S. House of Representatives*, 2d ed. (Indianapolis: Bobbs Merrill, 1970).

legislature 1 The lawmaking branch of a representative government. 2 The lawmaking branch of the government of the United States. Article I, Section 1, of the U.S. Constitution states that all legislative power shall be vested in the Congress. This means that the president is specifically denied the power to make laws. All his authority must be based either on expressed or implicit powers granted by the Constitution or on statutes enacted by the Congress. 3 The lawmaking branch of a state or local government. *Compare to* STATE GOVERNMENT.

REFERENCES

1 William K. Muir, Jr., *Legislature* (Chicago: University of Chicago Press, 1983).

3 Robert U. Goehlert and Frederick W. Musto, *State Legislatures: A Bibliography* (Santa Barbara, CA: ABC-Clio, 1985).

legitimacy 1 A characteristic of a social institution, such as a government or a family, whereby it has both a legal and a perceived right to make binding decisions for its members. Legitimacy is granted to an institution by its public—by that public conforming to established practices. In the federal government, the separation of powers allows each branch to judge the legitimacy of, and if necessary to take action to check, the acts of the others. Legitimacy is both a specific legal concept, meaning that something is lawful, and at the same time an amorphous psychosociological concept referring to an important element in the social glue that holds our societal institutions together. MAX WEBER, the most famous analyst of the legitimacy of governing structures, asserted that there were three pure types of domination: charismatic (in which the personal qualities of a leader command obedience); traditional (in which custom and culture yield acquiescence); and legal (in which people obey laws enacted by what they perceive to be appropriate authorities). **2** The quality of an administration that has come to power through free elections or established constitutional procedures.

REFERENCES
Peter G. Stillman, The concept of legitimacy, *Polity* 7 (Fall 1974);
Arthur J. Vidich, Political legitimacy in bureaucratic society: An analysis of Watergate, *Social Research* 42 (Winter 1975);
Ronald Glassman, Legitimacy and manufactured charisma, *Social Research* 42 (Winter 1975);
Robert Grafstein, The legitimacy of political institutions, *Polity* 14 (Fall 1981);
Claus Offe, Political legitimation through majority rule? *Social Research* 50 (Winter 1983);
Seymour Martin Lipset and William Schneider, Is there a legitimacy crisis? *Micropolitics* 3:1 (1983).

lese majesty A French term (*lèse-majesté*) literally meaning injured majesty, originally an offense against one's sovereign or ruler. Now it refers to an insolent or slighting behavior towards one's bureaucratic superiors.

lesser of two evils The least harmful of two potentially poor choices; the candidate that many citizens reluctantly prefer in an election.

levy **1** An assessment or collection of taxes. **2** The conscription of men for military service.

libel The creation and use of written materials that are so false and malicious that injury is caused to a person's reputation and he or she is subjected to ridicule, hatred, or contempt. The defense for allegations of libel is to prove that what was written was true. Libel comes from the Latin word *libellus*, meaning little book. When ancient Romans wanted to attack each other in writing, they would put their charges on posters for the public to read or on small scrolls to be passed from reader to reader. *Compare to* DEFAMATION OF CHARACTER; SLANDER.

REFERENCES
Leon Green, Political freedom of the press and the libel problem, *Texas Law Review* 56 (February 1978);
John Gruhl, The Supreme Court's impact on the law of libel: Compliance by lower federal courts, *Western Political Quarterly* 33 (December 1980);
Vivian Deborah Wilson, The law of libel and the art of fiction, *Law and Contemporary Problems* 44 (Autumn 1981);
Rodney A. Smolla, Let the author beware: The rejuvenation of the American law of libel, *University of Pennsylvania Law Review* 132 (December 1983).

liberalism **1** Originally, a political doctrine that espoused freedom of the individual from interference by the state, toleration by the state in matters of morality and religion, laissez-faire economic policies, and a belief in natural rights that exist independently of government. This is sometimes referred to as classical liberalism. While liberal concepts can be traced back to the Magna Charta of 1215 and through the writings of the major political theorists of the eighteenth-century European Enlightenment, by the nineteenth century liberalism had come to stand for a kind of limited governance whose policies most favored individual liberty and political equality. In this sense, the Founding Fathers were all liberals. **2** In this century, liberalism has come to stand for the advocacy of government programs for the welfare of individuals, because without such welfare state advantages the masses have little chance to enjoy the traditional freedoms long espoused by the political theorists. So a term that meant small government and low taxation in the last century has in this century come to mean big government and high taxation. One is reminded of Will Rogers' statement referring to the New Deal's domestic programs: "I can remember way back when a liberal was one who was generous with his own money."

REFERENCES
Louis Hartz, *The Liberal Tradition in America* (New York: Harcourt, Brace, and World, 1955);
Eric Voegelin, Liberalism and its history, *Review of Politics* 36 (October 1974);

liberal, limousine

Pamela Johnston Conover and Stanley Feldman, The origins and meaning of liberal/conservative self-identifications, *American Journal of Political Science* 25 (November 1981);

William A. Galston, Defending liberalism, *American Political Science Review* 76 (September 1982).

liberal, limousine A contemptuous term for a wealthy citizen who is a strong advocate of welfare state programs—that are paid for primarily by taxes on the middle class.

liberal, neo *See* NEOLIBERALS.

liberals, kneejerk A pejorative reference to liberals who, in the eyes of conservatives, automatically and unthinkingly respond favorably to causes espoused by the political left.

libertarianism A pure form of classical LIBERALISM, which asserts that a government should do little more than provide police and military protection; other than that, it should not interfere—either for good or ill—in the lives of its citizens. A major intellectual force advocating libertarianism was Ayn Rand (1905–1982), the objectivist philosopher who attacked welfare state notions of selflessness and sacrifice for a common good in novels such as *The Fountainhead* (1943) and *Atlas Shrugged* (1957). In 1980, a Libertarian party presidential candidate was on the ballot in all fifty states, and in 1984, in thirty-eight states. Thus far, the Libertarian party has had little impact on American politics.

REFERENCES

Monte Pasco, Libertarian longing, privatization, and federalism, *State Government* 55:4 (1982);

Murray N. Rothbard, *For A New Liberty: The Libertarian Manifesto* (Lanham, MD: University Press of America, 1985).

liberty 1 FREEDOM. 2 Freedom from government interference with private actions. *Compare to* CIVIL LIBERTY. 3 A naval term for an authorized short-term (usually less than twenty-four hours) absence from duty. 4 The Statue of Liberty in New York City.

REFERENCE

Harvey C. Mansfield, Jr., The forms and formalities of liberty, *Public Interest* 70 (Winter 1983).

Patrick Henry (1736–1799)
Demands Liberty or Death

The battle, sir, is not to the strong alone; it is to the vigilant, the active, the brave. Besides, sir, we have no election. If we were base enough to desire it, it is now too late to retire from the contest. There is no retreat, but in submission and slavery! Our chains are forged! Their clanking may be heard on the plains of Boston! The war is inevitable—and let it come! I repeat it, sir, let it come!

It is in vain, sir, to extenuate the matter. Gentlemen may cry peace, peace—but there is no peace. The war is actually begun! The next gale that sweeps from the north will bring to our ears the clash of resounding arms! Our brethren are already in the field! Why stand we here idle? What is it that gentlemen wish? What would they have? Is life so dear, or peace so sweet, as to be purchased at the price of chains and slavery? Forbid it, Almighty God! I know not what course others may take; but as for me, give me liberty, or give me death!

Source: Speech before the Virginia House of Burgesses, March 23, 1775.

Liberty Federation *See* MORAL MAJORITY.

Library of Congress The library established under a law approved on April 24, 1800, appropriating $5,000 "for the purchase of such books as may be necessary for the use of Congress." The library's scope of responsibility has been widened by subsequent legislation. One entity, the Congressional Research Service, functions exclusively for the legislative branch of the government. As the library has developed, its range of service has come to include both the entire government establishment in all its branches and the public at large, so it has become a national library for the United States and one of the great research libraries of the world. Since 1870, the library has been responsible for copyrights, which must be registered with its Copyright Office.

Library of Congress
101 Independence Avenue, S.E.
Washington, D.C. 20540
(202) 287–5000

lie *See* BIG LIE.

Lilienthal, David E. (1899–) Former chairman of the Tennessee Valley Authority (1941–1946) and the Atomic Energy Commission (1946–1950), who wrote widely of the advantages offered a democratic society by the intermingling of politics and administration.

REFERENCES

Lilienthal's major works include *TVA: Democracy on the March* (New York: Harper & Bros., 1944);
This I Do Believe (New York: Harper & Bros., 1949);
Big Business: A New Era (New York: Harper & Bros., 1953);
Change, Hope and the Bomb (Princeton, NJ: Princeton University Press, 1963);
The Journals of David E. Lilienthal, 6 vols. (New York: Harper & Row, 1964–1976).

limited government A government that is not all powerful. The United States is often said to be a limited government because it has only those powers assigned to it by the U.S. Constitution. Indeed, the Tenth Amendment specifically denies any additional powers to the federal government when it asserts that "the powers not delegated to the United States by the Constitution, nor prohibited by it to the States, are reserved to the States respectively, or to the people." However, the NECESSARY AND PROPER CLAUSE of the Constitution has allowed the federal government to expand its powers vastly over the years. *Compare to* CONSTITUTIONALISM.

REFERENCES

Carl J. Friedrich, *Limited Government: A Comparison* (Englewood Cliffs, NJ: Prentice-Hall, 1974);
Steven Kelman, Limited government: An incoherent concept, *Journal of Policy Analysis and Management* 3 (Fall 1983);
Lawrence R. Cima and Patrick S. Cotter, The coherence of the concept of limited government, *Journal of Policy Analysis and Management* 4 (Winter 1985).

limited war 1 A war in which at least one of the parties refrains from using all of its resources to defeat the enemy. This is in contrast to an all-out, no-holds-barred, total war. Limits are put on wars by the fear of the intervention of the opposition's nonbelligerent allies or by domestic opposition in one's own country. The Korean and Vietnam wars are examples of limited wars. The United States might have had greater success in both if it had not imposed limits on itself for fear of a greater war with China or the Soviet Union. 2 A war in which a government does not impose a total demand on its society and economy to further a maximum war effort. This is in contrast to a total war, in which all of the resources of the nation are put at the disposal of the military.

REFERENCES

William Vincent O'Brien, *The Conduct of Just and Limited War* (New York: Praeger, 1981);
Stephen Peter Rosen, Vietnam and the American theory of limited war, *International Security* 7 (Fall 1982).

Abraham Lincoln.

Lincoln, Abraham (1809–1865) The sixteenth president of the United States who led the North to victory during a Civil War that was forced upon him; who, in doing so, saved the union; and who, in an effort to deny resources to the enemy, abolished slavery in the

South. (The Thirteenth Amendment enacted after the Civil War would abolish slavery throughout the United States.) Lincoln's 1860 election to the presidency precipitated the secession of the southern states over the issue of slavery. Yet Lincoln's personal position on slavery was considered moderate for his times; he was willing to allow slavery in the South but opposed its extension to new territories. In his 1861 Inaugural Address, he told the seceded states that there would be no civil war unless they forced the issue:

> In your hands, my dissatisfied fellow country-men, and not in mine is the momentous issue of civil war. The government will not assail you. You can have no conflict without being yourselves the aggressors. You have no oath registered in heaven to destroy the government, while I shall have the most solemn one to "pre-serve, protect, and defend" it.

South Carolina did force the issue when it attacked the Union Army island fortress of Fort Sumter in Charleston harbor on April 12, 1861. Almost four years to the day, on April 9, 1865, the last effective army in the South, under General Robert E. Lee (1807–1870), surrendered to General Ulysses S. Grant (1822–1885) at Appomattox Court House in Virginia. (Grant would later be U.S. president from 1869–1877.) Five days later, on April 14, 1865, Lincoln was assassinated by an actor, John Wilkes Booth (1838–1865), while attend-ing a play at Ford's Theater in Washington, D.C.

Over the years, Lincoln's qualities of hon-esty (he was known as Honest Abe), his rise from humble origins (he was truly born in a log cabin), his dramatic death immediately follow-ing his greatest victory (the surrender of the South and the salvation of the union), his granting of freedom (*see* EMANCIPATION PROC-LAMATION) to millions of slaves (he was called the Great Emancipator), and his reverence for and eloquence on behalf of democratic govern-ment (*see* GETTYSBURG ADDRESS) have made him (along with George Washington) a secular saint in American political culture.

REFERENCES

David H. Donald, *Lincoln Reconsidered: Es-says on the Civil War Era* (New York: Vin-tage, 1961);

Stephen B. Oates, *With Malice Toward None: The Life of Abraham Lincoln* (New York: New American Library, 1977).

Lindblom, Charles E. (1917–   ) The leading proponent of the incremental approach to policy decision making. In his most famous work, "The Science of Muddling Through," *Public Administration Review* 19 (Spring 1959), Lindblom took a hard look at the ra-tional models of the decisional processes of government. He rejected the notion that most decisions are made by rational (total informa-tion) processes. Instead, he saw such deci-sions—indeed, the whole policymaking process—as dependent upon small incremental decisions that tend to be made in response to short-term political conditions. Lindblom's thesis, essentially, held that decision making was controlled infinitely more by events and circumstances than by the will of those in pol-icymaking positions. His thesis encouraged considerable work in the discipline on the boundary between political science and public administration—public policy. Lindblom re-stated his muddling thesis in "Still Muddling, Not Yet Through," *Public Administration Re-view* (January/February 1980).

REFERENCES

Lindblom's other major works include *Unions and Capitalism* (New Haven, CT: Yale Uni-versity Press, 1949);

Politics, Economics and Welfare, with Robert A. Dahl (New York: Harper & Row, 1953);

A Strategy of Decision, with David Braybrooke (New York: Free Press, 1963);

The Intelligence of Democracy: Decision-making through Mutual Adjustment (New York: Free Press, 1965);

Politics and Markets (New York: Basic Books, 1978);

The Policymaking Process, 2d ed. (Englewood Cliffs, NJ: Prentice-Hall, 1980).

For an analysis of his work, see Charles W. Anderson, The political economy of Charles E. Lindblom, *American Political Science Review* 72 (September 1978).

line-item budget   *See* BUDGET, LINE-ITEM.

line-item veto   *See* VETO.

line organizations Those segments of a larger organization that perform the major functions of the organization and have the most direct responsibilities for achieving organizational goals. *Compare to* STAFF.

linkage An international political strategy relating two or more issues in negotiations and then using one as a trade-off or pressure point.
REFERENCES
Helmut Sonnenfeldt, East-West relations: Linkage—A strategy for tempering Soviet antagonism, *NATO Review* 27 (February 1979);
Arthur A. Stein, The politics of linkage, *World Politics* 33 (October 1980).

linkage institution Any institution that is the means for the will of the people to get onto a government's agenda. Political parties, because they are the links between ordinary citizens and elected policymakers, are considered linkage institutions.
REFERENCE
Kay Lawson, ed., *Political Parties and Linkage: A Comparative Perspective* (New Haven, CT: Yale University Press, 1980).

litany A metaphor for a list of complaints, often repeated, as in the pleas of a prayer order or religious service.

litmus test The test that determines the alkaline or basic nature of a chemical solution and that has been applied to politics as an indicator of a politician's true ideological nature. Thus a stand or vote on any given issue may be considered a litmus test of whether the person in question is a real conservative, a true liberal, and so on.

little city hall A branch office of municipal government.
REFERENCE
Eric A. Nordlinger, *Decentralizing the City: A Study of Boston's Little City Halls* (Cambridge, MA: MIT Press, 1972).

little state department *See* STATE DEPARTMENT, LITTLE.

Lloyd-LaFollette Act of 1912 The federal statute that guarantees civilian employees of the federal government the right to petition the Congress, either individually or through their organizations. The act was the only statutory basis for the organization of federal employees until the Civil Service Reform Act of 1978. In addition, it provided the first statutory procedural safeguards for federal employees facing removal. It states that "no person in the classified civil service of the United States shall be removed or suspended without pay therefrom except for such cause as will promote the efficiency of such service and for reasons given in writing." *Compare to* GAG RULE/GAG ORDER.

loan guarantee An agreement by which a government pledges to pay part or all of the loan principal and interest to a lender or holder of a security in the event of default by a third-party borrower. The purpose of a guaranteed loan is to reduce the risk borne by a private lender by shifting all or part of the risk to the government. If it becomes necessary for the government to pay part or all of the loan's principal or interest, the payment is a direct outlay. Otherwise, the guarantee does not directly affect budget outlays. *See* CHRYSLER CORPORATION LOAN GUARANTEE ACT OF 1979.

lobby Any individual, group, or organization that seeks to influence legislation or administrative action. Lobbies can be trade associations, individual corporations, good-government public interest groups, or other levels of government. The term arose from the use of the lobbies, or corridors, of legislative halls as places to meet with and persuade legislators to vote a certain way. The right to attempt to influence legislation is based on the First Amendment to the U.S. Constitution which holds that the U.S. Congress shall make no law abridging the right of the people "to petition the government for a redress of grievances." Lobbying in general is not an evil; many lobbies provide legislatures with reliable first-hand information of considerable value. However, some lobbies have given the practice an undesirable connotation, because they often contribute money to political campaigns and offer special favors to elected and appointed officials. All such contributions and favors are given, of course, in the expectation of favorable treatment on some issue in the future. In effect, they are often thinly but effectively disguised BRIBES.

The most common forms of lobbying are testifying before a legislative hearing, formal and informal discussions with elected and appointed government officials, sending research results or technical information to appropriate officials, seeking publicity on an issue, drafting potential legislation, organizing letter writing campaigns, and so on.

REFERENCES

E. Pendleton Herring, *Group Representation Before Congress* (New York: Russell & Russell, 1929, 1967);

Suzanne Farkas, *Urban Lobbying; Mayors in the Federal Arena* (New York: New York University Press, 1971);

Donald H. Haider, *When Governments Come to Washington: Governors, Mayors, and Intergovernmental Lobbying* (New York: Free Press, 1974);

Charles T. Henry, Strategies for city lobbying in state legislatures, *Public Management* 56 (November 1974);

Jeffrey M. Berry, *Lobbying for the People* (Princeton, NJ: Princeton University Press, 1977);

Carol S. Greenwald, *Lobbying and Public Policy* (New York: Praeger, 1977);

John F. Manley, Presidential power and White House lobbying, *Political Science Quarterly* 93 (Summer 1978);

Kay L. Schlozman and John T. Tierney, *Organized Interests and American Democracy* (New York: Harper & Row, 1985).

Lobbying Act of 1946 The Federal Regulation of Lobbying Act of 1946, which requires that persons who solicit or accept contributions for lobbying purposes keep accounts, present receipts and statements to the clerk of the U.S. House of Representatives, and register with the clerk of the House and the secretary of the Senate. The information received is published quarterly in the *Congressional Record*. The purpose of this registration is to disclose the sponsorship and source of funds of lobbyists but not to curtail the right of persons to act as lobbyists. The constitutionality of the Lobbying Act

was upheld in *United States v Harriss,* 347 U.S. 612 (1954).

REFERENCE

Mary Kathryn Vanderbeck, First Amendment constraints on reform of the Federal Regulation of Lobbying Act, *Texas Law Review* 57 (October 1979).

local affairs, department of The generic name of a state agency with oversight responsibilities for local government. Sometimes local governments are required to submit audit and budget reports to such an agency, with the exact requirements varying from state to state.

local government Any government entity that is not clearly state or federal. This could include general local governments, such as counties, municipalities, and towns, as well as special-purpose local governments, such as school districts, port authorities, and fire districts.

REFERENCE

James W. Fesler, ed., *The 50 States and Their Local Governments* (New York: Knopf, 1967).

local option The authority given by a state to its localities to determine by a local referendum election a specific policy for that locality—for example, liquor sales on Sunday.

Lochner v New York 198 U.S. 45 (1905) The U.S. Supreme Court case that declared unconstitutional a New York law that sought to regulate the hours of employment in a bakery. The Court held that such regulation was not part of the police powers of the state and infringed on the constitutionally protected liberty of contract. This was overruled in *Bunting v State of Oregon*, 243 U.S. 426 (1917), which held that the regulation of working hours was a valid extension of police powers. The *Lochner* case is often considered the last gasp of judicial social Darwinism.

Locke, John (1632–1704) The English physician and philosopher whose writings on the nature of governance were a profound influence on the Founding Fathers. It is often argued that

John Locke.

the first part of the Declaration of Independence, which establishes the essential philosophic rationale for the break with England, is Thomas Jefferson's restatement of John Locke's most basic themes. Locke's *A Letter Concerning Toleration* (1689) anticipated American thought on religious toleration. Locke held that a policy of toleration was only logical because it permitted all of the religious groups to support the state, while the alternative of religious persecution and suppression only led to sedition and internal discord.

But Locke's most influential works by far were his *Two Treatises of Government* (1690), in which he rejected the notion that kings had a divine right to rule, made the case for a constitutional democracy, and provided the philosophic justification for revolution later used by the Americans. Locke wrote that man, who is "by nature free, equal, and independent," chose to live with others—to give up his "state of nature" to enter into a "social contract" to gain the security that is impossible in the "state of nature." He consents to live by the will of the majority, and it is for this purpose that governments are created. And a government formed by the people with their consent

can be dissolved by the people if their trust is betrayed. According to Locke:

> Whenever the legislators endeavor to take away and destroy the property of the people, or to reduce them to slavery under arbitrary power, they put themselves into a state of war with the people, who are thereupon absolved from any further obedience, and are left to the common refuge which God hath provided for all men against force and violence.

Compare to REVOLUTION; SOCIAL CONTRACT.

REFERENCES

Virginia McDonald, A guide to the interpretation of Locke the political theorist, *Canadian Journal of Political Science* 6 (December 1973);

Martyn P. Thompson, The reception of Locke's *Two Treatises of Government 1690–1705, Political Studies* 24 (June 1976);

Robert C. Grady II, Obligation, consent and Locke's right to revolution: "Who is to judge?" *Canadian Journal of Political Science* 9 (June 1976);

Richard Ashcraft, Revolutionary politics and Locke's *Two Treatises of Government*: Radicalism and Lockean political theory, *Political Theory* 8 (November 1980);

Mark Glat, John Locke's historical sense, *Review of Politics* 43 (January 1980);

J. H. Bogart, Lockean provisos and state of nature theories, *Ethics* 95 (July 1985);

Donald L. Doernberg, "We the people": John Locke, collective constitutional rights, and standing to challenge government action, *California Law Review* 73 (January 1985).

Lockhart v McCree 90 L.Ed. 2d 137 (1986) The U.S. Supreme Court case that held legal the exclusion from juries hearing capital cases those citizens who assert that they could never vote to impose the death penalty. This case upheld the use of so-called death qualified juries.

log cabin A reference to the oft-assumed humble origins of American politicians, especially presidential candidates. While most associated with Abraham Lincoln, the first presidential candidate to use the log cabin symbol was William Henry Harrison in 1840. He won in spite of the fact that his plebian past

logrolling

The log cabin symbol (here, on a handkerchief) helped elect William Henry Harrison to the presidency in 1840.

was considerably exaggerated. Until recently, the log cabin (or other symbol of early adversity) has been a significant factor in American elections. John Nance Gardner (1867–1967), vice president under Franklin D. Roosevelt from 1933–1939, was in 1959 presented with a birthday cake in the shape of the log cabin in which he was born. He then observed, "That log house did me more good in politics than anything I ever said in a speech."

REFERENCES

James D. Hart, They all were born in log cabins, *American Heritage* 7:5 (1956);

Edward Pessen, *The Log Cabin Myth: The Social Backgrounds of the Presidents* (New Haven, CT: Yale University Press, 1984).

logrolling   Mutual aid among legislators: you help me, I'll help you; you scratch my back, I'll scratch yours; you vote for my bill, I'll vote for yours. Logrolling is birling, a game of skill popular among lumberjacks, which calls for two people to cooperatively maintain their balance on a floating log as they spin it with their feet. Logrolling is usually associated with the passage of bills that benefit a legislator's constituency, pork barrel legislation, or bills that are of personal interest. Sam Taliaferro Rayburn (1882–1961), the three-time Speaker of the U.S. House of Representatives (1940–1946, 1949–1953, 1955–1961), summed it up when he told new congressmen, "If you want to *get* along, *go* along."

REFERENCES

Nicholas R. Miller, Logrolling, vote trading, and the paradox of voting: A game-theoretical overview, *Public Choice* 30 (Summer 1977);

Joe Oppenheimer, Outcomes of logrolling in the bargaining set and democratic theory: Some conjectures, *Public Choice* 34:3–4 (1979);

Bruce L. Benson, Logrolling and high demand committee review, *Public Choice* 41:3 (1983);

James M. Enelow, The stability of logrolling: An expectations approach, *Public Choice* 51:3 (1986).

long-arm statute   *See* STATUTE, LONG-ARM.

Long, Norton E. (1910–   )   The political scientist who wrote classic accounts of the political dimensions of public administration. The beginning of his article, "Power and Administration," *Public Administration Review* 9 (Autumn 1949), is perhaps the most poetic paragraph in the literature of public administration: "There is no more forlorn spectacle in the administrative world than an agency and a program possessed of statutory life, armed with executive orders, sustained in the courts, yet stricken with paralysis and deprived of power. An object of contempt to its enemies and of despair to its friends."

REFERENCE

Long's major essays have been collected in *The Polity* (Chicago: Rand McNally, 1962).

loose constructionist   *See* STRICT CONSTRUCTIONIST.

Los Angeles Department of Water and Power v Manhart   *See* CITY OF LOS ANGELES, DEPARTMENT OF WATER POWER V MANHART.

lottery   1 A form of decision making in which a choice is made by random selection of one entry from all entries submitted; the selection of one lot from among the entirety placed in a container. For example, draft selections in World Wars I and II were made from jars of numbers, each number having been assigned to a potential draftee. The intention of a lottery is to assure the absence of favoritism or special influence; it is a form of gambling in which the luck of the draw, so to speak, controls the selection of a winner. **2** State-sponsored and state-administered gambling undertaken as an alternative to raising taxes. Government lotteries have a long tradition in America. Many of the colonies were subsidized by lotteries. Even the Continental Congress authorized a lottery in 1776 to raise funds for the War of Independence. However, after a spate of scandals in the nineteenth century, the lottery fell into disfavor and disuse. The first of the modern state lotteries began in 1964 in New Hampshire. Since then, twenty-seven (plus the District of Columbia) states (by1987) have initiated lotteries, and over half of the U.S population now lives in states with lotteries. The lottery is praised by those who see it as a popular alternative to higher taxes and condemned by those who say it takes advantage of the poor who play it disproportionately, mostly lose, and thus subsidize the middle class, who would pay higher taxes if there were no lottery.

REFERENCES

James Brooks, State lotteries: Profits and problems, *State Government* 48 (Winter 1975);

Robert Blakey, State conducted lottery: History, problems, and promises, *Journal of Social Issues* 35 (Summer 1979);

John L. Mikesell and C. Kurt Zorn, State lotteries as fiscal savior or fiscal fraud: A look at the evidence, *Public Administration Review* 46 (July/August 1986).

Loving v Virginia   See MISCEGENATION LAW.

Lowi, Theodore J. (1931–   ) The leading critic of interest group pluralism, who is also noted for his classification of all public policies as either distributive, regulatory, or redistributive. His *The End of Liberalism: Ideology, Policy, and the Crisis of Public Authority* (New York: Norton, 1969; 2d ed., 1979) provided a provocative critique of the modern

democratic government and a condemnation of the paralyzing effects of interest group pluralism. Lowi asserted that public authority is parceled out to private interest groups, resulting in a weak, decentralized government incapable of long-range planning. These powerful interest groups operate to promote private goals; they do not compete to promote the public interest. Government then becomes not an institution capable of making hard choices among conflicting values but a holding company for interests. The various interests are promoted by alliances of interest groups, relevant government agencies, and the appropriate legislative committees. Lowi denied the very virtues that E. PENDLETON HERRING and other group theorists saw in their promotion of interest group pluralism. Lowi's analysis is a scathing indictment of a governing process in which agencies charged with regulation are seen as basically protectors of those being regulated. *See also* INTEREST GROUP THEORY; JURIDICAL DEMOCRACY; PUBLIC POLICYMAKING.

REFERENCES

Lowi's other works include *At the Pleasure of the Mayor: Patronage and Power in New York City, 1898–1958* (New York: Free Press, 1964);

American business, public policy, case-studies, and political theory, *World Politics* (July 1964);

ed., *Private Life and Public Order* (New York, Norton, 1968);

The Politics of Disorder (New York: Basic Books, 1971);

The Personal President: Power Invested, Promise Unfulfilled (Ithaca, NY: Cornell University Press, 1985).

loyal opposition   In a two-party system, the party out of power but loyal to the interest of the nation as a whole.

REFERENCE

Robert A. Dahl, ed., *Regimes and Opposition* (New Haven, CT: Yale University Press, 1973).

loyalty   Allegiance. A loyalty oath is an affirmation of allegiance. Allegiance may be given to a state or to any organization or religious group that may expect special commitment by its members to the interests of the organization or the group. When the interests of such groups are in conflict with one another, individuals who hold membership in both groups may find themselves, or be considered by others to be, conflicted in their loyalties; hence they may be thought inherently or potentially disloyal to one or the other. Many public employers may legitimately require their employees to swear or affirm their allegiance to the Constitution of the United States and to that of a particular state. *See also* COLE V RICHARDSON; CONNELL V HIGGINBOTHAM; ELFBRANDT V RUSSELL; GARNER V BOARD OF PUBLIC WORKS OF LOS ANGELES; KEYISHIAN V BOARD OF REGENTS; SHELTON V TUCKER.

REFERENCES

Morton Grodzins, *The Loyal and the Disloyal: Social Boundaries of Patriotism and Treason* (Chicago: University of Chicago Press, 1956);

Thomas W. Fletcher, The nature of administrative loyalty, *Public Administration Review* 18 (Winter 1958);

Paul E. Donnelly, The pervasive effect of McCarthyism on recent loyalty oath cases, *St. Louis University Law Journal* 16 (Spring 1972);

Paul M. Sniderman, *A Question of Loyalty* (Berkeley and Los Angeles: University of California Press, 1981).

Mark Twain on Loyalty

My kind of loyalty was loyalty to one's country, not to its institutions or its officeholders. The country is the real thing, the substantial thing, the eternal thing; it is the thing to watch over, and care for, and be loyal to; institutions are extraneous, they are its mere clothing, and clothing can wear out, become ragged, cease to be comfortable, cease to protect the body from winter, disease, and death. To be loyal to rags, to shout for rags, to worship rags, to die for rags—that is a loyalty of unreason, it is pure animal; it belongs to monarchy, was invented by monarchy; let monarchy keep it. I was from Connecticut, whose Constitution declares "that all political power is inherent in the people, and all free governments are founded on their authority and instituted for their benefit; and that they have at all times an undeniable and indefeasible right to alter their form of government in such a manner as they may think expedient."

Source: *A Connecticut Yankee in King Arthur's Court* (1889).

---

lulu A corruption of in lieu of; legislative slang for payments made to state legislators in lieu of expenses. Such lump-sum payments made it unnecessary for state lawmakers to suffer the inconvenience of submitting receipts for their expenses.

lunatic fringe The overzealous and fanatical members of any political party or social movement. The term was first applied by President Theodore Roosevelt—to impatient reformers.

M

McCardle, Ex parte *See* EX PARTE MCCARDLE.

McCarran Act *See* ALBERTSON V SUBVERSIVE ACTIVITIES CONTROL BOARD.

McCarthyism Extreme and irresponsible anticommunism. Senator Joseph R. McCarthy (1908–1957) of Wisconsin rose to fame and influence during the early 1950s by recklessly charging that individuals or organizations were communist or communist influenced. McCarthyism was not limited to McCarthy. The classic tactic of McCarthyism is the use of an unproven association with any individual, organization, or policy, which the accusor perceives as liberal or left and, as a result, either un-American or even treasonous. McCarthy himself grew so reckless with his accusations that he became one of the few senators in American history to be formally censured by the U.S. Senate.

Senator Joseph McCarthy (left) and Committee counsel Roy Cohn challenge Senator Ralph Flanders (standing) during the Army–McCarthy hearings.

Today, any actions by public officials that flout individual rights and imply guilt by association would be considered—by anyone sensitive to the concept of due process of law—as examples of McCarthyism. When President Harry S Truman was asked to comment on one of McCarthy's outbursts, he responded "No comment. The Senator is pathological and a liar, and I don't need to comment on that."
Also see DEMAGOGUE.

REFERENCES

Richard H. Rovere, *Senator Joe McCarthy* (Cleveland: World, 1959);

Robert Griffith, The political context of McCarthyism, *Review of Politics* 33 (January 1971);

Eleanor Lansing Dulles, Footnotes to history: A day in the life of Senator Joe McCarthy, *World Affairs* 143 (Fall 1980);

John G. Adams, *Without Precedent: The Story of the Death of McCarthyism* (New York: Norton, 1983);

David M. Oshinsky, *A Conspiracy So Immense: The World of Joe McCarthy* (New York: Free Press, 1983).

The Senate Resolution Censuring McCarthy

Resolved, That the Senator from Wisconsin, Mr. McCarthy, failed to cooperate with the Subcommittee on Privileges and Elections of the Senate Committee on Rules and Administration in clearing up matters referred to that subcommittee which concerned his conduct as a Senator and affected the honor of the Senate and, instead, repeatedly abused the subcommittee and its members who were trying to carry out assigned duties, thereby obstructing the constitutional process of the Senate, and that this conduct of the Senator from Wisconsin, Mr. McCarthy, is contrary to senatorial traditions and is hereby condemned.

Section 2. The Senator from Wisconsin, Mr. McCarthy, in writing to the chairman of the Select Committee to Study Censure Charges (Mr. Watkins) after the Select Committee had issued its report and before the report was presented to the Senate charging three members of the Select Committee with "deliberate deception" and "fraud" for failure to disqualify themselves; in stating to the press on November 4, 1954, that the special Senate session that was to begin on November 8, 1954, was a "lynch party"; in repeatedly describing this special Senate session as a "lynch bee" in a nationwide television and radio show on November 7, 1954; in stating to the public press on November 13, 1954, that the chairman of the Select Committee (Mr. Watkins) was guilty of "the most unusual, most cowardly thing I've heard of" and stating further: "I expected he would be afraid to answer the questions, but didn't think he'd be stupid enough to make a public statement"; and in characterizing the said committee as the "unwitting handmaiden," "involuntary agent" and "attorneys-in-fact" of the Communist Party and in charging that the said committee in writing its report "imitated Communist methods—that it distorted, misrepresented, and omitted in its efforts to manufacture a plausible rationalization" in support of its recommendations to the Senate, which characterizations and charges were contained in a statement released to the press and inserted in the *Congressional Record* of November 10, 1954, acted contrary to senatorial ethics and tended to bring the Senate into dishonor and disrepute, to obstruct the constitutional processes of the Senate, and to impair its dignity; and such conduct is hereby condemned.

Source: Senate Resolution 301, 83d Cong., 2d sess., December 2, 1954.

McCarthy v Philadelphia Civil Service Commission 424 U.S. 645 (1976) The U.S. Supreme Court case that upheld an ordinance requiring that city employees live within city limits. *Compare to* RESIDENCY REQUIREMENT.

McClellan Committee The Senate committee on Improper Activities in Labor-Management Relations, chaired by Senator John L. McClellan (1896–1977) of Arkansas. The committee's findings of violence and corruption spurred the passage of the Labor-Management Reporting and Disclosure (Landrum-Griffin) Act of 1959.

REFERENCES

For accounts of the committee's work by its legal counsel and chairman, see Robert F. Kennedy, *The Enemy Within* (New York: Harper & Row, 1960);

John L. McClellan, *Crime Without Punishment* (New York: Duell, Sloan and Pearce, 1962).

McCulloch v Maryland 4 Wheaton 316 (1819) The U.S. Supreme Court decision that upheld the implied powers granted to the Congress by the "necessary and proper" clause of the Constitution, upheld the supremacy of the national government in carrying out functions assigned to it by the Constitution, and established the doctrine of intergovernmental tax immunity. In stating that "the power to tax is the power to destroy," the Court held that the Bank of the United States was not subject to taxation by the State of Maryland. *Compare to* STRICT CONSTRUCTIONIST.

McDonald v City of West Branch, Michigan 80 L.Ed. 2d 302 (1984) The U.S. Supreme Court case that held that a discharged police officer could seek redress in court even though he had fully utilized the grievance procedure in his union's contract, culminating in an arbitrator's ruling that the discharge was warranted.

mace 1 A medieval weapon, usually a heavily studded club designed to be particularly threatening and destructive. 2 Political slang for forcing (with a figurative mace) public employees to make contributions to the party in power. 3 A legislature's symbol of authority; there is a mace in the U.S. House of Representatives. 4 A modern chemical spray weapon used to disable (but not kill) an opponent; often carried by police.

Machiavelli, Niccolo (1469–1527) An Italian Renaissance political philosopher and history's most famous and influential political analyst. His book of advice to would-be leaders, *The Prince* (1532), is the progenitor of all how-to-succeed books and is often considered the first real work of political science. Its exploration of how political power is grasped, used, and kept is the benchmark against which all subsequent analyses are judged. Machiavelli's amoral tone and detached analysis have caused him to be both soundly denounced as well as greatly imitated. For example, he asserted that "a prudent prince cannot and should not keep his word when to do so would go against his interest, or when the reasons that made him pledge it no longer apply." Such advice has made his name synonymous with political deception. But no other writer before or since has given the world such a brilliant lesson in how to think in terms of cold political power.

REFERENCES

Robert R. Sullivan, Machiavelli's balance of power theory, *Social Science Quarterly* 54 (September 1973);

J. G. Pocock, *The Machiavellian Moment: Florentine Political Thought and the Atlantic Republican Tradition* (Princeton, NJ: Princeton University Press, 1975);

Andrew T. Cowart, The Machiavellian budgeter, *British Journal of Political Science* 6 (January 1976);

Harvey C. Mansfield, Jr., Machiavelli's political science, *American Political Science Review* 75 (June 1981);

Mark Hulliung, *Citizen Machiavelli* (Princeton, NJ: Princeton University Press, 1983);

Donald McIntosh, The modernity of Machiavelli, *Political Theory* 12 (May 1984).

machine *See* POLITICAL MACHINE.

McNabb v United States 318 U.S. 332 (1943) The U.S. Supreme Court case that held that the federal courts could not convict someone of a crime because of a confession gained while the person was illegally detained; that is, held for interrogation for an unreasonable length of time without being charged with a crime or offered the opportunity for legal counsel. This ruling was extended to the states in *Mallory v Hogan*, 378 U.S. 1 (1964).

MAD Mutual assured destruction; a strategic policy of the United States. In 1965, U.S. defense officials concluded that it would be impossible to create a strategic superiority capable of preventing serious damage to the United States in case of enemy attack; therefore, the United States would no longer target only enemy military installations but would also target enemy population centers to maintain a "convincing capability to inflict unacceptable damage on an attacker."

REFERENCES

Samuel F. Wells, Jr., America and the "MAD" world, *Wilson Quarterly* 1 (Autumn 1977);

Robert Jervis, MAD is the best possible deterrence, *Bulletin of the Atomic Scientists* 41 (March 1985).

James Madison.

Madisonian model The basic framework for governance in the U.S. Constitution. It is republican as opposed to democratic, and has a strong system of CHECKS AND BALANCES. Historians have called this the Madisonian model because James Madison was so influential in advocating the basic concepts contained in the Constitution.

REFERENCES

James MacGregor Burns offers extensive critical analyses of the Madisonian model in two of his books. See *The Deadlock of Democracy: Four Party Politics in America* (Englewood Cliffs, NJ: Prentice-Hall, 1963);

Presidential Government: The Crucible of Leadership (Boston: Houghton Mifflin, 1965).

Also see George W. Carey, Separation of powers and the Madisonian model: A reply to the critics, *American Political Science Review* 72 (March 1978);

John Zvesper, The Madisonian system, *Western Political Quarterly* 37 (June 1984).

Madison, James (1751–1836) The fourth president of the United States (1809–1817),

often called the chief architect of (or the father of) the Constitution because he was (1) active in the call for the Constitutional Convention, (2) a major influence in creating a governing framework that stressed national supremacy; (3) a coauthor of the FEDERALIST PAPERS, which helped ensure ratification; (4) a major actor in the passage of the Bill of Rights; and (5) the author of a journal on the proceedings of the Constitutional Convention, which is history's prime source on the convention's deliberations. Madison is also one of America's preeminent political theorists. His intellectual framework for American government (incorporated into the Constitution) is known as the MADISONIAN MODEL. His theorizing on the nature of factions in FEDERALIST 10 is the beginning of interest group theory. There is no better example in world history of a political thinker so influential in his own lifetime—and since. *See also* COMMANDER-IN-CHIEF.

REFERENCES

For the standard biography, see Irving Brant, *James Madison*, 6 vols., (Indianapolis: Bobbs-Merrill, 1941–1961).

For Madison's role in the development and adoption of the Constitution, see Max Farrand, *Records of the Federal Convention* (New Haven, CT: Yale University Press, 1937), 3 vols;

James Madison, *Notes of Debates in the Federal Convention of 1787* (Athens: Ohio University Press, 1976);

Neil Riemer, *James Madison: Creating the American Constitution* (Washington, D.C.: Congressional Quarterly, 1986).

Magna Charta **1** The charter of liberties that English nobles forced from King John in 1215. **2** Any document offering fundamental guarantees of rights.

maiden speech A legislator's first speech to a legislative assembly upon first being elected to it. This is usually a moment of great significance to the speaker and great indifference to the audience.

mainstream The most advantageous of political positions, neither too far from the extremes of left and right. To be in the mainstream means to swim in the political center where most of the voters are to be found. A drier but parallel description is middle of the road.

majority, extraordinary *See* EXTRAORDINARY MAJORITY.

majority leader The chief strategist and floor spokesman for the party in nominal control in either house of a legislature. He or she is elected by party colleagues.
REFERENCES
Robert L. Peabody, *Leadership in Congress* (Boston: Little, Brown, 1976);
Sidney Waldman, Majority leadership in the House of Representatives, *Political Science Quarterly* 95 (Fall 1980).

majority of one A single individual, so long as he or she is in the right. Henry David Thoreau (1817–1862) wrote in *Civil Disobedience* (1849) that "any man more right than his neighbor constitutes a majority of one." And Calvin Coolidge (1872–1933), in accepting the Republican vice presidential nomination on July 27, 1920, said: "One with the law is a majority."

majority rule The underlying premise of democratic societies—that those with most of the people on their side should govern. The historic problem of majority rule has been protecting the minorities from oppression. This is why the founders created a REPUBLIC, a system of government one step removed from majority rule, and provided that the U.S. Constitution could only be changed by extraordinary majorities.
REFERENCE
Elaine Spitz, *Majority Rule* (Chatham, NJ: Chatham House, 1984).

majority whip In effect, the assistant majority leader in the U.S. House of Representatives or Senate. The whip helps marshal majority forces in support of party strategy. *Compare to* MINORITY WHIP; WHIP.

major player A slang phrase for someone, whether an individual, an organization, or a sovereign state, whose views must be taken into account on a policy issue.

make whole A legal remedy that provides for an injured party to be placed, as near as may be possible, in the situation he or she would have occupied if the wrong had not been committed. The concept was first put forth by the U.S. Supreme Court in the 1867 case of *Wicker v Hoppock*. In 1975, the Court held, in the case of *Albermarle Paper Company v Moody*, 422 U.S. 405, that Title VII of the Civil Rights Act of 1964 (as amended) intended a make whole remedy for unlawful discrimination.

Making of the President A series of bestselling books on the presidential election process written by Theodore H. White (1915–1986) on the campaigns of 1960, 1964, 1968, and 1972. White's reporting helped to change the nature of campaign press coverage. No longer could reporters just rewrite press handouts. White's *Making of the President* books set a new standard for political reporting, which had the juiciness of an inside story, the intimacy of a biography, and the perspective of history. White became the victim of the success of his behind-the-scenes format. He said, in 1972: "I used to specialize in getting behind-the-scenes stuff, but now the rooms are so crowded with reporters getting behind-the-scenes stories that nobody can get behind-the-scenes stories."

malaise The medical term for a vague feeling of illness that is used in other contexts to express a lassitude or ineffectiveness not traceable to a specific source and not exhibiting a specific set of symptoms. Malaise was President Jimmy Carter's word for the political uneasiness he found in America.

malaise, video Negative and cynical feelings toward the political system generated by television news reporting. This phenomenon was identified by Michael J. Robinson in "Public Affairs Broadcasting and the Growth of Political Malaise: The Case of 'The Selling of the Pentagon'," *American Political Science Review* 70 (June 1976).

malapportionment The skewed distribution of voters in a state's legislative or congressional districts. Prior to several landmark U.S. Supreme Court decisions in the early 1960s, malapportionment or maldistricting was the "normal" pattern of legislative apportionment throughout the nation. This tended to give sparsely populated rural districts a disproportionate say in state and national affairs. The Court held malapportionment to be unconstitutional in the 1964 cases of REYNOLDS V SIMS and WESBERRY V SANDERS.

Malek manual A guidebook concerning the operations of the federal personnel system prepared for Fred Malek, the manager of the White House Personnel Office during the early part of the Richard M. Nixon administration. Its Machiavellian character (asserting that "there is no merit in the merit system") gave it tremendous notoriety. Its purpose was to help the Nixon administration gain political control of the bureaucracy by quickly putting their people into as many merit positions as possible. It advocated little that has not been done by previous or subsequent administrations: its notoriety stemmed from its formal and systematic explanation of how to manipulate the system and the fact that it surfaced at a time when the now-defunct U.S. Civil Service Commission was under attack for political favoritism.

REFERENCES
For a dispassionate analysis, see Frank J. Thompson and Raymond G. Davis, The Malek manual revisited, *Bureaucrat* 6 (Summer 1977).
For Malek manual excerpts, see Frank J. Thompson, ed., *Classics of Public Personnel Policy* (Oak Park, IL: Moore, 1979).

malfeasance The performance of a consciously unlawful act on the part of a public official. *Compare to* MISFEASANCE.

Mallory v Hogan 378 U.S. 1 (1964) The U.S. Supreme Court case that held that the Fifth Amendment guarantee against self-incrimination applied to the states through the due process clause of the Fourteenth Amendment. Thus a prisoner has the right not to answer questions of police or prosecutors if the answers would be self-incriminating. This decision reversed *Twining v New Jersey,* 211 U.S. 78 (1908).

Malthus, Thomas Robert (1766–1834) The English economist whose *Essay on the Principle of Population* (1798) held that the world's population must ultimately outstrip food supply because, left unchecked, population increases geometrically, while food production increases arithmetically. Malthus wrote: "Almost everything that has been hitherto done for the poor has tended, as if with solicitous care, to throw a veil of obscurity over this subject and to hide from them the true cause of their poverty. When the wages of labour are hardly sufficient to maintain two children, a man marries and has five or six." Malthusian has since come to refer to any solution to the problem of population growth and famine that suggests the inevitability or even the utility of their relation to one another as the only effective way of controlling overpopulation.

REFERENCE
David Wells, Resurrecting the dismal parson: Malthus, ecology, and political thought, *Political Studies* 30 (March 1982).

mandamus/writ of mandamus A court order that compels the performance of an act.

339

mandate The perceived popular or electoral support for a public program, political party, or a particular politician. U.S. presidents who win elections by overwhelming majorities may rightly feel the vote was a mandate to carry out their proposed policies, but presidents who win by narrow margins may perceive no mandate to implement their programs. Thus a president's mandate or electoral margin can often have a significant effect on legislative proposals. The greater the mandate, the more deferential the Congress is likely to be. President Ronald Reagan was especially effective—with a Congress half controlled by the opposition party—because he won election and reelection by such large margins.

REFERENCES
Douglas A. Hibbs, Jr., President Reagan's mandate from the 1980 elections: A shift to the right? *American Politics Quarterly* 10 (October 1982);
Everett C. Ladd, On mandates, realignments, and the 1984 presidential election, *Political Science Quarterly* 100 (Spring 1985);
Michael D. Reagan, The Reagan "mandate," public law, and the ethics of policy change, *Congress and the Presidency* 12 (Autumn 1985).

mandating One level of government requiring another to offer—or pay for—a program as a matter of law or as a prerequisite to partial or full funding for either the program in question or other programs.

REFERENCES
Max Neiman and Catherine Lovell, Mandating as a policy issue—The definitional problem, *Policy Studies Journal* 9 (Spring 1981);
Max Neiman and Catherine Lovell, Federal and state mandating: A first look at the mandate terrain, *Administrative Science Quarterly* 14 (November 1983).

Manhart decision *See* CITY OF LOS ANGELES, DEPARTMENT OF WATER & POWER V MANHART.

Manhattan Project The federally financed research project during World War II that resulted in the development of the atomic bomb—the first major federal government in- volvement with science. The Manhattan Project cost about $2 billion then; about $10 billion in today's money.

REFERENCES
Leslie R. Groves, *Now It Can Be Told: The Story of the Manhattan Project* (New York: Harper & Row, 1962);
Richard Rhodes, *The Making of the Atomic Bomb* (New York: Simon & Schuster, 1987).

man in the street 1 The average person. 2 The point of view presumed to be held by an individual randomly selected from those passing any street corner. Interviews with these men (or women) on the street are often used by television news to air public opinion; but this should not be confused with a systematic effort at sampling opinion (*see* SAMPLE).

Mann Act of 1900 The federal law (also known as the White Slave Traffic Act) that prohibited transporting women across state lines for immoral purposes. The act was intended to stop interstate prostitution. The FBI, which was responsible for enforcement, so abused the act that public sentiment finally forced the Justice Department in 1940 to tell the FBI "that prosecutions in the future would be undertaken only in cases where commercialization was a factor."

REFERENCE
Mark Thomas Connelly, *The Response to Prostitution in the Progressive Era* (Chapel Hill: University of North Carolina Press, 1980).

man of the hour 1 The currently popular candidate. 2 The person whose abilities are critical to the success of something at a critical time. Harold J. Laski in *The American Presidency: An Interpretation* (New York: Harper, 1940) wrote that the hour of need has always seemed to bring forth the proper president:

> For there is at least one test of a system that is, I think decisive. There have been five considerable crises in American history. There was the need to start the new republic adequately in 1789; it gave the American people its natural leader in George Washington. The crisis of 1800 brought Jefferson to the presidency; that of 1861 brought Abraham Lincoln. The War of

1914 found Woodrow Wilson in office; the Great Depression resulted in the election of Franklin D. Roosevelt. So far, it is clear, the hour has brought forth the man. It is of course true, as Bagehot said, that "success in a lottery is no argument for lotteries."

man of the people 1 A politician of humble origins, such as Andrew Jackson, Abraham Lincoln, and Harry Truman. 2 A politician not of humble origins, such as Franklin D. Roosevelt, whose followers assert that he represents the interests of ordinary folks.

man on horseback 1 A military figure, such as Napoleon Bonaparte, who is a potential dictator if the civilian regime falters. 2 Any former military figure (usually a general) who aspires to civilian leadership. In American politics, the phrase was first applied to Ulysses S. Grant during his 1868 presidential campaign.

Mapp v Ohio 367 U.S. 643 (1961) The U.S. Supreme Court case that made the exclusionary rule (meaning that illegally gained evidence would be barred at trials) binding on all jurisdictions; thus evidence obtained by means of unreasonable searches and seizures would not be admissible in court. This overruled *Wolf v Colorado*, 338 U.S. 25 (1949). *Compare to* EX-CLUSIONARY RULE.

REFERENCE

Potter Stewart, The road to *Mapp v Ohio* and beyond: The origins, development, and future of the exclusionary rule in search-and-seizure cases, *Columbia Law Review* 83 (October 1983).

Marbury v Madison 1 Cranch 137 (1803) The preeminent U.S. Supreme Court case because of its famous declaration of the Court's power of judicial review—the power to declare federal legislation or executive actions unconstitutional and consequently unenforceable through the courts. It was in this case that Chief Justice John Marshall held that it was the duty of the judiciary to say what the law is, including expounding and interpreting that law. The law contained in the Constitution, he said, was paramount, and laws repugnant to its provisions must fall. He concluded that it was the province of the courts to decide when other law

was in violation of the basic law of the Constitution and, where this was found to occur, to declare that law null and void. This is the doctrine known as judicial review, which has become the basis for the Court's application of constitutional guarantees.

REFERENCES

William W. Van Alstyne, A critical guide to *Marbury v Madison*, *Duke Law Journal* 7 (February 1969);

Henry P. Monaghan, *Marbury* and the administrative state, *Columbia Law Review* 83 (January 1983).

The Case of *Marbury v Madison*

Thomas Jefferson was elected president in 1800. The race between Jefferson and the Federalist candidate, incumbent President John Adams, had been bitter. Between the election and the inauguration, lame duck President Adams appointed Secretary of State John Marshall to the post of chief justice of the Supreme Court. The lame duck Congress, which was controlled by the Federalists, passed a law giving Adams the power to appoint new justices of the peace for the District of Columbia, and Adams named loyal Federalists to these positions. Because of the pressure of time, however, Adams did not sign some of the commissions until the night before Jefferson's inauguration; thus they did not arrive on the desk of Secretary of State Marshall (soon to be chief justice) until after Jefferson became president. Jefferson then ordered his new secretary of state, James Madison, not to deliver them.

One of the midnight appointees whose commission Madison did not deliver was William Marbury. Marbury asked the Supreme Court, whose chief justice was now Marshall, to issue an order requiring Madison to deliver his commission: the Judiciary Act of 1789 had given the Supreme Court the power to issue orders requiring public officers to perform their duties, and it was on the strength of this act that Marbury made his request to the Court.

At the same time, the Court was under attack by the Jeffersonian majority in the Congress. This majority threatened to weaken the Federalist dominance of the Court and to impeach Federalist judges for alleged misconduct. Chief Justice Marshall wished to strengthen and protect the Court as an instrument of national power and saw in the Marbury case a politically acceptable way to do so. In his opinion on behalf of the Court, Marshall held that Madison could not be required to deliver Marbury's commission. The reason, he said, was that the provision of the

Judiciary Act giving the Court the power to require such action was unconstitutional. The jurisdiction of the Court was provided in the Constitution and could not, said Marshall, be enlarged by the Congress.

Source: Adapted from Samuel C. Patterson, Roger H. Davidson, and Randall B. Ripley, *A More Perfect Union: Introduction to American Government*, 3d ed. (Chicago: Dorsey, 1985), pp. 27–28.

marginal seat   A legislative district in which it is difficult to predict whether the incumbent will be reelected. Any district in which the winning candidate receives less than 55 percent of the vote is considered a marginal seat. *Compare to* DISTRICT, OPEN; SAFE SEAT.

REFERENCE

David Mayhew, Congressional elections: The case of the vanishing marginals, *Polity* 6 (Spring 1974).

marginal tax rate   The tax rate percentage applied to the last increment of income for purposes of computing federal or other income taxes.

marking up a bill   *See* BILL, MARKING UP A.

Marshall, John (1755–1835)   The revolutionary war soldier (he was actually in the same boat with George Washington as they crossed the Delaware River for the Battle of Trenton) who became the third chief justice of the Supreme Court and, by almost universal agreement, the one who did the most to establish the independent authority of the Court. From 1801 to 1835 he led the struggle for the Court to be the final arbiter of the Constitution and, by sheer force of will and legal cunning, made the federal judiciary a true check on the power of the other two branches and made the federal government supreme over the states. After many years on the bench, Marshall was able to say: "The acme of judicial distinction means the ability to look a lawyer straight in the eyes for two hours and not hear a damned word he says." For some of his landmark cases, *see* COHENS V VIRGINIA; DARTMOUTH COLLEGE V WOODWARD; FLETCHER V PECK; GIBBONS V OGDEN; MCCULLOCH V MARYLAND; MARBURY V MADISON.

John Marshall.

REFERENCES

Albert J. Beveridge, *The Life of John Marshall*, 4 vols. (Boston: Houghton Mifflin, 1919);

William M. Jones, ed., *Chief Justice John Marshall: A Reappraisal* (Ithaca, NY: Cornell University Press, 1956);

Robert K. Faulkner, *The Jurisprudence of John Marshall* (Princeton, NJ: Princeton University Press, 1968);

William E. Nelson, The eighteenth-century background of John Marshall's constitutional jurisprudence, *Michigan Law Review* 76 (May 1978);

Christopher Wolfe, John Marshall and constitutional law, *Polity* 15:1 (Fall 1982).

Marshall Plan   The economic aid program for post–World War II Europe proposed by George Catlett Marshall (1880–1959), U.S. Army chief of staff during the war. In 1947, President Harry S Truman made him secretary of State. In June of that year, Marshall proposed the European Recovery Program, a massive aid program that became known as the Marshall Plan. The plan worked so well and became so well known that the term entered the language and means any massive use of federal funds to solve a major social problem.

REFERENCES
Donald Hester, The Marshall Plan: A study of U.S. interests, values and institutions, *Orbis* 18 (Winter 1974);
Norton E. Long, A Marshall Plan for cities? *Public Interest* 46 (Winter 1977);
Charles P. Kindleberger, *The Marshall Plan Days* (London: Allen and Unwin, 1987).

Marshall v Barlow's, Inc. 436 U.S. 307 (1978) The U.S. Supreme Court case that interpreted the Fourth Amendment's prohibition on unreasonable searches to impose a warrant requirement on Occupational Safety and Health Administration inspections. The court ruled that such warrants do not require evidence establishing probable cause that a violation has occurred on the premises. Rather, a judge can issue an OSHA warrant upon a showing that the inspection follows a reasonable administrative or legislative plan for enforcing the Occupational Safety and Health Act.

Marxism   The doctrine of revolution based on the writings of Karl Marx (1818–1883) and Friedrich Engels (1820–1895) that maintains that human history is a history of struggle between the exploiting and exploited classes. Marx and Engels wrote the *Communist Manifesto* (1848) "to do for history what Darwin's theory has done for biology." The basic theme of Marxism holds that the proletariat will suffer so from alienation that it will rise up against the bourgeoisie, who own the means of production, and will overthrow the system of capitalism. After a brief period of rule by "the dictatorship of the proletariat," the classless society of communism would be forthcoming. While Marxism currently has a strong influence on the economies of the Second, Third, and Fourth worlds, its intent has never been fully achieved. Indeed, because Marx's writings are so vast and often contradictory, serious Marxists spend considerable time arguing about just what Marx "really" meant. Marx's magnum opus, *Das Kapital* (1867), is frequently referred to as the bible of socialism.

REFERENCES
Alfred Meyer, *Marxism: The Unity of Theory and Practice—A Critical Essay* (Cambridge, MA: Harvard University Press, 1959);
Sholomo Avineri, *The Social and Political Thought of Karl Marx* (Cambridge, England: Cambridge University Press, 1968);
Tom Bottomore, ed., *Dictionary of Marxism* (Cambridge, MA: Harvard University Press, 1985).

A Glossary of Major Marxist Concepts

alienation The process by which industrial workers become so disassociated and so frustrated over their lack of control over their work that they become ripe for revolution.

bourgeoisie The ruling class in capitalistic societies; those who own the means of production.

class society Any society in which the labor of one class is controlled by another.

class struggle The competition among social classes for control over labor and the means of production.

communism A classless society in which the workers are neither alienated nor exploited.

dictatorship of the proletariat The socialism that occurs immediately after the proletariat revolt against the capitalist oppressors; the transition stage between capitalism and communism.

expropriation The forcible seizure of significant assets, whether peasant lands seized by a feudal aristocracy or capitalistic factories seized by socialist workers.

means of production Any things, other than labor, used to make other things; for example, factories, machines, and land.

proletariat The exploited working class of a capitalistic society.

revolution The inevitable displacement of one ruling class by a lower class. In the final revolution, all classes will be abolished and communism will prevail.

socialism The temporary political rule of the proletariat after the overthrow of capitalism and before the transition to a classless communist society.

Mason-Dixon line   **1** Pennsylvania's southern border, where it meets the states of Delaware, Maryland, and West Virginia, that was established by a survey conducted by Charles Mason (1728–1786) and Jeremiah Dixon (died

1777) during 1763 to 1767. **2** The pre–Civil War demarcation between slave and free states—between North and South.

REFERENCE

A. Hughlett Mason and William Swindler, Mason and Dixon: Their line and its legend, *American Heritage* 15:2 (1964).

Massachusetts ballot *See* BALLOT, MASSACHUSETTS.

Massachusetts Board of Retirement v Murgia 427 U.S. 307 (1976) The U.S. Supreme Court case that held that a state statute requiring uniformed state police to retire at the age of fifty years was not a violation of equal protection. The Court ruled that the state had met its burden of showing some rational relation between the statute and the purpose of maintaining the physical condition of its police.

Massachusetts v Mellon, Frothingham v Mellon 262 U.S. 447 (1923) The U.S. Supreme Court case holding that federal taxpayers do not have standing to sue the government in federal court by virtue of the "injury" they bear due to taxation.

massive retaliation The stated policy of the Dwight D. Eisenhower administration during the late 1950s that it would respond to communist aggression with massive retaliation, meaning a nuclear attack. The policy evolved in the aftermath of the Korean War and the Harry S Truman administration's policy of not using nuclear weapons in a LIMITED WAR. Not wishing to get bogged down in another limited war and noting the conventional military superiority of the Soviet Union, it became U.S. policy to emphasize its military strength and to threaten an all-out nuclear war in response to either a conventional or a nuclear attack on the United States or its allies. It was Eisenhower's secretary of Defense, Charles E. Wilson, who called this policy the "new look" and stressed its economy by asserting that it would offer "a bigger bang for a buck." But soon after the John F. Kennedy administration took office in 1961, its secretary of Defense, Robert S. McNamara, asserted that a strategy of massive nuclear retaliation was "believed by few of our friends and none of our enemies." So a policy of FLEXIBLE RESPONSE was developed.

REFERENCE

Samuel F. Wells, Jr., The origins of massive retaliation, *Political Science Quarterly* 96 (Spring 1981).

mass party A POLITICAL PARTY in which membership is open to anyone. The United States has a tradition of mass or semimass parties—in contrast to elite (or cadre) parties, such as the Communist party of the Soviet Union, which only citizens meeting certain criteria are allowed to join.

master plan *See* COMPREHENSIVE PLAN/MASTER PLAN.

matching funds **1** Those funds provided for a specific purpose by one level of government as a condition for receiving additional funds for this same purpose from another level of government. Thus a state government may agree to pay 50 percent of the cost of a local capital improvement program if the local government provides the other 50 percent. **2** Funds provided by private foundations or government agencies that are contingent upon the donee organization raising equivalent funds from other sources. **3** Funding for presidential elections available on an optional basis to candidates who agree to abide by contribution and expenditure limits. Primary election campaigns are funded through the presidential primary matching payment account, and general election campaigns are funded through the presidential election campaign fund; these accounts are funded by taxpayers who take the option of earmarking one dollar of their tax liability for this purpose.

A primary election candidate may be eligible for matching funds, once $5,000 is raised in donations of $250 or less in each of twenty states. Thereafter, the fund matches each contribution of $250 or less until the total amount of public funds equals 50 percent of the candidate's primary expenditure limit. By requiring that private funds be raised in the primaries, the law seeks to insure that only serious candidates (i.e., those able to attract private contributors) may receive public funds.

In the general election, the nominees for president and vice president of the two major parties are automatically eligible for a flat stipend from the presidential election campaign fund. In 1980, Jimmy Carter and Ronald Reagan each received $29.4 million in the general election, but this figure is raised every four years according to the cost-of-living increase. No private contributions may be accepted by major party candidates who receive public funds in the general election, except for a specified amount from the national committees of their respective political parties. Third-party candidates may receive public funds in an amount proportionate to the votes received by that party in the previous presidential election, and candidates of newly organized parties may be eligible for retroactive public funds after the election if they receive at least 5 percent of the popular votes cast.

maximum feasible participation The requirement under the Economic Opportunity Act of 1964 that any community action program designed to help the poor have the maximum feasible participation of the people the program was designed to help. This was one of the most significant efforts ever of writing citizen participation requirements into federally funded programs.

REFERENCES

Lillian B. Rubin, Maximum feasible participation: The origins, implications and present status, *Annals of the American Academy of Political and Social Science* 382 (September 1969);

Daniel P. Moynihan, *Maximum Feasible Misunderstanding: Community Action in the War on Poverty* (New York: Free Press, 1969).

May Day 1 The day selected in 1889 by the International Socialist Congress as the day to publicize the eight-hour workday. Consequently, the American Federation of Labor organized a major demonstration on May 1, 1890. Since then, May Day has become a major holiday in socialist countries. 2 The day President Dwight D. Eisenhower proclaimed in 1955 as Loyalty Day.

Mayflower Compact The covenant for the governance of Plymouth Plantation signed by most of the male passengers aboard the ship, the *Mayflower*, on November 21, 1620. While not a constitution, it was a social compact for local government that has since been idealized as the foundation of American constitutional thinking.

REFERENCES

Samuel Eliot Morison, The Mayflower Compact, in *An American Primer,* ed. Daniel Boorstin (Chicago: University of Chicago Press, 1966);

Frank R. Donovan, *The Mayflower Compact* (New York: Grosset & Dunlap, 1968).

The Mayflower Compact

In the name of God, Amen. We whose names are underwriten, the loyall subjects of our dread soveraigne Lord, King James, by the grace of God, of Great Britaine, France, & Ireland king, defender of the faith, &c., haveing undertaken, for the glorie of God, and advancemente of the Christian faith, and honour of our king & countrie, a voyage to plant the first colonie in the Northerne parts of Virginia, doe by these presents solemnly & mutualy in the presence of God, and one of another, covenant & combine our selves togeather into a civill body politick, for our better ordering & preservation & furtherance of the ends aforesaid; and by vertue hearof to enacte, constitute, and fram such just & equall lawes, ordinances, acts, constitutions, & offices, from time to time, as shall be thought most meete & convenient for the generall good of the Colonie, unto which we promise all due submission and obedience. In witnes whereof we have hereunder subscribed our names at Cap-Codd the 11. of November, in the year of the raigne of our soveraigne lord, King James, of England, France & Ireland the eithteenth, and of Scotland the fiftie fourth. Anno: Dom. 1620.

Source: J. Mark Jacobson, *The Development of American Political Thought: A Documentary History* (New York: Appleton-Century-Crofts, 1932), p. 61.

---

mayor The elected chief executive officer of a municipal corporation; the chief ceremonial officer of a city. In most modest-sized and small cities, the office of mayor is a part-time job. Depending on whether the job of mayor is administratively strong or weak, the mayor may simply be the first among equals on a city

mayor-council system

council. While many big city mayors have become national figures, no mayor has ever been able to make the leap from city hall to the White House.

REFERENCES

Jeffrey L. Pressman, Preconditions of mayoral leadership, *American Political Science Review* 66 (June 1972);

Theodore J. Lowi, Why mayors go nowhere, *Washington Monthly* 3 (February 1972);

Russell D. Murphy, Whither the mayors? A note on mayoral careers, *Journal of Politics* 42 (February 1980).

mayor-council system A system of urban government with a separately elected executive (the mayor) and an urban legislature (the council) usually elected in partisan ward elections. It is called a strong mayor system if the office of mayor is filled by separate citywide elections and has such powers as veto, appointment, and removal. Where the office of mayor lacks such powers, it is called a weak mayor system. This designation does not take into account any informal powers possessed by the incumbent mayor, only the formal powers of the office. Hence Richard J. Daley (1902–1976) of Chicago was a strong mayor in a weak mayor system.

REFERENCES

Demetrius G. Jelatis, What can a "weak" mayor do? *Public Management* 55 (June 1973);

Paul Hain, Chris Garcia, and Judd Conway, From council-manager to mayor-council: The case of Albuquerque, *Nation's Cities* 14 (October 1975);

Barbara Ferman, Beating the odds: Mayoral leadership and the acquisition of power, *Political Studies Review* 3 (August 1983).

means test An income criterion used to determine if someone is eligible for government welfare or other benefits. For example, a family might be allowed certain welfare benefits only if its annual cash income is less than $10,609 (the federal government's present definition of poverty for a family of four). Means-tested entitlement programs are often compared to nonmeans-tested programs, such as social security, which citizens are entitled to without regard to their private means. It has even been suggested that one way of reducing the nation's social security liability is to subject future ben-

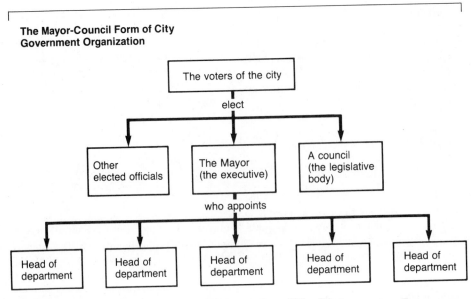

The Mayor-Council Form of City Government Organization

Source: Grover Starling, *Understanding American Politics* (Chicago: Dorsey, 1982), p. 354.

efits to a means test—that is, those people otherwise eligible for social security benefits would receive them only if their incomes were below a specified level.

REFERENCE

Alan Lewis, The comprehensibility of government forms and pamphlets with special reference to means tested benefits, *Policy and Politics* 7 (October 1979).

media event An activity undertaken as a means of generating publicity from the news media. The defining criterion for a media event is that it would not be done if cameras and reporters were not present. Examples include protest demonstrations scheduled for the convenience of the early evening television news programs or a walk through a poor or ethnic neighborhood by a candidate for public office to demonstrate meaningful (photogenic) concern. *Compare to* PSEUDOEVENT.

REFERENCE

Thomas R. Dye and Harmon Zeigler, *American Politics in the Media Age*, 2d ed. (Monterey, CA: Brooks/Cole, 1986).

mediation/conciliation Any attempt by an impartial third party to help settle disputes. A mediator has no power but that of persuasion; the mediator's suggestions are advisory and may be rejected by both parties. Mediation and conciliation tend to be used interchangeably to denote the entrance of an impartial third party into a labor dispute. However, there is a distinction. Conciliation is the less active term. It technically refers simply to efforts to bring the parties together so that they may resolve their problems themselves. Mediation, in contrast, is a more active term. It implies that an active effort will be made to help the parties reach agreement by clarifying issues, asking questions, and making specific proposals. However, the usage of the two terms has been so blurred that the only place where it is absolutely necessary to distinguish between them is in a dictionary.

REFERENCES

For a bibliography, see Edward Levin and Daniel V. DeSantis, *Mediation: An Annotated Bibliography* (Ithaca, NY: New York State School of Industrial and Labor Relations, Cornell University, 1978).

Also see J. Menier, The position of the mediator in the policy of administrative reform, *International Review of Administrative Sciences* 47:4 (1981);

Deborah M. Kolb, *The Mediators* (Cambridge, MA: MIT Press, 1983);

Arnold M. Zak, *Public Sector Mediation* (Washington, D.C.: Bureau of National Affairs, 1985).

mediation service An abbreviated way of referring to the Federal Mediation and Conciliation Service or state agencies performing a similar function.

Medicaid The federally aided, state-operated, and state-administered program that provides medical benefits for certain low-income people in need of health and medical care. Authorized by 1965 amendments to the Social Security Act, it covers only members of one of the categories of people who can be covered under the WELFARE cash payment programs—the aged, the blind, the disabled, and members of families with dependent children where one parent is absent, incapacitated, or unemployed. Under limited circumstances, states may also provide Medicaid coverage for children under twenty-one years of age who are not categorically related. Subject to broad federal guidelines, states determine coverage, eligibility, payment to health care providers, and the methods of administering the program.

REFERENCES

Randell R. Bovbjerg and John Holahan, *Medicaid in the Reagan Era: Federal Policy and State Choices* (Washington, D.C.: Urban Institute, 1982);

Kathleen N. Lohr and M. Susan Marquis, *Medicare and Medicaid: Past, Present, and Future* (Santa Monica, CA: Rand, 1984);

Pamela L. Haynes, *Evaluating State Medicaid Reforms* (Washington, D.C.: American Enterprise, 1985).

Medicare The national health insurance program for the elderly and the disabled authorized by a 1965 amendment to the Social Security Act. The two parts of Medicare—hospital insurance and medical insurance—help protect people sixty-five years of age and over from the high costs of health care. Also eligible for Medicare are disabled people under sixty-five who have been entitled to social security disability benefits for twenty-four or more consecutive months (including adults who are receiving benefits because they have been disabled since childhood). Insured workers and their dependents who need dialysis treatment or a kidney transplant because of permanent kidney failure also have Medicare protection.

REFERENCES

Max J. Skidmore, *Medicare and the American Rhetoric of Reconciliation* (University: University of Alabama Press, 1970);

Theodore Marmor, *The Politics of Medicare* (Chicago: Aldine, 1973);

Henry B. Sirgo, Congressional liaison operations during the Johnson administration: The case of Medicare, *Presidential Studies Quarterly* 15 (Fall 1985).

megatrends A term popularized by John Naisbitt in his 1982 book bearing the same title (New York: Warner Books). Megatrends are basic socio-economic-technological trends, which influence organizational strategies.

melting pot A sociological term that implies (1) that each succeeding wave of immigrants to the United States blends into the general society and (2) that this melting is ideally what should happen. The term originated in Israel Zangwill's (1864–1926) play *The Melting Pot* (1908), in which he wrote: "America is God's Crucible, the great Melting-Pot where all races of Europe are melting and reforming!" But studies have consistently shown that this "ain't necessarily so."

REFERENCE

For the leading analysis, see Nathan Glazer and Daniel Patrick Moynihan, *Beyond the Melting Pot*, 2d ed. (Cambridge, MA: MIT Press, 1970).

memorial A written request to a legislative body or an executive. Memorials are usually petitions by groups seeking to influence a proposed government action. All communications to the U.S. Congress from state legislatures, both supporting and opposing legislation, are embodied in memorials, which are referred to appropriate committees.

mending fences What legislators do when they return to their home districts to consult with constituents and generally look after their political interests.

mentor A trusted counselor. The term has become increasingly important in the context of organizational and political careers, as empirical evidence has shown that having an influential mentor is critically important to career advancement. The word comes from Homer's *The Odyssey*. When Odysseus set off for the war at Troy, he left his house and wife in the care of his friend, Mentor. When things got rough at home for Odysseus's family, Athena, the goddess of wisdom, assumed the shape of Mentor and provided Telemachus, the son of Odysseus, with some very helpful advice about how to deal with the problems of his most unusual adolescence.

REFERENCES

For modern applications, see Barbara Kellerman, Mentoring in political life: The case of Willy Brandt, *American Political Science Review* 72 (June 1978);

Kathy E. Kram, *Mentoring at Work: Developmental Relationships in Organizational Life* (Glenview, IL: Scott, Foresman, 1985);

Laura L. Vertz, Women, occupational advancement, and mentoring: An analysis of one public organization, *Public Administration Review* 45 (May/June 1985).

merchant of death 1 A private business that sells arms and munitions in quantities suitable for military use. The term was widely used in congressional investigations after World War I. 2 A government that sells military supplies and equipment.

REFERENCES

Robert H. Ferrell, The merchants of death, then and now, *Journal of International Affairs* 26:1 (1972);

Peter Wiles, Whatever happened to the merchants of death? Normal supply versus catastrophic demand, *Millennium: Journal of International Studies* 15 (Winter 1986).

meritocracy A word coined by Michael Young in *The Rise of Meritocracy, 1870–2033* (London: Thames and Hudson, 1958; Penguin,

1961). The book is about a governing class, both intelligent and energetic, yet sowing the seeds of its own destruction through its obsession with test scores and paper qualifications. Eventually, those deemed to have lesser IQs revolt. The slogan of the revolutionaries was "beauty is achievable by all." Today, meritocracy often refers to any elitist system of government or education, the grisly connotation of its original meaning effectively forgotten.

REFERENCE

Benjamin B. Ringer, Affirmative action, quotas, and meritocracy, *Society* 13 (January/February 1976).

Meritor Saving Bank v Vinson See SEX DISCRIMINATION.

merit system A public sector concept of staffing that implies that no test of party membership is involved in the selection, promotion, or retention of government employees and that a constant effort is made to select the best qualified individuals available for appointment and advancement. *Compare to* CIVIL SERVICE REFORM.

REFERENCES

For a classic analysis of why it ain't necessarily so, see E. S. Savas and Sigmund G. Ginsburg, The civil service: A meritless system? *Public Interest* 32 (Summer 1973).

Also see Nicholas P. Lovrich, Jr., et al., Do public servants welcome or fear merit evaluation of their performance? *Public Administration Review* 40 (May/June 1980);

Lawrence D. Greene, Federal merit requirements: A retrospective look, *Public Personnel Management* 11 (Spring 1982).

Merit Systems Protection Board (MSPB) The independent federal government agency, created by the Civil Service Reform Act of 1978, designed to safeguard both the merit system and individual employees against abuses and unfair personnel actions. The MSPB consists of three members, appointed on a bipartisan basis to seven-year nonrenewable terms. The MSPB hears and decides employee appeals and orders corrective and disciplinary actions against an employee or agency when appropriate. It also oversees the merit system

and reports annually to the Congress on how the system is functioning. Within the MSPB is an independent special counsel, appointed by the president for a five-year term. The special counsel has the power to investigate charges of prohibited personnel practices (including reprisals against whistle blowers), to ask MSPB to stop personnel actions in cases involving prohibited personnel practices, and to bring disciplinary charges before the MSPB against those who violate merit system law.

Merit Systems Protection Board
1120 Vermont Avenue, N.W.
Washington, D.C. 20419
(202) 653–7124

Merriam, Charles E. (1874–1953) The University of Chicago political scientist (and founding member of the CHICAGO SCHOOL) who was a major voice in the progressive reform movement, a member of the BROWNLOW COMMITTEE/PRESIDENT'S COMMITTEE ON ADMINISTRATIVE MANAGEMENT and the leading early advocate that BEHAVIORALISM be the dominant philosophy of the academic discipline of political science. Merriam's book *Non-Voting: Causes and Methods of Control*, with Harold F. Gosnell (Chicago: University of Chicago Press, 1924) is considered the foundation of all modern studies of voting behavior. Merriam remains influential because so many of his students (such as V. O. KEY, JR., DAVID B. TRUMAN, AND HAROLD D. LASSWELL) became giants in their own right and continued through their writings and their students to spread Merriam's philosophy of behavioralism.

REFERENCES

Leonard D. White, ed., *The Future of Government in the United States: Essays in Honor of Charles E. Merriam* (Chicago: University of Chicago Press, 1942);

Barry Dean Karl, *Charles E. Merriam and the Study of Politics* (Chicago: University of Chicago Press, 1974).

Merton, Robert K. (1910–) The sociologist who did pioneering work on the concepts of bureaucratic goal displacement and bureaucratic dysfunctions. His article, "Bureaucratic Structure and Personality," *Social Forces* 18 (1940), was the first major proclamation that Max Weber's ideal-type BUREAU-CRACY had inhibiting dysfunctions or characteristics that prevented it from being optimally efficient.

REFERENCES

Major works by Merton include *Social Theory and Social Structure* (New York: Free Press, 1949, rev. ed. 1957);

Reader in Bureaucracy (New York: Free Press, 1952);

The Sociology of Science: Theoretical and Empirical Investigations (Chicago: University of Chicago Press, 1973);

Sociological Ambivalence and Other Essays (New York: Free Press, 1976).

metropolitan government A central government for a metropolitan area. It is a consolidated government if all the existing local governments at the time of its formation are abolished. In contrast, under a pure federated government, each local unit retains its identity and some of its functions while other functions are transferred to the metropolitan government. However, there are so many variants and exceptions to this formula that it is impossible to generalize accurately about the structure of metropolitan governing arrangements.

REFERENCES

Joseph F. Zimmerman, *The Federated City: Community Control in Large Cities* (New York: St. Martin's, 1972);

Charles Adrian and Charles Press, *Governing Urban America*, 5th ed. (New York: Mc-Graw-Hill, 1977);

John C. Bollens and Henry J. Schmandt, *The Metropolis: Its People, Politics, and Economic Life*, 4th ed. (New York: Harper & Row, 1981).

Michels, Robert *See* IRON LAW OF OLIGARCHY.

Mickey Mouse 1 The pejorative term for many aspects of government administration. When Walt Disney's famous mouse made it big in the 1930s, he appeared in a variety of cartoon shorts that had him building something that would later fall apart (such as a house or boat), or generally going to a great deal of trouble for little result. So Mickey Mouse gradually gave his name to anything requiring considerable effort for slight results, including many of the Mickey Mouse requirements of bureaucracy. The term is also applied to policies or regulations felt to be needless, inane, silly, or mildly offensive. 2 Something that is insubstantial and is likely to fall apart or break down after slight use, perhaps from the first Mickey Mouse toys, watches, and dolls, which were of doubtful quality. Thus anything that is childish or a waste of energy. 3 College courses that are easy or trivial and not likely to provide any knowledge that is lasting or worthwhile.

micromanagement A pejorative term for too close supervision by policy makers in the implementation of programs. The Congress has been accused of micromanagement when it writes detailed rules governing programs into legislation thus denying line managers any real administrative discretion. But any manager is a micromanager if he or she refuses to allow subordinates to have any real authority or responsibility.

middle of the road *See* MAINSTREAM.

midterm election *See* ELECTION, MIDTERM.

military civil action *See* CIVIC ACTION.

military-industrial complex A nation's armed forces and their industrial suppliers. During his farewell address in 1961, President Dwight D. Eisenhower warned that "in the councils of government we must guard against the acquisition of unwarranted influence, whether sought or unsought, by the military-industrial complex. The potential for the disastrous rise of misplaced power exists and will persist." Malcolm C. Moos (1916–1982), Eisenhower's chief speechwriter during the second term, is usually credited with coining what has become Eisenhower's single most memorable warning: to "guard against . . . the military-industrial complex."

REFERENCES

Robert J. Art, Restructuring the military-industrial complex: Arms control in institutional perspective, *Public Policy* 22 (Fall 1974);

Jerome Slater and Terry Nardin, The "military-industrial complex" muddle, *Yale Review* 65 (October 1975);

Barry S. Rundquist, On testing a military industrial complex theory, *American Politics Quarterly* 6 (January 1978).

For comparative perspectives, see Vernon V. Aspaturian, The Soviet military-industrial complex—Does it exist? *Journal of International Affairs* 26:1 (1972);

Harlan W. Jencks, The Chinese "military-industrial complex" and defense modernization, *Asian Survey* 20 (October 1980);

Alex Mintz, Military-industrial linkages in Israel, *Armed Forces and Society* 12 (Fall 1985).

militia *See* NATIONAL GUARD.

Miller v California *See* ROTH • V UNITED STATES.

Milligan, Ex parte *See* WRIT OF HABEAS CORPUS.

Milliken v Bradley 418 U.S. 717 (1974)   The U.S. Supreme Court case holding that de facto racial segregation in the Detroit metropolitan area public schools, in which minorities were heavily concentrated in the city as opposed to the suburbs, was not unconstitutional since it did not develop from the specific activities of the suburban school districts or of any other public authority. The decision largely foreclosed court-ordered busing between cities and their suburbs.

Mill, John Stuart (1806–1873)   The English political reformer and philosopher best known for his classic argument in defense of civil liberties for those with diverse political opinions. In *On Liberty* (1859) he wrote: "Though the silenced opinion be in error, it may, and very commonly does, contain a portion of truth; and since the general or prevailing opinion on any subject is rarely or never the whole truth, it is only by the collision of adverse opinions that the remainder of the truth has any chance of being supplied."
REFERENCES
Richard W. Krouse, Two concepts of democratic representation: James and John Stuart Mill, *Journal of Politics* 44 (May 1982);

Fred R. Berger, *Happiness, Justice, and Freedom: The Moral and Political Philosophy of John Stuart Mill* (Berkeley and Los Angeles: University of California Press, 1984).

Mills, C. Wright (1916–1962)   The radical sociologist whose most famous book, *The Power Elite* (New York: Oxford University Press, 1956), asserted that the United States was basically ruled by a political, military, and business elite, whose decisional powers essentially preempted the democratic process. Most contemporary analyses of elitism in American governance have their intellectual foundations in Mills's work, even if Mills himself is not acknowledged.
REFERENCES
Joseph A. Scimecca, Paying homage to the father: C. Wright Mills and radical sociology, *Sociological Quarterly* 17 (Spring 1976);

Rick Tilman, The intellectual pedigree of C. Wright Mills: A reappraisal, *Western Political Quarterly* 32 (December 1979);

Hans H. Gerth, On C. Wright Mills (1962), *Society* 17 (January/February 1980);

Irving Louis Horowitz, *C. Wright Mills: An American Utopian* (New York: Free Press, 1983).

minimum wage   The smallest hourly rate that may be paid to a worker. While many minimum wages are established by union contracts, state laws, and organizational pay policies, minimum wage usually refers to the federal minimum wage law—the Fair Labor Standards Act (FLSA)—established by the Congress via FLSA amendments.
REFERENCE
Peter Linneman, The economic impacts of minimum wage laws: A new look at an old question, *Journal of Political Economy* 90 (June 1982).

ministerial function   Required action. In determining the liability of government agents for the consequences of their actions, courts have created a distinction between ministerial and discretionary functions. Though often blurred in specific cases, the distinction attempted to limit liability to acts done by the agents' volition (discretionary), in comparison to actions compelled by the Constitution, a statute, a charter, or other law (ministerial).

minority leader A legislative leader for the minority party. *Compare to* MAJORITY LEADER.

minority party Any political party in a legislature with less than a majority of the members of the legislature as its party's members. When the majority party has overwhelming numbers, the minority party is in a particularly powerless position. Late in the last century, an irate Democrat asked Speaker of the House Thomas B. Reed (1839–1902), "What becomes of the rights of the minority?" Reed replied: "The right of the minority is to draw its salaries, and its function is to make a quorum."
REFERENCE
Charles O. Jones, *The Minority Party in Congress* (Boston: Little, Brown, 1970).

minority set-asides *See* SET-ASIDES.

minority whip The legislator who performs the duties of whip for the minority party. *Compare to* MAJORITY WHIP; WHIP.

minor party A political party so small and uninfluential that it is not a major force in American politics. Support for minor parties is often localized, such as for the Liberal party in New York, or widely dispersed, such as for the Socialist party. Minor party movements are usually based on a single theme, such as prohibition or libertarianism, that is unable to gain widespread support. They differ from third parties in that a THIRD PARTY is a new party strong enough to possibly influence the outcome of an election. While there are significant differences between minor and third parties, in common usage they tend to be lumped together.
REFERENCES
John L. Hammond, Minor parties and electoral realignments, *American Politics Quarterly* 4 (January 1976);
John F. Freie, Minor parties in realigning eras, *American Politics Quarterly* 10 (January 1982).

Miranda **rights** The set of rights that a person accused or suspected of having committed a crime has during interrogation and of which he or she must be informed prior to questioning, according to the U.S. Supreme Court in its *Miranda v Arizona* decision. The act of informing a person of these rights is often called admonition of rights, or admonishment of rights. The information given is called the Miranda warning.
REFERENCE
John Gruhl, State supreme courts and the U.S. Supreme Court's post-Miranda rulings, *Journal of Criminal Law & Criminology* 72 (Fall 1981).

Miranda v Arizona 384 U.S. 436 (1966) The U.S. Supreme Court case that held that an arrested person must be warned of the right to be silent and the right to have a lawyer, who will be provided if the arrested person cannot afford one, as soon as the arrest is made. The Court stated that "the prosecution may not use statements . . . stemming from custodial interrogation of the defendant unless it demonstrates the use of procedural safeguards effective to secure the privilege against self-incrimination." When the police arrest individuals and "read them their rights," it is the rights embedded in the *Miranda* decision they refer to.
REFERENCE
Liva Baker, *Miranda: Crime, Law and Politics* (New York: Atheneum, 1983).

MIRV A multiple independently targeted reentry vehicle, the modern nuclear missile that breaks into as many as a dozen separate missiles, to hit as many separate targets, before it comes back to earth.
REFERENCES
Ronald L. Tammen, *MIRV and the Arms Race* (New York: Praeger, 1973);
Ted Greenwood, *Making the MIRV: A Study of Defense Decision Making* (Cambridge, MA: Ballinger, 1975).

miscegenation law Any law forbidding interracial marriages. The U.S. Supreme Court declared all such laws unconstitutional in *Loving v Virginia*, 388 U.S. 1 (1967).

misdemeanor A crime punishable by a jail term of less than a year. *Compare to* FELONY.
REFERENCE
Douglas W. Maynard, The structure of discourse in misdemeanor plea bargaining, *Law and Society Review* 18:1 (1984).

misery index The total of the rates of inflation and unemployment.

misfeasance The improper or illegal performance of an otherwise lawful act that causes harm to someone. Nonfeasance is a failure to perform at all. *Compare to* MALFEASANCE.
REFERENCE
R. C. Evans, Damages for unlawful administrative action: The remedy for misfeasance in public office, *International Comparative Law Quarterly* 31 (October 1982).

missile gap Presidential candidate John F. Kennedy's 1960 charge that the United States was behind the Soviet Union in nuclear missile production. Interestingly, after the election, the Kennedy administration discovered that there was no such gap after all. Because Kennedy's missile gap evaporated, the term is sometimes used to imply a nonexistent issue.
REFERENCE
James C. Dick, The strategic arms race, 1957–61: Who opened a missile gap? *Journal of Politics* 34 (November 1972).

Mississippi v Johnson 4 Wallace 475 (1867) The U.S. Supreme Court case that asserted that the Court could not interfere with the operations of the executive branch; it could not issue an injunction to restrain the president from enforcing the law.

Missouri plan The method of judicial selection, often referred to as a combination compromise, in which a nominating committee (appointed in part by the state bar, the governor, and the state's chief justice) nominates three candidates for each judicial vacancy. The governor then appoints one of them to the judgeship for at least a one-year term. At the next general election, he or she runs unopposed on a nonpartisan ballot. *Compare to* CALIFORNIA PLAN.

REFERENCES
Richard A. Watson and Rondal G. Downing, *The Politics of the Bench and the Bar: Judicial Selection under the Missouri Nonpartisan Court Plan* (New York: Wiley, 1969);
Marsha Puro, Peter J. Bergerson, and Steven Puro, An analysis of judicial diffusion: Adoption of the Missouri plan in the American states, *Publius* 15 (Fall 1985).

mister The proper form of address (established by custom, not by law) for the highest officials of the U.S. government. Thus the president should be called Mister President; the Speaker of the House, Mister Speaker; a cabinet secretary, Mister Secretary. The comparable title for a female officeholder is Madam, as in Madam President.

mixed economy An economic system that lies somewhere between laissez-faire capitalism and socialism. All of the industrialized countries of the free world have mixed economies, in that aspects of socialism lie side by side with free market capitalism. For example, the United Kingdom has a comprehensive system of socialized medicine within a basically capitalistic economy. In France, the telephone system is owned and operated by the government, while in the United States the telephone system is in private hands but heavily regulated by various levels of government.
REFERENCE
Andrew Shonfield, *In Defense of the Mixed Economy* (New York: Oxford University Press, 1984).

mobilization 1 Preparing for war or other emergencies through assembling and organizing national resources. 2 The process by which armed forces are brought to a state of immediate readiness for war or other national emergency. 3 The total process by which electoral support is generated for a candidate or issue; in effect, a marshaling of all the monetary, organizational, human, and political resources on behalf of the cause.
REFERENCES
1, 2 Paul Bracken, Mobilization in the nuclear age, *International Security* 3 (Winter 1978–79);

John D. Stuckey and Joseph H. Pistorius, Mobilization for the Vietnam War: A political and military catastrophe, *Parameters: Journal of the US Army War College* 15 (Spring 1985).
3 Benjamin Ginsberg and Robert Weissberg, Elections and the mobilization of popular support, *American Journal of Political Science* 22 (February 1978);
Eric M. Leifer, Competing models of political mobilization: The role of ethnic ties, *American Journal of Sociology* 87 (July 1981);
David Knoke, Political mobilization by voluntary associations, *Journal of Political and Military Sociology* 10 (Fall 1982).

Model Cities Program The most significant part of the Demonstration Cities and Metropolitan Development Act of 1966. It designated particular areas in demonstration cities for intensive coordinated federal programs. Though originally programmed for only a dozen or so cities as part of President Lyndon B. Johnson's Great Society, it quickly grew to include more than 150 cities. It was dismantled by the Richard M. Nixon administration. *Compare to* URBAN RENEWAL.

REFERENCES
Marshall Kaplan, *The Model Cities Program* (New York: Praeger, 1970);
Robert A. Aleshire, Power to the people: An assessment of the Community Action and Model Cities experience, *Public Administration Review* 32 (September 1972).

modus vivendi A Latin phrase meaning a temporary understanding pending a final agreement. It is the acceptance of a continuing working relation, with fundamental disagreements ignored or held in abeyance.

REFERENCE
Eugene V. Rostow, The next step in Soviet-American relations: Modus vivendi or peace? *Atlantic Community Quarterly* 23 (Summer 1985).

Monell v Department of Social Services, New York City 436 U.S. 658 (1978) The U.S. Supreme Court case that held that cities and municipalities may be held liable when their customs or official policies (in this case a mandatory maternity leave policy) violate a person's constitutional rights. *See also* OWEN V CITY OF INDEPENDENCE.

REFERENCE
Eric Schnapper, Civil rights litigation after *Monell*, *Columbia Law Review* 79 (March 1979).

monetary policy A government's formal efforts to manage the money in its economy in order to realize specific economic goals. Three basic kinds of monetary policy decisions can be made: (1) decisions about the amount of money in circulation; (2) decisions about the level of interest rates; (3) decisions about the functioning of credit markets and the banking system.

Controlling the amount of money is, of course, the key variable. In 1913, the United States passed into law the Federal Reserve Act, which created a strong central bank, the Federal Reserve. Like most central banks, the Federal Reserve is empowered to control the amount of money in circulation by either creating or canceling dollars. The implementation of money control is achieved through the process of putting up for sale or buying government securities, usually termed open-market operations, which means that the Federal Reserve competes with other bidders in the purchasing or selling of securities. The difference is that, when the Federal Reserve buys securities, it pays in the form of new currency in circulation. If it sells some of its securities, it decreases money available, since in effect it absorbs currency held by others. This does not mean, however, that the money stock fluctuates greatly. It steadily increases. It is in the margin of the increase that money supply has its impact. Through the use of the two other tools, the Federal Reserve can attempt to affect investments and loans. First, it can change its discount rate—the interest rate it charges other banks for loans of money that these banks can use to make loans. Second, it can change the reserve requirement—the amount of money a bank must have on hand in comparison with the amount of money it may have out on loan.

REFERENCES

Milton Friedman, The role of monetary policy, *American Economic Review* 58 (March 1968);

Douglas Fisher, *Money, Banking, and Monetary Policy* (Homewood, IL: Irwin, 1980);

Martin Feldstein, *Inflation, Capital Taxation and Monetary Policy* (Cambridge, MA: National Bureau of Economic Research, 1981);

John T. Woolley, Monetarists and the politics of monetary policy, *Annals of the American Academy of Political and Social Science* 459 (January 1982);

Nathaniel Beck, Domestic political sources of American monetary policy: 1955–1982, *Journal of Politics* 46 (August 1984).

money supply   The amount of money in the economy. There are several definitions of money. M1-A consists of currency (coin and paper notes) plus demand deposits at commercial banks, exclusive of demand deposits held by other domestic banks, foreign banks, and official institutions and the U.S. government. M1-B is M1-A plus other checkable accounts, including negotiable orders of withdrawal and automatic transfers from savings accounts at commercial banks and thrift institutions, credit union share draft accounts, and demand deposits at mutual savings banks. M2 consists of M1-B plus savings and small-denomination time deposits at all depository institutions, overnight repurchase agreements at commercial banks, overnight Eurodollars held by U.S. residents, other than Caribbean branches of member banks, and money market mutual fund shares. M3 is M2 plus large-denomination time deposits at all depository institutions and term repurchase agreements at commercial banks and savings and loan associations. The Federal Reserve Board (*see* FEDERAL RESERVE SYSTEM) is the greatest influence on the national money supply. A significant change in the money supply can herald a new policy on the part of the board or can function as a trigger for the board to implement policy changes.

REFERENCE

Ralph C. Bryant, *Controlling Money: The Federal Reserve and Its Critics* (Washington, D.C.: Brookings, 1983).

Monroe Doctrine   The assertion by President James Monroe in his 1823 State of the Union message that the Western Hemisphere was closed to colonization and aggressive actions by European powers. In return, the United States promised not "to interfere in the internal concerns" of Europe. The doctrine was actually formulated by Monroe's Secretary of State, John Quincy Adams (who would succeed Monroe as president). The Monroe Doctrine had strong rhetorical and political usage in the 1920s, on the eves of World Wars I and II, and in the debates that led up to the CUBAN MISSILE CRISIS, but its relevance is declining. After all, the United States had "interfered" extensively in Europe during the World Wars, and the Soviet Union has not been deterred from "colonizing" such Western Hemisphere countries as Cuba and Nicaragua.

REFERENCES

Ernest R. King, *The Making of the Monroe Doctrine* (Cambridge, MA: Belknap Press of Harvard University Press, 1975);

Jerald A. Combs, The origins of the Monroe Doctrine: A survey of interpretations by United States historians, *Australian Journal of Politics and History* 27:2 (1981);

David F. Ronfeldt, Rethinking the Monroe Doctrine, *Orbis* 28 (Winter 1985).

Monroe v Pape 365 U.S. 167 (1961)   The U.S. Supreme Court case that held that a person whose constitutional rights were violated by a police officer might be able to sue that officer personally for damages in federal court. However, the police officer might have official IMMUNITY, depending on what happened.

Montesquieu, Charles de   *See* CHECKS AND BALANCES.

Monthly Labor Review (MLR)   The journal of the U.S. Bureau of Labor Statistics, published since 1915. Its articles deal with labor relations, trends in the labor force, new laws and court decisions affecting workers, and so on. It lists the major labor agreements expiring each month and gives monthly current labor statistics on employment, unemployment, wages and prices, and productivity. Library of Congress no. HD8051 .A78.

Monthly Labor Review
Superintendent of Documents
441 G Street, N. W.
Washington, D.C. 20212

moon-ghetto metaphor The contrast between the great engineering feat of putting a man on the moon and the government's perennial but often futile efforts at solving the economic and social problems of urban ghettos. It is often posed as a question: If we can go to the moon, why can't we solve the problems of the ghetto? This metaphor has even escaped the confines of the urban ghetto. For example, in 1986 Ruth Westheimer, in an address at a convention of the American Society of Newspaper Editors, complained that "we can send a man to the moon, but we cannot prevent 1.5 million unwanted pregnancies each year."

REFERENCE
Richard R. Nelson, Intellectualizing about the moon-ghetto metaphor: A study of the current malaise of rational analysis of social problems, *Policy Sciences* 5 (December 1974).

moot 1 A hypothetical case used for purpose of discussion. 2 A legal case in which there is no controversy; that is, one in which any formal judgment can have no practical effect. 3 A legal issue that has already been decided.
REFERENCES
Don B. Kates, Jr., and William T. Barker, Mootness in judicial proceedings: Toward a coherent theory, *California Law Review* 62 (December 1974);
Richard K. Greenstein, Bridging the mootness gap in federal court class actions, *Stanford Law Review* 35 (May 1983).

Moral Majority A political organization of fundamentalist Christians founded in 1978 by television evangelist Jerry Falwell (1933–   ). This "majority" tended to support far Right Republican candidates; it opposed abortion and gay rights, supported mandatory school prayers, and generated considerable hostility from some members of the public—perhaps best summarized by a bumper sticker that read "The Moral Majority is Neither." In 1986, Falwell changed the name of his increasingly

attacked Moral Majority to the Liberty Federation. *Compare to* PEOPLE FOR THE AMERICAN WAY.
REFERENCES
John Kater, *Christians on the Right: The Moral Majority in Perspective* (New York: Seabury, 1982);
Michael Lienesch, Right-wing religion: Christian conservatism as a political movement, *Political Science Quarterly* 97 (Fall 1982);
Emmett H. Buell, Jr., and Lee Sigelman, An army that meets every Sunday? Popular support for the Moral Majority in 1980, *Social Science Quarterly* 66 (June 1985).

moral obligation bonds *See* BONDS, MORAL OBLIGATION.

moral victory An election defeat that is turned into a victory for principle by the very fact that the candidate ran and took a public stand. Consequently, the term is often used in an ironic or sarcastic sense.

Morgenthau, Hans J. *See* NATIONAL INTEREST.

morning hour The time set aside at the beginning of each legislative day in the U.S. Senate for the consideration of regular routine housekeeping business. (The "hour" is almost never used in the House of Representatives.) In the Senate it is the first two hours of a session following an adjournment, but it can be terminated earlier if the morning business has been completed. This business includes such matters as messages from the president, communications from the heads of departments, messages from the House, the presentation of petitions and memorials, reports of standing and select committees, and the introduction of bills and resolutions. During the first hour of the morning hour in the Senate, no motion to proceed to the consideration of any bill on the calendar is in order except by unanimous consent. During the second hour, motions can be made but must be decided without debate. Senate committees normally meet while the Senate is in its morning hour. Incidentally, morning hour or morning business can occur anytime of the day or night.

mortgage revenue bonds *See* BONDS, MORT-
GAGE REVENUE.

Moses, Robert (1881–1981) A New York
State and New York City official who had great
influence on the physical development of mod-
ern New York City and its environs. Moses is
often used as an example of the archetypal bu-
reaucratic entrepreneur, because he was able to
obtain so much power while serving in such
relatively "small" offices.
REFERENCES
For a critical biography, see Robert A. Caro,
*The Power Broker: Robert Moses and the
Fall of New York* (New York: Random
House, 1974).
For a more affectionate portrait, see Herbert
Kaufman, Robert Moses: Charismatic bu-
reaucrat, *Political Science Quarterly* 90
(Fall 1975).

most-favored nation An international trade
policy whereby countries agree to give each
other the most favorable of their trade conces-
sions given to foreign countries.
REFERENCES
Theodore C. Sorensen, Most-favored nation
and less favorite nations, *Foreign Affairs* 52
(January 1974);
Paul Lansing and Eric C. Rose, The granting
and suspension of most-favored-nation
status for nonmarket economy states: Policy
and consequences, *Harvard International
Law Journal* 25 (Spring 1984).

motion A request by a member of a legislature for any one of a wide array of parliamentary actions. One "moves" for a certain
procedure or for the consideration of a measure
or a vote, for example. The precedence of motions and whether they are debatable are determined by parliamentary law.

motion to recommit A motion to send a bill
back to the legislative committee that reported
it. Generally speaking, a motion to recommit,
if adopted, kills the bill unless the motion is
accompanied by specific instructions to report
it back to the floor, usually within a specified

time period, and with modifications, amendments, deletions, and so on.

motion to table *See* TABLE.

movers and shakers Those members of a
community who lead public opinion and are
active enough in politics or business that they
can make things happen. The term is often
used as an informal reference to a community's
power structure.
REFERENCE
Philip J. Troustine and Terry Christensen,
*Movers and Shakers: The Study of Commu-
nity Power* (New York: St. Martin's, 1982).

Daniel Patrick Moynihan.

Moynihan, Daniel Patrick (1927–   ) A
U.S. senator from New York elected in 1976,
former ambassador to the United Nations
(1975–76), former ambassador to India (1973–
1975), and former urban affairs advisor to
President Richard M. Nixon (1969–1973).
Moynihan first came to national attention in
1965 when, as an assistant secretary of Labor,
he wrote a report (The Negro family: The case
for national action) suggesting instability in
black families. For a full account of the ensuing
controversy, see Lee Rainwater and William
Yancey, *The Moynihan Report and the Politics*

muckrakers

of Controversy (Cambridge, MA: MIT Press, 1967). Moynihan once again ran afoul of black leaders when in 1970 he wrote in a memorandum to President Nixon stating that "the time may have come when the issue of race could benefit from a period of 'benign neglect.' " When the memorandum was leaked to the press, its misinterpretation once again made Moynihan a persona non grata with many members of the black community. Nevertheless, there are both black and white academics who now consider him a prophet of significant proportions.

REFERENCES

Despite his active public life, Moynihan has earned substantial scholarly reputation. His major works include *Beyond the Melting Pot,* with Nathan Glazer (Cambridge, MA: MIT Press, 1964; 2d ed., 1970);

Maximum Feasible Misunderstanding: Community Action in the War on Poverty (New York: Free Press, 1969);

The Politics of a Guaranteed Income (New York: Random House, 1973);

Coping: Essays on the Practice of Government (New York: Random House, 1973).

Also see Douglas Schoen, *Pat: A Biography of Daniel Patrick Moynihan* (New York: Harper & Row, 1979).

muckrakers President Theodore Roosevelt's term, taken from John Bunyan's (1628–1688) *Pilgrim's Progress* (1678), for a journalist who wrote exposés of business and government corruption. Some of the most famous muckrakers were Lincoln Steffens (1866–1935), Ida M. Tarbell (1857–1944), and Upton Sinclair (1878–1968). Today, anyone who writes an exposé of governmental corruption or incompetence might be called a muckraker.

REFERENCES

For anthologies of representative muckraking, see Harvey Swados, ed., *Years of Conscience: The Muckrakers* (New York: World, 1962);

Arthur Weinberg and Lila Weinberg, eds., *The Muckrakers* (New York: Capricorn, 1964).

Also see Stanley K. Schultz, The morality of politics: The muckrakers' vision of democracy, *Journal of American History* 52:3 (1968).

President Theodore Roosevelt First Puts the Muckrake into the Hands of Journalists

In Bunyan's *Pilgrim's Progress* you may recall the description of the Man with the Muckrake, the man who could look no way but downward with the muckrake in his hand; who was offered a celestial crown for his muckrake but who could neither look up nor regard the crown he was offered but continued to rake to himself the filth of the floor. Muckraking leads to slander that may attack an honest man or even assail a bad man with untruth. An epidemic indiscriminate assault upon character does no good but very great harm. Mudslinging is as bad as whitewashing. . . . Men with the muckrake are often indispensable to the well-being of society, but only if they know when to stop raking the muck.

Source: Speech of April 14, 1906.

---

muddling through *See* CHARLES E. LINDBLOM.

mugwumps 1 Those who desert their political party to support another candidate. 2 The Republicans who would not support the candidacy of James G. Blaine, the Republican nominee for president in 1884.

REFERENCES

Gordon S. Wood, The Massachusetts mugwumps, *New England Quarterly* 78:1 (1963);

Gerald W. McFarland, *Mugwumps, Morals & Politics, 1884–1920* (Amherst: University of Massachusetts Press, 1975).

Mulford v Smith *See* AGRICULTURAL ADJUSTMENT ADMINISTRATION.

municipal 1 Of local government concern—such as municipal bonds or municipal parks. 2 Of internal concern to a nation (as opposed to international). 3 Of concern to only one government, whether state or local. In Latin, *municipium* referred to any self-governing body within the Roman Empire.

Municipal Assistance Corporation Known as Big MAC, the financial instrumentality created in 1975 to refinance $3 billion of New York City loans to prevent the city from defaulting on its loans and technically going bankrupt.

municipal bonds *See* BONDS, MUNICIPAL/ TAX-EXEMPT MUNICIPAL BONDS.

municipal commercial paper Short-term promissory notes issued by local jurisdictions.
REFERENCE
Byron Klapper, Municipal commercial paper, *Governmental Finance* 9 (September 1980).

municipal corporation 1 The political entity created pursuant to state law by the people of a city or town for the purposes of local government. 2 Any formally created subnational government.
REFERENCE
Gerald E. Frug, The city as a legal concept, *Harvard Law Review* 93 (April 1980).

municipal court A local government court with exclusive jurisdiction over violations of municipal ordinances. State law may also grant limited jurisdiction in criminal and civil cases arising within the jurisdiction.

municipality 1 The municipal corporation. 2 The officials who manage the municipal corporation.

municipal law 1 Local legislation. 2 National law, as opposed to international law.

municipal ordinance A local law.

municipal revenue bonds State and local government debt securities, whose interest and principal are paid from the revenues of rents, tolls, or other user charges flowing from specific projects financed by the bonds.

Murray v Curlett *See* SCHOOL DISTRICT OF ABINGTON TOWNSHIP V SCHEMPP.

mx/missile experimental The U.S. intercontinental ballistic missile, formally called the Peacekeeper. While it is one missile, it has ten individually targeted warheads, which, combined, are 350 times the power of the U.S. atomic bomb that destroyed Hiroshima, Japan, in 1945.
REFERENCES
Herbert Scoville, Jr., *MX* (Cambridge, MA: MIT Press, 1981);
Lauren H. Holland and Robert A. Hoover, *The MX Decision: A New Direction in U.S. Weapons Procurement Policy* (Boulder, CO: Westview, 1985).

Myers v United States 272 U.S. 52 (1926) The U.S. Supreme Court case that presented the question of "whether under the Constitution the President has the exclusive power of removing executive officers of the United States whom he has appointed by and with the advice and consent of the Senate." The opinion of the Court was delivered by Chief Justice William H. Taft, a former U.S. president. Not surprisingly, he argued that the removal power is an executive power, vested by the Constitution in the president alone. In Taft's view, the power to dismiss the officials in the executive branch was necessary for presidential control of administration and the ability to make sure that the laws are faithfully executed. *See also* HUMPHREY'S EXECUTOR V UNITED STATES.

N

NAACP *See* NATIONAL ASSOCIATION FOR THE ADVANCEMENT OF COLORED PEOPLE.

NAACP v Federal Power Commission *See* NATIONAL ASSOCIATION FOR THE ADVANCEMENT OF COLORED PEOPLE V FEDERAL POWER COMMISSION.

NACo *See* NATIONAL ASSOCIATION OF COUNTIES.

Nader, Ralph (1934–   ) The archetypal champion of consumer rights whose various investigations have spawned dozens of new consumer laws and whose efforts form the backbone of the modern CONSUMER MOVEMENT. Nader, who also heralded a revival in public interest law, came to prominence in 1965 when his book *Unsafe at Any Speed* (New York: Grossman, 1965) attacked the auto industry for faulty designs. The clumsy effort by General Motors to discredit him backfired and made Nader, the David who forced the embarrassed GM Goliath to publicly apologize for hiring private detectives to dig up "dirt" on Nader's private life (there was none), into an overnight consumer advocate celebrity. Since then, Nader has continued as a reformer and has used his celebrity status to publicize the dangers of certain food additives, the hazards of radiation from television sets, the risks of nuclear power stations, and so on.

REFERENCES
Robert F. Buckhorn, *Nader: The People's Lawyer* (Englewood Cliffs, NJ: Prentice-Hall, 1972);
Hays Gorey, *Nader and the Power of Everyman* (New York: Grosset & Dunlap, 1975);
Arthur Snow, *Litigating Consumer Interests: An Economic Perspective on Ralph Nader* (Madison: University of Wisconsin Press, 1977).

Nader's Raiders People who work for any of Ralph Nader's Washington-based organizations, such as the Center for the Study of Responsive Law, Public Citizen, or the Center for Auto Safety, to investigate government regulatory efforts. The raiders are often college students on summer vacation.

National Academy of Public Administration (NAPA) An organization of more than three hundred distinguished practitioners and scholars in public administration, supported by a small staff, and dedicated to improving the role of public management. The academy was founded in 1967 (by all of the living past presidents of the American Society for Public Administration) to serve as a source of advice and counsel to government and public officials on problems of public administration; to help improve the policies, processes, and institutions of public administration through early identification of important problems and significant trends; to evaluate program performance and to assess administrative progress; and to increase public understanding of public administration and its critical role in a democratic society. *See* PUBLIC INTEREST GROUPS.
National Academy of Public Administration
1120 G Street, N.W.
Washington, D.C. 20005
(202) 347–3190

National Aeronautics and Space Administration (NASA) The federal agency created by the National Aeronautics and Space Act of 1958 whose principal statutory functions are to conduct research for the solution of problems of flight within and outside the earth's atmosphere and to develop, construct, test, and operate aeronautical and space vehicles; to conduct activities required for the exploration of space with manned and unmanned vehicles; to arrange for the most effective utilization of the scientific and engineering resources of the United States with other nations engaged in aeronautical and space activities for peaceful purposes; and to provide for the widest practicable and appropriate dissemination of information concerning NASA's activities and their results.

During its growth years, NASA led a charmed life—its work mesmerized the public and the press. Faced with squeezed budgets and an unwieldy combination of public bureaucracy and private contractors, NASA programs had great difficulties following the spectacular moon voyages. Its space shuttle program exposed more than a decade of poor leadership when, in January 1986, the shuttle *Challenger* exploded moments after launching. As NASA struggled to salvage the shuttle program and rebuild public confidence, the U.S. space program fell behind that of the USSR and consortiums of European nations.

National Aeronautics and Space
Administration
600 Independence Avenue, S.W.
Washington, D.C. 20546
(202) 453–1000

national anthem A country's official song of praise and loyalty. The U.S. national anthem is the "Star-Spangled Banner," the 1814 poem of Francis Scott Key (1779–1843) that was combined with the music of an English drinking song and, by an act of the Congress, officially designated the national anthem in 1931. (Irving Berlin's "God Bless America" has often been suggested as a more singable substitute.)

REFERENCES

For the best account of how Key came to write his famous poem see Walter Lord, *The Dawn's Early Light* (New York: Norton, 1972).

For a critique of its singability, see Caldwell Titcomb, Star-spangled earache, *New Republic* 192 (December 16, 1985).

The Star-Spangled Banner

I

Oh, say can you see by the dawn's early light
What so proudly we hailed at the twilight's last gleaming?
Whose broad stripes and bright stars thru the perilous fight,
O'er the ramparts we watched were so gallantly streaming?
And the rocket's red glare, the bombs bursting in air,
Gave proof through the night that our flag was still there.

Oh, say does that star-spangled banner yet wave
O'er the land of the free and the home of the brave?

II

On the shore, dimly seen through the mists of the deep,
Where the foe's haughty host in dread silence reposes,
What is that which the breeze, o'er the towering steep,
As it fitfully blows, half conceals, half discloses?
Now it catches the gleam of the morning's first beam,
In full glory reflected now shines in the stream:
'Tis the star-spangled banner! Oh long may it wave
O'er the land of the free and the home of the brave!

III

And where is that band who so vauntingly swore
That the havoc of war and the battle's confusion,
A home and a country should leave us no more!
Their blood has washed out their foul footsteps' pollution.
No refuge could save the hireling and slave
From the terror of flight, or the gloom of the grave.
And the star-spangled banner in triumph doth wave
O'er the land of the free and the home of the brave!

IV

Oh! thus be it ever, when freemen shall stand
Between their loved home and the war's desolation!
Blest with victory and peace, may the heav'n rescued land
Praise the Power that hath made and preserved us a nation.
Then conquer we must, when our cause it is just,
And this be our motto: "In God is our trust,"
And the star-spangled banner in triumph shall wave
O'er the land of the free and the home of the brave!

National Archives and Records Administration (NARA) The federal agency responsible for establishing policies and procedures for managing the records of the United States government. The NARA assists federal agencies in documenting their activities, administering their records management programs, and retiring their noncurrent records to Federal Records centers. The NARA also manages the Presidential Libraries system and is responsible for publishing legislative, regulatory, presidential, and other public documents. The NARA became an independent agency in the executive branch of the federal government in 1985. It is the successor agency to the National Archives Establishment, which was created in 1934 and subsequently incorporated into the General Services Administration as the National Archives and Records Service.

National Archives and Records
Administration
8th Street and Pennsylvania Avenue, N.W.
Washington, D.C. 20408
(202) 523–3220

National Association for the Advancement of Colored People (NAACP) The largest and historically most influential of the black interest groups. Founded in 1909, the NAACP is noted for its lobbying for civil rights laws and testing of civil rights cases in federal court. *Compare to* NATIONAL URBAN LEAGUE.

National Association for the Advancement
of Colored People
1025 Vermont Ave., N.W.
Washington, D.C. 20005
(202) 638–2269

National Association for the Advancement of Colored People v Alabama 357 U.S. 449 (1958) The U.S. Supreme Court case that held that a state may not force the disclosure of the names of members of an organization as long as that organization is lawful. While freedom of association is not expressly covered by the First Amendment, the court construed that it is implied from First Amendment safeguards for freedoms of expression and assembly.

National Association for the Advancement of Colored People v Federal Power Commission 425 U.S. 663 (1976) The U.S. Supreme Court case that held that the Federal Power Commission is authorized to consider the consequences of discriminatory employment practices on the part of its regulatees only insofar as such consequences are directly related to its establishment of just and reasonable rates in the public interest. To the extent that illegal,

duplicative, or unnecessary labor costs are demonstrably the product of a regulatee's discriminatory employment practices and can be or have been demonstrably quantified by judicial decree or the final action of an administrative agency, the Federal Power Commission should disallow them.

National Association of Counties (NACo) The major organization of county government and management officials. Founded in 1935, NACo provides research, reference, and lobbying services for its members. *See* PUBLIC INTEREST GROUPS.

National Association of Counties
440 1st Street, N.W.
Washington, D.C. 20001
(202) 393–6226

National Association of Schools of Public Affairs and Administration (NASPAA) An organization of academic programs in public administration and public affairs with a stated objective of advancing education and training in public affairs and public administration. Founded in 1970, NASPAA serves as a national center for information on programs and developments in public administration and functions as an accrediting agency for professional master's degrees in public administration. *See* PUBLIC INTEREST GROUPS.

NASPAA
1120 G Street, N.W.
Washington, D.C. 20005
(202) 628–8965

National Civic Review The monthly journal of the Citizens Forum on Self-Government/ National Civic League, first published in 1912. Until 1959 it was titled the *National Municipal Review*. Library of Congress no. JS39 .N3.

National Civic Review
55 West 44th Street
New York, NY 10036

national committee The formal governing structure of the major national political parties, consisting of fifty committeemen and fifty committeewomen (two from each state) elected by the various state committees and conventions along with state party chairs and other high-ranking party officials. The national committees seldom meet; their main task is to make arrangements for the national convention. While the national party chairperson is elected by the national committee, in reality he or she is often selected by the incumbent president or the party's presidential nominee. When there is no president or presidential candidate, as after a national election defeat, the national committee plays the key role in managing the fortunes of the party.

REFERENCE

Cornelius P. Cotter and Bernard C. Hennessy, *Politics Without Power: The National Party Committees* (New York: Atherton, 1964).

National Conference of State Legislatures (NCSL) The organization that in January 1975 replaced three previously existing organizations (the National Legislative Conference, the National Conference of State Legislative Leaders, and the National Society of State Legislators). The NCSL is the only nationwide organization representing all state legislators (seventy-six hundred) and their staffs (approximately ten thousand). It seeks to advance the effectiveness, independence, and integrity of the state legislature as an equal coordinate branch of government. It also fosters interstate cooperation and represents states and their legislatures before the Congress and federal agencies. *See* PUBLIC INTEREST GROUPS.

National Conference of State Legislatures
1050 17th Street
Denver, CO 80265
(303) 623–7800

national convention The assembly of delegates from the various state political parties who gather every four years to nominate candidates for president and vice president, to draft and vote on a party platform, and to use their time on national television to make their candidates and policies as attractive as possible to the American people. In recent years, with the increasing popularity of presidential primary elections and the opening up of caucuses, the national convention has often functioned merely to ratify the winner of the greatest number of delegates in the primary caucus states. But the convention's processes and traditions

remain available in case the primary season proves indecisive.

REFERENCES

Howard L. Reiter, Party factionalism: National conventions in the new era, *American Politics Quarterly* 8 (July 1980);

Donald S. Collat, Stanley Kelley, Jr., and Ronald Rogowski, The end game in presidential nominations, *American Political Science Review* 75 (June 1981);

James W. Davis, *National Conventions in an Age of Party Reform* (Westport, CT: Greenwood, 1983);

Paul W. David, Ralph M. Goldman, and Richard C. Bain, *The Politics of National Party Conventions*, rev. ed. (Washington, D.C.: University Press of America, 1984).

National Credit Union Administration (NCUA) The federal agency created in 1970 responsible for chartering, insuring, supervising, and examining federal credit unions and for administering the National Credit Union Share Insurance Fund.

National Credit Union Administration
1776 G Street, N.W.
Washington, D.C. 20456
(202) 357–1100

national debt The total outstanding debt of a central government. The national debt of the United States was $75 million in 1790. It reached its low point in 1835, when it was a mere $38,000. By 1981, it reached $1 trillion; but by 1986 this doubled to $2 trillion. The national debt is often confused with the nation's budget deficit in a given year. The debt is, in effect, the total of all the yearly deficits (borrowing) that have not been repaid, plus accumulated interest.

National Emergency Act of 1976 The law that terminated various emergency powers of the president that had been in effect since the 1930s. It established clear guidelines for the declaration of future national emergencies so such events will be decided jointly by the president and the Congress.

REFERENCES

Aaron S. Klieman, Preparing for the hour of need: The National Emergencies Act, *Presidential Studies Quarterly* 9 (Winter 1979);

National Endowment for the Arts/Humanities

Charles McC. Mathias, Jr., National emergencies and the Constitution, *Congressional Studies* 7 (Spring 1979).

National Endowment for the Arts/Humanities *See* NATIONAL FOUNDATION ON THE ARTS AND THE HUMANITIES.

National Energy Act of 1978 The federal statute composed of five separate pieces of legislation: (1) the National Energy Conservation Policy Act (established regulatory, grant, and loan programs to encourage conservation); (2) the Energy Tax Act (included provisions to reduce dependence on imported oil, increase conservation, and encourage development of solar energy); (3) the Natural Gas Policy Act (decontrolled the price of new natural gas); (4) the Public Utility Regulatory Policies Act (encouraged pricing of energy to reflect replacement costs); and (5) the Power Plant and Industrial Use Act (provided incentives for the increased use of coal). *See also* ENERGY ACT OF 1976.

National Environmental Policy Act *See* ENVIRONMENTAL POLICY/NATIONAL ENVIRONMENTAL POLICY ACT OF 1969.

National Foundation on the Arts and the Humanities An independent federal agency created in 1965 consisting of national endowments for the arts and humanities as well as the Federal Council on the Arts and Humanities.

The activities of the National Endowment for the Arts are designed to foster the growth and development of the arts in the United States. The endowment awards grants to individuals, to state and regional arts agencies, and to nonprofit organizations in the fields of architecture and environmental arts, crafts, dance, education, expansion arts, folk arts, literature, museums, music, media arts (film, radio, and television), theater, and the visual arts.

The activities of the National Endowment for the Humanities are designed to promote and support the production and dissemination of knowledge in the humanities, especially as it relates to the serious study and discussion of

The Denver Center Theatre Company's 1986 production of The Cherry Orchard *was supported by a grant from the National Endowment for the Arts.*

contemporary values and public issues. The endowment makes grants to individuals, groups, and institutions—schools, colleges, universities, museums, public television stations, libraries, public agencies, and private nonprofit groups—to increase understanding and appreciation of the humanities. It makes grants in support of research productive of humanistic knowledge of value to the scholarly and general public.

REFERENCES

Francis S. M. Hodsell, Supporting the arts in the eighties: The view from the National Endowment for the Arts, *Annals of the American Academy of Political and Social Science* 471 (January 1984);

James Bovard, Fast times at the Arts Endowment, *Policy Review* 29 (Summer 1984).

National Endowment for the Arts
1100 Pennsylvania Avenue, N.W.
Washington, D.C. 20506
(202) 682–5400

364

National Endowment for the Humanities
1100 Pennsylvania Avenue, N.W.
Washington, D.C. 20506
(202) 786–0438

National Governors Association (NGA) A
membership organization founded in 1908,
formerly the National Governors Conference,
that includes governors of the states, territories, and Puerto Rico. The NGA seeks to improve state government, addresses problems
requiring interstate cooperation, and endeavors
to facilitate intergovernmental relations at the
federal-state and state-local levels. See PUBLIC
INTEREST GROUPS.
REFERENCE
Carol S. Weissert, The National Governors'
    Association: 1908–1983, *State Government*
    56:2 (1983).

National Governors Association
444 North Capitol Street
Washington, D.C. 20001
(202) 624–5300

National Governors Conference *See* NA-
TIONAL GOVERNORS ASSOCIATION.

National Guard The military forces of the
states, which often are used for civil emergencies, such as major fires or floods. Normally,
under the command of each state's governor,
any or all of the state's individual guard units
may be called (by the U.S. Congress) into federal service at any time. Once a guard unit is
called into federal service, it is no longer subject to state control. The National Guard was
organized in 1916. Until that time, each state
had a volunteer militia.
REFERENCE
John K. Mahon, *History of the Militia and the
    National Guard* (New York: Macmillan,
    1983).

**National Industrial Recovery Act of 1933
(NIRA)** The federal statute that created a
massive program of public works and guaranteed employees "the right to organize and bargain collectively through representatives of
their own choosing . . . free from the interference, restraint or coercion of employers." The
act, which created the National Recovery

Administration (NRA) to administer its
provisions, was designed to establish self-
government of industry through codes of fair
competition, which tended to eliminate competitive practices. These codes (which fixed
hours, wages, and prices—in effect, overriding
the restrictions imposed by antitrust policies)
were the essence of the NIRA. Companies
adopting their industries' codes of fair practice
were entitled to display the Blue Eagle, a flag
or poster indicating compliance. The U.S. Supreme Court declared the act unconstitutional
in 1935 (*see* SCHECTER POULTRY CORPORATION
V UNITED STATES), but the Wagner Act (*see*
NATIONAL LABOR RELATIONS ACT OF 1935)
provided employees with even stronger collective bargaining guarantees.
REFERENCE
Ellis W. Hawley *The New Deal and the Prob-
    lem of Monopoly* (Princeton, NJ: Princeton
    University Press, 1966).

**National Institute for Occupational Safety
and Health (NIOSH)** The federal agency,
established under the provisions of the Occupational Safety and Health Act of 1970, responsible for formulating new or improved
occupational safety and health standards. Under the Occupational Safety and Health Act,
NIOSH has the responsibility for conducting
research designed to produce recommendations
for new occupational safety and health standards. These recommendations are transmitted
to the U.S. Department of Labor, which has
the responsibility for the final setting, promulgation, and enforcement of the standards.
National Institute for Occupational Safety
    and Health
1600 Clifton Road, N.E.
Atlanta, GA 30333
(404) 329–3771

national interest 1 Those policy aims identified as the special concerns of a given nation.
Violation of them either in the setting of domestic policy or in international negotiations
would be perceived as damaging to the nation's
future, both in domestic development and in
international competition. 2 In the context of
foreign policy, the security of the state. Theorizing about the national interest is often traced

back to NICCOLO MACHIAVELLI, who held that national advantage ought to be the goal of foreign policy. More recently, the national interest has been held to have two aspects: (1) minimum requirements involving a country's physical, political, and cultural integrity; and (2) variables within the total context of foreign policy. Hans J. Morgenthau (1904–1980) is the international relations scholar most associated with the notion that a nation's foreign policy must further a realistic national interest and be divested of a crusading idealistic spirit. Consequently, he became one of the severest critics of American involvement in Vietnam.

REFERENCES

Morgenthau's classic text is *Politics Among Nations: The Struggle for Power and Peace*, 5th ed. (New York: Knopf, 1948, 1973).

Also see Fred A. Sondermann, The concept of the national interest, *Orbis* 21 (Spring 1977);

Donald E. Nuechterlein, The concept of "national interest": A time for new approaches, *Orbis* 23 (Spring 1979);

Anthony Lake, Defining the national interest, *Proceedings of the Academy of Political Science* 34:2 (1981);

Alan Tonelson, The real national interest, *Foreign Policy* 16 (Winter 1985).

nationalism The development of a national consciousness; the totality of the cultural, historical, linguistic, psychological, and social forces that pull a people together with a sense of belonging and shared values. This development tends to lead to the political belief that this national community of people and interests should have their own political order, independent from and equal to all of the other political communities in the world. The modern nation-state was forged from such nationalistic sentiment, and most of the wars of the last two centuries have been efforts to find relief for a frustrated nationalism.

REFERENCES

Gale Stokes, The undeveloped theory of nationalism, *World Politics* 31 (October 1978);

Reginald C. Stuart, The origins of American nationalism to 1783: An historiographical survey, *Canadian Review of Studies in Nationalism* 6 (Fall 1979);

Ernst B. Haas, What is nationalism and why should we study it? *International Organization* 40 (Summer 1986).

Nationalism, New *See* NEW NATIONALISM.

nationality The legal relation between a person and a state, which implies a duty of allegiance on the part of the person and an obligation for protection on the part of the state. Nationality is not necessarily related to national origin. A person gains nationality via CITIZENSHIP. The concept is not restricted to people; thus corporations or ships have the nationality of the states that charter or register them.

REFERENCE

Philip L. White, What is a nationality? *Canadian Review of Studies in Nationalism* 12 (Spring 1985).

Nationality Act of 1940 *See* AFROYIM V RUSK.

nationalization The taking over by government of a significant segment of a country's private sector industry, land, transportation, and so on, usually with compensation to the former owners. Socialist governments tend to favor extensive nationalization. Indeed, the level of nationalization is an accurate measure of the degree of a nation's socialism. Ironically, even conservative and nonsocialist governments have resorted to nationalization, but in an effort to save a collapsing firm or service, rather than in ideological fervor. For example, the Conservative government of the United Kingdom nationalized part of Rolls-Royce in the early 1970s; and the U.S. government created AMTRAK (*see* NATIONAL RAILROAD PASSENGER CORPORATION). *Compare to* EXPROPRIATION.

REFERENCES

Eduardo Jimenez de Arechaga, State responsibility for the nationalization of foreign-owned property, *New York University Journal of International Law and Politics* 11 (Fall 1978);

Robert B. von Mehren and P. Nicholas Kourides, International arbitrations between states and foreign private parties: The Libyan nationalization cases, *American Journal of International Law* 75 (July 1981).

nationalization of the Bill of Rights *See* INCORPORATION.

National Journal A weekly monitor of activities in the federal bureaucracy, started in 1975. It contains detailed analyses of policies and programs as well as in-depth profiles of officials, interest groups, and programs. This journal is essential reading for all Washington insiders. Library of Congress no. JK1 .N28.
National Journal
1730 M Street, N.W.
Washington, D.C. 20036

National Labor Relations Act of 1935 (NLRA) Popularly known as the Wagner Act, this is the nation's principal labor relations law applying to all private sector interstate commerce, except railroad and airline operations (which are governed by the Railway Labor Act). The NLRA seeks to protect the rights of employees and employers, to encourage collective bargaining, and to eliminate certain practices on the part of labor and management that are harmful to the general welfare. It states and defines the rights of employees to organize and to bargain collectively with their employers through representatives of their own choosing. To ensure this, the act establishes a procedure by which workers can exercise their choice at a secret ballot election conducted by the National Labor Relations Board. Further, to protect the rights of employees and employers and to prevent labor disputes that would adversely affect the rights of the public, the Congress has defined certain practices of employers and unions as unfair labor practices. The NLRA is administered and enforced principally by the National Labor Relations Board, which was created by the act.

In common usage, the National Labor Relations Act refers not to the act of 1935 but to the act as amended by the Labor-Management Relations (Taft-Hartley) Act of 1947 and the Labor-Management Reporting and Disclosure (Landrum-Griffin) Act of 1959. The Wagner Act limits its coverage to those businesses that are engaged in interstate commerce in a substantial way; it was originally intended that its passage would spur the creation of "little" Wagner acts in the states. The Wagner Act also excluded some forms of labor, most pointedly, household and farm workers—this was intended to protect the South against labor organization by blacks.
REFERENCES
Paul Weiler, Promises to keep: Securing workers' rights to self-organization under the NLRA, *Harvard Law Review* 96 (June 1983);
Jules Bernstein and Laurence E. Gold, Midlife crisis: The NLRA at fifty, *Dissent* 32 (Spring 1985);
Paul C. Weiler, Milestone or tombstone: The Wagner Act at fifty, *Harvard Journal on Legislation* 23 (Winter 1986).

National Labor Relations Board (NLRB)
The federal agency created by the National Labor Relations Act of 1935 that administers the nation's laws relating to labor relations in the private and nonprofit sectors. (Some public sector organizations are also under its jurisdiction, most notably the U.S. Postal Service.) The NLRB is vested with the power to safeguard employees' rights to organize, to determine through elections whether workers want unions as their bargaining representatives, and to prevent and remedy unfair labor practices.
REFERENCES
James A. Gross, *The Making of the National Labor Relations Board: A Study in Economics, Politics, and the Law* (Albany: State University of New York Press, 1974);
James A. Gross, *The Reshaping of the National Labor Relations Board: National Labor Policy in Transition, 1937–1947* (Albany: State University of New York Press, 1981);
John R. Van de Water, New trends in NLRB law, *Labor Law Journal* 33 (October 1982);
Terry M. Moe, Control and feedback in economic regulation: The case of the NLRB, *American Political Science Review* 79 (December 1985).

National Labor Relations Board
1717 Pennsylvania Avenue, N.W.
Washington, D.C. 20570
(202) 632–4950

National Labor Relations Board v Bildisco & Bildisco 79 L.Ed. 2d 89 (1984)   The U.S. Supreme Court case that held that employers filing for reorganization in federal bankruptcy court may temporarily terminate or alter collective bargaining agreements even before the judge has heard their case. The Court also held that the termination or alteration may be made permanent if the employer can demonstrate to the judge that the agreement "burdens" the chances of recovery. In arriving at a decision, the Court said, the bankruptcy judge should determine if the company has made a "reasonable" effort to negotiate a less burdensome contract. If the negotiators are not able to arrive at a "satisfactory" solution, the judge still may cancel the contract.

National Labor Relations Board v Jones and Laughlin Steel Corp. 301 U.S. 1 (1937)   The U.S. Supreme Court case that upheld the National Labor Relations (Wagner) Act of 1935, which gave labor the right to organize and bargain collectively. The NLRB, created by the act to enforce its provisions, ordered the Jones and Laughlin Steel Corporation to reinstate some employees it had discharged because of their union activities. The corporation responded by challenging both the authority of the NLRB to issue such an order and the legality of the act itself. The court ruled that

> employees have as clear a right to organize and select their representatives for lawful purposes as the respondent to organize its business and select its own officers and agents. Discrimination and coercion to prevent the free exercise of the right of employees to self-organization and representation is a proper subject for condemnation by competent legislative authority.

National Labor Relations Board v Yeshiva University 444 U.S. 672 (1980)   The U.S. Supreme Court case that held that private university faculty members who were involved in the governance (management) of their institutions were excluded from the protections and rights offered nonmanagerial employees by the National Labor Relations Act.

REFERENCES

Joel M. Douglas, Distinguishing Yeshiva: A troubling task for the NLRB, *Labor Law Journal* 34 (February 1983);

Clarence R. Deitsch and David A. Dilts, *NLRB v Yeshiva University:* A positive perspective, *Monthly Labor Review* 106 (July 1983).

National League of Cities (NLC)   The organization, formerly the American Municipal Association, founded in 1924 by and for reform-minded state municipal leagues. Membership was opened to individual cities in 1947, and the NLC now has more than eleven hundred direct member cities. All U.S. cities with populations greater than five hundred thousand are NLC direct members, as are 87 percent of all cities with more than a hundred thousand residents. The NLC advocates municipal interests before the Congress, the executive branch, and the federal agencies, and in state capitals across the nation where other matters of importance to cities are decided. *See also* PUBLIC INTEREST GROUPS.

National League of Cities
1301 Pennsylvania Ave., N.W.
Washington, D.C. 20004
(202) 626–3000

National League of Cities v Usery 426 U.S. 833 (1976)   The U.S. Supreme Court case that held that the doctrine of federalism, as expressed in the Tenth Amendment, invalidates the 1974 amendments to the Fair Labor Standards Act (FLSA) extending minimum-wage and overtime provisions to state and local employees performing traditional government functions. This decision reversed the Court's decision in *Maryland v Wirtz*, 392 U.S. 183 (1968), which approved the extension of the FLSA to certain state-operated hospitals, institutions, and schools. *NLC v Usery* was, in turn, reversed in 1985 by *Garcia v San Antonion Metropolitan Transit Authority*.

National Mediation Board   The federal agency that provides the railroad and airline industries with specific mechanisms for the adjustment of labor-management disputes; that is, the facilitation of agreements through collective bargaining, investigation of questions of representation, and the arbitration and establishment of procedures for emergency disputes. Created by a 1934 amendment to the Railway

Labor Act, today the board's major responsibilities are (1) the mediation of disputes over wages, hours, and working conditions that arise between rail and air carriers and organizations representing their employees and (2) the investigation of representation disputes and the certification of employee organizations as representatives of crafts or of classes of carrier employees.

National Mediation Board
1425 K Street, N.W.
Washington, D.C. 20572
(202) 523-5920

National Municipal League A membership organization founded in 1894, long in the forefront of municipal reform efforts, that serves as a clearinghouse and lobby for urban concerns. Renamed National Civic League in 1987; publishes the *National Civic Review*.

REFERENCES
Frank Mann Stewart, *A Half Century of Municipal Reform: The History of the National Municipal League* (Berkeley and Los Angeles: University of California Press, 1950);
Alfred Willoughby, A short history of the National Municipal League, *National Civic Review* 58 (December 1969).

National Civic League
55 West 44th Street
New York, NY 10036
(212) 730-7930

national objective Those fundamental aims, goals, or purposes of a nation—as opposed to the means for seeking those ends—toward which a policy is directed and resources are applied.

National Organization for Women (NOW) The leading public interest group for women's issues; founded in 1966. NOW is dedicated to using politics (it both endorses and opposes candidates), education, and legal action to improve the political and economic status of American women. Compared to the League of Women Voters, which is nonpartisan, NOW is aggressively partisan.

National Organization for Women
1401 New York Ave., N.W.
Washington, D.C. 20005
(202) 347-2279

national planning 1 Comprehensive, national, societal planning, as opposed to local or regional planning. 2 Centralized, government-conducted or coordinated, economic planning and development. The concept has been highly controversial, because of its identification with socialistic and communistic approaches to government management of national economies. In the United States, concern for national planning really began with the development of national industries, like railroads, electric companies, and communications, whose needs for extensions beyond state and local regulatory boundaries called for some kind of national system of organization. In the 1980s, various approaches to national planning have been suggested for revitalizing the U.S. industrial economy. *Compare to* INDUSTRIAL POLICY.

REFERENCE
Don Lavoie, *National Economic Planning: What is Left?* (Washington, D.C.: Cato Institute, 1987).

National Planning Association (NPA) A nonpartisan, nonprofit organization founded in 1934 to encourage joint economic planning and cooperation by leaders from business, labor, agriculture, and the professions. Originally the National Economic and Social Planning Association, it changed to its present name in 1941.

National Planning Association
1616 P Street
Washington, D.C. 20036
(202) 265-7685

national policy A course of action or a statement of guidance adopted by a national government in pursuit of its objectives in a specific area. Thus there is often said to be a national policy for health, a national policy for education, and so on. All national policies are inherently vague and seldom fully achieved or even achievable. For example, the Employment Act of 1946 states it is national policy that the federal government promote full employment; and the Housing Act of 1949 states that all Americans should, as soon as possible, have a decent home.

National Railroad Adjustment Board The federal agency, created by a 1934 amendment

National Railroad Passenger Corporation

to the Railway Labor Act, with the responsibility for deciding disputes growing out of grievances or out of the interpretation or application of agreements concerning rates of pay, rules, or working conditions in the railroad industry.

National Railroad Adjustment Board
175 West Jackson Boulevard
Chicago, IL 60604
(312) 886–7300

National Railroad Passenger Corporation
The for-profit corporation, known as Amtrak, created by the Rail Passenger Service Act of 1970 to provide a balanced transportation system by improving and developing intercity rail passenger service.

REFERENCES

Theodore C. Forrence, Jr., Amtrak's legislative mandate: A time for rethinking, *Journal of Legislation* 8 (Summer 1981);

David C. Nice, Amtrak in the states, *Policy Studies Journal* 11 (June 1983).

AMTRAK
400 North Capitol Street, N.W.
Washington, D.C. 20001
(202) 383–3000

National Recovery Administration *See* NATIONAL INDUSTRIAL RECOVERY ACT OF 1933.

National Resources Planning Board The New Deal agency whose mission was to make recommendations to the president on the planned development and use of natural resources. The board began in 1934 as the National Resources Board and Advisory Committee, became the National Resources Committee in 1935, and the National Resources Planning Board in 1939. It had a broad mandate to cooperate with state and local agencies in planning for public works. This early example of a national planning agency was abolished as it had been created—by executive order (in 1943)—because the Congress rejected the president's request for its funding, calling it socialist, communist, fascist, and medieval.

REFERENCES

Philip W. Warken, *A History of the National Resources Planning Board, 1933–1943* (New York: Garland, 1979);

Marion Clawson, *New Deal Planning: The National Resources Planning Board* (Baltimore: Johns Hopkins University Press, 1981).

National Right to Work Committee An organization founded in 1955 that advocates legislation to prohibit all forms of forced union membership. Its National Right to Work Legal Defense Foundation, Inc., seeks to establish legal precedents protecting workers against compulsory unionism.

National Right to Work Committee
8001 Braddock Road
Springfield, VA 22160
(703) 321–9820

National Science Foundation (NSF) The federal agency created by the National Science Foundation Act of 1950 to (1) increase the nation's base of scientific knowledge and strengthen its ability to conduct scientific research; (2) encourage research in areas that can lead to improvements in economic growth, energy supply and use, productivity, and environmental quality; (3) promote international cooperation through science; and (4) develop and help implement science education programs. In its role as a leading supporter of all varieties of scientific research, NSF also has an important role in national science policy planning.

REFERENCE

James J. Zuiches, The organization and funding of social science in the NSF, *Sociological Inquiry* 54 (Spring 1984).

National Science Foundation
1800 G Street, N.W.
Washington, D.C. 20550
(202) 357–9498

national security 1 A condition of military or defense advantage. 2 A favorable foreign relations position. 3 A phrase used as justification to hide embarrassing or illegal activities on the part of a national government. *Compare to* CREDIBILITY GAP. 4 A defense posture capable of successfully resisting hostile or destructive action from within or without, overt or covert. *Compare to* SECURITY.

Contrasting Approaches to National Security

Item	Military Approach	Nonmilitary Approach
Bureaucratic base.	U.S. Department of Defense.	U.S. Department of State.
Method of settling differences.	Military threat and force.	Influence and persuasion.
Attitude toward security.	Can be achieved through greater numbers of more sophisticated weapons.	Cannot be achieved, since it is relative to the threat; increasing weapons increase tension, insecurity, and international instability.
Attitude toward international conflict.	Viewed in absolutes: win or lose, right or wrong.	Viewed in terms of conciliation and compromise.

Source: Adapted from Henry T. Nash, *American Foreign Policy*, 3d ed. (Chicago: Dorsey, 1985), p. 101.

REFERENCES

Richard D. Cotter, Notes toward a definition of national security, *Washington Monthly* 7 (December 1975);

Marcus G. Raskin, Democracy versus the national security state, *Law and Contemporary Problems* 40 (Summer 1976);

C. Maxwell Stanley, New definition for national security, *Bulletin of the Atomic Scientists* 37 (March 1981);

Lee H. Hamilton, National security and national defense, *Presidential Studies Quarterly* 15 (Spring 1985).

National Security Act The 1947 law that combined the U.S. army, navy, and air force into the National Military Establishment. It also created the National Security Council and the Central Intelligence Agency. Amendments to the act in 1949 replaced the National Military Establishment with the present Department of Defense and placed the National Security Council in the Executive Office of the President.

national security adviser The assistant to the president for national security affairs, who directs the staff of the National Security Council within the Executive Office of the President. Since the 1960s, there has been a large degree of institutional competitiveness between the national security adviser and the secretary of state over control of foreign policymaking.

REFERENCES

Thomas M. Franck, The constitutional and legal position of the national security adviser and deputy adviser, *American Journal of International Law* 74 (July 1980);

Zbigniew Brzezinski, *Power and Principle: Memoirs of the National Security Adviser, 1977–1981* (New York: Farrar, Straus, Giroux, 1983).

National Security Council (NSC) The organization within the Executive Office of the President whose statutory function is to advise the president with respect to the integration of domestic, foreign, and military policies relating to national security. The actual members of the council are the president, the vice president, and the secretaries of State and Defense. The council's staff is directed by the assistant to the president for national security affairs. In late 1986, revelations that the NSC was heavily involved with covert operations and functioning like a "little" CIA suggested that some NSC staff members went beyond their statutory authority (*see* IRAN-CONTRA AFFAIR). The ensuing scandal forced the Ronald Reagan administration to reorganize the NSC internally and substantially change its staff.

REFERENCES

I. M. Destler, National security management: What presidents have wrought, *Political Science Quarterly* 95 (Winter 1980–81);

R. Gordon Hoxie, The National Security Council, *Presidential Studies Quarterly* 12 (Winter 1982);

Arthur Cyr, How important is national security structure to national security policy? *World Affairs* 146 (Fall 1983);

Anna Kasten Nelson, President Truman and the evolution of the National Security Council, *Journal of American History* 72 (September 1985).

National Security Council
Old Executive Office Building
Washington, D.C. 20506
(202) 395–4974

national service **1** The concept that a nation's youth should serve the state for a set time period in a military or civilian capacity prior to completing higher education and starting a career. **2** A euphemism for CONSCRIPTION.

REFERENCE

1 Richard Danzig and Peter Szanton, *National Service: What Would It Mean?* (Lexington, MA: Lexington Books, 1986).

national supremacy The doctrine that national laws are superior to and take precedence over state laws. This is based upon (1) Article VI of the Constitution, which makes the Constitution the "supreme law of the land"; (2) landmark Supreme Court cases, such as *McCulloch v Maryland, Cohens v Virginia,* and *Gitlow v New York*; and (3) the military outcome of the Civil War.

National Technical Information Service (NTIS) The federal agency established in 1970 to simplify and to improve public access to Department of Commerce publications and to data files and scientific and technical reports sponsored by federal agencies. The service is the central point in the United States for the public sale of government-funded research and development reports and other analyses prepared by federal agencies, their contractors, or grantees.

National Technical Information Service
5285 Port Royal Road
Springfield, VA 22161
(703) 487–4600

National Transportation Safety Board (NTSB) The federal agency created by the Independent Safety Board Act of 1974 that seeks to assure that transportation in the United States is conducted safely. The board investigates accidents and makes recommendations to government agencies, the transportation industry, and others on safety measures and practices. The board also regulates the procedures for reporting accidents and promotes the safe transport of hazardous materials by government and private industry.

National Transportation Safety Board
800 Independence Avenue, S.W.
Washington, D.C. 20594
(202) 382–6600

National Urban League The nonpartisan community service agency, also called the Urban League, founded in 1911 and devoted to the economic and social concerns of blacks and other minorities. The NAACP and the National Urban League are the two major membership organizations that lobby for the interests of blacks. While the NAACP has been much concerned with the overall promotion of equal rights by lobbying for civil rights law and testing cases in the federal courts, the National Urban League (with 115 local units) has tended to concentrate its efforts on economic issues of importance to blacks.

National Urban League
1100 14th Street, N.W.
Washington, D.C. 20005
(202) 898–1604

Nation's Cities The monthly magazine of the National League of Cities; published since 1963. Library of Congress no. JS39 .N274.
Nation's Cities
1301 Pennsylvania Avenue, N.W.
Washington, D.C. 20004

nation-state **1** A country with defined and recognized boundaries whose citizens have common characteristics, such as race, religion, customs, language. **2** A country with defined and recognized boundaries and a diverse ethnic population (such as the United States) but whose citizens share political ideals and practices to such an extent that unity and internal peace prevail.

REFERENCES

Silviu Brucan, The nation-state: Will it keep order or wither away? *International Social Science Journal* 30:1 (1978);

David Luban, The romance of the nation-state, *Philosophy and Public Affairs* 9 (Summer 1980);

Seyom Brown, The world polity and the nation-state system: An updated analysis, *International Journal* 39 (Summer 1984).

NATO/North Atlantic Treaty Organization
An organization, also known as the Atlantic Alliance, consisting of the signatories of the 1949 North Atlantic Treaty, which unites Western Europe and North America in a commitment of mutual security. Article 5 states that "the parties agree that an armed attack against one or more of them in Europe or North America shall be considered an attack against them all." NATO was created at the height of the COLD WAR to contain Soviet expansionist tendencies. It seems to have worked, in that no member of NATO has ever been turned into a Soviet satellite. *Compare to* TRIPWIRE; WARSAW PACT.

REFERENCES

Cees Wiebes and Bert Zeeman, The Pentagon negotiations, March 1948: The launching of the North Atlantic Treaty, *International Affairs (Great Britain)* 59 (Summer 1983);

Nikolaj Petersen, Bargaining power among potential allies: Negotiating the North Atlantic Treaty, 1948–1949, *Review of International Studies* 12 (July 1986).

naturalization The granting of citizenship to someone who was previously an alien. Article I, Section 8, of the U.S. Constitution authorizes the Congress to enact uniform rules for naturalization. These rules are administered by the Immigration and Naturalization Service.

The North Atlantic Treaty Organization

Member (with year of accession)	Population (thousands, midyear 1983)	Armed Forces (thousands, total active midyear 1983)
Belgium (1949)	9,865	95
Canada (1949)	24,882	83
Denmark (1949)	5,115	31
France (1949)	54,604	493
Germany, Federal Republic of (1955)	61,543	495
Greece (1952)	9,898	185
Iceland (1949)	236	none
Italy (1949)	56,345	373
Luxembourg (1949)	366	0.7
Netherlands (1949)	14,374	103
Norway (1949)	4,131	43
Portugal (1949)	10,008	64
Spain (1982)	38,234	347
Turkey (1952)	49,115	569
United Kingdom (1949)	56,006	321
United States (1949)	234,193	2,136

Source: U.S. Department of State

natural law *See* LAW, NATURAL.

natural rights *See* INALIENABLE RIGHTS.

NCSL *See* NATIONAL CONFERENCE OF STATE LEGISLATURES.

NCUA *See* NATIONAL CREDIT UNION ADMINISTRATION.

Neagle, In re 135 U.S. 1 (1890) The U.S. Supreme Court case that held that the president had the right to authorize protection for federal judicial officers without a need for specific statutory authorization. The president did not have to cite the specific law that allowed him to appoint a deputy federal marshal (David Neagle) to protect a federal judge, because the president's actions are covered under his broad constitutional mandate to "take care that the laws be faithfully executed." Such instances are covered by what is called the prerogative theory of presidential power, which holds that a president can act on his own, without legislative authorization, because of his oath to "preserve, protect, and defend the Constitution of the United States."

Near v Minnesota *See* FREE PRESS CLAUSE.

Nebraska Press Association v Stuart *See* GAG RULE/GAG ORDER.

necessary and proper clause That portion of Article I, Section 8, of the U.S. Constitution (sometimes called the elastic clause) that makes it possible for the Congress to enact all "necessary and proper" laws to carry out its responsibilities. Chief Justice John Marshall in *McCulloch v Maryland* gave this clause broad effect when he wrote that "in the desire to remove all doubts respecting the right to legislate on that vast mass of incidental powers which must be involved in the Constitution if that instrument be not a splendid bauble" the framers included the necessary and proper or elastic clause.

neighborhood 1 A specific geographic area. 2 An informally designated subsection of a city having distinctive characteristics. 3 A community. While neighborhood and community tend to be used interchangeably, neighborhood has more of a geographic focus—the residents share a common area. Community, in contrast, implies that the population consciously identifies with the community and works together for common ends.

REFERENCE
William P. Hojnacki, What is a neighborhood? *Social Policy* 10 (September/October 1979).

neighborhood association An organization of residents of a neighborhood. In many American cities, neighbors in a particular area have formally organized into associations. These associations often play important political roles, lobbying local government to protect neighborhood interests at all levels of government. They often reflect a movement calling for a decentralization of local government. At the extreme are advocates for neighborhood self-sufficiency, who see economic and political power possible for poorer neighborhoods only to the extent they become independent of the dominant urban government.

REFERENCES
Milton Kolter, *Neighborhood Government: The Local Foundation of Political Life* (Indianapolis: Bobbs Merrill, 1969);
Howard W. Hallman, *The Organization of Neighborhood Councils: A Practical Guide* (New York: Praeger, 1977);
Richard C. Rich, The dynamics of leadership in neighborhood organizations, *Social Science Quarterly* 60 (March 1980);
Richard C. Rich, A political-economy approach to the study of neighborhood organizations, *American Journal of Political Science* 24 (November 1980);
Anthony Downs, *Neighborhoods and Urban Development* (Washington, D.C.: Brookings, 1981).

neo Something new about something old; a revival or a new variant of an older ideology.

neoconservatism A pragmatic form of traditional liberalism that accepts many elements of the welfare state but rejects many of the statist tendencies of "big government"; that is basically supportive of current domestic policies but wanting a more aggressive, more idealistic foreign policy; and that espouses responsible free enterprise but differs from traditional conservatism and the new Right in its rejection of government regulation of personal behavior in areas of morality, school prayer, abortion, and so on. Neoconservatism, as an intellectual force, evolved in the journal *Public Interest* during the late 1960s and early 1970s by writers who were formerly considered liberals. *Compare to* CONSERVATISM; LIBERALISM.

REFERENCES

Peter Steinfels, *The Neoconservatives: The Men Who Are Changing America's Politics* (New York: Simon & Schuster, 1979);

Irving Kristol, *Reflections of a Neoconservative: Looking Back, Looking Ahead* (New York: Basic Books, 1983).

For a comparative perspective, see Rob Kroes, ed., *Neo-Conservatism: Its Emergence in the USA and Europe* (Amsterdam: VU Uitgeuerij/Free University Press, 1984).

neoliberals Democrats who increasingly reject the Democratic party's traditional liberal agenda in favor of more pragmatic approaches to social problems, incorporating ideas from across the political spectrum. Neoliberal ideas will often be found in *The Washington Monthly*.

REFERENCES

Randall Rothenberg, *The Neo-Liberals: Creating the New American Politics* (New York: Simon & Schuster, 1984);

Charles Peters and Phillip Keisling, *A New Road for America: The Neoliberal Movement* (Lanham, MD: University Press of America, 1984);

Victor Ferkiss, Neoliberalism: How new? How liberal? How significant? *Western Political Quarterly* 39 (March 1986).

nepotism Any practice by which officeholders award positions to members of their immediate family. It is derived from the Latin *nepos*, meaning nephew or grandson. The rulers of the medieval church were often thought to give special preference to their nephews in distributing churchly offices, at that time, nephew being a euphemism for an illegitimate son. In this regard, James H. Boren (1925–   ), president of the humorously oriented International Association of Professional Bureaucrats, has observed that "Einstein's theory of relativity, as practiced by congressmen, simply means getting members of your family on the payroll."

neutral competence The concept that envisions a continuous, politically uncommitted cadre of bureaucrats at the disposal of elected or appointed political executives.

REFERENCES

Herbert Kaufman, Emerging conflicts in the doctrines of public administration, *American Political Science Review* 50 (December 1956);

Hugh Heclo, OMB and the presidency—The problem of "neutral competence," *Public Interest* 38 (Winter 1975).

neutrality In international law, the attitude of impartiality, during periods of war, adopted by third nations toward belligerents (the warring countries) and recognized by the belligerents. Nations declaring themselves neutral expect to be accorded rights of access to the belligerent countries for purposes of travel and trade, although when that trade has included materials necessary to the survival or the military effectiveness of the belligerent nation, such access has led to frequent debates. Thus declarations of neutrality have not been notably successful in preventing the ultimate involvement of neutral nations in the conflicts among belligerents.

REFERENCE

Walter L. Williams, Jr., Neutrality in modern armed conflicts: A survey of the developing law, *Military Law Review* 90 (Fall 1980).

neutral state In international law, a nation that pursues a policy of neutrality (noninvolvement) during a war.

Newburgh conspiracy *See* COUP D'ÉTAT.

New Deal The domestic programs and policies of the administration of President Franklin D. Roosevelt (1933–1945). The New Deal marked the beginning of big government in America—its domestic programs would literally touch the lives of every citizen. And the

Mail Carriers of Today, *by Frank Bergman, was one of many post office murals executed under the New Deal's Public Works of Art Project.*

political coalition it formed of the urban working classes, the farmers, the ethnic blocs, the southerners, and the liberal intellectuals still embraces important elements of the Democratic party. For New Deal legislation, *see* HUNDRED DAYS.

REFERENCES

Arthur M. Schlesinger, Jr., *The Coming of the New Deal* (Boston: Houghton Mifflin, 1959);

Irving Louis Horowitz, From the New Deal to the New Federalism: Presidential ideology in the U.S. from 1932 to 1982, *American Journal of Economics and Sociology* 42 (April 1983);

Michal R. Belknap, The New Deal and the emergency powers doctrine, *Texas Law Review* 62 (August 1983);

Walter F. Mondale, The legacy of the New Deal: The role of government in American life, *Minnesota Law Review* 68 (December 1983).

new federalism   *See* FEDERALISM, NEW.

New Freedom   The domestic programs and policies of the administration of President Woodrow Wilson (1913–1921). In contrast to Theodore Roosevelt's New Nationalism, which urged regulation as the basic government policy toward big business, Wilson's New Freedom,

following ideas suggested by Louis Brandeis (*see* BRIEF, BRANDEIS), favored rigorous antitrust action to break up large industrial combinations.

REFERENCE

Arthur S. Link, *Wilson: The New Freedom* (Princeton, NJ: Princeton University Press, 1956).

New Frontier   The policies and programs of the administration of President John F. Kennedy (1961–1963). He first used the phrase when he accepted his party's nomination at the Democratic National Convention in 1960, saying in part: "The New Frontier of which I speak is not a set of promises—it is a set of challenges. It sums up not what I intend to offer the American people, but what I intend to ask of them."

REFERENCE

Robert J. Williams and David A. Kershaw, Kennedy and Congress: The struggle for the New Frontier, *Political Studies* 27 (September 1979).

new industrial state   John Kenneth Galbraith's concept (from his 1967 book of the same name) that holds that modern organizations have become so complex that traditional leaders are no longer able to make major decisions. They can only ratify the decisions made for them by a technostructure of specialists, who may be more interested in maintaining themselves than in generating profits.

New Jersey plan The proposals put before the Constitutional Convention of 1787 by William Paterson of New Jersey, which called for equal representation of the states in a unicameral legislature. *Compare to* CONNECTICUT COMPROMISE.

Newlands Reclamation Act of 1902 The federal law that provided that funds from the sale of public lands would be used for irrigation and reclamation projects. This was one of the essential pieces of legislation in the development of the conservation movement.

new look *See* MASSIVE RETALIATION.

New Nationalism The domestic programs and policies urged by Theodore Roosevelt in his Progressive party campaign of 1912 against Woodrow Wilson and Republican incumbent, William Howard Taft. The New Nationalism accepted the reality of large business combinations but called for their regulation in the public interest. *Compare to* NEW FREEDOM.

new Right *See* RIGHT, NEW.

news management 1 The informal efforts of an administration to direct and control the reporting of its activities by the news media. 2 The use of professional public relations staffs by political and administrative leaders who seek extensive media coverage and a specific media image. News management includes scheduling press conferences in time to make the evening news broadcasts, denying (or granting) access to unfavorable (or favorable) reporters, allowing (or not allowing) reporters to cover military stories, planting stories with favored reporters, and anything else that makes it easier or harder for honest and fair news coverage to proceed. All administrations at all jurisdictional levels attempt to manage news to one extent or another. They will usually deny that they are doing so.

REFERENCES

John Mecklin, Managing the news in Vietnam, in *The Politics of the Federal Bureau-*

cracy, ed. Alan A. Altshuler (New York: Dodd, Mead, 1975);

Frank Cormier, James Deakin, and Helen Thomas, *The White House Press on the Presidency: News Management and Co-Option* (Lanham, MD: University Press of America, 1983);

Harvey G. Zeidenstein, News media perceptions of White House news management, *Presidential Studies Quarterly* 14 (Summer 1984).

new town 1 Any large-scale, integrated housing, industrial, and cultural development created as a self-contained community. Examples of new towns in the United States include Reston, Virginia, and Columbia, Maryland. 2 British term for garden city towns built under the New Towns Act of 1946.

REFERENCE

Robert K. Whelan, New towns: An idea whose time has passed? *Journal of Urban History* 10 (February 1984).

New York Times Magazine v Sullivan 376 U.S. 254 (1964) The U.S. Supreme Court case that held that a state cannot, under the First and Fourteenth amendments, award damages to a public official for defamatory falsehood relating to his official conduct unless he proves "actual malice"—that the statement was made with the knowledge of its falsity or with reckless disregard of whether it was true or false.

REFERENCES

Anthony Lewis, *New York Times v Sullivan* reconsidered: Time to return to "the central meaning of the First Amendment," *Columbia Law Review* 83 (April 1983);

Richard A. Epstein, Was *New York Times v Sullivan* wrong? *University of Chicago Law Review* 53 (Summer 1986).

New York Times v United States *See* FREE PRESS CLAUSE.

NGA *See* NATIONAL GOVERNORS ASSOCIATION.

nihilism A philosophy that professes a belief in literally nothing. This seems contradictory, because a professed belief in nothing is at least a positive statement of belief. Nihilists most specifically believe in the total rejection of organized social life. Nihilists, who have historically often been associated with terrorists and anarchists, seem to have a desire to go back to Thomas Hobbes's original state of nature, where life was "solitary, poor, nasty, brutish, and short."

REFERENCE

Irving Kristol, Capitalism, socialism, and nihilism, *Public Interest* 31 (Spring 1973).

Nineteenth Amendment   The 1920 amendment to the U.S. Constitution that gave women the right to vote. *Compare to* SUFFRAGE.

Ninth Amendment   The amendment to the U.S. Constitution that reads, "the enumeration in the Constitution, of certain rights, shall not be construed to deny or disparage others retained by the people." This amendment reflects the framers' view that the powers of government are limited by the rights (*see* INALIENABLE RIGHTS) of the people and that, by expressly enumerating certain rights of the people in the Constitution, the framers did not intend to recognize that government had unlimited power to invade other rights. Indeed, in *Griswold v Connecticut,* some justices sought to change the amendment's status as a rule of construction to one of positive affirmation and protection of the right to privacy.

REFERENCES

Jordon J. Paust, Human rights and the Ninth Amendment: A new forum of guarantee, *Cornell Law Review* 60 (January 1975); Raoul Berger, The Ninth Amendment, *Cornell Law Review* 66 (November 1980).

NIRA   *See* NATIONAL INDUSTRIAL RECOVERY ACT OF 1933.

Nixon Doctrine   The U.S. foreign policy enunciated by President Richard M. Nixon at a press conference on Guam on July 25, 1969, that sought to minimize the role of the United States as world policeman. The central thesis of the doctrine is that "America cannot—and will not—conceive all the plans, design all the programs, execute all the decisions and under-

take all the defense of the free nations of the world. We will help where it makes a real difference and is considered in our interest."

REFERENCES

Stephen P. Gibert, Implications of the Nixon Doctrine for military aid policy, *Orbis* 16 (Fall 1972); Werner Kaltefleiter, Europe and the Nixon Doctrine: A German point of view, *Orbis* 17 (Spring 1973).

Richard M. Nixon.

Nixon, Richard M. (1913–   )   The only man ever to be forced to resign (in 1974) from the office of president of the United States in the face of almost certain conviction by the Senate of the House impeachment charges of "high crimes and misdemeanors." This was in response to the scandals of WATERGATE.

After navy service in World War II, Nixon was elected to the U.S. House of Representatives (from California) in 1946 and 1948. As a member of the House Un-American Activities Committee, he developed a reputation as a virulent anticommunist. In 1950, California sent him to the Senate. The Republicans selected him as Dwight D. Eisenhower's vice presidential running mate in 1952. After being twice elected vice president (1952 and 1956), he ran as the Republican nominee for president in 1960 against the Democratic candidate, John F. Kennedy, and lost by a narrow margin. He returned to California and ran for governor in 1962. Soundly defeated, he announced his retirement from politics. But in the wake of public dissatisfaction with the Vietnam War, he won the Republican nomination and the presidency in 1968.

While it must be conceded that Nixon did some positive things in foreign policy, such as winding down U.S. involvement in Vietnam, opening diplomatic relations with Communist China, and accomplishing détente with the Soviet Union; and in domestic policy, by signing initiatives from the Democratically controlled Congress on environmental policy, workplace safety, and public service jobs. But his political duplicity will mark his place in history. His second-term efforts to centralize management of the federal bureaucracy in the White House would, if they had not been stopped by the Watergate affair, have transformed American national government. Nixon was able to avoid being tried for his Watergate crimes because his hand-picked successor, GERALD R. FORD, granted him a pardon for any crimes he may have committed while in office. *See also* CHECKERS SPEECH; STAND PAT; UNITED STATES V NIXON.

REFERENCES

For Nixon's version, see Richard Nixon, *RN: The Memoirs of Richard Nixon* (New York: Grosset & Dunlap, 1978).

For more objective versions, see Theodore H. White, *Breach of Faith: The Fall of Richard Nixon* (New York: Atheneum, 1975);

Bob Woodward and Carl Bernstein, *The Final Days* (New York: Simon & Schuster, 1976);

J. Anthony Lukas, *Nightmare: The Underside of the Nixon Years* (New York: Viking, 1976);

James David Barber, The Nixon brush with tyranny, *Political Science Quarterly* 92 (Winter 1977–78).

For the most comprehensive biography of Nixon's early career, see Stephen E. Ambrose, *Nixon: The Education of Politician 1913–1962* (New York: Simon & Schuster, 1987).

The Richard M. Nixon Administration

Major Accomplishments

- The opening of relations with China.
- Détente with the Soviet Union.
- The creation of the Office of Management and Budget to give greater control over the bureaucracy.
- The introduction of revenue sharing.

Major Frustrations

- The continuation of the Vietnam War.
- The Watergate scandal and Nixon's ultimate resignation, unprecedented among American presidents.
- The scandal surrounding Vice President Spiro Agnew and his forced resignation.

The Articles of Impeachment Against Richard M. Nixon

Article I

In his conduct of the office of President of the United States, Richard M. Nixon, in violation of his constitutional oath faithfully to execute the office of President of the United States and, to the best of his ability, preserve, protect, and defend the Constitution of the United States, and in violation of his constitutional duty to take care that the laws be faithfully executed, has prevented, obstructed, and impeded the administration of justice, in that:

On June 17, 1972, and prior thereto, agents of the Committee for the Re-election of the President committed unlawful entry of the headquarters of the Democratic National Committee in Washington, District of Columbia, for the purpose of securing political intelligence. Subsequent thereto, Richard M. Nixon, using the powers of his high office, engaged personally and through his subordinates and agents, in a course of conduct or plan designed to delay, impede, and obstruct the investigation of such unlawful entry; to cover up, conceal and protect those responsible; and to conceal the existence and scope of other unlawful covert activities.

Article II

Using the powers of the office of President of the United States, Richard M. Nixon, in violation of his constitutional oath faithfully to execute the office of President of the United States and, to the best of his ability, preserve, protect, and defend the Constitution of the United States, and in disregard of his constitutional duty to take care that the laws be faithfully executed, has repeatedly engaged in conduct violating the constitutional rights of citizens, impairing the due and proper ad-

ministration of justice and the conduct of lawful inquiries, or contravening the laws
governing agencies of the executive branch
and the purposes of these agencies.

Article III

In his conduct of the office of President of the
United States, Richard M. Nixon, contrary to
his oath faithfully to execute the office of
President of the United States and, to the
best of his ability, preserve, protect, and defend the Constitution of the United States,
and in violation of his constitutional duty to
take care that the laws be faithfully executed,
has failed without lawful cause or excuse to
produce papers and things as directed by
duly authorized subpoenas issued by the
Committee on the Judiciary of the House of
Representatives. . . . In refusing to produce
these papers and things, Richard M. Nixon,
substituting his judgment as to what materials were necessary for the inquiry, interposed the powers of the Presidency against
the lawful subpoenas of the House of Representatives, thereby assuming to himself functions and judgments necessary to the
exercise of the sole power of impeachment
vested by the Constitution in the House of
Representatives.

   In all of this, Richard M. Nixon has acted in
a manner contrary to his trust as President
and subversive of constitutional government,
to the great prejudice of the cause of law and
justice, and to the manifest injury of the people of the United States. Wherefore Richard
M. Nixon, by such conduct, warrants impeachment and trial, and removal from office.

Source: Report of the Committee on the Judiciary, U.S.
House of Representatives, August 20, 1974.

NLC *See* NATIONAL LEAGUE OF CITIES.

NLRB *See* NATIONAL LABOR RELATIONS
BOARD.

noblesse oblige A French term meaning nobility obliges; the notion that the nobility has a
special obligation to serve society. It has often
been suggested that wealthy Americans out of
a sense of noblesse oblige enter politics in a
noble effort to serve their fellow citizens. Don't
believe such nonsense. While it was once true
that the sons of wealthy American families
took noblesse oblige seriously (the Roosevelts
are a good example), today the children of the
very wealthy tend to enter politics for the same
reasons other people do—because it's fun, it
offers ego gratification, and, most important,
because it satisfies their desire for power. When

someone asked the multimillionaire presidential candidate John F. Kennedy why he wanted
to be president, he candidly replied, "Because
that is where the power is."

no first use A strategic policy, publicly proclaimed, of not being the first to use nuclear
weapons in a potential war. The United States
has never proclaimed this as a policy. Some
argue that such a policy would be desirable,
because it would help prevent an escalation to
nuclear war, but others contend that it would
give the Soviets an unreasonable advantage in
Europe, because of their overwhelming numerical advantage with conventional ground
forces. While it has never been officially
stated, the only way the United States and
NATO could probably stop a full-scale Warsaw
Pact attack on Western Europe is through the
use of nuclear weapons.

REFERENCES

Vincenzo Tornetta, The nuclear strategy of the
   Atlantic Alliance and the "no-first-use" de-
   bate, *NATO Review* 30 (December 1982);
John D. Steinbruner and Leon V. Sigal, eds.,
   *Alliance Security: NATO and the No-First-
   Use Question* (Washington, D.C.: Brook-
   ings, 1983);
Lawrence D. Weiler, No first use: A history,
   Bulletin of the Atomic Scientists 39 (Febru-
   ary 1983).

nolo contendere A Latin phrase meaning no
contest; a defendant's formal answer in court
to a charge in a complaint or an indictment,
stating that he or she will not contest the
charge but neither admits guilt nor claims innocence. Both guilty and nolo contendere pleas
can be followed by a judgment of conviction
without a trial and by a prison sentence. The
main difference lies in their potential use as
evidence in a related civil suit. During any subsequent civil proceeding, a guilty plea can constitute evidence that relevant facts have been
admitted; a nolo contendere plea cannot. *Compare to* SPIRO T. AGNEW.

nomination 1 The announcement of a name
or slate of names for action by any governing
body charged with selection. 2 An appoint-

ment to federal office by the executive branch of the U.S. government, subject to Senate confirmation. **3** A political party's designation of a particular person as their candidate for a particular public office.
REFERENCES
Richard D. Bingham, John P. Frendreis, and James M. Rhodes, The nominating process in nonpartisan elections: Petition signing as an act of support, *Journal of Politics* 40 (November 1978);
Gerald M. Pomper, New rules and new games in presidential nominations, *Journal of Politics* 41 (August 1979).

nonaligned countries Nations that have deliberately chosen not to be politically or militarily associated with either the West or the Soviet bloc. This word has lost much of its meaning, because many of the self-professed nonaligned nations (such as Cuba and Libya) are aligned with the Soviet Union.
REFERENCE
Leo Mates, The concept of non-alignment, *India Quarterly* 39 (January–March 1983).

Nonaligned Movement A formal association of Third World nations designed to promote the political and economic interests of developing and dependent nations. It supports efforts to remove colonial rule and stands behind the U.N. General Assembly's 1974 Declaration on the New International Economic Order, calling for transfer of economic resources to the Third World.
REFERENCES
William M. LeoGrande, Evolution of the non-aligned movement, *Problems of Communism* 29 (January–February 1980);
Anton Vratusa, Prospects of the non-alignment movement, *International Studies* 20 (January–June 1981).

nonintervention The policy that one nation should not intervene in the domestic life (the internal affairs) of another. This is an especially touchy international concern when the stronger of two nations (such as the United States) has had a history of interfering in the domestic policies of nations in a particular region (such as Latin America).
REFERENCE
Yale H. Ferguson, Reflections on the inter-American principle of nonintervention: A search for meaning in ambiguity, *Journal of Politics* 32 (August 1970).

nonpartisan election *See* ELECTION, NON-PARTISAN.

norms **1** The average or standard behavior for members of a group. The norm is what is normal. **2** The socially enforced requirements and expectations about basic responsibilities, behavior, and thought patterns of members in their organizational roles. *Compare to* RECIPROCITY. **3** In psychological testing, tables of scores from a large number of people who have taken a particular test.
REFERENCES
2 Herbert B. Asher, The learning of legislative norms, *American Political Science Review* 67 (June 1973);
William H. Panning, Rational choice and congressional norms, *Western Political Quarterly* 35 (June 1982).

Norris-LaGuardia Act of 1932 The federal statute that removed from the federal courts the power to prevent coercive activities by unions if such actions did not involve fraud or violence. The act was significant because it finally allowed unions to exert effective economic pressures against employers. It also declared yellow-dog contracts to be unenforceable. A yellow-dog contract is a preemployment agreement by an employee that he or she would not join a union. Why were they called yellow dog? Because only a yellow dog would sign one. Many states have little Norris-LaGuardia acts that cover industries not engaged in interstate commerce.

North-South dialogue Economic discussions between the North (the rich, industrialized, developed countries generally located in the Northern Hemisphere) and the South (the poor, developing countries located mainly in the Southern Hemisphere.

REFERENCES
Edward Heath, North-South dialogue and the quest for peace, *NATO Review* 28 (August 1980);

Hans-Henrik Holm, A banner of hope? North-South negotiations and the new international development strategy for the eighties, *Cooperation and Conflict* 16 (December 1981);

Michael W. Doyle, Stalemate in the North-South debate: Strategies and the new international economic order, *World Politics* 35 (April 1983).

no-show jobs Government positions for which the incumbent collects a salary but is not required to report to work. While no-show jobs are illegal, they are not uncommon.

notary public A semi-public official who can administer oaths, certify the validity of documents, and perform a variety of formal witnessing duties. A *notarius* was a person who took notes during legal actions in ancient Rome. Since then, notarization, a notary's certification of documents, has been a required part of legal proceedings in all Western European-oriented countries. Almost 4 million citizens are notaries in the United States. State requirements to be a notary vary greatly. Some states require examinations; others demand only the endorsement of a small number of local citizens. Many judges and state legislators are EX OFFICIO notaries.

NOW *See* NATIONAL ORGANIZATION FOR WOMEN.

NPA *See* NATIONAL PLANNING ASSOCIATION.

NRC *See* NUCLEAR REGULATORY COMMISSION.

NSC *See* NATIONAL SECURITY COUNCIL.

NSF *See* NATIONAL SCIENCE FOUNDATION.

NTIS *See* NATIONAL TECHNICAL INFORMATION SERVICE.

NTSB *See* NATIONAL TRANSPORTATION SAFETY BOARD.

nuclear freeze A policy of mutually stopping the testing, production, and deployment of nuclear weapons by all sides. The U.S. House of Representatives approved a resolution calling for an "immediate, mutual, and verifiable freeze" in 1983; but all nuclear freeze motions have been defeated in the Senate.

REFERENCES
Joshua Muravchik, The perils of a nuclear freeze, *World Affairs* 145 (Fall 1982);

Howard Stoertz, Jr., Monitoring a nuclear freeze, *International Security* 8 (Spring 1984);

James M. McCormick, Congressional voting on the nuclear freeze resolutions, *American Politics Quarterly* 13 (January 1985).

nuclear-free zone A country or region whose armed forces do not have nuclear weapons. A declaration of being a nuclear-free zone is sometimes seen as a way of inhibiting other nations from using nuclear weapons on the nuclear-free zone in the event of war. Some American cities have local laws declaring their jurisdictions to be nuclear-free zones, but this is more an expression of revulsion towards nuclear weapons than foreign policy, which only the federal government makes.

REFERENCE
Robert K. German, Nuclear-free zones: Norwegian interest, Soviet encouragement, *Orbis* 26 (Summer 1982).

nuclear nonproliferation The policy of stopping the spread of nuclear weapons to non-nuclear nations. The United States, since 1945, has followed a policy of nonproliferation, seeking to reduce the incentives for nonnuclear nations to adopt nuclear weapons and seeking to control the flow of weapons-grade nuclear materials.

REFERENCES
Lewis A. Dunn, *Controlling the Bomb: Nuclear Proliferation in the 1980s* (New Haven, CT: Yale University Press, 1982);

Richard T. Kennedy, Common sense and nonproliferation, *Society* 20 (September/October 1983).

Nuclear Non-Proliferation Treaty The 1968 treaty on the nonproliferation of nuclear weapons, signed by 115 nations. It calls for nuclear nations not to transfer nuclear weapons and for nonnuclear nations not to adopt them. The uses of nuclear energy for peaceful purposes are not covered by the treaty.

REFERENCES

D. M. Edwards, International legal aspects of safeguards and the non-proliferation of nuclear weapons, *International and Comparative Law Quarterly* 33 (January 1984);

Joan Johnson-Freese, Interpretations of the Nonproliferation Treaty: The U.S. and West Germany, *Journal of International Affairs* 37 (Winter 1984).

Nuclear Regulatory Commission (NRC) The federal agency within the U.S. Department of Energy that licenses and regulates the uses of nuclear energy to protect the public health and safety and the environment. It does this by licensing individuals and companies to build and operate nuclear reactors and to own and use nuclear materials. The NRC makes rules and sets standards for these licenses and also inspects the activities of the licensed individuals and companies to ensure that they do not violate the safety rules of the commission. The NRC was created in 1975 under provisions of the Energy Reorganization Act of 1974 and supplanted the Atomic Energy Commission (AEC), which had performed similar functions since 1946. The AEC was created to separate civilian and military uses of nuclear energy. But this battle has effectively been lost now that the NRC has responsibilities for both military and civilian uses of nuclear power.

REFERENCES

Jeffrey S. Klein, The nuclear regulatory bureaucracy, *Society* 18 (July/August 1981);

George T. Mazuzan and J. Samuel Walker, *Controlling the Atom: The Beginnings of Nuclear Regulation, 1946–1962* (Berkeley and Los Angeles: University of California Press, 1985).

Nuclear Regulatory Commission
1717 H Street, N.W.
Washington, D.C. 20555
(202) 492–7000

nuclear winter A theoretical climatic change caused by the effects of smoke from a full nuclear exchange among the superpowers. Because the smoke would blot out most of the earth's sunlight for weeks or months after a nuclear war, most plant and animal life that survived the initial blast would be subsequently destroyed.

REFERENCES

Thomas F. Malone, International scientists on nuclear winter, *Bulletin of the Atomic Scientists* 41 (December 1985);

Paul R. Ehrlich, Carl Sagan, Donald Kennedy, and Walter Orr Roberts, *The Cold and the Dark: The World after Nuclear War* (New York: Norton, 1985).

nullification *See* JOHN C. CALHOUN.

nuncio A diplomat from the Vatican who represents the Pope.

O

OAS *See* ORGANIZATION OF AMERICAN STATES.

OASDI *See* OLD AGE, SURVIVORS, AND DISABILITY INSURANCE.

obiter dictum A Latin term meaning an incidental remark; a portion of a written court opinion not germane to the case at hand; in effect, a digression. Consequently, an obiter dictum is not considered binding as a precedent; but it does provide a clue to a court's rationale and judicial philosophy.

An OSHA inspector conducts a workplace investigation.

obscenity *See* ROTH V UNITED STATES.

Occupational Safety and Health Act of 1970 The federal government's basic legislation, also called the Williams-Steiger Act, for providing for the health and safety of employees on the job. The act created the Occupational Safety and Health Review Commission, the Occupational Safety and Health Administration, and the National Institute for Occupational Safety and Health.

REFERENCES

George C. Guenther, The significance of the Occupational Safety and Health Act to the worker in the United States, *International Labor Review* 105 (January 1972);

Judson MacLaury, The job safety law of 1970: Its passage was perilous, *Monthly Labor Review* 104 (March 1981).

Occupational Safety and Health Administration (OSHA) A federal agency established by the Occupational Safety and Health Act of 1970. The OSHA develops and promulgates occupational safety and health standards, develops and issues regulations, conducts investigations and inspections to determine the status of compliance with safety and health standards and regulations, and issues citations and proposes penalties for noncompliance. The assistant secretary of Labor for occupational safety and health has responsibility for occu-

pational safety and health activities. OSHA has ten regional offices. *See also* MARSHALL V BARLOW'S, INC.

REFERENCES

Frank J. Thompson, The substitution approach to intergovernmental relations: The case of OSHA, *Publius* 13 (Fall 1983);

Benjamin W. Mintz, *OSHA: History, Law and Policy* (Washington, D.C.: Bureau of National Affairs, 1985);

Ann P. Bartel and Lacy Glenn Thomas, Direct and indirect effects of regulation: A new look at OSHA's impact, *Journal of Law & Economics* 28 (April 1985).

Occupational Safety and Health Administration
U.S. Department of Labor
Washington, D.C. 20210
(202) 523-8017

Occupational Safety and Health Review Commission (OSHRC) An independent adjudicatory agency established by the Occupational Safety and Health Act of 1970 to adjudicate enforcement actions initiated under the act when they are contested by employers, employees, or representatives of employees. Within OSHRC are two levels of adjudication. All cases requiring a hearing are assigned to an OSHRC administrative law judge, who decides the case. Each such decision is subject to discretionary review by the three OSHRC members upon the motion of any one of the three. However, approximately 90 percent of the decisions of the judges become final without any change whatsoever.

Occupational Safety and Health Review
    Commission
1825 K Street, N.W.
Washington, D.C. 20006
(202) 634-7943

OECD *See* ORGANIZATION FOR ECONOMIC COOPERATION AND DEVELOPMENT.

OFCCP *See* OFFICE OF FEDERAL CONTRACT COMPLIANCE PROGRAMS.

off-budget federal agencies Agencies, federally owned in whole or in part, whose transactions have been excluded from the budget totals under provisions of law (e.g., the Federal Financing Bank). The fiscal activities of these agencies are not included in either budget authority or outlay totals but are presented in an appendix to the federal budget.
REFERENCE
James T. Bennett and Thomas J. DiLorenzo, *Underground Government: The Off-Budget Public Sector* (Washington, D.C.: Cato, 1983).

office-block ballot *See* BALLOT, MASSACHUSETTS.

Office of Federal Contract Compliance Programs (OFCCP) The agency within the Department of Labor delegated to ensure (1) that there is no employment discrimination by government contractors because of race, religion, color, sex, or national origin; and (2) that there is affirmative action to employ Vietnam era veterans and handicapped workers.

Office of Federal Contract Compliance
    Programs
Department of Labor
200 Constitution Avenue, N.W.
Washington, D.C. 20210
(202) 523-9475

Office of Management and Budget (OMB) The office that supplanted the Bureau of the Budget in the Executive Office of the President on July 1, 1970. The OMB (1) assists the president in the preparation of the budget and the formulation of fiscal policy; (2) assists in developing coordinating mechanisms to expand interagency cooperation; (3) assists the president by reviewing the organizational structure and management procedures of the executive branch to ensure that they are capable of producing the intended results; (4) supervises and controls the administration of the budget; (5) clears and coordinates departmental advice on proposed legislation and makes recommendations about presidential action on legislative enactments; (6) assists in the development of regulatory reform proposals; and (7) assists in the consideration, clearance, and, where necessary, the preparation of proposed executive orders and proclamations.
REFERENCES
Larry Berman, *The Office of Management and Budget and the Presidency, 1921–1979* (Princeton, NJ: Princeton University Press, 1979);
Bruce E. Johnson, From analyst to negotiator: The OMB's new role, *Journal of Policy Analysis and Management* 3 (Summer 1984);
Frederick C. Mosher, *A Tale of Two Agencies: A Comparative Analysis of the General Accounting Office and the Office of Management and Budget* (Baton Rouge: Louisiana State University Press, 1984);
Shelley Lynne Tomkin, Playing politics in OMB: Civil servants join the game, *Presidential Studies Quarterly* 15 (Winter 1985).

Office of Management and Budget
Executive Office Building
Washington, D.C. 20503
(202) 395-3080

Office of Personnel Management (OPM) The central personnel agency of the federal government, created by the Civil Service Reform Act of 1978. The OPM took over many of the responsibilities of the U.S. Civil Service Commission, including central examining and employment operations, personnel investigations, personnel program evaluation, executive development, and training. The OPM administers the retirement and insurance programs for federal employees and exercises management leadership in labor relations and affirmative action. As the central personnel agency, the OPM develops policies governing civilian employment in executive branch agencies and in certain agencies of the legislative and judicial branches. It also delegates certain personnel powers to agency heads, subject to OPM standards and review.

Office of Personnel Management
1900 E Street, N.W.
Washington, D.C. 20415
(202) 632-7700

Office of Policy Development The president's primary advisory group on domestic issues. It assists the president in the formulation, coordination, and implementation of economic and domestic policy. In 1970, President Richard M. Nixon established the Domestic Council, a nineteen-member body, "as a domestic counterpart to the National Security Council." In 1977, President Jimmy Carter supplanted it with the Domestic Policy Staff. In 1981, President Ronald Reagan changed it to the Office of Policy Development. The primary changes have been in title.

REFERENCES

Raymond J. Waldman, The Domestic Council: Innovation in presidential government, *Public Administration Review* 36 (May/June 1976);

Ronald C. Moe, The Domestic Council in perspective, *Bureaucrat* 5 (October 1976);

John Helmer and Louis Maisel, Analytical problems in the study of presidential advice: The Domestic Council staff in flux, *Presidential Studies Quarterly* 8 (Winter 1978);

Margaret Jane Wyzomirski, A domestic policy office: Presidential agency in search of a role, *Policy Studies Journal* 12 (June 1984).

Office of Policy Development
1600 Pennsylvania Avenue, N.W.
Washington, D.C. 20500
(202) 456–6515

Office of Science and Technology Policy The unit within the Executive Office of the President, created by the National Science and Technology Policy, Organization, and Priorities Act of 1976, that serves as a source of scientific, engineering, and technological anal-

ysis and judgment for the president with respect to major policies, plans, and programs of the federal government.

Office of Science and Technology Policy
Old Executive Office Building
Washington, D.C. 20506
(202) 395-4692

Office of Technology Assessment (OTA) The legislative branch's support office created by the Technology Assessment Act of 1972 to help the U.S. Congress anticipate and plan for the consequences of uses of technology. The OTA provides an independent and objective source of information about the impacts, both beneficial and adverse, of technological applications, and identifies policy alternatives for technology-related issues.

REFERENCE

Barry M. Casper, The rhetoric and reality of congressional technology assessment, *Bulletin of the Atomic Scientists* 34 (February 1977).

Office of Technology Assessment
600 Pennsylvania Avenue, S.E.
Washington, D.C. 20510
(202) 224-8713

officialese *See* GOBBLEDYGOOK/OFFICIALESE/ FEDERALESE/BAFFLEGAB.

off the record A politician's statement that is not to be quoted or attributed. Behind every off the record statement is the implied threat that the speaker has the right to deny ever having said it.

off year 1 Any year in which there is not a presidential election. 2 Any year in which a politician loses an election. 3 Any year in which a government's tax revenues decline.

Old Age, Survivors, and Disability Insurance (OASDI) A federal program created by the Social Security Act that taxes both workers and employers to pay benefits to retired and disabled people, their dependents, widows, widowers, and children of deceased workers. *Compare to* SOCIAL SECURITY.

Older Americans Act of 1965 (OAA) The federal law that aids and encourages state and local programs to meet the needs of the elderly by providing community service jobs for the elderly, supporting volunteer programs by and on behalf of the elderly, forbidding age discrimination in programs supported by federal funds, and so on. The OAA is administered mainly by the Administration on Aging of the U.S. Department of Health and Human Services.

old guard **1** Very conservative Republicans; reactionary Republicans. **2** The most determined STALWARTS of a political party; the diehards of any organization. The phrase refers to Napoleon's Imperial Guard at the Battle of Waterloo. When asked to surrender, legend has it that they responded: "The guard dies but does not surrender." While their exact words have often been disputed by historians, there is no dispute that they futilely died. An old guard is often known by its efforts to slow down, or transform, inevitable changes.

oligarchy **1** Rule by a political elite who govern mainly for the benefit of themselves and their class. **2** Rule by a self-appointed elite, who wield informal but effective power because of wealth or position. **3** Minority rule. *Compare to* IRON LAW OF OLIGARCHY.

REFERENCES

Bruce H. Mayhew and Roger L. Levinger, On the emergence of oligarchy in human interaction, *American Journal of Sociology* 81 (March 1976);

Thomas R. Dye, Oligarchic tendencies in national policy-making: The role of the private policy-planning organizations, *Journal of Politics* 40 (May 1978);

Mark R. Beissinger, The age of the Soviet oligarchs, *Current History* 83 (October 1984).

OMB *See* OFFICE OF MANAGEMENT AND BUDGET.

ombudsman An official whose job is to investigate the complaints of the citizenry concerning public services and to assure that these complaints will reach the attention of those officials at levels above the original providers of service. The word is Swedish for a representative of the king. Ombudsmen and ombuds-

women are now found in many countries at a variety of jurisdictional levels. Many of the functions of ombudsmen in American state, and local, and national governments are performed by members of their respective legislatures as CASEWORK.

REFERENCES

Stanley V. Anderson, ed., *Ombudsmen for American Government?* (Englewood Cliffs, NJ: Prentice-Hall, 1968);

Carolyn Stieber, Talking back: States and ombudsmen, *State Government* 55:2 (1982);

Larry B. Hill, The citizen participation-representation roles of American ombudsmen, *Administration and Society* 13 (February 1982);

Robert D. Miewald and John C. Comer, The complaint function of government and the ombudsman, *State and Local Government Review* 16 (Winter 1984).

For a comparative perspective, see William B. Gwyn, The ombudsman in Britain: A qualified success in government reform, *Public Administration* 60 (Summer 1982).

Omnibus Claims Bill *See* CALENDAR, PRIVATE.

Omnibus Crime Control and Safe Streets Act of 1968 The federal government's major effort to improve local police forces. It provided for grants to improve local law enforcement, for weak gun control measures, for the admissibility of voluntary confessions even if there is a delay in arraignment or failure to inform suspects of their rights, and for the confirmation by the U.S. Senate of all future FBI directors.

one man, one vote *See* REYNOLDS V SIMS.

one-minute speeches Addresses by U.S. House of Representative members at the beginning of a legislative day. The speeches may cover any subject but are limited strictly to one minute. By unanimous consent, members may also be recognized to address the House for longer periods after completion of all legislative business for the day. Senators, by unanimous consent, are permitted to make speeches of a predetermined length during MORNING HOUR.

387

open convention A national nominating convention that starts without any candidate having a lock on the nomination because of the possession of a sufficient number of committed delegates.

open-end program An ENTITLEMENT PROGRAM for which eligibility requirements are determined by law (e.g., Medicaid). Actual fiscal obligations and the resultant outlays are limited only by the number of eligible persons who apply for benefits and the benefits paid to them.

open-market operations The purchase and sale in the open market by the Federal Reserve System of various securities, chiefly marketable federal government securities, for the purpose of implementing Federal Reserve monetary policy. Open-market operations, one of the most flexible instruments of monetary policy, affect the reserves of member banks and thus the supply of money and the availability and cost of credit.

open primary *See* PRIMARY, OPEN.

open seat An open district (*see* DISTRICT, OPEN).

open shop Any nonunion work organization. The term also applies to work organizations with unions but that do not make union membership a condition of employment. Historically, an open shop was one that tended to discriminate against unions.

open system Any organism or organization that interacts with its environment, as opposed to a closed system which does not.
REFERENCE
Michael Keren, Ideological implications of the use of open systems theory in political science, *Behavioral Science* 24 (September 1979).

operating budget *See* BUDGET, OPERATING.

opinion The formal announcement of a decision by a court, often giving the reasons for the decision. While a judge can deliver an opinion about any aspect of a case at almost any time, an opinion usually appears only in connection with final decisions in appeal proceedings.

opinion, advisory A statement by a judge or regulatory agency about a question that has been informally submitted. The U.S. federal courts never issue advisory opinions. *Compare to* DECLARATORY JUDGMENT.
REFERENCES
W. Michael Reisman, Accelerating advisory opinions: Critique and proposal, *American Journal of International Law* 68 (October 1974).

opinion, concurring The opinion of a judge who agrees with a decision, but who explains his or her agreement on grounds different from those used by the other judges.

opinion day The day, usually a Monday, on which the U.S. Supreme Court gives its opinions in open court on cases it has considered.

opinion, dissenting A minority opinion.

opinion, full A lengthy written opinion presenting in detail the reasons and reasoning leading to a decision.

opinion leaders 1 The minority of the population who take an active interest in political affairs, who regularly talk about political issues with their friends, coworkers, and family, and who therefore tend to influence public opinion. In what is called the two-step flow theory, opinion leaders function as mediators between the news media and the public. But as access to news via television becomes more and more pervasive, people will tend to rely less and less on these traditional leaders and more and more on the media itself. 2 Those political figures who are able to significantly influence the attitudes of the general public on political issues. 3 Journalists and the experts journalists tend to consult on specialized matters, who often have the public's attention via the media to state their opinions on the facts at hand.
REFERENCES
For the classic early studies of opinion leadership, see Paul F. Lazarsfeld, Bernard R. Berelson, and Hazel Gaudet, *The People's*

Choice, 2d ed. (New York: Columbia University Press, 1948);

Bernard R. Berelson, Paul F. Lazarsfeld, and Paul N. McPhee, *Voting* (Chicago: University of Chicago Press, 1954).

Also see Mark R. Levy, Opinion leadership and television news uses, *Public Opinion Quarterly* 42 (Fall 1978);

Joan S. Black, Opinion leaders: Is anyone following? *Public Opinion Quarterly* 46 (Summer 1982);

Benjamin I. Page and Robert Y. Shapiro, Presidents as opinion leaders: Some new evidence, *Policy Studies Journal* 12 (June 1984).

opinion, majority The opinion of most of the judges hearing a case. The majority opinion is the opinion of the court. In a U.S. Supreme Court case, the chief justice, if he or she has voted with the majority, designates the justice who will write the majority opinion; if the chief justice has voted with the minority, then the senior associate justice designates who will write the opinion.

REFERENCES

Elliot E. Slotnick, The chief justices and self-assignment of majority opinions: A research note, *Western Political Quarterly* 31 (June 1978);

Elliot E. Slotnick, Who speaks for the Court? Majority opinion assignment from Taft to Burger, *American Journal of Political Science* 23 (February 1979);

Elliot E. Slotnick, Judicial career patterns and majority opinion assignment on the Supreme Court, *Journal of Politics* 41 (May 1979);

Gregory J. Rathjen, Conventional wisdoms don't die easily: Judicial career patterns and the context of majority opinion assignment, *Journal of Politics* 42 (November 1980).

opinion, memorandum A brief written statement of the reasons for a decision, without detailed explanation.

opinion, minority The dissenting opinion of one or more judges who disagree with the decision of a court. On the U.S. Supreme Court, dissenting opinions have sometimes been extremely significant because they have so often established the intellectual framework for subsequent reversals of decisions. Chief Justice Charles Evans Hughes (1862–1948) observed that dissents are "appeals to the brooding spirit of the law, to the intelligence of another day." And Associate Justice Felix Frankfurter (1882–1965) concluded that "in this Court, dissents have gradually become majority opinions."

REFERENCE

Alan Barth, *Prophets with Honor: Great Dissents and Great Dissenters in the Supreme Court* (New York: Knopf, 1974).

opinion, per curiam An opinion issued by a court as a whole, without indication of individual authorship.

opinion poll *See* PUBLIC OPINION SURVEY.

opinion vote The coalition vote of the majority of judges on an appeals court, whose opinion becomes law.

REFERENCE

Saul Brenner, Minimum winning coalitions on the U.S. Supreme Court: A comparison of the original vote on the merits with the opinion vote, *American Politics Quarterly* 7 (July 1979).

OPM *See* OFFICE OF PERSONNEL MANAGEMENT.

order, cease and desist *See* CEASE-AND-DESIST ORDER.

order, executive *See* EXECUTIVE ORDER.

ordinance A regulation enacted by a local government. It has the force of law but must be in compliance with state and national laws. It is issued under the authority derived from a grant of power (such as a city charter) from a sovereign entity (such as a state).

Organization for a Better Austin v Keefe
See PRIOR RESTRAINT.

Organization for Economic Cooperation and Development (OECD) The only international organization comprising all industrial democracies. The OECD countries have one-fifth of the world's population and account for more than 80 percent of the world's trade. Founded in 1960 to replace the Organization for European Economic Cooperation, the organ of the Marshall Plan for European recovery, the OECD extended international economic consultation beyond Europe to North America and the Pacific. The OECD provides for joint analysis of economic trends and for efforts to harmonize international economic practices and improve assistance to the developing countries. The OECD headquarters are in Paris.

Organization of American States (OAS) The world's oldest regional association. Since the first international congress of American countries held in Washington in 1889, the Western Hemisphere republics have maintained a system of cooperation in cultural, social, economic, and political fields. The 1948 treaty creating the OAS intensified this cooperation and reaffirmed the mutual defense commitment undertaken in the Inter-American Treaty of Reciprocal Assistance (Rio Treaty) signed in 1947.

> Organization of American States
> Pan American Union Building
> 17th Street and Constitution Avenue, N.W.
> Washington, D.C. 20006
> (202) 458–3841

original intent What the 1789 framers of the U.S. Constitution really meant; what they really intended, by their words, phrases, and sentences used in the document. The original intent of the framers is often a debatable issue, often espoused by STRICT CONSTRUCTIONISTS, and often a CODE WORD (or phrase) for conservative attempts to reverse Supreme Court decisions on social policy and individual rights. *Compare to* LEGISLATIVE INTENT.

original jurisdiction The authority of a court to initially hear a case.

origination clause That portion of Article I, Section 7, of the U.S. Constitution that requires that "all bills for raising revenue [mean-

ing taxes] shall originate in the House of Representatives."

OSHA *See* OCCUPATIONAL SAFETY AND HEALTH ADMINISTRATION.

OSHRC *See* OCCUPATIONAL SAFETY AND HEALTH REVIEW COMMISSION.

Ostrogorskii, Moisei (1854–1919) The Russian political scientist (whose name is also translated as Ostrogorski and Ostrogorsky) whose studies of the American and British party systems mark him as the first major analyst of comparative political party organization. The works of Robert Michels and Maurice Duverger, among others, follow from Ostrogorskii's pioneering analyses.

REFERENCE
Ostrogorskii's most significant work is *Democracy and the Organization of Political Parties* (Garden City, NY: Anchor, 1902, 1964).

OTA *See* OFFICE OF TECHNOLOGY ASSESSMENT.

other body 1 A reference to the U.S. Senate by a member of the House of Representatives. 2 A reference to the House by a member of the U.S. Senate.

oval office 1 The oval-shaped White House office of the president of the United States. Although the oval office was built in the 1930s as part of an expansion of the west wing of the White House, the term did not come into general usage until the Richard M. Nixon administration. Until then the president's office was just called the president's office. 2 The presidency itself, as in "The order comes from the oval office."

REFERENCES
Hedley Donovan, Overcoming the isolation of the oval office, *Atlantic Community Quarterly* 19 (Summer 1981);

Arnold J. Meltzner, ed., *Politics and the Oval Office: Towards Presidential Governance* (San Francisco: Institute for Contemporary Studies, 1981).

In recent years the oval office has become synonymous with presidential power.

overbreadth doctrine The judicial policy that holds that laws be declared unconstitutional because of their overbreadth (meaning that they reach too far) if they attempt to punish activities protected by the Constitution (such as free speech) even as they seek to engage in otherwise legitimate regulation.

REFERENCE

Martin H. Redish, The Warren Court, the Burger Court, and the First Amendment overbreadth doctrine, *Northwestern University Law Review* 78 (December 1983).

Overseas Citizens Voting Rights Act of 1975 (OCVRA) *See* BALLOT, ABSENTEE.

oversight, congressional The total means by which the U.S. Congress monitors the activities of executive branch agencies to determine if the laws are being faithfully executed. Oversight takes many forms. The most obvious are the annual congressional hearings on agency budget requests, in which agency activities have to be justified to the satisfaction of the Congress. But any member of the Congress or a congressional committee can instigate an investigation. Most of these investigations are small matters properly falling under the rubric of CASEWORK. But if something more significant turns up worthy of a larger inquiry, an appropriate committee or subcommittee always has the right to initiate a further examination. The entire Congress is in effect a permanently sitting grand jury always waiting to hear of improper acts by executive branch agencies so that hearings can be launched and witnesses called. Some members of the Congress are so zealous in their oversight concerns that they will go to the trouble of traveling all over the world (at government expense) to see how federal programs and policies are operating. These visits are derisively called junkets; but they are an important part of the oversight process. Some members of the Congress simply cannot understand why it is necessary to vote for money for American forces in NATO unless they first visit Europe and make a thorough investigation of the situation.

REFERENCES

For oversight by the U.S. Congress, see Morris S. Ogul, *Congress Oversees the Bureaucracy: Studies in Legislative Supervision* (Pittsburgh: University of Pittsburgh Press, 1976);

Dean L. Yarwood, Oversight of presidential funds by the appropriations committees: Learning from the Watergate crisis, *Administration and Society* 13 (November 1981);

Mathew D. McCubbins and Thomas Schwartz, Congressional oversight overlooked: Police patrols versus fire alarms, *American Journal of Political Science* 28 (February 1984);

Robert J. Art, Congress and the defense budget: Enhancing policy oversight, *Political Science Quarterly* 100 (Summer 1985).

For comparable oversight activities by state legislatures, see Keith E. Hamm and Roby D. Robertson, Factors influencing the adoption of new methods of legislative oversight in the U.S. states, *Legislative Studies Quarterly* 6 (February 1980);

Carol S. Weissert, State legislative oversight of federal funds, *State Government* 53 (Spring 1980);

Ralph Craft, Successful legislative oversight: Lessons from state legislatures, *Policy Studies Journal* 10 (Autumn 1981);

William Lyons and Larry W. Thomas, Oversight in state legislatures: Structural-attitudinal interaction, *American Politics Quarterly* 10 (January 1982).

For municipal oversight activities by city councils, see Cortus T. Koehler, Policy development and legislative oversight in council-manager cities: An information and communications analysis, *Public Administration Review* 33 (September/October 1973);

Glenn Abney and Thomas P. Lauth, Councilmanic intervention in municipal administration, *Administration and Society* 13 (February 1982).

oversight, executive *See* EXECUTIVE OVERSIGHT.

oversight, political The use of the legislative oversight function for partisan advantage. Political oversight often happens when the executive and legislative branches of a government are controlled by opposing parties, when its purpose may be to embarrass the administration. Of course, whether an oversight action is simply in the interest of good government or whether it is a play in a game of partisan one-upmanship is in the eye of the beholder.

REFERENCES

For the politics of legislative oversight, see Leon Halpert, Legislative oversight and the partisan composition of government, *Presidential Studies Quarterly* 11 (Fall 1981);

Alan Rosenthal, Legislative oversight and the balance of power in state government, *State Government* 56:3 (1983);

Marcus E. Ethridge, A political-institutional interpretation of legislative oversight mechanisms and behavior, *Polity* 17 (Winter 1984);

Bert A. Rockman, Legislative-executive relations and legislative oversight, *Legislative Studies Quarterly* 9 (August 1984).

overt operations The collection of intelligence information openly, without concealment. *Compare to* COVERT OPERATIONS.

Owen v City of Independence 445 U.S. 622 (1980) The U.S. Supreme Court case expanding an earlier ruling in *Monell v Department of Social Services, New York City* concerning individuals' suits against cities (under 42 U.S. Code, Section 1983) for damages in connection with the violation of constitutional rights. The Court held that a municipality cannot rely upon a "good faith" defense in such cases, since "the knowledge that a municipality will be liable for all of its injurious conduct, whether committed in good faith or not, should create an incentive for officials who may harbor doubts about the lawfulness of their intended actions to err on the side of protecting citizens' constitutional rights."

P

PAC *See* POLITICAL ACTION COMMITTEE.

Paine, Thomas (1737–1809) The Revolutionary War pamphleteer whose *Common Sense* (1776) became a sensational "best seller" and helped crystallize sentiment for a total break with England. As a member of George Washington's army during the darkest days of retreat at Valley Forge, Paine in the first of a series of pamphlets entitled *The American Crisis* (1776) wrote his immortal justification of why the Americans should persevere with the war effort:

> These are the times that try men's souls. The summer soldier and the sunshine patriot will, in this crisis, shrink from the service of his country; but he that stands it *now*, deserves the love and thanks of man and woman. Tyranny, like hell, is not easily conquered; yet we have this consolation with us, that the harder the conflict, the more glorious the triumph. What we obtain too cheap, we esteem too lightly; 'tis dearness only that gives everything its value. Heaven knows how to put a proper price upon its goods; and it would be strange indeed, if so celestial an article as *freedom* should not be highly rated.

REFERENCES
Audrey Williamson, *Thomas Paine: His Life, Work, and Times* (New York: St. Martin's, 1973);
Jack P. Greene, Paine, America and the "modernization" of political consciousness, *Political Science Quarterly* 93 (Spring 1978).

pair Historically, a gentlemen's agreement between two lawmakers on opposite sides to withhold their votes on roll-call votes so that the absence of either will not affect the outcome of the recorded vote. In the House, live pairs and general pairs are used. When a vote is taken, the names of members paired are printed in the *Congressional Record* with a record of the vote. A live pair indicates how a member would have voted; a general pair does not. *Compare to* VOTE TRADING.

palace guard Once upon a time, the armed guards who protected the body of the king; now the staff aides who protect a president's (or any high executive's) time and sometimes make worse the inherent isolation of the office.
REFERENCES
For an analysis of such protection during the Richard M. Nixon presidency, see Dan Rather and Gary Paul Gates, *The Palace Guard* (New York: Harper & Row, 1974).
Also see Joseph A. Pika, White House boundary roles: Marginal men amidst the palace guard, *Presidential Studies Quarterly* 16 (Fall 1986).

Palmer raids *See* RED SCARE.

Panama Canal treaties The 1977 documents signed by the Republic of Panama and the United States that transferred ownership of the Panama Canal from the United States to Panama by the year 2000 and that guaranteed the permanent neutrality and operation of the canal. The treaties were ratified by a plebiscite in Panama in 1977 and by the U.S. Senate in 1978. *Compare to* DECONCINI RESERVATION.
REFERENCES
Steve C. Ropp, Ratification of the Panama Canal treaties: The muted debate, *World Affairs* 141 (Spring 1979);
James M. McCormick and Michael Black, Ideology and Senate voting on the Panama Canal treaties, *Legislative Studies Quarterly* 8 (February 1983);
Craig Allen Smith, Leadership, orientation, and rhetorical vision: Jimmy Carter, the "New Right," and the Panama Canal, *Presidential Studies Quarterly* 16 (Spring 1986).

Panama Refining Co. v Ryan 293 U.S. 388 (1935) The U.S. Supreme Court case invalidating Section 9(c) of the NATIONAL INDUSTRIAL RECOVERY ACT OF 1933, which allowed the president to exclude from interstate commerce oil produced in excess of state regula-

393

tions. The Court held that the section was an unconstitutional delegation of legislative power to the executive in contravention of the separation of powers. This was the first New Deal statute rejected by the Court as an unconstitutional delegation of power. Known as the hot oil case, because it involved oil illegally produced or withdrawn from storage, it is considered a harbinger of the Court's negative attitude toward the New Deal that would be more fully expressed in SCHECHTER POULTRY CORPORATION V THE UNITED STATES.

paper tiger　A Chinese expression for someone or some institution that is not as strong or powerful as appearances or reputation would suggest.

pardon　An executive's granting of a release from the legal consequences of a criminal act. This may occur before or after indictment or conviction. The U.S. president's power to pardon people for federal offenses is absolute except for convictions in impeachment cases. A pardon prior to indictment stops all criminal proceedings. This is what happened when President Gerald Ford pardoned Richard M. Nixon in 1974 for all offenses that he "has committed or may have committed or taken part in while President." Ford's forgiving of Nixon's complicity in the Watergate scandals, for which several dozen of Nixon's associates went to jail, probably cost Ford the presidential election in 1976. State governors have comparable powers to pardon individuals for state crimes; but some governors must share their pardoning authority with the state senate or a parole board.

REFERENCE

Leslie Sebba, The pardoning power—A world survey, *Journal of Criminal Law & Criminology* 68 (March 1977).

pardon, absolute　A pardon that restores a person to his or her legal position prior to the crime in question.

pardon, conditional　A pardon that becomes effective only when the person involved meets stipulated conditions.

REFERENCE

Patrick R. Cowlishaw, The conditional presidential pardon, *Stanford Law Review* 28 (November 1975).

pardon, general　*See* AMNESTY.

Pareto optimality　An equilibrium point reached in a society when resource allocation is most efficient; that is, no further changes in resource allocation can be made that will increase the welfare of one person without decreasing the welfare of other persons.

REFERENCES

Peter Coughlin, Pareto optimality of policy proposals with probabilistic voting, *Public Choice* 39:3 (1982);

John C. Goodman and Philip K. Porter, Majority voting and Pareto optimality, *Public Choice* 46:2 (1985).

Pareto's law　The contention that the pattern of income tends to become distributed in the same proportion in every country no matter what political or taxation conditions exist. Thus the only way to increase the income of the poor is to increase overall production.

REFERENCES

Vincent J. Tarascio, The Pareto law of income distribution, *Social Science Quarterly* 54 (December 1973);

E. C. Pasour, Jr., Pareto optimality as a guide to income redistribution, *Public Choice* 36:1 (1981).

Pareto, Vilfredo (1848–1923)　The Italian economist and sociologist who pioneered the application of mathematical techniques to the study of political and social problems. Because Pareto wrote widely of the inevitability of elites and masses in any society, he became a significant intellectual influence on the development of Italian fascism. Pareto's most important work on politics, *The Mind and Society* (New York: Harcourt Brace Jovanovich, 1916, 1923), dealt with his theory of the circulation of elites. Ruling elites seek to perpetuate themselves by closing off power from new talent from the masses. This frustrated leadership talent eventually organizes the masses to overthrow the old elite and becomes the new elite.

Then the cycle repeats. *Compare to* C. WRIGHT MILLS.

REFERENCES

Sally Cook Lopreato, Toward a formal restatement of Vilfredo Pareto's theory of the circulation of elites, *Social Science Quarterly* 54 (December 1973);

Warren J. Samuels, *Pareto on Policy* (New York: Elsevier Scientific, 1974);

Vincent J. Tarascio, Pareto: A view of the present through the past, *Journal of Political Economy* 84 (February 1976);

Renato Cirillo, *The Economics of Vilfredo Pareto* (Totowa, NJ: Cass, 1979);

Roy Gardner, The strategic inconsistency of Pareto liberalism, *Public Choice* 35:2 (1980).

parish **1** The term for a county in Louisiana. **2** An ecclesiastical district; a local church and its members. **3** An administrative district in some countries.

parity Equality; essential equivalence.

parity, employment The long-term goal of all affirmative action efforts, which will be achieved after all categories of an organization's employees are proportionately representative of the population in the organization's geographic region. Employment parity exists when the proportion of protected groups in the external labor market is equivalent to their proportion in an organization's total work force without regard to job classifications. Occupational parity exists when the proportion of an organization's protected group employees in all job classifications is equivalent to their respective availability in the external labor market.

parity, farm A price, guaranteed by the government, designed to allow a farmer to maintain a purchasing power equal to a previous base period. In theory, the parity price that the government is willing to pay gives a farmer a fair return on investment when contrasted with cost. Since the 1930s, the federal government has been using price supports (accompanied by production controls) to stabilize the prices of agricultural commodities. In this context, a price support is a guarantee to buy farm products at set prices. The U.S. Congress determines general parity support prices, while parity prices for specific commodities are the responsibility of the U.S. Department of Agriculture.

parity, nuclear A vague term for maintaining a rough equivalency in nuclear forces. If a superpower goes below parity, it is yielding "superiority" to the other side, something that both the United States and the Soviet Union have stated they will never tolerate for themselves.

REFERENCES

Warner R. Schilling, U.S. strategic nuclear concepts in the 1970s: The search for sufficiently equivalent countervailing parity, *International Security* 6 (Fall 1981);

Michael Don Ward, Differential paths to parity: A study of the contemporary arms race, *American Political Science Review* 78 (June 1984).

parity, wage The requirement that the salary level of one occupational classification be the same as for another. The most common example of wage parity is the linkage between the salaries of police and firefighters. Over two thirds of all cities in the United States have parity policies for their police and firefighters.

REFERENCE

Paul A. Lafranchise, Sr., and Michael T. Leibig, Collective bargaining for parity in the public sector, *Labor Law Journal* 32 (September 1981).

Parkinson's law C. Northcote Parkinson's (1909–) famous law that "work expands so as to fill the time available for its completion." It first appeared in his *Parkinson's Law and Other Studies in Administration* (Boston: Houghton Mifflin, 1957). With mathematical precision, he "discovered" that any public administrative department will invariably increase its staff an average of 5.75 percent per year. In anticipation of suggestions that he advise what might be done about this problem, he asserted that "it is not the business of the botanist to eradicate the weeds. Enough for him if he can tell us just how fast they grow."

parliamentarian

REFERENCES

Alfred C. Villaume, Parkinson's law and the
United States bureau of prisons, *Contempo-
rary Crises: Crime, Law and Social Policy* 2
(April 1978);

Bruce D. Porter, Parkinson's law revisited:
War and the growth of American government, *Public Interest* 60 (Summer 1980).

parliamentarian The official charged with
advising the presiding officer of a legislature
regarding questions of procedure.

REFERENCE

Prentice Bowsher, The Speaker's man: Lewis
Deschler, House parliamentarian. *Washington Monthly* 2 (April 1970).

parliamentary inquiry A question about a
legislative body's rules or procedures. Parliamentary inquiries almost always take precedence over any other business of the legislature.

parliamentary procedure The rules by
which a deliberative meeting or legislature conducts itself in an orderly fashion according to
established precedents.

REFERENCES

In the United States, the most commonly followed parliamentary procedures are *Robert's Rules of Order*, written (in response to
an unruly church meeting) by Henry Martyn Robert (1837–1923), a U.S. army officer. First published as the *Pocket Manual of
Rules of Order for Deliberative Assemblies* in
1876, it has since been revised many times.
For more comprehensive rules, see Lewis
Deschler, *Deschler's Rules of Order* (Englewood Cliffs, NJ: Prentice-Hall, 1976).

parliamentary system A means of governance whose power is concentrated in a legislature, which selects from among its members
a prime minister and his or her cabinet officers.
The government—that is, the prime minister
and the cabinet—stays in power so long as it
commands a majority of the parliament. When
the government loses its majority (loses a vote
of confidence), elections must be held within a
prescribed time period (or at least every five
years in British practice). The main differences
between a parliamentary system (which most
of the democratic countries of the world use)
and the American system are (1) the ease with
which parliamentary systems of government
can be changed if they fall out of favor with a
majority in the legislature and (2) the lack of
checks or balances in a parliamentary system.
In a parliamentary system, the legislative and
the executive branch are one. The prime minister represents the legislature and, through
them, the voters. The major check on his or
her power is the constant possibility that his or
her party will lose its working majority. *Compare to* CABINET GOVERNMENT.

REFERENCES

Ivor Jennings, *Parliament*, 2d ed. (London:
Cambridge University Press, 1969);

Vernon Bogdanor, ed., *Representatives of the
People? Parliamentarians and Their Constit-
uents in Western Democracies* (Brookfield,
VT: Gower, 1985).

parole 1 The freedom granted to a convicted
offender after he or she has served a period of
confinement and so long as certain conditions
of behavior are met. *Compare to* PROBA-
TION. 2 The practice of releasing prisoners of
war upon their swearing not to take up arms
again during the war. This was a common practice during the early part of the American Civil
War.

REFERENCES

1 Gary Cavender, *Parole: A Critical Analysis*
(Port Washington, NY: Kennikat, 1982);
Harry E. Allen, *Probation and Parole in
America* (New York: Free Press, 1985).

participatory democracy *See* DEMOCRACY,
PARTICIPATORY.

partisanship Extreme partiality toward the
candidates, elected officials, and policies of a
particular political party. While partisanship is
the glue that holds political parties together,
this glue has been gradually losing much of its
strength in recent decades as the ranks of independent voters have grown (*see* PARTY IDEN-
TIFICATION). One who is nonpartisan is not
influenced by, affiliated with, or supportive of,
a political party. *Compare to* ELECTION,
NONPARTISAN.

REFERENCES

Susan E. Howell, The behavioral component of changing partisanship, *American Politics Quarterly* 8 (July 1980);

Martin P. Wattenberg, The decline of political partisanship in the United States: Negativity or neutrality? *American Political Science Review* 75 (December 1981);

David W. Brady and John Ettling, The electoral connection and the decline of partisanship in the twentieth century House of Representatives, *Congress and the Presidency: A Journal of Capital Studies* 11 (Spring 1984);

Warren E. Miller, Party identification and political belief systems: Changes in partisanship in the United States, 1980–1984, *Electoral Studies* 5 (August 1986).

party *See* POLITICAL PARTY.

party-column ballot *See* BALLOT, INDIANA.

party, doctrinal A minor party whose principles appeal to a loyal, if small, cadre of voters and that is stable enough to place presidential candidates on the ballot over several elections. Examples include the Libertarian party and the Socialist party.

party identification Loyalty to a political party; in terms of survey research the response to the question: "generally speaking, do you consider yourself to be a Republican, a Democrat, an Independent, or something else?" While party identification has long been the single most significant factor in determining electoral behavior, the impact of party identification on voting has been declining in the last two decades because of the weakness of the parties, the increase of voters who consider themselves independents, and the growth of issue voting.

REFERENCES

William G. Jacoby, Unfolding the party identification scale: Improving the measurement of an important concept, *Political Methodology* 8:2 (1982);

Charles H. Franklin and John E. Jackson, The dynamics of party identification, *American Political Science Review* 77 (December 1983);

Steven E. Finkel and Howard A. Scarrow, Party identification and party enrollment: The difference and the consequence, *Journal of Politics* 47 (May 1985).

For a comparative perspective, see Bruce E. Cain and John Ferejohn, Party identification in the United States and Great Britain, *Comparative Political Studies* 14 (April 1981).

Party Identification (percentage)

Year	Republicans	Democrats	Independents
1937	34	50	16
1950	33	45	22
1960	30	47	23
1964	25	53	22
1976	23	48	29
1984	35	39	26
1985	35	37	28
1986	33	40	27
1987	31	42	27

Source: *Gallup Report*

party leader **1** Any prominent politician in his or her party; often the highest member of the party holding elected office. **2** The candidate running for office at the head of his or her party's ticket. **3** A member of a legislature chosen by a party to advocate its policies and viewpoints on various issues. Party leaders play a prominent role in floor debates and help determine the legislative program. The leader of the party with the greater number of members is known as the majority leader. The leader of the party in the minority is known as the minority leader. The majority and minority leaders in the U.S. House of Representatives and in the Senate are elected party officials, not constitutional officers or officials of the Congress. *Compare to* MAJORITY LEADER.

REFERENCES

Lynn Muchmore and Thad L. Beyle, The governor as party leader, *State Government* 53 (Summer 1980);

Cornelius P. Cotter, Eisenhower as party leader, *Political Science Quarterly* 98 (Summer 1983).

party line 1 A disparaging term applied to statements of belief that parrot those of a particular group, rather than resulting from individual judgment. 2 A political party's formal position on questions of policy or ideology. When used in connection with American parties, it is considered a point of departure from which party members are free to deviate. When used in connection with a communist party, it is the official pronouncements that a party member must accept without deviation. 3 The figurative lines separating parties. 4 The line (or column) on a ballot listing a party's nominees. 5 The official point of view of an intelligence agency.

party platform *See* PLATFORM.

party, transient A minor party that emerges from a protest or secessionist movement, runs a candidate for president, and may never be heard from again; for example, the States' Rights (Dixiecrat) party of 1948.

party unity 1 The coming home of all of the party's faithful to rally around the party's candidates to prevail in the general election. After a harshly fought primary, there is invariably a call for party unity—to put private grumblings aside and forget the ill feelings generated by the usual rhetoric—for the greater good of defeating the other party. 2 The common support that all party members in a legislature are supposed to give to their party's legislative proposals. That party unity tends to be weak is shown by the *Congressional Quarterly Weekly Report* 41 (January 15, 1983) finding that the "average Democrat voted with the party 72 percent of the time in 1982; . . . the average Republican voted with the party . . . 71 percent of the time." Technically, a party unity vote is one in which a majority of one party opposes a majority in the other party. Party unity scores, such as those often reported by the *Congressional Quarterly Weekly Report* represent the percentage of times that a member of Congress votes with his or her party on such votes.

REFERENCES
Denis G. Sullivan, Party unity: Appearance and reality, *Political Science Quarterly* 92 (Winter 1977–78);

Jeffrey Elliott Cohen and David C. Nice, Party unity and presidential election performance: 1936–1980, *Presidential Studies Quarterly* 12 (Summer 1982).

party vote A vote in a legislative body that is basically along party lines. Members of one party vote one way, while the members of the other party vote the opposite way.

passion for anonymity *See* BROWNLOW COMMITTEE/PRESIDENT'S COMMITTEE ON ADMINISTRATIVE MANAGEMENT.

PATCO *See* AIR TRAFFIC CONTROLLERS' STRIKE.

paternalism 1 In the United States, a derogatory reference to an organization's "fatherly" efforts to better the lot of its employees. Historically, the U.S. labor movement has considered paternalistic efforts to be a false and demeaning charity, inhibiting the growth of union membership. In societies where there are well-established paternalistic traditions, the derogatory connotations of the word may be absent. Japan is undoubtedly the most paternalistic of all the major industrial societies. 2 A sexist attitude by males toward females; treating women as one would treat children. Men who conscientiously provide for the needs of women but who at the same time refuse to give women real responsibility or to respect them as free-thinking individuals may be said to be paternalistic. 3 An overconcern by government for the welfare of its citizens. Those who strongly believe in SELF-RELIANCE denounce a government's paternalistic interference with their lives.

REFERENCES
Clarence N. Stone, Paternalism among social service employees, *Journal of Politics* 39 (August 1977);
Albert Weale, Paternalism and social policy, *Journal of Social Policy* 7 (April 1978);
John Kleinig, *Paternalism* (Totowa, NJ: Rowman and Allanheld, 1983).

Paterson plan *See* NEW JERSEY PLAN.

patronage The power of elected and appointed officials to make partisan appointments to office or to confer contracts, honors, or other benefits on their political supporters. While subject to frequent attack from reformers, patronage has traditionally been the method by which political leaders assure themselves a loyal support system of people who will carry out their policies and organize voters for their continued political control. Patronage has always been one of the major tools by which executives at all levels in all sectors consolidate their power and attempt to control a bureaucracy.

The story is often told of Woodrow Wilson, a man not noted for his sense of humor, that when he was governor of New Jersey he received a phone call advising him that a good friend, a U.S. senator from his state, had suddenly died. He sat stunned at his desk when the phone rang again. It was a local politico who wanted the patronage appointment to replace the so-recently deceased Senator. He boldly told Wilson, "Governor, I would like to take the senator's place." Wilson waited a moment, then said, "Well, you may quote me as saying that's perfectly agreeable to me if it's agreeable to the undertaker." *Compare to* SPOILS SYSTEM. *See also* APPOINTMENT CLAUSE; BRANTI V FINKEL; CIVIL SERVICE REFORM; ELROD V BURNS; MALEK MANUAL; MYERS V UNITED STATES; NO-SHOW JOBS; PLUM BOOK; PREFERMENTS; SINECURE.

REFERENCES

Frank Sorauf, The silent revolution in patronage, *Public Administration Review* 20 (Winter 1960);

Martin and Susan Tolchin, *To the Victor: Political Patronage from the Clubhouse to the White House* (New York: Random House, 1971);

W. Robert Gump, The functions of patronage in American party politics: An empirical reappraisal, *Midwest Journal of Political Science* 15 (February 1971);

Michael Johnston, Patrons and clients, jobs and machines: A case study of the uses of patronage, *American Political Science Review* 73 (June 1979);

Kenneth J. Meier, Ode to patronage: A critical analysis of two recent Supreme Court decisions, *Public Administration Review* 41 (September/October 1981);

Thomas G. Dagger, Political patronage in public contracting, *University of Chicago Law Review* 51 (Spring 1984).

patronage, social The ability of a chief executive to use the prestige aspects of his or her office to wine and dine and otherwise personally impress critical political actors whose support is desired. Because this depends as much upon force of personality as anything else, some executives, such as Ronald Reagan, have been far more successful at getting political mileage out of social patronage than others.

pay as you go 1 The automatic withholding of income tax liabilities by means of a payroll deduction. 2 A FISCAL POLICY calling for a BALANCED BUDGET. 3 A pension plan in which employers pay pension benefits to retired employees out of current income.

paying your dues The experiences that one must have before being ready for advancement. In effect, you have to pay your dues before you can be perceived as a legitimate occupant of a higher position. Many political activists must pay their dues by performing good works for their party before they can be considered "serious" candidates for higher positions.

PBGC *See* PENSION BENEFIT GUARANTY CORPORATION.

Peace Corps A program established by the Peace Corps Act of 1961 to help peoples of other countries in meeting their needs for skilled workers. The Peace Corps was the most successful and lasting of the foreign policy initiatives of the John F. Kennedy administration. It was made an independent agency by Title VI of the International Security and Development Cooperation Act of 1981. The Peace Corps consists of a Washington, D.C., headquarters; three recruitment service centers supporting fifteen area offices; and overseas operations in more than sixty-two countries. To fulfill the Peace Corps mandate, Americans of all ages and walks of life are trained for a nine-to-fourteen-week period in the appropriate local language, the technical skills necessary for their particular job, and the cross-cultural

peanut politics

A Peace Corps volunteer offers advice to a mother concerning her malnourished children in Torodi, Niger.

skills needed to adjust to a society with traditions and attitudes different from their own. Volunteers serve for two years, living among the people with whom they work.

REFERENCES

Robert E. Wood and Steven Cohn, Peace Corps volunteers and host country nationals: Determinants of variations in social interaction, *Journal of Developing Areas* 16 (July 1982);

Gerard T. Rice, *The Bold Experiment: JFK's Peace Corps* (Notre Dame: University of Indiana Press, 1985).

Peace Corps
806 Connecticut Avenue, N.W.
Washington, D.C. 20526
(202) 254–5010

peanut politics   **1** Petty, insignificant, sometimes lowdown political acts. By analogy, a peanut politician is one so unimportant that he or she never deals with "big" issues. **2** The politics of Jimmy Carter. While the use of the peanut in reference to politics goes back well into the last century, President Jimmy Carter, who was formerly in the peanut business, gave it new life.

pecking order   Relative order of power. Ever since social psychologists discovered that chickens have a pecking order—the strongest or most agressive fowl pecks a chicken weaker than it, and that one pecks another, and so on—the term has been used to describe the comparative ranks that humans hold in their social organizations. No aspect of our society is immune to the pecking order's fowl antics. According to President Lyndon B. Johnson's former press secretary, George E. Reedy, in *The Twilight of the Presidency* (Cleveland, OH: World, 1970):

> The inner life of the White House is essentially the life of the barnyard, as set forth so graphically in the study of the pecking order among chickens which every freshman sociology student must read. It is a question of who has the right to peck whom and who must submit to being pecked. There are only two important differences. The first is that the pecking order is determined by the individual strength and forcefulness of each chicken, whereas in the White House it depends upon the relationship to the barnyard keeper. The second is that no one outside the barnyard glorifies the chickens and expects them to order the affairs of mankind. They are destined for the frying pan and that is that.

Pendleton Act of 1883   The Act to Regulate and Improve the Civil Service of the United States that introduced the merit concept into federal employment and created the U.S. Civil Service Commission. While it was termed a commission, it was by no means independent. It was an executive agency that for all practical purposes was subject to the administrative discretion of the president. The act gave legislative legitimacy to many of the procedures developed by the earlier, unsuccessful, Civil Service Commission during the Ulysses S. Grant administration. *See also* CIVIL SERVICE REFORM ACT OF 1978.

REFERENCES

David H. Rosenbloom, ed., *Centenary Issues of the Pendleton Act of 1883: The Problematic Legacy of Civil Service Reform* (New York: Dekker, 1982);

Paul P. Van Riper, The Pendleton Act—A centennial eulogy, *American Review of Public Administration* 17 (Spring 1983).

Pennhurst State School v Halderman 67 L.Ed. 2d 694 (1981)   The U.S. Supreme Court case that held that federal law did not give the mentally retarded in state institutions substantive rights to "appropriate treatment" in the "least restrictive" environment. However, in the words of the Court, "whenever a state accepts retarded individuals into its facilities, it cannot create or maintain those facilities in a manner which deprives those individuals of the basic necessities of life." Thus if a government confers a right on its citizens, it must also arrange to pay for it.

Pension Benefit Guaranty Corporation (PBGC) The federal agency that guarantees basic pension benefits in covered private plans if they terminate with insufficient assets. Title IV of the Employee Retirement Income Security Act of 1974 (ERISA) established the corporation as a self-financing, wholly owned government corporation governed by a board of directors consisting of the secretaries of Labor, Commerce, and the Treasury.

> Pension Benefit Guaranty Corporation
> 2020 K Street, N.W.
> Washington, D.C. 20006
> (202) 778–8800

pension fund socialism Peter F. Drucker's term for the phenomenon that is turning traditional thinking about the "inherent" and historical separation of capital and labor upside down—namely, that the "workers" of the United States are rapidly and literally becoming the owners of the nation's industry through their pension fund investments in diverse common stocks. According to Drucker, pension funds "own at least 50—if not 60—percent of equity capital."

REFERENCES

Peter F. Drucker, *The Unseen Revolution: How Pension Fund Socialism Came to America* (New York: Harper & Row, 1976);

Peter F. Drucker, Pension fund "socialism," *Public Interest* 42 (Winter 1976).

Pentagon The building that has become the symbol of the U.S. Department of Defense. In 1941 it was proposed by the army as an alternative to the erection of a variety of temporary buildings. In less than four days, plans were made for a mammoth three-story facility to house forty thousand people. The pentagonal design derived from the fact that the original construction site was bounded by five existing roads. Immediately after the Pearl Harbor at-

tack, a fourth floor was added to the plan, and later a fifth. While parts of the building were occupied as early as eight months after ground-breaking, it wasn't finished until January 15, 1943.

The five-story, five-sided building has five concentric rings connected by ten spoke-like corridors ranging out from the inner, or A, ring. The combined length of the corridors is seventeen and a half miles, and the total floor space is more than six million square feet. The length of each of the five outer walls is 921 feet and the structure is just over seventy-one feet high. Because of the unique design of the building, it should take no more than ten minutes to walk between any two extremities.

Pentagon Papers An unedited and unexpurgated record of the step-by-step judgments that brought American involvement in Vietnam to its peak point by the end of the Lyndon B. Johnson administration. A historian's dream because of the raw data involved, this essentially shapeless body of material was destined to become a cause célèbre when forty-seven volumes of these secret documents were leaked in 1971 to the *New York Times* and the *Washington Post* by Daniel Ellsberg (1931–   ), a former Defense Department employee. The Richard M. Nixon administration got an injunction to prevent their publication, but in the case of *New York Times v United States,* 403 U.S. 317 (1971), the Supreme Court dissolved the injunction and the papers were published beginning June 13, 1971. Ellsberg was then charged with espionage, but the case was dismissed when it was shown that the administration authorized a burglary to steal Ellsberg's medical records from his psychiatrist's office.

REFERENCES

Jerald Gold, Allan M. Siegel, and Samuel Abt, eds., *The Pentagon Papers: As Published by the* New York Times (New York: Bantam, 1971);

Louis Henkin, The right to know and the duty to withhold: The case of the Pentagon Papers, *University of Pennsylvania Law Review* 120 (December 1971);

George McT. Kahin, The Pentagon Papers: A critical evaluation, *American Political Science Review* 69 (June 1975).

Pentagon Reorganization Act of 1986 *See* JOINT CHIEFS OF STAFF.

peonage Forced labor to pay off an indebtedness—as opposed to slavery, in which those forcing the labor also own the body of the laborer. The Thirteenth Amendment prohibits all such involuntary servitude.

People for the American Way A nonpartisan mass organization created to help "stem the rising tide of religious bigotry and intolerance in American electoral politics." Its policies are basically supportive of the Bill of Rights and in opposition to the new Right (*see* RIGHT, NEW). It was started by TV producer Norman Lear (1922–   ) in 1980 as a counter to organizations such as the MORAL MAJORITY.

People for the American Way
1424 16th Street, N.W., Suite 601
Washington, D.C. 20036
(202) 462-4777

per capita A Latin phrase meaning by heads. In a per capita election, each member has one vote.

per capita tax 1 A tax on each head. 2 The regular payment made on the basis of membership by a local union to its national organization.

peremptory challenge The right of either side in a jury trial to reject a prospective juror without giving any reason. The number of peremptory challenges available varies with state law.

Perez v Brownell *See* AFROYIM V RUSK.

perjury The intentional making of a false statement as part of testimony by a sworn witness in a judicial proceeding on a matter material to the inquiry.
REFERENCES
William J. Rogers, Perjury: The forgotten offense, *Journal of Criminal Law & Criminology* 65 (September 1974);

Terence F. MacCarthy and Kathy Morris Mejia, The perjurious client question: Putting criminal defense lawyers between a rock and a hard place, *Journal of Criminal Law & Criminology* 75 (Winter 1984).

perjury, subornation of The intentional causing of another person to commit the crime of perjury by persuasion, bribery, or threats.

Perkins, Frances (1882–1965) The secretary of Labor, 1933–1945, and the first woman to hold a cabinet post in the U.S. government.
REFERENCE
George Martin, *Madam Secretary: Frances Perkins* (Boston: Houghton Mifflin, 1976).

personal income tax *See* TAX, PERSONAL INCOME.

Personnel Administrator of Massachusetts v Feeney 442 U.S. 256 (1979) The U.S. Supreme Court case that held that a state law operating to the advantage of males by giving veterans lifetime preference for state employment was not in violation of the equal protection clause of the Fourteenth Amendment. The Court found that a VETERANS' PREFERENCE law's disproportionate impact on women did not prove intentional bias.

Peter principle The principle promulgated by Laurence J. Peter in his worldwide best seller, *The Peter Principle: Why Things Always Go Wrong,* with Raymond Hull (New York: Morrow, 1969). The principle holds that "in a hierarchy every employee tends to rise to his level of incompetence." Corollaries of the Peter principle hold that "in time, every post tends to be occupied by an employee who is incompetent to carry out its duties." In answer to the logical question of who then does the work that has to be done, Peter asserts that "work is accomplished by those employees who have not yet reached their level of incompetence." *See also* REALPOLITIK.

petition 1 Any formal request to a public agency or official. The First Amendment guarantees the right of citizens to communicate with the government without hindrance. *Compare to* ROUND ROBIN.   2 A request of a court to take some specific judicial action.   3 A usual requirement for placing a candidate on a ballot, for initiating a referendum on laws, and for seeking a recall of an elected official. The petition process usually requires that a certain percentage of a jurisdiction's voters sign the petition document.

REFERENCES

1   Stephen A. Higginson, A short history of the right to petition government for the redress of grievances, *Yale Law Journal* 96 (November 1986).
3   Max Neiman and M. Gottdiener, The relevance of the qualifying stage of initiative politics: The case of petition signing, *Social Science Quarterly* 63 (September 1982).

petition, congressional   A request or plea sent to one or both chambers of the U.S. Congress from an organization or private citizen's group asking for support of particular legislation or for favorable consideration of a matter not yet receiving congressional attention. Petitions are referred to appropriate committees for appropriate action. *Compare to* MEMORIAL.

Philadelphia plan   An equal opportunity compliance program created under Executive Order 11246 of 1965 that requires bidders on all federal and federally assisted construction projects exceeding $500,000 to submit affirmative action plans setting specific goals for the utilization of minority employees. The plan went into effect on July 18, 1969, in the Philadelphia area and affected six of the higher-paying construction trades.

REFERENCE

Robert P. Schuwerk, The Philadelphia plan: A study in the dynamics of executive power, *University of Chicago Law Review* 39 (Summer 1972).

Phillips curve   A graphic presentation of the theory, put forth in 1958 by the British economist A. W. Phillips, holding that there is a measurable and direct relation between unemployment and inflation. In short, as unemployment declines, wages and prices rise.

REFERENCE

A. G. Hines, The Phillips curve and the distribution of unemployment, *American Economic Review* 62 (March 1972).

picket fence federalism   *See* FEDERALISM, PICKET FENCE.

picketing   1 A political demonstration in which demonstrators walk about a symbolic area (e.g., in front of the White House) carrying signs with political messages. Picketing of this kind is often done to gain media attention for some issue.   2 An act that occurs when one or more persons are present at an employer's business in order (1) to publicize a labor dispute, (2) to influence others (both employees and customers) to withhold their services or business, or (3) to demonstrate a union's desire to represent the employees of the business being picketed. The U.S Supreme Court held, in the case of *Thornhill v Alabama,* 310 U.S. 88 (1940), that the dissemination of information concerning the facts of a labor dispute was within the rights guaranteed by the First Amendment. However, picketing may be lawfully enjoined if it is not peaceful, is for an unlawful purpose, or is in violation of a state or federal law.

pigeonholing   The virtual killing of a bill by a congressional committee by refusing to vote on whether or not to allow it to go to the entire House of Representatives or Senate for consideration. The committee figuratively puts the bill in a pigeonhole, and there it stays. Typically, over 90 percent of all bills referred to congressional committees are pigeonholed.

pinko   *See* RED.

PIRG   *See* PUBLIC INTEREST RESEARCH GROUP.

Pittsburgh Press Co. v the Pittsburgh Commission on Human Relations 413 U.S. 376 (1973)   The U.S. Supreme Court case that held that a municipal order forbidding newspapers to segregate job announcements according to sex when gender is not a required qualification did not violate the constitutional freedom of the press.

plaintiff The person who initiates a civil lawsuit.

planned unit development (PUD) A generic name for local governments' requirement that developers include in their development plan such public facilities as streets, schools, and parks. It is a legal designation and requires a set process if the developer or subsequent owners desire to change the original plan.

planning The formal process of making decisions for the future of individuals and organizations. There are two basic kinds of planning: strategic and operational. Strategic planning, also known as long-range, comprehensive, integrated, overall, and managerial planning, has three dimensions: the identification and examination of future opportunities, threats, and consequences; the process of analyzing an organization's environment and developing compatible objectives along with the appropriate strategies and policies capable of achieving those objectives; and the integration of the various elements of planning into an overall structure of plans so that each unit of the organization knows in advance what must be done, when, and by whom. Operational planning, also known as divisional planning, is concerned with the implementation of the larger goals and strategies that have been determined by strategic planning; with improving current operations; and with the allocation of resources through the operating budget. *See also* NATIONAL RESOURCES PLANNING BOARD.

REFERENCES

For city planning, see Anthony Sutcliffe, *The History of Urban and Regional Planning* (New York: Facts on File, 1981);

Marilyn Spigel Schultz and Vivian Loeb Kasen, *Encyclopedia of Community Planning and Environmental Management* (New York: Facts on File, 1981);

Donald A. Krueckeberg, ed., *Introduction to Planning History in the United States* (New Brunswick, NJ: Center of Urban Policy Research, Rutgers University, 1983);

David C. Slater, *Management of Local Planning* (Washington, D.C.: International City Management, 1984).

For strategic planning, see Douglas C. Eadie, Putting a powerful tool to practice use: The application of strategic planning in the public sector, *Public Administration Review* 43 (September/October 1983);

Robert B. Denhardt, Practitioner's corner: Strategic planning in state and local government, *State and Local Government Review* 17 (Winter 1985).

planning programming budgeting system (PPBS) A budgeting system that requires agency directors to identify program objectives, to develop methods of measuring program output, to calculate total program costs over the long run, to prepare detailed multiyear program and financial plans, and to analyze the costs and benefits of alternative program designs. The system was developed in the U.S. Department of Defense during the late 1950s. In the 1960s, the PPBS took the budgeting world by storm. It began by insisting that it could interrelate and coordinate the three management processes constituting its title. Planning would be related to programs that would be keyed to budgeting. To further emphasize the planning dimension, the system pushed the time horizon out to half a decade, requiring five-year forecasts for program plans and cost estimates. It placed a whole new emphasis on program objectives, outputs, and alternatives and stressed the new watchword of evaluation—the effectiveness criterion. Finally, the PPBS required the use of new analytical techniques from strategic planning, systems analysis, and cost-benefit analysis to make government decision making more systematic and rational.

President Lyndon B. Johnson made the PPBS mandatory for all federal agencies in 1965. Johnson—at the height of his political powers after his landslide election win—envisioned PPBS as the steering mechanism for his Great Society programs. Greatly concerned about the lack of objectives being formulated in the federal government, the nonconsideration of ends, and the preoccupation with means, the woeful lack of analysis and planning, and the lack of viable alternatives, Johnson embraced PPBS as the method and system that would ensure the success of his new programs. The PPBS became the preeminent budgeting system in U.S. government.

By 1970, the PPBS, as a formal system, was expanding in some jurisdictions, contracting in others. Opposition to the system came from various quarters, especially from bedeviled agency administrators and staff who experienced one difficulty after another in complying with the PPBS's submission requirements. The system was formally abandoned in the federal govenment when the Richard M. Nixon administration discontinued it in 1971. State and local governments, in the meantime, were rapidly modifying their PPBS programs and installing hybrid versions. Whatever happened to the PPBS? The answer, in short, is that jurisdictions all over the nation modified it to fit their needs.

REFERENCES

Allen Schick, The road to PPB: The states of budget reform, *Public Administration Review* 26 (December 1966);

David Novick, The origin and history of programming budgeting, *California Management Review* 11 (Fall 1968);

Aaron Wildavsky, Rescuing policy analysis from PPBS, *Public Administration Review* 29 (March/April 1969);

Allen Schick, A death in the bureaucracy: The demise of federal PPB, *Public Administration Review* 33 (March/April 1973);

W. R. Cook, Whatever happened to PPBS? *International Review of Administrative Sciences* 52 (June 1986).

platform   A statement of basic principles put forth by a political party, usually at its national convention, to be adopted by its candidates in the election campaign. The platform, which does not formally bind either the party or its candidates, also contains specific short-term goals or proposals for legislation, known as planks. The planks of a party's political platform are often hotly contested at a national convention, as party ideologists seek to nail down their favorite planks and supporters of the likely nominees strive to keep the platform so general that it will have wide appeal.

REFERENCES

Paul T. David, Party platforms as national plans, *Public Administration Review* 31 (May/June 1971);

Donald Bruce Johnson, ed., *National Party Platforms*, vols. 1 and 2 (Urbana: University of Illinois Press, 1978);

Richard C. Elling, State party platforms and state legislative performance: A comparative analysis, *American Journal of Political Science* 23 (May 1979);

Alan D. Monroe, American party platforms and public opinion, *American Journal of Political Science* 27 (February 1983).

Plato (427–347 BC)   The Greek philosopher who, because of his *The Republic* (370 BC), is often considered to be the first political scientist. *The Republic* is the Western world's first systematic analysis of the political process and the reason for a state. Plato provided an intellectual rationale for the "divine right of kings" even before Christianity sanctioned the notion. To Plato, only an elite of philosopher kings or "guardians" had the political wisdom necessary to govern; a wisdom that could be transmitted to others by selective breeding. Thus a just society would be one where each knew his place—with the guardians on top (*compare to* BIG LIE). Because Plato wrote his philosophy in the form of dialogues in which Socrates directs discussion among varying groups of people, questioning them rather than asserting his own positions, there are a multitude of interpretations of the meanings Plato himself would have intended had he stated them in more systematic form. Programs suggested in *The Republic*, for example, may appear contradicted by programs discussed in *The Laws*.

REFERENCES

John F. Wilson, *The Politics of Moderation: An Interpretation of Plato's Republic* (Lanham, MD: University Press of America, 1984);

George Klosko, *The Development of Plato's Political Theory* (New York: Methuen, 1986).

play in Peoria   To be acceptable in a Peoria-like American city: traditional, middle sized, and more-or-less homogenous, the mainstream of traditional social attitudes. Politicians often ask themselves of proposed national policies, "will it play in Peoria?"

play politics To put personal political or partisan advantage over the public interest. No competent politician would ever admit to playing politics; such reprehensible activities are only engaged in by the political opposition. Besides, one person's play may be another's astute furtherance of the public interest.

plea A defendant's formal answer in court to a charge contained in a complaint or indictment. The three possible pleas are guilty, not guilty, or nolo contendere (no contest). If a defendant stands mute, says nothing, it is considered a plea of not guilty.

plea bargaining The negotiations between a prosecutor and a criminal defendant's legal counsel over the severity and number of charges to which the defendant will plead guilty in exchange for the dropping of more serious charges or a promise to ask the court for a less severe sentence. Plea bargaining has grown to be an essential element in the American criminal justice system. Without it, the courts would be overwhelmed with demands for trials, which are both expensive and time consuming. However, the plea-bargaining process may not be in the best interests of the defendant or of justice, particularly when the threat of an even harsher sentence is used to produce a guilty plea that may not itself be justifiable. Nevertheless, plea bargaining is the normal, the most usual, process of criminal case disposition, because the overwhelming majority of criminal defendants accept a plea bargain in lieu of going to trial. The U.S. Supreme Court in *Bordenkircher v Hayes*, 434, U.S. 357 (1978), agreed that prosecutors should have broad discretion in negotiating pleas.

REFERENCES

John H. Langbein, Torture and plea bargaining, *University of Chicago Law Review* 46 (Fall 1978);

Albert W. Alschuler, Plea bargaining and its history, *Columbia Law Review* 79 (January 1979);

Albert W. Alschuler, Implementing the criminal defendant's right to trial: Alternatives to the plea bargaining system, *University of Chicago Law Review* 50 (Summer 1983);

Stephen J. Schullhofer, Is plea bargaining inevitable? *Harvard Law Review* 97 (March 1984);

Ronald A. Harris and J. Fred Springer, Plea bargaining as a game: An empirical analysis of negotiated sentencing decisions, *Policy Studies Review* 4 (November 1984).

For comparative perspective, see Philip A. Thomas, Plea bargaining in England, *Journal of Criminal Law & Criminology* 69 (Summer 1978).

plebiscite 1 A direct vote on an important issue by the entire electorate of a nation. 2 Any means of expression for popular opinion. In this sense, a REFERENDUM is a plebiscite. 3 Informally, a vote for a party or an individual associated with a particular policy. For example, some historians have contended that the 1920 national election, when the Democrats supported U.S. membership in the League of Nations (and lost), while the Republicans opposed it (and won), was a plebiscite on whether the United States should join the league.

plenary session Any meeting of a legislature, convention, and so on, with all members present.

Plessy v Ferguson *See* SEPARATE BUT EQUAL.

plum 1 Something thought to be especially desirable. 2 A political appointment. 3 Any advantage obtained as a political reward. The term is an abbreviated version of the phrase "shake the plum tree," which in the nineteenth century was slang for the dispensing of political largess.

plum book The book *Policy and Supporting Positions,* first published in 1960, which lists high-level jobs in the U.S. government. The plum book is often viewed as a list of political jobs available to a new administration to which it can make appointments. The available jobs include a large variety of positions exempt from competitive civil service rules as well as vacancies in the judiciary and jobs in the legislative branch filled by presidential appointment. The plum book is prepared by the Committee on Post Office and Civil Service of the House of Representatives after every presidential election and is printed quadrennially by the Government Printing Office. *See also* PATRONAGE.

plural executive 1 The de facto arrangement of most state governments because most GOVERNORS share executive authority with other independently elected officers, such as a secretary of state, treasurer, attorney general, or auditor. 2 Any formal arrangement whereby more than one individual or office shares executive power.

pluralism 1 Cultural diversity in a society stratified along racial lines. This concept was developed by John S. Furnival to describe the unstable colonial domination of an alien minority over an indigenous majority. *Compare to* PLURALISM, CULTURAL. 2 Any political system in which there are multiple centers of legitimate power and authority—for example, medieval Europe, where the various monarchies and the Catholic church had power in different spheres of society. *Compare to* PLURALISM, POLITICAL. 3 In the U.S. context, a theory of government that attempts to reaffirm the democratic character of society by asserting that open, multiple, competing, and responsive groups preserve traditional democratic values in a mass industrial state. In democratic theory, pluralism is distinguishable from GENERAL WILL theory, which posits the capacity to incorporate mass aims in a single conception of the public purpose. Thus traditional democratic theory, with its emphasis on individual responsibility and control, is transformed into a model that emphasizes the role of competitive groups in society. Pluralism assumes that power will shift from group to group as elements in the mass public transfer their allegiance in response to their perceptions of their individual interests. However, power-elite theory argues that, if democracy is defined as popular participation in public affairs, then pluralist theory is inadequate as an explanation of modern U.S. government. Pluralism, according to this view, offers little direct participation, since the elite structure is closed, pyramidal, consensual, and unresponsive. Society is divided into two classes: the few who govern and the many who are governed; that is, pluralism is covert elitism, instead of a practical solution to preserve democracy in a mass society. *See also* INTEREST GROUP LIBERALISM.

REFERENCES
1 John S. Furnival, *Colonial Policy and Practice* (New York: New York University Press, 1956).
3 The classic pluralist work is Robert Dahl, *Who Governs?* (New Haven, CT: Yale University Press, 1961).
For the classic statements of the elitist view, see C. Wright Mills, *The Power Elite* (New York: Oxford University Press, 1956);
William G. Domhoff, *The Higher Circles: The Governing Class in America* (New York: Random House, 1970).
Also see Robert A. Dahl, *Pluralist Democracy in the United States* (Chicago: Rand McNally, 1967);
William E. Connally, ed., *The Bias of Pluralism* (New York: Atherton, 1971);
David B. Truman, *The Governmental Process* (New York: Knopf, 1951, 1971);
David A. Nichols, Pluralism and post-pluralism in the study of public policy, *Polity* 10 (Winter 1977);
Robert A. Dahl, Pluralism Revisited, *Comparative Politics* 10 (January 1978);
Bruce Berg, Public choice, pluralism and scarcity: Implications for bureaucratic behavior, *Administration & Society* 16 (May 1984).

James Madison Provides a Political Justification for Pluralism

The other point of difference is, the greater number of citizens and extent of territory which may be brought within the compass of republican than of democratic government; and it is this circumstance principally which renders factious combinations less to be dreaded in the former than in the latter. The smaller the society, the fewer probably will be the distinct parties and interests composing it; the fewer the distinct parties and interests, the more frequently will a majority be found of the same party; and the smaller the number of individuals composing a majority, and the smaller the compass within which they are placed, the more easily will they concert and execute their plans of oppression. Extend the sphere, and you take in a greater variety of parties and interests; you make it less probable that a majority of the whole will have a common motive to invade the rights of other citizens; or if such a common motive exists, it will be more difficult for all who feel it to discover their own strength, and to act in unison with each other. Besides other impediments, it may be remarked that, where there is a consciousness of unjust or dishonourable purposes, communication is always checked by distrust in proportion to the number whose concurrence is necessary.

Hence, it clearly appears, that the same advantage which a republic has over a democracy, in controlling the effects of faction, is enjoyed by a large over a small republic—is enjoyed by the Union over the States composing it. . . .

The influence of factious leaders may kindle a flame within their particular States, but will be unable to spread a general conflagration through the other States. A religious sect may degenerate into a political faction in a part of the Confederacy; but the variety of sects dispersed over the entire face of it must secure the national councils against any danger from that source. A rage for paper money, for an abolition of debts, for an equal division of property, or for any other improper or wicked project, will be less apt to pervade the whole body of the Union than a particular member of it; in the same proportion as such a malady is more likely to taint a particular county or district, than an entire State.

In the extent and proper structure of the Union, therefore, we behold a republican remedy for the diseases most incident to republican government.

Source: Federalist 10.

---

pluralism, cultural **1** The belief that a nation's overall welfare is best served by preserving ethnic cultures, rather than by encouraging the integration and blending of cultures. This is in contrast to the assimilationist belief that all immigrants should take their turn in a national MELTING POT and come out homogenized. **2** A social and political condition in which diverse ethnic groups live in relative peace and harmony.

REFERENCES
Nathan Glazer, Pluralism and the new immigrants, *Society* 19 (November/December 1981);

Nathan Glazer and Ken Young, eds., *Ethnic Pluralism in the United States and Britain* (Lexington, MA: Lexington Books, 1984).

pluralism, political A governing arrangement with a SEPARATION OF POWERS, such as in the United States. Because power is distributed among several entities, which can check each other if need be, no single institution is all powerful or sovereign.

plurality The number of votes cast for a candidate who obtains the greatest number of votes, though not a majority, in a contest of more than two candidates.

pocket veto *See* VETO, POCKET.

Pointer v Texas *See* CONFRONTATION CLAUSE.

point of no return **1** That point in a voyage when it is just as far to go on to the destination as it is to return to the place of origin. **2** In policy analysis, the point at which it is just as costly in terms of money, prestige, time, and so forth, to go on with a decision as it is to reverse it. Shakespeare's Macbeth (*Macbeth*, Act 3, Scene 4) arrives at a similar policy analysis after he has embarked on his series of murders:

I am in blood
Stepp'd in so far that, should I wade no more,
Returning were as tedious as go o'er.

point of order An objection raised by a participant that a formal meeting is departing from rules governing its conduct of business. The objector cites the rule violated; the chair sustains the objection if correctly made. Order is restored by the chair's suspending proceedings until it conforms to the prescribed order of business.

polarization The political views on an issue taken to extremities; a situation where the degree of opposition appears to make compromise or rational adjudication of differences impossible. There are perennial discussions about how the United States is becoming increasingly polarized between those who would abolish abortion and those for freedom of choice, between those who favor school busing for integration and those who don't, and between those who favor protectionist policies and those for free trade.

REFERENCES

M. Stephen Weatherford, The politics of school busing: Contextual effects and community polarization, *Journal of Politics* 42 (August 1980);

David C. Nice, Polarization in the American party system, *Presidential Studies Quarterly* 14 (Winter 1984);

Martin P. Wattenberg, The Reagan polarization phenomenon and the continuing downward slide in presidential candidate popularity, *American Politics Quarterly* 14 (July 1986).

police Paramilitary state and local government organizations whose most basic responsibilities include maintaining public order and safety (through the use of force if necessary), investigating and arresting persons accused of crimes, and securing the cooperation of the citizenry. The term police, while referring to all law enforcement officers in general, is usually a reference to municipal law enforcement officers. County officers are sheriffs; state officers are usually called the state police, state troopers, or highway patrol. There is no national police force in the United States. The Federal Bureau of Investigation functions as a national police force only in direct response to crimes in violation of federal law. *Compare to* CONSTABLE.

REFERENCES

George L. Morse, ed., *Police Forces in History* (Beverly Hills, CA: Sage Publications, 1975);

William Preston, Cops and bosses: The origins of American police work, *Civil Liberties Review* 5 (May/June 1978).

police power The inherent power of a state to use physical force if needed to regulate affairs within its jurisdiction in the interests of the safety and welfare of its citizens. Police power goes far beyond the criminal justice system; it is the legal basis by which governments regulate such areas as public health, safety, and morals.

police review board A panel of ordinary citizens given the formal authority by their municipality to review specific acts of police officers about which citizens have complained and to make recommendations for disciplinary or other administrative actions. The most common issue before police review boards is whether, in a given instance, police have used excessive or unwarranted force.

REFERENCE

James R. Hudson, Police review boards and police accountability, *Law and Contemporary Problems* 36 (Autumn 1971).

police state **1** A totalitarian society in which citizens are heavily supervised by police forces, both open and secret. A police state is an inherent tyranny, which rules by explicit or implied terror and which denies its citizens many of the most obvious civil liberties. In a police state, sheer force replaces the legal system and due process of law. **2** A reference to the United States when it is felt that the government is violating basic freedoms and abusing the Bill of Rights.

REFERENCES

1 Brian Chapman, *Police State* (New York: Praeger, 1970).

2 David Wise, *The American Police State: The Government Against the People* (New York: Random House, 1976).

policy A statement of goals that can be translated into a plan or program by specifying the objectives to be obtained. Goals are a far more general statement of aims than are objectives. Goal-objective ambiguity may exist for a variety of reasons. The original sponsors of the policy or program may not have had a precise idea of the end results desired. Formal statements of objectives may be intentionally ambiguous, if such vagueness makes it easier to obtain a consensus on action: value judgments underlying the objectives may not be shared by important groups. Consequently, the end result intended may be perceived by some as implying ill effects for them. So explicit statements of objectives, which tend to imply a specific assignment of priorities and commitment of resources, may be purposely avoided. *Compare to* PUBLIC POLICY.

REFERENCE
Eugene J. Meehan, Policy: Constructing a definition, *Policy Sciences* 18 (December 1985).

policy analysis A set of techniques that seeks to answer the question of what the probable effects of a policy will be before they actually occur. A policy analysis undertaken on a program that is already in effect is more properly called a program evaluation (*see* EVALUATION, PROGRAM). Nevertheless, the term is used by many to refer to both before- and after-the-fact analyses of public policies. All policy analysis involves the application of systematic research techniques (drawn largely from the social sciences and based on measurements of program effectiveness, quality, cost, and impact) to the formulation, execution, and evaluation of public policy to create a more rational or optimal administrative system.

REFERENCES
Aaron Wildavsky, *Speaking Truth to Power: The Art and Craft of Policy Analysis* (Boston: Little, Brown, 1979);
William N. Dunn, *Public Policy Analysis: An Introduction* (Englewood Cliffs, NJ: Prentice-Hall, 1981);
Geoffrey Vickers, The assumptions of policy analysis, *Policy Studies Journal* 9, Special Issue no. 2 (1980–81);
Peter W. House, *The Art of Public Policy Analysis* (Beverly Hills, CA: Sage, 1982);
John S. Robey, *Public Policy Analysis: An Annotated Bibliography* (New York: Garland, 1982);
Robert U. Goehlert and Fenton S. Martin, *Policy Analysis and Management: A Bibliography* (Santa Barbara, CA: ABC-Clio, 1984).

The Policy Analysis Process

1. *Initiation*
   - Creative thought about a problem.
   - Definition of objectives.
   - Design of innovative options.
   - Tentative and preliminary exploration of concepts, claims, and possibilities.
2. *Estimation*
   - Thorough investigation of concepts and claims.
   - Scientific examination of impacts of continuing to do nothing and of each considered intervention option.
   - Normative examination of likely consequences.
   - Development of program outlines.
   - Establishment of expected performance criteria and indicators.
3. *Selection*
   - Debate of possible options.
   - Compromises, bargains, and accommodations.
   - Reduction of uncertainty about options.
   - Integration of ideological and other nonrational elements of decision.
   - Decisions among options.
   - Assignment of executive responsibility.
4. *Implementation*
   - Development of rules, regulations, and guidelines to carry out decision.
   - Modification of decision to reflect operational constraints, including incentives and resources.
   - Translation of decision into operational terms.
   - Setting of program goals and standards, including schedule of operations.
5. *Evaluation*
   - Comparison of expected and actual performance levels according to established criteria.
   - Assignment of responsibility for discovered discrepancies in performance.
6. *Termination*
   - Determination of costs, consequences, and benefits for reductions or closures.
   - Amelioration as necessary and required.
   - Specification of new problems created during termination.

Source: Adapted from Gary Brewer and Peter deLeon, *The Foundations of Policy Analysis* (Chicago: Dorsey, 1983), p. 20.

Policy Analysis The quarterly journal of the Graduate School of Public Policy of the University of California, Berkeley. This journal ceased publication in 1981 and was succeeded by the JOURNAL OF POLICY ANALYSIS AND MANAGEMENT.

policy analyst An individual, usually trained in economics, law, political science, or public administration, who is employed to study the effects of proposed or actual public policy.

REFERENCES

Yehezkel Dror, Policy analysts: A new professional role in government service, *Public Administration Review* 27 (September 1967);

Hank C. Jenkins-Smith, Professional roles for policy analysts: A critical assessment, *Journal of Policy Analysis and Management* 2 (Fall 1982).

Policy and Supporting Positions *See* PLUM BOOK.

policymaking *See* PUBLIC POLICYMAKING.

Policy Review A conservative quarterly on policy issues published since 1977. Library of Congress no. H1 .P69.

Policy Review
The Heritage Foundation
214 Massachusetts Avenue, N.W.
Washington, D.C. 20002

policy sciences A problem-solving orientation that cuts across all disciplines to deal with the most important societal decisions. It is more than applied social science; it is a new science, encompassing all that is involved with policy formulation and execution. It began as a post–World War II effort to distinguish between (1) an objective conception of social science (which rejected public purposes and goals) and (2) the pragmatic approach of policy practitioners (who insisted on the priority of experience and application as the sole basis for education and research). HAROLD D. LASSWELL, a pioneer in the concept, said that these sciences "study the process of deciding or choosing and evaluate the relevance of available knowledge for the solution of particular problems."

REFERENCES

Lasswell's work includes *The Policy Sciences*, ed. with David Lerner (Stanford, CA: Stanford University Press, 1951);

The emerging conception of policy sciences, *Policy Sciences* 1 (Spring 1970).

Also see Garry D. Brewer, The policy sciences emerge: To nurture and structure a discipline, *Policy Sciences* 5 (September 1974);

Peter deLeon, Policy sciences: The discipline and the profession, *Policy Sciences* 13 (February 1981);

Arie Halachmi, The relationship between political science and policy sciences, *Political Science Review* 20 (January/March 1981).

Policy Sciences An international journal devoted to the improvement of policymaking, policy analysis, and policymaking methodology; published since 1970. Library of Congress no H1 .P7.

Policy Sciences
Martinus Nijhoff Publishers
P.O. Box 211
3300 AH Dordrecht
The Netherlands

policy studies A phrase used to describe interdisciplinary academic programs that focus on aspects of public policy.

REFERENCES

Stuart Nagel and Marian Neef, What is and what should be in university policy studies? *Public Administration Review* 36 (July/August 1977);

William D. Coplin, ed., *Teaching Policy Studies: What and How* (Lexington, MA: Lexington Books, 1978);

Stuart Nagel, ed., *Encyclopedia of Policy Studies* (New York: Dekker, 1983).

Policy Studies Journal/Policy Studies Review Journals of the Policy Studies Organization. The *Policy Studies Journal,* published since 1972 (Library of Congress no. H1 .P72), concentrates on agenda setting and policy implementation; the *Policy Studies Review,* published since 1981 (Library of Congress no. H97 .P66), is more concerned with policy analysis, program evaluation, and quantitative methods.

Policy Studies Organization
361 Lincoln Hall
University of Illinois
Urbana, IL 61801

polis 1 The Greek word for city. 2 The Greek concept of a political community. *Compare to* POLITY.

political 1 Having to do with the state and its governing institutions. 2 Having to do with the processes by which people gain and use power in social settings, whether the setting is the city, a factory or office, or the family.

REFERENCE

Eugene F. Miller, What does "political" mean? *Review of Politics* 42 (January 1980).

political action Any organized attempt to influence the political process, from lobbying legislators to seeking the election (or defeat) of particular candidates.

political action committee (PAC) An organization whose purpose is to raise and then distribute campaign funds to candidates for political office. Because federal law restricts the amount of money a corporation, union, trade association, or individual can give to a candidate, PACs have evolved as the major means by which significant contributions can influence an election. The PACs were developed by labor unions during and after World War II to acknowledge and encourage the new, potentially significant, political power of the American labor movement and to separate specific labor interests from larger public interests in the effort to blunt public criticism of "big labor's" political influence (*see* COMMITTEE ON POLITICAL EDUCATION).

There are two kinds of PACs: (1) the segregated fund type, which is wholly accountable to its parent organization and may not solicit funds from the public; and (2) the nonconnected political committee, which raises money from the general public (mostly by direct mail) to independently support candidates—that is, to spend money on a candidate's behalf because federal law limits the amounts that candidates and parties can spend on their own.

The PACs were encouraged by the FEDERAL ELECTION CAMPAIGN ACT OF 1971 and its amendments, which sought to curtail the political campaign abuses disclosed by the Watergate scandals. But PACs have proved too popular, in a sense. There were 608 PACs in 1975; by 1982, that number jumped to 3,371. By 1987, the number exceeded 4,000. Their sheer numbers and the vast amounts of money they spend have greatly escalated the costs of running for office. Now, members of the U.S. Congress are more dependent upon large amounts of campaign money from PACs than they once were on the relatively small amounts of money from the traditional "fat cats" and special interests—who are as influential as ever, because they now have their own PACs. *Compare to* TARGETING.

REFERENCES

Elizabeth Drew, *Political Money: The Road to Corruption* (New York: Macmillan, 1983);

Lawton Chiles, PACs: Congress on the auction block, *Journal of Legislation* 11 (Summer 1984);

The Top Ten PACs in the 1984 National Elections

Political Action Committee	Dollars Contributed
National Conservative Political Action Committee	$16,258,217
National Congressional Club	5,172,546
Fund for a Conservative Majority	4,873,853
Republican Majority Fund	4,200,983
Realtors Political Action Committee	3,905,734
American Medical Association	3,713,984
NRA Political Victory Fund	3,172,401
Ruff Political Action Committee	2,981,095
Fund for a Democratic Majority	2,697,970
National Education Association	2,299,751

Source: *The National Journal* (November 11, 1984)

Frank J. Sorauf, Who's in charge? Accountability in political action committees, *Political Science Quarterly* 99 (Winter 1984–85);

J. David Gopoian, What makes PACs tick? An analysis of the allocation patterns of economic interest groups, *American Journal of Political Science* 28 (May 1984);

Larry J. Sabato, *PAC Power: Inside the World of Political Action Committees* (Washington, D.C.: Brookings, 1985);

John R. Wright, PACs, contributions and roll calls: An organizational perspective, *American Political Science Review* 79 (June 1985);

Mark F. Masters and Gerald D. Keim, Determinants of PAC participation among large corporations, *Journal of Politics* 47 (November 1985).

political activism   Organized efforts outside of the regular channels of political influence undertaken specifically to change or direct policy. *Compare to* ACTIVIST.

political amateurs   Political activists who get involved with a candidate or issue out of an ideological or personal commitment. Political amateurs are often known by their reluctance to compromise and by being more interested in fighting the good fight than in winning. While they are not permanently committed, not visibly accountable, and not predictable actors in the political process, they may still be important in a given campaign.

REFERENCE

James Q. Wilson, *The Amateur Democrat: Club Politics in Three Cities* (Chicago: University of Chicago Press, 1962).

political ambiguity   The purposeful use of words, phrases, or acts that are susceptible to multiple interpretation to seek the support of differing constituencies. This is why many members of legislatures avoid roll-call votes, offer hazy statements on policy issues, and make vague campaign promises. From the politician's point of view, ambiguity is a time-tested strategy that works; unless, of course, the voters are sophisticated enough to see through it.

REFERENCES

Kenneth A. Shepsle, The strategy of ambiguity: Uncertainty and electoral competition,

American Political Science Review 66 (June 1972);

Benjamin Page, The theory of political ambiguity, *American Political Science Review* 70 (September 1976).

political animal   Aristotle's term for the nature of man, in *Politics;* that aspect of human behavior that requires community organization. Some people see such a nature as prior to basic principles and to individual judgment. It is thus a term of praise when it is seen as a capacity for compromise and effective action, and of criticism, when it is perceived as destructive to fundamental values.

REFERENCE

Leo Rauch, *The Political Animal: Studies in Political Philosophy from Machiavelli to Marx* (Amherst: University of Massachusetts Press, 1981).

political apathy   Indifference to politics as demonstrated by a failure to vote or to take an interest in public affairs. On the one hand, apathy indicates contentment or at least the lack of discontent with the political process. But it can also be argued that apathy is an indication of despair and the lack of a sense of political efficacy.

REFERENCE

Stephen Earl Bennett, *Apathy in America, 1960–1984: Causes and Consequences of Citizen Political Indifference* (Ardsley-on-Hudson, NY: Transnational, 1986).

political appointee   A person given a job in government mainly because of political connections (or occasionally because of preeminence in a specific field) as opposed to a person who gains his or her job through the merit system. While a political appointee is any patronage appointment, the phrase tends to be reserved for high-level managerial positions, which elected officials use to take over the bureaucracy. *See also* BRANTI V FINKEL; ELROD V BURNS; SPOILS SYSTEM.

REFERENCES

William M. Timmins, Relations between political appointees and careerists, *Review of Public Personnel Administration* 4 (Spring 1984);

political assessment

James P. Pfiffner, Political appointees and
career executives: The democracy-
bureaucracy nexus in the third century,
Public Administration Review 47 (January-
February 1987).

political assessment *See* ASSESSMENT.

political business cycle *See* BUSINESS CY-
CLE, POLITICAL.

political campaign **1** A formal effort established by law to obtain elective office; the
contest for popular support between rival candidates that occurs prior to an election. Aspi-
rants to public office once took their campaigns
to the people; now they take them to the television station. Much of any major political
campaign is fought via competing thirty-
second spots for consumers who have learned
to take their politics in the same way they learn
to "vote" for their favorite deodorant, toilet
tissue, and denture glue. **2** Any effort to obtain a political objective by convincing relevant
individuals or groups of its importance, as in
lobbying.

REFERENCES
1   Gerald M. Pomper, Campaigning: The art
      & science of politics, *Polity* 2 (Summer
      1970);
     Robert S. Strauss, What's right with U.S.
      campaigns, *Foreign Policy* 55 (Summer
      1984).

political capital Influence of the kind that
will further a politico's ambitions. Just as the
private sector uses capital in the form of money
or property to create more wealth, the political
world has its own "coins" with which to buy
political wealth. A politician makes political
capital by doing favors for others, by exposing
a scandal that embarrasses the opposition, and
so on. Political capital, like any currency, can
be saved; and when the time is right, the debts
can be called in.

political clearance The process by which
qualified applicants for both patronage and
merit system appointments are hired only after
there is an appropriate indication of partisan

political sponsorship. While it is illegal to require political clearance for merit system appointments, it remains a common practice.

political club A local civic organization that
focuses on maintaining the fortunes of particular political party but that also engages in social, educational, and charitable works that
will indirectly advance the interests of the
party.
REFERENCES
James Q. Wilson, *The Amateur Democrat:
    Club Politics in Three Cities* (Chicago: Uni-
    versity of Chicago Press, 1962);
Alan Ware, Why amateur party politics has
    withered away: The club movement, party
    reform, and the decline of American party
    organizations, *European Journal of Political
    Research* 9 (September 1981).

political commissar **1** In the Soviet Union,
a civilian assigned to a military unit to insure
that its commanders follow the policies of the
government. **2** By analogy, any representation of a central executive assigned to line
agencies to insure that new employees and their
policies are politically acceptable. The Richard
M. Nixon administration placed political com-
missars in many federal agencies to assure that
new appointees, both patronage and merit system, had POLITICAL CLEARANCE.

political committee As defined by the Federal Election Commission, any committee,
club, association, or group of persons that for
the purposes of influencing federal elections
receives contributions or makes expenditures
in excess of a thousand dollars during a calendar year.

political consultants Advertising specialists
who are for hire to sell political candidates.
The underlying premise is that a political personality can be sold in the same way as songs
or soft drinks. Adlai Stevenson (1900–1965),
who was the Democratic party candidate for
president in 1952 and 1956, at the dawn of the
television age, said in accepting his party's
nomination on August 18, 1956, that "the idea
that you can merchandise candidates for high

office like breakfast cereal . . . is . . . the ultimate indignity to the democratic process." Indignity it may be, but it hasn't stopped most major candidates of both parties from suffering such in the hope of being elected—for their image if not for their substance. Mark Hanna's (1837–1904) management of William Mc-Kinley's presidential campaign is generally pointed to as the beginning of the modern form of national political advertising. The introduction of the idea of "Madison Avenue" in the Stevenson-Eisenhower campaign of the 1950s is generally thought to be the beginning of the professionalization of the process. *Compare to* IMAGE MAKERS.

REFERENCES

Joe McGinniss, *The Selling of the President, 1968* (New York: Simon & Schuster, 1969);

Larry J. Sabato, *The Rise of Political Consultants: New Ways of Winning Elections* (New York: Basic Books, 1981);

Kathleen Hall Jamieson, *Packaging the President: A History and Criticism of Presidential Campaign Advertising* (New York: Oxford University Press, 1984).

political corruption *See* CORRUPTION, POLITICAL.

political culture A community's attitudes toward the quality, style, and vigor of its political processes and government operations. The only way to explain the extreme variations in public bureaucracies is by the cultural context of the host jurisdictions. The quality of bureaucratic operations varies for a variety of reasons—not the least of which is the substantial disagreement on just what constitutes a quality operation. But the quality or style of operations is determined only in the lesser part by critics and public officials; the crucial determinant is the political will of the community. It determines the values to be applied to any given public problem; helps establish the obligations of the public role; and establishes the parameters of activities an official may participate in. Even when corruption is rife, it is the political culture that sets the limits and direction of such corruption. *Compare to* POLITICAL SOCIALIZATION.

REFERENCES

Robert R. Alford, *Bureaucracy and Participation: Political Cultures in Four Wisconsin Cities* (Chicago: Rand McNally, 1969);

Jay M. Shafritz, Political culture: The determinant of merit system viability, *Public Personnel Management* 3 (January/February 1974);

John G. Peters and Susan Welch, Politics, corruption and political culture: A view from the state legislature, *American Politics Quarterly* 6 (July 1978);

John R. Johannes, Political culture and congressional constituency service, *Polity* 15 (Summer 1983);

Michael Johnson, Corruption and political culture in America: An empirical perspective, *Publius* 13 (Winter 1983).

For a comparative perspective, see David Nachmias and David H. Rosenbloom, *Bureaucratic Culture: Citizens and Administration in Israel* (New York: St. Martin's, 1978);

Gabriel A. Almond and Sidney Verba, eds., *The Civic Culture Revisited* (Boston: Little, Brown, 1980).

political culture, Elazar's The division of American political culture into three major subcultures: the individualistic, the moralistic, and the traditional. A viable classification of the various American political cultures was not achieved until the mid-1960s with the work of Daniel J. Elazar of Temple University. Elazar classified the political subcultures of the United States (and of the individual states) by examining three sets of factors for each locality studied; (1) the sources of political culture, such as race, ethnicity, and religion; (2) the manifestations of political culture, such as political attitudes, behavior, and symbols; and (3) the effects of political culture, such as political actions and public policies. In this manner, he was able to identify the political subcultures for each of several hundred American communities.

The individualistic political culture "holds politics to be just another means by which individuals may improve themselves socially and economically." In the moralistic political culture, politics is conceived "as a public activity

political economy

centered on some notion of the public good and properly devoted to the advancement of the public interest." The traditionalistic political culture is reflective of "an older precommercial attitude that accepts a substantially hierarchical society as part of the ordered nature of things, authorizing and expecting those at the top of the social structure to take a special and dominant role in government."

REFERENCES

Ira Sharkansky, The utility of Elazar's political culture: A research note, *Polity* 2 (Fall 1969);

Daniel J. Elazar, *American Federalism: A View from the States*, 2d ed. (New York: Crowell, 1972);

Charles A. Johnson, Political culture in American states: Elazar's formulation examined, *American Journal of Political Science* 20 (August 1976).

political economy The conjunction of politics and economics; the field of study of relations between the economy and the state before either political science or economics became distinct disciplines. Political economy is a public policy concern because of the primacy of economic prosperity to U.S. governments. Not only does the government account for one third of the gross national product, it also regulates the basic economic conditions of society: for example, it can specify production of a product, regulate the wages of the production workers, prescribe working conditions, and establish standards for and inspect the quality of the finished product. *See also* ECONOMIC POLICY; FISCAL POLICY.

REFERENCES

Norman Frohlick and Joe A. Oppenheimer, *Modern Political Economy* (Englewood Cliffs, NJ: Prentice-Hall, 1978);

Barry M. Mitnick, *The Political Economy of Regulation* (New York: Columbia University Press, 1980);

Norton E. Long, The city as a local political economy, *Administration and Society* 12 (May 1980);

P. M. Jackson, *The Political Economy of Bureaucracy* (Totowa, N.J.: Rowman and Allanheld, 1983).

political efficacy A citizen's belief (1) that he or she can understand and participate in political affairs and (2) that the political system will be responsive. Angus Campbell, Philip E. Converse, Warren E. Miller, and Donald E. Stokes in their classic analysis of voting behavior, *The American Voter* (New York: Wiley, 1960), found that there existed a very high positive correlation between an individual's "sense of political efficacy" and his inclination to vote. Those with a high sense of political efficacy almost always voted; those with a low sense of political efficacy tended to vote only in about half the instances when there was an opportunity to vote.

REFERENCES

Harrell Rodgers, Toward explanation of the political efficacy and political cynicism of black adolescents: An exploratory study, *American Journal of Political Science* 18 (May 1974);

Steven E. Finkel, Reciprocal effects of participation and political efficacy: A panel analysis, *American Journal of Political Science* 29 (November 1985).

political executive 1 An individual, such as a president, governor, or mayor, whose institutional position makes him or her formally responsible for the governance of a political community. He or she gains this responsibility through election by the people and can have it taken away by not being reelected, by being impeached, or by being recalled. 2 A high-level patronage appointee. 3 The institutions of a government responsible for governing; the totality of the departments, agencies, and bureaus of a government.

REFERENCE

2 Hugh Heclo, Political executives and the Washington bureaucracy, *Political Science Quarterly* 92 (Fall 1977).

political machine 1 Historically, an informal organization that controlled the formal processes of a government through corruption, patronage, intimidation, and service to its constituents. A political machine usually centered on a single politician—a boss—who commanded loyalty through largess, fear, or affection. The phrase is usually pejorative, because the machine works to achieve political control through those who run the machine, rather than through the popular will. The classic story of a political machine concerns Tammany Hall in New York City. John P. O'Brien (1873–1951), the newly installed mayor in 1932, was asked who his new police commissioner would be. He responded: "I haven't had any word on that yet." Tammany Hall soon gave him the "word." 2 A grudging compliment to a modern political campaign or organization that is effectively managed—with or without some of the elements of the traditional political machine.

REFERENCES

1   Harold F. Gosnell, *Machine Politics: Chicago Model*, 2d ed. (Chicago: University of Chicago Press, 1968);

Raymond E. Wolfinger, Why political machines have not withered away and other revisionist thoughts, *Journal of Politics* 34 (March 1972);

Kenneth D. Wald, The electoral base of political machines: A deviant case analysis, *Urban Affairs Quarterly* 16 (September 1980);

Kenneth R. Mladenka, The Urban Bureaucracy and the Chicago political machine: Who gets what and the limits to political control, *American Political Science Review* 74 (December 1980);

Bertram M. Gross and Jeffrey F. Kraus, The political machine is alive and well, *Social Policy* 12 (Winter 1982);

Harvey Boulay and Alan DiGaetano, Why did political machines disappear? *Journal of Urban History* 12 (November 1985).

political obligation   1 The mutual responsibilities that citizens and states have to each other.   2 The informal sense of debt that one political actor may have toward another because of past favors. Someone under political obligation is expected to return the favor at an appropriate time.

REFERENCES

John P. Plamenatz, *Consent, Freedom and Political Obligation,* 2d ed. (New York: Oxford University Press, 1968);

Richard E. Flathman, *Political Obligation* (New York: Atheneum, 1972);

John Dunn, *Political Obligation in its Historical Context* (New York: Cambridge University Press, 1980).

political party   An organization that seeks to achieve political power by electing members to public office so that their political philosophies can be reflected in public policies. American political parties are inherently decentralized entities. While they annually engage in statewide and local campaigns of greatly varying intensity, they organize to mount national campaigns only in presidential election years. It has often been said that the party system is the oil that makes the constitutional machinery work. Throughout their history, Americans have taken to political parties with great enthusiasm in spite of the fact that George Washington in his Farewell Address of 1796 warned his fellow citizens "in the most solemn manner against the baneful effects of the spirit of party." Washington and the other founders hoped to create a partyless government. Their failure to do so led to the Twelfth Amendment, which changed the means by which the ELECTORAL COLLEGE elects the president.

EDMUND BURKE two centuries ago provided the first modern definition of a political party: "a body of men united for promulgating by their joint endeavors the national interest, upon some particular principle in which they are all agreed." JOSEPH A. SCHUMPETER disagreed. To him a party was not a group, in the Burkean sense, "who intend to promote public welfare." His party was "a group whose members propose to act in concert in the competitive struggle for political power." Most modern analysts would agree that they are both right; both principle and power are major motivations for people to join parties.

REFERENCES

John F. Hoadley, The emergence of political parties in Congress, 1789–1803, *American Political Science Review* 74 (September 1980);

Joseph A. Schlesinger, On the theory of party organization, *Journal of Politics* 46 (May 1984);

Xandra Kayden and Eddie Mahe, Jr., *The Party Goes On: The Persistence of the Two Party System in the United States* (New York: Basic Books, 1985);

Joseph A. Schlesinger, The new American political party, *American Political Science Review* 79 (December 1985);

David R. Mayhew, *Placing Parties in American Politics: Organization Electoral Settings and Government Activity in the Twentieth Century* (Princeton, NJ: Princeton University Press, 1986);

Leon D. Epstein, *Political Parties in the American Mold* (Madison: University of Wisconsin Press, 1986).

For a comparative perspective, see Maurice Duverger, *Political Parties: Their Organization and Activity in the Modern State,* 3d ed. (New York: Wiley, 1964);

Joachim Raschke, Political parties in Western democracies, *European Journal of Political Research* 11 (March 1983).

political question 1 An issue that a court chooses not to decide because it is the judgment of the court that the issue is inappropriate for a judicial determination; the question is better left to another, more political, branch of government. For example, in *Colegrove v Green*, 328 U.S.549 (1946), the U.S. Supreme Court denied federal jurisdiction over cases of legislative malapportionment because it felt the issue was a political question. However, the Court later reversed itself in BAKER V CARR. 2 The doctrine of self-imposed restraint on the part of the Supreme Court, through which it defers to the judgment of the legislature and executive branches when a political question is at issue. Such questions include decisions to recognize foreign governments, and determinations of when amendments to the Constitution have been ratified. For example, in *Coleman v Miller,* 307 U.S. 433 (1939), the Supreme Court held that the efficacy of a constitutional amendment's ratification by a state following a previous rejection by that same state is a political question, for determination by the Congress. *Compare to* JUSTICIABILITY. 3 A question that is understood as having no clear-cut, technical answer, and hence, as subject to debate among holders of competing opinions.

REFERENCES

2 Stephen Wexler, The "political question" doctrine: A decision not to decide, *Ethics* 79 (October 1968);

Michael E. Tigar, Judicial power, the "political question doctrine," and foreign relations, *UCLA Law Review* 17 (June 1970).

Martin H. Redish, Judicial review and the "political question," *Northwestern University Law Review* 79 (December/February 1984–85).

political rights 1 All of the implicit (constitutionally guaranteed) and implied (by national law) rights of a citizen in a free society. 2 Whatever rights a dictatorial government allows it citizens to have.

political science The academic discipline that studies political phenomena; originally, the contention by eighteenth-century theorists that the political behavior of individuals as well as states could be subjected to the same criteria of analysis as natural phenomena. While this idea can be traced back certainly to Plato and Aristotle, its development in Enlightenment thought rested on the transfer of conceptions of a mechanical celestial universe to the universe of human action. The constitution—the makeup—of governments could thus be defined in the form of mechanisms that limit and control the judgment and authority of individual leaders. The modern enlargement of that conception of science has led to recurring debates over the study of the mechanisms of government, the behavior of the governed, and the actions of those who govern—debates that assert either the applicability of scientific study or the relevance of the political arts of leadership that cannot be subjected to scientific analysis. While the growth of psychology, sociology, and the other social science disciplines have expanded our understanding of what a science of politics might be, the essential role of individual choice pointed out by Aristotle has kept the debate—science or art—alive.

The playwright George Bernard Shaw (1856–1950) gave early voice to what has become the standard complaint: that "political science, the science by which civilization must live or die, is busy explaining the past whilst we have to grapple with the present. It leaves the ground before our feet in black darkness whilst it lifts up every corner of the landscape behind us."

REFERENCES

Albert Somit and Joseph Tanenhaus, *American Political Science: A Profile of a Discipline* (New York: Atherton, 1964);

Heinz Eulau, Understanding political life in America: The contribution of political science, *Social Science Quarterly* 57 (June 1976);

John Dreijmanis, Political science in the United States: The discipline and the profession, *Government and Opposition* 18 (Spring 1983);

Ada W. Finifter, ed., *Political Science: The State of the Discipline* (Washington, D.C.: American Political Science Association, 1983).

Political Science Quarterly Founded in 1886, the oldest continuously published journal of political science in the United States. Library of Congress no. H1 .P8.

Political Science Quarterly
Academy of Political Science
2852 Broadway
New York, NY 10025

political socialization The transition from generation to generation of the ethos of a political system by the conscious and unconscious instilling of the values of a political culture. This is one of the most critical political processes; it starts in the home and continues in public school civics classes. ARISTOTLE thought that the real constitution of a society was to be found in the political attitudes of the people. Without these supportive predispositions in the psyche of the society, their paper manifestations—such as a written constitution—would be worthless and ineffective no matter how well written. He was right. W. S. Gilbert (1836–1911) in the Gilbert and Sullivan comic opera *Iolanthe* (1892) anticipated twentieth-century social science findings on political socialization when he wrote:

> I often think it's comical,
>   How nature always does contrive
> That every boy and every gal
>   That's born into the world alive,
> Is either a little Liberal,
>   Or else a little Conservative.

Factors Affecting Political Behavior

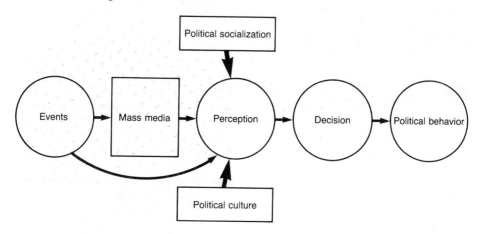

Source: Grover Starling, *Understanding American Politics* (Chicago: Dorsey, 1982), p. 153.

REFERENCES

Fred I. Greenstein, *Children and Politics* (New Haven, CT: Yale University Press, 1965);

Fred I. Greenstein, A note on the ambiguity of "political socialization": Definitions, criticisms, and strategies of inquiry, *Journal of Politics* 32 (November 1970);

M. Kent Jennings and Richard Niemi, *The Political Character of Adolescence: The Influence of Families and Schools* (Princeton, NJ: Princeton University Press, 1974);

Richard Dawson, Kenneth Prewitt, and Karen Dawson, *Political Socialization* (Boston: Little, Brown, 1977);

Charles H. Franklin, Issue preferences, socialization, and the evolution of party identification, *American Journal of Political Science* 28 (August 1984);

Timothy E. Cook, The bear market in political socialization and the costs of misunderstood psychological theories, *American Political Science Review* 79 (December 1985).

political stability The ability of a political system to maintain an equilibrium; to retain the support of its people for government policies within a stable range; to avoid radical and sudden changes in the premises of its political and economic systems. The United States has long been considered a country of great political stability. West Germany is considered very stable today; but during the three decades from the beginning of World War I to the end of World War II, it was a glaring example of instability.

REFERENCES

Claude Ake, A definition of political stability, *Comparative Politics* 7 (January 1975);

Bert Useem and Michael Useem, Government legitimacy and political stability, *Social Forces* 57 (March 1979).

political subculture 1 One of Daniel Elazar's political subcultures. *See* POLITICAL CULTURE, ELAZAR'S. 2 The specific political subculture of an ethnic group, which differs in significant ways from the dominant political culture of the community.

REFERENCE

Charles R. Foster, Political culture and regional ethnic minorities, *Journal of Politics* 44 (May 1982).

political system The institutions and processes that allow the citizens of a polity to make, implement, and revise public policies. According to DAVID EASTON, the political system essentially consists of those interactions through which values (such as equality and security) are authoritatively allocated for a society. Easton's model of the political system can be thought of as an input-output box, which takes in political demands and supports and puts out public policies, such as laws, court decisions, and regulations. These outputs then return, to influence the system as feedback.

political warfare A constant policy of taking political action against the interests of another power in the expectation that the opposing nation will be worn down by the constant demands of internal and international political problems. Political warfare is a major weapon in the cold war arsenal.

REFERENCE

Joseph Miranda, Political warfare: Can the West survive? *Journal of Social, Political and Economic Studies* 10 (Spring 1985).

politician 1 One who makes a career of seeking or serving in elective or appointive public office; one devoted to the service of a polis, a political community; one engaged in the professional practice of politics. 2 A political party boss; someone engaged in politics for personal gain. Any public service done is purely incidental. 3 According to Ambrose Bierce in *The Devil's Dictionary* (1911), "an eel in the fundamental mud upon which the superstructure of organized society is reared. When he wriggles he mistakes the agitation of his tail for the trembling of the edifice. As compared with the statesman, he suffers the disadvantage of being alive." This long-standing antipathy to politicians was recognized by President John F. Kennedy when he said: "Mothers all want their sons to grow up to be president, but they don't want them to become politicians in the process." *Compare to* STATESMAN.

REFERENCES

Stimson Bullitt, *To Be A Politician*, rev. ed. (New Haven, CT: Yale University Press, 1977);

Ann R. Tickamyer, Politics as a vocation, *Pacific Sociological Review* 24 (January 1981).

politician, honest "One who, when he is bought, will stay bought." This definition is usually credited to Simon Cameron (1799–1889), who as Abraham Lincoln's first secretary of War administered his office so corruptly that Lincoln appointed him minister to Russia just to get him out of town.

politico 1 An elected official. 2 A politician who is mainly concerned with reelection, patronage, and personal advancement and enrichment. 3 An unofficial hanger-on and mover and shaker (*see* MOVERS AND SHAKERS) of the political process, such as a campaign worker, a wealthy contributor, or a political consultant. 4 A role adopted by legislators that is a pragmatic mix between EDMUND BURKE's notions of trustee and delegate.

REFERENCES

2 Matthew Josephson, *The Politicos: 1865–1896* (New York: Harcourt, Brace, 1938).

4 Roger H. Davidson, *The Role of the Congressman* (New York: Pegasus, 1969).

The Legislator as Politico

The classical dichotomization of the concept of representation in terms of independent judgment and mandate was unlikely to exhaust the empirical possibilities of representational behavior. In particular, it would seem to be possible for a representative to act in line with both criteria. For roles and orientations need not be mutually exclusive. Depending on circumstances, a representative may hold the role orientation of trustee at one time, and the role orientation of delegate at another time. Or he might even seek to reconcile both orientations in terms of a third. In other words, the representational-role set comprises the extreme orientations of trustee and delegate and a third orientation, the politico, resulting from overlap of these two. Within the orientational range called politico, the trustee and delegate roles may be taken simultaneously, possibly making for role con-

flict, or they may be taken seriatim, one after another as legislative situations dictate.

Source: John C. Wahlke, Heinz Eulau, William Buchanan, and Leroy C. Ferguson, *The Legislative System: Explorations in Legislative Behavior* (New York: Wiley, 1962), pp. 277–78.

---

politics 1 The art and science of governance; the means by which the will of the community is arrived at and implemented; the activities of a government, politician, or political party. 2 The pursuit and exercise of the political power necessary to make binding policy decisions for the community and to distribute patronage and other government benefits. 3 The socialization of conflict. According to E. E. Schattschneider in *The Semi-Sovereign People* (New York: Holt, Rinehart & Winston, 1960):

> The political process is a sequence: conflicts are initiated by highly motivated, high-tension groups so directly and immediately involved that it is difficult for them to see the justice of competing claims. As long as the conflicts remain *private* . . . no political process is initiated. Conflicts become political only when an attempt is made to involve the wider public. Pressure politics might be described as a stage in the socialization of conflict.

Compare to PRIVATIZATION OF CONFLICT. 4 The policymaking aspect of government in contrast to its administration. 5 The interpersonal negotiation that leads to consensus within, and action by, groups. *Compare to* ART OF THE POSSIBLE.

REFERENCES

1 James E. Combs and Dan Nimmo, *A Primer of Politics* (New York: Macmillan, 1984).

2 For the classic work on the politics of distribution, see Harold D. Lasswell, *Politics: Who Gets What, When, How* (New York: Peter Smith, 1936).

5 Andrew Kakabadse, *The Politics of Management* (New York: Nichols, 1984).

John Adams on the Study of Politics

The science of government is my duty to study, more than all other sciences; the arts of legislation and administration and negotiation ought to take place of, indeed to exclude, in a manner, all other arts. I must study politics and war, that my sons may have liberty to study mathematics and philosophy. My sons ought to study mathematics and philosophy, geography, natural history and naval architecture, navigation, commerce, and agriculture, in order to give their children a right to study painting, poetry, music, architecture, statuary, tapestry and porcelain.

Source: 1780 letter to Abigail Adams.

politics-administration dichotomy The belief, growing out of the progressive and civil service reform movements, that the spoils system and political interference in administration eroded the opportunity for administrative efficiency. Consequently, the policymaking activities of government ought to be wholly separated from the administrative functions; administrators need an explicit assignment of objectives before they can begin to develop an efficient administrative system. Public administration theorists in the early part of this century argued that politics and administration could be distinguished, in the words of FRANK J. GOODNOW, as "the expression of the will of the state and the execution of that will."

Paul Appleby (1891–1963) became the leading critic of this theoretical insistence on apolitical government processes when he asserted that it went against the grain of the American experience. Appleby in *Big Democracy* (New York: Knopf, 1945) held that it was a myth that politics was separate and could somehow be taken out of administration. Political involvement was good—not evil, as many of the progressive reformers had claimed—because political involvement in administration acted as a check on the arbitrary exercise of bureaucratic power. In the future, those who would describe the political ramifications and issues of administration would not begin by contesting the politics-administration dichotomy as incorrect or irrelevant; rather, they would begin from the premise, so succinctly put by Appleby, that "government is different because government is politics." Today, most public administration theorists accept the notion that politics and administration are inherently and inevitably intertwined. *See also* WOODROW WILSON.

REFERENCES

The politics-administration dichotomy is traditionally traced to two sources. See Wood-

row Wilson, The study of administration, *Political Science Quarterly* 2 (June 1887); Frank J. Goodnow, *Politics and Administration: A Study in Government* (New York: Macmillan, 1900).

Also see Edwin W. Stene, The politics-administration dichotomy, *Midwest Review of Public Administration* 9 (April/July 1975);

James H. Svara, Dichotomy and duality: Reconceptualizing the relationship between policy and administration in council-manager cities, *Public Administration Review* 45 (January/February 1985);

Laurence J. O'Toole, Jr., Doctrines and developments: Separation of powers, the politics-administration dichotomy, and the rise of the administrative state, *Public Administration Review* 47 (January/February 1987).

For a comparative perspective, see Peter A. Hall, Policy innovation and the structure of the state: The politics-administration nexus in France and Britain, *Annals of the American Academy of Political and Social Science* 466 (March 1983).

politics, germ theory of *See* HERBERT BAXTER ADAMS.

politics, peanut *See* PEANUT POLITICS.

politics, power *See* POWER POLITICS.

politics, practical *See* PRACTICAL POLITICS.

polity **1** An organized society, such as a state. **2** The governing structures of a political community. **3** The Aristotelian (*see* ARISTOTLE) notion of the constitution, written or unwritten, that governs a body of people. *Compare to* POLIS.

Polity The scholarly quarterly of the Northeastern Political Science Association; published since 1968. Library of Congress no. JA3 .P65.

Polity
Thompson Hall
University of Massachusetts
Amherst, MA 01003

poll **1** The counting of votes in an election. Poll is derived from *polle*, an old Teutonic word meaning the top or crown of the head. In a head-counting situation in the olden days, someone would stand on high and count the tops of heads. **2** The place (usually plural: polls) where people vote. **3** The result of an election in terms of vote count. **4** Private and informal (meaning not legal or binding) surveys of public opinion or of the opinions of any group. *Compare to* PUBLIC OPINION SURVEY; SAMPLE.

REFERENCES

4 Charles Roll, Private opinion polls, *Proceedings of the Academy of Political Science* 34:4 (1982);

Seymour Sudman, The presidents and the polls, *Public Opinion Quarterly* 46 (Fall 1982);

Seymour Sudman, The network polls: A critical review, *Public Opinion Quarterly* 47 (Winter 1983);

Burns W. Roper, Are polls accurate? *Annals of the American Academy of Political and Social Science* 472 (March 1984);

M. Margaret Conway, The use of polls in congressional, state and local elections, *Annals of the American Academy of Political and Social Science* 472 (March 1984).

pollbook A register of eligible voters. Today, a pollbook is more likely to be a printout from a computer.

Pollock v Farmer's Loan & Trust Co. *See* SIXTEENTH AMENDMENT.

polls, exit Interviews with voters (asking how they voted) just after they have finished voting and are exiting the polling places. This information is then aggregated, and projections of who has won or lost are made. As with all polls, an exit poll might select a scientific sample of the voting population or it might sample the MAN IN THE STREET (those interviews so loved by local TV news programs). Consequently, the reliability of exit polls can vary enormously. The reporting of exit poll results in presidential elections has become controversial because the United States is geographically divided into four time zones. Sometimes

the winner is projected on the basis of exit polling by the news media on the East Coast many hours before the polls close on the West Coast. This seems to have discouraged many voters on the West Coast from voting at all, to the adverse interest of many state and local candidates.

REFERENCES

Ronald J. Busch and Joel A. Lieske, Does time of voting affect exit poll results? *Public Opinion Quarterly* 49 (Spring 1985);

Burns W. Roper, Early election calls: The larger dangers, *Public Opinion Quarterly* 49 (Spring 1985);

Richard Salant, Projections and exit polls, *Public Opinion Quarterly* 49 (Spring 1985);

Seymour Sudman, Do exit polls influence voting behavior? *Public Opinion Quarterly* 50 (Fall 1986).

pollster A person or organization that conducts public opinion polls. Thus a pollster could be the individual interviewer or the organization he or she works for. Pollsters are used both by the media, which make the results public, and by campaign organizations, which often base their strategy and tactics on them—and which may make their results public if it is to their advantage to do so. *See also* GEORGE HORACE GALLUP; ELMO ROPER.

REFERENCES

Albert H. Cantril, The press and the pollster, *Annals of the American Academy of Political and Social Science* 427 (September 1976);

Bruce Altschuler, Ethics and the new style candidate pollster, *Journal of Political Science* 11 (Spring 1984).

poll, straw A test of the opinions of a voting group deliberately intended to have no effect but to suggest to members of the group the direction in which opinion might be headed.

poll tax *See* TAX, POLL.

pollwatcher An individual who, on behalf of a candidate or a party, observes the voting process on election day to encourage proper procedures and to report irregularities.

popular sovereignty **1** The concept that ultimate political authority resides with the people. This concept is at the heart of American government; the notion that the people are sovereign is inherent in the Declaration of Independence and in the Constitution.   **2** In the pre-Civil War debates on slavery, popular sovereignty was advocated by the South; in this context it referred to the right of new states coming into the union to decide the issue of slavery on an individual basis. Because the western lands preparing for statehood were said to be "squatted upon" by its new residents, this option for slavery was also called "squatter sovereignty."

REFERENCE

1   Paul Keither Conkin, *Self-Evident Truths: Being a Discourse on the Origins and Development of the First Principles of American Government—Popular Sovereignty, Natural Rights, and Balance and Separation of Powers* (Bloomington: Indiana University Press, 1974).

popular vote   *See* VOTE, POPULAR.

populism   **1** A general term for any of a variety of mass political movements that began in both Europe and the United States toward the end of the nineteenth century. Populism is noted for mobilizing the poorer sectors of a society, often rural people who have suffered the dislocations of industrialization and urbanization, against existing institutions. In this sense, both fascism and national socialism (the nazism of Hitler's Germany) have their origins in populist movements—which, however, came under control of charismatic leaders. But any political movement that has mass popular backing and is generally perceived to be acting in the interests of the people can be called populist.   **2** A recurring political theme in the United States that stresses the role of government in defending small voices against the powerful and the wealthy. As a political force, populism, which grew out of a farmers' protest movement in the 1890s, is ideologically ambiguous. Economically, it has been decidedly to the Left, with its concerns for government aid for the little people. But at the same time, it has been decidedly to the Right on social issues, because its core support has often come from religious fundamentalists.

REFERENCES

Norman Pollack, ed., *The Populist Mind* (Indianapolis: Bobbs Merrill, 1967);

Raymond J. Cunningham, ed., *The Populists in Historical Perspective* (Boston: Heath, 1968);

Edward Schwartz, Populism: A tradition in search of a movement, *Social Policy* 10 (March/April 1980);

Alan Crawford, Right-wing populism, *Social Policy* 11 (May/June 1980);

Margaret Canovan, *Populism* (New York: Harcourt Brace Jovanovich, 1981);

Margaret Canovan, Two strategies for the study of populism, *Political Studies* 30 (December 1982).

pork   Government largess obtained not on merit or because of legal entitlement but because of political patronage.

pork barrel   **1** Favoritism by a government in the allocation of benefits or resources; legislation that favors the district of a particular legislator by providing for the funding of public works or other projects (such as post offices or defense contracts) that will bring economic advantage to the district and political favor for the legislator.   **2** The treasury of a state or national government when it is perceived as a means of providing funds for local interests regardless of their utility to the nation as a whole.

REFERENCES

James T. Murphy, Political parties and the pork barrel: Party conflict and cooperation in House Public Works Committee decision making, *American Political Science Review* 68 (March 1974);

Walter Shapiro, The two party pork barrel, *Washington Monthly* 9 (November 1975);

Gregory A. Daneke, Those pork barrel blues: The new politics of water resource planning and management, *Midwest Review of Public Administration* 11 (June 1977);

Kenneth A. Shepsle and Barry R. Weingast, Political preferences for the pork barrel: A generalization, *American Journal of Political Science* 25 (February 1981);

William Hartung, Star wars pork barrel, *Bulletin of the Atomic Scientists* 42 (January 1986).

pork chopper A patronage appointee who has a government job requiring slight work; one who is put on the payroll as a payoff for past services.

position classification The use of formal job descriptions to organize all jobs in a civil service merit system into classes on the basis of duties and responsibilities, for the purposes of delineating authority, establishing chains of command, and providing equitable salary scales.

REFERENCE

Jay M. Shafritz, *Position Classification: A Behavioral Analysis for the Public Service* (New York: Praeger, 1973).

position paper A formal statement of opinion or of proposed policies on political or social issues; often issued by candidates for public office, public interest group, unions, and so on.

positive economics Economic analysis that limits itself to what is, rather than to what ought to be.

REFERENCE

James R. Wible, Friedman's positive economics and philosophy of science, *Southern Economic Journal* (October 1982).

positive law A law passed by a legislature—as opposed to COMMON LAW or natural law, (*see* LAW, NATURAL), which are not.

posse comitatus 1 A Latin phrase meaning the power of the county. The term refers to the authority of a sheriff to gather a posse when temporarily needed to enforce the law. 2 A secret far-Right, paramilitary, political organization, whose members resist paying federal taxes because they believe taxation is an unwarranted intrusion on their civil liberties.

Postal Rate Commission The federal agency created by the Postal Reorganization Act of 1970 whose major responsibility is to submit recommended decisions to the U.S. Postal Service on postage rates, fees, and mail classifications. The commission also has appellate jurisdiction to review Postal Service determinations to close or consolidate small post offices.

Postal Rate Commission
1333 H Street, N.W.
Washington, D.C. 20268
(202) 789–6800

Postal Reorganization Act of 1970 The federal statute that converted the Post Office Department into an independent establishment—within the executive branch of the government—to own and operate the nation's postal system, known as the United States Postal Service. The act also provided for collective bargaining by postal workers, the first instance of true collective bargaining in the federal service.

REFERENCES

John J. Morrison, *Postal Reorganization: Managing the Public's Business* (Boston: Auburn, 1981);

Nicole Woolsey Biggart, The Post Office as a business: Ten years of postal reorganization, *Policy Studies Journal* 11 (March 1983).

Postal Service, United States (USPS) The federal government corporation that provides mail processing and delivery services to individuals and businesses within the United States. It is also the responsibility of the Postal Service to protect the mails from loss or theft and to apprehend those who violate postal laws. The Postal Service is the only federal agency whose employees are governed by a process of collective bargaining, which permits negotiations over wages. The chief executive officer of the Postal Service, the postmaster general, is appointed by the nine governors of the Postal Service, who are appointed by the president, with the advice and consent of the Senate, for overlapping nine-year terms. The ambiguous legal status of the Postal Service has been the source of political controversy since it was established in 1970. It does not report to the president and is only indirectly responsible to the Congress. There have been a number of bills introduced in recent congresses to return the Postal Service to the status of a regular executive department.

REFERENCES

George L. Priest, The history of the postal monopoly in the United States, *Journal of Law & Economics* 18 (April 1975);

Jean M. Berg, The postal subsidy: The need to continue funding of the Postal Service, *Journal of Legislation* 8 (Summer 1981);

Simcha B. Werner, The political reversibility of administrative reform: A case study of the United States Postal Service, *Public Administration* 60 (Autumn 1982);

Joel L. Fleishman, *The Future of the Postal Service* (New York: Praeger, 1983);

M. Elliot Vittes, Value trade-offs and productivity: The transpoliticization of the U.S. Postal Service, *Policy Studies Review* 4 (January 1985).

Disgruntled Postal Worker Resigns

William Faulkner (1897–1962), the American novelist who won the Nobel Prize for literature in 1949, was the postmaster at the University of Mississippi post office from 1921 to 1924. His letter of resignation said: "As long as I live under the capitalistic system I expect to have my life influenced by the demands of moneyed people. But I will be damned if I propose to be at the beck and call of every itinerant scoundrel who has two cents to invest in a postage stamp. This sir, is my resignation."

---

postindustrial society A phrase coined by Daniel Bell to describe the new social structures evolving in modern societies in the second half of the twentieth century. Bell holds that the "axial principle" of postindustrial society is the centrality of theoretical knowledge as the source of innovation and policy formation for the society. Hallmarks of postindustrial society include a change from a goods-producing to a service economy, the preeminence of a professional and technical class, and the creation of a new intellectual technology.

REFERENCES

Daniel Bell, *The Coming of Post-Industrial Society: A Venture in Social Forecasting* (New York: Basic Books, 1973);

Stanley Rothman and S. Robert Lichter, Power, politics, and personality in "postindustrial society," *Journal of Politics* 40 (August 1978);

Seymour Martin Lipset, ed., *The Third Century: America as a Post-Industrial Society* (Chicago: University of Chicago Press, 1979);

Laurence Veysey, A postmortem on Daniel Bell's postindustrialism, *American Quarterly* 34 (Spring 1982).

postmaster A federal government official in charge of a local post office.

postmaster general 1 The chief executive officer of the U.S. POSTAL SERVICE appointed by its nine-member board of governors. 2 The cabinet-level federal official in charge of the Post Office Department until it was reorganized into the U.S. Postal Service by the Postal Reorganization Act of 1970. Because of the large number of patronage jobs available in the old Post Office Department, the postmaster general tended to be the informal patronage chief of any administration.

Potomac fever An overwhelming desire to obtain or retain a high-status job, elective or appointive, in Washington, D.C., which sits on the banks of the Potomac River.

REFERENCE

Fred R. Harris, *Potomac Fever* (New York: Norton, 1977).

poverty Defined by the U.S. Bureau of the Census in 1986 as an annual cash income of less than $11,203 for a family of four. This is the subsistence approach. Another way is to approach poverty in terms of relative deprivation, in which the poor are those with less than most others, even if everyone's economic level is well above subsistence level. Poverty has long been perceived as a natural, a normal, condition for some members of a society. The *New Testament* teaches that "ye have the poor always with you" (Matthew 26:11). But in more recent times, poverty has come to be thought of as an essentially unnatural or undemocratic condition that measures the weakness of a society that claims equality for all of its citizens. *Compare to* WAR ON POVERTY; LEADERSHIP.

REFERENCES

N. A. Barr, Empirical definitions of the poverty line, *Policy and Politics* 9 (January 1981);

Sheldon Danziger and Peter Gottschalk, The measurement of poverty: Implications for antipoverty policy, *American Behavioral Scientist* 26 (July/August 1983);

Martha S. Hill, The changing nature of poverty, *Annals of the American Academy of Political and Social Science* 479 (May 1985).

poverty trap The dilemma that families on means-tested welfare benefits often face. The welfare system is such that they chance losing benefits if their income rises; consequently, they are discouraged from seeking employment that pays only marginally better than welfare alone—employment that might have eventually taken them off the welfare rolls.

Powell v Alabama *See* GIDEON V WAINWRIGHT.

power The ability or the right to do something; the ability to exercise authority over others. The term implies a hierarchy of control of stronger over weaker. John R. P. French and Bertram Raven, in "The Bases of Social Power," (see references) suggest that there are five major bases of power: (1) expert power, which is based on the perception that the leader possesses some special knowledge or expertise; (2) referent power, which is based on the follower's liking, admiring, or identifying with the leader; (3) reward power, which is based on the leader's ability to mediate rewards for the follower; (4) legitimate power, which is based on the follower's perception that the leader has the legitimate right or authority to exercise influence over him or her; and (5) coercive power, which is based on the follower's fear that noncompliance with the leader's wishes will lead to punishment. Subsequent research on these power bases has indicated that the first two (expert and referent power) are more positively related to subordinate performance and satisfaction than the last three (reward, legitimate, and coercive power).

REFERENCES

The French and Raven study is in *Studies in Social Power,* ed. Dorwin Cartwright (Ann Arbor: Institute for Social Research, University of Michigan, 1959).

Also see Norton E. Long, Power and administration, *Public Administration Review* 9 (Autumn 1949);

David C. McClelland, The two faces of power, *Journal of International Affairs* 24 (1970);

R. G. H. Siu, *The Craft of Power* (New York: Wiley, 1979);

Karen Van Wagner and Cheryl Swanson, From Machiavelli to Ms.: Differences in male-female power styles. *Public Administration Review* 39 (January/February 1979);

Jeffrey Pfiffer, *Power in Organizations* (Marshfield, MA: Pitman, 1981);

James MacGregor Burns, Power and politics, *Society* 18 (May/June 1981).

power base A politician's most dependable support. It is a vague phrase, which could mean a home state or district, a wing of the party, or a cadre of fat-cat campaign contributors.

power broker **1** A person who controls a bloc of votes that can be delivered in exchange for a price. The price in this case could be a promise of appointive office, the acceptance of a specific policy, the placement of a favored candidate on the ticket, or plain old-fashioned money. **2** Someone who is so trusted by the contesting sides of an issue that he or she can broker an agreement. **3** An *éminence grise*—who runs government from behind the scenes. *See* ROBERT MOSES.

power-elite theory *See* C. WRIGHT MILLS; PLURALISM.

power, inherent **1** An authority that is an integral part of sovereignty and that, while not expressly stated, is implied by the nature of government and necessary for a government to function. **2** A power not expressly granted by the U.S. Constitution but that came about through the NECESSARY AND PROPER CLAUSE.

power of attorney A legal document authorizing one person to act as attorney for, or in the place of, the person signing the document.

power of the purse **1** A purse (a money bag) generalized to mean a treasury or other source of funding. The power to control the distribution of funding for public expenditure has been the basis of disputes between executives and legislatures for centuries. **2** The ability of political figures to direct government appropriations to the programs they favor. Under Article I, Section 7, of the U.S. Constitution, the power of the purse belongs to the House of Representatives because "all bills for raising revenue shall originate" there.

REFERENCES

Richard F. Fenno, Jr., *The Power of the Purse: Appropriations Politics in Congress* (Boston: Little, Brown, 1966);

Gerald E. Frug, The judicial power of the purse, *University of Pennsylvania Law Review* 126 (April 1978).

power politics A translation of the German word *Machtpolitik*, referring to an aggressive foreign policy that substitutes threats and the actual use of military power for international law; in short, the notion that might makes right. *Compare to* REALPOLITIK.

REFERENCE

Ruth B. Russell, "Power politics" and the United Nations, *International Journal* 25 (Spring 1970).

power, public *See* PUBLIC POWER.

powers that be Those who must be obeyed; those who are in control of a state, a company, or other institution. This expression suggests that there are always forces or groups that exercise control, regardless of the legal or constitutional organization that establishes formal power. David Halberstam used the phrase to describe the masters of America's communications empires in *The Powers That Be* (New York: Knopf, 1979). But the phrase originates in the *Bible* (Romans 13:1): "Let every soul be subject unto the higher powers. For there is no power but of God: the powers that be are ordained by God."

power, two faces of The theory that political power is not always overt—that it is frequently covert and exercised in ways that are not readily observable. The other—hidden—face of power is often far more influential than the public face of power, exemplified by elected officials.

REFERENCE

For the classic analysis of the two faces of power, "neither of which the sociologists see and only one of which the political scientists see," see Peter Bachrach and Morton S. Baratz, Two faces of power, *American Political Science Review* 56 (December 1962).

practical politics **1** Expedient political actions; those that are on the edge of legality and morality. **2** Those political acts that go over the edge of legality and morality and are indeed illegal and immoral. **3** A cynical approach to political affairs.

preamble **1** The first paragraph of the U.S. Constitution, which begins "We the people . . . " and goes on to explain the reasons for the Constitution ("to form a more perfect union, establish justice, insure domestic tranquility . . . "). **2** An introduction to a legal document, such as an administrative agency rule or a statute, that explains why it was written. A preamble is not legally enforceable but may be referred to by the courts to ascertain the original intent.

precedent The legal principle that previous decisions influence future decisions unless explicitly overruled. It is the basis for stability in law, built on the expectation that judgments will be consistent with one another unless there is reason for change. According to Jonathan Swift (1667–1745) in *Gulliver's Travels* (1726), "It is a maxim among lawyers that whatever hath been done before may be done again: and therefore they take special care to record all the decisions formerly made against common justice and the general reason of mankind. These, under the name of *precedents*, they produce as authorities to justify the most iniquitous opinions."

REFERENCES

William M. Landes and Richard A. Posner, Legal precedent: A theoretical and empirical analysis, *Journal of Law and Economics* 19 (August 1976);

Gregory A. Caldeira, The transmission of legal precedent: A study of state supreme courts, *American Political Science Review* 79 (March 1985).

precinct **1** A local government subdivision for organizing the voting process, typically containing less than a thousand voters. As such, it is the basic unit of political party organizations. The precinct workers are the frontline troops in election campaigns. Modern political consultants often say: "There's a precinct worker in every home now. It's called a television." **2** A municipal subdivision for police administration, which may or may not be coterminous with election precincts.
REFERENCES
1 Raymond R. Wolfinger, The influence of precinct work on voting behavior, *Public Opinion Quarterly* 27:3 (1963);
Gerald H. Kramer, The effects of precinct-level canvassing on voter behavior, *Public Opinion Quarterly* 34:4 (Winter 1970).

precinct captain The person responsible for the interests of a political party in a voting precinct. Typical duties include supervising party volunteer workers, getting voters registered, cultivating voters by doing favors for them, and getting out the vote on election day.

preemption doctrine The legal principle that federal laws take precedence over state laws. This principle is grounded in the portion of Article VI of the U.S. Constitution that asserts that the Constitution "and all the laws of the United States which shall be made in pursuance thereof . . . shall be the supreme law of the land."
REFERENCES
Henry L. Bowden, Jr., A conceptual refinement of the doctrine of federal preemption, *Journal of Public Law* 22:2 (1973);
Nina J. Lahoud, Federal and New York State anti-boycott legislation: The preemption issue, *New York University Journal of International Law and Politics* 14 (Winter 1982);
Ronald D. Rotunda, The doctrine of conditional preemption and other limitations on Tenth Amendment restrictions, *University of Pennsylvania Law Review* 132 (January 1984).

preferments The modern version of HONEST GRAFT/DISHONEST GRAFT; the advantages politicians gain because of their position or connections. Examples include contracts to provide insurance on government property, contracts to supply government institutions, and retainers paid to a politician's law firm by an interested lobbyist. Mike Royko in *Boss: Richard J. Daley of Chicago* (New York: Dutton, 1971) reported that Mayor Daley was once asked by a real estate agent newly elected to the state legislature how he should conduct himself. Daley advised him, "Don't take a nickel; just hand them your business card." Preferments are often quietly solicited through seemingly innocent business cards.

preferred position doctrine The notion, not fully accepted by the U.S. Supreme Court, that First Amendment rights are more important than other parts of the Bill of Rights and thus have a preferred position.

Pregnancy Discrimination Act of 1978 An amendment to Title VII of the Civil Rights Act of 1964 that holds that discrimination on the basis of pregnancy, childbirth, or related medical conditions constitutes unlawful sex discrimination. The amendment was enacted in response to the Supreme Court's ruling in *General Electric Co. v Gilbert* that an employer's exclusion of pregnancy-related disabilities from its comprehensive disability plan did not violate Title VII. *Also see* CALIFORNIA FEDERAL SAVINGS AND LOAN ASSOCIATION V GUERRA.
REFERENCES
Andrew Weissmann, Sexual equality under the Pregnancy Discrimination Act, *Columbia Law Review* 83 (April 1983);
Reva B. Siegel, Employment equality under the Pregnancy Discrimination Act of 1978, *Yale Law Journal* 94 (March 1985).

prerogative theory of presidential powers *See* NEAGLE, IN RE.

prerogative theory of the presidency *See* PRESIDENCY, PREROGATIVE THEORY OF THE.

presidencies, two Aaron Wildavsky's division of the presidency into two differing spheres of influence: foreign policy and domestic policy. Wildavsky contended that presidential leadership in foreign policy will, generally speaking, find greater support among the public than leadership in domestic policy. To test his hypothesis, Wildavsky examined congressional action on presidential proposals from 1948 to 1964. For this period, the Congress approved 58.5 percent of the foreign policy bills; 73.3 percent of the defense policy bills; and 70.8 percent of general foreign relations, State Department, foreign aid bills, and treaties. During this same period, the Congress approved only 40.2 percent of the president's domestic policy proposals. Thus the two-presidencies thesis was confirmed. Wildavsky's work has spawned a bevy of research articles, none of which has materially diminished his original thesis.

REFERENCES

For the original presentation, see Aaron Wildavsky, The two presidencies, *Trans-Action* 4 (December 1966).

For subsequent analyses, see Lance T. LeLoup and Steven A. Shull, Congress versus the executive: The "two presidencies" reconsidered, *Social Sciences Quarterly* 59 (March 1979);

Lee Sigelman, A reassessment of the two presidencies thesis, *Journal of Politics* 41 (November 1979);

Frederick Paul Lee, "The two presidencies" revisited, *Presidential Studies Quarterly* 10 (Fall 1980);

Harvey G. Zeidenstein, The two presidencies thesis is alive and well and has been living in the U.S. Senate since 1973, *Presidential Studies Quarterly* 11 (Fall 1981);

Jeffrey E. Cohen, A historical reassessment of Wildavsky's "two presidencies," *Social Science Quarterly* 63 (September 1982);

George C. Edwards III, The two presidencies: A reevaluation, *American Politics Quarterly* 14 (July 1986).

presidency, American The U.S. institution and office of the presidency. The American president has been compared to an elective monarch, but there are few kings or queens

The seal of the U.S. president.

today who exercise the same degree of authority as does the president of the United States. He simultaneously holds several titles that are often split among two or more incumbents in monarchies and parliamentary democracies.

He is traditionally accorded the unofficial designation chief of state, a position that most closely parallels that of a king or queen in a monarchy. As such, the president is recognized as the symbolic embodiment of the United States and its citizens, and thus is accorded the same honors due a reigning sovereign. The president also performs many of the functions of a prime minister or premier in a parliamentary democracy. As chief executive, an office he holds under the Constitution, he presides over the cabinet and manages the executive branch. As political leader, he directs the operations of his party's national organzation and serves as leader of its members in the Congress. The Constitution also vests the president with the powers to make treaties and to appoint ambassadors, cabinet officers, and judges of federal courts, with the advice and consent of the Senate. He also holds the position of commander in chief of the armed forces. Unlike a prime minister, the president is not a member of the legislature, nor is his tenure in office dependent on the approval of a majority of the legislators. Elected by the citizens, he serves a definite term, from which he can be removed against his will only by the process of impeach-

The U.S. Constitution on the Presidency

Article I, Section 3,	Vice presidency; impeachment.
Article I, Section 7,	Veto.
Article II, Section 1,	Executive power; term of office; electoral college; vice presidency; qualifications; removal; compensation; oath of office.
Article II, Section 2,	Commander in chief; written opinions from executive department heads; reprieves and pardons; treaties; nominations and appointments.
Article II, Section 3,	State of the Union information; right to recommend measures to the Congress, to call special sessions of the Congress, to adjourn Congress if the two houses cannot agree on time of, to receive ambassadors and ministers, to take care that laws be faithfully executed, to commission officers of the United States.
Article II, Section 4,	Impeachment.
Article VI, Section 3,	Oath to support Constitution; no religious test.
Twelfth Amendment,	Modification of election process.
Twentieth Amendment, Section 1,	Date for end of term.
Twentieth Amendment, Sections 3, 4,	Death, disability, succession.
Twenty-second Amendment, Section 1,	Length of time in office.
Twenty-third Amendment,	District of Columbia's electoral vote.
Twenty-fifth Amendment,	Presidential succession.

Source: William J. Keefe, Henry J. Abraham, William H. Flanigan, Charles O. Jones, Morris S. Ogul, and John W. Spanier, *American Democracy: Institutions, Politics, and Policies,* 2d ed. (Chicago: Dorsey, 1986), p. 359.

ment. At the same time, his tenure is limited to two four-year terms or ten years, which distinguishes him from hereditary monarchs, who reign for life.

REFERENCES

Kenneth Davison, *The American Presidency: A Guide to Information Sources* (Detroit: Gale, 1983);

The American Presidency: A Historical Bibliography (Santa Barbara, CA: ABC-Clio, 1984);

Robert U. Goehlert and Fenton S. Martin, *The Presidency: A Research Guide* (Santa Barbara, CA: ABC-Clio, 1984).

Presidency, Center for the Study of *See* CENTER FOR THE STUDY OF THE PRESIDENCY.

presidency, hidden-hand *See* EISENHOWER, DWIGHT DAVID "IKE."

presidency, imperial A phrase that implies that the president of the United States has grown to be the head of an international empire as well as the head of a domestic political state. It suggests that the presidency has grown too powerful, that it has assumed more authority than is justified by its constitutionally granted powers. This suggestion is reinforced when the office takes on more and more of the trappings of traditional European monarchy. The high-water mark of these trappings occurred during the Richard M. Nixon administration, when the civilian White House guards were dressed in uniforms reminiscent of a Gilbert and Sullivan comic opera. The "imperial" uniforms were so ridiculed by the press that they were soon retired. The phrase imperial presidency is usually credited to the 1973 book of the same title by Arthur Schlesinger, Jr., (Boston: Houghton Mifflin). The book came out just as the Watergate scandal broke and all of the excesses of the Nixon administration were bared to the world. While Schlesinger's phrase was a convenient way to summarize Nixon's corrupting of the presidential office, the book, written before the scandal really broke, was not an attack on Nixon but rather an analysis of the gradual enhancement of presidential powers in modern times.

REFERENCES

George Reedy, *The Twilight of the Presidency* (Cleveland: World, 1970);

Alan F. Arcuri, The imperial presidency: The tug toward isolation, *Presidential Studies Quarterly* 7 (Spring/Summer 1977);

Thomas E. Cronin, A resurgent Congress and the imperial presidency, *Political Science Quarterly* 95 (Summer 1980);

R. Gordon Hoxie, The not so imperial presidency: A modest proposal, *Presidential Studies Quarterly* 10 (Spring 1980);

Louis W. Koenig, Reassessing the "imperial presidency," *Proceedings of the Academy of Political Science* 34:2 (1981).

presidency, literalist view of   *See* PRESIDENCY, RESTRICTED VIEW OF.

presidency, prerogative theory of the   Abraham Lincoln's belief supported by John Locke's *Second Treatise of Government* (1688) that, under certain conditions, the chief executive possesses extraordinary power to preserve the nation. This power, as Lincoln saw it, might not only exceed constitutional bounds but act against the Constitution. A president, according to this view, could at least for a short while assume dictatorial powers. Lincoln explained in his April 4, 1864, letter to A. G. Hodges that

my oath to preserve the Constitution to the best of my ability imposed upon me the duty of preserving, by every indispensable means, that government—that nation, of which that Constitution was the organic law. Was it possible to lose the nation and yet preserve the Constitution? By general law, life and limb must be protected, yet often a limb must be amputated to save a life; but a life is never wisely given to save a limb. I felt that measures otherwise unconstitutional might become lawful by becoming indispensable to the preservation of the Constitution through the preservation of the nation. Right or wrong, I assumed this ground, and now avow it.

presidency, restricted view of   A limited (or literalist) view of presidential power that holds, according to President William Howard Taft in *Our Chief Magistrate and His Powers* (New York: Columbia University Press, 1916), that "the president can exercise no power which cannot be fairly and reasonably traced to some specific grant of power or justly implied and included within such express grant as proper and necessary to its exercise." Furthermore (and directly contrary to President Theodore Roosevelt's stewardship view), "there is no undefined residuum of power which he can exercise because it seems to be in the public interest."

presidency, rhetorical   A description of the American presidency that refers to its ever-increasing reliance on rhetoric for political success, as opposed to its historic reliance on political parties and party organization. James Caeser, Glen Thorow, Jeffrey Tulis, and Joseph Bessette in "The Rise of the Rhetorical Presidency," *Presidential Studies Quarterly* 11 (Spring 1981) argue that, historically, leadership through rhetoric was suspect, that presidents rarely spoke directly to the people, and that, in any event, presidents relied much more heavily on party and political leadership in the Congress for their electoral and programmatic support. But today's presidents attempt to move mass opinion by speeches that exhort the public to support their policies and programs. Presidents are obliged to do this for three reasons: the modern doctrine of the presidency, which avers that the presidency is a place of moral leadership and should employ rhetoric to lead public opinion; the advent of the modern mass media, especially television, which facilitates the use of rhetoric; and the modern presidential campaign, which blurs campaigning and governing.

REFERENCE

Jeffrey K. Tulis, *The Rhetorical Presidency* (Princeton, NJ: Princeton University Press, 1987).

presidency, stewardship theory of the President Theodore Roosevelt's view that the president, because he represents and holds in trust the interests of all the people, should be free to take any actions in the public interest that are not specifically forbidden by the Constitution or statutory law. But he articulated this doctrine in his autobiography (Scribner, 1913) published after he left office. *Compare to* BULLY PULPIT.

president 1 The head of state in a republic. The powers of such presidents vary enormously. The president of the United States, because he is also the head of the government, has great powers. In contrast, most other presidents (such as those in the Soviet Union, Israel, and West Germany) have mainly ceremonial and informal authority. 2 One appointed or elected to preside over a formal assembly. 3 A chief executive officer of a corporation, board of trustees, university, or other institution.

Presidents of the United States

President	Age at Inauguration	Years Served	Party
George Washington (1732–1799)	57	1789–1797	Federalist
John Adams (1735–1826)	61	1797–1801	Federalist
Thomas Jefferson (1743–1826)	57	1801–1809	Democrat-Republican
James Madison (1751–1836)	57	1809–1817	Democrat-Republican
James Monroe (1758–1831)	58	1817–1825	Democrat-Republican
John Quincy Adams (1767–1848)	57	1825–1829	National Republican
Andrew Jackson (1767–1845)	61	1829–1837	Democrat
Martin Van Buren (1782–1862)	54	1837–1841	Democrat
William Henry Harrison (1773–1841)	68	1841–1841	Whig
John Tyler (1790–1862)	51	1841–1845	Whig
James K. Polk (1795–1849)	49	1845–1849	Democrat
Zachary Taylor (1784–1850)	64	1849–1850	Whig
Millard Fillmore (1800–1874)	50	1850–1853	Whig
Franklin Pierce (1804–1869)	48	1853–1857	Democrat
James Buchanan (1791–1868)	65	1857–1861	Democrat
Abraham Lincoln (1809–1865)	52	1861–1865	Republican
Andrew Johnson (1808–1875)	56	1865–1869	Republican
Ulysses S. Grant (1822–1885)	46	1869–1877	Republican
Rutherford B. Hayes (1822–1893)	54	1877–1881	Republican
James A. Garfield (1831–1881)	49	1881–1881	Republican
Chester A. Arthur (1830–1886)	50	1881–1885	Republican
Grover Cleveland (1837–1908)	47	1885–1889	Democrat
Benjamin Harrison (1833–1901)	55	1889–1893	Republican
Grover Cleveland (1837–1908)	55	1893–1897	Democrat
William McKinley (1843–1901)	54	1897–1901	Republican
Theodore Roosevelt (1858–1919)	42	1901–1909	Republican
William Howard Taft (1857–1930)	51	1909–1913	Republican
Woodrow Wilson (1856–1924)	56	1913–1921	Democrat
Warren G. Harding (1865–1923)	55	1921–1923	Republican

president, acting

President	Age at Inauguration	Years Served	Party
Calvin Coolidge (1872–1933)	51	1923–1929	Republican
Herbert Hoover (1874–1964)	54	1929–1933	Republican
Franklin D. Roosevelt (1882–1945)	51	1933–1945	Democrat
Harry S Truman (1884–1972)	60	1945–1953	Democrat
Dwight D. Eisenhower (1890–1969)	62	1953–1961	Republican
John F. Kennedy (1917–1963)	43	1961–1963	Democrat
Lyndon B. Johnson (1908–1973)	55	1963–1969	Democrat
Richard M. Nixon (1913–)	56	1969–1974	Republican
Gerald R. Ford (1913–)	61	1974–1977	Republican
Jimmy Carter (1924–)	52	1977–1981	Democrat
Ronald Reagan (1911–)	69	1981–	Republican

president, acting The title of the vice president of the United States when he is temporarily assuming the powers of the presidency under the provisions of the Twenty-fifth Amendment.

president elect The elected president of the United States, other than an incumbent president, from the time the election results are known in November until inauguration in January. This informal title is superfluous for a sitting president who wins reelection.

president emeritus Any living former president of the United States.

REFERENCE

John Whiteclay Chambers II, Presidents emeritus, *American Heritage* 30 (June/July 1979).

presidential character James David Barber's (1930–   ) theory of how a president's personality or character influences the success of his administration. Barber classifies all presidents according to whether they accept an active or passive role model for the presidency and whether their personal enjoyment of or emotional attitude toward the job of president is positive or negative. This puts all presidents into one of four quadrants: active-positive, active-negative, passive-positive, or passive-negative. Barber finds that the best presidents tend to be active-positive; they have great self-confidence, enjoy the give and take of politics, and are results-oriented. Examples include Franklin D. Roosevelt, Harry S Truman, and John F. Kennedy. In contrast, the worst presidents tend to be active-negative; they are often driven personalities with compulsive-aggressive behavior patterns and who are more interested in power than politics. Examples include Woodrow Wilson, Lyndon B. Johnson, and Richard M. Nixon. Barber's framework for evaluating presidents, while widely read and highly influential, has been severely criticized for being superficial, long-distance psychoanalysis.

REFERENCES

For Barber's basic presentation, see *The Presidential Character: Predicting Performance in the White House*, 3d ed. (Englewood Cliffs, NJ: Prentice-Hall, 1985).

For critiques of Barber's analysis, see Alexander L. George, Assessing presidential character, *World Politics* 26 (January 1974);

Michael Nelson, James David Barber and the psychological presidency, *Virginia Quarterly Review* 56 (Autumn 1980).

For applications of Barber's model, see William D. Pederson, Amnesty and presidential behavior: A "Barberian" test, *Presidential Studies Quarterly* 7 (Fall 1977);

John S. Latcham, President McKinley's active-positive character: A comparative revision with Barber's typology, *Presidential Studies Quarterly* 12 (Fall 1982);

Eric B. Herzik and Mary L. Dodson, Public Expectations and the presidency: Barber's "climate of expectations" examined, *Presidential Studies Quarterly* 12 (Fall 1982).

presidential commission *See* COMMISSION, PRESIDENTIAL.

Ever since the first televised presidential debates in 1960, candidates have tended to emphasize style over substance.

presidential debates Joint televised press conferences by the major party candidates for U.S. president. These head-to-head confrontations (which are not true debates) have become an expected part of each presidential election season. They have two main aspects: the pre-debate negotiations over whether there will be a debate, and the post-debate analysis of who did how well. The debates themselves, while compelling to watch, seldom offer anything new. The basic strategy is to hope the opponent will make a mistake. But few candidates have been as lucky as Jimmy Carter was in 1976, when his opponent, President Gerald Ford, boldly asserted that Poland was part of the free world. In the first of the modern presidential debates in 1960, Richard M. Nixon made the mistake of actually trying to debate, while his opponent, John F. Kennedy, concentrated on style and on presenting the correct presidential image. People listening to the debate on radio thought that Nixon had won, but Kennedy's style won him the television audience and the election. Ever since, presidential debates have been a game of style over substance.

REFERENCES

Alan I. Abramowitz, The impact of a presidential debate on voter rationality, *American Journal of Political Science* 22 (August 1978);

Kenneth D. Wald and Michael B. Lupfer, The presidential debate as a civics lesson, *Public Opinion Quarterly* 42 (Fall 1978);

Marilyn Jackson-Beeck and Robert G. Meadow, The triple agenda of presidential debates, *Public Opinion Quarterly* 43 (Summer 1979);

Lee Sigelman and Carol K. Sigelman, Judgments of the Carter-Reagan debate: The eyes of the beholders, *Public Opinion Quarterly* 48 (Fall 1984).

For a comparative perspective, see Robert E. Gilbert, Television debates and presidential elections: The United States and France, *Journal of Social, Political and Economic Studies* 7 (Winter 1982).

presidential election campaign fund The fund taxpayers may contribute to by checking a box on their federal income tax return. The tax form gives each taxpayer an opportunity to assign one dollar from their taxes (two dollars on a joint return) to pay for the public financing of presidential elections. Even though this does not increase their tax liability, only about 25 to 30 percent of all taxpayers contribute. *See* MATCHING FUNDS.

REFERENCE

Kim Quaile Hill, Taxpayer support for the presidential election campaign fund, *Social Science Quarterly* 62 (December 1981).

presidential electors The electors who compose the electoral college, which elects the president and vice president of the United States—the only elective federal officials not elected by a direct majority vote of the people. In the presidential election held the first Tuesday after the first Monday in November of every fourth year, each state chooses as many presidential electors as it has senators and representatives in the Congress. The District of Columbia also chooses three presidential electors. For an explanation of how presidential electors are selected and how they vote, *see* ELECTORAL COLLEGE.

presidential form of government A governing system in which the executive branch is separate from and independent of the legislature, as in the United States, in contrast to a parliamentary system, in which the executive is integrated with the legislature. *Compare to* CABINET GOVERNMENT.

presidential honeymoon *See* HONEYMOON PERIOD.

Presidential Libraries

President	Location	Phone
Hoover	West Branch, Iowa 52358	(319) 643–5301
Roosevelt	Hyde Park, New York 12538	(914) 229–8114
Truman	Independence, Missouri 64050	(816) 833–1400
Eisenhower	Abilene, Kansas 67410	(913) 263–4751
Kennedy	Boston, Massachusetts 02125	(617) 929–4500
Johnson	Austin, Texas 78705	(512) 482–5137
Nixon	(pending)	
Ford	Ann Arbor, Michigan 48109	(313) 668–2218
Carter	Atlanta, Georgia 30303	(404) 221–3942

presidential libraries Libraries containing the public papers and private memorabilia of past presidents of the United States. The libraries are open to the public. The custom, started by Franklin D. Roosevelt, is to establish regional archives of presidential documents and other papers, reflecting executive management of a particular presidency, for scholarly research. Papers of presidents prior to FDR are located either in the Library of Congress or in local archival collections.

REFERENCE

Robert F. Burk, New perspectives for presidential libraries, *Presidential Studies Quarterly* 11 (Summer 1981).

Office of Presidential Libraries
National Archives and Records
   Administration
Washington, D.C. 20408
(202) 523–3212

presidential mandate *See* MANDATE.

presidential primary matching account *See* MATCHING FUNDS.

presidential power 1 Executive power. Article II of the U.S. Constitution vests the executive power in the president. There is dispute among scholars about whether the executive power consists solely of those powers enumerated for the president or whether it includes also those powers that are implied in Article II. Most authorities lean toward the latter interpretation. The distinction between the president and the presidency—that is, between the individuals elected to the office and the power of the office itself—is essentially a modern distinction, which has its origins in the writings of political scientists of Woodrow Wilson's generation. The ability of individuals to effect the power of the office at given periods is distinguishable from the inherent powers of the office. The powers expressly granted to the president are few in number. He is commander in chief of the army and navy and of the state militias when they are called into the service of the United States. He may require the written opinion of his executive officers and is empowered to grant reprieves and pardons except in the case of impeachment, He has power, by and with the advice and consent of the Senate, to make treaties, provided that two-thirds of the Senators present concur. He also nominates and, by and with the advice and consent of the Senate, appoints ambassadors, other public ministers and consuls, justices of the Supreme Court, and other federal officers whose appointments are established by law. The president has the power to fill all vacancies that occur during the recess of the Senate. Those commissions expire unless the Senate consents to them when it reconvenes. The Constitution also directs the president to inform the Congress periodically on the state of the union and to recommend legislation that he considers necessary and expedient. He may, on extraordinary occasions, convene both houses of the Congress, or either of them, and, in case the two houses disagree about the time of adjournment, he may adjourn them to such time as he considers proper. The president also receives ambassadors and other public ministers, and commissions all officers of the United States. The president may veto acts of the Congress. A two-thirds vote of those present and voting is required in both the House and the Senate to override his veto. Finally, the president is instructed to "take care that the laws be faithfully executed."

In addition to these express powers, the president derives certain implied authority from the Constitution. This implied authority, like the express powers, has been in the past and remains today a subject of dispute and debate. Major implied constitutional powers flow from the president's authority as commander in chief. Though the Congress has the explicit power to declare war, the president has the authority not only to protect the nation from sudden attack but also to initiate military activities without a formal declaration of war. American presidents have used military force hundreds of times, but only on five occasions has the Congress declared war: the War of 1812, the Mexican War, the Spanish-American War, and the two World Wars. On all other occasions, it merely recognized, after executive initiatives, that hostilities did in fact exist. In recent years, the Congress has sought to define more clearly (most notably through the War Powers Resolution of 1973) the conditions under which presidents could take unilateral military action. **2 Persuasion.** Richard E. Neustadt's *Presidential Power* (New York: Wiley, 1960) asserts that a president's real powers are informal, that presidential power is essentially the power to persuade. *See also* LOUIS BROWNLOW; EDWARD S. CORWIN; PECKING ORDER; UNITED STATES V CURTISS-WRIGHT EXPORT CORPORATION; UNITED STATES V NIXON; YOUNGSTOWN SHEET AND TUBE CO. V SAWYER.

REFERENCES

Edward S. Corwin, *The President: Office and Powers*, 4th ed. (New York: New York University Press, 1957);

Wilfred E. Binkley, *The Man in the White House: His Powers and Duties* (Baltimore: Johns Hopkins University Press, 1970);

Robert S. Hirschfield, ed., *The Power of the Presidency*, 2d ed. (Chicago: Aldine, 1973);

Erwin C. Hargrove, *The Power of the Modern Presidency* (New York: Knopf, 1974);

Harold H. Bruff, Presidential power and administrative rulemaking, *Yale Law Journal* 88 (January 1979);

Richard Loss, Presidential power: The founders' intention as a problem of knowledge, *Presidential Studies Quarterly* 9 (Fall 1979);

George C. Edwards III, *Presidential Influence in Congress* (San Francisco: Freeman, 1980);

Bert A. Rockman, *The Leadership Question: The President and the American System* (New York: Praeger, 1984);

Theodore J. Lowi, Presidential power: Restoring the balance, *Political Science Quarterly* 100 (Summer 1985);

Louis Fisher, *The Politics of Shared Power: Congress and the Executive,* 2d ed. (Washington, D.C.: Congressional Quarterly, 1987);

Harry A. Bailey, Jr., and Jay M. Shafritz, eds., *The American Presidency: Historical and Contemporary Perspectives* (Chicago: Dorsey, 1988).

Alexander Hamilton on Presidential Power

There is an idea, which is not without its advocates, that a vigorous executive is inconsistent with the genius of republican government. The enlightened well-wishers to this species of government must at least hope that the supposition is destitute of foundation; since they can never admit its truth, without at the same time admitting the condemnation of their own principles. Energy in the executive is a leading character in the definition of good government. It is essential to the protection of the community against foreign attacks; it is not less essential to the steady administration of the laws; to the protection of property against those irregular and high-handed combinations which sometimes interrupt the ordinary course of justice; to the security of liberty against the enterprises and assaults of ambition, of faction, and of anarchy. . . .

A feeble executive implies a feeble execution of the government. A feeble execution is but another phrase for a bad execution; and a government ill executed, whatever it may be in theory, must be in practice, a bad government.

Taking it for granted, therefore, that all men of sense will agree in the necessity of an energetic executive, it will only remain to inquire, what are the ingredients which constitute energy? How far can they be combined with

> those other ingredients which constitute safety in the republican sense? And how far does this combination characterize the plan which has been reported by the convention?
>
> The ingredients which constitute energy in the executive are unity; duration; and adequate provision for its support; and competent powers.
>
> Source: Federalist 70

presidential press conference A formal meeting between a president and groups of representatives of the press. Prior to William McKinley, presidents met with individual reporters as they chose, or responded to pursuit. McKinley held the first group press meeting, and his successor, Theodore Roosevelt, used both individual and group meetings. By the 1920s, it was the custom for presidents to hold sporadic meetings with groups of reporters, using various methods of controlling the exchanges. Some presidents required that questions be submitted in advance; Herbert Hoover established the practice of distinguishing between what could or could not be quoted.

But the modern press conference began with Franklin D. Roosevelt, who, in his first one, established three classes of information: statements that could be directly quoted, statements that could be used for background but not directly attributed to him, and statements that were strictly off the record. Since none of the transcripts of the conferences were ever published, and since the president retained the power to exclude reporters from meetings, his control over the process was absolute. Roosevelt established regular meetings, and Harry S Truman continued the process; but only in the last year of the Truman administration were edited transcripts available for publication. Dwight D. Eisenhower, although under pressure to open press conferences to live television, insisted on allowing only edited films and radio transcripts, a fact that gave print news media and radio a distinct advantage over television news coverage, then in its infancy. His reason for exercising such control was the possibility that accidental statements could endanger national policy. John F. Kennedy's 1961 decision to move to live press conferences was a revolution in modern communications history and in the character not only of news confer-

ences but television news in general. Television made all public figures immediately quotable and without the protective controls their predecessors had enjoyed.

Since President Kennedy owed his election in large measure to his performance on televised debates with his opponent (Richard M. Nixon), he had no fear of using this medium to consolidate and extend his political support from the public. All presidents since Kennedy have used televised press conferences as part of an overall program of NEWS MANAGEMENT. By tradition, the first two reporters recognized at a presidential news conference are the representatives of the two major wire services, the Associated Press and United Press International.

REFERENCES

Jarol B. Manheim, The honeymoon's over: The news conference and the development of presidential style, *Journal of Politics* 41 (February 1979);

Jarol B. Manheim and William W. Lammers, The news conference and presidential leadership of public opinion: Does the tail wag the dog? *Presidential Studies Quarterly* 11 (Spring 1981);

William W. Lammers, Presidential press-conference schedules: Who hides, and when? *Political Science Quarterly* 96 (Summer 1981);

Jill McMillan and Sandra Ragan, The presidential press conference: A study in escalating institutionalism, *Presidential Studies Quarterly* 13 (Spring 1983).

presidential primary See PRIMARY, PRESIDENTIAL.

Presidential Studies Quarterly A scholarly journal published since 1972 that offers a historic, present, and projective view of the American presidency. It is published by the Center for the Study of the Presidency. Library of Congress no. JK501 .C44.

Presidential Studies Quarterly
208 East 75th Street
New York, NY 10021

presidential succession The order of successors to the U.S. presidency. Under Article II, Section 1, of the U.S. Constitution, the vice president exercises the power and duties of the president in the event of the president's death, resignation, disability, or removal from office. The Twenty-fifth Amendment, ratified by the required three-fourths of the states on February 10, 1967, provides (1) that a vice president who succeeds a president acquires all powers of the office; (2) that when the vice presidency is vacant, the president shall nominate a vice president who shall take office when confirmed by a majority vote of both houses of the Congress; (3) that when the president informs the Congress in writing that he is unable to discharge his duties and until he informs the Congress in writing otherwise, the vice president shall be the acting president; and (4) a procedure by which the Congress would settle disputes between a vice president and a president as to the latter's ability to discharge the powers and duties of his office.

Two vice presidents have been appointed under the provisions of the Twenty-fifth Amendment: Gerald R. Ford, installed on December 8, 1973 (to succeed Spiro T. Agnew), and Nelson A. Rockefeller, installed on December 16, 1974 (to succeed Gerald Ford, who had succeeded to the presidency with the resignation of President Richard M. Nixon on August 9, 1974). Nixon was the first president in history to resign from the presidency and Ford was the first to succeed to that office without being elected by the people. Prior to the Truman administration, the secretary of State was designated to become president if both a president and vice president vacated their offices. But the Presidential Succession Act of 1947 arranged for elected officials—first the Speaker of the House of Representatives, and then the Senate president pro tempore—to take over the office before unelected cabinet members.

REFERENCE

Arthur M. Schlesinger, Jr., On the presidential succession, *Political Science Quarterly* 89 (Fall 1974).

Line of Succession to the Presidency of the United States

1. Vice president.
2. Speaker of the House of Representatives.
3. Senate president pro tempore.
4. Secretary of State.
5. Secretary of the Treasury.
6. Secretary of Defense.
7. Attorney general.
8. Secretary of the Interior.
9. Secretary of Agriculture.
10. Secretary of Commerce.
11. Secretary of Labor.
12. Secretary of Health and Human Services.
13. Secretary of Housing and Urban Development.
14. Secretary of Transportation.
15. Secretary of Energy.
16. Secretary of Education.

---

presidential timber A potential president; someone who has the stuff out of which presidents are made; one who has enough political appeal to possibly get elected president. In a 1985 interview, Governor Richard Lamm of Colorado responded to suggestions that he might be presidential timber by saying: "Sure, I think I'm presidential timber. . . . The absurdity of that is that the average city councilman in Glendale also thinks he's presidential timber."

presidential transition The time between the election of a new U.S. president and his inauguration. Unless the incumbent is re-elected, there is always an element of tension and strain between the incoming and outgoing presidents, especially if they are from different parties and have been political opponents. The period of presidential transition was originally from the November election to March 4. But the Twentieth Amendment, the so-called LAME DUCK AMENDMENT, provided for a shorter transition. Now a new president is inaugurated on January 20.

REFERENCES

Laurin L. Henry, *Presidential Transitions* (Washington, D.C.: Brookings, 1960);

Carl M. Brauer, *Presidential Transitions: Eisenhower through Reagan* (New York: Oxford University Press, 1986);

James P. Pfiffner, *The Strategic Presidency: Hitting the Ground Running* (Chicago, IL: Dorsey, 1988).

President, Making of the See MAKING OF THE PRESIDENT.

president of the Senate The presiding officer of the U.S. Senate, normally the vice president of the United States. In his absence, a president pro tempore (president for the time being) presides. Normally, the vice president presides over the Senate only if an upcoming vote is expected to be close, because the U.S. Constitution (Article I, Section 3) provides that the vice president can vote only in the event of a tie.

president pro tempore The chief officer of the U.S. Senate in the absence of the vice president. The recent practice has been to elect to the office the Senator of the majority party with longest continuous service. In 1987, this was Senator John C. Stennis (1901–) of Mississippi, who first came to the Senate in 1947.

President's Committee on Administrative Management *See* BROWNLOW COMMITTEE/ PRESIDENT'S COMMITTEE ON ADMINISTRATIVE MANAGEMENT.

president, sitting The president currently in office; the incumbent president. A king sat on the throne, the symbol of power. By analogy, a president or any executive still in power is sitting on a figurative throne.

presiding officer 1 Any member of the U.S. Senate designated by the president pro tempore to preside during Senate sessions. Usually, only senators from the majority party preside, normally for one hour at a time. 2 Any formal chair of a meeting.

pressure group 1 Any organized group that seeks to influence the policies and practices of government. The difference between a pressure group and a lobby is that a pressure group is a large, often amorphous group that seeks to influence citizens as well as the political system; lobbyists are relatively small groups that seek to influence specific policies of government. Pressure groups are usually composed of committed amateurs. Lobbyists (usually full-time professional entreators) are often hired by pressure groups to help make their pressure more effective. 2 A less-than-kind way of referring to legitimate lobbying organizations. *Compare to* LOBBY.

REFERENCES
Norman Ornstein and Shirley Elder, *Interest Groups, Lobbying and Policymaking* (Washington, D.C.: Congressional Quarterly, 1978);
Kay Lehman Schlozman and John T. Tierney, More of the same: Washington pressure group activity in a decade of change, *Journal of Politics* 45 (May 1983).

pretrial detention The holding in custody, pending a trial, of someone suspected of committing a crime because there is evidence that the person meets specific conditions for the denial of bail.
REFERENCE
John S. Goldkamp, Questioning the practice of pretrial detention: Some empirical evidence from Philadelphia, *Journal of Criminal Law & Criminology* 74 (Winter 1983).

preventive detention Legally holding a person against his or her will because it is suspected that the person might commit a crime if allowed to go free. The Bail Reform Act of 1984, which permits preventive detention for those suspected of having committed a federal crime who might endanger the "safety of any other person and the community," was upheld by the U.S. Supreme Court in *United States v Salerno*, 95 L.Ed. 2d 697 (1987).
REFERENCES
J. Patrick Hickey, Preventive detention and the crime of being dangerous, *Georgetown Law Journal* 58 (November 1969);
Edward J. Shaughnessy, *Bail and Preventive Detention in New York* (Lanham, MD: University Press of America, 1982).

previous question An issue before the U.S. House of Representatives for a vote but superseded by another issue for the attention of the chamber. A motion for the previous question, when carried, has the effect of cutting off all debate and forcing a vote on the subject originally at hand. If, however, the previous question is moved and carried before there has been any debate on the subject at hand and the subject is debatable, then forty minutes of debate is allowed before the vote. The previous question is sometimes moved to prevent amendments from being introduced and voted on. The motion for the previous question is a debate-limiting device and is not allowed in the Senate.

Price, Don K. (1910–   ) A pioneering analyst of science policy and the first to assert that decisional authority inexorably flowed from executive to technical offices. Consequently, a major distinction had to be made between the legal authority to make a policy decision and the technical ability to make the same decision.

REFERENCES

Price's major works include *Government and Science* (New York: New York University Press, 1954);

The Scientific Estate (Cambridge, MA: Belknap Press of Harvard University Press, 1965).

price support *See* PARITY, FARM.

primary An election held before a general election to nominate a political party's candidates for office. In some states, other officials, such as delegates to party conventions, are also elected at this time. Primaries developed during the early twentieth century as part of the reform agenda of the progressive movement. It was argued that leaving the nomination process to the political party bosses was inherently undemocratic, that real democracy was possible only with rank-and-file participation, especially since nominations in jurisdictions where one party was dominant were often tantamount to election. Dates for primaries are set by the states and vary considerably. In some states, a separate primary is held by each of the principal parties. A major criticism of primaries is that those who vote in them tend to be unrepresentative not only of the general public but even of their party.

REFERENCES

For evidence of this, see J. Austin Ranney, The representativeness of primary electorates, *Midwest Journal of Political Science* 12 (1968);

Andrew J. DiNitto and William Smithers, The Representativeness of the direct primary: A further test of V. O. Key's thesis, *Polity* 5 (Winter 1972);

Bruce W. Robeck, The representativeness of congressional primary voters, *Congress and the Presidency: A Journal of Capital Studies* 11 (Spring 1984).

Types of Primaries, by State and Region

Northeast
- Connecticut, closed
- Delaware, closed
- Maine, closed
- Maryland, closed
- Massachusetts, closed
- New Hampshire, closed
- New Jersey, closed
- New York, closed
- Pennsylvania, closed

- Rhode Island, open*
- Vermont, open

Midwest
- Iowa, closed
- Kansas, closed
- Nebraska, closed
- Ohio, closed
- South Dakota, closed

- Illinois, open*
- Indiana, open*
- Michigan, open
- Minnesota, open
- North Dakota, open
- Wisconsin, open

Border
- Kentucky, closed
- Oklahoma, closed
- West Virginia, closed

- Missouri, open*

South
- Florida, closed
- North Carolina, closed

- Alabama, open*
- Arkansas, open*
- Georgia, open*
- Mississippi, open*
- South Carolina, open*
- Tennessee, open*
- Texas, open*
- Virginia, open*

- Louisiana, nonpartisan

West
- Arizona, closed
- California, closed
- Colorado, closed
- Nevada, closed
- New Mexico, closed
- Oregon, closed
- Wyoming, closed

- Hawaii, open
- Idaho, open
- Montana, open
- Utah, open

- Alaska, open-blanket
- Washington, open-blanket

*Voter must indicate party affiliation.

Source: Malcolm E. Jewell and David M. Olson, *American State Political Parties and Elections*, rev. ed. (Chicago: Dorsey, 1982), p. 110.

primary, advisory   A primary election that is not binding but is merely indicative of the voter's preferences.

primary, beauty contest   A presidential primary election in which voters elect a favored candidate in party caucuses and county and state conventions but do not elect national delegates. Michigan has a beauty contest primary.

primary, blanket   A primary election that allows voters to participate in the nominations of candidates from multiple parties on the same day by voting for a gubernatorial candidate of one party, a senatorial candidate from another party, a mayoral candidate from a third, and so on. Alaska and Washington state have blanket primaries.

primary, closed   A primary election in which a voter must declare (or have previously declared) a political party affiliation and vote only that party's ballot in the primary election. *Compare to* PRIMARY, OPEN.
REFERENCE
Steven H. Haeberle, Closed primaries and party support in Congress, *American Politics Quarterly* 13 (July 1985).

primary, contested   A primary election in which a candidate has some competition. An uncontested primary, in contrast, presents no competition to the candidate. Many political figures of both major parties, especially in legislative offices, are so entrenched with their party and constituents that it would be futile for another member of the same party to challenge them; so they run uncontested.
REFERENCE
Harvey L. Schantz, Contested and uncontested primaries for the U.S. House, *Legis-*

lative Studies Quarterly 5 (November 1980).

primary, direct   A primary election in which political party nominees are selected directly by the voters.

primary, divisive   A primary so hard-fought by the various party factions that it is difficult, if not impossible, to later create the PARTY UNITY needed for victory in the general election.
REFERENCES
Andrew Hacker, Does a "divisive" primary harm a candidate's election chances? *American Political Science Review* 59 (March 1965);
James E. Piereson and T. Smith, Primary divisiveness and general election success; A re-examination, *Journal of Politics* 37 (May 1975).

primary election   *See* PRIMARY.

primary, New Hampshire   Historically, the first primary election in the presidential election year and, consequently, a critically important one for generating the political and financial support that will allow candidates to continue. *Compare to* IOWA CAUCUS.
REFERENCE
Stuart Sprague, The New Hampshire primary, *Presidential Studies Quarterly* 14 (Winter 1984).

primary, nonpartisan   A primary election in which voters and candidates from all parties use a single ballot. This is common in judicial elections and in certain local elections. Runoff elections are often required if no candidate wins a majority of the vote. Louisiana is the only state with nonpartisan primaries for statewide and congressional offices.

primary, open   A primary election in which a voter may vote for the nomination of any of the candidates regardless of his or her political party affiliation. Open primaries often lead to strategic voting, where voters cross over to vote for the weaker opposition candidate.
REFERENCES
Ronald D. Hedlund, Meredith W. Watts, and David M. Hedge, Voting in an open pri-

mary, *American Politics Quarterly* 10 (April 1982);

Ronald D. Hedlund and Meredith W. Watts, The Wisconsin open primary: 1968–1984, *American Politics Quarterly* 14 (January–April 1986).

primary, preference A primary election in which the voters indicate their preference for particular candidates. Such indications may or may not be binding upon the states' delegates to the party's national convention. Some states automatically enter in their presidential preference primaries all candidates being seriously mentioned in the press. It then becomes the obligation of noncandidates to withdraw their names. No candidate's name stays on the ballot if he or she formally asks that it be withdrawn.

REFERENCE

Robert F. Sittig, Presidential preference primaries: The effect of automatic entry, *National Civic Review* 64 (June 1975).

primary, presidential The statewide elections that allow rank-and-file political party members to select (or to indicate preference for) delegates to their party's national nominating convention. Delegates may or may not be legally bound to support the candidate who wins the primary. Some delegates run already pledged to certain candidates, some run uncommitted. In 1984, about as many states used caucuses as used primaries. The primary game from the point of view of the candidate is to win so many delegates along the primary campaign trail that uncommitted delegates increasingly climb on the bandwagon as convention time approaches. The modern criteria for winning a primary is not that a candidate gain the most votes but that he or she does better than expected. Thus a dark horse can win even if he or she loses. And a front runner who literally wins the primary may lose if the win is not as big as expected.

REFERENCES

J. David Gopoian, Issue preferences and candidate choice in presidential primaries, *American Journal of Political Science* 26 (August 1982);

Tom W. Rice, The determinants of candidate spending in presidential primaries: Advice

for the states, *Presidential Studies Quarterly* 12 (Fall 1982);

Jack Moran and Mark Fenster, Voter turnout in presidential primaries: A diachronic analysis, *American Politics Quarterly* 10 (October 1982);

Barbara Norrander, Selective participation: Presidential primary voters as a subset of general election voters, *American Politics Quarterly* 14 (January–April 1986).

For the parallel process for the office of state governor, see Patrick J. Kenney, Explaining turnout in gubernatorial primaries, *American Politics Quarterly* 11 (July 1983);

Malcolm E. Jewell, Political money and gubernatorial primaries, *State Government* 56:2 (1983).

primary, regional A presidential primary in which all of the states in a region have primary elections on the same day. Although there are no formal regional primaries, whenever many states in a region have primaries on the same day it is, in effect, a regional primary. Many political analysts are against it, because it would give the winner too great of an advantage too early in the game; others are in favor of it for the same reason.

REFERENCE

Myron A. Levine, The case against regional primaries, *Presidential Studies Quarterly* 7 (Winter 1977).

primary, uncontested *See* PRIMARY, CONTESTED.

primary, white A primary election in which black participation was forbidden or discouraged. White primaries were common in the early part of the twentieth century in the South. The U.S. Supreme Court ruled that white primaries were illegal in *Smith v Allwright*, 321 U.S. 649 (1944).

prior restraint The power (which has usually been denied by the U.S. Supreme Court to the federal government) to prevent the publication of something or to require approval prior to publication. Generally speaking, any government effort to constrain any kind of freedom of expression is prior restraint and is prohibited

443

under the First Amendment. The major exception has been obscenity cases, but even there, according to the Supreme Court in *Organization for a Better Austin v Keefe,* 402 U.S. 415 (1971), the "government carries a heavy burden of showing justification for the imposition of such a restraint." *Compare to* FREE PRESS CLAUSE; PENTAGON PAPERS.

REFERENCES

Vincent Blasi, Toward a theory of prior restraint: The central linkage, *Minnesota Law Review* 66 (November 1981);

William T. Mayton, Toward a theory of First Amendment process: Injunctions of speech, subsequent punishment, and the costs of the prior restraint doctrine, *Cornell Law Review* 67 (January 1982);

John Calvin Jeffries, Jr., Rethinking prior restraint, *Yale Law Journal* 92 (January 1983).

For a comparative perspective, see Evan J. Wallach, Executive powers of prior restraint over publication of national security information: The UK and the U.S.A. compared, *International Comparative Law Quarterly* 32 (April 1983).

Privacy Act of 1974   The federal statute that reasserts the fundamental right to privacy as derived from the Constitution of the United States and that provides a series of basic safeguards for the individual to prevent the misuse of personal information by the federal government. The act provides for making known to the public the existence and characteristics of all personal information systems kept by every federal agency. It permits a person access to records containing personal information on him or her and allows the person control of the transfer of that information to other federal agencies for nonroutine uses. The act also requires all federal agencies to keep accurate accountings of transfers of personal records to other agencies and outsiders, and to make the accountings available to the individual. It further provides for civil remedies for the person whose records are kept or used in contravention of the requirements of the act.

Virtually all agencies of the federal government have issued regulations implementing the Privacy Act. These regulations generally inform the public how to determine if a system of records contains information on themselves, how to gain access to such records, how to request amendment of such records, and how to appeal an adverse agency determination on such a request. *See also* FREEDOM OF INFORMATION ACT OF 1966.

REFERENCES

Hugh V. O'Neill, The Privacy Act of 1974: Introduction and overview, *Bureaucrat* 5 (July 1976);

Freedom of Information Guide: Citizen's Guide to the Use of the Freedom of Information and Privacy Acts (Washington, D.C.: Want, 1982);

John F. Joyce, The Privacy act: A sword and a shield but sometimes neither, *Military Law Review* 99 (Winter 1982).

private bill   *See* BILL, PRIVATE.

private calendar   *See* CALENDAR, PRIVATE.

private law   A statute passed to affect only one person or group, in contrast to a public law.

private regardingness   An attitude on the part of some citizens that places their personal short-term benefit over the welfare of the community as a whole. *Compare to* PUBLIC REGARDINGNESS.

privatization   The process of returning to the private sector property (such as public lands) or functions (such as trash collection, fire protection) previously owned or performed by government. The Ronald Reagan administration and conservative Republicans in general tend to be in favor of privatizing those government functions that can be performed (in their opinion) less expensively or more efficiently by the private sector. In this context, privatization and reprivatization tend to be used interchangeably. Some extreme advocates of a wholesale privatization of government functions would even return social security, education, and public health to the private sector.

REFERENCES

Steve H. Hanke, The privatization debate: An insider's view, *Cato Journal* 2 (Winter 1982);

E. S. Savas, *Privatizing the Public Sector* (Chatham, NJ: Chatham, 1982);

David Heald, Will the privatization of public enterprises solve the problem of control? *Public Administration* 63 (Spring 1985);

Steve H. Hanke, Privatization: Theory, evidence, and implementation, *Proceedings of the Academy of Political Science* 35:4 (1985).

privatization of conflict E. E. Schattschneider's concept from *The Semi-Sovereign People* (New York: Holt, Rinehart & Winston, 1960) that there exists "a whole battery of ideas calculated to restrict the scope of conflict or even to keep it entirely out of the public domain." Consequently, "a tremendous amount of conflict is controlled by keeping it so private that it is almost completely invisible." This is in contrast to the socialization of conflict, Schattschneider's definition of POLITICS.

privilege 1 An advantage that a person or group has that others do not. 2 An exemption from a duty or obligation that others have. For example, attorneys often have the privilege of being exempt from jury duty. 3 The opportunity to make otherwise defamatory statements. For example, a senator cannot be held accountable in court for anything said on the floor of the Senate. Such remarks, no matter how scurrilous, are privileged. But the same thing said in another forum can bring a lawsuit for SLANDER. For example, when a senator read the still secret Pentagon Papers into the *Congressional Record,* the Supreme Court held that this was privileged speech in *Gravel v United States*, 408 U.S. 606 (1972). However, the Court held that a senator could be sued for statements made in a press release, because it does not represent speech on the floor of the Senate. See *Hutchinson v Proxmire*, 443 U.S. 111 (1979). 4 A basic right or implied set of rights. For example, the privilege of U.S. citizenship. 5 The obligation to withhold information. For example lawyers, priests, and physicians cannot be forced to divulge confidential discussions with clients, parishioners, and patients. *Compare to* EXECUTIVE PRIVILEGE. 6 Rights of members of the Congress as to the relative priority of the motions

and actions they may make in their respective chambers. Privileged questions concern legislative business. Questions of privilege concern legislators themselves (see PRIVILEGE, QUESTIONS OF).

privileged communication Information that a court cannot require disclosures of in evidence. Examples generally include (but may vary with local laws): communications between husbands and wives; physicians', psychologists', and lawyers' communications with their clients; and journalists' communications with their sources (*see* SHIELD LAWS). *Compare to* EXECUTIVE PRIVILEGE.

privileged questions Concerning the order in which bills, motions, and other legislative measures may be considered by the Congress. This order is governed by strict priorities. For instance, a motion to recommit can be superseded by a motion to table, and a vote would be forced on the latter motion only. A motion to adjourn, however, takes precedence over this one, and is thus considered of the highest privilege.

privilege, questions of Matters affecting members of the Congress individually or collectively. Questions affecting the rights, safety, dignity, and integrity of proceedings of the House of Representatives or of the Senate as a whole are questions of privilege of the House or Senate. Questions of personal privilege relate to individual members of the Congress. A member's rising to a question of personal privilege is given precedence over almost all other proceedings. An annotation in the House rules points out that the privilege of the member rests primarily on the Constitution, which gives him or her a conditional immunity from arrest and an unconditional freedom to speak in the House.

privileges and immunities clause 1 Article IV, Section 2, of the U.S. Constitution, which holds that "the citizens of each state shall be entitled to all privileges and immunities of citizens in the several states." This ensures that U.S. citizens from out of state have the same legal rights as local citizens in any state. 2 That portion of the Fourteenth Amendment that provides that "no state shall make or enforce any law which shall abridge the privileges and immunities of citizens of the United States." This was enacted in response to the BLACK CODES of some post-Civil War southern states, which denied blacks the same citizenship rights as whites. *See* HICKLIN V ORBECK; SLAUGHTER-HOUSE CASES.

probable cause A set of facts and circumstances that would induce a reasonably intelligent and prudent person to believe a particular person had committed a specific crime; reasonable grounds to make or believe an accusation. Probable cause is required to justify arrest and the beginning of prosecution. The U.S. Supreme Court established the criteria for probable cause in *Draper v United States*, 385 U.S. 307 (1959).

probate 1 The process of proving that a will is genuine and then distributing the property of an estate.   2 In some states, the name for a court that handles the distribution of decedents' estates (dead persons' property) and other matters.

probation 1 The freedom granted to a convicted offender as long as he or she meets certain conditions of behavior. Conditions typically include maintaining regular employment, abstaining from drugs and alcohol, and not associating with known offenders. Not committing another offense is always a condition of probation. *Compare to* PAROLE.   2 A period of service in a job during which the probationer is expected to prove his or her abilities to justify continued employment. Most civilian positions in government have mandatory probation periods. During this time, the employee usually has no seniority rights and may be discharged without CAUSE, as long as such a discharge does not violate laws concerning union membership and equal employment opportunity.

REFERENCES
1   Howard Abadivsky, *Probation and Parole: Theory and Practice* (Englewood Cliffs, NJ: Prentice-Hall, 1982);
Paul F. Cromwell, Jr., *Probation and Parole in the Criminal Justice System*, 2d ed. (St. Paul: West, 1985).

pro bono publico A Latin phrase meaning for the public good. Often abbreviated to pro bono, it usually stands for work done by lawyers without pay for some charitable or public purpose.

procedural rights The various DUE PROCESS protections that all citizens have against arbitrary actions by public officials.

Pro-choice groups are committed to electing politicians who support a woman's right to reproductive freedom.

pro choice A policy position of those who are not necessarily in favor of abortion but who are in favor of allowing each woman to decide the question for herself. *Compare to* PRO LIFE.
REFERENCE
William J. Voegeli, Jr., A critique of the pro-choice argument, *Review of Politics* 43 (October 1981).

proconsul 1 A governor of an ancient Roman province.   2 The highest administrator of a colonial or occupying power. The last American proconsuls, in effect if not in name, were General Douglas MacArthur (1880–1964) in postwar Japan and the U.S. High Commissioners in postwar Germany.
REFERENCE
2   Robert Wolfe, ed., *Americans as Proconsuls: United States Military Government in Germany and Japan, 1944–1952* (Carbondale: Southern Illinois University Press, 1984).

pro forma A Latin phrase meaning as a matter of form or a mere formality. The phrase applies to requirements or agreements that are presumed to have no real effect on behavior.

program 1 A major organizational, mission-oriented, endeavor that fulfills statutory or executive requirements and is defined in terms of the principal actions required to achieve a significant objective. A program is an organized set of activities designed to produce a particular result or a set of results that will have a certain impact upon a problem. 2 An announced plan of action that suggests an approach to a problem or that differentiates one political candidate from another.

progressive movement/progressive era A designation applied to the American experience with the consequences of urbanization and industrialization that affected Western society in the decades between 1890 and 1920. While the term has its origins in religious concepts that argued for the infinite improvability of the human condition, rather than ordained class distinctions, by the end of the nineteenth century it had come to mean a responsibility of classes for one another and a willingness to use all government and social institutions to give that responsibility legal effect. In the United States, the movement was associated with two extremes: the search for greater democratic participation by the individual in government, and the application of science and specialized knowledge and skills to the improvement of life.

Politically, the movement reached its national climax in 1911, with the creation of the Progressive party as a break between the Republican party professionals, who backed the incumbent, William Howard Taft, and the Republican opponents of machine politics and party regularity, who nominated former Republican president, Theodore Roosevelt. The split in the Republican party caused the Democratic candidate, Woodrow Wilson, to be elected. Wilson in fact represented many of the programs the Progressives had supported (banking reforms, antitrust laws, and business regulation), but he did not support many of the Progressive interests in national social policy. The New Deal inherited many of these latter concerns.

The progressives got their name from the fact that they believed in the doctrine of progress—that governing institutions could be im-

proved by bringing science to bear on public problems. It was a disparate movement, with each reform group targeting a level of government, a particular policy, and so on. Common beliefs included that good government was possible and that "the cure for democracy is *more* democracy." And to achieve this, they only had to "throw the rascals out." At the national level, they achieved civil service reform; at the state level, they introduced the direct primary, the initiative, the referendum, and the recall; at the local level, they spawned the commission and council-manager forms of government. And it was the progressive influence that initially forged the fledgling discipline of public administration. *See also* CIVIL SERVICE REFORM.

REFERENCES

Robert H. Wiebe, *Businessmen and Reform: A Study of the Progressive Movement* (Cambridge, MA: Harvard University Press, 1962);

Richard Hofstadter, *The Progressive Movement, 1900–1915* (Englewood Cliffs, NJ: Prentice-Hall, 1963);

John D. Buenker, *Urban Liberalism and Progressive Reform* (New York: Scribner, 1973);

Richard M. Bernard and Bradley R. Rice, Political environment and the adoption of progressive municipal reform, *Journal of Urban History* 1 (February 1975);

Martin J. Schiesl, *The Politics of Municipal Reform: Municipal Administration and Reform in America 1880–1920* (Berkeley and Los Angeles: University of California Press, 1977);

Robert M. Crunden, *Ministers of Reform: The Progressives' Achievement in American Civilization, 1889–1920* (New York: Basic Books, 1982);

Martin Shefter, Regional receptivity to reform: The legacy of the progressive era, *Political Science Quarterly* 98 (Fall 1983).

progressive tax *See* TAXATION, PROGRESSIVE.

prohibition 1 Legally forbidding the manufacture, transportation, sale, or possession of alcoholic beverages. 2 The specific period in American history when prohibition (as above)

Prohibition officials discovered this alcohol still mounted on an old car in an alley in Washington, D.C., 1922.

was national policy. It was enacted by the Eighteenth Amendment in 1919. But the "noble experiment" aroused such public protest and was so unenforceable that it was ended with the Twenty-first Amendment in 1933.

REFERENCES

John Kobler, *Ardent Spirits: The Rise and Fall of Prohibition* (New York: Putnam, 1973);

Norman H. Clark, *Deliver Us From Evil: An Interpretation of American Prohibition* (New York: Norton, 1976);

Sean Dennis Cashman, *Prohibition: The Lie of the Land* (New York: Free Press, 1981).

proletariat   In ancient Rome, those members of society who were so poor that they could contribute nothing to the state but their offspring. In the nineteenth century, Karl Marx (*see* MARXISM) used it to refer to the working class in general. Because of the word's political taint, it should not be used to refer simply to workers, but only to "oppressed" workers.

pro life   A policy position of those opposed to abortion, opposed to the U.S. Supreme Court's decision in ROE V WADE, and opposed to giving any woman the option of abortion. *Compare to* PRO CHOICE.

REFERENCE

Shane Andre, Pro-life or pro-choice: Is there a credible alternative? *Social Theory and Practice* 12 (Summer 1986).

proliferation   The spread of nuclear weapons to countries who did not previously possess them. The more countries that have nuclear weapons, the more likely it is that one will go off by accident—or on purpose.

REFERENCES

Leonard S. Spector, Nuclear proliferation: The pace quickens, *Bulletin of the Atomic Scientists* 41 (January 1985);

Bruce D. Berkowitz, Proliferation, deterrence, and the likelihood of nuclear war, *Journal of Conflict Resolution* 29 (March 1985).

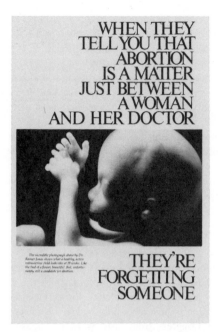

WHEN THEY
TELL YOU THAT
ABORTION
IS A MATTER
JUST BETWEEN
A WOMAN
AND HER DOCTOR

THEY'RE
FORGETTING
SOMEONE

This poster typifies a leading argument of pro-life advocates.

propaganda **1** A government's mass dissemination of true information about its policies and the policies of its adversaries. **2** Similar dissemination that is untruthful (sometimes called black propaganda). The concept was introduced into American political science after World War I when British news reports of German atrocities (both real and imagined) were indicted as having influenced American attitudes toward entry into the war. This fostered HAROLD D. LASSWELL's landmark analysis *Propaganda Technique in World War I* (Cambridge, MA: MIT Press, 1927, 1971). Ever since World War II, when the German Ministry of Propaganda broadcast one lie after another, the term has taken on a sinister connotation. **3** The manipulation of people's beliefs, values, and behavior by using symbols (such as flags, music, or oratory) and other psychological tools. **4** According to Sir Ian Hamilton, *The Soul and Body of an Army* (London: Edward Arnold, 1921), making the "enemy appear so great a monster that he forfeits the rights of a human being." This makes it emotionally easier to kill him. Hamilton further observes that

since the enemy cannot bring a libel action, "there is no need to stick at trifles."

REFERENCES

Jacques Ellul, *Propaganda: The Formation of Men's Attitudes* (New York: Knopf, 1965);

Richard W. Steele, Preparing the public for war: Efforts to establish a national propaganda agency, 1940–41, *American Historical Review* 75:6 (1970);

John B. Whitton, Hostile international propaganda and international law, *Annals of the American Academy of Political and Social Science* 398 (November 1971);

Jon T. Powell, Towards a negotiable definition of propaganda for international agreements related to direct broadcast satellites, *Law and Contemporary Problems* 45 (Winter 1982);

John Spicer Nichols, Wasting the propaganda dollar, *Foreign Policy* 56 (Fall 1984).

property tax *See* TAX, REAL-PROPERTY.

proportional representation An electoral system policy of allocating seats in a legislature or national nominating convention to the various interests, minorities, and parties in proportion to their strength in the electorate. Thus a group that is 10 percent of the electorate would be entitled to 10 percent of the legislative seats. Proportional representation systems require complicated voting practices (such as the Hare system) and are not widely used in the United States.

REFERENCES

Paul T. David and James W. Ceaser, *Proportional Representation in Presidential Nominating Politics* (Charleston: University of Virginia Press, 1980);

Robert Sugden, Free association and the theory of proportional representation, *American Political Science Review* 78 (March 1984);

Joseph Greenberg and Shlomo Weber, Multiparty equilibria under proportional representation, *American Political Science Review* 79 (September 1985).

Proposition 2$^1/_2$ A 1980 tax limitation measure approved by the voters of Massachusetts that requires local governments to lower property taxes by 15 percent a year until they reach $2^1/_2$ percent of fair market value.

REFERENCES

Sherry Tvedt, Enough is enough: Proposition $2^1/_2$ in Massachusetts, *National Civic Review* 70 (November 1981);

Lawrence Susskind and Cynthia Horan, Proposition $2^1/_2$: The response to tax restrictions in Massachusetts, *Proceedings of the Academy of Political Science* 35:1 (1983);

Helen F. Ladd and Julie Boatright Wilson, Who supports tax limitations: Evidence from Massachusetts' Proposition $2^1/_2$, *Journal of Policy Analysis and Management* 2 (Winter 1983).

Proposition 13/Jarvis-Gann Initiative A state constitutional amendment approved by California voters (it was put on the ballot as an initiative) in 1978 that rolled back and set ceilings on property taxes. Proposition 13 is an important landmark in a national tax-relief movement. *See also* TAX REVOLT.

REFERENCES

Jeffrey I. Chapman, *Proposition 13 and Land Use: A Case Study of Fiscal Limits in California* (Lexington, MA: Lexington Books, 1980);

Roger L. Kempt, *Coping with Proposition 13* (Lexington, MA: Lexington Books, 1980);

Terry Schwadron, ed., *California and the American Tax Revolt: Proposition 13 Five Years Later* (Berkeley and Los Angeles: University of California Press, 1984).

pro se A Latin term meaning in one's own behalf. Its expanded meanings are acting as one's own defense attorney in criminal proceedings; representing oneself.

prosecutor An attorney employed by a government agency whose official duty is to initiate and maintain criminal (and sometimes civil) proceedings on behalf of the government against people accused of committing criminal offenses. The prosecutor is the attorney acting on behalf of the government (the people) in a criminal case.

prosecutorial agency A federal, state, or local criminal justice agency of which the principal function is the prosecution of alleged offenders. Examples include the office of a local district attorney and the office of the U.S. attorney for a federal judicial district.

prosecutor, special A prosecutor appointed to consider the evidence in a case and, if necessary, to undertake the prosecution of a case that presents a possible conflict of interest for the jurisdiction's regular prosecutor. This usually happens in the federal government when someone who is or has been personally and professionally close to the U.S. attorney general must be investigated.

protectionism The use of government policy to determine the prices of foreign manufactured goods on domestic markets; a policy of high tariffs or low import quotas to protect domestic industries. Protectionism is the opposite of a free trade policy. Protectionist legislation is invariably proposed by members of the Congress from districts whose industries are adversely affected by foreign imports. Laid-off factory workers don't want to be talked to about the theoretical benefits of free trade; they want protectionist legislation that would put import duties on the foreign-made products that have cost them their jobs. *Compare to* FREE TRADE.

REFERENCES

Kenneth Durham, Protectionism and the financial structure of the world economy, *World Economy* 5 (December 1982);

Murray L. Weidenbaum, The high cost of protectionism, *Cato Journal* 3 (Winter 1983–84);

Lawrence A. Fox and Stephen Cooney, Protectionism returns, *Foreign Policy* 53 (Winter 1983–84);

Susan Strange, Protectionism and world politics, *International Organization* 39 (Spring 1985).

protocol 1 The generally accepted practices of international courtesy that have evolved over the centuries. 2 A supplementary international agreement or an annex to a treaty. 3 A preliminary draft of a treaty. 4 The conventions about computer software that allow different parts of a computer system and different computer systems to communicate.

proxy 1 A person authorized to request or fill out registration forms or to obtain an absentee ballot on behalf of another person. A proxy may not cast a ballot for another person. 2 A person who acts for another in a formal proceeding.

proxy war A war in which superpowers are involved on opposite sides as suppliers, supporters, and advisors to smaller states that are the actual combatants.
REFERENCE
Janice Gross Stein, Proxy wars—How superpowers end them: The diplomacy of war termination in the Middle East, *International Journal* 35 (Summer 1980).

PS See AMERICAN POLITICAL SCIENCE ASSOCIATION.

pseudoevent Historian Daniel J. Boorstin's (1914–) term for nonspontaneous, planted, or manufactured "news," whose main purpose is to gain publicity for the person or cause which arranged the "event." An orchestrated news LEAK and the releasing of TRIAL BALLOONS are typical pseudoevents. *Compare to* MEDIA EVENT.
REFERENCE
Daniel J. Boorstin, *The Image: A Guide to Pseudo-Events in America* (New York: Atheneum, 1961).

public administration 1 The executive function in government; the execution of public policy. 2 Organizing and managing people and other resources to achieve the goals of government. 3 The art and science of management applied to the public sector. Public administration is a broader term than public management, because it does not limit itself to management but incorporates all of the political, social, cultural, and legal environments that affect the managing of public institutions.
REFERENCES
Jay M. Shafritz, *The Facts on File Dictionary of Public Administration* (New York: Facts on File, 1985);
Jay M. Shafritz and Albert C. Hyde, eds., *Classics of Public Administration*, 2d ed. (Chicago: Dorsey, 1986);

Howard E. McCurdy, *Public Administration: A Bibliographic Guide to the Literature* (New York: Dekker, 1986).

Public Administration The leading British journal of public administration, sponsored by the Royal Institute of Public Administration; published since 1923. Library of Congress no. JA8 .P8.
Public Administration
Journals Department
Basil Blackwood
108 Cowley Road
Oxford OX4 1JF
England

Public Administration Review The leading American professional and scholarly journal on all aspects of managing public and nonprofit institutions; published by the American Society for Public Administration since 1940. Library of Congress no. JK1 .P85.
Public Administration Review
1120 G Street, N.W.
Washington, D.C. 20005

public affairs 1 Those aspects of corporate public relations that deal with political and social issues. 2 A more genteel-sounding name for a public relations department. 3 The totality of a government agency's public information and community relations activities. 4 An expansive view of the academic field of public administration. Accordingly, a graduate school of public affairs might include, in addition to degree programs in public administration, programs in police administration, urban studies, and so on.
REFERENCE
1 James E. Post, Edwin A. Murray, Jr., Robert B. Dickie, and John F. Mahon, Managing public affairs: The public affairs function, *California Management Review* 26 (Fall 1983).

public assistance Local government welfare programs. Such programs are a right, an entitlement, to those who meet specific criteria for the determination of need. They are often, as in the case of Aid to Families with Dependent Children and food stamps, heavily subsidized by the federal government. *Compare to* ENTI-TLEMENT PROGRAM.

REFERENCE

George Dellaportas, Effectiveness of public assistance payments (1970–1980) in reducing poverty reconsidered, *American Journal of Economics and Sociology* 45 (January 1986).

public bill *See* BILL, PUBLIC.

public broadcasting Nonprofit, noncommercial radio and television. The Public Broadcasting Act of 1967 amended the Communication Act of 1934 to create the Corporation for Public Broadcasting. This independent corporation has fifteen directors appointed by the president with the advice and consent of the Senate; no more than eight can be from the same party. Its purpose is to provide financial assistance and to arrange networks for educational programs. In 1970, it established the Public Broadcasting Service as a distribution channel for national public television programs. In 1971, it created National Public Radio for a parallel purpose. The Corporation for Public Broadcasting is funded annually by congressional appropriations.

REFERENCE

George H. Gibson, *Public Broadcasting: The Role of the Federal Government, 1912–1976* (New York: Praeger, 1977).

public choice economics An approach to public administration and politics based on microeconomic theory that views the citizen as a consumer of government goods and services. It would attempt to maximize administrative responsiveness to citizen demand by creating a market system for government activities in which public agencies would compete to provide citizens with goods and services. This might replace a portion of the current system, under which most administrative agencies in effect act as monopolies under the influence of organized pressure groups, which, the public choice economists argue, are institutionally incapable of representing the demands of individual citizens.

REFERENCES

Dennis C. Mueller, *Public Choice* (New York: Cambridge University Press, 1979);

Nicholas P. Lovrich and Max Neiman, *Public Choice Theory in Public Administration: An Annotated Bibliography* (New York: Garland, 1982);

Louis F. Weschler, Public choice: Methodological individualism in politics, *Public Administration Review* 42 (May/June 1982).

public defender An attorney employed by a government agency or subdivision whose official duty is to represent criminal defendants unable to hire private counsel.

public domain **1** Land owned by the government. **2** Any property right held in common by all citizens; for example, the content of U.S. government publications, expired copyrights, and expired patents. **3** The right of government to take property, with compensation, for a public purpose (*see* FIFTH AMENDMENT).

REFERENCES

1 Paul J. Culhane, *Public Lands Politics: Interest Groups Influence on the Forest Service and the Bureau of Land Management* (Baltimore: Johns Hopkins University Press, 1981).

2 David Lange, Recognizing the public domain, *Law and Contemporary Problems* 44 (Autumn 1981).

public employee Any person who works for a government agency. Public employees constitute the core of government in developed nations. They carry on the day-to-day business of government with expertise that is generally unavailable elsewhere in the society. Although many public service tasks are technical and highly structured, a substantial proportion of civil servants are inevitably engaged in making decisions that have an impact on public policy. For example, the use of affirmative action in the sense of quotas or goals has been an important political issue in the United States for almost two decades, yet it is a policy created by administrative fiat and has yet to be fully mandated either by legislation or executive order. The U.S. political system enhances the policymaking role of the public service in several ways. Elected officials often prefer to avoid making decisions on hotly contested political issues. In consequence, these matters are often thrust upon the judicial and administrative arms of government. And the Congress, recognizing both its own limitations and the expertise of career administrators, has in recent decades delegated authority in a vast array of policy areas to the bureaucracy.

Public Employees (in millions)

Government	1960	1984
Federal (civilian)	2,421	2,942
State	1,527	3,898
Local	4,860	9,595
Total	8,808	16,435

Source: *Statistical Abstract of the United States, 1986.*

public finance An imprecise term that refers to the totality (1) of the raising and spending of funds by governments and (2) of the management of government debt. *Compare to* FISCAL POLICY; MONETARY POLICY.

REFERENCES

Richard A. Musgrave and Peggy B. Musgrave, *Public Finance in Theory and Practice* (New York: McGraw-Hill, 1973);

Otto Eckstein, *Public Finance,* 4th ed. (Englewood Cliffs, NJ: Prentice-Hall, 1979);

Bernard P. Herber, *Modern Public Finance,* 5th ed. (Homewood, IL: Irwin, 1983).

public goods Commodities typically provided by government that cannot, or would not, be separately parceled out to individuals, since no one can be excluded from their benefits. Public goods, such as national defense, clean air, and public safety, are neither divisible nor exclusive. This definition applies only to pure public goods. Many goods supplied by governments (public housing, hospitals, and police protection) could be, and often are supplied privately.

REFERENCES

Mancur Olson, Jr., *The Logic of Collective Action: Public Goods and the Theory of Groups* (Cambridge, MA: Harvard University Press, 1965);

Joseph P. Kalt, Public goods and the theory of government, *Cato Journal* 1 (Fall 1981).

public hearing A meeting to receive public input—both informational and opinion—on a designated need, issue, problem, or pending policy or program. Public hearings are held by local, state, and national elected bodies (such as a U.S. Senate subcommittee or a board of county commissioners) and public agencies (e.g., the U.S. Environmental Protection Agency or a state highway department).

public interest A phrase used by those who seek to identify concerns generally considered to be private with concerns that are perceived to affect the public as a whole. This is the universal label in which political actors wrap the policies and programs that they advocate—but would any lobbyist, public manager, legislator, or chief executive ever propose a program that was not "in the public interest?" Because the public interest is generally taken to mean a commonly accepted good, the phrase is used both to further policies that are indeed for the common good and to obscure policies that may not be so commonly accepted as good. A considerable body of literature has developed about this phrase, because it represents an important philosophic point that, if found, could provide considerable guidance for politicians and public administrators alike.

REFERENCES

E. Pendleton Herring, *Public Administration and the Public Interest* (New York: Russell and Russell, 1936);

Glendon A. Schubert, *The Public Interest* (New York: Free Press, 1960);

Virginia Held, *The Public Interest and Individual Interests* (New York: Basic Books, 1970);

John Guinther, *Moralists and Managers: Public Interest Movements in America* (Garden City, NY: Anchor, 1976);

Barry M. Mitnick, A typology of conceptions of the public interest, *Administration & Society* 8 (May 1976);

A. W. McEachern and Jawad al-Arayed, Discerning the public interest, *Administration & Society* 15 (February 1984).

Public Interest The quarterly journal of public affairs that has been a major influence on

453

neoconservative thought; published since 1965. *See* NEOCONSERVATISM. Library of Congress no. H1 .P86.

Public Interest
National Affairs, Inc.
10 East 53d Street
New York, NY 10022

public interest groups **1** A national network of quasi-public voluntary associations. The so-called big seven include the Council of State governments (CSG), the National Governors Association (NGA), the National Conference of State Legislatures (NCSL), the National Association of Counties (NACo), the National League of Cities (NLC), United States Conference of Mayors (USCM), and the International City Management Association (ICMA). The CSG has several relevant affiliated organizations: the NGA; and associations of attorneys general, lieutenant governors, state budget officers, state purchasing officials, and state planning agencies. The various state leagues of municipalities are constituent bodies of the NLC. Furthermore, the American Society for Public Administration (ASPA), the National Academy of Public Administration (NAPA), and the National Association of Schools of Public Affairs and Administration (NASPAA) are the principal important voices in the intergovernmental network. More specialized are the associations of planning, personnel, and finance officials. **2** Organized pressure groups seeking to develop positions and to support national causes relating to a broader definition of the public good, as opposed to a specific social or economic interest. Such groups are often characterized by efforts to obtain a national membership and high participation. Examples of public interest groups are Common Cause, the Nader organizations, the League of Women Voters, the Sierra Club, and Consumer's Union. *See also* INTEREST GROUP THEORY.

REFERENCES

Jeffrey M. Berry, *Lobbying for the People: The Political Behavior of Public Interest Groups* (Princeton, NJ: Princeton University Press, 1977);

Peter W. Colby, The organization of public interest groups, *Policy Studies Journal* 11 (June 1983);

David P. Forsythe and Susan Welch, Joining and supporting public interest groups: A note on some empirical findings, *Western Political Quarterly* 36 (September 1983);

Constance Ewing Cook, Participation in public interest groups: Membership motivations, *American Politics Quarterly* 12 (October 1984).

public interest law That portion of a legal practice devoted to broad societal interests, rather than to the problems of individual clients. A public interest law firm provides services to advance or to protect important public interests (e.g., the environment or freedom of information issues) in cases that are not economically feasible or desirable for private law firms.

REFERENCES

Robert L. Rabin, Lawyers for social change: Perspectives on public interest law, *Stanford Law Review* 28 (January 1976);

Burton A. Weisbrod, *Public Interest Law: An Economic and Institutional Analysis* (Berkeley and Los Angeles: University of California Press, 1978).

public interest movement A loose phrase for the continuous efforts of public interest groups to gain the passage of legislation that will advance broad societal interests. The movement, whose origins can be traced back to the progressive era, consistently advances a heterogeneous public policy agenda through a threefold approach: (1) lobbying for legislation; (2) bringing civil suits in the federal courts, and (3) supporting political candidates who support their views.

REFERENCE

David Vogel, The public interest movement and the American reform tradition, *Political Science Quarterly* 95 (Winter 1980–81).

public interest research group (PIRG) One of the consumer advocacy organizations inspired by RALPH NADER that operate out of colleges and universities. While presumably nonpartisan, they tend to lobby in behalf of traditional liberal positions, and at least one chapter has even endorsed a presidential candidate.

REFERENCE

Ralph Nader and Donald Ross, *Action for a Change: A Student's Manual for Public Interest Organizing,* rev. ed. (New York: Viking, 1973).

public law **1** Legislative acts that deal with the public as a whole; statutes that apply to all citizens. **2** Legal actions initiated by a government agency on behalf of the public, as opposed to private civil actions initiated by a private party for personal benefit. **3** That branch of the law that deals with the relation between a government and its citizens.

REFERENCE

Walter B. Murphy and Joseph Tanenhaus, *The Study of Public Law* (New York: Random House, 1972).

public management A general term referring to a major segment of public administration. Typically, the phrase identifies those functions of public and nonprofit organizations that are internally oriented, such as personnel management, procedures management, and organizational control. Whereas policy management typically focuses on policy formation and the selection of basic strategies, public management focuses on the organizational machinery for achieving policy goals. Planning, organizing, and controlling are the major means by which a public manager shapes government services. These functions constitute the primary knowledge and skills of the public manager and are applied in the form of budgets, performance appraisals, management information systems, program evaluations, organizational charts, cost-benefit analyses, and similar tools. Public management also requires behavioral skills: communications, negotiation, motivation, leadership, and interpersonal skills.

REFERENCES

James Perry and Kenneth Kraemer, eds., *Public Management: Public and Private Perspectives* (Palo Alto, CA: Mayfield, 1983);

E. Samuel Overman, Public management: What's new and different? *Public Administration Review* 44 (May/June 1984).

Public Management (PM) The monthly magazine for city managers published by the International City Management Association since 1919. Library of Congress no JS39 .P97.

Public Management
1120 G Street, N.W.
Washington, D.C. 20005

public opinion **1** The GENERAL WILL; the aggregate of the individual feelings of a political community on a given issue; a force of such intangible power that it sets limits on what a government can do. American public opinion, while often tested in opinion polls, is really made known only through elections. **2** The mass media manipulated attitudes of an ill-informed public. According to Walter Lippman's classic analysis, *Public Opinion* (New York: Harcourt Brace Jovanovich, 1922), the media has increased the gap between citizens' stereotyped impressions of politics and the complex realities of politics by putting out selected simplified explanations of political phenomena. Lippman, in the best Burkean tradition (*see* EDMUND BURKE), was concerned that political leaders would defer too much to a basically ill-informed public and follow opinion instead of leading it. He would later write that "the notion that public opinion can and will decide all issues is in appearance very democratic. In practice it undermines and destroys democratic government. For when everyone is supposed to have a judgment about everything, nobody in fact is going to know much about anything."

REFERENCES

V. O. Key, Jr., *Public Opinion and American Democracy* (New York: Knopf, 1961);

Robert S. Erikson, Norman R. Luttbeg, and Kent L. Tedin, *American Public Opinion: Its Origins, Content, and Impact,* 2d ed. (New York: Wiley, 1980);

Harry Holloway and John H. George, *Public Opinion: Coalitions, Elites, and Masses,* 2d ed. (New York: St. Martin's, 1985).

public opinion leader *See* OPINION LEADER.

Public Opinion Quarterly The leading scholarly journal on voting behavior and opinion sampling; published since 1937. Library of Congress no. HM261 .A1P8.

Public Opinion Quarterly
Journals Fulfillment Department
University of Chicago Press
5801 S. Ellis Ave.
Chicago, IL 60637

public opinion survey A scientifically designed process to measure public opinion using a statistically sampled cross section of the population in question. Public opinion polls are used descriptively—for example, to describe public attitudes about crime in America; and predictively—for example, to project voting patterns in a forthcoming election or to gauge public support for a pending bond issue. *Compare to* POLL; SAMPLE.

REFERENCE

Herbert Asher, *Public Opinion Polling* (Washington, D.C.: Congressional Quarterly, 1987).

public policy Whatever a government decides to do or not to do. Public policies are made by authoritative actors in a political system, who are recognized because of their formal position as having the responsibility for making binding choices for the society. There are essentially two kinds of literature on public policy. One is process oriented and attempts to understand and explore the dynamic social and political mechanics and relations of how policies are made. The other is prescriptive and attempts to examine how rational analysis can produce better policy decisions.

REFERENCES

Raymond A. Bauer and Kenneth J. Gergen, eds., *The Study of Policy Formulation* (New York: Free Press, 1968);

Thomas R. Dye, *Understanding Public Policy*, 3d ed. (Englewood Cliffs, NJ: Prentice-Hall, 1978);

William J. Murin, Gerald Michael Greenfield, and John D. Buenker, *Public Policy: A Guide to Information Sources* (Detroit: Gale, 1981);

Kenneth M. Dolbeare, *American Public Policy: A Citizen's Guide* (New York: McGraw-Hill, 1982);

Stuart S. Nagel, *Public Policy: Goals, Means and Methods* (New York: St. Martin's, 1984).

Public Policy The quarterly journal of policy analysis of the Kennedy School of Government, Harvard University. This journal ceased publication in 1981 and was succeeded by the JOURNAL OF POLICY ANALYSIS AND MANAGEMENT.

public policymaking The totality of the decisional processes by which a government decides to act or not act to deal with a particular problem or concern. In seeking an explanation for the mechanisms that produce policy decisions or nondecisions, one is immediately confronted with two early, distinct, and opposite theories.

What might be called the rational decision-making approach generally has been attributed to Harold Lasswell's *The Future of Political Science* (New York: Atherton, 1963), which posited seven significant phases for every decision: (1) the intelligence phase, involving an influx of information; (2) the promoting or recommending phase, involving activities designed to influence the outcome; (3) the prescribing phase, involving the articulation of norms; (4) the invoking phase, involving establishing correspondence between prescriptions and concrete circumstances; (5) the application phase, in which the prescription is executed; (6) the appraisal phase, assessing intent in relation to effect, and (7) the terminating phase, treating expectations (rights) established while the prescription was in force.

The rejection of this approach was urged by Charles E. Lindblom, who proposed the incremental decision-making theory, popularly known as the science of muddling through. Lindblom sees a rational model as unrealistic. The policymaking process was above all, he asserted, complex and disorderly. Disjointed incrementalism as a policy course was in reality the only truly feasible route, since incrementalism "concentrated the policymaker's analysis on familiar, better-known experiences, sharply reduced the number of different alternative policies to be explored, and sharply reduced the number and complexity of factors to be analyzed."

The opposition of the rational and incremental models seemingly has produced no real obstacles for subsequent study of policymaking.

One later policy analysis scholar simply has contended that the reality of the policy process should not negate attempts to establish ideal models. Charles O. Jones, in *An Introduction to the Study of Public Policy*, 3d ed. (Monterey, CA: Brooks/Cole, 1984), finds that, while Lindblom's thesis accurately describes most policy processes, there is "no particular reason why those who want change should limit their actions because the system is 'incremental.'" A question then remains, How can one accept that the incremental model is the reality but use the rational model as a conceptual framework for policy analysis? There is no ready answer to such a question other than to go back to Jones. Scholars use the rational model because it affords a dissective capability that can be used to focus on policy specifics and stages, regardless of how well constructed or formulated any given decisions may be.

Another significant theorist, Theodore J. Lowi, holds that different models should be constructed for different types of public policies. His now classic article, "American Business, Public Policy, Case Studies and Political Theory" (*World Politics*, July 1964), argued that policy contents should be an independent variable and that there are three major categories of public policies: distribution, regulation, and redistribution. "Each arena tends to develop its own characteristic political structure, political process, elites, and group relations." As one might expect, distribution policies involve actions that provide services and products to individuals and groups; regulatory policies involve transfers or transactions that take from one party and provide to another.

It seems fair to conclude that there is no single policymaking process that produces all policies. Rather, there are numerous policy

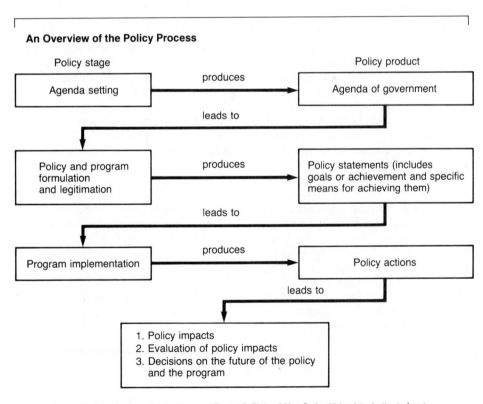

An Overview of the Policy Process

Source: Samuel C. Patterson, Roger H. Davidson, and Randall B. Ripley, *A More Perfect Union: Introduction to American Government*, 3d ed. (Chicago: Dorsey, 1985), p. 465.

processes, each capable of producing different policy contents and applicable only in a particular environment.

REFERENCES

Charles E. Lindblom, *The Policymaking Process* (Englewood Cliffs, NJ: Prentice-Hall, 1968);

Yehezkel Dror, *Public Policymaking Reexamined* (San Francisco: Chandler, 1968);

Carol H. Weiss, ed., *Using Social Research for Public Policy Making* (Lexington, MA: Lexington Books, 1977);

George C. Edwards III and Ira Sharkansky, *The Policy Predicament: Making and Implementing Public Policy* (San Francisco: Freeman, 1978);

James E. Anderson, *Public Policymaking* 3d ed. (New York: Holt, Rinehart & Winston, 1984);

Nelson W. Polsby, *Political Innovation in America: The Politics of Policy Initiation* (New Haven, CT: Yale University Press, 1984).

public power   Energy produced by government-owned and -operated power plants, such as those of the TENNESSEE VALLEY AUTHORITY in the East, and the Western Area Power Administration in the West. Only about 20 percent of the electricity annually produced in the United States is generated in publicly owned power stations, and most of this is sold to privately owned public utilities, which distribute it to households and businesses. Ever since the New Deal, when the federal government first got into the power-generating business, there has been considerable debate over whether the government should stay in it. The political Right tends to say no: Sell all the power plants to private investors. The political Left tends to say yes: Stay in it and build more.

The single most controversial area of public power is nuclear. While the federal government owns outright some nuclear plants (TVA, for example), it regulates them all through the NUCLEAR REGULATORY COMMISSION. With the development of nuclear weapons in the 1950s, the federal government actively encouraged utility companies to use nuclear power (*see* ATOMS FOR PEACE)—the safe and cheap power of the future. But as the 1979 accident at Three Mile Island in Pennsylvania and the 1986 accident at Chernobyl in the Soviet Union showed, nuclear power is not necessarily safe; nor has it proved inexpensive.

public-private partnerships   Joint efforts on the part of local governments and the business community to plan for, generate public support for, and pay for major social programs or construction projects that will be mutually beneficial.

REFERENCES

Dave Durenberger, Public-private partnerships: New meaning, new advocates, new problems, *National Civic Review* 73 (January 1984);

Jane H. Macon, Public/private partnership: A hope for the city's future, *National Civic Review* 74 (April 1985).

public regardingness   An attitude on the part of citizens in some income and ethnic groups that is broader than narrow self-interest; that, in marked contrast to the attitudes of others, takes the welfare of the community as a whole into account in decisions about voting and political support. Those who have a high degree of public regardingness would vote for higher school property taxes—even though they might not have children in public schools—because adequately financed schools are important for the general welfare of the community. *Compare to* PRIVATE REGARDINGNESS.

REFERENCES

James Q. Wilson and Edward C. Banfield, Public Regardingness is a value premise in voting behavior, *American Political Science Review* 58:4 (1964);

R. Durand, Ethnicity, "public regardingness," and referenda voting, *Midwest Journal of Political Science* 16 (May 1972);

Peter A. Lupsha, Social position and public regardingness; A new test of an old hypothesis, *Western Political Quarterly* 28 (December 1975).

public service   1 Participation in public life; voluntary acts for one's community. Jean Jacques Rousseau wrote in *Social Contract* (1762): "As soon as public service ceases to be the chief business of the citizens, and they would rather serve with their money than with their persons, the state is not far from its fall." **2** Government employment; the totality of a jurisdiction's employees; the totality of a nation's public sector employees. **3** What a government does for its community: police protection, trash collection, and so on. **4** A local public utility.

REFERENCE

2 John W. Macy, Jr., *Public Service: The Human Side of Government* (New York: Harper & Row, 1971).

public service corporation A private, regulated corporation that provides an essential service or commodity to the public, such as an electric or a gas utility company; not to be confused with public service organization or a publicly supported organization.

public utilities A legal designation encompassing those organizations producing essential services, usually in a monopolistic fashion; originally, a designation of services—like water, gas, and electricity—to large numbers of the public provided by private corporations and paid for by community users. The public nature yet monopolistic character of such corporations eventually subjected them to public scrutiny and regulation, if not public ownership. They are all characterized as public, now, despite differences in ownership, management, and regulation.

REFERENCES

William D. Berry, Utility regulation in the states: The policy effects of professionalism and salience to the consumer, *American Journal of Political Science* 23 (May 1979);

William T. Gormley, Jr., Policy, politics, and public utility regulation, *American Journal of Political Science* 27 (February 1983);

William T. Gormley, Jr., *The Politics of Public Utility Regulation* (Pittsburgh: University of Pittsburgh Press, 1985).

public utilities commission A state agency that regulates power companies, railroads, and so on. They typically set rates, hold hearings on the quality and level of services, and do economic analyses on regulated industries.

public welfare **1** Government support of and assistance to needy persons contingent upon their need. *Compare to* WELFARE. **2** A legal basis for government action. For example, a governor may be bound by a state constitution to protect the public welfare and thus to send National Guard troops to a major disaster site. **3** The general welfare of the United States. *Compare to* GENERAL WELFARE CLAUSE.

REFERENCES

1 Gilbert Y. Steiner, *Social Insecurity: The Politics of Welfare* (Chicago: Rand McNally, 1966);

Gilbert Y. Steiner, *The State of Welfare* (Washington, D.C.: Brookings, 1971);

Francis Fox Piven and Richard A. Cloward, *Regulating the Poor: The Functions of Public Welfare* (New York: Random House, 1972).

public works A generic term for government-sponsored construction projects. Initially, it was applied to any construction useful to the public, regardless of its potential for private profit. But the use of such projects as a means of providing employment during recession or as a potential for distribution of federal resources to states or cities has given the term a new meaning in economic planning. Since the New Deal, public works projects have sometimes been used in times of economic recession or depression to stimulate the economy (*see* PUMP PRIMING). Public works are also major elements in PORK BARREL legislation, designed to benefit an individual congressional district. *See also* BENEFIT DISTRICT.

REFERENCES

Ellis Armstrong, ed., *History of Public Works in the United States: 1776–1976* (Chicago: American Public Works, 1976);

F. Burke Sheeran, *Management Essentials for Public Works Administrators* (Chicago: American Public Works, 1976);

William E. Korbitz, ed. *Urban Public Works Administration* (Washington, D.C.: International City Management, 1976).

publius A Latin word meaning public man and the pen name (Publius) used by Alexander Hamilton, James Madison, and John Jay when writing the series of newspaper articles that became the FEDERALIST PAPERS. The three men were such obvious supporters of the proposed U.S. constitution that anonymity was desirable to make their arguments for ratification seem objective. Besides, it was then fashionable for a "gentleman" to use a pen name when writing for newspapers.

REFERENCE
George W. Carey, Publius—A split personality? *Review of Politics* 46 (January 1984).

Publius A journal of federalism that deals with all aspects of intergovernmental relations; published since 1971. It is called *Publius* in honor of the pen name used by the "godfathers" of American federalism. Library of Congress no. JK1 .P88.
> *Publius*
> Department of Political Science
> North Texas State University
> Denton, TX 76203

PUC *See* PUBLIC UTILITIES COMMISSION.

PUD *See* PLANNED UNIT DEVELOPMENT.

Pullman Strike *See* DEBS, IN RE.

pump priming 1 Pouring water into a dry pump to lubricate dry seals and valves to rapidly increase the efficiency of the pump, even though this may waste the initial water. 2 The concept, originating in the New Deal, of stimulating the economy during a time of economic decline by borrowing money to spend on public works, defense, welfare, and so on. In theory, the prosperity generated by such expenditures would increase tax revenues, which in turn would pay for the borrowing. *Compare to* JOHN MAYNARD KEYNES.

REFERENCE
W. O. Farber, State governments and pump priming, *State Government* 48 (Autumn 1975).

punitive damages Money awarded by a court to an organization or a person who has been harmed in a particularly malicious or willful way by another person or organization. This money is not necessarily related to the actual cost of the injury or the harm suffered. Its purpose is to punish the offender and to deter that sort of act from happening again, by serving as a warning.

puppet state 1 A country whose basic policies are controlled by another power. The modern use of the term dates from World War II, when the Germans established what the allies called puppet governments in the countries they conquered. The Soviet-dominated satellite states of Eastern Europe, while responsive to Soviet policies, have a level of independence far greater than the puppets of World War II. 2 In the perception of a super power, any small nation aligned with an opposing superpower.

Q

quartering of soldiers *See* THIRD AMENDMENT.

quasi-judicial agency An agency, such as a regulatory commission, that may perform many functions ordinarily performed by the courts. Its interpretation and enforcement of rules gives these rules the authority of law. It adjudicates (*see* ADJUDICATION) and may bring charges, hold hearings, and render judgments. Quasi is Latin for as if, or almost.

quasi-legislative Descriptive of the rule-making authority of administrative agencies. The authority of an administrative agency to make rules gives those rules the authority of law; that is, makes them enforceable as though they had been passsed by a legislature.

questions of privilege *See* PRIVILEGE, QUESTIONS OF.

quid pro quo A Latin phrase meaning something for something; initially meaning the substitution of one thing for another. In politics it suggests actions taken, because of some promised action in return.

quorum The number of members who must be in attendance to make valid the votes and other actions of a formal group. In the U.S. Supreme Court, a quorum is six. In the U.S. Senate and the House of Representatives, it is a majority of the membership. In the Committee of the Whole House, it is 100. If a point of order is made that a quorum is not present, the only business that is in order is either a motion to adjourn or a motion to direct the sergeant at arms to request the attendance of absentees.

quorum call A method of determining whether a legislative quorum is present by calling the roll of the legislature's members. In the U.S. Senate, a quorum call is used mainly as a kind of parliamentary "time out," while senators meet on and off the Senate floor to decide how to proceed on a particular piece of legislation. It is a routine way of suspending debate without recessing or adjourning the Senate. Usually, there are several quorum calls on any given day the Senate is in session. A call is triggered when a senator says, "I suggest the absence of a quorum," and the clerk of the Senate begins slowly to call the role of senators. Regular business resumes when a senator says, "I ask unanimous consent that further proceedings under the quorum call be dispensed with."

quorum call, notice In the Committee of the Whole House, a notice quorum call may be made by the chair when the point of order is made that a quorum is not present. If 100 members, which constitute a quorum in the Committee of the Whole House, appear within the specified time period, the notice quorum call is not recorded. If 100 members fail to appear, a regular quorum call, which is recorded, is made.

quotas *See* GOALS.

R

race 1 A grouping of human beings with common characteristics presumed to be transmitted genetically. Which characteristics are properly included has been a subject of debate. They range from physical characteristics that are immediately observable, such as color of hair, skin, and eyes, to the subtler aspects of intelligence and aptitudes. Some races have genetic susceptibility to certain diseases or physical disorders. 2 The human race as distinguished from other animals. 3 Ancestry, tribal, or national origin. The latter definition was common up to the middle of the twentieth century as a way of distinguishing among national groups and is traceable to eighteenth-century distinctions among people according to language. It became a method of attempting to define a hierarchy of races, with the so-called Anglo-Saxons at the top and others arranged along supposedly developmental lines. Friedrich Nietzsche's (1844–1900) conception of a superman or super race became a tragic caricature as used by Adolph Hitler (1889–1945) in his attempt to establish a German *volk* (people) destined to dominate the world. 4 In recent times, in American political language, race has come to designate issues or attitudes concerning blacks. Other minority groups are called ethnics or subcategories of ethnic, to satisfy government requirements for administration of certain programs (*see* RACE CATEGORIES). Race has thus moved from a term signifying high distinction or complex scientific differentiation to one that implies an unacceptable prejudice. **5** An election contest. **6** An armaments buildup, as in an arms race.

REFERENCES

4 Anne Wortham, *The Other Side of Racism: A Philosophical Study of Black Race Consciousness* (Columbus: Ohio State University Press, 1981);

Thomas S. Sowell, *The Economics and Politics of Race* (New York: Morrow, 1983);

George E. Simpson and J. Milton Yinger, *Racial and Cultural Minorities: An Analysis of Prejudice and Discrimination,* 5th ed. (New York: Harper & Row, 1985).

race categories The racial-ethnic categories that the Equal Employment Opportunity Commission requires for reporting purposes. These are *white, not of hispanic origin:* people having origins in any of the original peoples of Europe, North Africa, or the Middle East; *black, not of hispanic origin:* people having origins in any of the black racial groups of Africa; *Hispanic:* people of Mexican, Puerto Rican, Cuban, Central, or South American, or other Spanish culture origin, regardless of race; *American Indian or Alaskan native:* people having origins in any of the original peoples of North America and who maintain cultural identification through tribal affiliation or community recognition; *Asian or Pacific islander:* people having origins in any of the original peoples of the Far East, Southeast Asia, the Indian subcontinent, or the Pacific islands. These areas include China, Japan, Korea, the Philippine Islands, and Samoa.

The U.S. Supreme Court has also recognized additional race categories that are protected by the federal civil rights laws. In *Shaare Tefila Congregation v Cobb,* 95 L.Ed. 2d 594 (1987), it held that Jews could bring charges of

racial discrimination against defendants who were also considered caucasian. And in *Saint Francis College v Al-Khazraji,* 95 L.Ed. 2d 502 (1987), it held that someone of Arabian ancestry was protected from racial discrimination under the various civil rights statutes.

racism, institutional *See* INSTITUTIONAL DISCRIMINATION.

racist Any person or organization that either consciously or unconsciously practices racial discrimination or supports the supremacy of one race over others.

REFERENCES

Benjamin P. Bowser and Raymond G. Hunt, eds., *Impacts of Racism on White Americans* (Beverly Hills, CA: Sage, 1981);

John P. Fernandez, *Racism and Sexism in Corporate Life: Changing Values in American Business* (Lexington, MA: Lexington Books, 1981).

radical **1** Any political activist who advocates drastic changes in the operating premises of the nation—often, but not necessarily, by violent means. Radicals exist on both the extreme Left and extreme Right. Mark Twain said, "The radical of one century is the conservative of the next. The radical invents the views. When he has worn them out the conservatives adopt them." **2** After the Civil War, a Republican opponent of President Abraham Lincoln's policy of compassion for the defeated South.

REFERENCES

1 Saul Alinsky, *Rules for Radicals* (New York: Random House, 1972).

2 Glenn M. Linden, "Radicals" and economic policies: The Senate, 1861–1873, *Journal of Southern History* 32:2 (1966); Edward L. Gambill, Who were the Senate radicals? *Civil War History* 11:3 (1965).

Railroad Retirement Board The federal agency that administers retirement-survivor and unemployment-sickness benefit programs provided by federal laws for the nation's railroad workers and their families.

Railroad Retirement Board
844 Rush Street
Chicago, IL 60611
(312) 751–4776

Railroad Retirement Board
Washington Liaison Office
2000 L Street, N.W.
Washington, D.C. 20036
(202) 653–9540

Railway Labor Act of 1926 The federal statute, amended in 1934 to include airlines, that protects the collective bargaining rights of employees and established the National Railroad Adjustment Board to arbitrate grievances that arise from labor-management contracts in these industries.

REFERENCES

Leonard A. Lecht, *Experience under Railway Labor Legislation* (New York: AMS, 1955, 1968);

Herbert R. Northrup, The Railway Act: A critical reappraisal, *Industrial and Labor Relations Review* 25 (October 1971);

George S. Roukis, Should the Railway Labor Act be amended? *Arbitration Journal* 38 (March 1983).

RAND Corporation A leading think tank that consistently produces significant analyses of public policies and problems.

REFERENCE

Fred Kaplan, Scientists at war: The birth of the RAND corporation, *American Heritage* 34 (June/July 1983).

RAND Corporation
1700 Main Street
Santa Monica, CA 90406
(213) 393–0411

Randolph plan *See* VIRGINIA PLAN.

rank and file A colloquial expression for the masses. When used in an organizational context, it refers to those members of the organization who are not part of management; those who are the workers and have no status as officers. Rank and file was originally a military term, referring to the enlisted men who had to line up in ranks, side by side, and files, one behind the other. Officers, being gentlemen, were spared such indignities.

ranking member The member of a legislative committee who has the greatest seniority. The ranking member of the majority party often becomes the committee's chair. A ranking minority member is the senior committee member from the minority party.

Rawls, John (1921–) The American philosopher whose *A Theory of Justice* (Cambridge, MA: Harvard University Press, 1971) has become one of the most significant works of political theory in this century. Rawls's theory uses a hypothetical social contract to ascertain the degree of justice of various social arrangements. Rawls's readers are asked to hold information about their own social status behind a "veil of ignorance" and to make rational decisions based upon Rawls's two normative principles: (1) that each person has an equal right to basic liberties compatible with similar liberties for all others; and (2) that social-economic inequalities are to be such that they might benefit the least advantaged, assuming that offices and positions are fairly open to all. Rawls seeks to reassert a concept of natural rights, which holds some values (such as liberty) as absolute and others (such as right to equality) as secondary.

REFERENCES

Robert Paul Wolff, *Understanding Rawls: A Reconstruction and Critique of "A Theory of Justice"* (Princeton, NJ: Princeton University Press, 1977);

Steven D. Ealy, The justice of Rawls' original position, *Journal of Political Science* 9 (Fall 1981);

Philip Green, Equality since Rawls: Objective philosophers, subjective citizens, and rational choice, *Journal of Politics* 47 (August 1985).

reactionary One who would go back to outmoded ideas of the past. It is a derogatory reference to those political activists who are so discontent with maintaining the status quo that they yearn for a previous status quo. *Compare to* CONSERVATISM.

reading of bills *See* BILLS, READING OF.

Reagan Doctrine The media term for the Ronald Reagan administration's policy (in conjunction with the Congress) of militarily supporting guerrilla insurgencies against communist governments in Third World countries, such as Afghanistan, Angola, Cambodia, and Nicaragua.

REFERENCES

Stephen Rosenfeld, The Reagan Doctrine: The guns of July, *Foreign Affairs* 64 (Spring 1986);

Charles Krauthammer, Morality and the Reagan Doctrine, *New Republic* 195 (September 8, 1986);

Roger D. Hansen, The Reagan doctrine and global containment: Revival or recessional, *SAIS Review* 7 (Winter–Spring 1987).

Reaganomics *See* SUPPLY-SIDE ECONOMICS/ REAGANOMICS.

Reagan revolution **1** The resurgence of the Republican party in the 1980s under the leadership of President Ronald Reagan. **2** The radical changes in the nation's fiscal and tax policies under the Reagan administration, which redefined domestic priorities and curtailed federal programs designed to solve social problems. As Reagan often said: "Government is not the solution to our problems. Government is the problem." In other words, the national welfare would be better served with general economic prosperity, brought about by tax cuts (*see* SUPPLY-SIDE ECONOMICS/REAGANOMICS) than with expanded welfare programs.

REFERENCE

B. B. Kymlicka and Jean Matthews, *The Reagan Revolution?* (Chicago, IL: Dorsey, 1988).

Reagan, Ronald W. (1911–   )   The president of the United States since 1981 and the most personally popular president since Dwight D. Eisenhower. Reagan, a movie actor since the late 1930s, took part in the early introduction of Hollywood to labor organization and Democratic party politics. He became a successful television promoter of General Electric products in the 1950s and joined the Republican party. His active involvement in the ill-fated 1964 presidential campaign of Barry Goldwater made him a major voice in national Republican politics. This led to Reagan's elec-

Ronald Reagan.

tion as governor of California (1967–1975) and eventually to his successful 1980 presidential campaign against Jimmy Carter; and his even more successful 1984 campaign for re-election against Walter Mondale.

REFERENCES

Fred I. Greenstein, ed., *The Reagan Presidency: An Early Assessment* (Baltimore: Johns Hopkins University Press, 1983);

Robert Dallek, *Ronald Reagan: The Politics of Symbolism* (Cambridge, MA: Harvard University Press, 1984);

Garry Wills, *Reagan's America: Innocents at Home* (Garden City, NY: Doubleday, 1987).

The Ronald Reagan Administration

Major Accomplishments

- His first term congressional bipartisan coalition, which supported the administration on major domestic and foreign policy issues.
- The largest tax and budget cuts in U.S. history.
- The reduction of double-digit inflation to 3–5 percent.
- The invasion of Grenada.
- The Tax Reform Act of 1986.
- The appointment of the first woman (Sandra Day O'Connor) to the Supreme Court.

Major Frustrations
- Record budget deficits.
- An inability to reduce poverty and hardcore unemployment.
- The weak U.S. leverage in the Middle East and Central America.
- The Iran-Contra affair.

realignment 1 A new order of demonstrated political loyalties, whether of the electorate or of the parties and voting blocs in a legislature. A realignment could be a temporary response to a charismatic political figure, a one-time alliance on behalf of an issue, or, as the term is most often used, a permanent change in the electorate, such as when the South, which was once solidly Democratic, developed a two-party system—at least in national elections. The last major realignment in American national politics occurred in the 1930s, when Franklin D. Roosevelt forged the New Deal coalition, and the Democrats became the majority party. Everett Carll Ladd wrote in "On Mandates, Realignments, and the 1984 Presidential Election," *Political Science Quarterly* 100 (Spring 1985): "For two decades now, political scientists and other commentators have stumbled and sloshed around a conceptual swamp called realignment that we have created for ourselves. The main reason we have had such difficulty dealing with contemporary partisan realignment is that we have expected it to be like the one acted out in the 1930s—the great New Deal realignment." The question is still unanswered about whether Ronald Reagan has laid the political foundation for a realignment that will make the Republicans supplant the Democrats as the majority party. *See also* DEALIGNMENT; ELECTION, CRITICAL; SOUTHERN STRATEGY. 2 In international politics, the latest adjustments to diplomatic, military, or trade policies to reflect the current realities of international relationships. *Compare to* BALANCE OF POWER.

REFERENCES

1 John R. Petrocik, *Party Coalitions: Realignments and the Decline of the New Deal Party System* (Chicago: University of Chicago Press, 1981);

Barbara Sinclair, *Congressional Realignment, 1925–1978* (Austin: University of Texas Press, 1982);

Richard A. Champagne, Conditions for realignment in the U.S. Senate—Or what makes the steamroller start? *Legislative Studies Quarterly* 8 (May 1983);

Everett Ladd and Charles Hadley, *Transformation of the American Party System*, 2d ed. (New York: Norton, 1983);

David W. Brady, A reevaluation of realignments in American politics: Evidence from the House of Representatives, *American Political Science Review* 79 (March 1985).

2 Bruce D. Berkowitz, Realignment in international treaty organizations, *International Studies Quarterly* 27 (March 1983);

Dankwart A. Rustow, Realignments in the Middle East, *Foreign Affairs* 63 (1985).

realpolitik A German word, now absorbed into English, meaning realist politics. The term is applied to politics—whether of the organizational or societal variety—premised on material or practical factors rather than on theoretical or ethical considerations.

REFERENCES

Albert Somit, Bureaucratic realpolitik and teaching of administration, *Public Administration Review* 16 (Autumn 1956);

Nestor Cruz, "Realpolitik" and affirmative action, *Public Personnel Management* 9:3 (1980);

Patricia M. Wald, The realpolitik of judicial review in a deregulation era, *Journal of Policy Analysis and Management* 5 (Spring 1986).

real-property tax *See* TAX, REAL-PROPERTY.

reapportionment 1 A new apportionment (the assignment to a state of a new number of congressional seats) in response to changes in population as determined by the decimal census. The U.S. Congress takes the fixed size of the House of Representatives (435 members) and, after assigning one seat to each state as required by the Constitution, allots the remaining 385 on the basis of population. **2** A parallel apportionment of state legislature seats. *Compare to* GERRYMANDER; REDISTRICTING.

REFERENCES

Timothy G. O'Rourke, *The Impact of Reapportionment* (New Brunswick, NJ: Transaction, 1980);

Leroy Hardy, Alan Heslop, and Stuart Anderson, *Reapportionment Politics: The History of Redistricting in the 50 States* (Beverly Hills, CA: Sage, 1981);

Bruce E. Cain, *The Reapportionment Puzzle* (Berkeley and Los Angeles: University of California Press, 1984);

Q. Whitfield Ayres and David Whiteman, Congressional reapportionment in the 1980s: Types and determinants of policy outcomes, *Political Science Quarterly* 99 (Summer 1984).

reappropriation Legislative action to restore or extend the obligational availability, whether for the same or different purposes, of all or part of the unobligated portion of budget authority, which otherwise would lapse.

reasonable doubt *See* BEYOND A REASONABLE DOUBT.

rebellion *See* REVOLUTION.

recall **1** A procedure that allows citizens to vote officeholders out of office between regularly scheduled elections. For a new election to be called, a recall petition must be presented with a prescribed percentage of the jurisdiction's voters' signatures. **2** The rehiring of employees from a layoff. **3** The returning of defective products to their manufacturers (often via a retailer) either at the manufacturer's initiative or because of an order from a government regulatory agency enforcing a consumer protection law. *Compare to* REFERENDUM.

REFERENCES

1 Laura Tallian, *Direct Democracy: An Historical Analysis of the Initiative, Referendum, and Recall Process* (Los Angeles: People's Lobby, 1977);

Charles M. Price, Recalls at the local level: Dimensions and implications, *National Civic Review* 72 (April 1983).

recess **1** A break in a formal proceeding, such as a trial or hearing, that may last from a few minutes to a few hours. **2** A break in a legislative session. It is distinguished from adjournment in that it does not end a legislative day and so does not interfere with unfinished business. **3** The time between court sessions. For example, the U.S. Supreme Court is usually in recess during the summer months.

recess appointment **1** A presidential appointment to federal office of a person to fill a vacancy (that requires the advice and consent of the Senate to be filled) while the Senate is not in session. People appointed to office while the Senate is in recess may begin their duties before their names have been submitted to the Senate. However, the president must submit each such nomination when the Senate reconvenes, and the recess appointment expires at the end of the next session unless the Senate has confirmed each one by a majority vote. Moreover, the recess appointment expires and the office is declared vacant even earlier than the end of the next session if the Senate acts before that time to reject the nominee. **2** A similar appointment by a state governor.

recession A decline in overall business activity that is pervasive, substantial, and of at least several months' duration. Historically, a decline in real gross national product for at least two consecutive quarters of a year has been considered a recession. While the distinction between a recession and a depression is a matter of usage, recession is generally perceived as a temporary low point in a normal business cycle (*see* BUSINESS CYCLES), while a depression suggests more fundamental, underlying shifts in the economy—shifts that are likely to be permanent and to require basic changes. The last depression in the United States was the Great Depression of the 1930s.

reciprocity **1** The giving of privileges to the citizens of one jurisdiction by the government of another, and vice versa. **2** A mutuality in the terms of trade between two nations. **3** One of the key NORMS in a legislature, whereby members exchange favors in order to further their own, their constituents', and the public's interests.

REFERENCES

2 James J. Florio, Beyond reciprocity: The need for a new U.S. trade policy, *Journal of Legislation* 11 (Summer 1984).

3 Donald R. Matthews, *U.S. Senators and Their World* (Chapel Hill: University of North Carolina Press, 1960).

recommit to committee *See* COMMITTEE, RECOMMIT TO.

reconciliation The process used by the U.S. Congress to reconcile amounts for a fiscal year (determined by tax, spending, and debt legislation) with the ceilings enacted in the second required concurrent resolution on the budget for that year. Changes to laws, bills, and resolutions—as required to conform with the binding totals for budget authority, revenues, and the public debt—are incorporated into either a reconciliation resolution or reconciliation bill.

REFERENCES

Allen Schick, *Reconciliation and the Congressional Budget Process* (Washington, D.C.: American Enterprise, 1981);

Allen Schick, In Congress reassembled: Reconciliation and the legislative process, *PS* 14 (Fall 1981).

reconsider a vote *See* VOTE, RECONSIDER A.

record The written account of a legal or administrative case, containing the complete history of all actions taken concerning it.

record copy The copy of a document regarded by an organization as the most important or the key official copy.

recorded vote *See* VOTE, RECORDED.

recorder of deeds The local official responsible for filing public land records.

record, public A document filed with, or put out by, a government agency and open for public review.

red A communist, because the red flag is the international symbol of communism. This is why someone thought to be leaning toward communism might be called pink or a pinko.

red herring Originally, smoked herrings that people opposed to fox hunting might drag along a fox's trail to divert the hunting dogs to a false scent; by analogy, something used to divert attention from the real issue.

redistribution Taking from the rich and giving to the poor; domestic policies and programs whose goal is to shift wealth or benefits from one segment of the population to another. The welfare state is founded on the notion of redistribution. The basic mechanism for redistribution is taxation. However, the laws themselves can sometimes redistribute benefits. For example, tax loopholes benefit one group of taxpayers at the expense of others; and the Civil Rights Act, through equal employment opportunity mandates, gave economic benefits to one segment of the population at the theoretical expense of another. Redistribution is one leg of a three-part classification of all domestic public policies into distribution, regulation, or redistribution (*see* THEODORE J. LOWI). Redistribution is more popular with some classes of society than with others. As the playwright George Bernard Shaw (1856–1950) once said: "A government which robs Peter to pay Paul can always depend on the support of Paul."

REFERENCES

Brian R. Fry and Richard F. Winters, The politics of redistribution, *American Political Science Review* 64 (June 1970);

John D. Kasarda, The implications of contemporary redistribution trends for national urban policy, *Social Science Quarterly* 61 (December 1980);

Richard B. McKenzie, Taxation and income redistribution: An unsympathetic critique of practice and theory, *Cato Journal* 1 (Fall 1981);

Alexander Hicks and Duane H. Swank, Government redistribution in rich capitalist democracies, *Policy Studies Journal* 13 (December 1984);

Robert D. Plotnick and Richard F. Winters, A politico-economic theory of income redistribution, *American Political Science Review* 79 (June 1985).

redistricting 1 The action of a state legislature (or a court if the legislature fails to act) in redrawing congressional district boundaries in response to a reapportionment of congressional seats among the states. The Constitution requires (in Article I, Section 2) that an "enumeration," a census, be undertaken every ten years specifically for the purpose of adjusting the number of Congressional seats to which each state is entitled. This is a major means by which national political power peacefully follows the population as it shifts from one state or region to another. The reassignment of the numbers of congressional seats that each state will have is reapportionment; a state's redrawing of its congressional districts is redistricting. *Compare to* BAKER V CARR; GERRYMANDERING; REYNOLDS V SIMS. **2** A parallel process for state legislative districts.

REFERENCES

Charles S. Bullock III, The inexact science of congressional redistricting, *PS* 15 (Summer 1982);

J. David Gopoian and Darrell M. West, Trading security for seats: Strategic considerations in the redistricting process, *Journal of Politics* 46 (November 1984);

Richard Born, Partisan intentions and election day realities in the congressional redistricting process, *American Political Science Review* 79 (June 1985);

Peverill Squire, Results of partisan redistricting in seven U.S. states during the 1970s, *Legislative Studies Quarterly* 10 (May 1985).

redlining A practice allegedly followed by some urban financial institutions in which they refuse loans for home mortgages and improvements in areas thought to be poor risks. People living or wishing to live in these areas are denied such loans regardless of their particular financial situation. In consequence, the areas denied financing are unable to upgrade their housing and go into an economic decline. The term derives from the drawing of red lines around such areas on a map. Some states have laws prohibiting redlining.

REFERENCES

Peter Marcuse, The deceptive consensus on redlining: Definitions do matter, *Journal of American Planning Association* 45 (October 1979);

David I. Badain, Insurance redlining and the future of the urban core, *Columbia Journal of Law and Social Problems* 16:1 (1980);

Harriett Tee Taggart and Kevin W. Smith, Redlining: An assessment of the evidence of disinvestment in metropolitan Boston, *Urban Affairs Quarterly* 17 (September 1981);

Joe T. Darden, State anti-redlining laws: A comparative analysis, *State Government* 56:1 (1983).

Red Lion Broadcasting v FCC *See* FAIRNESS DOCTRINE.

red rash A job action by firefighters who, because they cannot legally strike, call in sick. When police suffer from this affliction, it is called the blue flu.

red scare **1** A time of unreasoning and unreasonable fear of communist subversion. **2** The period immediately following World War I and the Russian Revolution of 1917, when American hysteria over radicals, anarchists, and communists resulted in the wholesale arrest and often deportation of people thought to be subversive. The best known aspect of the red scare of this period was the "Palmer raids," conducted by agents of Attorney General A. Mitchell Palmer (1872–1936), in which thousands of citizens and aliens alike were arrested without specific charges. The raids were noted for their lack of due process and violations of civil liberties. They came to an end along with Palmer's presidential ambitions in 1920, when Palmer's predicted uprising of reds in an effort to overthrow the government never materialized. **3** The period of MCCARTHYISM after World War II.

REFERENCES

2 Robert K. Murray, *Red Scare: A Study in National Hysteria, 1919–1920* (New York: McGraw-Hill, 1964);

David R. Colburn, Governor Alfred E. Smith and the red scare, 1919–20, *Political Science Quarterly* 88 (September 1973).

red tape A symbol of excessive formality and attention to routine. It has its origins in the red ribbon with which clerks bound official documents in the nineteenth century. The ribbon has disappeared, but the practices it represents linger on. Herbert Kaufman, in *Red Tape: Its Origins, Uses and Abuses* (Washington, D.C.: Brookings, 1977), found that the term "is applied to a bewildering variety of organizational practices and features." After all, "one person's 'red tape' may be another's treasured procedural safeguard." Kaufman concluded that "red tape turns out to be at the core of our institutions rather than an excrescence on them."

REFERENCE

Raymond A. Rosenfeld, An expansion and application of Kaufman's model of red tape: The case of community development block grants, *Western Political Quarterly* 37 (December 1984).

referendum　A procedure for submitting proposed laws or state constitutional amendments to the voters for ratification. A petition signed by an appropriate percentage of the voters can force a newly passed law onto the ballot or it could be put on the ballot by the recommendation of the legislature. While only a minority of the states provide for statutory referenda, practically all states require them for constitutional amendments. Local governments also use the referendum, especially when the law requires that certain issues, such as capital project borrowing, must be submitted to the voters via referenda. *Compare to* RECALL.

REFERENCES

David Butler and Austin Ranney, *Referendums: A Comparative Study of Practice and Theory* (Washington, D.C.: American Enterprise, 1978);

John E. Filer and Lawrence W. Kenny, Voter reaction to city-council consolidation referenda, *Journal of Law & Economics* 23 (April 1980);

Robert M. Stein, Keith E. Hamm, and Patricia K. Freeman, An analysis of support for tax limitation referenda, *Public Choice* 40:2 (1983);

David B. Magleby, *Direct Legislation: Voting on Ballot Propositions in the United States* (Baltimore: Johns Hopkins University Press, 1984).

referral bill　*See* BILL, REFERRAL.

reflagging　*See* FLAG OF CONVENIENCE.

reform movement　**1** What an out-of-power political party often considers itself.　**2** Good government advocates of changes in governing structures.　**3** A loose term for efforts to weed out corruption in public office. New York Mayor Jimmy Walker (1881–1946) is usually credited with saying: "A reformer is a guy who rides through the sewer in a glass-bottom boat." In 1932, these reformers forced Walker to resign as mayor amid charges of vast corruption.　**4** The PROGRESSIVE MOVEMENT/ PROGRESSIVE ERA, which advocated municipal reforms, such as the council-manager form of government, civil service reform, the short ballot, and nonpartisan elections.

REFERENCES

Richard Hofstadter, *The Age of Reform: From Bryan to FDR* (New York: Knopf, 1955);

David Knoke, The spread of municipal reform: Temporal, spatial, and social dynamics, *American Journal of Sociology* 87 (May 1982);

Michael H. Frisch, Urban theorists, urban reform and American political culture in the progressive period, *Political Science Quarterly* 97 (Summer 1982).

Regents of the University of California v Allan Bakke　438 U.S. 265 (1978)　The U.S. Supreme Court case that upheld a white applicant's claim that he had been denied equal protection of the law because he was refused admission to the University of California Medical School at Davis when sixteen out of the school's one hundred class spaces were set aside for minority applicants. The Court ruled that Bakke, whose objective qualifications according to the school's admission criteria were better than those of some of the minority candidates who were admitted, must be admitted to the Davis Medical School as soon as possible; but that the university had the right to take race into account in its admissions criteria. The imprecise nature of taking race into account as one factor among many has created considerable confusion about voluntary affirmative action programs concerning employment.

Nonetheless, Bakke was admitted, did graduate, and is now a practicing physician *See also* DEFUNIS V ODEGAARD; REVERSE DISCRIMINATION; UNITED STEELWORKERS OF AMERICA V WEBER, ET AL.

REFERENCES

Allan P. Sindler, *Bakke, Defunis, and Minority Admissions: The Quest for Equal Opportunity* (New York: Longman, 1978);

Joel Dreyfuss and Charles Lawrence III, *The Bakke Case: The Politics of Inequality* (New York: Harcourt Brace Jovanovich, 1979);

J. Harvie Wilkinson II, *From Brown to Bakke: The Supreme Court and School Integration 1954–1978* (New York: Oxford University Press, 1979);

Laurence H. Tribe, Perspectives on *Bakke: Equal protection, procedural fairness, or structural justice? Harvard Law Review* 92 (February 1979);

Timothy J. O'Neill, *Bakke and the Politics of Equality: Friends and Foes in the Classroom of Litigation* (Middletown, CT: Wesleyan University Press, 1984).

regime   1 A form of government (republican, totalitarian, and so on).   2 The particular government in power; the group of people that constitutes the administration.   3 A system of governance (as opposed to anarchy).   4 Any generally accepted or customary procedures.

Regional Science Association (RSA)   An organization of academics and professionals (usually planners) concerned with urban and regional analysis.

Regional Science Association
3718 Locust Walk
University of Pennsylvania
Philadelphia, PA 19104
(215) 898–8412

register of eligibles   *See* CERTIFICATION OF ELIGIBLES.

register/registry   A book of public facts, such as births, deaths, and marriages. Other examples of public record books are the register of patents, the register of ships, the register of deeds, and the register of wills.

registration, voter   The process whereby a prospective voter is required to establish his or her identity and place of residence prior to an election to be declared eligible to vote in a particular jurisdiction. The reasons for registration are to prevent election day fraud by making it difficult for one person to vote at more than one location and to ensure that those who do vote have previously established that they are eligible residents. Prior to any major election, all political parties make significant efforts to get their potential supporters registered. In recent years, many jurisdictions have made major efforts to make it easier for citizens to register by combining registration with driver's license application, by allowing registration in supermarkets and shopping centers, and so on. *Compare to* VOTER REQUIREMENTS.

REFERENCES

Steven J. Rosenstone and Raymond E. Wolfinger, The effect of registration laws on voter turnout, *American Political Science Review* 72 (March 1978);

Robert S. Erikson, Why do people vote? Because they are registered, *American Politics Quarterly* 9 (July 1981);

Hulbert James, Maxine Phillips, and Donald Hazen, The new voter registration strategy, *Social Policy* 14 (Winter 1984);

Arnold Veditz, Voter registration drives and black voting in the South, *Journal of Politics* 47 (May 1985);

Bruce E. Cain and Ken McCue, The efficacy of registration drives, *Journal of Politics* 47 (November 1985);

M. Margaret Conway, *Political Participation in the United States* (Washington, D.C.: Congressional Quarterly, 1985).

regressive tax   *See* TAXATION, REGRESSIVE.

regulation   The rule-making process of those administrative agencies charged with the official interpretation of a statute. These agencies (often independent regulatory commissions), in addition to issuing rules, also tend to administer their implementation and to adjudicate interpretative disputes. The Interstate Commerce Commission in 1887 became the prototype of the modern regulatory agency. *See also* DELEGATION OF POWER; DEREGULATION; HUM-

PHREY'S EXECUTOR V UNITED STATES; INDE-
PENDENT AGENCY/REGULATORY COMMISSION;
NATIONAL ASSOCIATION FOR THE ADVANCE-
MENT OF COLORED PEOPLE V FEDERAL POWER
COMMISSION; RULE; UNITED STATES V STU-
DENTS CHALLENGING REGULATORY AGENCY
PROCEDURES.

REFERENCES

Eugene Bardach and Robert A. Kagan, *Going by the Book: The Problem of Regulatory Unreasonableness* (Philadelphia: Temple University Press, 1981);

Frederick C. Thayer, Jr., *Rebuilding America: The Case for Economic Regulation* (New York: Praeger, 1984);

Thomas K. McCraw, Regulation in America: A historical overview, *California Management Review* 27 (Fall 1984);

Kenneth J. Meier, *Regulation: Politics, Bureaucracy, and Economics* (New York: St. Martin's, 1985).

For current data on the various federal regulatory agencies, see the latest edition of the *Federal Regulatory Directory* (Washington, D.C.: Congressional Quarterly).

regulatory tax   *See* TAX, REGULATORY.

Rehabilitation Act of 1973   The federal law prohibiting discrimination against the handicapped by the federal government, by its contractors and subcontractors, and by any program or activity receiving federal financial assistance.

REFERENCE

Judith Welch Wegner, The antidiscrimination model reconsidered: Ensuring equal opportunity without respect to handicap under Section 504 of the Rehabilitation Act of 1973, *Cornell Law Review* 69 (March 1984).

Reid v Covert   *See* EXECUTIVE AGREEMENT.

relief/work relief   Terms that usually refer to the public assistance programs available during the depression of the 1930s. Relief, or direct relief, referred to straight welfare payments. Work relief referred to any of the numerous public works projects initiated specifically to provide jobs for the unemployed.

REFERENCE

Bruno Stein, *On Relief: The Economics of Poverty and Public Welfare* (New York: Basic Books, 1971).

religious test   A legal requirement that someone must profess faith in a particular religion to qualify for public office. This is expressly forbidden by that portion of Article VI of the U.S. Constitution that reads: "no religious test shall ever be required as a qualification to any office or public trust under the United States." Together with the First Amendment, this guarantee expresses the principle that church and government are to remain separate, and that citizens' religious beliefs are no indication of their patriotism or their ability and right to serve their country. Thus citizens need not fear that their religious affiliations or convictions will legally bar them from holding office.

rent   **1** Payment in compensation for temporary possession of land or property.   **2** The granting of the right of occupancy to land or property in exchange for regular payments.

rent control   Local laws that regulate the amount by which landlords can raise rents on residential rental properties. The U.S. Supreme Court in *Fisher v City of Berkeley,* 89 L. Ed. 2d 206 (1986), held that municipal rent control laws did not violate federal antitrust statutes.

REFERENCES

Stanley Kaish, What is "just and reasonable" in rent control? *American Journal of Economics and Sociology* 40 (April 1981);

Hugo Priemus, Rent control and housing tenure, *Planning and Administration* 9 (Autumn 1982).

rent strike   An organized refusal by the tenants of one landlord to pay their rent in an effort to force the landlord to do something, such as make repairs.

REFERENCE

Harry Brill, *Why Organizers Fail: The Story of a Rent Strike* (Berkeley and Los Angeles: University of California Press, 1971).

reorganization   Changes in the administrative structure or formal procedures of government that do not require fundamental constitutional change or the creation of new bodies not previously established by the legislature. Many reorganizations are undertaken for the purposes of departmental consolidation, executive office expansion, budgetary reform, and personnel administration—primarily to promote bureaucratic responsiveness to central executive control and, secondly, to simplify or professionalize administrative affairs.

Frederick C. Mosher in *Government Reorganizations: Cases and Commentary* (Indianapolis: Bobbs Merrill, 1967) held that the following generalities can be made about reorganizations: (1) that the tensions underlying reorganization efforts are already in existence and have been for some time; (2) that the majority of reorganization efforts are unsuccessful or only partially successful in reducing the tensions underlying them; (3) that understanding a single reorganization effort requires an understanding of the organization's prior history; and (4) that a reorganization effort is not a "one time thing" but a step in a progressive history.

There is often a strong relation between the organization of a legislature and that of its executive branch. According to Harold Seidman's *Politics, Position, and Power*, 3d ed. (New York: Oxford University Press, 1980),

> One could as well ignore the laws of aerodynamics in designing an aircraft as ignore the laws of congressional dynamics in designing executive branch structure. What may appear to be structural eccentricities and anomalies within the executive branch are often nothing but mirror images of jurisdictional conflicts within the Congress. Congressional organization and executive branch organization are interrelated and constitute two halves of a single system.

REFERENCES

For federal government reorganization, see
Harvey C. Mansfield, Federal executive reorganization: Thirty years of experience, *Public Administration Review* 29 (July/August 1969);
Rufus E. Miles, Jr., Considerations for a president bent on reorganization, *Public Administration Review* 37 (March/April 1977);

Richard Polenberg, Roosevelt, Carter, and executive reorganization: Lessons of the 1930s, *Presidential Studies Quarterly* 9 (Winter 1979);
Louis Fisher and Ronald C. Moe, Presidential reorganization authority: Is it worth the cost? *Political Science Quarterly* 96 (Summer 1981);
James G. Benze, Jr., Presidential reorganization as a tactical weapon: Putting politics back into administration, *Presidential Studies Quarterly* 15 (Winter 1985);
Peri E. Arnold, *Making the Managerial Presidency: Comprehensive Reorganization Planning, 1905–1980* (Princeton, NJ: Princeton University Press, 1986).
For state and local reorganization, see James L. Garnett, *Reorganizing State Government: The Executive Branch* (Boulder, CO: Westview, 1980);
James L. Garnett and Charles H. Levine, State executive branch reorganization: Patterns and perspectives, *Administration and Society* 12 (November 1980);
Glen Sparrow and Lauren McKinsey, Metropolitan reorganization: A theory and agenda for research, *National Civic Review* 72 (October 1983);
James Conant, State reorganization: A new model? *State Government* 58:4 (1986).

report The document setting forth a congressional committee's explanation of its action on a bill. Reports by the House of Representatives and the Senate are numbered separately and are designated H. Rept. and S. Rept. Conference reports are numbered and designated in the same way as regular committee reports. Most reports favor a bill's passage. Adverse reports are occasionally submitted, but more often, when a committee disapproves a bill, it simply fails to report it at all. When a committee report is not unanimous, the dissenting committee members may file a statement of their views, referred to as a minority report. Sometimes a bill is reported without recommendation; this means that the committee was divided on its merits.

representation election *See* AUTHORIZATION ELECTION.

representation, proportional *See* PROPOR-
TIONAL REPRESENTATION.

representative A member of the U.S. House
of Representatives or of a lower house in a
state legislature. *See* CONGRESSMAN/CONGRESS-
WOMAN; CONGRESS, MEMBER OF.

representative bureaucracy A concept originated by J. Donald Kingsley in *Representative
Bureaucracy* (Yellow Springs, OH: Antioch,
1944), which asserts that all social groups have
a right to participation in their governing institutions. In recent years, the concept has developed a normative overlay—that all social
groups should occupy bureaucratic positions in
direct proportion to their numbers in the general population.

REFERENCES
For analyses of this normative position, see
Samuel Krislov and David H. Rosenbloom,
*Representative Bureaucracy and the Ameri-
can Political System* (New York: Praeger,
1981);
Dennis Daley, Political and occupational barriers to the implementation of affirmative
action: Administrative, executive, and legislative attitudes toward representative bureaucracy, *Review of Public Personnel
Administration* 4 (Summer 1984).

representative government A governing
system in which a legislature freely chosen by
the people exercises substantial power on their
behalf. *See* EDMUND BURKE for the distinction
between representation and delegation.

Two Theories of Representative Government

In 1970, Senator Roman Hruska, a Republican from Nebraska, was speaking in the Senate on behalf of G. Harold Carswell, President
Richard M. Nixon's nominee to the U.S. Supreme Court. Judge Carswell, who in the end
was rejected by the Senate, was widely accused of being "mediocre," because so many
of his previous judicial decisions were poorly
written and inadequately reasoned. Hruska
sought to defend Carswell on the "mediocre"
issue. "Even if he were mediocre, there's a lot
of mediocre judges and people and lawyers.
They are entitled to a little representation,
aren't they?"

Then there is the oft-told story of President
Calvin Coolidge and his response to criticism
of a businessman he was considering for an
appointment to his cabinet. "But Mr. President," an associate objected, "that fellow's a
son of a bitch."

"Well," responded the president, "don't you
think they ought to be represented, too?"

---

reprivatization *See* PRIVATIZATION.

republic A Latin word meaning the public
thing; the state and its institutions; that form
of government in which sovereignty resides in
the people who elect agents to represent them
in political decision making. The United States
is a republic. The founders specifically wanted
a governing structure that was one step removed from a pure democracy. Yet they all
knew that many republics in history, such as
the Roman republic, had been replaced by des-
pots. Consequently, when Benjamin Franklin
was asked what sort of government had been
hatched at the Constitutional Convention, he
replied, "a republic, if you can keep it." He
knew that "keeping it" was far from certain.

REFERENCE
William R. Everdell, *The End of Kings: A
History of Republics and Republicans* (New
York: Free Press, 1983).

James Madison Advocates a Large Republic

A republic, by which I mean a government in
which the scheme of representation takes
place, opens a different prospect, and promises the cure for which we are seeking. Let us
examine the points in which it varies from
pure democracy and we shall comprehend
both the nature of the cure and the efficacy
which it must derive from the Union.

The two great points of difference between
a democracy and a republic are: first, the delegation of the government, in the latter, to a
small number of citizens elected by the rest;
secondly, the greater number of citizens, and
greater sphere of country, over which the latter may be extended.

The effect of the first difference is, on the
one hand, to refine and enlarge the public
views, by passing them through the medium
of a chosen body of citizens, whose wisdom
may best discern the true interest of their
country, and whose patriotism and love of
justice will be least likely to sacrifice it to temporary or partial considerations. Under such

473

a regulation, it may well happen that the public voice, pronounced by the representatives of the people, will be more consonant to the public good than if pronounced by the people themselves, convened for the purpose. On the other hand, the effect may be inverted. Men of factious tempers, of local prejudices, or of sinister designs, may, by intrigue, by corruption, or by other means, first obtain the suffrages, and then betray the interests, of the people. The question resulting is, whether small or extensive republics are more favorable to the election of proper guardians of the public weal; and it is clearly decided in favor of the latter by two obvious considerations:

In the first place, it is to be remarked that, however small the republic may be, the representatives must be raised to a certain number, in order to guard against the confusion of a multitude. Hence the number of representatives in the two cases not being in proportion to that of the two constituents, and being proportionally greater in the small republic, it follows that, if the proportion of fit characters be not less in the large than in the small republic, it will be more difficult for unworthy candidates to practice with success the vicious arts by which elections are too often carried; and the suffrages of the people being more free, will be more likely to center in men who possess the most attractive merit and the most diffusive and established character.

Source: Federalist 10

republican One who believes in a government where the people exercise their sovereignty through elected representatives. *Compare to* DEMOCRAT.

REFERENCE

David E. Marion, Alexander Hamilton and Woodrow Wilson on the spirit and form of a responsible republican government, *Review of Politics* 42 (July 1980).

Republican A member of the Republican party.

Republican party 1 The first American political party to develop in opposition to the Federalist Party in 1791. Led by Thomas Jefferson, this party later evolved into the Democratic-Republican party, which became the Democratic party in 1828. 2 The 1854 coalition of antislavery Whigs and Jacksonians that went on to win the presidency with Abraham Lincoln in 1860. It dominated national politics from the Civil War to the New Deal.

During that time, only two Democrats were elected president (Grover Cleveland and Woodrow Wilson). Since the New Deal, the Democrats have been the majority party, and the only times the Republicans were able to win the White House were (1) with a hero of World War II (Dwight D. Eisenhower), (2) in the wake of domestic disunity over Vietnam (Richard M. Nixon), and (3) in a contest against a Democratic president (Jimmy Carter) seemingly unable to control inflation or maintain a competent foreign policy (the Iranian hostage crisis). The question remains as to whether the Republican party under the leadership of Ronald Reagan has been able to break the Democratic party's majority to forge a new political REALIGNMENT with a Republican majority.

The Republican party has long been considered the conservative party in American politics. Under the leadership of President Reagan, the Republicans have favored increased spending on defense, decreased spending on domestic, educational, and welfare programs, and a general reduction in the size of government by curtailing government regulation and increasing the privatization of selected government programs.

REFERENCE

George H. Mayer, *The Republican Party, 1854–1966,* 2d ed. (New York: Oxford University Press, 1967).

Republican Party National Headquarters
310 1st Street, S.E.
Washington, D.C. 20003
(202) 863–8500

rescission A bill or a joint resolution that cancels in whole or in part budget authority previously granted by the U.S. Congress. Rescissions proposed by the president must be transmitted in a special message to the Congress, which must approve such proposed rescissions under procedures in the Budget and Impoundment Control Act of 1974 for them to take effect.

reservation 1 In the context of international relations, a nation's formal declaration that, while it accepts a treaty in general, it must modify or expand its terms before it is fully acceptable. Once the reservation is agreed to by the other party, it is then considered part of the original agreement. *See, for example,* DE-CONCINI RESERVATION. **2** Land set aside by a government for a specific purpose. **3** Any of the approximately four hundred land units reserved for American Indians and supervised by the Bureau of Indian Affairs of the U.S. Department of the Interior.

reserved powers The principle of American federalism embodied in the TENTH AMENDMENT of the U.S. Constitution that reserves for the states (or the people) the residue of powers not granted to the federal government or withheld from the states. Chief Justice Harlan F. Stone wrote in *United States v Darby Lumber* that the Tenth Amendment is "but a truism that all is retained which has not been surrendered."

reserve requirements The percentage of deposit liabilities that U.S. commercial banks are required to hold as a reserve at their Federal Reserve bank, as cash in their vaults, or as directed by state banking authorities. The reserve requirement is one of the tools of monetary policy. Federal Reserve officials can control the lending capacity of the banks (thus influencing the money supply) by varying the ratio of reserves to deposits that commercial banks are required to maintain.

residency requirement **1** The requirement that a citizen live in a jurisdiction for a specific length of time before being eligible to vote or hold public office. The U.S. Supreme Court held in *Dunn v Blumstein,* 405 U.S. 330 (1972), that a "durational" residency requirement to vote is unconstitutional. However, as a practical matter the Court recognizes the necessity of closing voter registration rolls thirty to fifty days before an election. **2** The requirement that a person be (or become) a resident of a jurisdiction to be eligible for employment with the jurisdiction. **3** The requirement that a person be a resident of a jurisdiction for a specific time period before becoming eligible for welfare benefits. The U.S. Supreme Court has ruled in *Shapiro v Thompson,* 394 U.S. 618 (1969), that jurisdictions cannot discriminate against newer residents in the provision of social benefits.

REFERENCES
1 Edward Tynes Hand, Durational residence requirements for candidates, *University of Chicago Law Review* 40 (Winter 1973);
2 Peter K. Eisinger, Municipal residency requirements and the local economy, *Social Science Quarterly* 64 (March 1983); Stephen L. Mehay and Kenneth P. Seiden, Municipal residency laws and local public budgets, *Public Choice* 48:1 (1986).
3 Eugene C. Durman, The impact of the elimination of residency laws on public assistance rolls, *Journal of Legal Studies* 4 (January 1975).

resident commissioner *See* DELEGATE.

residuals *See* BOLAND AMENDMENT.

res judicata A Latin term for a settled matter; a closed case. It means that a court has passed judgment on a case and consequently will not reexamine it.
REFERENCES
William H. Theis, Res judicata in Civil Rights Act cases: An introduction to the problem, *Northwestern University Law Review* 70 (January/February 1976);
David P. Currie, Res judicata: The neglected defense, *University of Chicago Law Review* 45 (Winter 1978).

resolution A congressional action, designated H. Res. or S. Res., that deals with matters entirely within the prerogatives of one house or the other. It requires neither passage by the other chamber nor approval by the president, and it does not have the force of law. Most resolutions deal with the rules of one house. They also are used to express the sentiments of a single house, as condolences to the family of a deceased member, or to give "advice" on foreign policy or other executive branch business.

resolution, joint A congressional action, designated H. J. Res. or S. J. Res., that requires the approval of both houses and the signature of the president, just as a bill does, and has the force of law if approved. There is no real difference between a bill and a joint resolution. The latter is generally used in dealing with limited matters, such as a single appropriation for a specific purpose. Joint resolutions also are used to propose amendments to the Constitution. They do not require presidential signature but become a part of the Constitution when three-fourths of the states have ratified them. *Compare to* CONCURRENT RESOLUTION.

responsibility, full *See* FULL RESPONSIBILITY.

restraining order, temporary *See* INJUNCTION.

restrictive covenant *See* COVENANT.

retained counsel A defense attorney selected and paid for by the defendant or other private person.

Retirement Equity Act of 1984 The federal law that broadens the conditions under which spouses receive retirement benefits. Under the act, spouses of employees who die after attaining eligibility for pensions are guaranteed a benefit beginning at age fifty-five; a prospective survivor must agree in a signed, notarized statement before a pension plan member can waive the option of providing a survivorship benefit (previously, the plan member had the sole right to decide); and the divorced spouse of a plan member is entitled to part of a pension, if stipulated in the separation papers or ordered by a judge.

revenue anticipation notes Forms of short-term borrowing used by a jurisdiction to resolve a cash flow problem occasioned by a shortage of necessary revenues or taxes to cover planned or unplanned expenditures.

revenue gainers/revenue enhancement 1 Euphemisms for tax increases. 2 The manipulation of existing tax laws (or methods) to increase revenues as opposed to the more straightforward approach of raising or creating new taxes.

revenue neutral A characteristic of a tax reform law whose net effect would be to neither increase nor decrease the total taxes raised. Instead, it would readjust tax burdens, presumably to make the overall tax system fairer or simpler.

revenue sharing The sharing of federal tax revenues among subnational levels of government. First proposed in its present form in the early 1960s by Walter Heller, then chairman of President John F. Kennedy's Council of Economic Advisers, revenue sharing was designed to arrest the rising fiscal burdens of many state and local governments. Part of its original rationale was the concern of some economists about the accumulation of federal budget surpluses. Given today's record federal deficits, this sounds a bit unreal; nevertheless, it was a true concern of the early 1960s. The theory was that a budget surplus would produce a fiscal drag on the economy and that the money ought to be put back into the economy in some efficient way. Revenue sharing was a natural. Another justification for revenue sharing was its ability to mitigate fiscal imbalances among the states, where variances in per capita personal income are significant. Finally, the argument was made that revenue sharing is economically justified by the federal government's monopolization of the most efficient and progressive tax source—the federal income tax.

In 1972, revenue sharing was introduced to the nation with the passage of the State and Local Fiscal Assistance Act. With the advent of the Ronald Reagan administration, general revenue sharing was subject to increased scrutiny. The General Revenue Sharing Program was allowed to expire in 1986. The burgeoning of federal budget deficits stands as one obstacle to renewal. Another obstacle seems to be the preference of the Reagan administration for some type of tax or revenue turn-back program, which would have the federal government relinquish its use of a specific tax or taxes in favor of state and local government adoption. A turn-back program seems to be viewed by the Reagan administration as a potentially more effective mechanism by which to devolve authority from the federal government to state and local governments.

REFERENCES

Sylvia V. Hewitt, A history of revenue sharing, *State Government* 46 (Winter 1973);

Paul R. Dommel, *The Politics of Revenue Sharing* (Bloomington: Indiana University Press, 1974);

Richard P. Nathan, Allen D. Manvel, and Susannah E. Calkans, *Monitoring Revenue Sharing* (Washington, D.C.: Brookings, 1975);

Will S. Myers, A legislative history of revenue sharing, *Annals of the American Academy of Political and Social Science* 419 (May 1975);

John P. Pelissero, State revenue sharing with large cities: A policy analysis over time, *Policy Studies Journal* 13 (March 1985).

reverse discrimination A practice generally understood to mean discrimination against white males in conjunction with preferential treatment for women and minorities. The practice had no legal standing. Indeed, Section 703(j) of Title VII of the Civil Rights Act of 1964 holds that nothing in the title shall be interpreted to permit any employer to "grant preferential treatment to any individual or group on the basis of race, color, religion, sex or national origin." Yet affirmative action programs necessarily put some white males at a disadvantage that they would not have otherwise had. Reverse discrimination is usually most keenly perceived when affirmative action policies conflict with older policies of granting preferments on the basis of seniority, test scores, and so on. The practice of reverse discrimination was finally given legal standing when the U.S. Supreme Court in *Johnson v Santa Clara County*, 94 L. Ed. 2d 615 (1987), upheld an affirmative action plan which promoted a woman ahead of an objectively more qualified man. Critics contended that this turned Title VII's requirement that there be no "preferential treatment" upside down because for the first time the Court sanctioned and gave legal standing to reverse discrimination. The whole matter may have been summed up by George Orwell in his 1945 novella, *Animal Farm*, when he observed that "All animals are equal, but some animals are more equal than others." *See also* DEFUNIS V ODEGAARD; REGENTS OF THE UNIVERSITY OF CALIFORNIA V ALLAN BAKKE; UNITED STEELWORKERS OF AMERICA V WEBER, ET AL.

REFERENCES
John Hart Ely, The constitutionality of reverse racial discrimination, *University of Chicago Law Review* 41 (Summer 1974);

Alan H. Goldman, Limits to the justification of reverse discrimination, *Social Theory and Practice* 3 (Spring 1975);

William T. Blackstone, Reverse discrimination and compensatory justice, *Social Theory and Practice* 3 (Spring 1975);

Joel Kassiola, Compensatory justice and the moral obligation for preferential treatment of discriminated groups, *Polity* 11 (Fall 1978);

Alan H. Goldman, *Justice and Reverse Discrimination* (Princeton, NJ: Princeton University Press, 1979);

Robert K. Fullinwider, *The Reverse Discrimination Controversy: A Moral and Legal Analysis* (Totowa, NJ: Rowman and Littlefield, 1980);

Ralph A. Rossum, *Reverse Discrimination: The Constitutional Debate* (New York: Dekker, 1980);

R. Kent Greenawalt, *Discrimination and Reverse Discrimination* (New York: Knopf, 1983).

Review of Politics A quarterly journal that emphasizes the philosophical and historical backgrounds of current politics; published since 1939. Library of Congress no. JA1 .R4.
Review of Politics
University of Notre Dame
Notre Dame, IN 46556

revolution 1 Any social, economic, agricultural, political, or intellectual change involving major transformations of fundamental institutions. Those institutions may be class structures (*see* MARXISM), economic structures (*see* INDUSTRIAL REVOLUTION), methods of producing food supplies (*see* GREEN REVOLUTION), ideas and approaches to knowledge (as in a scientific revolution), or systems of governance. Political revolutions in which one leader uses violent means to take power from another without transforming the system are also often called revolutions, although the use of the term since the eighteenth century has tended to be confined to fundamental change, rather than to changes in power. Political commentators who see major changes, say, from one presidential administration to another are often inclined to refer to the changes as a revolution (thus the Reagan revolution, the Roosevelt revolution) to indicate a large degree of supposed transformation. **2** A right of the citizens of a society to overthrow bad, incompetent, or unjust rulers—by violence if necessary—to establish a better government. The founders, heavily influenced by JOHN LOCKE, believed this strongly. Thomas Jefferson wrote in a letter to William Stevens Smith on November 13, 1787, that "the tree of liberty must be refreshed from time to time with the blood of patriots and tyrants. It is its natural manure." In this context, revolution is a right that helps insure proper government; that threatens only the government of tyrants. This right of revolution has often been turned into a religious obligation. Both the American Thomas Jefferson and the Iranian Ayatollah Khomeini (1901–   ) have preached that resistance to tyrants is obedience to God. The right of revolution serves as a continuous check on potential tyrants. According to Abraham Lincoln: "This country, with its institutions, belongs to the people who inhabit it. Whenever they shall grow weary of the existing government, they can exercise their constitutional right of amending it, or their revolutionary right to dismember or overthrow it." Unfortunately, as Franz Kafka (*see* KAFKAESQUE) is alleged to have warned: "Every revolution evaporates, leaving behind only the slime of a new bureaucracy." **3** Evolution. Americans have come to suspect revolutions and revolutionaries, even as they continue to revere their own. The association of the term with Marxism has led Americans to a more evolutionary concept of government change, one that denies anyone the right to overthrow the Constitution by force. While the concept of revolution by peaceful means is difficult for oppressed people to accept, here or anywhere else in the world, it has come to be the basis for the affirmation of American government as a successful system for carrying out the will of the people through established procedures.

Revolution must be contrasted with rebellion. Theoretically, those in rebellion seek power for its own sake. In seeking domination, they violate the structures of a civil society. In this context, the worst rebels are tyrannical rulers who have violated both their personal honor and their political mandates and thus deserve to be overthrown. The ability of those fighting to overthrow a government to sustain their cause ultimately affects whether history calls them revolutionaries or rebels—as the Confederate states discovered when they lost the American Civil War.

REFERENCES

Clarence Crane Brinton, *The Anatomy of Revolution,* rev. ed. (Englewood Cliffs, NJ: Prentice-Hall, 1952);

Hannah Arendt, *On Revolution* (New York: Viking, 1963);

Edward Hyams, *A Dictionary of Modern Revolution* (New York: Taplinger, 1973);

Marshall Smelser, An understanding of the American Revolution, *Review of Politics* 38 (July 1976);

Raymond B. Pratt, Toward a critical theory of revolution, *Polity* 11 (Winter 1978);

James Farr, Historical concepts in political science: The case of "revolution," *American Journal of Political Science* 26 (November 1982);

Robert Blackley, *Revolutions and Revolutionists: A Comprehensive Guide to the Literature* (Santa Barbara, CA: ABC–Clio, 1982);

D. H. Close and C. R. Bridge, *Revolution: The History of an Idea* (Totowa, NJ: Rowman and Allenheld, 1985).

Reynolds v Sims 377 U.S. 533 (1964) The U.S. Supreme Court case that established the criteria of one man, one vote for legislative apportionment. The Court held that legislative districts must be apportioned on the basis of population to comply with the equal protection of the laws guaranteed by the Fourteenth Amendment. In so ruling, it rejected the federal analogy, which suggested that one house of a state legislature (paralleling the U.S. Senate) could be apportioned on a basis other than population. It held that the analogy was invalid, because the political subdivisions of a state are not sovereign entities, as the states are. In holding that legislatures should "represent people, not trees, or acres," the Court did much to curb the rural bias of the state legislatures. *Compare to* BAKER V CARR.

REFERENCES
James A. Gazell, One man, one vote: Its long germination, *Western Political Quarterly* 23 (September 1970);
Gordon E. Baker, One man, one vote, and "political fairness"—Or how the Burger Court found happiness by rediscovering *Reynolds v Sims*, *Emory Law Journal* 23 (Summer 1974);
Barbara B. Knight, The states and reapportionment: One man, one vote reevaluated, *State Government* 49 (Summer 1976);
Bruce Adams, The unfinished revolution: Beyond one person, one vote, *National Civic Review* 67 (January 1978).

Reynolds v United States *See* FREE EXERCISE CLAUSE.

rider A provision that may have no relation to the basic subject matter of the bill it is riding on. Riders become law if the bills in which they are included become law. Riders on appropriation bills are outstanding examples, though technically they are banned. The U.S. House of Representatives, unlike the Senate, has a strict germaneness rule; thus riders are usually Senate devices.

right 1 The conservative, sometimes reactionary, elements of the political spectrum. The political Right in all countries tends to favor traditional free enterprise, capitalism, a strong military, a vigorous executive, and cultural conservatism. *See* LEFT for origin of term. 2 A legally enforceable power or privilege; or a power or privilege believed to have been conferred by God or nature, hence incapable of being subverted by man. *Compare to* CIVIL RIGHTS.

REFERENCES
1 Alan Crawford, *Thunder on the Right* (New York: Pantheon, 1980);
Gillian Peele, *Revival and Reaction: The Right in Contemporary America* (New York: Oxford University Press, 1985);
2 Stuart A. Scheingold, *The Politics of Rights* (New Haven, CT: Yale University Press, 1974);
Ronald M. Dworkin, *Taking Rights Seriously* (Cambridge, MA: Harvard University Press, 1977);
Steven B. Cord, Equal rights: A provable moral standard, *American Journal of Economics and Sociology* 38 (January 1979);
D. W. Haslett, The general theory of rights, *Social Theory and Practice* 5:3, 4 (1980).

rightful place The judicial doctrine that an individual who has been discriminated against should be restored to the job—to his or her "rightful place"—as if there had been no discrimination, and given appropriate seniority, merit increases, and promotions. *Compare to* MAKE WHOLE.

right, natural *See* LAW, NATURAL.

Right, new Traditional conservatism with an evangelical and intolerant edge to it. The new Right expresses the politics of resentment; it rejects much of government's involvement in the economy and with traditional welfare programs. It advocates a strong anticommunist foreign policy and traditional moral virtues regarding religion, school prayer, abortion, and pornography. The new Right believes so strongly in its views that it seeks various constitutional amendments and other changes in the law to foist its attitudes on all citizens. *Compare to* MORAL MAJORITY.

REFERENCES
Richard A. Viguerie, *The New Right: We're Ready to Lead* (Aurora, IL: Caroline House, 1981);
Pamela Johnston Conover, The mobilization of the new Right: A test of various explanations, *Western Political Quarterly* 36 (December 1983);
Nick Bosanquet, *After the New Right* (Brookfield, VT: Gower, 1983);
Desmond King, *The New Right: Politics, Markets, and Citizenship* (Chicago, IL: Dorsey, 1988).

right-of-way/easement The legal right to use the land of another, typically for right of passage of a person, vehicle, underground cables, and so on. In the case of scenic easement, it is the right to a view.

Right, radical Far Right conservatives, many of whom believe that those who advocate policies that differ from their own are motivated by treason. The radical Right is as intolerant of differing political opinions as is the radical Left.

REFERENCES
Seymour Martin Lipset, *The Politics of Unreason: Right-Wing Extremism in America, 1790–1977,* 2d ed. (Chicago: University of Chicago Press, 1978);
Edward L. Ericson, *American Freedom and the Radical Right* (New York: Ungar, 1982).

right to life The movement to reverse the present legal status of abortion in the United States. *See* ROE V WADE.

REFERENCES
Andrew H. Merton, *Enemies of Choice: The Right to Life Movement and Its Threat to Abortion* (Boston: Beacon, 1981);
Connie Paige, *The Right to Lifers: Who They Are, How They Operate, Where They Get Their Money* (New York: Summit, 1983).

right-to-work laws State laws that make it illegal for collective bargaining agreements to contain maintenance of membership, preferential hiring, union shop, or any other clauses calling for compulsory union membership. A typical right-to-work law might read: "No person may be denied employment and employers may not be denied the right to employ any person because of that person's membership or nonmembership in any labor organization." The Labor-Management Relations (Taft-Hartley) Act of 1947 authorized right-to-work laws in Section 14(b): "Nothing in this Act shall be construed as authorizing the execution or application of agreements requiring membership in a labor organization as a condition of employment in any State or Territory in which such execution or application is prohibited by State or Territorial law." The law does not prohibit the union or closed shop; it simply gives each state the option of doing so. Twenty states have done so to some degree: Alabama, Arizona, Arkansas, Florida, Georgia, Iowa, Kansas, Louisiana, Mississippi, Nebraska, Nevada, North Carolina, North Dakota, South Carolina, South Dakota, Tennessee, Texas, Utah, Virginia, and Wyoming.

REFERENCES
Ralph D. Elliott, Do right to work laws have an impact on union organizing activities? *Journal of Social and Political Studies* 4 (Spring 1979);
William J. Moore and Robert J. Newman, The effects of right-to-work laws: A review of the literature, *Industrial and Labor Relations Review* 38 (July 1985).

riot 1 Technically, actions by three or more people that create a clear and present danger to life or property. 2 Generally, any violent mass disturbance of the peace. A riot differs from an insurrection or a rebellion in that its primary purpose is disturbance in response to immediate circumstances, rather than a planned action focused on bringing about political change by attacking the governing regime.

REFERENCES
Samuel J. Raphalides, The president's use of troops in civil disorder, *Presidential Studies Quarterly* 8 (Spring 1978);
Mark Iris, American urban riots revisited, *American Behavioral Scientist* 26 (January/February 1983).

riot act A 1714 British statute for the suppression of riots that had to be read aloud to rioters before they could be legally ordered to dispense; thus the expression "read them the riot act." The first sentence of the act read: "Our sovereign Lord the King chargeth and commandeth all persons being assembled immediately to disperse themselves, and peaceably to depart to their habitations."

riot commission *See* KERNER COMMISSION.

ripper act Any legislative measure abolishing offices held by opposition partisans, thereby lessening the powers of administrative agencies controlled by opposition appointees, transferring the authority to grant contracts, and so on. All ripper acts are done in a spirit of partisanship and revenge.

rise above principle What a politician does when he or she compromises and agrees to measures that may be contrary to his or her professed principles but may better meet the perceived public need.

Robert's Rules of Order See PARLIAMEN-
TARY PROCEDURE.

Robinson-Patman Act of 1936 The federal
law that prohibits price discrimination and
other anticompetitive practices in business. It
forbids the seller from furnishing services or
an allowance to some of its customers unless
they are made available to all competing customers on proportionally equal terms. In addition, if sellers pay commissions or brokerage
fees to buyers, the buyers must actually perform some services to earn them. The act also
provides criminal sanctions for certain practices and for sales at unreasonably low prices if
the purpose is to destroy competition.
REFERENCE
Thomas W. Ross, Winners and losers under
the Robinson-Patman Act, *Journal of Law
& Economics* 27 (October 1984).

Robinson v California See CRUEL AND UN-
USUAL PUNISHMENT.

Roe v Wade 410 U.S. 113 (1973) The U.S.
Supreme Court case that (by a vote of seven to
two) made abortions legal in the United States
by ruling that governments lacked the power to
prohibit them. Associate Justice Harry Black-
mun wrote regarding this case that "freedom
of personal choice in matters of marriage and
family life is one of the liberties protected by
the due process clause of the Fourteenth
Amendment. . . . That right necessarily includes the right of a woman to decide whether
or not to terminate her pregnancy." This has
been one of the most controversial Supreme
Court decisions, heralded by some groups as a
landmark for women's rights and denounced
by others, especially the new Right, as the legalization of murder. The *Gallup Report* (Jan-
uary/February 1986) showed that Americans
were evenly divided between those who oppose
and those who support the *Roe v Wade* decision. *Compare to* GRISWOLD V CONNECTICUT.
REFERENCES
Kathleen A. Kemp, Robert A. Carp, and
David W. Brady, The Supreme Court and
social change: The case of abortion, *Western Political Quarterly* 31 (March 1978);
Susan B. Hansen, State implementation of Supreme Court decisions: Abortion rates since

Roe v Wade, Journal of Politics 42 (May
1980);
Charles A. Johnson and Jon R. Bond, Policy
implementation and responsiveness in non-
governmental institutions: Hospital abortion
services after *Roe v Wade, Western Political
Quarterly* 35 (September 1982);
Robert H. Blank, Judicial decision making
and biological fact: *Roe v Wade* and the un-
resolved question of fetal viability, *Western
Political Quarterly* 37 (December 1984).

Rogers Act of 1924 The federal statute that
created a merit-based career system for the
FOREIGN SERVICE of the U.S. Department of
State.

roll-call 1 The calling of the names of the
members of a legislature to determine whether
a quorum is present so that formal business
may be conducted. 2 An individually recorded vote of the members of a legislature. A
roll-call vote is in contrast to a voice vote, in
which there is no way to hold a legislator accountable for how he or she voted. Roll calls
have often been replaced by electronic devices,
but the effect is the same—the way each legislator voted becomes a matter of public record.
REFERENCES
2 David C. Kozak, Decision-making on roll
call votes in the House of Representatives, *Congress and the Presidency: A
Journal of Capital Studies* 9 (Autumn
1982);
Charles S. Bullock III and David W.
Brady, Party, constituency, and roll-call
voting in the U.S. Senate, *Legislative
Studies Quarterly* 8 (February 1983);
Thomas H. Hammond and Jane M. Fraser,
Judging presidential performance on
House and Senate roll calls, *Polity* 16
(Summer 1984);
Martin Thomas, Election proximity and
senatorial roll call voting, *American
Journal of Political Science* 29 (Febru-
ary 1985).

Roman law See LAW, ROMAN.

Roosevelt, Eleanor (1884–1962) The wife
of President Franklin D. Roosevelt. She was the
first First Lady to publicly play a major politi-

Eleanor Roosevelt.

Franklin D. Roosevelt.

cal role in her husband's administration. Her example has made her a major influence in the modern women's movement. She continued in public life after her husband's death, serving as a delegate to the United Nations and continuing as a significant voice in liberal causes and humanitarian issues.

REFERENCES

Joseph P. Lash, *Eleanor and Franklin* (New York: Norton, 1971);

Joseph P. Lash, *Eleanor: The Years Alone* (New York: Norton, 1972).

Roosevelt, Franklin Delano (1882–1945) The president of the United States (1933–1945) whose NEW DEAL policies are often said to have saved the capitalistic system, who led the nation through the Great Depression of the 1930s and to victory in World War II, and who is on every leading historian's list, along with Abraham Lincoln and George Washington, as one of the best U.S. presidents ever. Roosevelt entered public life as a member of the New York Senate (1910–1913). He became assistant secretary of the Navy (1913–1920) in the Woodrow Wilson administration, the unsuccessful Democratic nominee for vice president in 1920, and governor of New York (1929–1933).

Roosevelt reached the height of political power despite the fact that, after 1921, when he contracted polio, he was basically confined to a wheelchair. Yet because he was able to stand (with braces) to give speeches and because reporters were not allowed to take pictures that made him appear to be disabled, much of the American public was unaware of his handicapped condition—even though it was not a secret. But this did not stop his critics, who attacked him, his New Deal policies, and his wife, Eleanor, as being either socialist or fascist. The hatred of Roosevelt was so intense that his opponents were often too furious to pronounce his name; thus he was often called "that man in the White House." This reference is now used for any occupant of that house with whom one is exasperated.

REFERENCES

James MacGregor Burns, *Roosevelt: The Lion and the Fox* (New York: Harcourt Brace Jovanovich, 1956);

William E. Leuchtenberg, *Franklin D. Roosevelt and the New Deal, 1932–1940* (New York: Harper & Row, 1963);

James MacGregor Burns, *Roosevelt: The Soldier of Freedom* (New York: Harcourt Brace Jovanovich, 1970);

William E. Leuchtenberg, *In the Shadow of FDR: From Harry Truman to Ronald Reagan* (Ithaca, NY: Cornell University Press, 1985).

The Franklin D. Roosevelt Administration

Major Accomplishments
- The creation of the modern presidency (*see* BROWNLOW COMMITTEE).
- Made the Democratic Party the majority party in American politics; the last partisan realignment on which all analysts can agree.
- The hundred days of domestic legislation.
- The New Deal, which gave the United States a permanent mixed economy.
- Lend-lease military aid programs, which helped Britain to hold out against Germany until, after the Japanese attack on Pearl Harbor, the United States entered World War II.
- The mobilization of the nation to win World War II.
- His fireside chats—the use of radio to regularly communicate with the people.

Major Frustrations
- His failure to enlarge the U.S. Supreme Court (court packing).
- The persistence of the Great Depression until a wartime economy ended it.
- The removal of all Japanese–Americans (except those living in Hawaii) to internment camps during World War II.

Theodore Roosevelt.

John M. Blum, *The Republican Roosevelt* (Cambridge, MA: Harvard University Press, 1954);

Edmund Morris, *The Rise of Theodore Roosevelt* (New York: Coward, McCann, and Geoghegan, 1979).

Roosevelt, Theodore "Teddy" (1858–1919) The colonel who led the Rough Riders in Cuba during the 1898 Spanish-American War; who was the elected governor of New York on the basis of his war record; who was made vice president under William McKinley by the party bosses, who wanted him out of New York; and who became president after an assassin shot McKinley in 1901. Roosevelt, who won election in his own right in 1904, took an expansive view of the presidency (*see* BULLY PULPIT) and thus set the tone for most of the presidents to follow. He was the first to advocate consumer protection. *Also see* BIG STICK; NEW NATIONALISM; PRESIDENCY, STEWARDSHIP THEORY OF.
REFERENCES
Theodore Roosevelt, *An Autobiography* (New York: Macmillan, 1913);

The Theodore Roosevelt Administration

Major Accomplishments
- The Panama Canal.
- Peace between Russia and Japan in 1905, earning him the Nobel Peace Prize in 1906.
- Energetic trust busting.
- The Pure Food and Drug Act.
- The Department of Commerce and Labor.
- Conservation; the creation of national parks and forests.
- The Newlands Reclamation Act.

Major Frustrations
- The panic (recession) of 1907.
- The conservative-dominated Congress, which failed to pass much of his proposed domestic programs.
- The split in the Republican party between conservatives and progressives.

Roper, Elmo (1900–1971) One of the pioneers of modern small-sample, preelection, public opinion polling. Roper's technique came to prominence when he predicted Franklin D. Roosevelt's victory over Alfred Landon in the 1936 presidential election to within 1 percentage point of the actual vote. *Compare to* GEORGE HORACE GALLUP.

Rostker v Goldberg 453 U.S. 57 (1981) The U.S. Supreme Court case that held that the registration of males and not females for potential military draft was not in violation of the equal protection of the laws.

Roth v United States 354 U.S. 476 (1957) The U.S. Supreme Court case that asserted that obscenity was not protected free speech under the First Amendment because it was "utterly without redeeming social importance or value." But how is it to be determined whether some expression is obscene enough to forgo First Amendment protection? According to the Court, the test of obscenity is "whether to the average person, applying contemporary community standards, the dominant theme of the material taken as a whole appeals to prurient interest." This test of obscenity has been modified by the Court in *Miller v California*, 413 U.S. 15 (1973), when "contemporary community standards" were replaced by "national standards."

round robin A petition with the signatures arranged in a circle so there is no way to tell the order in which it was signed. This arrangement makes it difficult to single out the organizers of the petition for punishment.

Rousseau, Jean-Jacques (1712–1778) The Swiss-born French Enlightenment philosopher whose theories of democracy and the social contract were major influences on the American and French revolutions. His most important book, *The Social Contract* (1762), opens with the poignant: "Man is born free, and everywhere he is in chains." Rousseau found the free, natural man, the noble savage, good; but the institutions of society had corrupted him. The only form of social organization that could get man back to his state of natural liberty was direct democracy. Only this kind of popular sovereignty offered legitimacy; only the general will as expressed by the people could make valid law. Rousseau's notions fell on fertile intellectual ground. His basic ideas, that ordinary people had the right to govern themselves and had the right to overthrow kings who claimed a competing divine right, can be found in both the Declaration of Independence and the U.S. Constitution.

REFERENCES
Harvey F. Fireside, The concept of the legislator in Rousseau's *Social Contract, Review of Politics* 32 (April 1970);
Stephen G. Salkever, Rousseau and the concept of happiness, *Polity* 11 (Fall 1978);
Richard Fralin, The evolution of Rousseau's view of representative government, *Political Theory* 6 (November 1978);
Arthur M. Melzer, Rousseau's moral realism: Replacing natural law with the general will, *American Political Science Review* 77 (September 1983).

RSA *See* REGIONAL SCIENCE ASSOCIATION.

rubber-chicken circuit A gastronomic description of the political campaign trail.

rugged individualism *See* SELF-RELIANCE.

rule 1 A regulation made by an administrative agency. *See* RULE MAKING AUTHORITY. **2** A decision of a judge or presiding officer. **3** A standing order governing the conduct of business in the House of Representatives or Senate and listed in the chamber's book of rules. The rules deal with duties of officers, order of business, admission to the floor, voting procedures, and so on. **4** In the House, a decision made by its Rules Committee about the handling of a particular bill on the floor. The committee may determine under which standing rule a bill shall be considered, or it may provide a special rule in the form of a resolution. If the resolution is adopted by the House, the temporary rule becomes as valid as any standing rule. A special rule sets the time limit on general debate. It may also waive points of order against provisions of the bill or against specified amendments to the bill. It may even forbid all amendments or all amendments except those proposed by the legislative committee that handled the bill. In this instance, it is known as a closed rule, or gag rule, as opposed to an open rule, which puts no limitation on floor amendments. *Compare to* RULES, SUSPENSION OF.

REFERENCES

3   Charles B. Rangel, Use of congressional rules to delay progress in civil rights policy, *Journal of Legislation* 8 (Winter 1981).

4   Spark M. Matsunaga and Ping Chen, *Rulemakers of the House* (Urbana: University of Illinois Press, 1976);
    Bruce Oppenheimer, The Rules Committee: New arm of leadership in a decentralized House, in *Congress Reconsidered*, ed. Larry Dodd and Bruce Oppenheimer (New York: Praeger, 1977);
    Stanley Bach, Special rules in the House of Representatives: Themes and contemporary variations, *Congressional Studies* 8:2 (1981).

rule making authority   The powers, which have the force of law, exercised by administrative agencies. Agencies begin with some form of legislative mandate and translate their interpretation of that mandate into policy decisions, specifications of regulations, and statements of penalties and enforcement provisions. The exact process to be followed in formulating regulations is only briefly described in the federal Administration Procedure Act (APA). The APA does distinguish between rule making that requires a hearing and rule making that requires only notice and the opportunity for public comment (notice and comment). Whether the formal or informal procedure is to be used is determined by the enabling statute: the U.S. Supreme Court's decision in *United States v Florida East Coast Railway,* 410 U.S. 224 (1973), held that formal rule making need only be followed when the enabling statute expressly requires an agency hearing prior to rule formulation. The APA also requires that rules be published thirty days before their effective date and that agencies afford any interested party the right to petition for issuance, amendment,

or repeal of a rule. In effect, while the APA establishes a process of notice and time for comment, it accords administrative rule makers the same prerogatives as legislatures have in enacting statutes. There is, of course, the additional requirement that the rule enacted be consistent with the enabling statute directing the rule making.

REFERENCES

Daniel J. Gifford, Administrative rulemaking and judicial review: Some conceptual models, *Minnesota Law Review* 65 (November 1980);

Kenneth Culp Davis, Presidential control of rulemaking, *Tulane Law Review* 56 (April 1982);

William F. Kent, The politics of administrative rulemaking, *Public Administration Review* (September/October 1982);

William West and Joseph Cooper, The congressional veto and administrative rulemaking, *Political Science Quarterly* 98 (Summer 1983).

rule of four   The U.S. Supreme Court's policy of granting a petition for a writ of CERTIORARI if four or more justices consider a case to be worthy of review.

rule of law   A governing system in which the highest authority is a body of law that applies equally to all (as opposed to the rule of men, in which the personal whim of those in power can decide any issue). The idea of the desirability of a "government of laws, and not of men" can be traced back to Aristotle. The earliest American reference is in the 1779 Massachusetts Constitution. John Marshall also used this succinct legal description in *Marbury v Madison:* "The government of the United States has been emphatically termed a government of laws, and not of men. It will certainly cease to deserve this high appellation, if the laws furnish no remedy for the violation of a vested legal right."

REFERENCES

Edward A. Kent, *Revolution and the Rule of Law* (Englewood Cliffs, NJ: Prentice-Hall, 1971);

Richard F. Bensel, Creating the statutory state: The implications of a rule of law standard in American politics, *American Political Science Review* 74 (September 1980);

Harry N. Scheiber, Public rights and the rule of law in American legal history, *California Law Review* 72 (March 1984);

Carl-August Fleischhauer, The United Nations and the rule of law, *Aussenpolitik* 36:3 (1985).

rule of three The practice of certifying to an appointing authority the top three names on an eligible list. The rule of three is intended to give the appointing official an opportunity to weigh intangible factors, such as personality, before making a formal offer of appointment. The rule of one certifies only the highest-ranking person on the eligible list. The rule of the list gives the appointing authority the opportunity to choose from the entire list of eligibles.

rules of engagement Military or paramilitary directives that delineate the circumstances and limitations under which force can be used. For example, soldiers might be told to shoot only if they are fired upon first, or police might be told to use deadly force only when lives (as opposed to property) are in immediate danger.

rules, suspension of A time-saving procedure for passing bills in the U.S. House of Representatives. The wording of the motion, which may be made by any member recognized by the Speaker, is: "I move to suspend the rules and pass the bill." A favorable vote by two-thirds of those present is required for passage. Debate is limited to forty minutes, and no amendments from the floor are permitted. If a two-thirds favorable vote is not attained, the bill may be considered later under regular procedures. The suspension procedure is in order on the first and third Mondays and Tuesdays of each month.

run ahead of the ticket To get more votes in an election than the party's standard bearer. A candidate for the U.S. Congress runs ahead of the ticket when he or she gets more votes than the party's nominee for president.

runoff election *See* ELECTION, RUNOFF.

rustbelt Those parts of the northeastern and midwestern United States where traditional manufacturing industries are in decline, literally rusting away. Rustbelt is often used synonymously with snowbelt (*see* SUNBELT-SNOWBELT TENSION).

S

safe seat A legislative district in which the incumbent is virtually guaranteed reelection; normally a seat that is captured with 60 percent or more of the vote. This could be because of the candidate's strong political appeal, an overwhelming registration of voters from the candidate's party, or the candidate's many years of CASEWORK service to the district's citizens. In recent U.S. House of Representative elections, a majority of districts have been won by 65 percent or more of the vote. *Compare to* MARGINAL SEAT.

REFERENCES

Raymond E. Wolfinger and John Heifetz, Safe seats, seniority, and power in Congress, *American Political Science Review* 59:2 (1965);

Robert S. Erickson, Is there such a thing as a safe seat? *Polity* 8 (Summer 1976).

safety net President Ronald Reagan's term for the social welfare programs that, in his opinion, assure at least a subsistence standard of living for all Americans.

REFERENCES

Sar A. Levitan and Clifford M. Johnson, *Beyond the Safety Net: Reviving the Promise of Opportunity in America* (Cambridge, MA: Ballinger, 1984);

Martha R. Burt and Karen J. Pittman, *Testing the Social Safety Net* (Washington, D.C.: Urban Institute, 1986).

sagebrush rebellion A general term that covers any number of dissatisfactions—hardly a rebellion—that some people in the states of the American West have with the federal government's management and use of the federal lands within their borders. In general, they feel that the states should have more control over the lands and how they are used. The counterargument is that such lands are national trusts and can only legitimately be dealt with by representatives of the national government.

REFERENCES

Carroll B. Foster, The "sagebrush rebellion" and the Alaska Lands Bill in the U.S. Congress, *Legislative Studies Quarterly* 8 (November 1983);

Barney Dowdle, Perspective on the sagebrush rebellion, *Policy Studies Journal* 12 (March 1984);

Howard E. McCurdy, Public ownership of land and the "sagebrush rebellion," *Policy Studies Journal* 12 (March 1984);

Frank J. Popper, The timely end of the sagebrush rebellion, *Public Interest* 76 (Summer 1984).

Saint Francis College v Al-Khazraji See RACE CATEGORIES.

SALT Strategic arms limitation talks; the extensive negotiating sessions between the United States and the Soviet Union to promote balanced and verifiable limitations on strategic nuclear weapons. SALT I started in 1969; after two and a half years of negotiating, the parties signed the ABM treaty and an interim agreement, which presumably froze offensive weapons at existing levels for five years. SALT II, which began in 1972, sought to achieve a comprehensive agreement to replace the interim agreement. A SALT II treaty was signed by the United States and the Soviet Union in 1979; but U.S. Senate ratification of the treaty was indefinitely postponed on January 3, 1980, in response to the December 27, 1979, Soviet invasion of Afghanistan. Nevertheless, the United States abided by the terms of the treaty until 1986, when President Ronald Reagan asserted that Soviet violations made it impossible for the United States to continue doing so.

REFERENCES

Wolfgang Panofsky, *Arms Control and SALT II* (Seattle: University of Washington Press, 1979);

William C. Potter, ed., *Verification and SALT: The Challenge of Strategic Deception* (Boulder, CO: Westview, 1980).

sample Any deliberately chosen portion of a larger population that is representative of that population as a whole. Scientifically selected samples—random samples in which each person in a population has an equal chance of being selected—are the foundation of public opinion polling. The size of a sample can be very small in relation to the overall population. It is possible to accurately measure public opinion in a nation of over two hundred million with a sample of a few thousand—if the sample is properly selected. The pollsters often report that sample results are accurate to within plus or minus 3 or 4 percentage points. This may not be terribly helpful in a close race, but the cost of making the survey marginally more accurate by interviewing ten or twenty times as many subjects quickly becomes prohibitive. When opinion sampling was first introduced in the period between the World Wars, it was difficult for political leaders to believe that such a small portion of a large population could provide an accurate measure of the whole population. Now most politicians are true believers about sampling, and no major campaign is without its pollsters. This situation has created a larger danger: that those in or seeking public office will merely parrot their pollsters' perceptions of public opinion rather than forging new opinions. Modern sampling makes it all too easy to tell the public what they want to hear as opposed to what they need to hear. *Compare to* OPINION LEADER; PUBLIC OPINION.

REFERENCE

Donald P. Warwick and Charles A. Lininger, *The Sample Survey: Theory and Practice* (New York: McGraw-Hill, 1975).

A Famous Biased Sample

The devastating effect of biased sampling is illustrated by an incident that attracted national attention a third of a century ago. The summer before the 1936 presidential election, the *Literary Digest* undertook an extensive poll of the U.S. population to determine who the next president would be. The *Digest* did things in a big way. More than ten million double postcards were mailed to persons living in every county in the United States. The list was made up of names taken from every telephone book in the United States, from the rosters of clubs and associations, from state directories, lists of registered voters, mail order lists, and so on. The recipients were asked to indicate whether they intended to vote for Franklin D. Roosevelt or Alfred M. Landon for president. A sampling of ten million people established an all-time record, but the response was disappointing: only two million cards were returned. After tabulating the returned cards, the *Digest* predicted the election of Landon by a substantial majority. When the votes were counted, Governor Landon carried only two states. The debacle was fatal to the *Digest*. It went out of business shortly thereafter.

The gargantuan poll suffered from two fatal deficiencies. In the first place, the list was made up predominantly of people who had telephones or who belonged to clubs and associations. Millions of other citizens who did not enjoy the blessings of either a telephone or a membership were underrepresented in the sample; and these people composed a very different statistical universe from those who did. In the second place, the one-fifth of those polled who did respond doubtless also represented a different universe from the four-fifths who did not answer, thus contributing a further—and unmeasurable—source of error.

The *Digest* discovered the hard way that mere size of a sample carries no guarantee of producing a representative response. Only if care is taken to assure that the sample constitutes a true cross-section of the entire population can it be relied on to produce usefully accurate information.

Source: Adapted from Charles P. Kaplan and Thomas L. Van Valey, *Census '80: Continuing the Fact-finder Tradition* (Washington, D.C.: Department of Commerce, Bureau of the Census, 1980).

---

sampling error   The error caused by generalizing the behavior of a population from a sample of that population that is not totally representative of the population as a whole. For example, it is often reported that a specific survey of public opinion is accurate to plus or minus 4 percentage points. This 8 point spread represents the sampling error. There would be no sampling error if an entire population (e.g., 240 million Americans) were surveyed instead of a few thousand.

Samuelson, Paul Anthony (1915–   ) The Nobel Prize-winning economist who advanced the use of mathematics in economic analysis. His introductory textbook *Economics* (12th ed., New York: McGraw-Hill, 1985) has since 1947 been providing a Keynesian perspective to several generations of college students and has become a publishing phenomenon by selling over four million copies.

sanction   1 The penalties attached to a law to encourage people to obey it   2 Ratification by a higher (or another) authority.   3 Foreign policies that range in a continuum from the suspension of diplomatic or economic relations to outright military intervention, designed to force another nation to change its behavior.

REFERENCES

3   Margaret P. Doxey, *Economic Sanctions and International Enforcement*, 2d ed. (New York: Oxford University Press, 1980);

Gary Clyde Hufbauer and Jeffrey J. Schott, *Economic Sanctions in Support of Foreign Policy Goals* (Cambridge, MA: MIT Press, 1983);

James M. Lindsay, Trade sanctions as policy instruments: A re-examination, *International Studies Quarterly* 30 (June 1986).

sanctuary   1 A safe place.   2 A sacred or religious place.   3 The protection once offered by churches to those fleeing the secular law because of political or other crimes.   4 The 1980s movement to help illegal immigrants from Central America find refuge in the United States. *Compare to* ASYLUM.

REFERENCE
4   Renny Golden and Michael McConnell, *Sanctuary: The New Underground Railroad* (Maryknoll, NY: Orbis, 1986).

sanitary code   A local law that requires specific standards of cleanliness for establishments serving food, offering medical services, and so on.

sanitize   1 To make clean, to sterilize, or to disinfect.   2 To revise a document to prevent the identification (1) of sources, (2) of the actual person and places concerned, or (3) of the means by which it was acquired.

satellite   1 A small thing within the orbit of a larger one; a subservient attendant or follower.   2 A country informally dominated by another. For example, the communist states of Eastern Europe are generally considered to be satellites of the Soviet Union. However, no self-respecting country would ever formally admit to being a satellite, because that would imply that it is less than a sovereign nation.

satisficing   Herbert Simon's (1916–) term to explain his concept of "bounded rationality." Simon asserted that it is impossible to ever know all the facts that bear upon any given decision. Because truly rational research on any problem can never be completed, humans put bounds on their rationality and make decisions, not on the basis of optimal information, but on the basis of satisfactory information; that is by satisficing—choosing a course of action that meets one's minimum standards for satisfaction.

REFERENCES
James G. March and Herbert A. Simon, *Organizations* (New York: Wiley, 1958);
John Forester, Bounded rationality and the politics of muddling through, *Public Administration Review* 44 (January/February 1984);
Neil McK. Agnew and John L. Brown, Bounded rationality: Fallible decisions in unbounded decision space, *Behavioral Science* 31 (July 1986).

Saturday Night Massacre   The events of the evening of October 20, 1973, when President Richard M. Nixon ordered the firing of the first WATERGATE special prosecutor, Archibald Cox (1912–). Attorney General Elliot L. Richardson (1920–) refused to fire Cox as ordered; he immediately resigned instead. William D. Ruckelshaus (1932–), the Deputy Attorney General, also resigned rather than fire Cox. The number three man in the Justice Department, the Solicitor General, Robert H. Bork (1929–), then formally dismissed Cox. This created such a furor that a new special prosecutor, Leon Jaworski (1905–1982) was soon appointed. Jaworski's subsequent investigations were a major factor in Richard Nixon's resignation in 1974. The Saturday Night Massacre became significant again in 1987 when Bork was futilely nominated to the U.S. Supreme Court and both his critics and his supporters suggested that his actions on that night told much about his character.

SBA   *See* SMALL BUSINESS ADMINISTRATION.

scalawag   A derisive term for white southerners who became Republicans or who worked cooperatively with them during the period of reconstruction after the Civil War.
REFERENCE
Allen W. Trelease, Who were the scalawags? *Journal of Southern History* 29:4 (1963).

scandal   1 In religion, an offense committed by a holder of high office. The term has been popularized to cover the commission of any action considered a demeaning of the responsibilities of office by the holder of that office.   2 The exposure of corruption in public office. The corrupting nature of political power makes scandals inevitable. Remember Lord Acton's (1834–1902) maxim: "Power tends to corrupt; absolute power corrupts absolutely." The question to be asked of scandal is not why, but when. *See* IRAN-CONTRA AFFAIR; WATERGATE.
REFERENCES
Michael McMenamin and Walter McNamara, *Milking the Public: Political Scandals of the Dairy Lobby from L.B.J. to Jimmy Carter* (Chicago: Nelson-Hall, 1980);
Nicole Woolsey Biggart, Scandals in the White House: An organizational explanation, *Sociological Inquiry* 55 (Spring 1985).

scapegoating 1 The Old Testament ritual of selecting a goat to be sent into the wilderness symbolically bearing the sins of a whole community. 2 Shifting the blame for a problem or failure to another person, group, or organization—a common bureaucratic and political tactic.

REFERENCES

James Gallagher and Peter J. Burke, Scapegoating and leader behavior, *Social Forces* 52 (June 1974);

Jeffrey Eagle and Peter M. Newton, Scapegoating in small groups: An organizational approach, *Human Relations* 34 (April 1981).

Schattschneider, E. E. (1892–1971) A significant analyst of the role of political parties and pressure groups in American life. His *Politics, Pressures and the Tariff* (New York: Prentice Hall, 1935) established the intellectual framework for the next generation of political analysis on the role of pressure groups. Schattschneider argued for strong parties and was against direct primaries, which he felt to be destructive of party organization and inconsequential to the larger questions of democratic representation. In *Party Government* (New York: Holt, Rinehart, & Winston, 1942) he wrote that "democracy is not to be found *in* the parties but *between* the parties." Schattschneider clashed with many of his pluralistically oriented contemporaries because, as he wrote in his *The Semisovereign People* (New York: Holt, Rinehart, & Winston, 1960), the "flaw in the pluralist heaven is that the heavenly chorus sings with a strong upper-class accent." *See also* INTEREST GROUP THEORY; POLITICS; PRIVATIZATION OF CONFLICT.

REFERENCE

David Adamany, The political science of E. E. Schattschneider: A review essay, *American Political Science Review* 66 (December 1972).

Schechter Poultry Corporation v United States 295 U.S. 495 (1935) The U.S. Supreme Court case concerning the constitutionality of congressional delegations of authority that invalidated much of the NATIONAL INDUSTRIAL RECOVERY ACT OF 1933—then the heart of the New Deal's effort to fight the Great Depression. The Court held that the separation of powers provided for in the Constitution means that "Congress is not permitted to abdicate or to transfer to others the essential legislative functions with which it is vested." Consequently, legislative delegations would be constitutional only if the Congress "has itself established the standards of legal obligation." Based upon these premises, the Court held that the promulgation of a "live poultry code" under the National Industrial Recovery Act was constitutionally defective. Although *Schechter* has never been directly overruled, the courts have subsequently taken a more flexible view of legislative delegations. Had the *Schechter* rule been forcefully applied since 1935, the discretion exercised by the federal bureaucracy would have been severely constricted.

Schenck v United States *See* CLEAR AND PRESENT DANGER.

Scheuer v Rhodes 416 U.S. 232 (1974) The U.S. Supreme Court case that held that officers of the executive branch of state governments had a qualified immunity from civil suits for damages.

Schlafly, Phyllis *See* WOMEN'S LIBERATION MOVEMENT.

school district A SPECIAL DISTRICT for the provision of local public education for all children in its service area. An elected board, the typically governing body, usually hires a professional superintendent to administer the system. School districts, having their own taxing authority, are administratively, financially, and politically independent of other local government units.

School District of Abington Township v Schempp 374 U.S. 203 (1963) The U.S. Supreme Court case that held that school prayers or other religious exercises violated the establishment of religion clause of the First Amendment as applied to the states by the Fourteenth Amendment. *Murray v Curlett*, 374 U.S. 203 (1963), was decided at the same time on the same grounds. In *Engle v Vitale*, 370 U.S. 421 (1962), the Court also held unconstitutional a nondenominational prayer because it was inappropriate for school authorities to advocate an official prayer. In *Stone v Graham*, 449 U.S. 39 (1980), the Court forbade posting the Ten Commandments in classrooms; but in *Widmar v Vincent*, 454 U.S. 263 (1981), the Court allowed on First Amendment grounds that state university classrooms can be used for student religious group meetings.

REFERENCE

H. Frank Way, Jr., Survey research on judicial decisions: The prayer and bible reading cases, *Western Political Quarterly* 21 (June 1968).

school prayer *See* SCHOOL DISTRICT OF ABINGTON TOWNSHIP V SCHEMPP.

Schumpeter, Joseph Alois (1883–1950) An economist who developed theories of economic development and business cycles. While he held that the most frequently criticized elements of capitalism were largely responsible for the rapid advances in productivity and technology that capitalism has enjoyed, he also predicted that capitalism would eventually disappear because the traditional entrepreneur was becoming obsolete and the political factors that protected capitalism were being destroyed.

REFERENCES

See his *Capitalism, Socialism and Democracy*, 3d ed. (New York: Harper & Row, 1950).

Also see Laurence J. O'Toole, Jr., Schumpeter's "Democracy": A critical view, *Polity* 9 (Summer 1977).

Scott v Sandford *See* DRED SCOTT V SANDFORD.

SDI *See* STRATEGIC DEFENSE INITIATIVE.

search and seizure The ability of governments to look for, examine, and take as evidence the property and persons of citizens. The FOURTH AMENDMENT specifically forbids "unreasonable" searches and seizures. There is considerable debate and a multitude of court cases over what unreasonable means in the context. Criminal cases are often dismissed because "tainted evidence" (evidence obtained by

an unreasonable search or seizure) is inadmissible. *See also* EXCLUSIONARY RULE; MAPP V OHIO; WARRANT.

REFERENCES

Wayne R. LaFave, *Search and Seizure: A Treatise on the Fourth Amendment* (St. Paul, MN: West, 1978, 1984 supplement);

George E. Dix, Means of executing searches and seizures as Fourth Amendment issues, *Minnesota Law Review* 67 (October 1982).

SEATO The Southeast Asia Treaty Organization, the now expired mutual security pact signed in 1954 by Australia, France, New Zealand, Pakistan, the Philippines, Thailand, the United Kingdom, and the United States. SEATO was part of the post-World War II American strategy to contain communism (*see* CONTAINMENT); it was designed to be an Asian counterpart of NATO.

REFERENCE

Leszek Buszynski, SEATO: Why it survived until 1977 and why it was abolished, *Journal of Southeast and Asian Studies* 12 (September 1981).

SEC *See* SECURITIES AND EXCHANGE COMMISSION.

secession 1 Withdrawing one's membership in an organization. 2 The withdrawal of a polity from a large political union. 3 The now discredited notion that the American states retained so much of their sovereignty that they could withdraw from the union if they wished. This extreme states' rights position was rejected by the Abraham Lincoln administration; when the South tried to secede in 1861, the issue was settled by the Civil War.

REFERENCE

2 Harry Beran, Must secession be rebellion? *Politics* 18 (November 1983).

Second Amendment The amendment to the U.S. Constitution that provides for the freedom of the collective citizenry to protect itself—to have a "right to bear arms" against both disorder in the community and attack from foreign enemies. In America's frontier days, each person's own arms were vital to the national "militia" and were "necessary to the security of a free state." But in today's modern, urbanized society, military and police forces supplant the need for individual reliance upon firearms. The Supreme Court, as a result, has upheld state and federal laws prohibiting the carrying of concealed weapons, requiring the registration of firearms, and limiting the sale of specified firearms for other than military uses. *See also* GUN CONTROL.

REFERENCES

Ronald B. Levine and David B. Saxe, The Second Amendment: The right to bear arms, *Houston Law Review* 7 (September 1969);

Lawrence Delbert Cress, The origins and meaning of the right to bear arms, *Journal of American History* 71 (June 1984).

second-class citizen One who does not have all of the civil rights of other citizens. Historically, blacks were called, and because of segregation and discrimination often considered themselves to be, second-class citizens. But since the CIVIL RIGHTS MOVEMENT and the new laws that flowed from it, there can be no second-class citizens in the United States. Nevertheless, the phrase is still used in various contexts: by minorities who wish to emphasize economic disparities, by women who feel that they have not achieved social equity with men, by prisoners who complain they can't vote.

second reconstruction The CIVIL RIGHTS MOVEMENT and legislation of the 1960s. The first reconstruction, immediately after the Civil War, gave blacks their freedom from slavery. But the laws as enforced and customs as practiced did not allow for the full rights of citizens. That came in the 1960s, when public sentiment was aroused and legal action was taken to ensure equal rights for all Americans.

REFERENCES

Numan V. Bartley and H. D. Graham, *Southern Politics and the Second Reconstruction* (Baltimore: Johns Hopkins University Press, 1975);

Carl M. Brauer, *John F. Kennedy and the Second Reconstruction* (New York: Columbia University Press, 1977);

Steven F. Lawson, Preserving the second reconstruction: Enforcement of the Voting Rights Act, 1965–1975, *Southern Studies* 22 (Spring 1983).

second-strike capability The ability to survive a first military strike with sufficient resources to deliver an effective counterblow. This concept is usually associated with nuclear weapons. *Compare to* FIRST-STRIKE CAPABILITY.

Second World The socialist countries of Eastern Europe plus the U.S.S.R. *See* FIRST WORLD; THIRD WORLD; FOURTH WORLD.

secretariat 1 An office, headed by a secretary-general, that is responsible for the administrative affairs of a legislature or an international organization. 2 The United Nations secretariat, whose secretary-general is appointed to a five-year term of office by the General Assembly upon the recommendation of the Security Council.

REFERENCES

Y. Beigbeder, Current staff problems in UN secretariats, *International Review of Administrative Sciences* 46:2 (1980);

Seymour Maxwell Finger and Nina Hanan, The United Nations secretariat revisited, *Orbis* 25 (Spring 1981).

secretary 1 The head of a cabinet agency of the U.S. government; for example, the secretary of State, the secretary of Defense. 2 A diplomatic rank for those in positions that support the activities of the chief of a mission. For example, a first secretary is a career foreign service officer who is second in command to the ambassador, the second secretary is third in command, and so on. 3 A service person whose function is defined by an executive whom he or she supports. While such functions are often considered stenographic or clerical, the association of a secretary with an executive is a major relationship in carrying out the responsibilities of the executive, as well as in controlling access to executive judgment and responsibilities. The word comes from the Latin *secretarius*, meaning a confidential officer, one who can be trusted with secrets.

secretary-general The administrative head of a SECRETARIAT. The best-known secretary-

The Secretaries General of the United Nations		
Name	Country	Tenure
Trygve Lie	Norway	1946–1953
Dag Hammarskjold	Sweden	1953–1961
U Thant	Burma	1961–1972
Kurt Waldheim	Austria	1972–1982
Javier Perez de Cuellar	Peru	1982–present

general is that of the United Nations. Since the beginning of the United Nations, this office has been filled by a career diplomat from a country perceived as relatively neutral by both the Western alliance and the Soviet bloc.

REFERENCES

Y. Beigbeder, The operational, administrative, and political role of the secretary-general of the United Nations organization, *International Review of Administrative Sciences* 51 (1985);

Brian Urquhart, *A Life in Peace and War* (New York: Harper & Row, 1987).

secretary of State   1 The senior cabinet officer and chief foreign policy officer of the United States. The secretary of State (who is fourth in line of succession to the presidency after the vice president, the Speaker of the House of Representatives, and the president pro tempore of the Senate) directs the Department of State and all diplomatic missions abroad. While formally in charge of foreign policy, all post–World War II secretaries of State have had to, in effect, share power with other institutional and personal influences on the foreign policy-making process. Recent secretaries have often found themselves competing for foreign policy dominance with the secretary of Defense, the head of the Central Intelligence Agency, and the President's national security advisor. Overall, the secretary of State is only as strong or as influential as a president allows him or her to be. The only postwar secretaries to dominate the foreign policy-making process vis-à-vis the other actors were John Foster Dulles (1888–1959) under Dwight D. Eisenhower and Henry Kissinger (1923–   ) under Richard M. Nixon and Gerald Ford.   2 A state government official (elected in thirty-six states and appointed by the governor in fourteen states) who is responsible for official papers, the administration of elections, motor vehicle registration, business licensing and incorporation, and other jobs.

secretary of the Senate   The chief administrative office of the Senate, overseeing the duties of Senate employees, the education of the pages, the administration of oaths, the registration of lobbyists, and other activities necessary for the operation of the Senate.

Secret Service, United States   The federal agency created in 1860 that is authorized to detect and arrest any person committing any offense against U.S. laws relating to coins, currency, and other obligations, and securities of the United States and of foreign governments. In addition, subject to the direction of the secretary of the Treasury, the Secret Service is authorized to protect the person of the president of the United States, the members of his immediate family, the president elect, the vice president or other officer next in the order of succession to the presidency, the immediate family of the vice president, the vice president elect, major presidential and vice president candidates, former presidents and their wives during his lifetime, widows of former presidents until their deaths or remarriages, minor children of a former president until they reach age sixteen, and visiting heads of a foreign state or foreign government. *Compare to* G-MEN.

U.S. Secret Service
1800 G. Street, N.W.
Washington, D.C. 20223
(202) 535-5708

sectionalism Seeking to further the interests of a specific section of the country; defining a particular group of geographical political bodies in terms of a pressure group interest they have in common. The distinction between regions and sections in American history has sometimes rested on geographical common interests, such as rivers, woodlands, and other resources shared across state boundaries; and social, racial, and other cultural and historical concerns that tied them together as common political forces. The changing of such interests and their use of political rallying points has transformed, periodically, the meaning of both sectionalism and regionalism in American politics. Sectionalism is practiced by the congressional delegations of one part of the country presumably at the expense of the rest of the country. Nevertheless, astute practitioners of sectional politics will always be able to rationalize sectional programs as being in the overall national interest.

REFERENCES

Robert A. Garson, *The Democratic Party and the Politics of Sectionalism, 1941–1948* (Baton Rouge: Louisiana State University Press, 1974);

Richard F. Bensel, *Sectionalism and American Political Development, 1880–1980* (Madison: University of Wisconsin Press, 1984).

Securities and Exchange Commission (SEC) The federal regulatory commission created by the Securities Exchange Act of 1934 that oversees the nation's stock and financial markets. It seeks the fullest possible disclosure to the investing public and strives to protect the interests of the public and investors against malpractices in the securities and financial markets.

REFERENCES

Nicholas Wolfson, A critique of the Securities and Exchange Commission, *Emory Law Journal* 30 (Winter 1981);

Thomas K. McCraw, With consent of the governed: SEC's formative years, *Journal of Policy Analysis and Management* 1 (Spring 1982);

Bevis Longstreth, The SEC after fifty years: An assessment of its past and future, *Columbia Law Review* 83 (October 1983);

Larry Gene Pointer and Richard G. Schroeder, *An Introduction to the Securities and Exchange Commission* (Plano, TX: Business Publications, 1986).

Securities and Exchange Commission
450 5th Street, N.W.
Washington, D.C. 20549
(202) 272-3100

security 1 Being safe; a condition that results from protective measures that insure inviolability from hostile acts. **2** With respect to classified matter, a condition that prevents unauthorized persons from having access to safeguarded information or things. *Compare to* NATIONAL SECURITY.

security assistance The programs of various agencies of the U.S. government relating to international defense cooperation. Security assistance (sometimes called military assistance) has five components: (1) the military assistance program, in which defense articles and defense services are provided to eligible foreign governments on a grant basis; (2) international military education and training, which provides military training in the United States and U.S. territories to foreign military and civilian personnel; (3) foreign military sales, which provides credits and loan repayment guarantees to enable eligible foreign governments to purchase defense articles and defense services; (4) security supporting assistance, which promotes economic and political stability in areas where the United States has special foreign policy security interests; and (5) the peacekeeping operations programs, which funds the Sinai Support Mission and the U.S. contribution to the U.N. forces in Cyprus.

REFERENCES

Stephen B. Cohen, Conditioning U.S. security assistance on human rights practices, *American Journal of International Law* 76 (April 1982);

Gabriel Marcella, Security assistance revisited: How to win friends and not lose influence, *Parameters: Journal of the US Army War College* 12 (December 1982);

Harry J. Shaw, U.S. security assistance: Debts and dependency, *Foreign Policy* 50 (Spring 1983).

security certification The formal indication that a person has been investigated and is eligible for access to classified matter to the extent stated in the certification.

security classification A category to which national security information and material is assigned to denote the degree of damage that unauthorized disclosure would cause. There are three such categories: top secret, secret, and confidential.

security clearance An administrative determination that an individual is eligible for access to classified information.

Security Council The most powerful of the elements created by the United Nations Charter for dealing with questions of international peace and security. The Security Council has five permanent members (China, France, the Soviet Union, the United Kingdom, and the United States) and representatives of ten other nations, five of which are chosen each year for two-year terms. Each of the permanent members has a VETO over decisions of substance, which provides the major powers with protection against majority decisions in the larger U.N. GENERAL ASSEMBLY, where each member nation has only one vote.

REFERENCES

Robert S. Junn and Tong-Whan Park, Calculus of voting power in the UN Security Council, *Social Science Quarterly* 58 (June 1977);

Sydney D. Bailey, The UN Security Council: Evolving practice, *World Today* 34 (March 1978);

Istvan Pogany, The role of the president of the UN Security Council, *International and Comparative Law Quarterly* 31 (April 1982);

Louis B. Sohn, The Security Council's role in the settlement of international disputes, *American Journal of International Law* 78 (April 1984).

security risk 1 A public employee thought to be so susceptible to the influence of foreign agents that he or she cannot be trusted with continued employment or continued access to sensitive information. 2 Any disloyal or generally untrustworthy citizen.

seigniorage A government's profit from coinage; the difference between the value of the metal in the coin and its face value.

REFERENCE

Stanley Fischer, Seigniorage and the case for a national money, *Journal of Political Economy* 90 (April 1982).

selective incorporation *See* INCORPORATION.

selective service The process of conscription of male citizens into the armed forces used by the United States from 1940 until the creation of the all-volunteer force in 1972. However, all males turning eighteen years of age are required to register for selective service (all U.S. post offices have the forms), in case conscription once again becomes necessary.

REFERENCES

Herbert M. Kritzer, Enforcing the Selective Service Act: Deterrence of potential violators, *Stanford Law Review* 30 (July 1978);

Herbert C. Puscheck, Selective service registration: Success or failure? *Armed Forces and Society* 10 (Fall 1983).

self-government 1 Democratic government in which citizens participate in governance either directly or through their representatives. 2 HOME RULE; the autonomy possessed by substate jurisdictions.

self-incrimination clause That portion of the Fifth Amendment that holds that no person "shall be compelled in any criminal case to be a witness against himself." However, a witness may waive this privilege or have it waived by the court with a grant of immunity. This constitutional protection applies only to criminal prosecutions; the courts may still compel testimony that may adversely affect someone's economic interests or reputation. Although those accused may waive their rights under the Fifth Amendment, they generally must know what they are doing and must not be forced to confess, for any confession obtained by use of force or threat will be excluded from the evidence presented at trial. However, the Supreme Court has ruled that, even where an in-custody defendant initially exercises his or her right to remain silent, an incriminating statement procured after a significant time lapse and a fresh set of warnings operates as a waiver and is not violative of MIRANDA RIGHTS. Furthermore, if defendants or witnesses fail to invoke the Fifth Amendment in response to questions addressed to them while on the witness stand, such a failure may operate as a waiver of the right and they will not be permitted to object later to a court's admitting their statements into evidence on the basis that it was self-incriminating. The guarantee against self-incrimination applies only to testimonial actions. Thus it has been held that government actions, such as obtaining handwriting samples and blood tests, are not violative of the Fifth Amendment.

REFERENCES

Marshall Smelser, History of the right against self-incrimination, *Review of Politics* 31 (July 1969);

Leonard W. Levy, The right against self-incrimination: History and judicial history, *Political Science Quarterly* 84 (March 1969).

self-reliance **1** The title of Ralph Waldo Emerson's (1803–1882) 1841 essay, which urged readers to think for themselves, reminded them that "a foolish consistency is the hobgoblin of little minds," and observed that "an institution is the lengthened shadow of one man." **2** The notion that citizens should take care of their own economic needs and not be dependent upon the government for the necessities of life. This was President Herbert Hoover's philosophy of "rugged individualism," which called for economic freedom and opposed paternalistic government welfare programs—which he thought undermined character.

REFERENCE

2 Robert E. Goodin, Self-reliance versus the welfare state, *Journal of Social Policy* 14 (January 1985).

Herbert Hoover's Philosophy of Rugged Individualism

When the war closed, the most vital of all issues both in our own country and throughout the world was whether governments should continue their wartime ownership and operation of many instrumentalities of production and distribution. We were challenged with a peace-time choice between the American system of rugged individualism and a European philosophy of diametrically opposed doctrines—doctrines of paternalism and state socialism. The acceptance of these ideas would have meant the destruction of self-government through centralization of government. It would have meant the undermining of the individual initiative and enterprise through which our people have grown to unparalleled greatness.

The Republican party from the beginning resolutely turned its face away from these ideas and these war practices. . . . When the Republican party came into full power, it went at once resolutely back to our fundamental conception of the state and the rights and responsibilities of the individual. Thereby it restored confidence and hope in the American people, it freed and stimulated enterprise, it restored the government to its position as an umpire instead of a player in the economic game.

Source: Speech of October 22, 1928.

---

self-restraint *See* JUDICIAL SELF-RESTRAINT.

senate **1** The Latin word for a group of old men. A senate was the governing body of the ancient Roman Republic. **2** The upper chamber of the U.S. Congress. The House of Representatives does not, however, accept that the Senate is upper; it acknowledges the Senate only as a coequal chamber. The Roman origins of the word can be found in the constitutional provision that senators be at least thirty years old, while House members need only be twenty-five. Remember that two-hundred years ago, when life expectancy was far less than today, thirty was considered old. *Compare to* CONGRESS, UNITED STATES. **3** The upper chamber of a state legislature.

REFERENCES

2 Donald R. Matthews, *U.S. Senators and Their World* (Chapel Hill: University of North Carolina Press, 1960);

Norman J. Ornstein, Robert L. Peabody, and David W. Rohde, The contemporary Senate: Into the 1980s, in *Congress Reconsidered*, 2d ed., ed. Lawrence C. Dodd and Bruce I. Oppenheimer (Washington, D.C.: Congressional Quarterly, 1981);

George E. Reedy, *The U.S. Senate: Paralysis or a Search for Consensus* (New York: Crown, 1986).

Senate establishment   The inner club of senior, often southern, usually conservative senators that once dominated the U.S. Senate. This establishment disintegrated in the 1960s, as its members died or retired, as the Senate democratized some of its rules, and as new senators— more liberal and less deferential to their elders—were elected.

REFERENCES

William S. White, *Citadel: The Story of the United States Senate* (New York: Harper, 1956);

Joseph S. Clark, *The Senate Establishment* (New York: Hill and Wang, 1963);

Nelson W. Polsby, Goodbye to the inner club, *Washington Monthly* 1 (August 1969).

senator   One who serves as a legislator in the upper house of a legislature. For the qualifications of U.S. senator, *see* CONGRESS, MEMBER OF.

senatorial courtesy   The courtesy of the Senate applied to consideration of executive nominations. It means that nominations from a state are not to be confirmed unless they have been approved by the senators of the president's party from that state, with other senators following their lead (this is the courtesy) in the attitude they take toward such nominations.

senatorial saucer   *See* BICAMERAL.

senator, senior/senator, junior   The two senators from a state. Regardless of age, the senior senator is the one who was elected first; the junior senator is the one elected last.

senior executive service (SES)   The federal government's top management corps, established by the Civil Service Reform Act of 1978. The large majority of SES executives are career managers; there is a 10 percent governmentwide ceiling on the number who may be noncareer. In addition, about 45 percent of SES positions are career reserved; that is, they can be filled only by career executives. *See also* CIVIL SERVICE REFORM ACT OF 1978.

REFERENCES

Bernard Rosen, Uncertainty in the senior executive service, *Public Administration Review* 41 (March/April 1981);

Norton E. Long, The S.E.S. and the public interest, *Public Administration Review* 41 (May/June 1981);

Arthur L. Finkle, Herbert Hall, and Sophia S. Min, Senior executive service: The state of the art, *Public Opinon Quarterly* 10 (Fall 1981);

Michael A. Pagano, The SES performance management system and bonus awards, *Review of Public Personnel Administration* 4 (Spring 1984).

seniority, congressional   The custom whereby a member of the Congress who has served longest on the majority side of a committee becomes its chair or, if on the minority, its ranking member. Members are ranked from the chairman down, according to length of service on the committee. Modifications made during the 1970s' congresses caused the seniority rule to be less rigidly followed than previously. In both chambers, nominees for committee chairs are subject to public votes in caucus meetings of their party colleagues. Members who lose their seats in the Congress and then return (or who change committees) start at the bottom of the list again, except that they outrank those members beginning their first terms.

REFERENCES

Michael Abram and Joseph Cooper, The rise of seniority in the House of Representatives, *Polity* 1 (Fall 1968);

Nelson W. Polsby, Miriam Gallaher, and Barry Spencer Rundquist, The growth of the seniority system in the U.S. House of Representatives, *American Political Science Review* 63 (September 1969);

Barbara Hinckley, *The Seniority System in Congress* (Bloomington: Indiana University Press, 1971);

Albert D. Cover, Seniority in the House: Patterns and projections, *American Politics Quarterly* 11 (October 1983);

Sara Brandes Crook and John R. Hibbing, Congressional reform and party discipline:

The effects of changes in the seniority system on party loyalty in the U.S. House of Representatives, *British Journal of Political Science* 15 (April 1985).

sensitive position   A federal government job requiring access to classified (secret) documents and other information bearing on NATIONAL SECURITY.

separate but equal   The doctrine espoused by the U.S. Supreme Court in *Plessy v Ferguson,* 163 U.S 537 (1896), which held that segregated facilities for blacks, facilities that were considered equal in quality to those provided for whites, did not violate the equal protection clause of the Fourteenth Amendment. In *Brown v Board of Education,* the Court nullified this doctrine when it asserted that separate was "inherently unequal."

REFERENCES

David W. Bishop, *Plessy v. Ferguson:* A reinterpretation, *Journal of Negro History* 62 (April 1977);

Stephen J. Riegel, The persistent career of Jim Crow: Lower federal courts and the "separate but equal" doctrine, 1865–1896, *American Journal of Legal History* 28 (January 1984);

Ralph A. Rossum, *Plessy, Brown,* and the reverse discrimination cases: Consistency and continuity in judicial approach, *American Behavioral Scientist* 28 (July/August 1985).

separation of powers   The allocation of powers among the three branches of government so that they are a check upon each other. This separation, in theory, makes a tyrannical concentration of power impossible. The U.S. Constitution contains provisions in separate articles for three branches of government—legislative, executive, and judicial. There is a significant difference in the grants of power to these branches: the first article, dealing with legislative power, vests in the Congress "all legislative powers herein granted"; the second article vests "the executive power" in the president; and the third article states that "the judicial power of the United States shall be vested in one Supreme Court, and in such inferior courts as the Congress may from time to

time ordain and establish." *Compare to* CHECKS AND BALANCES; FEDERALIST 51.

REFERENCES

George W. Carey, Separation of powers and the Madisonian model: A reply to the critics, *American Political Science Review* 72 (March 1978);

Martin Diamond, The separation of powers and the mixed regime, *Publius* 8 (Summer 1978);

Lee H. Hamilton and Michael H. Van Dusen, Making the separation of powers work, *Foreign Affairs* 57 (Fall 1978);

Nathaniel L. Nathanson, Separation of powers and administrative law: Delegation, the legislative veto, and the "independent" agencies, *Northwestern University Law Review* 75 (February 1981);

Richard A. Brisbin, Jr., Separation of powers, the rule of law, and the study of political institutions, *Polity* 15 (Fall 1982).

James Madison on the Separation of Powers

But the great security against a gradual concentration of the several powers in the same department, consists in giving to those who administer each department the necessary constitutional means and personal motives to resist encroachments of the others. The provision for defence must in this, as in all other cases, be made commensurate to the danger of attack. Ambition must be made to counteract ambition. The interest of the man must be connected with the constitutional rights of the place. It may be a reflection on human nature that such devices should be necessary to control the abuses of government. But what is government itself but the greatest of all reflections on human nature? If men were angels, no government would be necessary. If angels were to govern men, neither external nor internal controls on government would be necessary. In framing a government which is to be administered by men over men, the great difficulty lies in this: you must first enable the government to control the governed; and in the next place oblige it to control itself. A dependence on the people is, no doubt, the primary control on the government; but experience has taught mankind the necessity of auxiliary precautions.

The policy of supplying, by opposite and rival interests, the defect of better motives, might be traced through the whole system of human affairs, private as well as public. We see it particularly displayed in all the subordinate distributions of power, where the constant aim is to divide and arrange the several offices in such a manner as that each may be a check on the other—that the private interest of every individual may be a sentinel over the public rights. These inventions of prudence cannot be less requisite in the distribution of the supreme powers of the State.

Source: Federalist 51.

sergeant at arms The officer charged with maintaining order in a formal meeting, under the direction of the presiding officer. The word *sergeant* is derived from the French word for servant. In the early British parliaments, a sergeant at arms enforced laws and arrested people. While a modern sergeant at arms may no longer be armed, the limited police powers remain. In the U.S. Senate, the sergeant at arms is the Senate's principal law enforcement and executive officer, responsible for the enforcement of all rules made by the Committee on Rules and Administration, for the regulation of the Senate wing of the Capitol, and for the Senate office buildings. The sergeant at arms in the House of Representatives tends to the security of the Capitol and House office buildings and is in charge of the mace, the symbol of legislative power and authority.

service contract An agreement between local units of government for one unit (usually larger) to provide a service for another (usually smaller). It is often called the Lakewood plan, because it was first extensively used between the County of Los Angeles and the City of Lakewood, California.

REFERENCES

Adrian Kuyper, Intergovernmental cooperation: An analysis of the Lakewood plan, *Georgetown Law Journal* 58 (March/May 1970);

Russell L. Smith and C. W. Kohfeld, Interlocal Service Cooperation in metropolitan areas: The impact of councils of governments, *Midwest Review of Public Administration* 14 (June 1980);

Martin J. Schiesl, The politics of contracting: Los Angeles County and the Lakewood plan, 1954–1962, *Huntington Library Quarterly* 45 (Summer 1982).

service fee **1** User charges for government services not fully paid for by general taxation. Examples include water fees from municipal governments and admission fees for national parks. **2** The equivalent of union dues that nonunion members of an agency shop pay the union for negotiating and administering the collective bargaining agreement.

SES *See* SENIOR EXECUTIVE SERVICE.

session The time between the convening and the adjournment of a legislature or court.

session, executive *See* EXECUTIVE SESSION.

session, special The formal convening of a legislature, outside of its constitutionally scheduled meetings, at the initiative of a chief executive. Article II, Section 3, of the U.S. Constitution gives the president the authority to call the entire Congress or either house into special seession "on extraordinary occasions." All state governors have similar authority. Prior to the ratification of the lame duck amendment in 1933, a new president came into office in March without a Congress in session until the next December. Early twentieth-century presidents often found it necessary to call special sessions to ask for new legislation at the opening of their administrations if they wanted to take advantage of the momentum of their election the previous November.

set asides Government purchasing and contracting provisions that set aside or allocate a certain percentage of business for minority-owned companies. The use of set asides was upheld by the Supreme Court in *Fullilove v Klutznick*.

REFERENCE

Felicity Hardee, *Fullilove* and the minority set aside: In search of an affirmative action rationale, *Emory Law Journal* 29 (Fall 1980).

Seventeenth Amendment The 1913 amendment to the U.S. Constitution that changed the electoral process for U.S. senators from selection by state legislatures to a popular vote. By the early 1900s, it had become a concern that, under the system of indirect election by state legislatures, many senators were indifferent to popular demands and obligated to corporations that could often influence their elections. Another objection to the selection of senators by legislatures was that often a state went unrepresented or only half-represented in the Senate because of the inability of many legislatures to agree on any one candidate.

Seventh Amendment The amendent to the U.S. Constitution that guarantees a jury trial in most federal civil suits.

REFERENCES

Charles W. Wolfram, The constitutional history of the Seventh Amendment, *Minnesota Law Review* 57 (March 1973);

Thomas M. Jorde, The Seventh Amendment right to jury trial of antitrust issues, *California Law Review* 69 (January 1981).

sex discrimination Any disparate or unfavorable treatment of a person in an employment situation because of his or her sex. The Civil Rights Act of 1964 (as amended by the Equal Employment Opportunity Act of 1972) makes sex discrimination illegal in most employment, except where a bona fide occupational qualification is involved. In 1980, after the federal courts had decided that sexual harassment was sex discrimination in a variety of cases, the Equal Employment Opportunity Commission issued legally binding rules clearly stating that an employer has a responsibility to provide a place of work that is free from sexual harassment or intimidation. In 1986, the Supreme Court reaffirmed this when in the case of *Meritor Saving Bank v Vinson,* 91 L. Ed. 2d 49, it held that sexual harassment creating a hostile or abusive work environment, even without economic loss for the person being harassed, was in violation of Title VIII of the Civil Rights Act of 1964.

REFERENCES

Dail Ann Neugarten and Jay M. Shafritz, eds., *Sexuality in Organizations* (Oak Park, IL: Moore, 1980);

Mary Coeli Meyer et al., *Sexual Harassment* (New York: Petrocelli, 1981);

U.S. Merit Systems Protection Board, *Sexual Harassment in the Federal Workplace: Is It a Problem?* (Washington, D.C.: Government Printing Office, 1981);

Patrice D. Horn and Jack C. Horn, *Sex in the Office: Power and Passion in the Workplace* (Reading, MA: Addison-Wesley, 1982).

Shaare Tefila Congregation v Cobb See RACE CATEGORIES.

shadow cabinet 1 The British practice of having the party out of power appoint party leaders to constantly review and criticize the performance of the various cabinet members. The American political parties have occasionally used this tactic in an effort to embarrass the administration in power. 2 The political party leaders out of power who would replace the current cabinet secretaries.

REFERENCE

Tom Bethell, Gentlemen-in-waiting: The democratic shadow cabinet, *Washington Monthly* 8 (April 1976).

Shangri-la *See* CAMP DAVID.

Shapiro v Thompson *See* RESIDENCY REQUIREMENT.

shared tax *See* TAX, SHARED.

Shays' Rebellion A futile armed revolt (1786–1787) led by Daniel Shays (1747–1825), a Revolutionary War officer, in New England to protest the discontent of small farmers over debts and taxes. The rebellion was never a serious military threat, but it raised concern over the inadequacy of the Articles of Confederation to handle internal disorders.

Shelton v Tucker 364 U.S. 479 (1960) The U.S. Supreme Court case that dealt with the question of whether public employees could have membership in subversive organizations, organizations with illegal objectives, and unions. Their right to join the latter was upheld. With regard to the former, it was held that there could be no general answer. Rather, each case has to be judged on the basis of whether a public employee actually supports an organization's illegal aims.

Sherbert v Verner 374 U.S. 398 (1963) The U.S. Supreme Court case that held it unconstitutional to disqualify a person for unemployment compensation benefits solely because that person refused to accept employment that would require working on Saturday, contrary to his or her religious beliefs.

sheriff The elected (in all states but Rhode Island) chief officer of a county law enforcement agency, usually responsible for law enforcement in unincorporated areas of the county and for the operation of the county jail. The sheriff—whose title comes from the Middle English *schirreff*, Old English *shire-reeve*, meaning the king's representative in a shire (an English county)—is also the officer of the local court who serves papers, enforces court orders, and so on.

Sherman Antitrust Act of 1890 The federal statute that held "every contract, combination in the form of trust or otherwise, or conspiracy, in restraint of trade or commerce . . . is hereby declared to be illegal." While the statute was directed at industrial monopolies, the courts used the act punitively against the budding union movement. Subsequent legislation (the Clayton Act of 1914) exempted unions from the Sherman Act prohibitions on the restraint of trade.

shield laws 1 Statutes that permit reporters to protect the confidentiality of their sources. While many states have shield laws to encourage people to talk freely to the press without fear that their identity will be publicly exposed, the federal government does not. 2 Any statute that shields victims or witnesses from questioning in open court—for example, statutes that protect the anonymity of children or statutes that prevent defense lawyers from asking rape victims about their previous and unrelated sexual activities.
REFERENCE
2 J. Alexander Tanford and Anthony J. Bocchino, Rape victim shield laws and the Sixth Amendment, *University of Pennsylvania Law Review* 128 (January 1980).

showboating The unusually dramatic behavior exhibited by members of the U.S. Congress and other legislators in their respective chambers when they know that they are being filmed or on live television.

silk stocking 1 Rich; often used to describe a wealthy legislative district. 2 A contemptuous reference to a person of wealth.
REFERENCE
James E. Alt and Janet Turner, The case of the silk-stocking socialists and the calculating children of the middle class, *British Journal of Political Science* 12 (January 1982).

Simpson-Mazzoli bill The reforms of immigration policy that, as incorporated in the Immigration Reform and Control Act of 1986, (1) provide for the granting of permanent residence status to illegal aliens who have continuously resided in the United States since 1982 and (2) impose strict legal penalties on employers who knowingly hire illegal aliens. The bill was considered in several sessions of the Congress before being passed and signed into law in 1986.
REFERENCES
Francis A. La Poll, The Simpson-Mazzoli Bill and employer sanctions: Political discriminatory impact and its minimization, *Stanford Journal of International Law* 19 (Summer 1983);
Katherine Terrell, The Simpson-Mazzoli Bill: Employer sanctions and immigration reform, *New York University Journal of International Law and Politics* 17 (Summer 1985);
B. Lindsay Lowell, Frank D. Bean, and Rodolfo O. de la Garza, The dilemmas of undocumented immigration: An analysis of the 1984 Simpson-Mazzoli vote, *Social Science Quarterly* 67 (March 1986).

sinecure Any position for which a salary is extracted but little or no work is expected. This was originally an ecclesiastical term, which meant a church office that did not require the care of souls, sinecure being Latin for without care.

sine die *See* ADJOURNMENT SINE DIE.

single-issue politics Situations in which decisions on political support or nonsupport are made on one factor to the exclusion of all others. The factor is usually quite specific, such as opposition to abortion, support for protectionist legislation to help a particular industry, and so on. *Compare to* ISSUE VOTING.

REFERENCES

Sylvia Tesh, In support of "single issue" politics, *Political Science Quarterly* 99 (Spring 1984);

Gregory Casey, Intensive analysis of a "single" issue: Attitudes on abortion, *Political Methodology* 10:1 (1984).

single-member district *See* DISTRICT, SINGLE-MEMBER.

single tax *See* HENRY GEORGE.

sinking fund Money put aside for a special purpose, such as to pay off bonds and other long-term debts as they come due or to replace worn-out or outdated machinery or buildings.

sitting president *See* PRESIDENT, SITTING.

Sixteenth Amendment The 1913 amendment to the U.S. Constitution that allows the federal government to tax income "from whatever source derived." This overturned the U.S. Supreme Court's decision in *Pollock v Farmer's Loan and Trust Co.*, 158 U.S. 601 (1895), which held that a direct income tax from the federal government was unconstitutional. The Supreme Court had earlier upheld the Civil War income tax in *Springer v United States*, 102 U.S. 586 (1881). The *Pollock* decision reversed *Springer*, which was, in turn, reversed by the Sixteenth Amendment.

REFERENCES

Arthur A. Ekirch, Jr., The Sixteenth Amendment: The historical background, *Cato Journal* 1 (Spring 1981);

John D. Buenker, The ratification of the federal income tax amendment, *Cato Journal* 1 (Spring 1981).

Sixth Amendment The amendment to the U.S. Constitution that sets forth specific rights guaranteed to persons facing criminal prosecution in federal courts—and in state courts by virtue of the Fourteenth Amendment. The right to a speedy and public trial requires that the accused be brought to trial without unnecessary delay and that the trial be open to the public. Intentional or negligent delay by the prosecution that prejudices the defendant's right to prepare a defense has been held as grounds for dismissal of the charges. Trial by an impartial jury supplements the earlier guarantee contained in Article III of the U.S. Constitution. The right to jury trial does not apply to trials for petty offenses, which the U.S. Supreme Court has suggested to be those punishable by six months confinement or less. In trials where a jury is used, the jury must be impartially selected, and no persons can be excluded from jury service merely because of their race, class, or sex.

The Sixth Amendment also requires that defendants be notified of the particular factual nature of the crimes they have been accused of committing, so that they can prepare their defense. This also means that the crime must be established by statute beforehand, so that all persons are on public notice about the existence of the prohibition. The statute must not be so vague or unclear that it does not inform people of the exact nature of the crime. Generally, those accused are entitled to have all witnesses against them present their evidence orally in court and to cross-examine them. Moreover, the accused is entitled to the aid of the court in having compulsory process issued, usually a subpoena, which orders into court as witnesses those persons whose testimony the accused desires at the trial.

Finally, the Sixth Amendment provides a right to be represented by counsel. For many years, this was interpreted to mean only that the defendant had a right to be represented by a lawyer if the defendant could obtain one. The Supreme Court has held, however, that the amendment imposes an affirmative obligation on the part of federal and state governments to provide at public expense legal counsel for those who cannot afford it (*see* GIDEON V WAINWRIGHT).

REFERENCE

Stephen G. Gilles, Effective assistance of counsel: The Sixth Amendment and the fair trial guarantee, *University of Chicago Law Review* 50 (Fall 1983).

slander Oral statements that are so false and malicious that injury is caused to a person's reputation. Slander is often confused with LIBEL (false and malicious written statements). For example, in a 1986 television show of *Saturday Night Live*, guest host Jimmy Breslin (1930–), a journalist, discussed his work. He jokingly told millions of people, "You call it slander. I call it getting paid." Breslin was wrong. Being a print reporter, he gets paid for "libel."

Slaughter-House cases 16 Wallace 36 (1873) The U.S. Supreme Court case that drew a sharp distinction between the rights of U.S. citizens and the rights of citizens of the various states. The Court held that civil rights were derived from state citizenship and thus were not protected by the U.S. Constitution (especially the Fourteenth Amendment) against state action. This ruling was the Supreme Court's first interpretation of the Fourteenth Amendment. The ruling has since been overruled, as the Court has gradually made most of the protections of the Bill of Rights applicable to the states. *See* INCORPORATION.

slip laws The first official publication of a bill enacted into law by the U.S. Congress. Each is published separately in unbound, single-sheet, or pamphlet form. Slip laws usually become available two to three days after presidential approval.

slush fund 1 Money collected by the military services in the nineteenth century by selling grease and other refuse (the slush). The resulting funds were used to buy small luxuries for the soldiers and sailors. 2 Discretionary funds appropriated by a legislature for the use of an agency head. 3 Private monies used for campaign expenses. 4 Funds used for bribery. 5 Secret funds. All slush funds because of their lack of formal accountability have an unsavory connotation—even when they are perfectly legal. *Compare to* CHECKERS SPEECH.

Small Business Administration (SBA) The federal agency created by the Small Business Act of 1953 whose purposes are to aid, coun-sel, assist, and protect the interests of small business; to ensure that small business concerns receive a fair portion of government purchases, contracts, and subcontracts, as well as of the sales of government property; to make loans to small business concerns, state and local development companies, and the business victims of floods or other catastrophes, or of certain types of economic injury; to license, regulate, and make loans to small business investment companies; to improve the management skills of small business owners, potential owners, and managers; to conduct studies of the economic environment; and to guarantee surety bonds for small contractors.

Small Business Administration
1441 L Street, N.W.
Washington, D.C. 20416
(202) 653–6554
(800) 368–5855 (toll free)

Smeal, Eleanor *See* WOMEN'S LIBERATION MOVEMENT.

Smith Act *See* ALIEN REGISTRATION ACT OF 1940/SMITH ACT.

Smith, Adam (1723–1790) The Scottish economist who provided the first systematic analysis of economic phenomena and the intellectual foundation for laissez-faire capitalism. In *The Wealth of Nations* (1776), Smith discusses an "invisible hand" that automatically promotes the general welfare as long as individuals are allowed to pursue their self-interest. It has become customary for organization theorists to trace the lineage of present-day theories to Smith's concept of the division of labor. Greater specialization of labor was one of the pillars of the invisible hand market mechanism, in which the greatest rewards would go to those who were the most efficient in the competitive marketplace. As Smith's work marks the beginning of economics as an identifiable discipline, he is often referred to as the father of economics. *See also* ABILITY TO PAY.

REFERENCES

Paul A. Samuelson, A modern theorist's vindication of Adam Smith, *American Economic Review* 67 (February 1977);

Warren J. Samuels, The political economy of Adam Smith, *Ethics* 87 (April 1977);

Andrew S. Skinner, Adam Smith and the American Revolution, *Presidential Studies Quarterly* 7 (Spring/Summer 1977);

Donald J. Devine, Adam Smith and the problem of justice in capitalist society, *Journal of Legal Studies* 6 (June 1977);

Peter Stein, Adam Smith's Jurisprudence: Between morality and economics, *Cornell Law Review* 64 (April 1979);

John W. Danford, Adam Smith, equality, and the wealth of sympathy, *American Journal of Political Science* 24 (November 1980).

Smithsonian Institution   The institution created by an act of the U.S. Congress in 1846 to carry out the terms of the will of James Smithson of England, who, in 1829, bequeathed his entire estate to the United States "to found at Washington, under the name of the Smithsonian Institution, an establishment for the increase and diffusion of knowledge among men." To carry out Smithson's mandate, the institution, as an independent trust establishment, performs fundamental research; publishes the results of studies, explorations, and investigations; preserves for study and reference over seventy million items of scientific, cultural, and historical interest; maintains exhibits representative of the arts, U.S. history, technology, aeronautics and space explorations, and natural history; participates in the international exchange of learned publications; and engages in programs of education and national and international cooperative research and training, supported by its trust endowments and gifts, grants and contracts, and funds appropriated to it by the Congress.

Smithsonian Institution
1000 Jefferson Drive, S.W.
Washington, D.C. 20560
(202) 357–1300

Smith v Allwright   See PRIMARY, WHITE.

Smith v Wade 461 U.S. 30 (1983)   The Supreme Court case that held that punitive damages can be awarded against public employees for reckless indifference to an individual's constitutional rights. It is not necessary for the plaintiff to prove actual malice or intentional violation. The decision expanded the liability of public administrators to punitive damages.

smoke-filled room   The stereotypical description of any place of political deal-making, where political bosses dictate the "will" of the people. In the old days when behind-the-scenes politicos got together to cut a deal or seal a nomination at a national convention, the room quickly filled up with the exhalations of their cigars and cigarettes. The slightly sinister connotations of "smoke filled room" first developed when the phrase was applied to the hotel room where the Republican party leaders decided on the nomination of Warren G. Harding in 1920.

REFERENCE

Wesley M. Bagby, The "smoke filled room" and the nomination of Warren G. Harding, *Mississippi Valley Historical Review* 41:4 (1955).

SMSA   See STANDARD METROPOLITAN STATISTICAL AREA.

Snepp v United States 445 U.S. 972 (1980)   The U.S. Supreme Court case that held that a former CIA agent was required to have the CIA's permission prior to the publication of information relating to his former employment.

REFERENCES

Joshua B. Bolten, Enforcing the CIA's secrecy agreement through postpublication civil action: *United States v. Snepp, Stanford Law Review* 32 (January 1980);

Diane F. Orentlicher, *Snepp v. United States*: The CIA secrecy agreement and the First Amendment, *Columbia Law Review* 81 (April 1981);

Jonathan C. Medow, The First Amendment and the secrecy state: *Snepp v. United States, University of Pennsylvania Law Review* 130 (April 1982).

snowbelt   See SUNBELT-SNOWBELT TENSION.

social contract   1 The philosophic notion that the obligations that individuals and states have toward each other originate in a theoretical social contract they have made with each other. If the state breaks the social contract, then grounds for revolution exist. This was an important consideration in the Declaration of Independence. *See the individual entries for the* SOCIAL CONTRACT THEORISTS. *Compare to* STATE OF NATURE. **2** The social welfare policies of a government. They are considered a contract because citizens have grown to expect and depend upon them.

REFERENCES
1 John B. Noone, Jr., The social contract and the idea of sovereignty in Rousseau, *Journal of Politics* 32 (August 1970);
   Claude Ake, Social contract theory and the problem of politicization: The case of Hobbes, *Western Political Quarterly* 23 (September 1970);
   William T. Bluhm, Freedom in *The Social Contract:* Rousseau's "legitimate chains," *Polity* 16 (Spring 1984).
2 D. Lee Bawden, ed., *The Social Contract Revisited* (Washington, D.C.: Urban Institute, 1984).

social contract theorists Thomas Hobbes (1588–1679), John Locke (1632–1704), and Jean-Jacques Rousseau (1712–1778). *See individual entries.*

social Darwinism Charles Darwin's (1809–1882) concept of biological evolution applied to the development of human social organization and economic policy. The major influence on American social Darwinism was the Englishman, Herbert Spencer (1820–1903), who spent much of his career working out the application of concepts such as "natural selection" and "survival of the fittest" to his ideas of social science. American social Darwinists, generally speaking, occupied a wide range of theories, from an absolute rejection of the idea of government intervention in social development to elaborate methods of developmental influence that could affect the various races (into which they believed civilization was divided).

REFERENCES
For the essays of America's most significant exponent of social Darwinism, William Graham Sumner (1840–1910), see *Social Darwinism: Selected Essays of William Graham Sumner* (Englewood Cliffs, NJ: Prentice-Hall, 1963).

For the classic history, see Richard Hofstadter, *Social Darwinism in American Thought,* rev. ed. (Boston: Beacon, 1955).
For recent applications, see Janna L. Thompson, The new social Darwinism: The politics of sociobiology, *Politics* 17 (May 1982);
Herbert Kaufman, *Time, Chance, and Organizations: Natural Selection in a Perilous Environment* (Chatham, NJ: Chatham House, 1985).

social democracy The democratization of all social institutions, as opposed to the democratization of only governing institutions. Compare to DEMOCRACY.

social equity A normative standard holding that equity, rather than efficiency, is the major criterion for evaluating the desirability of a policy or program.

REFERENCES
H. George Frederickson, ed., Social equity and public administration, *Public Administration Review* 34 (January/February 1974);
Arthur M. Oken, *Equity and Efficiency: The Big Tradeoff* (Washington, D.C.: Brookings, 1975).

social indicators Statistical measures that aid in the description of conditions in the social environment (e.g., measures of income distribution, poverty, health, physical environment).

REFERENCES
Raymond Bauer, *Social Indicators* (Cambridge, MA: MIT Press, 1967);
Barry Bozeman, Social science and social indicators—Problems and prospects, *Midwest Review of Public Administration* 8 (April 1974);
Robert Parke and David Seidman, Social indicators and social reporting, *Annals of the American Academy of Political and Social Science* 435 (January 1978).

social insurance Any benefit program that a state makes available to the members of its society in time of need and as a matter of right.

socialism A system of government in which many of the means of production and trade are owned or run by the government and in which many human welfare needs are provided directly by the government. Socialism may or may not be democratic. Socialism is one of the most "loaded" words in American politics. To the Right it represents the beginnings of communist encroachment on traditional American values and institutions. To the Left it represents the practical manifestation of America's pragmatic and generous spirit. But while American political culture will countenance limited socialistic measures, it will not tolerate socialistic rhetoric. Thus the social security program was labeled an insurance system when its proponents knew that it was always designed to be an income transfer program. On the whole, Americans abhor the symbol represented by the word *socialism*, but are very much in favor of limited socialistic measures (such as AFDC, OASDI, and TVA), so long as they are espoused as pragmatic responses to difficult problems. *Compare to* MARXISM; MIXED ECONOMY.

REFERENCE

Theodore J. Lowi, Why is there no socialism in the United States? A federal analysis, *International Political Science Review* 5:4 (1984).

socialism, creeping The gradual advance of socialist principles and practices into governing policies and institutions. The United States is often said to be a "victim" of creeping socialism because of the enactment of so many social welfare programs in this century.

socialization of conflict *See* POLITICS.

socialization, political *See* POLITICAL SOCIALIZATION.

socialized medicine 1 A medical care system in which the organization and provision of medical care services are under direct government control, and providers are employed by or under contract with the government. 2 A medical care system believed to be subject to excessive government control.

social security The popular name for the Old Age, Survivors, and Disability Insurance (OASDI) system established by the Social Se-

curity Act of 1935. At first, social security covered only retired private sector employees. In 1939, the law was changed to cover survivors when the worker dies and to cover certain dependents when the worker retired. In the 1950s, coverage was extended to include most self-employed persons, most state and local employees, household and farm employees, members of the armed forces, and members of the clergy. Today, almost all jobs are covered by social security. Disability insurance was added in 1954 to give workers protection against loss of earnings due to total disability. The social security program was expanded again in 1965 with the enactment of Medicare, which assured hospital and medical insurance protection to people sixty-five years of age and over. Since 1973, Medicare coverage has been available to people under sixty-five who have been entitled to disability checks for two or more consecutive years and to people with permanent kidney failure who need dialysis treatment or kidney transplants. Amendments enacted in 1972 provide that social security benefits increase automatically with the cost of living.

REFERENCES

For histories, see Edwin E. White, *The Development of the Social Security Act* (Madison: University of Wisconsin Press, 1963);

Roy Lubove, *The Struggle for Social Security: 1900–1935* (Cambridge, MA: Harvard University Press, 1968).

Also see Martha Derthick, *Policymaking for Social Security* (Washington, D.C.: Brookings, 1979);

Edward Wynne, *Social Security: A Reciprocity System under Pressure* (Boulder, CO: Westview, 1980);

Henry J. Aaron, *Economic Effects of Social Security* (Washington, D.C.: Brookings, 1982).

On the 1983 adjustments to OASDI, see Paul Light, *Artful Work: The Politics of Social Security Reform* (New York: Random House, 1985).

Social Security Administration The agency of the Department of Health and Human Services that administers the national program of contributory social insurance whereby employees, employers, and the self-employed pay contributions that are pooled in special trust funds.

Social Security Administration
6401 Security Boulevard
Baltimore, MD 21235
(301) 594–1234

soft money 1 Funds given by national political parties to their state and local parties for nonfederal uses, such as voter registration drives. The money is soft because its use is not watched carefully by the states and its collection by the national party is often unreported because of its nonfederal character. 2 Funds for a program that are not received on a recurring basis from a steady source. For example, grant or gift funds on a one-time or even a several-year basis are soft in comparison to the hard funds that come each year from a legislative appropriation.

solicitor general The official of the Department of Justice who is the actual attorney who represents the federal government before the U.S. Supreme Court and any other courts. It is the solicitor general who must approve any appeal that the U.S. government might take to an appellate court.

REFERENCE

Lincoln Caplan, *The Solicitor General and the Rule of Law* (New York: Knopf, 1987).

solid South A reference to the once solidly Democratic South (*see* v. o. key, jr.). The solid South was also solidly white, because most blacks were discouraged from voting by poll taxes, intimidation, and other means. Those few blacks who did vote tended to be Republican. This began to change with the New Deal of the 1930s and the Fair Deal of the 1940s and rapidly changed with the civil rights movement of the 1960s. The event that more than anything else broke the solid South was the advocacy of equal rights for blacks by the national Democratic party. Blacks have consequently become pivotal elements in the Democratic electorate of all southern states. Today the South is not solid for either major party.

REFERENCES

Jack Bass and Walter DeVries, *The Transformation of Southern Politics* (New York: Basic Books, 1976);

Jessica Brown, *The American South: A Historical Bibliography*, 2 vols. (Santa Barbara, CA: ABC-Clio, 1985);

Alexander P. Lamis, *The Two-Party South* (New York: Oxford University Press, 1986).

southern strategy The Republican party's efforts beginning in the late 1960s (1) to encourage significant numbers of traditional southern white Democratic voters to defect to the Republican party and (2) to appeal to Hispanic voters, especially in Texas, California, and Florida.

REFERENCES

Kevin Phillips, *The Emerging Republican Majority* (New Rochelle, NY: Arlington, 1969);

Reg Murphy and Hal Gulliver, *The Southern Strategy* (New York: Scribner, 1971).

sovereign immunity A government's freedom from being sued for damages in all but those situations in which it passes statutes allowing it. Amendments to the Administrative Procedure Act in 1976 allow suits to be filed against the federal government. *See also* IMMUNITY.

REFERENCE

Kenneth C. Davis, Sovereign immunity must go, *Administrative Law Review* 22 (April 1970).

sovereignty The quality of being supreme in power, rank, or authority. In the United States, the people are sovereign and government is considered their agent. The sovereignty of the sovereign states of the United States is largely a myth, however, because so much power on most crucial issues now lies with the federal government. The literature on sovereignty is immense and freighted with philosophy. *Compare to* TENTH AMENDMENT.

REFERENCES

Charles E. Merriam, Jr., *History of the Theory of Sovereignty Since Rousseau* (New York: Garland, 1900, 1972);

W. J. Stankiewicz, Sovereignty as political theory, *Political Studies* 24 (June 1976);

Julian H. Franklin, *John Locke and the Theory of Sovereignty* (Cambridge, UK: Cambridge University Press, 1978);

J. D. B. Miller, The sovereign state and its future, *International Journal* 39 (Spring 1984).

Spalding v Vilas 161 U.S. 483 (1896) The U.S. Supreme Court case granting absolute IM-MUNITY from civil suits for damages to the postmaster general of the United States and, by implication, to the heads of other federal departments. *See also* BARR V MATTEO; BUTZ V ECONOMOU; WOOD V STRICKLAND.

span of control The extent of an administrator's responsibility. The span of control has usually been expressed as the number of subordinates that a manager should supervise. Sir Ian Hamilton, in *The Soul and Body of an Army* (London: Arnold, 1921), asserted that the "average human brain finds its effective scope in handling from three to six other brains." A. V. Graicunas took a mathematical approach to the concept and demonstrated, in "Relationship in Organization," in *Papers on the Science of Administration*, ed. Luther Gulick and Lyndall Urwick (New York: Institute of Public Administration, 1937), that, as the number of subordinates reporting to a manager increases arithmetically, the number of possible interpersonal interactions increases geometrically. Building upon Graicunas's work, Lyndall F. Urwick boldly asserts, in "The Manager's Span of Control," *Harvard Business Review* (May/June 1956), that "no superior can supervise directly the work of more than five or, at the most, six subordinates whose work interlocks." Studies on the concept of span of control abound, but there is no consensus on an ideal span.

REFERENCE

Also see William G. Ouchi and James B. Dowling, Defining the span control, *Administrative Science Quarterly* 19 (September 1974).

Speaker The presiding officer of the U.S. House of Representatives, elected by its members. The U.S. Constitution (Article I, Section 2) says that the House "shall chuse their speaker and other officers." Although the membership may vote on officers as they do on any other question, in most cases it is strictly a party vote. Republicans and Democrats meet separately before the House organizes for a

Jim Wright (D-Texas) became Speaker of the House of Representatives in 1987.

new Congress and each chooses a slate of officers. These two slates are presented at the first session of the House, and the majority party slate is, of course, selected. The vote is viva voce (by voice), except for election of the Speaker. The Speaker (who, according to the Constitution, does not have to be an elected member, but always has been) presides over the House, appoints the chairs to preside over the committees of the Whole, appoints all special or select committees, appoints conference committees, has the power of recognition of members, and makes many important rulings and decisions in the House. He may vote, but usually does not, except in case of a tie. The Speaker and the majority leader determine administrative policies in the House, often confer with the president, and are regarded as spokesmen for the administration if they and the president belong to the same political party. Otherwise, they are major spokesmen for their own party.

REFERENCES

Donald R. Kennon, ed., *The Speakers of the U.S. House of Representatives: A Bibliography, 1789–1984* (Baltimore: Johns Hopkins University Press, 1986);

Tip O'Neill with William Novak, *Man of the House* (New York: Random House, 1987).

Speakers of the House of Representatives

Name	State	Tenure	Party
Frederick Muhlenberg	Pennsylvania	1789–1791	Federalist
Johnathan Trumbull	Connecticut	1791–1793	Federalist
Frederick Muhlenberg	Pennsylvania	1793–1795	Federalist
Jonathan Dayton	New Jersey	1795–1799	Federalist
Theodore Sedgwick	Massachusetts	1799–1801	Federalist
Nathaniel Macon	North Carolina	1801–1807	Democratic-Republican
Joseph B. Varnum	Massachusetts	1807–1811	Democratic-Republican
Henry Clay	Kentucky	1811–1814	Democratic-Republican
Langdon Cheves	South Carolina	1814–1815	Democratic-Republican
Henry Clay	Kentucky	1815–1820	Democratic-Republican
John W. Taylor	New York	1820–1821	Democratic-Republican
Philip P. Barbour	Virginia	1821–1823	Democratic-Republican
Henry Clay	Kentucky	1823–1825	Democratic-Republican
John W. Taylor	New York	1825–1827	Democratic
Andrew Stevenson	Virginia	1827–1834	Democratic
John Bell	Tennessee	1834–1835	Democratic
James K. Polk	Tennessee	1835–1839	Democratic
Robert M. T. Hunter	Virginia	1839–1841	Democratic
John White	Kentucky	1841–1843	Whig
John W. Jones	Virginia	1843–1845	Democratic
John W. Davis	Indiana	1845–1847	Democratic
Robert C. Winthrop	Massachusetts	1847–1849	Whig
Howell Cobb	Georgia	1849–1851	Democratic
Linn Boyd	Kentucky	1851–1855	Democratic
Nathaniel P. Banks	Massachusetts	1855–1857	American
James L. Orr	South Carolina	1857–1859	Democratic
William Pennington	New Jersey	1859–1861	Republican
Galusha A. Grow	Pennsylvania	1861–1863	Republican
Schuyler Colfax	Indiana	1863–1869	Republican
Theodore M. Pomeroy	New York	1869–1869	Republican
James G. Blaine	Maine	1869–1875	Republican
Michael C. Kerr	Indiana	1875–1876	Democratic
Samuel J. Randall	Pennsylvania	1876–1881	Democratic
Joseph W. Keifer	Ohio	1881–1883	Republican
John G. Carlisle	Kentucky	1883–1889	Democratic
Thomas B. Reed	Maine	1889–1891	Republican
Charles F. Crisp	Georgia	1891–1895	Democratic
Thomas B. Reed	Maine	1895–1899	Republican
David B. Henderson	Iowa	1899–1903	Republican
Joseph G. Cannon	Illinois	1903–1911	Republican
Champ Clark	Missouri	1911–1919	Democratic
Frederick H. Gillett	Massachusetts	1919–1925	Republican
Nicholas Longworth	Ohio	1925–1931	Republican
John N. Garner	Texas	1931–1933	Democratic
Henry T. Rainey	Illinois	1933–1935	Democratic
Joseph W. Byrns	Tennessee	1935–1936	Democratic
William P. Bankhead	Alabama	1936–1940	Democratic
Sam Rayburn	Texas	1940–1947	Democratic
Joseph W. Martin, Jr.	Massachusetts	1947–1949	Republican

Name	State	Tenure	Party
Sam Rayburn	Texas	1949–1953	Democratic
Joseph W. Martin, Jr.	Massachusetts	1953–1955	Republican
Sam Rayburn	Texas	1955–1961	Democratic
John W. McCormack	Massachusetts	1962–1971	Democratic
Carl Albert	Oklahama	1971–1977	Democratic
Thomas P. "Tip" O'Neill	Massachusetts	1977–1987	Democratic
Jim Wright	Texas	1987–Present	Democratic

special assessment A real estate tax on certain landowners to pay for improvements that will, at least in theory, benefit them; for example, a paved street. *See also* BENEFIT DISTRICT.

special committee *See* COMMITTEE, SELECT.

special district A unit of government typically performing a single function and overlapping traditional political boundaries. Examples include transportation districts, water districts, sewer districts.

REFERENCES

Neil D. McFeeley, Special district governments: The "new dark continent" twenty years later, *Midwest Review of Public Administration* 12 (December 1978);

Susan A. MacManus, Special district governments: A note on their use as property tax relief mechanisms in the 1970s, *Journal of Politics* 43 (November 1981);

Scott A. Bollens, Examining the link between state policy and the creation of local special districts, *State and Local Government Review* 18 (Fall 1986).

special election *See* ELECTION, SPECIAL.

special master A person appointed by a court to conduct an investigation or to carry out a court order; for example, a special master might supervise the sale of property that the court has ordered to be sold.

REFERENCE

Wayne D. Brazil, Special masters in complex cases: Extending the judiciary or reshaping adjudication? *University of Chicago Law Review* 53 (Spring 1986).

special prosecutor *See* PROSECUTOR, SPECIAL.

special relationship 1 The historic, military, cultural, and nostalgic relation between the United States and the United Kingdom that has emerged since World War II. While much touted by Winston Churchill (whose mother was American) and American politicians, the relation, while real, is often more expressed by political rhetoric than by true commonalities of interest. 2 In the general context of international relations, any interchange between nations where one of them expects special treatment from another because of historical, geographical, cultural, or political ties.

REFERENCES

1   Wm. Roger Louis and Hedley Bull, eds., *The Special Relationship: Anglo-American Relations Since 1945* (New York: Oxford University Press, 1986).

2   Elliot J. Feldman and Lily Gardner Feldman, The special relationship between Canada and the United States, *Jerusalem Journal of International Relations* 4 (1980);

Robert A. Pastor, U.S. immigration policy and Latin America: In search of a special relationship, *Latin American Research Review* 19:3 (1984).

special session *See* SESSION, SPECIAL.

speech and debate clause *See* IMMUNITY, CONGRESSIONAL.

speedy trial *See* TRIAL, SPEEDY.

spellbinder 1 A political speaker (or the speech itself) that can really hold an audience's attention, as if putting them under a bewitching spell. 2 A DEMAGOGUE with charismatic speaking abilities.

REFERENCE

Ann Ruth Willner, *The Spellbinders: Charismatic Political Leadership* (New Haven, CT: Yale University Press, 1984).

spillover effects/externalities   Benefits or costs that accrue to parties other than the buyer of a good or service. For the most part, the benefits of private goods and services inure exclusively to the buyer (e.g., new clothes, a television set). In the case of public goods, however, the benefit or cost usually spills over onto third parties. An airport, for example, benefits not only its users but spills over onto the population at large in both positive and negative ways. Benefits might include improved air service for a community, increased tourism, and attraction of new businesses, while costs might include noise pollution and traffic congestion.

REFERENCE

E. J. Mishan, The postwar literature on externalities: An interpretive essay, *Journal of Economic Literature* 9 (March 1971).

spin control   Efforts by an administration or an individual political actor to contain, deflect, and minimize an unraveling scandal or other embarrassing or politically damaging revelation. The purpose is to keep the situation from spinning out of control.

split ticket   *See* TICKET SPLITTING.

spoils system   The patronage practices of one's political opposition. The system got its name in 1832 when Senator William L. Marcy (1786–1854) asserted in a Senate debate that

> It may be . . . that the politicians of the United States are not so fastidious as some gentlemen are, as to declosing the principles on which they act. They boldly preach what they practice. When they are contending for victory, they avow their intention of enjoying the fruits of it. If they are defeated, they expect to retire from office. If they are successful, they claim, as a matter of right, the advantages of success. They see nothing wrong in the rule, that to the victor belong the spoils of the enemy.

The rhetoric of Senator Marcy notwithstanding, the spoils system did not come into full

President Cleveland ("Santa") surveys his supporters' chimneys in an 1892 send-up of the spoils system.

flower until a decade later. Martin Van Buren, who succeeded Andrew Jackson as president in 1837, continued with a moderate view of removals until the latter part of his term, when his unsuccessful campaign for reelection (against William Henry Harrison) demanded a more partisan strategy. He lost anyway. With a new party in the White House in 1841, spoils appointments became the norm, rather than the exception. The doctrine of rotation of office progressively prevailed over the earlier notion of stability in office. Presidents even began turning out of office appointees of previous presidents of the same party. President Millard Fillmore had dissident Whigs turned out in favor of "real" Whigs. When James Buchanan, a Democrat, succeeded Franklin Pierce, also a Democrat, it was announced that no incumbents appointed by Pierce would be retained. This development led William L. Marcy to remark, "They have it that I am the author of the office seeker's doctrine, that 'to the victor belong the spoils,' but I certainly should never recommend the policy of pillaging my

511

own camp." *Compare to* ANDREW JACKSON; PATRONAGE.

REFERENCES

Leonard D. White, *The Jacksonians* (New York: Macmillan, 1954);

Ivor Debenham Spencer, *The Victor and the Spoils: A Life of William L. Marcy* (Providence, RI: Brown University Press, 1959);

Martin and Susan Tolchin, *To the Victor . . . Political Patronage from the Clubhouse to the White House* (New York: Random House, 1971).

spook 1 A ghost. 2 Any spy, domestic or foreign, ours or theirs. 3 An employee of the Central Intelligence Agency. 4 A ghost writer; an anonymous political speech writer.

REFERENCES

2 Jim Hougan, *Spooks: The Haunting of America—The Private Use of Secret Agents* (New York: Morrow, 1978).

John Marks, How to spot a spook, *Washington Monthly* 6 (November 1974).

spot zoning *See* ZONING, SPOT.

Springer v United States *See* SIXTEENTH AMENDMENT.

squatter's rights The right to ownership of land merely by occupying it for a certain period. During the settling of the American West, this was a legal means of acquiring title to land. Today, squatting is generally not recognized as legal. But this has not stopped some urban social activists from squatting in abandoned housing, fixing it up somewhat, and then demanding ownership.

REFERENCE

Kevin C. Kearns, Urban squatting: Social activism in the housing sector, *Social Policy* 11 (September/October 1980).

SSI *See* SUPPLEMENTAL SECURITY INCOME.

staff 1 The subordinate employees of an organization. 2 Specialists who assist line managers in carrying out their duties. Generally, staff units do not have the power of decision, command, or control of operations. Rather, they make recommendations (which may or may not be adopted) to executives and line managers.

REFERENCE

James P. Pfiffner, White House staff versus the cabinet: Centripetal and centrifugal roles, *Presidential Studies Quarterly* 16 (Fall 1986).

staff, chief of 1 The military title for the officer who supervises the work of the other officers on a commander's staff. 2 A civilian supervisor of an overall management team who reports directly to the chief executive officer. 3 The top aid to the president of the United States. White House chiefs of staff have often been criticized for isolating the president from those who want to see him and for exercising enormous authority as a de facto deputy president when nobody elected them to that office. Presidents from Dwight D. Eisenhower to Ronald Reagan have had chiefs of staff; some have had greater power than others, and some functioned as a chief of staff without the title.

REFERENCE

Samuel Kernell and Samuel L. Popkin, eds., *Chief of Staff: Twenty-Five Years of Managing the Presidency* (Berkeley and Los Angeles: University of California Press, 1986).

staffer Originally, any full-time employee of a politician's campaign organization or elected public office. The term has grown to include all legislative committee staffs as well. Before World War I, the members of Congress outnumbered their full-time staff. Today, each senator has a paid staff of from thirteen to seventy-one members; they average thirty-six. House staffs average seventeen. In addition to helping with legislative matters and casework, each staffer is a personal political machine looking after the political fortunes of his or her boss. Congressional staff members have few employment rights (*see* CONGRESSIONAL EXEMPTION) and may be hired and fired at will.

Because staffer is an all-inclusive term equally applied to clerical and professional workers, it may be considered poor usage by those who rightly consider themselves more than just a staffer by virtue of their professional attainments. Nevertheless, diminutive and condescending as the term may be, it covers those who are clerical and those who are professional, those who are accomplished experts and those who are not, and those who are offended by the term as well as those who are not.

REFERENCES

Harrison W. Fox, Jr., and Susan Webb Hammond, *Congressional Staff: The Invisible Force in American Lawmaking* (New York: Free Press, 1975);

Arnold M. Howitt, The expanding role of mayoral staff, *Policy Studies Journal* 3 (Summer 1975);

Michael J. Malbin, *Unelected Representatives: Congressional Staff and the Future of Representative Government* (New York: Basic Books, 1980);

Ivan Kline, Use of congressional staff in election campaigning, *Columbia Law Review* 82 (June 1982);

Susan Webb Hammond, Legislative staffs, *Legislative Studies Quarterly* 9 (May 1984).

For a comparative perspective, see Michael T. Ryle, The legislative staff of the British House of Commons, *Legislative Studies Quarterly* 6 (November 1981);

Stanley Campbell and Jean Laporte, The staff of the parliamentary assemblies in France, *Legislative Studies Quarterly* 6 (November 1981);

Werner Blischke, Parliamentary Staffs in the German Bundestag, *Legislative Studies Quarterly* 6 (November 1981).

staff, personal 1 Those members of an organization who report directly to an executive, rather than through an intermediary, such as a chief of staff. Personal staff members could be relatively low-level, such as secretaries or chauffeurs, or high-level technical experts. 2 The staffs who serve individual legislators either in their capital offices or home state/district offices, as opposed to the staff of the legislative body or its committees. Personal staffs handle correspondence, publicity, CASEWORK, and local political affairs for the legislators.

staff principle The principle of administration that states that the executive should be assisted by officers who are not in the line of operations but are essentially extensions of the personality of the executive and whose duties consist primarily of assisting the executive in controlling and coordinating the organization and, secondly, of offering advice.

stagflation High unemployment and inflation, at the same time. This was something new in the 1970s because historically high unemployment tended toward deflation. *See also* PHILLIPS CURVE.

REFERENCES

Thomas D. Willett, The United States and world stagflation: The export and import of inflationary pressures, *Annals of the American Academy of Political and Social Science* 460 (March 1982);

Martin L. Weitzman, *The Share Economy: Conquering Stagflation* (Cambridge, MA: Harvard University Press, 1984);

Leon N. Lindberg and Charles S. Maier, *The Politics of Inflation and Economic Stagnation* (Washington, D.C.: Brookings, 1985).

stalking horse A politician who is a front for another. The phrase comes from hunting, when a hunter might literally hide behind his horse to better stalk his unsuspecting prey.

stalwarts 1 Faithful party followers. 2 Republican party loyalists during the last quarter of the nineteenth century. When Charles Guiteau shot President James A. Garfield in 1881 because the president had not given him a patronage appointment, he is supposed to have shouted, "I am a stalwart and Arthur is president now." Obviously, Guiteau, who was hanged the next year, felt that Chester Arthur, the vice president, would be more receptive to his petitions for office than Garfield had been. He wasn't.

REFERENCE

Allan Peskin, Who were the stalwarts? Who were their rivals? Republican factions in the gilded age, *Political Science Quarterly* 99 (Winter 1984–85).

stand A lawmaker's position, for or against, on a given issue or vote. A member of Congress can make his or her stand known in one of three ways: (1) by answering yea or nay on a roll-call vote, (2) by pairing with another legislator for or against, or (3) by announcing his or her position to the House or Senate.

standard consolidated statistical area (SCSA) A creation of the U.S. Census Bureau that combines contiguous standard metropolitan statistical areas to more accurately portray urban population patterns.

standard federal regions The geographic subdivisions of the United States established to achieve uniformity in the location and geographic jurisdiction of federal field offices as a basis for promoting coordination among agencies and among federal, state, and local governments and for securing management improvements and economies through greater interagency and intergovernmental cooperation. Boundaries were drawn and regional office locations designed for ten regions, and agencies are encouraged to adopt the uniform system when changes are made or new offices established.

standard metropolitan statistical area (SMSA) A creation of the U.S. Census Bureau to more accurately portray urban population; it includes the population in all counties contiguous to an urban county (i.e., one with a city over fifty thousand in a common total), if the population of those counties is involved in the urban county work force. Being designated an SMSA is important to cities and counties because only SMSAs are eligible for certain federal government grants.

standing 1 Permanent, as in a standing committee of the Congress; a standing rule; or a standing order. 2 A person's right to initiate legal action because he or she is directly affected by the issues raised. *See also* FLAST V COHEN; MASSACHUSETTS V MELLON, FROTHINGHAM V MELLON; UNITED STATES V RICHARDSON; VALLEY FORGE CHRISTIAN COLLEGE V AMERICANS UNITED FOR SEPARATION OF CHURCH AND STATE.
REFERENCES
Kenneth Culp Davis, The liberalized law of standing, *University of Chicago Law Review* 37 (Spring 1970);

William A. Fletcher, Standing to sue for members of Congress, *Yale Law Journal* 83 (July 1974);
Karen Orren, Standing to sue: Interest group conflict in the federal courts, *American Political Science Review* 70 (September 1976);
Kellis E. Parker and Robin Stone, Standing and public law remedies, *Columbia Law Review* 78 (May 1978);
Gene R. Nichol, Jr., Rethinking standing, *California Law Review* 72 (January 1984).

standing vote *See* VOTE, STANDING.

stand pat To accept a present situation; to maintain an existing policy. The phrase comes from poker, where it means you will play the cards initially dealt you and not draw additional cards in hopes of a better hand. Early in the twentieth century, to stand pat came to mean being REACTIONARY, especially in contrast to the progressives (*see* PROGRESSIVE MOVEMENT/PROGRESSIVE ERA). Nobody in American politics today is in favor of standing pat. There is a classic piece of film from the 1960 presidential campaign in which Richard Nixon, with his wife, Pat, seated behind him, energetically tells an audience that "we can't stand pat." Subsequently, to Mrs. Nixon's presumed relief, he changed that line to "America cannot stand still."

star chamber Secret judicial proceedings without any semblance of fairness or due process. The English Court of the Star Chamber (abolished in 1641) never used juries and often used torture.

stare decisis A Latin term meaning let the decision stand; the legal principle that once a precedent is established all similar cases should be decided the same way. *Compare to* PRECEDENT.
REFERENCE
Martin Shapiro, Toward a theory of *Stare Decisis, Journal of Legal Studies* 1 (January 1972).

stars and stripes 1 The flag of the United States. On June 14, 1777, the Continental Congress resolved "that the flag of the thirteen

The flag used in the American Revolution consisted of thirteen stars and stripes.

United States be thirteen stripes, alternate red and white; that the UNION be thirteen stars, white in a blue field, representing a new constellation." As new states came into the union, a star was added for each. **2** The newspaper published by and for the U.S. army. It was started during World War I, revived for World War II, and has continued ever since.

Star-Spangled Banner 1 The flag of the United States. **2** The NATIONAL ANTHEM of the United States.

star wars *See* STRATEGIC DEFENSE INITIATIVE.

state 1 A political unit having territory, population, and sovereignty over its internal and external affairs. **2** A component government in a federal system, such as an American state government. **3** One of the fifty states of the United States. In many federal laws, the term also includes the District of Columbia, the Commonwealth of Puerto Rico, and any territory or possession of the United States. **4** A short form of reference to the U.S. Department of State.

State, U.S. Department of The cabinet-level department of the federal government whose primary objective is the execution of foreign policy to promote the long-range security and well-being of the United States. The Department of State is the oldest of all cabinet departments. It was the first of three departments created in 1789; this makes the secre-

tary of State the ranking cabinet member.
REFERENCES
Bert A. Rockman, America's departments of State: Irregular and regular syndromes of policy making, *American Political Science Review* 75 (December 1981);
Barry Rubin, *Secrets of State: The State Department and the Struggle over U.S. Foreign Policy* (New York: Oxford University Press, 1985).

U.S. Department of State
2201 C Street, N.W.
Washington, D.C. 20520
(202) 647–4000

State and Local Fiscal Assistance Act *See* REVENUE SHARING.

State and Local Government Review A quarterly that emphasizes the administrative aspects of state and local government; published since 1968. Library of Congress no. JK2403 .S684.
State and Local Government Review
Carl Vinson Institute of Government
University of Georgia
Terrell Hall
Athens, GA 30602

state central committee The formal leadership body of a political party within a state. It is composed, variously, of representation of congressional districts, counties, or state legislative districts.

statecraft 1 The art and science of governance, of leadership, and of politics. **2** Machiavellian cunning or duplicity in government.
REFERENCE
George F. Will, *Statecraft as Soulcraft* (New York: Simon & Schuster 1983).

state department, little The president's foreign policy advisors, who work directly for him as part of the White House staff.

state government A subnational government in the United States that consists of its legislative, executive, and judicial branches and all departments, boards, commissions, and other organizational units thereof. It also includes any semiautonomous authorities, institutions of higher education, districts, and other agencies that are subject to administrative and fiscal control by the state through its appointment of officers, determination of budgets, approval of plans, and other devices. The state governments of the original independent colonies formed the union under the U.S. Constitution in 1787. The priority of these governments over the union was a claim that was finally ended by the Civil War, even though STATES' RIGHTS and the distinction between state and federal power remained highly controversial issues in American government well into the twentieth century.

REFERENCES

For comprehensive statistical data on state governments, see the latest edition of *The Book of the States* (Lexington, KY: Council of State Governments).

Also see Malcolm E. Jewell, The neglected world of state politics, *Journal of Politics* 44 (August 1982);

Robert S. Lorch, *State and Local Politics: The Great Entanglement* (Englewood Cliffs, NJ: Prentice-Hall, 1983);

John J. Harrigan, *Politics and Policy in States and Communities,* 2d ed. (Boston: Little, Brown, 1984).

Names of State Legislative Bodies

State	Both Bodies	Upper House	Lower House
Alabama	Legislature	Senate	House of Representatives
Alaska	Legislature	Senate	House of Representatives
Arizona	Legislature	Senate	House of Representatives
Arkansas	General Assembly	Senate	House of Representatives
California	Legislature	Senate	Assembly
Colorado	General Assembly	Senate	House of Representatives
Connecticut	General Assembly	Senate	House of Representatives
Delaware	General Assembly	Senate	House of Representatives
Florida	Legislature	Senate	House of Representatives
Georgia	General Assembly	Senate	House of Representatives
Hawaii	Legislature	Senate	House of Representatives
Idaho	Legislature	Senate	House of Representatives
Illinois	General Assembly	Senate	House of Representatives
Indiana	General Assembly	Senate	House of Representatives
Iowa	General Assembly	Senate	House of Representatives
Kansas	Legislature	Senate	House of Representatives
Kentucky	General Assembly	Senate	House of Representatives
Louisiana	Legislature	Senate	House of Representatives
Maine	Legislature	Senate	House of Representatives
Maryland	General Assembly	Senate	House of Delegates
Massachusetts	General Court	Senate	House of Representatives
Michigan	Legislature	Senate	House of Representatives
Minnesota	Legislature	Senate	House of Representatives
Mississippi	Legislature	Senate	House of Representatives
Missouri	General Assembly	Senate	House of Representatives
Montana	Legislature	Senate	House of Representatives
Nebraska	Legislature		(Unicameral)
Nevada	Legislature	Senate	Assembly
New Hampshire	General Court	Senate	House of Representatives
New Jersey	Legislature	Senate	General Assembly
New Mexico	Legislature	Senate	House of Representatives
New York	Legislature	Senate	Assembly
North Carolina	General Assembly	Senate	House of Representatives

State	Both Bodies	Upper House	Lower House
North Dakota	Legislative Assembly	Senate	House of Representatives
Ohio	General Assembly	Senate	House of Representatives
Oklahoma	Legislature	Senate	House of Representatives
Oregon	Legislative Assembly	Senate	House of Representatives
Pennsylvania	General Assembly	Senate	House of Representatives
Rhode Island	General Assembly	Senate	House of Representatives
South Carolina	General Assembly	Senate	House of Representatives
South Dakota	Legislature	Senate	House of Representatives
Tennessee	General Assembly	Senate	House of Representatives
Texas	Legislature	Senate	House of Representatives
Utah	Legislature	Senate	House of Representatives
Vermont	General Assembly	Senate	House of Representatives
Virginia	General Assembly	Senate	House of Delegates
Washington	Legislature	Senate	House of Representatives
West Virginia	Legislature	Senate	House of Delegates
Wisconsin	Legislature	Senate	Assembly
Wyoming	Legislature	Senate	House of Representatives

State Government The quarterly journal of the Council of State Governments; published since 1926. Library of Congress no. JK2403 .S7.

> State Government
> P.O. Box 11910
> Lexington, KY 40578

statehouse *See* CAPITOL.

state of nature What the social contract theorists assumed to be the condition of mankind before the establishment of a social contract and organized government. Thomas Hobbes found life in it to be "nasty, brutish, and short." Jean-Jacques Rousseau thought it idyllic. And John Locke wrote that "the state of nature has a law of nature to govern it, which obliges every one; and reason, which is that law, teaches all mankind who will but consult it, that, being all equal and independent, no one ought to harm another in his life, health, liberty or possessions."

REFERENCES
Robert A. Goldwin, Locke's state of nature in political science, *Western Political Quarterly* 29 (March 1976);
John Anglim, On Locke's state of nature, *Political Studies* 26 (March 1978).

state of the union message The annual message of the president of the United States to the Congress wherein he usually proposes legislative initiatives. Article II, Section 3, of the U.S. Constitution requires that the president "shall from time to time give to the Congress information of the state of the Union, and recommend to their consideration such measures as he shall judge necessary and expedient." George Washington and John Adams appeared before the two houses in joint session to read their messages. Thomas Jefferson discontinued the practice in 1801, transmitting his message to the Capitol to be read by clerks in both houses. Jefferson's procedure was followed for a full century. On April 8, 1913, Woodrow Wilson revived the practice of delivering the state of the union message in person. With the exception of Herbert Hoover, Wilson's example has been followed by subsequent presidents.

REFERENCE
Ronald D. Brunner and Katherine M. Livornese, The president's annual message, *Congress and the Presidency: A Journal of Capital Studies* 11 (Spring 1984).

state's attorney **1** The ATTORNEY GENERAL of a state. **2** A local prosecutor (e.g., a district attorney) who represents the state (the people) in a criminal trial.

State, secretary of *See* SECRETARY OF STATE.

state's evidence In a criminal trial, evidence or testimony on behalf of the state (the prosecution). State's evidence is what an accomplice to a crime gives to the state in a negotiated effort (*see* PLEA BARGAINING) to get a lesser personal penalty for the crime at issue.

statesman A respectful reference to a political leader of considerable national or international prominence. According to President Harry S Truman, "A statesman is a politician who's been dead ten or fifteen years." According to British Prime Minister Harold Mac-Millan (1894–1987), "When you're abroad you're a statesman; when you're home, you're just a politician." According to French President Georges Pompidou (1911–1974), "A statesman is a politician who places himself at the service of the nation. A politician is a statesman who places the nation at his service."
REFERENCES
John A. Gueguen, Reflections on statesmanship and the presidency, *Presidential Studies Quarterly* 12 (Fall 1982);
John W. Coffey, The statesmanship of Harry S Truman, *Review of Politics* 47 (April 1985).

states' rights **1** Those rights that, according to the U.S. Constitution, have been neither given to the federal government nor forbidden to the states. **2** A CODE WORD for opposition to federal civil rights legislation, federal land use policies (*see* SAGEBRUSH REBELLION), or other federal policies perceived to be violations of state sovereignty.
REFERENCES
For an analysis of the tension between states' rights and a strong national government among the Founding Fathers, see Alpheus T. Mason, ed., *The States Rights Debate: Antifederalism and the Constitution,* 2d ed. (New York: Oxford University Press, 1972).
Also see Zell Miller, A new definition of states' rights, *State Government* 49 (Winter 1976).

state trading nations Countries such as the Soviet Union, the People's Republic of China, and the countries of Eastern Europe that rely heavily on government entities, instead of private corporations, to conduct their trade with other countries.

state visit An official visit, attended by appropriate ceremonies, by one head of state (or government) to another.

statute A law passed by a legislature.
REFERENCE
Joseph T. Sneed, The art of statutory interpretation, *Texas Law Review* 62 (December 1983).

statute, long-arm A law that allows the courts in one state to claim jurisdiction over a matter in another state, often used in cases involving nonresident defendants.
REFERENCE
Mark P. Gergen, Constitutional limitations in state long-arm jurisdiction, *University of Chicago Law Review* 49 (Winter 1982).

statutes at large A collection of all statutes passed by a particular legislature (such as the U.S. Congress), printed in full and in the order of their passage.

statutes of limitations Laws that place limits on the time authorities have to charge someone with a crime after its commission, limits on the time someone has to contest a contract in a civil lawsuit, and so on.
REFERENCE
Charles F. Sawyer, Class actions and statutes of limitations, *University of Chicago Law Review* 48 (Winter 1981).

steel seizure case *See* YOUNGSTOWN SHEET AND TUBE CO. V SAWYER.

Steinem, Gloria *See* WOMEN'S LIBERATION MOVEMENT.

stewardship theory of the presidency *See* PRESIDENCY, STEWARDSHIP THEORY OF THE.

Stockman, David A. (1946–) President Ronald Reagan's director of the Office of Management and Budget from 1981 to 1985

David Stockman.

and who, in 1981, confessed to readers of the *Atlantic* (December 1981) that "None of us really understands what's going on with all these numbers." After presiding over the largest budget deficits in U.S. history (from fifty-eight billion dollars when he came into office in 1981 to two hundred billion dollars when he left in 1985), Stockman left office to accept a two million dollar advance to write a book denouncing large budget deficits and just about every federal official he had had the occasion to meet.

REFERENCES

For an expansion of the *Atlantic* article, see William Greider, *The Education of David Stockman and Other Americans* (New York: Dutton, 1982).

For Stockman's own inside story, see his *The Triumph of Politics: Why the Reagan Revolution Failed* (New York: Harper & Row, 1986).

For a critical biography, see John Groenya and Anne Urban, *The Real David Stockman* (New York: St. Martin's, 1986).

Stone v Graham See SCHOOL DISTRICT OF ABINGTON TOWNSHIP V SCHEMPP.

stonewall To hold one's ground and not give in to the opposition. The term has its roots in Confederate General Thomas Jonathan "Stonewall" Jackson (1824–1863), who was noted for standing "like a stone wall" and holding his ground in battle. It first came into modern political use as a tactic of the WATERGATE conspirators of the Richard M. Nixon administration. Ironically, a word that originated in the honorable acts of a brave general now refers to the dishonorable acts of politicians who refuse to cooperate with investigations of their corruptions.

strategic advantage The power relation between opponents that enables one side to effectively control the course of a military or political situation.

strategic defense initiative (SDI) The Ronald Reagan administration's effort to create a space-stationed defense against enemy missiles. It is popularly known as star wars, because its purported capabilities sound like a high-tech fantasy.

REFERENCES

Alvin M. Weinberg and Jack N. Barkenbus, Stabilizing star wars, *Foreign Policy* 54 (Spring 1984);

Rodney W. Jones and Steven A. Hildreth, Star wars: Down to earth, or gleam in the sky, *Washington Quarterly* 7 (Fall 1984);

James R. Schlesinger, Rhetoric and Realities in the star wars debate, *International Security* 10 (Summer 1985).

strategic planning *See* PLANNING.

strategic superiority The position of strategic military forces, usually meaning nuclear, in such numbers and in such placement as to be able to overwhelm the potential enemy in the event of war. In the nuclear era, this concept has lost much of its meaning because each of the major superpowers has a SECOND STRIKE CAPABILITY.

REFERENCE

Barry M. Blechman and Robert Powell, What in the name of God is strategic superiority? *Political Science Quarterly* 97 (Winter 1982–83).

strategic voting *See* VOTING, STRATEGIC.

strategy The art and science of developing and using political, economic, psychological, and military forces as necessary during peace and war; to afford the maximum support to policies to increase the possibility of a favorable outcome.

REFERENCES

Julian Lider, Towards a modern concept of strategy, *Cooperation and Conflict* 16 (December 1981);

Peter Paret, ed., *Makers of Modern Strategy from Machiavelli to the Nuclear Age* (Princeton, NJ: Princeton University Press, 1986).

street-level bureaucrats   *See* BUREAUCRATS, STREET-LEVEL.

strict constructionist   One who believes the U.S. Constitution should be interpreted narrowly and literally. Strict constructionists tend to be against judicial activism and in favor of judicial self-restraint. A loose constructionist, in contrast, believes that the Constitution should be interpreted liberally in order to reflect changing times. Chief Justice John Marshall first made the case for loose construction in *McCulloch v Maryland,* when he asserted:

"Let the end be legitimate, let it be within the scope of the Constitution, and all means which are appropriate, which are plainly adapted to that end, which are not prohibited, but consist with the letter and spirit of the Constitution, are constitutional." *Compare to* ORIGINAL INTENT.

REFERENCE

S. Sidney Ulmer, Supreme Court justices as strict and not-so-strict constructionists: Some implications, *Law & Society Review* 8 (Fall 1973).

strike   A mutual agreement among workers (whether members of a union or not) to a temporary work stoppage to obtain—or to resist—a change in their working conditions. The term is thought to have nautical origins because sailors would stop work by striking or taking down their sails. A strike or potential strike is considered an essential element of the collective bargaining process. Many labor leaders claim that collective bargaining can never be more than a charade without the right to strike. Major strikes have been declining in frequency in re-

One of the most bitter labor disputes in recent memory began when members of local P-9 struck against the George A. Hormel meat plant in Austin, Minnesota, in 1985.

cent years, as unions in both the public and private sectors have lost a large measure of economic clout and political support. Public employee strikes also have been declining for another reason as well. A great percentage of public sector strikes in the 1960s and early 1970s were over one issue: recognition of the union for purposes of collective bargaining. Because recognition strikes tend to be one-time issues and because many states have in the last two decades passed comprehensive public employee relations laws, public sector labor strife has been less than it once was. *See also* AIR TRAFFIC CONTROLLER'S STRIKE; BLUE FLU; BOSTON POLICE STRIKE OF 1919; GENERAL STRIKE; JURISDICTIONAL STRIKE; RED RASH.

REFERENCES

For histories, see P. K. Edwards, *Strikes in the United States, 1881–1974* (New York: St. Martin's, 1981);

Bruce E. Kaufman, The determinants of strikes in the United States, 1900–1977, *Industrial and Labor Relations Review* 35 (July 1982).

For public employee strikes, see Eugene H. Becker, Analysis of work stoppages in the federal sector, 1962–81, *Monthly Labor Review* 105 (August 1982);

Kurt L. Hanslowe and John L. Acierno, The law and theory of strikes by government employees, *Cornell Law Review* 67 (August 1982);

Peter A. Veglahn, Public sector strike penalties and their appeal, *Public Personnel Management* 12 (Summer 1983);

Timothy M. Gill, Public employee strikes: Legalization through the elimination of remedies, *California Law Review* 72 (July 1984).

strike force 1 A military force organized to undertake an offensive mission. 2 By analogy, a civilian government effort to attack some problem; commonly used by police and public prosecutors, as in a crime strike force.

strong mayor *See* MAYOR-COUNCIL SYSTEM.

structural-functional theory/structural-functionalism An approach in sociology in which societies, communities, and organiza-

tions are viewed as systems. Their particular features are then explained in terms of their contributions (their functions) in maintaining the system. Structural-functional analysis emphasizes the social system at the expense of, or as opposed to, the system's recognized political organizations, actors, and institutions. This approach is generally credited to Talcott Parsons.

REFERENCES

Talcott Parsons, *The Social System* (New York: Free Press, 1951);

Alexander J. Groth, Structural functionalism and political development: Three problems, *Western Political Quarterly* 23 (September 1970).

stump 1 To give campaign speeches in a great variety of locations in an electoral jurisdiction. Before empty soap boxes were commonly available, candidates would use a convenient tree stump, quite literally, as their political platform. The standard campaign speech, the one given on most occasions during a campaign, is the stump speech. 2 Any bombastic, exuberant, sometimes inflammatory, but always entertaining, political oratory.

REFERENCE

Richard Allen Heckman, The Lincoln-Douglas debates: A case study in "stump speaking," *Civil War History* 12:1 (1966).

Stump v Sparkman 435 U.S. 349 (1978) The U.S. Supreme Court case reaffirming the principle of *Bradley v Fisher*, 13 Wall 335 (1872), that judges have absolute immunity from liability in civil suits based upon their official acts.

REFERENCE

Irene Merker Rosenberg, *Stump v Sparkman:* The doctrine of judicial impunity, *Virginia Law Review* 64 (October 1978).

subcommittee A subset of a larger committee. Much of the business of the U.S. Congress is conducted in its approximately 230 subcommittees. These subcommittees give many junior members of the Congress their only opportunity to chair a committee—to "take an issue and run with it."

subgovernments

REFERENCES

Steven H. Haeberle, The institutionalization of the subcommittee in the United States House of Representatives, *Journal of Politics* 40 (November 1978);

Roger H. Davidson, Subcommittee government: New channels for policy making, in *The New Congress*, ed. Thomas E. Mann and Norman J. Ornstein (Washington, D.C.: American Enterprise, 1981);

Kenneth A. Shepsle and Barry R. Weingast, Policy consequences of government by congressional subcommittees, *Proceedings of the Academy of Political Science* 35:4 (1985).

subgovernments The COZY TRIANGLES/IRON TRIANGLES of congressional committees or subcommittees, agency executives, and interest group lobbyists that often dominate public policymaking in a given area. Subgovernments, with a relatively small number of participants which, as a group, can function pretty much autonomously, are often contrasted with ISSUE NETWORKS—large numbers of people with vastly varying degrees of interest, mutual commitment, and power to influence an issue. While a subgovernment or iron triangle is a relatively stable unit both for purposes of exercising power and political analysis, an issue network is so loose that it almost defies definition.

Feeding the Work of Subgovernments into Formal Institutions

Subgovernment

(bureaucrats, legislators, group representatives)

Identify problem   Choose option   Seek support

Proposal fed into

Executive   Congress

Relevant agency   White House   House   Senate

Office of Management and Budget   Formal lawmaking process   Formal lawmaking process

Formal processes for developing and clearing proposals

Transmittal to the Congress   Formal process for reaching agreement

Source: William J. Keefe, Henry J. Abraham, William H. Flanigan, Charles O. Jones, Morris S. Ogul, and John W. Spanier, *American Democracy: Institutions, Politics, and Policies,* 2d ed. (Chicago: Dorsey, 1986), p. 501.

REFERENCES

Lance deHaven-Smith and Carl E. Van Horn, Subgovernment conflict in public policy, *Policy Studies Journal* 12 (June 1984);

Keith E. Hamm, The role of "subgovernments" in U.S. state policy making: An exploratory analysis, *Legislative Studies Quarterly* 11 (August 1986).

subnational government State and local government.

REFERENCE

Joseph F. Zimmerman, ed., *Subnational Politics: Readings in State and Local Government,* 2d ed. (New York: Holt, Rinehart & Winston, 1970).

subornation of perjury *See* PERJURY, SUBORNATION OF.

subpoena 1 A written order issued by a judicial officer requiring a specified person to appear in a designated court at a specified time either to serve as a witness in a case under the jurisdiction of that court or to bring material to that court. 2 A formal order to appear before a legislature; usually a legislative committee. This has the same force of law as a subpoena issued by a judicial officer.

REFERENCES

Raoul Berger, Congressional subpoenas to executive officials, *Columbia Law Review* 75 (June 1975);

Michael Vitiello, The power of state legislatures to subpoena federal officials, *Tulane Law Review* 58 (November 1984).

subpresidencies The notion that the duties of the president of the United States can be grouped into logical and relatively independent categories of policies, actions, and political patterns, each representing a subpresidency. Examples include the foreign policy presidency, the economic policy presidency, the domestic policy presidency.

REFERENCE

Thomas E. Cronin, *The State of the Presidency,* 2d ed. (Boston: Little, Brown, 1980).

substantive bill clearance *See* CENTRAL CLEARANCE.

substantive law · The basic law of rights and duties (contract law, criminal law, accident law, law of wills), as opposed to procedural law (law of pleading, law of evidence, law of jurisdiction).

substitute A motion, an amendment, or an entire bill introduced in place of pending business. Passage of a substitute measure kills the original measure by supplanting it. A substitute may be amended.

Subversive Activities Control Board *See* ALBERTSON V SUBVERSIVE ACTIVITIES CONTROL BOARD.

A group of suffragists assemble on the steps of the U.S. Capitol.

suffrage The right to vote. Property ownership was commonly required for voters in the early years of the United States, but, by the time Andrew Jackson became president in 1829, universal white male suffrage had been effectively achieved. Since then, various constitutional amendments have been devoted to expanding the suffrage. In 1870, the Fifteenth Amendment held that suffrage shall not be denied "on account of race, color, or previous condition of servitude." In 1920, the Nineteenth Amendment held that citizens of either sex had the right to vote. In 1964, the Twenty-fourth Amendment prohibited the poll tax in federal elections. And in 1971, the Twenty-sixth Amendment lowered the voting age to eighteen years.

REFERENCES

Catherine Cole Mambretti, "The burden of ballot": The women's anti-suffrage movement, *American Heritage* 30 (December 1978);

Christine A. Lunardini and Thomas J. Knock, Woodrow Wilson and woman suffrage: A new look, *Political Science Quarterly* 95 (Winter 1980–81);

Anne Firor Scott and Andrew MacKay Scott, *One Half the People: The Fight for Woman Suffrage* (Urbana: University of Illinois Press, 1982).

Sugarman v Dougall 413 U.S. 634 (1973) The U.S. Supreme Court case that held that a ban on the employment of resident aliens by a state was unconstitutional because it encompassed positions that had little, if any, relation to a legitimate state interest in treating aliens differently from citizens. However, the Court also stated that alienage might be reasonably taken into account with regard to specific positions. *See also* AMBACH V NORWICK; CITIZENSHIP; FOLEY V CONNELIE; HAMPTON V MOW SUN WONG.

summit diplomacy *See* DIPLOMATIC SUMMIT.

summons 1 A written order issued by a judicial officer requiring a person who is a party to a lawsuit to appear in a designated court at a specified time. 2 A court order to appear as a witness in a case or for jury duty. 3 A traffic citation issued by a police officer.

sumptuary laws Laws that attempt to control the sale or use of socially undesirable, wasteful, or harmful products.

sunbelt-snowbelt tension The tension caused by the post–World War II era movement of jobs and population from states in the Northeast and the Midwest to the states of the South, Southwest, and West. Political power (in terms of congressional seats) and economic power (in term of jobs) continue to shift. *Compare to* RUSTBELT.

REFERENCES

Kirkpatrick Sale, *Power Shift* (New York: Random House, 1975);

Robert Jay Dilger, *The Sunbelt/Snowbelt Controversy: The War over Federal Funds* (New York: New York University Press, 1982);

Richard M. Bernard and Bradley R. Rice, *Sunbelt Cities: Politics and Growth Since World War II* (Austin: University of Texas Press, 1983).

The Sunbelt-Snowbelt Shift in Congressional Seats after the 1980 Census

Gaining States	Losing States
Arizona, +1	Illinois, −2
California, +2	Indiana, −1
Colorado, +1	Massachusetts, −1
Florida, +4	Michigan, −1
Nevada, +1	Missouri, −1
New Mexico, +1	New Jersey, −1
Oregon, +1	New York, −5
Tennessee, +1	Ohio, −2
Texas, +3	Pennsylvania, −2
Utah, +1	South Dakota, −1
Washington, +1	

sunset laws Laws that fix termination dates on programs or agencies. The laws were pioneered by Colorado, after a major lobbying effort by Common Cause. Many other jurisdictions have now enacted sunset laws. They require formal evaluations and subsequent affirmative legislation if the agency or program is to continue. Although the purpose of a finite life span of, say, five years is to force evaluation and to toughen legislative oversight, the effect is to subject programs to automatic termination unless the clock is reset. Despite its widespread popularity, such time bomb evaluation is not without risks. There are limits to the abilities of any legislature's staff to do the kind of thorough evaluation required to make sunset meaningful. And, of course, the political reality is that the evaluation might become a tool of bipartisan infighting. Requiring organizations to submit evaluation data for review and to justify their programs may amount to little more than burying the legislature in an avalanche of insignificant paper—something at which agencies have a demonstrated prowess. Furthermore, some agencies, such as police, prisons, and mental health institutions, will be rightly skeptical of the chances of their programs being shut down.

REFERENCES

Robert D. Behn, The false dawn of the sunset laws, *Public Interest* 49 (Fall 1977);

Ronald E. Gregson, Sunset in Colorado: The second round, *State Government* 53 (Spring 1980);

William Lyons and Larry W. Thomas, Legislative attitudes toward the feasibility of sunset legislation, *Midwest Review of Public Administration* 14 (March 1980);

William Lyons and Patricia K. Freeman, Sunset legislation and the legislative process in Tennessee, *Legislative Studies Quarterly* 9 (February 1984);

Mary K. Marvel, Sunset: An early evaluation, *Public Choice* 42:2 (1984).

sunshine laws Requirements that government agencies hold their formal business meetings open to the public. Many state and local governments have sunshine laws. The federal government's Sunshine Act of 1977 requires all independent regulatory commissions to give advance notice of the date, time, place, and agenda of their meetings. Closed meetings are allowed if circumstances warrant, but citizens have the right to take agencies to federal court if they feel that closed meetings were not justified.

REFERENCES

Jerry W. Markham, Sunshine on the administrative process: Wherein lies the shade, *Administrative Law Review* 28 (Summer 1976);

Thomas H. Tucker, Sunshine—The dubious new god, *Administrative Law Review* 32 (Summer 1980).

sunshine rules The rules adopted by the U.S. House of Representatives in 1973 and the Senate in 1975 that require committee meetings to be open to the public (including the press and lobbyists) unless a majority of the committee publicly votes to hold a closed, or executive, session.

super delegate *See* DELEGATE, SUPER.

supervisors, board of The governing body for a county government. Membership on the board is determined either by election or by ex officio appointment by other local officials.

REFERENCE

Gary W. Cox and Timothy N. Tutt, Universalism and allocative decision making in Los Angeles County board of supervisors. *Journal of Politics* 46 (May 1984).

supplemental bill *See* BILL, DEFICIENCY.

Supplemental Security Income (SSI) The federal program that assures a minimum monthly income to needy people with limited income and resources who are sixty-five years of age or older, blind, or disabled. Eligibility is based on income and assets. Although the program is administered by the Social Security Administration, it is financed from general revenues, not from social security contributions.

REFERENCES

Robert B. Albritton, Measuring public policy: Impacts of the Supplemental Social Security Income Program, *American Journal of Political Science* 23 (August 1979);

Marilyn Moon, Supplemental security income, asset tests, and equity, *Policy Analysis* 6 (Winter 1980).

supply-side economics/Reaganomics The belief that lower tax rates, especially on marginal income, encourages fresh capital to flow into the economy, which in turn generates jobs, growth, and new tax revenue. Because this concept was adopted by President Ronald Reagan and his advisors, it has been popularly called Reaganomics, even though Reagan's actual economic policies have been a melange of supply-side thinking, monetarism, old-fashioned conservatism, and even Keynesianism. While economist Arthur Laffer is generally credited with having "discovered" supply-side economics, the underlying premises of it were established almost two hundred years ago by Alexander Hamilton in Federalist 21. Hamilton argued that:

> It is a signal advantage of taxes . . . that they contain in their own nature a security against excess. They prescribe their own limit; which cannot be exceeded without defeating the end proposed,—that is, an extension of the revenue. When applied to this object, the saying is as just as it is witty, that, "in political arithmetic, two and two do not always make four." If duties are too high, they lessen the consumption; the collection is eluded; and the product to the treasury is not so great as when they are confined within proper and moderate bounds.

REFERENCES

R. T. McNamar, President Reagan's economic program, *Presidential Studies Quarterly* 11 (Summer 1981);

Robert Lekachman, *Greed Is Not Enough: Reaganomics* (New York: Pantheon, 1982);

Bruce Bartlett and Timothy P. Roth, eds., *The Supply-Side Solution* (Chatham, NJ: Chatham House, 1983);

Michael J. Boskin, *Reaganomics Examined: Successes, Failures, Unfinished Agenda* (San Francisco: Institute for Contemporary Studies, 1985);

C. Fred Bergsten and Henry R. Nau, The state of the debate: Reaganomics, *Foreign Policy* 59 (Summer 1985);

Charles E. Jacob, Reaganomics: The revolution in American political economy, *Law and Contemporary Problems* 48 (Summer 1985).

supremacy clause That portion of Article VI of the U.S. Constitution that asserts that the Constitution, treaties, and laws made on its behalf "shall be the supreme Law of the Land," implying that federal law will take precedence over state law.

REFERENCE

Louis E. Wolcher, Sovereign immunity and the supremacy clause: Damages against states in their own courts for constitutional violations, *California Law Review* 69 (March 1981).

Supreme Court, United States The highest United States court. Since 1869, the Court has been composed of the CHIEF JUSTICE of the United States and eight associate justices. The Congress, which governs its organization by legislation, has varied the number of associate justices from six to ten. The Congress now requires six justices for a quorum. The power to nominate the justices is vested in the president, and appointments are made by and with the advice and consent of the Senate. Article III, Section 1, of the Constitution further provides that "the judges, both of the supreme and inferior courts, shall hold their offices during good behavior, and shall, at stated times, receive for their services, a compensation, which shall not be diminished during their continuance in office."

The Constitution provides that "in all cases affecting ambassadors (to the United States), other public ministers and consuls, and those in which a State shall be party," the Supreme Court has original jurisdiction. This was modified by the Eleventh Amendment to preclude citizens from suing a state. Additionally, the Constitution provides that the Congress may regulate the appellate jurisdiction of the Court. The Congress has authorized the Supreme Court to, among other things, review decisions of the lower federal courts and the highest courts of the states. Because instances of original jurisdiction are rare, the overwhelming majority of cases heard by the Court are appeals from the federal and state court systems.

The internal review process of the Court has largely evolved by custom, while the procedures to be followed by petitioners to the Court are established in rules set forth by the Court. After individually examining each case submitted, the justices hold a private conference to decide which cases to schedule for oral argument, which to decide without argument, and which to dismiss. If at least four justices agree, a case will be taken by the Court for a decision, with or without argument. If oral argument is heard, a total of one hour is generally allowed the parties to argue the issues and respond to questions of the justices. Later, in conference, the justices make their decision by simple majority vote. A tie vote means that the decision of the lower court is allowed to stand. Such a vote could occur when one or three justices do not take part in a decision. When the justices

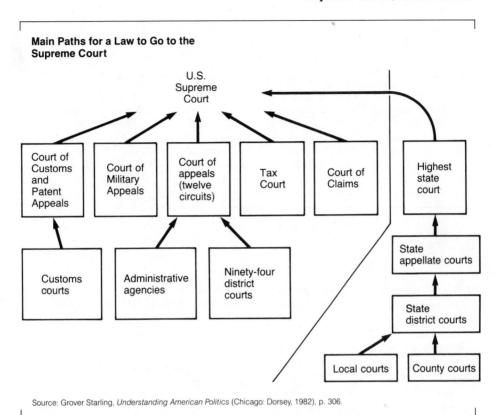

Main Paths for a Law to Go to the Supreme Court

Source: Grover Starling, *Understanding American Politics* (Chicago: Dorsey, 1982), p. 306.

have decided a case, the chief justice, if he voted with the majority, assigns an associate justice or himself to write the opinion of the Court. If the chief justice is in the minority, the senior associate justice in the majority makes the assignment. The individual justices may, of course, write their own opinions in any decision.

Article VI of the Constitution provides that the Constitution and the laws of the United States made "in pursuance thereof" shall be the supreme law of the land. Thus when the Supreme Court decides a case, particularly on constitutional grounds, it becomes guidance for all the lower courts and legislatures when a similar question arises. While the Court's greatest power is that of judicial review, this ability to negate acts of other branches of government is used sparingly. Whenever possible, the Court seeks other grounds if it is necessary to reverse a lower court decision. Each year, the Court receives for review nearly four thou-

sand decisions from lower state and federal courts. The justices examine each case submitted and agree to hear arguments on less than two hundred each term; another one hundred or so are disposed of by decision of the Court without oral argument; and the rest are either denied or dismissed. *Compare to* BRETHREN; JUDICIAL REVIEW.

REFERENCES

Robert G. McCloskey, *The American Supreme Court* (Chicago: University of Chicago Press, 1960);

Alexander M. Bickel, *The Least Dangerous Branch: The Supreme Court at the Bar of Politics* (Indianapolis: Bobbs Merrill, 1962);

Raoul Berger, *Congress versus the Supreme Court* (Cambridge, MA: Harvard University Press, 1969);

Congressional Quarterly, *Guide to the U.S. Supreme Court* (Washington, D.C.: Congressional Quarterly, 1979);

Supreme Court Justices, 1987

Name	Year of Birth	Home State	Law School	Appointment President	Year
William J. Brennan	1906	New Jersey	Harvard	Eisenhower	1956
Byron R. White	1918	Colorado	Yale	Kennedy	1962
Thurgood Marshall	1908	Maryland	Howard	Johnson	1967
Harry A. Blackmun	1908	Minnesota	Harvard	Nixon	1970
William H. Rehnquist	1924	Arizona	Stanford	Nixon	1972
John Paul Stevens	1916	Illinois	Chicago	Ford	1975
Sandra Day O'Connor	1930	Arizona	Stanford	Reagan	1981
Antonin Scalia	1936	New York	Harvard	Reagan	1986

Note: Justices are listed in order of appointment. In 1986, Ronald Reagan appointed William Rehnquist chief justice. There is one vacancy on the Court as this book goes to press.

D. Grier Stephenson, Jr., *The Supreme Court and the American Republic: An Annotated Bibliography* (New York: Garland, 1981); Lawrence Baum, *The Supreme Court,* 2d ed. (Washington, D.C.: Congressional Quarterly, 1984); Henry J. Abraham, *Justices and Presidents: A Political History of Appointments to the Supreme Court,* 2d ed. (New York: Oxford University Press, 1985); David M. O'Brien, *Storm Center: The Supreme Court in American Politics* (New York: Norton, 1986).

U.S. Supreme Court
1 First Street, N.E.
Washington, D.C. 20543
(202) 479–3000

supreme law of the land The U.S. Constitution, laws of the United States made "in pursuance of" the Constitution, and treaties made under authority of the United States. Judges throughout the country are bound by them, regardless of anything in separate state constitutions or laws.

surtax An additional tax, or surcharge, on what has already been taxed; that is, a tax on a tax. For example, if you must pay a thousand-dollar tax on a ten-thousand-dollar income (10 percent), a 10 percent surtax would be an additional hundred dollars.

REFERENCE
William L. Springer, Did the 1968 surcharge really work? *American Economic Review* 65 (September 1975).

survey research center *See* INSTITUTE FOR SOCIAL RESEARCH.

survey researcher *See* POLLSTER.

suspend the rules *See* RULES, SUSPENSION OF.

Swann v Charlotte-Mecklenburg Board of Education 402 U.S. 1 (1971) The U.S. Supreme Court case that decreed that extensive school busing could be used as part of a racial desegregation plan. This decision established the legal framework for all future school BUSING decisions.
REFERENCE
Bernard Schwartz, *Swann's Way: The School Busing Case and the Supreme Court* (New York: Oxford University Press, 1986).

symbol Something that stands for something else and may be respected or criticized as a sign of that which it represents. Since prehistory, people have been controlled by their leaders by means of taboos and rituals. The associated symbolism portends either terror or hope. Political leaders in the United States have evoked terror with dire predictions about the international communist conspiracy and hope with a call to arms to fight the war on poverty. Simlarly, U.S. business leaders evoke terror by reminding us of the perils of bad breath, dull teeth, and unsprayed body areas. These fears fade when the various sprays, creams, gels, and pastes are purchased and used. The public is assured that they, too, can be "beautiful people" it they take the right vitamin supplements, drive the appropriate car, and drink the correct diet cola or wine cooler. We are all subliminally (if not consciously) aware of the symbolism in political rhetoric and business advertising.

A political executive wishing to impose a sanction upon a congressional committee that is holding up the funding of his program might suggest that the committee is not acting in "the national interest." The notion of the national interest, while vague, is a powerful symbol because it represents a commonly accepted good. Because it is so widely revered, it has great legitimacy. By wrapping his program in a symbol of such weight and using that symbol punitively against legislators in opposition to his program, a political executive may succeed in influencing those legislators. The success or failure of such a gambit depends upon a variety of interrelated factors. How susceptible to this particular symbol are the legislators that he is trying to influence? Is the symbol of appropriate weight relative to the symbols of the opposition? While the political executive might wish to use a more powerful symbol, such a tactic might backfire. One does not fight the opposition's symbol of "economy and efficiency" by calling them "communist dupes."

REFERENCES

Thurman W. Arnold, *The Symbols of Government* (New Haven, CT: Yale University Press, 1935);

Murry Edelman, *The Symbolic Uses of Politics* (Urbana: University of Illinois Press, 1967);

Roger W. Cobb and Charles D. Elder, The political uses of symbolism, *American Politics Quarterly* 1 (July 1973);

Robert E. Goodin, Symbolic rewards: Being bought off cheaply, *Political Studies* 25 (September 1977);

David Kowalewski, The protest uses of symbolic politics, *Social Science Quarterly* 61 (June 1980).

symbolic speech Nonverbal behavior, such as hand movements, facial expressions, wearing certain items of clothing. Symbolic speech, as opposed to symbolic actions (which may be disruptive or destructive), is generally protected by the First Amendment. For example, the Supreme Court held in *Tinker v Des Moines School District*, 393 U.S. 503 (1969), that students who wore black armbands to protest the Vietnam War could not be punished because this was a "silent, passive expression of opinion" that was not disruptive.

syndicalism A theory of government that argues that trade unions should control the means of production and, ultimately, the government. *Compare to* FASCISM; MARXISM.

system 1 Any organized collection of parts united by prescribed interactions and designed for the accomplishment of a specific goal or general purpose. 2 The political process in general. 3 The establishment; the powers that be who govern; the domain of a ruling elite. 4 The BUREAUCRACY.

systems analysis The methodologically rigorous collection, manipulation, and evaluation of data on social units (as small as an organization or as large as a polity) to determine the best way to improve their functioning and to aid a decision maker in selecting a preferred choice among alternatives. The systems approach views social units as complex sets of dynamically intertwined, interconnected (and often unknown) elements, including inputs, processes, outputs, feedback loops, and the environments in which they operate. A change in any element of the system inevitably causes changes in its other elements. Norbert Wiener's (1894–1964) classic model of an adaptive system, from his 1948 book *Cybernetics: On Control and Communication in the Animal and the Machine* (Cambridge, MA: MIT Press), epitomizes the basic theoretical perspectives of the

table

systems school. Cybernetics, a Greek word meaning steersman, was used by Wiener to mean the multidisciplinary study of the structures and functions of control and information-processing systems in animals and machines. The basic concept behind cybernetics is self-regulation—biological, social, or technological systems that can identify problems, do something about them, and then receive feedback to adjust themselves automatically. Wiener, a mathematician, developed the concept of cybernetics while working on antiaircraft systems during World War II. While LUDWIG VON BERTALANFFY is considered the father of general systems theory, DAVID EASTON is credited with the first major application of systems in political science in his 1953 book, *The Political System* (New York: Knopf).

REFERENCES

Guy Black, *The Application of Systems Analysis to Government Operations* (New York: Praeger, 1968);

E. S. Quade and W. I. Boucher, eds., *Systems Analysis and Policy Planning* (New York: American Elsevier, 1968);

Ida R. Hoos, *Systems Analysis in Public Policy: A Critique* (Berkeley and Los Angeles: University of California Press, 1972);

David Easton, Systems analysis in political science today, *Policy Studies Review* 19 (January-March 1980);

Hugh J. Miser and Edward S. Quade, eds., *Handbook of Systems Analysis* (New York: Elsevier Science, 1985).

Norbert Wiener's Model of an Organization as an Adaptive System

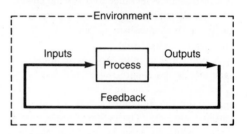

Source: Jay M. Shafritz and J. Steven Ott, *Classics of Organization Theory*, 2d ed. (Chicago: Dorsey, 1987), p. 235.

T

table   A legislative or procedural motion to suspend the consideration of a proposal. The motion to "lay on the table" is not debatable in either house of the U.S. Congress, and it is usually a method of making a final—and adverse—disposition of a matter. In the Senate, however, different language is sometimes used. The motion is worded to let a bill "lie on the table," perhaps for subsequent "picking up." This motion is more flexible, merely keeping the bill pending for later action, if desired.

tactics   1 The maneuvering of troops, ships, or aircraft on a battlefront in preparation for immediate combat. By analogy, a tactical weapon (as opposed to a strategic one) is any device available to a commander during the course of a battle. Nuclear weapons, while normally designed for strategic purposes, have also been designed for tactical use.   2 Short-term political actions; the day-to-day decisions that have to be made on the conduct of a political campaign, as opposed to its overall theme and approach.

REFERENCES

1   Richard Brandt and Thomas Nagel, The morality of tactical nuclear weapons: A philosophers' debate, *Parameters: Journal of the US Army War College* 11 (September 1981).

2   David C. Colby, A test of the relative efficacy of political tactics, *American Journal of Political Science* 26 (November 1982).

William Howard Taft.

Taft, William Howard (1857–1930) The only person to be both president of the United States (1909–1913) and chief justice of the Supreme Court (1921–1930). Taft, at 321 pounds, also holds the record as the largest of all presidents. While he was the handpicked successor of President Theodore Roosevelt, Taft quickly lost Roosevelt's support once in office. Roosevelt found him so unacceptably conservative that both men competed for the Republican nomination in 1912. When Roosevelt won the primaries but lost the nomination to Taft, he ran for president as a "Bullmoose" Progressive. This split the Republican vote and allowed Woodrow Wilson, the Democrat, to win. *See* PRESIDENCY, RESTRICTED VIEW OF.

REFERENCES

William Manners, *TR and Will: A Friendship that Split the Republican Party* (New York: Harcourt Brace Jovanovich, 1969);

Paolo Enrico Coletta, *The Presidency of William Howard Taft* (Lawrence: University Press of Kansas, 1973).

Taft Commission The 1912 Commission on Economy and Efficiency, chaired by the president, which called for a national budgetary sys-

tem. Its recommendations were incorporated into the BUDGET AND ACCOUNTING ACT OF 1921.

Taft-Hartley Act *See* LABOR-MANAGEMENT RELATIONS ACT OF 1947/TAFT-HARTLEY ACT.

Tammany Hall A building in New York City used by the Tammany Society (founded in 1789 and named after a Delaware Indian chief) and whose name became a symbol of all that is associated with political machines, because the New York County Democrats also met in the building.

REFERENCES

William Riordon, ed., *Plunkitt of Tammany Hall* (New York: Dutton, 1963);

Jerome Mushkat, *Tammany: The Evolution of a Political Machine, 1789–1865* (Syracuse, NY: Syracuse University Press, 1971);

Warren Moscow, *The Last of the Big-time Bosses: The Life and Times of Carmine de Sapio and the Rise and Fall of Tammany Hall* (New York: Stein and Day, 1971).

targeting A tactic used by political action committees (PACs) that has them identify (target) specific members of the U.S. Congress for defeat. They then channel campaign funds to the candidate's opposition, or spend funds on behalf of the opposition. The PACs that engage in this kind of negative campaigning have been called attack PACs.

tariff *See* DUTY.

task force 1 A temporary grouping of disparate military forces under a single commander to undertake a specific mission. 2 By analogy, a temporary interdisciplinary team within a larger organization charged with accomplishing a specific goal. Task forces are typically used in government when a problem crosses departmental lines. 3 A temporary government COMMISSION charged with investigating and reporting upon a problem. This meaning of task force has come into fashion at the expense of the more traditional government commission, because task force implies a more aggressive, more action-oriented, approach to seeking solutions to difficult social problems.

REFERENCES

2 Laurence V. Bass, *Management by Task Forces: A Manual on the Operation of Interdisciplinary Teams* (Mount Airy, MD: Lomond, 1975);

3 Nancy Kegan Smith, Presidential task force operation during the Johnson administration, *Presidential Studies Quarterly* 15 (Spring 1985).

tax A compulsory contribution exacted by a government for public purposes. This does not include employee and employer assessments for retirement and social insurance purposes, which are classified as insurance trust revenue. Taxes are generally perceived by a public to be legitimate if they are levied by that public's elected representatives. Indeed, one of the causes of, and principal rallying cries for, the American Revolution was that there should be "no taxation without representation" because "taxation without representation was tyranny." Consequently, practically all taxes at all levels of government are now enacted by popularly elected legislatures. While Benjamin Franklin wrote in 1789 that "in this world nothing is certain but death and taxes," and Oliver Wendell Holmes wrote in 1927 that "taxes are what we pay for civilized society," it remained for Margaret Mitchell to observe (in *Gone With the Wind*, 1936): "Death and taxes and childbirth! There's never any convenient time for any of them!" *See also* REVENUE GAINERS/REVENUE ENHANCEMENT; TAXATION.

tax abatement/tax remission The relinquishment of a tax that would ordinarily be due. For example, a local government might temporarily abate certain property taxes to encourage the renovation of slum housing.

taxable income Under federal tax law, either the gross income of businesses or the adjusted gross income of individuals minus deductions and exemptions—the income against which tax rates are applied.

tax amnesty A government's forgiving of the failure to pay taxes previously due if they are paid within an announced period. This saves the taxpayer the interest and penalties that would have been due and gains the government far more in revenues than it would obtain through normal enforcement. At least eighteen states have recently used tax amnesty programs to increase their income tax collections. The federal government has yet to have a tax amnesty program. Many complain that all such programs are inherently unfair to people who pay their taxes on time.

REFERENCES

John L. Mikesell, Tax amnesties as a tool for revenue, *State Government* 57:4 (1984);

William M. Parle and Mike W. Hirlinger, Evaluating the use of tax amnesty by state government, *Public Administration Review* 46 (May/June 1986).

tax anticipation notes *See* REVENUE ANTICIPATION NOTES.

tax assessment *See* ASSESSMENT.

taxation Government revenue collection. There are major differences between the federal and state-local revenue systems. The federal system has experienced a trend toward less diversity; over two-thirds of its general revenue are provided by the federal income tax and the several insurance trust funds (such as social security). State and local revenue systems, in contrast, depend on a greater variety of revenue sources (such as property taxes, income taxes, sales taxes, user charges, lotteries, and federal grants). While local governments still rely primarily on the property tax, their states—with a few exceptions—rely largely on the state personal income tax. In addition, state sales and business taxes provide a significant source of income. This melange of taxing authorities creates great disparities in the state-local tax burden. A resident of New York may pay hundreds or thousands of dollars in state income taxes while a resident of Texas—which has no state income tax—pays none. Virginians have to pay more than double the sales taxes paid by Vermonters. There are even greater variations in property taxes. Given two identical houses, one may be assessed at x dollars in one jurisdiction while the other may be taxed at three times that amount in another jurisdiction. *See also* ABILITY TO PAY; TAX, DIRECT/INDIRECT TAX; DUTY.

REFERENCES

Henry J. Aaron and Michael J. Boskin, eds., *The Economics of Taxation* (Washington, D.C.: Brookings, 1980);

Henry J. Aaron and Joseph A. Pechman, eds., *How Taxes Affect Economic Behavior* (Washington, D.C.: Brookings, 1981);

Susan B. Hansen, *The Politics of Taxation: Revenue without Representation* (New York: Praeger, 1983);

Joseph A. Pechman, *Who Paid the Taxes, 1966–85?* (Washington, D.C.: Brookings, 1985);

Carolyn Webber and Aaron Wildavsky, *A History of Taxation and Expenditure in the Western World* (New York: Simon & Schuster, 1986).

Comparative Tax Rates

Country	Percentage
Sweden	50.6%
Denmark	47.2
Norway	46.3
France	45.4
Netherlands	45.4
Belgium	45.4
Austria	42.0
Italy	40.6
Ireland	40.0
United Kingdom	38.6
West Germany	37.3
Finland	37.0
Canada	34.8
Greece	32.9
Switzerland	32.2
Portugal	31.2
Australia	30.0
United States	29.0
Japan	27.7
Spain	27.2

Note: Tax rates are totals paid by individuals to all levels of government (data from 1983–1984).

Source: Organization for Economic Cooperation and Development.

taxation, art of "So plucking the goose as to obtain the largest amount of feathers with the least possible amount of hissing." This definition is usually attributed to Jean-Baptiste Colbert (1619–1683), France's King Louis XIV's controller general of finance.

taxation, double *See* DOUBLE TAXATION.

taxation, progressive A tax policy in which people in each successively higher income bracket pay a progressively higher tax rate. The federal graduated personal income tax is the best example of progressive taxation.

REFERENCES

Efraim Sadka, On progressive income taxation, *American Economic Review* 66 (December 1976);

Gary H. Brooks, Correlates of progressive taxation in American states, *Journal of Political Science* 7 (Spring 1980).

taxation, proportional A tax policy in which people pay an identical percentage increase in their tax rates as their incomes rise. Some taxes that are actually proportional in structure, such as sales taxes or property taxes, function as regressive taxes when the tax paid is compared against income; the point being that people in a low-income bracket will pay a higher percentage of their incomes for sales tax than will people with higher incomes.

taxation, regressive A tax policy in which the effective tax rate falls as the tax base increases.

tax avoidance Avoiding taxes by planning one's personal finances to take advantage of all legal tax breaks, such as deductions and tax shelters. The very wealthy J. Pierpont Morgan

(1836–1913) provided the intellectual foundation of tax avoidance when he said, "No citizen has a moral obligation to assist in maintaining the government. If Congress insists on making stupid mistakes and passing foolish tax laws, millionaires should not be condemned if they take advantage of them." The Tax Reform Act of 1986 was designed to make tax avoidance more difficult by closing many tax loopholes. *Compare to* TAX EVASION.

REFERENCES

Alan Gunn, Tax avoidance, *Michigan Law Review* 76 (April 1978);

George Cooper, The taming of the shrewd: Identifying and controlling income tax avoidance, *Columbia Law Review* 85 (May 1985).

tax base The thing or value on which taxes are levied. Some of the more common tax bases include individual income, corporate income, real property, wealth, motor vehicles, sales of commodities and services, utilities, events, imports, estates, and gifts. The rate of a tax to be imposed against a given tax base may be either specific or ad valorem. Specific taxes raise a specific, nonvariable amount of revenue from each unit of the tax base (e.g., ten cents per gallon of gasoline). Ad valorem taxes are expressed as a percentage, and the revenue yield varies according to the value of the tax base (e.g., a mill levy against real property).

REFERENCE

D. A. Gilbert, Property tax base sharing: An answer to central city fiscal problems? *Social Sciences Quarterly* 59 (March 1979).

tax bracket *See* TAX RATE/TAX BRACKET.

tax, capital gains A tax on the profit made on the increase in value of capital assets (such as a house or stocks) when they are sold. Tax rates on capital gains may be lower than for personal income if the assets are held longer than a prescribed period. The TAX REFORM ACT OF 1986 eliminates the special treatment of capital gains for federal income tax purposes.

tax collections *See* TAX YIELD.

tax, corporate income A tax on the privilege of operating a business. Various deductions can be made for depreciation, capital gains, research and development costs, and so on, to determine taxable income.

tax credits The provisions of law that allow a dollar-for-dollar reduction in tax liabilities.

tax, direct/indirect tax A direct tax (e.g., an income tax): a tax paid to a government directly by a taxpayer; an indirect tax (e.g., a sales tax): a tax paid to a third party, who in turn pays it to a government. Article I, Section 9, of the U.S. Constitution holds that "no capitation, or other direct, tax shall be laid, unless in proportion to the census or enumeration herein before directed to be taken." This inhibited the enactment of the federal income tax until the Sixteenth Amendment of 1913 changed the Constitution to allow for direct taxation.

tax, earmarked A tax whose revenues must, by law, be spent for specific purposes. For example, a state gasoline tax may be earmarked for highway construction.

tax elasticity The relation between the percentage of tax revenue raised compared to the percentage of change in personal income. A perfectly elastic tax would always be able to collect the same percentage of the income of its jurisdiction's population.

REFERENCE

Eleanor D. Craig and A. James Heins, The effect of tax elasticity on government spending, *Public Choice* 35:3 (1980).

taxes, payments in lieu of Annual sums paid to local governments by tax-exempt organizations. For example, some universities make payments in lieu of taxes to their cities to help pay for such services as trash removal and police and fire protection.

tax, estate The federal and state taxes on a deceased person's property made prior to the estate's distribution to heirs.

REFERENCES

Byron L. Dorgan, The American estate tax: A death penalty, *State Government* 49 (Spring 1976);

Michael J. Graetz, To praise the estate tax, not to bury it, *Yale Law Journal* 93 (December 1983).

tax, estimated   That portion of income tax that individuals with other significant income than salaries must declare to the Internal Revenue Service and pay every three months.

tax evasion   Taking illegal and criminal actions to avoid paying one's tax obligations. *Compare to* TAX AVOIDANCE.

REFERENCES

Robert Mason and Lyle D. Calvin, A study of admitted income tax evasion, *Law and Society Review* 13 (Fall 1978);

Douglas J. Workman, The use of offshore tax havens for the purpose of criminally evading income taxes, *Journal of Criminal Law & Criminology* 73 (Summer 1982).

tax, excess profits   A supplement to corporate income taxes, usually imposed during a national emergency.

tax, excise   A tax on the manufacture, sale, or consumption of a product.

tax exemption   1 The immunity from taxation of certain activities and institutions. Such exemption may be temporary, such as a ten-year exemption to encourage new housing in a particular area, or permanent, as in the exemptions enjoyed by most schools and churches. 2 The immunity from taxation of certain kinds of income, such as child support payments and income from municipal bonds.

REFERENCE

1   John M. Quigley and Roger W. Schmenner, Property tax exemption and public policy, *Public Policy* 23 (Summer 1975).

tax-exempt municipal bonds   *See* BONDS, MUNICIPAL/TAX-EXEMPT MUNICIPAL BONDS.

tax exempts   1 Land, buildings, or businesses that do not pay taxes because of legal exemptions.   2 Investments, such as municipal bonds, that are tax free.   3 Nonprofit organizations that meet legal requirements for tax exemption.

REFERENCES

Douglas Laycock, Tax exemptions for racially discriminatory religious schools, *Texas Law Review* 60 (February 1982);

Dean M. Kelley, The Supreme Court redefines tax exemption, *Society* 21 (May/June 1984).

tax expenditure   The losses of tax revenue attributable to provisions of the federal tax laws that allow a special exclusion, exemption, or deduction from gross income or that provide a special credit, preferential rate of tax, or deferral of tax liability. When an individual or a corporation gets a tax subsidy, the federal government counts it as a tax expenditure. *Compare to* TAX LOOPHOLE.

REFERENCES

Stanley S. Surrey, *Pathways to Tax Reform: The Concept of Tax Expenditures* (Cambridge, MA: Harvard University Press, 1973);

Ronald F. King, Tax expenditures and systematic public policy: An essay on the political economy of the federal revenue code, *Public Budgeting & Finance* 4 (Spring 1984).

tax, exported   A tax paid by nonresidents of a community (e.g., a city wage tax paid by commuters).

tax, flat   A tax that charges the same rate to each taxpayer. The concept has been put forward in a variety of proposals for reform of the federal income tax. *Compare to* TAX REFORM ACT OF 1986.

REFERENCES

C. Lowell Harriss, Important issues and serious problems in flat-rate income taxation, *American Journal of Economics and Sociology* 43 (April 1984);

Robert E. Hall and Alvin Rabushka, *The Flat Tax* (Stanford, CA: Hoover Institution, 1985).

Tax Foundation   An organization devoted to nonpartisan research and public education on the fiscal aspects of government.
Tax Foundation
1808 Connecticut Avenue, N.W.
Washington, D.C. 20009
(202) 328-4500

tax incentive A provision in a tax law that encourages particular economic activity. For example, provisions for accelerated depreciation encourage businesses to buy new equipment; provisions that allow the deductibility of the interest on a home mortgage encourage people to buy houses.

REFERENCES

Barry P. Bosworth, *Tax Incentives and Economic Growth* (Washington, D.C.: Brookings, 1984);

Donald N. Steinnes, Business climate, tax incentives, and regional economic development, *Growth and Change* 15 (April 1984).

tax incidence The effects of a particular tax burden on various socioeconomic levels.

tax, income *See* TAX, PERSONAL INCOME.

tax-increment financing The ability of local government to finance large-scale development through the expected rise in the property tax to be collected after the development is completed. This permits the issuance of bonds based on the expected tax increase.

tax, inheritance A tax, usually progressive, on an individual's share of a deceased person's estate.

tax, license A tax exacted (either for revenue raising or for regulation) as a condition to the exercise of a business or nonbusiness privilege.

tax lien Legally executed charges on a property because of unpaid taxes. The lien can result in a foreclosure and tax sale; that is, the property can be forcibly sold to pay the taxes due.

tax loophole An inconsistency in the tax laws, intentional or unintentional, that allows the avoidance of some taxes. An intentional tax loophole is a TAX EXPENDITURE. A tax expenditure for one person is often viewed as a loophole by another. Tax loopholes are perfectly legal; but they have an unsavory reputation as the handiwork of special interest lobbyists. *Compare to* TRANSITION RULE.

REFERENCE

Boris I. Bittker, Income tax "loopholes" and political rhetoric, *Michigan Law Review* 71 (May 1973).

tax, marriage Not an actual tax, but the simple fact that under some income tax laws two wage earners who happen to be married to each other and file a joint tax return will often pay more in taxes than if they were single and filed separately.

REFERENCE

James A. Duran and Elizabeth C. Duran, The marriage tax, *Social Policy* 11 (March/April 1981).

tax, negative income A welfare program in which citizens with incomes below a specified level receive cash payments.

REFERENCES

Terry R. Johnson and John H. Pencavel, Forecasting the effects of a negative income tax program, *Industrial and Labor Relations Review* 35 (January 1982);

Barbara Devaney, Total work effort under a negative income tax, *Journal of Policy Analysis and Management* 2 (Summer 1983).

tax, personal income A tax based on ability to pay, in that the tax rate is applied against income. But income is more than just money; it is any asset that increases one's net worth; and yet income taxes are not necessarily a straight tax on all of one's income in a given year. Remember all those millionaires that the press annually discovers who do not pay any tax on their income? They are able to do this because it is not their large incomes that are subject to taxation, but their adjusted gross incomes. All taxpayers have the right to exclude certain kinds of incomes from their gross incomes for tax purposes. For example, interest from state and local bonds is exempt from federal taxation. Thus a millionaire whose sole income came from investments in such bonds would pay no federal income tax. The taxpayer may also subtract deductions and exemptions from taxable income. Then the taxpayer can deduct a host of expenses, as long as they are allowed by the tax laws: medical care, state and local taxes (if a federal return), home mortgage interest, and charitable contributions. A taxpayer can itemize deductions or take a minimum standard deduction, which is a pre-calculated weighted average. Progressive tax rates are then applied to the taxable income to determine how much tax is due.

All states but Florida, Nevada, South Dakota, Texas, Washington, and Vermont have personal income taxes, as do many cities. Residents of Baltimore, Cleveland, Detroit, New York, and Philadelphia, for example, must pay personal income taxes to three different governments: federal, state, and local.

REFERENCE

Jerold L. Waltman, *Political Origins of the U.S. Income Tax* (Jackson: University Press of Mississippi, 1985).

tax, personal property Tax on the assessed value of (1) tangible property, such as furniture, animals, or jewelry; or (2) intangible property, such as stocks and bonds.

REFERENCE

Steven J. Zellmer and Calvin A. Kent, Trends in the taxation of personal property, *State Government* 52 (Winter 1979).

tax, poll A tax required of voters, once widely used by southern states to discourage blacks from voting. The Twenty-fourth Amendment to the U.S. Constitution prohibits denial of the right to vote for federal officials because a person has not paid a tax. This amendment was designed to abolish the requirement of a poll tax which, at the time of its ratification, was imposed by five states as a condition to voting. The U.S. Supreme Court in *Harper v Virginia State Board of Elections,* 383 U.S. 663 (1966), subsequently held that poll taxes were unconstitutional under the equal protection clause of the Fourteenth Amendment, on the basis that the right to vote should not be conditioned on one's ability to pay a tax. Accordingly, poll taxes are now prohibited in all state and federal elections.

REFERENCE

Dick Smith, Texas and the poll tax, *Southwestern Social Science Quarterly* 45:2 (1964).

tax rate/tax bracket The percentage of taxable income (or of inherited money, things purchased subject to sales tax, and so on) paid in taxes. The federal income tax has a graduated tax rate. This means that the first ten thousand dollars of a person's taxable income might be taxed at a 20 percent rate (or two thousand dollars) and the next one thousand to two thousand dollars at a 25 percent rate. This percentage rate is what most people think of as their tax bracket.

tax, real-property Any tax on land and its improvements; usually referred to simply as property tax. This tax is the mainstay of most local governments; it provides nearly half of the revenues that local governments get from their own sources. To administer a property tax, the tax base must first be defined—that is, housing and land, automobiles, other assets, whatever. Then an evaluation of the worth of the tax base must be made—this is the assessment. Finally, a tax rate, usually an amount to be paid per hundred-dollar value of the tax base, is levied. Since the value of the tax base will appreciate or depreciate substantially over time, continuing assessments must be made.

Arguments for the property tax resemble a good news/bad news joke. The good news is that the property tax provides a stable revenue source and has a good track record as a strong revenue raiser. The bad news is that its stability can also be considered inflexibility, as it does not keep pace with income growth. The good news is that, since property is generally unmovable, it is hard to miss and, therefore, provides a visible tax base for relatively unskilled local tax offices to administer. The bad news is that the administration and assessment of property tax is at best erratic and at worst a horrendous mess. The result is that the property tax base tends to erode over time; that the property of the wealthy and the politically influential may be undervalued; that there is a strong incidence effect on newcomers; and that old people are being increasingly pressed to meet property tax burdens.

REFERENCES

Henry J. Aaron, *Who Pays the Property Tax? A New View* (Washington, D.C.: Brookings, 1975);

Diane B. Paul, *The Politics of the Property Tax* (Lexington, MA: Heath, 1975);

John H. Bowman and John L. Mikesell, The importance of property tax structural variations for effective tax reform: Barriers created by misconceptions, *State and Local Government Review* 12 (September 1980);

Jeffrey S. Slovak, Property taxes and community political structures, *Urban Affairs Quarterly* 16 (December 1980);

David Lowery, Tax equity under conditions of fiscal stress: The case of the property tax, *Publius* 14 (Spring 1984);

Dennis Hale, The evolution of the property tax: A study of the relation between public finance and political theory, *Journal of Politics* 47 (May 1985).

tax reform The recurrent effort to produce a more equitable tax system at all levels of government. As a process, it is never ending and full of semantic traps—for one person's tax reform often winds up as another's tax increase.

REFERENCES

Joseph A. Pechman, ed., *Options for Tax Reform* (Washington, D.C.: Brookings, 1984);

Henry J. Aaron and Harvey Galper, *Assessing Tax Reform* (Washington, D.C.: Brookings, 1985);

Michael Chiorazzi, Tax reform during President Reagan's first four years: A selective bibliography, *Law and Contemporary Problems* 48 (Autumn 1985).

Tax Reform Act of 1986 A comprehensive revision of the federal income tax law that collapses fourteen tax brackets into two (15 and 28 percent), eliminates most tax shelters and deductions (with the major exceptions of those for home mortgage interest, donations to charity, state and local income and property taxes), raises the personal exemption to two thousand dollars by 1988; and eliminates the special treatment of income from capital gains. The new law has been both praised and criticized for marking the federal government's retreat from using the tax code for economic and social engineering. Under the new law, investment decisions will, for the most part, have to be made on the merits of investments and not on their tax implications. While not a pure flat tax, the law is considered a victory for those who advocated simplifying the income tax rate structure. Because the act's large standard deduction (five thousand dollars for joint filees) and increased personal exemption, the law will have the effect of taking millions of low-income taxpayers off the rolls. Thus the act has been praised for being an important piece of antipoverty legislation.

REFERENCES

Joseph Pechman, *Federal Tax Policy,* 5th ed. (Washington, D.C.: Brookings, 1987);

Jeffrey H. Birnbaum and Alan S. Murray, *Showdown at Gucci Gulch: Lawmakers, Lobbyists, and the Unlikely Triumph of Tax Reform* (New York: Random House, 1987).

tax, regulatory A tax levied for another purpose than raising revenue.

tax revolt A nationwide grass roots movement, heralded by California Proposition 13, in 1978, to decrease or limit the rate of increase possible on property taxes. In a sense, this was a revolt by the middle class against the rising cost of government services, which created a period of fiscal stress for state and local government. The tax revolt, it is important to note, was not over the unfairness or uneven distribution of the tax burden but over the levels of taxation, especially on real estate, which were increasing dramatically in a period of double-digit inflation. By 1980, the tax revolt movement forced thirty-eight states to reduce or at least stabilize tax rates.

REFERENCES

Wilbur J. Scott, Harold G. Grasmick, and Craig M. Eckert, Dimensions of the tax revolt: Uncovering strange bedfellows, *American Politics Quarterly* 9 (January 1981);

David Lowery and Lee Sigelman, Understanding the tax revolt: Eight explanations, *American Political Science Review* 75 (December 1981);

Paul Peretz, There was no tax revolt! *Politics and Society* 11:2 (1982);

Marc P. Freiman and Patrick G. Grasso, Some conceptual comments on the 1978 "tax revolt," *Social Science Quarterly* 63 (September 1982);

Lee Sigelman, David Lowery, and Roland Smith, The tax revolt: A comparative state analysis, *Western Political Quarterly* 36 (March 1983).

tax, sales A tax on consumption, rather than income. This favorite of many state and local governments calls for a fixed tax rate, ranging from 2 to 9 percent, to be charged on most purchases. A variety of items tend to be excluded from sales taxation—for example, medicine and foods. The major criticism of the sales tax is equity. Sales taxes tend toward regressivity, in that higher-income groups pay a lesser percentage of their income in tax than do lower-income groups. To illustrate, a family of four with an annual income of eight thousand dollars would spend half of that in direct consumption and might pay a 5 percent sales tax of two hundred dollars, or 2.5 percent of their income. But another family of four with an eighty-thousand-dollar income will have a much lower percentage of direct consumption (say 25 percent) and, although they pay 5 percent on this amount (a thousand dollars), the proportion of their income taken by the sales tax is 1.2 percent—or half that of the lower-income family.

REFERENCES
Hui S. Chang, Functional forms and the estimation of a state's sales tax revenue: Tennessee as a case study, *Annals of Regional Science* 13 (July 1979);
Carl Shoup, The property tax versus sales and income taxes, *Proceedings of the Academy of Political Science* 35:1 (1983).

tax, self-employment The means by which persons who work for themselves are provided social security coverage. Each self-employed person must pay self-employment tax on part or all of his or her income to help finance social security benefits, which are payable to self-employed persons as well as to wage earners.

tax, severance A tax imposed by about half of the states for the privilege of "severing" natural resources, such as coal, from the land.

REFERENCES
Albert M. Church, *Taxation of Nonrenewable Resources* (Lexington, MA: Lexington Books, 1981);

Joseph P. Gilligan, Federal limits on state coal severance taxes, *Journal of Legislation* 8 (Summer 1981);
Bernard L. Weinstein, Who pays the severance tax? *Policy Studies Journal* 12 (March 1984).

tax, shared A tax imposed and administered by a higher level of government that it shares according to a predetermined percentage formula with lower units of government. For example, states commonly collect sales taxes and return a portion to counties and municipalities.

tax shelter An investment in which any profits are fully or partially tax free or that creates deductions and credits that reduce one's overall taxes.

tax, stamp A tax on certain legal documents, such as deeds, when it is required that revenue stamps be bought and put on the documents to make them valid. The British Parliament's Stamp Act of 1765 sought to increase revenues from the American colonies and helped trigger the movement toward revolution. This tax, which required stamps on legal papers, newspapers, pamphlets, almanacs, cards, and so on, was so resented and caused such turmoil that it was repealed in 1766.

REFERENCE
Edmund S. Morgan and Helen M. Morgan, *Stamp Act Crisis: Prologue to Revolution* (New York: Collier, 1963).

tax subsidy A tax advantage designed to encourage specific behavior that furthers public policy; for example, mortgage interest deductions to encourage citizens to buy houses and investment tax credits to encourage businesses to expand and create new jobs. *Compare to* TAX EXPENDITURE.

tax, transfer A tax on large transfers of property or money, which are made without something of value given in return. Often called a gift tax.

tax, unitary A business tax of a percentage of worldwide profits, not just profits earned in the taxing jurisdiction. For example, if a corporation has 20 percent of its payroll, property, and sales in a given state, that state might tax 20 percent of the corporation's worldwide income.

REFERENCE

Daniel L. Simmons, Worldwide unitary taxation: Retain and Rationalize, or block at the water's edge? *Stanford Journal of International Law* 21 (Spring 1985).

tax, value-added (VAT)   A type of national sales tax imposed by almost all Western European countries as a major source of revenue, levied on the value added at each stage of production and distribution of a product; sometimes called a business transfer tax. Proponents of VAT in the United States argue that VAT rewards efficiency and, thus, is superior to the corporate income tax in allocating economic resources; it can encourage savings and capital formation because it is a tax solely on consumption; it can help balance-of-payments problems because it can be imposed on imports and rebated on exports; and it can be a major new source of revenue for meeting domestic spending needs, especially social security costs. Opponents of VAT in the United States charge that it is a regressive tax (i.e., it falls most heavily on the poor); that it is inflationary, in that prices to consumers go up; and that it will be an additional tax, rather than a substitute for present taxes.

REFERENCES

L. L. Bravenec and Kerry Cooper, The flexibility of the value-added tax, *Texas Law Review* 55 (February 1977);

David Bruce Spizer, The value added tax and other proposed tax reforms: A critical assessment, *Tulane Law Review* 54 (December 1979);

Charles W. Baird, Proportionality, justice, and the value-added tax, *Cato Journal* 1 (Fall 1981);

Henry J. Aaron, ed., *The Value Added Tax: Lessons from Europe* (Washington, D.C.: Brookings, 1981).

tax, wage   Any tax on wages and salaries levied by a government. Many cities have wage taxes that have the indirect benefit of forcing suburban commuters to help pay for the services provided to the region by the central city.

tax, withholding   Sums of money that an employer takes out of an employee's pay and turns over to a government as prepayment of the employee's federal, state, or local tax obligations. *Compare to* FORCED SAVINGS.

tax yield   The amount of tax that could potentially be collected. Tax collections are the portion of the tax yield that is actually collected.

Teapot Dome   The Warren G. Harding administration scandal concerning naval oil reserves at Teapot Dome, Wyoming, and Elk Hills, California, that were leased to private parties without competitive bidding by Albert B. Fall (1861–1944), the secretary of the Interior (1921–1923). A Senate investigation resulted in Fall's later trial, conviction, and imprisonment for accepting bribes, and in the cancellation of the leases. Such an instance of a cabinet member being jailed for criminal behavior while in office would not be repeated until the WATERGATE scandals of the Richard M. Nixon administration.

REFERENCE

Burl Noggle, *Teapot Dome* (New York: Norton, 1965).

technocrat   An individual in a decision-making position of a technoscience agency whose background includes specialized technical training in a substantive field of science or technology. Sometimes used disparagingly.

REFERENCE

Raundi Halvorson, Technocrats on the firing line, *Fletcher Forum* 7 (Summer 1983).

Technology Assessment Act of 1972   *See* OFFICE OF TECHNOLOGY ASSESSMENT.

technoscience agencies   Those federal government agencies involved with science and technology policymaking. These agencies generate ideas for scientific research and technological development; sponsor research in universities, corporations, and federal laboratories; and direct deployment projects. Examples include the National Science Foundation, the National Aeronautics and Space Administration, the Department of Defense, and the Department of Energy.

technostructure A term that implies a growing influence of technical specialists in policy decisions. Technostructure is increasingly used as a technical term in the study of science and technology policymaking to refer to the technical decision-making structure in private and public organizations.

Forty dams operate in the TVA's water control system.

Ronald Reagan, the man in the teflon-coated suit.

teflon president A reference to Ronald Reagan because of his ability to avoid being blamed for the mistakes of his subordinates. He was so well liked that it was claimed "nothing sticks," much like Teflon brand no-stick cookware. The phrase was first used by Congresswoman Patricia Schroeder, a Democrat from Colorado, in 1983. While nothing else may have stuck, this phrase did—at least until the TOWER COMMISSION report of 1987.

telethon A many-hours-long television program that intersperses entertainment with appeals for charitable or political contributions.
REFERENCE
John W. Ellwood and Robert J. Spitzer, The Democratic national telethons: Their successes and failures, *Journal of Politics* 41 (August 1979).

teller vote *See* VOTE, TELLER.

Tennessee Valley Authority (TVA) The government-owned corporation created in 1933

that conducts a unified program of resource development for the advancement of economic growth in the Tennessee River Valley region. The authority's program includes flood control, navigation development, electric power production, fertilizer development, recreation improvement, and forestry and wildlife development. While its power program is financially self-supporting, other programs are financed primarily by appropriations from the Congress.

REFERENCES
For histories of the TVA, see David Lilienthal, *TVA—Democracy on the March* (New York: Harper & Row, 1944);

Philip Selznick, *T.V.A. and the Grass Roots* (Berkeley and Los Angeles: University of California Press, 1949);

E. M. Hugh-Jones, The Tennessee Valley Authority fifty years on, *Political Quarterly* 54 (July/September 1983);

Steven M. Neuse, TVA at age fifty—Reflections and retrospect, *Public Administration Review* 43 (November/December 1983).

Tennessee Valley Authority
400 West Summit Hill Drive
Knoxville, TN 37902
(615) 632-2101

Tennessee Valley Authority
Capitol Hill Office Building
412 1st Street, S.E.
Washington, D.C. 20444
(202) 245-0101

Tenth Amendment The last part of the Bill of Rights that holds that the "powers not dele-

541

gated to the United States by the Constitution, nor prohibited by it to the states, are reserved to the states respectively, or to the people." The Tenth Amendment embodies the principle of federalism, which reserves for the states the residue of powers not granted to the federal government or withheld from the states. In recent years, it has not served as much of a constraint on the expansion of the powers of the national government. *Compare to* RESERVE POWERS; TREATY.

REFERENCES
Kathryn Abrams, On reading and using the Tenth Amendment, *Yale Law Journal* 93 (March 1984);
James R. Alexander, State sovereignty in the federal system: Constitutional protections under the Tenth and Eleventh amendments, *Publius* 16 (Spring 1986).

term bonds *See* BONDS, SERIAL.

Terminiello v Chicago 337 U.S. 1 (1949) The U.S. Supreme Court case that held that a local ordinance calling for restrictions on free speech (if such speech was likely to cause a breach of the peace) was an unconstitutional infringement on the First Amendment guarantee of free speech.

terrorism 1 Highly visible violence directed against randomly selected civilians in an effort to generate a pervasive sense of fear and thus affect government policies. 2 Violence against representatives (police, politicians, diplomats) of a state by those who wish to overthrow its government; in this sense, terrorism is REVOLUTION—thus the cliché that one man's terrorist is another man's freedom fighter. 3 Covert warfare by one country against another; in effect, state-sponsored terrorism. 4 The acts of a regime that maintains itself in power by random or calculated abuse of its own citizens; in this sense, all oppression and dictatorial regimes are terrorist.

REFERENCES
Benjamin Netanyahu, ed., *Terrorism: How the West Can Win* (New York: Farrar, Straus, and Giroux, 1986);

Christopher Hitchens, Wanton acts of usage: Terrorism: A cliché in search of a meaning, *Harper's* 273 (September 1986);
Christopher H. Pyle, Defining terrorism, *Foreign Policy* 64 (Fall 1986).

that man in the White House *See* FRANKLIN DELANO ROOSEVELT.

Theory of Justice, A *See* JOHN RAWLS.

think tank A colloquial term for an organization or organizational segment whose sole function is research, usually in the policy and behavioral sciences. Some of the better-known think tanks include the RAND Corporation, the Brookings Institution, and the American Enterprise Institute.

REFERENCES
Paul Dickson, *Think Tanks* (New York: Atheneum, 1971);
Yehezkel Dror, Required breakthroughs in think tanks, *Policy Sciences* 16 (February 1984);
Peter R. Baehr, Think tanks—Who needs them? Advising a government in a democratic society, *Futures* 18 (June 1986).
For a comparative perspective, see Tyrus W. Cobb, National security perspectives of Soviet "think tanks," *Problems of Communism* 30 (November/December 1981).

Third Amendment The amendment to the U.S. Constitution that holds that "no soldier shall, in time of peace be quartered in any house, without the consent of the owner, nor in time of war, but in a manner to be prescribed by law." Prior to the Revolution, American colonists had frequently been required against their will to provide lodging and food for British soldiers. The Third Amendment prohibited the continuation of this practice. Ironically, during World War II many American soldiers were quartered in British homes—at the insistence of the British government.

Third House of Congress 1 Congressional conference committees, which so often allow for the passage of legislation by effecting critical compromises (*see* COMMITTEE, CONFERENCE). 2 The great number of lobbyists who constantly attend the congressional process; usually pejorative.

third party 1 A temporary political party that often arises during a presidential election year to affect the fortunes of the two major parties. A third party, in contrast to a MINOR PARTY, whose members tend to be ideologues, is often composed of independents and those disaffected from a major party who feel the country is ready for a new alternative. It often is hastily formed by a candidate who failed to win—and perhaps never had any prospect of winning—a major party presidential nomination. The best example of third party influence in a presidential election occurred in 1912, when the former president, Theodore Roosevelt, lost the Republican nomination to the sitting president, William Howard Taft, in spite of Roosevelt having won the primary elections. Roosevelt then ran as the candidate of the Progressive "Bull Moose" Party. This split the majority Republican vote and allowed the Democrat, Woodrow Wilson, to win with a plurality. 2 Technically, according to the Presidential Election Campaign Fund Act of 1971, a third party is a minor political party "whose candidate for the office of President in the preceding presidential election received, as the candidate of such party, 5 percent or more but less than 25 percent of the total number of popular votes received by all candidates for such office." Such a designation makes the party eligible for federal campaign funds.

REFERENCES
1 Daniel A. Mazmanian, *Third Parties in Presidential Elections* (Washington, D.C.: Brookings, 1974);
Frank Smallwood, *The Other Candidates: Third Parties in Presidential Elections* (Hanover, NH: University Press of New England, 1983);
Steven J. Rosenstone, Roy L. Behr, and Edward H. Lazarus, *Third Parties in America: Citizen Response to Major Party Failure* (Princeton, NJ: Princeton University Press, 1984);
D. Stephen Rockwood and others, *American Third Parties since the Civil War: An Annotated Bibliography* (New York: Garland, 1985).

Third World Those countries with underdeveloped but growing economies, and low per capita incomes, often with colonial pasts. Third World is often used interchangeably with or as a synonym for LDCs (less developed countries), the South, developing countries, and underdeveloped countries. India, Nigeria, Ecuador, and Morocco are examples. During the 1970s, a Fourth World was distinguished from the Third World to indicate those devel-

Major Third Parties in Presidential Elections

Year	Party Name	Percentage of Total Votes Cast
1832	Anti-Masonic (William Wirt)	8.0%
1848	Free Soil (Martin Van Buren)	10.1
1856	American Know Nothing (Millard Fillmore)	21.4
1860	Democratic Secessionist (John C. Breckinridge)	18.1
1860	Constitutional Union (John Bell)	12.6
1892	Populist (James B. Weaver)	8.5
1912	"Bull Moose" Progressive (Theodore Roosevelt)	27.4
1912	Socialist (Eugene V. Debs)	6.0
1924	Progressive (Robert M. LaFollette)	16.0
1948	States' Rights "Dixiecrats" (Strom Thurmond)	2.4
1968	American Independent (George Wallace)	13.5
1980	National Unity (John Anderson)	7.0

oping countries with little economic growth, few natural resources, slight financial reserves, and extremely low per capita incomes. Bangladesh, Ethiopia, and Sudan are examples. *See* FIRST WORLD; SECOND WORLD.

REFERENCES

Robert K. Olson, Third World: Ally or enemy? *Atlantic Community Quarterly* 17 (Summer 1979);

Bahgat Korany, The take-off of Third World studies: The case of foreign policy, *World Politics* 35 (April 1983);

H. A. Reitsma and J. M. G. Kleinpenning, *The Third World in Perspective* (Totowa, NJ: Rowman and Allanheld, 1985);

Jerry F. Hough, *The Struggle for the Third World: Soviet Debates and American Options* (Washington, D.C.: Brookings, 1986).

Thirteenth Amendment The 1865 amendment to the U.S. Constitution that prohibits slavery. This amendment is the only part of the Constitution that regulates purely private relationships and the first amendment to increase the jurisdiction of the federal government in discriminatory issues by overruling state law. With the secession of the southern states from the Union and the subsequent outbreak of the Civil War in April 1861, the controversy over slavery intensified. A necessary consequence of the southern states' secession was their forfeiture of representation in the Congress. As a result, congressmen advocating the abolition of slavery faced little opposition, and they were quick to act. On April 16, 1862, the Congress abolished slavery in the District of Columbia. In June, the law was extended to include all territories. In September 1862, President Abraham Lincoln, acting as commander in chief during a time of war, issued the Emancipation Proclamation, which became effective on January 1, 1863. The proclamation declared that all people held in slavery "are, and henceforth shall be, free; and the executive government of the United States, including the military and naval authorities thereof, will recognize and maintain the freedom."

The Emancipation Proclamation was contested on several grounds. Opponents strongly questioned the president's constitutional authority to issue such a decree. Others argued that, while the proclamation had freed the slaves in the seceded states, it had not, in effect, made slavery illegal. This left the status of border states and the already defeated Confederate states in question with regard to slavery. The Thirteenth Amendment was proposed and passed to quell the controversy over the constitutionality of the Emancipation Proclamation and to settle the issue of slavery in the United States forever.

REFERENCE

Carol A. Baldwin, The Thirteenth Amendment as an effective source of constitutional authority for affirmative action legislation, *Columbia Journal of Law and Social Problems* 18:1 (1983).

Thornhill v Alabama *See* PICKETING.

throw the rascals out An oft-heard campaign slogan of the party not in power. Sometimes all it really means is that it's time for a change of rascals.

REFERENCE

Arthur H. Miller and Martin P. Wattenberg, Throwing the rascals out: Policy and performance evaluation of presidential candidates, 1952–1980, *American Political Science Review* 79 (June 1985).

ticket splitting Voting for candidates of differing political parties for various offices, as opposed to voting for all of the candidates of a given party (a straight party ticket). Independents are most likely to split their tickets because they have no party loyalty. But even the party faithful split their tickets if provoked by unattractive candidates. To discourage voters from splitting their tickets, parties nominate someone to head the ticket (a candidate for president, governor, and so on) who might have sturdy COATTAILS and thus drag other members of the ticket along to victory. The last presidential coattail vote of any consequence was in 1964, when Lyndon B. Johnson's landslide victory carried a large number of new Democratic members of the Congress into office. In recent presidential elections, about 60 percent of all voters have voted split tickets. In 1984, there were split election outcomes (voting for a president of one party and a House member of another party) in 43.9 percent of the 435 congressional districts.

REFERENCES

Walter DeVries and V. Lance Tarrance, Jr., *The Ticket-Splitter: A New Force in American Politics* (Grand Rapids, MI: Eerdmans, 1972);

Frank B. Feigert, Illusions of ticket-splitting, *American Politics Quarterly* 7 (October 1979);

William H. Flanigan and Nancy H. Zingale, Ticket-splitting and the vote for governor, *State Government* 53 (Summer 1980);

William S. Maddox and Dan Nimmo, In search of the ticket splitter, *Social Science Quarterly* 62 (September 1981);

Alan R. Gitelson and Patricia Bayer Richard, Ticket-splitting: Aggregate measures versus actual ballots, *Western Political Quarterly* 36 (September 1983).

timocracy   The Aristotelian notion of a state in which one's political power is directly proportioned to one's wealth.

Tinker v Des Moines School District   *See* SYMBOLIC SPEECH.

Title VII   The backbone of the equal employment opportunity effort, part of the Civil Rights Act of 1964 as amended. Title VII prohibits employment discrimination because of race, color, religion, sex, or national origin and created the Equal Employment Opportunity Commission as its enforcement vehicle. The federal courts have relied heavily upon Title VII in mandating remedial action on the part of employers. *See also* CITY OF LOS ANGELES, DEPARTMENT OF WATER & POWER V MANHART; MAKE WHOLE; PREGNANCY DISCRIMINATION ACT OF 1978; SEXUAL DISCRIMINATION.

REFERENCES

George Rutherglen, Title VII class actions, *University of Chicago Law Review* 47 (Summer 1980);

Nestor Cruz, Abuse of rights in Title VII cases: The emerging doctrine, *Labor Law Journal* 32 (May 1981);

Elizabeth Bartholet, Application of Title VII to jobs in high places, *Harvard Law Review* 95 (March 1982).

titular leader   The nominal leader of a political party. In American politics, this phrase is generally reserved for defeated presidential candidates who remain the leader of their party, a leader in name only, until the party selects a new presidential nominee at its next national convention.

Alexis de Tocqueville.

Tocqueville, Alexis de (1805–1859)   The French historian who visited the United States in the early 1830s and went home to write *Democracy in America* (1835), a landmark description of American governance and a classic analysis of American political culture. According to Tocqueville, "The great advantage of the Americans is that they have arrived at a state of democracy without having to endure a democratic revolution; and that they are born equal instead of becoming so." While Tocqueville was the first to identify this notion of equality as the fundamental aspect in the development of American political culture, he also warned about the "tyranny of the majority," whereby minorities are forced into conformity by the "tyrannical" rule of the majority.

Tocqueville was quite taken with the American constitutional system, forty years old when he saw it, and was particularly impressed with the political independence of the judiciary and their power of judicial review, which he considered a stabilizing influence comparable to the position of privilege enjoyed by European aristocracy. "Within these limits the power vested in the American courts of justice of pronouncing a statute to be unconstitutional forms one of the most powerful barriers that have ever been devised against the tyranny of political assemblies." And it was Tocqueville who was the first to note that "there is hardly a political question in the United States which sooner or later does not turn into a judicial one."

REFERENCES

Hugh Brogan, Alexis de Tocqueville: The making of a historian, *Journal of Contemporary History* 7 (July/October 1972);

Delba Winthrop, Tocqueville on federalism, *Publius* 6 (Summer 1976);

Sanford Kessler, Tocqueville on civil religion and liberal democracy, *Journal of Politics* 39 (February 1977);

Cushing Strout, Tocqueville and republican religion: Revisiting the visitor, *Political Theory* 8 (February 1980);

Roger Boesche, Why could Tocqueville predict so well? *Political Theory* 11 (February 1983);

Eileen L. McDonagh, De Tocqueville's *Democracy in America:* A sociology of knowledge perspective, *Journal of Political Science* 12 (Spring 1985).

tokenism In the context of equal employment opportunity, an insincere EEO effort by which a few minority group members are hired to satisfy government affirmative action mandates or the demands of pressure groups.

REFERENCE

Donald G. Dutton, Tokenism, reverse discrimination, and egalitarianism in interracial behavior, *Journal of Social Issues* 32:2 (1976).

Torcaso v Watkins 367 U.S. 488 (1961) The U.S. Supreme Court case that held that a state requirement of a declaration of a belief in God as a qualification for office was unconstitutional because it invades one's freedom of belief and religion, guaranteed by the First

Amendment and protected by the Fourteenth Amendment from infringement by the states.

tort Legal harm done to another person that can be the cause of a civil court suit. For example, libel can be a tort.

REFERENCE

G. Edward White, *Tort Law in America* (New York: Oxford University Press, 1980).

totalitarianism A governing system in which a ruling elite holds all power and controls all aspects of society. No opposition is allowed, and power is maintained by internal terror and secret police. Nazi Germany and the Soviet Union under Stalin are two examples of totalitarian states. *Compare to* AUTHORITARIANISM; FASCISM; MARXISM.

REFERENCE

Waldemar Gurian, The totalitarian state, *Review of Politics* 40 (October 1978).

Tower Commission The President's Special Review Board established by President Ronald Reagan in the fall of 1986 to investigate the IRAN-CONTRA AFFAIR and the operations of the National Security Council. The commission, named for its chairman, John G. Tower, former U.S. Senator from Texas, had two other members: Edmund S. Muskie, former U.S. senator from Maine and former secretary of State; and Brent Scowcroft, national security adviser to President Gerald Ford. The commission's 1987 report found that President Reagan had been "disengaged" and "did not seem to be aware" of the White House foreign policy process; that the National Security Council had indeed arranged to trade arms for hostages with Iran and sought to use funds from the arms sale to illegally aid the CONTRAS in Nicaragua; and that certain members of the White House staff sought to cover up these facts as the Iran-contra affair evolved. The most immediate effects of the report was the resignation of Donald Regan, the president's chief of staff, and his replacement by Howard Baker, former U.S. senator from Tennessee.

REFERENCE

John Tower, Edmund Muskie, and Brent Scowcroft, *The Tower Commission Report* (New York: Bantam Books/Times Books, 1987).

town **1** An urban entity, with powers less than those possessed by cities. The powers of towns are strictly controlled by state statutes. **2** The New England town, which combines the role of both city and county. It usually contains one or more urban areas plus surrounding rural areas.

town meeting A method of self-government, suitable for only the smallest jurisdictions, where the entire citizenry meets to decide local public policy. The town meeting is still the governing body for 88 percent of all New England municipalities. According to Robert Preer—in "Town Meetings Don't Work," *Washington Post,* June 13, 1986—town meetings today are most likely to be controlled by special interests and the town's bureaucracy. Attendance is slight. Even though quorums are set at only 1 or 2 percent of registered voters, meetings are often cancelled because of the lack of a quorum. "Raises and promotions pass with ease because meetings are so often packed with employees and their families and friends." Preer concludes that the modern town meeting "is a microcosm of national politics. In both cases, power has shifted from an apathetic and unorganized public to special interests, the mass media, and a bureaucratic-technocratic elite."

REFERENCES

Jane J. Mansbridge, Town meeting democracy, *Dilemmas of Democracy,* ed. Peter Collier (New York: Harcourt Brace Jovanovich, 1976);

Frank M. Bryan, Does the town meeting offer an option for urban America? *National Civic Review* 67 (December 1978).

township A subdivision of a county traditionally having six miles on each side and varying in importance as a unit of government in

Residents of Northwood, New Hampshire, vote at an annual town meeting.

the sixteen states that have them. Townships in the Midwest are sometimes referred to as congressional townships because public land surveys in the last century initially labeled them thus on maps authorized by the Congress.

trade adjustment assistance *See* ADJUSTMENT ASSISTANCE.

trade union A labor organization that restricts its membership to skilled craft workers (such as plumbers and carpenters), in contrast to an industrial union, which seeks to recruit all workers in a given industry.
REFERENCE
Jack Barbash, Trade unionism from Roosevelt to Reagan, *Annals of the American Academy of Political and Social Science* 473 (May 1984).

tragedy of the commons A story illustrative of the principle that the maximization of private gain will not result in the maximization of social benefit. When herdsmen sought to maximize individual gain by adding more and more cattle to a common pasture, the common was overgrazed. The resulting tragedy was that no one was able to effectively use the common for grazing. The concepts involved with the tragedy of the commons apply to societal problems, such as pollution and overpopulation.
REFERENCES
Garrett Hardin, The tragedy of the commons, *Science* 162 (December 13, 1968);
Robert J. Smith, Resolving the tragedy of the commons by creating private property rights in wildlife, *Cato Journal* 1 (Fall 1981);
Hendrik Spruyt, The tragedy of the commons: The case against lifeboat ethics, *Coexistence* 22:2 (1985).

transfer payments Payments by a government made to individuals who provide no goods or services in return. All of the social welfare programs at all levels of government that provide subsistence income support are transfer payment programs. They are often referred to as entitlement programs because one becomes entitled to transfer payments if one meets criteria established by the authorizing legislation.

REFERENCES
Francine D. Blau, The use of transfer payments by immigrants, *Industrial and Labor Relations Review* 37 (January 1984);
John R. Hibbing, The liberal hour: Electoral pressures and transfer payment voting in the United States Congress, *Journal of Politics* 46 (August 1984);
Russell D. Roberts, Recipient preferences and the design of government transfer programs, *Journal of Law & Economics* 28 (April 1985).

transition quarter The three-month period (July 1 to September 30, 1976) between fiscal year 1976 and fiscal year 1977 resulting from the change from a July 1 through June 30 fiscal year to an October 1 through September 30 fiscal year, beginning with fiscal year 1977.

transition rule The euphemism for a TAX LOOPHOLE for special interests retained in the Tax Reform Act of 1986.

Transportation, U.S. Department of (DOT) The cabinet-level department established in 1966 that manages the nation's overall transportation policy. Under its umbrella are eight administrations, whose jurisdictions include highway planning, development, and construction; urban mass transit; railroads; aviation; and the safety of waterways, ports, highways, and oil and gas pipelines. In peacetime, the U.S. Coast Guard is part of the DOT.
U.S. Department of Transportation
400 7th Street, S.W.
Washington, D.C. 20590
(202) 366-4000

treason Disloyalty as defined by Article III, Section 3, of the U.S. Constitution. Treason is the only crime defined by the Constitution. (It "shall consist only in levying War against them [the United States], or in adhering to their enemies, giving them aid and comfort. No person shall be convicted of treason unless on the testimony of two witnesses to the same overt act, or on confession in open court.") The precise description of this offense reflects an awareness that persons holding unpopular views might be branded as traitors. Recent experience in other countries with prosecutions for conduct loosely labeled as treason confirms the wisdom of the authors of the Constitution in expressly stating what constitutes this crime and how it shall be proved. It was John Harington (1561–1612), an Elizabethan courtier, who wrote the most famous epigram on treason:

> Treason doth never prosper:
>   what's the reason?
> For if it prosper, none dare
>   call it treason.

REFERENCES

Rebecca West, *The New Meaning of Treason* (New York: Viking, 1964);

James Kirby Martin, Benedict Arnold's treason as political protest, *Parameters: Journal of the US Army War College* 11 (September 1981).

treason, high What the modern world considers TREASON. It was once distinguished from petit, or small, treason, which was the killing of someone to whom one owed obedience, such as a husband or overlord. Today, petit treason is treated as any other murder.

Treasury, U.S. Department of the One of the first cabinet-level departments of the United States. Created in 1789, the Department of the Treasury formulates and recommends financial, tax, and fiscal policies; serves as financial agent for the U.S. government; manufactures coins and currency; and enforces related laws. Its agencies include the Customs Service, the Bureau of Engraving and Printing, the Internal Revenue Service, the United States Mint, and the Secret Service.

U.S. Department of the Treasury
15th Street and Pennsylvania Avenue, N.W.
Washington, D.C. 20220
(202) 566-2000

treaty A formal international agreement between two or more sovereign states that establishes rights as well as obligations for the parties. In the United States, treaties, once they have been negotiated with foreign states, become, in effect, executive branch proposals that, to take effect, must be submitted to the Senate for approval by two-thirds of the senators present. Before acting on such foreign policy matters, senators usually send them to committee for scrutiny. Treaties are read and debated in the Senate, much like legislative proposals, but are rarely amended. After approval by the Senate, they must be ratified by the president. A ratified treaty binds the states as well as the federal government. Indeed, the Supreme Court held in *Missouri v Holland*, 252 U.S. 416 (1920), that a treaty may interfere with some of the rights reserved to the states by the Tenth Amendment.

But while a president cannot make a treaty without the Senate, can he abrogate one without their approval? This issue arose when President Jimmy Carter recognized the People's Republic of China effective January 1, 1979, and withdrew recognition from Taiwan effective the same date. Commensurate with this action, Carter announced that the 1955 National Defense Treaty with the Nationalist Chinese government of Taiwan would terminate on January 1, 1980, in accordance with the treaty's proviso permitting termination by either party with one year's notice. Carter obviously assumed that there existed presidential authority to abrogate treaties. Senator Barry Goldwater did not, and he filed an appeal with the federal district court that granted Goldwater and his colleagues from the Congress standing to sue. The Court then ruled President Carter's abrogation of the treaty unconstitutional. Eventually, the Supreme Court in *Goldwater v Carter*, 444 U.S. 996 (1979), ordered, without hearing argument, that the case be dismissed; thus upholding the president's power to terminate treaties.

REFERENCES

Gordon Hoxie, Presidential leadership and American foreign policy: Some reflections on the Taiwan issue, with particular considerations on Alexander Hamilton, Dwight D. Eisenhower, and Jimmy Carter, *Presidential Studies Quarterly* 9 (Spring 1979);

Raoul Berger, The president's unilateral termination of the Taiwan Treaty, *Northwestern University Law Review* 75 (November 1980);

L. Peter Schultz, *Goldwater v. Carter:* The separation of powers and the problem of executive prerogative, *Presidential Studies Quarterly* 12 (Winter 1982);

Alan M. Wachman, Carter's constitutional co-
nundrum: An examination of the president's
unilateral termination of a treaty. *Fletcher
Forum* 8 (Summer 1984).

triad The three legs of the U.S. nuclear deterrent: land-based intercontinental ballistic
missiles, submarine-launched ballistic missiles, and long-range strategic bombers. As
originally conceived, this diversification was
intended to insure the strongest possible defense and to disperse the enemy's attention;
each system was thought to be capable of an
independent retaliatory counterstrike against
the enemy. However, the increasing number
and sophistication of Soviet nuclear weapons
has reopened the discussion of the ability of
each leg of the triad to withstand a Soviet first
strike.
REFERENCES
David R. Anderton, *Strategic Air Command:
Two-Thirds of the Triad* (New York: Scribner, 1976);
Colin S. Gray, The strategic forces triad: End
of the road? *Foreign Affairs* 56 (July 1978).

trial The examination in a court of the issues
of fact and law in a case for the purpose of
reaching a judgment.
REFERENCE
Gordon Tullock, *Trials on Trial: The Pure Theory of Legal Procedure* (New York: Columbia University Press, 1980).

trial balloon A deliberate LEAK of a potential policy to see what public response will be.
The term comes from the meteorological practice of sending up a balloon to test weather
conditions. If public response is hostile, the
new policy proposal can be quietly dropped (or
deflated).

trial, bench A trial in which a judge decides
the issues at hand. Because no jury is used,
those involved must waive any constitutionally
or statutory rights to a jury trial.
REFERENCE
Susan C. Towne, The historical origins of
bench trial for serious crime, *American
Journal of Legal History* 26 (April 1982).

trial de novo The Latin term meaning a new
trial.

trial, jury A trial in which a jury determines
the issue of facts in a case.
REFERENCE
Nathalie M. Walker-Dittman, The right to
trial by jury in complex civil litigation, *Tulane Law Review* 55 (February 1981).

trial, nonjury A trial in which a judge determines the issues of fact and law in a case. This
is the same as a judge trial, bench trial, and
court trial.

trial, political 1 A highly publicized trial in
which standards of fair play and due process
are not followed and the verdict is predetermined by the state. 2 A highly publicized
trial in which the defendants and their supporters assert that they are being brought to trial
because of their political views, even though
all procedural safeguards and due processes
have been allowed. 3 A trial in which defendants specifically seek to generate community
support for an issue they espouse.
REFERENCES
Steven E. Barkan, Political trials and resource
mobilization: Towards an understanding of
social movement litigation, *Social Forces* 58
(March 1980);
Ronald Christenson, A political theory of political trials, *Journal of Criminal Law &
Criminology* 74 (Summer 1983).

trial, speedy The right of a defendant to
have a prompt trial, as guaranteed by the Sixth
Amendment provision that "in all criminal
prosecutions, the accused shall enjoy the right
to a speedy and public trial." Although the
federal constitution and the constitutions of almost all the states provide that the accused
shall enjoy the right to a speedy trial, the precise requirements are not clear. Most states and
the federal government (Speedy Trial Act of
1974) have enacted statutes setting forth the
time within which a defendant must be tried
following the date of arrest, detention, and first
appearance or the filing of charges in court. If
the accused is not brought to trial within the
specified period, the case is dismissed. Most

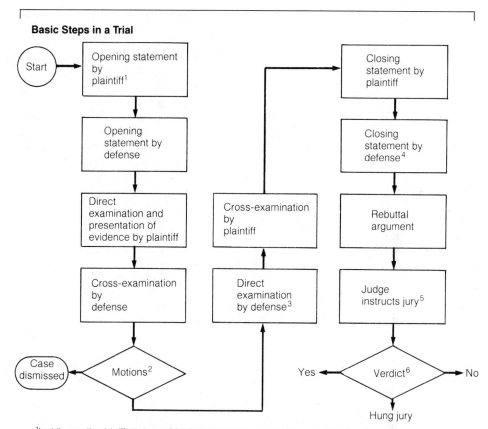

Basic Steps in a Trial

[1]In civil cases, the plaintiff attorney explains the evidence to be presented as proof of the allegations (i.e., unproven statement) in the complaint. In criminal cases, the prosecutor does this.

[2]If the plaintiff's basic case has not been established from the evidence introduced, the judge can end the case by granting the defendant's motion to dismiss.

[3]Defense questions its witnesses.

[4]Defense asks for a finding of not guilty in criminal cases or for defendant in civil cases.

[5]Finally the judge's instructions, sometimes called the charge, come to aid the jury in reaching its verdict. The judge instructs the jury in the law governing the case and reviews the evidence. The authority of the judge to comment on the facts of a case, as distinguished from the law involved, varies from state to state; federal judges have wide latitude. An important part of the charge deals with the burden of proof resting upon the prosecution. The jurors are told that the accused starts out with a presumption of innocence; they cannot convict unless satisfied of guilt beyond a reasonable doubt. If the judge is careless in his charge, or shows bias, the case may be overturned by a higher court.

[6]In most states, a unanimous decision is required one way or the other. If the jury cannot reach a unanimous decision, it is said to be a *hung jury*; the case may then be tried again.

Source: Grover Starling, *Understanding American Politics* (Chicago: Dorsey, 1982), p. 319.

statutes also provide a method for computing excludable delay—delay not counted for the purposes of determining if a trial is speedy. Examples of excludable delay include other proceedings concerning the defendant, such as a hearing on mental competency to stand trial, pending trials on other charges, probation or parole revocation hearings, continuances granted at the request of the defendant, and the absconding of the defendant. The speedy trial provision of the Sixth Amendment was made applicable to the states in *Klopfer v North Carolina*, 386 U.S. 213 (1967).

REFERENCES

Marc I. Steinberg, Right to speedy trial: The constitutional right and its applicability to the Speedy Trial Act of 1974, *Journal of Criminal Law & Criminology* 66 (September 1975);

Anthony G. Amsterdam, Speedy criminal trial: Rights and remedies, *Stanford Law Review* 27 (February 1975);

trickle-down theory

George S. Bridges, The Speedy Trial Act of 1974: Effect on delays in federal criminal litigation, *Journal of Criminal Law & Criminology* 73 (Spring 1982).

trickle-down theory **1** A basis for government policies that seek to benefit the wealthy in hopes that prosperity, in turn, will trickle down to the middle and lower economic classes. The term was first coined by humorist Will Rogers (1879–1935), when he analyzed some of the depression remedies of the Herbert Hoover administration and noted that "the money was all appropriated for the top in the hopes it would trickle down to the needy." **2** The belief that housing would be upgraded for all groups as they move into housing left vacant by other groups progressing up the economic ladder.

Trilateral Commission An organization of several hundred private citizens from Japan, Western Europe, and North America, which was created in 1973 for the purpose of debating the common political, economic, and security issues of the three regions. Many of the commission's activities make use of the number three: it meets for three days every nine months, rotating between the trilateral regions; its newsletter is called the *Trialogue;* and its task forces produce reports called Triangle Papers.
REFERENCE
Brad Roberts, The enigmatic Trilateral Commission: Boon or bane? *Millennium: Journal of International Studies* 11 (Autumn 1982).
    Trilateral Commission
    345 E. 46th Street
    New York, NY 10017
    (212) 661–1180

tripwire A military force situated on a defense line that is not expected to be able to hold off a major enemy assault but whose function is to buy time so that reserves can be brought into the battle or decisions can be made to use tactical or strategic nuclear weapons. The U.S. forces in NATO and Korea are often referred to as tripwires.

true bill *See* BILL, TRUE.

Truman, David B. (1913–   ) A political scientist and one of the most influential interest group theorists. Truman's principal work, *The Governmental Process* (New York: Knopf, 1951), views group interaction as the real determinant of public policy and as the proper focal point of study. Truman defines the interest group as "a shared attitude group that makes certain claims upon other groups in the society. If and when it makes its claims through or upon any of the institutions of government, it becomes a public interest group." Group pressure is assured through the establishment of lines of access and influence. Truman notes that the administrative process provides a multitude of points of access comparable to the legislature. What Truman provides for group theory is a complete description and analysis of how groups interact, function, and influence in the overall political system. Two types of groups are identified by Truman: existing groups and potential groups. The potential group is constituted by people who have common values and attitudes but do not yet see their interests being threatened. Once they do, Truman argues, they form a group to protect their interests.
REFERENCE
Joyce M. Mitchell and William C. Mitchell, Truman's *The Governmental Process:* A public choice perspective, *Micropolitics* 3:1 (1983).

Truman Doctrine The policy of the Harry S Truman administration of giving military and economic aid to those countries (Greece and Turkey, specifically) seeking to resist "totalitarian aggression." This doctrine, which was presented by President Truman in 1947 in his address to a joint session of the Congress in support of the Greek-Turkish aid bill, became a cornerstone of the U.S. policy of containment. *Compare to* NIXON DOCTRINE.
REFERENCES
John Lewis Gaddis, Was the Truman Doctrine a real turning point? *Foreign Affairs* 52 (January 1974);
Robert L. Messer, New evidence on Truman's Doctrine, *Bulletin of the Atomic Scientists* 41 (August 1985).

Harry S Truman.

Truman, Harry S (1884–1972)   The president of the United States (1945–1953) who (as vice president) became president upon the death of Franklin D. Roosevelt. It was Truman who made the decision to drop the first atomic bomb on Japan to quickly end World War II, whose foreign policy of communist CONTAINMENT is still the cornerstone of American foreign policy, and whose MARSHALL PLAN led to the economic recovery of Western Europe after World War II.

Truman started political life as part of the (Thomas J.) Pendergast political machine of Kansas City, Missouri. The machine arranged his appointment and then election to various county posts. While the machine sent him to the U.S. Senate in 1934, Truman's personal integrity remained unquestioned. Truman first gained national prominence during the early part of World War II, when he saved the federal government millions of dollars as chairman of a Senate watchdog committee on defense spending—the "Truman committee." This went far in making him acceptable to President Franklin D. Roosevelt as a vice presidential running mate in 1944. A true apostle of the New Deal, he tried with varying success to expand and sustain it with his own Fair Deal.

His greatest domestic triumph was his 1948 election as president in his own right. In spite of the fact that all the pollsters and political pundits predicted he would certainly lose to Thomas E. Dewey, the governor of New York, Truman won decisively.

REFERENCES

For Truman's two volumes of memoirs, see
Years of Decision (New York: Doubleday, 1955);
Trial and Hope (New York: Doubleday, 1956).
Also see Cabell Phillips, *The Truman Presidency: The History of a Triumphant Succession* (New York: Macmillan, 1966);
A. L. Hamby, *Beyond the New Deal: Harry S Truman and American Liberalism* (New York: Columbia University Press, 1973);
Robert J. Donovan, *Conflict and Crisis: The Presidency of Harry S Truman, 1945–1948* (New York: Norton, 1977);
Robert J. Donovan, *Tumultuous Years: The Presidency of Harry S Truman, 1948–1953* (New York: Norton, 1983).

The Harry S Truman Administration

Major Accomplishments

- The unconditional surrender of both Germany and Japan to end World War II.
- Laying of the political and economic foundations for Germany and Japan to become democratic allies in the postwar era.
- The National Security Act.
- NATO.
- The Marshall Plan.
- The cold war with the Soviet Union (an accomplishment, since the alternative was a hot war).
- The racial integration of the armed forces.

Major Frustrations

- The Korean War.
- The seizure of the steel industry (see YOUNGSTOWN SHEET AND TUBE CO. V SAWYER).
- His inability to get domestic reforms through the conservative coalition in the Congress.

---

trustee   The role that elected representatives adopt when they vote according to their conscience and best judgment, rather than according to the narrow interests of their immediate constituents. *Compare to* EDMUND BURKE; POLITICO.

trust funds Funds collected and used by the federal government for carrying out specific purposes and programs according to terms of a trust agreement or statute, such as the social security and the unemployment trust funds. Trust funds are administered by the government in a fiduciary capacity and are not available for the general purposes of the government. Trust fund receipts that are not anticipated to be used in the immediate future are generally invested in interest-bearing government securities and earn interest for the trust fund. A special category of trust funds called trust revolving funds is used to carry out a cycle of business-type operations, such as with the Federal Deposit Insurance Corporation.

truth squad A group of opposition party members who follow a candidate to tell their version of the truth about the candidate's campaign statements. The main purpose of a truth squad is to make an opposing candidate seem to be a liar.

turkey farm A government office with little work and slight, if any, responsibility. Government managers frequently find it easier to place troublesome or incompetent employees on turkey farms, rather than go through the hassle of ADVERSE ACTION proceedings.
REFERENCE
Richard E. Miller, Recipes for turkey turnover, *Bureaucrat* 8 (Winter 1979–80).

turnout The number of voters who actually vote, compared to the number of voters eligible to vote. Turnout is a significant indicator of

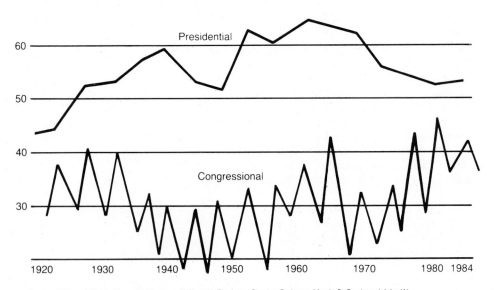

Turnout in Presidential and Congressional Elections, 1920–1984

Turnout of the electorate
Percent

Source: William J. Keefe, Henry J. Abraham, William H. Flanigan, Charles O. Jones, Morris S. Ogul, and John W. Spanier, *American Democracy: Institutions, Politics, and Policies,* 2d ed. (Chicago: Dorsey, 1986), p. 123.

voter apathy, though whether it also indicates voter alienation is hotly debated. Certainly turnout varies directly with socioeconomic status. A low turnout tends to favor Republicans, because Republicans are more likely to vote in any case. As a group, they have many of the attributes of conscientious voters—being older, more formally educated, and wealthier than Democrats. A large turnout tends to favor Democrats simply because they are the majority party. Theoretically, then, they should almost always win. But they don't because of ALIENATION from the political system, apathy (which is an indication of acquiescence with the status quo), or institutional blocks, such as voter registration (*see* REGISTRATION, VOTER), and the difficulties of absentee ballots. The highest turnouts are almost always for presidential elections. But even then, the United States has among the lowest turnouts in the Western world.

REFERENCES

Richard W. Boyd, Decline of U.S. voter turnout: Structural explanations, *American Politics Quarterly* 9 (April 1981);
Paul R. Abramson and John H. Aldrich, The decline of electoral participation in America, *American Political Science Review* 76 (September 1982);
John E. Jackson, Election night reporting and voter turnout, *American Journal of Political Science* 27 (November 1983);
William H. Flanigan and Nancy H. Zingale, *Political Behavior of the American Electorate,* 5th ed. (Boston: Allyn & Bacon, 1983).
For a comparative perspective, see Robert L. Morlan, Municipal vs. national election voter turnout: Europe and the United States, *Political Science Quarterly* 99 (Fall 1984);
G. Bingham Powell, Jr., American voter turnout in comparative perspective, *American Political Science Review* 80 (March 1986).

TVA *See* TENNESSEE VALLEY AUTHORITY.

Twelfth Amendment The 1804 amendment to the U.S. Constitution that required electors to vote separately for president and vice president. This was necessitated by the development of a national party system; something not an-ticipated by the framers. *See* ELECTORAL COLLEGE.

Twentieth Amendment *See* LAME DUCK AMENDMENT.

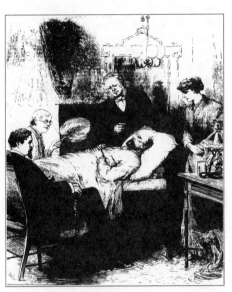

President Garfield was able to perform only one official act in the weeks after he was shot in 1881. The Twenty-fifth Amendment, passed nearly a century later, resolved the uncertainty regarding a president's inability to discharge his duties of office.

Twenty-fifth Amendment The 1967 amendment to the U.S. Constitution that provides for the vice president to become the acting president in the event that the president "is unable to discharge the powers and duties of his office."

In outlining the duties and functions of the president, the framers of the Constitution included provisions regarding the continuity of the executive. Article II, Section 1, reads in part: "In case of the removal of the president from office, or of his death, resignation, or inability to discharge the powers and duties of the said office, the same shall devolve on the vice president." In several respects, this provision of the Constitution is unclear, and eventually it presented a number of questions insufficiently answered by the document. For example, when President William Henry Harrison died in 1841, Vice President John Tyler was left unsure whether he should serve as an "acting" or "official" president of the United States. Although Tyler did ultimately take the oath of office as president, the decision to do so by no means met with unanimous approval. The controversy that ensued was, however, finally quieted when both houses of the Congress voted to recognize Tyler as the official president of the United States. The action taken by Tyler established the precedent followed by eight future vice presidents faced with similar circumstances: Millard Fillmore, Andrew Johnson, Chester Arthur, Theodore Roosevelt, Calvin Coolidge, Harry S Truman, Lyndon Johnson, and Gerald Ford—each of whom became president of the United States through succession.

Another uncertainty arose about presidential succession in cases when a president was unable to "discharge the powers and duties" of his office. Again, the Constitution provided no clear answer to the problem. In three instances in American history the president was considered unable to perform his duties. In all three cases, largely because of uncertainty over correct procedure, the vice president did not assume the incapacitated president's responsibilities.

The first occasion arose in 1881, when President James Garfield fell victim to an assassin's bullet. Garfield lingered for nearly eighty days, during which he was able to perform only one official act—the signing of an extradition paper. In 1919, President Woodrow Wilson suffered a severe stroke, leaving him largely disabled for the rest of his term. Finally, at least three times during his administration, President Dwight D. Eisenhower was considered unable to perform as president because of poor health. He chose to solve the problem by means of an informal working agreement with Vice President Richard M. Nixon, rather than an amendment to the Constitution. The Twenty-fifth Amendment provides a formal process for such situations.

The assassination of President John F. Kennedy and the succession of Vice President Lyndon B. Johnson in 1963 reminded the nation of yet another gap in the succession clause—the lack of a mechanism for choosing a vice president when the previous vice president succeeds

to the presidency. The framers foresaw the need to have a qualified vice president in office should the president die, but they neglected to establish a procedure whereby a vice presidential vacancy could be filled. The Twenty-fifth Amendment provides such a process. This procedure was first used in 1973, when President Richard M. Nixon nominated Gerald Ford to be vice president after Spiro Agnew resigned in disgrace. It was next (and last) used in 1974, when Ford nominated Nelson Rockefeller to be his vice president. This was the only time when both the offices of president and vice president were held by people who had not been elected to either one. *Also see* PRESIDENTIAL SUCCESSION.

REFERENCES

John D. Feerick, *The Twenty-Fifth Amendment: Its Complete History and Earliest Applications* (New York: Fordham University Press, 1976);

Stephen W. Stathis, Presidential disability agreements prior to the Twenty-fifth Amendment, *Presidential Studies Quarterly* 12 (Spring 1982).

Twenty-first Amendment The 1933 amendment to the U.S. Constitution that repealed the Eighteenth Amendment and Prohibition.

Twenty-fourth Amendment The 1964 amendment to the U.S. Constitution that prohibits the use of poll taxes by states.

Twenty-second Amendment The 1951 amendment to the U.S. Constitution that provides that no one person can be elected to the office of president more than twice. This was enacted to prevent any subsequent president from repeating Franklin D. Roosevelt's unparalleled record of being elected president four times (in 1932, 1936, 1940, and 1944).

Beginning with George Washington, the tradition of a two-term presidency was established. Thomas Jefferson followed Washington's precedent, as did succeeding presidents—until Franklin D. Roosevelt. Although the two-term tradition was regarded as an unwritten law prior to Roosevelt's extended administration, numerous attempts had been made throughout America's history to secure it through an amendment to the Constitution. It was not until the Eightieth Congress that an amendment to limit the president to two terms was finally successful. The Congress, convening in 1946, was the first to have a Republican majority since 1928. During the previous years, dominated by the Roosevelt administration, the Republicans had been unable to halt the president and his New Deal legislation. During the debates over the Twenty-second Amendment, the Republicans argued that Roosevelt had accumulated inappropriate power due to his long tenure as president. Ironically, when the Republicans finally had a president popular enough to be able to possibly get elected for a third term, Ronald Reagan, many, including Reagan, have expressed regret over the Twenty-second Amendment.

REFERENCE

Paul B. Davis, The results and implications of the enactment of the Twenty-second Amendment, *Presidential Studies Quarterly* 9 (Summer 1979).

Twenty-sixth Amendment The 1971 amendment to the U.S. Constitution that lowered the voting age to eighteen years.

Twenty-third Amendment The 1961 amendment to the U.S. Constitution that allots presidential electors to the District of Columbia. This allowed the people who lived in the same city as the president to vote for (or against) presidential candidates in national elections. When the Twenty-third Amendment was proposed in the Congress, the District of Columbia had over eight hundred thousand residents—a population greater than thirteen of the states. Those who lived in the nation's capital had all the obligations of citizenship, including payment of federal and local taxes and service in the armed forces, yet they were prevented from voting in national elections, since the Constitution reserved that privilege to residents of the states. Article II, Section 1, of the Constitution states that only "states" are eligible to appoint electors. The Twenty-third Amendment changed that.

two congresses *See* CONGRESS, MEMBER OF.

two-party system The political system in the United States, which, because of electoral provisions and cultural traditions, makes it almost impossible for a significant third party to emerge. Because most candidates for public office are chosen on the basis of single-member districts with plurality elections, where only one party's candidate can win, the party that comes in second can assert that it is the reasonable alternative. Third-party voters are made to feel that their vote is wasted. Each major party also has distinctive sectional strength; the second party, accordingly, is never wiped out. In addition, in spite of an abundance of rhetoric to the contrary, the United States is a society without great ideological disagreements. Political feeling tends toward the center. Consequently, third parties, which tend to be started by fringe groups, have little chance to attract significant numbers of voters. *Compare to* DUVERGER'S LAW.

REFERENCE

William H. Riker, The two-party system and Duverger's law: An essay on the history of political science, *American Political Science Review* 76 (December 1982).

The Persistent Two-Party System in America

The diversity and flexibility that characterize the two major parties also contribute to the preservation of the two-party system. The policy orientations of the parties are rarely so firmly fixed as to preclude a shift in emphasis or direction to attract emerging interests within the electorate. Moreover, each party is made up of officeholders with different views; almost any political group, as a result, can discover some officials who share its values and predilections and who are willing to represent its point of view. The adaptability of the parties and officeholders not only permits them to siphon off support that otherwise might contribute to the development of third parties but also creates a great deal of slack in the political system. Groups pressing for change know that there is always some chance that they can win acceptance for their positions within the existing party framework.

Source: William J. Keefe, *Parties, Politics, and Public Policy in America*, 3d ed. (New York: Holt, Rinehart & Winston, 1980), pp. 43–44.

Two Party System, Toward a More Responsible A 1950 report by the Committee on Political Parties of the American Political Science Association, *American Political Science Review* 44, supplement (September 1950), that called on the major American political parties to be "more responsible" in the sense of offering the public clear alternatives by adopting the kind of party discipline found in parliamentary systems. In this case, the party voted in would have a clear mandate to install its policies and, if the voters did not like these, they would know exactly who to vote out in the next election. This strong call to be more ideological fell on infertile intellectual ground. While this responsible party model has been much talked about by political scientists, politicians have all but ignored it. Nonetheless, the national government sometimes functions in the responsible party mode; particularly good examples would be the Eighty-ninth Congress (with Lyndon B. Johnson as president) and the Ninety-seventh Congress (with Ronald Reagan as president).

REFERENCES
Gerald M. Pomper, Toward a More Responsible Two-Party System? What, again? *Journal of Politics* 33 (November 1971);

Evron M. Kirkpatrick, "Toward a More Responsible Two-Party System": Political science, policy science, or pseudo-science? *American Political Science Review* 65 (December 1971);

Theodore J. Lowi, Toward a more responsible three-party system: The mythology of the two-party system and the prospects for reform, *PS* 16 (Fall 1983).

two presidencies *See* PRESIDENCIES, TWO.

two-step flow theory *See* OPINION LEADER.

tyranny of the majority *See* TOCQUEVILLE, ALEXIS DE.

tzar *See* CZAR.

U

Ullman v. United States 350 U.S. 422 (1956) The U.S. Supreme Court case that upheld the provisions of the Immunity Act of 1954, which authorized immunity from criminal prosecution for testimony in cases concerned with national security.

umbrella party An oft-used description of the major American political parties, because they unite a large variety of ideologies and interests under one overarching umbrella, the party itself. Because of this, they are sometimes also described as catchall parties.

unanimous consent A request of a legislative body made by a member that the entire body agree to a usually noncontroversial motion "without objection." This is a frequently used time-saving measure that avoids voting on minor procedural issues. For example, it is common for a U.S. senator to ask unanimous consent to insert a statement in the *Congressional Record*.

REFERENCE
Keith Krehbiel, Unanimous consent agreements: Going along in the Senate, *Journal of Politics* 48 (August 1986).

underclass That portion of the American population mired, from generation to generation, in a cycle of poverty.

REFERENCES
Ken Auletta, *The Underclass* (New York: Random House, 1982);

Gaither Loewenstein, The new underclass: A contemporary sociological dilemma, *Sociological Quarterly* 26 (Spring 1985).

underdog A candidate for elective office who is not leading in the polls; a candidate who starts a political campaign with a decided disadvantage; an apparent loser. Because underdogs often come from behind and win, candidates are seldom ashamed to admit that they are underdogs when it is obvious; besides, it might get them some sympathy votes. *Compare to* FRONT RUNNER.

REFERENCES
Stephen J. Ceci and Edward L. Kain, Jumping on the bandwagon with the underdog: The impact of attitude polls on the polling behavior, *Public Opinion Quarterly* 46 (Summer 1982);
Wolfgang J. Koschnick, Bandwagons and underdogs, *Society* 19 (September/October 1982);
John Orman, Media coverage of the congressional underdog, *PS* 18 (Fall 1985).

underground economy Economic activity that evades tax obligations; work done "off the books," for cash only. Examples of underground economic activity include a medical doctor accepting a cash payment from a patient and not recording the payment for income tax purposes; a carpenter doing work for a small business and accepting an in-kind payment, whose value is not recorded for income tax purposes; and, of course, traditional criminal activity. Underground in this context does not necessarily mean secret—except to the Internal Revenue Service.

REFERENCES
Richard J. McDonald, The "underground economy" and BLS statistical data, *Monthly Labor Review* 107 (January 1984);
Carol S. Carson, The underground economy: An introduction, *Survey of Current Business* 64 (May 1984).

undersecretary In the federal government, the official next in command after the cabinet secretary. The various assistant secretaries usually report to the undersecretary.

unemployment The totality of persons able and willing to work who are actively (but unsuccessfully) seeking to work at the prevailing wage rate. The unemployment rate is probably the most significant indicator of the health of the economy. Unemployment statistics are compiled monthly by the U.S. Bureau of Labor Statistics; these figures are obtained by surveys of a sample of all U.S. households. The Bureau of the Census, which actually conducts the surveys, defines an unemployed person as a civilian over sixteen years old who, during a given week, was available for work but had none, and (1) had been actively seeking employment during the past month, (2) was waiting to be recalled from a layoff, or (3) was waiting to report to a new job within thirty days. *Compare to* FULL EMPLOYMENT.

REFERENCES
Henry C. Kenski, The impact of unemployment on presidential popularity from Eisenhower to Nixon, *Presidential Studies Quarterly* 7 (Spring/Summer 1977);
John A. Garraty, *Unemployment in History: Economic Thought and Public Policy* (New York: Harper & Row, 1978);
Donald C. Baumer and Carl E. Van Horn, *The Politics of Unemployment* (Washington, D.C.: Congressional Quarterly, 1984).

unemployment benefits Specific payments available to workers from the various state unemployment insurance programs. Unemployment benefits are available as a matter of right (without a means test) to unemployed workers who have demonstrated their attachment to the labor force by a specified amount of recent work or earnings in covered employment. To be eligible for benefits, the worker must be ready, able, and willing to work and must be registered for work at a public employment office. A worker who meets these eligibility conditions may still be denied benefits if he or she is disqualified for an act that would indicate the worker is responsible for his or her own unemployment. In 1984 the national average weekly unemployment insurance payment was $123, which represented less than 36 percent of previous weekly wages.

Dorothea Lange's photographs from the Great Depression dramatized the plight of the unemployed.

REFERENCES

Joe A. Stone, The impact of unemployment compensation on the occupation decisions of unemployed workers, *Journal of Human Resources* 17 (Spring 1982);

Peter S. Saucier and John A. Roberts, Unemployment compensation: A growing concern for employers, *Employee Relations Law Journal* 9 (Spring 1984).

unemployment, cyclical Unemployment caused by a downward trend in the business cycle. It is assumed that those who are unemployed because of cyclical trends in the business cycle will be reemployed when the economy picks up. Cyclical unemployment is inherently temporary.

unemployment, hard-core The unemployment of people who, because of impoverished backgrounds or the lack of appropriate educa-

tion, have never been able to hold a job for a substantial time. Hard-core unemployment is unlikely to be affected by existing employment opportunities because of the health, mental condition, or education of the hard-core unemployed. Generally speaking, about 3 percent of the unemployed at any moment are probably unemployable and will remain so.

REFERENCE

Albert A. Blum, Hard-core unemployment: A long-term problem, *Business and Society* 22 (Spring 1983).

unicameral *See* BICAMERAL.

unified budget *See* BUDGET, UNIFIED.

unincorporated area An urban area that has not become a municipality and has no local government structure of its own other than its county.

unindicted coconspirator   **1** A person that a grand jury or public prosecutor recognizes as one of several conspirators to a crime, but who is not indicted and brought to trial.   **2** The thinly disguised reference to President Richard M. Nixon that appeared in indictments and other court records as Nixon's associates were brought to justice during the Watergate scandals.

union   **1** A labor union (*see* LABOR MOVE-MENT).   **2** The United States—which is a union of its component states.   **3** A single-purpose international organization; for example, a customs union.   **4** The merging of two or more countries to form a single new one. **5** That part of a national flag that signifies the union of two or more states; thus the blue part of the American flag on which are located the fifty white stars representing the fifty states in the union.

union calendar   *See* CALENDAR, UNION.

union shop   A union security provision found in some collective bargaining agreements that requires all employees to become members of the union within a specified time (usually thirty days) after being hired (or after the provision is negotiated) and to remain members as a condition of employment.

unitary government   *See* GOVERNMENT, UNITARY.

unitary tax   *See* TAX, UNITARY.

United Nations   **1** The World War II allies led by the United States and the United Kingdom who defeated the Axis powers of Germany, Japan, and Italy. The phrase united nations was devised by President Franklin D. Roosevelt and was first used in the Declaration of United Nations on January 1, 1942.   **2** The international peacekeeping agency that replaced the League of Nations. The U.N. charter, drawn up at a conference in San Francisco, was signed on June 25, 1945, by fifty nations; the United Nations formally came into existence on October 24, 1945, when a majority of the signatory nations had ratified the

charter. By the 1980s, it had three times the members it had when it started. The United Nations' business is conducted primarily through its GENERAL ASSEMBLY and SECURITY COUNCIL. The United Nations is funded by assessments on its member states by means of an elaborate formula; the United States annually contributes about one-third of the U.N.'s budget. Many U.N. activities are carried out by its specialized agencies, such as the International Atomic Energy Agency (founded in 1957), the International Civil Aviation Organization (founded in 1947), the International Labor Organization (founded in 1946), and the World Health Organization (founded in 1948).
REFERENCES
Richard J. Powers, United Nations voting
  alignments: A new equilibrium, *Western Political Quarterly* 33 (June 1980);
John F. Murphy, *The United Nations and the
  Control of International Violence: A Legal
  and Political Analysis* (Totowa, NJ: Allanheld, Osmun, 1982);
Jeane J. Kirkpatrick, The United Nations as a
  political system: A practicing political scientist's insights into UN politics, *World Affairs* 146 (Spring 1984);
Robert E. Riggs and Jack C. Plano, *The
  United Nations: International Organization
  and World Politics* (Chicago, IL: Dorsey,
  1988).

United Nations
New York, NY 10017
(212) 963–1234

United States Civil Service Commission The central personnel agency of the United States from 1883 through 1978. It was abolished by the Civil Service Reform Act of 1978. *See also* CIVIL SERVICE REFORM ACT OF 1978; MERIT SYSTEM PROTECTION BOARD; OFFICE OF PERSONNEL MANAGEMENT.

United States Civil Service Commission v National Association of Letter Carriers 413 U.S. 548 (1973) The U.S. Supreme Court case that upheld the Hatch Act's limitations on the political activities of federal employees. The *Letter Carriers* decision reaffirmed an earlier Court ruling, *United Public Workers v Mitchell*, 330 U.S. 75 (1947), that had held that the ordinary citizen rights of federal employees could be abridged by the Congress in the interest of increasing or maintaining the efficiency of the federal service. In the 1972 case that was being appealed (*National Association of Letter Carriers v United States Civil Service Commission,* 346 F. Supp. 578), the Court of Appeals for the District of Columbia Circuit declared the Hatch Act to be unconstitutional, because its vague and "overbroad" language made it impossible to determine what it prohibited. When this case was appealed to the Supreme Court, the Court reasoned that, despite some ambiguities, an ordinary person using ordinary common sense could ascertain and comply with the regulations involved. It also argued that its decision did nothing more than to confirm the judgment of history—that political neutrality was a desirable, or even essential feature, of public employment.

United States Code A consolidation and codification of the general and permanent laws of the United States arranged by subject under fifty titles, the first six dealing with general or political subjects, and the other forty-four alphabetically arranged from agriculture to war and national defense. The code is now revised every six years and a supplement is published after each session of the Congress.

United States Conference of Mayors (USCM) An organization of city governments founded in 1933. It is a national forum through which this country's larger cities express their concerns and actively work to meet U.S. urban needs. By limiting membership and participation to the 750 cities with over thirty thousand population and by concentrating on questions of federal-city relations, the conference seeks to become a focus for urban political leadership. *See* PUBLIC INTEREST GROUPS.

United States Conference of Mayors
1620 I Street, N.W.
Washington, D.C. 20006
(202) 293-7330

United States Court of Appeals *See* COURT OF APPEALS.

United States District Court *See* DISTRICT COURT/FEDERAL DISTRICT COURT/U.S. DISTRICT COURT.

United States Employment Service (USES) The federal agency within the U.S. Department of Labor that provides assistance to states and territories in establishing and maintaining a system of over twenty-five hundred local public employment offices. The USES was created by the Wagner-Peyser Act of 1933—a landmark acknowledgment that the federal government had a significant responsibility in aiding employment.

United States Government Manual An annual publication of the federal government that provides detailed information on all agencies of the executive, legislative, and judicial branches of government. The *Manual,* available from the GOVERNMENT PRINTING OFFICE, also includes the names of major federal officeholders.

United States International Trade Commission *See* INTERNATIONAL TRADE COMMISSION, UNITED STATES.

United States Reports The official record of cases decided by the U.S. Supreme Court. In citations, *United States Reports* is abbreviated to U.S. For example, the legal citation for the case of *Pickering v Board of Education* is 391 U.S. 563 (1968). This means that the case will be found on page 563 of volume 391 of the *United States Reports* and that it was decided in 1968. Prior to 1882, the *Reports* used the names of the court reporters. For example, the citation for *Marbury v Madison* is 1 Cranch 137 (1803). Cranch was the reporter from 1801 to 1815. *Compare to* L. ED.

United States Statutes at Large Bound volumes issued annually containing all public and private laws and concurrent resolutions enacted during a session of the Congress, reorganization plans, proposed and ratified amendments to the Constitution, and presidential proclamations.

United States Tariff Commission *See* IN-TERNATIONAL TRADE COMMISSION, UNITED STATES.

United States Treaties and Other International Agreements *See* EXECUTIVE AGREEMENT.

United States v Belmont *See* EXECUTIVE AGREEMENT.

United States v Brown 381 U.S. 437 (1965) The U.S. Supreme Court case that held that Section 504 of the Labor-Management Reporting and Disclosure (Landrum-Griffin) Act of 1959 was an unconstitutional BILL OF ATTAINDER in requiring that a person who was previously a member of the Communist party or convicted of criminal acts had to undergo a five-year "cleansing period" before he or she was eligible to hold an office in a labor union.

United States v Butler *See* AGRICULTURAL ADJUSTMENT ADMINISTRATION.

United States v Calandra *See* EXCLUSIONARY RULE.

United States v Curtiss-Wright Export Corporation 299 U.S. 304 (1936) The U.S. Supreme Court case defining the president's constitutional position in foreign affairs. In 1934 the Congress adopted a joint resolution authorizing the president by proclamation to prohibit the sale (within the United States) of arms to some South American nations. The president issued such a proclamation. Curtiss-Wright attacked such constraint on its business on the grounds that the joint resolution constituted an unconstitutional delegation of legislative authority to the president. The Supreme Court upheld the resolution and proclamation on the grounds that the Constitution created the "very delicate, plenary and exclusive power of the president as the sole organ of the federal government in the field of international relations" and that, in the international sphere, the president must be accorded "a degree of discretion and freedom from statutory restriction which would not be admissible were domestic affairs alone involved."

REFERENCE
Charles Lofgren, *United States v. Curtiss-Wright Export Corporation:* An historical reassessment, *Yale Law Journal* 83 (November 1973).

United States v Darby Lumber 312 U.S. 100 (1941) The U.S. Supreme Court case that upheld the Fair Labor Standards Act of 1938, which established minimum wages and maximum hours for workers in businesses engaged in, or producing goods for, interstate commerce.

United States v Guy W. Capps, Inc. *See* EXECUTIVE AGREEMENT.

United States v Harriss *See* LOBBYING ACT OF 1946.

United States v Havens *See* EXCLUSIONARY RULE.

United States v Jackson *See* CHILLING.

United States v Lovett 328 U.S. 303 (1946) The U.S. Supreme Court case that held that a congressional effort to dismiss three allegedly "irresponsible, unrepresentative, crackpot, radical bureaucrats" from the executive branch by passing legislation prohibiting the payment of their salaries amounted to an unconstitutional bill of attainder.

United States v Nixon 418 U.S. 683 (1974) The U.S. Supreme Court case dealing with President Richard M. Nixon's claim that the Constitution provided the president with an absolute and unreviewable EXECUTIVE PRIVILEGE; that is, the right not to respond to a subpoena in connection with a judicial trial. The court held that "neither the doctrine of separation of powers, nor the need for confidentiality of high-level communications, without more, can sustain an absolute, unqualified, presidential immunity from judicial process under all circumstances." The Court allowed there was a limited executive privilege that might pertain in the areas of military, diplomatic, or security affairs, and where confidentiality was related to the president's ability to carry out his constitutional mandates. This was the decision which, in effect, forced Nixon to resign as president.

REFERENCE

Philip B. Kurland, *United States v. Nixon: Who killed cock robin? UCLA Law Review* 22 (October 1974).

United States v Paradise The U.S. Supreme Court case, 94 L. Ed. 2d 203 (1987), that upheld a policy of temporary racial quotas for Alabama state trooper promotions.

United States v Richardson 418 U.S. 166 (1974) The U.S. Supreme Court case that held that a taxpayer did not have standing to challenge the Central Intelligence Act of 1949 on the grounds that one of its provisions violates Article I, Section 9, Clause 7, of the U.S. Constitution, which requires the government to publish from time to time a "regular statement and account of the receipts and expenditure of all public money." The Court reasoned that the challenger was unable to show any concrete injury, other than the federal taxes he paid. The challenger, however, could not show any such injury in the absence of published accounts of how the Central Intelligence Agency spent funds derived from taxation.

United States v Salerno See PREVENTIVE DETENTION.

United States v Salvucci See EXCLUSIONARY RULE.

United States v Seeger See CONSCIENTIOUS OBJECTOR.

United States v Students Challenging Regulatory Agency Procedures (SCRAP) 412 U.S. 669 (1973) The U.S. Supreme Court case granting standing to five law school students challenging an increase in freight rates sanctioned by the Interstate Commerce Commission, on the grounds that the increase might reduce the recycling of cans, which in turn, might pollute the national parks in the Washington, D.C., area and consequently injure the students who use these parks. The case sug-

gests that one who is injured by government activity has standing to challenge it in court.

United Steelworkers of America v Weber, et al. 443 U.S. 193 (1979); *Kaiser Aluminum & Chemical Corporation v Weber, et al.* The U.S. Supreme Court decision that upheld an affirmative action program giving blacks preference in selection of employees for a training program. Justice William Brennan, in delivering the majority opinion of the Court, stated that "the only question before us is the narrow statutory issue of whether Title VII forbids private employers and unions from voluntarily agreeing upon bona fide affirmative action plans that accord racial preferences." The Court concluded that the "Congress did not intend to limit traditional business freedom to such a degree as to prohibit all voluntary, race conscious affirmative action." Brennan went on to add that, because Kaiser's preferential scheme was legal, it was unnecessary to "define in detail the line of demarcation between permissible and impermissible affirmative action plans." See also AFFIRMATIVE ACTION; CIVIL RIGHTS ACT OF 1964; REGENTS OF THE UNIVERSITY OF CALIFORNIA V ALLAN BAKKE; REVERSE DISCRIMINATION; TITLE VII.

REFERENCES

David H. Rosenbloom, *Kaiser vs. Weber:* Perspective from the public sector, *Public Personnel Management* 8 (November/December 1979);

Bernard D. Meltzer, The *Weber* case: The judicial abrogation of the antidiscrimination standard in employment, *University of Chicago Law Review* 47 (Spring 1980);

William A. Simon, Jr., Voluntary affirmative action after Weber, *Labor Law Journal* 34 (March 1983);

Jerome L. Epstein, Walking a tightrope without a net: Voluntary affirmative action plans after *Weber, University of Pennsylvania Law Review* 134 (January 1986).

unit rule The requirement that state delegations to a national nominating convention must cast all of their votes for the issue or candidate that has the majority of the votes of the state delegates. Since 1972, both major political parties have put severe restrictions on the use of the unit rule.

REFERENCES
William P. Collins, Political behavior under the unit rule: A research note, *American Politics Quarterly* 8 (July 1980);
William P. Collins, Political participation under the unit rule: A research note, *Public Choice* 36:1 (1981).

unity of command The concept that each individual in an organization should be accountable to a single superior.

REFERENCE
Nobvo Takahasi, On the principle of unity of command: Application of a model and empirical research, *Behavioral Science* 31 (January 1986).

upper house That branch of a BICAMERAL legislature that tends, in contrast with the other house, to be both less representative of and less responsive to the public. (This is because upper houses have fewer members and longer terms of office than lower-house members.) The term comes from the fact that at one time many European parliaments had a house that represented the upper class, the aristocracy, and a "lower" house that represented the people.

Urban Affairs Quarterly A journal devoted to the social and political aspects of urban life; published since 1965. Library of Congress no. HT101 .U67.
> Urban Affairs Quarterly
> 2111 W. Hillcrest Drive
> Newbury Park, CA 91320

urban enterprise zone *See* ENTERPRISE ZONE/URBAN ENTERPRISE ZONE.

urban homesteading A local program that gives a family a substandard home in a distressed urban area on condition that the structure be renovated and lived in by that family. Sometimes these programs provide for low-interest home improvement loans or charge token amounts for the homes.

REFERENCES
James W. Hughes and Kenneth D. Bleakly, Jr., *Urban Homesteading* (New Brunswick, NJ: Center for Urban Policy Research, Rutgers University, 1975);
Anne Clark and Zelma Rivin, *Homesteading in Urban U.S.A.* (New York: Praeger, 1977);
Ann Burnet Schnare, *Household Mobility in Urban Homesteading Neighborhoods: Implication for Displacement* (Washington, D.C.: Government Printing Office, 1979).

Urban Institute A research organization and THINK TANK founded in 1968 to provide independent studies of, and solutions to, urban problems.
> Urban Institute
> 2100 M Street, N.W.
> Washington, D.C. 20037
> (202) 833–7200

Urban League *See* NATIONAL URBAN LEAGUE.

urban park movement Part of a growing movement in the years after the Civil War to make cities more beautiful. It sought to create municipal parks designed to appear natural (despite the roadways that wandered through them), waterways situated to provide restful vistas, and well-placed recreational facilities. The leading designer was Frederick Law Olmsted (1822–1903), who designed New York City's Central Park. He, like others who worked on such projects, gave city planning in the United States the elite, somewhat anti-industrial, character it was destined to have through the New Deal era. The major premise of the movement was that parks create an environment that helps ameliorate the immoral and squalid conditions of urban life occasioned by industrialization.

REFERENCES
Albert Fein, ed., *Landscape into Cityscape: Frederick Law Olmsted's Plans for a Greater New York City* (Ithaca, NY: Cornell University Press, 1968);
Galen Cranz, *The Politics of Park Design: A History of Urban Parks in America* (Cambridge, MA: MIT Press, 1982).

urban planning The formal process of guiding the physical and social development of cities and their regions. While urban planning is first of all a highly technical process, it is also highly politicized because the various com-

Frederick Law Olmsted was the leading exponent of the urban park movement. Above, Long Meadow in Olmsted's Prospect Park, Brooklyn, N.Y.

munity interests are always ready to fight for their version of beneficial change. *See also* PLANNING.

REFERENCES

James Q. Wilson, Planning and politics: Citizen participation in urban renewal, *Journal of the American Institute of Planners* 29 (November 1963);

Darwin Stuart, *Systematic Urban Planning* (New York: Praeger, 1976);

W. G. Roeseler, *Successful American Urban Plans* (Lexington, MA: Lexington Books, 1981).

urban renewal   The national program for urban redevelopment, started in 1949 to rejuvenate urban areas through large-scale physical projects. Originally a loan program primarily for housing, it was quickly transformed by political pressures into a grant program for redoing large sections of central business districts or other commercial areas. It has been severely criticized for its uprooting of communities, especially black neighborhoods, and replacing them with commercial developments. The Housing and Community Development Act of 1974 put urban renewal, model cities, and a variety of other categorical urban development programs under the Community Development Block Grant program administered by the Department of Housing and Urban Development.

REFERENCES

Martin Anderson, *The Federal Bulldozer: A Critical Analysis of Urban Renewal* (Cambridge, MA: MIT Press, 1964);

James Q. Wilson, ed., *Urban Renewal* (Cambridge, MA: MIT Press, 1966);

Roger Friedland, Corporate power and urban growth: The case of urban renewal, *Politics and Society* 10 (1980).

U.S.   *See* UNITED STATES REPORTS.

U.S.C. *See* UNITED STATES CODE.

USCM *See* UNITED STATES CONFERENCE OF MAYORS.

USDA *See* AGRICULTURE, U.S. DEPARTMENT OF.

user charges/user fees Specific sums that users or consumers of a government service pay to receive that service. For example, a homeowner's water bill, if based upon usage, would be a user charge.

REFERENCES

Calvin A. Kent, Users' fees for municipalities, *Governmental Finance* 1 (February 1972);

Selma Mushkin and Charles L. Vehorn, User fees and charges, *Governmental Finance* 6 (November 1977);

Bruce A. Weber, User charges, property taxes, and population growth: The distributional implications of alternative municipal financing strategies, *State and Local Government Review* 13 (January 1981).

USES *See* UNITED STATES EMPLOYMENT SERVICE.

USPS *See* POSTAL SERVICE, UNITED STATES.

usury laws Laws that limit the amount of interest financial institutions can charge their customers.

REFERENCES

Steven M. Crafton, An empirical test of the effect of usury laws, *Journal of Law & Economics* 23 (April 1980);

William J. Boyes, In defense of the downtrodden: Usury laws? *Public Choice* 39:2 (1982).

utopia 1 The Greek word meaning nowhere. 2 A model of a society that meets the needs of all of its citizens as they perceive those needs; in their terms, the perfect society. 3 A literary form that posits a carefully designed polity that will, by its character, raise contrasts with reality. While conceptions of ideal societies go back to ancient times, it was Sir Thomas More's 1516 book, *Utopia,* that gave the concept its modern name. Jonathan Swift's *Gulliver's Travels* (1726) provided the most comprehensive example by offering readers a whole collection of societies, all of them reflecting human behavior, sometimes at its worst.

REFERENCES

Lewis Mumford, *The Story of Utopias* (New York: Viking, 1922, 1962);

Lyman Tower Sargent, Utopianism in colonial America, *History of Political Thought* 4 (Winter 1983);

James Nendza, Political idealism in More's *Utopia*, *Review of Politics* 46 (July 1984).

V

VA *See* VETERANS ADMINISTRATION.

Valley Forge Christian College v Americans United for Separation of Church and State 70 L.Ed. 2d 700 (1982) The U.S. Supreme Court case that held that a taxpayers' organization dedicated to separation of church and state was without standing to challenge "no-

cost transfer of surplus" U.S. property to religious educational institutions.

value-added tax (VAT) *See* TAX, VALUE-ADDED.

Vance v Bradley 440 U.S. 93 (1979) The U.S. Supreme Court case that held that requiring officers of the U.S. Foreign Service to retire at the age of sixty years did not violate the equal protection component of the due process clause of the Fifth Amendment, even though other federal employees do not face mandatory retirement at such an early age.

Veblen, Thorstein (1857–1929)   The premier social critic of American society during the first decades of this century. His *The Theory of the Leisure Class* (New York: New American Library, 1899, 1954) introduced the concepts of "conspicuous consumption" and "conspicuous waste" as symbols of upper-class status. Considered the founder of institutional economics, he was convinced of the "triumph of imbecile institutions over life and culture."

REFERENCES

David Riesman, *Thorstein Veblen: A Critical Interpretation* (New York: Scribner, 1953);
Wesley Clair Mitchell, *What Veblen Taught* (New York: Viking, 1936; Kelly, 1964);
Joseph Dorfman, *Thorstein Veblen and His America* (New York: Viking, 1934; Kelly, 1972);
John P. Diggins, *The Bard of Savagery: Thorstein Veblen and Modern Social Theory* (Hassocks, Sussex, U.K.: Harvester, 1978);
Jerry L. Simich and Rich Tilman, *Thorstein Veblen: A Reference Guide* (Boston: Hall, 1985).

veep   A slang term for the vice president.

venire facias   A Latin term for *you should cause to come;* the writ that orders a sheriff to assemble a jury.

venireman   A member of a jury.

venue   **1** The locality in which a criminal trial takes place.   **2** The locality where a crime occurred. *Compare to* CHANGE OF VENUE.

verification   **1** A determination of the accuracy of something.   **2** A formal statement attesting to the truth of a theory or fact.   **3** The essence of an arms control agreement. This is a two-step process involving (1) an assessment before a treaty of whether the other side could violate the treaty and evade detection and

(2) the continuous monitoring of compliance after a treaty is signed and ratified.

REFERENCES

3   Stephen M. Meyer, Verification and risk in arms control, *International Security* 8 (Spring 1984);
Mark M. Lowenthal and Joel S. Wit, Politics, verification, and arms control, *Washington Quarterly* 7 (Summer 1984).

Veterans Administration (VA)   The federal agency, created in 1930, that administers benefits for veterans and their dependents. These benefits include compensation payments for disabilities or death related to military service; pensions for totally disabled veterans; education and rehabilitation; home loan guaranty; burial, including cemeteries, markers, flags; and a comprehensive medical program involving a widespread system of nursing homes, clinics, and more than 170 medical centers.

REFERENCE

Tom Daschle, Making the Veterans Administration work for veterans, *Journal of Legislation* 11 (Winter 1984).

Veterans Administration
810 Vermont Avenue, N.W.
Washington, D.C. 20420
(202) 233–4000

veterans' benefits   Any government advantages available to those who served in the armed forces of the United States that are not available to citizens who did not serve. Veterans' benefits may include government-supplied health care, advantageous home mortgage terms, and pensions.

REFERENCE

Allan L. Damon, Veterans' benefits, *American Heritage* 27 (June 1976).

veterans' preference   The concept that dates from 1865, when the Congress, toward the end of the Civil War, affirmed that "persons honorably discharged from the military or naval service by reason of disability resulting from wounds or sickness incurred in the line of duty, shall be preferred for appointments to civil offices, provided they are found to possess the business capacity necessary for the proper discharge of the duties of such offices." The 1865 law was superseded in 1919, when preference was extended to all "honorably discharged" veterans, their widows, and wives of disabled veterans. The Veterans' Preference Act of 1944 expanded the scope of veterans' preference by providing for a five-point bonus on federal examination scores for all honorably separated veterans (except for those with a service-connected disability, who are entitled to a ten-point bonus). Veterans also received other advantages in federal employment (such as protections against arbitrary dismissal and preference in the event of a reduction in force).

All states and many other jurisdictions have veterans' preference laws of varying intensity. New Jersey, an extreme example, offers veterans absolute preference; if a veteran passes an entrance examination, he or she must be hired (no matter what the score) before nonveterans can be hired. Veterans competing with each other are rank-ordered, and all disabled veterans receive preference over other veterans. Veterans' preference laws have been criticized because they have allegedly made it difficult for government agencies to hire and promote more women and minorities. Although the original version of the Civil Service Reform Act of 1978 sought to limit veterans' preference in the federal service, the final version contained a variety of new provisions strengthening veterans' preference. *See also* PERSONNEL ADMINISTRATOR OF MASSACHUSETTS V FEENEY.

REFERENCES

Charles E. Davis, A survey of veterans' preference legislation in the states, *State Government* 53 (Autumn 1980);

Charles E. Davis, Veterans' preference and civil service employment: Issues and policy implications, *Review of Public Personnel Administration* 3 (Fall 1982);

Gregory B. Lewis and Mark A. Emmert, Who pays for veterans' preference? *Administration and Society* 16 (November 1984).

veto **1** The Latin word for I forbid. **2** Disapproval by the president of a bill or joint resolution, other than one proposing an amendment to the Constitution. When the Congress is in session, the president must veto a bill within ten days, excluding Sundays, after he has received it, or it becomes law without his signature. When the president vetoes a bill, he returns it to the House of its origin with a message stating his objections. *Compare to* VETO OVERRIDE. **3** The right of any of the five permanent members of the United Nations Security Council (China, France, the United Kingdom, the United States, and the U.S.S.R.) under Article 27 of the U.N. charter to prevent any decision by withholding agreement. **4** The disapproval of proposed legislation by any chief executive who has formal authority to do so.

Presidential Vetoes and Congressional Overrides of Vetoes, 1961–1985

President	Vetoes	Overrides	Percentage Overridden
Kennedy (1961–1963)	21	0	0%
Johnson (1963–1969)	30	0	0
Nixon (1969–1974)	43	7	16.0
Ford (1974–1977)	66	12	18.0
Carter (1977–1981)	31	2	6.5
Reagan (1981–1985)	43	5	11.6

Source: Adapted from William J. Keefe, Henry J. Abraham, William H. Flanigan, Charles O. Jones, Morris S. Ogul, and John W. Spanier, *American Democracy: Institutions, Politics, and Policies,* 2d ed. (Chicago: Dorsey, 1986), p. 360.

veto, absolute

REFERENCES

2 Jong R. Lee, Presidential vetoes from
   Washington to Nixon, *Journal of Politics*
   37 (May 1975);
   Harry C. Thomson, The first presidential
   vetoes, *Presidential Studies Quarterly* 8
   (Winter 1978);
   Gary W. Copeland, When Congress and
   the president collide: Why presidents
   veto legislation, *Journal of Politics* 45
   (August 1983);
   Albert C. Ringelstein, Presidential vetoes:
   Motivations and classification, *Congress
   and the Presidency: A Journal of Capital
   Studies* 12 (Spring 1985).

3 Stephen Jacobs and Marc Poirier, The
   right to veto United Nations membership applications: The United States
   veto of the Viet-Nams, *Harvard International Law Journal* 17 (Summer 1976).

4 Gerald Benjamin, The diffusion of the
   governor's veto power, *State Government* 55:3 (1982).

veto, absolute   Any veto that is final because
there is no legal way to override it.

veto, congressional   *See* VETO, LEGISLATIVE.

veto, item   The executive power to veto separate items in a bill. Many state governors have
this authority; the president of the United
States does not, although President Ronald
Reagan repeatedly requested that the Congress
grant him this power. An item veto would allow a president to remove a RIDER from a bill
and thus make it more difficult for members of
the Congress to hold important legislation hostage to pork barrel or special interest provisions.

REFERENCES

For analyses of a possible presidential item
   veto, see Russell M. Ross and Fred
   Schwengel, An item veto for the president,
   Presidential Studies Quarterly 12 (Winter
   1982);
Judith A. Best, The item veto: Would the
   founders approve? *Presidential Studies
   Quarterly* 14 (Spring 1984);
R. J. Spitzer, The item veto reconsidered,
   Presidential Studies Quarterly 15 (Summer
   1985).

For how the item veto functions in the states,
   see Glenn Abney and Thomas P. Lauth, The
   line-item veto in the states: An instrument
   for fiscal restraint or an instrument for partisanship? *Public Administration Review* 45
   (May/June 1985);
James J. Gosling, Wisconsin item-veto
   lessons, *Public Administration Review* 46
   (July/August 1986).

Item Veto Powers of the State Governors

No Item Veto
- Indiana
- Maine
- Nevada
- New Hampshire
- North Carolina
- Rhode Island
- Vermont

Item Veto, Requiring Two-Thirds of Legislators Present to Override
- Massachusetts
- Montana
- New Mexico
- Oregon
- South Carolina
- Texas
- Virginia
- Washington
- Wisconsin

Item Veto, Requiring a Majority of Legislators to Override
- Alabama
- Arkansas
- Kentucky
- Tennessee
- West Virginia

Item Veto, Requiring Three-Fifths of Legislators to Override
- Delaware
- Illinois
- Maryland
- Nebraska
- Ohio

Item Veto, Requiring Two-Thirds of Legislators to Override
- Alaska
- Arizona
- California
- Colorado
- Connecticut
- Florida
- Georgia
- Hawaii
- Idaho
- Iowa
- Kansas

- Louisiana
- Michigan
- Minnesota
- Mississippi
- Missouri
- New Jersey
- New York
- North Dakota
- Oklahoma
- Pennsylvania
- South Dakota
- Utah
- Wyoming

Note: North Carolina's governor has no veto power at all. In West Virginia, two-thirds of all legislators are required to override budget and supplemental appropriations bills.

Source: Adapted from *The Book of the States* (Lexington, KY: Council of State Governments, 1986), pp. 37–38.

veto, legislative   A statutory measure that allows the president to put forth a proposal, subject to the approval or disapproval of the Congress. Either action must be taken usually within sixty or ninety days. The legislative veto may take the form of a committee veto, a simple resolution passed by either house, or a concurrent resolution.

The legislative veto was first provided for in the Economy Act of June 30, 1932, when the Congress authorized President Herbert Hoover to reorganize executive departments and agencies, subject to disapproval by a simple majority of either house within sixty days. Since 1932, several hundred pieces of legislation have included some version of the legislative veto. Until the War Powers Resolution of 1973, the legislative veto was used mainly for executive reorganization proposals. Then the War Powers Resolution unleashed a new conception of the legislative veto. For the first time, it became the only check on major presidential policy initiatives, such as war, as opposed to being an after-the-fact sanctioning of management reforms.

In 1983, the Supreme Court ruled in *Immigration and Naturalization Service v Chadha*, 454 U.S. 812 (1983), that the one-house (meaning either house) congressional veto violated the separation of powers and was therefore unconstitutional. The Court reasoned that the congressional veto bypassed the president because he was given no opportunity to sign or veto the measure at hand. The Congress

could accomplish the same ends and not violate the separation of powers by using the regular legislative processes to achieve its will; then the president would not be bypassed.

REFERENCES

For policy analyses of the congressional veto, see Joseph Cooper and Patricia A. Hurley, The legislative veto: A policy analysis, *Congress and the Presidency: A Journal of Capital Studies* 10 (Spring 1983);

Peter W. Rodino, Jr., The legislative veto and the balance of powers in Washington, *Parliamentarian* 65 (January 1984);

Robert S. Gilmour and Barbara Hinkson Craig, After the congressional veto: Assessing the alternatives, *Journal of Policy Analysis and Management* 3 (Spring 1984).

For analyses of the impact of the *Chadha* decision, see Joseph Cooper, Postscript on the congressional veto: Is there life after *Chadha? Political Science Quarterly* 98 (Fall 1983);

Laurence H. Tribe, The legislative veto decision: A law by any other name? *Harvard Journal on Legislation* 21 (Winter 1984);

Arthur H. Abel, *INS v. Chadha:* The future demise of legislative delegation and the need for a constitutional amendment, *Journal of Legislation* 11 (Summer 1984);

Emily S. McMahon, *Chadha* and the nondelegation doctrine: Defining a restricted legislative veto, *Yale Law Journal* 94 (May 1985).

For the legislative veto in the states, see Stephen F. Johnson, The legislative veto in the states, *State Government* 56:3 (1983);

David C. Nice, Sunset laws and legislative vetoes in the states, *State Government* 58 (Spring 1985).

veto override   A legislature's approval, usually by an extraordinary majority, of a bill that has been vetoed by the executive. If the president disapproves a bill and sends it back to the Congress with his objections, the Congress may override his veto by a two-thirds vote in each chamber. The Constitution requires a yea-and-nay roll call. The question put to each house is: "Shall the bill pass, the objections of the President to the contrary notwithstanding?"

REFERENCES

Charles W. Wiggins, Executive vetoes and legislative overrides in the American states, *Journal of Politics* 42 (November 1980);

Myron A. Levine, Tactical constraints and presidential influence on veto overrides, *Presidential Studies Quarterly* 13 (Fall 1983);

David W. Rohde and Dennis M. Simon, Presidential vetoes and congressional response: A study of institutional conflict, *American Journal of Political Science* 29 (August 1985).

veto, pocket The act of the president in withholding his approval of a bill after the Congress has adjourned—either for the year or for a specified period. When the Congress is in session, a bill becomes law without the president's signature if he does not act upon it within ten days, excluding Sundays, from the time he gets it. But if the Congress adjourns within that ten-day period, the bill is killed without the president's formal veto. In many cases, where bills have been sent to the president toward the close of a session, he has taken advantage of this provision and has held until after adjournment those measures of which he disapproved but which he did not wish to return with his objections to the Congress for its further action.

It is controversial whether a president may pocket veto a bill when the Congress adjourns between sessions of the same Congress. President Ronald Reagan, for example, exercised the pocket veto between the first and second sessions of the Ninety-seventh Congress and again during the intersession of the Ninety-eighth Congress. But in 1984, the U.S. Circuit Court ruled that a president may not pocket veto legislation between sessions of the Congress. The Reagan administration has appealed and a decision by the Supreme Court is awaited.

REFERENCES

Clement E. Vose, The memorandum pocket veto, *Journal of Politics* 26:2 (1964);

Edward M. Kennedy, Congress, the president, and the pocket veto, *Virginia Law Review* 63 (April 1977);

John W. Dumbrell and John D. Lees, Presidential pocket-veto power: Constitutional anachronism? *Political Studies* 28 (March 1980).

vice president The second highest elected official in the United States who succeeds to the presidency in the event of the death, removal, or resignation of the president of the United States. The vice president's only other constitutional responsibility is to preside over the U.S. Senate (except when it is trying a president for impeachment) and vote in the case of a tie.

John Adams (1735–1826), the first vice president, said: "My country has contrived for me the most insignificant office that ever the invention of man contrived or his imagination conceived." And Thomas R. Marshall (1854–1925), Woodrow Wilson's vice president, proclaimed that "the vice president of the United States is like a man in a cataleptic state: he cannot speak; he cannot move; he suffers no pain; and yet he is perfectly conscious of everything that is going on around him." John Nance Garner (1868–1967), the Texan who was Franklin D. Roosevelt's first vice president (1933–1941), said that "the vice presidency of the United States isn't worth a pitcher of warm spit." Spit is not the actual word he used for the bodily excretion he had in mind, but that is how the reporters cleaned it up. Recent presidents, however, have tended to give their vice presidents significant domestic and foreign policy assignments.

The presidency was seldom within the reach of early twentieth-century vice presidents because they tended to be obscure figures selected to balance tickets by representing states or regions whose votes were important to the presidential candidate. But television has changed the situation significantly. As their party's most visible candidates after four or eight years of highly visible public service, vice presidents now find themselves logical front runners. However, if the policies of the president they have served are unpopular, vice presidents seeking their party's nomination for president may have a particular difficulty disassociating themselves from those policies, especially under the watchful eyes of a president sensitive to criticism. Nine vice presidents have succeeded to the presidency upon the death (or resigna-

Vice Presidents of the United States

Vice President	Home State	Year Inaugurated	Party
John Adams*	Massachusetts	1789	Federalist
Thomas Jefferson*	Virginia	1797	Democratic-Republican
Aaron Burr	New York	1801	Democratic-Republican
George Clinton	New York	1805	Democratic-Republican
Elbridge Gerry	Massachusetts	1813	Democratic-Republican
Daniel D. Tompkins	New York	1817	Democratic-Republican
John C. Calhoun†	South Carolina	1825	Democratic-Republican
Martin Van Buren*	New York	1833	Democratic
Richard M. Johnson	Kentucky	1837	Democratic
John Tyler	Virginia	1841	Whig
George M. Dallas	Pennsylvania	1845	Democratic
Millard Fillmore*	New York	1849	Whig
William R. King	Alabama	1853	Democratic
John C. Breckinridge	Kentucky	1857	Democratic
Hannibal Hamlin	Maine	1861	Republican
Andrew Johnson*	Tennessee	1865	Republican
Schuyler Colfax	Indiana	1869	Republican
Henry Wilson	Massachusetts	1873	Republican
William A. Wheeler	New York	1877	Republican
Chester A. Arthur*	New York	1881	Republican
Thomas A. Hendricks	Indiana	1885	Democratic
Levi P. Morton	New York	1889	Republican
Adlai E. Stevenson	Illinois	1893	Democratic
Garret A. Hobart	New Jersey	1897	Republican
Theodore Roosevelt*	New York	1901	Republican
Charles W. Fairbanks	Indiana	1905	Republican
James S. Sherman	New York	1909	Republican
Thomas R. Marshall	Indiana	1913	Democratic
Calvin Coolidge*	Massachusetts	1921	Republican
Charles G. Dawes	Illinois	1925	Republican
Charles Curtis	Kansas	1929	Republican
John Nance Garner	Texas	1933	Democratic
Henry Agard Wallace	Iowa	1941	Democratic
Harry S Truman*	Missouri	1945	Democratic
Alben W. Barkley	Kentucky	1949	Democratic
Richard M. Nixon*	California	1953	Republican
Lyndon B. Johnson*	Texas	1961	Democratic
Hubert H. Humphrey	Minnesota	1965	Democratic
Spiro T. Agnew†	Maryland	1969	Republican
Gerald R. Ford*	Michigan	1973	Republican
Nelson A. Rockefeller	New York	1974	Republican
Walter F. Mondale	Minnesota	1977	Democratic
George Bush	Texas	1981	Republican

* Later became president.
† Resigned (see entries).

tion) of a president: John Tyler (1841), Millard Fillmore (1850), Andrew Johnson (1865), Chester A. Arthur (1881), Theodore Roosevelt (1901), Calvin Coolidge (1923), Harry S Truman (1945), Lyndon Johnson (1963), and Gerald Ford (1974). Others, such as John Adams, Martin Van Buren, and Richard Nixon, won election as president after completing terms as vice president.

REFERENCES

Stephen J. Wilhelm, The origins of the office of the vice presidency, *Presidential Studies Quarterly* 7 (Fall 1977);

Jay A. Hurwitz, Vice presidential eligibility and selection patterns, *Polity* 12 (Spring 1980);

Danny M. Adkison, The electoral significance of the vice presidency, *Presidential Studies Quarterly* 12 (Summer 1982);

Marie D. Natoli, Perspectives on the vice presidency, *Presidential Studies Quarterly* 12 (Fall 1982);

Joel K. Goldstein, *The Modern American Vice Presidency: The Transformation of a Political Institution* (Princeton, NJ: Princeton University Press, 1982);

Danny M. Adkison, The vice presidency as apprenticeship, *Presidential Studies Quarterly* 13 (Spring 1983);

Paul Light, *Vice Presidential Power* (Baltimore: Johns Hopkins University Press, 1984).

victim impact statements *See* BOOTH V MARYLAND.

Vietnam War The 1956 to 1975 war between the noncommunist Republic of Vietnam (South Vietnam) and the communist Democratic Republic of Vietnam (North Vietnam), which resulted in the victory of the North over the South and the unification of the two countries into the communist Socialist Republic of Vietnam on July 2, 1976. The United States first offered financial support to South Vietnam during the Dwight D. Eisenhower administration. Military assistance began with the John F. Kennedy administration in 1961. By 1963, the United States had sixteen thousand military "advisors" in South Vietnam. In 1964, the GULF OF TONKIN RESOLUTION allowed the ad-

A wounded U.S. paratrooper awaits evacuation. More than fifty-eight thousand Americans died in the Vietnam War.

ministration of LYNDON B. JOHNSON to expand U.S. involvement. By 1968, the United States had over one-half million men engaged in the most unpopular foreign war in American history. As a direct result, the Democrats lost control of the White House to Republican RICHARD M. NIXON. The Nixon administration's policy of Vietnamization called for the South Vietnamese to gradually take over all the fighting from the Americans. The Americans continued to pull out, and the South held off the North for awhile. As the American forces dwindled, the North got more aggressive and successful. Finally, the North's January 1975 offensive led to the South's unconditional surrender by April. More than fifty-eight thousand Americans died in the Vietnam War; another one hundred fifty thousand were wounded.

REFERENCES

Frances Fitzgerald, *Fire in the Lake: The Vietnamese and the Americans in Vietnam* (Boston: Atlantic-Little, Brown, 1972);

Stanley Karnow, *Vietnam: A History* (New York: Viking, 1983);

Tricia van Klaveron, Annotated bibliography: Books on Vietnam, *Teaching Political Science* 12 (Summer 1985).

vigilantes Citizens who take the law into their own hands and illegally administer what they consider to be justice (by murder, beatings, and so on) to those whom they feel would not be adequately punished by the normal operations of the criminal justice system.

REFERENCE

Kanti C. Kotecha and James L. Walker, Police vigilantes: Vigilantism is a corruption of the spirit, *Society* 13 (March/April 1976).

village **1** An unincorporated settlement within a county. **2** A small municipal corporation.

Village of Euclid v Ambler Realty Company *See* ZONING, EUCLIDIAN.

Virginia plan The proposals for abolishing the Articles of Confederation and creating a strong central government submitted to the Constitutional Convention in 1787 by Edmund Randolph (it is also called the Randolph plan, even though it was mostly written by James Madison) on behalf of the entire Virginia delegation. Many of the plan's elements eventually found their way into the Constitution; for example, a bicameral legislature, a national executive, a national judiciary, and legislative representation based on population as determined by a census.

REFERENCE

Calvin Jillson, The representation question in the federal convention of 1787: Madison's Virginia plan and its opponents, *Congressional Studies* 8:1 (1981).

VISTA *See* ACTION.

vital statistics The data on births, deaths, marriages, and so on, maintained by county governments.

viva voce voting Oral voting; a VOICE VOTE.

Voice of America The United States Information Agency's radio broadcasting service that transmits American news, public affairs, and cultural and musical programs to overseas audiences in forty-one languages; founded in 1942.

REFERENCE

James O. H. Nason, International broadcasting as an instrument of foreign policy, *Mil-*

lennium: Journal of International Studies 6 (Autumn 1977).

voice vote **1** A voting procedure in which those eligible to vote answer aye or nay in chorus. The presiding officer then decides the result. **2** UNANIMOUS CONSENT, or without objection.

voir dire **1** A French term meaning to speak the truth. **2** The formal examination of potential jurors by the judge and lawyers for the defense and prosecutions to learn if they are acceptable for jury service in the case at hand. **3** The preliminary examination of witnesses in a case to learn if they should testify. **4** An examination, out of the presence of the jury, of some issue or fact in a case.

REFERENCES

Barbara Allen Babcock, Voir dire: Preserving "its wonderful power," *Stanford Law Review* 27 (February 1975);

Anne Rankin Mahoney, American jury voir dire and the ideal of equal justice, *Journal of Applied Behavioral Science* 18:4 (1982).

Volstead Act of 1919 The law that provided for the enforcement of the Eighteenth (Prohibition) Amendment.

voodoo economics Presidential candidate George Bush's 1980 description of Republican primary opposition candidate Ronald Reagan's economic policy proposals. After joining Reagan as the vice presidential nominee on the 1980 (and the 1984) ticket, Bush thought he had better not say it any more. And he didn't.

vote, crossover A vote in an open primary election for a candidate of the opposition party. The usual motivation is to help gain a nomination for the opposition party's weakest candidate, but some crossover voting is also a sincere effort to support a favored candidate who just happens to belong to another party.

REFERENCES

Ronald D. Hedlund, Cross-over voting in a 1976 open presidential primary, *Public Opinion Quarterly* 41 (Winter 1977–78);

Steven D. Williams and Charles McCall, Crossover among Republican voters in a dominant Democratic setting, *Journal of Political Science* 11 (Fall 1983).

vote, floating Voters who constantly float from one political party to another instead of sticking to a single party and developing a strong sense of party identification.

REFERENCES

Douglas Dobson and Douglas St. Angelo, Party identification and the floating vote: Some dynamics, *American Political Science Review* 69 (June 1975);

W. Phillips Shively, The electoral impact of party loyalists and the "floating vote": A new measure and a new perspective, *Journal of Politics* 44 (August 1982).

vote of confidence In a parliamentary system of government, the formal approval that an administration needs from a majority of the legislature if it is to continue in power. A majority that has become disenchanted with the current government may call for a vote of no confidence to force the government to resign or to call an election. If the government wins the vote of confidence, it stays in power. *See* PARLIAMENTARY SYSTEM.

vote, popular The actual numbers of votes cast for the various presidential candidates in a national election, as opposed to the number of votes each wins in the ELECTORAL COLLEGE. There is always the concern with presidential elections that a candidate will win the popular vote but lose the election, because the electoral college vote is based on winning individual states.

Percentage of Popular Vote of Winners in Presidential Elections

President Elected	Year	Percentage
Harding	1920	60.4%
Coolidge	1924	54.0
Hoover	1928	58.1
Roosevelt	1932	57.4
Roosevelt	1936	60.8
Roosevelt	1940	54.7
Roosevelt	1944	53.4
Truman	1948	49.6
Eisenhower	1952	55.1
Eisenhower	1956	57.4
Kennedy	1960	49.7
Johnson	1964	61.1
Nixon	1968	43.4
Nixon	1972	60.7
Carter	1976	50.1
Reagan	1980	50.7
Reagan	1984	58.8

Source: *Statistical Abstract of United States, 1986.*

vote, protest A vote for a candidate who has no real chance of winning (e.g., a third-party candidate) to show unhappiness with the other options. More people talk of protest voting than actually do it, because once alone in the voting booth most people are reluctant to "throw their vote away." Consequently, most third-party candidates in national elections, such as George Wallace (1968) and John Anderson (1980), have higher preelection polls than postelection vote counts.

voter A citizen who indicates ballot choices in an election. Voter and elector tend to be used interchangeably; but there is a distinction. An elector has the right to vote. A voter is an elector exercising this right.

REFERENCE

Raymond Wolfinger and Steven Rosenstone, *Who Votes?* (New Haven, CT: Yale University Press, 1980).

voter, core One who votes in practically every election in which he or she is eligible. Core voters tend to be major party loyalists.

vote, reconsider a A motion to reconsider the vote by which an action was taken. It has, until it is disposed of, the effect of suspending the action. In the Senate, the motion can be made only by a member who voted on the prevailing side of the original question or by a member who did not vote at all. In the House, it can be made only by a member on the prevailing side. A common practice after close votes in the Senate is a motion to reconsider, followed by a motion to table the motion to reconsider. On this motion to table, Senators vote as they voted on the original question, to enable the motion to table to prevail. The matter is then finally closed, and further motions to reconsider are not entertained. In the Congress, as a routine precaution, a motion to reconsider usually is made every time a measure is passed. Such a motion almost always is tabled immediately.

vote, recorded A legislative vote upon which each member's stand is individually made known. In the Senate, this is accomplished through a roll call of the entire membership, to which each Senator on the floor must answer yea, nay, or (if he or she does not wish to vote) present. Since January 1973, the House has used an electronic voting system both for yeas and nays and for other recorded votes. The Constitution requires a recorded vote on the question of overriding a veto. In other cases, a recorded vote (or a recorded teller vote) can be obtained by the demand of one-fifth of the members present. *Compare to* VOTE, TELLER.
REFERENCE
Gary King, The significance of roll calls in voting bodies: A model and statistical estimation, *Social Science Research* 15 (June 1986).

vote, roll-call *See* VOTE, RECORDED.

voter, peripheral One who usually votes only in presidential elections, and not in state and local off-year elections.

voter registration *See* REGISTRATION, VOTER.

voter requirements Conditions that citizens must meet to be eligible to vote. Minimum requirements for voting in every state are citizenship of the United States and being eighteen years of age or older. Some states permit seventeen-year-olds to vote in primary elections if they will be eighteen by the date of the general election.

Voter, The American The landmark 1960 study (New York: Wiley) by Philip E. Converse, Warren E. Miller, and Donald E. Stokes (then of the Survey Research Center of the University of Michigan) that provided much

of the foundation of modern presidential voting analysis.
REFERENCES
For an update on the study, see Norman H. Nie, Sidney Verba, and John R. Petrocik, *The Changing American Voter* (Cambridge, MA: Harvard University Press, 1976).
For an appreciation of its influence, see Gerald M. Pomper, The impact of *The American Voter* on political science, *Political Science Quarterly* 93 (Winter 1978–79).

voter, undecided A citizen eligible to vote who has not yet made a decision on how to vote. The undecided vote is often large enough to confound the pollsters and to be the critical factor in close elections.
REFERENCE
Ian Fenwick, Frederick Wiseman, John F. Becker, and James R. Heiman, Classifying undecided voters in pre-election polls, *Public Opinion Quarterly* 46 (Fall 1982).

vote, standing A nonrecorded vote used in both the House and the Senate. A standing vote, also called a division vote, is taken as follows: those in favor of a proposal stand and are counted by the presiding officer; then members opposed stand and are counted. There is no record of how individual members voted. In the House, the presiding officer announces the numbers for and against. In the Senate, usually only the result is announced.

vote, straw An unofficial, nonbinding vote. It is derived from the adage that "straws show which way the wind blows."

vote, teller A means of voting in the House in which members file past tellers and are counted as for or against a measure but are not recorded individually. The teller vote is not used in the Senate. In the House, tellers are ordered upon demand of one-fifth of a quorum. This is forty-four in the House, twenty in the COMMITTEE OF THE WHOLE. The House also has a recorded teller vote procedure, introduced in 1971 (now largely supplanted by electronic voting), under which the individual votes of members are made public just as they would be on a yea-and-nay vote. *Compare to* VOTE, RECORDED.

REFERENCE
James A. Stimson, Teller voting in the House
of Representatives: The conservative screen-
ing hypothesis, *Polity* 8 (Winter 1975).

vote trading A legislative tactic in which one
legislator votes for a bill favored by a second
legislator, with the understanding that the second legislator will vote in favor of a bill advocated by the first legislator. Vote trading may
be explicit, where the two make an informal
agreement, or implicit, where the trade is the
result of an unspoken understanding. *Compare
to* PAIR; RECIPROCITY.

REFERENCES
James M. Enelow and David H. Koehler, Vote
trading in a legislative context: An analysis
of cooperative and noncooperative strategic
voting, *Public Choice* 34:2 (1979);
Richard D. McKelvey and Peter C. Orde-
shook, Vote trading: An experimental study,
Public Choice 35:2 (1980).

vote, voice *See* VOICE VOTE.

vote, write-in A vote for someone other than
one of the candidates on the official ballot.
While often legal, this is usually a futile protest
against the available candidates.

voting The exercise of the right of SUFFRAGE.
This is the only means by which most citizens
can participate in political decision making.

REFERENCES
Stanley Kelley, Jr., and Thad W. Mirer, The
simple act of voting, *American Political Science Review* 68 (June 1974);
Elizabeth Sanders, On the costs, utilities, and
simple joys of voting, *Journal of Politics* 42
(August 1980).

voting, absentee Voting by citizens who, for
whatever reasons, cannot go to their normal
polling places on election day and therefore
take advantage of state and federal laws that
allow them to vote in advance or by mail. *Compare to* BALLOT, ABSENTEE; FEDERAL POSTCARD
APPLICATION.

REFERENCE
Frank B. Feigert, Components of absentee
voting, *Polity* 4 (Summer 1972).

voting, approval An electoral process
whereby voters can vote for (approve of) as
many of the candidates as they desire but cannot cast more than one vote for each candidate.
Voters do not rank candidates, and the candidate with the greatest vote total wins. This voting system is rarely used but much discussed.

REFERENCES
Steven J. Brams and Peter C. Fishburn, Approval voting, *American Political Science
Review* 72 (September 1978);
Steven J. Brams, Approval voting: A practical
reform for multi-candidate elections, *National Civic Review* 68 (November 1979);
Peter S. Fishburn and Steven J. Brams, Efficacy, power, and equity under approval voting, *Public Choice* 37:3 (1981).

voting behavior 1 The total means by which
citizens express their opinions on political candidates and issues at the polls. 2 The subfield
of political science that seeks to discover (or
explain) voting patterns and trends.

REFERENCES
Gerald M. Pomper, *Voter's Choice: Varieties of
American Electoral Behavior* (New York:
Dodd, Mead, 1975);
Richard G. Niemi and Herbert F. Weisberg,
eds., *Controversies in American Voting Be-
havior* (San Francisco: Freeman, 1976).

voting, bloc Voting done in collusion with
others according to commonly agreed policies.
This can occur either in legislatures, when all
of the members of a party cast the same vote
or when a bipartisan coalition (such as the conservative coalition in the Congress) forms; or
in a general election, when all of the members
of an ethnic or interest group vote the same
way. In 1970, George C. Wallace won reelection as governor of Alabama by actively campaigning against the bloc vote. Because his
pronunciation of bloc and black were indistin-
guishable, he played to the white backlash vote
while being able to deny any racial attack.

voting, compulsory A legal requirement that
eligible voters vote. The Supreme Court has
held in *Lane v Wilson,* 307 U.S. 268 (1939),
that penalties for not voting are unconstitutional and a violation of the Fifteenth
Amendment.

REFERENCE
For a comparative perspective, see Galen Irwin, Compulsory voting legislation: Impact on voter turnout in the Netherlands, *Comparative Politics* 7 (October 1974).

voting, Hare system A single-transferable voting system of proportional representation in which electors vote for more than one candidate. Those candidates gaining a fixed number of votes are elected, while the surplus votes go to the voters' next choices. As the lowest polling candidates are eliminated, votes that went to them are transferred to other choices.

REFERENCE
Gideon Doron, Is the Hare voting scheme representative? *Journal of Politics* 41 (August 1979).

voting, issue *See* ISSUE VOTING.

voting, negative 1 Voting against, as opposed to voting for, something. 2 Voting against the party in power as a protest of its policies.

REFERENCES
Samuel Kernell, Presidential popularity and negative voting, *American Political Science Review* 71 (March 1977);
Michael M. Gant and Lee Sigelman, Anti-candidate voting in presidential elections, *Polity* 18 (Winter 1985).

voting, pocketbook Voting decided on the basis of personal economic issues; on whether a candidate's or an initiative's policies would cost the voter money in terms of additional taxes, fewer jobs, and so on.

REFERENCE
Michael S. Lewis-Beck, Pocketbook voting in U.S. national election studies: Fact or artifact? *American Journal of Political Science* 29 (May 1985).

voting, preferential A voting system in which electors indicate first, second, third, and so on, choices of candidates.

voting, proportional 1 PROPORTIONAL REPRESENTATION. 2 The option of assigning a portion of one's total vote to more than one candidate. The Hare system (*see* VOTING, HARE SYSTEM) is a variant of proportional voting.

voting, prospective Voting for a candidate on the assumption that he or she will advocate or implement specific policies in the future. Prospective voting is a major element in presidential elections. *Compare to* VOTING, RETROSPECTIVE.

voting residence A voter's DOMICILE, generally. However, the voting residence of an American voting pursuant to the Overseas Citizens Voting Rights Act and no longer domiciled in the United States is the place where the voter was domiciled immediately prior to departure from the United States. The Constitution originally left to the states the right to determine eligibility for voting. Consequently, residency in a state and registration as a voter became essential requirements for voting. In a series of steps, particularly over the last twenty years, the Supreme Court has moved in the direction of creating a national presumption of the right to vote, although a national registration still does not exist. *Compare to* RESIDENCY REQUIREMENTS.

voting, retrospective Voting for candidates on the basis of their past performance in political office. Restrospective voting is often a factor in returning incumbent legislators to office, because they have had time to be of service to their constituents, get public works for their district, and so on. *Compare to* VOTING, PROSPECTIVE.

REFERENCE
Morris P. Fiorina, *Retrospective Voting in American National Elections* (New Haven, CT: Yale University Press, 1981).

Voting Rights Act of 1965 The law that extended the elective franchise to millions of once-excluded members of minority groups, and arguably the most important civil rights legislation ever passed (with the possible exception of the Civil Rights Act of 1964). At the heart of the act are the Section 4 triggering formula, providing for automatic coverage of jurisdictions with low minority electoral participation, and the Section 5 requirement of preclearance of all voting law changes by such jurisdictions with the attorney general or the Federal District Court for the District of Columbia. Other sections authorize the appointment of federal examiners to enforce the right to vote and permit federal observers to monitor elections. The act, which was amended in 1970, 1975, and 1982, also bans literacy tests and requires bilingual elections in some jurisdictions. The constitutionality of the act was upheld by the Supreme Court in *South Carolina v Katzenbach,* 383 U.S. 301 (1966).

REFERENCES

Joseph F. Zimmerman, The federal Voting Rights Act: Its impact on annexation, *National Civic Review* 66 (June 1977);

Abigail M. Thernstrom, The odd evolution of the Voting Rights Act, *Public Interest* 55 (Spring 1979);

Howard D. Neighbor, The Voting Rights Act old and new: A forecast of political maturity, *National Civic Review* 72 (October 1983);

Alan Howard and Bruce Howard, The dilemma of the Voting Rights Act—Recognizing the emerging political equality norm, *Columbia Law Review* 83 (November 1983);

Gerald W. Jones, Redistricting and the Voting Rights Act; A limited but important impact, *National Civic Review* 73 (April 1984);

Lorn S. Foster, ed., *The Voting Rights Act: Consequences and Implications* (New York: Praeger, 1985).

voting, split ticket Voting for candidates of more than one party. *See* TICKET SPLITTING.

voting, straight ticket Voting only for candidates of the same party. Voting machines often allow voters to pull one lever to select the straight party ticket. Only 43 percent of all voters cast a straight ticket in 1984.

voting, strategic Voting that is not sincere but is intended to bring about some other result, such as when voters cross over in a primary to vote in favor of the weaker candidate of the opposition party or when legislators vote in favor of an amendment to a bill that they believe will cause its ultimate defeat.

REFERENCE

Alan Abramowitz, John McGlennon, and Ronald Rapoport, A note on strategic voting in a primary election, *Journal of Politics* 43 (August 1981).

Major Expansions of the Electorate and New Voting Rights

During most of American history, the states have determined qualifications for voting. Prior to the Civil War, most expansions of suffrage were limited to removing property qualifications for white males. The major changes in the Constitution and federal law are the following:

1870	The Fifteenth Amendment guaranteed suffrage to blacks (after it appeared that the Fourteenth Amendment had failed to do so).
1920	The Nineteenth Amendment guaranteed women the right to vote.
1961	The Twenty-third Amendment extended the right to vote in presidential elections to the District of Columbia.
1964	The Twenty-fourth Amendment provided that failure to pay a poll tax or any other tax cannot be used to deny the right to vote.
1965	The Voting Rights Act banned the use of tests or other similar devices to deny the right to vote in certain parts of the country, mainly the South; voting examiners were to handle registration of voters in these areas.
1970	The Voting Rights Act suspended literacy tests throughout the nation.
1971	The Twenty-sixth Amendment extended the vote to eighteen-year-olds.
1972	The U.S. Supreme Court ruled, in *Dunn v Blumstein,* 405 U.S. 330 (1972), that long residency requirements were unconstitutional.
1975	The Voting Rights Act required bilingual voting information in parts of twenty-four states.
1982	The Voting Rights Act was extended for twenty-five years.

Source: William J. Keefe, Henry J. Abraham, William H. Flanigan, Charles O. Jones, Morris S. Ogul, and John W. Spanier, *American Democracy: Institutions, Politics, and Policies,* 2d ed. (Chicago: Dorsey, 1986), p. 119.

voting, tactical Voting not for one's preferred choice but for a candidate that is more likely to win.
REFERENCE
George Tsebelis, A general model of tactical and inverse tactical voting, *British Journal of Political Science* 16 (July 1986).

voting, weighted A voting system in which each voter's vote is proportionate to something, such as shares of stocks owned or numbers of constituents represented.
REFERENCE
Bernard Grofman and Howard A. Scarrow,

Weighted voting in New York, *Legislative Studies Quarterly* 6 (May 1981).

voucher system A government program that issues redeemable vouchers to eligible citizens to purchase services on the open market. For example, housing vouchers have been suggested as an alternative to public housing and education vouchers have been suggested as an alternative to public education.
REFERENCE
Shawn Timothy Newman, Education vouchers and tuition tax credits: In search of viable public aid to private education, *Journal of Legislation* 10 (Winter 1983).

wage tax *See* TAX, WAGE.

Wagner Act *See* NATIONAL LABOR RELATIONS ACT OF 1935.

Waldo, (Clifford) Dwight (1913–) The preeminent historian of the academic discipline of public administration and the editor in chief of *Public Administration Review* from 1966 to 1977. Waldo first became an influence in public administration when he attacked the "gospel of efficiency" that so dominated administrative thinking prior to World War II. In his landmark book, *The Administrative State: A Study of the Political Theory of American Public Administration* (New York: Ronald, 1948), he asserted that the drive for efficiency has "occasionally served the end of those whose purposes might be regarded as more or less reprehensible if stated in another idiom."
REFERENCES
Waldo's other major works include *The Study of Public Administration* (New York: Random House, 1955);

Public Administration in a Time of Turbulence, ed. (Scranton, PA: Chandler, 1971);
The Enterprise of Public Administration (Novato, CA: Chandler and Sharp, 1980).
For biographies, see James A. Gazell, Dwight Waldo, public administration, and the "blooming buzzing confusion," *American Review of Public Administration* 16 (Summer/Fall 1982);
Brack Brown and Richard J. Stillman II, *The Search for Public Administration: The Ideas and Career of Dwight Waldo* (College Station: Texas A&M University Press, 1986).

Walz v Tax Commission of the City of New York *See* ESTABLISHMENT CLAUSE.

ward A subdivision of a city, often used as a legislative district for city council elections, as an administrative division for public services, or as a unit for the organization of political parties. A ward is often further divided (*see* PRECINCT).

ward heeler A local political functionary; someone who is involved with, but insignificant in, party affairs. A heeler is not worthy of much respect. The term comes from the way a dog is brought to heel by its master; ward heelers are known by their obedience to their masters.

war hawk *See* HAWK.

war on poverty The phrase used by the Lyndon B. Johnson administration for its 1960s Great Society programs designed to eliminate the causes and effects of poverty in the United States. After two decades, it is clear who won the war—poverty. But the fact that poverty has yet to be defeated takes nothing away from the great intentions and limited accomplishments of the "military" effort. The policy question to be asked is not whether the war was worth fighting (it was); but what would be the best strategies and tactics to employ the next time the nation makes a major effort to fight this perennial enemy.

REFERENCES

Roger H. Davidson, The war on poverty: Experiment in federalism, *Annals of the American Academy of Political and Social Science* 382 (September 1969);

Carl M. Brauer, Kennedy, Johnson, and the war on poverty, *Journal of American History* 69 (June 1982);

Charles A. Murray, The two wars against poverty: Economic growth and the Great Society, *Public Interest* 69 (Fall 1982).

war powers The legal authority to initiate war. The U.S. Constitution gives to the Congress the authority to declare war, but the president, as commander in chief, has implied powers to commit the military forces to action. In World War II, the last war the Congress actually declared, the Congress was called into emergency joint session by President Franklin D. Roosevelt the day after Pearl Harbor (December 8, 1941) and voted to declare war on Japan. More recently, the Congress, concerned with presidential military initiatives during the Vietnam War, has sought to place substantial controls on the president's power to commit American troops to combat. The War Powers

Resolution of 1973 clarifies the respective roles of the president and the Congress in cases involving the use of military forces without a declaration of war. The president "in every possible instance" shall consult with the Congress before introducing troops and shall report to the Congress within forty-eight hours. The use of the armed forces is to be terminated within sixty days (with a possible thirty-day extension by the president) unless the Congress acts during that time to declare war, enacts a specific authorization for use of armed forces, extends the sixty-to-ninety-day period, or is physically unable to meet as a result of an attack on the United States. At any time before the sixty days expires, the Congress may direct by concurrent resolution that American military forces be removed by the president.

REFERENCES

Harry C. Thomson, The War Powers Resolution of 1973: Can Congress make it stick? *World Affairs* 139 (Summer 1976);

W. Stuart Darling and D. Craig Mense, Rethinking the War Powers Act, *Presidential Studies Quarterly* 7 (Spring/Summer 1977);

Bennet C. Rushkoff, A defense of the War Powers Resolution, *Yale Law Journal* 93:7 (1984);

Michael J. Glennon, The War Powers Resolution ten years later: More politics than law, *American Journal of International Law* 78 (July 1984);

Cyrus R. Vance, Striking the balance: Congress and the president under the War Powers Resolution, *University of Pennsylvania Law Review* 133 (December 1984);

Michael Rubner, The Reagan administration, the 1973 War Powers Resolution, and the invasion of Grenada, *Political Science Quarterly* 100 (Winter 1985–86).

warrant **1** In criminal proceedings, a writ issued by a judge directing a law enforcement officer to do something; for example, to search some premises (a search warrant) or to arrest some person (an arrest warrant). Warrants are required because of the Fourth Amendment's assertion that the people be free from unreasonable searches and seizures. *Compare to* PROBABLE CAUSE. **2** A short-term obligation issued by a government in anticipation of revenue. The instrument (a draft much like a check), when presented to a disbursing officer, such as a bank, is payable only upon acceptance by the issuing jurisdiction. Warrants may be made payable on demand or at some time in the future. Local governments, in particular, have used delayed payment of warrants as a way to protect cash flow.

Warren Commission The commission established by President Lyndon B. Johnson to investigate the assassination of President John F. Kennedy in 1963. Chaired by Chief Justice Earl Warren (1891–1974), it concluded that Lee Harvey Oswald had acted alone in shooting the president. The ensuing Warren Report has since been completely discredited by subsequent congressional and other investigations. By the time there was consensus that Kennedy was killed by a conspiracy, too many years had passed, too many of the principles involved were dead by natural or other causes, and it was simply too late. Because of the ineptness of the Warren Commission, the question, Who killed President Kennedy? will never be satisfactorily answered.

REFERENCES

Sylvia Meagher, *Accessories after the Fact: The Warren Commission, the Authorities, and the Report* (New York: Vintage, 1967, 1976);

Sylvia Meagher, *Master Index to the J.F.K. Assassination Investigations: The Reports and Supporting Volumes of the House Select Committee on Assassinations and the Warren Commission* (Metuchen, NJ: Scarecrow, 1980);

Michael L. Lurtz, *Crime of the Century: The Kennedy Assassination from a Historian's Perspective* (Knoxville: University of Tennessee Press, 1982).

Warren, Earl (1891–1974) The chief justice of the United States from 1953 to 1969 who became the symbol of judicial activism and led the Court to many landmark decisions on desegregation, civil rights, First Amendment freedoms, and the rights of criminal defendants.

REFERENCES

G. Edward White, *Earl Warren: Paradoxes of a Public Life* (New York: Oxford University Press, 1982);

Bernard Schwartz, *Super Chief: Earl Warren and His Supreme Court—A Judicial Biography* (New York: New York University Press, 1983).

Warsaw Pact A multilateral military alliance formed by the Treaty of Warsaw, signed May 14, 1955, by the Soviet Union, Bulgaria, Czechoslovakia, East Germany, Hungary, Poland, and Romania. The pact was ostensibly created as a communist counterpart to NATO and to counter the threat of a remilitarized West Germany. In fact, the parties were already integrated into the Soviet military system through standard treaties of alliance concluded between 1945 and 1948. The pact has a joint

The Warsaw Pact

Members	Population (in thousands)	Armed Forces (in thousands)
Bulgaria	8,944	162
Czechoslovakia	15,420	205
German Democratic Republic	16,724	167
Hungary	10,691	105
Poland	36,556	340
Romania	22,649	189
U.S.S.R.	272,308	5,050

Note: Data are for midyear 1983.
Source: U.S. Department of State.

command under Soviet leadership, and all forces come under Soviet command in wartime.

REFERENCES

Richard A. Gabriel, ed., *NATO and the Warsaw Pact: A Combat Assessment* (Westport, CT: Greenwood, 1983);

David Holloway and Jane M. O. Sharp, eds., *The Warsaw Pact: Alliance in Transition* (Ithaca, NY: Cornell University Press, 1984);

David N. Nelson, ed., *Soviet Allies: The Warsaw Pact and the Issue of Reliability* (Boulder, CO: Westview, 1984);

Richard C. Martin, Warsaw Pact force modernization: A closer look, *Parameters: Journal of the US Army War College* 15 (Summer 1985).

Washington 1 The capital city of the United States. While Washington refers to the physical location of the federal government's central offices, it is frequently used as a collective noun to refer to the policymaking processes and actors of the national government (e.g., as in Washington said, . . . Washington decided, . . . or it is Washington's policy, . . .). 2 Washington State, located in the northwestern United States. 3 The District of Columbia, the "D.C." in Washington, D.C., which occupies the same territory as the capital city of Washington.

Washington became the site of the U.S. capital for a variety of reasons. Many members of the first congresses wanted to meet in a relatively remote place that would be free of possible intimidation by urban mobs. The North and South needed a compromise location, relatively convenient to each. In 1790, the decision was reached to locate the capital on the Potomac River. The newly elected first president, George Washington, would choose the exact site. Both Maryland and Virginia donated land on opposite sides of the Potomac. (The Virginia donation was returned to that state in the mid-nineteenth century). In 1791, President Washington engaged Pierre-Charles L'Enfant (1754–1825), a French military engineer who served in the Continental army, to lay out plans for the city on a grand scale. Even though L'Enfant was dismissed a short time later, in 1792, his original design for the city still dominates.

Citizens of the District of Columbia were not given voting rights until recently to emphasize the political neutrality of the federal establishment. The Twenty-third Amendment adopted in 1961 allows District residents to vote in presidential elections and to have three electoral votes. In 1970, the Congress granted the District a nonvoting delegate to the House of Representatives. In 1974, the Congress allowed voters living in the District to elect a mayor and a thirteen-member city council for limited home rule. Proposed constitutional amendments to give the District congressional representation as if it were a state or to make it the fifty-first state have yet to be adopted. Nor are they likely to be, as long as Republicans in the Congress and state legislatures can stop them. The District's population is overwhelmingly Democratic and would almost certainly send Democrats to the Congress if given the opportunity.

George Washington.

Washington, George (1732–1799) The plantation owner and land surveyor from Virginia who was the victorious commander of the American revolutionary army, the chairman of the Constitutional Convention of 1787, and first president of the United States (1789–1797). In each instance, Washington's service brought enormous benefits to his country and honor to himself. Washington is that rare case in which a man's mythic qualities of integrity, patriotism, and honor actually live up to what he was in real life. James Flexner was correct in calling Washington the "indispensable man." It seems fair to say that, were it not for Washington's character, personal presence, and dedication to republican principles, the history of the fledgling United States would have taken a radically different turn—for the worse. He is the closest thing the United States has to a secular saint—and deservedly so. *Compare to* LUCIUS QUINCTIUS CINCINNATUS; COUP D'ÉTAT.

REFERENCES

For the definitive four-volume biography, see James T. Flexner's *George Washington: The Forge of Experience, 1732–1775* (Boston: Little, Brown, 1965);

George Washington in the American Revolution, 1775–1783 (Boston: Little, Brown, 1968);

George Washington and the New Nation, 1783–1793 (Boston: Little, Brown, 1970);

George Washington: Anguish and Farewell, 1793–1799 (Boston: Little, Brown, 1972).

For a one-volume abridgement, see James T. Flexner's *Washington: The Indispensable Man* (Boston: Little, Brown, 1974).

Washington Monthly A journal that focuses on public policy and the bureaucracy; published since 1969. It is considered a major voice for neoliberalism. Library of Congress no. E838 .W37

Washington Monthly
1711 Connecticut Avenue, N.W.
Washington, D.C. 20009

Washington v Davis 426 U.S. 229 (1976) The U.S. Supreme Court case that held that, although the due process clause of the Fifth Amendment prohibits the government from invidious discrimination, it does not follow that a law or other official act is unconstitutional solely because it has a racially disproportionate impact. The Court ruled that, under the U.S.

Constitution (as opposed to Title VII of the Civil Rights Act of 1964), there must be discriminatory purpose or intent—adverse impact alone is insufficient.

Garry Trudeau's running commentary in **Doonesbury** *covered the Watergate scandal from hotel break-in to presidential collapse.*

Watergate The scandal that led to the resignation of President Richard M. Nixon. Watergate itself is a hotel-office-apartment complex in Washington, D.C. When individuals associated with the Committee to Reelect the President were caught breaking into the Democratic National Committee Headquarters (then located in the Watergate complex) in 1972, the resulting cover-up and national trauma was condensed into one word—Watergate. The term has grown to refer to any political crime or instance of bureaucratic corruption that undermines confidence in governing institutions.

The aftermath of Watergate brought about a major review of the presidency as an administrative institution. Much of the focus of public administration's development since the 1930s had been to concentrate power and control in the executive branch. Now that it had been accomplished, Watergate provided a dramatic lesson in what could happen if such centralized power were abused. The public administration community responded with its own review of Watergate. In response to a request from the Senate Select Committee on Presidential Campaign Activities, a special panel of the National Academy of Public Administration, chaired by Frederick C. Mosher, examined the situation and produced a report, *Watergate: Implications for Responsible Government* (New York: Basic Books, 1974), which provided a detailed indictment of the Nixon administration's abuses of executive and administrative authority and power. Educational institutions were urged to "focus more attention on public sector ethics." Although codes of ethics have been around for years, the panel concluded that more sophisticated and effective codes of conduct and standards were needed. *Also see* SATURDAY NIGHT MASSACRE.

REFERENCES

James L. Sundquist, Reflections on Watergate: Lessons for public administration, *Public Administration Review* 34 (September/October 1974);

Richard E. Neustadt, The constraining of the president: The presidency after Watergate, *British Journal of Political Science* 4 (October 1974);

Ronald E. Pynn, ed., *Watergate and the American Political Process* (New York: Praeger, 1975);

Roger C. Dunham and Armand L. Mauss, Waves from Watergate: Evidence concerning the impact of the Watergate scandal upon political legitimacy and social control, *Pacific Sociological Review* 19 (October 1976);

Howard J. Silver, Presidential power and the post-Watergate presidency, *Presidential Studies Quarterly* 8 (Spring 1978);

Richard W. Boyd and David J. Hadley, Presidential and congressional response to political crisis: Nixon, Congress, and Watergate, *Congress and the Presidency: A Journal of Capital Studies* 10 (Autumn 1983).

Don't Buy Books by Crooks

Because so many of the Watergate conspirators got lucrative book contracts to tell their sordid stories, a modest grass-roots movement, "don't buy books by crooks," arose in a futile effort to take the profit out of their crimes.

Author	Position in Nixon Administration	Served Time in Prison?	Book
Charles Colson	Special counsel to the president	yes	*Born Again* (New York: Bantam, 1977)
John Dean	White House counsel	yes	*Blind Ambition: The White House Years* (New York: Simon & Schuster, 1976)
John Ehrlichman	Chief domestic affairs advisor to the president	yes	*Witness to Power: The Nixon Years* (New York: Simon & Schuster, 1982)
H. R. Haldeman	White House chief of staff	yes	*The Ends of Power* (New York: Times Books, 1978)
Richard Kleindienst	Attorney general	sentence suspended	*Justice: The Memoirs of Attorney General Richard Kleindienst* (Ottawa IL: Jameson, 1985)
G. Gordon Liddy	White House aide	yes	*Will: The Autobiography of G. Gordon Liddy* (New York: St. Martin's, 1980)
Jeb Stuart Magruder	White House aide	yes	*An American Life: One Man's Road to Watergate* (New York: Atheneum, 1974)
Richard Nixon	President	pardoned	*RN: The Memoirs of Richard Nixon* (New York: Grosset & Dunlap, 1978)

Watergate analogy Ever since the Watergate scandal, political activities that seem to smell of corruption have had a ＿＿gate suffix added in analogy. Thus when the Ronald Reagan 1980 campaign organization was accused of "somehow" getting hold of President Jimmy Carter's debate briefing book, the affair was dubbed debategate. President Carter's problems with his brother's connection to Libya was called Billygate. Of course, ＿＿gate charges are often denounced as pseudogates.

REFERENCE

Tom Bethell, Breakfastgate: The FTC versus the cereal companies, *Policy Review* 16 (Spring 1981).

ways and means 1 A government's financial resources. 2 The methods by which a state gains its funds, supplies, and other necessities. The English House of Commons has had a Committee on Ways and Means at least since 1644. The U.S. House of Representatives has had a Ways and Means Committee since 1795. All national tax legislation must originate in the House Ways and Means Committee.

REFERENCE

John F. Manley, *The Politics of Finance: The House Committee on Ways and Means* (Boston: Little, Brown, 1970).

weapon system An imprecise term for a weapon and the components required for its operation. It can be as small as a rifle and its ammunition or as large as an aircraft carrier and its support ships.

Weber decision *See* UNITED STEELWORKERS OF AMERICA V WEBER, ET AL.

Weber, Max (1864–1920) The German sociologist who produced an analysis of an idealtype bureaucracy that is still the most influential statement—the point of departure for all further analyses—on the subject. Weber also pioneered the concepts of the Protestant ethic, charismatic authority, and a value-free approach to social research. *Also see* BUREAUCRACY; CHARISMA; LEGITIMACY.

REFERENCES

For Weber's major works, see Max Weber, *Protestant Ethic and the Spirit of Capital-*

ism, trans. Talcott Parsons (New York: Scribner, 1904–05, 1958);

H. H. Gerth and C. Wright Mills, eds., *From Max Weber: Essays in Sociology* (New York: Oxford University Press, 1946);

S. N. Eisenstadt, ed., *Max Weber on Charisma and Institution Building: Selected Papers* (Chicago: University of Chicago Press, 1968);

W. G. Runciman, ed., *Weber: Selections in Translation* (Cambridge, England: Cambridge University Press, 1978).

For critical and biographical studies, see Reinhard Bendix, *Max Weber: An Intellectual Portrait* (Garden City, NY: Doubleday, 1960);

L. M. Lachmann, *The Legacy of Max Weber* (San Francisco: Boyd and Fraser, 1971);

Lawrence A. Scaff, Max Weber's politics and political education, *American Political Science Review* 67 (March 1973);

Frank Parkin, *Max Weber* (London: Methuen, 1982).

welfare Public financial or in-kind assistance available to citizens as a matter of right if they meet eligibility requirements, such as a MEANS TEST of income or assets below a preset minimum. Welfare is not only for the poor; it can cover a wide range of people of various means. *See also* ENTITLEMENT PROGRAM; GOLDBERG V KELLY; RELIEF/WORK RELIEF.

REFERENCE

M. Donna Price Cofer, *Administering Public Assistance: A Constitutional and Administrative Perspective* (Port Washington, NY: Kennikat, 1982).

welfare clause *See* GENERAL WELFARE CLAUSE.

welfare state A governing system in which it is a public policy that government will strive for the maximum economic and social benefits for each of its citizens short of changing the operating premises of the society. The line between an extreme welfare state and socialism is so thin that its existence is debatable.

REFERENCES

Edward D. Berkowitz and Kim McQuaid, *Creating the Welfare State: The Political Econ-*

omy of Twentieth Century Reform (New
York: Praeger, 1980);

Roger A. Freeman, *The Wayward Welfare State*
(Stanford, CA: Stanford University, Hoover
Institution, 1981);

Theodore J. Lowi, The welfare state: Ethical
foundations and constitutional remedies,
Political Science Quarterly 101:2 (1986).

Welsh v United States *See* CONSCIENTIOUS
OBJECTOR.

Wesberry v Sanders 376 U.S. 1 (1964) The
U.S. Supreme Court case that, in holding that
congressional districts had to be substantially
equal in population, created the legal basis for
ending the rural bias in congressional representation. *Compare to* REYNOLDS V SIMS.

West Coast Hotel v Parrish 300 U.S. 379
(1937) The U.S. Supreme Court case that
upheld the minimum wage law of the State of
Washington by declaring that a minimum wage
law did not violate the freedom of contract provided by the due process clause of the Fourteenth Amendment. This case overruled the
Court's earlier decision, *Adkins v Children's
Hospital*, 261 U.S. 525 (1923), which held unconstitutional a federal law establishing minimum wages for women and children in the
District of Columbia.

Western Political Quarterly The scholarly
journal of the Western Political Science Association; published since 1948. Library of Congress no. JA1 .W4.

> *Western Political Quarterly*
> University of Utah
> 258 Orson Spencer Hall
> Salt Lake City, UT 84112

Whig party 1 An American political party
established in 1836 by opponents of Andrew
Jackson's policies. It elected presidents in 1840
(William Henry Harrison) and 1848 (Zachary
Taylor) but then divided over the slavery issue. By 1852 it had completely disintegrated.
2 The seventeenth-century English political
party whose goal was the transfer of power
from the king to parliament. In the nineteenth
century, it was succeeded by the Liberal party.

REFERENCE

1 Lynn L. Marshall, The strange stillbirth of
the Whig party, *American History Review* 72:2 (1967).

whip A fox-hunting term applied to a key
aspect of the legislative process. A whipper-in
keeps fox-sniffing dogs from straying by whip-
ping them back into the pack. The British Parliament first used the term, then shortened it
to whip, to describe those members of the legislature responsible for party discipline—for
literally rounding up the party members when
it was time for a vote.

While the U.S. Congress borrowed the term
from the British, it has been far less successful
in maintaining party discipline. The whips (of
the majority and minority parties) keep track
of all important political legislation and endeavor to have all members of their parties
present when important measures are to be
voted upon. When a vote appears to be close,
the whips contact absent members, advise them
of the vote, and determine if they wish to PAIR
vote. The whips assist the leadership in managing the party's legislative program on the
floor of the chambers and provide information
to party members about important legislative-
related matters. The office of whip is unofficial
and carries no special salary. *Compare to* MA-
JORITY WHIP.

REFERENCES

Randell B. Ripley, The party whip organizations in the United States, *American Political Science Review* 58:3 (1964);

Walter J. Oleszek, Party whips in the United
States Senate, *Journal of Politics* 33 (November 1971);

Lawrence C. Dodd, The expanded roles of the
House Democratic whip system: The 93rd
and 94th congresses, *Congressional Studies*
7 (Spring 1979);

Lynne P. Brown and Robert L. Peabody, Dilemmas of party leadership: Majority whips
in the U.S. House of Representatives,
1963–1982, *Congress and the Presidency: A
Journal of Capital Studies* 11 (Autumn
1984).

For a comparative perspective, see Donald
Searing and Chris Game, Horses for
courses: The recruitment of whips in the

British House of Commons, *British Journal of Political Science* 7:3 (1977).

whistle blower An individual who believes the public interest overrides the interests of his or her organization and publicly blows the whistle on corrupt, illegal, fraudulent, or harmful activity. *See* ERNEST A. FITZGERALD.
REFERENCES
Ralph Nader, Peter J. Petkas, and Kate Blackwell, eds., *Whistle Blowing: The Report of the Conference on Professional Responsibility* (New York: Grossman, 1972);
James S. Bowman, Whistle-blowing in the public service: An overview of the issues, *Review of Public Personnel Administration* 1 (Fall 1980);
James S. Bowman, Whistle blowing: Literature and resource materials, *Public Administration Review* 43 (May/June 1983).

white citizens' councils *See* CITIZENS' COUNCILS.

white flight 1 The movement of white residents from central cities. It was a common response to public school busing to achieve school racial integration. If they could afford it, whites would tend to move out of the central city and into the suburbs so that their children could attend neighborhood schools. White flight most often occurred when the school population became overwhelmingly black and when bus rides were deemed excessively long. 2 More recently, as in the case of Miami, it is the movement of English-speaking citizens from an area that has become increasingly Hispanic in language and culture.
REFERENCES
1 M. W. Giles, Douglas S. Gatlin, and Everett F. Cataldo, The impact of busing on white flight, *Social Science Quarterly* 55 (September 1974);
Charles T. Clotfelter, The Detroit decision and "white flight," *Journal of Legal Studies* 5 (January 1976);
Diane Ravitch, Social science and social policy: The "white flight" controversy, *Public Interest* 51 (Spring 1978);
William H. Frey, Central city white flight: Racial and nonracial causes, *American Sociological Review* 44 (June 1979).

White House The official residence of the president of the United States.
White House
1600 Pennsylvania Avenue
Washington, D.C. 20500
(202) 456–1414

White House Office The personal office of the president of the United States, containing the staff and facilities that allow the president to communicate with the Congress, his appointed agency heads, the press, and the public. *Compare to* EXECUTIVE OFFICE OF THE PRESIDENT.

White House tapes The recorded Oval Office conversations that were the main issue in *United States v Nixon:* Did the president have to turn over incriminating tape recordings to the special prosecutor? The Supreme Court said yes, and within days Richard M. Nixon had resigned as president. In 1986, Nixon was asked at a press luncheon what he thought was the greatest lesson of Watergate; he unrepentantly replied, "Just destroy all the tapes."
REFERENCE
Steven J. Brams and Douglas Muzzio, Unanimity in the Supreme Court: A game-theoretic explanation of the decision in the White House tapes case, *Public Choice* 32 (Winter 1977).

White House, that man in the *See* FRANKLIN DELANO ROOSEVELT.

White, Leonard D. (1891–1958) Author of the first public administration text, in 1926; author of the standard administrative histories of the United States government in the nineteenth century; and one of the most significant voices in the development of public administration as an academic discipline.
REFERENCES
White's major works include *Introduction to the Study of Public Administration* (New York: Harper & Row, 1926; 4th ed., 1955);
The City Manager (Chicago: University of Chicago Press, 1927);
The Federalists (New York: Macmillan, 1948);
The Jeffersonians (New York: Macmillan, 1951);

The White House Office, 1986

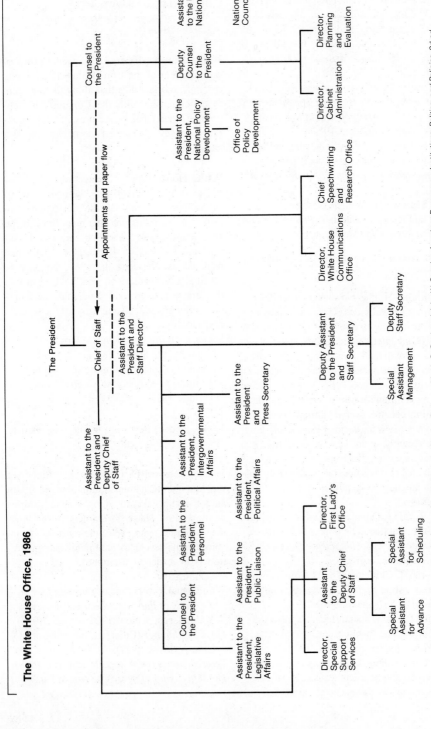

Source: William J. Keefe, Henry J. Abraham, William H. Flanigan, Charles O. Jones, Morris S. Ogul, and John W. Spanier, *American Democracy: Institutions, Politics, and Policies,* 2d ed. (Chicago: Dorsey, 1986), p. 398.

The Jacksonians (New York: Macmillan, 1954);

The Republican Era (New York: Macmillan, 1958).

For appreciations, see John M. Gaus, Leonard Dupree White 1891–1958, *Public Administration Review* 18 (Summer 1958);

H. J. Storing, Leonard D. White and the study of public administration, *Public Administration Review* 25 (March 1965).

white paper Any formal statement of an official government policy, with its associated background documentation.

white primary *See* PRIMARY, WHITE.

White, Theodore H. *See* MAKING OF THE PRESIDENT.

Widmar v Vincent *See* SCHOOL DISTRICT OF ABINGTON TOWNSHIP V SCHEMPP.

Wiener v United States 357 U.S. 349 (1958) The U.S. Supreme Court case holding that the president overstepped his constitutional authority in removing a member of the War Claims Commission for political reasons, since the commission had judicial functions. *See also* HUMPHREY'S EXECUTOR V UNITED STATES; MYERS V UNITED STATES.

Wildavsky, Aaron B. (1930–   ) The author of *The Politics of the Budgetary Process* (Boston: Little, Brown, 1964; 4th ed., 1984), which reveals the tactics public managers use to get their budgets passed and explains why rational attempts to reform the budgetary process have always failed. For this classic work alone, Wildavsky would have earned his place in the pantheon of public administration. However, Wildavsky has also made landmark contributions to the study of the U.S. presidency (*see* PRESIDENCIES, TWO), policy analysis, and program implementation and evaluation. Because of the volume, quality, and diversity of his work, Wildavsky is one of the nation's most widely read and influential academic analysts of public affairs.

REFERENCES

Wildavsky's other major works include *Presidential Elections,* with Nelson W. Polsby (New York: Scribner, 1964; 4th ed., 1976);

Implementation, with Jeffrey Pressman (Berkeley and Los Angeles: University of California Press, 1973; 2d ed., 1979);

Speaking Truth to Power: The Art and Craft of Policy Analysis (Boston: Little, Brown, 1979);

How to Limit Government Spending (Berkeley and Los Angeles: University of California Press, 1980);

The Nursing Father: Moses as a Political Leader (University: University of Alabama Press, 1984);

The New Politics of the Budgetary Process (Boston: Little, Brown, 1988).

Williams-Steiger Act *See* OCCUPATIONAL SAFETY AND HEALTH ACT OF 1970.

Woodrow Wilson.

Wilson, (Thomas) Woodrow (1856–1924) The president of the United States from 1913 to 1921. Wilson, who was president of Princeton University (1902–1910) and governor of New Jersey (1911–1913), was also a president of the American Political Science Association; he is considered one of the most influential early voices of both political science and public administration.

Wilson's 1885 classic analysis of American national government, *Congressional Government*, found Congress to be "predominant over its so-called coordinate branches" with congressional power parceled out to the various congressional committees. While the book immediately became, and remains, a landmark in the study of American politics, Wilson's analysis failed to see the revival of a strong energetic presidency—a development to which his presidency would make a great contribution.

It has become customary to trace the origins of the academic discipline of public administration to Wilson's 1887 article, "The Study of Administration." Wilson attempted nothing less than to refocus political science. Rather than be concerned with the great maxims of lasting political truth, he argued that political science should concentrate on how governments are administered. In his words: "It is getting to be harder to run a constitution than to frame one." It was in this essay that Wilson put forth the then radical notion that politics should be separate from administration. *See* POLITICS-ADMINISTRATION DICHOTOMY. *Compare to* NEW FREEDOM.

REFERENCES

Wilson's most enduring scholarly works are *Congressional Government: A Study in American Politics* (Boston: Houghton Mifflin, 1885; Baltimore: Johns Hopkins University Press, 1981);

The study of administration, *Political Science Quarterly* 2 (June 1887).

For appreciations of his contributions to public administration, see Louis Brownlow, Woodrow Wilson and public administration, *Public Administration Review* 16 (Spring 1956);

Richard J. Stillman II, Woodrow Wilson and the study of administration: A new look at an old essay, *American Political Science Review* 67 (June 1973);

Jack Rabin and James S. Bowman, eds., *Politics and Administration: Woodrow Wilson and American Public Administration* (New York: Dekker, 1984).

The standard biographies of Wilson are Ray Stannard Baker, *Woodrow Wilson: Life and Letters,* 8 vols. (Garden City, NY: Doubleday, 1927–1939);

Arthur S. Link, *Wilson,* 5 vols. (Princeton, NJ: Princeton University Press, 1947–   ). Link and others also edited Wilson's papers (1966–   ) for Princeton University Press.

The Woodrow Wilson Administration

Major Accomplishments

- The Federal Reserve System.
- The modern federal income tax.
- The Federal Trade Commission.
- The involvement of the United States in World War I on the side of Britain and France and against Germany.
- The League of Nations.

Major Frustrations

- His inability to mediate peace with warring European powers.
- U.S. intervention in the Mexican civil war.
- The Versailles Treaty, which ended World War I but sowed the seeds of World War II.
- His inability to have the Congress approve U.S. participation in the League of Nations.

---

window A military, diplomatic, or political term for a time frame when there is either an opportunity for achievement or a vulnerability to danger. For example, international developments may create a window of opportunity for a diplomatic breakthrough; or a new weapon system may be deployed to close a window of vulnerability.

REFERENCES

Robert H. Johnson, Periods of peril: The window of vulnerability and other myths, *Foreign Affairs* 61 (Spring 1983);

Richard Ned Lebow, Windows of opportunity: Do states jump through them? *International Security* 9 (Summer 1984).

withholding tax *See* TAX, WITHHOLDING.

witness A person who has knowledge of the circumstances of a case and who may present such knowledge as evidence in a court case. Under the Sixth Amendment, someone accused of a crime has the right to be confronted in court by witnesses to alleged crimes and compel the attendance of favorable witnesses. Forcing the attendance of witnesses who may not wish to testify is known as compulsory process. This was upheld by the Supreme Court in *Washington v Texas,* 388 U.S. 14 (1967).

REFERENCE

Jack Wenik, Forcing the bystander to get involved: A case for a statute requiring witnesses to report crime, *Yale Law Journal* 94 (June 1985).

witness, expert   A technical expert who, because of special knowledge, is allowed to testify at a trial not only about the facts of the case but also about conclusions that may be drawn by an expert from the facts.

REFERENCE

Sandra S. Evans and Joseph E. Scott, Social scientists as expert witnesses: Their use, misuse, and sometimes abuse, *Law and Policy Quarterly* 5 (April 1983).

Wolf v Colorado   See MAPP V OHIO.

women's liberation movement   The contemporary social, economic, and political efforts of women to achieve equality with men in all aspects of life. The movement was the major force behind the effort to get the Equal Rights Amendment ratified. The origins of the American women's liberation movement are often traced to a letter that Abigail Adams (1744–1818) wrote in 1776 to her husband, the future president John Adams, about American independence:

> I long to hear that you have declared an independency. And in the new code of laws which I suppose it will be necessary for you to make, I desire you would remember the ladies, and be more generous and favorable to them than your ancestors. . . . If particular care and attention is not paid to the ladies, we are determined to foment a rebellion and will not hold ourselves bound by any laws in which we have no voice or representation.

REFERENCES

Jo Freeman, The origins of the women's liberation movement, *American Journal of Sociology* 78 (January 1973);

Barbara Deckard Sinclair, *The Women's Movement,* 3d ed. (New York: Harper & Row, 1983);

Sylvia Ann Hewlett, *A Lesser Life: The Myth of Women's Liberation in America* (New York: Morrow, 1986).

Major Political Voices in the Modern Women's Movement

Berry, Mary Frances (1938–   )   A major scholar of the black experience in America who, as a member of the U.S. Commission on Civil Rights, has been a significant voice on civil rights and women's movement issues.

REFERENCES

Some of her recent books are *Black Resistance, White Law: A History of Constitutional Racism in America* (New York: Appleton-Century-Crofts, 1971);

Military Necessity and Civil Rights Policy: Black Citizenship and the Constitution (Port Washington, NY: Kennikat, 1977);

Long Memory: The Black Experience in America, with John W. Blassingame (New York: Oxford University Press, 1982).

Ferraro, Geraldine (1935–   )   The congresswoman from New York who was the Democratic nominee for vice president in 1984, the first woman to be placed on the national ticket of a major party.

REFERENCE

For her autobiography, see *Ferraro: My Story* (New York: Bantam, 1985).

Friedan, Betty (1921–   )   The author of *The Feminine Mystique* (New York: Norton, 1963), the book often credited with reviving the women's movement by raising the consciousness of women about the subtle forms of discrimination and victimization to which they were systematically subjected.

REFERENCE

Her latest book is *The Second Stage* (New York: Summit, 1981).

Ford, Betty (1918–   )   The wife of President Gerald Ford, who used her position as FIRST LADY to actively support the Equal

Rights Amendment and other issues of concern to the women's movement.

REFERENCE

For her autobiography, see *The Times of My Life* (New York: Harper & Row, 1978).

Schlafly, Phyllis (1924–   ) Not a member of the women's liberation movement but the leading conservative voice on the role of women in American society. Schlafly led the fight against the ratification of the Equal Rights Amendment, and won.

REFERENCE

For a biography, see Carol Felsenthal, *The Sweetheart of the Silent Majority: The Biography of Phyllis Schlafly* (Garden City, NY: Doubleday, 1981).

Smeal, Eleanor (1939–   ) A former president of the National Organization of Women (1977–1982; 1985–1987) and a major voice on women's movement issues.

REFERENCE

See her *Why and How Women Will Elect the Next President* (New York: Harper & Row, 1984).

Steinem, Gloria (1934–   ) A founder, in 1972, and editor of *MS* magazine; cofounder of the National Women's Political Caucus. Steinem has been a major media advocate of the women's movement.

REFERENCE

For her autobiography, see *Outrageous Acts and Everyday Rebellions* (New York: Holt, Rinehart & Winston, 1983).

Woodson v North Carolina See CRUEL AND UNUSUAL PUNISHMENT.

Wood v Strickland 420 U.S. 308 (1975) The U.S. Supreme Court ruling that created new standards for the immunity of public employees from civil suits for damages. The Court held that a school board member (and by implication other public employees) is not immune from liability for damages "if he knew or reasonably should have known that the action he took within his sphere of official responsibility would violate the constitutional

rights of the students affected, or if he took the action with the malicious intention to cause a deprivation of constitutional rights or other injury to the student."

REFERENCE

David H. Rosenbloom, Public administrators' official immunity and the Supreme Court: Developments during the 1970s, *Public Administration Review* 40 (March/April 1980).

workers' compensation Industrial accident insurance (also known as workmen's compensation) designed to provide cash benefits and medical care for a worker injured on the job and monetary payments to survivors for a worker killed on the job. This was the first form of social insurance to develop widely in the United States.

Workers' compensation was first developed in Germany and Great Britain in the 1880s. In 1908, the U.S. government created a program for certain federal employees. By 1920, all but a handful of states had laws encouraging workmen's compensation in private industry. There are now fifty-four different workers' compensation programs in operation: each of the fifty states and Puerto Rico has its own program and there are three federal workers' compensation programs—covering federal government and private employees in the District of Columbia and covering longshoremen and harbor workers throughout the country.

Before the passage of workmen's compensation laws, an injured employee ordinarily had to file suit against his or her employer and, in order to recover damages, had to prove that the injury was due to the employer's negligence. The first workmen's compensation laws during the early twentieth century introduced the principle that a worker incurring an occupational injury would be compensated regardless of fault or blame in the accident and with a minimum of delay and legal formality. In turn, the employer's liability was limited, because workmen's compensation benefits became the exclusive remedy for work-related injuries.

REFERENCES

Joel A. Thompson, Outputs and outcomes of state workmen's compensation laws, *Journal of Politics* 43 (November 1981);

James R. Chelius, The influence of workers' compensation on safety incentives, *Industrial and Labor Relations Review* 35 (January 1982).

workfare　Any public welfare program that requires welfare payment recipients to work (work + welfare = workfare) or to enroll in a formal job-training program.

REFERENCES

Linda E. Demkovich, Does workfare work? *National Journal,* July 14, 1981;

Valerie Englander and Fred Englander, Workfare in New Jersey: A five-year assessment, *Policy Studies Review* 5 (August 1985).

working class　All who work for wages, usually at manual labor. When the term is used politically, it tends to exclude managers, professionals, and anyone who is not at the lower end of the educational and economic scales.

REFERENCES

Andrew Levison, *The Working-Class Majority* (New York: Coward, McCann, and Geoghegan, 1974);

Maurice F. Neufeld, Daniel J. Leab, and Dorothy Swanson, *American Working Class History: A Representative Bibliography* (New York: Bowker, 1983);

Seymour Martin Lipset, Radicalism or reformism: The sources of working-class politics, *American Political Science Review* 77 (March 1983).

work to rule　A work slowdown in which all of the formal work rules are so scrupulously obeyed that productivity suffers. Those working to rule seek to place pressure on management without losing pay by going on strike. Work-to-rule protests are particularly popular in the public sector, where formal strikes may be illegal.

World Court　The International Court of Justice established by the United Nations Charter in 1945. The present World Court succeeded the Permanent Court of International Justice, established in 1920 by the League of Nations. Located in The Hague (Netherlands), the World Court consists of fifteen judges elected by the United Nations, each from a different country. Because the court has no powers of enforcement, it usually considers only cases brought before it by the disputing nations, themselves. Consequently, the World Court is not really a court but rather a panel for the arbitration of minor international disputes. How is "minor" defined here? It means that the case is of such significance (or insignificance) to a nation's vital interests that the nation is willing to let an "objective" third party resolve it. In 1986, the World Court ruled against the United States in a case concerning the CONTRAS brought before the court by the government of Nicaragua. But since the United States did not recognize the court's jurisdiction in this matter, the ruling had no effect—except that it was of considerable propaganda value to the government of Nicaragua.

REFERENCES

David S. Patterson, The United States and the origins of the World Court, *Political Science Quarterly* 91 (Spring 1976);

Jeffrey B. Golden, The World Court: The qualifications of the judges, *Columbia Journal of Law and Social Problems* 14:1 (1978);

Dana D. Fischer, Decisions to use the International Court of Justice: Four recent cases, *International Studies Quarterly* 26 (June 1982);

Louis B. Sohn, Broadening the advisory jurisdiction of the International Court of Justice, *American Journal of International Law* 77 (January 1983);

Richard Falk, The role of the International Court of Justice, *Journal of International Affairs* 37 (Winter 1984);

Abram Chayes, Nicaragua, the United States and the World Court, *Columbia Law Review* 85 (November 1985).

writ　A document issued by a judicial officer ordering or forbidding the performance of a specified act. Writs include arrest warrants, search warrants, subpoenas, and summonses.

write-in vote　*See* VOTE, WRITE-IN.

writ of certiorari　*See* CERTIORARI.

writ of habeas corpus A writ directing a person detaining a prisoner to bring him or her before a judicial officer to determine the lawfulness of the imprisonment. (Habeas corpus is Latin meaning you have the body.) This writ is one of the oldest protections of personal liberty and is considered fundamental to due process of law. Originally, the writ of habeas corpus was a pretrial device that enabled persons imprisoned pursuant to executive order to attack the legality of their detention. Subsequently, the concept of the writ has been expanded so that anyone whose freedom has been officially restrained may petition a federal court to test whether that restraint was legally imposed. In this manner of use, it has become an important means of postconviction attacks upon criminal convictions in state and federal courts. The Supreme Court has curtailed the availability of this device in state convictions by requiring full compliance with and exhaustion of state remedies before permitting the issuance of a writ of habeas corpus from a federal court.

Article I, Section 9, of the Constitution provides that "the privilege of the writ of habeas corpus shall not be suspended, unless when in cases of rebellion or invasion the public safety may require it." The privilege of the writ is significant because it guarantees that someone arrested will be brought before a judge and not simply be left to rot in prison. During the Civil War, President Abraham Lincoln temporarily suspended the writ of habeas corpus. But after the war, in *Ex parte Milligan*, 4 Wallace 2 (1866), the Supreme Court held that he had no authority to do so. This was the last attempt to suspend habeas corpus in the United States.

Because habeas corpus is a vital safeguard against unlawful imprisonment, it is strange that it is explicitly mentioned only in the context of its suspension; nowhere in the Constitution is this right affirmatively conferred. Nevertheless, there is a long-standing statutory authorization to federal courts to exercise the habeas corpus power. *See also* ABLEMAN V BOOTH.

REFERENCES

David L. Martin, When Lincoln suspended habeas corpus, *American Bar Association Journal* 60 (January 1974);

Neil D. McFeeley, A change of direction: Habeas corpus from Warren to Burger, *Western Political Quarterly* 32 (June 1979);

Jim Smith, Federal habeas corpus—A need for reform, *Journal of Criminal Law & Criminology* 73 (Fall 1982).

writ of mandamus *See* MANDAMUS/WRIT OF MANDAMUS.

Wygant v Jackson Board of Education 90 L. Ed. 2d 260 (1986) The U.S. Supreme Court case that held that white teachers could not be laid off to preserve the jobs of minority group members. The Court held that while "societal discrimination" was not sufficient reason for racially discriminatory layoffs, such layoffs might be permissible if it was a part of a "narrowly tailored" remedy for past patterns of discrimination by the employer. The Court was careful to distinguish between racially based layoffs and racially conscious hiring. The former imposes a greater burden on the individual excluded.

yankees 1 The United States in general; all U.S. citizens. 2 The northerners during the American Civil War. 3 The colonial settlers of New England. There are several explanations of the origin of the word. It was the theory of James Fenimore Cooper (1789–1851), the novelist who wrote *The Last of the Mohicans* (1826) and the *Deerslayer* (1841), that yankee is how the Indians pronounced *l'anglais*, the French word for the English. But other authorities, such as H. L. Mencken (1880–1956), contend that it is a corruption of Jan Kees, an unkind Dutch nickname, meaning John Cheese. The Dutch who first settled New York applied the name to the English who followed. By the mid-eighteenth century, the word was used to refer to any resident of the English colonies.

Yates v United States See DENNIS V UNITED STATES.

Yeshiva University decision See NATIONAL LABOR RELATIONS BOARD V YESHIVA UNIVERSITY.

yield 1 Profits as measured by a percentage of money invested. 2 The interest rate on funds deposited in a bank. 3 The net return of a tax after the expenses of collecting and administering it are deducted. 4 A parliamentary procedure whereby a legislator holding the floor allows another member to speak. This kind of yielding can be temporary (as in yielding for a question) or permanent (if the yielder must be officially recognized to speak again). 5 The energy produced by a nuclear explosion usually measured in terms of tons of TNT. For example, a nuclear explosion of one megaton is the equivalent to one million tons of TNT.

Yippies Members of the Youth International Party, which in the late 1960s became well known for civil disobedience in general and Vietnam War protests in particular. *Compare to* HIPPIES.

Youngberg v Romeo 457 U.S. 307 (1982) The U.S. Supreme Court case that held that involuntarily committed residents at public facilities for the mentally retarded have "constitutionally protected interests in conditions of reasonable care and safety, reasonably nonrestrictive confinement conditions, and such training as may be required by these interests."

Youngstown Sheet and Tube Co. v Sawyer 343 U.S. 579 (1952) The U.S. Supreme Court case involving the constitutionality of President Harry S Truman's executive order directing the secretary of Commerce to take possession of and operate the nation's steel mills in connection with a labor dispute that threatened to disrupt war production. By a vote of six to three, the Supreme Court held that the president exceeded his constitutional powers.
REFERENCES
John L. Blackman, Jr., *Presidential Seizure in Labor Disputes* (Cambridge, MA: Harvard University Press, 1967);
Chong-do Hah and Robert M. Lindquist, The 1952 steel seizure revisited: A systematic study in presidential decision making, *Administrative Science Quarterly* 20 (December 1975);
Maeva Marcus, *Truman and the Steel Seizure Case: The Limits of Presidential Power* (New York: Columbia University Press, 1977).

Seizing the Steel Mills

President Harry S Truman had a problem in 1952. We were in the midst of the Korean War and the American steel industry was about to be shut down by a strike. A prolonged strike would seriously impair defense production, hamper the war effort, and—if it lasted long enough—endanger the lives of the front-line soldiers. Because of federal wartime price controls, the steel companies had to get government approval for the price increase they felt was needed to meet the union wage demands. While the president was willing to grant "a reasonable price increase," he felt that the steel companies' requests were "entirely out of reason"—far more than was necessary to meet wage demands.

The president initially referred the dispute to the Wage Stabilization Board. While this delayed the strike, the board was unable to gain a settlement, and after a delay of more than three months, the strike was scheduled for April 9.

Truman waited until the afternoon of the day before the scheduled shutdown, and then issued Executive Order 10340 authorizing Secretary of Commerce Charles Sawyer to seize the steel mills. While government seizure sounds ominous, it did not mean confiscation but that the government would assume temporary custody: the same people who worked for and managed the steel plants would continue to do their jobs. The only point of the seizure was to insure uninterrupted production. As Truman told the American people in a radio address: "With American troops facing the enemy on the field of battle, I would not be living up to my oath of office if I failed to do whatever is required to provide them with the weapons and ammunition they need for their survival."

The steel companies obeyed the seizure order under protest and promptly took the issue to court. With almost unprecedented speed, the case reached the Supreme Court. In *Youngstown Sheet and Tube Company v Sawyer*, the justices ruled that the president had exceeded his constitutional powers. The Court did not deny that a president has the inherent power of seizure in cases of national emergency. But the Congress had specifically considered the possibility of this kind of dispute when it debated the Taft-Hartley Act just a few years before and, in the opinion of Justice Felix Frankfurter, "chose not to lodge this power in the president." While the Congress did not prohibit presidential seizure during industrial disputes, it had "expressed its will to withhold this power from the president as though it had said so in so many words." The president could have invoked the

eighty-day cooling-off period provided for in the act and then gone to the Congress to ask for legislation to deal with the emergency if no settlement was reached. But Truman chose to ignore the provisions of the act—perhaps because it had been passed over his veto.

When the Court's decision reached the president on June 2, he immediately canceled the seizure order and the strike commenced. On June 10, he formally asked the Congress for authority to again seize the steel plants and return them to production; but the Congress took no action. The strike ended on July 24, after lasting fifty-three days. And it ended only after Truman allowed government price controllers to grant a substantial increase in the price of steel, which was exactly what he had wanted to avoid.

Source: Adapted from David H. Rosenbloom and Jay M. Shafritz, *Essentials of Labor Relations* (Reston, VA: Reston/Prentice-Hall, 1985), pp. 95–97.

young Turks **1** Young army officers who sought reforms in the Ottoman empire in the decade prior to World War I. **2** Any newer members of an organization or party who seek to significantly reform it.

yuppy/yuppies Young upwardly mobile professional(s). The term suggests the pursuit of one's own career and the gratification of one's own taste or need, without regard for the interests of others. Yuppies have been an important factor in urban GENTRIFICATION.

REFERENCE

Michael Delli Carpini and Lee Sigelman, Do yuppies matter? Competing explanations of their political distinctiveness, *Public Opinion Quarterly* 50 (Winter 1986).

Z

zero-based budgeting *See* BUDGETING, ZERO-BASED.

zero out To totally destroy, budgetarily speaking.

zoning The process by which local government can designate the types of structures and activities for a particular area. Zoning began in the 1920s to protect neighborhoods from the encroachments of business and industry and to preserve their economic and social integrity. It involves a highly complex legal process, which is often impacted by local politics.

REFERENCES

Richard Babcock, *The Zoning Game: Municipal Practices and Policies* (Madison: University of Wisconsin Press, 1966);

Stanislaw J. Makielski, Jr., *The Politics of Zoning* (New York: Columbia University Press, 1966);

Seymour I. Toll, *Zoned America* (New York: Grossman, 1969);

Peter M. Degnan, Zoning and the judiciary: A policy of limited review, *Emory Law Journal* 30 (Summer 1981);

Kenneth Pearlman, Zoning and the First Amendment, *Urban Lawyer* 16 (Spring 1984).

zoning, aesthetic A zoning policy operating in the interests of beauty. According to Justice William O. Douglas's majority opinion in the Supreme Court case of *Berma v Parker,* 348 U.S. 26 (1954), "It is within the power of the legislature to determine that the community should be beautiful as well as healthy."

zoning, affirmative Land-use regulations that seek neighborhood development that will benefit the disadvantaged.

zoning, cluster A zoning policy that allows builders to reduce lot sizes below normal standards so that the "extra" land is retained as open space for the community.

zoning, Euclidian A zoning policy that keeps apartments and businesses out of single-home residential areas. This kind of zoning was adopted by Euclid, Ohio, and the subject of the Supreme Court case of *Village of Euclid v Ambler Realty Company,* 272 U.S. 365 (1926), which asserted that zoning was a valid exercise of local government powers.

zoning, exclusionary A zoning policy that specifically excludes some specified types of usages, such as home sites on lots smaller than an acre.

REFERENCES

Richard Babcock and Fred Bosselman, *Exclusionary Zoning: Land Use Regulation and Housing in the 1970s* (New York: Praeger, 1973);

Dennis A. LaRussa, Exclusionary zoning: An overview, *Tulane Law Review* 47 (June 1973);

Michael N. Danielson, The politics of exclusionary zoning in suburbia, *Political Science Quarterly* 91 (Spring 1976).

zoning, inclusionary A zoning policy that requires builders to provide (at reduced rates) a portion of new housing units for moderate and low-income families.

zoning, open-space A zoning policy requiring developers to provide a certain amount of open space, depending upon the size of their project.

REFERENCE

Jon A. Kusler, Open space zoning: Valid regulation or invalid taking, *Minnesota Law Review* 57 (November 1972).

zoning, spot Changing the zoning of a parcel of land without regard for the zoning plan of the entire area.

zoning variance A lawful deviation from normal zoning policy.

REFERENCE

David P. Bryden, The impact of variances: A study of statewide zoning, *Minnesota Law Review* 61 (May 1977).

Zorach v Clauson 343 U.S. 306 (1952) The U.S. Supreme Court case that upheld the New York City policy of allowing students, with their parents' written permission, to have religious instruction during the school day but away from school property. This practice was not considered a violation of the First Amendment's establishment of religion clause.

REFERENCE

Frank J. Sorauf, *Zorach v Clauson:* The impact of a Supreme Court decision, *American Political Science Review* 53 (September 1959).

The Constitution of the United States

Note: Margin notes explain certain constitutional passages.

We the People of the United States, In Order to form a more perfect Union, establish Justice, insure domestic Tranquility, provide for the common defense, promote the general Welfare, and secure the Blessings of Liberty to ourselves and our Posterity, do ordain and establish this Constitution for the United States of America.

Article I

Section 1. All legislative Powers herein granted shall be vested in a Congress of the United States, which shall consist of a Senate and House of Representatives.

> Provides for a Congress, a bicameral legislature, the first branch of government.

Section 2. The House of Representatives shall be composed of members chosen every second Year by the People of the several States, and the Electors in each State shall have the Qualifications requisite for Electors of the most numerous Branch of the State Legislature.

> Provides for a two-year term for members of the House of Representatives.

No person shall be a representative who shall not have attained to the Age of twenty five Years, and been seven Years a Citizen of the United States, and who shall not, when elected, be an Inhabitant of that State in which he shall be chosen.

> Describes qualifications for House members: citizenship, twenty-five years of age.

Representatives and direct Taxes shall be apportioned among the several States which may be included within this union, according to their respective Numbers, which shall be determined by adding to the whole Number of free Persons, including those bound to Service for a Term of Years, and excluding Indians not taxed, three fifths of all other Persons. The actual Enumeration shall be made within three Years after the first Meeting of the Congress of the United States, and within every subsequent Term

> Apportions representatives among states on basis of state population. Except for several small states, each representative today represents more than five hundred thousand people. A decennial (ten-year) census determines the number

---

Source of annotations: Adapted from William J. Keefe, Henry J. Abraham, William H. Flanigan, Charles O. Jones, Morris S. Ogul, and John W. Spanier, *American Democracy: Institutions, Politics, and Policies,* 2d ed. (Chicago: Dorsey, 1986), pp. 579–96.

of House seats to be awarded each state. States may win or lose seats following the census.

Gives governors authority to call an election to fill a House vacancy.

Provides for a Speaker of the House, chosen by the majority party, to preside over the chamber. The impeachment process (to remove federal officials from office) begins in the House of Representatives.

Provides for two senators from each state, a six-year term, one-third of Senate to be elected every two years. Since the passage of the Seventeenth Amendment, senators have been popularly elected—a democratizing reform.

Allows governors to make temporary appointments to fill Senate vacancies.

Describes qualifications for Senate members: citizenship, thirty years of age.

Allows vice president to vote to break a tie in Senate.

Provides for a presiding officer of the Senate. The president pro tempore is

of ten Years, in such Manner as they shall by Law direct. The Number of Representatives shall not exceed one for every thirty Thousand, but each State shall have at Least one Representative; and until such enumeration shall be made, the State of New Hampshire shall be entitled to chuse three, Massachusetts eight, Rhode-Island and Providence Plantations one, Connecticut five, New York six, New Jersey four, Pennsylvania eight, Delaware one, Maryland six, Virginia ten, North Carolina five, South Carolina five, and Georgia three.

When vacancies happen in the Representation from any State, the Executive Authority thereof shall issue Writs of Election to fill such Vacancies.

The House of Representatives shall chuse their speaker and other Officers; and shall have the sole Power of Impeachment.

Section 3. The Senate of the United States shall be composed of two Senators from each State, chosen by the Legislature thereof, for six Years; and each Senator shall have one Vote.

Immediately after they shall be assembled in Consequence of the first Election, they shall be divided as equally as may be into three Classes. The Seats of the Senators of the first Class shall be vacated at the Expiration of the second Year, of the second Class at the Expiration of the fourth Year, and of the third Class at the Expiration of the sixth Year, so that one third may be chosen every second Year; and if Vacancies happen by Resignation, or otherwise, during the Recess of the Legislature of any State, the Executive thereof may make temporary Appointments until the next Meeting of the Legislature, which shall then fill such Vacancies.

No Person shall be a Senator who shall not have attained to the Age of thirty Years, and been nine Years a Citizen of the United States, and who shall not, when elected, be an Inhabitant of that State for which he shall be chosen.

The Vice President of the United States shall be President of the Senate, but shall have no Vote, unless they be equally divided.

The Senate shall chuse their other Officers, and also a President pro tempore, in the Absence of the Vice President, or when he shall exercise the Office of the President of the United States.

traditionally the senior member of the majority party.

The Senate shall have the sole Power to try all Impeachments. When sitting for that Purpose, they shall be on Oath of Affirmation. When the President of the United States is tried, the Chief Justice shall preside; And no Person shall be convicted without the Concurrence of two thirds of the Members present.

Describes second stage of the impeachment process: Senate acts as a court to try a federal official impeached (accused) by the House. Conviction (and removal from office) requires two-thirds vote of members present. The impeachment process is a gun behind the door, a deterrent to the waywardness of federal officials.

Judgment in Cases of Impeachment shall not extend further than to removal from Office, and disqualification to hold and enjoy any Office of honor, Trust or Profit under the United States: but the Party convicted shall nevertheless be liable and subject to Indictment, Trial, Judgment and Punishment, according to law.

Section 4. The Times, Places and Manner of holding Elections for Senators and Representatives, shall be prescribed in each State by the Legislature thereof; but the Congress may at any time by Law make or alter such regulations, except as to the Places of chusing Senators.

Provides that congressional elections will be held on first Tuesday after first Monday in November in even-numbered years.

The Congress shall assemble at least once in every Year, and such Meeting shall be on the first Monday in December, unless they shall by Law appoint a different Day.

Provides for opening of congressional session. Changed by Twentieth Amendment to January 3.

Section 5. Each House shall be the Judge of the Elections, Returns and Qualifications of its own Members, and a Majority of each shall constitute a Quorum to do Business; but a smaller Number may adjourn from day to day, and may be authorized to compel the Attendance of absent Members, in such Manner, and under such Penalties as each House may provide.

Allows House and Senate to refuse to seat a member judged to be improperly elected. Requires majority of members to transact business. Allows each house to establish its own rules of procedure. Requires two-thirds vote to expel a member.

Each House may determine the Rules for its Proceedings, punish its Members for disorderly Behaviour, and, with the Concurrence of two thirds, expel a Member.

Each House shall keep a Journal of its Proceedings, and from time to time publish the same, excepting such Parts as may in their Judgment require Secrecy; and the Yeas and Nays of the Members of either House on any question shall, at the Desire of one fifth of those Present, be entered on the Journal.

Neither House, during the Session of Congress, shall, without the Consent of the other, adjourn for more than three days, nor to any other Place than that in which the two Houses shall be sitting.

Section 6. The Senators and Representatives shall receive a Compensation for their Services, to be ascertained by Law, and paid out of the Treasury of the United States. They shall in all Cases, except Treason, Felony and Breach of the Peace, be privileged from Arrest during their Attendance at the Session of their respective Houses, and in going to and returning from the same; and for any Speech or Debate in either House, they shall not be questioned in any other Place.

Provides for congressional salary to be established by members. Gives members freedom of speech and immunity from arrest. Immunity to contribute to the independence of the legislative branch.

603

Prevents a member of Congress from holding a position in another branch of government. Reaffirms principle of separation of powers.

No Senator or Representative shall, during the Time for which he was elected, be appointed to any civil Office under the Authority of the United States, which shall have been created, or the Emoluments whereof shall have been encreased during such time; and no Person holding any Office under the United States, shall be a Member of either House during his Continuance in Office.

Provides that tax legislation will originate in the House of Representatives but that the Senate may change it.

Section 7. All bills for raising Revenue shall originate in the House of Representatives; but the Senate may propose or concur with Amendments as on other Bills.

Provides for presidential veto, a basic element in the doctrine of checks and balances. Vetoed bill may be overridden (and thus become law) by a two-thirds majority in both houses. The president can "pocket veto" by refusing to sign a bill sent to him within the last ten days of a session.

Every Bill which shall have passed the House of Representatives and the Senate, shall, before it become a Law, be presented to the President of the United States; If he approve he shall sign it, but if not he shall return it, with his Objections to that House in which it shall have originated, who shall enter the Objections at large on their Journal, and proceed to reconsider it. If after such Reconsideration two thirds of that House shall agree to pass the Bill, it shall be sent, together with the Objections, to the other House, by which it shall likewise be reconsidered, and if approved by two thirds of that House, it shall become a Law. But in all such Cases the Votes of both Houses shall be determined by Yeas and Nays, and the Names of the Persons voting for and against the Bill shall be entered on the Journal of each House respectively. If any Bill shall not be returned by the President within ten Days (Sundays excepted) after it shall have been presented to him, the Same shall be a Law, in like Manner as if he had signed it, unless the Congress by their Adjournment prevent its Return, in which Case it shall not be a Law.

Provides that constitutional amendments adopted by Congress are not subject to presidential veto. They are ratified (or rejected) by state legislatures or state conventions.

Every Order, Resolution, or Vote to which the Concurrence of the Senate and House of Representatives may be necessary (except on a question of Adjournment) shall be presented to the President of the United States; and before the Same shall take Effect, shall be approved by him, or being disapproved by him, shall be repassed by two thirds of the Senate and House of Representatives, according to the Rules and Limitations prescribed in the Case of a Bill.

Lists the express or enumerated powers of Congress: to tax, borrow money, regulate commerce, provide for a monetary system, establish provisions for naturalization, establish lower federal courts, declare war, and maintain armed services.

Section 8. The Congress shall have Power To lay and collect Taxes, Duties, Imposts and Excises, to pay the Debts and provide for the common Defence and general Welfare of the United States; but all Duties, Imposts and Excises shall be uniform throughout the United States;

To borrow Money on the credit of the United States;

To regulate Commerce with foreign Nations, and among the several States, and with the Indian Tribes;

To establish an uniform Rule of Naturalization, and uniform Laws on the subject of Bankruptcies throughout the United States;

To coin Money, regulate the Value thereof, and of foreign Coin, and fix the Standard of Weights and Measures;

To provide for the Punishment of counterfeiting the Securities and current Coin of the United States;

To establish Post Offices and post Roads;

To promote the Progress of Science and useful Arts, by securing for limited Times to Authors and Inventors the exclusive Right to their respective Writings and Discoveries;

To constitute Tribunals inferior to the supreme Court;

To define and punish Piracies and Felonies committed on the high Seas, and Offences against the Law of Nations;

To declare War, grant Letters of Marque and Reprisal, and make Rules concerning Captures on Land and Water;

To raise and support Armies, but no Appropriation of Money to that Use shall be for a longer Term than two Years;

To provide and maintain a Navy;

To make Rules for the Government and Regulation of the land and naval Forces;

To provide for calling forth the Militia to execute the Laws of the Union, suppress Insurrections and repel Invasions;

To provide for organizing, arming, and disciplining, the Militia, and for governing such Part of them as may be employed in the Service of the United States, reserving to the States respectively, the Appointment of the Officers, and the Authority of training the Militia according to the discipline prescribed by Congress;

To exercise exclusive Legislation in all Cases whatsoever, over such District (not exceeding ten Miles square) as may, by Cession of particular States, and the Acceptance of Congress, become the Seat of the Government of the United States, and to exercise like Authority over all Places purchased by the Consent of the Legislature of the State in which the Same shall be for the Erection of Forts, Magazines, Arsenals, dock-Yards, and other needful Buildings;-And

To make all Laws which shall be necessary and proper for carrying into Execution the foregoing Powers, and all other Powers vested by this Constitution in the Government of the United States, or in any Department or Officer thereof.

Sets forth necessary and proper clause, also known as the elastic clause. Gives Congress many powers not expressly granted in Article I, Section 8.

Section 9. The Migration or Importation of such Persons as any of the States now existing shall think proper to admit, shall not be prohibited by the Congress prior to the Year one thousand eight hundred and eight, but a Tax or duty may be imposed on such Importation, not exceeding ten dollars for each Person.

Presages a ban on importation of slaves, which took effect in 1808.

The Privilege of the Writ of Habeas Corpus shall not be suspended, unless when in Cases of Rebellion or Invasion the public Safety may require it.

Protects basic human liberties. The writ of habeas corpus is the right of an imprisoned person to be brought before a judge to decide the legality of his or her detention. A bill of attainder is a legislative act declaring a person or persons guilty of a crime and meting out punishment for that crime. An ex post facto law is a criminal law that takes effect after the fact.

Gives Congress control of the purse strings of the nation. No legislative power is more important.

No Bill of Attainder or ex post facto Law shall be passed.

No Capitation, or other direct, Tax shall be laid, unless in Proportion to the Census or Enumeration herein before directed to be taken.

No Tax or Duty shall be laid on Articles exported from any State.

No Preference shall be given by any Regulation of Commerce or Revenue to the Ports of one State over those of another: nor shall Vessels bound to, or from, one State be obliged to enter, clear, or pay Duties in another.

No Money shall be drawn from the Treasury, but in Consequence of Appropriations made by Law; and a regular Statement and Account of the Receipts and Expenditures of all public Money shall be published from time to time.

No Title of Nobility shall be granted by the United States: And no Person holding any office of Profit or Trust under them, shall, without the Consent of the Congress, accept of any present, Emolument, Office, or Title, of any kind whatever, from any King, Prince, or foreign States.

Prohibits the states from making treaties with foreign nations, coining money, passing bills of attainder, or passing ex post facto laws.

Section 10. No State shall enter into any Treaty, Alliance, or Confederation; grant Letters of Marque and Reprisal; coin Money; emit Bills of Credit; make any Thing but gold and silver coin a Tender in Payment of Debts; pass any Bill of Attainder, ex post facto Law, or Law impairing the Obligation of Contracts, or grant any Title of Nobility.

No State shall, without the Consent of the Congress, lay any Imposts or Duties on Imports or Exports, except what may be absolutely necessary for executing its inspection Laws: and the net Produce of all Duties and Imposts, laid by any State on Imports and Exports, shall be for the Use of the Treasury of the United States; and all such Laws shall be subject to Revision and Controul of the Congress.

No State shall, without the Consent of Congress, lay any Duty of Tonnage, keep Troops, or Ships of War in time of Peace, enter into any Agreement or Compact with another State, or with a foreign Power, or engage in War, unless actually invaded, or in such imminent Danger as will not admit of delay.

Article II

Gives a broad grant of authority to the president. Presidential actions and court decisions have helped explain this vague grant of power.

Gives each state as many presidential electors as it

Section 1. The executive Power shall be vested in a President of the United States of America. He shall hold his Office during the Term of four Years, and, together with the Vice President, chosen for the same term, be elected, as follows:

Each State shall appoint, in such Manner as the Legislature thereof may direct, a Number of Electors, equal to the whole

Number of Senators and Representatives to which the State may be entitled in the Congress: but no Senator or Representative, or Person holding an office of Trust or Profit under the United States, shall be appointed an Elector.

has representatives and senators. Today, electors are popularly elected; a presidential candidate who wins a *plurality* of popular votes in a state wins *all* of that state's electoral votes.

The Electors shall meet in their respective States, and vote by Ballot for two Persons, of whom one at least shall not be an Inhabitant of the same State with themselves. And they shall make a List of all the persons voted for, and of the Number of Votes for each; which List they shall sign and certify, and transmit sealed to the Seat of the Government of the United States, directed to the President of the Senate. The President of the Senate shall, in the Presence of the Senate and House of Representatives, open all the Certificates, and the Votes shall then be counted. The Person having the greatest Number of Votes shall be the President, if such Number be a Majority of the whole Number of Electors appointed; and if there be more than one who have such Majority, and have an equal Number of Votes, then the House of Representatives shall immediately chuse by Ballot one of them for President: and if no Person have a Majority, then from the five highest on the List the said House shall in like Manner chuse the President. But in chusing the President, the Votes shall be taken by States, the Representation from each State having one Vote; A quorum for this Purpose shall consist of a Member or Members from two thirds of the States, and a Majority of all the States shall be necessary to a Choice. In every Case, after the Choice of the President, the Person having the greatest Number of Votes of the Electors shall be the Vice President. But if there should remain two or more who have equal Votes, the Senate shall chuse from them by Ballot the Vice President.

Provides for election of president and vice president. Replaced by Twelfth Amendment.

The Congress may determine the Time of chusing the Electors and the Day on which they shall give their Votes; which Day shall be the same throughout the United States.

No Person except a natural born Citizen, or a citizen of the United States, at the time of the Adoption of this Constitution, shall be eligible to the Office of President; neither shall any person be eligible to that Office who shall not have attained to the Age of thirty five Years, and been fourteen Years a Resident within the United States.

Describes qualifications for the presidency: natural-born citizen, thirty-five years of age, fourteen years a resident within the United States.

In Case of the Removal of the President from Office, or of his Death, Resignation, or Inability to discharge the Powers and Duties of the said Office, the Same shall devolve on the Vice President, and the Congress may by Law provide for the Case of Removal, Death, Resignation or Inability, both of the President and Vice President, declaring what Officer shall then act as President, and such Officer shall act accordingly, until the Disability be removed, or a President shall be elected.

Provides for vice president to succeed to the presidency in the event of the president's death (or resignation, as in the case of Richard M. Nixon). The Twenty-fifth Amendment deals with presidential disability.

The President shall, at stated Times, receive for his Services a Compensation, which shall neither be increased nor diminished during the Period for which he shall have been elected, and he shall not receive within that Period any other Emolument from the United States, or any of them.

Spells out president's oath of office.

Before he enter on the Execution of his Office, he shall take the following Oath of Affirmation:-"I do solemnly swear (or affirm) that I will faithfully execute the Office of President of the United States, and will to the best of my Ability, preserve, protect and defend the Constitution of the United States."

Provides for civilian supremacy by making the president commander in chief of the armed forces. Department heads appointed by the president. Collectively, they now compose the cabinet. A pardon permits the president to forgive persons for all offenses against the United States, except in cases of impeachment. A reprieve delays punishment.

Section 2. The President shall be Commander in Chief of the Army and Navy of the United States, and of the Militia of the several States, when called into the actual Service of the United States; he may require the Opinion, in writing, of the principal Officer in each of the executive Departments, upon any Subject relating to the Duties of their respective Offices, and he shall have power to grant Reprieves and Pardons for Offences against the United States, except in Cases of Impeachment.

Requires that presidential treaties and appointments be approved by the Senate—an important check and balance.

He shall have Power, by and with the Advice and Consent of the Senate, to make Treaties, provided two thirds of the Senators present concur; and he shall nominate, and by and with the Advice and Consent of the Senate, shall appoint Ambassadors, other public Ministers and Consuls, Judges of the supreme Court, and all other Officers of the United States, whose Appointments are not herein otherwise provided for, and which shall be established by Law; but the Congress may by Law vest the Appointment of such inferior officers, as they think proper, in the President alone, in the Courts of Law, or in the Heads of Departments.

Allows the president to make appointments while the Senate is not in session.

The President shall have Power to fill up all Vacancies that may happen during the Recess of the Senate, by granting Commissions which shall expire at the End of their next Session.

Gives a legislative power to the president in his messages to Congress describing his program and recommending the passage of legislation.

Section 3. He shall from time to time give to the Congress Information of the State of the Union, and recommend to their Consideration such Measures as he shall judge necessary and expedient; he may, on extraordinary Occasions, convene both Houses, or either of them, and in Case of Disagreement between them, with Respect to the Time of Adjournment, he may adjourn them to such Time as he shall think proper; he shall receive Ambassadors and other public Ministers; he shall take Care that the Laws be faithfully executed, and shall Commission all of the officers of the United States.

Prescribes removal of the president from office through impeachment proceedings.

Section 4. The President, Vice President and all civil Officers of the United States, shall be removed from Office on Impeachment for, and Conviction of, Treason, Bribery, or other High Crimes and Misdemeanors.

Article III

Section 1. The judicial Power of the United States, shall be vested in one supreme Court, and in such inferior Courts as the Congress may from time to time ordain and establish. The Judges, both of the supreme and inferior Courts, shall hold their Offices during good Behaviour, and shall, at stated Times, receive for their Services, a Compensation, which shall not be diminished during their Continuance in Office.

Establishes a Supreme Court, with other federal courts to be created by Congress. Federal judges, whose appointments must be confirmed by the Senate, to hold office for life, assuming good behavior.

Section 2. The judicial Power shall extend to all Cases, in Law and Equity, arising under this Constitution, the Laws of the United States, and Treaties made, or which shall be made, under their Authority;-to all Cases affecting Ambassadors, other public Ministers and Consuls;-to all Cases of admiralty and maritime Jurisdiction;-to Controversies to which the United States shall be a party;-to Controversies between two or more States; between a State and Citizens of another State;-between Citizens of different States;-between Citizens of the same State claiming Lands under Grants of different States, and between a State, or the Citizens thereof, and foreign States, Citizens or Subjects.

Describes the types of cases and controversies that make up the jurisdiction of federal courts: diplomatic cases, admiralty and maritime cases, controversies between two or more states, and cases between citizens of different states.

In all Cases affecting Ambassadors, other public Ministers and Consuls, and those in which a State shall be Party, the supreme Court shall have original Jurisdiction. In all the other Cases before mentioned, the supreme Court shall have appellate Jurisdiction, both as to Law and Fact, with such Exceptions, and under such Regulations as the Congress shall make.

Describes the types of cases that start in the Supreme Court. Original jurisdiction cases are rare. The Supreme Court is basically an appeals court, with cases appealed to it from state courts and lower federal courts.

The Trial of all Crimes, except in Cases of Impeachment, shall be by Jury; and such Trial shall be held in the State where the said Crimes shall have been committed; but when not committed within any State, the Trial shall be at such Place or Places as the Congress may by Law have directed.

Provides for the right to trial by jury.

Section 3. Treason against the United States, shall consist only in levying War against them, or in adhering to their Enemies, giving them Aid and Comfort. No Person shall be convicted of Treason unless on the Testimony of two Witnesses to the same overt Act, or on Confession in open Court.

Describes treason.

The Congress shall have Power to declare the Punishment of Treason, but no Attainder of Treason shall work Corruption of Blood, or Forfeiture except during the Life of the Person attainted.

Article IV

Section 1. Full Faith and Credit shall be given in each State to the public Acts, Records, and judicial Proceedings of every other State. And the Congress may by general Laws prescribe the Man-

Provides for state recognition of the civil rulings of other states.

ner in which such Acts, Records, and Proceedings shall be proved, and the Effect thereof.

Proscribes states discriminating against citizens of other states. Citizens of one state, for example, may acquire property in another state, engage in normal business there, and have access to that state's courts.

Section 2. The Citizens of each State shall be entitled to all Privileges and Immunities of Citizens in the several States.

Deals with extradition. A person accused of a crime who flees across a state line (under ordinary circumstances) will, when captured, be surrendered to the state from which he or she fled.

A Person charged in any State with Treason, Felony, or other Crime, who shall flee from Justice, and be found in another State, shall on Demand of the executive Authority of the State from which he fled, be delivered up, to be removed to the State having Jurisdiction of the Crime.

Made obsolete by the Thirteenth Amendment, which abolished slavery.

No Person held to Service or Labour in one State, under the Laws thereof, escaping into another, shall, in Consequence of any Law or Regulation therein, be discharged from such Service or Labour, but shall be delivered up on Claim of the Party to whom such Service or Labour may be due.

Describes procedures for admitting new states. Alaska and Hawaii were the last states admitted to the Union.

Section 3. New States may be admitted by the Congress into this Union; but no new State shall be formed or erected within the Jurisdiction of any other State; nor any State be formed by the Junction of two or more States, or Parts of States, without the Consent of the Legislatures of the States concerned as well as of the Congress.

The Congress shall have Power to dispose of and make all needful Rules and Regulations respecting the Territory or other Property belonging to the United States; and nothing in this Constitution shall be so construed as to Prejudice any Claims of the United States, or of any particular State.

Prescribes a republican form of government, in which the majority rules through the election of representatives.

Section 4. The United States shall guarantee to every State in this Union a Republican Form of Government, and shall protect each of them against Invasion; and on Application of the Legislature, or of the Executive (when the Legislature cannot be convened) against domestic Violence.

Article V

Provides for amending the Constitution: proposed by a two-thirds vote of both houses of Congress or by a convention called by Congress in response to the request of two-thirds of the states, ratified by three-fourths of the state legisla-

The Congress, whenever two thirds of both Houses shall deem it necessary, shall propose Amendments to this Constitution, or, on the Application of the Legislatures of two thirds of the several States, shall call a Convention for proposing Amendments, which, in either Case, shall be valid to all Intents and Purposes, as Part of this Constitution, when ratified by the Legislatures of three fourths of the several States, or by Conventions in three fourths thereof, as the one or the other Mode of Ratification may be proposed by the Congress; Provided that no Amendment which may be made prior to the Year One thousand eight hundred and eight shall in any Manner affect the first and fourth Clauses in the Ninth Section of the first Article; and that no State, without its Consent, shall be deprived of its equal Suffrage in the Senate.

tures or by constitutional conventions in three-fourths of the states.

Article VI

All Debts contracted and Engagements entered into, before the Adoption of this Constitution, shall be as valid against the United States under this Constitution, as under the Confederation.

This Constitution, and the Laws of the United States which shall be made in Pursuance thereof; and all Treaties made, or which shall be made, under the Authority of the United States, shall be the supreme Law of the Land; and the Judges in every State shall be bound thereby, any Thing in the Constitution or Laws of any State to the Contrary notwithstanding.

Provides that if a federal and a state law are in conflict, the federal law prevails.

The Senators and Representatives before mentioned, and the Members of the several State Legislatures, and all executive and judicial Officers, both of the United States and of the several States, shall be bound by Oath or Affirmation, to support this Constitution; but no religious Test shall ever be required as a Qualification to any Office or public Trust under the United States.

Prescribes support of the Constitution by state and national officials. Proscribes religion as a qualification for holding public office.

Article VII

The Ratification of the Conventions of nine States shall be sufficient for the Establishment of this Constitution between the States so ratifying the Same.

Describes adoption of the Constitution: consent of nine of the thirteen states.

Done in Convention by the Unanimous Consent of the States present the Seventeenth Day of September in the Year of our Lord one thousand seven hundred and Eighty seven and of the Independence of the United States of America the Twelfth. In witness whereof We have hereunto subscribed our Names.

The first ten amendments were ratified December 15, 1791, and form what is known as the Bill of Rights.

Amendment 1

Congress shall make no law respecting an establishment of religion, or prohibiting the free exercise thereof; or abridging the freedom of speech, or of the press; or the right of the people peaceably to assemble, and to petition the Government for a redress of grievances.

Describes constitutional liberties of citizens: freedom of religion, speech, press, association, assembly, and petition. Many of the most important and best-known Supreme Court decisions deal with the protection of these liberties.

Appendix A

Amendment 2

Empowers states to maintain an armed militia (national guard, in today's terminology).

A well regulated Militia, being necessary to the security of a free State, the right of the people to keep and bear Arms, shall not be infringed.

Amendment 3

Limits the army's right to place soldiers in private homes.

No Soldier shall, in time of peace be quartered in any house, without the consent of the Owner, nor in time of war, but in a manner to be prescribed by law.

Amendment 4

Requires a warrant (legal order from a judicial officer) to search a person's house or place of business.

The right of the people to be secure in their persons, houses, papers, and effects, against unreasonable searches and seizures, shall not be violated, and no Warrants shall issue, but upon probable cause, supported by Oath or affirmation, and particularly describing the place to be searched and the persons or things to be seized.

Amendment 5

Describes legal rights of citizens. A person accused of a serious crime must first be accused by a grand jury. No person can be tried twice for the same crime. Persons are protected from self-incrimination. Due process of law clause protects persons from arbitrary treatment by government.

No person shall be held to answer for a capital, or otherwise infamous crime, unless on a presentment or indictment of a Grand Jury, except in cases arising in the land or naval forces, or in the Militia, when in actual service in time of War or public danger; nor shall any person be subject for the same offence to be twice put in jeopardy of life or limb; nor shall be compelled in any criminal case to be a witness against himself, nor be deprived of life, liberty, or property, without due process of law; nor shall private property be taken for public use, without just compensation.

Amendment 6

Guarantees a defendant in a criminal case a trial without undue delay, a reasonable length of time to prepare his or her case, the right to be informed of the charges, and the right to confront hostile witnesses.

In all criminal prosecutions, the accused shall enjoy the right to a speedy and public trial, by an impartial jury of the State and district wherein the crime shall have been committed, which district shall have been previously ascertained by law, and to be informed of the nature and cause of the accusation; to be confronted with the witnesses against him; to have compulsory process for obtaining witnesses in his favor, and to have the Assistance of Counsel for his defense.

Amendment 7

Requires a jury trial in federal courts in cases involv-

In Suits at common law, where the value in controversy shall exceed twenty dollars, the right of trial by jury shall be preserved, and no fact tried by a jury, shall be otherwise reexamined in any Court of the United States, than according to the rules of the common law.

ing twenty or more dollars. Jury trial can be waived by the parties to the dispute, permitting a judge to settle the case.

Amendment 8

Excessive bail shall not be required, nor excessive fines imposed, nor cruel and unusual punishments inflicted.

Sets general limits on arbitrary government.

Amendment 9

The enumeration in the Constitution, of certain rights, shall not be construed to deny or disparage others retained by the people.

Does not limit the rights of the people to those specifically enumerated.

Amendment 10

The powers not delegated to the United States by the Constitution, nor prohibited by it to the States, are reserved to the States respectively, or to the people.

Limits the power of the national government. From one perspective, the Tenth Amendment is simply a truism.

Amendment 11
[Ratified February 7, 1795]

The Judicial power of the United States shall not be construed to extend to any suit in law or equity, commenced or prosecuted against one of the United States by Citizens of another State, or by Citizens or Subjects of any Foreign State.

Protects a state from being sued in the federal courts by a citizen of another state or by a citizen of a foreign country.

Amendment 12
[Ratified July 27, 1804]

The Electors shall meet in their respective states and vote by ballot for President and Vice-President, one of whom, at least, shall not be an inhabitant of the same state with themselves; they shall name in their ballots the person voted for as President, and in distinct ballots the person voted for as Vice-President, and they shall make distinct lists of all persons voted for as President, and of all persons voted for as Vice-President, and of the number of votes for each, which lists they shall sign and certify, and transmit sealed to the seat of the government of the United States, directed to the President of the Senate;-The President of the Senate shall, in the presence of the Senate and House of Representatives, open all the certificates and the votes shall then be counted;-The person having the greatest number of votes for President, shall be the

Changes the original method by which the president and vice president were selected by requiring presidential electors to cast separate ballots for these offices. If no presidential candidate receives a majority of the electoral votes (270 out of 538), the House of Representatives chooses from among the top three candidates. In this process, each state delegation casts one vote. If no vice presidential candidate receives a majority, the Senate chooses from among the top two candidates.

President, if such number be a majority of the whole number of Electors appointed; and if no person have such majority, then from the persons having the highest numbers not exceeding three on the list of those voted for as President, the House of Representatives shall choose immediately by ballot, the President. But in choosing the President, the votes shall be taken by states, the representation from each state having one vote; a quorum for this purpose shall consist of a member or members from two-thirds of the states, and a majority of all the states shall be necessary to a choice. And if the House of Representatives shall not choose a President whenever the right of choice shall devolve upon them, before the fourth day of March next following, the Vice-President shall act as President, as in the case of the death or other constitutional disability of the President.-The person having the greatest number of votes as Vice-President, shall be the Vice-President, if such number be a majority of the whole number of Electors appointed, and if no person have a majority, then from the two highest numbers on the list, the Senate shall choose the Vice-President; a quorum for the purpose shall consist of two-thirds of the whole number of Senators, and a majority of the whole number shall be necessary to a choice. But no person constitutionally ineligible to the office of President shall be eligible to that of Vice-President of the United States.

Amendment 13
[Ratified December 6, 1865]

Abolishes slavery.

Section 1. Neither slavery nor involuntary servitude, except as a punishment for crime whereof the party shall have been duly convicted, shall exist within the United States, or any place subject to their jurisdiction.

Section 2. Congress shall have the power to enforce this article by appropriate legislation.

Amendment 14
[Ratified July 9, 1868]

Accords former slaves full citizenship. As a result of decisions of the Supreme Court, state governments as well as the federal government are limited by the Bill of Rights. State governments must observe the principles of due process of law and grant all persons equal protection of the laws. This latter clause became the basis for the Su-

Section 1. All persons born or naturalized in the United States, and subject to the jurisdiction thereof, are citizens of the United States and of the State wherein they reside. No State shall make or enforce any law which shall abridge the privileges or immunities of citizens of the United States; nor shall any State deprive any person of life, liberty, or property, without due process of law; nor deny to any person within its jurisdiction the equal protection of the laws.

preme Court's decision outlawing segregated public schools in 1954 (*Brown v Board of Education of Topeka*).

Section 2. Representatives shall be appointed among the several States according to their respective numbers, counting the whole number of persons in each State, excluding Indians not taxed. But when the right to vote at any election for the choice of electors for President and Vice President of the United States, Representatives in Congress, the Executive and Judicial Officers of a State, or the members of the Legislature thereof, is denied to any of the male inhabitants of such State, being twenty-one years of age, and citizens of the United States, or in any way abridged, except for participation in rebellion, or other crime, the basis of representation therein shall be reduced in the proportion which the number of such male citizens shall bear to the whole number of male citizens twenty-one years of age in such State.

Threatens to reduce a state's representation in the House if they don't allow blacks to vote. This section of the Fourteenth Amendment was never applied.

Section 3. No person shall be a Senator or Representative in Congress, or elector of President and Vice President, or hold any office, civil or military, under the United States, or under any State, who, having previously taken an oath, as a member of Congress, or as an officer of the United States, or as a member of any State legislature, or as an executive or judicial officer of any State, to support the Constitution of the United States, shall have engaged in insurrection or rebellion against the same, or given aid or comfort to the enemies thereof. But Congress may by a vote of two-thirds of each House, remove such disability.

Disqualifies officials of the Confederacy from becoming federal officials, unless exempted by Congress.

Section 4. The validity of the public debt of the United States, authorized by law, including debts incurred for payment of pensions and bounties for services in suppressing insurrection or rebellion, shall not be questioned. But neither the United States nor any State shall assume or pay any debt or obligation incurred in aid of insurrection or rebellion against the United States, or any claim for the loss or emancipation of any slave; but all such debts, obligations and claims shall be held illegal and void.

Declares the federal Civil War debt legal.

Section 5. The Congress shall have power to enforce, by appropriate legislation, the provisions of this article.

Amendment 15
[Ratified February 3, 1870]

Section 1. The right of citizens of the United States to vote shall not be denied or abridged by the United States or by any State on account of race, color, or previous condition of servitude.

Section 2. The Congress shall have power to enforce this article by appropriate legislation.

Gives blacks the right to vote. Its passage had little effect at the time. The Voting Rights Act of 1965, arguably the most important civil rights legislation in

American history, brought black citizens into the electorate on a large scale; it delivered what the Fifteenth Amendment promised.

Amendment 16
[Ratified February 3, 1913]

Gives Congress the power to levy an income tax. A Supreme Court decision thus is nullified.

The Congress shall have power to lay and collect taxes on incomes, from whatever source derived, without apportionment among the several States, and without regard to any census or enumeration.

Amendment 17
[Ratified April 8, 1913]

Provides that senators be popularly elected. A democratizing reform.

The Senate of the United States shall be composed of two Senators from each State, elected by the people thereof for six years; and each Senator shall have one vote. The electors in each state shall have the qualification requisite for electors of the most numerous branch of the State legislatures.

When vacancies happen in the representation of any State in the Senate, the executive authority of such State shall issue writs of election to fill such vacancies: *Provided,* That the legislature of any State may empower the executive thereof to make temporary appointments until the people fill the vacancies by election as the legislature may direct.

This amendment shall not be so construed as to affect the election or term of any Senator chosen before it becomes valid as part of the Constitution.

Amendment 18
[Ratified January 16, 1919]

Prohibits liquor manufacture, sale, or transportation. The experiment failed; repealed by the Twenty-first Amendment.

Section 1. After one year from the ratification of this article the manufacture, sale, or transportation of intoxicating liquors within, the importation thereof into, or the exportation thereof from the United States and all territory subject to the jurisdiction thereof for beverage purposes is hereby prohibited.

Section 2. The Congress and the several States shall have concurrent power to enforce this article by appropriate legislation.

Section 3. This article shall be inoperative unless it shall have been ratified as an amendment to the Constitution by the legislatures of the several States, as provided in the Constitution, within seven years from the date of the submission hereof to the State by the Congress.

Amendment 19
[Ratified August 18, 1920]

The right of citizens of the United States to vote shall not be denied or abridged by the United States or by any State on account of sex. Congress shall have the power to enforce this article by appropriate legislation.

Gives women the right to vote.

Amendment 20
[Ratified January 23, 1933]

Section 1. The terms of the President and Vice-President shall end at noon on the 20th day of January, and the terms of Senators and Representatives at noon on the 3d day of January, of the years in which such terms would have ended if this article had not been ratified; and the terms of their successors shall then begin.

Changes the dates for the beginning of presidential and congressional terms from March to January, provides for succession to the presidency, and empowers Congress to extend the line of succession.

Section 2. The Congress shall assemble at least once in every year, and such meeting shall begin at noon on the 3d day of January, unless they shall by law appoint a different day.

Section 3. If, at the time fixed for the beginning of the term of the President, the President elect shall have died, the Vice-President elect shall become President. If a President shall not have been chosen before the time fixed for the beginning of his term, or if the President elect shall have failed to qualify, then the Vice-President elect shall act as President until a President shall have qualified; and the Congress may by law provide for the case wherein neither a President elect nor a Vice-President elect shall have qualified, declaring who shall then act as President, or the manner in which one who is to act shall be selected, and such person shall act accordingly until a President or Vice-President shall have qualified.

Section 4. The Congress may by law provide for the case of the death of any of the persons from whom the House of Representatives may choose a President whenever the right of choice shall have devolved upon them, and for the case of the death of any of the persons from whom the Senate may choose a Vice-President whenever the right of choice shall have devolved upon them.

Section 5. Sections 1 and 2 shall take effect on the 15th day of October following the ratification of this article.

Section 6. This article shall be inoperative unless it shall have been ratified as an amendment to the Constitution by the legislatures of three-fourths of the several states within seven years from the date of its submission.

Amendment 21
[Ratified December 5, 1933]

Repeals the Eighteenth Amendment.

Section 1. The eighteenth article of amendment to the Constitution of the United States is hereby repealed.

Section 2. The transportation or importation into any State, Territory, or Possession of the United States for delivery or use herein of intoxicating liquors, in violation of the laws thereof, is hereby prohibited.

Section 3. This article shall be inoperative unless it shall have been ratified as an amendment to the Constitution by conventions in several States, as provided in the Constitution, within seven years from the date of the submission hereof to the States by the Congress.

Amendment 22
[Ratified February 27, 1951]

Limits a president to two full terms plus two years of the previous president's term—in other words, ten years maximum.

Section 1. No person shall be elected to the office of the President more than twice, and no person who has held the office of President, or acted as President, for more than two years of a term to which some other person was elected President shall be elected to the office of the President more than once. But this Article shall not apply to any person holding the office of President when this article was proposed by the Congress, and shall not prevent any person who may be holding the office of President, or acting as President, during the term within which this Article becomes operative from holding the office of President or acting as President during the remainder of such term.

Section 2. This article shall be inoperative unless it shall have been ratified as an amendment to the Constitution by the legislatures of three-fourths of the several States within seven years from the date of its submission to the States by the Congress.

Amendment 23
[Ratified March 29, 1961]

Awards the District of Columbia three electoral votes.

Section 1. The District constituting the seat of Government of the United States shall appoint in such manner as the Congress may direct:

A number of electors of President and Vice President equal to the whole number of Senators and Representatives in Congress to which the District would be entitled if it were a state, but in no event more than the least populous State; they shall be in addition to those appointed by the States, but they shall be considered, for the purposes of the election of President and Vice President, to be electors appointed by a State; and they shall meet in the District and perform such duties as provided by the twelfth article of amendment.

Section 2. The Congress shall have power to enforce this article by appropriate legislation.

Amendment 24
[Ratified January 23, 1964]

Section 1. The right of citizens of the United States to vote in any primary or other election for President or Vice President, for electors for President or Vice President, or for Senator or Representative in Congress, shall not be denied or abridged by the United States or by any State by reason or failure to pay any poll tax or other tax.

Outlaws the poll tax as a requirement for voting in federal elections. The poll tax was a tax on the right to vote. In 1966, the Supreme Court outlawed poll taxes in all elections.

Section 2. The Congress shall have power to enforce this article by appropriate legislation.

Amendment 25
[Ratified February 10, 1967]

Section 1. In case of the removal of the President from office or of his death or resignation, the Vice President shall become President.

Prescribes the succession route to the presidency, provides for the selection of the vice president in the case of a vacancy in that office, and develops procedures to be used in the event of the president's inability to discharge the powers and duties of his office.

Section 2. Whenever there is a vacancy in the office of the Vice President, the President shall nominate a Vice President who shall take office upon confirmation by a majority vote of both Houses of Congress.

Section 3. Whenever the President transmits to the President pro tempore of the Senate and the speaker of the House of Representatives his written declaration that he is unable to discharge the powers and duties of his office, and until he transmits to them a written declaration to the contrary, such powers and duties shall be discharged by the Vice President as Acting President.

Section 4. Whenever the Vice President and a majority of either the principal officers of the executive department or of such other body as Congress may by law provide, transmit to the President pro tempore of the Senate and the Speaker of the House of Representatives their written declaration that the President is unable to discharge the powers and duties of his office, the Vice President shall immediately assume the powers and duties of the office as Acting President.

Thereafter, when the President transmits to the President pro tempore of the Senate and the Speaker of the House of Representatives his written declaration that no inability exists, he shall resume the powers and duties of his office unless the Vice President and a majority of either the principal officers of the executive department or of such other body as Congress may by law provide, transmit within four days to the President pro tempore of the Senate and the Speaker of the House of Representatives their written declaration that the President is unable to discharge the powers and duties of his office. Thereupon Congress shall decide the issue, assembling within forty-eight hours for that purpose if not in session. If the Congress, within twenty-one days after receipt of the latter written declaration, or, if Congress is not in session, within twenty-one days after Congress is required to assemble, determined by two-thirds vote of both Houses that the President is unable to discharge the powers and duties of his office, the Vice President shall continue to discharge the same as Acting President; otherwise, the President shall resume the powers and duties of his office.

Amendment 26
[Ratified June 30, 1971]

Gives eighteen-year-old citizens the right to vote in all elections.

Section 1. The right of citizens of the United States, who are eighteen years of age or older, to vote shall not be denied or abridged by the United States or by any State on account of age.

Section 2. The Congress shall have the power to enforce this article by appropriate legislation.

Equal Rights For Women
[Proposed March 22, 1972]

Proposes equal rights for women. Adopted by Congress. Not ratified.

Section 1. Equality of rights under the law shall not be denied or abridged by the United States or by any State on account of sex.

Section 2. The Congress shall have power to enforce, by appropriate legislation, the provisions of this article.

Section 3. This amendment shall take effect two years after date of ratification.

District of Columbia Representation
[Proposed August 22, 1978]

Proposes to give representation in Congress to the

Section 1. For purposes of representation in the Congress, election of the President and Vice President, and article V of this

Constitution, the District constituting the seat of government of the United States shall be treated as though it were a State.

Section 2. The exercise of the rights and powers conferred under this article shall be by the people of the District constituting the seat of government, and as shall be provided by the Congress.

Section 3. The twenty-third article of amendment to the Constitution of the United States is hereby repealed.

Section 4. This article shall be inoperative, unless it shall have been ratified as an amendment to the Constitution by the legislatures of three-fourths of the several States within seven years from the date of its submission.

Appendix

B

A Guide to Federal Government Documents: What They Are and How to Find Them

Government documents are materials that are published at government expense and by government authority. They are considered official publications of the government unit or organization that releases them. Most librarians use the term *government documents* to refer to publications of the United States Government: its executive branch, legislative branch, and judicial branch.

The prospective user of government documents is well advised to contact a government documents librarian or a reference librarian as the first step. There are good reasons for obtaining professional assistance early in the process. Libraries organize their government documents collections differently: some libraries shelve government documents in a separate section; others integrate them into their reference and general collections. For example, the library of Queens College in New York treats some government documents as books (and lists them in the general catalogue), others (the *Department of State Bulletin*, for example) as periodicals, and the majority according to a system of the U.S. Superintendent of Documents. In smaller libraries, the Library of Congress classification system is more likely to be used for government documents.[1] Moreover, the sheer volume of publications, the many government organizations that release publications, and the relatively frequent reorganization or renaming of government units, can make the task of locating documents difficult and time consuming for the first time user.

There is a wide network of government agencies, departments, bureaus, legislative committees, and courts that issue government documents. Some of these organizations are familiar: The president and the Executive Office of the President, the Congress, and the Supreme Court. However, many important government documents are issued by units of the government that are not as well known.

In the legislative branch, there are twenty-two standing (permanent) committees of the House of Representatives and fifteen standing committees of the Senate. While the names of some of the standing committees may be relatively familiar, probably most are not, nor are most of the special and select congressional committees, which are appointed for a limited time or purpose. Yet the hearings and reports of such bodies constitute a substantial portion of government documents issued in any given year.

In the executive branch are thirteen cabinet-level departments, each of which has subordinate agencies and bureaus. The Department of Health and Human Services, one of the

Written by Robert W. Gage, Graduate School of Public Affairs, University of Colorado at Denver, with the assistance of Louise Stwally, Government Documents Librarian, Auraria Higher Education Center.

largest domestic agencies, had four major operating divisions in the beginning of 1986: the Public Health Service, the Office of Human Development Services, the Health Care Financing Administration, and the Social Security Administration. The Public Health Service, one of the four major operating divisions, itself contains six large units, including the Centers for Disease Control, the Food and Drug Administration, and the National Institutes of Health. But such complex organization is not static—it changes frequently. Government reorganization is a common and ongoing process.

The executive branch also contains regulatory agencies, numerous commissions, independent offices and establishments, and—at any given time—a number of specially appointed task forces and fact-finding boards. Among these are the Veterans Administration, the U.S. Postal Service, the Securities and Exchange Commission, the National Aeronautics and Space Administration, the Nuclear Regulatory Commission, the Panama Canal Company, the Railroad Retirement Board, and the National Science Foundation, to mention only a few. Each of these agencies issues publications that become part of the stream of government documents printed by the Government Printing Office.

The content of government documents is as far-reaching as the network of organizations that issues these documents. Government documents take many forms: books, pamphlets, magazines, periodicals, and monographs. They are available in various media, including the printed page or microform, or they may be accessed through specialized clearinghouses and by means of on-line data bases.

Often, the most current information on popular topics will be found in government documents—indeed, this is one of the principal advantages of these documents. Topics include cancer research, working women, civil rights, outer-space explorations, solar energy, mass transit, American artists, and home gardening. Many government documents are published as popular pamphlets of the "how to" variety. For example, the Small Business Administration, an independent agency in the executive branch, has published a series of pamphlets on starting businesses. One of the more popular of this series is *Starting and Managing a Small Retail Camera Shop*.[2]

The printer of federal documents is the U.S. Government Printing Office. The GPO was established in Washington, D.C., in 1861, and is directed by an official called the Public Printer, who reports to the Congress of the United States. Prior to 1861, the government contracted with private printers for most of its publications, a system that became unmanageable as the national government increased in size and complexity after the Civil War. The system for government documents was improved in 1895, when the Office of the Superintendent of Documents was established in the Government Printing Office. The superintendent of documents (sometimes called the assistant public printer) was established to (1) sell government publications produced by or through the Government Printing Office; (2) distribute government publications to designated depository libraries; (3) compile catalogues and indexes of government publications; and (4) mail government publications for members of the Congress or for government agencies, as provided for in the law, or on a reimbursable basis.[3]

No organization in the world publishes more information than the U.S. government. The superintendent of documents currently sells seventeen thousand titles, and these are only a small portion of the publications used by the federal government. In addition to sales, the superintendent of documents distributes government documents free of charge to the over 1,350 libraries across the nation that have been designated as depository libraries. It compiles and publishes the *Monthly Catalogue of United States Government Publications* for users of government documents, the best known of four major indexes of U.S. government publications. The three others are the *Index to U.S. Government Periodicals*, the *American Statistics Index (ASI)*, and the *Congressional Information Service* (CIS) *Annual*.

Appendix B

In the early 1970s, following the expansion of the federal government under presidents John F. Kennedy and Lyndon B. Johnson, the *New York Times* noted that the superintendent of documents handled "an average of 30,000 orders a day, spurting to 60,000 during peak periods at the start of the school year, the Christmas season, and income tax time." Between 1947 and 1970 the publication, *Your Federal Income Tax*, had sold over fourteen million copies, topped only by *Infant Care,* which hit the fifteen million mark after twenty years.[4]

The increasing size of the U.S. government publications operations is apparent from the volume of printing done for the *Federal Register* alone. The *Federal Register,* published since March 14, 1936, is essentially a daily record of new administrative rules and regulations made by the departments and agencies of the executive branch of government. In 1936, the *Federal Register* contained 2,355 pages, a significant volume by standards of that time. In 1946, it contained 14,736 pages, an increase that reflected growth in government regulation during World War II. In 1972, at the end of the Korean War, the *Federal Register* contained 28,928 pages, approximately double that of the World War II era. By 1975, only three years later, it doubled again, reaching 60,221 pages![5] While it does not follow that all government printing increased by this magnitude, it is a strikingly good indicator of the massiveness of the printed output of the United States government.

Numerous state and local governments also publish government documents. The best single resource for locating publications of state governments is the *Monthly Checklist of State Publications,* compiled by the Library of Congress. The *Monthly Checklist* is a record of all state documents issued within a five-year period that have been received by the Library of Congress. Also, publications of foreign governments and of international organizations (such as the United Nations) or regional organizations (such as the European Economic Community, the Pan American Union, and the Latin American Free Trade Association) are readily available in most larger libraries.[6] For publications of the United Nations, see *UNDOC: Current Index.* This index is a key to recent United Nations publications and proceedings. The *UNDOC* is considered an essential source of basic information about political questions, international relations, international law, economic development, trade and commerce, social questions, statistics, transportation, human rights, world population, public administration, and other topics related to the United Nations' mandate.

Government publications are classified, using the superintendent of documents classification system, by the branch of government and agency or unit that issues them. Publications of the executive branch include those of the presidency, which are often highly visible—and popular. Publications of the Congress are much more voluminous than those of the executive branch. In comparison, judicial branch publications are more difficult to find and to use.

Executive Branch Publications

The publications of the executive branch include the presidential papers, publications of the central executive (the White House, the Executive Office of the President, and the Office of Management and Budget), and publications of the various departments and agencies.

The published papers of the President cover messages, speeches, and policy statements of the presidents and all communications to the Congress, whether delivered in person or in writing. Most presidential messages are printed, when delivered as documents of the Congress, in a section of the *Congressional Record* labeled President of the United States.

In response to a recommendation of the National Historical Publications Commission, the National Archives and Records Service began a consolidated series of publications in

624

1958 entitled *Public Papers of the Presidents of the United States*. The first edition contains public messages and statements of President Dwight D. Eisenhower. The text was selected from communications to the Congress, public addresses, transcripts of press conferences, public letters, messages to heads of state, and formal executive documents. Not all publishing of this kind is done by the government; notable compilations of presidential papers that have been prepared commercially are the *State Papers and Other Public Writings of Herbert Hoover* and the *Public Papers and Addresses of Franklin D. Roosevelt*. These are particularly valuable because they contain papers and letters not published in any government document.[7]

Many speeches of the presidents made over radio, television, or to unofficial gatherings contain important policy statements. Some are issued as pamphlets, some are printed in the *Congressional Record,* others appear as press releases of the U.S. State Department. Presidential speeches also appear regularly in the *Department of State Bulletin* and eventually are included in the *Public Papers of the Presidents*.

Proclamations and executive orders of the president are means by which the chief executive carries out legal and ceremonial duties of office. They range from detailed administrative procedures that carry the force of law to recognition of special occasions and ceremonies, such as Fire Protection Week or National Secretaries' Week. Proclamations and executive orders are published in the *Federal Register*. Cumulative editions have been published in the *Code of Federal Regulations*, Title 3, since 1936.

Publications of government agencies and offices that are part of the inner circle of presidential control and authority (the central executive) are grouped together in the superintendent of documents classification system. They include publications of the White House, the Office of Management and Budget, and specially appointed units, such as the President's Commission on the Assassination of President John F. Kennedy. Examples of regular publications of such units are the *Economic Report of the President* and the *Budget of the United States Government*.

Publications containing serial accounts of major presidential activities include the *Weekly Compilation of Presidential Documents*, considered by many to be the single most useful collection of presidential activities in the public record.[8] Other official documents, such as treaties and executive agreements, record actions taken by presidents. Activities of the president in foreign affairs are indexed under Presidential Documents in the *Department of State Bulletin*.

A number of general government publications provide an overview of government structure and operations. One of the best known is the *United States Government Manual*, which is the official handbook of the federal government. The manual contains descriptions of programs and activities of the executive, legislative, and judicial branches. It includes the independent agencies, boards, committees, and commissions, and the quasi-official agencies, such as the Smithsonian Institution and international organizations.

Publications of departments and agencies, despite their tremendous volume and scope, can readily be divided into (1) those dealing with foreign affairs and some aspect of defense and national security and (2) those dealing with domestic affairs.

In foreign affairs, important sources of information are treaties, executive agreements, diplomatic correspondence, reports and resolutions from international conferences, and State Department publications on regional problems. The State Department serial publications, such as *United States Treaties and International Agreements* and *Executive Agreement Series*, have subject indexes. They are widely used to locate basic information on foreign relations. The monthly *Department of State Bulletin* is available for more current treaty information. Prior to ratification, each treaty is transmitted to the Senate as a *Senate Executive Document*, which is probably the most easily obtained source for current treaty information.

Appendix B

Basic information on administrative operations of all agencies, foreign and domestic, is published in the *Federal Register* and in the *Code of Federal Regulations*. The latter is divided into fifty titles and is published with a user's guide, itself a seventy-page document. Rules and regulations occupy the largest portion of any issue of the *Federal Register*. Proposed rules are published to permit interested parties to comment on changes to existing regulations or on new rules that an agency is considering. A substantial part of the *Federal Register* is devoted to notices: changes in agency organization; advisory opinions; meetings of commissions, boards, and other bodies; and miscellaneous announcements.

Major government departments and agencies issue annual reports and periodicals, handbooks and yearbooks, and information publications for the sectors of American society to which each relates. Many publications are educational: these range from publications on the energy crisis to agricultural extension publications on how to make home preserves. Shopper's guides, handbooks for the home, gardening, and auto mechanics are covered in such publications. Many of these publications are listed in the *Consumer Information Catalogue* issued by the Government Printing Office.

Government departments and agencies issue many more publications than can be mentioned here. Indexes cited in the last part of this appendix should be consulted. For example, the *American Statistics Index* covers more than eight hundred federal government reports and periodicals on statistical matters alone. Statistical publications of the Bureau of the Census, the Bureau of Labor Statistics, and the Department of Energy are among those listed in this index.

Legislative Branch Publications

Congressional publications consist primarily of records of congressional activities, the largest part of which is devoted to floor proceedings in the Senate and in the House of Representatives and to committee hearings and reports. The systematic classification of congressional publications began with the first session of the Fifteenth Congress (1817). Different methods have been used to classify these publications.

Principal House and Senate documents and reports compose most of the collection referred to as the *Congressional Set* or the *Serial Set*. The serial number is a number applied to each book in a congressional series of publications, beginning with the Fifteenth Congress. These books also contain various miscellaneous reports, but do not contain the *Congressional Record*. Serial numbers afford a convenient method for locating publications in libraries that have extensive government documents collections, such as the Library of Congress and the National Archives.

A second classification, the numbers given to document volumes of each term and session of the Congress, is more familiar and widely used. Each congressional term has two sessions. Numbers indicating the term and session appear on the title page of congressional documents, as shown in Figure 1.

Users frequently wish to trace the history of a particular law from the time it is introduced as a bill to the point at which it is signed into law by the president. Or they may wish to locate a committee print containing expert testimony on a particular subject. Figure 2 traces the legislative process and lists the kinds of documents that are printed as records of that process.

The *Congressional Record* is the daily record of the proceedings of both houses of the Congress. The *Record* consists of four sections: the Proceedings of the Senate, the Proceedings of the House of Representatives, the Extensions of Remarks, and the Daily Digest. One will find an essentially verbatim record of speeches, debates, and voting in the *Record*, but not the text of bills and resolutions, committee hearings, or laws. These are printed

Figure 1. **Senate Committee Report**

Calendar No. 592

90TH CONGRESS	}	SENATE	{	REPORT
1st Session				No. 609

EXTENDING THE AMERICAN REVOLUTION BICENTENNIAL COMMISSION

OCTOBER 11 (legislative day, OCTOBER 10), 1967.— Ordered to be printed

Mr. DIRKSEN, from the Committee on the Judiciary,
submitted the following

REPORT

[To accompany H.R. 8629]

The Committee on the Judiciary, to which was referred the bill (H.R. 8629) to amend the act of July 4, 1966 (Public Law 89–491), having considered the same, reports favorably thereon with an amendment and recommends that the bill as amended do pass.

AMENDMENT

On page 2, after line 4, insert the following:

4. By deleting in section 2(b)(1) the word "Four" and inserting in lieu thereof the word "Six"; and by deleting in section 2(b)(2) the word "Four" and inserting in lieu thereof the word "Six".

PURPOSE OF AMENDMENT

The purpose of the amendment is to increase the Senate membership on the Commission from four members to six members, and to increase the House of Representatives membership on the Commission from four members to six members.

PURPOSE

The purpose of the proposed legislation, as amended, is fourfold: First, it would add the Secretary of Commerce as an exofficio member of the Commission; second,

[With certain exceptions, the Legislative Reorganization Act of 1970, requires the report to contain an estimate of the costs involved in the bill]

---

separately. The Extensions of Remarks section includes such material as excerpts from letters, telegrams, or articles related to speeches; and communications from state legislatures. The Daily Digest includes highlights of the legislative day as well as a summary of activities, including bills signed by the president. The *Record* also contains recurring information useful for basic references, such as a list of members of Congress, with state and party affiliation; and standing committees with names of members. When the Congress is

Figure 2. **How a Bill Becomes a Law**

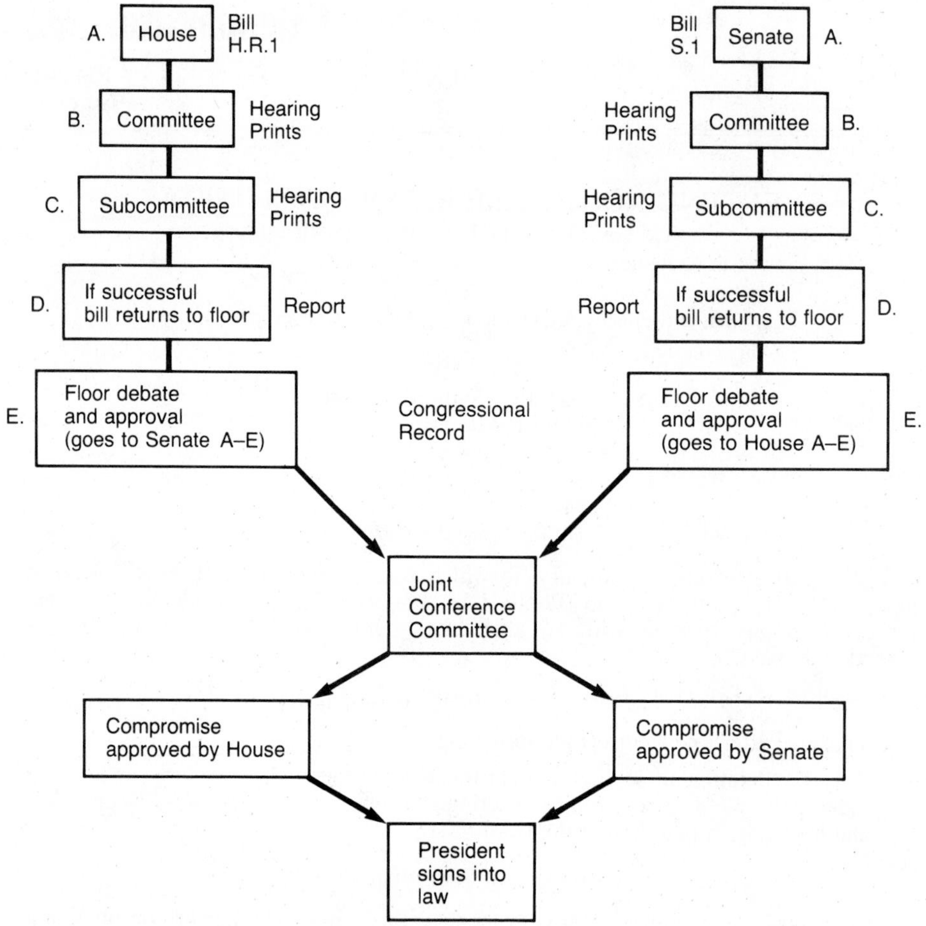

```
 A. | House |  Bill                    Bill  | Senate | A.
              H.R.1                     S.1

 B. | Committee |  Hearing      Hearing | Committee | B.
                   Prints       Prints

 C. | Subcommittee |  Hearing   Hearing | Subcommittee | C.
                      Prints    Prints

 D. | If successful |  Report   Report | If successful | D.
      bill returns to floor             bill returns to floor

 E. | Floor debate          Congressional    Floor debate   | E.
      and approval           Record          and approval
      (goes to Senate A–E)                   (goes to House A–E)

                    | Joint
                      Conference
                      Committee |

 | Compromise                         Compromise   |
   approved by House                  approved by Senate

                    | President
                      signs into
                      law |
```

Source: Auraria Library, Government Documents Section, Auraria Higher Education Center, Denver, Colorado.

in session, a visitor in the gallery can watch official reporters record the proceedings and debates.

The legislative process begins with the introduction of proposed legislation, called a bill. Bills may originate in either the House or the Senate, except for bills raising revenue, which by Article I, Section 7, of the U.S. Constitution must originate in the House. Bills are numbered consecutively from the beginning of each two-year term of the Congress. The house of origin is identified by a prefix (H.R. for House of Representatives, S. for Senate). Resolutions, which may be passed by either the House or the Senate, or concurrently, are similarly labeled. Resolutions do not have the force of law, but they are used to express an opinion on matters in which the chambers of the Congress take an interest.

The majority of bills and resolutions are printed only once. Since depository libraries are permitted to dispose of House and Senate bills one year after adjournment, most collections are incomplete. The Library of Congress has a complete collection of all printed versions of bills. For bills dated from 1979 to the present, a complete text is available in microfiche; for bills prior to 1979, a brief summary may be obtained from the *Digest of Public General Bills and Resolutions (Bill Digest)*. The *Bill Digest* was first published by the Legislative Reference Service of the Library of Congress in 1936.

When bills are introduced in either house, they are referred to committee. During consideration, the committee may hold hearings, which may or may not be printed. Hearings are transcripts of nonlegislative testimony. If reintroduced in a subsequent session of Congress, bills may have more than one set of hearings. Occasionally, committee hearings are printed as a part of larger reports.

Committee prints are documents compiled by a congressional research staff. Often these are independent studies requested by a committee from an outside source. They also may be activity reports or compilations of relevant material of general interest to proceedings. Committee hearings and prints are published as separate documents and usually are offered for sale by the superintendent of documents. When made public, committee hearings are distributed to depository libraries, which usually have respectable collections of back issues.

House and Senate reports contain the findings of committees explaining the rationale for recommending passage. The existence of a committee report on a bill indicates a recommendation for passage. No report means that a bill has been left to die in committee. Reports are indexed by number and can be found in the *Serial Set*. If a bill passes, it becomes known as an act, and is then referred to the other chamber of the Congress. By far the most useful source for locating committee and subcommittee hearings and prints is the *Congressional Information Service Index* (CIS). Committee hearings are issued in a much more consistent manner than committee prints. The process for distributing the latter remains inadequate.

The *Statutes at Large* is a chronological arrangement of acts (called slip laws) that have been signed by the president or have become law over a presidential veto. The *Statutes at Large* are compiled and indexed according to the term and session of the Congress in which they were passed into law. The *United States Code* is a codification and consolidation of the general and permanent laws of the nation. It is published every six years, and cumulative annual *Supplements* are available between editions. The commercial versions, the *U.S. Code, Annotated* and the *U.S. Code Service* provide more current editions.

Numerous other useful publications are issued by the legislative branch. Among these are the *House Manual* and the *Senate Manual*. These manuals contain the rules for each chamber, as well as regulations, statutes, and other material pertaining to operations and organization.

Judicial Branch Publications

Judicial publications include the published laws of the United States and the publications of the courts. Of all topical areas in government documents, judicial publications tend to be among the most specialized. Their use generally requires the assistance of someone with considerable knowledge of government organization. It is likely that the user will need a specialized law library or a legislative reference service. However, there are several things that the general user will find helpful in beginning a research project involving the courts. Beyond this, a legal textbook, such as Morris L. Cohen and Robert C. Berring, *How to Find the Law*, 8th ed. (St. Paul, MN: West, 1983), is recommended as a guide.

At the top of the federal court structure is the Supreme Court, the highest tribunal of the land. On the second level are the United States courts of appeals, and at the bottom of the pyramid are the United States district courts. Most court decisions published by the federal government are of these federal courts, although decisions of state courts are sometimes included. Published decisions may be divided into two groups: those published regularly, as the decisions are made, and those published as compilations of special topics.

Decisions of the following courts are published regularly: the Supreme Court of the United States, Court of Claims, Court of Customs and Patent Appeals, Customs Court, Commerce Court, Tax Court, and the United States Court of Military Appeals.[9] The reader wishing to locate the text of decisions from such courts will need to consult one of a number of serialized court reports. For the Supreme Court, the title of the series is *United States Reports*. The superintendent of documents began distribution and sale of the *Reports* to the public in 1922. Prior volumes were prepared solely for distribution to government officials. For the U.S. Court of Customs and Patent Appeals, decisions may be found in a number of specialized publications. Decisions on customs matters are published weekly in the *Customs Bulletin*. Decisions on patents are published in the *Official Gazette of the United States Patent Office* and cumulated into the *Decisions of the Commissioner on Patents and of U.S. Courts on Patent and Trademark Cases*. Each of the other federal courts listed above has its own publication for reporting decisions.

Because the law is a changing process, it is important to know what cases are valid and may be cited as authoritative. Case citations furnish a record for tracing a judicial history, similar to a legislative history of a particular law. The most complete system, *Shepard's Citations,* is published commercially. Another critically important reference source are digests of judicial decisions. Digests are indexes that classify judicial decisions by subject and that provide brief abstracts of each decision. The most comprehensive of the digests is the *American Digest System*. It claims to cover all standard written law reports of appellate courts from 1658 to date.

Using Government Documents

Few libraries with substantial numbers of government publications catalogue and shelve these publications in the same manner as they do privately published books and materials. They depend almost entirely on printed catalogues and indexes. Government publications often are shelved in one area as a separate collection. In many cases, few if any government publications will be found in the card (or public-access) catalogue. This presents some difficulty for the user, particularly the first-time user of government publications.

While all libraries in the country probably receive some government publications, certain designated libraries, called depository libraries, receive government publications directly from the superintendent of documents.[10] Among the depository libraries are fifty regional depository libraries, which permanently retain a complete collection of publications to provide interlibrary loan and reference service in their regions. Other depository libraries may dispose of documents over five years old. If a reader wishes to use an original publication, and it is over five years old, it will probably be necessary to obtain it from a regional depository library.

Depository libraries frequently assign responsibilities for their collections to a government documents librarian. The documents librarian and staff may provide users' guides for distribution. These are likely to include detailed instruction on the organization of that library's document collection, short descriptions of major indexes of government documents, and instructions on frequent requests, such as compiling a legislative history.

Other libraries are also likely to have collections of government publications. Nondepository libraries acquire publications from executive branch agencies and buy additional publications from clearinghouse systems, such as the National Technical Information Service

(NTIS) of the Department of Commerce. The NTIS is a central source for the public sale of reports on government-sponsored research, development, and engineering. These documents fall outside the depository system and are classified as technical or scientific documents. Other agencies that are sources of technical and scientific documents include the Defense Documentation Center (nonclassified documents); the National Aeronautics and Space Administration, which generates a significant portion of government technical literature and operates a bibliographic service known as Scientific and Technical Aerospace Reports (STAR); and the Educational Resources Information Center (ERIC), which is operated by the National Institute of Education in the Department of Education. The ERIC's data bank contains educational materials not easily located through primary educational journals or their indexes.

The most complete collections of government publications are housed in the Library of Congress; the most complete collection of maps is in the National Archives. Depository libraries receive some maps, most from the U.S. Geological Survey and the Defense Mapping Agency.

Many guides to government publications are available from the government and from commercial publishing houses. Three of these are particularly useful: the *Monthly Catalogue of U.S. Government Publications;* the *Index to U.S. Government Periodicals;* and the *Congressional Information Service* (CIS) *Annual.* A fourth guide, the *American Statistics Index* (ASI) is discussed in Appendix C.

The *Monthly Catalogue* has monthly, semiannual, and annual indexes and is considered to be a comprehensive index to nearly all U.S. government publications, with the exception of periodicals. In addition to the author, title, and subject index sections, it has key word indexes. A sample entry from the *Monthly Catalogue* is presented in Figure 3.

A number of indexes are published by commercial publishing houses. The *Cumulative Subject Index to the Monthly Catalogue of U.S. Government Publications, 1900–1971* has been issued in fifteen hardcover volumes. It provides one convenient index of publications issued during this period. A microfilm edition of the *Monthly Catalogue* also is available.

The *Index to U.S. Government Periodicals,* also published commercially, is the equivalent to the *Readers' Guide to Periodical Literature.* The *Index* contains subject and author listings for articles in over 170 of the most frequently used U.S. government magazines. This index is excellent for locating articles on current and specialized topics, such as age discrimination, Japanese management styles, jogging, and acid rain.

The *Congressional Information Service Annual,* also published by a commercial source, is the primary index to use in identifying information on congressional hearings, committee prints, House and Senate reports, and the other publications of the Congress. It outlines legislative histories for laws passed since 1970. Indexing is done by subject, by names of organizations or witnesses, by official and popular names of bills and laws, by bill numbers, and by public law numbers.

Notes

1. William A. Katz, *Introduction to Reference Work,* vol. 1, 2d ed. (New York: McGraw Hill, 1974), p. 321.

2. Small Business Administration, *Starting and Managing a Small Retail Camera Shop,* the Starting and Managing Series, vol. 17 (Washington, D.C.: Government Printing Office, October 1969).

3. Joe Morehead, *Introduction to United States Public Documents,* 2d ed. (Littleton, CO: Libraries Unlimited, 1978), p.45.

4. *New York Times,* November 28, 1971, p. 95.

Figure 3. **Sample Entry**

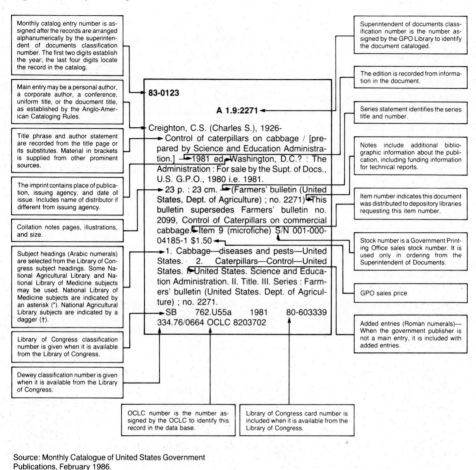

Monthly catalog entry number is assigned after the records are arranged alphanumerically by the superintendent of documents classification number. The first two digits establish the year; the last four digits locate the record in the catalog.

Main entry may be a personal author, a corporate author, a conference, uniform title, or the document title, as established by the Anglo-American Cataloging Rules.

Title phrase and author statement are recorded from the title page or its substitutes. Material in brackets is supplied from other prominent sources.

The imprint contains place of publication, issuing agency, and date of issue. Includes name of distributor if different from issuing agency.

Collation notes pages, illustrations, and size.

Subject headings (Arabic numerals) are selected from the Library of Congress subject headings. Some National Agricultural Library and National Library of Medicine subjects may be used. National Library of Medicine subjects are indicated by an asterisk (*). National Agricultural Library subjects are indicated by a dagger (†).

Library of Congress classification number is given when it is available from the Library of Congress.

Dewey classification number is given when it is available from the Library of Congress.

Superintendent of documents classification number is the number assigned by the GPO Library to identify the document cataloged.

The edition is recorded from information in the document.

Series statement identifies the series title and number.

Notes include additional bibliographic information about the publication, including funding information for technical reports.

Item number indicates this document was distributed to depository libraries requesting this item number.

Stock number is a Government Printing Office sales stock number. It is used only in ordering from the Superintendent of Documents.

GPO sales price

Added entries (Roman numerals)—When the government publisher is not a main entry, it is included with added entries.

OCLC number is the number assigned by the OCLC to identify this record in the data base.

Library of Congress card number is included when it is available from the Library of Congress.

83-0123

A 1.9:2271

Creighton, C.S. (Charles S.), 1926-
Control of caterpillars on cabbage / [prepared by Science and Education Administration.] —1981 ed. —Washington, D.C.? : The Administration : For sale by the Supt. of Docs., U.S. G.P.O., 1980 i.e. 1981.
23 p. : 23 cm. (Farmers' bulletin (United States, Dept. of Agriculture) ; no. 2271) This bulletin supersedes Farmers' bulletin no. 2099, Control of Caterpillars on commercial cabbage. Item 9 (microfiche) S/N 001-000-04185-1 $1.50
1. Cabbage—diseases and pests—United States. 2. Caterpillars—Control—United States. I. United States. Science and Education Administration. II. Title. III. Series : Farmers' bulletin (United States. Dept. of Agriculture) ; no. 2271.
SB   762.U55a   1981   80-603339
334.76/0664 OCLC 8203702

Source: Monthly Catalogue of United States Government Publications, February 1986.

5. Advisory Commission on Intergovernmental Relations, *State and Local Roles in the Federal System* (Washington, D.C.: Government Printing Office, April 1982), p. 58.

6. For publications of other international organizations, refer to the specific organization by title. Specialized commercial indexes for international relations also may be consulted for these publications.

7. Lawrence F. Schmeckebier and Roy B. Eastin, *Government Publications and Their Use*, 2d ed. (Washington, D.C.: Brookings, 1969), p.336.

8. Morehead, p. 219.

9. Schmeckebier and Eastin, p. 279.

10. For the kinds of documents not received by depository libraries, see Schmeckebier and Eastin (note 7), p. 130, or consult the government documents librarian in a depository library.

A Guide to Statistical Information on American Government

A wealth of quantitative information exists on statistical information relevant to the study of American government. Much of it is published by the federal government. Unfortunately, these data are found in many different publications, some voluminous, and locating the right source requires some planning and forethought.

For the most part, sources of statistical data can be accessed easily with some basic knowledge about indexes and abstracts. The information sources discussed here will likely be available in most college and university libraries and in major branches of public libraries. Two basic steps are involved in getting the numerical information you need. First, you must discover which publication has the required statistics; second, you must locate the publication, itself. The second step assumes you are familiar with libraries and how to search a catalogue (card or on–line) to see if the library carries the publication. Since much statistical information is found in government documents, you may initially need the help of a reference librarian to assist you in searching these publications.

The Statistical Abstract of the United States

The easiest place to begin is with the *Statistical Abstract of the United States,* a compendium published annually by the U.S. Bureau of the Census. It summarizes, in tabular form, a great deal of statistical data about political, economic, and social aspects of the United States. Of particular interest to American government are the sections on federal government finances and employment; state and local government finances and employment; elections; and law enforcement, federal courts, and prisons. Each table lists the source from which the data were taken, thus providing additional sources of information. Examples of the type of statistics published in the elections section are the votes cast for the president of the United States by major political parties from 1920 to 1984; these data are also available for each state and for Senate and House elections. The *Statistical Abstract* is widely available in libraries and is easy to use.

American Statistical Index

If the *Statistical Abstract* does not contain the needed data or suggest other sources, the *American Statistical Index* (*ASI*) should be consulted. The *ASI* is a guide to U.S. govern-

Written by Eileen Tynan, Graduate School of Public Affairs, University of Colorado at Denver.

ment publications that contain statistical information. It is published monthly, with an annual update, and comes in two parts: the *Index* and the *Abstracts*. The place to start is with the *Index*, which actually contains several indexes: (1) an index by categories; (2) an index by title; and (3), the most useful, an index by subjects and names. The index by categories is used when you need comparative data by a particular breakdown. Twenty-one separate categories are used. They consist of geographic breakdowns, such as by state, by city, and by county; economic breakdowns, such as by income, by industry, and by occupation; and demographic breakdowns, such as by age, by race, and by sex. Within each of the categories, nineteen subheadings are provided. One subheading is government, which covers statistical information on government in general, including finances, programs, personnel, and elections and voting. The title index is used when you know the title (or agency number) of a publication and you want to find out where its abstract is located.

The index by subjects and names is usually the place to start, as you go directly to the subject you are interested in, such as elections. An entry under this term briefly describes the contents of the publications indexed to the term. It also provides the accession number of the abstract. Next, turn to the volume of *Abstracts* for the same month and year of the *Index* you are using. Each abstract is arranged by accession number. When you locate the abstract of the publication you are interested in, you will see that it contains a description of the publication, including a description of the statistical data found in the document.

Your review of the abstract will determine if you want to get a copy of the publication. If so, you need the bibliographic data contained in the abstract. In addition to the title and the issuing agency, the superintendent of documents item number, which is useful in locating a government document, is provided. With the report title, agency, and item number, you should be able to search the library catalogue and the government documents catalogue to see if your library owns the publication. The publications indexed are also available from the Congressional Information Service on microfiche.

Bureau of the Census Publications

In addition to the *Statistical Abstract*, the Bureau of the Census, U.S. Department of Commerce, publishes two series useful in the study of American government. The *County and City Data Book*, published every five or six years, provides a variety of statistical information on counties, standard metropolitan statistical areas (SMSAs), cities, urbanized areas, and unincorporated places. One set of tables contains statistical information on elections and government. The *Census of Governments*, published in years ending in 2 and 7, contains statistics on government characteristics, such as revenues, payrolls, expenditures, organization, and labor-management relations for the federal government; and counties, places, minor civil divisions, and school and special districts for each state. In the years ending in 7, data on popular elected officials are provided for the United States, states, counties, and so on —as listed above.

The Bureau of the Census publishes a vast amount of statistical information about the United States. It makes available many printed reports, microfiche, public-use computer tapes, and special data tabulations. Two useful guides to census publications are the *Data User News*, published monthly, and the *Bureau of the Census Catalog of Publications*, published annually. A reference librarian can assist you in accessing census data, or you may be able to call or visit a local census office.

Statistical Reference Index (SRI)

Published by the Congressional Information Service (CIS), the *Statistical Reference Index* complements the *ASI*, since it indexes and abstracts statistical publications from sources other than the U.S. government. Like the *ASI*, it consists of two volumes, an *Index* and *Abstract*, and is used in the same manner. Also like the *ASI*, microfiche copies of the indexed publications are available from CIS, and many libraries own the microfiche collection.

Monthly Checklist of State Publications

The information sources discussed above are concerned with statistical data that are, for the most part, published by the federal government. The *Monthly Checklist of State Publications*, published by the Library of Congress, indexes state documents received by the library, arranged by state. An annual index is also published, which is arranged by subject. A brief description of the state publication is provided, which typically indicates whether statistical information is available in the publication. In addition, a subject heading called statistics can be reviewed for any suitable publications.

Congressional Information Service (CIS) Index

The *Congressional Information Service* (CIS) *Index,* which is published monthly, with an annual update, catalogues, indexes, and abstracts publications of the U.S. Congress. Like the *ASI* and the *SRI,* it consists of two volumes: *Index* and *Abstracts*. The *Index* can be searched by bill, report, and document number, and by subject and title. The *Index* entry provides a brief description of the publication and a number to be used in finding the appropriate abstract in the *Abstracts*. The abstract will let you know whether the indexed document contains statistical information. In addition to searching the *Index* by the subject you are interested in, check the category called statistical data: government, for a possible entry.

Privately Published Sources

The *Book of the States,* published biennially (most recent, 1984–1985) by the Council of State Governments, provides statistical data relating to state government. Categories covered are intergovernmental affairs, legislation, elections and constitutions, finances, and major state services.

The *Municipal Yearbook,* published by the International City Management Association, contains data on local government. The personnel issues section contains statistics on compensation (salary and fringe benefits) for a variety of local officials.

America Votes, a biennial publication of the Elections Research Center, Washington, D.C., provides data on federal and state elections.

Appendix

D

A Guide to On-Line Data Bases on American Government

What Is a Data Base?

A data base is simply information stored in computer-readable form. Most of them are not on-line; that is, not available to be immediately called up by a computer terminal. Millions of them are just sitting on floppy or hard disks or on magnetic tape on a shelf near somebody's computer. This is because most data bases are private and have no reason to be on-line all the time. Some public data bases are also private in that, although they belong to the public as a whole, they are not available for general use. Examples of such public data bases include those containing classified (secret) data for the U.S. Defense Department, those containing arrest records of alleged and convicted criminals, and those containing certain income tax records.

Public access data bases only became widely available in the 1970s. This happened usually for one of two reasons: the needs of research or the advancing technology of printing. The very first of the on-line data bases was created for medical and other technical research. Once the data base was in existence, it made sense to defray its costs by selling it to other users. At about this time, a revolution was occurring in the printing industry. More and more type was being set by computer. And what is a book, government report, or journal stored in a computer memory device, if not a data base? As more people, organizations, and especially libraries began to use computers, publishers saw a new market for their products. Thus the number of publicly available, on-line data bases began to explode.

Almost anything printed today can be made available on-line if there is a market for it. That market will grow as the number of personal computers in use grows. The day is coming when most technical reference books will be published only electronically—and be available only on-line. The world may run out of trees to make cheap paper, but it will never run out of electrons.

The on-line data bases currently available are just the beginning of a revolution that will see on-line resources supplant traditional research facilities. Simply put, one terminal with access to the nation's on-line data bases is an infinitely more productive instrument than an equivalent print facility with thousands of bound volumes—because all the data you seek can be called up from a data base in a few seconds, while it would take hours to find the equivalent information in bound volumes—assuming, of course, that you could easily locate the volumes you needed. Research using on-line data bases is not only more convenient and infinitely faster, it is more accurate. Because this is the essence of productivity, whether in school or business, the demand for on-line usage can only continue to increase.

Written by Louise Alexander.

The Data Base Industry

A data base is a product just like any other. If its owners feel there is a market for it, they will either seek a retail outlet or try to sell it themselves. On-line data base retailers are called vendors, or suppliers. At first they sold their products only to university and corporate libraries, where information scientists specially trained in information retrieval performed searches at the request of students, faculty, and researchers. But as more people obtained personal computers, the vendors realized that profits could be had by selling to them as well. Some vendors entered the market specifically as so-called consumer data base retailers. But unless they are private, all on-line data bases are for consumers. Some are just more expensive, more sophisticated, or more technical than others.

The on-line data base industry, because it is so new, is somewhat chaotic. This is particularly ironic when you consider that the industry's stock in trade, the computer and all that it holds and implies, is considered the essence of logic. There are many manufacturers of shoes, but they all use a common sizing system. One would think that people who deal with the logic of a computer would agree upon a common system of commands—a command language—to call up data from various data bases. But they have not done so. The situation now is much like the early railroad industry before there was agreement on a common gauge of track. Vendors want you to "ride" only on their "line," so they assure you that their data bases have the easiest-to-use command language. Actually, all the command languages are somewhat alike and not that difficult to learn. The problem is there are several dozen of them.

The situation cries out for standardization. And it will eventually come—not too many years from now. In the meantime, this lack of a command language should not cause a problem for you. The odds are that any one person will need to be familiar with only a few command languages. Most vendors offer more than one data base, all in the same command language.

As with any business, there are industry leaders; among data base vendors are the usual big three. By far the largest is Dialog Information Services, which offers the greatest variety of data bases and is known simply as Dialog throughout the on-line world. (Its previous name was Lockheed Dialog.) The two others are Bibliographic Retrieval Services and Pergamon Orbit Infoline, Inc. The former is almost always referred to as BRS; the latter as Orbit. Dialog, BRS, and Orbit are like large department stores offering something for every taste. The rest of the industry consists of specialty shops and business services. For example, Dow Jones (as you might expect) offers a dozen business-related data bases; NewsNet contains over a hundred specialized business newsletters; I. P. Sharp, Ltd., concentrates on numeric data bases; and so on.

**The Big Three On-Line
Data Base Vendors**

Bibliographic Retrieval Service
1200 Route 7
Latham, NY 12110
(518) 783-1161
(800) 833-4707 (toll free)

DIALOG
3450 Hillview Avenue
Palo Alto, CA 94304
(415) 858-2700

Pergamon Orbit Infoline, Inc.
8000 Westpark Drive
4th Floor

McLean, VA 22102
(703) 442–0900
(800) 421-7229 (toll free)

The United States government actually produces many data bases that others claim to produce. Is somebody lying? No. It's just that many government agencies sell data tapes that on-line producers sell either with minimal reshaping or with considerable reshaping. Deciding when a data tape, created by a government agency (such as the Bureau of the Census or the Bureau of Labor Statistics), has been reshaped enough to have a new creator is a point having only philosophic value. It is perfectly legal to buy federal government data tapes and do whatever you wish with them. Unlike privately produced data tapes, they are considered to be in the public domain and are not protected by copyright laws.

Sometimes a data base will go out of print, just like a book. In such cases, one of two things will happen. It can simply be taken off-line, because there is not sufficient demand—meaning profit to be had—for keeping it on-line. Or if it is simply too expensive to update, but there is still demand, it can become a closed file—kept on-line, but with frozen data.

One noteworthy benefit for consumers is that data base producers exhibit little loyalty to their vendors. Consequently, many data bases are offered by as many as a half-dozen suppliers. Remember, they are doing this to make money, and the more people who have access to their data bases, the greater their eventual royalties will be. So—shop around a bit. One supplier may offer the exact data base as another at 40 percent less. But be careful when you shop, because, while two vendors may offer the same data base, one may have it going back twice as many years as the other, or one may have the data organized in an easier-to-use format, or one may offer proprietary software that makes the data easier to manipulate.

On-line data bases are less expensive than they used to be, and this will continue to be true. When digital watches and pocket calculators first came on the market, they cost hundreds of dollars. But a decade later you could buy them for less than five dollars. The economics of on-line data bases are no different. As demand increases, the price will go down. Even today, on-line data base searching is a bargain—considering. While access to a data base might cost eighty or ninety dollars an hour, the time and cost of a typical search is less than a quarter of that. If it is worth twenty dollars to save days and days of traditional manual library searching, then it is money well spent. It is often said that one minute of on-line searching is equivalent to one hour of manual searching. The best way to get started with on-line searching is not to do it yourself but to consult the on-line librarian at any research library. Almost all major libraries will do searches for their patrons at or near their own cost.

Data Bases Dealing with Government

There are hundreds of data bases that deal with government, but most of the specialized ones, such as those containing patent information, agricultural research, and environmental studies, are not particularly useful for those interested in the political aspects of American governance. Listed below are easily available data bases containing statistical and bibliographic information on American government:

ABI/Inform (August 1971–present)   Designed to meet the information needs of executives by covering all phases of business and government. Articles from over four hundred U.S. and foreign journals are indexed and abstracted.

American Statistics Index (1973–present)   A comprehensive index of the statistical publications from more than four hundred central or regional issuing agencies of the U.S. government; provides abstracts and indexing of all federal statistical publications, including non-GPO publications, which contain social, economic, demographic, or natural resources data.

BLS Consumer Price Index (dates of coverage vary from record to record)   Contains time series of consumer price indexes calculated by the U.S. Bureau of Labor Statistics (BLS).

BLS Employment, Hours and Earnings (dates of coverage vary from record to record)   Contains times series on employment, hours of work, and earnings information for the United States organized by industry. National, state, and local data are provided.

BLS Labor Force (dates of coverage vary from record to record)   Contains time series on U.S. employment, unemployment, and nonparticipation in the labor force. The data are classified by a variety of demographic, social, and economic characteristics.

CIS (1970–present)   The machine-readable form of the Congressional Information Service's *Index to Publications of the United States Congress;* provides comprehensive access to the contents of the entire spectrum of congressional working papers published each year by the nearly three hundred House, Senate, and joint committees and subcommittees.

Comprehensive Dissertation Index (1861–present)   A definitive subject, title, and author guide to virtually every American dissertation accepted at an accredited institution since 1861, when academic doctoral degrees were first granted in the United States.

Criminal Justice Periodicals Index (1975–present)   Provides comprehensive cover-to-cover indexing of 120 administration of justice and law enforcement periodicals and journals.

Federal Index (October 1976–present)   Provides coverage of such federal actions as proposed rules, regulations, bill introductions, speeches, hearings, roll calls, reports, vetoes, court decisions, executive orders, and contract awards. The *Washington Post* and federal documents, such as the *Congressional Record, Federal Register,* and presidential documents, are indexed, as well as other publications covering government activities.

Federal Register Abstracts (March 1977–present)   Provides comprehensive coverage of federal regulatory agency actions as published in the *Federal Register,* the official U.S. government publication of regulations, proposed rules, and legal notices.

Government Printing Office Monthly Catalog (July 1976–present)   Contains records of reports, studies, fact sheets, maps, handbooks, conference proceedings, and so on, issued by all federal government agencies, including the Congress. Included are records of all of the Senate and House hearings on private and public bills and laws.

Legal Resource Index (1980–present)   Provides cover-to-cover indexing of over 660 law journals and five law newspapers plus legal monographs.

Magazine Index (1976–present)   Covers over 370 popular magazines.

National Newspaper Index (1979–present)   Provides front-to-back-page indexing of newspapers such as the *Christian Science Monitor,* the *New York Times,* and *The Wall Street Journal.*

National Criminal Justice Reference Service (1972–present)   Covers all aspects of law enforcement and criminal justice.

National Technical Information Service (1964–present)   Consists of government-sponsored research, development, and engineering plus analyses prepared by federal agencies, their contractors, or grantees.

PAIS International (1976–present)   The on-line version of the *Public Affairs Informa-tion Service*; contains references to information in all fields of social science including political science, banking, public administration, international relations, economics, law, public policy, social welfare, sociology, education, and social anthropology.

Social Scisearch (1972–present)   A multidisciplinary data base indexing every signifi-cant item from the one thousand most important science journals throughout the world and the social science articles selected from twenty-two hundred additional journals in the natural, physical, and biomedical sciences.

Sociological Abstracts (1963–present)   Covers the world's literature in sociology and related disciplines in the social and behavioral sciences.

United States Political Science Documents (1975–present)   Includes such specific areas as foreign policy, international relations, behavioral sciences, public administra-tion, economics, law and contemporary problems, world politics, and all areas of politi-cal science, including theory and methodology.

Appendix

E

Key Concepts Organized by Subject

Bureaucracy

administration
administrative law
administrative order
board/commission
bond
budgeting
bureaucracy
cease-and-desist order
certification of eligibles
civil service
Civil Service Reform Act of 1978
clientele
delegation of power
department
Ethics in Government Act of 1978
Federal Register
Freedom of Information Act of 1966
government corporation
Grace Commission
Hatch Act
Hoover Commission of 1947–49, 1953–55
independent agency/regulatory commission
merit system
nepotism
neutral competence
Office of Personnel Management
ombudsman
Parkinson's law
patronage

Pendleton Act of 1883
Peter principle
public administration
public management
quasi-judicial agency
quasi legislative
red tape
reorganization
representative bureaucracy
senior executive service
span of control
spoils system
sunset laws
veterans' preference

Civil Liberties

arraignment
arrest
backlash
bill of attainder
Brown v Board of Education of Topeka, Kansas
busing
civil disobedience
civil liberty
civil rights
clear and present danger
comparable worth
conscientious objector
cruel and unusual punishment
de facto
de jure
double jeopardy
due process of law
equal employment opportunity
establishment clause
exclusionary rule
ex post facto law
fairness doctrine
Fifth Amendment

First Amendment
Fourteenth Amendment
free exercise clause
free press clause
free speech clause
Gideon v Wainwright
human rights
indictment
Jim Crow
libel
Mapp v Ohio
Miranda rights
naturalization
Nineteenth Amendment
obscenity
Pentagon Papers
prior restraint
probable cause
procedural rights
reverse discrimination
Roe v Wade
second reconstruction
separate but equal
speech and debate clause
Thirteenth Amendment
Voting Rights Act of 1965
writ of habeas corpus

Congress

advice and consent
appropriation
authorization/authorizing legislation
bicameral
bill
calendar
casework
caucus
cloture
committee

Appendix E

Congress

Congressional Budget and Impoundment Control Act of 1974

Congressional Budget Office

constituency

cozy triangles/iron triangles

executive session

filibuster

fiscal year

gerrymander

hundred days

impoundment

issue networks

legislation

legislative history

legislative immunity

legislative intent

legislative liaison

legislative veto

lobby

logrolling

majority leader

minority leader

oversight, congressional

pair

parliamentary system

party leader

pork barrel

power of the purse

president pro tempore

quorum

reconciliation

resolution

rider

Senate establishment

seniority, congressional

Speaker

staffer

subgovernments

sunset laws

sunshine laws

unanimous consent
veto, congressional
veto, override
whip

The Constitution

amendment
antifederalists
Bill of Rights
commerce clause
concurrent power
Connecticut compromise
constituent power
constitution
elastic clause
enumerated powers
Equal Rights Amendment
federalism
federalists
full faith and credit
impeachment
implied power
incorporation
inherent power
judicial review
McCulloch v Maryland
Madison, James
Marbury v Madison
necessary and proper clause
New Jersey plan
nullification
preemption doctrine
representative government
republic
reserved powers
Shays' Rebellion
unitary government
Virginia plan

Appendix E

Courts

adjudication

administrative law

adversary system

amicus curiae

appeal

attorney general

bail

beyond a reasonable doubt

brief

capital punishment

certiorari

civil law

common law

contempt of court

court

court of appeals

court packing

defendant

district court/federal district court/U.S. district court

entrapment

felony

hearing

immunity

judge

judicial activism

judicial review

judicial self-restraint

judiciary

jurisdiction

jurisprudence

jury, grand

jury, trial

justice

justice of the peace

libel

misdemeanor

nolo contendere

opinion

parole

plaintiff

plea bargaining

political question

precedent

private law

public law

search and seizure

slander

solicitor general

standing

stare decisis

strict constructionist

Supreme Court, United States

tort

trial

warrant

Federalism

Advisory Commission on Intergovernmental Relations

Articles of Confederation

commerce clause

commonwealth

concurrent power

confederation

federalism

Federalist Papers

full faith and credit

grant

implied power

intergovernmental relations

interposition

interstate compacts

reserved powers

revenue sharing

states' rights

supremacy clause

Tenth Amendment

Appendix E

Foreign Policy

ambassador

appeasement

arms control

balance of power

balance of terror

bargaining chip

Bay of Pigs

bipartisanship

Brezhnev Doctrine

brinkmanship

build-down

Central Intelligence Agency

civil defense

cold war

constructive engagement

containment

contras

Cuban missile crisis

DeConcini reservation

détente

deterrence

diplomacy

dumping

Eisenhower Doctrine

embargo

entente

Finlandization

first-strike capability

foreign aid

good neighbor policy

Gulf of Tonkin Resolution

gunboat

hawk

Iran-contra affair

iron curtain

isolationism

limited war

linkage

Marshall Plan

massive retaliation

Monroe Doctrine

national interest

NATO/North Atlantic Treaty Organization

Nixon Doctrine

nuclear freeze

nuclear nonproliferation

Panama Canal treaties

Pentagon

Reagan Doctrine

SALT/Strategic Arms Limitations Talks

triad

Truman Doctrine

United Nations

Warsaw Pact

Political Economy

ability to pay

absolute advantage

adjustment assistance

antitrust laws

automatic stabilizer/built-in stabilizer

bailout

beggar-thy-neighbor policy

budget

business cycle, political

business cycles

capitalism

central bank

comparative advantage

consumer movement

cooling-off period

crowding out

deficit financing

discount rate

duty

economic policy

Federal Reserve System

fiscal policy

Appendix E

fiscal year
full employment
general welfare clause
gold standard
gross national product
industrial policy
inflation/deflation
invisible hand
Keynes, John Maynard
Laffer curve
laissez-faire
mixed economy
monetarism
monetary policy
open-market operations
Phillips curve
political economy
protectionism
public choice economics
public goods
public works
reserve requirements
Sixteenth Amendment
socialism
stagflation
supply-side economics/Reaganomics
taxation

Political Parties and Interest Groups

caucus
class action
coalition
corruption, political
delegate
Democratic party
direct mail
election

electoral college

faction

front runner

GOP

image makers

interest group liberalism

lame duck

Left

Left, new

mass party

melting pot

minor party

national committee

national convention

partisanship

party identification

party line

party unity

platform

political action committee

political campaign

political consultant

political machine

political party

populism

precinct

primary

progressive movement/progressive era

proportional representation

public interest groups

realignment

Republican party

Right

single-issue politics

suffrage

third party

two-party system

umbrella party

Appendix E

Political Theory

alienation

anarchism

aristocracy

Aristotle

authoritarianism

autocracy

checks and balances

citizenship

civil disobedience

conservatism

Declaration of Independence

democracy

dictator

divine right of kings

equality/egalitarianism

fascism

freedom

garrison state

general will

higher law

ideology

inalienable rights

justice

legitimacy

liberalism

limited government

Locke, John

Machiavelli, Niccolo

Marxism

nihilism

oligarchy

radical

revolution

Rousseau, Jean-Jacques

rule of law

separation of powers

social contract

sovereignty

utopia

Presidency

amnesty

appointment clause

Brownlow Committee/President's Committee on Administrative Management

cabinet

Camp David

central clearance

commander in chief

commission, presidential

Council of Economic Advisers

emergency powers

executive agreement

Executive Office of the President

executive order

executive privilege

Humphrey's Executor v United States

impeachment

impoundment

inherent power

jawboning

Joint Chiefs of Staff

National Security Council

news management

Office of Management and Budget

oval office

presidency, imperial

presidency, prerogative theory of

presidency, restricted view of

presidency, stewardship theory of

presidential character

presidential debates

presidential election campaign fund

presidential power

presidential press conference

presidential succession

primary, presidential

state of the union message

Twenty-fifth Amendment

United States v Nixon

veto

vice president
war powers
Warren Commission
Watergate
White House Office

Public Policy

administrative advocacy
affirmative action
agenda setting
benign neglect
citizen participation
cooptation
deregulation
econometric model
Employment Act of 1946
entitlement program
environmental policy/National Environmental Policy Act of 1969
evaluation, policy
gatekeeper
Great Society
gun control
incrementalism
issue-attention cycle
issue networks
moon-ghetto metaphor
New Deal
Office of Technology Assessment
Pareto optimality
parity, employment
parity, farm
parity, nuclear
pluralism
polarization
policy analysis
policy sciences
policy studies
program
public interest

public interest groups
public interest law
public interest movement
public policymaking
public regardingness
redistribution
regulation
social indicators
spillover effects/externalities
subgovernments
tax expenditure
tragedy of the commons
transfer payments
trickle-down theory
war on poverty
welfare state
white flight

State and Local Government

annexation
authority
benefit district
black power
bonds, municipal/tax-exempt municipal bonds
borough
bossism
California plan
city
city charter
city council
city-county consolidation
city manager
commission form of government
community development
council-manager plan/county-manager system
council of government
county
county commissioner
county seat

Appendix E

Dillon's rule

enterprise zone/urban enterprise zone

gentrification

ghetto

governor

home rule

Kerner Commission

local government

local option

mayor

metropolitan government

Missouri plan

Model Cities Program

movers and shakers

municipal

municipality

neighborhood

ordinance

precinct

redlining

rent control

sagebrush rebellion

secretary of State

sheriff

special district

state government

tax revolt

town

town meeting

township

urban homesteading

urban renewal

zoning

Voting and Elections

apportionment

at large

ballot

bandwagon effect

bellwether
candidate
coattails
election
electioneering
elector
electoral college
Federal Election Campaign Act of 1972
Federal Election Commission
federal postcard application
friends and neighbors effect
gender gap
gerrymander
incumbency effect
initiative
issue voting
League of Women Voters
mandate
matching funds
national convention
plurality
poll
pollster
reapportionment
recall
referendum
registration, voter
sample
stump
tax, poll
ticket splitting
underdog
vote, popular
voter
voting, approval
voting, bloc
voting, pocketbook
voting, strategic

List of Credits

A

Access, © 1986 Jimmy Margulies/The Houston Post. Reprinted by permission.

ACTION, Courtesy ACTION

Alphabet soup, Courtesy Franklin D. Roosevelt Library

USDA, Courtesy USDA

Arms control, © 1986 Ed Gamble/The Florida Times-Union/King Features Syndicate. Reprinted by permission.

Asylum, AP/Wide World Photos

B

Ballyhoo, AP/Wide World Photos

Jeremy Bentham, The Bettmann Archive, Inc.

Big stick, Courtesy Sagamore Hill National Historic Site

Black Panthers, AP/Wide World Photos

Bossism, Reproduced from *Thomas Nast: Cartoons and Illustrations,* Dover, 1974

C

President's cabinet, Courtesy The New-York Historical Society

Capital punishment, The Bettmann Archive, Inc.

Capitol, Library of Congress

Jimmy Carter, Courtesy Jimmy Carter Library

Child labor, International Museum of Photography at George Eastman House

Civil rights movement, AP/Wide World Photos

Correctional institution, Robert George Gaylord/EKM-Nepenthe

Court packing, Library of Congress

U.S. Customs Service, John Grafton, *New York in the Nineteenth Century,* Dover Publications, 1977

D

Huey Long, Bettmann Newsphotos

Donkey, Culver Pictures

Dynasty, AP/Wide World Photos

E

Elephant, Prints Old & Rare, San Francisco

List of Credits

Department of Energy, Courtesy Department of Energy

F

Fascism, Courtesy Architect of the Capitol

Fireside chat, Courtesy Franklin D. Roosevelt Library

Food stamps, Courtesy USDA

Gerald R. Ford, Courtesy Gerald R. Ford Library

Forest Service, Jim Hughes/USDA, Forest Service

Milton Friedman, AP/Wide World Photos

G

General Services Administration, Courtesy General Services Administration

Gentrification, Philip Jon Bailey/Stock, Boston

G-men, Museum of Modern Art/Film Stills Archive

Great Society, Drawing by Alan Dunn; © 1964 The New Yorker Magazine, Inc.

H

Health and Human Services, National Institutes of Health, NINCDS

Housing and Urban Development, Tony Maine/Chicago Theater Restoration Associates

I

Image makers, Museum of Modern Art/Film Stills Archive

Impeachment, Drawing by Lorenz; © 1964 The New Yorker Magazine, Inc.

Iran-contra affair, © 1987 Washington Post Writers Group. Reprinted by permission.

J

Jesse Jackson, Courtesy Operation PUSH, Chicago

Jim Crow, Elliott Erwitt/Magnum Photos, Inc.

K

John Maynard Keynes, The Bettmann Archive, Inc.

Martin Luther King, Jr., AP/Wide World Photos

L

League of Women Voters, Courtesy League of Women Voters

Locke, The Bettmann Archive, Inc.

Log cabin, Courtesy The New-York Historical Society

M

McCarthyism, AP/Wide World Photos

Patrick Moynihan, Courtesy Office of Senator Daniel P. Moynihan

N

NEA, © 1986 Nicholas De Sciose/Courtesy National Endowment for the Arts

New Deal, Courtesy University of Maryland Art Gallery

O

OSHA, Courtesy Occupational Safety and Health Administration

Oval Office, Bill Fitz-Patrick/The White House

P

Peace Corps, Courtesy Peace Corps

Presidency, Courtesy The White House

Presidential debates, AP/Wide World Photos

Pro-choice, National Abortion Rights Action League

Pro-life, Courtesy National Right to Life Committee

Prohibition, The Bettmann Archive, Inc.

R

Ronald Reagan, Courtesy The White House

S

Speaker, Courtesy Office of the Speaker of the House of Representatives

Spoils system, Prints Old & Rare, San Francisco

Stars and stripes, The Bettmann Archive, Inc.

David Stockman, AP/Wide World Photos

Strike, Paula Williamson

Suffrage, The Bettmann Archive, Inc.

T

Teflon president, © Conrad, Los Angeles Times. Reprinted by permission of Los Angeles Times Syndicate.

TVA, Courtesy Tennessee Valley Authority

Town meeting, *Foster's Daily Democrat*

25th Amendment, Prints Old & Rare, San Francisco

U

Unemployment, Photograph by Dorothea Lange, Courtesy Library of Congress

Urban park movement, Courtesy Olmsted National Historic Site, Brookline, Mass.

V

Vietnam War, AP/Wide World Photos

W

Washington, Painting by Gilbert Stuart

Watergate, Copyright 1974, G. B. Trudeau. Reprinted with permission of Universal Press Syndicate. All rights reserved.

The following portraits are reproduced from *Dictionary of American Portraits,* Dover Publications, 1967: John Adams/John C. Calhoun (Daguerrotype by Mathew Brady; Courtesy Library of Congress)/Calvin Coolidge (Library of Congress)/Eugene V. Debs (Courtesy Tamiment Institute Library)/Dwight D. Eisenhower (Library of Congress)/James A. Garfield (Courtesy National Archives, Brady Collection)/Warren G. Harding (Library of Congress)/Herbert Hoover (Library of Congress)/Andrew Jackson (Library of Congress)/Thomas Jefferson (Painting by Rembrandt Peale; Courtesy Princeton University)/Andrew Johnson (Engraving by Alexander H. Ritchie)/Lyndon B. Johnson (Library of Congress)/John F. Kennedy (Courtesy The White House)/Abraham Lincoln (Photograph by Alexander Hesler)/James Madison (Painting by Asher B. Durand)/John Marshall (Painting by Rembrandt Peale; Courtesy Virginia Museum of Fine Arts, The Glasgow Fund)/Richard M. Nixon/Eleanor Roosevelt (Library of Congress)/Franklin D. Roosevelt (Library of Congress)/Theodore Roosevelt/William Howard Taft (Library of Congress)/Harry S Truman (Courtesy Harry S Truman Library)/Woodrow Wilson (Courtesy The New-York Historical Society).

ABOUT THE AUTHOR

Jay M. Shafritz is a professor in the Graduate School of Public and International Affairs at the University of Pittsburgh. Previously he taught at the University of Colorado at Denver, the University of Houston at Clear Lake City, and the State University of New York at Albany. He served as the Director of the Executive Development Program at NASA–Johnson Space Center from 1980 to 1986, was a consultant to the Department of State's Bureau of Personnel, and was a National Association of Schools of Public Affairs and Administration Fellow to the Department of Housing and Urban Development.

He is the author, coauthor, and editor of more than two dozen books on politics and government including *Classics of Public Administration, Classics of Organizational Theory,* and several dictionaries including the *Facts on File Dictionary of Public Administration.* Dr. Shafritz received his M.P.A. from Baruch College of the City University of New York and his Ph.D. in political science from Temple University.

A NOTE ON THE TYPE

The text of this book was set in 9/11 Times Roman, a film version of the face designed by Stanley Morison, which was first used by *The Times* (of London) in 1932. Part of Morison's special intent for Times Roman was to create a face that was editorially neutral. It is an especially compact, attractive, and legible typeface, which has come to be seen as the "most important type design of the twentieth century."

Composed by Weimer Typesetting Co., Inc., Indianapolis, Indiana

Printed and bound by Arcata Graphics/Halliday, West Hanover, Massachusetts